ENCYCLOPEDIA OF CONTEMPORARY FRENCH CULTURE

ENCYCLOPEDIA OF CONTEMPORARY FRENCH CULTURE

Edited by
**Alex Hughes and
Keith Reader**

London and New York

First published 1998
by Routledge
11 New Fetter Lane, London EC4P 4EE
29 West 35th Street, New York, NY 10001

Typeset in Sabon by Routledge
Printed and bound in Great Britain by TJ International Ltd, Padstow, Cornwall

British Library Cataloguing in Publication Data
A catalogue record for this book is available from the British Library

Library of Congress Cataloging-in-Publication Data
Encyclopedia of contemporary French culture / edited by
Alex Hughes and Keith Reader
p.   cm.
Includes bibliographical references and index.
1. France—Civilization—1945– —Encyclopedias. 2. France—Popular
culture–Encyclopedias. I. Hughes, Alex. II. Reader, Keith.
DC33.7.E53 1998 97–31879 CIP
944.08'03—dc21

ISBN 0–415–13186–3

Contents

Editorial team

List of contributors

Elza Adamowicz
Queen Mary and Westfield College London

Dennis Ager
Aston University

Robert Aldrich
University of Sydney

Laurence Bell
University of Surrey

Jennifer Birkett
University of Birmingham

Michael Bishop
Dalhousie University

Craig Blunt
University of Birmingham

Sophie Boyron
University of Birmingham

William C. Calin
University of Florida

Kay Chadwick
University of Liverpool

Susan Collard
University of Sussex

Tom Conley
Harvard University

Martyn Cornick
University of Birmingham

Béatrice Damamme-Gilbert
University of Birmingham

Hugh Dauncey
University of Newcastle upon Tyne

Richard Derderian
University of North Carolina

Philip Dine
Loughborough University

David Drake
Middlesex University

David Ellison
University of Miami

Elizabeth Ezra
University of Stirling

Patrick ffrench
University College London

Jill Forbes
University of Bristol

Cathy Fowler
Southampton Institute

Johnnie Gratton
University College Dublin

Vérène Grieshaber
University College London

Renate Günther
University of Sheffield

Ron Hallmark
University of Birmingham

Seán Hand
Oxford Brookes University

Linda Hantrais
Loughborough University

Peter Hawkins
University of Bristol

Susan Hayward
University of Exeter

Owen Heathcote
University of Bradford

Nicholas Hewitt
University of Nottingham

Lynn A. Higgins
Dartmouth College (USA)

Gill Howie
Liverpool University

Alex Hughes
University of Birmingham

Simeon Hunter
United Kingdom

Laïla Ibnlfassi
London Guildhall University

Kate Ince
University of Birmingham

Brian Jenkins
University of Portsmouth

Christopher Johnson
Keele University

Roger Kain
University of Exeter

Debra Kelly
University of Westminster

Michael Kelly
University of Southampton

William Kidd
University of Stirling

Eleonore Kofman
Nottingham Trent University

Raymond Kuhn
Queen Mary and Westfield College

David Looseley
University of Leeds

Lucy McKeever
Sunderland University

Mark McKinney
Miami University

Jean Mainil
University of Nottingham

Margaret Majumdar
University of Glamorgan

John Marks
Loughborough University

Bill Marshall
University of Southampton

Ann Miller
Leicester University

Pam Moores
Aston University

† Peter Morris
Aston University

François Nectoux
Kingston University

Patrick O'Donovan
University College Cork

George Paizis
University College London

Alan Pedley
University of Exeter

Ian Pickup
University of Birmingham

Gérard Poulet
University of Exeter

Phil Powrie
University of Newcastle upon Tyne

Keith Reader
University of Newcastle upon Tyne

† Jo Reed
University of Birmingham

Mireille Rosello
University of Nottingham

Gerard Paul Sharpling
University of Birmingham

Michael Sheringham
Royal Holloway, University of London

Max Silverman
University of Leeds

Annie Sparks
Royal Holloway, University of London

Judith Still
University of Nottingham

Walter A. Strauss
Case Western Reserve University

Anthony Sutcliffe
University of Leicester

Valerie Swales
University of Portsmouth

Joe Szarka
University of Bath

Carrie Tarr
Thames Valley University

Ursula Tidd
University of Salford

Chris Tinker
University of Birmingham

D. A. Trotter
University of Wales, Aberystwyth

Steven Ungar
University of Iowa

Joëlle Vitiello
Macalester College, Saint Paul

Khursheed Wadia
University of Wolverhampton

Peter Wagstaff
University of Bath

Fiona Warne
University of Birmingham

Colville Wemyss
MA, University of St Andrews

Steve Wharton
University of Bath

Nicola White
Kingston University

Carol Wilcox
South Kent College

James Williams
University of Kent at Canterbury

Jan Windebank
University of Sheffield

Michael Worton
University College London

Preface

In an age when France has consolidated its position as the leading European destination for English-speaking holiday-makers, tourists and second-home-owners, retained its prestige as the international capital of gastronomy, wine production, chic and sex appeal, and bred film directors to rival Hollywood and singer-songwriters without equal on the world stage, it has also become an object of profound suspicion for many non-French commentators on the intellectual life. French ideas are produced in a faddish and fashion-conscious climate, we are often told, prominent philosophers and social theorists are treated with absurd veneration and their obscure, portentous, jargon-infested diction threatens to run riot through the human sciences, undermining otherwise secure British and North American bastions of clarity, good sense and methodological rectitude. It could of course be that the prevailing enthusiasm for France as a source of pleasure is closely linked to this distrust of French ideas: while *volupté* and *jouissance* belong quite properly in the restaurant, the bedroom or the cinema, they have no place in the library or the lecture theatre. Could it be that French intellectuals enjoy themselves too much and too openly in the eyes of their Anglophone detractors, and that their writings are therefore easily seen by such critics as an attempt to seduce and corrupt our impressionable young? In order to begin answering questions of this kind we clearly need a new kind of reference work – one which talks about wine and psychoanalysis, movie-makers and *maîtres-à-penser*, Piaf and Piaget.

The entire field of contemporary French culture is alive with myths and counter-myths about France and Frenchness. While some of these are produced at home and then exported, others originate abroad – in British tabloid newspapers, say, or on North American campuses – and are then imported into France. So much that is fascinating about contemporary France is transmitted by gossip, hearsay and the insider talk of various professional groups that it has until now been difficult for the would-be demythologizer to lay down a firm factual foundation for his or her enquiry. Things are even more problematic for the newcomer. Basic documents are often surprisingly difficult to find, and divisions between 'high' and 'popular' culture, or between the hexagon and the wider world of *francophonie*, have often meant that students and general readers have had to visit far-flung sections of their local reference library in order to begin assembling a comprehensive picture of France today. What Keith Reader, Alex Hughes and their team of contributors have produced in this splendid new *Encyclopedia* is a huge multi-dimensional snapshot of a culture that has reinvented itself with dizzying rapidity in the last half-century and shows no sign of slowing down. The range of their book is astonishing. With a single movement, the reader is able to travel from the world of screen goddesses (Aimée, Bardot, Deneuve) to the world of jet-setting intellectual demiurges (Baudrillard, Bourdieu, Derrida), from *Elle* to Eluard, from nuclear power to pornography, from agriculture to athletics, from the structure of Pierre Reverdy's verse to the labyrinthine and recursive structures of the new European legislation. All those who study modern French and Francophone cultures will be in debt to Hughes and Reader. Dangerous and delectable France has been mapped as never before between the covers of this cornucopian volume.

Malcolm Bowie

Introduction

Our *Encyclopedia of Contemporary French Culture* reflects the growing interest in French cultural studies that is a feature of the current academic and intellectual scene. Its existence echoes, in other words, the trend towards a broadening of the syllabus for further and higher education programmes in French, away from the once sacrosanct duo of language and canonical literature, to incorporate such areas as cinema, political and social institutions, gender-based studies and critical theory. More generally, it will be relevant to students of areas such as above who do not necessarily have a particular interest in French culture *per se*. French cinema remains the dominant Western national industry outside the United States; French political history and institutions, given France's place since 1789 as the first modern nation-state, exercise a continuing fascination; feminist theory, and critical theory more generally, are frequently nowadays thought of as characteristically French developments. Our text presupposes no knowledge of the French language, nor indeed of France's history and institutions beyond what might be expected of the educated lay reader of a quality daily paper or news weekly, so that its usefulness will extend well outside the domain of French studies.

The *Encyclopedia of Contemporary French Culture* is intended, above all, to break new ground. Our project, in producing it, has been to create a reference volume which, unlike the standard works of reference that exist within the context of French studies, brings together material relating to French (and francophone) culture defined in its very broadest sense. Areas covered, and connected, by the *Encyclopedia*'s palette of essay texts include art, cinema, economic issues, education, food and wine, intellectual life, linguistic issues, literature, media, music, performing arts, politics and society, transport, and technology. While the chronological period taken in by the *Encyclopedia* ranges from the end of World War II in 1945 to the present day, we have sought to weight the contents of many of our overview articles towards the latter. However, some pre-1945 material has been included where developments in contemporary French society would be difficult or impossible to understand without it.

The *Encyclopedia* is composed of pieces of varying lengths, ranging from fairly extensive short essays to thumbnail sketches. Longer entries are 'facts-fronted' and have lists of texts for further reading, some of which are accompanied by a short note explaining their content and/or relevance. Essays and entries are carefully cross-referenced, either in the text or in the *see also* section at the end of the entry. The purpose of this is to permit the *Encyclopedia*'s readers to pursue their own 'paths' through the texts contained in the volume, teasing out connections that might not perhaps otherwise have been self-evident.

In an enterprise of this kind, it is impossible to be all-inclusive. The selection of entries contained in the *Encyclopedia* reflects this fact, and reflects a number of decisions which we, as editors, in consultation with our editors at Routledge, found ourselves having to make. We decided, for example, that it was important that the *Encyclopedia* should address francophone culture, as well as the cultural life of mainland France and its overseas *départements* and territories (DOM-TOMs such as Martinique, Guadeloupe and La Réunion), and that it should avoid doing so in a tokenistic manner. Issues of space meant, however, that we could not engage with the culture(s) of *la francophonie* – the totality of French-speaking areas – as comprehensively as with that of France itself. We concluded, therefore, regretfully, that only those francophone countries which are geographically close to the *Hexagone* or which, for a variety of reasons, enjoy close cultural links with France, should be the object of scrutiny in our volume. We also decided that aspects of francophone culture should be the subject of long essay pieces, whose inclusion and detail would obviate the need for a proliferation of shorter entries devoted to a single francophone writer/artist/cultural phenomenon. The inclusion/omission of entries devoted to postwar writing in France also gave us pause for thought. Many excellent guides to modern and contemporary French and francophone literature already exist, most notably the recently reissued *Oxford Companion to Literature in French* (which also, and significantly, includes for the first time in its existence a number of pieces on cultural studies topics). In view of this fact, we elected to base the 'literature' component of the *Encyclopedia* primarily on essay pieces devoted to different textual genres/forms (for example, autobiography, committed literature, detective fiction, the *nouveau roman*, poetry, short-story writing, etc.), rather than to offer a comprehensive set of short entries focused on individual writers. This is not to say that we have not included entries of this latter type; their inclusion is, however, a function of the contents of the longer essay pieces in which 'high' and 'popular' literary forms are discussed. The shorter individual entries relating to literature have, in other words, been the object of systematic selection. An illustration of this is our inclusion of a good many short entries devoted to postwar French drama. Here, our strategy reflects the fact that i) theatre-related matters are the subject of several of the longer entries in our volume, and ii) drama is less comprehensively 'covered' in reference works dealing with French literary production than other literary genres. It is our hope that the emphasis which our *Encyclopedia* places on performing arts in France will encourage research work in this area, of which there would seem currently to be a dearth.

Because, as we explained above, our target readership stretches well outside the realm of French studies, we have translated the titles of all books mentioned in the *Encyclopedia*, except in cases where the title is either self-evident or untranslatable. If an 'official' translation exists and is still (as far as we have been able to ascertain) in print, then we have preceded the French title by its English equivalent. We have left the titles of the films in the original French, however, except where a standard translation, recognized in Britain and the US, exists. We have elected not to translate most film titles because different translations of the same title often exist in Britain and America, and our sense is that including our own translation would serve simply to confuse readers.

The entries inevitably contain numerous references to institutions of various kinds which it was impossible, for reasons of space, to describe or define. The bemused reader with a reading knowledge of French may find a single-volume reference work, such as the *Petit Larousse encyclopédique* or the invaluable *Quid?*, helpful in clarifying these.

Please note that places and dates of birth have been included wherever the information was readily available.

Alex Hughes
Keith Reader

Acknowledgements

We should like to thank all our contributors for their commitment to this project. We are particularly grateful to those among them who produced entries dealing with the more 'out-of-the-way' areas on which expertise was not always widely available. Colville Wemyss, Fiona Cairns and Denise Rea at Routledge have been helpful and long-suffering editors, and provided first-rate counsel and practical assistance. Finally, each of us thanks the other for moral support, constructive criticism and endless patience.

Classified contents list

All of the entries in the *Encyclopedia* are categorized under the most appropriate subject heading(s). Some entries appear under more than one heading where relevant.

Architecture

architecture
architecture under Mitterrand
Bercy
conservation zones
Le Corbusier
Malraux act
Marais plan
Montparnasse Tower
Pompidou Centre and the Forum des Halles
renovation projects

Cultural institutions/phenomena

Académie Française
arts funding (including regional)
cultural policy
cultural topography (Paris)
iconography
Lang, Jack
libraries
literary prizes
maisons de la culture
Malraux, André
publishing/l'édition
youth culture

Economy

agriculture
Attali, Jacques
banks
dirigisme
economy
employment
European economic integration
Fourastié, Jean
informal economy
management style
manufacturing industry
minimum wage
multinational companies

nationalization and privatization
planning system
public works
regional economic development
service industry
Tapie, Bernard
trade
transport
unions

Education and research

education ministry
education, primary
education, secondary: *collèges*, *lycées*, etc.
education, the state and the church
educational elitism: the *grandes écoles*
student revolt of 1986
universities

Fashion and design

Cardin, Pierre
Chanel, Coco
Dior, Christian
fashion
Gaultier, Jean-Paul
Lacroix, Christian
Rykiel, Sonia
Saint Laurent, Yves

Film

Adjani, Isabelle
Aimée, Anouk
Ardant, Fanny
Autant-Lara, Claude
Auteuil, Daniel
avance sur recettes
Balasko, Josiane
Bardot, Brigitte
Baye, Nathalie
Bazin, André

Food and drink

abortion/contraception

In 1945, French women had little control over their fertility and their reproductive processes. Laws passed in the early 1920s had prohibited not only abortion, but also the dissemination of information concerning contraception and the distribution of contraceptive material. During World War II, the **Vichy** regime firmly established motherhood as women's lot, equating abortion with treason against the state and guillotining an abortionist, Marie-Louise Giraud. In the decades following the war, a series of campaigns against the pro-natalist climate which prevailed in France eventually afforded French women the kind of sociosexual rights in force in other European countries. Change was, however, slow in coming.

In the late twentieth century, French women have full and free access to a range of contraceptive methods, and can obtain an abortion (an IVG, or *interruption volontaire de grossesse*) within the first ten weeks of their pregnancy. Abortion is reimbursable by social security and, in the wake of **AIDS** and growing public concern about unwanted pregnancies, pro-contraceptive publicity is no longer subject to restriction. That this is the case is due to campaigning activities mounted in the postwar period by diverse groups and movements, such as the Mouvement pour le Planning Familial (the French Family Planning Association, initially formed by Evelyne Sullerot and Marie-Andrée Weill-Hallé), the Mouvement pour la Libération de l'Avortement et la Contraception or MLAC (the Association for the Liberation of Abortion and Contraception), the Groupe Information Santé (Health Information Group) and Choisir (Choice). These activities, whose aim was to generate reform of the 1920s laws, took off in the 1950s, with support from the parliamentary Left and Centre Left, from elements of the left-wing and the women's press, and from numerous women's associations. They derived further impetus with the emergence, in the late 1960s and early 1970s, of the Mouvement de la Libération des Femmes (the MLF, or French Feminist Movement). In 1971, for example, the MLF demonstrated in favour of the liberalization of abortion. A manifesto signed by 343 women in the public eye, and published by *Le Nouvel Observateur* on 5 April, declared that they had had illegal abortions and called for free access to abortion and contraception. In 1972, French feminists, including lawyer Gisèle Halimi, used the Bobigny *procès* – the trial of four women accused of procuring a backstreet abortion – to draw public attention to the consequences of the repressive status quo. In 1973, feminist women joined with doctors and unionists to form MLAC.

Key laws marking French women's gradual acquisition of control over their bodies include:

- the *loi Neuwirth* (19 December 1967), a law which was proposed by the Gaullist *député* Lucien Neuwirth and which set in train a liberalization of contraception completed by a further law of 4 December 1974;

- the *loi Veil* (17 January 1975), which legalized abortion; and
- the *loi Roudy* (31 December 1982), which legislated to authorize state reimbursement of IVG.

The existence of these laws reflects the extent to which reform of legislation about women's sexual rights had elicited widespread popular support in France by the mid-1960s. This is not to say that such support was (or subsequently became) total. Numerous anti-abortion groups exist in France (e.g. SOS Tout-Petits and Laissez-les Vivre), and commando-style attacks on abortion clinics (by groups such as Trève de Dieu), have proliferated in the 1990s.

ALEX HUGHES

See also: demographic developments; feminism (movements/groups)

Further reading

Duchen, C. (1986) *Feminism in France from May '68 to Mitterrand*, London: Routledge & Kegan Paul (a history of post-1968 French feminism, which foregrounds the key role the pro-abortion/contraception struggle played in feminist campaigns of the period).
——(1994) *Women's Rights and Women's Lives in France 1944–1968*, London and New York: Routledge (an invaluable account of French's women's history in the postwar period, which illuminates their relationship with issues of motherhood, fertility and control over their bodies).
Mossuz-Lavau, J. (1991) *Les Lois de l'amour: les politiques de la sexualité en France*, Paris: Payot (an excellent overview of the evolution of legislation relating to sexuality and gender in postwar France).

Académie Française

The Académie Française, founded by Richelieu in 1635, is one of the five academies that make up the Institut de France which is housed in a splendid building on the Quai Conti in Paris. The Académie's role was to promote the improvement of the French language, primarily through the establishing of standard vocabulary through a dictionary, of which eight editions have so far appeared. The forty members, known as *immortels*, elect replacements when a death occurs, but the election must be approved by the head of state. Any writer may apply, and the Academy has always included distinguished authors: however, the list of great writers not belonging to the Academy is lengthy. The first woman to be elected was Marguerite **Yourcenar** in 1980, and occasionally foreign writers of French are included. On formal occasions academicians wear an embroidered uniform with cocked hat and carry a sword. An important function of the Academy is to award eighty prestigious **literary prizes** as well as 200 charitable grants, funded by the numerous bequests made to the Academy over the centuries.

JO REED

See also: linguistic regulation; women's/lesbian writing

Acquart, André

b. 1922, Vincennes

Artist and stage designer

One of the pioneers of stage design as an integral part of theatre productions, working most notably in the 1950s and 1960s with directors **Blin**, **Vilar**, **Terzieff**, Miquel and **Rétoré** on texts as varied as Shakespeare, Brecht and **Genet**, Acquart's designs are typified by abstraction and an experimental approach.

ANNIE SPARKS

See also: theatre

Further reading

Couty, D. and Rey, A. (eds) (1995), *Le Théâtre*, Paris: Bordas (general chapters on changing scenography in postwar period, including mentions of Acquart's work).

Actes Sud

Publishing house

Incorporating the century-old publisher Papiers, this Parisian publishing house, under the direction of Claire David, is responsible for publishing a large number of contemporary theatrical texts in France, often in collaboration with theatres staging the plays. It is responsible for over thirty new titles a year, and for the 'Répliques' series of texts, edited for education by Michel **Vinaver**.

ANNIE SPARKS

See also: publishing/*l'édition*; theatre

Adamov, Arthur

b. 1908, Kislovodsk, Caucasia;
d. 1970, Paris

Playwright and writer

Famous for his experimental, often confrontational approach, Adamov's absurdist dream plays such as *La Parodie* (Parody) and Brechtian-style, grotesque political satires such as *Off Limits* were staged by **Planchon**, **Vilar** and **Serreau**.

ANNIE SPARKS

See also: theatre; Theatre of the Absurd

Further reading

Abirached, R. (ed.) (1983) *Lectures d'Adamov*, Tübingen: Gunter Narr (essays).
Bradby, D. (1975) *Adamov*, London: Grant and Cutler (bibliography).

Adjani, Isabelle

b. 1955, Paris

Actor

Adjani's career was launched in a 1975 François **Truffaut** film, *L'Histoire d'Adèle H*. During the 1980s she mixed comic roles and the enigmatic, tormented and sexually confused *femme fatale*, culminating in *Camille Claudel* (1988), produced by Adjani and directed by Bruno Nuttyens and, in 1994, Patrice **Chéreau**'s *La Reine Margot*. Often called the only French star, her mythical status has been magnified by a secretive private life, coupled with a relatively small number of films (an average of one a year since 1975). She was the 1987 president of the Commission d'Avance sur Recettes. In May 1997 she chaired the jury at the Cannes Film Festival.

PHIL POWRIE

See also: *avance sur recettes*; cinema; stars

Further reading

Roques-Briscard, C. (1987) *La Passion d'Adjani*, Lausanne: Favre (hagiographic biography).

advertising

The importance of advertising within contemporary French popular culture has grown considerably since 1945, and the forms of advertising discourse have been evolving alongside changes in technology and communication. Controversy as to its cultural and ethical value has long been a feature of ideological debate in France.

Advertising's massive expansion since 1945 can be linked initially to the emergence of the consumer society and the economic confidence of the 1950s and 1960s and, later, to increased commercial competition alongside massive media expansion. Total advertising expenditure represents 1.25 per cent of the French gross domestic product and the sector employs on a regular basis an estimated 50,000 people. Although this is small compared with countries such as the United States, the French advertising sector has continued to grow even during periods of recession. However, the late twentieth century is seeing a period of turmoil. The long-established tradition of agencies such as Havas and Publicis has enabled the sector successfully to resist infiltration by foreign competitors, so that the largest French advertising groups – EURO-RSCG (the result of a 1991 merger between Havas-EUROCOM, and RSCG: Roux-Séguéla-Cayzac-Goudard), Publicis and BDDP: Boulet-Dru-Dupuy-Petit – still command the largest share of the national market, but their position on the international market remains modest.

Following a succession of changes in the regulation and funding of the broadcasting media, advertising (which had started to appear from 1968 on state-owned radio stations and **television** channels) became a major source of funding for both television and radio in the 1980s (particularly affecting the fast-expanding private stations and channels), thereby vastly extending its influence as a means of mass communication. Even in the case of state-owned television channels, advertising revenue has grown faster than licence revenue, taking the maximum advertising time per hour to twelve minutes in 1995. As a social practice, advertising has itself started to attract media attention (the **M6** television channel offers a popular weekly programme *Culture pub*), and *publicitaires* (admen) have gained in social recognition via such figures as Jacques Séguéla of RSCG (who masterminded the 1988 **Mitterrand** presidential campaign) and Bernard Cathelat of the Centre de Communication Avancée (Centre for Advanced Communication), linked to the group Havas, who has published many books on *socio-styles* or *styles de vie* (lifestyles), outlining a sociological method for analysing consumer motivations.

Advertising is a communication process which involves a number of social actors: advertisers (manufacturing or service industries, state or other public agencies, etc.), advertising agencies which create the advertising messages, the media (the five traditionally recognized *grands médias*: **cinema**, press, radio, television and 'outdoors' which includes bill boards, to which one must add the new electronic technologies, particularly relevant to France since the launching of Minitel) and the consumers as target audience. The growing importance of a category of intermediate companies, the *centrales d'achat*, such as Carat France, who purchase the crucial advertising space and time and negotiate between advertisers, agencies and media companies, is one of the more striking organizational changes which have affected this sector in France since the 1960s. The reliance of advertising on the media to deliver commercial messages, and, conversely, the increasing financial dependence of the media on advertising revenue, raise the issue of whose voices are heard and compete for influence in society. The new practice of advertisers sponsoring programmes is likely to extend their influence. The idea of public space and public service (which has been an important concept in the cultural history of France and which is echoed in the French term for advertising, *publicité*) is often seen by critics as losing out to commercial forces.

Advertising as a discourse is one of the most pervasive means of mass communication and lies at the heart of popular culture; its omnipresence ensures that all members of society receive advertising messages in the course of their most mundane activities and, as such, these messages are a powerful indicator of a society's values and practices. Whether advertising is seen as a mirror of society or as capable of shaping attitudes and inhibiting or initiating social change has always been a fiercely debated ideological question. A number of laws regulate advertising – for instance when it involves children or where it concerns particular types of products or services. Advertising of tobacco was banned in 1991 (Evin law) and alcohol advertising subjected to restrictions. The Sapin law of 1993, aimed at preventing political and economic corruption, introduced strict financial rules affecting advertising groups. The BVP (Bureau de Vérification de la Publicité) and the CSA (Conseil Supérieur de l'Audiovisuel) are the main bodies concerned with the regulation and fairness of advertising. Comparative advertising was made legal in 1992 but is strictly regulated.

In the 1950s, Roland **Barthes** pioneered academic interest in popular discourses by his bold semiological analyses published in *Mythologies*; meanwhile, the forms of advertising discourse have evolved and become increasingly sophisticated as both creators and receivers of messages have become conversant with the codes of this communication process. Since advertising messages are ephemeral and dependent on media space and time, the optimum conditions of reception necessitate a frequent renewal of forms and techniques. Initially a discourse that spoke directly to passive consumers and attempted to persuade them with arguments for the superiority of a product or a service, it has gradually resorted to more subtle forms of seduction: an attractive lifestyle or highly desirable but often unreachable qualities such as glamour, beauty or a return to an ideal state of nature are presented, by means of visual juxtaposition and semantic transfer, as irresistibly within the consumer's grasp. A new form of seduction which seeks to entertain the receiver signals a shift in the positions of the participants in the process of mass communication: potential consumers are invited to partake in a narrative (a brief **soap** opera) or a humorous scenario, or to solve a puzzle, the product or service sometimes only performing an accessory function. The need to provide instant viewer's interest, given the cost of advertising space, is thus generating new forms

of exchange and interactive behaviour. The multiplicity of art forms contributing to the increasingly sophisticated production of messages (video clips, computer-produced images and graphics, special visual effects, electronically mixed jingles), while providing an experimental ground for musicians and artists, is also pointing at a redistribution of boundaries between discourses. Advertising is increasingly intertextual. It has been described as an unstable and parasitic discourse which feeds on the whole range of cultural forms of expression of a society. The culture of advertising, meanwhile, is becoming internationalized; the cost of producing advertising films for television is so high that agencies seek to produce messages which can be recognized and decoded everywhere in the world for products (such as cars or training shoes) which are equally available everywhere. The now frequent use of internationally acclaimed film stars, athletes or supermodels adds to this process of globalization. Analysing the specificity of French advertising discourse is thus becoming less relevant. Although French agencies are proud of some of their creative achievements, the sophistication of some of the British advertisements from the 1960s onwards has been rarely matched, it seems, by their French (or North American) counterparts. However, there are a number of ways in which the national environment is relevant.

Borrowings from other cultural discourses, including high culture, demonstrate the ability of French advertisements to rely readily on a shared cultural heritage transmitted through the education system. The French as a nation have always enjoyed games involving language: advertising slogans constitute an immensely rich field where language-specific creativity is deployed and where the receiver's attention is engaged with riddles and puns or highly organized rhythms and sound patterns. It is also a good experimental ground for new modish words: advertisements promptly pick up on shared but elusive linguistic innovations, even if regulators will occasionally attempt to intervene in the process (the case of the 1994

Toubon law banning the use of foreign words in advertising is a good example).

National stereotypes frequently used to promote certain foreign products will clearly depend on a specifically French perception of, for instance, Italian, English or American behaviour patterns.

More importantly, gender stereotyping needs to be considered in the light of French cultural practices. Nudity, particularly female (and increasingly, since the 1970s, male), is used considerably more in French advertising than it is in Britain or the United States (but probably less than in some Scandinavian countries). This is often seen as reflecting French people's less puritanical outlook and their easy relationship with the body; none the less, the casual and constant representation of people as sex objects cannot be ignored as irrelevant. More controversial is the subservient, not to say degrading, role often assigned to women in French advertising discourse. The objective situation of women in French society has changed considerably since 1945. French advertising seemed for several decades impervious to this new situation, but since the 1970s a number of changes have become visible. Society's changed perception of gender roles and sexuality has found many echoes; particularly in the 1980s, when Yvette **Roudy**, the Ministre de la Condition Féminine, started a campaign protesting against the humiliating representation of women in advertising and a deliberate attempt was made to convey both men and women in a new light: images of caring or domesticated fathers, and assertive businesswomen displaying their new social confidence in traditionally male environments and occupations, began to appear. However, given the capacity for advertising discourse to function intertextually and its increasing use of humour, which is one of the hallmarks of the new styles of advertisements, many of these examples can arguably be interpreted as more of a playful acknowlegement that gender relations have become high-profile than a genuine attempt to reflect women's changed reality and aspirations to social equality. Reversals of (or allusions to) old stereotypes, allowing the receiver to engage

humorously with a scene from which he or she can feel detached, do little to change deeply ingrained perceptions. Judging by the dominant messages conveyed by advertisements in **women's magazines,** there is little evidence that the late twentieth century is offering new perspectives on gender (and indeed race and **class**) representation. French feminist organizations seem reluctant to intervene.

Advertising as a prime vehicle of mass communication and mass culture has been at the heart of the cultural debate in France since 1945. More than in many Western countries, it has been held in utter contempt for its vulgarity or accused of being manipulative and degrading by successive generations of intellectuals scornful of mass culture generally. Its link with capitalism has been one of the reasons for its low esteem among left-wing intellectuals, but official **cultural policy** under the Gaullist regime also denied it any value, favouring all forms of high culture which it tried to disseminate among the masses. The first signs of a change came in the 1980s, when some high-profile intellectuals started to embrace the new Americanized way of life. The younger generations are particularly open in their enjoyment of the newly shared media and advertising culture, as is demonstrated by the success of '*la nuit des publivores*' (an all-night event where advertisements from all over the world are shown to a jingle-chanting audience). However, advertising and its easily attainable pleasures is still regarded with deep suspicion by sections of the more educated French population.

BÉATRICE DAMAMME-GILBERT

See also: alchohol/cigarettes/drugs; anglomanie/franglais; feminism (movements/groups); radio (state-owned)

Further reading

Barthes, R. (1973) *Mythologies*, St Albans: Paladin. (French edition (1957) Paris: Seuil.)
Brochand, B. and Landrevie, J. (1993), *Le*

Publicitor, Paris: Dalloz (a mine of information on French advertising).

Chapman, R. and Hewitt, N. (eds) (1992) *Popular Culture and Mass Communication in Twentieth-Century France*, Lampeter: Edwin Mellen Press (contains several articles presenting different perspectives on French advertising).

Cornuéjols, C. (1992) 'Gender Roles in French Advertisements in the 1980s', *French Review*, 66, 2: 201–21 (an upbeat review of changes).

Grunig, B. (1990), *Les Mots de la publicité*, Paris: Presses du CNRS (a detailed analysis of French advertising slogans).

agriculture

French agriculture is by far the most important in Europe. A radical policy of modernization was implemented from the 1950s, later associated with Europe's Common Agricultural Policy (CAP). The strategy has been successful, but its consequences include a series of social problems such as regional desertification, the ageing of farming communities and the disappearance of debt-ridden small farms, together with a deterioration of the rural environment. Recent reforms of the CAP and the gradual opening of agricultural markets to international competition signal the ultimate failure of the 'modern family farm' model which was at the root of the policy consensus since the 1950s.

French agriculture is diverse. There is little common ground between large wheat producers such as Champagne, where extensive cultivation of fields extends way over the horizon, creating one of the most deserted landscapes to be found in Europe; specialized vineyards in Burgundy; and areas in the Alp foot-hills or around the Massif Central, where ageing communities die out, still practising mixed production in small farms. A common feature, however, is that all of the above are beset with problems and conflicts born of a rapid and brutal modernization process which has changed the face of French agriculture beyond recognition.

These often assume an importance in French political life which may seem disproportionate to the actual social weight of agriculture. But the lateness of the modernization process, the continued pace of rural exodus, and nostalgia for a fast-disappearing 'traditional' society, form part of the cultural background of a majority of the adult population; hence the frequent support given to farmers in their protest actions.

The cultural relevance of agriculture is still considerable. French children still learn the adage pronounced by Sully, a minister of King Henry IV, according to whom '*Labourage et pâturage sont les deux mamelles de la France*' ('Ploughing and grazing are breasts feeding France'). France was indeed the corn-belt of Europe in the seventeenth century. However, it fell behind in the early twentieth century, withdrawing into a protectionist stance and lacking in investments. Then the French countryside took on the forms which have been used by writers such as Giono, in *Regain*, or Pagnol, in his *L'Eau des collines* novel or in recollections such as *La Gloire de mon père*. Both, in different ways, set their writing in an early twentieth-century Provence left behind by a fast-changing urban France.

Prospects for French agriculture changed in the 1950s. Modernization policies were pursued by successive governments, supported by the main farmers' union, the FNSEA. This consensual approach aimed to preserve the family farm unit by providing the means to modernize. Policies were organized around market stabilization strategies, cheap finances (through the Crédit Agricole), processing and marketing tools (especially through co-operatives which developed considerably since the 1960s), the restructuring of land property (for instance, *remembrement* (reassembling) seeks to create larger fields through land exchanges in order to facilitate mechanization), and hefty subsidies for drainage, hedge cutting, etc. The CAP reinforced this approach, guaranteeing and subsidizing internal prices and protecting European production against imports through a common tariff barrier. The system was soon eating most of the EU budget, creating huge stocks and benefiting mostly the larger farm businesses but also providing a fragile lifeline to the smaller family units. These policies were successful on a purely quantitative level. Undercapitalized and antiquated in the 1940s, French agriculture changed into a highly productive and technically up-to-date industry which, in the early 1990s, provided more than a quarter of EU production – this proportion rises to more than a third for **wine**, not surprisingly. France has also become the world's second agricultural exporter, behind the USA.

However, this technical success has its darker side. Ultimately, the original aims of the postwar modernization programme have not been achieved – the medium-sized family farm is disappearing and the environmental, social and cultural costs of ensuring food security are considerable. In environmental terms, requirements of modern, mechanized agriculture, compounded with subsidized drainage, hedge-cutting and soil 'improvement', have caused a complete change of landscape and a general deterioration of biological diversity in many regions. The concepts of *terroir* or *pays* (a sub-regional geographical areas forming an ecological, historical, cultural and agricultural unit) have lost their relevance, despite a recent fashionable comeback. At a social level, the consequences of modernization policies have been severe. The number of farms and the size of the workforce are still falling. The population active in agriculture was reduced from 3.9 to 2.1 million people between 1962 and 1975, and continued to fall thereafter to only 1.2 million in 1993. It can be expected to fall further, since more than half of French farmers were aged 50 or more in the early 1990s, and the average farm surface area is only 28 hectares (against 65 hectares in Great Britain). Therefore, rural exodus still affects more remote regions, with local services slowly disappearing and whole areas becoming deserted.

These trends have accelerated further with changes in the CAP since the early 1980s. Despite numerous protests, from specialized fruit growers to cattle owners (particularly affected in 1996 by bovine spongiform encephalopathy, or 'Mad Cow Disease'), the highly protective system is being dismantled. The resistance of farmers has a long history – for instance the *Révolte des Vignerons* (Winemakers' Revolt) in the south of France in 1907, quelled by the army, is still in farmers' memories, and their descendants violently clashed with police forces again in 1975–6 against the EC market regulations. Protests against imports of Spanish fruit or British lamb have been part of life for decades, as smaller farmers, often heavily in debt, find themselves unable to survive – their feeling of betrayal towards agricultural policy's failure to maintain the family farm model of the 1950s explains brutal flare-ups which are sometimes difficult to understand from abroad.

FRANÇOIS NECTOUX

See also: *dirigisme*; economy; European economic integration; European Union

Further reading

Flockton, C. and Kofman, E. (1989) *France*, London: Paul Chapman (this includes a succinct description of the modernization process of agriculture).

Mendras, H. (1970) *La Fin des paysans*, Paris: Armand Colin (this remains one of the best accounts of the sociological consequences of modernization).

Weber, E. (1979) *Peasants into Frenchmen*, London: Chatto & Windus (this analysis of the ways in which rural agricultural societies became part of France in the nineteenth century has become a classic work).

AIDS

AIDS (Acquired Immune Deficiency Syndrome) is known as *Sida* (*Syndrome Immunodéficitaire Acquis*) in French, and is the terminal outcome of infection with the Human Immunodeficiency Virus (HIV) – *Virus Immunodéficitaire Humain* (VIH).

Since the discovery of the HIV virus by

Professor Luc Montaigner in 1983, the word AIDS (*Sida*) has been indelibly imposed on to human consciousness, and interpersonal contact and conduct irrevocably affected. Although originally believed to target specific 'risk groups' such as intravenous drug users, haemophiliacs and homosexuals, AIDS is now known to be a danger to all and a particular problem when compounded by poverty, be it in the Old, New or Third World.

By the end of this century, the World Health Organization (WHO) estimates that there will be between 20 and 40 million victims of HIV infection worldwide, with some 90 per cent of the cases in the Third World. Of all European countries, France is the most affected by AIDS – 1995 figures give total reported cases of HIV infection as 36,982, with some 60.8 per cent of these having died; the same estimates give four new cases of infection in Paris per day.

French government reaction and campaigns could arguably be described as slow, perhaps due to the traditional Republican respect of the individual coupled with a reluctance to admit to the existence of smaller groups within the *République unie et indivisible* (the united and indivisible Republic). It was not until 1988, for example, that the government established the Agence Nationale de Recherches sur le Sida (ANRS) to co-ordinate research into the syndrome. Its activities include the launch of the 1991 *Analyse des Comportements Sexuels en France*, a telephone enquiry involving some 20,000 people aged between 18 and 69 followed up by a longer questionnaire completed by the 25 per cent or so reporting sexual conduct judged to put them at risk from the virus. Before this, in 1988, the first ever advertising campaigns for condoms were produced in France. Previous pro-natalist legislation had banned all such material.

It was left instead to interested groups in the voluntary sector to become involved earlier. 1983, for example, saw the creation of Vaincre Le Sida (VLS), the first anti-AIDS group, followed by Aides, founded in 1984 by **Foucault's** partner Daniel Defert.

In 1986, AIDS in France became a notifiable disease, and 1987 saw the first sales of AZT, a drug which helps to fight some effects of HIV infection. Despite a later Anglo-French *Concorde* trial indicating potential mitigating effects of AZT in its treatment of symptoms, the drug continues to be used, more often as part of a 'cocktail' intended to prevent the HIV virus reproducing itself.

Interestingly, the whole question of AIDS as it appears in France has not been polarized by the press as it has been by British journalists, who have created 'innocent' (haemophiliacs, children . . .) and 'guilty' (homosexuals, drug users . . .) victims; it has not tended to be used as an excuse to 'gay-bash' or to pick on minorities owing to France's attitudes towards the public and private life of the individual.

Perhaps the most notorious situation relating to AIDS in France is that of the *affaire du sang contaminé*, which arose in 1985 when it was revealed that the delay in the launch of American testing kits in France until such a time as French ones could be commercialized had resulted in the contamination of blood transfusion stocks and in the subsequent infection of haemophiliacs. One year later, in 1986, the French **social security** system agreed to take on 100 per cent of medical costs incurred by those suffering from AIDS. Those judged responsible for the *affaire* – ministers, doctors and civil servants – were severely criticized. The principal protagonists, including Dr Michel Garetta (former Director of the national Blood Transfusion Service), were sentenced to prison (sentences were confirmed in July 1993). Coincidentally, two more HIV antibody tests were withdrawn in the same year.

More general public awareness was increased on the evening of 7 March 1994. An event unique in French history saw all television channels (and some in Belgium and Luxembourg) transmitting *Sidaction*, a series of programmes about AIDS and those affected by it. This received widespread press coverage and arguably contributed to greater knowledge of the syndrome. The experiment was repeated on 30 November 1995 – the eve of World AIDS Day (1 December). The success of the March 1996 *Sidaction* was almost negated by the difference of approach favoured by members of radical proponents of **gay activism**, ACT-UP.

AIDS has also led to the establishment of groups aimed at preventing the spread of the disease. The Syndicat National des Entreprises Gaies (SNEG) was founded in 1990 and acts as a means of making information on prevention available to its membership of some 600 who, as the organization's name suggests, are gay- and lesbian-run companies. Their activities are not exclusively directed at this base, however – SNEG worked closely with the Ministry of Health in the elaboration of the summer 1995 AIDS awareness poster campaign.

The presence of AIDS worldwide has had an indelible effect on human behaviour and conduct. In its position as the AIDS capital of Europe, France has not always acted with sensitivity or alacrity, leaving activists and those most directly affected to act as the government's conscience. While at the forefront of research into the discovery of AIDS, France still has further to go in dealing with the repercussions.

STEVE WHARTON

See also: gay writing; Guibert, Hervé

Further reading

ACT-UP Paris (1994) *Le Sida: combien de divisions?*, Paris: Éditions Dagorno (a good overview of the motivations and activities of ACT-UP, written by those most directly involved).

INSEE (1993) 'Le Sida en France 1982–1992', in *Données sociales 1993* [Social Statistics 1993], Paris: Hachette (a dispassionate, 'scientific' discussion of the spread of AIDS in France and of various associated factors).

Martet, C. (1993) *Les combattants du Sida* Paris: Flammarion (the history of ACT-UP in France from one of its founder members).

Paillard, B. (1994) *L'Épidémie – carnets d'un sociologue*, Paris: Stock (a sociologist

recounts his experiences from direct interviews with AIDS sufferers and their families).

Wharton, S. (1996) 'The Pink Economy in France', in Cross, M. (ed.) (1996) *Voices of France*, London: Cassell (an overview of the activities of SNEG).

Aimée, Anouk

b. 1932, Paris

Actor

She appeared as an idealized love-object in Astruc's *Le Rideau cramoisi* of 1953, but is better remembered for her roles for Fellini (*La dolce vita* of 1960 and *8½* of 1963), **Demy** (*Lola* of 1961) and above all Claude Lelouch – *Un homme et une femme* of 1966, the best-known incarnation of her as a sensuous creature of destiny. Her recent screen appearances have been few and far between, and she probably last came to the attention of a British public when she was married to Albert Finney.

KEITH READER

See also: cinema

alcohol, cigarettes, drugs

The consumption of alcohol and cigarettes has frequently played a considerable role in popular conceptions of French society – traditional representations of the French have portrayed them as addicted to *gros rouge* (cheap red wine) and Gauloises. The use of drugs, or *toxicomanie*, has become an issue in France rather later in the contemporary period than *alcoolisme* and *tabagisme*, which, (in the case of drink at least) had a long tradition as an object of concern over public **health** and morals. Evolving cultures of alcohol and tobacco consumption seem to have been influenced by specifically French factors such as the nationalization of the cigarette industry or the electoral importance of rural wine- and tobacco-producing areas, whereas the French experience of drugs seems less influenced by national factors.

The French remain consistently among the highest consumers of alcohol in the European Union. Postwar alcohol consumption has prolonged stereotypical images of the French as quaffers of *petits blancs*, *gros rouge*, *apéro* and *pousse-café* (liqueurs), although with some modifications. In an echo of earlier moral panics about *absinthe*, Pierre **Mendès France** initiated a campaign in 1954 against the alcohol-distilling lobbies, even drinking milk in a prime-ministerial photo call. The atavistic criticisms of PMF's 'unmanliness' which ensued can be seen now to reinforce the argument that the government's aim in controlling the production of low-grade alcohol was as much about modernizing society as it was about freeing the economy or limiting alcoholism. More recently, alcohol consumption has diversified, with opportunities for foreign travel, greater mobility and advertising. Young people have been progressively tempted by Coca-Cola, and new refreshments compete with traditional drinks, either replacing alcohol, or combining with other foreign products in exotic mixes such as *Whisky-Coca*. Yet **wine** remains a major industry, important economically for exports and socially as a provider of employment. It is important to realize that the wine industry produces different types of wine, from aristocratic elite vintages (indicators of *distinction sociale*) to *co-opérative* supermarket reds sold from plastic tanks. Wine drinking covers a multitude of social experiences, whose common denominator is found only in individuals' 'rights' to alcohol abuse and in the fact that drinking American sodas contributes (for some) to turning France into *'une société Coca-Cola'*.

In **Godard**'s 1959 film *A bout de souffle* (Breathless), Jean-Paul **Belmondo** is hardly ever without a cigarette hanging provocatively from his lips, and the girl he pursues is American and blonde – *une blonde américaine* – more attractive than the other women – *les brunes françaises* – who no longer interest him. The story of *tabagisme* in France since 1945 seems

determined by two dynamics: first the move from French *clopes* (slang: cigaretttes) of sometimes dubious quality towards imported American cigarettes of Virginian tobacco; and second, the increasingly negative image of smoking conveyed by medicine. The Société (Nationale) d'Exploitation Industrielle des Tabacs et Allumettes (SEITA) was formed in 1935 to impose government control on the tobacco industry and its tax revenues. During the 1940s and 1950s SEITA Gauloises and Gitanes held a virtual monopoly over smokers which was only relaxed by an increasing availability of American cigarettes, fuelled by the popularity of everything Hollywood and by growing affluence. Embattled by rising tobacco prices and by intense competition, and despite the marketing of *blondes françaises* and low-nicotine cigarettes to compete with US brands which allowed the company to maintain a profitable 45 per cent market share, SEITA was privatized in 1995. Since Marlboros are now France's favourite cigarettes, this privatization perhaps represented the state's final admission that France had finally 'smoked herself American'. The separation between the state and the tobacco industry was also encouraged by perceptions of the government's embarrassing links to an industry with perceived social costs. Effective from January 1993, the *loi Evin* banned tobacco **advertising** and smoking in public places to reduce the burden of smoking illnesses on the health system, but discouraging tobacco consumption diminished tax returns on cigarette sales, reducing the usefulness of SEITA as a national company. The *loi Evin* has been unsuccessful in stopping advertising and in constraining smokers to respect non-smoking areas, mainly because the French believe that to smoke is an inalienable right.

It is more difficult to identify a *spécificité française* in the use and regulation of drugs. Concerning, *la toxicomanie* and the use of *stupéfiants* (narcotics), French society and government entertain complicated opinions about tolerance and *non-permissivité* which, as with the smoking of cigarettes, centre around notions of individual rights. Drug taking first became widespread arguably only in the liberalization of society which followed **May 1968**. Figures show that numbers of drug addicts remained relatively stable during 1946–66, rising rapidly with the use of cannabis, morphine and heroin in the late 1960s and 1970s. In 1989, cannabis was taken by 64 per cent of users, heroin by 33 per cent and cocaine by 2 per cent, although since the late 1980s, when ecstasy and crack became available, their popularity has increased rapidly. Drug taking appears to be a mainly youthful and male phenomenon, since only one in ten users is female and more than 80 per cent are aged between 16 and 30. In the public mind, drug taking is generally held to be a problem affecting urban youth, as illustrated by **Tavernier**'s 1991 film *L627*, which dramatizes the work of a narcotics police team in Paris. In this perspective, although in reality more widespread, drug taking is perceived to be yet another problem of *la banlieue* and of underprivileged **youth culture** born from *exclusion*. Government policy towards drugs has been confused and somewhat ineffective, much work being done by private rather than state organizations, and with the rise of **AIDS** there has been amalgamation of the problems of HIV sufferers and drug addiction, distorting public perceptions.

A final irony of France's experience of alcohol, cigarettes and drugs is that the French are renowned for their costly overconsumption of medicines, particularly tranquillizers of all kinds. While still accepting the traditional drugs of alcohol and nicotine, French society seems yet to come to terms with newer habits of illicit drugs and of prescription pill-popping.

HUGH DAUNCEY

Further reading

Délégation Générale à la Lutte Contre la Drogue (1994) *La Demande sociale de drogues*, Paris: La documentation française (the official approach).

Ehrenberg, A. (ed.) (1992) *État des lieux, textes réunis*, Paris: Éditions Descartes (personal viewpoints).

Algerian war

Immediately preceded by France's catastrophic defeat in the Indochina conflict (1945–54), the Algerian war (1954–62) was the climax of the traumatic French experience of **decolonization**. France's oldest and most important colony, Algeria was home to a million settlers (known as the *pieds-noirs*), together with some 9 million 'Muslims' of Arabo-Berber origin. This large European presence underlay the determination of successive governments to resist Algerian nationalism with massive military force, a strategy further rationalized in terms of the territory's unique legal status as three, theoretically fully integrated *départements* of the Republic. Measures taken included the building of electrified fortifications along Algeria's frontiers with Morocco and Tunisia, the forcible relocation of large sections of the indigenous population, and the mobilization of nearly 3 million metropolitan conscripts over the course of the eight-year campaign against the revolutionary Front de Libération Nationale (FLN). The principal victims of what became a brutal guerrilla war were Algerian civilians (up to a million of whom may have died), with the FLN at least as willing as the French army to use coercion whenever persuasion failed. With neither obvious fronts nor set-piece battles, the war reached a crux with the so-called Battle of Algiers of 1956–7, in which paratroopers made systematic use of torture and summary execution to crush the FLN's bombing networks. Although such tactics enabled the French to achieve military dominance, they also encouraged support for the nationalist cause both within Algeria and abroad. The army's response was a campaign of political 'activism' which culminated, in May 1958, in the collapse of the ineffectual Fourth Republic and the return to power of the country's wartime 'saviour', General Charles de **Gaulle**. De Gaulle, backed by the **armed forces** in the belief that he would safeguard *Algérie française* (French Algeria), quickly realized that the war was politically unwinnable and set about ridding the country of what had become a threat to the Republic and a barrier to postwar reconstruction. Skilfully exploiting his personal prestige, the semi-presidential constitution of the new Fifth Republic, and his incomparable mastery of the mass media, de Gaulle was able finally to break the settler and military stranglehold on Algerian policy. His declaration of the Algerians' right to self-determination on 16 September 1959 was a watershed, prompting armed challenges to his authority by the forces of colonial reaction. Having faced down the *pieds-noirs* during the so-called 'Week of the Barricades' in January 1960, he would overcome an attempted army putsch in April 1961. Subsequent negotiations with the FLN led to a ceasefire on 19 March 1962, with Algerian independence being declared a few months later.

PHILIP DINE

Further reading

Droz, B. and Lever, E. (1982) *Histoire de la guerre d'Algérie, 1954–1962*, Paris: Éditions du Seuil (the best French-language introduction to the war).

Horne, A. (1977) *A Savage War of Peace: Algeria, 1954–1962*, London: Macmillan (still the standard English-language history of the conflict).

Stora, B. (1992) *La Gangrène et l'oubli: la mémoire de la guerre d'Algérie*, Paris: La Découverte (an examination of the difficulties still faced by France and Algeria in coming to terms with the war).

Althusser, Louis

b. 1918, Birmandreïs, Algeria;
d. 1990, La Verrière, Yvelines

Marxist philosopher

A Catholic militant in his youth, Althusser received his political education as a prisoner of war and in 1948 joined the French Communist Party (PCF). As a philosopher at the École Normale Supérieure, he influenced a generation of young people, who responded with enthusiasm to his attempt to revitalize the stultified Marxist theory of the 1950s. Applying his theory of symptomatic reading to the classic texts of **Marxism**, analysing gaps and silences, unanswered questions, as well as answers to unasked questions, he attempted to construct the conceptual system Marx himself had not been able to complete.

Rejecting the interpretation of Marxism as an ethical humanism, which dominated European Communist parties after the Twentieth Congress of the Soviet Communist Party, Althusser denied any continuity with Hegelian philosophy, stressing Marxism's revolutionary originality. In *For Marx* (*Pour Marx*) and *Reading Capital* (*Lire le Capital*), he applied principles learned from the Bachelardian school of historical epistemology to demonstrate that Marxism was a new development, inaugurating the science of history, through an epistemological break with previous ideological, non-scientific thinking. As a science, it was subject only to scientific criteria of validity, not to political pressures. Knowledge production was a process confined solely to the domain of thought, which he defined as theoretical practice. This position owed much to Spinoza's notion that truth contained its own norms of validity, but ran counter to orthodox communism's reflection theory of knowledge, which Althusser rejected as empiricist.

Only scientific knowledge had the status of knowledge; all else was dismissed as ideology, though in his key 1970 essay, 'Ideology and the Ideological State Apparatuses' ('Idéologie et appareils idéologiques d'État'), Althusser admitted that ideology was more than mere lack of knowledge or error. Not only was ideology a social practice, the mode in which individuals operated within the Ideological State

Apparatuses, it was also the vehicle whereby individuals were constituted into subjects, as 'supports' for the reproduction of class relations of production. The theory of the constitution of the subject owed much to Jacques **Lacan**.

Influenced also by **structuralism**, the Althusserian social formation was constituted by combinations of elements, apart from human beings, who did not create these structures nor determine their meaning, but had their own meaning determined by them; history was not made by men, but was a 'process without subject or end(s)'. His theory of overdetermination, rejecting vulgar economic determinism, acknowledged the complexity of real social processes, although it failed to explain the transition from one mode of production to another.

Despite the influence of militant French Maoism, Althusser remained in the PCF. Modifying his position on the autonomy of theory, he adopted a view of philosophy as 'class struggle in theory' from the late 1960s. Politics played a more important role in his theoretical analyses, though his own political involvement receded, until, following the Left's failure in the 1978 elections, he openly criticised the PCF in *What Must Change in the Party* (*Ce qui ne peut plus durer dans le parti communiste*). Dogged by depressive illness, Althusser played no further part in public life after killing his wife in 1980. By then, he had already renounced most of his theoretical principles, though not his faith in the communist movement.

MARGARET MAJUMDAR

See also: class; May 1968; parties and movements

Further reading

Boutang, Y. M. (1992) *Louis Althusser: la formation du mythe (1918–1956)*, Paris: Grasset (first volume of Althusser's biography).

Elliott, G. (1987) *Althusser, the Detour of Theory*, London and New York: Verso (major overview of Althusser's work).
——(ed.) (1994) *Althusser: A Critical Reader*, Oxford and Cambridge, MA: Blackwell (contains bibliography of Althusser's writings, and essays assessing his work and influence).
Kaplan, E. A. and Sprinker, M. (eds) (1993) *The Althusserian Legacy*, London and New York: Verso (assessment of Althusser's legacy from a variety of perspectives).
Majumdar, M.A. (1995) *Althusser and the End of Leninism?*, London and East Haven, CT: Pluto (examines the changes in Althusser's thought, with particular emphasis on the central question of Leninism).

Amont, Marcel

b. 1929, Bordeaux

Singer, real name Jean-Pierre Miramon

Having studied at the Conservatoire, Marcel Amont performed in light operas and musical comedies before turning to cabaret in the 1950s. His very successful career as a solo singer includes appearances at Bobino and the Olympia, tours throughout France and abroad and work on television and in films. Hit songs include the humorous *Un Mexicain* (A Mexican) and *Ping-Pong*.

IAN PICKUP

See also: song/*chanson*

anglomanie/franglais

Anglomania began in the eighteenth century with an enthusiasm for all things English, particularly literature and institutions. This resulted in a massive importation of anglicisms into the vocabulary of French. The trend culminated in R. Étiemble's satirical denunciation of this development in *Parlez-vous franglais?* (1964). He feared that French was evolving into a bastardized Atlantic pidgin and pressed for official action. The French government has attempted to stem this inflow, but with little measurable success.

JO REED

See also: linguistic regulation; Toubon law

Annales

A journal (full title *Annales d'histoire: économies, sociétés, civilisations*) founded by the historians Lucien Febvre and Marc Bloch in 1929, but particularly influential in the postwar period. Influenced by the sociology of Émile Durkheim, and in its turn influential on the work of such as **Foucault**, *Annales* and the school of historiography that bears its name concentrate on 'the study of socio-economic structures and collective phenomena, not on that of events' (*Quid?*). Emmanuel **Le Roy Ladurie** is the best known of figures recently associated with the journal.

KEITH READER

Anouilh, Jean

b. 1910, Bordeaux;
d. 1987, Lausanne

Playwright

Anouilh's works have been among those most performed in the postwar period, and continue to form a popular part of the contemporary repertoire in private and public theatre alike. Many have been played in long runs by famous directors, including most notably **Barsacq** and **Barrault** in the 1940s and 1950s, and today form part of the **Comédie-Française**'s modern repertoire. His plays are noted for their variety in style and subject matter, from comedy-inspired language to history and tradition in

Medea (*Médée*) and *Antigone*. Many of his highly successful works are also noted for their existentialist, philosophical tone and were written at the same time as the works of **Sartre** and **Camus**, the former of whom included Anouilh's plays in his consideration of playwrights as 'forgers of myths' in a 1946 lecture (Bradby 1991), Anouilh's plays are existentialist inasmuch as they exploit the notion of role-playing, with characters representing their role, hence their actions and choices, in terms of inevitability. *Antigone*, first performed in 1944, *The Lark* (*L'Alouette*), and his 1959 *Becket* are good examples of this. However, Anouilh cannot be considered a political playwright *per se*, even though plays such as *Antigone* were particularly successful with wartime Parisian audiences who were quick to relate the psychological struggle in the play to their own personal struggle and choices under occupation. Influenced as a young writer by the work of Pirandello, Anouilh was interested in playing with illusion and reality, hence the use of masks and 'types' as the characters in his work. The latter gave him ample scope for subject matter, ranging from ancient classics to the modern day, since the ideas, situations and attitudes they embodied were timeless and applicable to the human condition no matter what the historical or social setting. Many of his works deal with moral choices and the limitations imposed upon his characters which influence their behaviour. This 'psychological' aspect of his plays, combined with the light, well-crafted tone of his dialogue, has made them great successes with postwar audiences.

ANNIE SPARKS

See also: existentialist theatre; theatre

Further reading

Bradby, D. (1991) *Modern French Theatre 1940–1990*, Cambridge: Cambridge University Press (contains a chapter on philosophical melodrama, dealing with Anouilh's work alongside that of Sartre and Camus).

Vier, J. (1976) *Le Théâtre de Jean Anouilh*, Paris: SEDES.

anthropology and ethnology

As an academic discipline anthropology was established relatively late in France. Despite a distinguished tradition of 'armchair' anthropology (Durkheim, Mauss, Lévy-Bruhl), specialized fieldwork was not undertaken until the 1930s, symbolically inaugurated with the famous Dakar–Djibouti expedition in 1931–3. This first generation of fieldworkers was instrumental in the notable expansion of French anthropology in the postwar years.

The development of anthropology in postwar France cannot be properly understood without reference to the sociology of Durkheim and Mauss earlier in the century. In his later work Émile Durkheim (d. 1917) made extensive use of ethnographic data in his attempt to formulate a universal theory of social cohesion, and ethnological interests featured strongly in the research team that formed around his journal, *L'Année sociologique*. It was, however, Durkheim's nephew and close collaborator, Marcel Mauss (d. 1950), often called the 'father' of French ethnology, who came to specialize in the discipline and who made a crucial contribution to its academic provision in the university. The phenomenally erudite Mauss was an inspirational teacher to many of the first generation of professional ethnologists; he was also author of the remarkable *The Gift* (*Essai sur le don*), one of the most influential texts in twentieth-century anthropology. The main thesis of the essay is that exchange in non-Western cultures does not have the utilitarian and individualist functions it possesses in industrial capitalist societies. The exchange of gifts in traditional societies is a collective phenomenon, and must be viewed as a 'total social fact' to the extent that it involves not only economic, but also moral, religious, legal and cultural-aesthetic considerations. As such, gift exchange is an important agent of social cohesion, ensuring the integration of different social groups and the resolution of potential conflict between them.

The influence of Mauss's theory of the gift extends well beyond the academic disciplines of sociology and anthropology, and is discernible in much contemporary French thought. In anthropology, the most important mediator of Mauss and the Durkheimian school in the postwar period is Claude **Lévi-Strauss**. While the fieldwork initiated in the 1930s was providing French ethnology with a growing empirical base, the discipline suffered from a distinct lack of theorization. Lévi-Strauss's originality was to combine the insights of Mauss's theory of exchange with binary models borrowed from structural linguistics, as demonstrated in his first major work, *The Elementary Structures of Kinship* (*Les Structures élémentaires de la parenté*), published in 1949. His work on kinship structures not only brought a new level of theoretical sophistication to French ethnology, but also suggested a wider programme of research for the discipline. Since Durkheim and Mauss, ethnological studies had focused primarily on aspects of religion and ritual, notable examples including Alfred Métraux's studies of voodoo practices in Haiti or Marcel Griaule's work on Dogon cosmology. Lévi-Strauss's venture into the highly technical domain of kinship relations moved the focus from religion to social organization, traditionally the preserve of British anthropology. Significantly, when after 1950 he himself began to specialize in the anthropology of religions, Lévi-Strauss concentrated on myth rather than ritual, on non-Western thought rather than non-Western religion.

Lévi-Strauss's attempt to construct a rigorous theoretical framework for French anthropology needs to be viewed in the context of a general realignment of the *sciences humaines* (human sciences) in postwar France. Lévi-Strauss contributed actively to this realignment in that he presented ethnology as no longer the adjunct of sociology, as it had been for Durkheim and even for Mauss, but as a discipline in its own right, with its own distinct objects, methods and goals. More than this, he expanded the conventional definition of the discipline by substituting the term '*anthropologie*' for the more common '*ethnologie*', distinguishing between three stages or moments of anthropological inquiry: ethnography, the preliminary collection of data in the field; ethnology, the synthesis of data provided by ethnography; and anthropology, the comparative analysis of ethnological material, leading to a general theory of human society. Lévi-Strauss's redefinition of the scope of anthropology meant that it was not restricted to the so-called 'primitive' societies which had traditionally been the object of ethnology. It also meant that the previous subordination of ethnology to sociology was reversed, sociology becoming in effect a subsidiary component of anthropology.

The implications of Lévi-Strauss's ambitious programme for anthropology were obviously more general than its historically ambivalent relationship with sociology. This programme placed anthropology at the very centre of the human sciences, also challenging more firmly established disciplines such as history and philosophy. The new historian Fernand **Braudel**'s famous article 'La longue durée', published in 1958, was allegedly written in response to Lévi-Strauss's *Structural Anthropology* (*Anthropologie structurale*), the seminal collection of essays on the scope and methods of the new anthropology. For his part, the philosopher and historian Michel **Foucault** anticipated the dissolution and absorption of philosophy into other disciplines, presenting his 'archaeology' of the human sciences as an attempt to view our own cultural history with the sense of defamiliarization and distantiation achieved in Lévi-Strauss's anthropology.

Despite the undisputed influence of Lévi-Strauss, it would be wrong to attribute these interdisciplinary effects of anthropology solely to his individual initiative. The special status of ethnology in the years following the war can be explained by a number of factors specific to that context. The devastation caused by the war was psychological as well as physical: for the second time in the century Europe had unleashed destructive forces which had enveloped the world, and the wave of **decolonization** which followed the war was both a

reminder of European responsibility and a symptom of the decline of the former colonial powers. These events caused many to question the pre-eminence of European culture and consciousness and also to criticize its ethnocentrism. In this context it was therefore logical that ethnology, as a privileged mediator of non-Western cultures, should become the special focus of such questioning and criticism. Indeed, in the 1950s ethnology came to be regarded as a 'new humanism', with a wider vision of humanity than the traditional philosophical version of humanism, whose conception of the individual subject was culture-specific and thus far from achieving the universality it claimed. The resultant sense of the diversity of human existence was also accompanied by an acute awareness of the increasing homogenization of the post-colonial world, subject as it was to the continuing influence of Western civilization. Again, ethnology became the repository of alternative values, values different to those of an increasingly consumerist and materialistic society. This mood and these ideas were eloquently expressed in Lévi-Strauss's autobiographical account *Tristes tropiques*, published in 1955 in Jean Malaurie's aptly named *Terre humaine* series. The book struck a chord not only among the French intelligentsia but also with a wider literate public, thus confirming ethnology's position as the human science most attuned to the complexities and ambiguities of the modern world.

Lévi-Strauss's successful promotion of anthropology has sometimes tended to overshadow the achievements of his other French colleagues, whose contribution to the discipline has often been no less distinguished (Bastide, Balandier, Dumont, Griaule, **Leiris**, Métraux). Nevertheless, it was Lévi-Strauss who was the most influential in bringing an anthropological perspective to the wider intellectual debates which have traditionally been so important in France, and it was his formulation of a structural anthropology which inspired the movement known as **structuralism**. At the same time, his version of anthropology did not go unchallenged. One notable criticism within the discipline came from ethnologists such as the

Africanist Georges Balandier, who argued that while Lévi-Strauss's structural analysis might be appropriate to the small-scale communities he had studied in the rainforests of Brazil – societies with relatively little contact with the outside world – it was entirely inappropriate to the analysis of, for example, the substantially larger and rapidly changing societies of the African continent. The implication of this criticism was that anthropology should resist the temptation to idealize the exotic culture as an isolate untouched by history and instead attempt to understand the difficult process of the adaptation of traditional cultures to the modern world.

CHRISTOPHER JOHNSON

Further reading

Bonte, P. and Izard, M. (eds) (1992) *Dictionnaire de l'ethnologie et de l'anthropologie* [*Dictionary of Ethnology and Anthropology*], Paris: PUF (some useful entries on the history of French anthropology, with detailed biographies of its most eminent figures).

Lévi-Strauss, C. (1967) *Les Structures élémentaires de la parenté*, Paris and La Haye: Mouton & Co./Maison des Sciences de l'Homme. Translated J. H. Bell, J. R. von Sturmer and R. Needham (1969) *The Elementary Structures of Kinship*, Boston: Beacon Press.

——(1955) *Tristes tropiques*, Paris: Plon. Translated J. and D. Weightman (1984) *Tristes tropiques*, Harmondsworth: Penguin.

——(1958) *Anthropologie structurale*, Paris: Plon. Translated C. Jacobson and B. Grundfest Schoepf (1977) *Structural Anthropology 1*, Harmondsworth: Penguin.

Mauss, M. (1950) *Essai sur le don*, in *Sociologie et anthropologie*, Paris: PUF. Translated W. D. Halls (1990) *The Gift*, London and New York: Routledge.

Apostrophes

Television programme

A book programme, produced and presented by Bernard Pivot, on Antenne 2 (now **France 2**) on Friday evening, from January 1975 to June 1990 (724 programmes in all). This award-winning chat show, attracting audiences ranging from two to six million viewers, was credited with a highly significant and controversial influence on intellectual life (which was much criticized by Régis **Debray**). An appearance on *Apostrophes* could make or break a new book: the impact on sales was immediately visible in bookshops on Saturday morning. Pivot's appeal lay in his fair-minded independence, pitching discussion at a level accessible to a mass audience.

PAM MOORES

architecture, urban planning and housing after 1945

French architecture was traditionally inspired by a very strong classical tradition sustained by the state-backed École des Beaux-Arts in Paris, After about 1900, an alternative, modern architecture sprang up, partly on the basis of new, industrial techniques led by reinforced concrete. After 1914, classical styles largely disappeared, but they were replaced by eclectic treatments rather than by distinctively modern design, despite the efforts of leading modern architects such as Auguste Perret and **Le Corbusier**. Slow French economic growth in the 1930s contributed to this lack of clear progress. Even after 1945, reference to the past was implicit in many new buildings and planned layouts. The result was often inspired by order and symmetry, and sensitive, human treatment sometimes suffered.

Under the **Vichy** regime (1940–4), architecture looked back to traditional French society. After the **Liberation**, only the devastated areas saw much new construction, and a great deal of this echoed or recreated earlier building, using what were known as 'regionalist' styles. Perret's rebuilt Le Havre (1945–63), with its geometrical plan, big axial avenues and modular concrete buildings, was the country's biggest and best example of modern planning and architecture until the 1960s. Its monochrome concrete surfaces, horizontal emphases and repetition were tolerable in Perret's impressive plan, but their dull and inferior application to anonymous housing estates across France were no substitute for a mature competence in modern architecture. Public buildings drew heavily on concrete-related materials and styles, and on metal components like those developed by Jean Prouvé. Overall, concrete elevations and their related glazing often recalled 1930s design until the late 1950s. The main novelty was an enhanced gigantism, behind which lay the inspiration of reinforced concrete.

The biggest area of divergence from this conformity was church architecture. Following a long tradition, church architects sought originality and strong statements after 1945. Especially influential was Auguste Perret's concrete, towered church of St-Joseph, Le Havre, built between 1949 and 1956. Powerful, ribbed vaults and soaring, angular towers gave many churches a timeless quality which looked awkward or quaint alongside the new housing blocks. Many of the churches now completed had been started in the 1930s and design adjustments were often made, especially to the interiors. Churches had little influence on the rest of contemporary architecture, therefore, and became even more detached as time passed. Le Corbusier's Notre-Dame-du-Haut, at Ronchamp (1951–5), and the convent of La Tourette (1957–60), were isolated masterworks by an architect who built little secular work after the early 1950s.

An architecture of mass housing did not develop extensively until the 1950s, when the country made strenuous efforts to make up its serious housing backlog, signalled by the shacks and shanty towns around the big cities, and the crowded inner slums. Public housing was the main solution. Le Corbusier's expensive, experimental housing blocks (unités d'habitation) failed to multiply, but French architects and engineers perfected industrial methods of construction. The main guidance here was provided by the Ministry of Reconstruction and Urbanism, which had been given the task of producing mass housing after the war. The traditional concrete specialist, Marcel Lods (1891–1978), was widely followed, even though his work was redolent of the 1930s. The result was a diffusion of mass designs which (ironically) represented a triumph for Le Corbusier's post-1930 Radiant City urban concepts, without the accompanying detail and quality. French pre-eminence in reinforced concrete since before the war, combined with a lack of expertise in modern architecture after it, produced standardized treatments which were often tedious. The resulting simple, symmetrical blocks offered little scope to the architect and the layouts were generally repetitive, with geometrical effects spreading over wide areas, together with minimal landscaping and few public buildings. Most of the flats were in slabs but there were also many towers, demonstrating French prowess in reinforced concrete but revealing a lack of social planning. Individual towers were sometimes used to liven up slab estates, but this scarcely qualified as creative architecture. In the 1950s and 1960s much of the new suburban housing was in the form of grands ensembles (large multi-storey housing estates) such as the notorious Sarcelles, north of Paris. Developed with repetitive towers and slabs, they were laid out on geometrical lines. Housing up to 40,000 people, they created a new urban environment which soon disturbed the French public. Ironically, much of the inspiration for this mass architecture came from the eighteenth century, whose symmetry and rationalism were applied to popular housing by French architects in the absence of a training in modern design.

Similar designs were built in the French colonies of North Africa. A high-rise tradition was lacking here, but the French architects applied the same techniques as in France, except that Arab forms and detailing were often included. Climatic factors were fully considered and the blocks were grouped together to create shade. Public buildings often acknowledged local forms, with arcades, white surfaces and, often, arched openings and loggias. Apartments built for rich Europeans were visibly open to air and light and they had a luxurious appearance, like the Liberté block of luxury flats in Casablanca (1961). Most of the architects, though trained in France, specialized in colonial work and continued into the 1960s after independence.

By the 1960s, prefabrication was highly developed and architectural repetition became even more pronounced. Curved and asymmetrical layouts became more common in the 1960s, but the volume of the structures tended to increase at the same time. Industrialized concrete techniques were now being applied to the building of blocks of flats on a scale unrivalled in Europe. New public buildings were now almost without exception in a modern style. In Paris, the UNESCO building (1958), the exhibition hall at the Défense (1958), and the ORTF headquarters (1963) featured simple, efficient modernism and geometrical forms in gigantic structures. These projects emphasized the growing international role of Paris, but they soon influenced public buildings elsewhere in France. Urban renewal often emphasized space, geometry and height, with the gigantic Part-Dieu scheme in Lyon crowned in 1974 by the awesome, cylindrical Tour du Crédit Lyonnais. This phase of gigantism on geometrical lines still tended to reveal some of the deficiencies of French architects in modern design and in the later 1960s architectural education was reformed to make its products more adaptable. From 1969, President Georges **Pompidou** encouraged modern architecture through his influence on big competitions such as that for the **Pompidou Centre** in Paris. The president especially favoured tall towers, and by the 1970s a number of these broke the traditional flat skyline in Paris and the big provincial cities like Lyon. Meanwhile, Le Corbusier at last achieved national recognition as the guiding spirit of French architecture in the 1960s. André Wogensky's Hauts-de-Seine pre-

fecture at Nanterre (1967) epitomized his new influence.

French economic difficulties after 1973 created a complex context for new architecture. Modernism, its reputation tarnished by much of the cheap housing of the 1960s, and the tall Paris office towers like the Tour Montparnasse (1973), was partly replaced by cheapened versions of traditional and vernacular styles. The conservation of historic districts under the **Malraux** act of 1962 created a new interest in the old. Popular preference for small, individual houses was reflected on the outskirts of growing towns and in the new towns (*villes nouvelles*) planned around Paris. The École des Beaux-Arts was reformed in 1968 in the wake of the Paris student demonstrations. Its new structure of eight largely independent teaching units in Paris, with a number of provincial centres, encouraged variety and independence in the early 1970s. However, modernism, which had only just made its mark, did not completely disappear, and pure **postmodernism** on American lines did not develop in France. As in the last century, national traditions provided the main lines of continuity. Even the cheapest buildings, such as blocks of flats and offices, moved away from brutal repetition to smoother, asymmetrical, varied treatments incorporating water and greenery. Colour was given a bigger role than before 1970, though grey and white monochrome lived on, with primary colours used in panels or blazes. The ubiquitous grey marble floor slab set the tone for many a new public building, not least in Carlos Ott's new Paris opera house (1984). Preformed concrete components, often emphasized by the expansion gaps between them, remained common.

Overall, French architecture absorbed the new respect for the past which grew up in France, as elsewhere in Europe. The Pompidou Centre at Paris – designed by Renzo Piano and Richard Rogers after a big international competition, and completed in 1977 – was blatantly modern but its failure to create a school in France reflected the big shift in opinion. The 'new modern architecture' which grew up from around 1975 was based on ideas of tradition and an organic relationship between site and adjoining buildings. A human scale was sought, and new buildings were often attached directly to existing frontages. Steel, often combined with glass in atria and canopies, was used more often and more visibly, and reinforced concrete was used in a more restrained fashion. High-quality bricks were often used to stress artisanal traditions, as in Paul Chemetov's huge brick apartment house at the Porte de Pantin (1981). Elsewhere, brick panels were often set in concrete frames, emphasizing a human scale. The Catalan architect, Ricardo Bofill, who built widely in Paris in the 1970s for public clients, exaggerated this historicism while seeking a rich social life, via an architectural theatricality. His Espaces d'Abraxas (1978–83), a concrete neoclassical estate at Noisy-le-Grand, won worldwide acclaim for its expressionist romanticism, and influenced many French housing architects, though mainly in the direction of visual effects. The greatest scope was in the new towns, where French architects had much freedom. Best described as 'neo-modern', the new approach both modernized and humanized France's multi-storey cities, being applicable to both old and new districts. In effect, it allowed history to reinforce the French urban habitat. However, many French architects continued to work in close association with the state, as they had since the war, and the observer could detect a degree of repetition in schemes across the country.

Outside the city centres, in the new towns, and in the small towns of traditional France, a shift occurred from the early 1970s towards the individual house and away from the block of flats. American influence helped to ensure that, even when built by large developers, these received varied treatment. The decline of public sector building between the 1970s and the 1990s produced growing numbers of these individual houses, with the architects of both developers and private clients recreating traditional forms, often reminiscent of rural life.

Commercial buildings, which multiplied from the later 1950s, conformed to the tradition of continuous frontages and constant heights, together with, in many cases, traditional materials. Residential buildings made some use of traditional materials and forms, with mansard roofs returning to favour. The persistence of nineteenth-century building regulations contributed to this result and encouraged conservatism among architectects. President **Mitterrand**'s Parisian Grands Projets in the 1980s and the early 1990s combined modern architecture with respect for the historic Parisian environment. The eight major projects announced in 1982 were gradually complemented by other schemes. The styles varied, but the neo-modern was the dominant theme. Their scale varied from I. M. Pei's deferential pyramid at the Louvre (1988) to J. O. von Spreckelsen's great arch at the Défense (1989), whose grandeur was much valued.

French architecture since 1945 has witnessed the persistence of a national, historic tradition, tempered by an imported modernism. From the 1970s, a return to tradition took place, while the best features of modern architecture were retained or adapted. The resulting continuity allowed French architecture to retain the best of the past while encouraging good design. The design emphasis switched from individual buildings to ensembles, and by the 1980s a new urban aesthetic had emerged, based on intimate space with a hint of an older tradition in which people were the masters of their cities, rather than the victims of brutal modernity.

ANTHONY SUTCLIFFE

See also: architecture under Mitterrand; Liberation and épuration

Further reading

Basdevant, D. (1971) *L'Architecture française des origines à nos jours*, Paris: Hachette (full historical survey until the 1970s).

Béhar, M. and Salama, M. (1985) *Paris nouvelle*, Paris: Regirex France (review of recent designs).

Besset, M. (1967) *New French Architecture*, London: The Architectural Press (national review of the dull French modernism of the 1960s).

Evenson, N. (1979) *Paris: A Century of Change*, New Haven and London: Yale University Press (long-run view of architecture in its planning context).

Jullian, R. (1984) *Histoire de l'architecture en France de 1889 à nos jours: un siècle de modernité*, Paris: Philippe Sers (traces French modernism back to the nineteenth century).

Lesnikowski, W. (1990) *The New French Architecture*, New York: Rizzoli (stresses variety and brilliance).

Sutcliffe, A. (1993) *Paris: An Architectural History*, London and New Haven: Yale University Press (comprehensive review of the development of architecture in Paris between 1500 and the 1990s; largely echoed by provincial architecture).

Vayssière, B. (1988) *Reconstruction déconstruction: le hard french ou l'architecture française des trente glorieuses*, Paris: Picard (extensive review of French mass architecture between 1945 and 1975, stressing domination by concrete).

architecture under Mitterrand

For François Mitterrand, '*le premier des arts*' was architecture; indeed, his personal fascination for this subject is clearly discernible in his writing. This private 'passion' was to have a very striking influence on his presidency, most obviously in the form of what were known as the Grands Travaux or Grands Projets Culturels, a programme of architectural projects in Paris which constitute one of the most visible and durable aspects of his legacy.

Mitterrand's Grands Travaux consisted of a programme of about a dozen major architectural projects in Paris, three of which had in fact been initiated under Giscard d'Estaing: the Institute of the Arab World, the Science Museum at La Villette and the Musée d'Orsay. The first of these, inaugurated in 1987, is a cultural centre whose stated objective was to foster the understanding in France of the culture of the Arab world, defined in its broadest sense, since more than twenty Arab countries participated in this joint venture, in partnership with the French state. The Musée d'Orsay, also inaugurated in 1987, is a museum of art from the mid-nineteenth to early twentieth centuries, created by converting the old Orsay station which had been abandoned after the war. The third project instigated by Giscard and then completed under Mitterrand is the Cité des Sciences at La Villette, inaugurated in 1986, just days before the legislative elections that led to the first period of political 'cohabitation' in France. This was also an architectural conversion, involving in this case the central building of the new abattoir commissioned under de Gaulle but then not completed due to changing market conditions. It is surrounded by a new 'urban' park, designed by the Franco-Swiss architect, Bernard Tschumi; commissioned under Mitterrand, it is classified separately as another of his Grands Travaux, though the President is said to have had very little involvement in its conception or execution, and indeed, is rumoured to have disliked it intensely. A third project on the same site is the Cité de la Musique, designed by French architect Christian de Portzamparc, in two separate units, one housing the new Conservatoire and rehearsal studios, and the other containing a museum of music, a concert hall and amphitheatre, a multimedia library and exhibition area. This was not inaugurated until January 1995, having been given the lowest priority of all the projects, paradoxically, because of the cross-party support for it.

The music complex at La Villette was originally also to have incorporated another project, for a new 'popular' opera house, but in fact a more central site on the Place de la Bastille was then chosen, essentially for symbolic reasons. The Opéra-Bastille, designed by the Canadian-Uruguayan architect Carlos Ott, was inaugurated for the Bicentenary celebrations in 1989, but did not open to the public until the following year. There was intense opposition to this project on aesthetic, financial and technical grounds, and Mitterrand, who did not like the design, nearly abandoned it on several occasions. It has remained the subject of much controversy surrounding its cost, its technical qualities and its programming policy, and it is undoubtedly one of the least well received of the Grands Travaux.

Conversely, the project which is now considered as being the most successful is the one with which Mitterrand was most closely involved personally: the Grand Louvre. Mitterrand confessed to having long been 'obsessed' with the idea of modernizing the Louvre, where the lack of space and funds prevented the proper functioning of the museum; he was determined to force the departure of the Ministry of Finance from the Richelieu wing of the building, in what he saw as a symbolic battle between money and culture. His appointment, without competition, of the Chinese-American architect Ieoh Ming Pei to take on the project, was much attacked for its allegedly personalized and 'arbitrary' nature, though public criticism was in fact fuelled less by this apparent autocracy than by Pei's 'revolutionary' design for a glass pyramid in the Cour Napoléon to mark the new central entrance. The 'battle of the pyramid', which was launched by *France-Soir* in January 1984, did not die down until over a year later when a life-size model, erected on the proposed site, persuaded opponents that it would not be the 'aberration' that many had predicted. Indeed, the pyramid has since become probably the most admired architectural project of the Mitterrand presidency, and has attracted record numbers of visitors.

An offshoot of the Grand Louvre was the construction of another new building to house the displaced Ministry of Finance. In order to minimize potential technical problems that might indirectly cause delays to the Grand Louvre project, thereby jeopardizing its completion, Mitterrand allowed Jacques **Chirac** as mayor of Paris to exert a major influence over the choice of site at Bercy, which suited his plan to redevelop the eastern half of the city according to his '*Plan de l'est parisien*'. Given the intended function of the building, the architectural competition was open to French architects only, and it was won by Paul Chemetov

and Borja Huidobro, whose design was much criticized for what was often described as its neo-Stalinist style, which Mitterrand himself described as being that of a motorway toll. The Ministry finally moved into its new location in 1989, after a bitter struggle involving Chirac's Finance Minister from 1986–1988, Édouard **Balladur**, who was reluctant to move; this enabled the Richelieu wing of the Louvre to be inaugurated by 1993, year of the bicentenary of the Convention's decision to turn the royal palace into a national museum.

The other architectural project in which Mitterrand took a particular personal interest was the Arche de La Défense; all the previous presidents of the Fifth Republic had discussed plans to build a major monument on this site, but it was Mitterrand who made this a reality. An international competition was won by Danish architect Johan Otto von Spreckelsen whose design for a huge white marble arch (or cube as it was first called) met with almost unanimous acclaim from specialists and non-specialists alike. Built on top of four main pillars sunk underground, it had to be slightly turned at an angle from the 'triumphal route' leading down to the Arc de Triomphe and the Champs Élysées, because of existing underground service networks. It was initially designed to house a vast communications centre, abandoned by the Chirac government in 1986, when private investment had to be sought to ensure the future of the building, which is now essentially occupied as office space. It was inaugurated during the Bicentenary celebrations in 1989, and the roof of the arch was used for the G7 meeting that took place on this occasion. Since then, the roof has housed the Fondation des Droits de l'Homme, officially inaugurated on 26 August, anniversary of the Declaration of the Rights of Man.

Mitterrand's re-election to the presidency in 1988 gave him the confidence to launch another major architectural project, this time for a vast new modern library. A limited competition was held, which was won by French architect Dominique Perrault, whose design consisted of four L-shaped glass towers facing inwards towards each other, symbolizing open books, round a sunken garden. The site was once again chosen partly out of deference to Chirac, since the Ville de Paris offered to give the site free of charge, because it wanted to use the new library as the central focus of a whole new redevelopment in this area, known as the Seine Rive-Gauche. The Bibliothèque Nationale de France was officially inaugurated by Mitterrand in 1994, but not opened to the public (and then only partially) until December 1996, at which point Chirac decided to extend the library's full name by adding that of François Mitterrand. Two other less important projects were also planned for the second presidency: the renovation of the Galerie de l'Évolution in the Muséum d'Histoire Naturelle, which was completed in 1994, and the International Conference Centre to be built on a site on the Quai Branly, near the Eiffel Tower. This project was the only one to fall foul of conflicts with the Ville de Paris, and had to be abandoned in 1993.

Besides these major projects in Paris, many others were also carried out in the provinces, but they were not really part of the presidential programme; they were partly funded by the Ministry of Culture in partnership with local authorities which, usually under the auspices of ambitious mayors, emulated the central model of cultural gestures, by initiating the construction of major cultural projects that would not only satisfy the increasing demand from the electorate for cultural facilities in their areas, but also act as vehicles for urban development. These projects outside Paris were instigated by the state largely to offset criticisms by decentralizers of excessive resources being concentrated into the capital, and they enabled the defenders of the Grands Travaux to argue that the central 'example' was the most effective model for irrigating the country with cultural initiatives.

The significance of the Grands Travaux has been extensively discussed in the press and, to a lesser degree, in academic research. The widely accepted presentation is that of Mitterrand as the *président-pharaon* (pharaoh-president), building monuments to his own glory, in a revival of the old French monarchical tradition

of building in the capital, in order to establish and enhance the personal image of the head of state. That the president chose to leave his most personal and controversial mark on the Louvre, the symbolic heart of French national culture, simply reinforced this view of Mitterrand as a 'megalomaniac' with an overriding ambition to be remembered in history through the construction of these prestigious monuments. Moreover, the fact that he was able to carry out such a massive programme of architectural projects, on a scale unprecedented since the days of Haussmann, was made possible, according to this interpretation, by the almost unlimited powers supposedly available to the president of the Fifth Republic, who is frequently portrayed as 'an elected monarch', able to dictate policy without having to contend with any significant constraints.

However, this construal of the Grands Travaux makes assumptions about the president's motives and the extent of his powers, both of which can be contested. First, with regard to his ambitions, the quest for personal glory is in no way an accurate reflection of the mood that initially inspired them: Mitterrand's greatest concern in initiating the Grands Travaux was to leave a cultural stamp on his presidency, and the architectural projects were intended as prestigious 'cultural gestures', designed to drive a much broader cultural policy, pursued in parallel under the authority of Jack **Lang** as Minister of Culture. Indeed, all the architectural projects (except for the new Ministry of Finance, which was simply an offshoot of the Grand Louvre) had a cultural function of some sort, which was in each case conceived as a response to a widely perceived and often long-standing demand from the public and from professionals in the field. It was also Mitterrand's ambition to use these cultural projects to bring about an architectural revival in the capital, enabling new talents to come forward and express themselves in a burst of artistic creativity. Indeed, Mitterrand had often deplored the quality of publicly funded architecture in France, and he hoped that the Grands Travaux would play an exemplary role in setting new architectural standards and expectations. This would also have the effect of focusing international architectural attention on Paris, thereby restoring the city's supposedly declining status as a cultural Mecca. But there was a further dimension to the architectural revival about which Mitterrand spoke often before his election, and this was the role it would play in humanizing 'the city' and making it more 'civilized', a notion which he claimed was central to his idea of socialism. His architectural projects would therefore also, in theory at least, be informed by a wider concern with urban design and planning that was, and continues to be, a major preoccupation of architects and planners alike with regard to the city of Paris and its future development. However, this 'urban' dimension was in the event very considerably eclipsed by the cultural demands, and the president was much criticized for emphasizing the monumental and neglecting the concerns of the **suburbs**, for example with regard to the choice of sites. It is also true that there was undoubtedly, over the years, a certain shift in his ambitions with regard to the Grands Travaux: the library project was conceived and executed in a context of supreme political self-confidence at the beginning of his second period of office, which for many marked the beginning of a decline into the excesses and abuses of power that branded him a nepotist, a liar and a despot.

Second, the extent to which the very complex decision-making processes involving the Grands Travaux were associated personally with the president himself has been greatly exaggerated. Similarly, the often crucial role and influence of political advisers, technicians and other professionals has been almost totally ignored in the attempt to portray Mitterrand as having behaved in the manner of an absolute monarch. Recent research, however, has shown that the president would not have been able to undertake or complete the Grands Travaux had he not been actively supported and advised in this venture by certain informally constituted groups, who were not simply behaving as courtiers, but who saw in Mitterrand's programme the opportunity to realize their own independently elaborated projects. For the 'cultural community', as represented, essentially, in the person of Jack Lang, this meant providing the capital with better cultural facilities. For local planners (mainly those working from the local authority agency, the Atelier Parisien d'Urbanisme or APUR), it meant a chance to redevelop certain parts of the city according to their own existing plans that would otherwise have remained on the drawing board. For many involved in local cultural politics, behind the rhetoric of political opposition, the presidential projects represented a unique opportunity to provide the local electorate with facilities that would be paid for by the state rather than out of local taxes. Indeed, it could even be argued that the case of the Grands Travaux, rather than representing the presidential expression of pure sovereign power, showed, on the contrary, how these groups were able to *use* the president's own ambitions to pursue their own agendas. More accurately, given the heterogeneous nature of the different projects in the programme, the Grands Travaux should be seen as an example of an osmosis between the presidential ambitions and their harnessing by the actors in the relevant policy area to suit their own specific demands.

Thus, the widely accepted view of the Grands Travaux as the expression of Mitterrand's monarchical ambitions and powers can be reassessed as a gross misrepresentation, and yet it is a view which will almost certainly continue to hold sway, not only due to the limited dissemination of academic research, but also because of the ease with which this view lends itself to caricatural representation in the media, and the appeal of this sort of image to the public in general. Besides, it is a view which has clearly served the political interests of Mitterrand's critics both on the Right and the Left, and it is for this reason that the Grands Travaux will continue to be a controversial aspect of his legacy.

SUSAN COLLARD

Further reading

Clément, C. (1982) *Rêver chacun pour l'autre* [Dreaming for Each Other]: Paris, Fayard (a somewhat dithyrambic collection of essays on first-term Socialist cultural politics, Chapter 5 of which is particularly relevant).

Collard, S. (1998) *The Politics of François Mitterrand's Architectural Projects in Paris*, Basingstoke: Macmillan (forthcoming).

Ardant, Fanny

b. 1949, Saumur

Actor

Her career took off as the heroine of **Truffaut**'s *La Femme d'à côté* (1981), in which she starred with **Depardieu**. Truffaut's *Vivement dimanche!* (1983) was a showcase for Ardant. She also appeared in three 1980s films by **Resnais** (*La Vie est un roman*, *L'Amour à mort*, *Mélo*). She once more starred alongside Depardieu in Yves Angelo's *Le Colonel Chabert*, a 1994 literary heritage film echoing her role in Schlöndorff's 1984 Proust adaptation, *Swann in Love*. Both films exemplify her languorously romantic acting style.

PHIL POWRIE

See also: cinema; stars

armed forces

From 1945 through to the present day, the French armed forces have undergone repeated and significant changes at a conceptual level and in terms of the tasks which they have been asked to perform. French forces have been involved in a variety of conflicts in many different theatres, most notably the counter-guerrilla wars in Indochina (1945–54) and Algeria (1954–62), but also in the abortive Suez expedition of 1956, in rapid interventions designed to maintain sta-

bility in former French colonies in sub-Saharan Africa, in humanitarian interventions in Bosnia and Rwanda, and as part of the international coalition of forces in the Gulf War.

France has been a permanent, if somewhat maverick, member of the Western Alliance – withdrawing from NATO's integrated command structure in 1966 while continuing to co-operate at a lower level. France, along with Britain and the United States, is one of only three NATO countries to possess an independent nuclear deterrent, the main impetus behind its acquisition being the (then) President de **Gaulle**'s determination to assert, if only on a symbolic level, French strategic independence, to wean the army from its colonial preoccupations, seen as outdated, and to transform it into a modern fighting force with a more European focus.

French military forces had enjoyed a long tradition of apolitical neutrality; the Army was known as *la grande muette* (the great silent one) on the grounds that it did not interfere in political affairs. This tradition was shattered during the **Algerian war** at the time of the Generals' Putsch of 1961, when some of the most decorated and trusted men in France's armed forces openly rebelled against the regime, angered at what they saw as de Gaulle's desire to 'abandon' Algeria. The failure of the putsch was in no small part due to the reluctance of the reservists and those carrying out their compulsory period of military service in Algeria to join the revolt. From 1997 onwards, however, compulsory national service was phased out, reflecting, in part, the lowering of tension brought by the end of the Cold War. This also suggests a change of attitudes. Service in the armed forces has usually been seen as a way of ensuring that the army did not become too detached from the nation whose values it was supposed to defend, and as a moral contract between the citizen and the nation – a duty incumbent upon the citizen who, in return, received the rights and protection which citizenship conferred.

CRAIG BLUNT

See also: decolonization; nuclear power

Further reading

Ambler, J. S. (1966) *The French Army in Politics 1945–1962*, Ohio: Ohio State University Press (very good on the Algerian and Indochinese conflicts and the rancour of the professional military establishment).

Girardet, R. (ed.) (1964) *La Crise militaire française 1945–1962*, Paris: Armand Colin (a good study in French along similar lines to Ambler's, but with a slightly different emphasis).

Aron, Jean-Paul

b. 1925, Strasbourg;
d. 1988, Paris

Philosopher and historical anthropologist

Aron worked across various disciplines, including philosophy, history, sociology and epistemology. His principal works are: *Essais d'epistémologie biologique*, *Anthropologie du conscrit français* (which he co-authored), *The Art of Eating in France* (*Le Mangeur du XIXe siècle*), *La Bourgeoisie, le sexe et l'honneur*, and (with Roger Kempf) *Le Pénis et la démoralisation de l'Occident*, a stunning exposé of the bourgeois discourse of morality in post-revolutionary France (1820–50). In *Les Modernes* (The Moderns), a series of witty and highly scathing attacks on the major intellectual figures of postwar France (**Sartre**, **Lévi-Strauss**, **Lacan**, **Barthes**, etc.), he decried the power and influence of the French media and teaching institutions. Aron (who was based at the École des Hautes Études en Sciences Sociales in Paris) achieved national fame in 1987 when, in a highly publicized interview for the *Nouvel Observateur* entitled 'Mon Sida' (My AIDS), he became the first celebrity in France to declare publicly that he was HIV positive. This act was in direct response to Michel **Foucault**'s 'shameful' decision not to reveal he had **AIDS**. Aron wrote several novels and a col-lection of plays, producing for television histories of medicine and inventions. He was Raymond Aron's nephew.

JAMES WILLIAMS

See also: gay writing; television

Aron, Raymond

b. 1905, Paris;
d. 1983, Paris

Intellectual and journalist

Aron was one of the most prominent of France's postwar intellectuals. Educated at the École Normale Supérieure, where he was close to **Sartre**, he also studied in Germany, and it was his first-hand observation of the Nazi seizure of power which led to his enduring fascination with the nature of historical explanation, the claims of political ideology and the menace of totalitarianism. After the war, which he spent in London with the Free French, he sought to combine academic scholarship with political (though not, apart from a brief period in the late 1940s, party) engagement. Although he wrote widely in the fields of sociology and international relations, it was as a dedicated opponent of the philosophical claims of **Marxism**, and the political record of communism, that he made his name. His attack on the Marxist sympathies of the French intelligentsia in *The Opium of the Intellectuals* (*L'Opium des intellectuels*) (1955) – much admired in America and England – led most French progressives, including Sartre, to view him as nothing more than a crude Cold War conservative. In fact he was an independent-minded liberal, who supported Algerian independence and criticized aspects of de **Gaulle**'s nationalist foreign policy. His unorthodoxy, and his isolation, were further demonstrated by his response to the 1968 Events, which he mocked in *The Undiscoverable Revolution* (*La Révolution introuvable*) as a psychodrama with no historical meaning. In 1978, as the intellectual credibility of communism finally crumbled in France, the cause of liberal democracy suddenly became fashionable – and so did its chief spokesman. Aron wrote a well-regarded **autobiography** and acquired the status of national guru which had earlier belonged to his student friend, and subsequent adversary, Sartre.

PETER MORRIS

See also: educational elitism: the *grandes écoles*

Arp, Jean

b. 1887, Strasbourg;
d. 1966, Basle

Artist

Arp was a modernist pioneer sculptor, and a founder member of the 1916 Zurich Dada group. Expressionism provoked his interest in abstract form with only oblique reference to the real world. He abandoned traditional skills in favour of the idea of artist as artificer. In his works, for example, *Portrait of Tristran Tzara* (1916), form, following the elements of cubism, becomes determined by the laws of chance and force (air currents, gravity) rather than the artist's choice. After 1930, his contemplative three-dimensional **sculptures**, for example, *Human Concretion in Oval Bowl* (1935), began to reflect the face of nature and growing forms.

VALERIE SWALES

Arrabal, Fernando

b. 1932, Melilla, Spanish Morocco

Playwright and director

Arrabal is best known as the writer of ritualistic, turbulent plays noted for their disregard for convention, influenced by grim personal experience of war and family tragedy, e.g. *Le*

Cimetière des voitures and *Picnic on a Battlefield* (*Pique-Nique en campagne*).

ANNIE SPARKS

See also: theatre

Further reading

Bérenguer, A. (1977) *L'Exil et la cérémonie dans le premier théâtre d'Arrabal*, Paris: Union Générale d'Éditions (analysis of works).

art brut

The company of art brut was formed in 1948 to manage Jean **Dubuffet**'s immense collection of 'raw art' (*l'art brut*) at the Galerie Drouin. Other founder members were André Breton and Michel Tapié. The group's major exhibition, 'L'Art Brut Préféré aux Arts Culturels', was held in November 1948. Following Surrealism and also the tradition of the irrational of Alfred Jarry, Dubuffet sought inspiration in the art of children and the mentally unstable, and in accidental marks and graffiti on walls and pavements. Encrusted, muddy pigment, trowelled, scrawled and scratched into parodies of the heroic metaphors of the romantic tradition, contribute to postwar realism's commentaries on the brutalism of contemporary society and the careerist intellectual; for example, *The Cow with the Subtle Nose* (1954).

VALERIE SWALES

See also: painting

art criticism

Art criticism in France since 1945 has shown two distinct trends, embodied first in the writings of the 'professional' art critics, and second in the writings of intellectuals whose discussion of the visual arts is simply part of their wider body of work.

'Professional' art criticism in the years immediately following World War II was largely influenced by a resurfacing of the prewar abstraction/representation debate in the visual arts, which meant that critics took sides, were combative, and rhetorical in approach and became promoters of the art they had engaged with. Michel Tapié and Julien Alvard, for example, were both militant apologists for abstract art, the French counterparts of Clement Greenberg in the United States, creating trends as much as discussing them. With his 1951 exhibition, 'Les Signifiants de l'informel', Tapié defined, launched and thereafter promoted the **art informel** movement. The critic Pierre Restany, initially at least, also argued for abstract art, allying himself with the Lyrical Abstraction movement created in 1947 and promoting the work of this group of painters. The absence of a well-argued, intellectually committed philosophical foundation for the opinions of these *critiques de métier* was illustrated when Restany, in 1960, without apparent hesitation, changed sides in the abstraction/figuration debate. Defining a number of disparate artists (Yves **Klein**, Hains, Arman, **Tinguely** *et al.*) as Nouveaux Réalistes and promoting their work himself, Restany now declared himself an opponent of abstract art. A familiarity with the opportunities of the art market appears to have been a determining factor in the positions taken up by critics such as Restany, who, like Tapié, was creating a product and selling it. Restany has been regarded as the most representative French exponent of the type of criticism dominating the period 1950–70, of which Greenberg as the promoter of Abstract Expressionism in America is probably the best-known practitioner.

A parallel trend in French art criticism since the war stems from the tendency of intellectuals in France to turn their attention to the visual arts as part of their principal project. While the most influential art criticism of this type, grounded in **structuralism** and **poststructuralism**, has come to the fore since the 1960s, the model of the philosopher engaging with the fine arts was defined by Jean-Paul **Sartre** in the immediate postwar years. His admiration for **Giacometti**, as well as his attacks on Surrealism, stemmed from his existentialist position, and found expression in his 1948 essay on Giacometti for the catalogue of the sculptor's first postwar exhibition as well as in his critical endorsements of the work of Jean **Dubuffet**, **Wols**, Calder and Masson. In the same period, Merleau-Ponty gave a phenomenological account of the work of artists such as Cézanne.

From the late 1950s on, important critical writing on art became increasingly grounded in theory. An offshoot of Saussure's structural linguistics – which saw the basic unit of any language, including the visual, as sign – this approach to the image enabled French academics to move between different disciplines – sociology, literature, philosophy, **psychoanalysis** and the visual arts – and to free themselves from the traditional stylistic boundaries of academic discourse. Thus Michel **Foucault** analyses Velasquez's *Las Meniñas*, Jacques **Lacan** discusses Holbein's *The French Ambassadors*, Roland **Barthes** writes essays on Dutch painting and Cy Twombly, and Jean-François **Lyotard** produces articles on **Duchamp**, Barnett Newman and Daniel **Buren**. The 1980s saw a two-volume study of Francis Bacon by **Deleuze** and a book on the graphic art of Antonin **Artaud** by **Derrida**. Derrida's poststructuralism also informs his collection of essays, *Truth in Painting (La Vérité en peinture)* of 1978. Analyses of the visual arts can also be seen in the work of **Baudrillard** and Julia **Kristeva**. This approach, based on a response to the visual image in terms of signs, where the emphasis is on the reading of the art work itself rather than the documentation surrounding it, is perhaps the most distinctive feature of contemporary art criticism in France.

CAROL WILCOX

See also: structuralism

Further reading

Bryson, N. (ed.) (1991) *Calligram*, Cambridge: Cambridge University Press (examples of contemporary art criticism, including essays by Barthes, Baudrillard, Lebensztejn and Bonnefoy).

Gee, M. (ed.) (1993) *Art Criticism Since 1900*, Manchester and New York: Manchester University Press (chapters on general issues in criticism and on art criticism in France between the wars and postwar).

art galleries/museums

The idea of offering public access to hitherto private collections was to have social implications unimaginable in 1793 when the Louvre was transformed from a royal palace into the first national museum in Europe. It was not until the late nineteenth century and the rise of the historical sciences, notably art history, that the public art gallery/museum became a recognized social institution, albeit one that excluded any innovatory art that might challenge the French establishment. The official policy in France remained unchanged until just before World War II, although of course many small privately owned art galleries in Paris regularly exhibited and promoted avant-garde art during this period. The closed-door policy of the public art galleries was reflected in the closed spaces of their architecture and in the sober atmosphere they generated. Apollinaire, in fact, wanted to burn down the Louvre and Proust saw it as an elitist microcosm isolated from the world.

A change in French policy after the war was illustrated in 1947 by the opening of the Musée National d'Art Moderne, then housed in the Palais de Tokyo, with its collection of twentieth-century avant-garde art. Despite this change in attitude, the concept of the museum's function, as essentially a preserver of the artistic legacy of the past, and the elitist image that went with it, remained unquestioned until the 1960s, when the prevailing ethos forced the institution to open up to a wider public and a wider range of activities.

The Amsterdam Stedelijk Museum and the Berne Kunsthalle, which **Christo** 'wrapped' in 1968 encouraged by its director, were pioneering forces shaping the new museology which aimed at desanctifying and democratizing the public's experience of art.

The same ideas informed the policies of the curator of the Moderna Museet in Stockholm, Pontus Hulten, who was able to implement them on a grand scale when the Musée National d'Art Moderne (MNAM) was rehoused in Beaubourg in 1977.

Beaubourg, or the Centre Georges Pompidou, to give it its official name, was the architectural incarnation *par excellence* of this new spirit. President Georges **Pompidou**, a keen collector of modern art, had decided in 1969, in line with the prevailing ideology, to create a multipurpose cultural centre, and Richard Rogers and Renzo Piano were the architects chosen to bring his project to fruition. Their late-modernist structure incited controversy as well as admiration. Its design encouraged public participation in cultural activities, while its flexibility invited collaboration between the museum and the artists themselves. This resulted, for example, in the adaptation of exhibition spaces to contemporary artistic practice such as installation art. At the same time it promoted itself as multifunctional, a place of entertainment, incorporating restaurants and bars, children's play areas/workshops as well as a place for research and study with its cinema, library, bookshops, music, lectures and debates. These activities are currently organized by its four main departments. Beaubourg represented a turning point in museum design and thereby, in a sense, succeeded in reasserting the artistic vitality Paris had lost when New York usurped its place as art capital of the world. In terms of numbers of visitors, it was an immediate success.

A similar conception of the museum's function seems to have informed President **Mitterrand**'s appointment of I. M. Pei as the architect of the new 'open' entrance space for the Louvre and its undergound network of service areas, made available when the Ministère des Finances moved out of part of the building. It was completed in 1988 in time for the Bicentenary celebrations of the Revolution that had given birth to the museum. The choice of a glass pyramid to cover the new entrance was practical as well as symbolic, in that it allowed light to penetrate by day, adding to the openness of the new user-friendly area in which the visitor is informed by wall-mounted texts and video monitors of the options available in the museum. In conception, it recalls the vast ground-floor information area at Beaubourg, while the physical transparency of both buildings mirrors the transparency and honesty of their intentions. The same cannot be said for the Musée d'Orsay, at least in the view of those who support the 'Beaubourg' ideology.

Pompidou's immediate presidential successor, **Giscard d'Estaing**, took the decision in 1977 to have the old Gare d'Orsay turned into a museum for nineteenth-century art. The success of Beaubourg may explain the timing of this decision, as a conversion plan had been mooted some four years earlier. It fell to Mitterrand, elected president in 1981, to see this project through to its conclusion (and thereby to claim it as one of his Grands Projets, along with the Pyramide du Louvre). Appropriately, art of the period 1848 to 1914 (from the beginning of the Second Empire to the outbreak of World War I) was to be displayed in this turn-of-the-century building. To defenders of the 'Beaubourg' idea, however, Gae Aulenti's conversion of the interior into the traditional palace of separate spaces, divided off by grandiose structures which eclipsed Victor Laloux's original architecture, was a retrograde step. She admits, moreover, that the decorative features, pastiches of Egyptian and neoclassical motifs, were not intended as references to nineteenth-century cultural traditions. This may be condemned as artistic dishonesty or accepted as **postmodernism**. The curators have also been accused of promulgating a neo-conservative interpretation of nineteenth-century art, with the work of avant-garde artists once rejected by the official salons virtually hidden on the top floor, while the so-called

pompier (more 'popular', not to say vulgar) paintings are among the first art works seen by the public as it enters on ground floor level.

This restatement of the museum as a 'palace of rooms' is also evident in the 1985 conversion of the Hotel Salé in the Marais quarter of Paris into the Musée Picasso. Because the conversion specified a minimum number of changes to the original *hôtel particulier* built for a rich merchant in 1656, its obviously bourgeois layout defines a space that clearly contradicts the spirit of the avant-garde that **Picasso**'s work consistently embodied.

While the thinking behind the Musée Picasso and Orsay conversions appears to reinstate a retrograde museum culture, this is only partially counterbalanced by the alternative conception of the museum represented by the **Pompidou Centre**. Research has shown that the typical Beaubourg visitor is still a member of the educated middle class and that the working classes are poorly represented. Cultural barriers are clearly more complex in origin and much harder to break down than the architects of the Beaubourg idea originally thought.

CAROL WILCOX

See also: architecture under Mitterrand

Further reading

Davis, D. (1990) *The Museum Transformed*, New York: Abbeville Press (a study of the effect of Beaubourg on museums worldwide, with excellent photographs and a foreword by Jack Lang).

Lumley, R. (ed.) (1988) *The Museum Time Machine*, London and New York: Routledge (a collection of essays presenting different perspectives on the changing face of the museum).

art informel

Mathieu is historically significant for his role in delineating art practices along the Paris–New

York axis in the 1940s and 1950s. Two pairs of terms were used to name this difference: American artists were referred to as *expressionistes abstraits*, while Mathieu and his colleagues styled themselves *expressionistes lyriques*. The subdivision of action painting, usually used to refer to Pollock's work, was paralleled in France by the term *'informel'*. The difference was insistently revealed by a show at Nina Dausset's gallery in 1951 entitled *Véhémences confrontées*, at which **Bryen**, Capogrossi, De Kooning, Hartung, Mathieu, Pollock, Riopelle, Russel and **Wols** were represented. The reliance upon Merleau-Ponty's notion of the body as inseparable from the self (a refusal of the mind/body problem present in philosophy since Plato), and the addition of suggestive ideogrammatic symbols related to the Surrealist notion of 'automatic drawing', distinguish the French work from similar experiments in the US. Other artists whose work may be styled *'Informel'* include Degottex, Hantaï, and Soulages.

SIMEON HUNTER

See also: painting

Artaud, Antonin

b. 1896, Marseille;
d. 1948, Ivry-sur-Seine

Actor, director and writer

Antonin Artaud's writing has had a significant influence on postwar French culture. He is best known for his **Theatre of Cruelty**, a notion developed in his collection of essays *The Theatre and its Double* (*Le Théâtre et son double*). The scope of his writing extended from Surrealist poetry in the early 1920s to the film script for the first Surrealist film, *The Shell and the Clergyman* (*La Coquille et le clergyman*), directed by Germaine Dulac and released in 1927. He wrote and directed one full-length play, *The Cenci* (*Les Cenci*) in 1935, based on P. B. Shelley's play of the same name,

and he also turned to politics in his *Revolutionary Messages* (*Messages révolutionnaires*) of 1936, writing of the hopelessness of French youth and their opposition to bourgeois capitalism. His prose writing is peopled with marginal characters, such as Heliogabalus, the effeminate 14-year-old boy emperor of Rome who was assassinated and cast into the River Tiber, and Van Gogh, whom Artaud defended against criticisms of madness. Towards the end of his life, he wrote three radio plays, the last of which was entitled *To Have Done with the Judgement of God* (*Pour en finir avec le jugement de Dieu*). His language became increasingly impassioned and aggressive, often breaking with referentiality, and he frequently accompanied his performances with shouts and screams.

As a result of Artaud's unstable mental condition, his writings were not taken seriously until *The Theatre and its Double* was translated posthumously into English in 1958, and became widely read by writers and practitioners. There are evident parallels between Artaud's theatre of cruelty and the New Theatre of postwar France. Both movements aimed to exploit the full range of expressive means in the theatre, rather than to focus predominantly on the spoken word, and both tried to tear the audience away from all recognized social conventions. However, if something of Artaud's aesthetics can be felt through **Genet**'s sense of religious ritual, **Beckett**'s density of language and **Ionesco**'s rupture of discourse and referentiality, renewed interest in Artaud can be seen as largely retrospective, a way of explaining the cruelty and violence which was already seeping into the theatre. Nevertheless, actors such as Jean-Louis **Barrault** acknowledged Artaud's influence on aspects of actor training, such as double breathing, which provided a continued impetus to the postwar theatre.

Despite Artaud's highly developed theatrical aesthetics, he wrote few major works of his own. It has been suggested that Artaud's detailed prescriptions for a modernist theatre are unattainable and inaccessible. Michel **Foucault**, in *Madness and Civilization* (*Folie* *de déraison*), has expressed the view that Artaud is an artist without works, which is a sign of madness itself. Meanwhile, **Derrida**, in *Writing and Difference* (*L'Écriture et la différence*) sees Artaud's failure as the logical outcome of any rebellion against the Western metaphysical tradition. In attempting to bypass the legacy of God the Father, Artaud created a scene of non-representation, a non-theological space which arose from the act of parricide conducted against the tyranny of the Father's Word.

GERARD PAUL SHARPLING

See also: theatre

Further reading

Sontag, S. (ed.) (1976) *Antonin Artaud: Selected Writings*, trans. H. Weaver, New York: Farrar, Straus and Giroux (a representative selection from all Artaud's major writings; the introductory essay by the editor summarizes some of the key points in the poststructuralist debate on Artaud.)

ARTE (Association Relative aux Télévisions Européennes)

Television channel

ARTE is a public sector Franco-German cultural television channel created by agreement in 1990 between President **Mitterrand** and Chancellor Kohl, which began transmissions in 1992.

On the French side, the origins of ARTE lay in the creation in 1986 of la Sept (Société d'Édition de Programmes de Télévision, renamed Société Européenne de Programmes de Télévision in 1989), whose mission was to develop cultural and educational television programming for pan-European transmission on the French direct broadcasting satellite Télédiffusion 1. While the satellite was not a

commercial success, the French state still retained its commitment to the concept of a European cultural channel and sought a partner for the new venture. The Franco-German agreement on the creation of ARTE represented another instance of co-operation between the two states at the heart of the European Union. In the audiovisual field it followed on from the bilateral technological collaboration on satellite broadcasting during the late 1970s and 1980s.

The headquarters of ARTE are symbolically located near the Franco-German border in Strasbourg. The ownership of the channel is equally shared between La Sept/ARTE (France) and ARTE Deutschland TV (Germany). La Sept/ARTE is jointly owned by the French state and three public sector broadcasting companies, of which the television company **France 3** is the biggest single shareholder. France's stake in ARTE is funded from a combination of licence revenue and direct state subsidy.

Following the collapse of the commercial channel La **Cinq** in 1992, the French government allocated the fifth terrestrial network to ARTE. Programme transmission began on French and German cable networks in the same year. Since late 1994, ARTE has shared the fifth network with the educational channel La Cinquième, with the former transmitting in the evening from 7 p.m. until 3 a.m. ARTE's programme output consists of high culture, including **documentaries**, magazine programmes, music and feature films. Despite its free availability on a terrestrial network, its audience share in France is minuscule.

Two main criticisms have been directed against ARTE: first, the undesirability of the 'ghettoization' of cultural output on a specialist channel; and second, the high cost per viewer to the public purse of such elitist programming. Defenders of ARTE emphasize the originality of the channel. It is the first transnational television channel in Europe resulting from co-operation between two countries; there is an acceptance of the principle of bilingual programming; and ARTE's production and programming are innovative, with the channel providing free to the viewer a range of contemporary cultural and intellectual output not generally available on other channels. The next stage in ARTE's development – and a test of the commitment of both governments to the project – is to transform itself into a truly pan-European cultural service capable of attracting a significant audience share in a competitive, multi-channel, digital environment.

RAYMOND KUHN

See also: television

Further reading

Kuhn, R. (1995) *The Media in France*, London: Routledge (the first full-length study of the French media in English).

arts funding (including regional)

Financial support for the arts in France comes from four sources: the Ministry of Culture, other ministries, local government and private sponsorship.

The culture ministry contributed 19.8 per cent of overall public spending on the arts in 1993. Its remit is wide-ranging: **theatre** and shows, music and **dance**, **cinema**, books and reading, visual arts, archives, heritage and museums. Until 1981, its spending rarely exceeded 0.5 per cent of state spending. But in the late 1960s, a target figure of 1 per cent was adopted by the arts world, which **Mitterrand** promised to reach. Accordingly, the ministry's budget was doubled in 1981, passing from 0.47 to 0.75 per cent (5.99 billion francs) and continued to rise in the ensuing years, though 1 per cent was only ever reached fleetingly. Furthermore, the costly presidential building projects absorbed much of the increase and, alongside existing institutions like the **Pompidou Centre**, continue to do so because of their high operating costs. The ministry's budget for 1995 fell from 0.93 to 0.91 per cent; but in

his 1995 presidential campaign **Chirac** restored the 1 per cent target and the following September Léotard, his Culture Minister, proposed a budget for 1996 of 15.54 billion francs to meet it.

Various other ministries, including Education and Foreign Affairs, fund the arts, accounting for 27.4 per cent of public spending in 1993. But the biggest spender is local government, whose arts provision has risen steadily since the 1960s, due to the commitment of particular authorities, the introduction of contractual agreements with central government, and decentralization measures. In 1993, local arts spending made up 50.3 per cent of public expenditure and is expected to rise to around two-thirds by the year 2000. Although regions and departments have begun to play a bigger part (2.0 and 7.4 per cent respectively in 1993), the lion's share comes from *communes* (40.9 per cent in 1993).

While public funding totalled 73.3 billion francs in 1993, business sponsorship has traditionally contributed little. The setting up of ADMICAL (Association for the Development of Industrial and Commercial Patronage) in 1979 and the subsequent introduction of tax and other incentives partly remedied this, though income from private business remains relatively small (1–1.6 billion francs in 1992). Various types of approved private foundations, including the state-initiated Fondation de France, also provide funds. Plans for a new, autonomous Heritage Foundation were announced by the government in 1993.

DAVID LOOSELEY

See also: architecture under Mitterrand; cultural policy

Further reading

Looseley, D. L. (1995) *The Politics of Fun: Cultural Policy and Debate in Contemporary France*, Oxford and Washington, DC: Berg (traces the ups and downs of public arts funding).

Ministry of Culture (1996) *Chiffres clés 1995: statistiques de la culture*, Paris: Document-ation Française (full statistics on funding and other matters).

Wangermée, R. and Gournay, B. (1991) *Cultural Policy in France*, Strasbourg: Council for Cultural Co-operation (a detailed 1988 sur-vey of arts provision).

athletics

France, in the person of Pierre de Coubertin (1863–1937), did much to resurrect the Olympic Games (Athens 1896), but a national body devoted exclusively to athletics – the Fédération Française d'Athlétisme – was creat-ed only in 1920 (its predecessor, dating from 1887, having embraced other sports as well). Paris hosted the Olympic Games in 1924. France's success in athletics was rather limited before the Atlanta games of 1996 (which saw a marked improvement), but a small number of outstanding world record-holders and Olympic champions have emerged from the 1960s onwards, including Guy Drut (110 m hurdles), Michel Jazy (middle distances), Pierre Quinon and Thierry Vigneron (both pole vault), Colette Besson and Marie-Jo Pérec (both 400 m).

IAN PICKUP

See also: sport and education

Further reading

Gardien, A., Houvion, M., Prost, R. and Thomas, R. (1982) *L'Athlétisme*, Paris: PUF (a technical analysis of athletic events).

Atlan, Jean-Michel

b. 1913, Constantine, Algeria;
d. 1960, Paris

Artist and poet

Atlan, a philosophy teacher, received no formal art training. Arrested for Resistance activities in 1942, he escaped deportation by simulating insanity. He was interned in St Anne mental hospital, where he produced *Le Sang profond* (Blood's Depths), a collection of illustrated poems. After the war he joined the Surréalisme Révolutionnaire group and contributed to the avant-garde reviews *Réalités nouvelles* and *Cobra*. His early figurative paintings combine landscapes and animal images (*Paysage*) and Old Testament subjects (*Le Lion de Judah*, *Salomé*), which testify to his Jewish roots. He developed violent abstract forms, combining the magical and the erotic (*Miroirs de l'Asie*), and explored the relations between writing and **painting**.

ELZA ADAMOWICZ

Atlan, Liliane

b. 1932, Montpellier

Playwright and poet

A Jewish writer whose work deals with the his-tory and suffering of her people and the atroc-ity of war, often employing fantasy rather than grim realism to tell the tale. Her major works include *Monsieur Fugue*, first staged in 1967 at the Comédie de St-Étienne.

ANNIE SPARKS

See also: theatre

Further reading

Oswald, P.-J. (1971) *Les Musiciens, les émigrants*, Paris: Honfleur (biographical analysis).

Attali, Jacques

b. 1943, Algiers, Algeria

Writer, economist and political adviser

An economist and polymath intellectual, a graduate from the École Nationale d'Administration (ENA), and the author of numerous socioeconomic and historical essays, Attali was Special Adviser to President **Mitterrand** from 1981 to 1989, and helped shape the foreign and European policies of the president. In 1990 he became Director of the newly formed European Bank for Reconstruction and Development, providing financial support to Eastern Europe. He resigned in 1993 amidst allegations of over-spending and lax management. His long memoirs, *Verbatim*, were criticized for plagiarism and for not always being trustworthy.

FRANÇOIS NECTOUX

Further reading

MacShane, D. (1994) 'Misjudgements', *Critical Quarterly*, 36, 3 (an analysis of the reasons why Attali never fitted the Anglo-Saxon financial world).

Attoun, Lucien

birthdate not known

Broadcaster, actor and director

As well as for his acting and directing roles, Attoun is known for founding the Théâtre Ouvert company in Paris, with his wife Micheline, in 1971, in order to promote contemporary playwrights through readings, performance and publication. The company, permanently based since 1981 at the Jardin d'Hiver, Paris, was made the first Centre Dramatique National devoted to new writing in 1987.

ANNIE SPARKS

See also: theatre

Further reading

G. C. (1992) 'Théâtre Ouvert – vingt et un ans de théâtre d'essai et de création', in P. Laville (ed.) *Théâtre 1991–1992*, Paris: Hachette.
Meureuze, D. (1986) 'A la recherche des auteurs', *Avant-Scène* 797 (article on the Attouns).

Audiberti, Jacques

b. 1899, Antibes;
d. 1965, Paris

Playwright and writer

A playwright of carnavalesque, wordy plays, many dealing with concepts of good and evil, which were mainstays of 1950s and 1960s Parisian arts theatre, e.g. *Le Mal Court* (Evil Runs About) and *Le Cavalier seul* (The Lone Cavalier).

ANNIE SPARKS

See also: theatre

Further reading

Farcy, G.-D. (1988), *Les Théâtres d'Audiberti*, Paris: Presses Universitaires de France (analysis of work).

Aufray, Hugues

b. 1932, Neuilly-sur-Seine

Singer-songwriter, real name Jean Auffray

Aufray appeared in nightclubs on the Left Bank in Paris before forming a skiffle group in the

1960s under the influence of Joan Baez, Pete Seeger and, above all, Bob Dylan, some of whose early songs he sang in imaginative French translations by Pierre **Delanoë**. Important on the French musical scene for his importation of American folk music and as an exponent of protest songs, he has enjoyed something of a revival in the 1990s.

IAN PICKUP

See also: song/chanson

Auriol, Vincent

b. 1884, Revel;
d. 1966, Paris

Politician

Vincent Auriol was a leading member of the French Socialist Party (SFIO) in the interwar period and held the Finance ministry in Léon Blum's 1936 Popular Front government. His resolute opposition to the **Vichy** regime ensured his prominence in the postwar period. As president of the Constituent Assembly he played a central role in the complicated drafting of the constitution of the Fourth Republic. His status as Father of the Constitution led the National Assembly to elect him, by a large majority, president of the new Republic, an office which held few real powers but had a potential for influence which Auriol was fully to exploit in the turbulent politics of the late 1940s. The Republic was attacked on its Left by the powerful Communist Party and on its Right by de **Gaulle**'s anti-system Rassemblement pour la France. Auriol used such authority as his office possessed, and also his insider's familiarity with the tortuous procedures of French parliamentary politics, to shore up the authority of the fragile governmental coalitions which struggled to cope with problems at home and abroad. His posthumously published diaries show the extent of his interventionism. He left office in 1954, but returned to prominence in 1958 as one of the Socialist leaders who backed the return to power of de Gaulle. He soon turned against the latter's style of leadership. and in 1962 campaigned strongly against the proposal for a directly elected presidency on the grounds that it was incompatible with Republican democracy. The electorate did not agree with him.

PETER MORRIS

See also: parties and movements

Aurore, L'

Newspaper

An important popular daily in the 1950s. Created in 1942, this right-wing newspaper reached its peak circulation of over 400,000 copies in the mid-1950s. In 1951, cotton giant Marcel Boussac bought a 74 per cent shareholding in the paper. *L'Aurore*'s popularity declined through the 1960s and 1970s, and financial problems forced Boussac to sell, in 1978, to Marcel Fournier (of retailer Carrefour). He passed *L'Aurore* on to press baron Robert **Hersant**, who allowed it to decline, gradually merging it with *Le Figaro*. Although *L'Aurore* as such disappeared in 1984, an edition of *Le Figaro* continues to carry its name.

PAM MOORES

See also: national press in France

Autant-Lara, Claude

b. 1901, Luzarches

Director

The archetypal Fourth Republic film director, Autant-Lara's denunciations of bourgeois hypocrisy often, as in *Douce* of 1943, show a savage awareness of class differences. His penchant for literary adaptations and co-operation with screenwriters Jean Aurenche and Pierre

Bost, as on *Le Diable au corps* of 1946 or *Le Blé en herbe* of 1954, earned him the scorn of the *Cahiers du cinéma* critics, above all **Truffaut**. Yet *La Traversée de Paris* (1956) was one of the first determinedly non-heroic treatments of the Occupation, and his move across the political spectrum, from Communist Party member after the war to National Front MEP in the 1980s, was clearly the result of cynical opportunism as much as of any major ideological change.

KEITH READER

See also: cinema; *cinéma de qualité*; parties and movements

Auteuil, Daniel

b. 1950, Algiers, Algeria

Actor

His career began in 1977 with comic roles. He became well-known for his role as Ugolin in **Berri**'s 1986 diptych *Jean de Florette/Manon des sources*, for which he received a César and a BAFTA award. Apart from the nineteenth-century criminal in Girod's *Lacenaire* (1990) and Henry of Navarre in **Chéreau**'s *La Reine Margot* (1994), his roles in the 1990s were mainly of middle-class males in emotional trouble, exemplified in 1992 in **Sautet**'s *A Heart in Winter* (*Un Coeur en hiver*), where he played opposite Emmanuelle **Béart**, his real-life partner during the 1980s after he had been her screen suitor in *Manon des sources*.

PHIL POWRIE

See also: cinema

autobiography

A widespread interest in autobiography (a person's account of his or her life which usually emphasizes the origins and development of personal identity) has been a notable feature of

French culture since World War II and particularly since the 1970s.

The increasing prominence of autobiography in France is a multifaceted cultural phenomenon. At one level it represents belated recognition for a neglected body of major texts, including Rousseau's *Confessions* and Stendhal's *Life of Henry Brulard* (*Vie de Henry Brulard*), which had been relegated to the periphery of the literary field. New critical methods spawned by **structuralism** generated an interest in the workings of narrative, and questioned the established parameters of literary genres. Autobiography, with its combination of fact and fable, found its place in an expanded canon, and drew serious critical attention to other forms such as memoirs, essays, biographies and diaries. However, this new-found fascination with the first person singular placed a premium on the investigation of subjective reality and its complex determinants, rather than on personal effusions. As such, the rising tide of interest in the autobiographical reflects the wider impact of the human sciences – **psychoanalysis**, linguistics, semiotics, structural anthropology, sociology, feminist theory – in French culture generally. It is no coincidence that a crucial figure in twentieth-century French autobiography, Michel **Leiris**, was a poet adept at dissecting words, a trained ethnographer, and a lifelong devotee of psychoanalysis. The rise of autobiography reflects new ways of locating the sources of identity – in gender, ideological representations, history, ethnicity, the body, as well as in the dynamics of personal relations. It goes hand in hand with the questioning of old categorizations and divisions of experience into individual and collective, public and private, personal and historical. If it represents an emphasis on the experiential, the prestige of autobiography reflects new ways of placing *le vécu* (lived experience) at the heart of human understanding and cultural endeavour.

The rise of autobiography may seem paradoxical given the structuralist proclamation of the death of the author and the demise of the sovereign self, key themes in contemporary French culture. But in fact, the general model of the subject, as opposed to the self, which emerged in such quarters as linguistic theory centring on enunciation, **Lacan**ian psycho-analysis with its emphasis on the illusory nature of the ego, or **Cixous**'s account of gendered subjectivity and language, paved the way for an increasingly self-aware and sophisticated mode of autobiographical writing attuned to the dispersion of a multiply constituted subjectivity. The inherently hybrid character of autobiography, at the crossroads of the referential and the fictional, and capable of finding expression in a wide range of media, visual (film, photograph, video) as well as verbal, becomes a distinct advantage. In the 1990s it has given autobiography a central position in a number of important cultural currents. These include the focus on the *récit de vie* (life history) which has led to new experiments in oral testimony, biography and travel writing, and the focus on the ordinary and the everyday, associated with such theoreticians as Henri **Lefebvre** and Michel de **Certeau**. In these contexts autobiography, while by no means supporting die-hard individualism, does have a positive role in renegotiating the place of the subjective in wider social and intellectual formations.

Although it had been published just before the war, Michel Leiris's *Manhood* (*L'Age d'homme*) only made its real impact when reissued in 1946 with an essay which has come to be seen as a manifesto for a new kind of literary enterprise. 'The Autobiographer as Torero' ('De la littérature considérée comme une tauromachie') underlined the work's radical structural and thematic innovations. The first modern autobiographer to break with chronology, Leiris had structured his self-investigation around certain obsessional motifs organized in associative patterns. Crucially, Leiris underlined the risk-taking candour of the confessional autobiographer, willing to 'tell all', and thus to expose himself to vilification, as the matador exposes himself to the bull's horns. The element of risk gave autobiography the edge over other forms of literary expression which seemed merely footling in the face of the horrors of war. In its authenticity, autobiographi-cal writing could constitute a form of that *engagement* which Jean-Paul **Sartre** was calling for on the part of intellectuals.

In fact, Leiris's autobiographical project, to be pursued for the rest of his life, notably in the four-volume cycle (1948–76) *The Rules of the game* (*La Règle du jeu*), partly inspired Sartre's own passionate interest in human lives, which first found full expression in his biography of Charles Baudelaire, also published in 1946 and in fact dedicated to Leiris. Sartre's next biographical subject was the homosexual writer Jean **Genet**. This was partly on the strength of Genet's 1948 *The Thief's Journal* (*Journal du voleur*), a major autobiographical work, which, as in Leiris's case, combined a high degree of awareness of the pitfalls and challenges of autobiography with a radical approach to narrative and time. Sartre himself embarked on an autobiography in the early 1950s, but by the time it was published to great acclaim in 1964 as *Words* (*Les Mots*), two other important autobiographies had been published by members of his circle, Simone de **Beauvoir**'s 1958 *Memoirs of a Dutiful Daughter* (*Mémoires d'une jeune fille rangée*) and André **Gorz**'s 1958 *The Traitor* (*Le Traître*). These were to be followed by Violette **Leduc**'s *La Bâtarde*, an important autobiography by a writer close to Beauvoir. While all these autobiographies have common features which can be associated with **existentialism** (for example, a concern with betrayal and bad faith), Sartre's *Words* is in a class of its own. Witty and fast-moving, it injects a strong dose of parody into the autobiographical proceedings, while in fact, as critical analysis has shown, disguising a complex structure of argument behind a loosely chronological surface.

A decade later, three works published in 1975 can be seen as the next milestone in the evolution of autobiography in France. First, a brilliant critical work by Philippe Lejeune, *Le Pacte autobiographique* (The Autobiographical Contract), placed autobiography at the top of the literary critical agenda. Well-versed in contemporary literary theory, Lejeune combined a concern for rigorous formal criteria with an approach favouring close textual reading. In a series of subsequent works Lejeune refined and broadened his critical approach, serving as an indispensable interpreter of the manifold developments which have occurred in French autobiography in the last twenty-five years or so.

Roland Barthes by Roland Barthes (*Roland Barthes par Roland Barthes*) and Georges **Perec**'s *W or the Childhood Memory* (*W ou le souvenir d'enfance*), both from 1975, broke new ground. **Barthes**'s text, featuring alphabetically ordered fragments, and a narrative voice oscillating between first and third person pronouns, adapted concepts from Lacanian psychoanalysis and used autobiography to explore a new vision of the human subject. In Perec's case, chapters from an autobiographical narrative sifting through a meagre stock of childhood memories alternate with chapters from a fictional story written when Perec was an adolescent. Progressively it emerges that both narratives point to a horror neither can name: the annihilation of the author's mother in Auschwitz. Posthumous texts published since Perec's early death in 1982 reveal the extent of his interest in developing new kinds of autobiographical project geared to exploring the borders of individual and collective experience.

The upsurge of interest in autobiography in the late 1970s had a direct impact on the *nouveau roman* group of novelists. Although, in the heyday of the structuralist assault on humanism, the new novelists had appeared to banish subjectivity, the '*retour du sujet*' (return of the subject) spearheaded by Barthes's later work prompted Alain **Robbe-Grillet** to write *Le Miroir qui revient* (The Return of the Mirror) and two subsequent volumes where autobiography and fantasy fuse in a manner particularly characteristic of what was to become known as *autofiction* (see below). Nathalie **Sarraute**'s outstanding 1983 *Childhood* (*Enfance*) used the established stylistic and thematic range developed in her fiction to probe childhood memories. With *The Lover* (*L'Amant*), published in 1984, Marguerite **Duras** used memories of an illicit affair as the sounding-board for a haunting exercise in memory and fantasy which clarified the autobiographical basis of her fictional

work. Similarly, Claude **Simon**'s 1989 *L'Acacia* (The Acacia) consolidated a distinct autobiographical turn in his work.

The 1980s saw the emergence of several writers whose work bears the strong impact of the revival of autobiography. To some degree they can be seen as exponents of *autofiction*, a label coined by Serge **Doubrovsky** for novels where the narrator-protagonist bears the author's real name. Works of *autofiction*, including those of Robbe-Grillet mentioned above, and Doubrovsky's *Un Amour de soi* (Self-Love), often involve the reader in games with truth and fiction, blurring the border between autobiographical revelation and fictional creation. But for younger writers like Annie **Ernaux**, Hervé **Guibert** and Patrick **Modiano**, the ludic dimension of *autofiction* serves more authentically autobiographical ends. For Guibert, in *To the Friend Who Did Not Save My Life* (*A l'ami qui ne m'a pas sauvé la vie*) the fusion of the diary mode (which also undergoes a revival at this time), autobiographical narrative and novelistic effects creates a medium in which he can explore the experience of being HIV positive. Ernaux has moved from autobiographical novels to works where biography – that of her father in *Positions* (*La Place*), that of her mother in *Une Femme* (A Woman) – provide the framework for autobiographical self-scrutiny. In her 1993 *Journal du dehors* (A Diary of the Outside), autobiographical writing becomes the medium for an exploration of '*le quotidien*' (the everyday), the zone of immediate daily experience where the balance between freedom and constraint in the rhythm of individual existence can be gauged.

This turn towards everydayness, to the texture of individual lives, present or past, can be linked to another of the alliances autobiography has forged. Historians of private life, sociologists of collective memory, ethnographers who investigate their own society rather than exotic ones, have opened up new ways of exploiting the archive of everyday existence that individuals and institutions assemble in the shape of documents, photographs and artefacts bearing the trace of human identity. The autobiographical works of Marguerite **Yourcenar**, consisting of explorations in her family history, reflect what the historian Arlette **Farge** calls '*le goût de l'archive*' (the taste of the archive) as do such mixed-media autobiographical ventures, involving texts and photographs, as Anne Duperey's *Le Voile noir* (The Black Veil) and Anne-Marie Garat's *Photos de famille* (Family Photos). Another symptomatic sign of the key role of autobiography in contemporary French culture is the prominence of new forms of biographical essay where biography becomes a form of indirect autobiography, as in Pierre Michon's influential *Vies minuscules* (Minuscule Lives) or the volumes in the series 'L'Un et l'autre' ('The One and the Other') edited by the psychoanalyst J.-B. Pontalis. The flourishing Association pour le Patrimoine Autobiographique, founded in 1992 to encourage the creation and dissemination of life-archives, and the collective creation and discussion of autobiographical works, is further testimony to the fact that the rise of autobiography reflects a widespread fascination with life histories and individual testimony which is a phenomenon affecting a broad cross-section of French society.

MICHAEL SHERINGHAM

See also: gay writing; Lacan, Jacques; structuralism; women's/lesbian writing

Further reading

Barthes, R. (1975) *Roland Barthes par Roland Barthes*, Paris: Éditions du Seuil. Translated R. Howard (1977) *Roland Barthes by Roland Barthes*, New York: Hill and Wang.

Keefe, T. and Smyth, E. (eds) (1995) *Autobiography and the Existential Self: Studies in Modern French Writing*, Liverpool: Liverpool University Press (a useful collection of essays on Sartre, Beauvoir, Camus, Genet, Leduc and Guibert).

Leiris, M. (1939, 1946) *L'Age d'homme*, Paris: Gallimard. Translated R. Howard (1968) *Manhood*, London: Cape.

Lejeune, P. (1975) *Le Pacte autobiographique*, Paris: Éditions du Seuil (an immensely influential book which contains a seminal account of the idea of an autobiographer's contact with the reader, and excellent close textual readings of Rousseau, Gide, Leiris and Sartre).

——(1989) *On Autobiography*, Minneapolis: University of Minnesota Press (a selection of Lejeune's writings covering the full range of his writings on autobiography).

Perec, G. (1975), *W ou le souvenir d'enfance*, Paris: Denoël. Translated D. Bellos (1988) *W or the Childhood Memory*, London: Collins-Harvill.

Sarraute, N. (1983), *Enfance*, Paris: Gallimard. Translated B. Wright (1984) *Childhood*, London: John Calder.

Sartre, J.-P. (1964) *Les Mots*, Paris: Gallimard. Translated I. Clifton (1964) *Words*, London: Hamish Hamilton.

Sheringham, M. (1993) *French Autobiography: Devices and Desires: Rousseau to Perec*, Oxford: Clarendon Press (a comprehensive critical analysis of the French autobiographical canon via such topics as the reader's role, the use of incidents, existentialist autobiography and the function of memory).

avance sur recettes

Instituted in 1960 by the state in the face of the film industry's financial crisis caused by declining audiences, this form of selective financing benefits 20 per cent of the films made and represents 5 per cent of investment in production. It targets films of quality (experimental, *auteur*, heritage films) and is attributed to a producer or film-maker upon the successful acceptance of his or her script by a government-appointed commission. Not a subsidy, this advance is to be repaid. However, of the films benefiting from this system since 1960, less than 10 per cent have paid off the loan in full, and only 50 per cent in part.

SUSAN HAYWARD

See also: cinema; National Cinematographic Centre

Avignon and summer arts festivals

Cultural life in the field of the performing arts (including theatre and dance) is particularly vibrant in the summer months, thanks to the establishment over the last fifty years of a series of festivals, of which Avignon is certainly by far the biggest and most famous.

The Avignon festival was founded in 1947 by Jean **Vilar** with the intention of making theatre available to a public wider than the traditional Parisian audience. At a time when the general trend in French politics and culture was towards decentralization, the festival became a popular centre with audiences from all over France, especially the south. Jean Vilar's productions in the Cour d'Honneur of the Palais des Papes (Papal Palace), and those which followed him there, have included some memorable stagings, which have become theatrical reference points. These include Vilar's *Richard II* in 1947, and his *Prince of Homburg* starring Gérard **Philipe** and Jeanne **Moreau** in 1951; Bob Wilson's *Einstein on the Beach* in 1976; Peter **Brook**'s *Mahabharata* in 1985, Vitez's *The Satin Slipper* (*Le Soulier de satin*) in 1988, and **Chéreau**'s *Hamlet* in 1989. Famous dancers and **choreographers** have also staged productions in the Cour d'Honneur, which has become the most prominent performance space used at the official Avignon festival. By 1996, the official festival had grown to take in twenty-nine venues, with thirty theatre productions – plus lectures, musical theatre, some thirty concerts and five exhibitions – attracting an audience of between 120,000 and 130,000 over the three weeks of the festival.

Avignon is funded by state, town and ticket sales: in 1996, the total budget amounted to 45 million francs, of which 24.5 million came from subsidy (12.5 million from the state and 12 million from the region). A total of 86.6 million is spent during the Avignon festival, 44.2 million of which is spent on events connected with the festival, and 42.4 million within the town by festival-goers.

The equivalent of the Avignon 'fringe' festival – the 'Off', as it is known – has been running alongside the official festival for some thirty years. In 1982, Alain Léotard founded the association Avignon Public Off, to co-ordinate and provide a structure for the numerous young troupes wanting to take part in the Avignon season, issuing a programme of all events happening outside the official festival. Today, it encompasses productions in ninety-five performance spaces, with 482 productions from eighteen countries, taking place from 10 a.m. to 2 a.m. all over town. The 'Off' includes a wide range of arts, ranging from **circus** performance to cabaret, as well as numerous theatre creations, with a particular emphasis on contemporary writers. Villeneuve-lès-Avignon, home to the state-funded writer's centre La Chartreuse, also launched its own festival in 1996 to run at the same time as the Avignon festival, with over thirty events.

As well as being motivated by the desire to diffuse culture more widely, towns around France have also realized, as these figures illustrate, that for the municipality a festival is likely to be beneficial both for reputation and for business. 'Festivalomania' has resulted in a plethora of festivals appearing and disappearing, celebrating music, dance, theatre and other art forms all over France. All are fighting for the subsidy without which it is very difficult to make a festival financially viable. Avignon, too, has to struggle to make its money stretch: although artistically the aim is to present as wide a range of productions as possible, the number of events has in fact decreased from the levels of 1995 (forty-three spectacles) to around 30–35 each year. Festival director Bertrand Faivre d'Arcier recently criticized those municipalities which, he says, are inspired to run a festival for touristic rather than for artistic reasons. Whether this is true or not, it is certainly undeniable that 'festivalomania' exists in France, with over 600 performing arts festivals recognized by the Ministry of Culture. Although Avignon is by far the biggest cultural festival, others are also worthy of note. Pau, for example, was founded by Roger Hanin in 1966 to help promote the work of young troupes, also the philosophy of the Alès festival of 'Jeune Théâtre', which specializes in new talent, in the past providing a forum for now famous names such as Jérôme **Deschamps** or the Royal de Luxe theatre company. The annual Cannes film festival is celebrated for its Palme d'Or awards. Aix-en-Provence hosts a renowned festival of lyric music, particularly Mozart, which attracts an international audience. The city of Paris also hosts a summer arts festival, the Quartiers d'Été, funded by the city and state and directed by Patrice Martinet. Other notable theatre festivals during May and June are Théâtre en Mai, held in Dijon since 1991; Les Turbulences at La Maillon in Strasbourg; the St Herblain festival near Nantes, the Lille-based circus Festival du Prato and the Printemps des Comédiens in Montpellier. Paris is also home to the autumn arts festival, the Festival d'Automne, which traditionally attracts big-name productions from practitioners such as Peter Brook, Bob Wilson and other famous directors, as well as a range of **dance**, musical and cinematic events. Major film festivals take place in Cannes, La Rochelle, Deauville (devoted to American cinema) and Créteil, near Paris (devoted to the work of women film-makers).

ANNIE SPARKS

See also: Azama, Michel; cinema; theatre; women directors

Further reading

Bradby, D. (1991) *Modern French Drama 1940–1990*, Cambridge: Cambridge University Press (see the chapter on Vilar).

Faivre d'Arcier, B. (1993) 'De la fonction culturelle du festival', in *Festivals, création, tourisme et image*, Paris: Les Cahiers Espace.

——(1996) 'Ici on fait du théâtre d'art', *Le Figaro* 9, 7.

Festivals et Expositions (1996) Paris: Ministry of Culture (a government publication, with listings of theatre and other arts festivals).

Festive France: Festivals, Sound and Light, Shows, Events, Paris: Maison de la France (an annually published listing).

Azama, Michel

b. 1947, Catalonia

Playwright

A master in modern arts and former professional actor, Azama has written numerous plays, including *Vie et mort de Pier Paolo Pasolini* (Life and Death of Pier Paolo Pasolini), *Croisades* (Crusades) and *Aztèques* (Aztecs). From 1989 to 1992 he was resident writer at the Centre Dramatique National in Dijon. Since 1993, he has been literary adviser to the Centre National des Écritures Contemporaines at La Chartreuse, Villeneuve-les-Avignon. He edits its theatre journal for authors, *Les Cahiers du Prospéro*.

ANNIE SPARKS

See also: theatre

Aznavour, Charles

b. 1924, Paris

Singer-songwriter,
real name Varenagh Aznavourian

Immediately after the war, Aznavour wrote only the words of songs in collaboration with Pierre Roche, but later wrote both words and music of songs performed by Édith **Piaf**, Eddie Constantine and Juliette **Gréco**. Eventually succeeding as a solo artist from the mid-1950s, he enjoyed much success in the United States and the United Kingdom. Hit songs include *For Mamma* (*La Mamma*), which was written with R. Gall, and *Comme ils disent* (As They Say).

IAN PICKUP

See also: song/*chanson*

B

Badinter, Élisabeth

b. 1944, France

Historian

After pursuing studies in sociology and psychology, Badinter turned to history, which she has taught in a number of Paris's tertiary educational institutions. In the 1980s and 1990s, she has published works dealing with gender and sexual/political issues. These include *The Myth of Motherhood: An Historical View of the Maternal Instinct (L'Amour en plus: histoire de l'amour maternel XVIIe–XXe siècle)*, *Man/Woman: The One is the Other (L'Un est l'autre)*, *Qu'est-ce qu'une femme?* (What is a Woman?), and *XY: On Masculine Identity (XY, de l'identité masculine)*. She has also written biographical historical works.

ALEX HUGHES

See also: feminist thought

Badinter, Robert

b. 1928, Paris

Lawyer and politician

A prominent humanitarian lawyer, Badinter became Justice Minister in the first government of the **Mitterrand** presidency (1981). He was the architect of the abolition of the death penalty, widely regarded as the most significant measure of the Mitterrand years – a reform with which his name has been indelibly associated. He is married to Élisabeth **Badinter**.

KEITH READER

See also: parties and movements

Baker, Josephine

b. 1906 Saint Louis, USA;
d. 1975

An expatriate African-American singer and dancer, Baker rose to great fame in the 1920s as the star of the *Revue Nègre*, a music-hall show, and the Folies Bergères. Her signature song was *J'ai deux amours (Paris et mon pays)*. She starred in a silent film, *La Sirène des tropiques* (1927), and two popular French sound films, *Zouzou* (1934) and *Princesse Tam-Tam* (1935). Often shown in photographs wearing nothing but a string of banana skins around her waist, she is thought by many to evoke the exoticism (and eroticism) of the Jazz Age in Paris between the world wars.

ELIZABETH EZRA

See also: dance

Balasko, Josiane

b. 1952, Paris

Actor and director

Originally a member of Le Splendid café theatre troupe, she acted in a number of their plays which were eventually made into films, for example Poiré's *Le Père Noël est une ordure* (1982). She was best known in the 1980s for her role as Depardieu's lover in Blier's *Trop belle pour toi* (1989), as well as for a number of her own comic films, for example *Les Keufs* in 1987. Her *French Twist* (*Gazon maudit*), in which she plays a lesbian, was the second-best-selling film of 1995 in France.

PHIL POWRIE

See also: cinema

Further reading

Vincendeau, G. (1996) 'Twist and Farce', *Sight and Sound* 6, 4: 24–6 (an appraisal).

Balladur, Édouard

b. 1929, Smyrna, Turkey

Politician

Balladur served in the Conseil d'État before becoming an adviser to Premier Pompidou in 1966. He was President Pompidou's chief of staff in 1973–4 and director of a major industrial group from 1977 to 1984. As Finance Minister in the 1986–8 Chirac government, he was responsible for a major privatization and deregulation programme. He was elected to parliament in 1988 and 1993 and, following the victory of the parties of the right in 1993, was appointed prime minister by President Mitterrand. He was able to use this position to challenge his fellow Gaullist, Chirac, in the 1995 presidential election but was eliminated in the first ballot.

LAURENCE BELL

See also: parties and movements

Major works

Balladur, É. (1992) *Dictionnaire de la réforme*, Paris: Fayard (the author's own neo-conservative prescriptions).

Further reading

Zemmour, É. (1995) *Balladur: immobile à grands pas*, Paris: Grasset.

Balthus

b. 1908, France;
d. 1997, France

Artist, real name Balthasar Klossowski de Rola

Balthus is a painter working independently in the figurative tradition within the European context. Isolated from the main current of contemporary art, but influenced by Gustave Courbet (1819–77) and Piero della Francesca (1410/20–92), his work is naturalistic and non-improvised. Using the figure as symbolic, his images portray the claustrophobia of male sexual fantasy. The dominant theme is the private obsession of the nude or exposed adolescent girl sprawled or bent over, inviting sexual violence, as in *La Chambre* (1954). His paint surfaces have become increasingly worked, his images highly structured, reminiscent of the densely decorated and impastoed surfaces of the Byzantine fresco.

VALERIE SWALES

See also: painting

banks

The banking system in France has been slow to develop. Main high-street banks (Crédit Lyonnais, Société Générale and BNP) were nationalized in 1945, and most of the remaining ones, including investment banks, were nationalized in 1981. A slow deregulation process started in the 1960s, whose impact was only significantly felt in the 1980s, especially after the 'Big Bang' liberalization in 1985. A movement towards privatization started in 1986. The recent growth and liberalization of the banking system has encountered considerable difficulties, especially in regulatory terms, with large banks such as Crédit Lyonnais suffering from speculative investment strategies.

FRANÇOIS NECTOUX

See also: economy; nationalization and privatization

Barbara

b. 1930, Paris;
d. 1997, Paris

Singer-songwriter,
real name Monique Serf

Having served a long apprenticeship in Parisian cabarets and in Belgium, Barbara performed, in the late 1950s and early 1960s, songs written by others (including **Brassens** and **Brel**) before making her reputation with her own songs. The archetypal *femme fatale* on stage, Barbara captivated her audiences with such songs as *Nantes*, *Mes hommes* (My Men) and *Pierre*. An influential performer, she is noted for an individual style on the piano.

IAN PICKUP

See also: song/*chanson*

Barclay, Eddie

b. 1921, Paris

Composer, bandleader and
record-company owner,
real name Édouard Ruault

Originally a **jazz** pianist, Eddie Barclay formed his own record company in order to record his own band. By the sixties, the Barclay label had attracted such important names as Charles **Aznavour**, Léo **Ferré**, Jacques **Brel**, Claude **Nougaro** and Jean **Ferrat**. Barclay himself was one of the most powerful figures in French show business from the 1950s until 1979, when his company was taken over by Polygram.

IAN PICKUP

See also: song/*chanson*

Bardèche, Maurice

b. 1907, Dun-sur-Auron

Writer

Bardèche is an avowedly Fascist writer, imbued by his brother-in-law Robert Brasillach's execution at the **Liberation** with a lifelong passion to redeem and spread his ideals. He staunchly defended collaboration in the *Lettre à François Mauriac* of 1947, and founded the **publishing** house Les Sept Couleurs and the journal *Défense de l'Occident*, from 1952 to 1982 the epicentre of the intellectual extreme Right in France. Since the rise of **Le Pen** and the increasing influence of rightist ideologies worldwide, his prominence has waned, but he remains important as the last surviving major link between the far Right of today and the Occupation.

KEITH READER

See also: *Hussards*

Bardot, Brigitte

b. 1934, Paris

Actor

More than any of the other French female **stars**
– indeed any female star in the world except
Marilyn Monroe – she is associated with a sexuality at once threatening and fascinating
through its very naivety and candour. The
Bardot star persona, from the 'sex kitten' of the
1950s to the animal-besotted St Tropez recluse
of today, has long outlived her acting career,
which came to an end in 1973. **Vadim**'s *And
God Created Woman* (*Et Dieu créa la femme*)
of 1956 is by far her best-known screen role,
though her dramatic capabilities were better
revealed by **Clouzot** in *La Vérité* of 1960 and
Godard in *Le Mépris* three years later.

Keith Reader

See also: cinema; stars

Barrault, Jean-Louis

b. 1910, Le Vésinet;
d. 1994, Paris

Director

Barrault was one of the most influential postwar theatre directors, whose directorial work
explored the idea of 'total' theatre, experimenting with scene, music, dancing, comedy and
acrobatics, with emphasis on the actor's role
and physical expression. He is often referred
to, in this sense, as a disciple of **Artaud**,
although his special interest in the actor also
stems from theatre traditions pioneered by
Copeau and the prewar Cartel directors, especially Dullin, Barrault's teacher in the 1930s.
Barrault's concept of theatre thus combined
spiritual and physical desire for 'total' expression like that of Artaud, but was firmly rooted
in humanist, down-to-earth practices.

A gifted **mime** artist working in Dullin's

workshops at the age of 20, where he was
encouraged by **Decroux**, Barrault began to
impress audiences, among them Artaud, who
praised his skilled gesture and movement in
mimodrames. Between 1935 and 1939, his
experimentation also included the formation of
the collective Le Grenier des Augustins with
Jean **Dasté**, which included **Vilar** and Artaud
among its regulars.

At the same time, he also began to work in
the **cinema**, again winning acclaim for his
mime abilities (as in Carné and **Prévert**'s *Les
Enfants du Paradis* of 1945). He also became a
Comédie-Française *sociétaire* in 1940, where,
as well as acting, he directed the celebrated
1943 production of Claudel's *The Satin Slipper*
(*Le Soulier de Satin*). He was to develop a fruitful director–author relationship with Claudel
as a result, lasting into the 1950s and 1960s.

In 1946 he founded the Compagnie
Renaud-Barrault with his actor wife Madeleine
Renaud, based for ten years at the independent
Marigny theatre. In 1959, Barrault took on
directorship of the Odéon theatre. During this
period he directed notable productions of classics and new works from authors such as
Ionesco, as well as productions of non-dramatic material, including *The Trial* (*Le Procès*) and
The Castle (*Le Château*), based on Kafka,
exploring his version of notions of 'total' theatre. He also invited young directors such as
Roger **Blin** to direct controversial works by
authors such as **Beckett** and **Genet**. Between
1966 and 1968, he also took on the directorship of the Théâtre des Nations, a home for
experimental international theatre from
Grotowski, **Brook** and the Living Theatre
among others.

After **May 1968**, Barrault was dismissed
from the Odéon for discussing issues with students occupying the theatre rather than opposing them on behalf of the authorities. His company moved to an old wrestling hall near
Clichy, the Élysée Montmartre, where they
staged *Rabelais*, a production based on the
latter's works in a liberating new theatre arena.
In 1972 the company moved to the Théâtre
d'Orsay, where it constructed a portable theatre space, and performed a varied repertoire,

alongside companies such as the **Grand Magic Circus**, also permitted to perform here. In 1981, the company moved its portable theatre to the Théâtre du Rond-Point, where it remained until Barrault's death.

ANNIE SPARKS

See also: theatre; Theatre of the Absurd; theatres, national

Further reading

Whitton, D. (1987) *Stage Directors in Modern France*, Manchester: Manchester University Press (contains a useful chapter on 'total' theatre).

Barre, Raymond

b. 1924, St-Denis-de-la-Réunion

Politician

A former professor of economic history and European Commissioner, Barre was appointed prime minister in 1976 by President **Giscard d'Estaing** and, in response to economic recession, undertook a policy of budget cuts and industrial rationalization. His blunt pedagogical style did not endear him to the public. In opposition in the 1980s, however, his plain speaking came to be appreciated as a mark of independence and sincerity. First elected to parliament in 1978, he stood in the presidential election of 1988, but was eliminated in the first ballot. Identified with the centrist component of the conservative coalition, he was elected mayor of Lyon in 1995.

LAURENCE BELL

See also: parties and movements

Major

Barre, R. (1981) *Une Politique pour l'avenir*, Paris: Plon (here Barre defends his economic record in government and outlines his proposals for the [then] future).

Further reading

Grendel, F. (1978) *Raymond Barre ou les plumes du paon*, Paris: Régine Deforges (a short, laconic, journalistic sketch written during Barre's premiership).

Barrière, Alain

b. 1935, La Trinité-sur-Mer, Morbihan

Singer-songwriter, composer, real name Alain Bellec

Alain Barrière's Breton roots have left their imprint on his compositions, which are often characterized by their vague, suggestive qualities but also by their wistful treatment of the theme of love. He remained extremely popular in the 1960s and 1970s. Hit songs include *Plus je t'entends* (The More I Hear You), *Ma vie* (My Life) and *Tu t'en vas* (You Are Going Away).

IAN PICKUP

See also: song/*chanson*

Barsacq, André

b. 1909, Feodossia, Crimea;
d. 1973, Paris

Stage designer and director

A designer for Dullin, Copeau, and **Dasté**, Barsacq became director at the Théâtre de l'Atelier in 1940. His productions demonstrated an emphasis on linking design and direction closely to the text. He was a founder member of the directors' union.

ANNIE SPARKS

See also: theatre

Further reading

Bibliothèque Nationale (1978) *André Barsacq, cinquante ans de théâtre*, Paris: Bibliothèque Nationale (exhibition catalogue).

Barthes, Roland

b. 1915, Cherbourg;
d. 1980, Paris

Writer and literary critic

Barthes reshaped literary studies between the 1950s to 1980 by championing innovative practices ranging from the new novel (*nouveau roman*) and **structuralism** to semiology and the study of affect from love to mourning. At the Sorbonne between 1935 and 1941, he studied classics and theatre before tuberculosis ended his hopes of a university teaching career. It was while undergoing treatment for tuberculosis during the Occupation that Barthes first published short essays on culture and tragedy, André Gide's *Journal*, and the style of Albert **Camus**'s *The Stranger* (*L'Étranger*).

In August 1947, a piece in *Combat* was the point of departure for the essay published six years later as *Writing Degree Zero* (*Le Degré zéro de l'écriture*). Barthes drew in this first book on definitions of prose and poetry that Jean-Paul **Sartre** in 1947 had set forth in *What is Literature?* (*Qu'est-ce que la littérature?*) for his programme of **committed literature**. But, whereas Sartre rejected poetry in favour of a transparent prose that propelled the writer through language and into the world, Barthes's notion of writing (*écriture*) set between lan-

guage and style asserted a morality of form over literary genres. Similar concerns for moral dimensions of writing in Barthes's 1954 monograph on the nineteenth-century historian, Jules Michelet, prophesied the introspection, mixing of genres, and fragmentation of the *Roland Barthes by Roland Barthes* (*Roland Barthes par Roland Barthes*) that Barthes contributed twenty-one years later to the same series, known informally as *X par lui-même*.

In *Mythologies* (1957), Barthes explored the mass cultures of postwar France across high and low expressions, ranging from **advertising** campaigns for margarine and the face of Greta Garbo to the annual **Tour de France** bicycle race and Citroën model DS automobile. Alongside the insights provided by individual texts, *Mythologies* disclosed a predilection for system and theory that spanned traditional rhetoric and emergent structuralism. Over the next decade, Barthes wrote increasingly against the grain of academic criticism. In *Sur Racine* (1963), he recast critical terms borrowed from **psychoanalysis** and linguistics into a direct challenge to the writings of the Sorbonne specialist, Raymond Picard. If, as Barthes once confessed, he wrote *On Racine* (*Sur Racine*) because he had never really taken to Racine's tragedies, his oppositional stance towards classical tragedy and academic criticism matched the contentiousness of the future *soixante-huitards* who were to question a cultural heritage (*patrimoine*) with which they could not identify. By 1968, Barthes's writings – along with those of Claude **Lévi-Strauss**, Michel **Foucault** and Jacques **Lacan** – had captured the imaginations of youths, students and intellectuals smitten by the force of the moment. At the same time, Barthes's frequent contributions to journals such as ***Tel quel***, *Communications* and *Critique* solidified his ties to a Parisian avant-garde linked with structuralism.

S/Z (1970) marked a turning point in Barthes's critical practices by breaking Balzac's twenty-five-page story, 'Sarrasine', down into 561 units of meaning (*lexies*) interspersed with a number of critical asides. The result was a close analysis that revealed as much about the reader and reading process as it did about the

text in question. Rather than simply dissecting the form and structure of Balzac's story, *S/Z* plotted how the interaction of text and reader fashioned meaning around a set of codes open to variation from reader to reader and from one reading to the next. In sum, *S/Z* illustrated the extent to which a turn towards introspection had replaced Barthes's earlier involvement with the structuralist dream of a science of literature.

In 1973's *The Pleasure of the Text* (*Le Plaisir du texte*), Barthes explicitly practised the concepts of text and writing that he had theorized elsewhere. In place of expository prose, terse aphorisms in alphabetical order enhanced the disjointedness of a fragmentary writing whose form was closer to the texts of Pascal and La Rochefoucauld than to those of **Greimas**, Lévi-Strauss and Propp. Newly fashioned binaries such as readerly/writerly texts and texts of pleasure/bliss (*texte lisible/texte scriptible* and *texte de plaisir/texte de jouissance*, respectively) recast Barthes's critical vision into a mode that was personalized and intuitive. Two years later, *Roland Barthes* dispersed the first person pronoun into an unstable mix of essay, **autobiography** and fiction seemingly adapted from Lacan's account of subjectivity constructed by an ongoing interplay of imaginary and symbolic modes.

1977's *A Lover's Discourse* (*Fragments d'un discours amoureux*) illustrated the full extent to which Barthes's writings of the previous decade had redirected structural analysis towards a personalized semiology concerned less with the science or analysis of literature than with the critical self or subject. *A Lover's Discourse* none the less developed a critical reflection on language that fashioned the persona of the lover through utterances (*énonciations*) whose confessional nature once again played off conventions of genres by overlapping essay, novel and autobiography. It is no small irony that *Camera Lucida* (*La Chambre claire*), Barthes's note on **photography**, was published less than two months before his death in March 1980: the signs of time's passage that Barthes sought in the faces of the subjects depicted in the book's photos were a way

of contending with his mother's death in 1977. What Barthes expressed as the *studium/punctum* binary set language and culture against the perceived detail that broke through language to disclose the reality of death. *La Chambre claire* was, then, both an essay or meditation on photography and a book of mourning, whose parallels with Marcel Proust's *Remembrance of Things Past* (*A la recherche du temps perdu*) were hard to misconstrue.

Throughout his career, numerous short texts set Barthes's major writings within the extended engagement with ideas and culture that he conveyed to his students at the École Pratique des Hautes Études and École des Hautes Études en Sciences Sociales. Focusing on subjects as diverse as wrestling, *frites*, Schubert's last compositions and the art of Cy Twombly, Barthes combined the traits of intellectual and sensualist, ever open to what Stephen Heath has aptly termed the 'dizziness of displacement'. This openness – an offshoot of Gide's *disponibilité* – remains the long-term legacy of the texts he wrote and the personal example he lived.

STEVEN UNGAR

Further reading

Calvet, L.-J. (1995) *Roland Barthes*, Bloomington: Indiana University Press (biography).

Heath, S. (1974) *Vertige du déplacement: lecture de Barthes*, Paris: Fayard (a French-language study by Barthes's major British exegete).

Lavers, A. (1982) *Roland Barthes: Structuralism and After*, Cambridge: Harvard University Press (concise presentation of writings through the mid-1960s).

Roger, P. (1986) *Roland Barthes, roman*, Paris: Grasset (a fictionalized biography).

Thody, P. (1977) *Roland Barthes: A Conservative Estimate*, London: Macmillan (uneven, but provocative).

Ungar, S. (1983) *Roland Barthes: The Professor Desire*, Lincoln: University of Nebraska Press (a major analytic study).

Bataille, Georges

b. 1897, Puy-de-Dôme;
d. 1962, Paris

Intellectual and writer

The work of Georges Bataille is seemingly composed of contradiction. Early texts, from the late 1920s, such as 'W.C.', 'L'Anus solaire' (Solar Anus) and 'L'Oeil pinéal' (The Pineal Eye) can be read as a violent reaction, informed by a reading of Nietzsche and Freud, to a pious and conformist youth. His influential journal *Documents* (1929–31) engaged in an ethnography of the everyday, directly contrasting high and low culture or Western and non-Western society, in order to arrive at a 'base materialism'. The 1935 *Contre-Attaque* movement to which he adhered was an anti-Fascist and anti-Stalinist resistance to the Popular Front that involved a short-lived collaboration with Surrealism. His recognition of the Durkheimian principles of the College of Sociology, which he co-founded in 1937 with Michel **Leiris** and Roger Caillois, was implicitly contested by his parallel formation of *Acéphale*, a conspiratonal and 'headless' society devoted to the realization of ritual transgression and sacrifice. These essentially collaborative manifestations of the sacred in contemporary life collapsed with the advent of the war, giving way to an intense internalization of sacred experience culminating in the 1943 *Inner Experience* (*L'Expérience intérieure*). His new journal, *Critique*, founded in 1946 and still in existence, stands in direct contrast to the short-lived *Documents* with its challenge to academic classification, being based on extended book reviews. At the same time, their heterogeneous nature (the areas covered being 'literary creation, philosophy and historical, scientific, political and economic knowledge') sought to contest the orthodoxies of **existentialism**. Cutting across these critical works, in turn, was an equally transgressive production of novels and stories, culminating in *L'Abbé C* (published in 1950 but set during the war) and *Blue of Noon* (*Le Bleu du ciel*), published in

1957 (but finished in 1935), the same year as *Literature and Evil* (*La littérature et le mal*), a collection of essays which had appeared in *Critique*, and *Eroticism* (*L'Érotisme*). This last text, probably Bataille's best known, and (if we can say this) the summation of his work, presents eroticism and its relation to transgression and death as central to the human condition. The recovery of this eroticism, repressed by Christian culture, is the task of an atheism. Such tensions and transgressions are defined by Bataille himself as the contradiction between solidity, involving the orthodox isolation and analysis of an object, and sovereignty, a key term in Bataille which designates a rejection of preservation and reserve in favour of the dynamics of excess and expenditure. On a personal level, sovereignty may be experienced and celebrated via the mucosity of the body, the extremity of the emotions and the uselessness of human activity (play, crime, eroticism, poetry); on an economic level, as Bataille attempts to show in *The Accursed Share* (*La Part maudite*), this involves replacing a scarcity model with the notion of the circulation of excess. Such designations indicate, of course, how the idea of contradiction is ultimately inadequate to the task of reading and applying Bataille. His work has enormously influenced poststructuralist theorizing.

SEÁN HAND

See also: erotic writing; literary journals; poststructuralism

Further reading

Hollier, D. (1990) *Beyond Architecture*, Cambridge: MIT Press (a theoretical, involved attempt to realize the implications of Bataille's theories for the notion of critical discourse).

Surya, M. (1987) *Georges Bataille: la mort à l'oeuvre*, Paris: Séguier (the essential biography).

Bataille, Nicolas

birthdate not known

Director and actor

Bataille is most noted for his directing work during the 1930s and 1940s of experimental Surrealist plays, by authors such as **Ionesco**, including the first performances of Ionesco's still-running *The Bald Primadonna* (*La Cantatrice chauve*). After the war, he worked mainly in the small theatres of the Latin Quarter.

ANNIE SPARKS

See also: theatre; Theatre of the Absurd

Baudrillard, Jean

b. 1929, Reims

Intellectual and social theorist

Baudrillard has become one of the most influential and controversial intellectual figures in postwar France. He is often seen as one of the major thinkers of **postmodernism**, a label which, however, he rejects.

His work has explored the world of objects and, latterly, the contemporary tendency of the world to become a pure object; the 'revenge of the crystal' as he calls it. This 'objective' world resists human strategy, becoming a prosthesis of the human body. It is a world of seduction, simulation, hyperreality and 'fatal' strategies. His first important works, including *The Object System* (*Le Système des objets*), initiate the important themes of the interpretation of objects and of a concentration on consumption rather than production. He is convinced that consumer society is a new and completely distinctive phase of capitalism. Influenced by Marx, the situationists, Marcuse, Lewis Mumford, **Barthes**, McLuhan and **Lefebvre**, he develops a sophisticated analysis of a new spatial system of objects, technology and media.

This system creates a 'seductive' and transparent coherence which makes humanist ideologies incoherent. In this way he develops McLuhan's celebrated statement that 'the medium is the message'. Baudrillard is never really satisfied with a **Marxist** notion of alienation and turns increasingly in the 1970s towards 'pataphysics', a science fiction of 'imaginary solutions'. He has remained an admirer of J. G. Ballard since writing an appreciative review of *Crash* in 1976, and his own writing has begun to incorporate elements of science fiction and poetry. By the mid-1970s he dispensed with alienation and any notion of an alternative mode of production, and in *Symbolic Exchange and Death* (*L'Échange symbolique et la mort*) the influence of Mauss and **Bataille** is evident. The pataphysical 'solution' offered to counter the world of simulation is that of a return to a 'symbolic' order. Marxist critique can only think in terms of a contradiction between use-value and exchange-value. Mauss's analysis of the symbolic violence of the gift, on the other hand, helps Baudrillard to think in terms of a Symbolic Order which challenges the seduction of hyperreality. He also draws on Bataille's notions of excessive expenditure and sacrifice, at times evincing a nostalgia for 'primitive' symbolic exchange. Baudrillard is scathing about what he sees as the project of modernity, premissed as it is upon the paradigms of progress and accumulation. The poetic mode becomes for Baudrillard a way of rejecting the principle of accumulation, and as such it is a principle that he applies to his own work. In interviews, he has alluded to his peasant origins, and points to the principle of discretion and conservation of productive energy as the converse of excess. Poetry as a pared-down form respects this principle of discretion, and can even, as Saussure shows in his notebooks on anagrams, point towards its own disappearance. In the 1980s and 1990s Baudrillard largely effaced the distinctions between theory, poetry and **autobiography** in his work. He has published three volumes of aphorisms which are drawn from his own journals. It is here that he presents a concise summary of his own development, from pataphysician at 20 to 'viral and metaleptic' at 60.

JOHN MARKS

See also: situationism

Further reading

Gane, M. (1991) *Baudrillard's Bestiary: Baudrillard and Culture*, London: Routledge (a clear and wide-ranging introduction to Baudrillard's work).
——(ed.) (1993) *Baudrillard Live: Selected Interviews*, London: Routledge (these interviews provide an illuminating insight into Baudrillard's main ideas).

Baye, Nathalie

b. 1948, Maineville

Actor

Baye's career began in 1970. She has made films with many of the major directors: **Blier** (*Beau-père*), **Pialat** (*La Gueule ouverte*), **Godard** (*Sauve qui peut (la vie)*, *Détective*, in which she starred with her then-partner Johnny **Hallyday**), **Truffaut** (*L'Homme qui aimait les femmes*, *La Chambre verte*) and **Tavernier** (*Une semaine de vacances*). She has tended to play sensitive women, but received a César as best actress for the uncharacteristic role of prostitute in Swaim's *La Balance* (1982). She also received awards for best supporting actress in 1981 and 1982.

PHIL POWRIE

See also: cinema

Bazaine, Jean

b. 1904, Paris

Artist

Bazaine's work searches for a national, not a nationalist identity. He works with the automatism of the abstract expressionists but heightens the process to an ethic of exercise and rhythm. Until the 1940s, blue and red dominate the canvas. With later work, such as *Chicago* (1965) and *Naissance* (1975), Bazaine pursues a lengthy engagement with the ambition to capture the forces of nature and universal correspondences. The tachist surface reveals a furiously dynamic world, perpetually on the move yet held in balance by an imposed severe discipline, as in *Vent sur les pierres* (1971).

VALERIE SWALES

See also: painting

Bazin, André

b. 1918, Paris;
d. 1958, Paris

Film critic

An influential film critic post-1945, and the co-founder in 1951 of *Cahiers du cinéma*, Bazin introduced three crucial interrelated issues into film theory debates: genre, the phenomenological dimension of cinematic practices, and cinema as language.

Genre had hitherto been a neglected question and much of the post-1960s writing on it among Anglo-Saxon critics owes a lot to Bazin. The question of genre was introduced into theoretical debate by Bazin through his investigation into the relationship between film-maker and film product. A primary purpose behind this investigation was an attempt to dissolve the high art/low art divide then much in evidence in critics' dismissive attitude towards popular American genres. Bazin argued against the binary divide which dismissed Hollywood cinema as formulaic, suggesting that although Hollywood directors had little say over the production practice, none the less their films merited historical and contextual analysis as signs of their times. Thus popular generic cinema (Westerns, thrillers, etc.) entered into the forum of critical debate.

Bazin's second important contribution lies in his argument against a pure cinema aesthetic and for a phenomenological dimension of cinema. He claimed that cinema allows us to see time and that, unlike earlier aesthetics of cinema (the avant-garde of the 1920s) – which placed cinematic practices outside reality (by seeking to resolve the question of time and space through the fragmentation of the real) – its true aesthetics are firmly grounded in the revelation of the identity between reproduction and expression (the staging of the real world for the camera), and the conjuncture between the ontological (the essence of things) and the psychological (the perception of things).

Closely linked to this phenomenological approach was Bazin's notion of an aesthetic realism which he based in his concept of cinema as language. Bazin argued for a naturalism of the image that refuses all a priori knowledge or analysis of the world. To this effect, he advocated the merits of deep focus and the long take over the principles of montage (a fast editing style that produces a priori meaning through the collision of images). Deep focus occurs when all planes within the lens's focus are in sharp focus. This in turn makes long takes possible. There is no need to edit to make movement (movement takes place within the frame). According to Bazin, deep focus makes a greater objective realism possible. It allows for a more open reading of the image than the fast editing style of montage. It does not subject the spectator to the ideological nature of montage, but secures instead the principle of aesthetic realism.

This insistence on the readability of the image meant that the concept of *mise-en-scène* (the staging of shots) was central to Bazin's notion of cinematic language. For him, *mise-en-scène* meant the staging of the real world for the camera, creating an ontological realism that the spectator could then read without being manipulated. The implication of Bazin's notion of *mise-en-scène* is the self-effacement

of the individual film-maker. Paradoxically, the *Cahiers du cinéma* group took an opposing view of this concept, arguing through their *politique des auteurs* (a polemical debate surrounding the concept of auteurism) that *auteur* status could be achieved through the concept of *mise-en-scène*. Bazin disassociated himself from this romantic aesthetic of the film-maker as *auteur*, that is, as an individual separate from the modes and conditions of production.

SUSAN HAYWARD

See also: cinema

Major works

Bazin, A. (1967) *What is Cinema?*, Berkeley: University of California Press (collected essays on cinema theory). (French edition (1962: *Qu'est-ce que le cinéma*, Paris.

BCBG (*bon chic bon genre*)

Class type

An approximate French equivalent of preppy style or the Sloane Ranger. To be BCBG it helps greatly to live in the triangle known as 'NAP' – Neuilly-Auteuil-Passy – the exclusive residential areas between the sixteenth *arrondissement* of Paris and the Bois de Boulogne.

KEITH READER

See also: class

Béart, Emmanuelle

b. 1964, St-Tropez

Actor

The daughter of singer Guy **Béart**, her career took off as Manon in **Berri's** *Manon des* *sources* (1986), for which she received a César as best supporting actress. After several slight films in the late 1980s, she became a familiar face as the middle-class woman preyed upon by emotionally fragile men, whether **Piccoli**'s artist in **Rivette**'s *La Belle Noiseuse* (1991), the violin repairer of **Sautet**'s *A Heart in Winter* (*Un Coeur en hiver*) (1992), played by her then real-life partner, Daniel **Auteuil**, or the jealous husband in **Chabrol**'s *L'Enfer* (1994).

PHIL POWRIE

See also: cinema; stars

Béart, Guy

b. 1930, Cairo, Egypt

Singer-songwriter,
real name Guy Behar

Having written songs for others (**Patachou**, Juliette **Gréco**), Guy Béart formed his own record company (Temporel) and in the 1960s produced a highly successful variety show on French television, *Bienvenue* (Welcome), before concentrating on his own career as a performer. His (often 'intellectual') songs show tremendous variety but are strongly influenced by **folk** music. Hits include *La Vérité* (The Truth), *Qui suis-je?* (Who Am I?) and *Le Messie* (The Messiah). He is the father of Emmanuelle **Béart**.

IAN PICKUP

See also: song/chanson

Beauvoir, Simone de

b. 1908, Paris;
d. 1986, Paris

Writer, philosopher and
political activist

Simone de Beauvoir is a major figure in post-

World War II culture. Her main contribution to cultural capital is usually considered to be her pioneering work on gender, *The Second Sex* (*Le Deuxième Sexe*), yet she is also a key figure in the French postwar variety of **existentialism**, an important novelist and autobiographer, and a founder member of *Les Temps Modernes*, with which she was closely involved through the late 1940s and 1950s.

Beauvoir was born into an upper-middle-class family. Her mother Françoise was a provincial, devout Catholic. Her father, Georges, was an atheistic Parisian with aristocratic leanings and strong right-wing sympathies. Beauvoir attended an intellectually inadequate, Catholic private school until she was 17, a regrettable start to a career for an intellectual of her calibre. Family fortunes dwindled and, to train for a teaching career, she began studying for two *licences* (undergraduate degrees) and the *agrégation* (qualification to teach in secondary and higher education) in philosophy. In 1929 Beauvoir formed a lifelong partnership and intellectual collaboration with Jean-Paul **Sartre**. She was placed second in the *agrégation* and Sartre, a student at the prestigious École Normale Supérieure (see **educational elitism: the *grandes écoles***), gained first place. This result may explain why Beauvoir consistently valued Sartre's philosophical abilities over her own. Despite her undoubted talent for philosophy, Beauvoir insisted that her principal ambition was to write. Nevertheless, much of her writing has a philosophical character.

In 1938 she submitted a collection of short stories, *When Things of the Spirit Come First* (*Quand prime le spirituel*), to **Gallimard** and Grasset for publication. Both publishers refused it at the time, probably because of its focus on women's experience, particularly of sexuality, and its critique of the bourgeoisie. Beauvoir's first published novel, *She Came to Stay* (*L'Invitée*), was published in 1943. Its Hegelian epigraph, '*chaque conscience poursuit la mort de l'autre*' (each consciousness pursues the death of the other), neatly encapsulates the novel's central theme – the conflict involved in self–other relations. Among Beauvoir's writing, these early novels are unusual because the historical and political dimensions of intersubjectivity are neglected. In her subsequent fiction of the 1940s – *The Blood of Others* (*Le Sang des autres*) and *All Men are Mortal* (*Tous les hommes sont mortels*) – the existentialist aspects of *She Came to Stay* are explored more fully within broad historical frameworks. Beauvoir's realization of her own historicity can be explained by her firsthand experience of the daily realities of war, living in Paris during the German Occupation. In the second volume of her memoirs, *The Prime of Life* (*La Force de l'âge*), Beauvoir noted of this period, '*l'Histoire m'a saisie pour ne plus me lâcher*' (History took hold of me and never let me go thereafter). During the war, she corresponded extensively with Sartre, and kept a diary. Her *Lettres à Sartre* (Letters to Sartre) and *Journal de guerre* (War Diary) were both published in 1990.

During the 1940s, Beauvoir published two significant philosophical texts: *Pyrrhus et Cinéas*, which is a companion theoretical text to *The Blood of Others*, and *The Ethics of Ambiguity* (*Pour une morale de l'ambiguité*). In these essays, although working broadly within the same existentialist framework as Sartre, Beauvoir rejects the conflictual analysis of self–other relations of *Being and Nothingness* (*L'Être et le néant*), in favour of examining the practical possibilities of reciprocal intersubjective relationships. In *The Ethics of Ambiguity*, Beauvoir argues that aspects of an individual's situation, such as gender, race, class and age, are crucial to how an individual assumes and is able to assume his or her freedom. In her ground-breaking *The Second Sex*, Beauvoir offers a constructionist, materialist account of women's gendered identity, five years after women gained the right to vote in France. Politically isolated during the escalating Cold War period when it was published, *The Second Sex* was later largely out of step with post-1968 psychoanalytically influenced feminism which embraced female essentialism. Nevertheless, it proved highly influential because of its broad scope of analysis and its focus on the materiality of gendered identity. Beauvoir did not iden-

tify herself as a feminist until the mid-1960s.

In 1954, she won the Prix Goncourt for *Les Mandarins*, a telling portrait of the situation of the French Left during the immediate postwar period in France. In 1956, Beauvoir began writing *Memoirs of a Dutiful Daughter* (*Mémoires d'une jeune fille rangée*), the first of four volumes of memoirs. These offer an invaluable political and cultural account by a left-wing intellectual of France and of the many countries which Beauvoir visited from the 1930s to the early 1970s. They also constitute a rare case study of the life of a French female intellectual of Beauvoir's generation.

During the **Algerian war**, Beauvoir became politically active. She supported Algerian **decolonization** and publicized the case of Djamila Boupacha, a young Algerian tortured by the French military. Her late fiction of the 1960s, *Les Belles Images* and *The Woman Destroyed* (*La Femme rompue*), focuses more extensively on the situation of women. *Les Belles Images* is also a sophisticated narrative which parodies the discourse of the technocratic bourgeoisie of the 1960s. In *Old Age* (*La Vieillesse*), published in 1970, Beauvoir studied another controversial issue – the experience of ageing. Throughout the 1970s, Beauvoir campaigned on feminist issues, such as **abortion**. Her last book, *Adieux: A Farewell to Sartre* (*La Cérémonie des adieux*), is an account of the last ten years of Sartre's life. For many, Beauvoir remains 'the emblematic intellectual woman of the twentieth century' (Moi 1994).

URSULA TIDD

See also: autobiography; feminist thought; literary prizes

Major works

Beauvoir, S. de (1949) *Le Deuxième Sexe*, Paris: Gallimard. Translated H. Parshley (1972) *The Second Sex*, Harmondsworth: Penguin.

——*Les Mandarins* (1954) Paris: Gallimard.

Translated L. M. Friedman (1960) *The Mandarins*, London: Fontana.

——*Mémoires d'une jeune fille rangée* (1958) Paris: Gallimard. Translated J. Kirkup (1963) *Memoirs of a Dutiful Daughter*, Harmondsworth: Penguin.

——*La Force de l'âge* (1960) Paris: Gallimard. Translated P. Green (1965) *The Prime of Life*, Harmondsworth: Penguin.

Further reading

Bair, D. (1990) *Simone de Beauvoir: A Biography*, London: Jonathan Cape (the most extensive biography of Beauvoir, published unfortunately prior to the publication of her controversial correspondence with Sartre and war diary).

Fallaize, E. (1988) *The Novels of Simone de Beauvoir*, London: Routledge (scholarly feminist study; focuses especially on Beauvoir's narrative strategies and remains unsurpassed as a study of her fiction).

Heath, J. (1989) *Simone de Beauvoir*, Hemel Hempstead: Harvester (valuable feminist Lacanian discussion of Beauvoir's memoirs and some of her fiction).

Moi, T. (1994) *Simone de Beauvoir: The Making of an Intellectual Woman*, Oxford: Blackwell (scholarly, stimulating and wide-ranging examination of Beauvoir's trajectory as an intellectual and writer; essential reading).

Simons, M. A. (ed.) (1995) *Feminist Interpretations of Simone de Beauvoir*, Pennsylvania: Pennsylvania State University Press (wide-ranging collection of essays on Beauvoir's philosophy).

Bébête-Show

Television programme

The *Bébête-Show* was a political satire programme broadcast on the main commercial television channel **TF1** between 7.50 p.m. and 7.55 p.m. each evening, just before the main news programme. It was first transmitted during the 1988 presidential election campaign and its final broadcast took place just after the 1995 presidential elections. Its most famous character was Kermitterrand, a frog-like puppet of President **Mitterrand** based on Kermit in *The Muppets*. The success of the *Bébête-Show*, with a nightly audience of between 8 and 13 million viewers, gave rise to other satirical programmes featuring puppets, notably *Les Guignols de l'info* on **Canal Plus**.

RAYMOND KUHN

Bécaud, Gilbert

b. 1927, Toulon

Singer-composer,
real name François Silly

Having worked as Jacques Pills's pianist, Bécaud wrote songs with Pierre **Delanoë** before making a triumphal appearance at the Olympia in 1954. An outstanding stage performer known as *Monsieur 100 000 volts*, Gilbert Bécaud remains popular today, and with some justification claims to be the most widely sung composer in popular music worldwide. Hits include *What Now My Love?* (*Et maintenant*) and *La solitude, ça n'existe pas* (There's no Such Thing as Loneliness).

IAN PICKUP

See also: song/*chanson*

Becker, Jacques

b. 1906, Paris;
d. 1960, Paris

Director

Becker began his film-making career as assistant to **Renoir** before the war. His postwar work has a light yet penetrating comic touch in some ways reminiscent of a less garrulous **Rohmer**, as in *Rue de l'Estrapade* of 1953. He is best known for *Casque d'or* of the previous year, a tale of Parisian underworld passion set in 1902, which gives Simone **Signoret** one of her greatest roles. Many, however, would consider his last film, *Le Trou* (1960), about a betrayed prison escape, to be his master-work.

KEITH READER

See also: cinema

Further reading

Vey, J.-L. (1995) *Jacques Becker ou la fausse évidence*, Lyon: Aléas (a decent thematic overview).

Beckett, Samuel

b. 1906, Dublin, Ireland;
d. 1989, Paris

Writer and playwright

Samuel Beckett was a leading postwar writer of fiction and drama. His work, because of its range and inventiveness, encapsulates several of the dominant trends of contemporary writing and, as such, it leads us to probe the symbolic value of literary discourse. For Beckett, questions of self are intimately intertwined with questions of language. Many of his texts are written in both French and English, and his translations/rewritings of his own works are fundamental to his exploration of writing.

Born into the settled Protestant middle classes, Beckett received an education in keeping with his standing at Trinity College, Dublin, which provided the bedrock of his knowledge of European languages and of his extensive reading in literature and philosophy. His early writings, including the novel *Murphy*, reflect his exposure to modernist influences, in particular that of Joyce, whom he came to know during an initial period of residence in Paris in 1928–30. Between 1928 and 1937, when he settled in Paris, he developed an enduring interest in **painting**, on which he wrote widely. His decision to leave Ireland permanently was motivated in part by an awareness that his focus as a writer depended on recovering a sense of freedom and of intellectual purpose. On the fall of France in 1940, Beckett left Paris, but returned soon afterwards and became active in the Resistance in 1941, before going into hiding in the south of France in 1942. In 1945, he received the Croix de Guerre for his Resistance work.

Beckett's first writings in French date from the late 1930s. In 1938, *Murphy* was published. Beckett published no further fiction (except for a piece in *Les Temps modernes* in 1946) until the appearance of *Molloy* in 1951. By that time, he had written his major trilogy of novels – *Molloy*, *Malone Dies* (*Malone meurt*) from 1951, and the *Unnamable* (*L'Innommable*) from 1953 – a number of shorter works and the play *Waiting for Godot* (*En attendant Godot*). This play was first performed in a production by Roger **Blin** in 1953. Beckett's extraordinary fame dates from this time. The publication of the trilogy and the performance of *Endgame* (*Fin de partie*) in 1957, again in a production by Blin, consolidated his reputation as one of the leading avant-garde writers of the day, closely associated with the **Theatre of the Absurd**. His works were published by **Minuit** and Beckett was also identified as pursuing a line of experimentation related to that of the *nouveau roman*.

Beckett's work from this time provoked a critical response (notably on the part of figures such as Maurice **Blanchot** and Alain **Robbe-Grillet**) that decisively influenced its reception. The ceaseless movement of his writing, manifest in its range, but also in its engagement with processes of writing as a means of generating fiction, emerges as the characteristic of a body of work which is deprived not of meaning as such, but of a secure centre or reference point. The impact of the work depends as much on its humour as on its restless speculative urge.

From the mid-1950s, Beckett's increasing prominence led to a range of media projects, including an experiment in **cinema**, namely *Film* (1964). His first radio play, *All That Fall* (*Tous ceux qui tombent*) was broadcast in 1957. Later works, including *Cascando* (his earliest radio play in French, broadcast in 1963), incorporate music as well as text. *Eh Joe* (*Hé Joe*), of 1966, was his first work for **television**. The later works for this medium, including ... *But the Clouds* ... (... *que nuages* ...) of 1976, and *Quad* (1981), are characterized by stylized patterns of repetition and variation, and by the progressive effacement of speech.

In the 1960s, Beckett's work was dominated by the **theatre**. From 1962's *Happy Days* (*Oh les beaux jours*) onwards, English tended to be the original language of his plays. Following the first performance of *Play* (*Comédie*) in 1963, Beckett himself was closely involved in productions of his work. Several Paris productions, including a staging of *Happy Days* in 1963, led him to collaborate with Madeleine **Renaud** and Jean-Louis **Barrault**. His later plays, including *Not I* (*Pas moi*) of 1973, *Footfalls* (*Pas*) of 1976, and *Rockaby* (*Berceuse*) of 1981, prominently feature the use of monologue. The award of the Nobel prize for literature (1969) came at a time when Beckett was strongly involved in the theatre, though in this period he also published a wide range of increasingly fragmented fiction. *How It Is* (*Comment c'est*) appeared in 1961. Shorter prose texts were collected in *No's Knife* and in *Têtes mortes* (1967), and further pieces in *For to End Yet Again and Other Fizzles* (*Pour finir encore et autres foirades*) from 1976.

The presence of monologue is a salient feature also of the later prose texts, which include the second 'trilogy' of *Company* (*Compagnie*), *Ill Seen Ill Said* (*Mal vu mal dit*) – published in French, in 1979 and 1982 respectively – and *Worstward Ho* (*Cap au pire*), published in English in 1983. In these texts, an overt concern with narration and with identity emerges from the use of monologue. Beckett's writing, which dwells increasingly on the obstacles to complete and enduring self-identification, reveals a fascination with stories, with listening as well as speaking. These stories matter because they generate a sense of bafflement that proves inexhaustibly compelling.

PATRICK O'DONOVAN

See also: existentialist theatre

Further reading

Cohn, R. (1980) *Just Play: Beckett's Theater*, Princeton: Princeton University Press (a detailed treatment of recurring elements in Beckett's drama).

Hill, L. (1990) *Beckett's Fiction: In Different Words*, Cambridge: Cambridge University Press (a sophisticated exploration of difference as a feature of Beckett's writing).

Kalb, J. (1989) *Beckett in Performance*, Cambridge: Cambridge University Press (a useful scrutiny of the staging of Beckett's plays and of his own work in the theatre).

Knowlson, J. (1996) *Damned to Fame: The Life of Samuel Beckett*, London: Bloomsbury (a detailed account of Beckett's life as a writer).

Pilling, J. (ed.) (1994) *The Cambridge Companion to Beckett*, Cambridge: Cambridge University Press (a valuable survey of each aspect of Beckett's activity).

Begag, Azouz

b. 1957, Lyon

Writer

Azouz Begag became known in the 1980s as a beur writer and spokesperson on the **suburbs** and immigrant culture. A lecturer in economics at Lyon University, he published two lively semi-autobiographical novels in the 1980s – *The Kid from the Chaâba* (*Le Gone du Chaâba*), documenting the contradictions between primary school and immigrant shanty-town life experienced by a young boy of Algerian origin; and *Béni ou le paradis privé* (Béni, or Private Paradise), focusing on the troubled identity of a beur adolescent – before concentrating on children's fiction. His political fable, *Les Chiens, aussi* (Dogs Too), published in 1995, demands action against **racism** to prevent civil unrest.

CARRIE TARR

See also: beur writing; beurs; immigration

Beineix, Jean-Jacques

b. 1947, Paris

Director

A visually brilliant film-maker, in *Diva* (1981) Beineix was arguably the first French director to make a postmodern *film noir français*. The layered textures and stylized nature of his images, the use of unusual locations, a dense soundtrack – these are the major aesthetic signs of his work; for example *Betty Blue* (37,2 *degrés le matin*) (1986). Uneven success with the box office and audiences result from the difficult, even prurient and at times sexually obsessive nature of his thematics, such as in *La Lune dans le caniveau* (1982). An aggressive film-maker imagistically, he brings power and strength to the *mise-en-scène*, which can lead to an underdevelopment of the plot, a surface beauty that leaves the deep (mostly [hetero]sexual) tensions of the narrative hanging fire, as in *Roselyne and the Lions* (*Roselyne et les Lions*) (1988).

SUSAN HAYWARD

See also: cinema

Belghoul, Farida

b. 1958, Paris

Writer and director

Farida Belghoul was a key figure in the political activism and cultural production of the **beurs** in the 1980s. The eldest child of Algerian immigrants, she wrote and directed two influential short films: the semi-autobiographical 1981 production *C'est Madame la France que tu préfères?* (Do You Prefer Madame France?), made in 1981, about the double life of a beurette student, and the more experimental 1983 work *Le Départ du père* (The Father's Departure). Her novel *Georgette!* (1986) vividly evokes the inner turmoil of a little girl torn between Algerian and French values and culture.

CARRIE TARR

See also: beur cinema; beur writing; immigration

Bellon, Lolleh

b. 1925, Bayonne

Actor and playwright

After achieving theatrical and cinematic acclaim, especially for her classical roles at the Renaud-Barrault company in the 1960s, Bellon is now known for her sensitive writing approach, dubbed 'feminist' by some critics. *Les Dames du Jeudi* (Thursday's Women) in 1976 was her first play; others include *Le Coeur sur la main* (Open-Handed) and *Une absence* (Absence).

ANNIE SPARKS

See also: Barrault, Jean-Louis; Renaud, Madeleine; theatre

Bellon, Yannick

b. 1934, Biarritz

Director, producer,

screenwriter and editor,
real name Marie-Annick Bellon

One of the first women to attend the Institut des Hautes Études Cinématographiques (IDHEC), Yannick Bellon worked as an editor, documentary film-maker and television director, turning to feature films after **May 1968**. Her most successful films address feminist topics: *La Femme de Jean* (1974) questions women's subordination and *L'Amour violé* (1978) courageously examines rape. Sometimes criticized as overly didactic, her films deal with controversial social issues in an accessible style, as in her study of a woman with cancer, *L'Amour nu* (1981), and a man's bisexuality, *La Triche* (1984).

CARRIE TARR

See also: Bellon, Lolleh; feminism (movements/groups); women directors

Belmondo, Jean-Paul

b. 1933, Neuilly-sur-Seine

Actor

'Bébel' is in the middle of the trilogy of great male stars between Gabin and **Depardieu**. He made some sixty films between 1958 and 1988, and his career broadly has three strands: New Wave actor, best known for two key films, Godard's 1959 *A bout de souffle* (*Breathless*) and *Pierrot le fou* (1965); comic actor in action films, such as Lautner's *Flic ou voyou?* (1978), and *Le Professionnel* (1981); and respected character actor in two of Lelouch's films – the nostalgic *Itinéraire d'un enfant gâté* (1987), for which Belmondo received a César, and *Les Misérables* (1995).

PHIL POWRIE

See also: cinema; Nouvelle Vague; stars

Further reading

Durant, P. (1993) *Belmondo*, Paris: Laffont (biography).

Ben Jelloun, Tahar

b. 1944, Fez, Morocco

Writer and poet

Although he has published various collections of poems and case studies of sexual dysfunction of immigrant workers in France, Ben Jelloun is best known for his novels. His first, *Harrouda* (Harrouda), written in 1973, is a historical novel about the author's home cities, Fez and Tangier. The 1980s texts *The Sand Child* (*L'Enfant de sable*) and its sequel *The Sacred Night* (*La Nuit sacrée*), for which he was awarded the Prix Goncourt in 1987, narrate the tortuous psychological journey towards female identity of a girl raised as a boy. Ben Jelloun's writing style draws extensively on the oral tradition and the tale. He departed from the theme of Maghrebi culture in *State of Absence* (*L'Ange aveugle*), a novel about the Sicilian Mafia.

LAÏLA IBNLFASSI

See also: francophone writing (fiction, poetry): North Africa; literary prizes

Further reading

M'Henni, M. (ed.) (1993) *Tahar Ben Jelloun: stratégies d'écriture*, Paris: L'Harmattan (a selection of essays in French dealing with Ben Jelloun's work).

Benmussa, Simone

b. 1932, Tunis

Feminist writer and director

The literary manager at the Renaud-Barrault company in the 1960s and 1970s, and editor of its *Cahiers* until 1989, Benmussa is currently best known for her feminist standpoint, directing pieces confronting patriarchal boundaries and images, including **Cixous**'s plays, her own plays, and many by authors including Nathalie **Sarraute**, Henry James and Edna O'Brien.

ANNIE SPARKS

See also: Barrault, Jean-Louis; Renaud, Madeleine; theatre; women's/lesbian writing

Major works

Benmussa Directs (1989) Methuen: London (a book of two plays directed by Benmussa accompanied by an essay by her on her work).

Benveniste, Émile

b. 1902, Aleppo, Syria;
d. 1976, Versailles

Linguist

One of the greatest French linguists of the twentieth century, he taught at the École Pratique des Hautes Études and later at the Collège de France. He was active in both Indo-European comparative grammar and general linguistics, developing and sometimes challenging Saussure's views. His work on personal pronouns, verbal tenses and subjective aspects of language has been particularly influential amongst semioticians.

BÉATRICE DAMAMME-GILBERT

See also: Barthes, Roland; linguistic/discourse theory; structuralism

Further reading

Asher, R. E. (ed.) (1994) *Encyclopedia of Language and Linguistics*, Oxford and New York: Pergamon Press (gives a thorough account of his work and a bibliography).

Bercy

The run-down Bercy area of Paris, formerly the centre for wine-traders, was developed by the Ville de Paris under Jacques **Chirac**'s mayorship as part of the *Plan de l'Est parisien*. It includes the municipal Palais Omnisports de Bercy (POPB) inaugurated in 1984; a new park, opened in 1995, to be linked across the Seine by a footbridge to the Bibliothèque Nationale de France; and the new building designed by Paul Chemetov and Borja Huidobro for the new Ministry of Finance, which was one of the Grands Projets of François **Mitterrand**. The name 'Bercy' is now commonly used to refer to this ministry.

SUSAN COLLARD

See also: architecture under Mitterrand

Bérégovoy, Pierre

b. 1925, France;
d. 1993, Nevers

Politician

Bérégovoy was the archetypal Socialist politician of working-class origins, a gas board employee who rose through the ranks to become successively Finance Minister and, in 1992, prime minister. On the Right of his party and unstinting in his implementation of austerity policies, he was badly demoralized by the crushing Gaullist victory of 1993 and, it is rumoured, by **Mitterrand**'s subsequent neglect. It was on May Day 1993, in the Burgundy town of Nevers of which he was mayor, that he shot himself – a suicide that caused deep distress throughout France and undoubtedly contributed to the tarnishing of Mitterrand's reputation in his final years.

KEITH READER

See also: parties and movements

Berger, Michel

b. 1947, Paris;
d. 1992, France

Singer-songwriter,
real name Michel Hamburger

Having worked for Bourvil – and with Véronique Sanson (he produced her first two records), Françoise Hardy (for whom he wrote Message personnel [Personal Message]) and his future wife France Gall (La Déclaration d'amour [Declaration of Love]) – Michel Berger wrote the highly successful rock musical Starmania (1979) which featured Daniel Balavoine and Fabienne Thibeault. A new version (produced by Berger and Luc Plamondon) was staged in 1988 and the musical was still breaking box-office records in 1996. A notable producer, Berger eventually gained recognition as a solo artist before his premature death in 1992.

IAN PICKUP

See also: song/chanson

Berri, Claude

b. 1934, Paris

Director and producer

He began making films in 1961, but only became well-known as a director with Tchao Pantin (1983), starring Coluche. He is best known for his successful heritage diptych (adapted from Pagnol), Jean de Florette/Manon des sources (1986), and further literary adaptations, in which he specializes and which he often also produces, such as Germinal (1993). He is a key producer, with many commercial successes, for example Annaud's The Bear (L'Ours) from 1988, and his Duras adaptation, The Lover (L'Amant) of 1992.

Further reading

Frodon, J.-M. and Loiseau, J.-C. (1987) Jean de Florette: la folle aventure du film, Paris: Herscher (the book of the film, including an account of Berri's previous career).

PHIL POWRIE

See also: cinema

Besnehard, Daniel

b. 1954, Bois-Colombes

Playwright

A dramaturg at the Comédie de Caen from 1978 to 1985 he has been the general secretary/dramaturg at the Nouveau Théâtre d'Angers since 1986. Often dealing with recent history and covering diverse themes, his plays include Mala Strana and Arromanches (both directed by Yersin in the 1980s), and Clair de Terre (Earthlight), directed by Rétoré in 1989. He often works with the Théâtre Ouvert and has acted in films.

ANNIE SPARKS

See also: Attoun, Lucien; theatre

Besset, Jean-Marie

b. 1959, Carcassonne

Playwright

Besset is the author of many plays, including *Villa Luco, Ce qui arrive et ce qu'on attend* (Actuality and Expectation) and *Grande École*. Having spent much time in New York, his work is more influenced by anglophone traditions than many of his contemporaries in France. He also translates: notably works by Alan Bennett, Michael Frayn and Tom Stoppard.

ANNIE SPARKS

See also: theatre

Besson, Luc

b. 1959, Paris

Director

A very anti-establishment director, Besson aims technically to compete with American action films (he quotes as his inspiration Sam Peckinpah). His work, which is visually and sonically pulsating, cuts across genres but dominant themes of loneliness, suffering and displacement resonate throughout. A new moralist of the cinema (in the tradition of **Renoir**), he exposes the negative connotations of commodity fetishism: consumer goods as signs of death. Against this he opposes his modest heroes with their vision of self-fulfilment, the value of which is based in a purely personal aesthetic: music in *Subway* (1985) deep-sea diving in *The Big Blue* (*Le Grand Bleu*) in 1988, violence in *Nikita* (1990) and *Léon* (1995). *The Fifth Element* (*Le Cinquième Élément*), starring Bruce Willis and with costumes by **Gaultier,** was released in 1997.

SUSAN HAYWARD

See also: cinema

beur cinema

The term *cinéma beur* was coined in the mid-1980s as a result of the sudden appearance on French cinema screens of films dealing with the effects of **immigration** from the point of view of the **beurs**, members of the 'second-generation' North African community in France. Despite attempts to limit the application of the term, it has been used to cover militant-activist shorts and **documentaries** made on Super 8 and 16 mm for distribution within the immigrant community (the bulk of early beur film and video production), commercial feature films about the beurs made by beur and other French film-makers, and films about the effects of immigration and the '*retour au pays*' made by francophone North African film-makers. Current debates about the usage of the word 'beur' and the emergence of a *cinéma de banlieue* mean that the term may no longer be productive.

Critical attention has focused primarily on the feature films of the 1980s, which achieved box office success through addressing contemporary issues of ethnicity and identity in a popular realist style, far removed from the 'miserabilism' of 1970s films dealing with immigration. Foreshadowed by Serge Le Péron's *Laisse béton* (1984), these included *Thé à la menthe* (1985) by Algerian film-maker Abdelkrim Bahloul, and *Le Thé au harem d'Archi Ahmed* (1985) and *Bâton rouge* (1986) by second-generation Algerian film-makers Mehdi **Charef** and Rachid Bouchareb, respectively. These films popularized a new type of 'immigrant' figure: the charming, streetwise (male) youth, tormented by his fragmented identity, certainly, but able to shake off adversity with some degree of humour. The films articulate common themes: the problematic relationship with the culture of the immigrant parents, represented positively through the mother figure, but negatively through the silenced or absent father figure; and the difficulty of survival in racist metropolitan France. They are set primarily in the inner city and/or run-down suburban housing estate (though *Bâton rouge* extends the quest for identity to the United States), but the protagonists' involvement in delinquency and drugs is played down, as is the role of French **racism** and the police in maintaining a racist society. The use of narrative structures based on close friendships between beur and white French working-class youths in *Le Thé au harem* and *Bâton rouge* can be seen as a bid for acceptance and integration into French society. At the same time, the narrative closures of these films offer little hope for a future multicultural society: the couple (mixed-race or otherwise) is not allowed to form, and the central character either returns to Algeria (*Thé à la menthe*), gets arrested (*Le Thé au harem*) or resorts to fantasy (*Bâton rouge*).

Both Charef and Bouchareb's second films depart from the tone set by the first beur features, bringing the question of immigration and identity into sharper focus at the cost of box office success. *Miss Mona* (1987) centres on the downfall of a poverty-stricken but pure-hearted illegal immigrant who is enticed into prostitution through his friendship with transvestite Miss Mona. *Cheb* (1991) explores the alienation experienced by two Westernized young beurs abandoned in a hostile, unfamiliar Algeria, a theme also addressed by Algerian film-maker Mahmoud Zemmouri. It was left to white French film-makers to sustain the representation of the streetwise young beur anxiously seeking integration, in comedies like Serge Meynard's *L'Oeil au beurre noir* (1987) and Philippe Galland's *La Thune* (1991).

In the mid-1990s, a new generation of film-makers of North African origin started making films with a wider range of beur and beurette roles in more complex immigrant family set-ups, less involved in relationships with white characters. Malik Chibane's *Hexagone* (1994), made on a shoestring budget outside the usual production circuits and shot on location using a local cast of amateur actors, was called 'the first film to be made by beurs for beurs'. It addresses familiar issues through its mini-narratives involving unemployed beur youths negotiating petty crime, drugs, generational conflict and racism, but it also emphasizes the central characters' subjectivity and refuses to address a white audience through the incorporation of white characters. Chibane stresses the problematic identity of beurettes, too; a theme previously glimpsed in the work of Farida Belghoul, and further articulated in Zaïda Ghorab-Volta's autobiographical low-budget feature *Souviens-toi de moi* (1996). In *Douce France* (1995), Chibane ostensibly returns to the foregrounding of a white/beur male friendship (though the beur is a harki), but it is the independent young beur/Algerian women characters who dominate the last section of the film, while the representation of the parents' generation uses cultural difference as a site of local colour and nostalgia rather than threat. *Bye bye* (1995), by Franco-Tunisian film-maker Karim Dridi, provides another affectionate representation of the extended immigrant family, although the exploration of the two brothers' identity crisis, faced with drug dealing and racism in downtown Marseille or the 'return' to Tunisia, is not overly optimistic. The central focus of Ahmed Bouchaala's melodramatic *Krim* (1995), structured through the friendship between the eponymous protagonist and his (white) prison cell mate, is the new role of the beur as father to, and saviour of, his long-lost drug-addicted daughter.

The release of these films coincided with a series of white-authored films about the *banlieue*, which address issues of identity and ethnicity without the same complex representations of ethnic minority cultures and subjectivities. Thomas Gilou's *Raï* (1995) reworks the familiar tropes of beur cinema, while Jean-François Richet's *État des lieux* (1995) and Mathieu Kassovitz's *La Haine* (1995) represent the *banlieue* as multicultural melting pot but foreground their white protagonists rather than problematizing black and beur identities. There is still a need for a plurality of representations of contemporary France by ethnic minority film-makers.

Cinéma beur as a label appeared to have given way to the *cinéma de banlieue*, but its passing should not be regretted if it means that an increasing number of film-makers are making films about France as a multiethnic society and beur film-makers are accepted within mainstream French cinema.

Carrie Tarr

See also: beur writing; francophone cinema: North Africa; suburbs

Further reading

CinémAction/ hommes & migrations (1990) special issue 56 (July) *Cinéma métis: de Hollywood aux films beurs* (an early overview).

beur comics

Comics by **Beurs**, or Maghrebi-French (i.e. French of North African Arabic or Berber descent), usually focus on France as a post-colonial, multiethnic nation. The most prominent Maghrebi-French cartoonist is Farid Boudjellal, an artist of Algerian heritage who has published numerous individual comic books and collaborative works. His comics sometimes draw on the fantastic substance of traditional Arabic tales, e.g. *Djinn* (Genie) and on humour and caricature, e.g. the four-album *Juif–Arabe* (Jew–Arab) series, but he is also known for his realist-style saga that tells the story of the Slimani family, which emigrated from Algeria to France, recounted in *L'Oud* (The Oud), *Le Gourbi* (The Hovel), *Ramadân*, *Gags à l'harissa* (Harissa-Flavoured Gags) and *Jambon-Beur: les couples mixtes* (Ham-Beur/Butter: Mixed Couples). In his comics, Boudjellal tackles the complex issues at the heart of **immigration** and Maghrebi-French cultural hybridity, by examining mixed couples, gender roles, the composition of **Islam in France** and anti-Maghrebi **racism**. His *Ramadân* won the Résistance prize at the 1989 Angoulême national comics festival.

Cartooning by Maghrebin artists who take **immigration** issues in France as their subject matter dates back at least to the 1970s, and includes Saladin's *Les migrations de Djeha: les nouveaux immigrés* (The Migrations of Djeha: The New Immigrants), whose principal character, an immigrant to France named Djeha, was borrowed from North African folk tales.

Saladin's comic book and Boudjellal's *Les soirées d'Abdulah: Ratonnade* (Abdulah's Evenings:RatHunt/Beating up an Arab) exemplify an initial crop of comics that depicted the lives of single, male Maghrebi immigrant workers. A subsequent Beur moment in comics occurred in the early to mid-1980s, when Maghrebi-French cartoonists, who had grown up in France and called it home came of age, participated in the effervescence of the Beur political and cultural movement and began to address the concerns of their own generation. Cartoonists who then shared time in the spotlight included Rasheed, Sabeurdet and Larbi Mechkour, an artist who drew *Les Beurs* (The Beurs), a series of humorous sketches, dosed with fantasy, about life in the housing projects (storyline by Boudjellal). Since that period, few comic books by Maghrebi-French artists have made it into print, excepting those of Boudjellal. However, other comic books of note include *Homicide*, a hallucinatory murder story set in Marseille, drawn by Kamel Khelif (storyline by Amine Medjdoub), and *Le Monde merveilleux des Barbus* (The Marvellous World of the Bearded Ones), which satirizes the Islamic movement and was drawn by Slim, an exiled Algerian cartoonist living in France.

MARK McKINNEY

See also: beur writing; comic strips/cartoonists

Further reading

Douglas, A. and Malti-Douglas, F. (1994) *Arab Comic Strips: Politics of an Emerging Mass Culture*, Bloomington, IN: Indiana University Press (includes analyses of comics by Boudjellal, Mechkour and Slim).

McKinney, M. (1997) '*Métissage* in Post-Colonial Comics,' in A. G. Hargreaves and M. McKinney (eds) *Post-Colonial Cultures in France*, London: Routledge, pp. 169–88 (a study of the post-colonial thematic in comics by Boudjellal, Mechkour, and others).

beur music

Music has been a refuge and a springboard for the **beurs** (second-generation immigrants of North African origin), often confined to the **suburbs** and to a life of deprivation and exclusion, with its vicious circle of unemployment and delinquency.

The 1960s and 1970s saw the birth of a multitude of Arab groups who were attracted by Western rock. Kabyle musicians Idir and Djamel Allam went on successful tours in France. The 1980s saw the birth of 'franco-beur' rock. Two groups, first Rocking Babouche and then **Carte de séjour** from Lyon's ghettos at Rilleux-le-Pape, chose music as a means of integration as well as of protest at a society which excluded them. But the pop industry was reluctant to give them contracts, so they resorted to creating their own company to press their first LP. Carte de séjour were the forerunners of musicians, songwriters and performers who created musical hybrids at the crossroads of musical traditions (**jazz**, **rock**, funk, raï, Afro-Andalusian), and paved the way for culturally hybrid bands like **Mano Negra** and Les **Négresses vertes**.

The end of the 1980s saw the rise of beur music. One of the original voices from this decade is Karim **Kacel**, who expressed the troubled existence of the suburbs (*banlieues*). An important landmark is the Bobigny festival in January 1986, where the stars of Algerian raï Cheb Mami, Cheb **Khaled** and Raina Raï sang. The early 1990s saw beur music blossoming in France. The group Zebda from Les Isards, a northern suburb of Toulouse, offered a mixture of rock, funk and *chaâbi* which replaced raï in their idiom. In their albums *L'Arène des rumeurs* (Arena of Rumours) and *Le Bruit et l'odeur* (The Noise and the Smell), they denounce the shortcomings of French society but still offer a message of hope. In more pessimistic mood is Big Brother Hakim who spent his childhood in Bagnolet and Belleville. Essentially a drummer moved by *chaâbi*, American soul, reggae and jazz rock, he turned to **rap** and became a master of improvisation, remaining close to Islamic values. In 1993 he created the group Jungle Gala, one of the most original voices in rap in Paris. There is a definite feeling of *fin-de-siècle* in his solo offering of 1995, *Même le diable ne peut plus m'aider* (Even the Devil Can't Help Me Any More), where the misery and spleen of a drug addict are laid bare. Finally, the group Alliance Ethnic from the Cité du Plateau in Creil have used in their 1995 album *Simple et funky* a form of rap which is less harsh – as the title indicates – and puts the emphasis on the joy of making beur music.

GÉRARD POULET

See also: francophone popular music: North Africa; immigration; slang/*argot*/*verlan*; suburbs

beur radio

Radio Beur (1981–92) was among the hundreds of private radio stations, and one of several dozen minority stations, created after the 1981 decision by the newly elected Socialist government to end the state monopoly over radio and television. For over a decade Radio Beur entertained and informed thousands of listeners from Paris's North African immigrant community who previously had little access to news or music over the airwaves. With some 121,500 listeners in the Paris region, according to a 1991 IPSOS poll, Radio Beur claimed the largest audience of any minority station in France (CSA 1991: 121). During its eleven-year history Radio Beur broadcast scores of native North African performers as well as aspiring second-generation North African artists, commonly known as **beurs**. Former station members also claimed that Radio Beur was the largest organizer of concerts in the North African community. Its most successful concert, at the Zénith in 1985, drew some 7,000 people. Some station members credited Radio Beur with much of the success enjoyed by Algerian raï music in France since the mid-1980s.

Radio Beur's programmes covered a great

variety of subjects. Shows such as *Triptye* featured literature and cinema; *Canoun* and *Tafsuf* took up Berber language and culture. *Juridiquement vôtre*, hosted by two lawyers, helped inform listeners about their rights by discussing pertinent topics and allowing callers to ask specific legal questions. Many of Radio Beur's programmes depended on listener participation. For example, *Les Beurs et la plume* gave listeners the opportunity to compose and present their own poetry. *Flipper* was a show directed at and hosted by North African youth (CSA 1987: 86–7; 1991: 96, 98). In addition to these programmes, the station created its own literary prize for promising North African novelists, published a collection of poems, *Les Beurs et la plume* (1985) and an account of the anti-government demonstrations in Algeria, *Octobre à Alger* (1988).

Yet in June 1992, only five years after receiving its first twenty-four-hour frequency on 98.2 FM, Radio Beur disappeared from the airwaves. Like many volunteer-based, non-profit minority stations, Radio Beur had become a victim of its own success. The growing prominence of Radio Beur within the North African community and among French institutions unleashed and intensified centrifugal forces long present within the station. Rivalries between station members, problems of corruption, and the tendency of some station administrators to exploit ambiguities in Radio Beur's membership lists and voting practices, ultimately led to the station's demise. The decision of the Conseil Supérieur de l'Audiovisuel (CSA), responsible for authorizing and regulating broadcasting rights in France, to reject Radio Beur's frequency application, in favour of Beur FM, a commercial station created by one of Radio Beur's founding members and long-time administrators, brought an untimely end to an unprecedented, eleven-year adventure (Derderian 1995).

RICHARD L. DERDERIAN

See also: francophone popular music: North Africa; radio (private/free)

Further reading

CSA (1987) Radio Beur frequency application, no. 3407.
——(1991) Radio Beur frequency application, no. 91PA A045.
Derderian, R. L. (1995) 'Radio Beur, 1981–1992: l'échec d'un multiculturalisme à la française?', *Hommes & Migrations* 1191 (October): 55–9.

beur writing

The coming-of-age of the beur generation in France in the 1980s was accompanied by a significant volume of new writing by and about the **beurs**, particularly in the form of semi-autobiographical novels. Since 1983, date of the publication of Mehdi **Charef**'s groundbreaking first novel, *Le Thé au harem d'Archi Ahmed*, over thirty authors of Maghrebin origin have been published and the corpus is still evolving. However, the status of their writing, variously classified as Maghrebi French or 'immigrant' by academics, critics, publishers and booksellers, is problematic. Debates on this issue have tended to obscure the specificity of their articulation of voices from the periphery at the same time, paradoxically, as they have marginalized authors who are not beurs, like Leïla **Sebbar**, Nina Bouraoui and Ahmed Zitouni, who also write about the situation of the beurs in France.

Beur writing has been assessed for its value as social document rather than on its literary merits, partly because the writers are young, many have produced only one novel, and many novels rework clusters of similar themes. In working through the traumas generated by the historical and socioeconomic circumstances of their upbringing, caught between the values of the (predominantly) Arabo-Islamic culture of their immigrant parents and the Western culture to which they aspire but from which they are excluded, beur writers have produced *témoignages* (testimonies) valued for their ethnographic veracity rather than their aesthetic value. Yet such a summary evaluation would not do justice to the range and quality of beur writing. On the one hand, it shows a variety of forms, including short stories, poems, plays and essays, as well as novels which depart from the semi-autobiographical format and texts which freely use a mix of genres. On the other hand, striking stylistic qualities in the handling of language, humour and modes of narration can be identified in many of the texts, as in the work of Farida **Belghoul**, Leïla Houari, Ahmed Kalouaz and Ramdane Issaad.

Certain key themes can be traced across a number of texts. The fundamental problematic of language, naming and identity is raised in the titles of novels, such as Sakinna Boukhedenna's *Journal 'Nationalité: immigré(e)'* (1987), Akli Tadjer's 1984 publication *Les ANI du 'Tassili'* (where ANI stands for Arabes Non Identifiés), Tassadit Imache's 1989 work *Une Fille sans histoire* (An Ordinary Girl) and Soraya Nini's 1993 *Ils disent que je suis une beurette!* (They Say I'm a Beurette!), while titles like Azouz **Begag**'s *Le Gone du Chaâba* (which mixes Lyonnais slang with Arabic), Belghoul's *Georgette!* (a sign of the narrator's inability to enunciate her own name) and Ferrudja Kessas's anglicized *Beur's Story* (1990) provide further indications of the perceived limitations of the French language for the expression of the author's concerns. These texts demonstrate an ability to articulate a variety of types of language, including popular speech forms, **slang** and backslang, English, Arabic and Berber borrowings, and heavily accented spoken French. The immediacy of this hybrid language, to be found in particular in the work of Moussa Labkiri, Tadjer, Begag and Belghoul, constitutes one of the 'pleasures' of beur writing.

Many, though not all, of the texts are semi-autobiographical *romans d'apprentissage*, which focus on the struggle of a central character of the same age and gender as the author to come to terms with the double marginalization experienced by being at odds with both parental culture and the majority culture. Critical descriptions of the school and the housing estate or project form the backdrop to narratives relating the protagonists' anguished negotiation of relationships with peer groups and family, both in the early works of Charef and Begag and in novels of the 1990s like Brahim Benaïcha's *Vivre au paradis: d'une oasis à un bidonville* (Life in Paradise . . .) and Djura's *Le Voile du silence* (The Veil of Silence). Representations of the parents are generally informed by an intense love–hate relationship, and the role of the Arab father is particularly problematic, especially in female-authored novels which challenge traditional Maghrebin gender roles. Many of these texts also demystify aspirations of a '*retour au pays*' (homecoming) through accounts of travels to the Maghreb, as in Houari's 1985 novel *Zeïda de nulle part* (Zeïda, from Nowhere), which confirm that the beur generation has no place there.

A structuring element of most beur-authored texts is French **racism** and its effects. Racist murders are the starting point for the elaboration of the subjectivity of the central protagonists in Nacer Kettane's 1985 text *Le Sourire de Brahim* (Brahim's Smile), which invokes the events of 17 October 1961, when peaceful Algerian demonstrators died at the hands of the French police, Ahmed Kalouaz's *Point kilométrique 190* (1986) which reworks the incident in which Habib Grimzi was thrown from a train by three French legionnaires, and Charef's 1989 novel *Le Harki de Mériem* (Mériem's Harki), which traces the origins of conflict to French colonial rule in Algeria. In the more autobiographical texts, confrontations with unemployment, crime, drugs, prison and death, as in Mehdi Lalloui's *Les Beurs de Seine* (1986), are attributable to French racism. These texts therefore invite their French readers to acknowledge the beurs' pain and aspire towards a more just, integrated French society.

Beur writing proposes a new, critical look at both French and Maghrebin society. While it may not constitute a 'minor literature' as proposed by **Deleuze** and **Guattari**, its foregrounding of voices from the margins calls into question dominant assumptions about French culture and identity.

CARRIE TARR

See also: autobiography; beur cinema; immigration

Further reading

Bonn, C. (ed.) (1995), 'Littératures des immigrations 1: un espace littéraire émergent', *Études littéraires maghrébines*, Paris: L'Harmattan (includes recent articles on beur writing).

Hargreaves, A. (1991) *Voices from the North African Community in France: Immigration and Identity in Beur Fiction*, Oxford: Berg (a useful account of beur writing in the 1980s).

Laronde, M. (1993) *Autour du roman beur, immigration et identité*, Paris: L'Harmattan (a semiotic approach to selected novels, including those of Sebbar and Zitouni).

beurs

The word *beur* was coined in the late 1970s by young 'second-generation' immigrants of North African origin living in the Parisian **suburbs** (*banlieues*), and is usually understood to have been derived from *verlan* (backslang) for *arabe*. Originally adopted to counteract the negative connotations of *arabe* and *musulman* in France (the result of France's former colonial role in the Maghreb), the word also usefully indicated the hybrid identity of the 'second generation', born or brought up in France but neither fully French nor fully Arab (or Berber).

The product of increased family **immigration** in the 1970s, the beurs were often torn between the Islamic values and expectations of their working-class Maghrebin parents and the majority culture, a situation exacerbated by conflicting nationality laws and the growth of **racism**. Many members of the North African community in France now experience the word *beur* – once an empowering term – as a pejorative, homogenizing label imposed by the majority. As Mouloud says in *Bye bye*, '*Ne m'appelez pas Beur, le mot me fait horreur*'. Alternatives like the cumbersome *d'origine maghrébine* or *issu de l'immigration maghrébine*, the often inaccurate *arabo-français*, or the alternative *verlan* word *Rebeu*, indicate the continuing problematic status of beurs and beurettes in relation to contemporary French culture and identity.

The emergence of the word *beur*, coinciding with the appearance of Radio Beur in 1981, is linked with the political and cultural mobilization of the 'second generation'. Their first protests against French racism, unjust laws, deportation orders and police violence were Rock Against Police concerts. When **Mitterrand**'s new administration granted immigrants the right to free association, the resulting movement laid the foundation for beur activism and promoted beur creativity in music, writing, cinema, theatre, dance and fashion. The need for action against institutionalized racism was highlighted by the police shooting of a beur activist, Toumi, in the Minguettes estate (Vaux-en-Velin) in 1983. A March Against Racism and for Equality, organized by local youths and the priest Christian Delorme, set off from Marseille to Paris, where it mobilized 100,000 demonstrators and was received by President Mitterrand. Significantly, the media renamed it the March of the Beurs, marking a high point in the beurs' visibility and acceptability but also the recuperation of the word and the movement.

The march was followed by attempts to organize on a national level and by Convergence 84, a multiethnic demonstration in favour of equality and citizenship. Plagued by internal dissent, hopes for a national beur-led organization were dashed by the setting-up of SOS Racisme, France-Plus and the JALB (Jeunes Arabes de Lyon et sa Banlieue), headed by Djida Tazdaït. SOS Racisme, funded by the Socialists and headed until 1992 by Harlem **Désir** (of West Indian origin), successfully mobilized a multiethnic youth movement with its slogan '*Touche pas à mon pote*' (Hands off my mate), but focused on combating the rise of **Le Pen** and the Front National rather than addressing the specific grievances of the beurs. France-Plus, led by Arezki Dahmani, tried to mobilize the beurs as an electoral force and lobby for citizenship rights, but its policy of integration at the expense of any distinctive ethno-cultural agenda appealed primarily to Maghrebins of higher socioeconomic status.

Though a handful of beurs may have achieved national prominence, particularly in the arts, the 900,000 beurs aged 18–30 living in the *cités* (housing estates or projects) are still marginalized by high levels of unemployment, housing problems, delinquency and drug abuse. Barriers to integration appear to lie not in their bicultural heritage but in the obstacles placed in their way by the majority culture.

CARRIE TARR

See also: beur radio; immigration; slang/*argot*/*verlan*; suburbs

Further reading

Bouamama, S. (1994) *Dix ans de marche des beurs*, Paris: Épi/Desclée de Brouwer.

Hargreaves, A. G. (1995) *Immigration, 'Race' and Ethnicity in Contemporary France*, London: Routledge (essential contextual reference work).

Hargreaves, A. G. and McKinney, M. (1997) *Post-colonial Cultures in France*, London and New York: Routledge (includes chapters on aspects of beur cultural production).

Sans Frontière (1985) special issue 92–3 (April/May), *La 'Beur' génération*.

Billetdoux, François

b. 1927, Paris;
d. 1991, Paris

Playwright and novelist

Billetdoux's work was first produced in the 1950s art theatres, and he is noted for his sharp dialogue and unconventional outlook. His plays include *Tchin-Tchin* (Cheers) and *Réveille-Toi, Philadelphie* (Wake up, Philadelphia), completed in 1988.

ANNIE SPARKS

See also: theatre

Further reading

Lhôte, J.-M. (1988) *Mise en jeu François Billetdoux*, Paris: Actes Sud Papiers (considerations on his approach).

Binoche, Juliette

b. 1964, Paris

Actor

Although her first starring role was in **Téchiné**'s *Rendez-Vous* (1985), her early career is linked with **Carax**, who modelled her for *The Night is Young* (*Mauvais Sang*) in 1986, and *Les Amants du Pont-Neuf* (1991). She became an international star in Kaufman's adaptation of Kundera's *The Unbearable Lightness of Being* (1987), **Malle**'s *Damage* (1992) and **Kieslowski**'s *Three Colours: Blue* (1993). With her cool exterior, which is also apparent in **Rappeneau**'s *The Horseman on the Roof* (*Le Hussard sur le toit*) of 1995, she is an updated **Deneuve**, the 1990s image of French femininity, as Lancôme's use of her for their 1995 perfume suggests. In March 1997, she won an Academy Award for her role as a French-Canadian nurse in Anthony Minghella's English-language *The English Patient*.

PHIL POWRIE

See also: cinema; stars

Birkin, Jane

b. 1947, London

Actor

Her career of some fifty-five films (to 1994)

began in 1966, and is infamously remembered for an erotic song (followed by a film in 1975) *Je t'aime moi non plus*, with her partner, Serge Gainsbourg. She played liberated and often promiscuous women in the 1970s, taking on more serious roles in the 1980s: **Rivette**'s *L'Amour par terre* (1983) and *La Belle Noiseuse* (1991), **Tavernier**'s *Daddy Nostalgie* (1989) and, especially, **Varda**'s diptych, a portrait of her (*Jane B par Agnès V*) and a fiction (*Kung Fu Master*) (both 1987).

PHIL POWRIE

See also: cinema

Blanc, Michel

b. 1952, Courbevoie

Actor and director

His moustachioed mousiness makes him the perfect foil to **Depardieu**, with whom he had begun his career in **café theatre**. Best known as a comic actor, notably in **Blier**'s *Tenue de soirée* of 1986, he reveals tragic capabilities in Patrice Leconte's *Monsieur Hire* (1989), as the reclusive tailor fatally infatuated with Sandrine **Bonnaire**. He has also directed films, notably the comedy of mistaken cinematic identity, *Grosse Fatigue* of 1994.

KEITH READER

See also: cinema

Blanchot, Maurice

b. 1907, France

Critic and writer

Notwithstanding the writing's opacity and the wilful obscurity surrounding the life, Blanchot has come to be considered one of the most influential critics of the period. After an involvement with violent nationalist journalism

during the 1930s, Blanchot turned to and into literature. Surviving a political and human disaster that seemed to mark the end of history, literature is experienced as committed *for itself*. In *The Space of Literature* (*L'Espace littéraire*) of 1955, 1969's *Infinite Conversation* (*L'Entretien infini*) and *Writing of the Disaster* (*L'Écriture du désastre*) from 1980, Blanchot explores how literature is the only reality left for language and subjectivity, the only authentic arena for the anonymity and ethics of being.

SEÁN HAND

Blier, Bertrand

b. 1939, Paris

Director

Blier, a key director of the 1980s, makes provocative comedies tinged with black humour. He has frequently used **Depardieu**, whose combination of masculine aggressivity and 'femininity' allows Blier to question received ideas. In *Trop belle pour toi* (1989), which received a César, Depardieu, married to Carole Bouquet, the Chanel ideal of femininity, falls in love with the 'ordinary' **Balasko**, subverting notions of iconic beauty, while misogynistically (but consciously so) cocking a snook at **feminism**.

PHIL POWRIE

See also: cinema

Blin, Roger

b. 1907, Neuilly;
d. 1984, Paris

Director and actor

A director of **Beckett**'s work, including the original production of *Waiting for Godot*, and of **Genet**'s plays, such as *The Screens* (*Les*

Paravents). Blin worked with many young authors and was noted both for his disregard for traditional theatrical boundaries and for his willingness to experiment.

ANNIE SPARKS

See also: theatre

Further reading

Aslan, O. (1988) *Roger Blin*, Cambridge: Cambridge University Press (biography and analysis of work).

Bloc, André

b. 1896, Algiers, Algeria;
d. 1966, New Delhi

Artist and engineer

Bloc favoured close collaboration between architects, painters and sculptors. He founded the reviews *Architecture d'aujourd'hui* and *Art d'aujourd'hui*, and was president of the group Espace, which was created in 1951 to integrate and synthesize the arts. His monumental sculptures in polychrome or polished metal include: *Signal* in Paris, to mark the centenary of reinforced concrete in 1949; a mosaic for a student hostel at Caracas University; the tomb of the Iranian musician Abolhassan Saba; and public **sculpture** in Brasilia. His sculpture-furniture demonstrates the linking of fine and decorative arts.

ELZA ADAMOWICZ

Bocuse, Paul

b. 1926, Collonges-au-Mont-d'Or

Chef

Bocuse is France's most celebrated chef and has

been proprietor of a restaurant in his native village near Lyon since 1959. He is the first master chef to spend more time promoting his cuisine, through international visits, television appearances and publications, than in his kitchen, and boasts of being paid as much as the film star Alain **Delon**. He was an ardent fan of President **Giscard d'Estaing**, in whose honour he created a truffle soup with champagne. Asked what he would have prepared for the Communist leader Georges **Marchais**, he wittily suggested a broth of Jerusalem artichokes – a far more downmarket vegetable.

KEITH READER

See also: gastronomy

Bohringer, Richard

b. 1942, Moulins

Actor

Father of the actor Romane Bohringer, he began his career in 1971, but became well-known only in 1981 with **Beineix**'s *Diva*. He is prolific, with some forty-five films between 1981 and 1994 for directors as diverse as **Besson**, Deville, Issermann and Mocky. He has a streetwise image, and tends to play cold and enigmatic loners. He received Césars for best supporting actor in Amar's *L'Addition* (1984) and best actor for Hubert's *Le Grand Chemin* (1987). He was the laconic wife-killing star of Leconte's *Tango* (1993), and has also published a fictionalized autobiography, *C'est beau une ville la nuit: blues* (1988).

PHIL POWRIE

See also: cinema

Bonal, Denise

b. 1921, Oued El Alleug, Algeria

Actor and playwright

A successful radio and theatre actor, who since 1968 has become one of the better-known women playwrights in France. Her plays often handle issues such as family conflict, and use everyday language. Examples are *Légère en août* (Free in August), *Passions et Prairie* (Passions and Meadows) and *Portrait de Famille* (Family Portrait).

ANNIE SPARKS

See also: theatre

Bondy, Luc

b. 1948, Zürich

Director

Bondy is a Swiss theatre director working mainly in Germany, Belgium and France, who is best known for his psychological approach to drama. He has directed classics and contemporary works by authors including Botho Strauss and Arthur Schnitzler, as well as many operas.

ANNIE SPARKS

See also: performing arts in francophone countries: Belgium; theatre

Bonnaire, Sandrine

b. 1967, Gannat

Actor

Her career began in a key film of the 1980s, Pialat's 1983 *To Our Loves* (*A nos amours*), for which she received a César. She worked with Pialat in two more films in the 1980s: *Police* (1985) and *Sous le Soleil de Satan* (1987). She received a second César in 1985 for her role as a loner in Varda's *Vagabonde* (*Sans toit ni loi*), another key 1980s film. Her roles in Sautet's *Quelques jours avec moi* (1988) and, more particularly, Rivette's monumental *Jeanne la Pucelle* (1994), confirmed her as one of France's leading female actors.

PHIL POWRIE

See also: cinema

Bonnefoy, Yves

b. 1923, Tours

Poet, translator and critic

In some ways, Bonnefoy is the first important poet in modern France whose career was not shaped by Surrealism. He writes with great precision and concentration and thus reiterates the traditional French insistence on discipline, which has characterized most French poetry from the seventeenth century through Valéry and Saint-John Perse. The poetic lines are often Alexandrines, as in classical French practice. Bonnefoy studied philosophy, translated poems and a number of plays by Shakespeare, as well as Yeats and Seferis. He is also an important critic of poetry and art. His first volume of verse, *On the Motion and Immobility of Douve* (*Du mouvement et de l'immobilité de Douve*), from 1953, sets the tone for his poetry. Douve is a landscape, a river and a person; in any case, an animated female form of nature, made present and concrete, combining the aspects of becoming and being. This also means a consciousness of the presence of dying in the midst of living. It is a 'poetry that speaks only of presences – or absences'. The principal later collections of poetry are *Yesterday's Desert Dominion* (*Hier régnant desert*) from 1958, *Words in Stone* (*Pierre écrite*) from 1965, *In the Lure of the Threshold* (*Dans le leurre du seuil*) from 1975, *In the Shadow's Light* (*Ce qui fut sans lumière*) from 1987 and *The Beginning and the End of the Snow* (*Début et fin de la neige*), followed by *Where the Arrow Falls* (*Là où retombe la flèche*) both from 1991.

WALTER A. STRAUSS

See also: poetry

Boulez, Pierre

b. 1925, Montbrison

Composer, conductor and theorist

Pierre Boulez is unquestionably the most powerful force and the most trenchant intellect in contemporary music. He was educated in mathematics in Lyon and went to Paris to study with Olivier **Messiaen** at the Conservatoire and with René Leibowitz (a pupil of Schönberg). Boulez's uniquely forceful personality became manifest early in his *Sonatine* for flute and piano and his first piano sonata, both written at the age of 20. In those early years, Boulez often rebelled against his mentors and models (Messiaen, Schönberg, Stravinsky) in order to carve out his own musical language. It is also worth noting that Boulez, very broadly cultured, always manifested an extraordinary capacity to link music with the other arts (the poetry of Mallarmé and **Char**, the novels of Joyce, the painting of Klee).

His experience as an organizer and conductor dates back to his association with Jean-Louis **Barrault** and the subsequent series of concerts in Paris known as *Domaine Musical*, beginning in 1959, in which the public was first exposed to a systematic presentation of the major composers of the twentieth century. Many of these composers (Stockhausen, Maderna) were colleagues at the international summer school for new music in Darmstadt. Boulez's official conducting career began with the Vienna Philharmonic in Salzburg in 1962, continued in London with the BBC Orchestra, and in the United States with the Cleveland Orchestra and the New York Philharmonic.

As a composer, he is primarily a problem-solver. Frequently that means that his works are only provisionally 'finished', either because there are problems that still need resolution or because the developing experience as a composer/conductor constantly enlarges and modi-fies the perspective that he has adopted towards a composition in progress. In this respect, he has genuine affinities with Mallarmé.

The most frequently performed work of Boulez in the years 1950–75 was *Le Marteau sans maître* (1952–7), notable for its Balinese sonorities and based on three poems by René Char. His largest orchestral work is the celebration of Mallarmé entitled *Pli selon pli* (1957–62), which encapsulates three Mallarmé poems of chamber proportions within its larger orchestral framework, also centred on Mallarmé. In the 1950s Boulez carried the process of serialization to a point of saturation (all aspects of composition were serially organized, not merely pitch), in the two-piano works aptly entitled *Structures I* and *II*. During those years Boulez also came into contact with John Cage and aleatoric music, but the differences between the two composers quickly became clear: whereas Cage was moving towards silence and anarchy, Boulez used 'chance' in a disciplined way, always emphasizing problems of structure. In the works since 1975, random events are strictly circumscribed in such works as *Rituel in memoriam Bruno Maderna* for eight orchestral groups, and *Domaines* for clarinet and six instrumental groups. It is evident in these later works that Boulez has a refined lyric sensibility that in many of his earlier works had been overshadowed by structural exigencies. The most important of his most recent works, lyrical as well as theatrical, are *Répons* for six instrumental soloists, instrumental ensemble and electro-acoustical equipment (including loud speakers), and '... *explosante-fixe* ...' (a quotation from André Breton) for a similar ensemble with flutes dominant. These works are the product of Boulez's experience as a texture and colour-oriented conductor and of his musical research undertaken at IRCAM (Institut de Recherche et de Coordination Acoustique/Musique), which he founded in 1976 in Paris. Thus, in these recent works, Boulez's musical language has been enriched and 'amplified' by electronic distribution (not production) of sound across the auditorium. In this sense, Boulez is also a pioneer in the modern tendency towards the spatialization of sonority.

Boulez is without a doubt the most important champion of twentieth-century music. His own compositions, as well as his musical analyses, are a '*pays fertile*' (the title of his book on Paul Klee), in which the play of imagination and discipline generates a perpetually fascinating tension between rigorous structure and the labour of the imagination, and thus enacts the drama of the intellect harnessing the sensibility.

WALTER A. STRAUSS

See also: concert music

Major works

Boulez, P. (1968) *Notes of an Apprenticeship*, New York: Knopf.
——(1971) *Boulez on Music Today*, Cambridge: Harvard University Press.
——(1986) *Orientations*, Cambridge: Harvard University Press.

Further reading

Jameux, D. (1991) *Pierre Boulez*, Cambridge: Harvard University Press (the most comprehensive and detailed study of his works in English translation).

Bouquet, Michel

b. 1925, Paris

Actor

Famous for performances in 1940s productions of **Anouilh** and **Camus** plays, for his work with Jean **Vilar** at the Théâtre National Populaire, and for roles in many important Pinter productions, Bouquet teaches acting at the Paris Conservatoire. He has also played many film roles.

ANNIE SPARKS

See also: theatre

Further reading

Bouquet, M. (1988) *La Leçon de comédie, entretiens avec J.-J. Vincensini*, Paris: Librairie Séguier (interviews).

Bourdet, Gildas

b. 1927, Le Havre

Director and playwright

Bourdet is a director of the regional theatre in Le Havre, a town which provides the reference for many of the productions he directs and designs. Formerly a proponent of **collective creation** in the 1970s, he also writes. Plays include *Les Derniers Détails* (The Last Details) and *Station service* (Service Station).

ANNIE SPARKS

See also: regional writing: Breton; theatre

Bourdieu, Pierre

b. 1930, Denguin, Basses-Pyrénées

Sociologist

One of the main themes in Bourdieu's work as a sociologist is the attempt to articulate the relationship between an individual's 'subjectivity', and the 'objective' world of social phenomena. In this way, he has sought to overcome the dichotomy between the subjective and the objective in sociology. He has called the attempt to understand the ways in which these two areas are inextricably bound together 'genetic **structuralism**'. Bourdieu has become one of France's foremost postwar intellectuals, having been appointed to a Chair of Sociology at the Collège de France in 1982. However, unlike fellow intellectuals such as **Foucault** and **Derrida**, he does not operate solely as a 'theorist'. Throughout his career he has combined empirical research and fieldwork with a theoretical, philosophical reflection on the methodological and more general questions raised by this research. His first work developed out of two years spent as a conscript in the French army during the **Algerian war**. He published *The Algerians* (*Sociologie de l'Algérie*) in 1958. This and subsequent publications on Algeria were largely descriptive, but also provided analytical sections which point towards the key themes of later work. For example, he looks at the way in which peasants and the urban proletariat experience technological and industrial development as a new experience of time. Time as part of a lived relation to the natural world is lost, which serves to illustrate the problematic relationship between 'subjective hopes' and 'objective chances'. Bourdieu has also described himself in this period as a 'blissful structuralist', referring primarily to his analysis of the binary oppositions which structure the Kabyle house as a microcosm which is pregnant with social meaning. In subsequent work, Bourdieu has tended to reject structuralism as a method which is too 'objectivist', seeing it as overly reliant on the model. However, he has also rejected the 'subjectivist' illusion of ideology as an overt and conscious project of class domination. Instead, he has tried to steer a path through these illusions by looking at 'practice' and 'strategy'. Strategy allows for individual human intervention against the model. As far as practice is concerned, Bourdieu attempts to construct a sociology which takes into account contingency and agency. Another tool used to overcome the subjectivism/objectivism dichotomy is the concept of the 'habitus'. The habitus is literally the mediating link between the subjective world of individuals and the objective world in which they must live. It has connotations of habit and habituation, rather than consciously learned social rules. Habitus may also be

regarded as a sort of grammar of actions and tastes by which the dominant class distinguishes itself from the dominated class. In a conscious decision to turn the ethnographer's gaze away from conventional 'exotic' objectives, he has worked with the concept of habitus in relation to a world he knows well, that of French academics. In *Homo Academicus* (1984), he carries out qualitative sociological research on the French university system. Bourdieu shows that cultural capital is a means of achieving social domination. Culture is the object both about which, and over which, people fight.

JOHN MARKS

See also: anthropology and ethnology; class

Further reading

Jenkins, R. (1992) *Pierre Bourdieu*, Key Sociologists series, London: Routledge (a clear and concise introduction to Bourdieu's work).

Robbins, D. (1991) *The Work of Pierre Bourdieu: Recognizing Society*, Milton Keynes: Open University Press (an extensive introduction to Bourdieu's work).

Braque, Georges

b. 1882, Argenteuil-sur-Seine;
d. 1963, Paris

Artist

With **Picasso**, Braque evolved analytic and synthetic Cubism from 1908. Also, he explored colour lithography from the 1940s. From the mid-1930s, the human figure returned and his work grew more cryptically personal and less literally representational of material things, as in *Duet* (1937). In the occupation period Braque's stripped canvas rejected lyricism in favour of unequivocal severity of line and colour – for instance, *The Grey Table* (1942).

His *Studio Series* (1949–56) comprised eight canvases, the result of a long process of thought over several years. Harmonious relationships are sought as plain objects, crowding the image, metamorphose and lose their identity as they merge through the pleasure of associations.

VALERIE SWALES

See also: painting

Brassens, Georges

b. 1921, Sète;
d. 1981, Paris

Singer-songwriter

Brassens, along with **Brel**, was one of the most successful and enduring figures in French *chanson* during the 1950s and 1960s. The son of a builder, he arrived in Paris from Sète in 1939, where he initially lived with his aunt. Brassens worked for Renault, but was called up during the **Vichy** era for the German forced-labour programme. He absconded and was sheltered by Jeanne Planche, to whom he dedicated two songs. Surrounded by his closest friends, he continued to live with Jeanne and her husband until her death in 1968. Although Joha (Püppchen) Heiman was his lifetime companion, he never wished for a formal marriage certificate, as he explained in 'La Non-Demande en mariage' (The Non-Proposal of Marriage).

In 1952 **Patachou** finally convinced him to perform his own songs. From early on he was conscious of his 'Mauvaise Réputation' (Bad Reputation), describing himself later as 'Le Pornographe du phonographe' (The Pornographer of the Gramophone). Although Brassens was accused of vulgarity, with half of his songs being censored between 1952 and 1964, his vocabulary actually draws more on Villon and Rabelais than on twentieth-century **slang**. There are, in fact, no contemporary swear words in 'La Ronde des jurons' (Dance of the Swear Words). Brassens liked simply to amuse his audience, and if anything was likely to shock it was perhaps what lay behind the songs. These deal with timeless subjects such as love, e.g. 'La Première Fille' (The First Girl); women, both admirable ('Saturne') and treacherous ('Concurrence déloyale' ['Unfair Competition']); fidelity and the cult of friendship, e.g. 'Les Copains d'abord' (Friends First); generosity, e.g. 'Chanson pour l'Auvergnat', a song dedicated to a native of the Auvergne; and death and the passing of time, e.g.'Boulevard du temps qui passe' (The Boulevard of Passing Time).

His particular brand of anarchy rejected dogmatism and collectivism. In 'Les Deux Oncles' (The Two Uncles), he effectively put Resistance fighters and collaborators in the same basket. Conscious of both his mother's pious Catholicism and his father's atheism, he could never believe positively in God, as in 'Le Mécréant' (The Infidel). He did not consider it was his place to participate in the social debates launched by the **May 1968** movement, but did write against the revanchist tendencies in postwar France that ensured that French women who slept with German soldiers had their heads shaved in public ('La Tondue').

Brassens, a voracious reader and music lover, was greatly influenced by swing and its exponents, especially Charles **Trenet** and Ray Ventura. He did not wish to mask the relationship between words and music with an artificial orchestral accompaniment, so continued to play his guitar on stage. Brassens did not seek to communicate with his audience through gestures, and was often likened to a big bear trapped in a cage. None the less, he did bring the intimacy of the cabaret to the music hall. Although Brassens particularly disliked recordings of live performances, one which survives is his 1973 concert at Cardiff University. He set the words of other poets to music, including those of his friend, Paul Fort. His songs have been translated and sung in English, most notably by Jake Thackeray.

CHRIS TINKER

See also: song/*chanson*

Major works

Brassens, G. (1993) *Les Chansons d'abord* (collected song lyrics).

Further reading

Calvet, L.-J. (1993) *Georges Brassens*, Paris: Payot (biographically oriented study).

Braudel, Fernand

b. 1902, France;
d. 1985, Paris

Intellectual

Perhaps France's most influential postwar historian, Braudel was from 1956 the editor of the journal *Annales*, was instrumental in the setting-up of the sixth section of the École Pratique des Hautes Études (later the institutional bastion of **structuralism**), and founded the Maison des Sciences de l'Homme, later to be the powerbase of **Bourdieu**. His institutional importance is fully matched by that of his writing. *La Méditerranée* of 1947 (on the sixteenth century) and 1979's *Civilisation matérielle, économie et capitalisme (XVe–XVIIIe siècle)* are two of the century's major works of history. Braudel was elected to the **Académie Française** shortly before his death.

KEITH READER

Brel, Jacques

b. 1929, Brussels;
d. 1978, Paris

Singer-songwriter

Brel, together with **Brassens**, is regarded as one of the great icons of postwar *chanson*. Following a middle-class Catholic education in Brussels, Brel escaped his father's cardboard-box factory, to make his debut in 1953 at the Théatre des Trois Baudets in Paris. He initially adopted a lyrical voice in the songs of the 1950s, combining religious and moral zeal with youthful romanticism, typified in 'Quand on n'a que l'amour' (If We Only Have Love), earning from Brassens the nickname *l'Abbé Brel* (Abbot Brel).

Following a heightened sense of pessimism and disillusionment towards the end of the 1950s, especially where women and love were concerned, as in 'Ne me quitte pas' (If You Go Away), Brel's lyricism was eclipsed by the development of two additional voices. The first satirized middle-class society in songs such as 'Les Bourgeois' (The Bourgeois), and 'Les Flamandes' (The Flemish Women) which made him unpopular in Flanders. Brel's attack was, however, of more universal significance, addressing those who fall into immobility, deny their intelligence and individuality, and refuse to be existentially committed in life. The second voice was developed in a series of invented characters which served to renew his hope of finding the perfect love ('Madeleine', 'Titine', 'Les Bonbons').

The optimism generated in these dramatic songs faded by 1968 with the triumph of death and time, as in 'J'arrive' (I'm Coming). Songs such as 'Les Bonbons 67', the sequel to 'Les Bonbons', degenerated into parody and the burlesque, as characters could no longer hold on to any serious goal in life. Resigned to a more realistic notion of love, as in 'La Chanson des vieux amants' ('The Song of the Old Lovers'), the lyrical narrator returned, escaping nostalgically back towards an idealized childhood. Given the pessimism and escapism of his 1967–8 work, it is perhaps not coincidental that Brel decided to stop his concert tours.

During the 1970s, he went on to star as Don Quixote in the musical *Homme de la Mancha* (*Man of La Mancha*), produced and acted in several films, and developed a passion for sailing and flying, all before settling in the

Marquesas Islands with his companion Maddly Bamy. Following this long absence, Brel returned in 1977, shortly before his early death from cancer, with a sell-out comeback album, *Brel*, which reflected both the themes of his earlier songs and his subsequent evolution away from France. Not only was the narrator dissatisfied with society, as in 'Jaurès' and 'Les Flamingants' (extreme Flemish nationalists), but his faith in love was at an all-time low and his view of women often corresponded to an angel–whore dichotomy ('Knokke-le-Zoute Tango'). The cult of male friendship did, however, offer some consolation ('Jojo'). Much of Brel's originality lies in his theatrical stage performances, where he developed his facial and gestural expression to the full. English versions of his songs formed the basis of an American musical, *Jacques Brel is Alive and Well and Living in Paris*, and have since been recorded by many artists, including Scott Walker and Marc Almond.

CHRIS TINKER

See also: francophone popular music: Europe; song/*chanson*

Major works

Brel, J. (1982) *Tout Brel*, Paris: Laffont (collected song lyrics).

Further reading

Todd, O. (1984) *Jacques Brel: une vie*, Paris: Laffont (biography).

Bresson, Robert

b. 1901, Bromont-Lamothe

Director

Bresson is a film-maker whose cinematic writ-

ing is unlike any other – elliptical, hermetic, making extensive use of close-ups less for psychological insight (a term foreign to him) than as windows on the soul. A Catholic, he has also been described as a Jansenist, and his later films, such as *Le Diable, probablement* (1977) and *L'Argent* (1983), bear the trace of a spirituality, at once resigned and refined, that could not inappropriately be described as Oriental.

His early films make comparatively conventional use of actors and dialogue, and it was not until *Diary of a Country Priest* (*Le Journal d'un curé de campagne*) in 1951 that the distinctiveness of his style came to the fore. This adaptation of the Bernanos novel counterposes the young priest's writing of his diary to his voice on the soundtrack reading it aloud. The result is an unprecedented stress on the materiality of writing and of the priest's agony. Bresson has famously said that if a sound can replace an image then the image should be done away with. His work from this film onwards can be understood as a sustained development of that idea.

He was to return to the work of Bernanos with *Mouchette* in 1967, but two other works of that period, the Dostoevskian *Pickpocket* of 1959 and *Au hasard, Balthazar* (1966), are more remarkable. *Pickpocket* presents its central character's compulsive thieving as the means by which he attains (a kind of) salvation, in a narrative reversal of *Un condamné à mort s'est échappé* of 1956. Michel the pickpocket finds grace through imprisonment as grace finds Fontaine, the hero of the earlier film, and enables him to escape from a German wartime prison. Both films are extraordinarily gripping on the level of narrative suspense, whereas the narration of *Balthazar* is such a tissue of ellipses and paradoxes that it often baffles audiences. The eponymous central character is a donkey, for whom the film constructs a kind of spiritual odyssey, in the extreme example of Bresson's refusal of the notion of the actor and espousal of the 'model' from whose pro-filmic behaviour any taint of emotional manipulation is to be rigorously expunged. The deadpan quality this gives his films – which is doubtless why **Tati** said that he would like to work with him – achieves an iconic effect similar to the flattening-out of the image in early medieval art. Very few of his 'models' go on to prolonged screen careers, so uniquely draining is the experience of working with him. Bresson is at once the most spiritual and the most material of film-makers, an influence on **Godard** but also on Martin Scorsese (*Raging Bull*). There is scarcely another director whose work is so instantly and consistently recognizable.

KEITH READER

See also: Catholicism and Protestantism; cinema

Major works

Bresson, R. (1975/88), *Notes sur le cinématographe*, Paris: Gallimard/Folio (Bresson's aphoristic distillations of his views on the true essence of cinema).

Further reading

Arnaud, P. (1986), *Robert Bresson*, Paris: Cahiers du cinéma (a well-illustrated phenomenological study, articulating the films' formal properties with their theological implications).

Schrader, P. (1972), *Transcendental Style in Film: Ozu, Bresson, Dreyer*, Berkeley, Los Angeles and London: University of California Press (a monograph by Scorsese's main scriptwriter, situating Bresson's work within a wider context of spiritual art).

Sémolué, J. (1993), *Bresson*, Paris: Flammarion/Cinémas (a careful and well-documented overview).

Brialy, Jean-Claude

b. 1933, Aumale, Algeria

Actor and producer

Brialy has acted in some ninety films since 1957, but is best known as a key actor of the **Nouvelle vague** (New Wave), especially for **Chabrol**'s *Le Beau Serge* and *Les Cousins* (both 1959), also acting in films by **Godard, Malle, Rivette, Truffaut** and **Varda**. An important role is the ageing fetishist of **Rohmer**'s *Claire's Knee* (*Le Genou de Claire*) in 1970. Among his secondary roles, there is the judge of **Tavernier**'s *Le Juge et l'assassin* (1976), and the bourgeois of Buñuel's *The Phantom of Liberty* (*Le Fantôme de la Liberté*) in 1974 and Chabrol's *L'Inspecteur Lavardin* (1986).

PHIL POWRIE

See also: cinema

Brook, Peter

b. 1925, London

Director

One of the best-known international directors to have made Paris his base in recent decades, Peter Brook remains to this day renowned for his experimental approach to theatre, as well as his love of the epic theatre world encompassed by the Elizabethan theatre. The founder of the CIRT (Centre International de Recherches Théâtrales) in 1968, Brook moved to Paris to begin his experimental workshops with international backing and an international team of actors. Before moving to France, he had enjoyed a prestigious directorial career at the Royal Shakespeare Company, notably for his 1962 *King Lear*, although his interest in the avant-garde and experimental was evident in his **Theatre of Cruelty** season (influenced by **Artaud**) in 1964 and his good relationship with the experimental Polish director Grotowski. Shortly after setting up the CIRT, he also produced perhaps his most famous production – Shakespeare's *A Midsummer Night's Dream* in 1970. This, like many of his projects, retained an earthy, real quality rather than a dreamlike one, while questioning existing principles and practices. At this time, the CIRT was deep in a period of experimentation with gesture and movement, and was generally concerned with sensitizing the team of actors in order to break down existing barriers and create an environment in which creation would be the organic result of improvisation and experiment, rather than of directorial imposition. While not abolishing language as a means of communication, Brook encouraged his team to consider other means at their disposal, rather than relying on meaningless, lifeless words. Brook's team created *Orghast*, a poetic, abstract work for an Iranian festival, and the following year embarked upon an important improvisation tour in Africa which was to influence its subsequent work heavily. The democratic layout of its shows, performed on a carpet with the audience sitting around the edge, is reflected to this day in the performance space and seating plan in Brook's Les Bouffes du Nord theatre, which he acquired in 1974. Brook and his team produced many notable productions there in the 1970s and 1980s, including *Timon of Athens*, *The Cherry Orchard* and *Ubu aux bouffes*, as well as his famous and ground-breaking production of the *Mahabharata* in 1985, based on a script by Jean-Claude **Carrière**. Since then, Brook has continued to work with international theatrical traditions; for example, in *The Tempest* in 1990, which explored African cultures. He began covering new territory with the '*cycle de cerveau*' (brain cycle) of plays in 1992, with *The Man Who Mistook His Wife for a Hat* (*L'Homme qui prenait sa femme pour un chapeau*), based on Oliver Sacks' book of the same name and exploring the nature of mental illness. His more recent production, *Qui est là* (Who's There), in 1995, examined different directorial and theatrical approaches through Shakespeare's *Hamlet*.

ANNIE SPARKS

See also: theatre

Further reading

Bradby, D. and Williams, D. (1988) *Director's Theatre*, London: Macmillan (Chapter 6 deals with Brook).

Williams, D. (1988) *Peter Brook – A Theatrical Casebook*, revised edition 1991, London: Methuen.

Bryen, Camille

b. 1902, Nantes;
d. 1977, Paris

Artist, poet and illustrator

Bryen took part in Dada and Surrealist activities in the 1930s and 1940s. His 'objects of symbolic function' are assemblages of disparate elements brought together according to an inner logic. He wrote poems (*Opoponax*) and produced works in gestural automatism (*Hépéril*). He collaborated in the avant-garde review *Réalités nouvelles* and participated in exhibitions of **art informel** including *HWPSMTB* in 1948 and *Signifiants de l'Informel* in 1958. In 1952 Bryen and **Audiberti** published *L'Ouvre-Boîte, colloque abhumaniste* (The Tin-Opener: An Abhumanist Colloquium), where they defined their philosophy of *abhumanism* as 'the world without man . . . the world as it is at the beginning, before it has been compartmentalized, classified, humanized'.

ELZA ADAMOWICZ

Seee also: painting

Buffet, Bernard

b. 1928, France

Artist

Buffet acquired a successful reputation in the

1940s and 1950s. His figurative painting represented aspects of **Sartre**'s existentialist theory in a literalist and highly schematic manner, which was popular with a large section of the French public. An example is *Self Portrait* (1954).

VALERIE SWALES

See also: existentialism; painting

Buren, Daniel

b. 1938, France

Artist

In the 1967 exhibition at the Musée d'Art Moderne in Paris, Buren represented himself through a stylistically reduced signature of vertical red and white stripes on identically sized canvases, which he has continued to reproduce. In a 1970 essay, Buren rejected the art object as illusion and proposed the reality of the visuality of the painting as a system. For Buren, neutrality of composition and absence of style negate all formal problems and thereby offer complete rupture with the mythification of art. Visual repetition in differently scaled locations becomes for this artist a method for questioning the proposition of the work. Following **Althusser**, theory becomes a specific form of revolutionary art practice.

VALERIE SWALES

See also: painting

Butor, Michel

b. 1926, Mons-en Baroeul

Writer

In his 1955 essay, 'Le Roman comme recherche', Butor defined the novel as the writer's (and reader's) search for new forms, new techniques for writing novels that would both express and create new realities. Butor has been a leader in inventing new genres for fiction, drawing from the visual, musical and other arts.

Butor's career falls into three overlapping explorations. Four novels correspond to the early *nouveau roman*: while his 1954 *Passage de Milan* (Passage to Milan), the 1956 *Passing Time* (*L'Emploi du temps*), *Degrees* (*Degrés*), published in 1960, and *Second Thoughts* (*La Modification*) of 1957 retain identifiable protagonists and narrative point of view, their structures are experimental. The importance of character diminishes progressively, and narrative is simply the framework or excuse for formal innovation. Each story traces permutations within a complex architecture of time and space. A change in consciousness is often both the character's fate and the goal of the fiction as a whole.

In 1962 and 1967, *Mobile* (*Mobile: étude pour une représentation des États-Unis*) and *Portrait de l'artiste en jeune singe* (Portrait of the Artist as a Young Monkey) move into postnarrative fiction. Plot and characters disappear, and the reader receives less guidance in finding coherence. Five volumes of *Matière de rêves* (The Stuff of Dreams) experiment with dream logic. *Mobile, Description of San Marco* (*Description de San Marco*) and other works use places – their particular features and associated mythologies – as points of departure for fictional meditations. This most extensive and continuing domain of his oeuvre emphasizes inventing alternative forms by generating fiction from dream, painting, opera, typography, maps and geography, and inventories. Texts are compared to mobiles (such as those by Calder), where readers must move about within seemingly random arrangements of elements. Butor seeks maximum engagement of his readers' intellectual and imaginative resources.

Butor is also known for his critical essays, collected in four volumes of *Répertoires*. Here he pursues the crossover potential among varying art forms – fiction (Roussel, Mallarmé, Faulkner, Proust, science fiction, and other precursors), visual arts (Hokusai), music

(Beethoven) – and the ways other arts can provide new departures for writing.

Butor's work is unified by his casting of the reader as detective, as researcher, as decipherer, and ultimately as creator of the fiction. His own extensive travels provide generators and thematic material for his books. He never stops disrupting habits of reading and perceiving, exploring ways to write spatially, poetically, symbolically, rhythmically, and visually – not just narratively – and he reflects continuously on the nature of writing.

LYNN A. HIGGINS

Further reading

Lydon, M. (1980) *Perpetuum Mobile: A Study of the Novels and Aesthetics of Michel Butor*, Edmonton: University of Alberta Press (analysis of Butor's approach to writing).

Raillard, G. (ed.) (1974) *Butor: colloque de Cerisy*, Paris: UGE (talks by and about Butor).

Spencer, M. C. (1974) *Michel Butor*, New York: Twayne (overview of Butor's writing career; also contains bibliography).

World Literature Today (1982) 56, 2 (journal issue on Butor).

C

cable and satellite television

The importance of developing the new media of cable and satellite as part of France's hi-tech communications revolution featured prominently on the media policy agenda of both Socialist and Gaullist governments throughout the 1980s. However, the era of multichannel cable television has been slow to arrive. By the late 1990s only about 10 per cent of French households were hooked up to a cable network. Satellite television had fared even less well, with only a handful of households equipped to receive the output of the technologically oversophisticated French direct-broadcasting satellites Télédiffusion 1 and 2. However, in the late 1990s the development of digital television looked set to give a boost to satellite television in France.

RAYMOND KUHN

See also: television

Further reading

Lunven, R. and Vedel, T. (1993) *La Télévision de demain*, Paris: Armand Colin (a detailed analysis of the new media technologies of cable and satellite).

Cabrel, Francis

b. 1953, Agen

Singer-songwriter

With his *occitan* (Southern French) accent, nostalgic and sometimes melancholy songs, Francis Cabrel has espoused good causes, for example, leukaemia with *Il faudra leur dire* (They Must be Told), and has defended his atavistic roots with *Les Chevaliers cathares* (The Cathar Knights). But the so-called *ermite d'Astaffort* (hermit of Astaffort) is perhaps most important as an outstanding lyricist, charismatic stage performer and stout defender of *la chanson française* (French song).

IAN PICKUP

See also: song/*chanson*

café theatre

Since its beginnings in the 1960s, café theatre – performed cabaret-style in cafés – has grown from a marginalized art form to one worthy of its own section in Paris events guides and a significant place at the Avignon festival, with a repertoire ranging from the classics to one-man stand-up comedy shows, and a reputation for creativity and nonconformism. Often forced to work with limited resources and space, like many parts of the fringe theatre scene in London or off-off-Broadway in New York, today's café theatres usually work six days a week putting on perhaps three productions a night in venues which simultaneously serve food and drink. The numerous venues operating in Paris include the Café d'Edgar, La Vieille Grille (one of the first venues in the 1960s), Les Blancs-Manteaux and the Café de la Gare, all operating in premises which are to all intents and purposes still cafés, adapted to the theatre they house to a greater or lesser extent.

The first Parisian café theatre, the now defunct Royal, was founded in February 1966 by one of the genre's key practitioners, Bernard da Costa, followed by the first provincial venue, L'Œnyx in Bordeaux, a year later. Supposedly inspired by the idea of a French variation of 'off-off-Broadway', practitioners such as da Costa and Romain Bouteille (who began at La Vieille Grille) aimed to found a theatrical arena where actors and authors could operate in freedom, putting on their own productions. Hence, as well as producing many classics, café theatre has also been an ideal space for new writing and contemporary authors and performers, with room to experiment. Indeed it is the fact that café theatre often involves a close, egalitarian relationship between performers and audience which led **Anouilh** to praise it as an institution and to allow many of his plays to be performed by its practitioners. Alongside other great writers such as **Arrabal**, whose works were regularly performed by them, café theatres also fostered many now famous authors and actors, among them **Coluche**, **Depardieu**, Vitor Haïm and **Michel**.

By May 1967, café theatre had begun to emerge as a separate heading in many events guides for the capital, and by 1968 had become so accepted by the theatre world that **Vilar** took the opportunity to welcome it to the Avignon festival – it now makes up a substantial proportion of the total number of productions performed there, particularly in the 'Avignon Public Off' festival. The Marais theatre festival in Paris finally followed suit in 1971, by which time new government subsidies were also being awarded to practising compa-

nies such as the Sans Souci in Paris. By the 1980s, café theatre was an extremely popular genre, which had become closely linked in people's minds with the cabaret, sketch and one-man-show scene which seemed to account for a large number of productions. Café theatre is now, in many ways, a term synonymous with this type of entertainment, although strictly speaking its scope and repertoire are as wide as ever.

Annie Sparks

See also: Avignon and summer arts festivals; theatre

Further reading

da Costa, B. (1978) *Histoire du café-théâtre*, Paris: Buchet/Chastel (an anecdotal history of the café theatre)

café-concert

The *café-concert* (*caf'conc'*) – a café where singers and other artistes entertained customers – became popular in France in the 1860s. By 1890 there were some 200 in Paris alone. The forerunners of twentieth-century cabarets (e.g. of the Left and Right Bank in Paris in the 1960s), the *café-concerts* provided popular entertainment and are important, historically, as establishments where the public listened to music rather than joining in the singing of popular songs.

Ian Pickup

See also: cultural topography (Paris); song/*chanson*

Cahiers du cinéma

Journal

Launched by **Gallimard** on 1 April 1951 as the

successor to *La Revue du cinéma* (1946–9), *Cahiers du cinéma* contributed, with journals such as *Positif* and *Image et son*, to the rise of film culture in France in the immediate postwar period. Edited by Jacques Doniol-Valcroze, J.-M. Lo Duca and André **Bazin** and, from 1955, by Éric **Rohmer**, it became celebrated, retrospectively, as the breeding ground for the **Nouvelle Vague** film-makers **Truffaut, Godard, Chabrol** and **Rivette**, as well as Rohmer himself, all of whom wrote for *Cahiers* before making their first films. The journal became the focus of the *politique des auteurs*, adumbrated by Truffaut in the article 'Une Certaine Tendance du cinéma français' (see February 1954 issue), which defended the role of the director as 'author' of a film and attacked the 'tradition de qualité' then dominant in French cinema. It also enabled the Hollywood output of the 1940s and 1950s to be classified and taken seriously, and established the reputation of Hollywood directors such as Hitchcock and Hawks, despised or neglected up to that time. In this way it defined a new attitude to both making and viewing films. The second important, though less well-known aspect of *Cahiers du cinéma*'s influence in the 1950s was the promotion of prewar and postwar European directors such as **Renoir**, Gance, Ophuls, Murnau and Dreyer, and its support for independent film-makers like **Tati** and **Melville**. *Cahiers* thus defended cinema as an important cultural form when it was increasingly threatened by the rise of **television**, and bequeathed to British critics in *Movie*, and American critics such as Andrew Sarris, the outlines of the 'auteur theory' which was to dominate film criticism for a generation.

Cahiers du cinéma made a second major contribution to film theory and practice during and after **May 1968**. It supported Henri **Langlois** in his resistance to a Gaullist government takeover of the Cinémathèque in 1968, and it published the proceedings of the États généraux du cinéma (States General of the Cinema) held at the time of the May Events. Under the editorship of Jean-Louis Comolli and Jean Narboni it became strongly politicized, publishing an important series of articles on the relationship between fiction and documentary, and between technology and ideology, as well as extensive translations of the writings of Eisenstein. Its Maoist editorial line caused the withdrawal of financial backing from Daniel Filipacchi and, ultimately, a sharp decline in circulation, which was brought to an end, in 1974, by a *retour au cinéma* under the joint editorship of Serge **Daney** and Narboni. At this point, *Cahiers* was redesigned and relaunched for an upmarket, knowledgeable, but more general, readership. Today, with a circulation of some 60,000, *Cahiers du cinéma* remains the most influential film journal published in France.

JILL FORBES

See also: cinema; documentaries; Gaulle, Charles de

Further reading

de Baecque, A. (1991) *Cahiers du cinéma: histoire d'une revue*, 2 vols, Paris: Cahiers du Cinéma (essential reading on the life and times of *Cahiers*).

Camus, Albert

b. 1913, Mondovi, Algeria;
d. 1960, Villeblevin

Writer, playwright and essayist

Camus's death in an automobile accident foreshortened a career characterized by a remarkable range of literary and journalistic output. Not only was Camus the author of important and widely read novels, the creator and director of numerous plays, and a philosophical essayist/polemicist, but he was deeply engaged in the events of his time, first as an investigative journalist in Algeria, then as the editor of the Resistance journal *Combat*, and finally as a regular writer for the first incarnation of the widely diffused *L'Express*. Along with Jean-Paul **Sartre**, Camus lived the life of the committed writer, the *écrivain engagé*. Like Sartre and, later, Michel **Foucault**, Camus did not hesitate to enlist in humanitarian causes and take sides in social conflicts. Often influential and effective in his interventions, Camus had to endure one great disappointment: the progressive unravelling of Algeria, his native land. Camus sought an accommodation between the French colonial establishment and its revolutionary opponents, espousing the peaceful creation of a middle ground, but he died two years before Algerian independence, an embittered outsider in a progressively escalating conflict.

Camus began his writing career with two slender volumes entitled *The Wrong Side and the Right Side* (*L'Envers et l'endroit*) and *Nuptials* (*Noces*), written in 1937 and 1938 respectively. The collected stories of *L'Envers et l'endroit* are the first of Camus's works to develop the theme of the absurdity of human existence, notably in 'La Mort dans l'âme' (Death in the Soul), an autobiographical piece on the author's encounter with an unknown person's death in Prague. The central subject of the collection as a whole is the irresolvable contradiction between the beauty of nature and the reality of human misery and death. *Nuptials* emphasizes uniquely the first of these polarities, and can be read as an exalted prose poem to the luminous setting of Algeria.

Written for the most part in 1939 and 1940 in Algeria and published in 1942, *The Outsider* (*L'Étranger*) is the first of Camus's works to achieve notoriety in French intellectual circles. In the first part of this short novel, the hero (or, better, anti-hero), a man of French extraction named Meursault, kills an Arab on the beach without apparent motive, urged on in his act by the blinding rays of the sun. The second part of the narrative relates his trial, in which he is accused more for not crying at his mother's funeral than for killing a fellow-human. Like *The Myth of Sisyphus* (*Le Mythe de Sisyphe*), a 1942 essay which tells of the cyclical travails of a mortal condemned to roll an immense rock up a steep cliff, only to watch it roll down again, *L'Étranger* sets the absurdity of the

human condition against the backdrop of a Greek mythical universe.

Camus's fame continued to spread with the appearance of his plays in Paris theatres, especially *Caligula*, a consummate study of cruelty and evil first performed in Paris in September 1945 with Gérard **Philipe** in the title role. In 1947 came *The Plague* (*La Peste*), an allegorical novel whose protagonist, Dr Rieux, emblematizes a distinctly non-heroic, modest mode of action in the face of the plague's destruction. The plague is itself a multilevelled symbol of massive and meaningless death which, among other things, no doubt refers to World War II – the 'art' of total warfare and the building of concentration camps.

Camus's meditations on the war and its aftermath led to the publication of his most controversial work, *The Rebel* (*L'Homme révolté*), in 1951. In this long and sometimes ponderous treatise, Camus criticizes both Christianity and **Marxism** and proposes his own conception of 'Mediterranean thought' (based on moderation, on the Greek golden mean). The work was attacked by Sartre for its philosophical naivety, and this attack seems to have had a profound effect on Camus, who for five years wrote virtually nothing of note. In 1956, however, he published *The Fall* (*La Chute*), perhaps his most brilliant work. As concise as *L'Étranger* but much more ironical in tone, *La Chute* is a masterful condemnation of the moral evasions and deluded self-satisfaction that characterize the contemporary human being. It is also probable that the protagonist of *La Chute*, a 'fallen' lawyer named Jean-Baptiste Clamence, is in part an unflattering self-portrait of Camus himself.

The final works of Camus's career are the elegant short stories entitled *Exile and the Kingdom* (*L'Exil et le royaume*), published in 1957, the year in which he received the Nobel Prize for literature, and *The First Man* (*Le Premier Homme*), a fragmentary autobiographical novel set in Algeria and published for the first time thirty-four years after the author's death.

Now that the postwar debates surrounding **existentialism** have lost their immediacy, now that the quarrel between Sartre and Camus has faded into the shadows of anecdotal oblivion, what remains is Camus's talent as a stylist, especially in the novel and short story. His spare descriptions and cogent characterizations, his sense of rhetorical effect (especially his considerable gift as an ironist), will ensure him a place of distinction in twentieth-century French literary history.

DAVID ELLISON

See also: autobiography; decolonization; existentialist theatre

Further reading

Brée, G. (1959) *Camus*, New Brunswick, NJ: Rutgers University Press (the best early overview of Camus's literary works).

Ellison, D. (1990) *Understanding Albert Camus*, Columbia: University of South Carolina Press (synthetic study of Camus's novels, plays and philosophical essays).

Freeman, E. (1971) *The Theatre of Albert Camus: A Critical Study*, London: Methuen (the best account to date of the entirety of Camus's theatrical production).

Lottman, H. (1979) *Albert Camus: A Biography*, Garden City, NJ: Doubleday (by far the most detailed account of Camus's life).

Camus, Renaud

b. 1946, Chamalières

Writer, also writes under the names of Jean-Renaud Camus, Denis Duparc, Tony Duparc and Denis Duvert

One of the most interesting of the writers to be heavily influenced by **Barthes**'s theories, Camus's most important book is *Tricks*, a volume of 'autobiographical' memoirs of gay cruising, prefaced by Barthes. He has also published many gay-centred texts and 'travelogues' in which he plays with intertextuality in its

myriad forms: allusion, parody, plagiarism, quotation, reference, rewriting. His project is a writing of the self which renders obsolete the distinction between the novelistic and the autobiographical.

MICHAEL WORTON

See also: autobiography; gay writing

Canal Plus

Television channel

Established in 1984 by the Socialist government, Europe's first terrestrial pay-TV channel overcame early teething problems to become a huge commercial success. Funded by viewer subscription and mostly transmitted in scrambled form, the channel concentrates on feature films and 'live' coverage of sport. Pursuing a strategy of vertical integration and multimedia diversification, Canal Plus has become actively involved in film and television production, decoding technology and satellite transmission. It is a major sponsor of the French film industry. The company has helped establish pay-TV in other European countries and is set to become a key player in the development of digital television in Europe.

RAYMOND KUHN

See also: francophone television: Europe; television

Canard enchaîné, Le

Newspaper

This satirical weekly newspaper, which attracts 400,000 regular readers, and was first published by Maurice Maréchal in 1915 in reaction to wartime propaganda, is notoriously iconoclastic. The title plays on *canard*, which means 'duck' (as evident in cartoon ducks and wordplay), but is also slang for 'newspaper' or 'false report'. The 'chained duck' symbolizes rebellion against censorship and exposure of falsehood. The paper's investigative journalism and revelations of scandal have damaged many political careers. Owned by its journalists, *Le Canard* is staunchly independent, refusing advertising. Although it leans to the Left, this does not restrict the scope of its humour. The language is familiar, rich in political allusions and often cryptic.

PAM MOORES

See also: national press in France

Carax, Léos

b. 1960, Paris

Director

Carax is influenced by (post-)modern style and the *vidéo-clip*. His *alter ego* Denis Lavant – a very different sort of Jean-Pierre **Léaud** to his **Truffaut** – stars in all his three films to date: *Boy Meets Girl* of 1984, *Mauvais sang* of 1986 and (with Juliette **Binoche**) *Les Amants du Pont-Neuf* of 1991, a visually dazzling tale of love on the Paris bridge, which went massively over budget and was criticized for its aestheticization of poverty.

KEITH READER

See also: cinema; post-modernism

Cardin, Pierre

b. 1922, Venice, Italy

Fashion designer

Cardin studied architecture, then turned to dressmaking. After World War II, he worked for Paquin's fashion house in Paris, and for Schiaparelli. In 1947, he designed Christian **Dior**'s collection. In 1952, he opened his own fashion house. He participated in the creation of the 'New Look' for women, and was the first high-fashion designer to introduce a ready-to-wear line in 1960, inventing the sack-dress (*la chasuble*), the collarless look, and the poncho coat. He experimented with fabrics and technology, vinyl, and participated in designing clothes for the 'Space Age'. In 1962, he created his first menswear line.

JOËLLE VITIELLO

See also: fashion

Cardinal, Marie

b. 1929, Algiers, Algeria

Writer

Cardinal's reputation was established when she published *La Clé sur la porte* (Open Door) in 1972 and consolidated with the appearance, in 1975, of *The Words to Say It* (*Les Mots pour le dire*). Both texts are autobiographical fictions, reflecting Cardinal's concern with issues such as marital/family life, motherhood and the situation of women. The latter records the psychoanalytic process by means of which Cardinal defeated the mental and physiological problems that dogged her in the 1950s and 1960s. It speaks also of her bond with her native Algeria and of her difficult relationship with her mother. The complexities of the mother–daughter tie are the focus of *Devotion and Disorder* (*Les Grands Désordres*), a tale of a parent's experience of a daughter's drug addiction, published in 1987. Cardinal's involvement in collaborative projects with other feminists has generated *The Right to Choose* (*La Cause des femmes*), co-written in 1973 with Gisèle Halimi, and *Autrement dit* (In Other Words) in 1977. Born out of discussions with Annie **Leclerc**, this focuses on *The Words to Say It* and on women's relationship to history, language and the body.

ALEX HUGHES

See also: Algerian war; autobiography; women's/lesbian writing

Further reading

Cairns, L. (1992) *Marie Cardinal: Motherhood and Creativity*, Glasgow: University of Glasgow French and German Publications (a comprehensive, gender-oriented examination of Cardinal's writing).

Carrière, Jean-Claude

b. 1931, Colombières sur Orb

Scenarist, dramaturg and adaptor

Best known for his screenplays for famous directors such as Louis **Malle** and Luis Buñuel, whom he worked with for nineteen years, Carrière is renowned in the theatre for his work as a dramaturg and adaptor, especially for Jean-Louis **Barrault** and Peter **Brook**, whose *Mahabharata* he translated and adapted in 1985.

ANNIE SPARKS

See also: cinema; theatre

Carte de séjour

A 1980s beur rock group from Lyon, they are a voice of the second generation of North African immigrants. They made an extraordinary impact with the 1985 hit, *Sweet France* (*Douce France*), an ironical remake of **Trenet**'s song, performing at La Concorde for a meeting for SOS Racisme. They separated in 1988, but their leader, Rachid Taha, has carried on with a solo career.

GÉRARD POULET

See also: beur music; beurs; Désir, Harlem, and SOS Racisme; francophone popular music: North Africa

Cartier-Bresson, Henri

b. 1908, Chanteloup

Photographer and artist

After studying painting, Cartier-Bresson took up photography in 1931. His early work was extremely influential for the rigorous harmony and balance of form of his compositions, but it was as a photojournalist with the agency Magnum Photos that he had the greatest impact, fusing the artistic and the documentary into what became known as 'modern photography'. His photographs often focus on unexpected juxtapositions, and he famously refused to reframe or crop an image once it was taken. Since 1973, he has devoted himself essentially to drawing.

MICHAEL WORTON

See also: photography

Casarès, Maria

b. 1922, La Corogna, Spain;
d. 1996, Paris

Actor

Casarès is noted for powerful interpretations of tragic roles, especially in the 1940s and 1950s, at the **Comédie-Française** and Théâtre National de Paris, for directors such as **Chéreau**, **Blin** and Sobel. She has also worked with film directors Carné and **Bresson**.

ANNIE SPARKS

See also: theatre

Further reading

Laville, P. (1989) 'Maria Casarès, une vie de théâtre', *Acteurs*, November/December (analysis of her career).

Catholicism and Protestantism

France's Catholic culture stretches back some 1,500 years to the baptism of Clovis, King of the Gauls (the ancestors of the French), who embraced Catholicism in AD 496. For centuries the nation was officially Catholic, defined as *la fille aînée de Rome* (the elder daughter of Rome); the Catholic church was all-powerful, and other religions (such as Protestantism) were persecuted. However, these close ties between the Catholic church and the French state were weakened after the 1789 French Revolution: first, the 1801 Concordat demoted Catholicism from its status as the official religion of France to the religion of the majority; and second, in 1905, the Law of Separation of Churches and State formalized the principle of *laïcité* (secularism), according to which the state publicly neither recognizes nor subsidizes any religion, but yet guarantees the freedom of all private religious expression.

The diversification of France's religious framework is now recognized and accepted; it reflects the nation's increasingly mixed and complex society, and is characterized both by religions long-established in France (such as Protestantism and **Judaism**) as well as by those of more recent implantation (especially **Islam**, France's second religion in terms of the number of faithful). Religion today no longer enjoys the same status or the same degree of power and influence as in previous times, but this is not to say that it no longer has any impact on, or any role to play in, contemporary society. Indeed, expectations of religion (in whatever form) remain significant in a nation faced with an ever-increasing list of social problems and moral issues, for which successive political voices seem to have found no real solution.

Catholicism in France is in decline in terms of both its institutional structures and its traditional religious practice. Ordinations of new priests have fallen far below the number who retire or die in office each year, with just 171 ordinations in 1994 in contrast to 1,033 in 1950, a crisis of recruitment which means that around 60 per cent of priests are aged over 60. The total number of priests fell from 43,000 in 1948 to 25,000 in 1994, the most significant decline occurring after the events of **May 1968**, and only a third of France's 38,200 parishes have their own priest, with many priests required to oversee several parishes at once. With fewer priests to call on, the church has placed increasing responsibilities on France's deacons, of whom some 1,000 have been ordained since 1969, and who, unlike priests, are not required to be celibate, while lay Catholics also are now more widely employed in ceremonial celebration. But this has only provided the church with a small pool of additional workers and mass can still only be celebrated by a priest.

Religious practice has declined considerably since 1945, even in those regions which traditionally constitute the bedrock of French Catholicism, including Brittany, the Vendée, the Pyrenees, the Basque country and Savoy. Overall, 80 per cent of French people declare themselves Catholics, but the number regularly attending Sunday mass fell from 30 per cent of Catholics in 1950 to just 10 per cent (equating to four million faithful) in 1994, while many French are Catholic in name but never attend church. Furthermore, the number of those who turn to the church largely on ceremonial or seasonal occasions is also in decline: Catholic baptisms fell from 91 per cent of births in 1958 to 51 per cent in 1990, while Catholic marriages fell from 79 per cent of ceremonies in 1958 to 51 per cent in 1990; and few take communion at Easter, the yardstick by which Catholic practice is generally measured.

Although traditional religious practice is in decline, the French do retain a degree of religious culture characterized by their knowledge of a scale of religious references. France respects the Christian calendar alongside Republican and secular festivals such as the 14 July celebrations, and surveys reveal that 20 per cent of French overall possess a bible, missal, crucifix and rosary, while significant numbers can recognize and define the principal Christian figures and feast days and recite the major prayers. Secularism, it seems, has not eradicated religious culture; recognition of its importance in the complete socialization of the nation's children is evidenced by increasing calls for the teaching of religious history (but not theology) within the state education system. Moreover, Catholicism's pre-eminence in French religious culture was clearly illustrated in January 1996, when the secular state turned to the Catholic church for its celebration of the life of former President François **Mitterrand**.

The changing typology of French society, characterized by the effect of **immigration** and by an increase in the number of non-standard family structures, must be taken into account in any assessment of the impact of the Catholic church in France. The church's appeal has been particularly affected by its attitude to modern society. In some respects, it has evolved considerably: the church now accepts that it operates within a secular, multicultural society and many have welcomed its instrumental role in the defence of human (and especially immigrant) rights in the post-1945 period, in which it has joined with France's other representative religions. But, for many Catholics, the church operates within structures which remain too rigid, hierarchical and male-dominated, and considerable support is voiced for the ordination of married priests, the full integration of divorcees into the church and an increase in the role and powers granted to women. Moreover, many Catholics believe that the church retains an outdated social language and does not sufficiently respect individual conscience in the moral sphere, particularly on matters of sexual health and welfare where dogma continues to reject assisted fertility, abortion and artificial contraception, even when this may prevent **AIDS**. Two-thirds of Catholics (including 80 per cent of those under 25) reject the church's declarations on sexuality, preferring to regard the church's voice as simply one form of guidance among many, rather than the sole moral authority.

The institutional and practical decline of the French Catholic church is tempered, however, by evidence of a resurgence of spiritual enquiry and faith. Sixty-three per cent of the French claim to believe in God, although this cannot be taken to represent identification with a religion. But what is certain is that many Catholics

(especially the young) now choose to express their faith privately or differently, and to find a religious identity and a way to God other than through the traditional church. In particular, France's forty or so Catholic charismatic movements (numbering some 200,000 active members) represent rare examples of a religious revival, of Catholicism in expansion. The faith therefore survives, in spite of the institution's decline.

Although the Protestant church in France has also seen a fall in religious practice, it has not experienced the same rate of decline as the Catholic church and enjoys a relatively stable existence. A persecuted religion before 1789, Protestantism has become France's third religion, with about one million practising faithful (representing 1.8 per cent of the French population), variously distributed across France but particularly established in Alsace-Moselle, the Cévennes, the Rhône valley and the Paris region. The French Protestant church operates as a decentralized and democratic federal structure. Its principal structure is the French Protestant Federation, created in 1905 at the time of the formal secularization of the French state, which groups fifteen churches, including the Reform church (by far the largest Protestant group in France) and the Lutherans, and accounts overall for nine out of ten Protestants. Churches within the Federation remain autonomous, but unite to promote their common interests and a shared message on social, ethical and political matters. Evangelical Protestants (principally Baptists) have their own umbrella organization, the French Evangelical Federation, created in 1969.

Protestantism does not dismiss the notion of free will or the individual moral responsibility of its believers and, unlike Catholicism, does not condemn or retreat into authoritarian dogma in the sexual domain. Moreover, as an institution, the Protestant church's structures correspond more closely to the everyday lives of its members than those of the Catholic church. For example, it operates within a less rigid hierarchical structure within which 15 per cent of its priests are women and 20 per cent are divorced, a degree of flexibility which explains why the Protestant church has not suffered the same crisis of recruitment as the Catholic church. Furthermore, the Protestant church gives greater recognition to the role and status of lay members than the Catholic church, including them in the decision-making process. Such flexibility and openness is clearly attractive, as illustrated by the 3 per cent of the population (1.8 million people) who declare an affinity with Protestantism, among whom are some 450,000 Catholics disenchanted with the Vatican's dialogue. Many originally Protestant values have passed into the public domain to the extent that contemporary French society, through its promotion of secularism, liberalism, individualism and tolerance of others, now generally adheres to values inherited from the Reformation. In this respect, it can be argued that France has become 'Protestant', in attitude if not in religious practice.

The secularization of public life in France has changed how the Catholic and Protestant churches see both themselves and each other. Secularism has not forced the churches into the background, but has granted them a voice unobstructed by state interference and left them free to pronounce on a wide range of social and political issues. The two churches will regularly co-operate in such activity (alongside France's other religious groups), believing that they have a right and a duty to comment on governmental projects particularly where human rights are at stake. For instance, in 1991 the Gulf War prompted a joint statement of opposition to conflict and to the proliferation of weapons, while the churches' involvement in the 1993 debate on immigration and nationality law led indirectly to the modification of some of the more restrictive legislation. Both churches also work with the state, acting as advisers on its ethical committees. Such ecumenical activity is to be welcomed, although it is much less visible in the theological domain where, despite the creation of Catholic–Protestant mixed groups (such as the ecumenical community at Taizé), the two churches remain poles apart on certain issues (for example, the ordination of women priests).

In a quantitative sense, then, Christianity in France is in decline; but in a qualitative and symbolic sense there is evidence of an enduring religious sentiment and interest, and even of a new religiosity. Only 12 per cent of the French declare themselves committed atheists, which suggests that, for the remainder, there is still room for some degree of religious focus in their lives, although this may not necessarily be channelled through any institution. The future for Catholicism and Protestantism as individual religions is difficult to gauge. What does seem likely, however, is that 'God' will acquire many new faces as the churches implode and religions proliferate.

KAY CHADWICK

See also: abortion/contraception; Croix, La; education, the state and the church

Further reading

Cholvy, G. (1994) La Religion en France de la fin du XVIIIe siècle à nos jours, Paris: Hachette (an excellent and accessible thematic overview of France's principal religions).

Gisel, P. (1995) Encyclopédie du protestantisme, Paris: Cerf (an extensive survey, clearly written in the form of short but comprehensive articles).

Imbert, J. (1990) L'Église catholique dans la France contemporaine, Paris: Economica (a general introduction to the structures, role and ideology of the French Catholic church).

Makarian, C. (1996) 'Les Catholiques de France', Le Point 1252 (an analysis of the evolution of French Catholic identity and attitudes).

Michelat, G. (1995) Les Français sont-ils encore catholiques?, Paris: Cerf (an analysis of surveys and statistics relating to Catholic religious practice and culture).

Richardot, J.-P. (1992) Le Peuple protestant français, Paris: Laffont (a classic study of Protestantism in France).

Secrétariat général de l'Épiscopat (1994) L'Église catholique en France: documents pour la presse, Paris: Bayard (a collection of short thematic articles describing the structures and social ideas of the French Catholic Church).

Caubère, Philippe

b. 1950, Marseille

Playwright, director and actor

An improviser and actor at the **Théâtre du Soleil** – roles included Molière in **Mnouchkine's** 1979 film and Abdallah in *L'Age d'or* (The Golden Age) – he left to pursue his own creative projects during the 1980s. His 1993 production of *Les Marches du palais* (Steps of the Palace) incorporated seven years' improvisation and creation.

ANNIE SPARKS

See also: theatre

Certeau, Michel de

b. 1925, France;
d. 1986, France

Historian of ideas

By professional formation a historian of religion, de Certeau studied four areas of experience. He specialized, first, in the history of the disappearance of mysticism from the fifteenth up to the seventeenth centuries. For him, it was clear that the growth of rational science indeed 'repressed' but never eradicated belief, a concept and a practice basic to the drive to live. That is why, second, his work on the inventions of 'everyday life' addressed the productive – and subversive – areas of human practice. And third, de Certeau's work on heterology, or the science of the other, embraces movement across and through different cultural spheres: the other (i.e. what defies understanding and is welcomed because it is unknown) inaugurates ethical and creative movement in the world

about us. Finally, the results of **psychoanalysis** have the virtue of telling us how the imagination copes with the world and its history. This important dimension in de Certeau's formation is yoked to his work on historiography, the other and inventiveness. He has been known in France not as a magisterial voice, but as a vital and nomadic consciousness. His works are only now finding an international audience.

TOM CONLEY

Césaire, Aimé

b. 1913, Basse-Pointe, Martinique

Poet and playwright

Césaire was born in Martinique and educated in Paris, where he became acquainted with the leading intellectual from Senegal, Léopold Senghor. It was the discovery of *négritude* (Césaire coined the term) and close contact with the Surrealist movement, especially the support of André Breton, that gave Césaire's life a new poetic and political direction. He published *Return to My Native Land* (*Cahier d'un retour au pays natal*) in 1939 and thus began his liberation from the patterns of Western culture in favour of a 'black consciousness'. His poetry is rich in images (a sign of Surrealist influence), particularly those drawn from his native fauna and flora. His political activity has been left-wing (Communist Party until 1956), and he served as mayor of Fort-de-France. In addition to his first volume of poetry, there are also significant collections, such as *Les Armes miraculeuses* (Miraculous Weapons) in 1946 and *Cadastre* (1961). There are also several plays, notably *A Season in the Congo* (*Une saison au Congo*) from 1966, plus a political essay entitled *Discourse on Colonialism* (*Discours sur le colonialisme*). Césaire is generally acknowledged to be the outstanding black francophone poet.

WALTER A. STRAUSS

See also: francophone writing (fiction, poetry): DOM-TOMs; poetry

Chaban-Delmas, Jacques

b. 1915, Paris

Politician

A wartime Gaullist, Chaban-Delmas was also a Gaullist member of the National Assembly for the Gironde from 1946 to 1993 and mayor of Bordeaux from 1947 to 1995. He was, nevertheless, close to the *Radical* tradition. Several times minister under the Fourth Republic, he was president of the National Assembly in 1958–69, 1979–81 and 1986–8. Appointed prime minister in 1969, his 'New Society' programme antagonized the right wing of the Gaullist party and led President **Pompidou** to dismiss him in 1972. He stood in the presidential election of 1974, but was deserted by the **Chirac**-led wing of the party and gained only 15.1 per cent of the vote.

LAURENCE BELL

See also: Gaulle, Charles de; parties and movements

Further reading

Rouanet, P. (1974) *Le Cas Chaban*, Paris: Laffont (a biography which focuses on his relations with de Gaulle and on his premiership.)

Chabrol, Claude

b. 1930, Paris

Director

With sixty-five films between 1958 and 1993, Chabrol is one of the more prolific (and less dis-

cerning) directors to have emerged from the **Nouvelle Vague** (New Wave), where he made key films, e.g. *Le Beau Serge* (1959) and *Les Cousins* (1959). His best early film is the Hitchcockian *Le Boucher* (1970). His later 1970s films are lacklustre, but *Les Fantômes du chapelier* (1982) was the beginning of a renewal, followed by *Cop au vin* (*Poulet au vinaigre*) in 1984, *L'Inspecteur Lavardin* (1986), the underestimated *Masques* (1987), starring **Noiret**, and *La Cérémonie* (1995).

PHIL POWRIE

See also: cinema

Chagall, Marc

b. 1887, Vitebsk, Russia;
d. 1985, St-Paul, Alpes-Maritimes

Artist

Chagall's characteristic work emerged after contact with post-impressionism in 1908. He spent time in Paris between 1910 and 1914, where he met with Robert Delaunay (1885–1941) and Guillaume Apollinaire (1880–1918). He resided in Paris from 1923 but lived in the United States from 1941 to 1947, returning to France in 1948. His work demonstrated an imaginative realism, as in *I and the Village* (1911), and the image is composed in disc-like arrangements reminiscent of Delaunay. Memories of personal history, rural origins and Jewish religion are juxtaposed to convey a sense of the supernatural with scale and vibrant colour, following an internal truth of visual metaphor. His intensely personal and symbolic work, for example, *The Cock with Lovers* (1947–50), became increasingly lyrical.

VALERIE SWALES

See also: painting

Chalem, Denise

birthdate unknown

Author and actor

Inspired by **Vitez**, her teacher at the Conservatoire National d'Art Dramatique, Chalem has written (and directed) a number of stage plays, such as *A cinquante ans, elle découvrait la mer* (At Fifty She Discovered the Sea), as well as screenplays for television. She has enjoyed a successful stage, television and film acting career, working with directors such as Jean-Pierre **Vincent** at the Théâtre National de Chaillot.

ANNIE SPARKS

See also: theatre

Chanel, Coco

b. 1883, Saumur;
d. 1971, Paris

Fashion designer,
real name Gabrielle Chanel

Orphaned at the age of 6, Chanel was a dancer in Pau before becoming a *modiste* in Paris. She designed clothes for women volunteering in the First World War and, in 1920, introduced her trademark suits of jersey wool, simple lines, sober tones, and above-the-knee hemlines. By 1924, hers was the most successful fashion house in Paris. Famous for her first perfume, Chanel No. 5, the simple black dress, her trousers, the black and beige pump (shoe), and jersey berets for women, she retired in 1938, but made a comeback in 1954.

JOËLLE VITIELLO

See also: fashion

Char, René

b. 1907, Isle-sur-la-Sorgue, Vaucluse;
d. 1988, Paris

Poet

Char was perhaps the most important poet of the postwar years and the most interesting and prolific poet to come out of the Surrealist movement, which he left in the late 1930s. He was active in the Resistance in his native Provence and also became a close friend of Albert **Camus**. His poetic work moves back and forth between poems, prose poems and aphoristic writing, there is a strong affinity with Greek culture, especially through the pre-Socratic philosopher Heraclitus. Char's friendship with the artists **Picasso**, **Braque**, Miró, and **Giacometti** resulted in remarkable illustrations of his numerous poetic volumes. Of the volumes of poetry, 1948's *Fureur et mystère* (Fury and Mystery) is particularly important as the first major collection of his poems, including the very striking collection of aphorisms, 'Feuillets d'Hypnos' (Hypnos Waking). Of the subsequent publications, *Lettera amorosa* (1953) and 1955's *Recherche de la base au sommet* (Search for Top and Bottom) and *La parole en archipel* (Speech in Archipelago) (1961) are worth mentioning. The complete works of Char have been published in Éditions de la Pléïade in 1983. The poems are rich in images, as one might expect of a poet who was schooled by the Surrealists, yet they are more compact and concentrated. Perhaps the best characterization of Char's work, in terms of aspiration and accomplishment, might be the title of his 1951 volume, *A une sérénite crispée* (To a Tensed Serenity).

WALTER A. STRAUSS

See also: poetry

Charef, Mehdi

b. 1952, Maghnia, Algeria

Writer and director

Mehdi Charef was the first beur to write a successful semi-autobiographical novel about the problems facing 'second-generation' Maghrebin immigrants in the shanty towns and housing estates of metropolitan France. *Le Thé au harem d'Archi Ahmed* (1983), centring on streetwise, unemployed Madjid, '*paumé entre deux cultures*' (stranded between two cultures), became a successful beur film, enabling Charef to direct other features, including *Miss Mona* (1987), charting the doomed friendship between an illegal immigrant and a lonely French transvestite. His second novel, *Le Harki de Mériem* (Mériem's Harki), published in 1989, addresses the painful effects of internal divisions between Algerians and *harkis*.

CARRIE TARR

See also: Algerian war; beur cinema; beur writing; beurs; immigration

Charlie Hebdo

Magazine

A satirical weekly, created in 1970, in the wake of a flurry of alternative publications born of the climate of protest manifest in **May 1968**. Rebellious and anti-establishment, *Charlie Hebdo* has regular skirmishes with the authorities. Cartoon sketches are its central weapon, especially those of Cabu, Gébé, Siné and Wolinsky. Falling readership and accumulating law suits caused the paper to cease publication in May 1981, but the original team of contributors, with François Cavanna and Georges Bernier (alias Professeur Choron) at the helm, relaunched the paper in July 1992, joined by a new generation of cartoonists: Tignous, Luz and Charb. By the mid-1990s, the paper boasted 200,000 readers.

PAM MOORES

See also: comic strips/cartoonists; national press in France

Chartreux, Bernard

b. 1942, Nancy

Playwright

A dramaturg at the Théâtre des Nanterre-Amandiers, Chartreux is known for his contemporary adaptations of foreign and ancient works, and his social documentary plays such as *Violences à Vichy* (Violence in Vichy) and the adaptation *Les Derniers sur la peste* (The Latest on the Plague).

ANNIE SPARKS

See also: theatre

Chawaf, Chantal

b. 1943, Paris

Writer

In all her writings, from the 1974 publication *Retable/La Rêverie* (Retabulum/Dreaming) onwards, Chawaf pursues a mode of *écriture* which strives to stay in touch with the (feminine) body and its experiences/unconscious, reforge the material links between words and their objects obliterated by/within the (masculine) linguistic order, and effect a return to the pre-Oedipal/verbal. Sensuous, fluid and poetic in their style, speaking of themes such as bodily being, desire, sexuality and parent–child relations, Chawaf's texts are regularly read in the context of *écriture féminine*. Her publications include *Le Soleil et la terre* (Sun and Earth) of 1977, 1986's *Elwina, le roman fée* (Elwina, the Fairy Tale Novel) and *Rédemption* from 1989.

ALEX HUGHES

See also: Montrelay, Michèle; psychoanalysis; women's/lesbian writing

Further reading

Hannagan, V. (1990) 'Reading as a Daughter: Chantal Chawaf Revisited', in M. Atack and P. Powrie (eds) *Contemporary French Fiction by Women*, Manchester: MUP (an account of Chawaf's explorations of the mother–daughter relation, and of its effect upon her writing practice).

Chéreau, Patrice

b. 1944, Lézigné

Director and actor

One of the most influential theatre directors in France today, as well as a well-respected film director, Chéreau's reputation for creation and innovation is influential enough to attract large audiences. Known for his perfectionist approach and his energy, in contemporary terms he is noted especially for his collaboration with popular playwright Bernard-Marie **Koltès** during the 1980s, whose work he championed, promoted and directed. His actor-director revival of *Dans la solitude des champs de coton* (In the Solitude of the Cotton Fields), in November 1995, was a sell-out success, partly due to the popularity of Chéreau's and Koltès's work.

Before 1969, his directorial career, beginning at Sartrouville, saw him become noted for his Brechtian approach to stage, text and actors. A defender of the notion of the theatre as art and a lover of Italian theatre, he also worked for a short time at the Piccolò Theatre in Milan, until, in 1970, he began co-director with **Planchon** at the Théâtre National Populaire in Villeurbanne, forming a creative partnership with professionals such as Richard **Peduzzi**, with whom he still works today. His most famous production of this period, with Peduzzi, was his 1973 *La Dispute* by Marivaux, which critic Bernard **Dort** described as 'wild-cat Marivaux'. Alongside his theatre direction, Chéreau also directed a series of musical works, including Offenbach's *The Tales of Hoffmann* in 1974, a spectacular Wagner's *Ring* in 1976 and Alban Berg's *Lulu* in 1979.

By the late 1970s, he had also developed an interest in author Jean-Paul **Wenzel**, whose *Loin d'Hagondange* (Far from Hagondange) he directed in 1977. At around the turn of the decade, he also began making inroads into a new film career, which was to inspire (but also disappoint) him until his films *L'Homme Blessé* (The Injured Man), co-written with Hervé **Guibert** and released in 1983, and *La Reine Margot* in 1994.

In 1982, he directed an acclaimed production of Ibsen's *Peer Gynt*, and became director of the Théâtre de Nanterre-Amandiers, where he set up a film and theatre school and promoted new writing, particularly the plays of Koltès. Between 1982 and 1988, Chéreau mounted four of his works, as well as acclaimed productions of **Genet**'s *The Screens* (*Les Paravents*), German author Heiner Müller's *Quartett*, and a particularly praised Chekhov's *Platonov* in 1987. Following the death of Koltès, whom Chéreau had come to regard at the greatest playwright of his era, he left Nanterre to work independently, pursuing a career in cinema and theatre.

ANNIE SPARKS

See also: cinema; theatre; Théâtre du Quotidien

Further reading

'Patrice Chéreau' (1986), *Les Voies de la création théâtrale* 14, Paris: CNRS (essential reading).

Chevalier, Maurice

b. 1888, Paris;
d. 1972, Paris

Singer and actor

Maurice Chevalier's career spanned three-quarters of a century. Having started in partnership with **Mistinguett**, who launched his career, he became one of France's best-loved singers and crooners of this century, with such songs as *Valentine*. He also had success in England and America as a singer and in films. Although suspected of collaborationist sympathies after World War II – partly because of *La Chanson du maçon* (The Mason's Song) – his career continued to blossom well into old age.

IAN PICKUP

See also: song/*chanson*

child care

France has one of the most generous systems of assistance for parents requiring child care in Europe. Nearly all children aged 3 to 5 attend free nursery school. Furthermore, for many nursery and primary school children, provision is made at school for very inexpensive before- and after-hours care. All official paid child care is tax-deductible, and for those employing carers in their own homes the state takes responsibility for the employee's social contributions. There are also subsidies for all forms of paid child care for children up to 6 years old. Public crèches are available for the youngest children, but many working parents use childminders.

JAN WINDEBANK

See also: family

Chirac, Jacques

b. 1932, Paris

Politician

Chirac was elected president of the Fifth Republic in May 1995 after a long political career which had included two spells as prime minister and an eighteen-year stint as leader of the neo-Gaullist party the Rassemblement pour la République (RPR, or Rally for the Republic) Although his family came from the rural Corrèze, Chirac grew up in Paris, where his father worked for a bank. He studied at the Institut d'Études Politiques and saw military service in Algeria. Having briefly flirted with such diverse causes as communism and French Algeria, Chirac in the early 1960s placed his driving ambition at the service of the new Fifth Republic, and in particular of de **Gaulle**'s long-serving prime minister Georges **Pompidou**, in whose private office he served between 1962 and 1967. Pompidou had a high regard for the drive and intelligence of the man he called the 'bulldozer'. He backed Chirac's successful campaign to be elected deputy for a Corrèze constituency in 1967 and immediately appointed him under-secretary of state for employment. Chirac was thus at his master's side in the **May 1968** crisis, and when Pompidou became president in 1969 a year later his career took off. As Minister of the Interior during the 1974 presidential contest which followed Pompidou's death, the general public first witnessed the ruthlessness which would become Chirac's hallmark. He sabotaged the chances of the official Gaullist candidate **Chaban-Delmas** and backed the non-Gaullist conservative **Giscard d'Estaing**, who, once elected, promptly appointed him prime minister. In 1976, however, he resigned office and turned his formidable energies to the pursuit of the presidency. He became president of the Rassemblement pour la République, a mass neo-Gaullist movement, and between 1977 and the 1981 presidential election he waged open war on Giscard, whom he correctly regarded as an obstacle to his ambitions, and whom he accused of disloyalty to the principles of Gaullism. One high point of the war was his victory, against Giscard's candidate, in the 1977 battle for the Paris town hall, a victory which over the next eighteen years gave him a vast patronage machine.

Although his first shot at the presidency, in 1981, ended with his elimination on round one, his 18 per cent share of the vote showed that the RPR was a viable political force, and the coolness of his second-round endorsement of Giscard helped ensure the latter's defeat at the hands of the Socialist **Mitterrand**. To Giscard and his supporters it was another betrayal; to Chirac it vindicated his claim to the leadership of the French Right. The 1980s were, however, to be a difficult decade. His ability to represent French nationalism was challenged by the emergence of a hard Right under **Le Pen**, and he was regarded by commentators, and political rivals, as being at once demagogic and superficial. His flirtation with the fashionable liberal economics of the 1980s sat ill with the interventionist and welfarist agendas of the Gaullism he had hitherto championed. In 1986, he became prime minister for the second time in the cohabitation government formed after the victory of the Right in the parliamentary elections. For all his acceptance of the single European market (another break with his past) and introduction of a privatization programme, it was another unhappy time in office. His coalition government was divided; mass student opposition forced the withdrawal of a bill to reform higher education: liberal opinion was made uneasy by the government's attempts to regain control of the **immigration** agenda from Le Pen. As candidate for the 1988 presidential elections he had to face the opposition of President Mitterrand, a politician just as ruthless as himself (and considerably more subtle), who constructed a highly effective profile as the guardian of national unity against the alleged extremism of his prime minister. On round two of the election, Chirac was soundly beaten.

Still master of Paris, and still (despite internal rumblings) boss of the RPR, Chirac was starting to look like yesterday's man. After the triumph of the Right in the 1993 parliamentary elections, he refused to become prime minister for the third time and had the mortification of seeing his then best political friend Édouard **Balladur** (who took the job) acquire massive popularity. By the time he announced his third presidential bid in November 1995, his prospect looked bleak. His continuing grip on the RPR machine, however, combined with his skills as a baby-kissing campaigner and his improbable status as an outsider to enable him to come from behind. His campaign speeches

emphasized the Gaullist principle of strong leadership (to combat unemployment), the European vision of a single currency, and the Republican myth of social equality (via generous welfare payments). Though commentators regarded Chirac's programme as self-contradictory, it promised enough things to enough people to allow him to see off the Balladur challenge on round one and to win a comfortable victory over the Socialist **Jospin** on round two.

His presidency began with the controversial decision to resume French nuclear testing in the South Pacific and with a mass outbreak of strikes in response to his government's attempt to reduce the cost of the social security budget and prepare France for the single European currency. The former spoke to the great tradition of Gaullist grandeur, the other to the new political economy of the European Union. Chirac's presidency underwent a striking reverse when the Socialists, under Jospin, won the parliamentary elections he called in a would-be pre-emptive strike in 1997.

PETER MORRIS

See also: Constitution of the Fifth Republic; nationalization and privatization; parties and movements

Further reading

Giesbert, F.-O. (1987) *Jacques Chirac*, Paris: Éditions du Seuil (the standard political biography).

choreographers

French choreographers could until recently be divided into two easily distinguished categories: those working in ballet and those working in contemporary dance. However, these genres are now less polarized and separate, in keeping with developments on the wider international dance scene. As French contemporary dance has also been influenced by a wide variety of dance and other sources, rather than following specific schools, a multiplicity of styles co-exist within it. Any overview of French choreography must delineate its major unifying concerns, indicate the contributions of established leading choreographers and highlight members of the rising choreographic generation.

French choreographers draw on a wide variety of dance styles and techniques from abroad that were developed prior to the **dance** boom of the 1980s. A number also came to dance late, having studied another artistic or physical displine, and increasingly they bring various cultural heritages to bear on their work. Choreographers are also generally well-informed, absorbing ideas from literature, **cinema** and popular music. From this multiplicity of sources arises a multiplicity of choreographic visions. New French dance is increasingly claiming the term *danse d'auteur* (author's dance) to encompass this desire to avoid imitative trends. Two other widespread choreographic preoccupations are *le langage du corps* (the desire to reintegrate the humanity of the dancer and the communicative power of the dance) as a reaction against earlier abstract postmodern dance styles, and a general enthusiasm for theatricality and visual spectacle.

Such attention to the spectacle was also evident directly after World War II, when the only French choreographers of international standing were Serge Lifar, director of the Paris Opéra Ballet until 1959, and Roland Petit, director of the Ballet des Champs-Elysées and then founder of the Ballet de Paris in 1948.

When Serge Lifar first took over the Paris Opéra in the 1930s, he inherited a company which had lost much of its former glory. Lifar managed to return audiences to the Opéra through various reforms of the company, and by staging a wide variety of ballets that appealed to public taste and displayed his own, and his principal dancers' talents. His desire to demonstrate the independence of dance from music is shown in work such as the classical *Giselle* and his own original ballets: the mythic *Icaré* (Icarus) and *Phèdre* (Phaedra), and the fairy-tale *Snow White* (*Blanche-Neige*).

Roland Petit, a pupil of Lifar's, had an even greater sense of the theatre. After leaving the Paris Opéra in 1944, he created a succession of works, collaborating with fashionable designers and painters. The most noted of his works are *Le Jeune Homme et la mort* (Death and the Young Man) and *Carmen*. Petit rehearsed the former ballet (which had a modern scenario devised by Cocteau) to **jazz** music, but in performance substituted Bach, creating a striking contrast between old and new. In *Carmen*, he created a stunning vehicle for his ballerina wife, Zizi Jeanmaire, which exploited her unusual physique and included a seduction scene that was controversially long.

The blurring of boundaries between ballet and modern dance that began to occur mid-century is seen in the work of France's most prominent choreographer, Maurice Béjart. Although ironically Béjart has spent most of his career based in Belgium and Switzerland, he reached the status of a pop star during the 1970s, capable of filling the enormous Palais des Sports. His first successful work was a version of *The Rite of Spring* (*Le Sacré du printemps*), which elicited an invitation to move to Brussels. Since then he has created a large number of ballets employing an eclectic range of ideas, including strong religious and moral themes. These cover homosexuality and other provocative subjects, as well as creating large-scale realizations of orchestral scores (such as Beethoven's for the *9th Symphony*) in which his male dancers are often featured most prominently. In 1970 Béjart founded the MUDRA school in Brussels, which has become a training ground for many young French artists; but in 1987, after conflicts with the management, his company moved to Lausanne.

Another choreographer, who trained and performed with Béjart and whose work occupies the middle ground, is Maguy Marin, director of the Lyon Opéra Ballet. Marin first achieved success with her **Beckett**-inspired work *May B*, in which she shows her formidable gift for creating unforgettable images of humanity. These images are often tinged with naivety and humour, as in *Cinderella* (*Cendrillon*) and *Groosland* in which costumes enlarge dancers to enormous proportions.

Over the last twenty-five years, government

policy on dance has actively sought to encourage primarily the creator's role, dramatically increasing the number of working choreographers. It is therefore becoming more common for leading contemporary choreographers to be asked to work with ballet companies, either to create new work or to remount important pieces so they are not lost. Recent examples at the Paris Opéra include Jean-Claude Gallotta's reworking of his sporadically incomprehensible, yet simultaneously seductive fable *Ulysse* (Ulysses), and Philippe Decouflé's restaging of another surreally costumed world, *Decodex*. Leading contemporary choreographers as these, and Daniel Larrieu, Karine Saporta and Dominique Bagouet (before his premature death from **AIDS**), are also recognized by higher government subsidy.

Among the many less-established choreographers who are gaining critical acclaim, a few deserve particular mention. These include Régis Obadia and Joelle Bouvier, whose duet *Welcome to Paradise* and video work have drawn much praise for their exploration of a physical language which delves into the depths of an emotional interior world; Josef Nadj, whose signature work remains the quirky and humorous *Canard pékinois* (Peking Duck); and Claude Brumachon, who took three prizes in the 1988 Bagnolet competition and continues to make a succession of works which appeal through their effective gestural language, such as *Texane* and *L'Avalanche*.

Despite doubts that such growth can be maintained, it is clear from this brief outline that French choreographers are currently creating a wealth of new work that reflects a visual bias and spans a broad range of styles and sources.

FIONA WARNE

See also: dance; dance troupes

Christo

b. 1935, Gabrovo, Bulgaria

Artist, real name Christo Javacheff

Christo, the artist best known for 'wrapping' large objects, collaborates with his wife, Jeanne-Claude. He worked in Paris between 1958 and 1964, and began to make temporary wrapped objects in 1958. He packaged his first public building, the Teatro Nuovo, Spoleto, in 1968. He also wrapped part of the Australian coast (*Wrapped Coast*) in 1969, and a Parisian bridge (*Pont Neuf Wrapped*) in 1985. Perhaps his most significant project, however, is the *Wrapped Reichstag* in Berlin. Conceived in 1977 and financed entirely by Christo himself, it represents several years of effort by the artist, involving the teamwork of politicians and people from communities in both East and West Berlin. The project was finally realized in 1994: the building was presented in its wrapped state for fourteen days, a luminous, billowing volume of high-strength woven fabric, demanding recognition of the form beneath. Although this was almost five years after the fall of the Berlin Wall, *Wrapped Reichstag* stands as a metaphorical statement in memory of the significance of the Reichstag as an enduring symbol of democracy.

VALERIE SWALES

cinema

Since the world's first commercial screening of a moving picture, in Paris on 28 December 1895, cinema has occupied a place of particular significance in French culture, illustrated by the interest in it shown by intellectuals from the Surrealists through **Sartre** to **Robbe-Grillet**. Paris, thanks to its cultural hegemony, along with the importance of state support for the arts in France, can be described as the world capital of cinema as art form, and the French industry maintains a level of autonomy and distinctiveness that are the envy of others in Europe.

At the end of World War II, that last statement in particular would have appeared highly dubious. The consequences of Occupation were not all negative for the cinema: competition from American films disappeared and the free-wheeling artisanal proliferation of the 1930s industry was replaced by tighter organization and greater government support (as well as intervention). After the **Liberation**, however, the renewed availability of American films and the loss of many key figures who had left for the United States or been ostracized for collaboration left the French industry in a somewhat weakened state.

The cinema of the fifteen years after the Liberation has tended to enjoy a bad press, reviled by *Cahiers du cinéma* for its dependence on traditional studio values and **literary adaptations**. The term *cinéma de qualité* in this context is indeed a highly pejorative one. The work of directors such as Claude **Autant-Lara** and René **Clément** may appear hidebound by comparison with the **Nouvelle Vague**, but the performances of actors such as Gérard **Philipe** and Simone **Signoret** remain powerful in such films as Autant-Lara's 1946 *Le Diable au corps* and Jacques **Becker**'s 1952 *Casque d'or*, respectively. Autant-Lara's regular scriptwriters, Jean Aurenche and Pierre Bost, scorned by **Truffaut** in particular for their conservative dependence on literary pretexts, have recently come to the fore again through their work for Bertrand **Tavernier**, and much of the so-called 'heritage cinema' of the 1980s and 1990s, such as the films of Claude **Berri**, owes a good deal to their example.

One reason for the relatively low esteem in which Fourth Republic cinema has tended to be held may be that it now appears as marking a low-water mark – a period of recovery and consolidation rather than innovation – between the 'golden age' of prewar classic cinema and the arrival of the Nouvelle Vague. A number of key classic directors lost their earlier momentum (René Clair, more strikingly Marcel Carné); the greatest of all, Jean **Renoir**, spent his postwar career largely in the United States. The 1950s saw the burgeoning of a number of directors – Bresson, Melville, Tati – who were to become major figures, but, even more significantly, the appearance in the pages

of *Cahiers du cinéma* of pieces by **Chabrol**, **Godard**, **Rohmer** and Truffaut.

The transition from criticism to film-making was made much easier by the greater availability of lightweight film-making equipment and the introduction, in 1959, of a government-funded scheme of advances to film-makers (*avances sur recettes*). The low-budget explosion of the Nouvelle Vague that began in that year owed much to these factors as well as to the use, by Chabrol and **Malle**, of private means and inheritances. Since the movement never defined itself or, unlike (for example) the Surrealists, established criteria for membership, its extent is impossible to determine precisely. Even the term was originally used, by the journalist Françoise **Giroud**, to refer to changes within French society as a whole rather than specifically to the cinema. De **Gaulle**'s coming-to-power paradoxically coincided with a large-scale modernization and industrialization of French society, in which American culture – cars, music and, of course, films – played an important part. Increased sexual frankness (within still tight censorship limits) was incarnated by Jeanne **Moreau** and above all by Brigitte **Bardot**, and although the Nouvelle Vague directors and those closely associated with them (such as **Demy** and **Resnais**) had no defining political position, they tended to be united in opposition to the **Algerian war**.

The relationship between these film-makers and the world of literature was a more complex one than might appear. They saw the adaptation of literary classics as profoundly uncinematic, but drew with relish upon the American pulp novels of such as David Goodis and William Irish. Resnais worked initially from scripts by **Duras** and Robbe-Grillet, and it can be argued that these changes in cinematic writing brought by the Nouvelle Vague had much in common with what was going on in the field of literary theory and the *nouveau roman*. The 1960s and 1970s saw, in the wake of **May 1968** and the rise of the French 'new Left', the ascendancy of Marxist theory in the pages of *Cahiers* as in the film-making practice of Godard, though the lavish sentimentality of

Claude Lelouch's 1966 *A Man and a Woman* (*Un homme et une femme*) reached a far wider audience and was arguably the most influential French film of its period.

The 1970s saw a flattening-out in the drop in cinema attendances, experienced by France as by every other country with the spread of television, and under the presidency of **Giscard d'Estaing** a marked liberalization of censorship, political and sexual. Television/cinema co-productions became more frequent, and in 1976 460 films were screened on French television. The Nouvelle Vague directors – now with less and less in common – and their allies continued to dominate this period, though its biggest-grossing French film was Gérard Oury's *Les Aventures de Rabbi Jacob* of 1973, starring Louis de **Funès** – a reminder that comedy, often of a not particularly sophisticated kind, has always been the most successful genre at the French box office.

The rise of television and the concentration of cinemas in towns and cities – marked in a still largely rural country like France – between them ensured a shift, starting in the mid-1970s and pronounced ever since, back towards the large-scale spectacular 'evening-out' style of film. Berri, **Rappeneau** and **Chéreau** (whose 1994 Dumas adaptation *La Reine Margot* enjoyed great success) are names emblematically associated with the 'heritage film' – as that label suggests something like a revival of the *cinéma de qualité*. The other tendency to have asserted itself from the mid-1980s is the 'Forum des Halles' genre of designer movie associated with **Beineix**, **Besson** and **Carax**. These costly types of film undoubtedly owed much to the larger share of French income devoted to cultural production under the regime of **Mitterrand** and **Lang**. The erosion of the barriers between 'high' and 'popular' culture characteristic of what has variously been called the 'postmodern' or the 'middle-brow' is a theme common to the otherwise very disparate kinds of film-making that have dominated production in France over the past decade or so. Nobody better epitomizes this than Gérard **Depardieu** – director of an adaptation of Molière's *Tartuffe* (1984), but also co-

star of the raucously Poujadist low comedy *Les Anges gardiens* (1995), Jean-Marie **Poiré**'s follow-up to *Les Visiteurs* of 1993 which was one of the biggest-grossing French films ever.

White males do not – contrary to appearances so far – have the French cinematic field entirely to themselves. The annual Women's Film Festival at Créteil remains an important event, and woman directors such as Christine Pascal and Brigitte Royan attract attention on the *art et essai* circuit (roughly equivalent to the Regional Film Theatres in Britain). Recently, the **beur cinema** and the *cinéma de banlieue* have been drawing wider audiences – signs doubtless of an encroaching malaise within French society after the hopes of the 1968 generation and the disappointments of the second Mitterrand term in particular. Unlike the Nouvelle Vague as these films in many respects are, they nevertheless present two significant points of comparison with it. They engage with France's social problems urgently, and generally on a low budget, where the 'Forum des Halles' film-makers often (as with Carax's *Les Amants du Pont-Neuf*) romanticized them; and they mark a return of the influence of Hollywood cinema. What the laconic monochrome of Howard Hawks and Samuel Fuller was to the early Godard or Truffaut, the work of John Cassavetes and Spike Lee is to beur and *banlieue* cinema. Quentin Tarantino, meanwhile, proclaims the influence of Godard's *Bande à Part* on *Pulp Fiction*, and the Jack Lang who waxed sulphurous about the influence of Hollywood cinema shortly after becoming Culture Minister is delighted to present a state decoration to the no-less-delighted Sharon Stone. The Atlantic is more than ever a two-way street . . .

It would be easy to wax overenthusiastic about the future of French cinema. In 1994, French films' share of the domestic market fell below 30 per cent for the first time, and co-production is clearly only a partial counterweight to the hegemony of Hollywood. Yet state support continues to be the envy of the British, and French film (increasingly available on video) is more and more taught on secondary and higher education courses, where it appears increasingly as an integral part of the national culture.

KEITH READER

See also: Marxism and Marxian thought; postmodernism

Further reading

Billard, P. (1995) *L'Age classique du cinéma français*, Paris : Flammarion (a very long, thoroughly documented history, with indispensable chronological and statistical appendices).

Forbes, J. (1992) *The Cinema in France: After the New Wave*, Basingstoke and London: Macmillan/British Film Institute (a comprehensive and socially aware history, with much valuable information on important films unavailable in English-speaking countries).

Frodon, J.-M. (1995) *L'Age moderne du cinéma français*, Paris: Flammarion (a long and well-documented history; features invaluable chronological and statistical appendices).

Hayward, S. (1993) *French National Cinema*, London and New York: Routledge (a well-documented chronological overview, with valuable information on the industry).

Passek, J.-L. (ed.) (1987) *Dictionnaire du cinéma français*, Paris: Larousse (a useful one-volume reference to leading actors and film-makers).

Williams, A. (1992) *Republic of Images*, Cambridge, MA and London: Harvard University Press (stresses formal and stylistic elements and is good up to the Nouvelle Vague, but much sketchier thereafter).

cinéma de banlieue

The label given to a number of films that attracted attention in mid-1990s France through their depiction of the class and ethnic tensions, often issuing in rioting, that were common in the French **suburbs**. The best-known example, a major international success clearly influenced by black American cinema, is Matthieu Kassowitz's *La Haine* (1995), but works by beur directors and independent French film-makers also form an important part of the category.

KEITH READER

See also: beur cinema; beurs; cinema

cinéma de qualité

La tradition de qualité, sometimes referred to as *la qualité française*, is the term used to refer to a style of French film-making dominant in the late 1940s and 1950s.

The term became common currency thanks to François **Truffaut**'s seminal article, 'Une Certaine Tendance du cinéma français', published in *Cahiers du cinéma* in 1954, which criticized the influence of scriptwriters and the approach known as *le réalisme psychologique* (psychological realism) on the output of post-war French cinema. Typical of this trend, in Truffaut's opinion, were films such as Jean Delannoy's *La Symphonie pastorale* (1946), Claude **Autant-Lara**'s *Le Diable au corps* (1946), René **Clément**'s *Jeux interdits* (1951), Yves Allégret's *Manèges* (1949) and Marcello Pagliero's *Un Homme marche dans la ville* (1950). He also singled out for particular attack the writers Jean Aurenche and Pierre Bost, whose **literary adaptations** not only reduced the status of the director to that of 'the chap who puts the frame round the story', but also promoted an ideology of anticlericalism and pseudo-radicalism which frequently involved the invention of scenes not contained in the original works, and whose intention was to be faithful to the spirit rather than the letter of the original work of literature. Truffaut's polemic is, rightly, seen as the manifesto of the **Nouvelle Vague** which considered the director to be the true author of a film. Nevertheless, there was another source of *la tradition de qualité* which has subsequently come to seem as important, if not more important, than the influence of powerful scriptwriters. French cinema in the 1950s was a highly corporatist and hierarchical industry, dominated by technicians and, especially, by lighting cameramen. There was 'une véritable dictature de l'opérateur' (dictatorship of the cameraman) which the director Louis Daquin slightly mischievously attributed to the talent and charisma of German Jewish producers and cameramen, such as Eugen Schüfftan, who emigrated to France before World War II, and who had not only trained an entire generation of French technicians but had imbued them with their perfectionism and sense of mission. It was undoubtedly the combination of powerful technicians and scriptwriters that gave the mainstream French cinema of the immediate postwar years a certain homogeneity. This is based not just on photographic perfection (*un certain glacis de la lumière*), but also on a clearly developed idea of the function of cinema which, in its most extreme form, as Truffaut complained, amounted to a world-view. Although the *tradition de qualité* ceased to dominate the cinema after the advent of the Nouvelle Vague, it continued to flourish in **television**, for which the Buttes Chaumont Studios continued to produce highly polished literary adaptations well into the 1960s.

JILL FORBES

See also: cinema

Cinq, La

Television channel

This privately owned commercial television channel was established in 1986. Funded wholly from advertising revenue, it competed for the mass audience primarily with **TF1** with an output composed of general entertainment programming, imported series and news. For most of its existence it was run by a consortium dominated by the press mogul Robert **Hersant** and the Italian media entrepreneur Silvio Berlusconi, before being taken over briefly by

Hachette. Despite several reforms of programme scheduling and the high reputation of its news coverage, the channel failed to attract advertisers. It went into liquidation in 1992.

RAYMOND KUHN

See also: television

circus

Since the war, the nature of circus has changed immeasurably in France, a fact which has influenced international perceptions of the limits of circus performance. Traditionally a family-run industry, with very little cross-company contact or professional solidarity, and reliant on traditional circus acts such as animals and clowns, circus found itself left behind by the modern industrial age. Not only did urbanization leave little room for big tops in the cities, but circus families were not great self-promoters and floundered under increasingly commercial pressures. The old circus families of performers were literally dying out, and by the 1960s circus companies were beginning to realize that they would need to evolve to survive so, in 1968, Jean Richard was helped by the traditional circus family Grüss to set up a musical and animal-led circus, buying up the Cirque Pinder and relaunching the Médrano circus, installing his showground at the Porte de Pantin. Despite surviving only until 1978, Richard remained an influential figure in the decades of change to follow. Other precursors of modern circus included Jules Cordières at the Palais des Merveilles, and Geraldine Chaplin and Jean-Baptiste Therré's Le Cirque Imaginaire. By 1978, the French government had stepped in to help the ailing circus industry, creating the Association (and *fonds*, or fund) pour la Modernisation du Cirque (Association for Circus Modernization). Educational measures had already begun: by 1974, the Grüss family had helped Sylvia Montfort to create a Conservatoire for circus and **mime** studies, and the École Nationale du Cirque had opened. The result was a new breed of young circus performers from outside the traditional families. After training, their options were several: they could join a traditional family circus; work for one of the school directors; work in the theatre (which had become increasingly interested in the idea of popular performers); or go into street theatre. Alongside these options, however, a number of the new circus artists set up their own companies. From the Cirque du Bidone, renowned in the 1970s for its nomadic, hippie approach, sprang several young companies which became internationally well-known, including Archaos, with its appeal to urban audiences through its machines and apparent chaos. Other names such as Roncalli, Zingaro, Plume and Docteur Paradis also became synonymous with the new circus generation. In 1981 they set up the Artistes Associés pour la Recherche et l'Innovation au Cirque to help and promote their profession. With their new enthusiasm and fresh approach, introducing the mystery, illusion and drama that was evident in the theatre of the time, young companies succeeded in attracting audiences back to the circus: the traditional ones also benefited from this renewed interest. The three most influential circus companies are still the equestrian Zingaro theatre, Archaos and the commercial Cirque du Soleil.

ANNIE SPARKS

See also: theatre

Further reading

Goudard, P. (1993) *Écrits sur le sable*, Paris: Artistes Associés pour la Recherche et l'Innovation au Cirque (a lively account of the development of postwar circus).

civil rights

France has a proud history of enshrining civil rights in her constitutions. The Constitutions of the Fourth and Fifth Republics (1946, 1958) make reference to the 1789 Declaration of the Rights of Man, and the Republic proclaims the fundamental rights of liberty and equality. However, aspects of French politics and society – such as centralized political control of the police and judiciary – have given rise to concern over civil rights as they apply in practice.

In the 1950s, little concern was arguably paid in practice to civil rights, except perhaps over French use of torture in the **Algerian war** (1954–62) and the brutal repression of pro-Algerian demonstrations in Paris (1961). In addition to concern over the independence of police and judiciary under de **Gaulle,** much of the French police's bad reputation stems from the disturbances of **May 1968.** The violence of the riot police created animosity between the public and forces of law and order which is still prevalent, periodically renewed by events such as the **student revolt of 1986.** During the 1970s, liberalization of society led to developments which increased individuals' civil rights, albeit with occasional attempts by government to maintain control. In 1973, the post of *Médiateur* (Ombudsman) facilitated contacts between the administration and individuals, and in 1974 France signed the European Convention (but omitted to allow individuals to appeal to the European Court of Human Rights). In 1975, the *loi Veil* legalized abortion, symbolizing the progress made in the 1970s by **feminism** and gay rights. In 1978 the Commission Nationale de l'Informatique et des Libertés (National Computing and Freedoms Commission) was created, notably allowing access to administrative documents. In reaction to May 1968, the *loi anti-casseurs* (anti-vandal law) of 1970 gave the authorities greater powers over demonstrations, and in 1980 the *loi Sécurité et Liberté* was introduced to combat the 'insecurity' fostered by anti-Jewish terrorism in Paris and Corsican nationalism.

After 1981, it was expected that civil rights would be strengthened by a Socialist administration more attentive to individual freedoms. Indeed, the 1980s saw a number of reforms of legislation, including in 1981 the repeal of the 'anti-vandal' and 'security and liberty' laws and abolition of the guillotine and of the Court of State Security. The Socialists attempted to suppress unauthorized police phone-tapping and unnecessary identity checks and to make the police and *gendarmes* more accountable. During *cohabitation* (1986–8), the Right introduced an 'anti-terrorist law' and tightened control of immigration, reversing Socialist ambitions. Increasingly during the 1990s attention has focused less on civil rights in the context of law and order (despite various continued misuses of phone-tapping) and more on the threats to citizens' freedoms posed by *la fracture sociale* (social division) of economic hardship and by the challenges of multicultural society: initiatives such as the *Revenu Minimum d'Insertion* (RMI, or minimum guaranteed income) have helped address the problems of exclusion, but the rights of immigrants to freedom and equality are under continuing threat.

HUGH DAUNCEY

See also: abortion/contraception; immigration; legal system; racism/anti-semitism

Further reading

Questiaux, N. (1991) 'Liberties in France: A Balance Sheet of the 1980s', *French Politics and Society* 9, 3–4: 18–31 (useful overview).

Cixous, Hélène

b. 1937, Oran, Algeria

Writer and literary theorist

Although an Algerian whose first language is German, Cixous is thought of as a French literary theorist. Her father, who died in 1948, was a Sephardic Jew whose family moved from Spain to Algeria and her mother, an Ashkenazi Jew, settled in Algeria after her family had fled the rise of Nazism in 1933. Observing the affects of French colonialism, Cixous was also witness to anti-semitism both from the French, when the **Vichy** government refused licence to her father to continue practising medicine, and

from the Algerian Arabs. Her experiences may explain her interests in the relation between politics and writing, the construction of subject identity, the politics of sexual difference and, more generally, the representation of 'otherness'. With some simplification we can distinguish three phases of her work.

The first phase, commencing with the 1967 publication of the novel *Le Prénom de Dieu* (God's First Name) and her doctoral thesis on James Joyce (1968), focuses on the materiality of writing, the idea of the 'exile' as a critical figure of cultural resistance and on 'epiphany' as a moment of transformation. This theoretical occupation with the relation of culture, politics and writing was reflected in her appointment as *chargée de mission* to found the experimental University of Paris VIII at Vincennes in 1968. Her experimental novel *Inside* (*Dedans*) of 1969, awarded the Prix Médicis, is structured according to a number of oppositions or differences and this attentiveness to the structure of language and meaning led Cixous to investigate the unconscious processes involved in writing and reading in *Le Troisième Corps* (The Third Body) of 1970, *Les Commencements* (Beginnings) in 1970 and *Neutral* (*Neutre*) from 1972.

In the 1970s, along with theorists such as **Kristeva**, **Barthes**, **Irigaray** and **Derrida**, she pursued literary questions concerning the narrative voice and these took her, via poststructuralist linguistic analysis and **Lacanian psychoanalysis**, to her second-stage analysis of the complexity and instability of subjectivity in its relation to the dominant, phallic, order. In *First Names of No One* (*Prénoms de Personne*) and *Portrait du soleil* (Portrait of the Sun), both from 1974, Cixous moved from the Hegelian idea that recognition is constitutive of subject identity. Armed with **Bataille**'s rendering of an open psychic economy, she named the psychic economy of contract 'debt', violent appropriation and property as masculine and the economy of gift as feminine.

Sorties (Exits) and *The Laugh of Medusa* (*Le Rire de la Méduse*) both from 1975, have become canonized within feminist literary criticism for the clarity with which they state the epistemological project of feminist **poststructuralism**. We can see repeated the influence of Hegel's Phenomenology of Spirit and its Derridean deconstruction in her insistence that one term in any relationship attempts to dominate, control or even obliterate the other, that (feminine) otherness is necessary but threatening to the formation of (masculine) subject identity. Beyond this, she suggested, one should think of the subject as primarily bisexual and the *jouissance* of the psychic economy as polymorphously perverse, and try to figure 'an economy without reservation' which is performed as, or speaks through, *écriture féminine*. While Cixous believed that either sex can write in this way, she retained the gendered name to mark two facts: that women would benefit from a subversion of the Symbolic Order and that women, due to enculturation, are more likely to identify with it as they have a more positive relation to desire. Works such as *Breaths* (*Souffles*) and *The (Feminine)* (*LA*), from 1975 and 1976 respectively, were an attempt to demonstrate this affirmative relation to desire but also led to the criticism that she was exploiting cultural definitions of 'feminine' values and the identification of the feminine (gender) with women (sex). Clearly Cixous was aware that the analysis of stable subject identity as an effect of the masculine Symbolic Order left her with two problems. The first, of practical import, was that feminists, radical or otherwise, often proclaimed the concept 'woman' as though it held stable reference. For this reason, Cixous helped establish Des Femmes publishing house and was active in **Psych et Po**, a group dedicated to psychoanalytic and revolutionary theories of oppression but antagonistic to the 'humanist' feminism associated with *Questions féministes*. Second, she had to conceive a psychic economy 'outside' the dominant, binary, patriarchal order without using terms produced within that order; work undertaken by the Centre de Recherches en Études Féminines. Influenced in the main by the writings of the Brazilian Lispector, Cixous embarked upon the third stage of her work, which can be characterized loosely as the exploration of the representation of difference,

a move from the 'scene of the unconscious' to 'the scene of history'.

In her work with the **Théâtre du Soleil**, the early modernist themes are woven with the sense of the historical-political nature of the Symbolic Order. Firmly within the tradition of cultural theory, Cixous on the one hand decries the cultural logic of industrialization and colonial expansionism, but on the other risks eulogizing cultural otherness as 'the otherness of the other', with theatrical space posited as the place for showing the problems of identity and for the enactment of pluralism as many and varied voices. Thus, it could be said that, just as Cixous previously looked for the resolution of the conflictual relationship between men and women in the imaginary, a psychic economy without reservation, here she looks for a utopic reconciliation of conflict in 'an economy of love and gift' exemplified in other, more exotic, cultures. The problematic aspect of the latter position revolves around three things: the conflation of psychoanalytic and monetary definitions of the term 'economy', Cixous's attempt to give positive content to utopic reconciliation and the placing of this at the level of a general *libidinal* economy. It does appear that certain naturalist, if not essentialist, assumptions are an integral part of her work. Because she is working within cultural theory, it should come as no surprise that transformation, we find finally, is an individual, 'epiphanic', aesthetic act.

GILL HOWIE

See also: feminist thought; literary prizes

Major works

Cixous, H. (1975) *Le Rire de la Méduse*, Paris: L'Arc pp. 39 – 54. Translated K. Cohen and P. Cohen (1976) in E. Marks and I. de Courtivron (eds) (1981) *New French Feminisms*, Brighton: Harvester Press.
Cixous, H. and Clement, C. (1975) *La Jeune Née*, Paris: Union Générale d'Éditions, '10/18'. Translated B. Wing (1986) *The*

Newly Born Woman, Minneapolis: University of Minnesota Press.

Further reading

Conley, V. A. (1992) *Hélène Cixous*, London and New York: Harvester Wheatsheaf (a key critical analysis).

Sellars, S. (ed.) (1988) *Writing Differences: Readings from the Seminar of Hélène Cixous*, Milton Keynes: Open University Press (collected pieces).

——(ed.) (1994) *The Hélène Cixous Reader*, London: Routledge.

Shiach, M. (1991) *Hélène Cixous: A Politics of Writing*, London and New York; Routledge (a highly lucid study).

class

Class is a fundamental social category, expressing the relationships within and between large groups, each of which is characterized by a common economic condition. Class therefore provides an important cultural identity, as the focus for social solidarities and for the complex relationship between individuals and their social environment. It ranks along with nation and gender as one of the most powerful sources of identity.

Class identities embody the domination of particular classes at particular times, and the struggles and strategies of classes to secure or improve their relative social power. For most of the nineteenth and twentieth centuries France has been acutely conscious of its class conflicts, and the decade which preceded World War II was one of the most class-conscious periods in its history. To a large extent these conflicts were suppressed during the Occupation, and they continued to be repressed by common consensus at the **Liberation**. The extent to which class identities were subordinated in the work of national reconstruction is one of the most remarkable features of the period. However, class conflicts re-emerged with

renewed vigour in 1947, and have been a feature of fluctuating prominence since that time, with a second peak in the early 1970s after the **May 1968** events. Class considerations inform the material conditions in which culture is produced, the forms and hierarchies of cultural production, and the images and narratives which it presents.

In so far as it depends on a degree of surplus, whether of time or money or other resources, culture has usually been associated with social elites, and the term 'culture' itself is often restricted to mean certain preferred leisure pursuits of the wealthiest classes. The dominant French Republican tradition has, however, usually presented a more universalistic aspiration, and has shown a concern to 'democratize' or broaden the class base of culture in three dimensions: what may be depicted, what activities are recognized as cultural, and who can gain access to culture.

The written and visual forms of culture since the nineteenth century have prided themselves on widening the range of what may be depicted in respectable culture, including the most harrowing depictions of life in the lower depths of society. The class-conscious realist classics of Balzac, Stendhal, Flaubert, Hugo and Zola have remained popular, and are frequently adapted for stage or screen, whether as period pieces, like **Berri**'s *Germinal* of 1993 (after Zola), or in modernized settings, like Lelouch's *Les Misérables* of 1996 (after Hugo).

Class differences are most frequently explored in realist mode, in works such as Claire Etcherelli's novel *Élise or the Real Life* (*Élise ou la vraie vie*) of 1967 or Chatiliez's film *La Vie est un long fleuve tranquille* (1988). Both of these show class differences intersecting with ethnic differences, an increasing preoccupation in France as the layering of education, wealth and status have concentrated immigrant communities in the least-favoured économic sectors and geographical zones. However, the avant-garde culture of the 1960s and 1970s exhibited class in other aesthetic modes, often less sentimentally, as in Buñuel's film *The Discreet Charm of the Bourgeoisie* (*Le Charme discret de la bourgeoisie*) of 1972,

Mnouchkine's **Théâtre du Soleil** production of *1789* (1970), or in **Coluche**'s one-man comedy shows, with the distinctive comic persona of the 'ordinary bloke' (*le mec*).

Often the portrayal of class has been associated with the Left, as in the poems and film scripts of Jacques **Prévert**, the paintings of Fernand **Léger** or the novels of Louis Aragon. It was a feature of the 'socialist realist' movement of the late 1940s and early 1950s, promoted by the Communist Party and exemplified in the novels of André Stil, or the paintings of André Fougeron, whose subjects were the struggles of dockers, miners and other industrial workers. But class has also been a focus of the more conservative 'heritage' culture, exemplified in Berri's films *Jean de Florette* and *Manon des sources* (1986), which examine the hierarchies of rural society and the onset of modernization. Whatever their ideological preferences or personal aspirations, French audiences remain fascinated by images and narratives of class.

The providers of culture have, however, sought not only to satisfy their audiences, but also to widen them, attempting to draw in the 'popular' or working classes, which since the 1950s have had significant amounts of disposable income. In the process, they have also been led to reappraise and widen the notion of what might legitimately count as culture. In practice, if not in theory, these two concerns have usually been in conflict, the aims of 'democratizing culture' cutting across those of 'cultural democracy'. And, since 1945, both tendencies have had weighty advocates.

Both the Fourth and Fifth Republics pursued policies of state support for the arts, encouraging more popular access to the established founts of culture: to libraries, museums and galleries, theatres, and even, with the Cinémathèque, to cinemas. Then early attempts at decentralization were followed by **Malraux**'s *maisons de la culture* of the 1960s, attempting to expand the number of these centres of cultural excellence. This process was accelerated through the huge expansion of the Ministry of Culture in the **Mitterrand** presidencies, under the impulsion of Jack **Lang**. However, in most of these attempts to bring culture to the people, the benefits were largely reaped by the well-to-do middle classes.

The opposite approach, of valorizing the culture of the people, was largely aimed at giving recognition to existing cultural activities of the industrial and rural working classes, and enabling them to develop their critical and creative abilities. Its most articulate early advocates were the People and Culture (*Peuple et culture*) association, formed of left-wing Catholics and communist activists. From 1945 onwards they arranged cultural events in workplaces, church halls and community centres, and organized film clubs, festivals and other local initiatives. Gradually their work was taken up by adult education networks and from the 1960s by the new category of 'cultural animators' (*animateurs*), first at municipal level, and then under Jack Lang by the Ministry of Culture. The state imprimatur on a wider concept of culture, including, for example, folk crafts, popular music, and **comic strips** (*bandes dessinées*), has typically met with a mixed response, being widely resented for co-opting and institutionalizing activities which had their origins in resistance to the dominant bourgeois cultural values.

Since 1945, French intellectuals have developed many approaches to class, ranging from Marxist theories of class struggle as the motor of history, through debates on whether economic changes were transforming or entrenching the class structures, to the subordination or abandonment of class in favour of other social preoccupations such as race, gender, sexuality or ecology. Class has usually been euphemized in governmental discourse, even under Socialist governments, but class issues continue to be reflected in social problems of unemployment, homelessness, urban decay and the like, and the figures of proletariat and 'lumpenproletariat' (underclass) lurk under the preferred notions of inequality (*les inégalités*), insecurity (*la précarité*) and exclusion.

MICHAEL KELLY

See also: Catholicism and Protestantism; constitution of the Fifth Republic; literary adaptations; Marxism and Marxian thought

Further reading

Forbes, J. and Kelly, M. (eds) *French Cultural Studies: An Introduction*, Oxford: Oxford University Press (explores the relationship between culture and its social context since the late nineteenth century, dealing at several points with class and its representation).

Mendras, H. and Cole, A. (1991) *Social Change in Modern France: Towards a Cultural Anthropology of the Fifth Republic*, Cambridge: Cambridge University Press (focuses on the social history of France and the breakup of traditional class structures).

Rigby, B. (1991) *Popular Culture in Modern France: A Study of Cultural Discourse*, London: Routledge (traces notions of popular culture since the 1930s, examining the debates around it and its class associations)

Clément, Catherine

b. 1939, France

Feminist thinker, writer and journalist

The author of works on the history of psychoanalysis, Freud and **Lacan** – whose theory she defends in the 1981 publication *Vies et légendes de Jacques Lacan* (Lives and Legends of Jacques Lacan) – Clément has also written (in 1979) a study of opera as a patriarchal production, *Opera, or the Undoing of Women* (*L'Opéra ou la défaite des femmes*), and a collection of Marxist-orientated essays on literature, art, film and opera, entitled *Miroirs du sujet* (Mirrors of the Subject). This latter work, published in 1975, dissects the relationships between ideology, culture, sociosymbolic structures and the subject. Clément is best known for the essay which she co-wrote in 1975 with Hélène **Cixous**, *The Newly Born Woman* (*La Jeune Née*). She is also the author of several novels.

ALEX HUGHES

See also: feminist thought; psychoanalysis; women's/lesbian writing

Clément, René

b. 1913, Bordeaux;
d. 1995, France

Director

One of the leading film-makers of the Fourth Republic in particular, Clément's prolific output lacks any strong thematic unity and thus brought him into disfavour with the **Cahiers du cinéma** critics. *Jeux interdits* won an Oscar in 1953 and remains a major filmic evocation of childhood, while *Plein Soleil* (1960) gave Alain **Delon** his first major role. He was probably the first major French director to realize the benefits of co-production, working in Italy and London as well as in France.

KEITH READER

See also: cinema

Clouzot, Henri-Georges

b. 1907, Niort;
d. 1977, Paris

Director

The sourest and most acid of French film-makers; it is no accident that **Chabrol** paid homage to Clouzot in 1994 by filming his last project, *L'Enfer*. He became notorious under the Occupation for the poison-pen drama *Le Corbeau* (1943), for which he was briefly banned, but is nowadays better known for the savage tension of *Le Salaire de la peur*, which gave Yves **Montand** one of his major roles in 1953, and 1955's *Les Diaboliques*, a drama of jealousy and murder in a private school worthy of Hitchcock. *Les Diaboliques* is quoted in Adrian Lyne's *Fatal Attraction* and has been remade by Jeremiah Chechnik in Hollywood – a good illustration of the influence French cinema can exert on American cinema, as well as vice versa.

KEITH READER

See also: cinema

Cohn-Bendit, Daniel

b. 1945, Frankfurt, Germany

Student activist and writer

Cohn-Bendit was the figure most indelibly associated with **May 1968**, when, as a sociology student at Nanterre, he advocated non-sectarian, broad-based direct action in a frequently jesting style that earned him the loathing of the PCF (Parti Communiste Français) as well as of the Gaullist regime, which deported him to Germany in the middle of the crisis. His greatest coup was perhaps to reappear at the Sorbonne barely a week afterwards, disguised in false beard and dark glasses. Yet his clowning was the vehicle for a profound, and often self-critical, political seriousness which has never abandoned the values of May 1968. He is currently a Frankfurt city councillor for the Green Party and a Euro MP.

KEITH READER

See also: Gaulle, Charles de; universities

Major works

Cohn-Bendit, D. (1988), *Nous l'avons tant aimée, la Révolution*, Paris: Éditions du Seuil/Points (twentieth-anniversary interviews and reassessments with key 1968 activists).

Collard, Cyril

b. 1957, Paris;
d. 1993, Paris

Writer and director

A novelist, poet, scriptwriter and film-maker, Collard achieved international celebrity with his prizewinning film of his novel *Savage Nights* (*Les Nuits fauves*) (1992) in which he played the lead alongside Romane Bohringer. Like his earlier novel *Condamné amour* (Love Condemned) and journal *L'Ange sauvage* (The Savage Angel), it charts the protagonist's alternation between tempestuous relationships with women and impassioned male affairs. Through his promiscuous, drug-using and defiantly HIV-positive characters, Collard combines 1970s hedonistic nonconformity with sexual and racial violence and *fin de siècle* nihilism and disintegration. He died of **AIDS** as *Savage Nights* was acclaimed at the 1993 Cannes festival.

OWEN HEATHCOTE

See also: cinema; gay cinema; gay writing

Further reading

Delannoy, P. (1995) *Cyril Collard: l'ange noir*, Paris: Éditions du Rocher (readable biography).

Médioni, G. (1995) *Cyril Collard*, Paris: Flammarion (portrait of Collard through interviews with family, friends and colleagues).

collective creation

In post-**May 1968** theatre, some **theatre** groups wanted to respond to the revolutionary mood of the times by assuming a political role in the type and subject matter of their productions as well as operating democratically as a company.

Collective creation, as the resulting practice

became known, was pioneered by companies such as Ariane **Mnouchkine's Théâtre du Soleil**, its leading exponent. Each member of the company played an equal role in conceiving and executing the production, receiving equal pay. Rather than working from established texts, collective creation relied on lengthy improvisation periods and research from all company members into the subject matter of the work. Famous productions included the Théâtre du Soleil's celebrated *1789*, *1793* and *L'Age d'or* (The Golden Age), which aimed to break down barriers between audience and players as well as those of job descriptions within the company: all took their turn ticket-collecting (even Mnouchkine), sweeping the stage, and discussing the production with the public after the show. Individual areas of expertise – for example, the skill of a stage designer or lighting director – were recognized, but ideas and suggestions were welcome from any company member.

The Théâtre de l'Aquarium, also at the Cartoucherie, Vincennes, was equally noted for its collective creations. The first of these, *Les Guerres Pichrocholines* (The Pichrocholean Wars), in 1967, was based on an episode in Rabelais, and actually preceded the first Soleil collective creation. Led by Jacques Nichet, the company was noted for its expert handling of documentary material which it adapted into theatrical events, for example in *Marchands de ville* (Town Traders) and the later *La Soeur de Shakespeare* (Shakespeare's Sister). The Théâtre National de Lorraine, which specialized in regionally based, politically based collective creations such as *Splendeur et misère de Minette la bonne Lorraine* (Splendour and Misery of Minette, the Good Woman of Lorraine). This handled the troubles of the Lorraine iron-ore industry through a detective-story plot depicting a girl caught up in American-style gang warfare.

André Bernedetto's Nouveau Théâtre d'Avignon was also noted for its collective creations dealing with the Mediterranean area, often performed outside, using both professional and amateur actors.

Although collective creation was successful in establishing new techniques and attitudes, presenting ideas and material in a revolutionary theatrical way, the lengthy lead periods needed for improvisation and research were time- and cost-consuming, and often financially impractical. Creation by committee, always a difficult proposition, was also a significant contributory factor in the decline of collective creation by the end of the 1970s. Companies like the Théâtre du Soleil returned to text-based productions, applying to these many of the useful techniques collective creation had taught them.

ANNIE SPARKS

See also: theatre

Further reading

Bradby, D. (1991) *Modern French Drama 1940–1990*, Cambridge: Cambridge University Press (see the chapter on collective creation).
Whitton, D. (1988) *Stage Directors in Modern France*, Manchester: Manchester University Press (see the chapter on Mnouchkine).

Coluche

b. 1944, Montrouge;
d. 1986, Opio, Alpes-Maritimes

Comedian and actor,
real name Michel Colucci

The comedian, film actor and activist known as Coluche attained instant notoriety when the **ORTF** aired his send-up mocking **racism** on the part of a 'normal' petit-bourgeois *mec* to millions of viewers awaiting results of the May 1974 presidential elections. Six years later, Coluche draped a *tricolore* sash over his bib overalls during his own brief presidential campaign. In 1983, he earned a César for his performance in Claude **Berri's** *Tchao Pantin*. Subsequently he helped to launch the *restaurants du coeur* to provide free meals for the unemployed and homeless. He died in a motorcycle accident in 1986.

STEVEN UNGAR

See also: cinema

Further reading

Boggio, P. (1991) *Coluche*, Paris: Flammarion (biography).
Ungar, S. (1996) 'The Coluche Effect', in S. Ungar and T. Conley (eds) *Identity Papers: Contested Nationhood in Twentieth Century France*, Minneapolis: University of Minnesota Press (relates two early satirical sketches to Coluche's performance in *Tchao Pantin*).

Comédie-Française

Founded in 1680 by Louis XIV, the Comédie-Française is the oldest of France's five national theatres, operating as a society of self-managing performers, or *sociétaires*. Its repertoire is based on classics and major modern works. Jean-Pierre Miquel has been general administrator since 1993.

ANNIE SPARKS

See also: theatre; theatres, national

comic strips/cartoonists

Bande dessinée (henceforth BD) is a visual and narrative art form. The term (literally 'drawn strip') is normally translated either as 'comic strip', suggesting the origins of the Anglo-Saxon version of the medium in American newspapers, or as 'graphic novel', which captures one key feature of the medium: a story told in pictures, not a text illustrated by pictures. A further defining feature is sequentiality: whereas a single painting may evoke or condense a narrative, a BD frame is not intended to be read in isolation.

The respectability of the 'ninth art' was consecrated by the opening in 1991 of the Centre National de la Bande Dessinée et de l'Image in Angoulême, which has hosted the annual Salon de la Bande Dessinée since 1977. Since the 1960s, francophone BD has emerged as an adult genre, no longer limited in its subject matter to adventure stories or **science fiction** and becoming more experimental in its form.

In the immediate postwar period, francophone BD was essentially destined for a youthful readership: the Belgian journals *Tintin* and *Spirou* were both firmly within a conservative Catholic ideological tradition, and the magazine *Vaillant*, produced by the French Communist Party, shared with them the aim of combating the influence of American pulp culture on French youth.

The founding of the journal *Pilote* in 1959 set in train the evolution of BD towards a more adult readership. The influence of the American underground and of the taboo-breaking climate of **May 1968** led to a revolt against classical narrative and figurative codes (the influence of Hergé's *ligne claire*, implying clear outlines and realist decors still predominated), and a move towards an adult treatment of eroticism and politics. A breakaway group from *Pilote* founded *Charlie mensuel* in 1969, and a further group of ex-*Pilote* artists including Brétécher founded *L'Écho des savanes* in 1972. Gotlib founded *Fluide glacial* in 1975. Throughout the 1970s there was a proliferation of BD journals and fanzines, often ephemeral. Of these journals, only *Fluide glacial* and *A suivre*, along with *Spirou* for children, survived into the 1990s, as hard-cover albums became the dominant format for the publication of BD. The response by the major BD publishers such as Dargaud and Casterman to the fall in sales (which began with the economic crisis of the late 1980s) has been an increased reliance on series, such as the best-selling *XIII* saga by van Hamme and Vance, with its enigmatic superhero and thriller format, and on the work of well-known (often dead) authors: the *Astérix* albums represent a quarter of the annual sales of Dargaud.

BD shares some of the codes of **cinema** in terms of framing, composition and use of high or low angles. Montage conventions can also be described in cinematic terms: establishing shots may open a sequence then give way to medium shots and close-ups, dialogues may follow a shot–reverse-shot sequence, and links between shots may involve zooming in on a detail or following the gaze of a character into what was off-screen space in the previous shot.

The two media diverge, however, in their representation of time and space. In BD, time relations are translated into spatial terms. The conditions of reception of the two media are thus fundamentally different: in film, shots are viewed sequentially, whereas in BD they are viewed simultaneously. A BD is necessarily both linear and tabular: the reader may move from one frame to the next, but cannot help but apprehend at the same time the surrounding frames. Any page, or double page, offers a number of possible trajectories for the reader. On a page which offers narrative continuity and spatial logic in consecutive frames, there may be, for instance, a sense of movement along the diagonals or a sense that the emotional tone is set by a close-up in the centre. A character may gaze at another within a frame but also beyond the frame. Frames will relate to each other through visual rhymes and resonances and through symmetry. In *Nogegon* by François and Luc Schuiten, symmetry is the structuring principle: it operates at the level of the frame, of each page *and* of the album as a whole.

The medium offers multiple possibilities for the manipulation of space–time relationships. In *Tintin in Tibet* (*Tintin au Tibet*), Hergé maintains spatial continuity in the mountainous background across three frames as his characters, who appear in the foreground in each frame, trudge on through the day. In *The Crow That Wore Trainers* (*Le Corbac aux baskets*), Fred takes up a whole page with a grand staircase. A grid of regular frames is superimposed on to the staircase, and the same characters appear on the page several times as they

approach from different directions. The reader can see that two characters are in conversation with each other at the same time as we can see that they have not yet met.

The relationship of audience/reader knowledge to the knowledge of characters within the diegesis operates differently in BD and in film. Off-screen space is by definition invisible to the spectator of a film for the duration of a shot, but in a BD whatever is hidden from view in one frame may be seen elsewhere on the page. The effect of prior reader knowledge of what is to happen can be used to ironic effect: even as we read Captain Haddock's adamant refusal to leave the comfort of his home at the start of *Tintin au Tibet*, our eye is attracted by the next frame, where he steps compliantly on to the airport tarmac.

In BD the size and shape of frames is variable and may be used to reinforce the impact of the narrative: a horizontal frame filling the whole width of the page is used, for example, to show Tintin and Haddock adrift in the ocean. Horizontal frames tend to slow the narrative down, where a succession of vertical frames will speed it up. A long shot may be given added drama by the addition of an insert: usually a close-up of a character or object. Some artists, such as Brétécher, prefer to use a regular pattern. The uniformity of the frames enables her to gain maximum effect from the slightest change in the position of her protagonists, and to represent both their immobilism and the obsessive rituals of their lives. The image can go beyond the frame: in Guido Crépax's *Le Point de non retour* (The Point of No Return), the chaos and brutality of battle are expressed by diagonal borders which divide the page into triangular frames, the points of which echo the soldiers' swords threatening their fleeing victims, whose heads, arms and legs spill over from one frame into the next. The political cartoonist Wolinski uses no frames at all, and so does not have to set his characters against any kind of background. He draws only enough of each character to evoke the manner – hectoring, self-satisfied or sycophantic – in which the flood of words, unconstrained by a speech bubble, is delivered.

The enunciative stance of BD draws upon some of the codes of classic cinema in order, in some cases, to transgress them: Tintin gazes out at the reader from the cover of *The Castafiore Emerald* (*Les Bijoux de la Castafiore*), as do some of the bewildered soldiers in Tardi's *La Guerre des Tranchées* (Trench Warfare). The artist Bilal draws himself in *La Croisière des oubliés* (The Crusade of the Forgotten Ones) and gives himself a speech bubble justifying the drawing style of the frames on the page. Authors vary in the extent to which they make use of *récitatif* (voice-over): some, such as Hergé, consider descriptive prose to be redundant in a visual narrative, and limit their use of it to brief indications of changes in time and place. Others, such as Charlier and Giraud in the western saga of the adventures of Blueberry, take the opportunity to underline the epic quality of their subject matter with a certain grandiloquence of tone. There may be a disjunction between what is written in the *récitatif* and what is shown: Tardi juxtaposes extracts from speeches of generals and politicians with images of the horror of war.

Unlike cinema, BD is silent and immobile. It has, however, a number of resources for evoking sound and movement. The 'soundtrack' of BD consists both of onomatopoeic words, whose thickness varies according to the loudness of the sound, and of dialogue contained in speech bubbles. Speech bubbles and onomatopoeia occupy space within (or overlapping) the frame, and may become visual elements in their own right: Giraud uses a speech bubble to obscure the face of a character in a 'Blueberry' album which is all about spying and hiding. The narrative may, though, be carried by pictures alone: *Arzach* by Moebius is thirty-two pages long and has only one speech bubble at the very end.

BD is discontinuous. Ellipsis occurs not just between actions but within them, and readers must complete the movement in their imagination. The codes of BD are therefore different from those of the animated cartoon, which recomposes all the stages of a movement, frame by frame. BD can convey great energy by portraying only the most extreme stage of a movement.

The issue of realism is posed differently for BD and film: since BD does not involve mechanical recording, it does not have to have any relationship to the external world at all. In practice, although many artists reject the meticulously encoded documentary realism of the *ligne claire*, it is hard to imagine a BD that would be completely non-representational and still fulfil the criterion of being narrative art. The medium allows for spectacular departures from the laws which govern the natural world: villages may float in the air, strange pyramidal structures may engulf cities, and the detailed architectural façades drawn by François Schuiten may suddenly reveal themselves not to belong to three-dimensional buildings but to be based on a two-dimensional illusion. A significant current in BD aims at a form of realism which is based on the faithful reproduction of the iconography of film genres such as the western or the film noir, the latter most often in black and white with an expressionist use of shadows and contrast. Colour is not necessarily used in BD to enhance the effect of realism, but may add an emotional tonality to the frame. Colour is normally added in the final stages of the process of production of a BD, often not by the artist but by a colourist. Artists such as Bilal and Barbier have worked directly in coloured paint, however, with no prior drawing.

The maturity of the medium is not in any doubt. A work like *Partie de chasse* by Christin and Bilal, in which officials of Eastern bloc countries settle scores during a weekend at a hunting lodge, is acknowledged as a masterpiece of narrative and visual art by the critics of the serious press, although in general media coverage of BD is scant and its status remains that of a minority cult interest rather than a mainstream art form. The future of BD is uncertain: publishers are unwilling to take risks with untried authors and, in the absence of the outlet for new creative work formerly provided by the journals, conservatism threatens to stifle the industry. Its best hope may lie in the resurgence of small publishing collectives which will free authors and readers from the tyranny of the series and the superhero.

ANN MILLER

See also: beur comics; youth culture

Further reading

Bilal, E. and Christin, P. (1983) *Partie de chasse*, Paris: Dargaud.
Fred (1994) *Le Corbac aux baskets*, Paris: Dargaud.
Hergé (1960) *Tintin au Tibet*, Paris, Casterman.
Peeters, B. (1991) *Case, planche, récit: lire une bande dessinée*, Paris: Casterman (formal analysis).
Sadoul, N. (1989) *Entretiens avec Hergé*, Paris: Casterman (interviews).
Tardi (1993) *C'était la guerre des tranchées*, Paris: Casterman.
Tisseron, S. (1990) *La Bande dessinée au pied du mot*, Paris: Aubier.

committed literature

This term describes a movement encompassing fiction and non-fiction which was inspired by the underground press and clandestine publishers during the Occupation.

Wartime prototypes of *littérature engagée* – the adjective translates into English as both 'engaged' and 'committed' – were typically collective efforts among various left-wing groups united by circumstance against the censorship imposed by the Nazis and those in France who collaborated with them. Later forms and expressions were determined less by the specific experience of the Occupation than by the longer French tradition of the writer or artist responding to his or her historical moment in a wide public sphere.

A first major attempt to extend collective wartime efforts following the **Liberation** began in late 1944 when Jean-Paul **Sartre**, Simone de **Beauvoir** and Maurice Merleau-Ponty launched *Les Temps modernes* as an alternative to the more or less apolitical ('disengaged') *Nouvelle Revue française*, which had dominated French literary monthlies between the wars.

Between January and June 1946, *Les Temps modernes* ran a series of articles written by Sartre in response to the general question, 'What is literature?' These articles, republished in book form a year later, served as a manifesto of the programme of an engaged literature that – in line with a tradition going back to Plato's *Republic* – excluded **poetry**, whose sonorous and semantic density Sartre saw as an obstacle between the writer and the world of historical change. Sartre's exclusion of poetry made clear the extent to which his preferred medium was a transparent prose whose mission he prescribed as being that of protecting individual and collective freedom by disclosing any and all threats to it. Yet, because this exclusion asserted engagement as a conscious choice on the part of the writer, the Sartrean programme set forth in *What is Literature?* was arguably less concerned with literature as an end in itself than with the practice of an engaged writing whose objective was to transform the writer into a (bad) conscience of his or her historical age.

The Sartrean programme set forth in *What is Literature?* drew its theoretical grounding from distinctions between prose and poetry defended earlier by Paul Valéry, and by virtue of a parallel distinction set forth by Stéphane Mallarmé. At the same time, Sartre's characterization of the writer as the bad conscience of his or her age evoked the turn-of-the-century figure of the public intellectual (one thinks first, here, of Émile Zola and 'J'accuse') linked to the Dreyfus Affair. It is this second sense of *littérature engagée* (i.e. of a literature linked to debating social and political issues in a public sphere) that evolved beyond the Sartrean programme of the late 1940s into a wider practice of a socially responsible mode of writing that ranged from novel and essay to theatre and – Sartre's exclusions notwithstanding – poetry.

Two further points need to be made here. First, this broader model of *littérature engagée*, equated with the figure of the public intellectual, goes back at least as far as the period between the wars to include writers such as Roger Martin du Gard, Julien Benda, Paul Nizan, André **Malraux** and Emmanuel Mounier. (Even André Gide published a 1938 collection of essays entitled *Littérature engagée*). Second, a considerable debate surrounds the question of whether the writer expresses commitment indirectly, by depicting issues of political involvement, or instead by a more direct personal involvement ranging from essay and/or editorial to the picket line, demonstration and similar activism. To restate the question even more pointedly, one might ask whether commitment is an attribute of the writing or of the writer. Debate surrounding the nature of committed literature extended between 1945 and 1970 beyond Sartre's early postwar paradigm toward a sense of the term as political involvement on the part of Left-leaning writers and artists.

Involvement in this wider sense was, in turn, equated with position-taking (*prise de position*) on specific matters and – often – removed from formal partisan affiliation. One consequence of this wider practice was that committed literature came increasingly to include non-literary forms of writing such as journalism and the topical essay. This evolved sense of committed literature as committed writing was driven by what Simone de Beauvoir aptly referred to in her memoirs as the 'force of circumstance'. Throughout the 1950s and 1960s, debates in literary journals, as well as in newspapers, lecture halls and congresses, centred on how the committed writer might best respond to the issues ranging from France's colonial policies in Indochina and Algeria to the 1956 Soviet suppression of Hungary, Fidel Castro's takeover in Cuba, American military presence in Vietnam, and the question of Israel's territorial claims in the Middle East.

A definite anti-totalitarian shift on the Left in the mid-1970s was prompted by the publication of Alexander Solzhenitsyn's *Gulag Archipelago*. This shift was soon enhanced by the visibility of a post-**May 1968** generation of 'new' philosophers such as Bernard-Henri **Lévy** and André **Glucksmann**, who increasingly appropriated the role of public intellectual for-

merly held by Sartre and his contemporaries. On the domestic front, since the 1970s, young figures of popular song and film such as **Renaud** and **Coluche** raised public awareness concerning racism and the homeless.

A related shift since the mid-1970s stemmed from practices of committed literature in support of identity issues involving **feminism** and **decolonization** as well as practices that raised awareness concerning oppressed minorities such as gays and Jews. These writings recalled earlier texts by writers such as Albert Memmi, Jean **Genet**, Frantz **Fanon** and Albertine **Sarrazin** that illustrated persistent prejudice and oppression as obstacles to be recognized and overcome.

STEVEN UNGAR

See also: Algerian war; existentialism; gay writing; racism/anti-semitism; women's/lesbian writing

Further reading

Judt, T. (1992) *Past Imperfect: French Intellectuals, 1944–56*, Berkeley: University of California Press (traces evolving attitudes of leftist intellectuals towards Soviet Russia; critical and provocative).

Schalk, D. (1979) *The Spectrum of Political Engagement: Mounier, Benda, Nizan, Brasillach, Sartre*, Princeton: Princeton University Press (a key reference for interwar practices and their postwar evolution).

Stoekl, A. (1992) *Agonies of the Intellectual: Commitment, Subjectivity, and the Performative in the Twentieth-Century French Tradition*, Lincoln: University of Nebraska Press (essential background reading).

Compagnons de la chanson, Les

Singers

Originally made up of nine singers when formed in 1944, the Compagnons de la chanson spent two years singing with Édith **Piaf** after the war (for example, *The Three Bells* (*Les Trois Cloches*)), but gained more fame on their own in France and abroad. The Compagnons survived many changes of musical fashion, without deviating from their rigid harmonic style and without seeing their popularity wane. The group split up in 1980 after the death of one of its members.

IAN PICKUP

See also: song/*chanson*

concert music

The situation of concert (defined here as orchestral) music in France is marked by the problems besetting orchestral music in the rest of the Western world. One should not really regard it as a crisis; it is rather a profound sociological and aesthetic change that has characterized music since 1945.

In the first place, musical audiences are diminishing; partly as the result of the popularity of recordings, partly as a result of a reduction of interest and the power of discrimination. Much of this deterioration is due to the fact that the grand continuity of musical education, from the classical period until the dawn of modernity, towards 1910, has been disrupted. Audiences tend to be either hostile or impatient toward the avant-garde music of the earlier part of the twentieth century, although a number of works by Bartók, Stravinsky and Berg have entered the concert repertory; but the important music written after 1945, with very few exceptions, has not even been played widely, and therefore audiences are not likely to become interested. Since it is generally difficult for young composers to get a hearing in the concert hall or on radio stations specializing in classical music, they have found a viable solution by composing for smaller ensembles that can be formed in conservatories and around universities; and the obvious result of this situation means small but dedicated audiences. Another fact to be taken into consideration is that this music is frequently diffi-

cult to perform and requires special understanding in order to play it at all. These aesthetic considerations, along with the economic realities of concert halls and orchestras that are obliged to cater to and satisfy upper-middle-class consumers (even when these organizations are subsidized by the state), are keeping contemporary music in a precarious state of insecurity, and the future of concert music is by no means reassuring.

In some respects, one might say that the nineteenth century, in which concert music became a major modern ritual (like opera) primarily patronized by the wealthy middle class, came to an end by the time World War I began, and certainly by the time World War II ended. The nineteenth century marked the triumph of the symphony in the concert hall; and in some way, the situation of concert music in our time parallels the dilemma of the symphony after Mahler. Moreover, it is worth noting that Debussy and Ravel, the leading French contemporaries of Mahler, were simply not interested in writing symphonies. It is arguable that, after 1945, the symphony ceased to exist as a compositional genre (there are, however, some noteworthy exceptions); in its wake, symphonic music also suffered neglect, sometimes disdain, on the part of the new generation of composers. Among the group of French composers, formerly known as Les Six, who lived beyond 1945, one might say that their principal work had been done before 1939. This is largely true of Milhaud and Honegger. In the case of Francis Poulenc (1899–1963), we must nevertheless note the fact that his three operas – *Les Mamelles de Tirésias* (1944), a setting of Apollinaire's play; *Dialogues des carmélites* (1953–6), based on a text by Georges Bernanos; and *La Voix humaine* (1958), using a libretto by Jean Cocteau – are impressive achievements. The *Dialogues* have been widely performed, with much success.

The most original of the younger composers that came to (limited) prominence after 1945 is Henri Dutilleux (1916–), who is actually in the succession of Debussy and Ravel and at the same time open to serial techniques. As a result, his works are full of original touches, harmonic as well as structural. Two individual traits that are constantly encountered in his works are the predilection for titles and subtitles either derived from Baudelaire or reminiscent of the enigmas of the *correspondances* central to symbolist poetry; and the design of developing thematic transformations throughout his compositions for which the title *Métaboles* is splendidly appropriate. The title of that composition (1962–4) could as easily have been *Métamorphoses*, which means more or less the same thing. Dutilleux has written two symphonies (1951 and 1959): the second one, 'Le double', utilizes an instrumental group of twelve soloists along with the orchestra but keeps the two groups independent from each other and thus explores the sonorities that can be produced by this arrangement. A later work, *Timbres, espace, mouvement* (1977–8) reinforces the notion implicit in Dutilleux's work since the 1950s that his dominant interest lies in sonority and in the problem of the spatialization of music, which is one of the major preoccupations of the music of the second half of the twentieth century (Stockhausen, **Boulez**, Ligeti, Carter and Birtwistle come to mind).

The most important composer by far to come out of the Jeune France movement of the 1930s, and certainly one of the most important shapers of music of the last fifty years, has been Olivier **Messiaen** (1908–92); most of the experimental composers in France were his students at the Conservatoire (Boulez, Barraqué, **Xenakis**). Messiaen's compositional journey has been from organ composition to orchestral works, plus a large and important body of piano works, stretching over a period of more than sixty years. The symphonic piece that made his name famous as an orchestral composer was the Turangalîla-Symphonie (1946–8), a ten-movement work requiring large orchestral forces, including a piano soloist, ondes Martenot and enlarged percussion. The characteristic 'signatures' of this large work are the unusual rhythms and sonorities, many of them derived from Hindu musical practice; the overall sound comes close to a kind of super-gamelan (many contemporary composers have made attempts to find Western equivalents of the Balinese

gamelan). In *Chronochromie* (Time Colour), ten years later, as the title indicates, these timbral effects are treated with greater sophistication and economy; and by that time a new ingredient that is to be found in most of Messiaen's later works, namely the use of birdsong, has become an important part of his orchestral palette. (Messiaen always insisted that certain chords were 'coloured'.) The same thing is true of the *Sept Haïkai, esquisses japonaises* (1963), scored mainly for wind and percussion, and *Couleurs de la cité céleste*, in the same year, which dispenses with strings altogether. It is also true of the remarkable *Et exspecto resurrectionem mortuorum* (1964). The two last-mentioned works are indices of the profound attachment of Olivier Messiaen to his Catholic faith. It can be said without exaggeration that every one of his works is a celebration of Catholic belief and doctrine, and that music is the language in which this belief can best be expressed. During the following years Messiaen was at work on a huge work for large chorus and orchestra entitled *La Transfiguration de Notre-Seigneur Jésus-Christ*; a few years later came a very large symphonic work, *Des canyons aux étoiles*, which is also a tribute to the landscape (and birdsong) of the western United States. The most striking final work is the four-hour opera *Saint François d'Assise* which occupied Messiaen between 1975 and 1983 and which was performed at the Paris Opéra in the following year. It is clear that a work about the saint who preached to the birds had always been dormant in Messiaen; the opera is most impressive and constitutes, in some ways, a summary of Messiaen's musical and religious commitment. It is subtitled 'Scènes franciscaines' and, instead of relying on plot, it is panoramic. The static quality of this opera is typical of Messiaen's music, which is predicated to transcend time and to 'intimate' the presence of eternity within its musical duration. The opera was followed by a large orchestral work, *Éclairs sur l'au-delà* (Illuminations of the Beyond).

The example of Messiaen's orchestral music points up the fact that the conception of writing for the orchestra was rapidly changing after 1945; and these ideas, quickly transmitted to his more impatient and radical pupils, have enriched the concert repertoire in France since 1945. It is necessary, however, to make one proviso: obviously the notion of 'concert music' is now somewhat different from what it was during the first half of this century, the seeds having been planted in the years 1908–20 by Stravinsky and the Viennese twelve-tone composers. As a matter of fact, virtually all of the younger composers have been exposed to serial composition and have been clearly marked by it. Because of the new interest in sonorities and timbre, most of the newer compositions are for specialized ensembles, usually limited in number, and 'unorthodox' from the point of view of the normal concert-hall expectations. Younger composers in France have been fascinated by the possibilities of the music of Asia, particularly the gamelan; and many of them encountered the influence of Edgard Varèse, who opened the way for large percussion works as well as construction in terms of blocks of sound. Another influence in the 1950s is that of John Cage and aleatoric ('chance') music; and of course the advent of *musique concrète* in the laboratories of Pierre Schaeffer at the RTF (Radio et Télévision Française) during the same period. This experimentation with artificially created soundscapes and patterns led naturally into the technologically more sophisticated regions of electronic music; almost all experimental composers tried electronic composition – and usually left it behind.

Among the more important composers of that generation, two deserve brief mention, and one is absolutely central to an adequate comprehension of what has been accomplished in the second half of the century. Iannis Xenakis studied with Messiaen, and is in many ways closer to Varèse, in view of the strongly percussive nature of his music. He is also known for his 'stochastic' method, a method of devising structures by mathematical means, using the calculus of probability. Many of his larger works, such as *Metastasis* and *Pithoprakta*, are remarkable in their powerful new sonorities. In *Nomos gamma* the orchestra is deployed among the audience, and there are numerous

compositions for tape and for smaller groups, most of them highly intriguing.

Jean Barraqué (1928–73), another disciple of Messiaen and a serial composer of remarkable talent, died too early to accomplish his lifetime ambition to set to music extensive excerpts of Hermann Broch's novel *The Death of Virgil*; a few excerpts were completed. It will be a matter of time before Barraqué's extremely difficult music can reach a larger public; however, his final completed work, a clarinet concerto, offers a good index of Barraqué's impressive abilities.

But the central figure is Pierre **Boulez**, certainly the most important composer/conductor/theorist of the century. After his graduation from the Conservatoire (where Messiaen was his major teacher), he immediately manifested his uncompromisingly austere and brilliant intellectual and compositional genius by creating a number of works that carried serialism to its final conclusion – total serialization of all the compositional aspects of music – particularly the two books of *Structures* for two pianos (1951–61). His orchestral works during those years make use of texts by René **Char**: *Le Visage nuptial* and *Le Soleil des eaux*. The most famous and important of these Char settings is for a small ensemble, *Le Marteau sans maître*, the work that made him internationally famous as a composer. The largest Boulez orchestral work is *Pli selon pli* (1957–62), a powerful *hommage* to Mallarmé, with whom Boulez has many affinities (discipline, frequent revision, precision, clarity and a strong lyricism that is often veiled by these severe compositional constraints). In the 1960s, Boulez became internationally acclaimed as a conductor. His compositions went forward at a somewhat slower pace; now he was absorbing the impact of aleatoric music, which he nevertheless kept under strict compositional control. Outstanding large-scale works in this category are *Figures-Doubles-Prismes* for large orchestra, *Éclat/Multiples*, *Domaines* (for clarinet and six instrumental groups) and *Rituel in memoriam Maderna* for eight orchestral groups. Since 1977, with the Foundation of IRCAM (Institut de Recherche et de

Coordination Acoustique/Musique), Boulez has been active in research into experimental techniques and acoustical problems (in addition to a lively conducting schedule). The two most impressive outgrowths of this activity (besides the creation of the Ensemble Intercontemporain to perform these works) have been *Répons* for six instrumental soloists, instrumental ensemble and electro-acoustic equipment. In this work, which requires a spatial arrangement altogether different from the ordinary concert hall, the conductor and the electronic engineer are placed at the centre, the instrumental ensemble is located in front of the conductor, and the audience is seated around the hall, the soloists being situated on the periphery, along with six loudspeakers. The task of the electronic expert is to distribute and manipulate the sound, so that the music is literally deployed within a spatial site. One of his most recent works is similar in nature, ' . . . *explosante-fixe* . . . ', once again with the disposition of the audience in a space of electronically distributed sound. These works point toward a radically new conception of how music can be produced, and requires a new way of listening – all of these factors being a sort of synthesis of what most contemporary experimental music has been trying to achieve.

WALTER A. STRAUSS

See also: song/*chanson*

Further reading

Griffiths, P. (1994) *Modern Music: A Concise History*, New York: Thames and Hudson (most concise overview of modern music presently available).

Hodeir, A. (1961) *Since Debussy: A View of Contemporary Music*, New York: Grove Press (an older, but still interesting study of the major modern composers).

conservation zones

Conservation zones (*secteurs sauvegardés*) were introduced in 1962 by national legislation known today as the **Malraux act**, after André **Malraux**, the then Minister for Cultural Affairs, its chief sponsor. They are areas designated in historic towns (some seventy-five) within which the historic architectural and urban heritage is not only protected but also positively enhanced. Some spectacularly beautiful enhancement schemes have been effected within *secteurs sauvegardés* (as in the Marais, Paris) but, due to lack of finance and political opposition to the radical nature of the works, they have not brought about the general renaissance of the French urban past which André Malraux intended.

ROGER KAIN

See also: Marais plan; renovation projects

constitution of the Fifth Republic

The constitution of the Fifth Republic was drawn up by Charles de **Gaulle** and Michel Debré in the summer of 1958 and gained massive public approval in a referendum held on 28 September 1958. The constitution marked a significant break with the principles and practices of French Republican institutions and its radicalism was emphasized by a controversial amendment in 1962 which introduced the direct election of the president of the Republic. Over time, however, it has acquired a significant degree of political legitimacy.

The immediate origins of the 1958 constitution lay in the inability of the weak coalition governments of the Fourth Republic to resolve the bitter war with the Front de la Libération Nationale (FLN, or National Liberation Movement) and the supporters of French Algeria. By 1958, sections of the French **armed forces** were on the verge of open rebellion and the authority of the civil power was crumbling. Faced with this crisis, the majority of the party leaders reluctantly accepted the return to power of General de Gaulle, whom they saw as the only man capable of solving the **Algerian war** without turning France into a military dictatorship. For de Gaulle, however, Algeria was only a symptom of what he regarded as the fundamental weakness in French politics, namely the absence of strong government and the excessive power of the political parties. Ever since the military and political collapse of 1940, de Gaulle had believed that only by the exercise of leadership could France survive as an independent nation. He was thus determined to use the opportunity provided by his return to power to reshape France's political insitutions. He took personal control of the drafting of the constitution, made sure that the parties were barred from any significant say in its contents, and excluded parliament from the ratification process by appealing directly to the electorate via a referendum.

The principal innovations of the 1958 constitution were the strengthening of the powers of the president and the weakening of parliament's role to disrupt government. The president was given a range of prerogative powers designed to enable him to control the political situation – the right to declare a state of emergency, to dissolve the National Assembly, to make nominations to senior positions in civil and military offices as well as to the office of prime minister – and his authority was emphasized by the statement in Article 5 that he represents national unity and is responsible for the proper working of the constitutional powers. At the same time, the powers of the National Assembly were reduced. Its ability to harass government was curtailed, the length of its sessions was reduced, its monopoly over legislation was broken by the introduction of referenda and by the creation of a Constitutional Council able to veto laws deemed unconstitutional. Strengthening the presidency and curtailing the National Assembly marked a clear break with the principles of democratic Republicanism, which argued that the National Assembly was the sole repository of the national will and that a strong presidency was incompatible with political liberty.

It is, however, important to note that the 1958 constitution did not challenge other key elements in the constitutional code of French Republicanism. It states that the Republican form of regime is not subject to revision and that the Tricolour flag (the symbol of the French Revolution) is the national flag. It also reaffirms the secular nature of the state and includes in the preamble the 1789 Declaration of the Rights of Man and the Citizen as extended by the 1946 constitution of the Fourth Republic. To these essentially symbolic continuities should be added the more politically charged clauses respecting the core principle of French Republicanism that the executive power should be responsible to the Legislature. The constitution establishes a prime minister and government who are responsible for the formulation and implementation of policy, and who cannot continue in office without the confidence of the directly elected National Assembly. It is true that the president appoints the prime minister; but the text clearly implies that the power to remove him or her resides with the National Assembly. It also lays down that constitutional revision is the prerogative of the Legislature.

The 1958 text thus provides both for parliamentary government and for a 'two-headed' executive, and in doing so left unanswered the key question, 'Who rules?' That it did so reflects the fact that the constitution is a compromise between de Gaulle's vision of the president as national leader and the Republican's insistence that democracy was only safe when government was accountable to parliament. Each side could appeal to the lessons of historical memory – de Gaulle to the impotence of the presidency in 1940, parliament to the rape of the Second Republic by Louis Napoleon in 1851. It was the latter fear which explains why the 1958 constitution made no provision for the election of the president of the Republic by universal suffrage. So long as the Algerian war continued, de Gaulle and the parties were willing to stand by the 1958 compromise. Once it ended, the real battle for the constitution began. De Gaulle was determined to base presidential power not simply on his own charisma (which by definition was not transferable to anyone else) but on the legitimacy of universal suffrage. He thus introduced, by a dubious procedure, a constitutional amendment establishing a directly elected presidency. To almost all the political parties, this represented an unacceptable assault on Republican democracy. Secure in the knowledge that, with the Algerian crisis over, de Gaulle was no longer necessary, they attacked him in the only way they could by voting a censure motion on his government. De Gaulle promptly responded by exercising his constitutional right to dissolve the National Assembly. After a highly charged election campaign, de Gaulle won a comfortable (though not overwhelming) majority for his referendum and, shortly afterwards, an overwhelming vote in the parliamentary elections.

The constitutional expert Maurice Duverger said of the 1962 amendment that it gave the president no new powers, but that it gave him power. By this he meant that the president henceforth possessed a democratic mandate at least as strong as that of the National Assembly. Over the next two decades, the pre-eminence of the president, and the subordinate status of the prime minister, became entrenched in practice and acceptable in theory, particularly once the democratic Left under **Mitterrand** decided to work with, rather than against, the system. Thus there have been relatively few changes to the constitution, apart from the 1974 amendment extending to parliamentarians the right to appeal to the Constitutional Council and various measures designed to incorporate European Community legislation into constitutional law. The biggest test to the constitutional convention established in 1958–62 came in 1986 when the incumbent President Mitterrand lost control of the National Assembly to his conservative opponents led by Jacques **Chirac**. In what became known as the 'cohabitation' experience (which would be repeated in 1993–5 with Mitterand and **Balladur** and again, this time with Chirac as president and Lionel **Jospin** as prime minister, following the left-wing coalition's victory in the 1997 parliamentary election), the president effectively gave up control of the domestic policy agenda to the prime minister but maintained his status as guardian of the constitution and head of national defence. Cohabitation demonstrated, first, that the exercise of the full extent of presidential powers depended on a supportive parliamentary majority and, second, that the Gaullist reading of the constitution was not the only one. The fact that the Fifth Republic constitution could survive, first, the victory of its former opponents and, second, the breakdown of the president/parliament axis on which since 1962 it had worked, is a tribute to its flexibility. It is now second only to the Third Republic as France's longest-lasting constitution since the Revolution.

PETER MORRIS

See also: legal system; parties and movements

Copi

b. 1939, Buenos Aires;
d. 1987, Paris

Humorist, writer, designer
and performer
real name Raúl Damonte

The writer and performer of his own humorous, sometimes shocking short plays, including *L'Homosexuel ou la difficulté de s'exprimer* (Homosexuals or the Difficulty of Self-Expression) in 1971, and his 1988 *Une Visite Inopportune* (An Untimely Visit). This last play, under direction from **Lavelli**, is about his own death.

ANNIE SPARKS

See also: theatre

Cormann, Enzo

b. 1954, Coublevie

Playwright,
real name Bernard Vergnes

A contemporary and frequently performed
playwright, known for his experimentation
with style and form, particularly monologue.
He is a regular collaborator at the Théâtre
Ouvert. Works include *Noises*, *Corps Perdus*
(Lost Bodies), *Sang et Eau* (Blood and Water),
Takiya! Tokaya! and *Âmes Soeurs* (Sister
Souls).

ANNIE SPARKS

See also: Attoun, Lucien; theatre

Cousin, Gabriel

b. 1918, Droué

Poet and playwright

An ex-sports teacher, who at the age of 40
began writing plays dealing predominantly
with themes such as war, famine and capitalism. He founded a research centre in Grenoble
in 1972, and has experimented with other
artistic forms, such as puppetry, radio drama
and 'total theatre'.

ANNIE SPARKS

See also: theatre

Cousse, Raymond

b. 1942

Writer, actor and playwright

Cousse was a novelist until the 1980s, when he
began to write for the theatre. He is best
known for his dramatic monologues, which he
often performs himself, such as *These Childish
Things* (*Enfantillages*) and *Strategy for Two
Hams* (*Stratégie pour deux jambons*), based on
one of his novels. His writing is influenced by

the **Theatre of the Absurd**, especially **Beckett**,
with whom he corresponded regularly.

ANNIE SPARKS

See also: theatre

Major works

Cousse, R. (1989) *New French Plays*,
Methuen: London (edited by C. Schumacher,
with a translation of *These Childish Things*).

Cresson, Édith

b. 1934, Paris

Politician

Édith Cresson holds the distinction of being the
first woman prime minister of France and of
holding that office for the shortest time in the
history of the Fifth Republic. Born to a well-off
Parisian family, she broke with her background
and became a devoted lieutenant of François
Mitterrand, who would be her patron throughout her political career. She held a series of ministerial offices in the Socialist governments of
the 1980s and established a regional base as
deputy mayor of Châtellerault (Indre et Loire).
Her appointment as prime minister in 1991
owed less to her ministerial achievements, or to
her clout in the Socialist Party, than to her
closeness to Mitterrand and to the latter's
determination to be rid of the incumbent,
Michel **Rocard**. It proved to be a disastrous
miscalculation by both Mitterrand and
Cresson. The new prime minister was unable to
impose her authority on the members of her
government or on the male-dominated preserve
of the higher administration, whose fury she
aroused by insisting that its training school, the
École Nationale d'Administration, should be
moved from Paris to Strasbourg. Although she
was unquestionably the victim of sexism – and
of the sudden decline in the popularity of the
Socialist Party – she lacked communication and

administrative skills and rapidly became the most unpopular prime minister of modern times. Following disastrous regional elections in May 1992, the Socialist Party bosses insisted that she be replaced; in a demonstration of how weak Mitterrand's political authority had become, he reluctantly agreed. It was the end of Cresson's political ambitions, although she received the consolation prize of a portfolio in the Commission of the **European Union** in 1994.

PETER MORRIS

See also: educational elitism: the *grandes écoles*; parties and movements; women and politics

Croix, La

Newspaper

A Catholic daily founded in 1883, and now published by Catholic press group Bayard. This quality newspaper provides broad news coverage, as well as exploring religious matters. Particular importance is attached to debate and dialogue, giving rise to a substantial letters column. Once very right-wing and closely linked to the Catholic hierarchy, in 1956 *La Croix* dropped the crucifix from its front page and has become more open-minded. Christian values are defended, but without religion becoming all-pervasive. Most readers are provincial (75 per cent) and are regular subscribers (93 per cent). In line with declining religious practice, circulation has fallen below 100,000 copies in the 1990s.

PAM MOORES

See also: Catholicism and Protestantism; national press in France

Crozier, Michel

b. 1922, Ste-Ménéhould, Marne

Sociologist

Famous principally for the analysis of French politics and society developed in 1970 in *La Société bloquée* (Stalemated Society), where he portrayed French culture as tolerant of internal pressures for long periods but periodically suffering crises of change and modernization, Crozier has provided insightful studies of politics, society and bureaucracy. The term '*société bloquée*', borrowed from Stanley Hoffmann's description of France as a 'stalemate society', has succeeded in explaining how rigidities and lack of transparency have fostered upheavals such as **May 1968**. Crozier has developed detailed analyses of the French civil service, ranging from his 1964 study *Le Phénomène bureaucratique* (The Bureaucratic Phenomenon) and the 1979 *On ne change pas la société par décret* (Society Does Not Change by Decree), to the 1987 *État modeste, État moderne* (Modest State, Modern State), which influenced government thinking on the reform of the state in the 1990s.

HUGH DAUNCEY

cultural policy

Cultural policy signifies the central and, increasingly, local government measures that are taken to protect and encourage the arts and heritage. These measures concern four areas. The first two are time-honoured spheres of state intervention in France: preserving the national heritage (*conservation du patrimoine*), and providing professional training (*formation*) in such skills as music, the fine arts, conservation and museum management. But at specific moments in its recent history, policy has become more voluntarist, seeking to widen access to the arts (*démocratisation*) or to facilitate the production of new works (*création*). Since 1959, such voluntarism has been the mission of a specific ministry and, since the 1980s, the subject of debate.

Prior to 1959, it is not really appropriate to

speak of a cultural policy at all. With the exceptions of the Popular Front in 1936 and the governments of 1944–7, the liberalism of the Third and Fourth Republics implied an 'arm's length' relationship with the arts, the state's role being largely confined to conservation and training. Furthermore, in official parlance the term 'cultural' had not yet replaced the narrower '*beaux-arts*' (fine arts). *Beaux-arts* came under the gigantic **education ministry** and was overshadowed by it. Little money was spent on the arts and scant attention paid to extending their constituency or commissioning innovative new work. In the standard history, this non-intervention is frequently criticized, though Marc Fumaroli has argued that the greatness of France's cultural achievements during the period belies this view. Nevertheless, abstention came to an end with the Fifth Republic, when de **Gaulle** created a separate department in 1959, the Ministry of State in charge of Cultural Affairs, under a prestigious incumbent, André **Malraux**.

Cultural policy now took on the appearance of a national crusade. Convinced that the heritage of great art was the only salvation for humankind in a godless world and for a divided nation spiritually diminished by mass leisure, Malraux saw his mission in the quasi-religious, unitarian terms which have characterized ministerial discourse ever since. More prosaically, the term *action culturelle* (cultural action) was coined to describe that mission which, as defined in a decree of July 1959, implied three forms of voluntarism.

One was the traditional sphere of conservation, where a number of important measures were taken: the cleaning of Parisian buildings; a programme for restoring historic monuments; the well-known **Malraux act**, creating urban **conservation zones**; and a massive inventory of France's monuments and artistic treasures. But the new ministry also ventured into less traditional territory. Contrary to past practice, Malraux took some tentative steps towards encouraging creation, such as the **avance sur recettes** (1959) which aids innovative new films; or the National Centre for Contemporary Art (1967) which bought bold

new work by little-known visual artists. Malraux's chief form of voluntarism, however, involved democratization, which the left-wing governments of 1936 and 1944–7 had made the touchstone of their short-lived interventionism. Malraux went further, most notably by launching an ambitious programme of regional arts centres, the *maisons de la culture*.

His originality and achievements should not, however, be exaggerated. First, the rapid economic, industrial and technological changes France was undergoing were already foregrounding the cultural in a way governments could not ignore. Indeed, against this backcloth, Malraux's policies appear somewhat modest if not retrograde. His department still retained some of the old *beaux-arts* ways, and his unashamedly disdainful conception of mass leisure already seemed to come from a bygone age. His budget also remained too small to enact many of his ambitions. Furthermore, the upheaval of **May 1968** lambasted his largely unsuccessful democratization policies as bourgeois and paternalistic, though with hindsight what it chiefly highlighted was that they were out of touch. With de Gaulle's resignation in April 1969, Malraux too stood down.

There followed a period of instability for cultural policy, the ministry repeatedly changing its name, status and minister. Under President **Pompidou** (1969–74), 'cultural action' became 'cultural development', according to which the state's responsibility was to encourage the creativity of all in the name of quality of life and economic progress. This implied a more modern, pluralistic definition of culture, embracing the media, the cultural industries and the rich diversity of grassroots practices. Little, however, altered in the ministry's remit. When President **Giscard d'Estaing** came to power in 1974, its standing and its budget declined, though this was partly compensated by the rise in local government spending on the arts, encouraged via a system of contractual agreements with central government called 'cultural charters'. Similarly encouraged were corporate sponsorship and the rapidly expanding cultural industries, in the hope that the market and new technologies would allow reduced state intervention. Yet both Pompidou and Giscard opened up a new sector of state spending by initiating the presidential Grands Projets (grand projects): magnificent new cultural facilities for Paris such as the **Pompidou Centre** and the Musée d'Orsay. By thus scaling down expenditure on local projects while concentrating resources on Paris, Giscard gave the new Socialist Party (Parti Socialiste) under François **Mitterrand** a platform upon which to build an alternative strategy. With his election to the presidency in May 1981, culture became a government priority and the Mitterrand years (1981–95) represent the second great age of cultural policy.

This strategy was based on three priorities: 'irrigation' (e.g. a bill on creative-arts education in schools), decentralization and creation. To pursue it, Mitterrand appointed a controversial **theatre** activist, Jack **Lang,** to the Ministry of Culture (as it was now known) and doubled his budget. In his first budget speech, Lang appeared to lay the high Malraucian conception of culture to rest, building on the notion of cultural development instead. He particularly stressed the need for France to be irrigated by creativity and invention if economic stagnation was to be vanquished. Everything, he claimed, is cultural and, accordingly, everything would be a priority. Unsurprisingly, this non-selective policy was enacted with mixed results.

On decentralization, Lang was reluctant to devolve to local authorities the new funds he had just acquired. Instead, he extended the mid-1970s charters, rechristened 'conventions for cultural development'. He also set up a controversial new Directorate for Cultural Development within his ministry, whose mission was to develop local contacts and encourage the amateur creativity of different communities. Another approach was the emphasis on festive occasions, such as the Fête de la Musique, a national music day introduced in 1982, which urged amateur and professional musicians to make music in the streets. As for creation, Lang ostentatiously protested about American cultural 'imperialism' and spoke up for French creative activities of every kind, particularly those formerly neglected by the state:

rock and pop, comic strips, circus, even French cuisine, earning the policy the pejorative nickname, *le tout-culturel* (everything-cultural). He also began to stress the economic benefits of cultural industries such as **fashion** and of new technologies such as video, computer games or musical software, while new mechanisms to encourage private sponsorship were devised. In the meantime, Mitterrand too was supporting French creation by launching the most extensive programme of Grands Projets so far, designed to promote architectural design, improve access and provide new employment opportunities. The programme included the Louvre Pyramid, the monumental arch of La Défense and a controversial 'popular' opera house at La Bastille.

These new measures, heavily publicized by Lang, did not go unnoticed. Opposition parties complained of the escalating costs of the Grands Projets, neglect of the national cultural heritage, and failure to produce the promised bill on creative-arts education. Many on Left and Right also deplored Mitterrand's high-handed authorization of private **television** channels. Even so, when Lang left office in March 1986 after the Socialist Party's electoral defeat, his successor, the Centrist François **Léotard,** largely continued his work, developing Lang's sponsorship measures by a new act in 1987, and introducing the eagerly awaited creative-arts education bill in 1988. He also prioritized the national cultural heritage and extended the private television sector by selling off **TF1.** In turn, when Lang returned after Mitterrand's 1988 re-election, he left much of Léotard's work intact, continuing to foreground the national heritage, while Mitterrand rounded off his Grands Projets with an expensive new plan for a national library, the Bibliothèque Nationale de France.

Lang left office again in March 1993. Like Léotard, his successors – the Gaullist Jacques Toubon (1993–5) in the Balladur government, President **Chirac**'s first Culture Minister, the Centrist Philippe Douste-Blazy (1995–97) – and the Socialist Catherine Trautmann (1997–) did not substantially undo his achievements which, despite the uproar they initially caused, have been absorbed into the status quo. Toubon's main accomplishments were reinforcing the use of the French language and seeing off the American assault on French audiovisual 'protectionism' during the 1993 GATT (General Agreement on Tariffs and Trade) negotiations, both of which were consistent with Lang's anti-Americanism; as were Douste-Blazy's bid in February 1996 to strengthen the EU directive protecting European audiovisual production, 'Television without frontiers', and his introduction of an obligatory 40 per cent quota of French music on domestic radio in January 1996.

The history of French cultural policy since 1959 is, therefore, one of continuity more than change. A number of persistent themes in fact define its distinctiveness. Part of that distinctiveness is of course the ministry's very existence. This has not been seriously challenged for years, doubtless because of an underlying political consensus about the importance of culture to national identity. A second continuity is the problematic relationship between policies for culture and those concerning the two major influences on cultural life today: education and television. Any cultural policy ignores these influences at its peril. Yet the French education system has traditionally been reluctant to find time for creative activities in schools beyond a theoretical minimum. There are, therefore, those who regret the administrative separation of culture and education in 1959, for neither the Léotard law of 1988 nor a short-lived Ministry of Education and Culture under Lang in 1992–3 adequately addressed the problem. The periodic separation of culture from 'communication', the department responsible for broadcasting, has created similar difficulties, to say nothing of Mitterrand's readiness to privatize broadcasting irrespective of the cultural cost.

One last continuity involves the definition of culture itself, despite a semblance of change under Lang. Much of the hostility he incurred concerned the confusion about aesthetic values which le tout-culturel was deemed to have caused. And yet the distribution of his budgets actually changed little, the lion's share still going to high-cultural activities. Consequently, the need which some identify to design an entirely new policy is still largely intact (as demonstrated by Douste-Blazy's decision in February 1996 to appoint a commission for that purpose). Recent developments in communication and information technologies have brought about new patterns of cultural consumption enabling the French to take their cultural pleasures in the privacy of their homes. It remains to be seen how far these patterns can be reconciled with the ministry's deepest raison d'être, which is to perpetuate a shared national culture.

DAVID LOOSELEY

See also: architecture under Mitterrand; arts funding (including regional); Toubon law; libraries

Further reading

Fumaroli, M. (1991) L'État culturel: essai sur une religion moderne, Paris: Fallois (a polemical but stimulating historical essay).

Looseley, D. L. (1995) The Politics of Fun: Cultural Policy and Debate in Contemporary France, Oxford and Washington, DC: Berg (a broad history since 1936 and a close study of the Mitterrand era).

Mesnard, A.-H. (1990) Droit et politique de la culture, Paris: PUF (a thorough technical analysis of cultural policy legislation).

Rigaud, J. (1995) L'Exception culturelle: culture et pouvoirs sous La Cinquième République, Paris: Grasset (a moderately polemical essay by a cultural administrator).

Wangermée, R. and Gournay, B. (1991) Cultural Policy in France, Strasbourg: Council for Cultural Co-operation (a detailed, informative, outsider's assessment).

cultural topography (Paris)

Paris, like all capital cities, evolved certain geographical districts in which cultural activity was privileged and dominant, depending upon such features as proximity to the university and its attendant **publishing** houses, the provision of artisanal premises which could be used as artists' studios, and a supply of cheap accommodation, bars and restaurants. In the postwar period, the traditional cultural areas continued to operate, albeit with increased or diminished importance.

Montmartre, for example, was massively important in the first years of the century as the centre of the avant-garde under the leadership of its impresario Apollinaire, and in the inter-war years as the headquarters of a radically conservative bohemianism, uniting figures such as Vlaminck, Aymé, Céline, MacOrlan, Dorgelès, Carco, and illustrators and engravers like Gus Bofa, Chas Laborde and Daragnès. Later it still played host to writers and artists, but had considerably less impact, overshadowed by the 'pleasure and crime' of the Place Pigalle and the tourism on the Place du Tertre. Similarly, Montparnasse, which had been a major centre of the visual arts in the last half of the nineteenth century, had welcomed the Cubists when they left Montmartre just before World War I, and was the principal stage for the *années folles* of the 1920s, still retained its cafés and some of its personalities, but was considerably diminished in importance. The major, and last, beneficiary of this process of cultural topographic evolution was also the most permanent: the Quartier Latin, and, especially, St-Germain-des-Près.

From the Middle Ages onwards, the Quartier Latin, with the university and the publishing industry which sprang up around it, was the capital's major cultural centre. In the nineteenth century, joined by the École des Beaux-Arts, it was the context for the dramas of intellectual and artistic ambition of the young Bohemians described in Murger's *Scènes de la vie de bohème*. In the twentieth century, however, importance shifted to St-Germain-des-Près, still dominated by Bohemians and poets, most notably Apollinaire and Léon-Paul Fargue, but increasingly, in the 1930s, by politically committed intellectuals of both Left and Right, with each faction having its preferred café. After the **Liberation**, this tendency became accentuated, to the extent that St-Germain-des-Près achieved considerable, but ambiguous, prominence, even in the popular press. Its left-wing intellectual tradition was maintained by the phemomenon of **existentialism**, whose more serious protagonists used the Café de Flore and the Deux Magots as places to write and debate, and by the dissident communists of the Groupe de la Rue St-Benoît, including Marguerite **Duras** and Edgar **Morin**. The Right continued to occupy its traditional headquarters in the Brasserie Lipp, on the other side of the Boulevard St-Germain, but its younger members, especially the *Hussards*, congregated in the Rhumerie Martiniquaise. The originality of St-Germain-des-Près in the postwar period, however, was that it combined this intellectual and literary activity with an explosion of youth and popular culture, predominantly orchestrated by Boris **Vian**, who played the same role in the 1940s as that played by Apollinaire in the 1900s. The Quartier Latin had become a centre of **youth culture** during the Occupation through the activity of the 'Zazous' and, largely under Vian's influence, this activity became concentrated on St-Germain-des-Près after the war, particularly through the 'caves', of which Le Tabou, opened in 1947, was the prototype: primitive nightclubs which combined American dance, cabaret performance and **jazz**, and in which young Parisians mixed with established writers and intellectuals. While this youth culture proved to be the most vibrant, but also the most ephemeral, ingredient in this cultural mixture, the other two elements, jazz and cabaret, proved more durable. Initially under Vian's influence, Paris increasingly, through the clubs in St-Germain-des-Près, became with New York the foremost jazz centre in the world, welcoming both New Orleans and bebop styles. The young performers in Vian's 'caves' rapidly moved on to the Left Bank music hall, Bobino, and evolved a new style of French popular music, the *chanson Rive Gauche*, which, through singers like Juliette **Gréco**, Léo **Ferré**, Georges **Brassens** and Marcel **Mouloudji**, is still prominent.

Parisian cultural history after the 1950s,

however, is the story of the disappearance, or at best dispersal, of these centres of cultural dominance. The early Left Bank music hall stars moved to the Right Bank, from Bobino to L'Olympia; jazz became available all over the city; and intellectual and literary activity was no longer exclusively situated in one quartier. The reasons for this evolution are both technical and to do with the status of writers and intellectuals. If politically committed intellectuals needed to meet so frequently in particular venues, it was as much to communicate essential ideas and information as to socialize, and that communication was facilitated by, for example, the proliferation of the telephone in France in the 1960s and 1970s. At the same time, technical changes in the print media and the challenges presented to them by the audio-visual media, altered both the modes of communication and the patterns of sociability of the writers and intellectuals. At the same time, the vigour of Parisian cultural centres was diminished by the changing status of the intellectual: freelance or Bohemian intellectuals require places to congregate; professional intellectuals, less so. From the 1950s onwards, there was a marked professionalization of the French intellectual, by which most of the major protagonists operated within the university system. At the same time, the expansion of the University of Paris in the 1960s to Nanterre and Vincennes, and subsequent expansion to other areas of Paris following the Edgar Faure reforms, definitively removed an important monopoly from the Quartier Latin, reinforced by the relocation to the provinces of Grandes Écoles like the École Polytechnique and ENA. This devolution of university activity within the capital was accompanied by a devolution of theatrical activity: both the serious and the popular Parisian theatres, mainly situated on the Right Bank and the Grands Boulevards, have been joined by major theatrical ventures outside of the centre of the city: Les Amandiers at Nanterre, Peter **Brook**'s Bouffes du Nord, the Théâtre de la Villette and the Théâtre Gérard **Philipe** at St-Denis. In this way, if the traditional notion of urban centres of cultural activity has permanently changed, that change

has been accompanied by an erosion of a monopoly which can only be fruitful.

NICHOLAS HEWITT

See also: cultural policy; music venues; theatre

Further reading

Hewitt, N. (1996) 'Shifting Cultural Centres in Twentieth-Century Paris', in M. Sheringham (ed.) *Parisian Fields*, London: Reaktion Books (an account of Paris's cultural topography and its economy).

Cuny, Alain

b. 1908, St-Malo;
d. 1994, Paris

Actor

A great tragic actor, with a rich career in theatre and film. He is especially remembered for his mystic interpretations of Claudel, including his own film of *L'Annonce faite à Marie* (The Good News to Mary) in 1991.

ANNIE SPARKS

See also: theatre

Further reading

Simon, A. (1989) *Alain Cuny: le désir de paroles*, Lyon: La Manufacture (interviews with Cuny).

cycling

Cycling is one of France's most popular sports and the annual road race, the **Tour de France**, attracts millions of spectators. The sport is governed by the Fédération Française de Cyclisme, which was founded in 1945 (its predecessor dates from 1881). While track cycling is much less lucrative, road racing in France is highly commercialized and a huge caravan of sponsors and reporters follows the Tour and the so-called 'Classics' (Paris–Roubaix, Paris–Tours, Paris–Nice, etc.). Outstanding French cyclists of the postwar period include Louis Bobet, Jacques Anquetil, Bernard Thévenet, Laurent Fignon and Bernard Hinault, all winners of the Tour de France on more than one occasion.

IAN PICKUP

See also: sport

Further reading

Noret, A. and Thomas, R. (1980), *Le Cyclisme*, Paris: PUF (an account of the history, development and organization of cycling in France).

D

Da Silva, Éric

b. 1957, Gennevilliers

Playwright, actor and director

The director of L'Emballage Theatre in Paris, Da Silva's career spans twenty years, including **collective creations**, the production of his own plays and the translations of several classics for the Théâtre de la Bastille and Théâtre de Gennevilliers. His plays include *No Man's Man* and *Je ne pourrais pas vivre, si je croyais que je faisais du mal* (I Couldn't Live if I Thought I Was Doing Wrong).

ANNIE SPARKS

See also: theatre

Daeninckx, Didier

b. 1949, Paris

Writer

Born in the working-class district of St-Denis on the northern outskirts of Paris, Daeninckx worked as a printer and local journalist before publishing in 1984 his first successful thriller *Meurtres pour mémoire* (Murders for The Record). His best fiction explores, within the thriller framework, the mechanisms of collective memory and amnesia relating to inglorious episodes in recent French history such as the **Algerian war** or the Occupation – see *La Mort n'oublie personne* (Death Forgets Nobody) of 1989. More recently, his essays have traced the hidden links between extreme Right and extreme Left, promoting his view of an essentially corrupt world occasionally redeemed by individual decency.

JILL FORBES

See also: detective fiction

dance

The dance heritage of France is an extremely rich and long-standing one which dates back to the reign of Louis XIV, where the court ballet reached its height. However, the history of dance in France this century has been somewhat chequered, often leaving French dance trailing behind recent developments in Germany, Britain and (particularly) America, especially with regard to the rise of modern and contemporary dance forms. None the less, the second half of the century has seen a dramatic turn around, enabling dance to have become reputedly the second most popular activity in France after football.

To understand this rapid expansion and the multifaceted nature of the current French dance scene, it is important to address three issues: the dominant role of classical ballet up to the end of the first half of this century; the consequent difficulties encountered by modern dancers mid-century; and the various changes in circumstance that precipitated a contemporary dance boom in the following decades.

Before the 1970s, dance in France was equated with the Paris Opéra and a solid network of ballet companies attached to the regional opera houses, while outside the cities there was a strong tradition of folk dancing. After 1945, the Paris Opéra under Serge Lifar had mostly regained its reputation, while Roland Petit and the dancer Jean Babillée also contributed to the general well-being of French ballet. In addition to remounting the classics, they paid great attention to the appearance of their works, employing artists, designers and couturiers of repute to create stunning visual spectacles that were popular and accessible to new audiences and which reinvigorated classical dance with a neoclassical aesthetic which, while being highly entertaining, ultimately presented few challenges to conservative notions of good taste.

Ballet was entrenched within national culture to the point of being seen as essentially French. Therefore modern dance, which was essentially a revolt against the rules and norms of classical ballet, struggled to gain acceptance both from the establishment and from audiences. Although France had been at the forefront of the revolutionary modern art movements at the beginning of the century and (in dance) had played enthusiastic host to many of the international pioneers of modern dance, the strength of the balletic establishment made it virtually impossible, in the early decades of the postwar period, for modern dancers to challenge. The dynamic focus of the art world was no longer France, but America. Even visits to Paris by the internationally renowned American dancers Martha Graham and Jose Limon were met with unfavourable responses in the 1950s. With no official recognition from the government until 1982, contemporary dance existed on the margins, with scarcely ten companies in existence in the whole of France prior to 1970.

It is generally agreed that the cultural upheaval caused by the events of **May 1968** provided a more fertile ground for contemporary dance not only to establish itself, but also to become a positively flourishing, vibrant and multifaceted art form with a distinctive character of its own on the world dance stage, as well as filling theatres regularly at home. French writers commenting on this phenomenon are fairly unanimous in attributing the rapid expansion of *la danse contemporaine* since 1968 to four general factors.

First, repeated visits to the Théâtre de la Ville in Paris of leading international dance figures such as Martha Graham, Merce Cunningham, Alwin Nikolais and, later, Pina Bausch simultaneously showed up the sorry state of French dance during the 1960s and 1970s, while also generating interest in modern dance and its ideas among audiences. By the end of the 1970s, ticket sales at the Théâtre de la Ville in Paris had risen hugely.

Stylistically, the 'abstraction' of the Americans, evident in particular in Cunningham's ideas about choreography, were major influences on the beginnings of a flourishing French dance scene, and still remain so today. The annual visits to France made by Pina Bausch since the late 1970s have also contributed equally strong aesthetic ideas that bring 'neo-expressionism' and theatricality into the choreographic arena. Whereas generally across the anglophone dance world these two aesthetic standpoints are viewed as being diametrically opposed and distinct from each other, French choreographers have been unafraid to absorb and combine aspects from both schools in original ways.

Second, it is perhaps unsurprising that French audiences of the 1970s should welcome American dancers and choreographers in the post-1968 climate, given that the events of May that year led to a new wave of enthusiasm among the French middle classes for American culture, in particular its youth-oriented and hippie movements (which arrived in France in the early 1970s as the baby boomers came of age). With these cultural changes came a new, more relaxed attitude to the body, and a disillusionment with the bastions of the cultural establishment. In the sphere of dance, this translated into a move away from ballet towards new forms of dance that were more 'free'. Furthermore, in the climate of poststructuralist communication, the body offered a new possibility for conveying meaning. This focus on the body was also catered for in the therapeutic techniques and Oriental disciplines of various martial arts which became popular at this time. In accordance with these general shifts in public attitudes in France, the first summer dance festivals and events catered to the taste of the new large young dance audiences, rather than the bourgeois elites who had frequented the ballet.

Third, although May 1968 represents a watershed, there had already existed French modern dancers working, teaching and striving to gain a voice in French culture. In the atmosphere post-1968, the new audiences generated by international dance performances, together with positive government attitudes towards contemporary dance, opened up new possibilities for dance performances by this early generation of modern dancers. The work of pioneers such as Loudolf Child, Karin Waehner, Jean Weidt and the Dupuys, which had previously struggled to survive in a climate that was hostile, was now set in a new, non-marginal context where gaining an audience, students and recognition was not nearly as difficult as it had been. Their importance should not be overstated, however.

The recent generation of French choreographers owes far more to influences outside of French dance and its history. Jean-Claude Gallotta, a major figure in the French dance scene, comes, like many of his choreographic contemporaries, from a different branch of the arts. Therefore he draws on various artistic sources and philosophical ideas to inspire his choreography, preferring to acknowledge the influences of American techniques, such as that of Merce Cunningham, as a dance source rather than the work or teachings of any French dance pioneers.

Finally, it is undoubtedly the case that the French government can claim a large share of the credit for the French dance boom of the 1980s. Indeed, in comparison with other European countries, the French state has been generous in its funding increases and effective in implementing new cultural policies for dance. The government's changing commitment to dance is apparent in the increasing status of dance within the Ministry of Culture over the last few decades. Dance moved from being a department within a department in 1966, through various changes until the Délégation à la Danse was created in 1987. This functions independently, although it is still grouped with the music department. These organizational changes within the Ministry of Culture have effected changes far away from the corridors of power.

The first significant developments occurred after 1968, when a decentralization policy for dance was sketched out following the pattern developed earlier for the establishment of national drama centres dispersed around the various regions of France. Although the regional dance centres in the main cater for contemporary dance, other forms – such as modern and classical ballet, and baroque dance – are also represented. The first regional dance company installed was the Ballet Théâtre Contemporain at Amiens, followed in the 1970s by five others. Such companies now number seventeen. These centres were set up in addition to the regional opera houses, as partnerships between the choreographer, the local town hall and the performance venue, as a means of spreading dance events around the whole of France.

Another early initiative by the government was the backing in 1969 of the inaugural choreographic festival at Bagnolet, which has become a major international choreographic festival attracting representatives from countries across the world. It serves as a nursery for French choreographic talent and indicates the government's awareness and support for this type of event, of which there are now several: Avignon, Bagnolet, Montpellier, Val de Marne and the Lyon Biennale ranking as the most important. A notable feature of these festivals is the breadth of styles and dance forms which are staged. As well as Western forms of stage dance, Oriental and Asian forms such as

Butoh, Barata Natyam and Kathak are represented, as well as flamenco, folk dance and various forms of street dance, especially hip-hop and break dancing. Some of these events also encompass workshops, pre- and post-performance talks and video showings that allow non-professional dancers, students and the general public to participate more fully, and further develop their interests in dance.

As a result of these circumstances, France has witnessed a remarkable expansion of dance activities over the last few decades which reached its height in the dance boom of the 1980s, and in particular when 1988 was designated as *l'année de la danse*. This expansion has not only been quantitative, but has qualitatively fostered the talents of a whole generation of new choreographers who have felt free to absorb inspiration from a wealth of sources, and to combine apparently antithetical dance ideas in forms that bear witness to a developing cultural diversity in France. With the changes of political climate in the last five years, there has been some shrinkage of dance activities, but as Jack **Lang** has said, 'dance is an irreversible movement' (see Adolphe 1992). It is to be hoped not only that the momentum of the 1980s can be maintained but also that, artistically, French dance will be able to regenerate itself through what could be more difficult times ahead.

FIONA WARNE

See also: Avignon and summer arts festivals; choreographers; cultural policy; dance troupes; poststructuralism

Further reading

Adolphe, J. M. (1992) 'La Nouvelle Danse française', in W. Sorrell (ed.) *The Dance Has Many Faces*, Chicago: Acapella Books (a very good overview of French modern dance with parallel articles on British and German situations as well as chapters outlining the ideas of the pioneers of modern dance through the century).

Au, S. (1988) *Ballet and Modern Dance*, London: Thames and Hudson (a concise, very readable historical overview).

Clarke, M. and Crisp, C. (1973) *Ballet: An Illustrated History*, New York: Universe Books (useful for sections relating to French ballet).

Dance Theatre Journal (1989), 7,1 (summer), London: Laban Centre (this issue was entirely devoted to contemporary French dance).

Lambert, É. (ed.) (1983) *Fous de danse*, Paris: Autrement, série Mutations no. 51 (lots of short articles on a wide variety of dance-related topics).

Robinson, J. (1988) *L'Aventure de la danse moderne en France 1920–1970*, Paris: Diffusion Chiron (in-depth history of pre-dance-boom moderns in France).

dance troupes

While the position of **choreographers** in France is relatively stable, the position of dancers is often much less fortunate, unless they belong to a permanent subsidized company. In terms of the overall distribution, organization and economic situation of ballet and contemporary **dance** companies in France, the role of the Paris Opéra (and Paris in general) as home to dance companies is still an important one, despite the decentralization programme which has continuously promoted regional dance centres alongside the established opera houses to counteract Parisian dominance.

The organization and situation of dance companies in France is quite different from the British situation, where all the major ballet and contemporary companies have identities of their own which are distinct from their commissioned choreographers. In France, a company's identity is generally synonymous with that of their choreographer (often reflected in the company sharing the choreographer's name), because the choreographer's status has been somewhat privileged, and dancers are often employed on a temporary project basis. France does not have a large-scale touring contemporary dance company like Britain's Rambert Dance Company, for example. The stars of France's modern dance world are certainly the choreographers, not the performers.

Among French dance companies, the Paris Opéra has been the focus for theatre dance for several hundred years, and still retains its vital importance today, especially now it is the sole resident of the Palais Garnier Theatre. After a stormy period under Rudolf Nureyev in the 1980s which was not without its highlights, under the directorship of Patrick Dupond the company has found itself tackling not only twentieth-century ballets from the Diaghilev period alongside classics such as *Swan Lake* but also following the example of Nureyev in proving that the stars of the Opéra are equal to the challenges of modern choreography.

In addition to the Paris Opéra, France was also one of the first countries to establish a strong organization throughout the country for ballet in the nine regional opera houses, or the Ballets des Maisons d'Opéra. However, the quality is variable, as full-length performance opportunities are often rare. This results in dancers lacking performance confidence and creates companies that are uneconomically run. Four of the original opera companies have been given new impetus by being redesignated as national choreographic centres. Of these, the Ballet du Rhin in Mulhouse is gaining a good reputation for staging rarely seen works of this century, while the Ballet de Nancy produces classical works on a smaller scale. The Ballet du Nord has expanded its Balanchine repertory to American work and Petit's Ballet de Marseille creates mixed programmes.

Ballet's Parisian orientation is also reflected across genres, with over 60 per cent of the 286 dance companies (both state-subsidized and independent), counted by the Centre National d'Action Musicale (CENAM) in its guide to dance of 1989, working in and around Paris despite the decentralization programme of the last few decades. The decentralization policy relocated some companies, and recommissioned others, to add to the nine municipal ballet companies. The first regional dance company to be installed was the Ballet Théâtre

Contemporain at Amiens in 1969, followed in the 1970s by Théâtre du Silence at La Rochelle, the Ballet du Rhin, Ballets Félix Blaska in Grenoble, the Ballet de Marseille and the Centre National de Danse Contemporaine at Angers. In 1984, the decentralization policy was reinforced and there are now almost twenty national choreographic centres as well as several choreographers and their groups designated as 'associate creators' in various *maisons de la culture*.

To encourage companies to relocate, adequate rehearsing and performing facilities were provided and the policy backed financially by local, regional and national government. In exchange, the companies undertake three-year renewable contracts to make a certain number of new works and to give usually around thirty performances annually. Companies are also responsible for promoting dance across their region through workshops and teaching engagements and by performing in otherwise culturally deprived areas.

While the government funds about 120 dance companies, every year 300–350 funding requests are received. Consequently, many contemporary companies are transitory in nature due to economic difficulties. Therefore, professional dancers often do not enjoy the job security and pension rights of colleagues employed by regional centres and opera houses. Building up a national repertory in these circumstances is very difficult but, conversely, this problem also creates positive cross-fertilization of styles and ideas between companies and choreographers.

In addition to economic insecurities, the close involvement of the government in dance matters means political changes directly affect dance companies. With the National Front taking over three town halls in the south of France, Angelin Prélocaj (whose company was recently given the status of Ballet National Contemporain de Toulon and a base at Chateauvallon's Theatre of Dance and Image) has resigned, along with the theatre's director, in protest at the ultra-right wing's victory in the town hall.

The most stable and well-known contemporary companies are therefore those headed by the leading choreographers, who are often based at national choreographic centres. These include Jean-Claude Gallotta's company Le Groupe Émile Dubois, Philippe Decouflé's Companie DCA, Daniel Larrieu's Askrakan and the Lyon Opéra Ballet headed by Maguy Marin, with Bouvier and Obadia's L'Esquisse quickly becoming a recognizable force on the scene. The groups of other leading choreographers, such as those of Karine Saporta, Odile Duboc, François Raffinot, Hervé Robbe and Catherine Diverrés, take the name of their choreographer.

Therefore, French dance companies depend very much upon the profile and reputation of their choreographer to gain secure funding, but, once established, enjoy fairly stable conditions and a high degree of artistic freedom.

FIONA WARNE

See also: choreographers; dance

Daney, Serge

b. 1944, Paris
d. 1992, Paris

Film critic

Daney was one of France's most individual and influential writers on film. His work, for *Cahiers du cinéma* and *Libération*, is the most substantial interrogation of the difference between watching a film on the big screen and on television or video, as suggested by the titles of his two collections of essays – *The Zapper's Salary* (*Le Salaire du zappeur*) and *Devant la récrudescence des vols de sacs à main* (a reference to the notice displayed in cinemas warning against thieves). His career as film writer and tennis correspondent for *Libération* was curtailed by his death from AIDS.

KEITH READER

See also: cinema

Dasté, Jean

b. 1904, Paris;
d. 1994, St-Étienne

Actor and director

An ex-pupil of Copeau known for his honest, direct approach and a strong supporter of decentralized theatre, Dasté founded France's second Centre Dramatique National in St-Étienne in 1947 and directed it until his retirement in 1970.

ANNIE SPARKS

See also: theatre

Further reading

Dasté, J. (1977) *Voyage d'un comédien*, Paris: Stock (observations on theatre by Dasté).

Debray, Régis

b. 1940, Paris

Intellectual

From his Marxist-Leninist period in the 1970s, through his work as Third World adviser to President **Mitterrand** in the 1980s and thence to his important work on the evolution of the media and the different kinds of ideas and discourses they enable, Debray has been one of the most prominent French thinkers of the last quarter-century. His widely divergent work centres around a series of key themes: the importance of the nation-state; that of the weapons with which it defends and the mediations through which it articulates itself; the necessarily compromised status of the intellectual; and an abiding nostalgia for the now-displaced *culture du verbe*. His imprisonment in Bolivia for three years (the original sentence was thirty) from 1967 focused much attention on *Revolution in the Revolution?* (*Révolution* *dans la révolution?*), a theoretical justification of the Castro-Guevarist strategy of guerrilla warfare. His denunciation of the power exercised by the media over French intellectual life, in *Writers, Teachers, Celebrities* (*Le Pouvoir intellectuel en France*) of 1979, served as the starting point for a sustained examination of different types of mediation and their evolution from 'logosphere', via 'graphosphere', to the contemporary 'videosphere' (*Vie et mort de l'image* of 1992, *L'État séducteur* of 1993). His 1990 defence of an idealized de **Gaulle**, *Charles de Gaulle: Futurist of the Nation* (*A demain de Gaulle*) rests on his admiration for de Gaulle as *homme du verbe* and on their shared belief in the centrality of the nation-state. His novel *La Neige brûle* (The Snow is Burning) won the Prix Femina in 1977.

KEITH READER

See also: literary prizes; Marxism and Marxian thought; May 1968

Further reading

Reader, K. (1995) *Régis Debray*, London: Pluto Press (the only monograph on his life and work).

decolonization

Decolonization is the process whereby the European colonial powers, including France, retreated from their overseas empires in the postwar period, sometimes under peaceful circumstances but often as a result of long and bloody wars.

Although frequently compared unfavourably with Britain's relatively orderly withdrawal from her overseas empire after World War II, French decolonization can by no means be equated simply with the successive wars in Indochina (1945–54) and Algeria (1954–62). For, while the violence in France's two principal colonies cannot be ignored, neither should the real achievements of French decolonization

in sub-Saharan Africa and elsewhere be overlooked. Both the relative successes and the conspicuous failures of French decolonization may be understood in terms of the specificity of the French colonial project on the one hand and the impact on the empire of World War II on the other.

It is a convenient commonplace to contrast the pragmatic mercantilism and indirect rule commonly held to have been the twin foundations of the British imperial edifice, and the assimilationist rhetoric and centralizing practice constitutive of the French colonial enterprise. Rooted in notions of civilizing mission, the much-vaunted project of creating 'the France of a hundred million Frenchmen' may have remained largely mythical, but nevertheless was to constitute an important psychological barrier to decolonization after 1945. Yet, paradoxically, the French colonies had never previously generated anything to compare with the popular imperial enthusiasm so familiar in the British context. Neither private capital nor willing settlers proved to be forthcoming in the volumes necessary for effective colonial consolidation. So, for instance, Algeria, France's foremost colony, would throughout be dominated by the **armed forces** – for whose colonial regiments (and especially the Foreign Legion) it became a spiritual home – and settlers of Spanish, Italian, Maltese and various other non-French origin.

However, the role played by the French empire after the fall of France in June 1940 was radically to transform the perceptions of French policy-makers and the general public alike. In the wake of the armistice, and more particularly General de **Gaulle**'s historic appeal to the French to continue their struggle, the colonies took on a new importance. The rallying to the Free French cause of dependencies in the Indian subcontinent, the Pacific Ocean and sub-Saharan Africa provided de Gaulle with his first real political base, and constituted a potent symbol of national continuity and resistance. With the Allied landings in North Africa in November 1942, France's territories in the Maghreb became a springboard for the forthcoming attack on the southern flank of Hitler's 'fortress Europe' and thus, ultimately, for the **Liberation** of France itself (with colonial troops, both 'European' and 'native', playing a significant part in the Free French contribution to the Allied war effort). De Gaulle's subsequent establishment in Algiers of the French Committee of National Liberation (CFLN), which became the Provisional Government of the French Republic (GPRF), was to provide another powerful symbol of imperial continuity.

The role of the empire, real and symbolic, in the liberation of the 'mother country' encouraged the emergence of an unprecedented colonial consensus after the war. The necessity of maintaining France's overseas territories in order to re-establish the nation's 'great power' status became an article of faith for many veterans of the internal and external Resistance. However, what these policy-makers failed to appreciate was that the colonized peoples of the French empire had drawn directly contradictory conclusions from the wartime spectacle of French military defeat, Occupation and division. Where prewar colonial nationalists had tended to favour legal routes to reform within the French empire, their more militant postwar replacements now looked to full independence. Moreover, they were increasingly prepared to take up arms to achieve this outcome. On the French side, the fact that many soldiers were to be involved in a succession of campaigns spread over a quarter of a century and three continents led to a marginalization and, crucially, a politicization of the officer corps which would ultimately constitute a serious threat to the very existence of the Republic.

Thus, just as the other European powers – led by the British in India – began loosening their military, political and emotional bonds with their colonies, France sought to reimpose its authority on an empire permanently altered by its wartime loss of control. De Gaulle's own thinking on the future of the empire became apparent with the conference organized for the governors of France's tropical African colonies in Brazzaville (Congo) in January 1944. The complete absence of representatives of the African populations of these territories was indicative of the paternalist vision which

inspired the conference's real, but strictly limited rethinking of France's colonial vocation. For what was proposed at Brazzaville was not independence, but rather a measure of administrative decentralization which might eventually lead to limited self-government within a notionally federal structure.

This top-down attempt at colonial modernization was variously prompted by the insights of reformers, the agitation of the increasingly well-organized nationalists and, especially, the avowed hostility to continued colonial rule, in the French empire as elsewhere, of the United States. The new French Union envisaged a rosy colonial future in which 'associated states' would freely consent to continued French control in return for political and economic concessions. However, such thinking was fatally outmoded in an age when the self-affirmation of the colonized peoples was daily becoming more apparent. Leading French intellectuals such as Jean-Paul **Sartre** were instrumental in drawing attention to the political implications of cultural movements such as the *négritude* championed by Léopold Sédar Senghor in Senegal and Aimé **Césaire** in Martinique, while the elected representatives of newly enfranchised colonial voters such as Félix Houphouët-Boigny in the Ivory Coast and Lamine Gueye in Senegal gave a fresh voice to colonial aspirations. Other signs of the strength of the decolonizing 'winds of change' blowing in this period included some particularly vicious clashes between colonizers and colonized, of which the most bloody – and most ruthlessly suppressed – occurred in the Sétif region of Algeria in May 1945 and Madagascar in 1947–8. However, it was in Indochina that the opposition to France's attempted reimposition of its colonial authority was to manifest itself most violently.

Having lost effective control of its Southeast Asian 'protectorate' with the Japanese invasion in July 1941, French armed forces were unable to participate in the liberation of the territory in August–September 1945. This role fell instead to the indigenous nationalist resistance, supported, very ironically in the light of later developments, by the United States. On 2

September 1945, the Viet Minh's leader Nguyen Ai Quoc, better known as Ho Chi Minh, proclaimed the independence from France of the Republic of Vietnam; a move which, following the breakdown of negotiations between the two sides, was to lead directly to war. After an eight-year jungle conflict, the French army was catastrophically defeated at **Dien Biên Phu** on 7 May 1954. Although the peace agreements that sealed the French withdrawal were signed before the end of July, neither Vietnam nor France would be at peace for long: Vietnam would soon be obliged to engage the military might of the United States as the priorities of the Cold War replaced the latter's erstwhile decolonizing zeal; France, for its part, would end one colonial war only to embark on another.

The **Algerian war** represents the greatest failure of French colonial policy after 1945. The effective autonomy enjoyed by the governing coalition of settlers and soldiers in Algeria meant that even the most moderate reforms belatedly proposed by Paris could without difficulty be blocked or circumvented on the ground. In the face of such intransigence, the Algerian nationalists – including many who, like future president Ahmed Ben Bella, had wartime experience in the French army – had little option but to launch an armed struggle for independence. When the war of national liberation finally began on 1 November 1954, Algeria's special status as France's most economically, politically, administratively and psychologically assimilated overseas territory meant that the government of Pierre **Mendès France**, recently elected precisely to extricate France from the débâcle in Indochina, opted without hesitation to use force in response to the nationalists' demands. Such was the determination of François **Mitterrand** (Minister of the Interior at the time) to defend *Algérie française* that he ordered the mobilization of conscripts for military service in Algeria, something which had never been done in Indochina. Once set on this course, it proved impossible for the chronically unstable governments of the Fourth Republic to overcome the momentum generated by the war, as the **Mollet** adminis-

tration's involvement in the Suez fiasco of 1956 graphically demonstrated. So, whereas Morocco and Tunisia were permitted to accede to independence with relative ease in 1956, France's principal colony was to remain gripped by a conflict which is still a source of heated debate in France and which may straightforwardly be linked to the vicious civil war being waged in Algeria today between the successors to the FLN and Islamic fundamentalists.

It was only with de Gaulle's return to power in 1958 that a way out of the Algerian impasse became possible. The ability of de Gaulle accurately to identify the stalemate in Algeria, coupled with his determination to shift metropolitan public opinion decisively away from an imperial conception of French *grandeur* and towards a modern and Europe-centred one, meant that he was ultimately able to prevail over the supporters of *Algérie française*. De Gaulle was undoubtedly helped in this task by the series of revelations which had been made concerning the abhorrent 'pacification' methods used by the army in Algeria – often by returning conscripts and relayed by sections of the French press, despite strict government censorship – and which led to concerted antiwar campaigning by such contrasting intellectuals as Sartre and François Mauriac.

The Évian agreements which eventually concluded the war included temporary guarantees for preferential French access to newly discovered oil and gas deposits in the Sahara desert, as well as the continued use of certain military and naval installations. They also included provisions for the future of Algeria's European population. However, the scorched-earth policy implemented by the European terrorists of the Organisation Armée Secrète (OAS) rendered inevitable the exodus of a million settlers in considerable confusion and panic. Never envisaged by de Gaulle or his negotiators, this massive transfer of population was only made possible by the booming French economy. In a period of full employment, the *pieds-noirs* were assimilated remarkably rapidly into metropolitan French society.

If the Évian agreements proved to be a dead letter, de Gaulle's attempts at orderly decolonization were more successful in sub-Saharan Africa, where they have resulted in the maintenance of a real economic and cultural influence, often as well as a significant military presence. While the truly federal 'French Community' outlined by de Gaulle never came into being, its notional existence allowed the rapid achievement of full independence by the territories involved, while continued French economic and technical assistance have provided the basis of the modern project of co-operation most often referred to nowadays as *la francophonie*. In a few cases, of course, the avowed French project of assimilation was actually carried through, with such fragments of the colonial empire as Martinique and Guadeloupe now firmly established as fully integrated overseas *départements* or territories (DOM-TOMs).

PHILIP DINE

Further reading

Ageron, C.-R. (1991) *La Décolonisation française*, Paris: Armand Colin (a concise French-language account).

Clayton, A. (1994) *The Wars of French Decolonization*, London: Longman (best and most up-to-date English-language account).

Hargreaves, J. (1996) *Decolonization in Africa*, 2nd edition, London: Longman.

Kahler, M. (1986) *Decolonization in Britain and France: The Domestic Consequences of International Relations*, Princeton, NJ: Princeton University Press.

Marseille, J. (1986) *Empire colonial et capitalisme français: histoire d'un divorce*, Paris: Albin Michel.

Pervillé, G. (1991) *De l'empire français à la décolonisation*, Paris: Hachette.

Ruscio, A. (1987) *La Décolonisation tragique, 1945–1962*, Paris: Messidor/Éditions Sociales.

Decroux, Étienne

b. 1898, Paris;
d. 1991, Boulogne

Actor and mime expert

An actor famous for pioneering physical theatre and **mime**, who worked with many famous theatre directors including Copeau and **Barrault**, as well as in films such as Carné's *Les Enfants du Paradis*. After the war, he opened his own school, and produced famous *mimodrames* such as *Les Arbres* (The Trees), *L'Usine* (The Factory) and *Le Combat antique d'Antoine et Cléopatre* (The Ancient Struggle between Antony and Cleopatra).

ANNIE SPARKS

See also: theatre

defence and security

French security policy since 1945 has paralleled France's modernization, mirroring changes in **foreign policy** and moves towards European union. The nuclear deterrent and conventional capabilities created by de **Gaulle** and their associated security strategies have driven important developments in French society and political culture. In the post-Cold War international system, France is attempting to redefine its security stance.

In the late 1940s and early 1950s, France recognized that, despite traditional enmity with Germany, the USSR was now the foe. This culture shift was not universally shared, particularly by some on the Right, but French support for NATO (1949) illustrated new realities. During incipient European integration, France's ambiguous (and finally fatal) attitude towards the EDC (1954) showed persisting mistrust of Germany and French desire for independent control over her **armed forces**. Until after the **Algerian war** (1954–62), defence required forces capable of waging colonial wars: in Indochina (1947–54) the professional army lost at **Dien Biên Phu** (1954); in Algeria, the use of *appelés* (young conscripts) to support professional troops changed public perceptions of the conflict. After defeat in Indochina and withdrawal from Algeria, de Gaulle used the technological modernization of defence through the **Force de frappe** to restore army self-esteem. The technological effort devoted to France's nuclear capability catalysed many aspects of industry and the economy, and the importance of the president as final arbiter of deployment reinforced defence as a 'reserved domain' of the presidency and further rigidified political authority. France has retained strong links with former colonies and has thus maintained the capability to intervene in African conflicts (such as Chad in 1984).

Deterrence has underpinned French defence policy since the 1960s, at the cost of maintaining land-, air- and sea-based missiles, conventional forces and young national servicemen, although the conventional forces have been subsidized by a highly developed arms industry. The vaunted independence of nuclear capability has enabled foreign policy, based on *indépendance nationale* from superpowers and on the safety of France. In the 1960s, the importance of sovereignty was illustrated by France's withdrawal from operational participation in NATO (1966) and by the (proposed) strategy of *tous azimuts* (360-degree) targeting for nuclear weapons (1968), intended to show total freedom. Security has been seen as a choice between independence (an extreme being the *sanctuarisation* of France), and collaboration with other countries (usually within NATO). In the 1970s, **Giscard d'Estaing** tried to compromise with *sanctuarisation élargie* (enlarged strategic space), attack against which would be attack against France herself, but Gaullist doctrines continued. Under **Mitterrand**, stand-alone policy persisted (conceding to NATO over Pershing-II and Cruise, and with minor Franco-German military co-operation), and some priorities changed after German reunification. In the 1990s, reviews of strategy and strict control of defence spending have identified needs such as spatial reconnaissance and communications. The planned withdrawal of national service in the last few years of the millennium, giving a smaller and cheaper professional army, illustrates new financial and strategic realities, the changing place of defence in French society and a transformation of citizens' relationship to the nation.

HUGH DAUNCEY

See also: decolonization; European Union

Further reading

Aldrich, R. and Connell, J. (eds) (1989) *France in World Politics*, London: Routledge & KeganPaul (the beginnings of current debates).

Deguy, Michel

b. 1930, Paris

Poet, translator, critic and theorist

Deguy is in many ways a truly experimental poet. His earliest interest was philosophy, which he taught from 1953 to 1968. He regards poetry as a mode of knowledge – for example, *Actes* (Deeds) of 1966 – and wishes to make it reflect the ambiguity of our world; hence he can call ruins a 'spiritual contour' in one of his poems. The earliest collections are *Fragments du cadastre* (Fragments of Land Survey) in 1960, 1962's *Poèmes de la presqu'île* (Poems of the Peninsula) and *Biefs* (Canal-Levels) of 1964, followed by the collection with the suggestive title of *Ouï dire* (Hear Say) in 1966. In later collections, such as *Figurations* (1969), he proposes a new kind of poem, the *poème sourd* (mute poem), gravitating between prose and verse as a means of providing a meeting ground for language and philosophy.

WALTER A. STRAUSS

See also: poetry

Deixonne law

Passed in the National Assembly in 1951, this law, named after a *Député* from Brittany, signalled the first postwar concession to regionalism, symbolized by language, and ensured that for the first time since the Revolution regional languages – as opposed to foreign languages like German – could be taught in the public educational system. The law allowed the teaching of only four regional languages (Basque, Breton, Catalan, Occitan) for up to three hours per week, although success in them could not count towards passing the *baccalauréat*. The ministerial circular applying the law's provisions did not appear until 1969; Corsican had to wait until 1974, and other regional languages have followed slowly since.

DENNIS AGER

See also: language and the French regions; regional writing: Breton; Occitan

Delanoë, Pierre

b. 1918, Paris

Lyricist, real name Pierre Leroyer

Having been programme director of the radio station Europe 1 from 1955 to 1960, Pierre Delanoë wrote the words of songs for Gilbert Bécaud (*Nathalie*, *L'Orange*) and later for a whole host of popular singers including André Claveau, the Compagnons de la chanson, Hugues Aufray, Michel Sardou and Gérard Lenorman. He is one of the most prolific and admired French lyricists of the postwar period.

IAN PICKUP

See also: song/*chanson*

Deleuze, Gilles

b. 1925, Paris;
d. 1995, Paris

Intellectual and philosopher

Deleuze was, along with Michel Foucault and Jacques Derrida, one of the most celebrated poststructuralist thinkers in France. He gained his *agrégation* in philosophy in 1948, and in 1969 he was appointed professor of philosophy at Vincennes.

Deleuze began his career by writing a series of monographs on philosophers, such as Hume, Kant, Bergson, Nietzsche and Spinoza, along with studies of Proust and Sacher-Masoch. He traces an alternative pathway through the history of philosophy with these figures, finding something 'untimely' or 'non-philosophical' in each of them. For example, Spinoza and Nietzsche introduce the question of the body into philosophy; Proust challenges the idea that the mind is naturally inclined towards truth, claiming that only the sign can shock thought out of its habitual stupor; and the figure of Nietzsche is pivotal in this period as a radically anti-dialectical, pluralist thinker who is suspicious of stable identities.

In the second period of his career, Deleuze began to develop his own philosophy of difference and multiplicity. In *Difference and Repetition (Différence et répétition)* he drew upon an eclectic series of philosophical, literary and scientific sources to produce non-linear studies of meaning which questioned the dominance of the category of 'sameness' and identity. In the 1970s Deleuze entered into a period of collaboration with the radical psychiatrist and psychoanalyst Félix Guattari, and the writing of *Anti-Oedipus (L'Anti-Œdipe)*, the first volume of a two-volume study of 'capitalism and schizophrenia', which was published in France in 1972, constituted a practical experiment with the identity of the author. As Deleuze commented in the late 1970s, 'we do not work together, we work between the two'. *L'Anti-Œdipe* emerged from the questions posed by the events of May 1968 in France, and provided the authors with temporary fame. They argue that desire is prior to representation, in that it constantly escapes and 'deterritorializes' the Oedipal model. Deleuze and Guattari have subsequently been criticized for idealizing the anarchic, 'desiring' potential of the schizophrenic. The second volume of the capitalism and schizophrenia project, published in 1980, concentrated on the study of 'rhizomatic', acentred structures.

In the third phase of his career, throughout the 1980s and up to his suicide in 1995, Deleuze continued to collaborate occasionally with Guattari. He also turned increasingly to aesthetic questions, publishing a study of the painter Francis Bacon and a well-received two-volume study of cinema in the mid-1980s. Deleuze returns to Bergson to show how cinema at its best can correspond to a new type of thought which resists the spatializing tendency of the intellect; the 'movement-image' of early cinema and the 'time-image' of postwar cinema represent new ways of thinking aesthetically. In 1991 Deleuze published his final major work, *What is Philosophy?* (*Qu'est-ce que la philosophie?*), which was, appropriately enough, a collaboration with Guattari. Demonstrating the continuing influence of Nietzsche, they argue that the true objective of philosophy is neither communication nor reflection, but rather the creation of concepts.

JOHN MARKS

See also: cinema; poststructuralism; psycho-analysis

Further reading

Boundas, C. V. (ed.) (1993) *The Deleuze Reader*, Oxford: Columbia University Press (an edited collection of important extracts, with an informative introduction to Deleuze's work).

Delon, Alain

b.1935, Paris

Actor

One of the great **stars**, his career has been inter-

national from the start, with major roles in films by Visconti and Antonioni in the 1960s. He is best known as the archetypal hero of the police thriller, the best example being **Melville's** cult *Le Samourai* (1967). By the 1970s, his roles were stereotyped, and it was not until the late 1970s that he found roles worthy of his considerable talents: the hero of Losey's *Monsieur Klein* (1976), Baron Charlus in Schlöndorff's *Swann in Love* (1984), the hero of **Blier's** *Notre Histoire* (1984) and **Godard's** *Nouvelle Vague* (1990).

PHIL POWRIE

See also: cinema

Delors, Jacques

b. 1925, Paris

Politician

A Christian Socialist, Delors began his career at the Bank of France (1945–62), worked at the Planning Commissariat (1962–9) and acted as adviser on social affairs to Gaullist premier **Chaban-Delmas** (1969–72). He joined the Parti Socialiste in 1974. Never a member of the National Assembly, he was elected to the European parliament in 1979. As Finance Minister between 1981 and 1984 he endorsed the adoption of a policy of monetary 'rigour', and as president of the European Commission from 1985 to 1995 he was a tireless advocate of European integration. Mooted as a possible Socialist candidate for the 1995 presidential election (with a strong chance of winning), he finally declined to stand.

LAURENCE BELL

See also: **banks**; European Union; Gaulle, Charles de; parties and movements

Major works

Delors, J. (1994) *L'Unité d'un homme*, Paris:

Odile Jacob (a series of interviews with a journalist).

Delphy, Christine

b. 1941, France

Feminist academic

Christine Delphy has been one of the leading activists in the French women's liberation movement and close to Simone de **Beauvoir**. Her work has focused on the feminist 'discovery' of housework as being the material basis of women's oppression and therefore central to understanding the nature of patriarchy. Delphy is firmly social constructionist in her approach and she has sought to combat the 'essentialist' feminist ideas of **Psych et Po**, more often associated with French feminism, particularly through her editorship of the journal *Questions féministes*.

JAN WINDEBANK

See also: feminism; feminist thought

Further reading

Jackson, S. (1996) *Christine Delphy*, London: Sage (a discussion of the development of Delphy's theoretical perspective).

Demarcy, Richard

b. 1942, Bosc-Roger en Roumois

Playwright, adaptor and director

Founder of the Naïf Théâtre Atelier for contemporary creation in 1972, Demarcy's plays deal with myth, and social and historical observations, such as the Portuguese Civil War in *Quatre Soldats et un accordéon* (Four Soldiers

and an Accordion) and social decay in *La Nuit du père* (Night of the father). His adaptations include Lewis Carroll's *Hunting of the Snark* (*Disparitions*) and Pessoa's *Ode Maritime*.

ANNIE SPARKS

See also: theatre

Major works

Demarcy, R. (1973) *Éléments d'une sociologie du spectacle*, Paris: Union Générale d'Éditions (Demarcy's published thesis).

demographic developments

After Germany, France is (with Italy and the United Kingdom) one of the largest **European Union** (EU) member-states in terms of population size. In 1995, total population had reached over 58 million, representing an increase of some 18 million in half a century. France remains, however, much less densely populated than its north European neighbours: with an average of nearly 106 inhabitants per square kilometre, it is one of the least densely populated EU member-states. Its density is less than half that of the United Kingdom, and well under a quarter that of the Netherlands. Although, by the 1990s, over 80 per cent of French people lived in towns, and Paris continued to dwarf other major cities, France is also less urbanized than its neighbours.

Over the postwar period, procedures for recording, monitoring and evaluating population size and structure have been refined. In France, the Institut National d'Études Démographiques (INED) and the Institut National de la Statistique et des Études Économiques (INSEE) were established in the mid-1940s to co-ordinate national data collection and report to the government on demographic matters. These organizations are responsible for conducting regular population censuses and surveys and for carrying out demographic studies. France has a long tradition of concern about population decline, and policy makers are interested in tracking and understanding growth and change in the composition of population by age, sex, marital and socio-occupational status and ethnic origin.

Many of the features characteristic of the French population in the twentieth century were already present at the turn of the century. Compared with its neighbours, France was well advanced in the demographic transition from high to low mortality and birth rates, primarily as a result of voluntary birth control and medical and social advances in the care of infants and young children. In less than a century, life expectancy at birth has increased by thirty years: at birth, men in France may expect to live almost to the age of 74, and women to 82 (the largest age difference between men and women among EU member-states). Over the same time span, infant mortality rates have fallen dramatically from above 160 to below 6.5 deaths per 1,000 live births.

The second half of the twentieth century has been marked by fluctuations in family building patterns. In the immediate postwar years, France shared with its neighbours a significant increase in birth rates, described as the 'baby boom'. A peak was reached in 1946 for total fertility rates, with 2.98 children per woman. From the mid-1960s, the birth rate fell, and family size decreased. In the 1990s, France was still above the European average, with a fertility rate of 1.66, but below the replacement level needed to ensure continued population growth. The fall in birth rates has been attributed to a number of factors, in particular the widespread use of effective forms of contraception combined with changing aspirations. By the 1990s, fewer couples were choosing to have two children than one child, but France remained above the European average for the proportion of couples with three and four children. While most French women are producing a smaller number of children, fewer women are remaining childless: about 10 per cent of the women born in the early 1940s will have no children, compared with 20 per cent half a century earlier.

The continued growth in population size can be explained by the combined effect of the reduction in mortality rates, the increase in the number of women of child-bearing age (the baby boomers) and **immigration**. Between 1955 and 1971, during the years of economic expansion (*les trente glorieuses*), immigration was encouraged to bolster the workforce. It was fuelled by **decolonization**, particularly in 1962 with the repatriation from Algeria following independence. From 1974, as France entered recession in the wake of the oil crises, restrictions were introduced to curb immigration, resulting in the stabilization of the foreign population, which accounted for 6.3 per cent of total population in the mid-1990s.

The effect of declining birth rates at a time of increasing life expectancy was to stimulate population ageing. The second half of the twentieth century has seen continuing change in the age structure of the population as the baby boomers move through the generations. The proportion of young people (under 20) has fallen slightly from 29.5 per cent in 1946 to 26.8 per cent in 1993, while the population over 60 (statutory retirement age) has risen from 16.0 to 19.7 per cent, and that over the age of 75 from 3.4 to 6.3 per cent. The proportion of the population of working age (20 to 59 years), after falling between 1965 and 1975, has regained its 1950 level with 53.6 per cent. Because of the intensity of the baby boom, the full effect of population ageing will not, however, be felt in France until the year 2020, when the baby boomers have reached retirement age. Already by the mid-1990s, care for older people was recognized as a growing social problem. Because female life expectancy is greater than that of men, women are over-represented among older people. They are also less likely to have contributed to occupational pension schemes and are, therefore, expected to place an increasingly heavy financial and physical burden on a diminishing population of working age.

LINDA HANTRAIS

See also: abortion/contraception; family; social policy; social security; women and employment; women and social policy

Further reading

Eurostat, *Demographic Statistics*, Luxembourg: Office for Official Publications of the European Communities (an annual publication providing data on demographic trends across the European Union).

INED, *Population et sociétés*, Paris: INED (a regular monthly publication providing succinct updates on population issues).

INSEE (1996) *Données sociales 1996: la société française*, Paris: INSEE (an analytical and statistical account of demographic trends in France, with a focus, in this issue, on the twentieth century).

Demy, Jacques

b. 1931, Pontchâteau;
d. 1990, Paris

Director

Demy was the only major postwar French director of musical films. Most famous of these is *Les Parapluies de Cherbourg* (1964), with Catherine **Deneuve**, in which every line of 'dialogue', grand-opera fashion, is sung. Michel Legrand's music was a key element in this and other Demy musicals (*Les Demoiselles de Rochefort* of 1967). For many, however, his finest work is to be found in the non-musical dramas *Lola* (1961) and *La Baie des anges* (1963), starring Anouk **Aimée** and Jeanne **Moreau** respectively. His love of the seaport towns of western France, such as Nantes (the setting for *Lola*) and Cherbourg, makes him a regionalist poet of the cinema. His wife Agnès **Varda** devoted a documentary farewell to him – *Jacquot* (also known as *Jacquot de Nantes*) – in 1991.

KEITH READER

See also: cinema

Deneuve, Catherine

b. 1943, Paris

Actor

She began her career as the rather insipid 'girl next door' in **Demy**'s *Les Parapluies de Cherbourg* (1964), but was soon to reveal greater dramatic potential as the schizophrenic blonde in peril in Roman Polanski's meta-Hitchcockian *Repulsion* of the following year. It was in her work for **Truffaut** (*La Sirène du Mississippi* in 1969) and Luis Buñuel – *Belle de jour* of 1967 and *Tristana* of 1970 – that her icy self-possession hinting at intense disturbance beneath the surface was most fully realized. Her 1970s career lacked consistency and featured a number of comedies that were neither commercial nor critical successes, but her dramatic potential came to the fore with the approach of middle age. Opposite **Depardieu** in Truffaut's *Le Dernier Métro* of 1980 she showed real poise and command, as the theatre director's wife keeping the show running and her Jewish husband safe in the cellar – a resolution of the conflicts and contradictions of Occupation, which doubtless contributed greatly to her status as national icon. The following year she gave a moving performance (for **Téchiné** in *Hôtel des Amériques*) as the woman imprisoned by her love for a man now dead. Téchiné's *Ma saison préférée* of 1993 gave her one of her most demanding dramatic roles, as a surgeon whose marriage and family relationships are in crisis. The extent to which her once scandalous persona as mother of illegitimate children with Roger **Vadim** and Marcello Mastroianni has mellowed and become accepted is illustrated by the choice of her to succeed Brigitte **Bardot** as the model for 'Marianne', the icon of the French Republic, in 1985.

KEITH READER

See also: cinema; stars

Denis, Claire

b. 1948, Paris

Director, screenwriter and actor

Claire Denis achieved international success in 1988 with her first film, *Chocolat*, a semi-autobiographical reflection on growing up in colonial Cameroon. Subsequent films further address the dispossessed black (male) subject: *S'en fout la mort* (1990), an obsessive study of illegal cock-fighting in Rungis, and *J'ai pas sommeil* (1993), based on mass murderer Thierry Paulin, a gay transvestite African Caribbean with **AIDS**. In two low-budget art films, *US Go Home* (1994) and *Nénette et Boni* (1997), Denis focuses engagingly on relationships between teenage brother and sister. Her style owes much to close collaboration with actors and with camerawoman Agnès Goddard.

CARRIE TARR

See also: women directors

Depardieu, Gérard

b. 1948, Châteauroux

Actor

Depardieu is the heir to Jean Gabin and Jean-Paul **Belmondo**. Famous for his energy, he has sometimes made as many as five films a year in his thirty-year career of some seventy-five films (to 1996). His image is complex: he stars in auteurist films, big-budget spectaculars, popular comedies. In his early career, his roles were mainly comic and proletarian, the best example being **Blier**'s provocative *Les Valseuses* (1974), a consciously misogynistic road/buddy movie, informed by the rebellious post-**May 1968** spirit of the **café theatre**, in which Depardieu and **Dewaere** play delinquents or *loubards*. Depardieu starred in a number of Blier films subsequently: *Buffet froid* (1979), *Trop belle*

pour toi (1989), *Merci la vie* (1991) and, especially, *Tenue de soirée* (1986), a remake of the *ménage à trois* of *Les Valseuses*, again with **Miou-Miou**, and Michel **Blanc** replacing Dewaere. (Depardieu, his aggressive masculinity sufficiently well-anchored, plays a gay drag queen.) Other more popular comic triumphs are the three extremely successful films with Pierre Richard, directed by Veber: *La Chèvre* (1981), *Les Compères* (1983) and *Les Fugitifs* (1986). He also acted in auteur cinema, with roles in several films by **Duras**, **Resnais**, **Truffaut** (*Le Dernier Métro* in 1980, for which he received a César, and *La Femme d'à côté* from 1981, in which he starred with **Ardant**), and especially **Pialat** (*Loulou* in 1980; *Police* in 1985; *Sous le soleil de Satan* in 1987). In such films he is the 'suffering macho man' (Vincendeau 1993: 351), playing on a masculine aggressivity tempered by his often-proclaimed 'femininity'. Predictably, his least favourite film, judging from the vituperative comments in his *Lettres volées* (1990), is Ferreri's *La Dernière Femme* (1976), where he plays an aggressive male who refuses to understand **feminism** and castrates himself. He has said that his favourite film is Vigne's *Le Retour de Martin Guerre* (1982), where he is Nathalie **Baye**'s lover in the context of rural medieval France. The return to the land or to 'authentic' roots forms a strong part of his star image from the 1980s, evidenced in **Berri**'s *Jean de Florette* (1986), and other heritage spectaculars (Berri's *Germinal* of 1993; Angelo's *Le Colonel Chabert* of 1994). His complex star image can be seen in the combination of several films made in 1990–1: one of the best-selling French films, **Rappeneau**'s *Cyrano de Bergerac*, in which he plays the swaggering hero with a melancholic sensitive side; another literary adaptation, Berri's *Uranus*, in which he is a loud-mouthed café owner with literary pretensions; an American comedy, Weir's *Green Card*; and a French comedy, Lauzier's *Mon père ce héros*, where he is both father and mother to his adolescent daughter, a film remade in Hollywood with him as star in 1994.

PHIL POWRIE

See also: cinema; stars

Major works

Depardieu, G. (1990) *Lettres volées*, Paris: Livre de Poche (a semi-autobiography in the form of letters addressed to parents, industry colleagues and others; originally published 1988).

Further reading

Gray, M. (1991) *Depardieu: A Biography*, London: Warner Books.
Vincendeau, G. (1993) 'Gérard Depardieu: The Axiom of Contemporary French Cinema', *Screen* 34, 4: 343–61 (a brilliant star analysis).

Derrida, Jacques

b. 1930, Algiers

Philosopher

The most celebrated and influential of contemporary French philosophers. Derrida studied at the prestigious École Normale Supérieure in Paris and was a teacher there for some twenty years (1964–84) before moving to the École Pratique des Hautes Études in 1984. He was the founding president of the Collège Internationale de Philosophie in 1983 and has also held a number of visiting professorships in the USA.

Like most philosophers of his generation, Derrida was thoroughly acquainted with the German phenomenological tradition (Hegel, Husserl, Heidegger) which had been the principal source of inspiration for existentialism. His first published work in 1962 was an important introduction to the translation of Edmund Husserl's *Origin of Geometry*. *Voice and Phenomenon* (*La Voix et le phénomène*), also on Husserl, followed in 1967. Derrida's reading of Husserl had little in common with ortho-

dox existentialist interpretations, however, and was in certain respects closer to the preoccupations of **structuralism**. Two ground-breaking works were also published in 1967: *Of Grammatology* (*De la grammatologie*) and *Writing and Difference* (*L'Écriture et la différence*). Derrida's thinking in these texts crystallized around the concept of writing. His argument, best exemplified in the systematic and scholarly demonstration of *De la grammatologie*, was that throughout the history of Western thought writing had consistently been cast in a role subordinate to that of speech. Whereas speech was associated with reason and rationality (Greek: *logos*), the voice being closer to the inner 'truth' of individual consciousness, writing was viewed as an artificial extension or supplement to the voice, an auxiliary technology employed by human reason but not essential to it. Derrida's critique of this repression of writing or 'logocentrism' takes the form of close readings of thinkers representing different 'moments' of the logocentric tradition: Plato, Leibniz, Rousseau, Saussure, **Lévi-Strauss**. In each case he shows how arguments predicated on the exclusion of writing are in fact essentially dependent upon it. In addition to this, he proposes a more fundamental form of 'writing' that is the precondition of both speech and writing and indeed all cultural and communication systems.

Derrida's choice of Saussure, and especially of Lévi-Strauss, as examples of logocentric philosophy clearly had a polemical side, given the intellectual predominance of structuralism in France at the time. While Derrida recognized the important theoretical contribution of structuralism, he was critical of its reductionism. More generally, he questioned the claims of structuralism and the human sciences to have transcended the problems of traditional philosophy, arguing that the very discourse of the human sciences was dependent on unexamined presuppositions inherited from that tradition. Derrida's critique of the human sciences provided philosophy with a powerful alternative to the humanist-existentialist critique, whose success in checking the advance of structuralism had been limited; historically, it could be said to mark the beginning of **poststructuralism**.

It was not only the content of Derrida's theory of writing and his critique of logocentrism that was so influential in the intellectual debates of the late 1960s, but equally his style of analysis, the critical approach he called 'deconstruction'. Deconstruction involved a rigorous working through of the argumentative and rhetorical structures of the texts selected as examples or 'symptoms' of the logocentric tradition. Here, it was not so much a question of demolishing a philosophical opponent as revealing the problematic tensions and contradictions within a given text. At the same time, deconstruction involved a reflexive and critical awareness of its own discourse, and a systematic resistance to the reification and instrumentalization of its concepts. The result is that much of Derrida's writing has a rhetorical quality that distinguishes it from more conventional philosophical discourse. This rhetorical dimension is most apparent in the more experimental texts of the 1970s, such as *Dissemination* (*La Dissémination*), *Glas* and *The Post Card* (*La Carte postale*). The text of *Glas*, for example, consists of two parallel columns; one a reading of Hegel, the other of the writer Jean **Genet**. While separate, the two commentaries converge and interfere in their exploration of the themes of biology, sexuality, the family and the state, the reading of Genet in particular depending on a complex system of puns and linguistic assimilations. Similarly unconventional is the quasi-autobiographical account that opens *La Carte postale*, offering an extremely sophisticated meditation on Freud, reproduction and communications technologies through its narrative of the author's repeated attempts to contact his distant partner.

As these brief examples indicate, a preoccupation with language and literature is central to Derrida's philosophy. While his deconstructive readings of philosophical texts practise the kind of close linguistic commentary normally associated with literary analysis, he frequently turns to literary texts (Genet, Baudelaire, Mallarmé) as a source of philosophical reflection. For Derrida, what is interesting about complex symbolic systems such as language and fiction is their autonomy and mutability, their non-finalization and flexibility, which allows for the perpetual creation of new possibilities. Derrida's recourse to literature is thus an integral part of his deconstruction of Western metaphysics, which has consistently sought to regulate or repress the subversive effects of fiction and rhetoric. The importance of the literary in Derrida's work also explains his prodigious success in the domain of literary criticism, especially in English-speaking countries. While this has produced some interesting results, it has also led to misunderstanding and misinterpretation, contributing to the sometimes hostile reception of Derrida's work among philosophers suspicious of the 'continental' tradition he is seen to represent.

Some critics have pointed to the lack of ethical and political concerns in Derrida's thought, a criticism quickly dispelled by even a casual perusal of his texts: his early engagement with the ethical philosophy of Emmanuel **Levinas** in *L'Écriture et la différence*; his deconstructive reading of the psychology of nuclear politics in *Psyché: inventions de l'autre* (Psyche: Inventions of the Other); his analysis of Heidegger's politics in *Of Spirit* (*De l'esprit*), and the problem of the institutionalization of knowledge in the university in *Du droit à la philosophie* (On the Right to Philosophy); his reflections on the significance of Marx in a 'post-Marxist' world (in *Spectres de Marx)* – all of these readings testify to the enduring significance of the political and the ethical in Derrida's work. That work has been, and will doubtless continue to be, a subject of controversy among more orthodox philosophers. Few, however, would contest the importance of Derrida's contribution to late twentieth-century philosophy.

CHRISTOPHER JOHNSON

Major works

Derrida, J. (1967a) *De la grammatologie*, Paris:

Éditions de Minuit. Translated G. C. Spivak (1976) *Of Grammatology*, Baltimore: Johns Hopkins University Press.

——(1967b) *L'Écriture et la différence*, Paris: Éditions du Seuil. Translated A. Bass (1978) *Writing and Difference*, London: Routledge.

——(1972) *La Dissémination*, Paris: Éditions du Seuil. Translated Barbara Johnson (1981) *Dissemination*, Chicago: University of Chicago Press.

——(1974) *Glas*, Paris: Éditions Galilée. Translated J. P. Leavey Jr and R. Rand (1984) *Glas*, Lincoln: University of Nebraska Press.

——(1979) *La Carte postale: de Socrate à Freud et au-delà*, Paris: Flammarion. Translated A. Bass (1987) *The Post Card: From Socrates to Freud and Beyond*, Chicago: University of Chicago Press.

——(1987a) *De l'esprit: Heidegger et la question*, Paris: Éditions Galilée. Translated G. Bennington and R. Bowlby (1989) *Of Spirit: Heidegger and the Question*, Chicago: University of Chicago Press.

——(1987b) *Psyché: Inventions de l'autre*, Paris: Éditions Galilée.

——(1990) *Du droit à la philosophie*, Paris: Éditions Galilée.

——(1993) *Spectres de Marx*, Paris: Éditions Galilée. Translated P. Kamuf (1994) *Specters of Marx*, Routledge: London.

Further reading

Norris, C. (1987) *Derrida*, London: Fontana (a clear, informed and intelligent overview of Derrida's thought).

Desarthe, Gérard

b. 1945, Paris

Actor and director

Desarthe is famous for his interpretations of major roles for famous directors, notably in Chéreau's 1981 *Peer Gynt*, Jourdheuil's 1978

Jean-Jacques Rousseau and **Planchon**'s 1980 *Dom Juan*. His directorial career began with an acclaimed production of *Le Cid* in 1988.

ANNIE SPARKS

See also: theatre

Further reading

Temkine, R. (1989) 'Gérard Desarthe toujours plus outre', *Europe (le théâtre ailleurs autrement)* 726 (article on Desarthe's work).

Deschamps, Jérôme

b. 1947, Neuilly-sur-Seine

Playwright, actor and director

Deschamps is the creator of popular shows noted for their visual comedy and scenic experimentation. They include *Baboulifiche* and *Papavoine* (created for **Vitez**) in 1974, *La Famille Deschiens* in 1979 and *C'est magnifique* with Macha Makeiff in 1994.

ANNIE SPARKS

See also: theatre

Further reading

Makeiff, M. (1996) *C'est magnifique*, Paris: Actes Sud (illustrated album of the show).

Désir, Harlem, and SOS Racisme

b. 1959, Paris

Anti-racism activist

Harlem Désir became a national figure in the

mid-1980s as the president of SOS Racisme, an anti-racist organization founded in 1984. Through marches, demonstrations, concerts and, especially, a badge containing the words *Touche pas à mon pote* (Hands off my pal), it raised awareness of **racism** and inequality. Criticized in the late 1980s for being a media creation and too closely attached to the Socialist Party, it subsequently concentrated less on high-profile events and more on local action. At the same time, it shifted its focus from *le droit à la différence* (the right to difference) to claims for equality through integration. On standing down as president of SOS Racisme, Désir eventually became a *secrétaire national* of the Socialist Party.

MAX SILVERMAN

See also: immigration

Major works

Désir, H. (1987) *SOS désirs*, Paris: Calmann-Lévy (account of the early history of SOS Racisme).

detective fiction

Detective fiction – *le roman policier* or *polar* – is a product of modernity. This is reflected in the comparatively recent development of the genre, in the mass readership it has attracted, in its tendency to appear in series and in its rich relationship with **cinema**, **comic strips** and **television**. Murder as a means to an end offers an inexhaustible instrument with which to explore social and moral contradictions between myth and reality with regard to the sanctity of the individual, rights of property and the mechanics of social privilege. Its ancestry in France can be traced to Balzac, Sue and Hugo, but the founder of the genre is Edgar Allan Poe. In the Anglo-Saxon world Conan Doyle's Holmes brought the genre into the twentieth century, as, in France, did the adventures of Maurice Leblanc's Arsène Lupin. The interwar years saw the flowering of the problem novel (*roman à clé*) – whose most famous exponent is Agatha Christie – where the narrative takes the form of an intellectual puzzle set within a defined social and physical space. In France, it was promoted primarily by Hachette in the pioneering series Le Masque. The adventures of **Simenon**'s world-famous hero Maigret lasted from 1931 to 1972 and were innovatory in that the hero was a senior police officer whose enquiries added both a psychological depth and a social breadth to the traditional detective novel. The post-World War II period is dominated by the *roman noir*, a coming-together of the detective story and aspects of the western. Here, the mystery tends to evolve during the course of the narrative and the hero is more active, providing greater possibilities to exploit the urban landscape's social detail, and shifting the emphasis more to an exposure and a neutralization of evil. In 1945 La Série noire, led by Marcel Duhamel, introduced Hammett, Chandler and others, but Léo Malet's private eye Nestor Burma contributed an aesthetic dimension to the style of his American colleagues. The last subgenre to evolve was the suspense novel, which focuses on the state of mind of the victim or the criminal. The novels of the team of Boileau and Nercejac proved particularly successful in adaptation for the cinema. Doggedly ignored by 'serious' critics until the 1970s, the genre has since attracted the attention of major literary figures. It has its own centre in Paris, there are popular fan clubs and journals, as well as dictionaries of characters and terms. New writers, like **Daeninckx**, Pennac, and the innovative series Le Poulpe, are developing the genre to explore the experiences of alienation, oppression and social contradictions.

GEORGE PAIZIS

Further reading

Deleuse, R. (1991) *Les Maîtres du roman policier*, Paris: Bordas, Les Compacts (contains a comprehensive bibliography of the topic).

Dubois, J. (1992) *Le Roman policier ou la modernité*, Paris: Nathan (historical development of the genre with special reference to France).

Lacassin, F. (1974) *Mythologie du roman policier*, Paris: UGE, 10/18 (a basic starting point for a comprehensive look at the genre).

Deutsch, Michel

b. 1948, Strasbourg

Playwright, poet and essayist

Classed as a member of the **Théâtre du Quotidien** in the 1970s, Deutsch is a member of **Vincent's** dramaturgy collective at the Théâtre National de Strasbourg, and a writer of poetry and criticism for the review *Aléa*. His philosophical, social documentary-style plays include *Convoi* (Convoy), the three-part *Féroé, la nuit*, (Féroé, at Night) and *La Négresse bonheur* (Negress Happiness).

ANNIE SPARKS

See also: theatre

Major works

Deutsch, M. (1990) *Inventaire après liquidation*, Paris: L'Arche (texts and interviews).

Devers, Claire

b. 1955, Paris

Director

With only three films to her name, none the less she is indisputably an important film-maker. Devers broke into film-making in 1986 through her highly controversial, award-winning film *Black and White* (*Noir et blanc*), about a male sadomasochistic relationship. Made in black and white, it was her graduating film from the Institut des Hautes Études Cinématographiques (IDHEC). Her films interweave the sociopolitical with the sexual, and the dangerous narratives of her films expose spectator expectation and address female fantasy. Essays on voyeurism and the technology of surveillance, her films offer an uncompromising female eye on male sexuality and the tensions inherent in a homosocial hegemony – giving a new dimension to the generic concept of film noir, which is so traditionally a male director's province (see 1992's *Max et Jérémie*).

SUSAN HAYWARD

See also: cinema; women directors

Dewaere, Patrick

b. 1947, St-Brieuc;
d. 1982, Paris

Actor

A product, like his screen partners **Depardieu** and **Miou-Miou**, of the **café theatre**. His role in **Blier's** *Les Valseuses* of 1974 gave him a *voyou* image he took a long time to shake off. His best work, apart from the Blier films, was for Alain Corneau (*Série noire* of 1979) and **Téchiné** (*Hôtel des Amériques* of 1981). He took his own life, reputedly because of an unhappy relationship with Miou-Miou, in 1982.

KEITH READER

See also: cinema

Dib, Mohammed

b. 1920, Tlemcen, Algeria

Writer and poet

At various times a school teacher, interpreter

and rug designer, Dib published a trilogy in the 1950s: *La Grande Maison* (The Great Mansion), *L'Incendie* (The Fire) and *Le Métier à tisser* (The Weaving Loom). In this trilogy Dib denounced the humiliations of life under colonial rule from a communist perspective. He has lived in France since his expulsion from Algeria in 1959. In *Who Remembers the Sea* (*Qui se souvient de la mer*), published in 1962, Dib's style became more oriented towards an oneiric discourse. *La Danse du roi* (The King's Dance) and *Habel*, published in 1968 and 1977 respectively, depict the **Algerian war** of liberation from a Surrealist angle. Dib's collections of poems deal with the themes of exile, erotic sexuality and the psychological journey within the self.

LAÏLA IBNLFASSI

See also: francophone writing (fiction, poetry): North Africa

Further reading

Déjeux, J. (1977) *Mohammed Dib, écrivain Algérien*, Quebec: Naaman (full-length study of Dib and his work in French).

Diên Biên Phu

The battle of Diên Biên Phu in early 1954 effectively marked the end of French colonial interests in Indochina. After regaining nominal jurisdiction over its prewar possessions in southeast Asia following the Allied defeat of Japan in 1945, France was immediately faced with the prospect of being unable to implement it. The Vietnamese nationalists under Ho Chi Minh had gained control of northern Indochina and, after attempts at a negotiated settlement had failed, over seven years of war ensued which were draining both financially and psychologically for the French forces and government, in spite of military assistance from the United States. On 13 March 1954, Viet Minh forces began a siege of French military

positions in the valley of Diên Biên Phu in northwestern Vietnam, bombarding the French from the mountains around the valley. The French finally surrendered on 7 May 1954, just as talks on the future of Indochina were about to begin in Geneva, leaving the French government in a desperately weak position at the negotiations which resulted in the north–south partitioning of Vietnam.

COLVILLE WEMYSS

See also: decolonization; Mendès France, Pierre

Further reading

Leifer, M. (1996) *Dictionary of the Modern Politics of South-East Asia*, 2nd edition, London and New York: Routledge.

Dior, Christian

b. 1905, Granville;
d. 1957, Montecatini, Italy

Fashion designer

Born into a wealthy Norman family, Dior wanted to study architecture, opened an art gallery, and mingled with avant-garde artists such as **Picasso** and **Matisse**. After the 1929 economic crash ruined his family, he learned to sketch, and in 1938 he designed Robert Pinguet's collection. With the help of investor Marcel Boussac, Dior opened his own fashion house in 1947. His 'Corolle' silhouette revolutionized the fashion industry. In 1954, he created his 'H' line with loose tunics. After his death, the Dior company added a ready-to-wear Miss Dior boutique (1967) and a men's line (1970).

JOËLLE VITIELLO

See also: fashion

director's theatre

This term is used to describe director-dominated **theatre**, a phenomenon particularly prominent in France in the postwar period. During the twentieth century, the role of the director in French theatre has achieved extremely high status. Although during the last century and even at the beginning of this one, the theatre director, or in those days the 'producer', was considered to be little more than an orchestrator of actors and scenes, the situation today is very different, with directors wielding considerable creative input as well as financial power, especially in the public theatre. The role of director today has been influenced by several traditions. Prewar theatre in France saw the rise of Copeau and the Cartel directors (including Dullin, Jouvet, Pitoëff and **Dasté**), who believed in the importance of the director as an interpreter of the author's text, helping the actors to develop their role as part of the production. Copeau and others wielded additional influence thanks to the theatre schools they ran. The second influence to affect the role of the director in France is that of the more avant-garde, revolutionary approach which began with **Artaud** and his **Theatre of Cruelty**. In his wake, theatre came to rely less on text and more on a complex web of sign systems based on the visual and the active as much as the aural. French theatre and its directors began to experiment with non-text-based theatre, and the boundaries to which theatre could be pushed. As a result, text was no longer the only source of theatrical creation: the directors became central to the co-ordination of experimentation with stage, movement and visual imagery, and added their own artistic input. The arrival of Brecht on the French theatre scene after the war was also an important influence. **Planchon** was especially noted for his interest in experimenting with Brechtian theatre.

While directors such as **Brook** and **Barrault** could be said to be influenced by both the Copeauesque and Artaudian traditions, Planchon and **Vilar**, two of the best-known postwar directors, are certainly more influenced by Copeau and the Cartel, as well as by Brecht. Meanwhile, Ariane **Mnouchkine** at the **Théâtre du Soleil** and Patrice **Chéreau** could be said to fall more into the Brechtian and Artaudian schools of direction. Thus it is difficult to describe today's directors as descendants of any single tradition: it would be more accurate to say that postwar directors have drawn on all of them in varying proportions, while experimenting with the boundaries of theatre and imposing their own creative style. While directors continue to be extremely influential in French theatre, it is difficult to class them into any kind of school or movement: each has his/her own strong, and individual, voice.

Director's theatre in France reached its peak in the 1960s and 1970s. During the 1950s, the great decentralization movement had meant that Centres Dramatiques Nationaux had begun to be established around the country. Each was run by a director, usually the theatre's artistic director, who became administratively responsible too, thus wielding considerable power over how money was spent and on which productions. By the 1960s and 1970s, directors had gained such power that they were in almost total charge of most of France's theatres. Artistically, they were in a position to choose how to spend subsidies: often this meant working on texts upon which they could impose their own creative stamp and tread new ground, which frequently led to non-theatrical texts being used. **Vitez**, for example, is famed for his adaptations of non-dramatic texts such as Aragon's *Les Cloches de Bâle* (staged as *Catherine*). It was not uncommon, for example, for directors to cut, alter or reorganize the author's text to suit their own creative purpose, or to choose a repertoire which deliberately reflected their own creative interests. Even in the 1990s, the tradition persists that one refers to 'Planchon's' rather than to 'Molière's' *Tartuffe*, crediting directors with the major creative input in much the same way as they are treated in the cinema.

The 1970s also saw the emergence of the **collective creation** movement, in which the playwright was rendered entirely redundant, as theatre companies began devising their own creations from research and improvisation. In this case, the director theoretically held no more power than any other member of the company; in practice, it would be fair to say, directors such as Mnouchkine still had considerable input into productions. The 1980s, however, saw the return to text as a source of theatre, with directors such as Planchon, Vitez, Mnouchkine and Chéreau continuing to dominate the theatrical scene until the end of the decade (and beyond in the case of Mnouchkine and Chéreau). Directors continue to wield considerable power financially in public theatre and creatively, although the re-emerging importance of text-led theatre has led to renewed recognition of partnership with authors (for example, Mnouchkine and **Cixous**, Chéreau and **Koltès**, or **Minyana** and Cantarella). While the director today continues to occupy an important position in the theatre world, the relationship between director and author is shifting back towards a creative partnership, in which the text retains its own voice.

ANNIE SPARKS

See also: theatres, national

Further reading

Bradby, D. and Williams, D. (1988) *Directors' Theatre*, London: Macmillan (see Chapters 1, 3, 4 and 6 especially).
Whitton, D. (1987) *Stage Directors in Modern France*, Manchester: Manchester University Press (essential reading).

dirigisme

The concept of *dirigisme* denotes the type of state intervention in economic life which developed in France in the postwar period and which dominated French economic thinking until the 1980s. *Dirigiste* policies have been carried out by Left and Right alike. This is because *dirigisme* does not necessarily imply a critique of the capitalist system or a socioeco-

nomic ideology which rejects the market. Rather, *dirigiste* policies are based on the notion that the state is in a better position than market forces to secure the long-term health of the French capitalist economy, particularly in terms of investment.

JAN WINDEBANK

See also: economy; nationalization and privatization

Further reading

Fenton, F. (1992) *L'État et le capitalisme au XXe siècle*, Paris: PUF (a concise account of the rise and relative decline of French *dirigisme*).
Kuisel, R. (1981) *Capitalism and the State in Modern France*, Cambridge: Cambridge University Press (a discussion of the traditional relationship between state and market in France)

documentaries

The documentary tradition in France has had a chequered career. The first documentaries date back to 1895 and the Lumière brothers' travelogues and scenes from daily life. During the silent period, many film-makers came into feature films via the training ground of documentaries; however, the soaring cost of production during the 1930s, with the advent of sound technology and the impact of the Depression, brought this training process to a virtual halt until the late 1940s. Arguably the heydays of the French documentary are the 1950s and 1960s, even though important contributions to its development were still being made during the 1970s and 1980s. The 1970s in particular must be singled out because the documentary shifted from occupying a putatively objective position to adopting an investigative and often strongly politicized one. Presently the impact of the French documentary tradition is most strongly felt, on an international level, in

African nations and, on a more parochial level, in regional film collectives established post-1980 in a governmental effort at decentralization.

In terms of the documentary's history in the sound era, the revival of the genre after its slump in the 1930s was due to the effects of the Occupation (1940–4). Audiences, disgruntled at the abolition of the double-feature pro-gramme, obliged the (then) organizing body for the film industry, the Comité d'Organisation des Industries Cinématographiques (COIC), to find a way of providing value for money. COIC identified the documentary as one inexpensive source of entertainment and directed state funding to finance documentaries and shorts that were ostensibly non-propagandistic. This investment provided a system of apprenticeship for the next generation of film-makers (e.g. Jacques Cousteau, Jacques **Becker**, Jean **Rouch**). It also instigated a training tradition that culminated (in the late 1950s) on the one hand in the feature cinema known as the **Nouvelle Vague** (New Wave), and on the other in the documentary cinema known first as *ciné-ma direct* and later as *cinéma vérité*. Both types of cinema were famous for their location shooting, hand-held camera work, grainy, real-ist filming, and – where the documentary is concerned – on-site sound recording.

Cinéma vérité was the first identifiable doc-umentary movement in French cinema and one that sought to obtain the closest possible rela-tionship to objective realism. It was, then, the first movement to address questions of representation even though, earlier, individual film-makers had also investigated the role and ideological function of documentary and its relationship to history (e.g. the fairly isolated examples of Vigo and **Renoir** in the 1930s, **Resnais** in the 1940s and early 1950s). *Cinéma vérité* was strongly influenced by the visual codes of live TV and the principles of ethnog-raphy (thanks mostly to Rouch's work), and it is this movement that has been quite wide-spread in its influence on African documentary traditions.

Post-**May 1968**, the radicalizing effect on the documentary of the various debates on the Left around the politics of representation

(whose history, what is truth, who is the speak-ing voice, and so on) and also the effects of the democratization of the camera (low-cost video and lightweight cameras) meant that different voices were being heard and different issues put up on screen: women's voices, those of blacks and **beurs**, questions of reproductive rights, **racism** and integration. Contemporary history was no longer the safe mythology of heroes. Now, the complexities of the Occupation and its effects on the French population were given a full airing: for example, Marcel **Ophuls**'s *The Sorrow and the Pity* (*Le Chagrin et la pitié*) of 1971. This documentary tradition is the one that has fed into the regional docu-mentary cinema of France.

SUSAN HAYWARD

See also: beur cinema; cinema; women directors

Further reading

CinémAction (1995) 76, special issue on the French documentary (a review of its history and major trends).

Doillon, Jacques

b. 1944, Paris

Director

A film-maker distinctive in his rigorous use of close-ups and framing, often suggesting intense social and emotional isolation. Like André **Téchiné** he may be looked upon as 'a poet of the alternative family' (to quote Jill Forbes) – a judgement borne out by *La Pirate* of 1984, an agonized bisexual love triangle, and *La Vie de famille* of the following year, recounting the fraught journey to Spain of a man and his daughter, in which understanding comes about only when the two address each other through video recordings.

KEITH READER

See also: Birkin, Jane; cinema

Doisneau, Robert

b. 1912, Gentilly;
d. 1994, Paris

Photographer

Most famous for *Le Baiser de l'Hôtel de Ville* (The Kiss) which came to symbolize the eternal romantic allure of Paris, Doisneau was one of the great photographers of Paris's changing urban landscape, his true passion and genius being for the recording of everyday life in the **suburbs** (*banlieue*). Working in the tradition of Baudelaire's 'Artist of modern life', he charted the progressive destruction by government planning policies of the soul of the southern Paris suburbs.

MICHAEL WORTON

See also: photography

Dort, Bernard

b. 1929, Metz;
d. 1994, Paris

Theatre critic

Best known for his part in France's discovery of Brecht, as well as for his editorial work on the well-known theatre journals, *Théâtre populaire* and *Travail théâtral*, Dort is the author of *Lecture de Brecht* (Reading Brecht), published in 1972.

ANNIE SPARKS

See also: theatre

Douai, Jacques

b. 1920, Douai

Singer, real name Gaston Tranchant

Often perceived as the standard-bearer of traditional and contemporary French folk-songs, Jacques Douai projects an image in the troubadour tradition, promoting in particular the poetic dimension of popular song. Along with his wife, Thérèse Palau (the leader of a dance group known as La Frairie), he toured France, Canada and America in order to reach an increasingly wide public, particularly in the 1960s and 1970s.

IAN PICKUP

See also: song/*chanson*

Doubrovsky, Serge

b. 1928, Paris

Intellectual, literary critic and writer

The author of studies on Corneille, Proust, literary theory and autobiography, Doubrovsky is himself a prolific autobiographer. He prefers, however, to label his self-narratives – which include *Fils* (Son/Strands), *Un Amour de soi* (Self-Love) and *Le Livre brisé* (The Broken Book) – *autofictions*. This is because his stated intention is to produce texts which, although they relate authentic episodes from their author's life, display literary qualities and formal/stylistic characteristics owing more to the novel genre than that of autobiography 'proper'. In 1989, Doubrovsky won the Prix Médicis for *Le Livre brisé*.

ALEX HUGHES

See also: autobiography; literary prizes

Further reading

Doubrovsky, S., Lecarme, J. and Lejeune, P. (eds) (1993) *Autofictions et cie*, Paris: Cahiers RITM (collection of essays on *autofiction*).

Doutreligne, Louise

b. 1948, Roubaix

Playwright

The writer of prizewinning texts for theatre, radio and film during the 1980s and 1990s, Doutreligne's theatre works include *Femme à la porte cochère* (Woman at the Carriage Entrance) and *Les Jardins de France* (France's Gardens).

ANNIE SPARKS

See also: theatre

Du Bouchet, André

b. 1924

Poet, translator and critic

He spent his early years in the United States (Amherst College, Harvard University). In France he worked on the review *L'Éphémère* and translated Shakespeare, Hölderlin, G. M. Hopkins, Pasternak and Paul Celan. There are also essays on painting and poetry and a study of the work of **Giacometti**. The poetry is sparse and tightly constructed, avoiding abstractions and making considerable use of typographical spacing, mindful of the blank areas of the page, the ultimate model being Mallarmé's *A Throw of the Dice* (*Un Coup de dés*). It is as if Du Bouchet were making a clean slate of things. The major collections are *Dans la chaleur vacante* (In the Vacant Heat) from 1961, *Ou le soleil* (Or the Sun) in 1968, *Laisses* (Leashes) and *L'Incohérence* from 1975 and 1979, *Rapides* (1980) and *Axiales* (1992).

WALTER A. STRAUSS

See also: poetry

Dubillard, Roland

b. 1923, Paris

Actor and playwright

A 1950s **radio** actor, author of radio plays, and adaptor of numerous anglophone works, his theatre plays include *Où boivent les vaches* (Where the Cows Drink), adapted from an earlier radio piece, *Naïves Hirondelles* (Naive Swallows) and *La Maison d'os* (House of Bones).

ANNIE SPARKS

See also: theatre

Further reading

Wilkinson, R. (1989) *Le Théâtre de Roland Dubillard: essai d'analyse sémiotique*, Berne: Peter Lang (critical analysis).

Dubuffet, Jean

b. 1901, Le Havre;
d. 1985, Paris

Artist

Jean-Philippe-Arthur Dubuffet was a full-time painter from 1942, and in 1949 he published the essay 'Art Brut Preferred to the Civilized Arts'. He acquired a collection of **art brut** of children, the insane or the untrained and naive, unadulterated by culture, and founded the Compagnie de l'Art Brut (1948–51) with André Breton. Highly influenced by the Surrealists, he attempted to capture the essence of freedom of expression, but was accused of imitating outsider's art. Crude, scatological images, roughly worked and scratched in thick paint, of the female body, cows, the surface of the earth (for example, *Blood and Fire, Body of Women* from 1950), were seen as powerful figurative images of matter, texture and colour.

From 1967 he worked in polystyrene, as in *Cabinet lologique*.

VALERIE SWALES

See also: painting; sculpture

Duchamp, Marcel

b. 1887, Blainville;
d.1968, Neuilly-sur-Seine

Artist

The brother of the painter Jacques Villon and the sculptor Raymond Duchamp-Villon, and a member of the Parisian avant-garde and the Surrealist movement, Duchamp was also a champion chess player and was ranked sixth in the 1925 French chess championships. His iconoclastic work rejected painting and he worked with found objects (*objets trouvés*) and visual puns to redefine artistic modes of production. In 1916 he first produced his 'Readymades', such as the urinal *Fountain* (*Fontaine*), and from 1915 to 1923 worked on one of his most famous compositions, *The Bride Stripped Bare by her Bachelors, Even* (*La Mariée mise à nu par ses célibataires, même*), also known as the *Large Glass*. He often worked in America, especially during World War II, and took American nationality in 1955. He is considered to have influenced conceptual art, especially in the United States.

DEBRA KELLY

See also: painting; sculpture

Dufy, Raoul

b. 1877, Le Havre:
d. 1953, Forcalquier, Basses Alpes

Artist

Dufy is principally known for his decorative style, often portraying the leisured life of the French upper classes at the races, regattas and on the French Riviera. He was influenced by **Matisse** and the Fauves, which led to his use of simplified forms and bright palette. He also designed ceramics, textiles (including dresses with Paul Poiret), tapestries and illustrated books. Dufy created a large decorative composition, the *Electricity Fairy* (*La Fée électricitée*), for the 1937 International Exhibition.

DEBRA KELLY

See also: painting

Dumazedier, Joffre

b. 1915

Sociologist

An intellectual and advocate of democratic popular culture. He helped to found the organization Peuple et Culture (People and Culture) at the Liberation. His best-known book, *Towards a Society of Leisure?* (*Vers une civilisation du loisir?*) of 1962, earnestly promotes the value of popular culture in the development of the person, while attacking commercial culture for its escapism. For Dumazedier, 'leisure . . . should be the occasion when high social and personal ideals are pursued and reinforced' (Rigby 1991).

KEITH READER

Further reading

Rigby, B. (1991) *Popular Culture in Modern France*, London and New York: Routledge.

Dupin, Jacques

b. 1927, Privas, Ardèche

Poet and critic

Jacques Dupin is associated with the review *L'Éphémère* (like **Du Bouchet**). He has been in close and regular contact with painters and painting and has written books on Miró and **Giacometti**. He moves along poetic paths similar to Yves **Bonnefoy**: unaffected by Surrealism and classically oriented, with strong affinities to Mallarmé, tending also toward hermeticism in his poetry. There is also a notable impact of **Char**'s poetry on Dupin. His collections are *Gravir* (Climbing) from 1963 and *L'Embrasure* (1969) – the poems are highly concentrated and concise, frequently difficult to access, yet characterized by great verbal richness and strong energy, often in the form of anguish. He occupies an important place among the poets who came into prominence after World War II and who represent, by and large, a return to a new dispensation in the history of French classicism.

WALTER A. STRAUSS

See also: poetry

Duras, Marguerite

b. 1914, Giadinh, Indochina;
d. 1996, Paris

Writer, essayist, playwright
and director, real name
Marguerite Donnadieu

A prodigious writer and film-maker whose career spanned over fifty years, Duras was one of the most important, fascinating and influential cultural figures in postwar France. Her unique literary style and constant experimentation with form resulted in a complex oeuvre of remarkable diversity. Alert to the unconscious workings of language and committed to the absolutes of love and passion, Duras took her readers and viewers to the boundaries of the unthinkable and unsayable. Although she encountered much hostility throughout her career, particularly from the Right, her brutal honesty, force of personality and radical vision

helped to redefine the very nature of the female artist and intellectual in France.

Duras's childhood in French Indochina left her with an ineradicable sense of injustice: her father died when she was 4 years old and her mother – who always favoured her elder brother – was sold unworkable land by corrupt French officials. Ironically, Duras's first text, *L'Empire français* (The French Empire), a collaboration with Philippe Roques published under her maiden name and the fruit of two years spent at the Colonial Office in Paris from 1937 to 1939, extols the virtues of French colonial expansion. Her first, fairly conventional novels appeared during the war, but she temporarily abandoned writing to become a Communist activist. Upon leaving the Communist Party acrimoniously in 1950, she published *The Sea-Wall* (*Un barrage contre le Pacifique*), a harsh, neo-realist tale of growing up in Indochina, clearly autobiographical in inspiration. With the minimalist style and blank, seemingly non-expressive prose of *The Square* (*Le Square*) and *Moderato cantabile*, Duras became associated with the *nouveau roman*, although her themes of female alienation, self-destructive, violent desire and potential madness already set her firmly apart. She achieved international fame in 1959 with her screenplay for Alain **Resnais**'s *Hiroshima, mon amour*, with its famous refrain, 'You are killing me, you are doing me good', and produced in the mid-1960s her major long novels, *The Ravishing of Lol V. Stein* (*Le Ravissement de Lol V Stein*) and *The Vice-Consul* (*Le Vice-Consul*). The first, featuring an unreliable male narrator who finds himself 'ravished' and progressively 'unmanned' by the eponymous heroine, is written in a fragmentary, abstract and non-linear style, and it inspired Jacques **Lacan** to write a famous 'homage' (his only article on a contemporary writer), in which he celebrated Duras as a writer of 'clinically perfect madness'. This provoked, in turn, a stream of psychoanalytic readings of Duras's work, notably Marcelle Marini's attempt to chart the territories of silence and unexplained narrative lacunae (or 'blanks') that 'resonate with' and 'speak' the feminine (e.g. the mute beggar woman in *Le Vice-Consul*). Throughout this period, Duras also established herself as a major dramatist, producing adaptations both of her own novels, such as *Whole Days in the Trees* (*Des journées entières dans les arbres*) and *L'Amante anglaise*, and of classic works, such as Strindberg's *The Dance of Death*. The culmination of her work in **theatre** was *Savannah Bay*, a play written in 1982 for Madeleine **Renaud** about the apocalyptic impact of sexual passion and the vital necessity of bearing witness.

Duras was briefly a member of the revolutionary action committee of students and writers set up at the Sorbonne during the events of **May 1968**. Yet, after reaching with *L'Amour* a kind of limit point, she began to devote her energies almost exclusively to film-making. *Nathalie Granger* (1972), based around a young girl's refusal to speak, exemplified the attraction Duras's marginal status had for established stars (here Jeanne **Moreau**), and it encouraged a temporary and highly ambivalent association with **feminism** evident in her published interviews in 1974 with Xavière Gauthier, *Woman to Woman* (*Les Parleuses*). *La Femme du Gange* and *India Song* (1974/1975) rework elements from Duras's 1960s novels to create a dense network of intertextual echoes commonly referred to as the 'India Cycle'. Both films are composed of slow, long takes which are often repeated and have no direct relation with the intricately layered, plurivocal soundtrack. The actors such as Delphine **Seyrig** are asked simply to 'figure' – rather than act – their rôles. *Son nom de Venise dans Calcutta désert*, which uses the same soundtrack as *India Song* but this time over frozen images of an abandoned château, revealed that Duras's underlying ambition was not merely to reappropriate her literary work – which, she claimed, had been betrayed in commercial adaptations – but also to destroy the very foundations of cinema. *Le Camion* (1979), centred around a dialogue with Gérard **Depardieu** about a film that 'could have been made' of a female hitch-hiker, marked the first occasion that Duras entered her own work as Duras. Not only did it refuse any essentialist

notion of a female writing of the body, but it also established a new, defiantly heterosexual and ultimately sadomasochistic, aesthetic, or *malheur merveilleux* (magical misery). The four-part series of shorts comprising *Césarée*, *Les Mains négatives*, and two versions of *Aurélia Steiner* (about the Holocaust), where Duras recites haunting poetic texts over stark, quasi-documentary images of Paris and the Seine estuary, represents the pinnacle of her work in film. In *Green Eyes* (*Les Yeux verts*), where she theorizes her cinematic practice, Duras fully recognizes the seductive power of her voice – low and gravelly – when delivered over a limited range of neutral 'master-images'. The logical conclusion to her experiments in minimalism was the short *L'Homme atlantique*, the second half of which presents a black screen and her own voice interrogating an unnamed male 'you'.

In 1980, Duras returned to fiction proper with *The Seated Man in the Passage* (*L'Homme assis dans le couloir*), a slim volume which elaborates in graphic detail the violent erotic subtext of *Le Vice-Consul* and heralds the arrival in her literary work of an explicit first-person narrator-*voyeuse*. *L'Été 80* (Summer 1980) was Duras's first experiment in *écriture courante* (literally 'running writing'), her answer to *écriture féminine* and an apparent transcription of anything personal, social or political that 'passes' during the scene of writing. Contingent and potentially all-inclusive, *écriture courante* was taken by many as proof of Duras's stated ethical commitment to alterity. *L'Été 80* also introduced Yann Andréa, a gay man half her age with whom she formed a lasting relationship and who featured in her films and novels, often as Yann or 'YA, homosexual' (most obviously in *Yann Andréa Steiner*). A new set of thematics had begun to emerge: homosexual/heterosexual relations, explicit incestuous desire (explored at length in *Agatha*), selfhood, collaboration and ageing. The sparse *The Malady of Death* (*La Maladie de la mort*), which stages an aggressive encounter between a female narrator and another anonymous male 'you' (by implication, also the reader), offered a brilliant deconstruction of sexual difference, fantasy and transferential desire. *The Lover* (*L'Amant*), an autobiographical novel of consummate skill and linguistic mastery structured around the photographic image of a young girl's crossing of the Mekong river, won the Prix Goncourt in 1984 and achieved record-breaking sales, aided by a stunning personal performance on *Apostrophes*. From being an obscure, 'difficult' author for a chosen few, Duras soon became France's most widely translated living writer. There followed a series of 'prose poems' of almost uniform length; each, however, stunningly different, as if she was deliberately outplaying her new readers' expectations. While *The War: A Memoir* (*La Douleur*), based on her wartime experiences in Paris, caused much controversy, particularly in its depiction of the torture of a French collaborator, it nevertheless consolidated her public links with François **Mitterrand**, with whom she had served in the Resistance. *Blue Eyes, Black Hair* (*Les Yeux bleus cheveux noirs*) was a brave study of an impossible love between a gay man and a straight woman, which avoided the new conventions of Duras's self-ironizing textuality by lacking, for instance, a first-person female narrator or scene of self-naming. *Emily L.*, a 'pure' novel and a *tour de force* examination of human fears and emotions, developed further Duras's erotic, intertextual relations with what she termed her 'Great Men' (e.g. Proust, Henry James, Robert Musil).

During the mid- to late 1980s, Duras, now a virtual icon of the Mitterrand Left, worked intensively in the media, particularly journalism (her 'Outside'), and she pronounced publicly on subjects ranging from politics and drugs to **football**. Her reputation began to suffer through overexposure, however, and she was widely attacked for her article in *Libération* entitled 'Sublime, forcément sublime Christine V.', where she heroized Christine Villemin as the entirely justifiable murderer of her son although the case was still *sub judice*. In 1988 Duras suffered a nearly fatal coma and underwent a tracheotomy, yet she still continued to write, publishing *Summer Rain* (*La Pluie d'été*) and *The North China Lover* (*L'Amant de la Chine du nord*), her narrative reworking of a filmscript of *L'Amant* originally intended for Jean-Jacques Annaud. Her final text, *C'est tout* (That's All), was almost ignored when it appeared, yet its physical staging of her own death distinguishes it as one of Duras's most searing and uncompromising works.

JAMES WILLIAMS

See also: autobiography; cinema; feminist thought; literary prizes; Marxism and Marxian thought; psychoanalysis; television; women directors; women's/lesbian writing

Further reading

Andréa, Y. (1983) *MD*, Paris: Éditions de Minuit (a moving and compelling account of the background to Duras's writing of *La Maladie de la mort*, including her hospitalization during treatment for detoxification).

Cohen, S. D. (1993) *Women and Discourse in the Fiction of Marguerite Duras: Love, Legends, Language*, London: Macmillan (a finely argued feminist reading of Duras's work).

Hill, L. (1993) *Marguerite Duras: Apocalyptic Desires*, London: Routledge (an excellent introduction to the complexities of Duras's work).

Kristeva, J. (1987) 'The Pain of Sorrow in the Modern World: The Works of Marguerite Duras', *PMLA* 102, 2 (the most powerful argument yet made that Duras's literary work is one of irremediable pain symptomatic of the postwar period).

Lacan, J. (1987) 'Homage to Marguerite Duras', trans. Peter Connor, in *Duras on Duras*, San Francisco: City Lights Books.

Marini, M. (1977) *Territoires du féminin: avec Marguerite Duras*, Paris: Éditions de Minuit (a pioneering psychoanalytical reading of Duras's longer novels).

Vircondelet, A. (1996) *Marguerite Duras: vérités et légendes*, Paris: Éditions du Chêne (most up-to-date and detailed biography of Duras, lavishly illustrated).

Williams, J. S. (1997) *The Erotics of Passage:*

Pleasure, Politics, and Form in the Later Work of Marguerite Duras, Liverpool: Liverpool University Press (a study of all aspects of Duras's work post-1977, including her cinematic practice of montage, her engagement with **gay writing** and culture, and her collaborative project with Andréa).

Durif, Eugène

b. 1950, Lyon

Poet and playwright

Durif is the author of arts and literary reviews, adaptations, poems and plays. His *Conversation sur la montagne* (Conversation on the Mountainside) and *Le Petit Bois* (The Little Wood), put on at the Théâtre National Populaire in 1991, both feature the long monologues that characterize his work. His works are regularly performed by the Théâtre Ouvert.

ANNIE SPARKS

See also: theatre

Duteil, Yves

b. 1949, Paris

Singer-songwriter

A popular singer-songwriter, who had his first hit in 1974 with *le Petit Pont de bois* (The Little Wooden Bridge), followed by others such as *Tarentelle* (Tarantella), *Prendre un enfant par la main* (To Take a Child by the Hand) and *La Langue de chez nous* (The Language of Our Country), which won the poetry prize of the **Académie Française**. An interesting lyricist whose songs sometimes verge on the oversentimental.

IAN PICKUP

See also: song/*chanson*

Duvert, Tony

b. 1945, Villeneuve-le-Roi

Writer

Duvert has been described as perverse and as a writer of evil. While his largely autobiographical work centres on the questions of juvenile sexuality and sexual transgression, notably paedophilia, he presents his marginal world as a world of innocence. However, this moral category is a provocatively ambiguous one in his work: in his 1976 *Journal d'un innocent* (Diary of an Innocent), the 'innocent' with whom he has sex is a mentally retarded adolescent. In his essays, he repeatedly inveighs against 'heterocracy', which he defines as a social system in which heterosexuality is posited – and imposed – as a universal.

MICHAEL WORTON

See also: autobiography; gay writing

E

economy

The French economy was radically transformed after World War II. Economic stagnation in the 1930s, caused in part by the conservative attitudes of businessmen and bankers, had resulted in France lagging behind its nearest neighbours in 1945 in terms of its degree of industrialization and modernization. A large proportion of the population still worked in agriculture (using very outdated farming methods), and small businesses, which were equally unproductive, proliferated. The traditional image of France was thus of a rural *France profonde* (depths of France) dominated by artisans, small shopkeepers and the peasantry. The economic history of France in the latter half of the twentieth century is thus, on the one hand, a tale of how state intervention helped to turn the economy around to make the country one of the top five industrial nations of the world, but on the other hand, the story of how the state was to become the scapegoat for the country's economic ills as the ideology of economic liberalism took hold in France.

After World War II, France's first priority was to develop its backward economy by modernizing **agriculture** in order to liberate the agricultural workforce for labour in the factories which themselves were to be made more productive and more efficient. This task was not left up to the market, however, which had come to be despised after the Great Depression. Instead, a consensus existed in the country around the idea that it was the responsibility of the state to plan economic development and to assist industrialists. It was at this time that institutions such as the Commissariat Général du Plan were set up. The 1950s and 1960s were therefore set to become the heyday of French state intervention in and protection of the economy, or *dirigisme*. Indeed, the years 1945 to 1974 are known as the *Trente Glorieuses* because economic growth rates were so spectacular during this period and social and economic change so dramatic. Equally, increases in real wages were significant and the living standard of the population rose accordingly. After the 1950s, industrialization and urbanization gathered momentum and consumption patterns altered. The consumer society was born. However, the extent to which state intervention brought about this situation is a debatable issue: some argue that similar levels of economic growth would have occurred even without so much state intervention because France's economic success was based on technological progress and a favourable international environment in which raw materials were cheap and competition was not as yet coming from the newly industrializing countries of the Pacific Rim.

All good things come to an end, however, and this spectacular success also came to a faltering halt. The first signs that all was not well came in **May 1968**. The strikes and demonstrations which took place during that month, especially among the younger generation, were an expression of the fact that French social structures had not kept pace with economic change. Nevertheless, the social discontent manifested in 1968 was soon to be overshadowed by the economic troubles which were to hit the country in 1974, when the first oil crisis heralded a profound and irreversible change in the international economic climate. The immediate effect of the oil crisis was to send French energy prices soaring because of the dependence of the country on imported energy sources. However, in the longer term, the oil crisis led to an increase in the price of raw materials as developing countries and ex-colonies, particularly those with rich reserves of raw materials, saw that they could exert economic power over their former masters. This rise in the price of raw materials coincided with countries in new areas of the world, such as southeast Asia, beginning to industrialize and challenge countries such as France in traditional industrial sectors: heavy industry, shipbuilding and textiles, for instance.

It was in the wake of the first oil crisis that the role of the state in assisting and subsidizing the French economy began to be called into question. The 1974 oil crisis caused recession, but the high cost of energy caused inflation and hence the entirely new phenomenon of 'stagflation'. Raymond **Barre**, who became prime minister in 1976, was one of the first to suggest that state intervention might actually harm the French economy. He declared that one of France's principal economic problems was that industry had been too heavily subsidized and protected by the state and, like a spoilt child, it had become lazy and uncompetitive. Therefore, he proposed that state aid for industry should be limited to those 'sunrise' companies which would constitute France's future, and 'lame duck' industries should go to the wall. Equally, Barre was of the opinion that lax monetary policy in the past had made French industry complacent. If costs in France rose too much and made French goods internationally uncompetitive, then the currency would be devalued in order to make them competitive again. Barre, along with **Giscard d'Estaing**, was one of the authors of the European Monetary System, designed to impose a degree of monetary discipline on France and force it to be cost-competitive with its nearest neighbours and rivals. Thus, it was in the late 1970s that France had its first (albeit limited) taste of economic liberalism.

However, the second oil shock hit in 1979 and the ensuing recession disrupted Barre's plans. Unemployment rose steadily, reaching over 1.5 million by the presidential elections in 1981 which the Socialist François **Mitterrand** won. In office, the Socialists, aided by the Communists, set about introducing a radical Socialist alternative to Barre's strategy, swimming against the tide of liberalism which was sweeping across America and Britain. The Socialists were elected on a programme based on *la rupture avec le capitalisme*; that is, a complete break with the capitalist system. To this end, they introduced a sweeping round of nationalizations of the banking sector and the largest industrial groups. The Socialists believed that Barre was wrong to let whole sections of French industry disappear and that it was necessary to make France industrially self-sufficient again. They also spent vast amounts of money on job creation. For a year, their plan worked, in the sense that French unemployment stabilized while in competitor countries the rate was increasing dramatically.

None the less, as the recession continued, the Socialists found themselves in an untenable position since the cost of their policies far outstripped the state's ability to pay. Particularly because of constraints imposed by Europe, the Socialists were forced to abandon their original policies. Mitterrand turned his back on *la rupture avec le capitalisme* and instead began to work towards putting France at the centre of a more integrated European Community. Thus, by 1984 the country was back on the road towards economic liberalism and the reduction of state intervention. Between 1984 and 1986, the Socialists reduced public spending and, although not going so far as to privatize any of the nationalized industries, public sector companies were instructed to behave as if they were in the private sector. Privatizations had to wait until Jacques **Chirac** took over as prime minister in 1986. Influenced by the policies of

Reagan in the United States and Thatcher in Britain, Chirac set about a major programme of privatizations. He proclaimed the virtues of a less interventionist but more efficiently run state, and his programme stressed the need to denationalize the **banks**, privatize nationalized companies, deregulate prices, create more flexibility among the workforce and limit public expenditure so as to be able to reduce taxation and provide more incentive for entrepreneurs.

By 1988, the French had experienced both a radical left-wing and a radical right-wing government within the space of seven years. Nevertheless, it appeared to the general public that neither experiment had had the desired effect – namely, to reduce unemployment and increase standards of living. In the presidential elections of that year, Mitterrand put himself forward as the candidate of compromise, promising neither to renationalize recently privatized industries, nor to pursue further privatizations. This won him the election. However, the Socialist government of 1988 to 1993 was never popular with the electorate, even though from 1989 to 1991 the French economy grew well and unemployment fell before going into the recession sparked off by the Gulf war. Ironically, this was because the Socialist government applied strict monetary policies to the country, keeping wages down and avoiding a credit boom in order check inflation. This was proof indeed that the Socialists had learned the lessons of liberalism. However, it also meant that the electorate did not benefit from the fruits of economic growth to the extent which they might have done.

It is apparent, therefore, that by the end of the century France had transformed its economy, not only in terms of modernization, but also in terms of the role that the state plays in the workings of the economy. This is no longer a question of ideology, since right-wing and left-wing parties alike propose strikingly similar policies, all of which advocate an acceptance of the rules of the capitalist market and a limitation of the powers of the state. The concern on both sides of the political divide, however, is that France might be in the grip of a process of deindustrialization and might slip eventually into the second rank of industrial nations.

JAN WINDEBANK

See also: employment; European Union; nationalization and privatization

Further reading

Flockton, C. and Kofman, E. (1989) *France*, London: Paul Chapman (an account of French economic and social development from a geographical perspective).

Holmes, G. and Fawcett, C. (1983) *The Contemporary French Economy*, Basingstoke: Macmillan (an overview of French economic development from 1945 to the early 1980s; includes text in French).

Jeanneney, J.-M. (1989) *L'Économie française depuis 1967*, Paris: Éditions du Seuil (a discussion of the forces influencing French economic development since the late 1960s).

Szarka, J. (1992) *Business in France: An Introduction to the Economic and Social Context*, London: Pitman (an overview of the French business environment of the late 1980s).

écriture féminine

The term *écriture féminine* describes a mode of writing which is deemed to overcome women's alienation from/in the order of language, and to give voice to repressed feminine difference. The concept came to the fore in the 1970s.

Since the 1970s, a number of French feminists have denounced the gender bias they perceive to exist within language, and have argued that the patriarchal, male-centred nature of the linguistic realm militates against symbolic self-definition by and for women. Elements of their argumentation recall the complex psychoanalytic writings of Jacques **Lacan**. Lacan suggests that women, by virtue of their different, unconscious relation to the phallus, enjoy a problematic and alienated relationship with the order of language, also described more broadly as the Symbolic Order. French feminist theorists such as Luce **Irigaray** (a psychoanalyst, linguistician and philosopher) and Hélène **Cixous** (an academic and creative writer), both of whom address the issue of women's relation to language and discourse, are certainly indebted to Lacanian theory. However, unlike Lacan, neither woman believes the exclusion of the feminine by and in the linguistic domain to be irremediable. Both have produced texts in which they indicate that there may in fact be linguistic and writing practices which allow its articulation – see Irigaray's *This Sex Which is Not One* (*Ce sexe qui n'en est pas un*) of 1977, and Cixous's *The Newly Born Woman* (*La Jeune Née*) from 1975. Consequently, both women have been associated with the related notions of *écriture féminine* and *parler femme*, although neither uses these terms extensively in her own theoretical writings.

Before the precise nature of 'feminine' linguistic practices can be explored, it is useful to establish why Irigaray and Cixous were ready to claim in the 1970s that women are excluded and banished by the patriarchal linguistic order. Irigaray's broad-ranging discussions of linguistic issues address language in its everyday, communicative mode, as well as more particularized forms of language and discourse. One of her more accessible arguments (Irigaray 1987) is that all of those language systems which, like French, involve grammatical genderization are somehow intrinsically 'sexist'. This is because the feminine gender is consistently associated within them with nouns connoting inferiority/'otherness', while nouns connoting superiority are gendered masculine. Moreover (in French, at least), seemingly 'neutral' expressions – *il pleut*, for instance – in fact privilege the masculine. In her more speculative, abstract writings, Irigaray denounces the phallic/masculine bias present specifically within the language of rational, philosophical thought (which she views as occupying a key place within Western culture). She considers this form of language to be underpinned by certain, central 'male' principles; principles such as linearity and non-contradiction. She suggests that these principles,

because they exclude ambivalence and ensure that meaning remains single and stable, may be symbolically equated with 'monolithic', masculine sexuality rather than with women's libidinal organization – which she theorizes as plural and multiple. She argues that rational, philosophical discourse relies on a goal-oriented syntactical model (subject-verb-object) which is alien to women, because 'female sexuality is not unifiable, it cannot be subsumed under the concept of subject – which brings into question all the syntactical norms' (Irigaray 1977b). Cixous analyses philosophical discourse and the secondary discourses it has engendered – including literary discourse – in a comparable way. She considers these signifying systems to be governed by an either/or logic and by a system of hierarchized binary oppositions (activity/passivity, black/white, nature/culture, etc.), which can be traced back always to the unequal couple man/woman and to the inequalities of the patriarchal value system. This argument is advanced in an early section of her highly influential 1975 essay, *La Jeune Née*.

According to Irigaray, the 'reinscription' of the repressed feminine within the masculine Symbolic, linguistic order necessitates a radical linguistic project, a *travail du langage*. On the one hand, women must mount an assault on the representations of femininity which masculine discourse offers them. This assault must take the form of an ironic 'rewriting' of such representations. The parodic, 'mimetic' strategy she envisions will, she argues, reveal (potentially) a 'feminine' operation within language (Irigaray 1977a). Furthermore, women must evolve a new kind of writing practice aimed at disrupting the 'phallicity' of (rational) discourse. The disruption Irigaray recommends rests upon a modification of structural and stylistic discursive features. If 'male' language is characterized by a linear, logical syntactical organization, then, says Irigaray, a feminine linguistic mode, a *langage autre*, must be one whose style and structure allows fixed significations to be subverted. The language she has in mind would 'undo the unique meaning of words, of nouns, which still regulates all discourse' and 'would have nothing to do with the syntax we have used for centuries' (Irigaray 1977b). Its plurality and multivalence, since they stand in a metaphorical relation to the non-unified form of women's genital anatomy and to the decentred, multiple nature of female pleasure, may be considered to be 'vulvomorphic', i.e. to bear the 'mark' of the female body. It is important to note that Irigaray's vision of 'vulvomorphic' discourse is not based on the concept of a linguistic mode that would 'speak' the female body directly. Such discourse, for Irigaray, is not in any way predestined by anatomy. It constitutes, rather, 'a *symbolic* interpretation of that anatomy' (Gallop 1983).

In her explorations of language, Cixous concurs that the creation of explosive modes of discourse represents the means by which the feminine can be (re)born into/from within the phallocentric Symbolic Order. She argues in parts of *La Jeune Née* that the type of language she envisions – a language whose refusal to repress feminine difference marks it out as 'bisexual' – need not necessarily be the province of women alone. Male writers such as Jean **Genet**, she claims, are capable of producing texts in which the feminine is decipherable. However, in other sections of her study she seems to reverse her position and to move into 'essentialist' mode. She implies that women are in fact far more likely to produce the kind of discourse in question. This is because, unlike men, they are psychically more open to bisexuality. She suggests, moreover – far more emphatically than Irigaray may be taken to do – that a direct link can and does exist between the female body and libido and the pluralistic *écriture* which she recommends (Cixous 1975). Cixous's vision of feminine language/writing is summarized comprehensively in her essay 'The Laugh of the Medusa'. In spite of her claim that it is impossible to define a feminine mode of writing, because such writing eludes the discursive and conceptual limits of the patriarchal system, she outlines in this essay certain of its key characteristics. These are:

- its poetic quality;
- its open-ended heterogeneity;
- its connection with orality and with the

voice (specifically the voice of the archaic Mother); and

- its function as a space of decensorization, in and via which woman can access her (forbidden) sexuality and unconscious.

In summary, both Irigaray and Cixous privilege forms of language characterized by ambiguity, polyvalence and poetic quality. Both women relate these 'feminine' linguistic and discursive forms, however symbolically, to the sexuality and anatomy of the female subject. This latter connection is not without its problems. As a result of it, both theorists have been accused of biologistic essentialism; that is, of endeavouring (dangerously) to ghettoize women within their bodies and within their (biological) 'natures'. Materialist, socialist feminists – those belonging to the *Questions féministes* group, for example – were particularly keen in the 1970s to level accusations of this type. The discussions of language and discourse produced by Irigaray and Cixous may also be considered to be elitist and overly abstract. This is in part because they are the product of an intellectual training and context which is alien to many readers. Further, they seem in their evocations of 'womanspeak' to take no account of (racial, cultural, social) differences *between* women, and of the way in which these differences can or might affect linguistic practice. Finally, and most pertinently perhaps, Cixous's and Irigaray's notions of what, in formal, stylistic and syntactical terms, constitutes 'the feminine' may be viewed as wholly arbitrary. None the less, their writings on language have proved highly influential. These writings have been exploited not least by contemporary feminist literary critics – especially Anglo-American critics – eager to scrutinize women's creative productions for evidence of sexual/textual 'difference'.

French women authors who, rightly or wrongly, have been associated by critics with the practice of *écriture féminine* include Chantal **Chawaf**, Marguerite **Duras**, Jeanne **Hyvrard**, Marie **Redonnet** and Monique **Wittig**. In the writings of these authors, issues such as feminine sexuality and desire and the female body play a key role. All of them, moreover, have developed unusual, formally innovative, textual and narrative strategies. In the work of Chawaf – see, for instance, *Le Soleil et la terre* (Sun and Earth) from 1977 – we find a sustained focus on the link between bodily experience and language, and a structuring of sentences which privileges the fluid, the convoluted and the mellifluous over the rational, the ordered, the univocal. In the writings of Marguerite Duras – notably *Moderato Cantabile* (1958) and 1964's *Le Ravissement de Lol V Stein* (*The Ravishing of Lol V Stein*) – 'blanks', 'silences' and the *non-dit* (the unsaid) disrupt narrative coherence and flow, creating an elliptical, illogical narrating mode. Monique Wittig's avowed textual project is to create a 'political', anti-patriarchal language, rather than a gender-specific 'women's writing'. However, her *Les Guérillères* (1969) and *The Lesbian Body* (*Le Corps lesbien*) from 1973 have been taken (by virtue of their accounts of new relations between women and between the sexes, and their startlingly experimental nature) to represent key examples of *écriture féminine*.

If French women writers of the 1970s and early 1980s engaged upon avant-garde textual practices which echoed and exemplified the notion of a poetics of the feminine, in more recent times, French *écrivaines* appear to be effecting a return to more conventional, realist narrative modes.

ALEX HUGHES

See also: Kristeva, Julia; feminism; feminist press; feminist thought; women's/lesbian writing

Further reading

Cixous, H. (in collaboration with C. Clément) (1975) *La Jeune Née*, Paris: Union Générale d'Éditions. Translated B. Wing (1986) *The Newly Born Woman*, Manchester: Manchester University Press.
——(1976) 'The Laugh of the Medusa', *Signs* 1–4. Translated in I. de Courtivron and E. Marks (eds) (1981) *New French Feminisms*, Brighton: Harvester Press.
de Courtivron, I. and Marks, E. (eds) (1981) *New French Feminisms*, Brighton: Harvester Press (a selection of a variety of French feminist texts, translated into English; an invaluable introduction to French feminism).
Gallop, J. (1983) 'Quand nos lèvres s'écrivent: Irigaray's Body Politic', *Romanic Review* 74. Reprinted 1988 *Thinking through the Body*, New York: Columbia University Press (an interesting account of the role of the body in Irigarayan thought, which assumes a certain theoretical sophistication on the part of the reader).
Irigaray, L. (1977a) *Ce Sexe qui n'en est pas un*, Paris: Éditions de Minuit. Translated C. Porter with C. Burke (1985) *This Sex Which is Not One*, Ithaca: Cornell University Press.
——(1977b) 'Women's Exile' (interview with Couze Venn), *Ideology and Consciousness* 1.
——(1987) *Le Sexe linguistique*, special issue of *Langage* 85.
Jones, A. R. (1986) 'Writing the Body: Towards an Understanding of *écriture féminine*', in E. Showalter (ed.) *The New Feminist Criticism: Essays on Women, Literature and Theory*, London: Virago (an excellent introduction to theories of feminine writing).
Mitchell, J. and Rose, J. (eds) (1982) *Feminine Sexuality: Jacques Lacan and the École Freudienne*, Basingstoke and London: Macmillan (translation of Lacan's essays on feminine sexuality, prefaced by two illuminating introductory essays glossing Freudian and Lacanian psychoanalytic theory).
Moi, T. (1985) *Sexual/Textual Politics*, London: Methuen (a sophisticated but accessible comparative account of Anglo-Saxon and French feminist theory).
Schiach, M. (1991) *Hélène Cixous: A Politics of Writing*, London: Routledge (essential reading for students of Cixous's work).
Sellars, S. (1991) *Writing and Sexual Difference*, Basingstoke and London: Macmillan (a broad-ranging introduction to post-1968 French women's writing and its preoccupations, set in the conceptual context of French feminist theory and its influences).

education ministry

The central and regional services of the education ministry form the backbone of the public education service. They devise policy, and then supervise and monitor all operations within this heavily centralized system. The ministry is also a major force within French economic life, as one out of every eighteen members of the working population is employed by it (three out of four of whom are teachers). All full-time teachers in state institutions in France are civil servants.

Established in its present headquarters in the rue de Grenelle in 1860 as the Ministère de l'Instruction Publique, the ministry has been reorganized many times since, and its precise function has been redefined. It became the Ministère de l'Éducation and acquired its proud 'National' epithet in 1932. The government appointed in May 1995 added responsibility for the transition from classroom to workplace, in its full title of Ministère de l'Éducation Nationale, de l'Enseignement Supérieur, de la Recherche, et de l'Insertion Professionnelle. In this case, the minister himself is flanked by three secretaries of state: one for schools, one for higher education and one for research. Rue de Grenelle (as it is generally known), assisted by its national advisory bodies, is responsible for national policy with regard to curriculum design, school organization, examinations and awards, and educational development, and also for the recruitment, appointment, promotion and remuneration of teaching and other staff in state schools and universities. In addition, a network of decentralized subsidiary departments oversees the application of national policy at local level.

In each of the twenty-eight académies (educational subdivisions) of France and her overseas départements, the minister is represented by the recteur and his staff, and by the two regional inspectorates, which together have local administrative responsibility for: supervising national examinations and awards, assessing the performance of schools and standards of teaching, monitoring the implementation of national policy, encouraging innovation, and dealing with staff counselling, promotion, development and training.

In the early 1980s, decentralization policies resulted in duties traditionally discharged by the ministry being devolved upon local government. The regions acquired responsibility for future planning, building and maintenance of the lycées (senior high schools), while the départements were given similar powers with regard to the collèges (junior high schools). In each case, however, the ministry remained responsible for the allocation of teaching posts and for staff remuneration. In addition, it continues to exercise control of higher education through the pluri-annual contracts it signs with universities, together with scrutiny of their senior staff appointments, and through the sanctioning of the diplomas awarded by the grandes écoles.

RON HALLMARK

See also: educational elitism: the grandes écoles; education, secondary: collèges, lycées, etc.

Further reading

Auduc, J.-L. and Bayard-Pierlot, J. (1995) Le Système éducatif français, 4th edition, Créteil: Centre Régional de Documentation Pédagogique (a succinct, but comprehensive account of the system; a revised edition is published every year).

Durand-Prinborgne, C. (1994) L'Éducation nationale, une culture, un service, un système, 2nd edition, Paris: Nathan (a well-informed discussion of the presiding philosophy, and of the organization in context).

education, primary

Schooling in France is compulsory from 6 to 16 years of age. Elementary schools teach children aged from 6 to 11. However, primary education in France cannot be discussed without consideration of the wholesale nursery provision, which, though optional, involved some 80 per cent of 2- to 5-year-olds in 1995 (35 per cent of 2-year-olds, and over 99 per cent of those 3 and over). Nursery classes are formally programmed into the planning of the initial educational process.

Schooling from 2 to 11 is organized into three successive periods (*cycles*), in principle by age groups. The first period consists of the nursery classes for the *petits* (the infants, aged 2 to 4), the *moyens* (intermediates, aged 4 to 5) and the *grands* (the seniors, aged 5 to 6). The second period encompasses the first three years of elementary school, defined as the *cours préparatoire* (CP), the preparatory year, for 6- to 7-year-olds, and the *cours élémentaire 1ère et 2ème années* (CE 1 and 2 – elementary years one and two, for 7- to 8- and 8- to 9-year-olds, respectively). The last two years of elementary school, called the *cours moyen, 1ère et 2ème années* (CM 1 and 2 – intermediate years one and two, for 9- to 10- and 10- to 11-year-olds), constitute the third period. The boundaries between periods are not, however, rigid. There is an overlap between the top class of nursery education (*section grande*) and the first year of the elementary school (*cours préparatoire*), to ensure continuity and facilitate integration; and, to take account of different rates of development and individual learning capacities, it is possible to complete each *cycle* in two or three years.

No set syllabus is laid down for nursery education, but its aims are said to be 'to help the child to develop and become active; to arrive at an awareness of the outside world, and to relate to and communicate with others'. Methods are based upon play – whether organized or independent – and a gradual introduction to the three Rs. The second and third *cycles* are designed to 'ensure a grasp of the skills basic to all learning (oral communication, reading and arithmetic) as well as the development of the child's intellect, sensitivities, physical potential and and manual dexterity'. They must also introduce the child to fine arts and music.

The curriculum to be followed in pursuit of these aims is laid down centrally by the **education ministry**. In terms of the circular of

March 1995, which defines the second period as the *cycle des apprentissages fondamentaux* (period for learning the basics), the following weekly hourage is prescribed: nine hours of French, 5 hours of mathematics, 4 hours devoted to 'exploration of the world' and civics, 6 hours of PE, sport and art, and 2 hours of directed work (conceived as an opportunity for the teacher to help pupils develop independent work habits). The 'directed work' is to take place in half-hour sessions at the end of each full school day. The curriculum for the third period, the *cycle des approfondissements* (period of more advanced learning) is similar, but adds an additional half-hour of mathematics instead of half an hour of PE, sport or art. With effect from 1995, modern foreign languages were introduced into the elementary school curriculum: one hour of French per week in CE 2 and one and a half-hours maximum in CM 1 and 2 were to be sacrificed to this end. Begun on a voluntary basis for the first year, this teaching is designed to be extended to all schools as training and resources permit.

The balance and design of the school week (26 hours, spread typically over 9 half-days) and of the school year remain a matter of debate. The subject was raised again by the report of the Fauroux Committee on education in June 1996. In 1992, when the teaching week was reduced from 27 hours, the same annual total of classroom time (972 hours) was maintained by adding extra days to the academic year. In 1995–6, three experiments with different weekly patterns of primary education were being conducted in different areas of the country.

Since the early nineteenth century, primary education has been the responsibility of the *commune* and its local council. In this respect, the decentralization legislation of the 1980s meant little change to the status quo. It is the duty of the local authorities at that level to provide and maintain state schools and support facilities (such as school canteens), and also to engage and pay maintenance staff, or such auxiliary classroom staff as may be required to help with the younger children (*Agents Spécialisés des Écoles Maternelles* or ASEM).

For its part, the state, via the education ministry, appoints and pays the teaching staff. The latter are no longer trained in the Écoles Normales that were set up, on the basis of one per *département*, by the Guizot law (1833), and fulfilled this function until the late 1980s. As from 1990, teachers in state schools are mainly the products of the Instituts Universitaires de Formation des Maîtres. Recruitment to these is selective, and candidates must have obtained the *licence* or equivalent before entry. In the course of their studies there, during which they may be paid, intending teachers prepare for and sit the competitive examination for the Certificat d'Aptitude au Professorat des Écoles, as well as spending periods on observation and teaching practice in schools.

Declining numbers of pupils in elementary schools from the 1960s to the 1990s, together with population loss in country areas, have had both good effects and bad. On the one hand there has been a reduction in average class sizes in state elementary schools from 30 in 1960 to 22 in 1995; on the other, it has meant the threat of school closures, and the creation of inter-*commune* groups in rural areas to protect and run a local school.

To complete the picture, mention should be made of the distinctive provision made since the 1980s to cater for groups with special learning difficulties, whether the handicapped, taught in small groups in the *classes de perfectionnement* attached to some elementary schools, or the non-francophone children of recent immigrants, for whom were devised the beginners' classes – *classes d'initiation* (CLIN) – within the context of the special centres set up to this end (Centres d'Études pour la Formation et l'Information sur la Scolarisation des Enfants de Migrants or CEFISEM).

RON HALLMARK

See also: education, the state and the church; education, secondary

Further reading

Auduc, J.-L. and Bayard-Pierlot, J. (1995) *Le Système éducatif français*, 4th edition, Créteil: Centre Régional de Documentation Pédagogique (an official account of the system, incorporating the most recent changes; a revised edition is published each year).

Vasconcellos, M. (1993) *Le Système éducatif*, Paris: Éditions La Découverte (a more systematic critique with historical perspective).

education, secondary: collèges, lycées, etc.

After completing primary education, pupils attend a junior high school (*collège*) from the age of 11 to 15 or so, and then choose to pursue further study in a senior high school (*lycée*), or to enter the world of work via, for instance, an apprenticeship training centre (*centre de formation de l'apprentissage*). For their own part, *lycées* are of two kinds: general and technological, which offer a three-year course leading to the general and technological *baccalauréats*; and professional which, in addition to preparing pupils for the professional *baccalauréat*, provide courses leading to a range of more practical, work-orientated qualifications.

Until 1995, the four years of junior high school study (known as classes 6, 5, 4 and 3 respectively) were divided into two periods (*cycles*): classes 6 and 5 formed the observation period (*cycle d'observation*), while classes 4 and 3 were known as the period of career and study choice (*cycle d'orientation*). In all four years, pupils followed a curriculum determined nationally, consisting of French, mathematics, a first modern language, history and geography, civics, life and earth sciences, technology, music, and physical education. Physical sciences and a second foreign language were added in classes 4 and 3, together with a choice of options from Latin, Greek, extra technology or extra modern language teaching.

However, the 1990s are witnessing a major

reform of the *collèges*. A pilot scheme to this effect was launched in 1994–5 in 368 schools across the country, and all other institutions were to follow suit in 1995–6. On this basis the progressive renewal of the four-year cycle will be complete in 1998–9.

The aims are to make the curriculum more flexible and more responsive to individual needs, and to provide appropriate extra teaching support for pupils in difficulty, thereby keeping pupils in the mainstream of the system as long as possible. To this end, the two *cycles* are transformed into three: class 6 becomes the observation period, with special arrangements for remedial teaching for pupils in difficulty, and a focus on the consolidation of basic skills and knowledge; classes 5 and 4 are henceforth the period of more developed learning (*cycle d'approfondissement*), where a more flexible timetable will enable greater individual choice; and class 3 becomes the period of career and study guidance (*cycle d'orientation*), where resources will be put into a major counselling and information effort. The redefinition of the *cycles* involves a delay in the timing of crucial decisions on a pupil's progress (proceed, repeat the year, choice of study/career path, such as via the 'general' stream in the *lycée*, or the less highly rated technological stream, or professional studies).

A diploma (the *brevet des collèges*) marks the successful completion of junior high school studies. It is awarded on the basis of marks gained in classes 4 and 3, together with written examinations in French, maths and history/geography.

Pupils able and willing to continue their studies in a general and technological high school (*lycée général et technologique*) do so with the aim of achieving the broad-based diploma awarded at the end of three years of further study, the *baccalauréat*. This aims to provide a good general education, as well as to enable successful candidates to embark upon higher education. An initial year (known as *seconde*) based upon common core subjects, to which are added options chosen by the student, is the prelude to increasing specialization over a further two years (*première* and *terminale*) in

terms of one of the three general subject categories (literary studies, economics and social studies, and science) or four defined technological areas (industrial science and technology, laboratory science and technology, medical sciences, tertiary-sector science and technology). The curriculum remains broadly based throughout, however: even in *terminale*, a specialist in mechanical engineering (within the general area of industrial science and technology) must cope with maths, history/geography, a foreign language, philosophy, and physical education, in addition to his or her chosen specialism.

The *lycée professionnel* (formerly, *lycée d'enseignement professionnel* and, before that, *collège d'enseignement technique*) is open mainly to students from class 3 of the *collèges* who wish, or have been advised or directed, to seek practical qualifications which will give direct entry to the job market. To this end, two-year sandwich courses lead to the Certificat d'Aptitude Professionnelle (CAP) or the Brevet d'Études Professionnelles (BEP). After this point, however, it is possible to go on to attempt a *baccalauréat professionnel*, whose twenty-nine specialisms lead directly to the world of work; or, indeed, by taking a year's reconversion course, to take a technological *baccalauréat*. It should also be pointed out that some students take advantage of their professional *baccalauréat* to follow courses in higher education, particularly in advanced technical departments (*sections de techniciens supérieurs* – see below).

Student numbers in the *lycées* have increased dramatically over the last forty years of the twentieth century, from 800,000 in 1960 to more than 2.3 million in 1995. This expansion looks set to continue, in view of the national objective of bringing 80 per cent of the age group to *baccalauréat* level by the year 2000 (in 1995, almost 63 per cent of the age group achieved the diploma). Hence efforts have been made to adapt what was originally a general, cultural diet for the elite to the needs of much wider audience. In 1969, the *baccalauréat technique* (renamed *technologique* in 1986) was created, and the *baccalauréat professionnel* was introduced the same year. The reform of the *lycée* curriculum, launched in 1992 and completed in 1995, should be viewed in the same perspective. The trend is now for *lycées* to become *polyvalents*, that is to say to to develop all three strands within the same institution, so as to facilitate interchange and mitigate the relative disfavour which which the non-generalist strands (especially the 'professional' strand) are viewed.

Mention should also be made of two branches of higher education to which some *lycées* are host: the *sections de techniciens supérieurs* (STS) and the *classes préparatoires aux grandes écoles* (CPGE). The former provide two-year courses leading to an advanced technical diploma in a range of options, sometimes linked to the needs of local industry, and designed to produce qualified supervisors and middle managers. The latter prepare candidates for the competitive examinations upon which recruitment to the elitist preserve of the *grandes écoles* is based.

Since the 1989 Education Act, all schools are required to produce an institutional plan showing how the sum total of their activities – curricular and extracurricular – combine to make up the school's distinctive contribution to achieving the aims and objectives laid down nationally. Such a plan, if sufficiently impressive, may ensure additional funding.

RON HALLMARK

See also: educational elitism: the *grandes écoles*; universities

Further reading

Auduc, J.-L. and Bayard-Pierlot, J. (1995) *Le Système éducatif français*, 4th edition, Créteil: Centre Régional de Documentation Pédagogique (an up-to-date guide to the system; a revised edition is produced every year).

Ministère de l'Éducation Nationale, de l'Enseignement Supérieur et de la Recherche (1996) *De la 6e au BAC*, Paris: Les Dossiers de l'Office National de l'Information sur les Enseignements et les Professions (ONISEP) (subtitled 'how to help your child succeed', it is a practical guide for parents to the workings of the system).

Vasconcellos, M. (1993) *Le Système éducatif*, Paris: Éditions La Découverte (gives a good perspective on how the system developed into its current form).

education, the state and the church

The French constitution guarantees equal access to educational opportunity for all citizens. Public education is free and secular, and its provision is an obligation upon the state. Yet, in the 1990s, almost 1 in 5 children is taught in a private – that is to say, for the most part (92 per cent) Catholic – school. Nowadays, despite traditional antagonism between the public and private sectors, the vast majority of private institutions enjoy a contractual relationship with the state, which gives them access to state funding. Given transfers at crucial moments of failure, educational progression or choice of stream, it has been estimated that as many as 1 in 3 pupils may, during their school careers, take advantage of the 'freedom of choice' represented by the private sector (*l'école libre*).

Until the Revolution, virtually all education was under the control of the church. The abolition of this monopoly in 1789 heralded more than a century of strife, as the state strove to take control of education in the face of stern opposition from the church, which considered teaching as one of its basic missions. Successive governments laboured to build up the capital and manpower resources, building and opening schools, and setting up training colleges for lay teachers (*écoles normales*) where anticlericalism was rife. While the church's authority was on the whole consolidated under the Restoration and the First and Second Empire, state control was eventually established under the Third Republic, in a series of measures associated in particular with Jules Ferry, minister from 1879 to 1883. In 1881–2, primary education was made compulsory, and free state schooling was introduced. In 1886, it was ruled that state education was to be dispensed exclusively by lay teachers, and religious education was replaced in the curriculum by 'moral and civic education'. Hence, the framework for a basic free, secular, compulsory state system was in place well before the formal separation of church and state in 1905 and the closure of the religious schools run by teaching Orders.

Catholic education did not disappear, however: two acts of parliament, the Guizot law (1833, for primary education) and the famous Falloux law of 1850 (for secondary education), had recognized the right of any authorized person or body to open and run a school, and hence endorsed the 'freedom' of families to choose the form of education for their children. These provisions remain in force today. Current relationships between the state and private education are regulated by acts of the Fifth Republic (the Debré law of 1959 and the Guermeur law of 1977) which offered private institutions a choice between independence outside the state system (where their income would be derived from fees), complete integration or association by contract. The last of these has been the choice of the overwhelming majority of such institutions. Under the two forms of contract that exist, the state assumes responsibility for the payment of staff salaries and teaching materials, and the competent local authorities (under decentralization) are required to make a contribution to overheads and running costs. In return, the state retains control over staff appointments, curriculum and the creation of new establishments, as places at private schools are counted in terms of the planning of resources. Contracting institutions must guarantee equal opportunity of access for all, irrespective of race or religion.

Antagonism remains deep-seated, however, and intermittently resurfaces. In 1982–4, attempts by the Socialist government to implement President **Mitterrand**'s election promise to make education 'a unified, secular public service' saw battle again joined along traditional lines. The proponents of secularism, led by the Comité National d'Action Laïque (CNAL), restated their opposition to the perpetuation of the 'dual' provision fostered by the current system of contracts; the defenders of 'freedom of choice', with the Comité National de l'Enseignement Catholique (CNEC) to the forefront, opposed any suggestion of integration or assimilation with the state system. After mass demonstrations by both camps, the proposed legislation was withdrawn as it was proving so socially divisive.

Yet traditional Catholic religious positions are not alone in posing a challenge to secularism in today's multicultural society. In 1989, when three girls were suspended from school in Creil for wearing the traditional Muslim headscarf (*chador*) during lessons – on the grounds that this represented a breach of the obligatory secular stance (*laïcité*), to which all state educational establishments are bound by law – there ensued counter-claims of racial and cultural discrimination. In an attempt to preserve tradition, in such a way as to rebut such claims, and also to cater for the right to freedom of conscience which the Conseil d'État, when consulted, was anxious to affirm, François Bayrou, the government minister, eventually issued a circular distinguishing between 'discreet' signs of religious allegiance (which are to be tolerated) and 'ostentatious symbols' which, amounting to proselytism, are potentially divisive and are therefore banned. Schools were instructed to incorporate a clause to this effect in their house regulations, though ultimately it was left to heads of schools to police this regulation and pronounce in individual cases.

RON HALLMARK

See also: Catholicism and Protestantism; education, primary; education, secondary: *collèges, lycées*, etc.; immigration; Islam; racism/-anti-semitism

Further reading

Durand-Prinborgne, C. (1994) *L'Éducation nationale: une culture, un service, un système*,

2nd edition, Paris: Nathan (this contains good, succinct sections on the private sector in context, and the current state of issues).

Gilsou-Bézier, F. (1989) *Connaissance du système éducatif français*, Paris: Éditions Castella (an especially useful source for the legislative framework of the system).

Langouet, G. and Léger, A. (1991) *Public ou privé? Trajectoires et réussites*, Paris: Éditions Publidix – Éditions de l'Espace Européen (an up-to-date study of trends and social contexts).

Parias, L.-H., Rémond, R., Rouche, M., Lebrun, F., Venard, M., Quéniart, J., Mayeur, F. and Prost, A. (1981/2) *Histoire général de l'enseignement et de l'éducation en France*, published under the direction of L.-H. Parias, preface by R. Rémond, 4 vols, Paris: Nouvelle Librairie de France (a well-documented general history; volume 3 traces the nineteenth-century struggle).

Le Monde (1984) 'L'École privée: les vrais enjeux', *Le Monde*, 3 March (an excellent review of the issues and of the state of play at the time of the attempt at major reform).

educational elitism: the grandes écoles

A very distinctive aspect of the French higher education system, the *grandes écoles* are a range of small, highly selective, mainly independent institutions which exist in parallel to the **universities** and form the privileged training ground of top politicians, civil servants, and chief executives in modern-day France.

It is difficult to generalize about the *grandes écoles* because they are both so numerous (well over 150) and so diverse in legal status, specialist fields, regimes and modes of finance. Their dominant role in the late twentieth century does not mean that they are modern foundations. Many of the most prestigious among them date from the nineteenth (or even eighteenth) century: the École des Ponts et Chaussées was founded in 1747, and others go back to the Revolution or the Empire. On the

other hand, perhaps the most famous of all, the École Nationale d'Administration (ENA), with its awesome reputation for turning out, not only top civil servants, but also senior diplomats, politicians and presidents of the Republic, was established as recently as 1945.

Some establishments are privately financed, others are publicly funded by Ministries of State (Defence, Agriculture, Transport, etc.), while yet others come under public commercial bodies such as the Chambers of Commerce. Some charge fees, some are free, some even confer salaried status upon their entrants, usually subject to an undertaking to enter state employment upon graduation: as *fonctionnaires-stagiaires*, entrants to the four Écoles Normales Supérieures receive about 8,000 francs per month. Lengths of courses vary (though three years would be the norm), as does the timing of recruitment.

However, various features are shared by most of these institutions. Although they have expanded over the last twenty years, they remain, unlike the universities, small and exclusive, with rarely many more than a thousand or so students. Given the increasing demand for such prestigious studies, and the lure of job prospects upon graduation, they can afford to be highly selective on entry. In most cases, this selection is based upon competitive examinations requiring special preparation, typically in the Classes Préparatoires aux Grandes Écoles (CPGE), which form part of the post-*baccalauréat* provision in the big *lycées* and to which entry is itself selective. The CPGE represent two years of intensive, highly competitive and stressful study of one of three main branches of learning – humanities, economics or science – without any guarantee of success. Students often have to – or choose to – repeat a year, and by no means all obtain places in the end; but the jobs to which successful candidates may aspire at the end of study in a *grande école* – senior, highly paid, executive posts in the civil service or the private sector – are such that increasing numbers of applicants come forward each year.

As well as being small and selective, the *grandes écoles* are also professionally orientated.

Their statutes are often defined, not in terms of the disciplines they teach, but of the end product: the École Polytechnique, for example, is committed to 'give its students a general and scientific education which will equip them for highly qualified positions of responsibility in the scientific, technical or economic sectors in state civil or military departments and the public services, and more generally in the activities of the Nation as a whole'. Active professionals and industrialists assist in the design of syllabuses and in their updating, and are often involved in the teaching. Practical placements form an essential part of the curriculum in many cases. The value of an individual school's diploma, for which, in addition, each graduand is ranked in order within the year's cohort, is assessed partly in terms of the jobs and salaries commanded by its graduates. A fierce sense of loyalty is engendered within the student bodies, which, after graduation, continue to pursue activities on behalf of the institution through networks of alumni.

Amid all the diversity indicated above, it is possible to identify certain significant groupings. The four Écoles Normales Supérieures, which admit some 3,000 students in all, train top-level researchers, teachers and more generally administrators in a range of basic disciplines (including literature and the arts, the sciences and technology). The engineering schools (École Nationale Supérieure des Mines, des Ponts et Chaussées, des Télécommunications, etc.) provide senior managers and technical experts for the public services and for industry. The title 'engineer' is prestigious and highly sought-after in France, and the right to confer this title is strictly regulated. L'École des Hautes Études Commerciales (HEC) and the various Écoles Supérieures de Commerce train business executives, accountants, financial consultants, etc. Finally, a clutch of establishments prepare their students specifically (though not exclusively) for careers in government administration: the ENA (referred to above) and the nine Instituts d'Études Politiques.

With their unabashed elitist approach, the upper-middle-class bias of their social composition, their tendency to teach conformist atti-tudes, and their capacity for internal self-perpetuation, the *grandes écoles* have come under increasing criticism in the 1980s and 1990s. There is no doubt about their influence in French society, however, or the stranglehold they have on senior posts in both the public and private sectors. A survey in 1993 revealed that, in the 200 leading French companies, 73 per cent of the top executives were products of the *grandes écoles*; almost 50 per cent of them were diplomates of either ENA or the École Polytechnique.

RON HALLMARK

See also: education, secondary: *collèges*, *lycées*, etc.

Further reading

Fauconnier, P. (1992) 'Le Vent de la révolte: les grandes écoles dans le colimateur', *Le Nouvel Observateur*, 21 May 1992.

Gaillard, J.-M. (1987) *Tu seras président, mon fils. Anatomie des Grandes Écoles et malformations des élites*, Paris: Éditions Ramsay (critique of the training provided, and of its inadequacy to meet the challenges of the year 2000).

Ministère de l'Éducation Nationale, de l'Enseignement Supérieur et de la Recherche (1996) *Après le BAC: réussir ses études. Le Guide des études supérieures 1996*, Paris: Les Dossiers ONISEP (up-to-date review of the options and procedures).

electronic revolution

The electronic revolution affects many areas of French life. According to President **Chirac**, its most important realization, the information revolution, will be the third such major upheaval for mankind, following the agricultural and the industrial revolutions. The Minitel telephone-based information system, started early, is popular and widespread; computer-based learning has been massively supported in education; in entertainment, **television**, video, games and CDs have become normal features of everyday life; the information society – bringing together information, entertainment and the exchange of opinion and channelled through new information highways – is being prepared through specific government (and to a lesser extent commercial) action. Perhaps more so than in other countries, 'language engineering' has played a significant part: the specific problems and role of French language have been at the forefront of official concern, although French is inventing neologisms to cope.

The French Teletel network, Minitel, was formed in 1980 as a response to Prestel, but followed an original approach widening provision from business to the general public. France Télécom provided minicomputers free to telephone subscribers, and incidentally gave massive support to the French computer industry. Individuals and commercial enterprises were encouraged to set up their own servers, and are paid for whatever service they make available with money collected on their behalf through phone bills. The approach had enormous success, with 6.5 million interactive terminals by 1995, and 25,000 on-line services ranging from newspapers to bulletin boards, from sober bank transactions and the booking of tickets for trains or concerts to *messageries roses*, enabling usually erotic pictures and messages to be anonymously accessed and exchanged – with no public outcry. Giving access to everybody and familiarizing users with computer screens, Minitel popularized the electronic revolution and brought home how useful and indeed interesting and entertaining technology could be. Even by 1985, some 42 per cent of Minitel time was devoted to games and messages, while during 1994 the French made 1,913 million calls, used the system for 110 million hours and spent 6.6 billion francs. However, the system has remained almost exclusively French, and hopes of France leading the world were not realized.

Computer-based learning has been massively supported in education: computers have been given to schools, and widespread training offered to teachers. As in most countries, however, the incredible speed of change has reduced the value of early large-scale initiatives, and computers have not yet become either required or integral parts of the learning process. In entertainment, television, video and games have become normal features of everyday life. **Cable and satellite television** have provoked the creation of new French TV channels, although much that is on offer is in English. CD-Roms, both for educational and entertainment purposes, and both audio and audiovisual, have followed earlier forms of electronic diffusion. Laser shows have transformed Paris for official celebrations as well as for concerts. Arcade games and consoles are enormously popular with the young, and sales of multimedia PCs are booming.

Government and other public authorities, rather than private industry, have led the way, developing information highways – cable, satellite transmission and the Internet. The French public has become used to many outward signs of electronic technology – constantly changing municipal notice-boards in every town's pedestrian area, driverless trains on light passenger railways, destination boards on buses. Behind these outward signs, industrial and particularly transport technology is heavily dependent on computerization and such international developments as the Global Positioning System. But the French tradition of high protectionist barriers and centralized methods of control has offended European competition laws, and more significantly may find it difficult to withstand the anarchic explosion of the Internet or the commercial pressures from non-French manufacturers.

Perhaps more so than in other countries, 'language engineering' has been a significant element in the electronic revolution. The stakes are high: President Chirac is on record in December 1995 as saying, 'if, in the new media, our language, our programmes, our inventions are not significantly present our future generations will be both economically and culturally marginalized'. Language engineering is the concern of the language industries, concerned with the creation and manipulation of (monolingual and multilingual) text, documents of any size from memos to encyclopedias, mixtures of text and images. These industries have many profitable outlets: simple word processing, office management, automatic translation, full-text information held in data banks, and a whole range of software for finding it. Most of these applications, and particularly the databases, use American English, and indeed the enormous economic and commercial power of American industry and media across the world impose the use of this lingua franca; consequently much effort in France has been deployed on language planning. As far as possible, government organizations like the Délégation Générale à la Langue Française must discover French terms to replace American ones and enforce their use; American must be translated to French in every aspect of communication media; and as far as possible French software and hardware should be supported. There have been some successes: the ubiquitous suffix *-ique* (*informatique*, *bureautique*, *robotique*) is fruitful in neologisms; words like *logiciel* (software), *convivial* (user-friendly), *baladeur* (walkman) have become common usage. But the inventiveness of people has another outlet: writing on screens, as in Minitel, has created a whole new shorthand and spelling, with *k* replacing *qu*, *c* replacing *c'est*, and words telescoped: *oqp* stands for *occupé* (busy).

DENNIS AGER

See also: economy; linguistic regulation; music industry; pop video

Further reading

Ager, D. E. (1996) *Language Policy in Britain and France: The Processes of Policy*, London: Cassell (examines the processes used in France for language planning, together with the policy itself).

Noreiko, S. F. (1993) 'New words for new technologies', in Sanders, C. (ed.) *French Today: Language in Its Social Context*, Cambridge: Cambridge University Press, (a useful gloss of the relationship between language and the electronic revolution in France).

Elkabbach, Jean-Pierre

b. 1937, Oran, Algeria

Broadcaster

He is an *éminence grise* of French **television**, where he became director of news at Antenne 2 in 1977. It was during an interview with him in the run-up to the 1978 legislative elections that Georges **Marchais** lost his cool and endeared himself to much of the audience by instructing him to 'Shut up, Elkabbach!' ('Taisez-vous, Elkabbach!' – later to be the title of Elkabbach's autobiography). Eased out under the Socialists, he has since 1992 been director of the channels **France 2** and **France 3**.

KEITH READER

See also: television

Elle

Women's magazine

Elle has been one of the most innovative of French women's weekly magazines since 1945. It was founded in 1945, by the Défense de la France group, upon the initiative of its first editor, Hélène Gordon-Lazareff, who had returned from the USA to an effervescent France which was keen to consume, communicate and be entertained. Gordon-Lazareff saw it as her mission to establish an *haut de gamme* (luxury) women's magazine to respond to these three desires. Hence, from the start, *Elle* represented an original women's magazine in terms of the luxury quality of paper, use of quadrochromatic colour, state-of-the-art printing techniques, the use of well-known photographers to produce sophisticated images and the frank, humorous tone with which all subjects deemed female were discussed. In the 1950s, *Elle* saw itself as the 'bible' for women who aspired to be in the forefront of social, cultural and political change: the typical *Elle* reader was young, middle-class and Paris-based. By 1960, *Elle*'s annual circulation figure stood at over 650,000.

As a self-proclaimed progressive magazine, after **May 1968** *Elle* adopted the less radical, feminist ideas surrounding women's sexuality and personal liberation and began campaigning in favour of an extension of women's rights: for **abortion/contraception**; for extended maternity rights and facilities for public **child care**; for the employment rights of part-time workers, etc. Not only did *Elle*'s campaigning take place within its pages but also through organized events of which the show-piece was the États Généraux de la Femme, held at Versailles in November 1970. This congress brought together politicians, academics, trade unionists, doctors, civil servants and employers to discuss a number of themes chosen as a result of a nationwide survey, organized by the magazine, to establish women's foremost concerns. The aim of the congress was to present those in power with a detailed picture of the aspirations of French women. Undoubtedly, though, it constituted an effective means of marketing the magazine beyond its established Parisian readership and the magazine achieved high sales between 1970 and 1974.

By 1975, gloomy economic forecasts and competition from the specialist periodical press and other media led to plummeting sales and hence the adoption of another marketing formula – that of the unisex magazine, which included news stories, political and economic analyses, serious cultural features and reviews. This approach failed, however, and the magazine's takeover by the Filipacchi group marked a return, at the beginning of the 1980s, to the tried and tested formula of femininity. In the 1980s and 1990s, *Elle* survived in a fiercely competitive market, not due to success in France but because of its foreign editions which now number twenty-five. It no longer bears the hallmark of originality and innovation it once did.

KHURSHEED WADIA

See also: feminism (movements/groups); women's magazines

Further reading

Bonvoisin, S-M and Maignien, M. (1986) *La presse féminine*, Paris: PUF (a useful introduction to the women's periodical press).

Presse et Statistiques (1994), Paris: SJTI (statistical information relating to the press).

Wadia, K. (1991) 'Women's Magazines: Coming to Terms with Feminism Post-May 1968', *French Cultural Studies* 2, 6 (an examination of the influence of second wave feminism upon the ideology and discourse of femininity as encountered in women's magazines).

Éluard, Paul

b. 1895, St-Denis, Paris;
d. 1952, Charenton-le-Pont

Poet, real name Eugène Grindel

He has the distinction of being the foremost poet of the Surrealist movement and the most celebrated of the Resistance poets. In keeping with the objectives of Surrealism, his poetry abounds in images, and yet the effect of the poetry is virtually 'classical' because of Éluard's gift for elegant control and sensuousness. Almost all of the poetry celebrates the fascination of Woman and the erotic power she exercises over men. One often has the impression that Éluard is continuing the grand tradition of troubadour poetry. In the years of the Resistance, the subject matter of the poems widens to include the themes of fraternity and liberty. The enormous quantity of poetry written over a period of thirty-five years is collected in the Pléiade edition of his *Poésies complètes* (1968). Éluard was a close friend of **Picasso** and knew most of the Cubist and Surrealist painters well; they often illustrated his works.

WALTER A. STRAUSS

See also: poetry

employment

In the postwar period, France has undergone a major transformation both in the composition of its workforce and in the nature of the employment which the economy offers the population. From an economy in which the majority of workers were men, working full-time in stable jobs, often in industry or **agriculture**, France has moved to a position in which women are as likely as men to be employed in the labour market, the service sector provides two-thirds of all jobs and the notion of a stable job for life is becoming a thing of the past.

In the first years after World War II, a significant proportion of the French working population were still engaged in agriculture. Indeed, France remained a much more agricultural country than its main economic competitors. However, the rapid industrialization which the country experienced in the 1950s drew large numbers of individuals away from their farming activities and into the towns and factories. This pool of indigenous, cheap unskilled labour was a major boost to French industrial output and prosperity in this period. That said, indigenous labour was not sufficient to respond to the massive labour requirements of the country at that time and the French economy relied heavily on migrant workers. Alongside this industrialization of the French economy, an equally important change was taking place which itself demanded new workers. This was the tertiarization of the economy, meaning the rapid expansion of service-sector jobs in shops, offices, schools, hospitals and the like. Many of the new jobs created in the service sector in the 1960s and 1970s were taken by women. Therefore, during the years of expansion, new categories of workers, in particular women and migrants, were called upon

to make up the shortfall of indigenous male workers for the expanding French economy. However, when the world recession hit France in 1974 and unemployment began its inexorable rise, these new categories of workers did not simply return whence they had come, be that another country or the 'kitchen sink'. The active population of France had undergone a radical and irreversible transformation.

The only problem concerning employment in the 1950s and 1960s had been labour shortage. All this changed dramatically after 1974, when unemployment became an integral, if unwelcome part of French life. From an average of 200,000–300,000 during the years of economic growth, by 1976 the number of unemployed had reached the 1 million mark, by 1981 it had reached 1.5 million, until by the 1990s the figure was stuck at over 3 million. During the first years of recession after 1974, it was thought by the government that a return to growth would immediately reduce the unemployment figures to acceptable levels. However, as the 1970s and 1980s wore on, it became clear that two factors inhibited significant reductions in unemployment, even when economic growth returned. The first was the phenomenon of 'jobless growth'. If the rate of economic growth is strong, but nevertheless remains below the level of productivity increases in the economy, significant numbers of jobs will not be created and therefore such growth will be 'jobless'. Second, even if economic growth does create jobs, these do not necessarily keep pace with the increase in the number of those seeking jobs.

Indeed, there is a certain amount of debate concerning the solutions to the unemployment question in France. Right-wing politicians and commentators often argue that French labour costs are too high and that these costs result from the **minimum wage** (SMIC) and the cost to employers of social security contributions. This acts as a disincentive for companies to take on workers. Most politicians, however, pin their hopes for a reduction in unemployment on France becoming more successful and competitive in the world. In the meantime, successive governments have set up schemes to encourage employers to hire the unemployed, particularly young people, by relieving them of the social security contributions which they pay on behalf of their employees. Although unemployment in and of itself is a serious social problem, the unevenness of its distribution throughout the French population worsens matters. Geographically speaking, traditional industrial regions such as the north and the east of the country are most badly affected. In social terms, women, immigrants, the unskilled, the young and the over-50s are all disproportionately affected by unemployment.

For those who manage to remain in a job, the experience of work has changed dramatically since the 1970s. Whereas in the years of expansion jobs were permanent, and often for life, the economic crisis led to the development of 'flexibility' in the labour market with a wide range of differing conditions for labour being on offer. Although a core of employees with secure long-term jobs stills exists in France, an increasing proportion of the population find themselves working on short-term contracts and/or as part-time employees. For some, such jobs are merely a temporary expedient, but for others, their entire work life consists in going from one insecure job, or 'petit boulot', to another. Furthermore, the average person's working life is becoming shorter as young people stay on in education for longer periods of time and individuals continue to retire earlier. This generational concentration in the distribution of work, however, coupled with an increasingly aged population, means that an ever-dwindling active population is keeping a growing army of the inactive, whether young or old.

JAN WINDEBANK

See also: economy; immigration; social security

Further reading

Bouvier, P. (1991) *Le Travail*, Paris: PUF (a concise account of the way in which work is structured in contemporary France).

Grangeas, G. and Le Pagé, J.-M. (1992) *Les Politiques de l'emploi*, Paris: PUF (a neat description of state policy towards employment and unemployment in France).

Équipe, L'

L'Équipe, France's best-known and oldest sports newspaper (it celebrated its fiftieth birthday in February 1996), is published daily except Sunday and has a weekly magazine which is also devoted exclusively to sport. With a readership often in excess of half a million, *L'Équipe*, which uses the most advanced technology available, is noted for the range of sports that it covers and for its esoteric style, often relying heavily on specialized vocabulary, literary allusions, pun and wordplay.

IAN PICKUP

See also: national press in France; sport

Ernaux, Annie

b. 1940, Lillebonne

Writer

Ernaux's literary corpus, initiated by the 1974 novel *Cleaned Out* (*Les Armoires vides*), focuses particularly on the theme of social **class**. The only daughter of working-class parents, a number of the autobiographical fictions she published in the 1980s – *Positions* (*La Place*), *Une Femme* (A Woman) and *La Femme gelée* (The Frozen Woman) – address the gulf between the 'classe dominée' into which Ernaux was born and the 'classe dominante' to which university education permitted her to accede, and the consequences of the kind of social metamorphosis Ernaux herself underwent. While she is by no means a militant feminist, gender-role formation and (female) sexuality also feature as key themes in Ernaux's writing, dominating *Ce qu'ils disent ou rien* (What They Say or

Nothing), published in 1977, and 1991's more recent *Passion simple* (Simple Passion). One of France's leading contemporary women writers, Ernaux's latest work includes *Journal du dehors* (A Diary of the Outside) and *La Honte* (Shame).

ALEX HUGHES

See also: autobiography; women's/lesbian writing

erotic writing

In the decades following the war, authors of erotica had to contend with a prolongation of the moral order imposed by **Vichy**, and with a climate of repression which made publication problematic. From the mid-1970s onward, the situation became less restrictive, and in the late twentieth century French erotic literature appears to be flourishing. Any review of post-war erotico-literary production in France needs to focus upon those texts which, if they occasionally or even regularly employ the motifs of commercial pornography, nevertheless transcend the limitations of a crudely pornographic model (see Frappier-Mazur 1988). Additionally, such a review must take account, not only of the sociohistorical landmarks punctuating the evolution of the erotico-literary genre and the publishers associated with that genre, but also of the diverse 'categories' of erotica it has engendered.

In the introduction to her very useful anthology, *Écrire d'amour,* Claudine Brécourt-Villars isolates laws passed in 1930, 1939, 1949, 1958 and 1967 as generative of the controls to which the publication of erotica was subjected in France for the first thirty years of the postwar period (Brécourt-Villars 1985). She cites also, as significant moments in the evolution of the erotico-literary field, 1964 (a year which witnessed a 'new erotic offensive') and 1970 (the year in which an 'unprecedented wave of erotica' burst upon the literary scene). Her essay makes the further point that if literary erotica managed to survive in postwar France, this was because it was defended by the country's intelligentsia. This fact is evidenced by the enthusiasm for the works of Sade displayed in the writings of authors such as **Beauvoir**, Georges **Bataille**, **Blanchot** and **Lacan**. Indicative also of intellectual support for erotico-literary freedom is the way in which public and literary figures voiced their opposition, in 1945 and 1973, to the prosecutions of the Denoël publishing house (Henry Miller's French publishers) and of Régine Deforges, whose *maison d'édition* L'Or du Temps specialized in erotica.

Deforges is not the only specialist publisher whose name springs to mind in the context of literary erotica. *Éditeurs* in this field include Éric Losfeld, a Surrealist who published erotic works clandestinely ('sous le manteau') and officially; Claude Tchou, whose Cercle du Livre Précieux series included erotic 'classics' and new texts; and Jean-Jacques Pauvert, whose efforts to bring out new editions of the works of Sade encountered legal obstacles in the 1950s. Yet other publishers specializing in the erotico-literary domain are Christian Bourgois, La Jeune Parque, Spengler, and Zulma. As Brécourt-Villars indicates, after 1964 mainstream *maisons d'édition* such as **Gallimard** also began to publish erotic fiction (Brécourt-Villars 1985).

For review purposes, we can divide postwar erotic writing into two key subsections – male- and female-authored erotic discourse – and subdivide these bodies of writing into a further series of categories. According to Anne-Marie Dardigna's study *Les Châteaux d'Éros*, a good many postwar, male-authored, heterosexually oriented erotic texts – the creations of writers such as **Leiris**, Klossowski and Mandiargues – associate the erotic with the mystical and the metaphysical, and/or privilege quasi-religious motifs such as transgression and profanation (Dardigna 1980). The fusion of the erotic and the metaphysical/spiritual is likewise a central theme in Bataille's influential 1957 essay *Eroticism* (*L'Erotisme*), as it is in his own prewar erotic tales. The first modern writers to connect sexual liberation to an *affirmation du Mal*, suggests Dardigna, were the Surrealists.

While most of the erotico-literary works emerging from the Surrealist movement predated 1945, postwar texts associated with it include André Pieyre de Mandiargues's tales of sadism *Le Musée Noir* (The Black Museum), published in 1946 and Leiris's *Aurora*, which appeared in the same year. In these works, and in later erotic texts such as Klossowski's *Roberte ce soir* (Roberte This Evening) and **Robbe-Grillet**'s *La Maison de rendez-vous*, the female body (argues Dardigna) regularly becomes the key locus of ritualized profanation and obliteration. Clearly, the same is not true of texts in which male homosexuality is the focus. In the immediate postwar period, the gay writers whose work focused most explicitly on masculine homoeroticism were **Genet** and **Jouhandeau**: neither offers wholly empowering visions of gay male love/sexuality. Genet's accounts of homoerotic transgression were long viewed as radical texts, but in recent times critics have addressed the way in which their images of homosexual abjection mesh with heterosexual prejudice (see Rifkin 1995; Robinson 1995). In and after the late 1960s, texts by authors such as Renaud **Camus**, Yves **Navarre**, Tony **Duvert** and Hervé **Guibert** offered constructions of gay sexuality which departed from the model contained in the writings of Genet.

Within the generic field of postwar women's erotic discourse, various subcategories exist. On the one hand, there are those texts which reveal scant evidence of a 'politicization' of women's erotic experience. Such works generally refrain from questioning gender norms/relations, and tend to employ the motifs of male-authored erotica/pornography (see Hughes and Ince 1995). This body of writing is exemplified by Pauline Réage's *Story of O* (a pseudonymous work which appeared in 1954 and whose female authorship remains in doubt) and the *Emmanuelle* series, launched in 1960. On the other hand, the 1960s, 1970s and 1980s witnessed the publication of a series of more complex female-authored erotico-literary productions. These works place women's eroticism against the backdrop of social and gender relations (see Frappier-Mazur 1988), and/or attest to a feminist awareness initiated by the publication of Beauvoir's *The Second Sex* and reinforced by post-**May 1968**, neo-feminist reconsiderations of questions of sexuality, language and representation. Often exercises in textual innovation, they interrogate, implicitly or explicitly, sexual power relations, erotic norms and the modalities of their representation. Among this group of texts may be included the accounts of lesbian love offered by Violette **Leduc** and by the more radical Hélène **Cixous** and Monique **Wittig**; **Duras**'s *The Seated Man in the Passage* (*L'Homme assis dans le couloir*); as well as Christiane **Rochefort**'s *Warrior's Rest* (*Le Repos du guerrier*) and the highly ironic, male-narrated *Quand tu vas chez les femmes* (Excursions into Womankind). Other contemporary women authors associated with the erotico-literary domain are: Vanessa Duriès, whose allegedly autobiographical account of S/M love, *The Ties That Bind* (*Le Lien*), was published shortly before her death in 1993; Alina **Reyes**, best known, perhaps, for the erotic novels *The Butcher* (*Le Boucher*) and *Behind Closed Doors* (*Derrière la porte*); and Benoîte **Groult**.

ALEX HUGHES

See also: feminism (movements/groups); gay writing; literary censorship; publishing/*l'édition*; women's/lesbian writing

Further reading

Alexandrian (1995) *Histoire de la littérature érotique*, Paris: Payot (a wide-ranging, personal discussion of erotic writing in France).

Brécourt-Villars, C. (1985) *Écrire d'amour*, Paris: Ramsay (an anthology of French women's erotic writing, with a useful introductory essay).

Dardigna, A.-M. (1980) *Les Châteaux d'Éros*, Paris: Maspero (an exploration of the narrative, representational and ideological characteristics of modern French male-authored erotic writing).

Frappier-Mazur, L. (1988) 'Marginal Canons: Rewriting the Erotic', *Yale French Studies* 75 (an interesting analysis of French women's reinscriptions of sexual/textual models established by the male erotico-literary tradition).

Hughes, A. and Ince, K. (eds) (1995) *French Erotic Fiction*, Oxford: Berg (a series of essays on contemporary French women's erotic writing).

Rifkin, A. (1995) 'From Renaud Camus to the Gay City Guide', in M. Sheringham (ed.) *Parisian Fields*, London: Reaktion Books (an essay containing useful insights into gay male erotic writing).

Robinson, C. (1995) *Scandal in the Ink*, London: Cassell (a study of modern gay and lesbian writing in France).

Etcherelli, Claire

b. 1934, Bordeaux

Writer

Etcherelli's best-known novel, *Élise or the Real Life* (*Élise ou la vraie vie*) was published in 1967 and won the Prix Femina. In realist mode, it tells of the relationship between its heroine and an Algerian, Arezki, which forms in the factory where both characters work and develops against the backdrop of the **Algerian war**. Key themes/experiences charted in the text are class identity/oppression, sexism, racism and the growth of political awareness. In the 1970s, Etcherelli published two other novels – *A propos de Clémence* (About Clémence) and *Un Arbre voyageur* (The Travelling Tree) – which focus on postwar French society, and also edited a volume of anti-racist poems.

ALEX HUGHES

See also: literary prizes; racism/anti-semitism; women's/lesbian writing

Further reading

Atack, M. (1990) 'The Politics of Identity in *Élise ou la vraie vie*', in M. Atack and P. Powrie (eds) *Contemporary French Fiction by Women*, Manchester: Manchester University Press (a lucid account of Etcherelli's treatment, in *Élise*, of identity and self-awareness, which stresses the political potential, for feminism, of realist literary practice).

Europe 1

Radio station

Created in 1955, this general-interest station (long wave and FM) was one of the big three *radios périphériques*, tolerated by the French state, but transmitting from the Sarre, just outside the national borders. Its innovative style (news flashes, variety shows and game programmes involving listeners) has influenced all other stations over the years. Although its audience share is waning, it still attracts at least 10 per cent of France's listeners. In 1986 it set up a subsidiary popular music station, Europe 2 (FM), which attracts over 5 per cent of the national audience. Its studios are at 26 bis, rue François Ier, 75008 Paris.

ALAN PEDLEY

See also: francophone radio: Europe; radio (private/free)

European economic integration

France is at the core of the European economic integration project. This process finds its origins in a political strategy aimed at avoiding conflicts in Europe, and it has gained impetus from the 1986 Single European Act and the 1992 Maastricht Treaty. The liberal ideology and economic strategies which have underpinned recent developments in the **European Union** are seen as having heavy social costs, however, and enthusiasm for integration has cooled significantly.

The European economic integration project has always been overtly political – the French 'fathers' of Europe, such as Monnet and Schuman, who initiated the first steps through the European Coal and Steel Community treaty in 1951, sought to avoid the economic isolation of defeated Germany and a repeat of the errors of the Versailles Treaty after World War I. The signing of the Rome Treaty was followed by the coming to power of de Gaulle in 1958, and the French attitude to European integration became quite complex, with France staunchly promoting national independence within a 'Europe of States', but continuing to advocate economic integration for the benefit of French economic interests. Traditions of protectionism started to be dismantled with the abolition of internal EC duties in 1968, but the Common Agricultural Policy (CAP) ran into difficulties with de Gaulle's refusal to agree to agricultural policies not acceptable to French farmers. During the 1970s, European economic integration made relatively little progress except via the emergence of new tools of political co-operation, such as the European Council and the creation in 1979 of the Exchange Rate Mechanism. With de Gaulle out of power, France also accepted the UK's membership. Public opinion was then highly favourable to European economic integration. During the 1980s, France again found itself at the forefront of European economic integration efforts. After a brief period of coolness, President Mitterrand firmly backed European integration as the only way to achieve an autonomous economic space, accepting the Single European Act in 1986 (which forced sea changes in French trade and administrative practices) and supporting the Maastricht Treaty in 1992.

Europe has benefited the French economy, helping to switch and develop export markets in industrial sectors and services and helping to develop French agriculture into the most powerful agriculture in Europe. Since the mid-1980s the pursuit of European integration has encouraged governments to apply a liberal economic strategy combining anti-inflation policy, rigorous budgetary strategy, high interest rates and accelerated deregulation. The relentless pursuit of this strategy, dubbed *La Pensée unique*, is widely held responsible for France's

social ills, especially its very high unemployment and the weakening of social cohesion (the *fracture sociale*), as well as for putting a question mark over the future of French 'Public Services' and its welfare system. Despite this deep unease and outright rejection by a significant part of the population, governments have persevered in their policies, so that France can be alongside Germany in the first wave of countries to adopt the single European currency, the Euro, in 1999.

FRANÇOIS NECTOUX

See also: Delors, Jacques

Further reading

Dyker, D. A. (ed.) (1992) *The National Economies of Europe*, 2 vols, London: Longman (volume 1 includes a general analysis of economic integration; volume 2 contains a chapter on the role of the French economy in Europe).

Lipietz, A. (1991) 'Governing the Economy in the Face of International Challenge', in: J. F. Hollifield and G. Ross (eds) *In Search of New France*, London: Routledge (a broad survey of the consequences of the opening of the French economy).

European Union

France played a founding role in early European integration and has since aimed to lead the development of European union, usually in partnership with Germany, and arguably to her own advantage. Despite general political support for integration, French European policy has occasionally provoked some domestic division between partisans of supranational integration and supporters of a more Gaullist 'Europe of Nations'.

As a signatory of the Treaty of Rome (1957), France had already participated in the Council of Europe (1949) and the ECSC (1950). Although lack of French support sabotaged a proposed European Defence Community (1954), France fostered *rapprochement* with Germany to prevent future conflict, and the Common Market was easily ratified by parliament, only the Communists voting against *en bloc*. Under the presidency of de **Gaulle** (1958–69), France adopted a critical attitude towards European integration, basing her policy on the primacy of national sovereignty. The French *Plan Fouchet* (1962) argued for a 'Europe of States' driven by high politics rather than by economic and technical convergence and with a 'European' rather than 'Atlanticist' character. The failure of this vision, French withdrawal from NATO (1966) and de Gaulle's vetoes of British entry (1963, 1967) slowed integration, but reinforced France's dominance (with Germany) at the heart of policy.

In the 1970s and 1980s, after **Pompidou**'s 'Oui' to the UK (1973), partnerships between **Giscard d'Estaing** and Schmidt (who reputedly conversed in English on European matters) and **Mitterrand** and Kohl furthered the growth of the Community. During 1985–93, the presidency of the Commission was assumed by Jacques **Delors** (previously French Finance and Economics minister and, subsequently, a potential presidential candidate), further heightening French public awareness of Europe. In 1992 debate over Maastricht reopened domestic political divisions between integrationists, and those fearing loss of sovereignty (notably the Socialist Jean-Pierre Chevènement and the neo-Gaullists Philippe **Séguin** and Charles **Pasqua** of the RPR). The Treaty was accepted by parliament, supported by the Left and the Centre-Right UDF, but with divided neo-Gaullists mainly abstaining. This split in the Centre-Right coalition was echoed in the referendum, which accepted Maastricht by only 1 per cent.

France has benefited from her status as a founding member of the European Union and has used her central role to derive advantage from European policies: French **agriculture**, iron and steel, aerospace and the regions have profited in particular. France has also been conscious of the symbolic and practical benefits to be gained from aspects of European union, such as the siting of parliament in Strasbourg, the predominance of French administrative procedures in the European Commission and the major role of the French language in much European bureaucracy. Under the **Chirac** presidency, latent Euroscepticism has been encouraged by difficulties in shadowing the German economy and by disquiet over aspects of GATT, ERM and Bosnia, although governments have seemed committed to traditional French support for Europe.

HUGH DAUNCEY

See also: European economic integration

Further reading

Kramer, S. P. (1994) *Does France Still Count? The French Role in the New Europe*, Westport, CN: Praeger (a short clear overview, with some background on evolving issues).

Eurovision Song Contest

The much-maligned Eurovision Song Contest, which in its early days provided some of the first live, trans-Europe television links, has seen a number of French successes, including those of André Claveau, with **Delanoë** and Giraud's 1958 *Dors mon amour* (Sleep My Love), and Isabelle Aubret, first with Vic and Valade's *Un premier amour* (A First Love) in 1962, and then with *La Source* (The Spring) in 1968, by Djian, Bonnet and Faure. Another notable French success was that of France **Gall** with Serge **Gainsbourg**'s *Poupée de cire, poupée de son* (Wax Doll, Rag Doll) in 1965.

IAN PICKUP

See also: song/*chanson*

Eustache, Jean

b. 1938, Pessac;
d. 1981, Paris

Director

Eustache's suicide deprived France of one of its major film-makers. The **documentary** style of his approach, as with *Le Cochon* of 1970, reaches its apotheosis in *The Mother and the Whore* (*La Maman et la putain*) of 1973. More than three and a half hours of triangular emotional and sexual agonizing, in the literal sense of that word, in the flats and bars of St-Germain-des-Prés give Bernadette Lafont and above all Jean-Pierre **Léaud** perhaps their greatest roles. The film is an endlessly suggestive epitaph for the 'generation of **May 1968**.'

KEITH READER

See also: cinema

Événement du jeudi, L'

Magazine

A weekly news magazine, created by Jean-François Kahn in 1984. Left of centre and iconoclastic, it was the most personalized of news magazines, reflecting its founder's originality and candour. Investigative journalism, in-depth dossiers, broad cultural coverage, cartoons and sensational headlines (verging on bad taste) brought success. Initially, editorial freedom was secured by limiting dependence on **advertising**, setting a high cover price, and involving readers and journalists as shareholders. Financial problems arose in the early 1990s, and in 1995 the arrival of new director and majority shareholder Thierry Verret saved the paper from bankruptcy, and radical changes were introduced. Circulation in 1995 fell to below 170,000 copies per week.

PAM MOORES

See also: comic strips/cartoonists; national press in France

existentialism

'Existentialism' is the name given to the philosophical, literary and artistic movement centred in postwar Paris. Early signs of the flowering of existentialism that swept French literature, philosophy and art in the wake of the 1940–4 German Occupation first appeared a decade earlier, in French translations of, and commentaries on, writings by the philosophers Edmund Husserl and Martin Heidegger. Between 1945 and 1949, a range of writers, artists and philosophers, energized by metaphysical questions of identity and the meaning of life, drew on the euphoria of the **Liberation** and the despair following revelations of the Nazi genocide perpetrated on European Jews and other minorities in order to produce work that can be classed as existentialist. Over the same period, what began as a topic of specialized concern among philosophers evolved into a wider cultural sensibility and fashion.

As if overnight, Jean-Paul **Sartre** and Albert **Camus** were cast as proponents of a new intellectual movement and as role models of an existentialist chic characterized by a taste for black turtle neck jerseys and smoky subterranean **jazz** clubs such as Le Tabou in St-Germain des Prés. Debates over Sartre's *Being and Nothingness* (*L'Être et le néant*) and Camus's *The Myth of Sisyphus* (*Le Mythe de Sisyphe*) carried over from the lecture hall to the café where the writer/jazz trumpeter Boris **Vian** and the cabaret singer/actor Juliette **Gréco** ruled.

In its narrowest sense, existentialism is a philosophical system whose focuses include human freedom – defined as our capacity to reinvent our own meaning, constantly, via future-oriented projects – and the anguish that accompanies our awareness of it. Broader expressions of postwar existentialism drew not only on key concepts such as being-for-itself, bad faith (that is, the refusal of freedom) and the absurd supplied by the philosophical writings of Sartre and Camus, but also on a mix of literary and philosophical texts concerned with subjective experience from Descartes and Dostoevsky to Kafka and **Malraux**. A related tradition drew on the writings of Racine,

Kierkegaard and Nietzsche in order to raise similar questions with regard to the silence, absence and death of God. Where Sartre was steadfastly atheistic, other philosophers such as Gabriel Marcel and Emmanuel Mounier asserted a Christian existentialism.

Literary expressions of postwar existentialism ranged well beyond the meditations on the human condition contained in Sartre's 'Roads to Freedom' trilogy and Camus's *The Plague* (*La Peste*). Samuel **Beckett**'s early fiction in French – *Molloy, Malone Dies* (*Malone meurt*) and *The Unnameable* (*L'Innommable*) – as well as his theatre, as in *Waiting for Godot* (*En attendant Godot*), and that of Eugène **Ionesco**, such as *The Bald Primadonna* (*La Cantatrice charuve*) and *The Chairs* (*Les Chaises*), often pushed this meditation to the point of laughter, especially when the vision that grounded this laughter was one of meaninglessness. Among the poets of the period associated to a greater or lesser degree with an existentialist sensibility, Francis **Ponge**'s 1942 *The Nature of Things* (*Le Parti pris des choses*) drew on Husserl's notion of a return to things in themselves, while René **Char** evolved from a figure of wartime resistance into a devoted reader of Heidegger. In the tradition of experimentation linked to Baudelaire and Rimbaud, Antonin **Artaud** and Henri **Michaux** used word and image to explore the fluid boundaries of identity, space and place through automatism, travel and drugs.

Artists and sculptors likewise contributed to the new postwar existentialist sensibility. Where Jean Fautrier completed 'Hostages', a series of bas-relief portraits that evoked the sombre violence of the Occupation, Jean **Dubuffet** used thick oil paste to depict human figures that emerged directly from the elements of their physical environment. The striking results mixed an imagery of caricature with a sophisticated use of tone and texture with ties to primitivism, **art brut** and outsider art. The elongated human figures on heavy pedestals sculpted by Alberto **Giacometti** came closest to conveying the pained sense of existentialist subjectivity set into the ground of being. A similar heaviness was enhanced by anonymity in sculptures by Germaine Richier, whose faceless figures seemed paralysed in mid-gesture by an oppressive space that closed in on them.

Among writers, thinkers and artists associated with existentialism, differences of philosophical and literary origin were soon exacerbated by political and ideological divergences. Sartre, in particular, found himself increasingly isolated, as his defence of Soviet Communism under Joseph Stalin set him at odds first with Camus and later with long-time philosophical colleagues Raymond **Aron** and Maurice Merleau-Ponty. Between 1945 and 1960, the Sartrean programme of **committed writing** (*littérature engagée*), set forth in his monthly review *Les* **Temps modernes**, established itself as a model of social and political activism whose contributors and fellow travellers addressed issues of gender, as in Simone de **Beauvoir**'s *The Second Sex* (*Le Deuxième Sexe*), sexuality (the plays and novels of Jean **Genet**) and race, as in Frantz **Fanon**'s *The Wretched of the Earth* (*Les Damnés de la terre*).

The same activist concerns among proponents of *littérature engagée* led them over a longer duration to denounce France's colonial occupation of territories in Indochina, sub-Saharan Africa and – above all – North Africa. Alongside Sartre's personal role during the 1954–62 period of debate over Algerian self-determination, the propensity to take a public stand extended among *sartriens* and *sartriennes* from the 1956 Hungarian revolt and Castro's takeover of Cuba to the 1967 Arab–Israeli war, Russia's 1968 suppression of the Prague Spring in Czechoslovakia, and mid-1970s feminist movement in France. In retrospect, the equation of personal identity and commitment in a public sphere remains a strong legacy of early postwar existentialism among left-wing intellectuals such as Marguerite **Duras**, Michel **Foucault** and Gilles **Deleuze**, as well as the new **philosophers** (*nouveaux philosophes*) Bernard-Henri **Lévy** and André **Glucksmann** of the late 1970s and early 1980s.

STEVEN UNGAR

See also: Algerian war; cultural topography (Paris); existentialist theatre; feminism (movements/groups); Theatre of the Absurd

Further reading

Howells, C. (ed.) (1992) *The Cambridge Companion to Sartre*, Cambridge: Cambridge University Press (a collection of essays which approach Sartrean philosophical thinking from a range of angles).

Poster, M. (1975) *Existential Marxism in Postwar France*, Princeton, NJ: Princeton University Press (this puts existentialism in its historical context).

Ungar, S. (1989) '1945 (October 15): First Issue of *Les Temps modernes*, Sartre's Postwar Journal: "Revolution or Revolt?" ', in D. Hollier (ed.) *A New History of French Literature*, Cambridge, MA: Harvard University Press (an essay contextualizing the postwar emergence of existentialism as a cultural, literary and philosophical movement, which focuses particularly on the roles played by Sartre, Camus and *Les Temps modernes*).

Wilson, S. (1993) 'Paris Post War: In Search of the Absolute', in Frances Morris (ed.) *Paris Post War: Art and Existentialism, 1945–55*, London: Tate Gallery (essay on art and existentialism).

existentialist theatre

The existentialist theatre, led by the philosophy's main exponents, **Sartre** and **Camus**, involved a series of plays in the 1950s and 1960s which sought to deal with issues arising from major existentialist themes. The Absurd, the need to resist or revolt against it, and the isolation, guilt and need for political responsibility engendered by it, are all preoccupations of Sartre's and Camus's theatre works, and also those of Jean **Anouilh**, who shares some of the themes, if not all of the political opinions, of Sartrean theatre. In terms of theme, the **Theatre of the Absurd** which followed existentialist theatre in the 1950s and 1960s dealt with similar material; **Beckett's** *Waiting for Godot* (*En attendant Godot*), for example, is a prime example of the Absurd which features in existentialist philosophy. However, it is in the absurdist form it epitomizes that it exemplifies the radical difference in approach between the Absurdists and their existential predecessors. Whereas the Theatre of the Absurd employed absurdity not only in subject matter but also in structure and form, many existentialist plays rely on a formal, classical structure and dialectic. Hence, while many of Sartre's plays, such as *In Camera* (*Huis Clos*) and *Dirty Hands* (*Les Mains Sales*), discuss the issue of choice in defining oneself, the need for recognition and the need to revolt against absurdity, these ideas are formulated in a classical, structured way more reminiscent of Greek tragedy than of a new genre. This is due, partly, to a conscious effort to attempt to establish a new form of tragedy for the modern day, combining the ancient ritual of classical drama (inspiration also for pre-war predecessors such as Giraudoux) with a new form of tragedy, based on the necessity of choice discussed from an existentialist viewpoint. Both Sartre and Camus sought to show the tragedy inherent in Absurdity and the necessary tragedy of choice in the life of mankind. However, whereas Sartre believed in the individual's responsibility to resist Absurdity for himself or herself, Camus believed that mankind should rebel collectively, and that an individual response was inadequate (an idea expressed in *Caligula*).

Existentialist theatre has always been popular with educated Parisian middle-class audiences, especially at the time the plays were written, many before subsidized state theatre arrived in France, when authors were obliged to rely on the goodwill of one of the private theatres. Perhaps because they used finely crafted language and situations to expound their philosophies and theories, Sartre's and Camus's works, even if they presented sometimes less than rounded characters and dramatic techniques, were as successful when first performed as they are today. Certainly during the Occupation and the years which followed, their individualist spirit and strength of purpose and ideals appealed to Parisian audiences. With the advent of state funding, they also saw themselves established as regular members of the subsidized theatre's popular repertoire, and continue to be performed frequently to this day.

ANNIE SPARKS

See also: theatre; theatres, national; theatres, private

Further reading

Bradby, D. (1991) *Modern French Drama 1940–1990*, Cambridge: Cambridge University Press (Chapter 3 deals with modern philosophical theatre).

Freeman, E. (1971) *The Theatre of Albert Camus*, London: Methuen.

McCall, D. (1969) *The Theatre of Jean-Paul Sartre*, Columbia: Columbia University Press.

Express, L'

Magazine

France's first weekly news magazine, *L'Express* was created by Jean-Jacques **Servan-Schreiber** and Françoise **Giroud** in 1953, initially as a supplement to *Les Échos* (owned by the former's father). Inspired by Pierre **Mendès France**, *L'Express* was a politically outspoken, left-wing title, campaigning for peace and **decolonization** during the wars in Algeria and Indochina. Influential and avant-garde, it was often at the centre of controversy. When **Sartre** wrote in its columns about Henri Alleg's account of torture in Algeria at the hands of French paratroopers, the authorities seized the whole issue of the magazine. Famous writers such as Albert **Camus** and François Mauriac were associated with *L'Express*, and it served as a training ground for many leading journal-

ists of the late twentieth century: Pierre Viansson-Ponté, Jean Daniel, Claude Imbert, Michèle Cotta . . .

In 1964 Servan-Schreiber, a great admirer of all things American, decided to transform *L'Express*, adopting the smaller news magazine format, and a more commercial approach, while toning down political content. Unhappy with the changes, Jean Daniel resigned, and was soon leading rival title, *Le Nouvel Observateur*. The new *L'Express* was such a success that it multiplied its sales fourfold in a decade (from 153,000 copies per week in 1965 to 605,000 in 1974); readers were attracted by the clear synthesis of the week's events. In 1970, Servan-Schreiber began actively to pursue a political career. Fearing for the paper's independence, Claude Imbert and a number of colleagues (including Georges Suffert, Olivier Chevrillon and Jacques Duquesne) resigned, and were soon launching another rival, *Le Point*. In 1977 Servan-Schreiber sold *L'Express* to international financier Sir Jimmy Goldsmith, and with Raymond **Aron** as political director, it moved markedly to the right. Differences of opinion with Goldsmith over presentation of the leading presidential contenders in 1981 led to the departure of Olivier Todd, Jean-François Revel and Albert du Roy. In 1987 Goldsmith sold to the Compagnie Générale d'Électricité; job losses and a succession of presidents and directors followed. It is a testimony to the resilience and intrinsic merits of the magazine that, despite a turbulent history of internal conflict and changing leadership, it has sustained its popularity.

From the highly original, left-wing title of the 1950s, *L'Express* has changed to become a conformist, more institutionalized publication in the 1990s, with its reputation for innovation shifting from the political to the commercial sphere. Successful marketing strategies have led to an exceptionally high number of readers taking out subscriptions, often in response to offers of free gifts or discounts (although critics argue that this undermines its image). Readers are predominantly male city-dwellers, in middle or senior management positions, and with above average disposable income (an attraction for advertisers). Since 1992, *L'Express* has collaborated with *Le Point*, for commercial, technical and administrative purposes, although both titles retain editorial independence and a distinct identity. Circulation of over 560,000 copies per week in 1995, considerably higher than for rival news magazines, confirms its continuing success.

PAM MOORES

See also: Algerian war; national press in France

F

Fabius, Laurent

b. 1946, Paris

Politician

Academically accomplished and urbane, Fabius joined the Parti Socialiste (PS) in 1974. Viewed as the ambitious 'spiritual son' of **Mitterrand** and his possible successor, he has been a *député* since 1978 and was Minister for the Budget in 1981–3 and Minister for Industry and Research in 1983–4. As prime minister in 1984–6, he symbolized Mitterrand's policy U-turn towards market liberalism, although he projected a technocratic image. He was president of the National Assembly from 1988 to 1992. He gained the leadership of the PS in 1992, but was ousted in 1993 following the party's electoral *débâcle*. His support for **Jospin** in the 1995 presidential election was somewhat lukewarm. He remains a leading Socialist.

LAURENCE BELL

See also: parties and movements

Major works

Fabius, L. (1990) *C'est en allant à la mer*, Paris: Éditions du Seuil (outlines his vision of modern socialism).
——(1995) *Les Blessures de la vérité*, Paris: Flammarion (attempts to take stock of the Socialists' experience in government).

family

The notion of the family has two interconnected meanings. The first, more restricted meaning of 'family' is the individuals who come together to form a home and is akin to the concept of household. The second refers to the kinship group – that is, those who share the same blood relatives. In the postwar period in France, it is the family as described in the first of these definitions that has undergone major changes.

During the first twenty years after World War II, a certain convergence of family forms took place in France around a model of early marriage and the married couple subsequently living together with two children independently from older generations. Prior to that, on the one hand, the peasantry and *petite bourgeoisie* in certain regions had tended to restrict their family size to one child, while on the other hand, the large family with four or more children had been common among working-class families in industrial regions. Furthermore, in the 1950s and 1960s, divorce rates were low, as were rates of **employment** for mothers of young children. Couples living together without being married were also an extraordinary and morally reprehensible phenomenon. However, the mood of the country at the end of the 1960s, and particularly after **May**

1968, did much to change notions of the family in France. Indeed, the 'nuclear' family model was portrayed as constraining, particularly for young adults and for women.

Thus, from the 1970s onwards, the 'family' underwent a number of far-reaching transformations. First, the nature of marriage changed. French couples began to marry later, often after a period of living together or, indeed, they started increasingly not to marry at all, opting instead for *unions libres*. Furthermore, marriage has become increasingly unstable, with divorce rates standing at around 1 in 3 of all marriages, depending on the region of the country. Although for a certain time it was thought that marriage remained a popular institution because of the number of remarriages after divorce, the marriage rate had gone into decline in France by the 1990s. As a result of increased divorce rates, two new forms of families thus developed: the single- parent family (*la famille monoparentale*) and the reconstituted family (*la famille recomposée*), made up of stepbrothers and sisters and/or half-brothers and -sisters. The increase in divorce and marriage instability may be bemoaned by some, but to others it is simply the logical extension of the changes in the nature of marriage in France which took place in the first half of the twentieth century. At that time, marriage became less an institution whose primary function was to perpetuate the family line and transmit property across the generations, and more an institution based entirely on the affection and love existing between two partners. It is clear that the former, traditional model of marriage is more stable than the latter 'companionship' family model.

Second, the nuclear family of the immediate postwar period was based on a strict division of labour between husband and wife. For many (if not all) couples, the model of 'man the breadwinner' and 'woman the homemaker' did hold true. However, from the 1970s onwards, the nature of women's employment patterns changed. In the 1950s and 1960s, mothers in France tended to give up work on the birth of their children and only return once their children were independent – if they returned at all.

From the 1970s onwards, mothers in France began to work for longer and longer proportions of their child-rearing years. Indeed, it was discovered in the 1982 census that it was more common for families with children to have two working parents than to have one. The economic dependence of a woman on a man, the remaining economic function of the nuclear family in the 1950s and 1960s, was therefore disappearing.

The increase in women's participation in the labour market, coupled with later marriage, the prospect of marriage instability and the greater availability of birth control measures, have all contributed to a steep decline in the birth rate in France since World War II. The 'baby boom' after the war in France is well-known. Indeed, until the 1970s the average number of births per French woman was over two. That is, it was at a rate which would not only replace, but rejuvenate, the population. However, from the 1970s onwards, the French birth rate began to drop below the replacement rate of two children per woman. Indeed, demographic decline is a question which has traditionally preoccupied French governments and a number of incentives are provided by the state to make the lives of parents easier and thus encourage them to have larger families. However, some argue that certain of these measures – for example, the state making it easier for mothers to go out to work – encourage the limiting of family size and are thus counterproductive. None the less, it should be stressed that France remains one of the more fecund countries in the **European Union**.

Although the birth rate has fallen in France, the population continues to grow because of its increased longevity. This more aged population, in which one marriage partner (usually the woman) outlives the other, often lives alone. Kin groups are more dispersed than in the past, which means that elderly relatives are less likely to move in with their children when they are widowed or become infirm. This phenomenon, coupled with later marriage and higher rates of divorce, means that 'families' (or, perhaps more accurately, 'households') containing a single person are set to become the dominant family form in France, particularly in large towns and cities. However, there is also evidence to suggest that, as grown-up children find it increasingly difficult to find employment, they are staying at home for longer and longer periods with their parents.

JAN WINDEBANK

See also: abortion/contraception; child care; demographic developments; marriage/cohabitation; women and employment; women and social policy

Further reading

Hantrais, L. (1982) *Contemporary French Society*, Basingstoke: Macmillan (a discussion of the developments in French society from 1945 to the late 1970s; includes texts in French).

Fanon, Frantz

b. 1925, Fort-de-France, Martinique; d. 1961, Bethesda, USA

Psychiatrist and writer

A psychiatrist and writer turned militant nationalist and socialist revolutionary, Fanon's *The Wretched of the Earth* (*Les Damnés de la terre*) of 1961 earned him international attention. Converted to the cause of self-determination for Algeria through his work as director of the psychiatric hospital at Blida-Joinville between 1953 and 1956, his understanding of clinical alienation disclosed the depersonalization suffered by Algerians under French colonial rule.

In *Black Skin, White Masks* (*Peau noire, masques blancs*), in 1952, Fanon had already criticized the human consequences of encounters with **racism** he had known in Martinique and France by linking the interplay of self-consciousness and recognition in Hegel's *Phenomenology of Mind* and the dynamics of

prejudice analysed by **Sartre** in *Anti-Semite and Jew* (*Réflexions sur la question juive*) in order to account for the torment of black women and men subjected to racism under the culture of colonial rule. Long before he advocated militancy and revolution, Fanon denounced racism as part of a more general cultural system to be resisted and overcome.

By the time he died in 1961, Fanon had evolved from a supporter of the *négritude* movement linked to Aimé **Césaire** and the journal *Présence africaine* to a proponent of socialist revolution in Africa whose views on violence were in line with those taken up in the United States by individuals associated with the Black Power movement. After resigning his post at Blida-Joinville, Fanon attended the 1956 Congress of Black Writers and Artists in Paris before moving to Tunis, where he wrote for the Algerian National Liberation Front newspaper, *El Moudjahid*. In 1960, he was appointed ambassador of the Provisional Algerian Government to Ghana. The same year, he contracted leukaemia and completed *The Wretched of the Earth* before dying outside Washington DC, where he had been sent for medical treatment.

There were, in David Caute's apt words, three successive Fanons: the de-alienated man of *Black Skins, White Masks*, the Algerian citizen of *A Dying Colonialism* (*L'An Cinq de la révolution algérienne*) of 1959, and the committed socialist revolutionary of *The Wretched of the Earth*. Among these, the most enduring remains the final Fanon who came to see the 'wretched of the earth' of Third World peasantry alluded to in the opening line of the *Internationale* as the class of authentic revolution in Africa. Renewed interest in Fanon's writings, in evidence since the mid-1980s has resituated them with regard to theories of the post-colonial and a revised politics of identity.

STEVEN UNGAR

See also: Algerian war; decolonization

Further reading

Bhabha, H. (1994) 'Interrogating Identity: Frantz Fanon and the Postcolonial Prerogative', in *The Location of Culture*, London and New York: Routledge (essay by Fanon's leading post-colonial exponent).

Caute, D. (1970) *Frantz Fanon*, New York: Viking (essential reading).

Gendzier, I. (1973) *Frantz Fanon: A Critical Study*, New York: Pantheon (a critical study and biography).

Farge, Arlette

b. 1941, France

Feminist historian and journalist

Focusing in the main on the eighteenth century, Farge's work foregrounds women's history. Her publications include *Le Miroir des femmes* (Women's Mirror), *La Vie fragile: violence, pouvoir et solidarité à Paris au XVIIIe siècle* (Fragile Life: Violence, Power and Solidarity in Eighteenth-Century Paris) and *Dire et mal dire: l'opinion publique au XVIIIe siècle* (Public Opinion in Eighteenth-Century France). She works at the Centre National de la Recherche Scientifique (CNRS) in Paris.

ALEX HUGHES

See also: feminist thought

fashion

France's leading role in the international fashion industry, and the special status of fashion in French society, make this apparently epiphenomenal activity of significance in understanding French culture. Fashion also has an economic importance which belies its ephemeral nature, and as political and social correctness spreads in France the work of some designers has provoked polemical comment.

It is useful to consider what is understood by *la mode* in France: first, fashion is the industry and society of *la haute couture*; second, fashion as *le prêt à porter* is what is worn by people in everyday life; third, fashion is informal leisurewear, or streetwear – clothing worn as a kind of inverted badge of social distinction. Each of these reflexes of fashion has produced companion corpuses of clothing in **cinema** and **photography** especially, and also in literature. The place of fashion in French intellectual life is indicated by the way in which it has inspired literary critics and philosophers such as Roland **Barthes** and Gilles Lipovetsky: Barthes formulated a semiotic analysis of a corpus of articles from the women's fashion magazines *Jardin des modes* and *Elle*, elaborated in 1967 in *The Fashion System* (*Système de la mode*), and Lipovetsky has interpreted modern democracy in the light of fashion and trends.

Arguably the first connotation of fashion in France is *haute couture*. Historically, European and American fashion has been dominated by French style and expertise, and an important component of the contemporary image of La Maison France (France plc) is her production of luxury clothing, perfume, accessories and toiletries. Not for nothing is the fashion, wine and spirits conglomerate owning Givenchy (Louis-Vuitton-Moët-Hennessey or LVMH) now one of France's largest companies: fashion houses are controlled by big businesses – YSL is owned by the petrochemicals giant Elf-Sanofi. Surprisingly, given the high profile of the industry, fashion houses of *couture-création* (fabrication and design) number only twenty or so, of which only Azzedine Alaïa remains independent. The *haute couture* industry employs some 30,000, and overall (taking account of the production of *prêt à porter* and accessories) French fashion has an annual turnover of 20 billion francs. Contemporary French culture has been irrigated by the trickle-down glitter of the fashion houses of Balenciaga (founded 1937), Balmain (1945), **Cardin** (1950), **Chanel** (1924), **Dior** (1947), Givenchy (1951), **Lacroix** (1987), Lapidus (1949), Nina Ricci (1932), Patou (1919), Yves **Saint Laurent** (1962) – and others – who, in providing products for the rich, have influenced fashion in society in general. In the 1980s and 1990s, newcomers such as **Gaultier** arguably started to blur distinctions between the fashion of *la grande société* (high society) and that of ordinary French citizens. Ironically, French *haute couture* has long been dependent on foreign designers such as Gianfranco Ferré at Dior, Karl Lagerfeld and, most recently, the Britons Galliano (Givenchy, then Dior), McQueen (Givenchy) and McCartney (Lagerfeld), and since the 1970s a Japanese influence has derived from Kenzo and Issey Miyake. French fashion is linked closely to the visual arts, continuing the cross-fertilization established by **Cartier-Bresson** in photography and, in cinema, by Chanel who provided costumes for **Renoir**'s *La Règle du jeu*, and Cocteau's postwar *La Belle et la bête* (Beauty and the Beast). In 1997, Gaultier's futuristic frocks adorned, for example, **Besson**'s *The Fifth Element* (*Le Cinquième Élément*). Fashion also plays a key role in the world of French **publishing**, in the form of top-of-the-range **women's magazines** such as *Jardin des modes* (circulation 12,000) and *Vogue* (84,000). Another crucial element of the fashion industry, often forgotten, is perfume. The perfume trade employs some 30,000 in 220 companies, the largest of which are linked to major fashion houses such as Patou, Dior and Givenchy. Despite the continuing celebrity of supermodels and designers, the *haute couture* industry is now, however, questioning its future, facing public scepticism about its ethics and role: Balenciaga reputedly lost faith in fashion because 'there was no-one left to dress', and the managing director of YSL has predicted that *haute couture* will disappear at the death of Yves Saint Laurent himself.

The rise of *prêt à porter* clothing, derived from high-society fashion, is one of the ways in which fashion has become progressively democratized in postwar France; this branch of the industry employs some 50,000 in 2,000 companies. Azzedine Alaïa, Balenciaga, Cerruti, Gaultier, Kenzo, Lagerfeld, **Rykiel** and Mugler all produce lines carrying their own labels (*griffé*) for the general public beyond the diminishing 3,000 or so clients worldwide for *haute couture*. This aspect of fashion has been spread by high readership women's magazines such as *Elle* (circulation 340,000), and **Marie-Claire** (544,000), and well-known mail-order clothing companies such as *Les Trois Suisses* (8 million) and *La Redoute* (6 million) have helped 'decentralize' the experience of fashion from its source in the Place Vendôme in Paris, governed by the Chambre Syndicale de la Couture Parisienne, to the furthest reaches of provincial France (*la France profonde*). Since the 1980s, Les Trois Suisses has popularized styles by Rykiel, Gaultier and Alaïa and, in 1996, La Redoute celebrated its thirtieth anniversary by bringing YSL's famous women's dinner jacket (*le smoking* – itself launched in 1966) to a mass market for the first time. As well as mail order, an important role in the spread of fashion styles and a salient feature of the everyday experience of buying clothes has been the famous *grands magasins* (department stores). Stores like Prisunic, Printemps and Galeries Lafayette have popularized styles and designs launched by the fashion houses at accessible prices. As the antithesis of *haute couture*, the famous Tati shops have provided low-price clothing for the masses (the best-known branch is in the Paris working-class/immigrant quarter of of Barbès-Rochechouart), even if in the 1990s they have offered a special range of styles designed by Azzedine Alaïa significantly entitled *La rue c'est à nous* (The street is ours). Another quantitatively important aspect of everyday fashion is the role played by hypermarkets, such as Leclerc and Mammouth, in providing value-for-money apparel for the man and woman in the street.

The extension of 'Parisian' style through *prêt à porter griffé*, the influence of *haute couture* on the clothes industry in general (*la confection*), and social and geographical mobility and prosperity have attenuated some disparities in clothing worn by the French. Concomitant with the modernization of French society it is now rarer to see the little old ladies, *toutes de noir vêtues* (all in black), who symbolized the Latin urban–rural divide, now arguably in retreat. Although regional singularities of dress have all but disappeared (save for self-conscious displays of 'folklore' destined for tourists), fashion and style nevertheless remain reasonable indicators in France of some aspects of social status. Typical examples of socially indicative items of clothing range from the famous *bleu de travail* (workmen's overalls) to the pearl necklaces, Hermès bags, scarves, hairbands and American penny-loafers favoured by well-to-do young women from the *16e arrondissement* or the Neuilly-Auteuil-Passy suburbs of Paris. The initials 'NAP' have indeed become an acronym describing a particular style, associated with a subclass of the category **BCBG** (*bon chic bon genre*). BCBG attire is demonstrated notably in some fields of **university** education, where students in law faculties, institutions of political studies and some *grandes écoles* use more formal dress codes to differentiate themselves from the majority of other students.

More than simply categorizing a social class and its sartorial characteristics, descriptions of dress-style, such as rocker (Johnny **Hallyday**), hippie and punk, refer to French incarnations of American and British music-related youth culture and their associated vestimentary clichés. More specifically French, however, is the *baba-cool* style. Originating in the questioning of authority and dominant modes of behaviour prevalent in the 1960s, *baba-cool* fashion is environmentally friendly, politically correct and informal, attesting to the continuing echoes of **May 1968** throughout the 1970s and beyond. In the 1980s and 1990s, street style influenced by American **rap** and hip-hop music has been adopted by **youth culture** and by French bands such as Nique ta mère (NTM) and their fans. Large numbers of alienated young French people, often of immigrant origin, express their anomie in their choice of music and an aggressively informal style of dress (baseball caps, trainers, sports, blousons). The distinctions between formal and informal dress have been lessening progressively as French society has become less rigid since the 1960s. It has been claimed that one of the major effects of May 1968 was that some peo-

ple stopped feeling obliged to present themselves at work in a suit and tie.

In 1947, Dior's exuberant use of material was considered by some as immoral; more recently, Colonna's deconstructed clothes have drawn criticism for evoking the poverty of utility clothing. More generally, fashion in France seems to be becoming increasingly politicized, both in the sense understood by YSL in 1971 with his 'Mourning for Vietnam' collection, but also in the way new sensibilities about inequality, race and revisionism are undermining designers' freedom of expression by making individuals aware of the semiotics of clothing. Thus Gaultier's use of nuns, Eskimos and Hasidic Jews as inspirations for his designs has provoked controversy; in 1994, a debate with Lagerfeld at the Sorbonne turned sour as students challenged his constant use of status logos and his influence on culture; in 1995, near the fiftieth anniversary of the liberation of Auschwitz, the Comme des Garçons collection of pyjama stripes shown by shaven-headed models provoked a furore. The popularity of the French-born black Muslim model Adia in the mid-1990s constitutes an exception in the sorority of mainly white supermodels, which in turn represents an inequality in France's multi-ethnic society. However, Gaultier used only black models for his 1997 show, in protest at apparent xenophobia among many French people, and within the fashion industry.

The proportion of households' disposable income spent on clothing is in constant decline (in 1970, 9.6 per cent; 1995, 5.4 per cent), despite the increased financial autonomy of adolescents and the consequent rise in specially marketed lines of fashion clothing such as Naf-Naf (founded in 1973) and Chevignon (1979). The fashion industry in the 1990s has reflected French society's new desire for a blend of individualism and conformism after the more radical individualism of the 1980s. The cyclical, intertextual nature of fashion (interweaving old styles with new modes) engages it in constant dialogue with the past; French fashion is in many ways the product of recurrent French preoccupations with eroticism, exoticism, spectacle, the mixing of genres and deconstruction.

Arguably since Dior's 'New Look' of 1947 which luxuriously 're-feminized' women's dress after the austerity of the war, much of French fashion exploits the tension between seduction and the socially correct with a postmodern playfulness perhaps best encapsulated by Dim's slogan for colourful clothes: *La vie est trop courte pour s'habiller triste* (Life is too short to wear dull clothes).

Despite the industry's problems, as with so many other aspects of French culture, fashion is seen by the French as a means of exhibiting French genius; the fact that army, traffic warden and Air France uniforms have all been redesigned by major fashion houses illustrates the emblematic importance of style. More institutionally, the 'Colbert Committee', set up in 1954 by the perfumer Guerlain with the aim of communicating French luxury, quality and elegance to the world, now links seventy companies drawn from the most famous establishments of the fashion, art and leisure industries. The prevalence of such cultural *colbertisme* (protectionism) was indicated in 1995 when President **Chirac** was criticized by Lacoste (the famous French designer of polo shirts) for publicly wearing a shirt made by his US competitor Ralph Lauren. Moreover, the fact that a president can appear in such attire reveals how far the formal and the informal and the public and private spheres are blurring in France.

HUGH DAUNCEY

See also: demographic developments; economy; educational elitism: the *grandes écoles*

Further reading

Barthes, R. (1990) *The Fashion System*, trans. M. Ward and R. Berkeley, Berkeley: University of California Press (French edition (1967): *Système de la mode*, Paris: Seuil) (a semiotic analysis of *la mode*).

Herpin, N. (1986) 'L'Habillement, la classe sociale et la mode', *Économie et statistique* 188 (May) (a useful reading on fashion and style as social indicators).

Lipovetsky, G. (1994) *The Empire of Fashion: Dressing Modern Democracy*, Princeton, NJ: Princeton University Press (a reading of modern democracy in the light of fashion and trends).

Zeldin, T. (1983) 'How to be Chic', in *The French*, London: Collins (a cultural analysis).

fast food

Le fast-food is as rife in France as anywhere else in the Western world. The meal of choice for many young French is *un Macdo*, though indigenous chains such as Love Burger or Flunch provide competition. Latterly, big-name chefs such as Paul **Bocuse** or Michel **Guérard** have joined the trend with pre-prepared meals (frozen or vacuum-packed), whose quality is generally deemed to be excellent.

KEITH READER

See also: gastronomy

feminism (movements/groups)

In France, as elsewhere, 'feminism' in fact comprises a diversity of feminisms, of which most stand committed to transforming society through the eradication of sexist domination and the promotion of sexual equality.

French feminism of the 'second wave' (a convenient term used to describe the cluster of women's activities from the 1960s to the present) emerged at the time of the events of **May 1968**, although the gradual reform of women's status from 1944 onwards, together with increasing publications, in the 1950s and early 1960s, on the position of French women, had laid the groundwork for an independent women's movement in the late 1960s.

During the events of May 1968, women participated widely in demonstrations, occupations and meetings. However, in this upheaval, their voices were drowned, their role downgraded to one of mere support to male comrades. From the frustration and anger, experienced by women activists at this time, emerged the realization that if women were to be seen and heard they would have to speak and act for themselves. Following May 1968, small and large women's groups formed, mainly in **universities**, but also in workplaces and neighbourhoods. However, it was sensationalist actions which brought feminists to the public gaze. In August 1970, some ten women laid a wreath at the Arc de Triomphe, in Paris, in remembrance of someone more unknown than the soldier – his wife. This 'perfidious' action (more than any monument, the Arc de Triomphe represented a French universal male order, glorifying only the heroes of war) attracted press attention, with *France-Soir*'s lead story referring to the women as representatives of the Mouvement de Libération des Femmes (MLF).

The title 'MLF' covered numerous groups acting in concert over certain issues such as the legalization of **abortion**. However, from the beginning, the MLF accommodated a variety of currents which were not in agreement on fundamental questions of theory (e.g. the basis of femininity; whether or not class constituted a more fundamental and important category than sex) and practice (co-operation with parties and groups of the Left; separatist action). The three principal currents within the MLF were the Féministes Révolutionnaires, the *lutte des classes* (class struggle) current and **Psych et Po** (Psychanalyse et Politique).

Féministes Révolutionnaires came to prominence within the MLF towards the end of 1970. Within it were collectives organized around publications such as *Histoires d'elles* or *Questions féministes* and also lesbian groups such as Les Gouines Rouges (Red Dykes) and Les Polymorphes Perverses. Of all MLF currents, it was most influenced by post-1950s North American feminism, believing that the total overthrow of patriarchy alone would signal an end to women's oppression and that, in order to achieve this, women would have to act separately, without men. Some argued further that only a lesbian position would survive the persistent assault of patriarchy and capitalism. It was the Féministes Révolutionnaires who engaged in the most spectacular actions which grabbed media attention: for instance, disrupting a conference on the theme of 'Woman' organized by the magazine *Elle* in November 1970, and demonstrating against Mother's Day in May 1972. However, the influence of Féministes Révolutionnaires was relatively short-lived, as the current struggled to survive, within the MLF, against attacks from Psych et Po and against a background of intra-current conflict between lesbian and heterosexual groups.

The 'class struggle' current was largely made up of women who were members of Far Left Maoist and Trotskyist groups. One of the best known of these groups to emerge in the mid-1970s was the Trotskyist collective which published *Les Pétroleuses*. As far as 'class struggle' feminists were concerned, capitalism remained the principal enemy and collaboration with left-wing groups or parties was necessary even though it was admitted that women also had to struggle against specifically male power and domination. It was the 'class struggle' current which provided the thrust behind the formation of feminist neighbourhood groups (*groupes de quartier*) and workplace groups (*groupes femmes d'entreprises*) which, in turn, founded and supported organizations such as the Mouvement pour la Libération de l'Avortement et la Contraception (MLAC). From 1974, the 'class struggle' current attempted to redefine the MLF as an organized, hierarchically structured force capable of influencing French politics but failed against resistance from the Féministes Révolutionnaires. By 1977, many members of the 'class struggle' current were moving away from the MLF to form a new Marxist-feminist organization, Mouvement Autonome des Femmes.

The third main current, Psych et Po, born in 1968 from the marriage between Marxism and **psychoanalysis**, separated itself from feminists within the MLF, declaring that feminists were a bourgeois avant-garde which sought merely to conserve the dominant capitalist order but in an inverted form, replacing male power with female power. Psych et Po argued that the only way of revolutionizing society and ending the oppression of women was by disrupting the

Symbolic Order and subverting bourgeois language through which people understood and identified with the world in which they lived. Thus, from 1972, Psych et Po began to wage an anti-feminist campaign, through its **publishing** empire (bookshops and periodicals) and 'research associations', in a bid to 'save' the MLF. The campaign culminated in 1979, with legal action on Psych et Po's part, whereby the title MLF was registered as the group's commercial trade name. From here on, the MLF became synonymous with Psych et Po and feminists were legally barred from representing it.

The conflicts within the MLF considerably weakened the movement. By 1981, when a new Socialist government established the Ministry for Women's Rights, it was not difficult for a state-inspired reformist feminism to usurp the space once occupied by an autonomous and dynamic MLF.

KHURSHEED WADIA

See also: écriture féminine; feminist thought; feminist press; Roudy, Yvette

Further reading

De Courtivron, I. and Marks, E. (eds) (1981) *New French Feminisms*, Brighton: Harvester Press (an anthology of over fifty French feminist texts, translated into English; includes a good introduction and selected bibliography).

Duchen, C. (1986) *Feminism in France: From May '68 to Mitterrand*, London: Routledge & Kegan Paul (to date, the best account, in English, of second wave feminist thought and activism in France).

Picq, F. (1993) *Libération des femmes: les années-mouvement*, Paris: Éditions du Seuil (an interesting retrospective assessment of the French Women's Liberation Movement by one of its well-known activists).

feminist press

Written by women for women, newspapers, magazines, intellectual journals, pamphlets and books within the category of 'feminist press' were initially linked with the Women's Liberation Movement (Mouvement de Libération des Femmes or MLF) in the 1970s and early 1980s, and have since contributed to the creation of a feminist culture within the spheres of intellectual, social, economic and political life.

A decade of feminist struggle, from 1968, produced an explosion of feminist writing and the foundation of numerous publications with varying aims, content and style. By the end of the 1970s, it is estimated that thirty-five titles (excluding regional, neighbourhood and workplace publications) were in circulation nationally. Their emergence responded to a need and desire for theoretical debate, the exchange of practical information and analysis of issues such as sexual liberation, homosexuality, rape, **prostitution**, violence against women, the representation of women in writing and visual forms of communication and of equality in the workplace. These periodicals and newspapers, of both a general and more specialist orientation, nearly always represented a particular political current within the MLF.

The category of general publications included, among many: *Le Torchon Brûle*, an autonomous publication which aimed to reflect the views of all MLF groups; *Les Pétroleuses* and *Les Cahiers du féminisme,* published by groups within the MLF's *lutte des classes* current; *Histoires d'elles, Questions féministes* and *Les Nouvelles Féministes,* set up by groups within the current *Féministes Révolutionnaires*; *Le Quotidien des femmes* and *Des Femmes en mouvement,* both published by the group **Psych et Po** (*Psychanalyse et Politique*). Among the specialist feminist publications were the gay and lesbian review *Masques*, the history review *Pénélope*, the cartoon magazine *Ah Nana* and *Sorcières*, published by Éditions Stock, which dealt with one specialist feminist theme per issue. As the majority of feminist newspapers and magazines relied upon unpaid editorial teams and operated on meagre budgets, their publication was irregular and sales took place at demonstrations, meetings and feminist bookshops. A few, however, such as *Les Cahiers du féminisme* and *Questions féministes* managed to attract regular subscribers while *Le Quotidien des Femmes* and *Des Femmes en Mouvement* appeared to benefit from the unlimited private funds of **Psych et Po**'s main helmswoman, Antoinette Fouque, although both titles eventually folded due to lack of readers.

The precarious finances of the majority of these publications meant that many only survived during a short period. While it was never the intention or hope that these publications should reach a mass readership (in their heyday an estimated 150,000 women bought at least one title), their influence has not been negligible. First, they provided the mainstream press, and especially **women's magazines** such as *Elle* and *Marie-Claire*, with bold new themes and ideas and inspired the launch of *F Magazine*, in 1978, which was aimed at a large feminist readership. Second, their provocative tone and the challenge that they presented to trade unionists and women in the mainstream Left led publications such as *Antoinette* – the women's magazine of the Confédération Générale du Travail (CGT) – to reconsider women's issues in a new light. The magazine's editors began to take an oppositional stance to the trade union's male leaders, which finally led to the dismissal of the entire editorial team in 1983, when it refused to withdraw support for the Polish trade union, Solidarity, as instructed by the CGT's leadership. Women in the Confédération Française Démocratique du Travail (CFDT) also began to be active around feminist issues, and 1977 saw the publication of Jeannette Laot's *Stratégie pour les femmes*.

As far as the two main parties of the Left were concerned, a number of Communist women formed a group, in 1978, which published the feminist magazine *Elles voient rouge* and in the Socialist Party, the feminist publication *Mignonnes allons voir sous la rose* was launched after the party's 1977 Nantes congress. Both publications were used by their editors and supporters to question sexist thinking and practices within their respective parties, eventually leading to the departure of the women concerned from both parties.

The 1970s were also marked by the establishment of about a dozen feminist **publishing** houses, including Psych et Po's Des Femmes publishing venture, which gave women the opportunity to (re)discover and create their own champions in real life and fiction. Campaigning feminist writers included Annie **Leclerc**, Gisèle Halimi, Christine **Delphy** and Monique **Wittig**, while writers such as Marguerite **Duras**, Christiane **Rochefort** and Nathalie **Sarraute** contributed original styles and substance to French literature. Furthermore, this period saw the publication of the first histories of French feminism and the MLF, and introduced the public to certain hallmarks of *écriture féminine* such as Hélène **Cixous**'s *The Laugh of the Medusa* (*Le Rire de la méduse*), Julia **Kristeva**'s *About Chinese Women* (*Des Chinoises*) and Luce **Irigaray**'s *Speculum of the Other Woman* (*Speculum de l'autre femme*) and *This Sex which Is not One* (*Ce sexe qui n'en est pas un*).

From the mid-1980s, feminist publication has increasingly entered the mainstream as women's studies have become a feature of the higher education curriculum, as big publishers (e.g. **Seuil**, Stock and Éditions Syros) have established their own 'women's series' and as trade unions, professional and political organizations have gradually attached more importance to women's sections or committees. However, the relative acceptance of feminist publications within the mainstream has not occurred without the exaction of a price, which is that the most original and uncompromising type of publications (*Histoires d'elles* or *Pénélope*) have gradually disappeared. Those which have survived (*Cahiers du féminisme* and *Nouvelles Questions féministes*) or which have been set up in recent years (*Clio: histoire, femmes et société* and *Résonances-Femmes*) have done so either because they have adopted a more 'serious' and less doctrinaire tone or because they have achieved and maintained academic respectability.

KHURSHEED WADIA

See also: *écriture féminine*; feminism (move-ments/groups); feminist thought; parties and movements; publishing *l'edition*

Further reading

Burke, C. (1978) 'Report from Paris: Women's Writing and the Women's Movement', *Signs* 3, 4: 843–55 (useful appraisal of feminist writings).

De Courtivron, I. and Marks, E. (eds) (1981) *New French Feminisms*, Brighton: Harvester Press (brings together over fifty French femi-nist texts, translated into English; also has a good introduction and selected bibliography).

Duchen, C. (1986) *Feminism in France: From May '68 to Mitterrand*, London: Routledge & Kegan Paul (the best account, in English, of French second wave feminist thought and activism).

Picq, F. (1993) *Libération des femmes: les années-mouvement*, Paris: Éditions du Seuil (one of its well-known activists assesses ret-rospectively the French Women's Liberation Movement).

feminist thought

A good working definition of feminist thought has been provided by the philosopher Michèle Le Doeuff: 'Depuis deux siècles, une féministe est une femme qui ne laisse à personne le soin de penser à sa place; de penser, tout court, et plus particulièrement de penser ce que c'est la condition féminine, ou ce qu'elle devrait être' ('For the last two hundred years, a feminist has been a woman who lets no one do her thinking for her: thinking full stop, but more especially, thinking about what women's condition is, or what it ought to be'; Le Doeuff 1989).

The number of French women fitting this definition rose steadily throughout the first half of the twentieth century, as educational and career opportunities expanded. The right to vote (granted in 1944) transformed the possi-bilities of the feminine condition. Economic expansion in the 1960s provided the conditions to turn the possibilities into reality. More women were taking up new roles as producers as well as consumers in the market economy, just as that economy and its culture were undergoing the radical political and philosoph-ical critique that shaped the revolutionary events of **May 1968**. Women, experiencing what for many was the novelty of acting for the first time as independent economic subjects, found themselves in a cultural politics where the agenda had been set by Marx, Freud and **Lacan**, and the dominant discourses were those of **Barthes**, **Foucault** and **Derrida**. The women's groups who came together in the aftermath of the May events to form the MLF (Mouvement de Libération des Femmes) developed within and against those radical masculine doctrines and the consciousness of the theoretical dimen-sion of practice which is the distinctive mark of contemporary French feminism. Their activities over the subsequent years, foregrounding and challenging masculinist bias in the production of thought, and creating opportunities for women to participate fully in all areas of intel-lectual activity, have transformed the cultural landscape in France. In the process, they have also made a distinctive contribution to the course of feminism elsewhere in Europe and America.

For most Anglo-American feminists, who know France chiefly through the bias of humanities departments, the work of Julia **Kristeva**, Luce **Irigaray** and Hélène **Cixous** (often known only partially and belatedly, through translations) are synonymous with French feminist thought. The real situation is more complex. Feminist thought nowadays operates within a multitude of disciplines: philosophy, sociology, linguistics, literature, **psychoanalysis**, history and politics. Within France, perceptions of the importance of differ-ent individuals and groups have varied, as intellectual fashions and emphases change. Outside France, this fashion-effect has been compounded by the inevitable distortions pro-duced by the special interests of academic and **publishing** networks.

Postwar feminist thought begins, famously,

with Simone de **Beauvoir**. Trained as an academic philosopher, she devoted her first energies to developing the themes of **existentialism** within the terms set by Jean-Paul **Sartre**. Early Beauvoirian existentialist essays are *Pyrrhus et Cinéas* (1944) and *The Ethics of Ambiguity* (*Pour une morale de l'ambiguïté*) of 1947. The ground-breaking *The Second Sex* (*Le Deuxième Sexe*), published in 1949, transformed the terms of the discussion of the woman question, with its exploration of the situation of the female subject in Western culture, and its challenging presentation of woman as the object constructed by men's fictions and sciences and by the male-determined rituals and conventions of **family** and social life. Beauvoir argued for the need to remake the heterosexual couple, to produce a better life for both men and women, and for the importance of women seeking economic independence to free themselves from the chains of domesticity. In her later novels and autobiographical writings, she pursued her analysis in terms which always situated the personal in its wider political context. Her political activism in conjunction with Sartre, from the 1950s onwards, also produced political commentaries – see, for example, *The Long March* (*La Longue Marche*), published in 1957, relating her visit to Mao's China.

Not until the mid-1960s did Beauvoir characterize herself as feminist; but her distinctive intellectual style, with its rationalist analysis, left-wing commitment, engagement with practical moral and political issues and constant return to personal experience as the ground of understanding has left a clear mark on succeeding feminist thinkers. The direct influence of *The Second Sex* is apparent in, for example, Benoîte **Groult**'s *Ainsi soit-elle* (1975), a polemic account of the marginalization of women in everyday life. The work of Christine **Delphy** ploughs a distinctive furrow within the tradition. An academic sociologist active in the feminist movement in the late 1960s and early 1970s, and one of the founder members of the MLF, as well as of the campaign for the legalization of abortion, Delphy continues in the 1990s to produce theory linked closely to prac-

tical social action. She founded the radical feminist collective *Questions Féministes* (1977), and after the split in the collective on the issue of radical lesbianism (whose separatist doctrines she opposed, including those of her erstwhile collaborator Monique **Wittig**), she co-founded *Nouvelles Questions Feministes*, with continuing editorial support from Beauvoir. A Marxist, Delphy nevertheless conceives women's oppression not in terms of class struggle but as primarily a struggle against patriarchy, which is conducted in the first instance within the family, where unpaid female labour is expropriated by the (male) head of household. Delphy's doctrine of materialist feminism views gender as a social construct rather than a natural category, and she is opposed to psychoanalytical theories which look for definitions of the difference of the female subject in terms which invite biological essentialism. Her 1976 essay 'Protofeminism and Anti-Feminism' ('Proto-Féminisme et anti-féminisme') was a refutation of Annie **Leclerc**'s much-hyped *Parole de femme* (1974), a lyrical celebration of the 'natural' difference of woman which urged women to abandon attempts to compete on masculine terrain and seek instead to valorize female discourse (giggles and gossip), the female reproductive capacity and the domain of domesticity.

Julia Kristeva, a former member of the influential **Tel quel** collective, whose work builds on that of Barthes, Bakhtin and **Lacan**, defines her intellectual project as the exploration of the positioning of the subject in language. Her work has enriched feminist thinking with the fresh dimensions it has brought to consideration of the relationship between language and meaning. In her *Revolution in Poetic Language* (*La Révolution du langage poétique*) of 1974, Kristeva drew together linguistics, philosophy and psychoanalysis for an analysis of the revolutionary subject in post-Mallarmean literature. She set out her discussion of language and meaning (and, especially, the subversion of meaning) in gender terms, presenting the production of meaning as involving the interaction of two types of signifying process. The *semiotic*, pre-linguistic, involves the imprinting of the child with social and familial structures mediated through the maternal body. The *symbolic* has to do with sign and syntax and with linguistic and social laws, and is said to be a paternal function. In its explanations of some of the difficult new concepts it was inventing, Kristeva's early work used some very traditional metaphors based on gender (for example, the traditional association of women and nature), which her later work has reassessed. But even at that early stage, she developed the metaphors in ways that were productive for feminist political positions. See, for example, *About Chinese Women* (*Des Chinoises*), published in 1974; *Polylogue*, 1977). *The Powers of Horror: An Essay in Abjection* (*Pouvoirs de l'horreur*) of 1980 is a powerful critique of the conventional association of woman with nature and its monstrous repressions; which has produced, Kristeva argues, the Western fear of the archaic mother.

The work of Luce **Irigaray** is conceived in sustained opposition to the philosophical and psychoanalytic masters who organize the academy. It challenges the masculinist terms of their logic, questions their right to lay down the laws of debate, and sets up in opposition radically different feminine sets of images for thought. *Speculum of the Other Woman* (*Speculum de l'autre femme*), published in 1974, addresses itself to the question of what constitutes feminine difference, which it describes as the burning question of our age. Freud is dismissed for having assimilated the formation of the feminine subject to a system expressed in terms of the phallus, and is attacked for the contradictions and ill-disguised self-interest of his logic. Plato is swept up in the condemnation, as one of the originating masters of masculine thought. *Marine Lover of Friedrich Nietzsche* (*Amante marine de Friedrich Nietzsche*) from 1980 attacks this other significant pole of contemporary Western philosophy, as yet another emblem of the sameness of masculine thought, always reducing feminine Other to its mirror. Irigaray attacks specifically Nietzsche's celebration of the will to power, his emphasis on recurrence, the sharp binary oppositions that his thought imposes, and its aspirations to possess its object. Against these, she places the preoc-

cupation with change, difference, inclusiveness, openness and sharing, which she claims as the property of feminine thought. *Marine Lover* is a major text for reading Irigaray's famous association of the feminine with fluidity (the mobile, all-embracing, creative sea) and, again, her opposition to the rationalist tradition. This time it is Socrates who is called to the tribunal, along with his modern heir. Re-evaluation of modes of thought carries with it the re-evaluation of personal relationships. *This Sex Which Is not One* (*Ce sexe qui n'en est pas un*) of 1977 collects important essays on feminine sexuality and writing, including a reconsideration of mother/father roles. A fresh version of the bonds between mother and daughter appears in *And One Does Not Move Without the Other* (*Et l'une ne bouge pas sans l'autre*) of 1979. More empirical investigations into the different ways men and women use language figure in, for example, *Sex and Gender Through Language* (*Sexes et genres à travers les langues*) published in 1990, and *Je, tu, nous* (1990).

The reputation of Hélène **Cixous**, founder in 1977 of the influential Centre d'Études Féminines, rests principally in her creative writing, which itself constitutes an exploration into key theoretical issues concerned with the nature of the feminine subject, and the relation to writing of feminine desire and the female body (*écriture féminine*). Her work is closely associated with the psychoanalytic theory of the group **Psych et Po**. But her thinking on the relations of body, history and language, and also her distinctive style, is at least as heavily indebted to the Irish modernist James Joyce, on whom she wrote her thesis. The images and structures of her writing embody the search theorized by Kristeva and Irigaray for a mode of writing that models what is characterized as the specific nature of feminine desire – see, for example, *The Laugh of the Medusa* (*Le Rire de la Méduse*) from 1975, 'Coming to Writing' *and Other Essays* (*La Venue à l'écriture*) from 1977, and *The Newly Born Woman* (*La Jeune Née*) of 1975. The play *Portrait de Dora* (1976) turns back against Freud the content and form of the case study in which he tried to pin down the 'hysteric' Dora in the imprisoning categories of his psychoanalysis. More recent plays go beyond the perspective of women's repression to explore in the wider perspective more general questions of identity and freedom in language and history.

A more traditional approach to academic philosophy appears in the work of Michèle Le Doeuff, who has highlighted the institutional barriers to women's careers in the academic institutions. *Hipparchia's Choice* (*L'Étude et le rouet*), from 1989, sets her own work in the tradition of Mary Wollstonecraft and Simone de Beauvoir, and defines her own philosophical approach as contestatory, exploratory, analytical and rationalist. Like Irigaray's, but in more conventional and accessible terms, her texts explore statements on women by male philosophers and demonstrate their theoretical weaknesses. Le Doeuff's language is also that advocated by Catherine **Clément**, teacher of philosophy and former professional diplomat, who, in *La Jeune Née*, played devil's advocate to Cixous, arguing that rationalist speech, being more generally comprehensible, was politically more effective than hysterical and lyrical discourse. Clément's study of opera – *Opera, or the Undoing of Women* (*L'Opéra ou la défaite des femmes*) from 1979 – offers a feminist critique of the myths of feminine hysteria carried in the libretti, and an analysis of the relation of myths and music.

The transformations in academic history effected by the *Annales* school helped prepare the ground for a new generation of women historians, of whom the doyenne is Michelle Perrot, general editor of the *Histoire des femmes* (1990–2). History blends with philosophy in the work of Élisabeth **Badinter**, which has brought fresh perspectives to the discussion of motherhood. More recently, Badinter used the historical perspective to contribute to the debate on the 'crisis' in masculine identity generated by the rise of feminism.

JENNIFER BIRKETT

See also: abortion/contraception; autobiography; feminism (movements/groups); Marxism and Marxian thought; women's/lesbian writing

Further reading

Jackson, S. (1996) *Christine Delphy*, London: SAGE Publications (a richly detailed account of an important sociological body of work).

Lechte, J. (1990) *Julia Kristeva*, London: Routledge (a rewarding overview of Kristeva's work).

Marks, E. and de Courtivron, I. (eds) (1981) *New French Feminisms: An Anthology*, Brighton: Harvester Press (the first collection of its kind, offering short extracts with, by and large, insufficient context for the new reader to evaluate them; nevertheless, it retains its value).

Moi, T. (1987) *French Feminist Thought: A Reader*, Blackwell: Oxford (a compendium of well-presented substantial extracts from a broad range of writers, with a useful introduction).

——(1994) *Simone de Beauvoir: The Making of an Intellectual Woman*, Oxford and Cambridge, MA: Blackwell (readable and scholarly; in the Beauvoirean tradition, it situates the private subject in the public sphere).

Oliver, K. (1995) *Womanizing Nietzsche: Philosophy's Relation to the Feminine*, New York and London: Routledge (includes useful sections on the implications for social structures of Kristeva's and Irigaray's work on the family triangle).

Whitford, M. (1991) *Luce Irigaray: Philosophy in the Feminine*, London and New York: Routledge (the standard text).

Fernandez, Dominique

b. 1929, Neuilly-sur-Seine

Writer, essayist and critic

The son of the literary critic and collaborator Ramon Fernandez, Fernandez is a prolific novelist, distinguished Italianist, travel writer, and literary and music critic. He began writing psychobiographies of Pavese and Eisenstein based on Freudian theories of sublimation (a method he also applied to Mozart and Michelangelo). His most interesting novels are *L'Étoile rose* (The Pink Star), a magisterial portrayal of postwar gay culture in France and America, published in 1978; *Dans la main de l'ange* (In the Hand of the Angel), winner in 1982 of the Prix Goncourt, which retraces the tragic itinerary of Pasolini; and *La Gloire du paria* (The Glory of the Pariah), a 1987 examination of the value of human suffering caused by **AIDS**. While Fernandez believes in the normality of homosexuality, he also claims that AIDS restores to gay men an outlaw status fundamental to artistic creativity. In *Le Rapt de Ganymède* (The Abduction of Ganymede), an excellent literary and cultural history of gay representation published in 1989, he argues that only when homosexuality is an object of contestation does it become a properly creative subject for literature. By turns baroque, sober, subtle and fastidious, Fernandez's style is distinguished by its impressive probity.

JAMES WILLIAMS

See also: gay writing; literary prizes

Further reading

Robinson, C. (1995) *Scandal in the Ink: Male and Female Homosexuality in Twentieth-Century French Literature*, London: Cassell (includes a sensitive discussion of all aspects of Fernandez's gay writing)

Ferrat, Jean

b. 1930, Vaucresson

Singer-songwriter,
real name Jean Tenenbaum

A leading anti-establishment figure in French *chanson*, particularly during the 1960s, Ferrat earned initial recognition in 1954 with the populist *Ma Môme* (My Girl). He expressed his

Communist sympathies in *En groupe, en ligue, en procession* (In Groups, in League, in Procession). His father's detention in the Nazi concentration camps inspired *Nuit et Brouillard* (Night and Fog). Ferrat's output is often romantic, as in *Je vous aime* (I Love You), *Potemkine*, and environmentally aware; for example, in *La Montagne* (*The Mountain*). He has paid tribute to **Vian**, **Brassens** and Lorca, as well as Aragon, whose poetry he set to music.

CHRIS TINKER

See also: song/*chanson*

Ferré, Léo

b. 1916, Monaco;
d. 1993, Italy

Singer-songwriter

Although Ferré is widely regarded as a cornerstone of French *chanson*, he was anxious to portray himself as a marginalized figure, a banner for left-wing intellectuals and anarchists. Marked by an oppressive education at a Catholic boarding school in Italy, Ferré went to Paris in 1936 to study political science and law. At the end of the war he became an announcer and pianist at Radio-Monte-Carlo, and by 1949 was performing in cabarets. He had initial success with *Jolie Môme* (Pretty Girl), and *Merde à Vauban* (Down with Vauban), a poem by Pierre Seghers.

While Ferré wanted to appeal to, and be understood by, a wide audience, with references to the culture and language of the masses, as in *Épique Époque* (Epic Era), he also identified himself as part of a more poetic tradition, for example in *Étang chimérique* (Imaginary Pond). He published a largely autobiographical novel, *Benoît misère*, and his writing has often been compared to that of the symbolists and Surrealists. Ferré's musical tastes are equally eclectic, ranging from the popular tango, *Mister Giorgina* (dedicated to his accordionist), and accordion waltz, *C'est le printemps* (It's Springtime), to the more classical influences of Debussy and Ravel. Ferré's earlier work contains relatively simple melodies and harmonies, but during the 1970s he wrote much longer, heavier and ambitious pieces, such as *Il n'y a plus rien* (There is Nothing Left).

From early on, Ferré was an anti-conformist who aggressively challenged authority and the system (*La Mafia*). His targets included the Catholic church and the Pope – for example, *Monsieur Tout-Blanc* (Mr Whiter-Than-White). Closely associated with the anarchist movement, he participated in the angry protests of the **May 1968** movement, condemning state injustice, as in *Ni Dieu ni maître* (Without God or Master) and *Thank You Satan*. While he argued against collective action in principle, he expressed solidarity with the protesters by performing a series of low-priced concerts in 1970 at the Salle de la Mutualité in Paris.

Although Ferré could preach angrily at his audiences, he was also capable of a more serious and tender tone. An animal lover, he was deeply affected by the death of his pet chimpanzee (*Pépée*). Such sensitivity may also be identified in Ferré's songs about love – both ephemeral, as in *Avec le temps* (As Time Passes), and enduring, for example in *Ça te va* (It Suits You) – although his writing was also often charged with explicit sexual imagery, like in *La Lettre* (The Letter). The song *Amour-Anarchie* (Love-Anarchy) perhaps best defines Ferré, whose criticism of society stemmed from a fundamental love for humanity. The image of himself he chose to project was of an accursed poet who embraced melancholy and solitude, wandering the streets of Paris by night (*Paris-Spleen*).

Among his innovations, Ferré recorded long, self-contained texts; prose poems which he declaimed rather than sang, such as *Les Amants tristes* (The Sad Lovers). He also set the poetry of Aragon, Baudelaire and Apollinaire to music, introducing them to a wider sudience.

Although Ferré was perhaps not as mainstream as **Brel** and **Brassens**, his music was popular with the disaffected French youth – for example, *Salut Beatnik!* (Hi Beatnik!)).

CHRIS TINKER

See also: song/*chanson*

Major works

Ferré, L. (1993) *La Mauvaise Graine* [The Bad Seed], Paris: Paris (collected texts, poems and songs).

Further reading

Fléouter, C. (1996) *Léo*, Paris: Laffont (biography).
Letellier, C. (1993) *Léo Ferré, l'unique et sa solitude*, Paris: Nizet (biographically oriented study).

Figaro, Le

Newspaper

Leading right-wing quality broadsheet, *Le Figaro* is a morning newspaper and France's oldest national daily. Launched as a weekly by Hippolyte de Villemessant in 1854, it became a daily in 1866. Publication was interrupted from November 1942 to August 1944 as a result of the Occupation, but after the **Liberation** *Le Figaro* flourished, as many right-wing rivals had now disappeared.

Under Pierre Brisson's leadership (1936–64), the newspaper gained a reputation for editorial independence despite a succession of owners. However, Brisson's death in 1964 provoked a series of crises culminating in the purchase of *Le Figaro* by Robert **Hersant** in 1975, and the subsequent departure of numerous journalists (including Raymond **Aron**, who had written for *Le Figaro* for many years). Staff were unhappy with the new owner's political ambitions, editorial interference and ruthless management style.

Circulation fell, but in the early 1980s conservative dissatisfaction with the Socialist government led to a rise in *Le Figaro*'s fortunes. New Saturday supplements also proved successful: *Le Figaro magazine* created in 1978, *Le Figaro Madame* in 1980, and *TV magazine* since 1987. The aim is to appeal to the whole family by covering a wide range of interests. There are economic and literary supplements, and *Figaroscope*, a guide to events in the Paris area. The paper contains practical pages, offering advice on tourism, sales bargains, and classified advertisements, especially for jobs and property. Readers are predominantly from the professional middle and upper classes, with above average income. Consequently, *Le Figaro* is attractive to advertisers and, depending on the economic climate, **advertising** accounts for up to 70 per cent of its revenue. Compared to *Le Monde, Le Figaro* provides fuller financial and business information, much appreciated by industrialists, businessmen and investors. It has a reputation as tribune of the right-wing intelligentsia, thanks to supplement *Le Figaro littéraire* and regular contributions from members of the prestigious **Académie Française** such as Jean d'Ormesson and Alain Peyrefitte.

Politically, *Le Figaro* is extremely conservative, and was closely associated with the Gaullist Rassemblement pour la République, having well-known RPR politicians among its staff. However, overt bias in favour of Jacques **Chirac** in the 1988 presidential election, at the expense of other right-wing candidates, led to falling sales, and *Le Figaro* was forced to moderate its tone and move towards the Centre. This was demonstrated in the appointment of Franz-Olivier Giesbert, formerly of *Le Nouvel Observateur*, as editorial director, and the reduction in prominence of hard-liner Max Clos.

In 1995, although outsold by *Le Parisien*, *Le Figaro* was the leading upmarket daily, with an average circulation of 391,533 copies. However, financial problems resulting from questionable business decisions, such as the investment in new printing facilities at Roissy in 1988, prompted Hersant to fire group director Philippe Villin in 1994 and, following Hersant's death in April 1996, questions surround *Le Figaro*'s future.

PAM MOORES

See also: national press in France; parties and movements

Fini, Léonore

b. 1918, Buenos Aires, Argentina;
d. 1996, Paris

Artist, theatre designer and illustrator

Brought up in Trieste, Fini received little formal art training. Influenced by Italian Mannerism, German Romanticism, and Surrealism, her paintings, executed in meticulous detail, suggest enigmatic dreams. Although close to the Surrealists she was not a formal member of the group. Her often hallucinatory compositions present images of mysterious rituals in theatrical spaces, female warriors (*La Chambre noire*), hybrid creatures half-female, half-animal (*Les Mutantes*), and a number of self-portraits (*Le Bout du monde*). Drawing from the hermetic tradition, she explored images of petrification (*Mémoire géologique*) and decomposition and regeneration (*Sphinx Regina*). She designed **theatre** sets and costumes, including *Bérénice* for **Barrault** and *The Maids* (*Les Bonnes*) for **Genet**.

ELZA ADAMOWICZ

Finkielkraut, Alain

b. 1949, Paris

Writer and essayist

Finkielkraut is a writer who, having been influenced by philosophers such as Michel **Foucault** and Emmanuel **Levinas,** has written a number of trenchant essays whose common theme is to attack the false premises on which the supposed 'liberties' of the modern individual have been based. After a series of works on Jewish identity and memory, he achieved notoriety principally for his attack on modernity in *The Undoing of Thought* (*La Défaite de la pensée*). Here he develops his critique of postmodern culture, reflecting a major concern of his (shared with several contemporary intellectuals) that 'non-thought' threatens the continuity of French cultural identity.

MARTYN CORNICK

Major works

Finkielkraut, A. (1982) *L'Avenir d'une négation*, Paris: Éditions du Seuil.
——(1983) *Le Juif imaginaire*, Paris: Éditions du Seuil.
——(1988) *The Undoing of Thought* [*La Défaite de la pensée*], London: Claridge.
——(1992) *Comment peut-on être croate?*, Paris: Gallimard.

Flammarion

Publishing house

Flammarion was founded in 1876 by the publisher Ernest Flammarion (1846–1936). Among the popular authors it launched were Daudet, Zola, Gyp and, later, Henri Troyat and Guy des Cars. It publishes novels, academic works and art books, as well as affordable and popular collections such as 'J'ai lu' (3,850 titles 1958–94), 'Père Castor' (for children) and 'GF-Flammarion' (600 titles of French literature).

MARTYN CORNICK

See also: publishing/*l'édition*

Further reading

Martin, H.-J., Chartier, R. and Vivet, J.-P. (eds) (1986) *Histoire de l'édition française*, vol. 4, *Le Livre concurrencé 1900–1950*, Paris: Promodis (essential reading).
Parinet, E. (1992) *La Librairie Flammarion (1875–1914)*, Paris: IMEC.

folk music

The word *folklore* in French, as its derivative *folklorique* attests, has always had a derogatory connotation. Music scholars would preferably refer to *musique traditionnelle* or *musique ethnique*. This domain extends to *chansons*. French folk-song's heritage is rich and its diversity reflects France's geographical and linguistic variety. If this heritage still nourishes the collective mentality through familial, parochial and educational channels (sea shanties, Christmas carols, drinking songs, lullabies, etc. from different regions), the creative sources of new folk-songs are more likely to be found at the periphery: Brittany, Basque and Occitan country, Alsace.

The folk music revival in the 1960s and 1970s coincided with the creation, under **Malraux** of the *maisons de la culture* . After the events of **May 1968,** folk music's green messages appealed to the generation of *soixante-huitards* (literally 'sixty-eighters'; young people who followed for a while the ecological and libertarian ideal, away from consumer society). Their audience was also exposed to Bob Dylan, Joan Baez and Leonard Cohen, as well as to the country-and-western repertoire through Hugues **Aufray,** who specialized in adapting them in French. Folk clubs appeared everywhere.

The folk group of the period was Malicorne, formed in 1974 by a whole group of musicians who mastered traditional instruments (spinet, dulcimer, hurdy-gurdy), while at the same time introducing modern arrangements. Their best album was *Almanach*, and they triumphed at the Cambridge Folk Festival in July 1975, but the group fell apart, separated in 1981 and attempted a comeback with their last album, *Les Cathédrales de l'industrie* (The Cathedrals of industry), in 1987. Another well-known group was La Bamboche from Berry, musically talented and full of humour and *joie de vivre*. Roger Siffer in Alsace reinvented with humour the heritage of his region.

A special case must be made for Occitan and Breton folk-singers. South of the Loire valley, folk music became the instrument or the context of a revival of Occitan cultural identity, with Marti, Patric and Joan Pau Verdier. In Brittany, Alan Stivell led the rise of Celtic folk and pop, followed by Glenmor and Gilles Servat, whose *Blanche Hermine* (White Ermine) became the hymn of minorities neglected by central government. The Breton folk-singers survived the doldrums of the 1980s and early 1990s, in which folk music in France seemed to have declined, drawing their strength from their traditional Celtic musical heritage mixed with modern idioms. Since 1994, there are signs of a revival in folk music in France, and again some regions with a strong singular cultural identity are providing the talents: Brittany (with Tri Yann and Dan Ar Braz), the Basque country (with Peio Serbielle), Alsace and Corsica.

GÉRARD POULET

See also: regional music; regionalism; song/*chanson*

Further reading

Coulomb, S. and Varrod, D. (1987) *Histoires de chansons 1968–1988*, Paris: Balland (an informative survey, with some entertaining pages on 'Le Folk à travers les âges').

Krümm, P. and Ribouillault, C. (1995) 'Les Musiques traditionelles en France', in *Musiques en France*, Paris: ADPF (a brief overview, with a very useful bibliography on traditional instruments and folk-songs).

football

Football has been an extremely popular sport in France since the late nineteenth century (Le Havre, the first club, was founded in 1872) but it was only in 1984 that the country, captained by Michel Platini, won its first major trophy when it hosted the European Nations' Championship. France also won the Olympic title in the same year. Although it has been rocked by scandals in the 1990s (allegations of drug taking among players, of financial irregularities and bribes, and the embarrassment of seeing the country's first European Club Champions, Olympique de Marseille, relegated after match-fixing bribes were shown to have been offered), French football none the less retains its high profile in the media and the French Football Federation boasts something in excess of 1.7 million registered players. Paris-St Germain's victory in the 1996 European Cup Winners' Cup and the national team's showing in Euro 96 did much to repair the damage. The country hosted the World Cup in 1998.

IAN PICKUP

See also: sport

Further reading

Mercier, J. (1979), *Le football*, Paris: PUF (an account of the history, development and organization of football in France).

foreign policy

Foreign policy since 1945 has contributed much to defining public perceptions of France and Frenchness in France, as well as to creating a distinctive profile for France internationally. Postwar, French foreign policy has negotiated **decolonization** and post-imperial diplomacy, partnership with Germany in developing the **European Union** and (partly thanks to **defence and security** policy based on nuclear deterrence) independence vis-à-vis the Cold War superpowers. Foreign policy is still strongly marked by de **Gaulle**, whose vision of France in the 1960s initially moulded contemporary French international relations by suggesting that France was not herself without *grandeur*.

Until the 1960s, foreign policy was mainly concerned with establishing a relationship with the US, co-operating with Germany in face of the USSR and reconsidering the Empire (renamed *Union française*), under pressure of colonial unrest. French pride was initially hurt by Allied underevaluation of France's part in victory, the rejection of French representation at Yalta and Potsdam, the proposal to run liberated France through an Allied military government, and by the grudging inclusion of France in the administration of Germany. Marshall aid heightened French sensitivity towards the United States, and exacerbated divisions between the Communists (ordered by Moscow to oppose it) and parties more mistrustful of the USSR. With the establishment of NATO (1949) and the ECSC (1952), the way was cleared to France's founding role in the EEC (1957), marking an opening of the protected French economy. Simultaneously came crisis in colonial Algeria, and the return of de Gaulle. Following humiliating disengagement from Indochina (1954), de Gaulle tortuously negotiated Algerian independence (1962), after an **Algerian war** costly in financial, political and human terms. French culture was marked by the resettlement of approximately 1 million *pieds noirs* (European Algerians) and by the trauma suffered in the 'savage war of peace' by more than 3 million conscripts, as well as by the political divisions created by decolonization.

After losing Algeria, France developed her deterrent force and structured foreign and defence policies around *indépendance nationale*. Gaullism favoured a multipolar international system, a Europe of nation-states and a network of francophony; these aims were furthered through encouraging nationalism (for example, Quebec), by reluctant European integration (including veto of British entry because of feared Atlanticism), and by links with former colonies. **Giscard d'Estaing** pursued *mondialisme* (internationalism), expressed in intervention in francophone African countries, contributions to North–South debates, action in favour of disarmament while maintaining strong military capability, and *rapprochement* with Germany in Europe. Under **Mitterrand** and **Chirac**, France has continued support of European integration, and in the context of global interdependence and economic rigour has started to reassess its ambitions of total independence. Nevertheless, much of French diplomatic rhetoric and public opinion is still heavily coloured by France's *grandeur*, and by mistrust of the perceived US military, financial and cultural hegemony, although France did participate as a minor allied partner in the Gulf War. French foreign policy is still trying to build France a home in the post-colonial, post-Cold War international system.

HUGH DAUNCEY

See also: European economic integration; parties and movements

Further reading

Cerny, P. G. (1980) *The Politics of Grandeur*, Cambridge: Cambridge University Press (the definitive treatment of the implications of Gaullist foreign policy).

Forrester, Viviane

b. 1925, Paris

Literary critic, historian and writer

A creative writer and feminist literary critic whose work has focused on Anglo-Saxon women authors, especially Virginia Woolf, Forrester's best-known work is *La Violence du calme* (The Violence of Calm). Published in 1980, this study offers a radical critique of history, as generative of a culture of coercion and repression.

ALEX HUGHES

See also: feminist thought; women's/lesbian writing

Foucault, Michel

b. 1926, Poitiers;
d. 1984, Paris

Intellectual historian

Michel Foucault stands among the most important philosophers and writers in postwar France. His work explores at least six interrelated areas: art and literature as what describes a space outside of cognition and reason; madness as that which defines the way a culture and its history can be understood; the symptomatic relation of word to things in classical and modern culture; the clinical 'gaze' as a determiner of relations of societal and sexual difference; sexuality as the very basis for study of ideology; the history of penality as the area in which is mapped out the birth of the modern or 'disciplinary' state.

Foucault's *Death and the Labyrinth: The Work of Raymond Roussel* (*Raymond Roussel*) and 'This is Not a Pipe' ('Ceci n'est pas une pipe') constitute a dictionary and an exemplary indicator of his style of analysis. In the former, published in 1963, the novelist is seen as providing a language of extreme platitude which in fact makes the reader aware of an extraordinary violence that inhabits the literary cliché. Roussel makes us aware, says Foucault, of a 'lacunary reserve', like the unconscious, that inhabits all language, and that is paradoxically neutral or of 'zero-degree' inflection in modern writing. Similarly, 1968's 'Ceci n'est pas une pipe' suggests that the word–image relations in Magritte's **paintings** attest to an imponderable paradox of identity and difference of language and visual form. What is indicated in an act of deixis (*ceci* or 'this . . . ') is not, as an image,

what is either stated or written in the discourse describing it. Yet, too, it is, since the trick of the painter is to present a pipe, or a lure, that inhabits the 'pipe' which is before our eyes. Foucault shows that whenever the memory of ideograms and pictograms is recalled, as they are with Roussel and Magritte, meaning and institutions that are built on the illusion of conventional communication begin to totter.

In *The Order of Things* (*Les Mots et les choses*), published in 1966, Foucault maps out a history of constitutive differences of the kind begun in his work on art and literature. Its sweeping vision leads the reader from the early modern realm of linguistic analogy, in which words and the objects to which they referred shared a common substance and malleability, to the regime of representation, in which words 'stand for' or are the procurative agents for things that are no longer there or present. This radical change, begun with the advent of seventeenth-century science (and felt in the gap between, for example, Montaigne of the 1580s and Descartes of the 1640s), inaugurates the modern world. It leads forward to the age of the psychoanalyst and the ethnologist.

Foucault designed his study to show how relations of identity are constitutive of the modern subject. In its companion volume, *Madness and Civilization* (*Folie et déraison*), which was his doctoral thesis, and was published in 1961, Foucault begins in roughly the same areas and reaches similar conclusions, except that the approach is cued to relations of difference. How madness is defined, and then how it is legislated and managed, become the counterpart to his work on sameness. Van Gogh and **Artaud** become in this work what the analyst and the anthropologist were in *The Order of Things*. They crown a work that begins with the Erasmian drive to bring madness into civilization, and illustrates how madness becomes implicated with practices of incarceration in the Classical Age, then finds itself reborn and renamed in the growth of the human sciences.

The backdrop of these two studies indicates why Foucault's greatest work, the 1975 *Discipline and Punish* (*Surveiller et punir*), was subtitled a 'history of modern times'. In this work, the author studies what he calls the history of the relation of the body to the soul by way of institutions designed to impose pain, suffering, retribution and amendment. The history of the prison, like that of alterity, stands at the basis of political and military institutions. Noteworthy, however, is that Foucault offers a history of the articulation of space in the prison, military barracks, hospital, asylum and secondary school. He shows that these architectures tell much through their 'form of content' as much as through what they elsewhere try to impose or convey in their language. This book was part of a political commitment on Foucault's part to institutional reform and, to a more radical degree, liberation in general. His work did not ever separate its inaugural drive – its eros and its politics – from its conclusions. *Surveiller et punir* in fact made manifest an ethics that had been less immediately visible in the earlier writings.

Foucault's last works take up many of the same themes encountered in the studies of the years 1962–76. In the four-volume collection of *Sayings and Writings* (*Dits et écrits*) published in 1994, the reader encounters Foucault in his most resonant voice. In so far as he had defined his work not only as writing but also as an ongoing political and social practice, the interview, the short news item, the occasional article, the book review and other ephemera become crucial elements in his labours. *Dits et écrits* transforms what readers have felt Foucault's work to have been by showing us the conditions – the spaces and places, the resistances and the stakes – in which his work, be it on sexuality, incarceration, the invention of the self, or the author as a mode of classification, was elaborated. Few historians of the same stripe have ever wedded such inclusive sense of labour and praxis to their lives. Foucault stands as one of the greatest exponents and barometers of radical shifts in approaches to understanding and rethinking the history of Western culture. This work goes much further than the three volumes of *The History of Sexuality* (*Histoire de la sexualité*), which were published between 1976 and 1984

and which, conceivably by virtue of Foucault's own homosexuality, are his best-known books.

Tom Conley

See also: anthropology and ethnography; Aron, Jean-Paul; poststructuralism; psychoanalysis

Further reading

Dreyfus, H. and Rabinow, P. (1982) *Michel Foucault*, Brighton: Harvester Press (contains an interview with Foucault and is a lucid treatment of the shift from archaeology to genealogy in his work).

Eribon, D. (1989) *Michel Foucault 1926–1984*, revised edition 1991, Paris: Flammarion (a very thoroughly researched biography).

Macey, D. (1993) *The Lives of Michel Foucault*, London: Hutchinson (a comprehensive overview of Foucault's life and work).

Fourastié, Jean

b. 1907, St-Benin-d'Azy, Nièvre; d. 1990

Economist

Fourastié's socioeconomic analysis of the modernization of France after 1945 revealed the scale of change that occurred during the Fourth Republic and early years of the Fifth. The title of his 1976 book, *Les Trente glorieuses*, became shorthand for the years that had transformed France from an archaic, rural, agricultural society into a modern, technological, industrial nation. In 1945 Fourastié had joined the new Commissariat Général au Plan, facilitating the modernization he later described as an 'invisible revolution', and much of his academic work looked at the sociological implications of economic growth, examining inequalities, for instance, in *Le Jardin du voisin* (The Neighbour's Garden) published in 1980.

Fourastié devoted considerable time to teaching, notably at the Conservatoire national des Arts et Métiers and at Sciences Po (the Paris political science institute), and wrote for *Le Figaro*. In 1968, he was elected to the Académie des Sciences Morales et Politiques.

HUGH DAUNCEY

See also: economy

France 2

Television channel

This national television company came into existence in 1975 as a result of the breakup of the state broadcasting organization, l'Office de Radiodiffusion-Télévision Française (ORTF). Funded by a mix of licence-fee and advertising revenue, the channel remained part of the public sector throughout the various broadcasting reforms of the 1980s. Its programme output remains subject to detailed public service-type regulations and is monitored by a state-appointed regulatory authority, the Conseil Supérieur de l'Audiovisuel (Higher Audiovisual Council). Originally called Antenne 2, the company was renamed France 2 in 1992.

RAYMOND KUHN

See also: television

France 3

Television channel

Known as France Régions 3 (FR3) until 1992, this television company came into existence in 1975 as a result of the breakup of the state broadcasting organization, l'Office de Radiodiffusion-Télévision Française (ORTF). It was originally intended to be a channel for both the regions and French **cinema**. Funded mainly from licence-fee revenue plus some **advertising**, the channel remained part of the public sector throughout the various broadcasting reforms

of the 1980s. Its programme output remains subject to detailed public-service regulations and is monitored by a state-appointed regulatory authority, the Conseil Supérieur de l'Audiovisuel (Higher Audiovisual Council).

RAYMOND KUHN

See also: television

France Culture

Radio station

This is one of the state-owned Radio France's six national stations available on FM stereo in all parts of France (for frequency details, see Télérama's *Guide de la radio* or regional newspapers). Since 1963 (when it was created), France Culture has been fulfilling its ambitious mission, which is to disseminate culture (especially art, literature, science, history, philosophy, **theatre** and politics), develop creative projects in the field of radio and to reflect key movements in the world of ideas. This nonstop service (programmes are repeats between 1 a.m. and 7 a.m.) offers news, documentaries, debates, drama and music (classical as well as jazz).

ALAN PEDLEY

See also: radio (state-owned)

France Musique

Radio station

France Musique is one of the state-owned Radio France's six national stations broadcast on FM stereo throughout France (for frequency details, see Télérama's *Guide de la radio* or regional press). Created in 1963, this quality music station broadcasts a large number of live regional, national and international concerts and recitals. Music from all periods and cultural origins is often supported by introductions, explanations and discussions, which gives the station both an educational and a pluralistic flavour. Some recently created rivals in the private sector (e.g. Radio Classique) have affected listening figures.

ALAN PEDLEY

See also: radio (state-owned); television/spectacle guides

France-Dimanche

Newspaper

A sensational Sunday publication of long standing. Created at the end of World War II, it was apparently intended to cheer up the population. Dramatic headlines and extensive use of colour photographs entice the reader to share in the secrets of well-known personalities, their health, financial problems and love life. Appealing to the emotions, *France-Dimanche* provides escapist entertainment for a popular audience. It is produced by a limited number of journalists using various pseudonyms; news content and intellectual input are minimal. Typical readers are elderly, or women between 35 and 50 years of age. In the mid-1990s, circulation was stable at around 650,000 copies per week.

PAM MOORES

See also: national press in France

France-Inter

Radio station

Radio France's general-interest station, broadcast twenty-four hours a day, on long wave (162 kHz, 1852m), medium wave and FM (see local press or Télérama's *Guide de la radio* for frequency details). Created in 1947 as Paris-Inter, it was renamed in 1964. Catering for all tastes and most ages, this family station, while still commanding more than an 11 per cent share of the national audience, has been steadi-

ly losing listeners to the more specialized private and local stations bursting on the scene with the audiovisual deregulation of the 1980s. Current affairs, drama, interviews, phone-ins and music of all kinds feature prominently.

ALAN PEDLEY

See also: radio (state-owned); television/spectacle guides

France-Soir

Newspaper

The only mass-circulation national daily in postwar France, *France-Soir* regularly sold over a million copies in the 1950s. Created by Pierre Lazareff in 1944, it continued the traditions of prewar *Paris-Soir*, and sensationalism, human interest stories and extensive use of photography brought success in the popular market. The events of **May 1968**, together with Lazareff's death in 1972, marked a turning point: circulation declined steadily thereafter. Robert **Hersant** bought the paper in 1976, as a second Gaullist title to complement the more upmarket *Le Figaro*. Despite a succession of new initiatives, however, losses continue to accumulate.

PAM MOORES

See also: Gaulle, Charles de; national press in France

François, Claude

b. 1939, Ismaïlia, Egypt;
d. 1978, Paris

Lyricist and singer

Claude François established himself as one of the major figures of the French *yé-yé* (1960s pop) generation with hit songs such as *Si j'avais un marteau* (*If I Had a Hammer*). 'Clo-Clo', as he was known, appealed to adolescent audiences, often singing imported French versions of American hits. The incarnation of the glitzy showman on stage, Claude François will be best remembered in the Anglo-Saxon world as the co-author (with Thibault; music by Revaux) of *Comme d'habitude*, which in translation became the Sinatra classic *My Way*.

IAN PICKUP

See also: song/*chanson*

François, Guy-Claude

b. 1940, Berck

Stage designer

A designer at the **Théâtre du Soleil** since the 1960s, he worked on countless famous productions, including *L'Age d'or* in 1975 and *Mephisto* in 1978. He has also worked in cinema with James Ivory and Bertrand **Tavernier**, and acts as adviser to architects of public buildings, such as the **Pompidou Centre**.

ANNIE SPARKS

See also: collective creation; theatre

francophone cinema: Belgium

If the size of France has played a large part in the country's success in the **cinema**, it has also influenced the cinema of other francophone countries. Thus the linguistic border which Belgium shares with France has enabled its francophone community to produce larger-scale co-productions that are guaranteed a respectable market share. This involvement of France is significant, since Belgium's three official languages (French, Dutch and German) fragment what is already a very small market. These linguistic divisions make it necessary to divide 'Belgian' cinema into francophone/Belgian and Dutch/Belgian, and only a handful of directors (such as Delvaux and Henri Storck) have worked in both languages.

The above scenario would seem to suggest that France 'facilitates' the cinema of francophone Belgium. However, the relationship between the two countries has ranged from one of colonization (some of the first films to be made in Belgium were those by Alfred Machin, a Frenchman specifically sent by Pathé to produce films for the Belgian audience) to cultural 'exchange' (mainly through personnel abandoning the first country to work in the second – for example, Jacques Feyder, Raoul J. Lévy and Charles Spaak).

While its relationship with France has provided both advantages and disadvantages, Belgium's position within Europe has had a similar impact on its cinema. On the one hand, any sense of a 'Belgian specificity' is obscured by the country's role as centre of the new Europe. On the other hand, perhaps also because of its geographical position, Belgium has a long history as an enthusiastic host and sponsor of world cinema, with its Cinémathèque, its festivals and film schools all ensuring its place on world cinema's map.

Though Belgium is evidently a country which is far from hostile to cinema, its own national product has been hard to export, with the few actual successes coming from films which use the European auteur or art-cinema models (such as Jaco Van Dormael's *Toto le héros* in 1993). Meanwhile, much critical success has been gained through small-scale experimental work. There is a strong **documentary** tradition in Dutch/Belgian cinema (illustrated in the work of Henri Storck, Robbe de Hert or Frans Buyens) and this feeds into a wider preoccupation in both linguistic groups with 'reality'. Thus the *quotidien* is observed in microscopic detail by Boris Lehman and Manu Bonmariage, or analysed for its intersection with the fictional by Chantal Akerman (specifically *Jeanne Dielman 23 quai du Commerce 1080 Bruxelles* of 1975) or André Delvaux.

Apart from their use of 'European' genres (art and auteur cinema), and perhaps because of the lack of good scriptwriting, many Belgian directors have turned to their pictorial heritage for inspiration. The influence of **painting** can be seen in the preoccupation of many directors with Belgian landscape (Jean-Jacques Andrien,

Boris Lehman), the success of animation from the 1940s onwards (Belgium being the home of Tintin, Astérix and the Smurfs) and, finally, what could be seen as a truly Belgian genre – the *film sur l'art*. The latter can be described as a film which takes an artist or work of art as its subject.

CATHERINE FOWLER

See also: comic strips/cartoonists; francophone performing arts: Belgium; francophone writing (fiction, poetry): Belgium

Further reading

Bolen, F. (1978) *Histoire authentique (anecdotique, folklorique et critique) du cinéma belge*, Bruxelles: Éditions Memo & Codec (historical overview).

Davay, P. (1967) 'Belgium', in A. Lovell (ed.) *Art of the Cinema in Ten European Countries*, Strasbourg: Council for Cultural Co-operation.

Jungblutt, G., Leboutte, P. and Païni, D. (1990) *Une encyclopédie des cinémas de Belgique*, Paris: Éditions Yellow Now (comprehensive work of reference).

francophone cinema: North Africa

National cinemas in the countries of the Maghreb (Algeria, Morocco and Tunisia) were only able to develop after independence from French colonial rule (Tunisia and Morocco in 1956, Algeria in 1962), and their relationship with France and the French cinema industry continues to be problematic. Irrespective of differences in political systems and conditions of production, which range from state control in Algeria to private funding in Morocco, with Tunisia occupying an intermediary position, opportunities for film-making in North Africa are limited. North African films are in competition for audiences with Egyptian cinema on the one hand and Hollywood on the other. As a result, many North African film-makers have turned to France (and Europe) for training, funding, technical support and aid for distribution and exhibition. Ironically, therefore, given that metropolitan French audiences generally show little interest in Arabic culture, as many as one in two North African film-makers live and work in 'exile' in France or Belgium (particularly since the increase in fundamentalist terrorism in Algeria), and a large proportion of francophone North African films are (co-)produced in France and address a European arthouse and festival audience rather than an indigenous popular audience in the Maghreb.

The first Carthage Pan-African Film Festival was held in 1966, and the first features by North African film-makers were heroic narratives of revolt informed by the national liberation struggle against French colonialism and foreign exploitation, the volume of which eventually gave rise to the term 'couscous Western'. A major figure to emerge from this period was Algerian film-maker Mohamed Lakhdar-Hamina, who won the best first film award at Cannes with *Le Vent des Aurès* (1967) and the 1975 Palme d'Or for *Chronique des années de braise* (1974), a moving drama about the war of independence. Like other films of the 1970s, Abdellatif Ben Ammar's *Sejnane* began to address more contemporary social issues: the power of the state and the new ruling classes; the condition of the peasants; urban misery; and the condition of women (a topic also addressed in films like Assia Djebar's 1978 *Nouba*). Merzak Allouache's ground-breaking *Omar Gatlato* (1976) replaced the conventional hero with the figure of an ordinary Algerian youth, and the success of its down-to-earth realism allowed Algerian cinema to develop in less conformist ways.

A key theme of films of the 1970s was emigration and the problems faced by immigrant workers in France, represented in what critics have referred to as a 'miserabilist' style. Ali Ghalem's two films, *Mektoub?* (1969) and *L' Autre France* (1976), portray a young Algerian desperately seeking work and the exploitation of Algerian workers. Other examples include

Nacer Ktari's *Les Ambassadeurs* (1977), an exploration of the effects of French racism on the community of North Africans living in the Goutte d'Or district of Paris, Ali Akika and Anne-Marie Autissier's *Voyage en capital* (1977), a comparison between the lives of a (male) working-class immigrant and a (female) middle-class student born in France, and Ahmed Rachedi's *Ali au pays des mirages* (1979), a study of the aspirations and nightmares of an immigrant crane-operator. Since the advent of **beur cinema** in the 1980s, there have been few films by North Africans about **immigration** in France apart from Okacha Touita's intense realist dramas, including *Les Sacrifiés*, (1982), a dramatization of the fate of a young immigrant driven mad by the struggle between the FLN and the MNA which tore apart the Algerian community in Paris during the **Algerian war**. Allouache captures the tone of beur cinema in *Un amour à Paris* (1988), centring on the doomed love affair between a Jewish Algerian girl and a beur who fancies himself as the first beur cosmonaut, and returns to analysing contemporary beur and *banlieue* (suburb) culture in *Salut cousin!* (1996).

The film-maker of the 1980s who most successfully uses humour to problematize and critique Algerian mores and cultural identity is Mahmoud Zemmouri, now resident in France. His first black comedy, *Prends dix mille balles et casse-toi* (1980), explores the cultural conflicts produced when an immigrant family accepts the French government's offer of funding to return 'home' and discovers that their sons cannot adapt to Algerian village life. *Les Folles Années du twist* (1983) refuses the heroic narrative of the national liberation struggle, focusing instead on the pragmatic survival tactics of two lovable rogues, while *De Hollywood à Tamanrasset* (1990) dramatizes the intrigues of an Algerian community who model their behaviour on their favourite American film and TV stars.

However, in the 1980s North African film-makers generally turned away from explicitly political topics, disillusioned by the intransigence of the nationalist movements and influenced by both economic factors and Western ideological values. Some sought commercial success by using international stars and settings, like Moroccan film-maker Souhel Ben Barka's *Blood Honeymoon* (1979), starring Irène Pappas and Laurent Terzieff, and *Amok* (1984), a film about apartheid starring Miriam Makeba. Others sought international recognition through a personal cinema linked to the quest for identity and/or through self-consciously auteurist topics and techniques. Nouri Bouzid's *L'Homme de cendres* (1987) and Lakhdar-Hamina's *La Dernière Image* (1986) are specifically rooted in their director's childhood experiences, while Mahmoud Ben Mahmoud's *Traversées* (1982) and Nacer Khemir's *Les Baliseurs du désert* (1986) evoke a universal sense of alienation and mystery.

In the 1990s, a number of film-makers introduced debates about Islam, and about sexuality and the body, into North African cinema. Allouache's *Bab El Oued City* (1993) and Malik Lakhdar-Hamina's *Automne – octobre à Alger* (1991) offer critiques of the current crisis in Algeria, while in Tunisia Nouri Bouzid's *Bezness* (1992) addresses the pernicious effects of sex tourism, and Moufida Tlatli's *Les Silences du palais* (1994) and Ferid Boughedir's 1990 *Boy of the Terraces (Halfaouine)* – both scripted by Bouzid – explore various interdicts on the body. *Halfouine*, which recounts the coming of age of a 12-year-old boy amid very intimate domestic scenes, has been the biggest box office hit in Tunisia since the invention of motion pictures.

CARRIE TARR

See also: francophone performing arts (North Africa); francophone writing (fiction, poetry); North Africa; suburbs

Further reading

Malkmus, L. and Armes, R. (1991) *Arab and African Filmmaking*, London: Zed Books.
—— (1981) 'Cinémas du Maghreb', *CinémAction* 14.

—— (1982) 'Cinémas de l'émigration 3', *CinémAction* 24.

—— (1987) 'Les Cinémas arabes', *CinémAction et Grand Maghreb*, Paris: Institut du Monde Arabe.

francophone cinema: Switzerland

This small industry is largely known outside Switzerland by the names of two directors. Claude Goretta's 1976 adaptation of Pascal Lainé's popular novel *The Lacemaker* (*La Dentellière*) helped to make a major star of Isabelle **Huppert**, and his biopic of Rousseau, *Les Chemins de l'exil* (1977), paid oblique tribute to the greatest of Swiss-born actors by casting Michel Simon's son François in the main role. Alain Tanner has specialized in dulcet post-**May 1968** satires such as *La Salamandre* of 1971, starring Bulle Ogier, and 1973's *Le Retour d'Afrique*, which parodies the enthusiastic Third Worldism characteristic of its time.

KEITH READER

See also: cinema; francophone performing arts: Switzerland; francophone writing (fiction, poetry): Switzerland

francophone performing arts: Belgium

The first major literary figures of Belgian origin were closely related to the **theatre** (Maeterlinck was awarded the Nobel prize for literature in 1911 and his *Pelléas et Mélisande* was immortalized by Claude Debussy). Yet, despite its famous origin, twentieth-century Belgian theatre of French expression has not emerged as a major genre. Belgium has produced major playwrights but no identifiable school of drama. The relative non-identity of a Belgian drama of French expression can be accounted for in a number of diverse ways. Major figures avoid categories and cannot easily be inscribed

in the context of international movements. Enjoying a complex relationship with their country of origin, its languages and its tumultuous history (including the Question Royale and the 'linguistic wars' which split the nation in two), Belgian theatre remains individualistic and is often centred around the problems of language, memory and history.

Avant-garde theatre has not thrived in Belgium, and Belgian drama of French expression as a whole has had to compete with two popular genres: plays written in dialect reflecting local interests, and popular productions of French (Georges Feydeau's) *vaudevilles* or Belgian comedies such as *Le Mariage de Melle Beulemans* (Miss Beulemans' Wedding), performed for the first time in 1910. Not surprisingly, playwrights had to look elsewhere for an audience. After World War II, despite the state funding of Belgian theatres, many playwrights of Belgian origin looked to Paris for an audience: Parisian blockbusters of Belgian manufacture include Suzanne Lilar's *Le Burlador*, Jean Mogin's 1950 play *A chacun selon sa faim* (According to One's Hunger), and Michel de Ghelderode's *La Ballade du grand macabre* (The Macabre Ballad) of 1953.

The 1960s saw productions from two major playwrights: Paul Willems and Jean Sigrid. In *Il pleut dans ma maison* (It Is Raining in My House), first performed in 1962, Willems reveals a lyrical theatre where the barriers between life and death, between reality and dream, are shown to be porous. His 1967 production, *La Ville à voile* (The Sailing City), is also obsessed with the past, but here a much less optimistic view is expressed: language fails to conjure up a past and a history, and the main character's dream 'sailing city' (i.e. Antwerp) will never emerge from its ashes. Sigrid's plays, 1959's *Les Cavaliers* (The Horseriders), *Mort d'une souris* (Death of a Mouse) in 1968, and *L'Espadon* (The Swordfish) from 1976, focus on a search for identity, and his 1977 production *L'Auto-Stoppeur* (The Hitchhiker) experiments with a dysfunctional chronology.

On the international scene, the most famous and original Belgian playwright is René **Kalisky**. The author of plays first performed in the 1970s and 1980s, he translated into an experimental form traumatic events of the twentieth century (Stalinism, Nazism, Fascism). His most acclaimed productions include *Jim le téméraire* (Jim the Reckless), *Le Pique-Nique de Claretta* (Claretta's Picnic), *Dave au bord de mer* (Dave at the Seaside), *La Passion selon Pier Paolo Pasolini* (Passion According to Pier Paolo Pasolini) and *Falsch*. Kalisky's theatrical aim is to destabilize conventional ways of representing and reading a dramatic plot, as well as to undermine traditional notions of identity by multiplying the possibilities of the text (which he calls *le surtexte*, 'the supertext') and the performance (which becomes *le surjeu*, superacting; see his *Du surtexte au surjeu*).

JEAN MAINIL

See also: francophone cinema: Belgium; francophone writing (fiction, poetry): Belgium; theatre

Further reading

Frickx, R. and Trousson, R. (eds) (1989) *Lettres françaises de Belgique*, vol. 3 *Le Théâtre*, Louvain-la-Neuve (a comprehensive list of plays by Belgian authors, including summaries, history of performances and bibliographies).

Quaghebeur, M. (1990) *Lettres belges entre absence et magie*, Bruxelles: Éditions Labor (a comprehensive analysis of drama, including chapters on Willems, Kalisky, Baal, Sigrid and Louvet).

francophone performing arts: Indian Ocean

The islands of the Indian Ocean – Madagascar, Mauritius, Reunion and the Seychelles – are home to populations of very varied ethnic origins, and their differing cultural traditions are reflected in the diversity and richness of the performing arts in the area. Common to all the islands is a tradition of storytelling, with recitation of folk-tales transmitted orally and, more recently, collected and transcribed in local languages and in French. These, along with riddles and proverbial forms such as the *sirindanes* of Mauritius, often form the basis of public celebrations of folklore in all the islands.

Popular music and **dance** traditions are more differentiated: Mauritius and Reunion share the *sega*, a Creole song form accompanied by a rolling rhythm – usually in 6/8 tempo – provided by percussion instruments and associated with a sensual form of dancing. This was repressed as subversive and licentious in the years of slavery, but it is now the dominant local **folk music** of both islands, and is often used for tourist promotional purposes. Since the mid-1970s in Reunion, there has been a revival of a related form, the *maloya*, closer to its African and Malagasy origins, which in its pure form uses a chant–response pattern and purely percussion accompaniment. A contemporary, very successful example is the troupe of Gramoune Lélé, a sprightly 65-year-old former sugar refinery worker who has toured the 'world music' festivals of France and Europe. The style has been taken up by Creole poets such as Danyel Waro, as a vehicle for social and political protest, and further refined by local groups such as Ziskakan, militantly autonomist in inspiration, who have added sophisticated electro-acoustic instrumentation and subtle Creole lyrics by literary figures such as Axel Gauvin and Carpanin Marimoutou. A younger generation, exemplified by the group Baster, has incorporated Western influences such as reggae to produce a pop music with a distinctive rhythmic style.

Madagascar has followed a similar pattern in developing the resources of its folk music to produce a popular style internationally acceptable in 'world music' circles. Rossy and his group have had an international recording career since the mid-1980s sponsored by the British singer-songwriter Peter Gabriel; and, more recently, Justin Vali, specialist of the distinctively Malagasy bamboo harp, has toured in Europe, as have the group Salala, inheritors of a Protestant tradition of a cappella close harmony singing.

The development of **dance** in the islands is similarly diverse. Apart from the troupes of *sega* dancers from Mauritius and Reunion, both islands have well-established schools of Indian dance, and Reunion also has some locally subsidized amateur companies of modern dance and ballet. Madagascar has had its own national folk troupe, Imadefolk, directed from 1975 onwards by Odeamson as a touring theatre group and continued by his daughters as the *Landyrolafotsy* troupe. Popular drama in Malagasy languages, often sung, has always attracted a wide audience, as in the *hira gasy* form. In recent years, the novelist Michèle Rakotoson has succeeded in staging as-yet-unpublished French-language plays in Antananarivo, such as *Sambancy*, which was a prizewinner in the Radio France Internationale play competition in 1980; and a new generation of women playwrights is returning to French after the period of 'Malgachization', such as Charlotte Rafenomanjato, Suzanne Ravoaja and Josette Rakotondradany.

Mauritius and Reunion have had thriving theatres at least since the early years of the nineteenth century, and the theatre in the Mauritian capital Port-Louis has recently been restored with the help of grants from francophone sources. Popular drama has none the less relied principally on Creole in recent times, the language accessible to the broadest spectrum of its audience. The most successful Mauritian dramatist, Dev Virahsawmy, published a series of plays in the 1980s, some of them in trilingual versions, using Mauritian Creole, Reunionnais Creole and French. In Reunion, the Théâtre Vollard, under the direction of Emmanuel Genvrin, has been the most prominent theatre group, with a series of original historical dramas combining Creole and French, such as *Étuves* (Steamrooms) in 1988, recreating the Revolutionary period in Reunion, and Creole adaptations of Jarry's *King Ubu* (*Ubu roi*) in 1979 and *Ubu colonial* (1994). The troupe has regularly visited the Théâtre International de Langue Française in Paris and the Festival des Francophonies in Limoges. Other Réunionnais theatre groups, such as the Théâtre Talipot of St-Pierre, directed by Philippe Pelen, are attempting a dramatic synthesis of the diverse cultural traditions of the Indian Ocean area in ambitious multimedia productions such as *Mâ* in 1995.

Cinema, not surprisingly the Cinderella of the performing arts in such an isolated part of the francophone world, has maintained a presence in Reunion: a thriving animation school at the Village-Titan in the Port area and a tradition of local cineclubs, the Fédération Abel Gance. This serves to promote the embryonic regional film production, such as the work of the pioneering Malagasy film-maker Ignace Solo Randrasana, and his first feature film *Ilo tsy very*, a Malagasy–Algerian co-production, about the bloody anti-colonial insurrection of 1947. The local **television** stations, the state-controlled RFO and the private companies Canal Réunion, TV4 and TV Sud, also produce local documentaries, for instance, on the multicultural music festival Kabaréunion in 1995.

In general, the multicultural, multilingual variety of contemporary performing arts in the Indian Ocean islands can be seen as a vibrant example of post-colonial and postmodern creativity which, while enjoying the benefits of francophone support networks, is developing a hybrid culture which is capable of transcending the limits of French as a world language.

PETER HAWKINS

See also: francophone popular music: DOM-TOMs; francophone writing (fiction, poetry): Indian Ocean; theatre

francophone performing arts: North Africa

Dramatic performance in the three countries of the Maghreb (Algeria, Tunisia, Morocco) is marked by its multiple cultural inheritance: an Arabic, Berber and Islamic tradition, to which has been added the culture and language of France, the colonial power from which independence was only relatively recently won (by

Tunisia and Morocco in 1956, and by Algeria in 1962). The situation generated by this multiple inheritance for individuals and for creative art is modelled in Assia Djebar's 1985 novel *Love, Fantasia* (*L'Amour, la fantasia*), in terms which foreground issues relating to public and private performative expression. The Algerian-born cultural subject inherits indigenous performance traditions related to the body, and primarily spectacular: the parades, feasts and festivals of tribal tradition, equestrian displays for men (the fantasia), and, for women, the **dance**. Oral performance is similarly gender-divided: ululation for women and, for men, the chanting of the Koran and all forms of discursive speech. In Djebar's text, the acquisition of French produces a transformation of subject position which in its turn transforms cultural performance. French introduces both female and male speakers into the equalizing discourse of bourgeois subjectivity, into a post-Revolutionary history both democratic and secular, which redraws familiar boundaries of action and speech. Djebar herself has largely confined her explorations to the novel; in Maghrebin culture, religious and social obstacles to female expression have been especially potent in the domain of **theatre**. (In the 1950s, when the middle-class public first came to the theatre, special performances were held for women.) Male Maghrebin writers, however, have found in the multiple resources of the postwar francophone stage, with its alliance of spectacle and word, the ideal vehicle to project the tensions and transformations attendant on the birth of their nations.

European theatre has been a cultural presence in the Maghreb from the beginning of the twentieth century: French touring groups were playing in Algeria as early as 1830. In the 1920s and 1930s, Egyptian theatre troupes introduced the French classical repertoire, especially the comedies of Molière. These led to adaptations, and thereafter some original creations in literary Arabic and in the spoken dialects. But the effective genesis of Maghrebin drama was in the 1950s and 1960s, when the energies of political liberation met up with the subversions of an avant-garde politically

engaged European theatre. Writers, actors and directors who have been key figures in the new movement worked in Paris with **Vitez**, **Chéreau** and **Serreau**.

Since independence, negotiation with the bilingual performance tradition has seen two distinct phases. In the 1960s, building a national drama, both in French and in literary Arabic, was a key part of establishing national cultural identities. The *International Theatre Directory* (1973) testifies to some success in developing the institutional infrastructure for theatre in the Western mode. In Algeria, where theatre became a nationalized monopoly in 1963, the Théâtre National Algérien ran five theatres (in Algiers, Oran, Constantine, Sidi-bel-Abbès and Annaba). Five other theatres were managed and subsidized by the municipal authorities, and the Petit Théâtre in Algiers was given over to the youth of the FLN. Morocco boasted two theatres, in Casablanca (founded 1922) and Rabat. Tunisia had one professional theatre, the Théâtre Municipal de Tunis, built in 1903, occupied by the Troupe Municipal de Tunis, which was founded in 1953. In the 1950s, both Tunis and Morocco created drama centres. The *Directory of Theatre, Dance and Folklore Festivals* (1979) registers a complementary interest in developing the festival. This was particularly evident in Tunis, after the decentralization of drama in the mid-1960s, and was encouraged by the Tunisian National Tourist Office. Nineteen annual festivals, throughout the regions, offer a mixed diet of folklore, theatre, dance and equestrian shows. The International Festival of Carthage, held in the Roman amphitheatre, was founded in 1964 to introduce the Tunisian public to 'the styles of classic expression in the West', but soon made equal space for national productions. In the second stage, the emphasis has been chiefly on the national, focusing on plays in modern literary Arabic, Arabic dialects and Berber.

Francophone drama has developed differentially in the three countries of the Maghreb. Morocco has a strong tradition of popular and ritual drama, but literary drama is overshadowed by the novel. In the 1950s, a few dramatists had work performed in the country

(Abdelkader Ben Hachmy, Ahmed Belhachmi). Most recently, however, francophone dramatists have found their audiences and publishers in France. Abdelkébir Khatibi's *The Veiled Prophet* (*Le Prophète voilé*) was performed in 1979. Tahar **Ben Jelloun**'s *La Fiancée de l'eau* (Water Bride), staged in April 1984 at the Théâtre Populaire de Lorraine, evokes the tensions of the village communities left behind by the migrant workers.

In Tunisia, Arab tradition is more important than francophone influence in all areas of literature, despite the country's relative openness to Western culture. The popular plays of Habib Boularès were usually written and staged in Arabic, but *Le Temps d'El Boraq* (The Time of Dreams), staged in Tunis in November 1969, was published in French and Arabic versions in 1979. The members of a Tunisian family in a fishing village, shaken by contemporary social conflicts, articulate their very different aspirations and interests (the educated children, with their urban ambitions and socialist values; the parents, with their reluctance to abandon their patriarchal Islamic conservatism, the basis of a hard-won and precarious sense of security). An uneasy compromise is reached, at the expense of the women. Realistic, often comic language alternates with lyrical dream-voice episodes, with voices and persons speaking in isolation or caught back into communion, forced to exchange discourses by the pressure of history, figured in the simple plot. The linguistic anarchy models the ferment produced by the introduction of Western subject positions, represented as critical and revolutionary, into traditional hierarchies. Fawzi Mellah's *Néron ou les oiseaux de passage* (Nero or Birds of Passage) from 1975, and *Le Palais du non-retour* (The Palace of No Return) of 1975, use violent satirical melodrama to denounce a **decolonization** process which has left Western capitalism more firmly entrenched in the Third World. The Western audience written into the text is harangued from the stage for its collusion in genocide. Mohammed Moncef Métoui's *Messieurs . . . je vous accuse* (Gentlemen . . . You Stand Accused), an attack on the effects of absolute power, European influence and *fran-cophonie* in Tunisia, was published in France (in French) in 1982.

Most francophone dramatic activity has come from Algeria – the work of writers who operate either in Algeria when conditions permit, or otherwise in France and the rest of Europe, playing both to immigrant communities and to avant-garde European audiences. There is keen ideological debate whether the activity of Maghrebin writers who made France their primary base (**Camus**, for example) can be included in the history of Maghrebin culture. In any event, the most significant dramatic activity begins in the period 1955–70, stimulated by the call of the Algerian Front de Libération Nationale (FLN) on 20 August 1956, for plays, poems and prose in support of the armed struggle. Mustapha Kateb became director of the Troupe du FLN in 1958, and during the **Algerian war** toured the world with his militant productions. Director of the Théâtre National Algérien (at independence) and joint organizer of the Institut National d'Art Dramatique (INAD) from 1964 to 1973, he withdrew in 1972 in opposition to the decentralization of the theatre, and then returned as head of the national theatre at the end of the 1980s. INAD reopened in 1986. Dramatists in the 1950s and 1960s concentrated on topics related to the war: from Henri Kréa (pseudonym of Cachin), who published *Le Séisme* (Earthquake) in 1958 and *Théâtre algérien* (Algerian Theatre) in 1962, to Kadour M'Hamsadji's 1959 *La Dévoilée* (Woman Without a Veil), Mouloud Mammeri's *Le Foehn ou la preuve par neuf* (The Foehn), staged in 1967, and Assia Djebar and Walid Garn's *Rouge l'aube* (Red the Dawn), performed in Arabic and then published in French in 1969.

The most important work has been that of Kateb **Yacine**, initially in collaboration with the director Jean-Marie Serreau, who helped introduce Brecht to Parisian theatre in the 1950s. Banned in the 1950s for their criticism of French colonial policies, Kateb's first plays turned to Greek theatre (Aeschylus) as much as to Brecht for inspiration and techniques to harness the national imagination to political issues. The trilogy published as *Le Cercle des représailles* (1959) is an exercise in militant mythologizing: *Le Cadavre encerclé* (Corpse Surrounded), first performed in Carthage and Brussels in 1958 and in Paris in 1959; and the fairy-tale/farce *La Poudre d'intelligence* (Cleverness Dust) and *Les Ancêtres redoublent de férocité* (Savage Ancestors), both staged in Paris in 1967. In the trilogy, Kateb uses sound and lighting to spectacular effect, marries a lyrical and symbol-laden rhetoric to realist dialogue, and disrupts narrative time with dream discontinuities and flashback, in order to rouse the emotions of the audience. At the same time, he gives a central place to a chorus and its leader to comment on and analyse the action. In these plays, humanity is always collectivized and the group is the real focus of performance. The individual 'heroes' (male and female) who carry the action forward are stereotyped in the Brechtian fashion and their activity is always referred to the interests of the group – a familiar feature, after Kateb, of Maghrebin drama. Kateb returned to Algeria in 1972 to experiment with political theatre in popular Arabic, under governmental auspices. *Mohammed, prends ta valise* (Mohammed, Pick Up Your Suitcase), first played in Algerian Arabic (Birkadem 1971), toured in France February to June 1972, in migrant workers' hostels and *maisons de la culture*. *L'Homme aux sandales de caoutchouc* (The Man in Rubber Sandals), which sets choruses of French workers, Chinese, and Black American revolutionaries around an epic history of anti-colonial struggle in Vietnam, was performed first in Algiers and then at the Théâtre du Cothurne in Lyon, in 1971. The mayor of Lyon cut the theatre's subsidy. *La Voix des femmes* (Women's Voice) – staged in 1972 in spoken Arabic, which uses female voices to celebrate an amalgam of ancestral and socialist values, was staged in French in Tlemcen, also in 1972. From 1977, Kateb's iconoclasm encountered renewed hostility from the Algerian political and religious authorities. *Le Bourgeois sans culotte, ou le spectre du Parc Monceau* (The Middle-Class Revolutionary, or the Ghost of the Parc Monceau) is a satire written in French for the

Bicentenary and performed at the Avignon Festival of 1989, juxtaposing the politics of 1789 with the colonial experience of Indochina and New World.

Since the early 1970s, Algerian drama has moved away from the themes of war and independence into social satire, gender issues and international liberation. With few exceptions, plays performed in Algeria have been in Algerian Arabic; francophone writers find their audiences in France. Noureddine Aba, whose plays have been presented on ORTF as well as in the live theatre, handles psychological and epic modes with equal skill. *L'Annonce faite à Marco, ou à l'aube et sans couronne* (The Annunciation to Marco, or Uncrowned at Dawn) (1983), set in a village cafe in Algeria in the summer of 1957 and mixing colloquial French with snatches of Arabic, shows how divided interests and loyalties fuel both sides of the conflict. *Tell el Zaatar s'est tu à la tombée du soir* (Silence at Nightfall in Tell el Zaatar), from 1981, is a spectacular dramatization of the history of the Palestinian tragedy, charting the displacement of the inhabitants of Palestine by the Balfour declaration, their exploitation by the United States, Britain and the oil sheikhs, and the continuing resistance by individuals, guerrilla groups and terrorists, backed finally by international popular uprisings. A cast of dozens of episodic characters fills a sequence of tableaux casting backwards and forwards in time, using film and sound recordings, the full gamut of lighting and explosive sound effects, music and dance. The action is held together by a love story, which recounts the persistence of personal and national loyalties down the generations, and by a framing technique drawn, with a novel twist, from the most traditional mode of Arab performance art. A tale-teller from Algeria himself turns into a frame for another narrator, a woman, who tells the full story – in this fight for liberation, the women take up the word, as they took up the guns. There is the same recognition of women's changed role, established through the war of independence, in Mohammed **Dib**'s black comedy, performed at the Avignon Festival in 1977, *Mille houras pour une gueuse*

(Cheers for the Skirt). The female voice comes to the foreground, urging on the despairing revolutionaries, marching alongside them and, in a striking reversal of the traditional nurturing maternal role, abandoning individuals to die, when necessary, for the sake of the Revolutionary cause. New ground has now been broken by the first woman dramatist, Fatima Gallaire, whose work explores the efforts of post-Revolutionary women to free themselves from the hierarchies of the patriarchal family, mediated by a colluding matriarchy – for example, *Princesses, ou ah! vous êtes venus ... là où il y a quelques tombes* (Princesses, or You've Come Among the Tombs), staged in New York in 1988 and Paris in 1991, and *Les Co-Épouses* (Joint Wives) performed in Paris in 1991).

JENNIFER BIRKETT

See also: Avignon and summer arts; decolonization; festivals; francophone cinema: North Africa; francophone performing arts (Indian Ocean); francophone writing (fiction, poetry): North Africa

Further reading

Auclaire-Tamaroff, E. and Auclaire-Tamaroff, B. (1986) *Jean-Michel Serreau: découvreur de théâtres*, Paris: A l'Arbre Verdoyant (a text that includes numerous references to Serreau's collaboration in the development of North African drama, especially his work with Kateb).

Corvin, M. (1991) *Dictionnaire encyclopédique du théâtre*, Paris: Bordas (an invaluable and up-to-date reference book, with useful detail on the socioeconomic conditions of theatrical performance as well as particular works and writers).

Déjeux, J. (1992) *La Littérature maghrébine d'expression française*, Paris: PUF and (1993) *Maghréb. Littératures de langue française*, Paris: Arcantère Editions (the indispensable reference works for a summary but informative overview and discussion of all aspects of Maghrebin writing).

Tomiche, N. (1993) *La Littérature arabe contemporaine*, Paris: Maisonneuve et Larose (a rich and informative work; needs to be read in conjunction with any reading of francophone culture in the Maghreb to obtain some insight into the cultural negotiations involved).

francophone performing arts: Switzerland

The performing arts in French-speaking Switzerland began to come into their own in the mid-nineteenth century. The *Romands* were noted for attempts, in the lineage of Rousseau, to popularize a theatre in which song and dance were an integral part. In the first part of the twentieth century, many theatrical companies were created in keeping with this spirit; René Morax's Théâtre du Jorat (1908), for instance, was founded in a barn. Plays shown in such spaces incorporated music, like *Le Roi David* (1921), with a score by Honegger, and exploited popular themes, like *Tell* (1914), with music by Gustave Doret. Contemporary traditional theatre has benefited from the international renown of German-speaking Swiss authors such as Dürrenmatt and Frisch, especially through the increase in funding available.

After World War II, new companies were founded to complement existing municipal theatres. Most notable examples are: La Compagnie des Faux-Nez (Lausanne, 1948) under Charles Apothéloz; the Théâtre de Carouge (1957), which merged in 1972 with the Théâtre de l'Atelier (Geneva, mid-1960s); the Théâtre de Poche (Geneva, late 1940s), which became the Nouveau Théâtre de Poche; and the Théâtre Populaire Romand or TPR (Neuchâtel in 1959, and now based in La Chaux-de-Fonds). French-Swiss theatre is often experimental or, at least, untraditional by Parisian standards. Themes tend to be surreal or farcical – for example, Henri Dublüe's 1962 *Le Procès de la Truie* (The Trial of the Sow),

Louis Gaulis's *Capitaine Karagheuz* (1960) – or are centred on issues of Swiss identity. Contemporary theatre has developed these characteristics in plays by, and adaptations of, contemporary writers in other genres (Anne Cuneo, Éric Schaer, Amélie Plume, Michel Viala).

Substantial patronage from the Swiss Art Council (*ProHelvetia*) led to the creation in 1991 (in conjunction with the Swiss Society of Authors, or SSA) of the Parloir Romand, an organization encompassing five companies (Arsenic, Osses, TPR, St-Gervais and Yverdon). New plays can be showcased through the Parloir, thereby gaining a degree of international recognition (see, for instance, the work of Claude Delarue and Jean-Daniel Coudray). In the 1990s the SSA has also supported the showing of new plays at the Théâtre du Grütli in Geneva. The merging of different art forms within Swiss theatre helps transcend language and socioeconomic barriers, and is in keeping with the Swiss spirit of popular art. **Mime**, self-evidently not restricted to one linguistic area, is very popular: the famed school founded by the mime Dimitri is in Italian-speaking Ticino, and the international fame of the *Mummenschanz* transcends more than mere language barriers. Physical performance is traditional, as illustrated by the work of Émile Jaques-Dalcroze, the creator of *danse rythmique* (now part of the *romand* primary school curriculum). **Poetry**, literature, music (from the traditional *Ranz des vaches* to the modernism of Honegger and Frank Martin), **dance**, film, mime, puppetry (Théâtre des Marionnettes de Genève) and **circus** (*Knie*) all feed into the diversity of the Swiss performing arts, and the collaboration of Ramuz and Stravinsky in 1918 on the *Histoire du Soldat* (The Soldier's Tale) is an illustrious early example. Today dance and theatre are closely linked, with the Béjart school (*Rudra-Atelier*) in Lausanne teaching not only dance and kendo, but also percussion, singing, theatre and music, so as to produce performers whose understanding of dance as a language is not restricted to choreographic annotations. The Arsenic Theatre's director, Jacques Gardel, collaborated with Linga to produce *Alma Mahler*, benefiting from the open attitude of companies created by ex-Béjart dancers (Linga, Buissonière, Nomades).

The most spectacular and popular merging of performance arts occurs every twenty-five years for the Fête des Vignerons in Vevey. The last festival of this kind was in 1977 and was written by Henri Dubluë, with a musical score from Jean Balissat and costumes by Jean Monod. The 1977 Fête was directed by Charles Apothéloz, a doyen of mainstream art theatre who also successfully directed other popular celebrations: *La Pierre et l'esprit* (1975) (The Stone and the Spirit), *La Fête du blé et du pain* (1978) (The Feast of Corn and Bread) and *Terre nouvelle* (1979) (New Land). No performance in Switzerland can equal the scale of the Fête des Vignerons, originally a parade that became partly a stationary show in the nineteenth century. It has grown in size over the years to become, in 1977, a two-week-long spectacle (coinciding with National Day) comprising more than 4,000 performers in an open-air arena (seating 15,800) overlooking Lake Léman. The performers were non-professional (a choice made by Apothéloz, after the snub received by organizers of the previous Fête, in 1955, when the Corps de Ballet of the Paris Opéra refused to participate in the parade), and comprised more than 1,000 children. The representation of the four seasons featured modern and popular dance, poetry, music (from orchestra to Alpenhorn), and traditional, patriotic *romand* songs (including the *Ranz des vaches*) sung tearfully by the whole audience. Such spectacles are the apotheosis of the performing arts in Switzerland.

VÉRÈNE GRIESHABER

See also: francophone cinema (Switzerland); francophone performing arts (Belgium); francophone writing (poetry, fiction): Switzerland

Further reading

Louis, N. and Béatrice, P. (eds) (1993) *Théâtre*

en Suisse: Visions, Société Suisse du Théâtre (SST).

Mimos (quarterly journal of the Société Suisse du Théâtre).

Schweizer Theaterjahrbuch (an annual publication).

francophone popular music: DOM-TOMs

Martinique and Guadeloupe, the two Caribbean DOMs (*départements d'outre-mer*, or 'overseas departments'), share the same cultural identity. Although French is the official language, Creole is the vehicle for artistic expression. In musical terms their culture is rooted in West Indian, therefore West African heritage.

In the 1960s and 1970s public entertainment generally took place in the *paillottes*, straw huts often located on the seaside. Local groups or individual artists would come and play traditional West Indian rhythms, live of course. In the 1980s a new musical form creatively fusing old idioms and contemporary forms of swing, **rock** and funk emerged: the zouk. The seminal exponent group Kassav' exported it to France, to Africa and to the world, and with this new form came coincidentally the decline of the *paillottes*, and the appearance of nightclubs with heavy acoustic equipment and play-back facilities (to the point where live music entertainment had more or less disappeared). In the early 1990s, Kali and his group in Martinique were the exception that confirmed the play-back rule. But, apart from the fact that market forces imposed exile to mainland France on the ambitious local zouk or jazz-biguine groups, things were changing. Besides the official temples (Maison des Arts et de la Culture, in Pointe-à-Pitre, Guadeloupe, and Le Carbet in Fort-de France, Martinique), bars and clubs open their doors to their local zouk artists. In Guadeloupe, where it all began, you can hear Patrick St Eloi and Jean Michel Rotin, as well as the most established stars like Zouk Machine, Energy and Tanya St Val. In Martinique, one finds Kwak and Taxi-Kreole (exponents of pure zouk), Max Ramsay and the group Malavoi, which explore the biguine and sounds of the 1950s reborn. After years of neglect, some traditional forms of music and events on these islands are back in force; for example, the *gwo-ka* as well as the *lewoz*, where workers on the sugar plantations would sing of their troubled existence and commemorate their African roots. These *vie neg* styles (Creole for 'old Negroes') bear witness to the vitality of traditional music and are an antidote to the invasion of ragamuffin music imported by exiles from France or Jamaica.

Further south along the Atlantic coast, French Guiana is a singular country which, from an old penal colony, became a high-technology capital without much transition; a disparate group of immigrants from Brazil, Surinam, Haiti, Europe came to the new Eldorado. Each community endeavours to keep its own cultural identity. There is an extraordinary musical patchwork – American tradition, Creole koesco and biguine, **jazz** sessions and Brazilian-style carnival – and the organic link between these traditions is reggae. Compared to the French West Indies, there is no singular or original feature such as the zouk, but French and/or Creole are used by a myriad of artists, who explore a variety of genres from progressive music (Azica), reggae (Marcel Blood, Wailing Roots, Nikko), traditional Guianese (Ayne Gabrielle), latino-jazz (Jorland), latino-african (Gilda Rey), to *chanson* (Edward Blasse) and bossa nova (José Ultet).

In the Indian Ocean, the island of Reunion – a French territory since 1638, which became a DOM in 1946 – offers an even wider form of *métissage* of cultures. As it developed over two centuries, immigrants came: slaves from Africa, colons from Europe, traders from China, India, Madagascar and the Middle East. The specificity of Reunion is born out of this clash of cultures. Compared to his/her West Indian cousin, the *Réunionnais* is more inhibited; he/she has so many cultures to contend with, but the common language apart from the official French is the popular Creole (which is used almost exclusively for the lyrics of any musical expression). Reunion music is born of tradition akin to the other Indian Ocean islands (Mauritius, Seychelles), a mixture of binary and ternary rhythms. The two seminal styles of music on the island are *maloya* (synthesis of traditional music from Madagascar and East Africa) and *sega* (black African dance and music mixed with white European rhythms and instruments). Up to the 1980s, *sega* was officially encouraged, while *maloya* became the protest voice of political opposition and, until 1981, was censored. During the **Mitterrand** era, *maloya* became the focus of the young generation, and local groups like the Camaleons, TI Fock and Ziskakan, as well as the more established figures (Danyel Waro and Gramoun Lélé, Jacques Farreyrol and Bernadette Ladauge), have syncretized the ancient art of *maloya* and modern electric support to create an authentic Reunion sound. This musical explosion in terms of production is a sign of extraordinary vitality and diversity.

New Caledonia has seen the rise of Kanak cultural identity and has received the financial support of both the DAC (official French cultural office) and the ADCK (local structure). Too often ignored by the Caldoches (Europeans who represent one-third of the whole population), the musical heritage of this island is now systematically explored and mixed with modern-day techniques. The concept of kaneka (rhythms of the Kanaks) appeared in 1986 as a variation of a Pacific reggae with traditional percussion instruments. Almost all local artists sing in French and in one of the twenty-eight different Kanak languages: Lifou, Drehu, Laai . . . This mode of pop music is only beginning to flourish.

French Polynesia has 200,000 inhabitants disseminated across 130 small islands over 4 million square kilometres, with Tahiti at the centre of cultural and musical enterprise. The mixture of races and cultures over the centuries is even more inextricable and reflected in the languages used by the most successful artists established in Tahiti: French, Spanish, Tahitian, Rarotongian, Creole and...English. The richness of traditional music and instruments

(ukelele, Tahitian guitar) is enthusiastically mixed with French *variété*, Californian pop, rock and jazz, and (inevitably) reggae, to form a powerful eclectic sound where ancestral Taupiti celebrations are perpetuated.

GÉRARD POULET

See also: francophone performing arts: Indian Ocean; francophone writing (fiction, poetry): DOM-TOMs; francophone writing (fiction, poetry): Indian Ocean; parties and movements in francophone countries: DOM-TOMs; song/*chanson*

Further reading

Hidalgo, F. (1993) 'La Réunion, l'ile à grand spectacle', *Chorus* 4: 106–8 (an informative retrospective of forty years of music on the island).

Zone Franche (eds) (1995) *Sans visa*, Paris (700 pages of rich information on the music of the francophone connection throughout the world).

francophone popular music: Europe

Belgium and Switzerland are the main sources of popular music in francophone Europe, in terms of both production and distribution.

Politically and culturally, Belgium's two main communities – Flemish and French-speaking – live in dynamic tension rather than in harmony. The French-speaking community mainly inhabits Brussels and southern Belgium (Wallonie). In popular music terms, Jacques **Brel** has put Belgium on the map since 1959. His monumental presence overshadowed a rich pattern of young talent, some of it ephemeral, such as Philippe Anciaux, Paul Louka in Charleroi, Hustin, Watrin and Piérot. Others mentioned below have lasted longer and still participate in the present scene. The survival of *la chanson* as one of the most popular and authentic expressions of French-speaking Belgian identity encounters many obstacles: the geographical context is too restricted, there are few venues which offer regular slots to pop, *variété* or **rock** artists, the record/CD market is small, media support weak, and foreign impact important. Even the home audience often expressed attachment to pop artists only after success in France. In general terms, production and distribution of cultural products is concentrated in the hands of non-French-speaking multinationals, and the danger of uniformity of music culture across the planet is all too real: francophone pop music represents under 3 per cent of the world recording market. Nevertheless, there is a framework to support artists of the Communauté Française de Belgique (CFB) from Wallonie and Brussels. Funding exists to support participation in main festivals in what is usually known as the *espace francophone*: in France, the Printemps de Bourges, the Francofolies de La Rochelle and the Chaînon-Manquant in Tours; elsewhere, the Festival International d'Été de Québec, the Francofolies de Montréal and the Coup de Coeur Francophone, all in Montreal; in Switzerland, the Paléo Festival de Noyon. Such participation is vital because of the decline of local events since the heyday of the 1960s and 1970s.

While Brel was enjoying success in France, in Brussels some assertive voices were heard, such as Freddy Zegers, Jules Beaucarne and Salvatore Adamo. At the same time, rock and roll surged through both linguistic communities – three francophone groups were The Cousins, Wallace Collection and, in the 1970s, Machiavel – together with a general trend towards social and regional protest songs. Representative voices of that period are André Bialek and Claude Semal, who gave perhaps a more accurate image of contemporary Belgian identity than Brel himself in *Plat Pays* (1960). More socially aware were Christiane Stefanski, Guy Harmel and Ann Gaytan, among others. Young talent of the 1970s has since established itself in the 1980s and 1990s, such as Philippe Lafontaine, Maurane and Pascal Charpentier. Of these, Maurane had success in France,

Quebec and Switzerland. Her songs, full of humour, tenderness and energy, are appreciated there as much as at the Cirque Royal in Liège. She heads a new generation of artists, including Pierre Rapsat, Stella, Odieu, Marka and the Frères Mansion who, year after year, attempt to renew style and repertoire. In the 1990s, the extraordinary voices of Zap Mama and Khadja Nin, from Zaire and Burundi, impose their private worlds and rhythm on the old colonial metropolis, on Montreal and in the USA.

The Festival International de la Chanson Française in Spa was a fertile forum for new talent between 1963 and 1984. Since then, hopefuls must attend festivals in France, Quebec or Switzerland or start at the Botanique in Brussels in the shadow of established artists, as in the festival of September 1993 ('*Le Botanique fait la rentrée chanson*'). On the airwaves, the Anglo-American steamroller prevails: there is no prescribed quota for French songs as in France and Quebec, even though, for a while, Pierre Collard-Bovy had a radio show dedicated to Belgian artists. Popular venues in Brussels are: the Os à Moelle, the Samaritaine and the Soupape and, in Liège, Les Forges, Georges Fassotte or Six Corale, where the new generation can be heard – Audrey Englebert, Etienne Dontaine, Légétime Démence, Pascal Vyvère and Vaya Con Dios.

The French-speaking community in Switzerland has a long singing tradition and its essential voice is undoubtedly Michel Bülher. In the mould of Brel and **Brassens**, he is the rebellious troubadour who questions our times and echoes the uneasy hopes of the *Suisse romande* youth. His 1993 album, *L'Autre Chemin* (The Other Path), shows consistency in his message over twenty years, even if some lyrics are in the more trendy idiom of *rap suisse*. A sign of the times is that Évasion, the company which had produced Swiss-French singers since the 1950s, went bankrupt in 1995. In an eclectic musical environment, where **jazz** is particularly fertile, a few artists are perpetuating francophone song: for example, Sens Unik (a group of young rappers), Carlos and his band, Valérie Lou and Sakharyn. They remain a minority with little airtime on local French-speaking radio.

However, two annual events are used as a forum for artists from the francophone world in a variety of musical styles: one is exclusively francophone (the Francomanias in Bulle, since 1990) and the other the Paléo-Festival at Noyon, which gives a substantial slot for French performers and repertoire. Switzerland is a microcosm of European cultural diversity. There is evidence of this cross-fertilization in the work of Stephan Eicher, a German-speaking Swiss gypsy now highly successful on the international scene singing in French, English and German.

GÉRARD POULET

See also: music festivals

Further reading

Chenot, F. (1994) 'Brel et après', *Chorus* 6: 110–18 (on pop music in French-speaking parts of Belgium; informative and well illustrated).

CMCFB (eds) (1995) *Dictionnaire de la chanson francophone belge*, Brussels (seminal work on the history of French-speaking songs in Belgium since 1830).

Dumortier, G. (ed.) (1993/4) *Consonances, dissonances* (two special numbers of a termly review published by the Ministry of Culture for the French-speaking community; in 1993, *Spécial Chanson*, and in 1994 *Spécial Rock*, constitute a series of pertinent, critical articles written by local experts).

Zone Franche (eds) (1995) *Sans visa*, Paris (indispensable guide to music styles of the *espace francophone* and the world, giving up-to-date information, addresses of artists, associations, venues and agencies for relevant countries).

francophone popular music: North Africa

The Maghreb (Morocco, Tunisia and Algeria) is a land of ancient civilizations where successive contributions from Mediterranean neighbours have produced a burgeoning and conflictual context, favourable to a rich and varied musical texture. Three main languages commonly used are Arabic, Berber and French. The French colonial presence varied in length in its three countries: 44 years in Morocco, 75 years in Tunisia and 132 years in Algeria. Since then, throughout North Africa (though less markedly in Algeria), francophone musical expression has mainly been imported and native talents have remained loyal to their ancestral roots and traditional languages: Arabic and Berber.

In Morocco the African-Andalusian musical tradition is the dominating influence. Evidence of this can be found in the numerous *Écoles de Musique* (Oujda, Meknes) or Instituts de Musique (Fez, Tétouan, Tangier), which specialized in that type of music, originally from Granada and Córdoba. The language of instruction might sometimes be French, as in the Institut National de Musique et de Danse in Rabat, but the musical idiom is not.

Apart from this central tradition, represented in the 1990s by Bajedoub Mohamed, there are many other influences that never really converge in the creation of an authentic Moroccan sound: Berber, Jewish, Middle Eastern, Bambara and International *variété*. Nevertheless, in the 1970s Nass El Ghowan and Jil Jilala were instrumental in attempting a characteristic Moroccan style. A younger generation (the Bouchnak brothers, for example) emulated their Algerian neighbours in promoting their own version of raï, and today the leading artist is Cheb Mimoun El Oudji from Oujda. The Berber tradition is centred in Agadir with Ahihi Moulay Ahmed and Izenzaren.

Any Moroccan talent that wishes to use French as a vehicle of expression tends to end up in France. The best example of this kind is Sapho. Born in Marrakesh in the Jewish community, she came to France in 1968 and brought with her the memories of the rich sounds of her childhood. If at first she rejected her background to embrace the values and culture of the Western world, using **rock** and **jazz** to express her torn experience and her sense of revolt, in 1987 she added rhythms which are close to those of the *gnawas*, 'musician-thera-pists' who entrance the crowds in Casablanca and Marrakesh using traditional drums, Bambara-style. Idolized in Japan, she has invented a kind of ethno-rock, merging her dis-parate roots – Jewish and Maghrebin culture and French language.

Tunisia is also a land of extraordinary musi-cal vitality rooted in long tradition and influ-enced by a Turkish presence established for 100 years as well as Andalusian *nouba*. In the 1960s, apart from the academic *malouf*, more popular styles were developed like the recita-tive *fondo*. The 1970s saw the beginning of a rich period in the singing tradition, illustrated by Lofti Bouchenak (who gave concerts in France) and Ahmed Hamza. Ridha Hjouini from Tunis is the only artist of the 1980s and 1990s who performs in French as well as in Arabic and is the prolific writer of more than 3,000 songs. The new trends are the *bisquit* (from the French *biscuit*) meaning 'commercial' and the *mezwed* (whose name is derived from the Breton bagpipe). Popular Tunisian tunes rarely cross the Mediterranean.

After 1962, Algeria experienced an ebullient period, when a strictly state-controlled cultural policy of Arabization, and of instruction in Andalusian traditional musical style (perceived as 'politically correct'), did not prevent some artists from exposing their modern-day Algerian-style pop music, mainly in Algiers and Oran. The new styles emerged from the poorer suburbs. Around Oran there was a modern ver-sion of raï, created in the 1920s and from the Algiers casbah, the *chaâbi*, a sort of Algerian traditional blues, which pervaded this young country whose population more than doubled in twenty years. The central planning of cultur-al policy became more marked in 1965, with the arrival of Boumedienne as president, but, nevertheless, the international pop and rock movement did permeate somehow, and the introduction of the acoustic guitar allowed a new breed of artists (Aït-Menguellet, and Idir with his famous hit, *A vava Inouva*) to express outside official channels the troubled existence and aspirations of Algerian youth. Fifteen years later, at the end of the 1970s, a new breed

nourished on traditional raï but exposed to rock, pop and reggae came on the scene from the same suburbs of Oran. This was a social phenomenon first, then a musical movement which grew clandestinely to express in its vital-ity the spirit of a whole generation, at once joy-fully exuberant and freely melancholic. They called themselves *chebs* (meaning 'young'), they crossed the sea, and took Paris and France by storm in 1986, adding an extraordinary dimension to the French musical landscape.

GÉRARD POULET

See also: beur music; francophone performing arts (North Africa); francophone writing (fic-tion, poetry): North Africa

Further reading

Coulomb, S. and Varrod, D. (1987) *Histoires de chansons 1968–1988*, Paris: Balland (some entertaining and pertinent pages on the upsurge of raï love music in France in 1986).

Seck, N. and Clerfeuille, S. (1993) *Les Musiciens du beat africain*, Paris: Bordas (essential guide to African artists of renown from North to South Africa, alphabetically classified, usefully completed by a concise presentation of the different musical styles, e.g. raï).

francophone radio: DOM-TOMs

Radio audiences in the *départements d'outre-mer* (DOM) and the *territoires d'outre-mer* (TOM), France's overseas departments and ter-ritories, depend mainly on programmes broad-cast by Radio France Outre-Mer (RFO, whose headquarters are at 5 avenue du Recteur Poincaré, 75016 Paris), which employs a full-time staff of over 1,000. This subsidiary of Radio France, whose official title is the Société Nationale de Radio et de Télévision Française d'Outre-Mer, was created in 1982. Short-wave radio broadcasts to former French colonies began as early as 1931, on the occasion of the opening of the Colonial Exhibition in Paris. In 1955, DOM-TOM radio services were taken over by a new organization, SORAFORM (Société de Radiodiffusion de la France d'Outre-Mer), which became OCORA (Office de Coopération Radiophonique) in 1964. From 1975 to 1982, the service was controlled by FR3, the television channel.

There are nine RFO stations, each available on FM networks: Martinique, Guadeloupe, Guyane, Réunion, St Pierre-et-Miquelon, Polynésie (Tahiti), Nouvelle-Calédonie, Wallis-et-Futuna and Mayotte. Since 1991 RFO programmes have been broadcast via the Télécom 2B satellite. Programmes are planned centrally (but 75 per cent are produced locally) and concentrate on reflecting local culture, traditions and social and economic affairs. Programmes retransmitted from Radio France stations are provided free to RFO. Advertising on RFO stations has been authorized since 1984 – in 1993, 14.5 per cent of RFO's total revenue came from advertising – but the major part of its income (over 70 per cent) was provided by the *redevance* (radio and television licence-fee payments). The state occasionally contributes subsidies.

In most overseas departments and territories, France-Inter programmes are also available on FM. There is also a popular private *périphérique* radio station, Radio Antilles, which is available to most French Caribbean listeners (Guadeloupe and Martinique), and transmits from the nearby British island of Montserrat.

Overseas francophone listeners can also tune into France's world service news broadcasts on short wave, many of which are in French. This service, which has an estimated regular audience of 30 million, is provided by RFI (Radio France Internationale), another subsidiary of Radio France. France's world service dates back to 1935: RFI was created in 1975 and became an autonomous organization in 1983.

ALAN PEDLEY

See also: francophone radio: Europe; parties and movements in francophone countries: DOM-TOMs

francophone radio: Europe

According to the most recent estimates, over 61 million Europeans use French as their first language. Many more can understand it and speak it as a second language. Radio, which is unaffected by national frontiers, makes a significant contribution to the maintenance of *francophonie*, which extends in Europe beyond French borders into Belgium, Switzerland and Luxembourg.

France's 23 national radio stations (including networks), 39 state-owned local radio stations and estimated 1,600 private local radio stations provide the bulk of francophone radio in Europe. Some of these stations, the so-called *radios périphériques*, do not even transmit from within French borders: RTL (formerly known as Radio Luxembourg), the most popular station in France since 1982 (with 17.6 per cent of the national audience), has its long and short-wave transmitters in the Duchy. Europe 1, the other main private *périphérique* station (attracting 10 per cent of French radio listeners), transmits from the Sarre in Germany. Both these long-wave stations are listened to by many Belgians, Swiss and Luxembourgers. In the southern half of France, two other private *périphérique* stations broadcast non-specialized programmes similar to those of RTL and Europe 1: RMC (Radio Monte-Carlo), claiming over 4 per cent of the national audience, and Sud Radio, which transmits from the Principality of Andorra.

The French state broadcasting company, Radio France, also runs a non-specialized national station, France-Inter (commanding 11.2 per cent of the national audience), both on FM and long wave, so capturing many listeners in Belgium, Switzerland, Luxembourg and even Britain. Radio France also runs five other national stations of a more specialized nature:

France Info, **France Culture, France Musique,** Radio Bleue and FIP. Radio France's local stations cover all corners of the country, from Lille (Fréquence Nord) to Bayonne (Pays Basque), from Quimper (Bretagne Ouest) to Bastia (Corse Frequenza Mora).

In addition to the *périphérique* stations there are a number of private national networks which are more specialized: NRJ, Fun, Nostalgie, Europe 2, Skyrock, Chérie FM, RFM, M40, Metropolys-Maxximum, Super-Loustic, Montmartre, Notre-Dame, Fourvière, TSF, RTL 2 and Radio Classique. These stations are tending to progress in terms of audience at the expense of the non-specialist stations.

Outside France, the largest number of French speakers is to be found in Belgium (about 4.5 million). Before World War II, radio broadcasting was in the hands of a private company, INR (Institut National Belge de Radiodiffusion) – founded in 1930, it ran two stations, one broadcasting in Flemish and the other in French. In 1945, the INR was granted a monopoly of broadcasting and became a state-owned concern. Following a period of growing tension between the two main cultural and linguistic groups in Belgium, a law created two distinctive autonomous organizations in 1960: RTBF (Radio-Télévision Belge de la Communauté Française) for Walloon/French speakers and BRT for Flemish speakers.

These two state-owned companies could not originally carry advertising. During the 1970s they were increasingly challenged by private pirate radio stations and RTL. This led the Belgian government to legalize private radio at the local level. In 1987, BRT and RTBF were allowed to take advertising. BRT runs four FM stations; RTBF runs three FM stations and one station on medium wave. Despite the spread of television into virtually every Belgian home in the 1980s, radio listening has increased (the average of 2.5 hours a day in 1980 became 3.5 hours in 1990), even more than TV viewing (2 hours in 1980, 2.25 hours in 1990).

In Switzerland, where there are nearly 1.25 million French speakers, broadcasting has been in the hands of the SRG (Schweizerische Rundfunk Gesellschaft) since 1931, when it

was created by the Swiss Confederation as a private company enjoying a monopoly of broadcasting, controlled by the state. It is subdivided into three regional/linguistic organizations: the RDRS (for German speakers), the SSR (Société Suisse de Rediffusion et Télévision) and RDSI (for Italian speakers). French-language radio programmes are provided by Radio Suisse Romande (RSR), which is based at Lausanne (40 avenue du Temple, Case Postale 78, 1010 Lausanne). RSR runs three stations: RSR-La Première, RSR-Espace 2 and RSR-Couleur 3. It is financed partly by revenue produced by the licence fee and partly by income from advertising. The latter is strictly controlled: commercial breaks must not exceed 8 per cent of any single day's broadcasting. The SSR monopoly was broken for the first time in 1979 by Radio 24, and further concessions have been granted to a number of local private radio stations since that time.

While managing reasonably well to hold its own in the face of the ever-increasing popularity of television, radio listening in francophone Switzerland compares unfavourably with the other two major linguistic areas of the country. While Italian speakers average 156 minutes of listening per day, and German speakers average 198, French speakers only manage 133.

ALAN PEDLEY

See also: francophone radio: DOM-TOMs; radio (private/free); radio (state-owned)

Further reading

Albert, P. and Tudesq, A.-J. (1987) *Histoire de la radio- télévision*, Paris: PUF (a concise historical overview).

Boon, M., Ryst, A. and Vinay, C. (1990) *Lexique de l'audiovisuel*, Paris: Dalloz (general reference work).

Chevalier, P.-A. (1993) 'Le Paysage médiatique helvétique', Swiss Embassy.

Debbasch, C. (1985) *Radio et télévision en Europe*, Paris: Éditions du CNRS (a useful survey of the European scene).

Études de radio-télévision, Brussels: RTB (annual review, useful for updating European context).

Landam, G. (1986) *Introduction à la radiodiffusion internationale*, Paris: Davoze (a good basic guide to international broadcasting).

francophone television: DOM-TOMs

Francophone television in the French overseas departments and territories (DOM-TOMs) comes from three main sources: the public sector company Société National de Radio et de Télévision Française d'Outre-Mer (RFO), which operates two channels; local private television companies; and pay-TV on the **Canal Plus** format.

In terms of audience share, the most important broadcaster by far is RFO. This company was originally established by the 1982 broadcasting statute (the *loi Fillioud*) as a subsidiary of the state broadcasting companies, Radio France and FR3, but was transformed into a separate self-standing programme company by the 1986 audiovisual statute (the *loi Léotard*). RFO is funded primarily from licence-fee income, supplemented by state grants and **advertising** revenue. It has three zones of transmission. The Atlantic zone comprises Martinique, French Guiana, Guadeloupe and St-Pierre-et-Miquelon; the Indian Ocean zone consists of Reunion and Mayotte; and the Pacific zone includes New Caledonia, Polynesia, and Wallis and Futuna. Its first channel, RFO 1, broadcasts programmes from the schedules of **TF1**, France Télévision and **ARTE** as well as some locally produced output, especially news. The second channel, RFO 2, transmits the programme schedule of **France 2.** In the early 1990s, thanks to developments in satellite technology, the programme schedules of both channels were lengthened and reception improved. RFO's audience share is upwards of 70 per cent across the DOM-TOMs.

Having lost its long-standing monopoly, however, RFO is facing increasing competition for viewers with the establishment of new sources of television programming. In the early 1990s, several local private television companies were licensed by the national regulatory authority, the Conseil Supérieur de l'Audiovisuel (Higher Audiovisual Council). The most popular private television channels in the DOM-TOMs include: Antenne Réunion, whose main shareholder is the Bourbon sugar company; Archipel 4 in Guadeloupe; Télévision Caraïbe Internationale and Antilles Télévision in Martinique; and Antenne Créole Guyane. In addition, encrypted pay-TV channels, in which Havas DOM is a major shareholder, have very quickly established themselves in the market. These include: Canal Réunion, Canal Antilles in Guadeloupe and Martinique, Canal Guyane, Canal Calédonie and Canal Polynésie. Finally, there are assorted pirate television stations, including Canal 10 and TV-Éclair in Guadeloupe and TV Freedom in Reunion, broadcasting illegally to small but often very faithful audiences.

There is little doubt that the pay-TV stations will attract enough subscribers to be a viable commercial enterprise. In contrast, the advertising-funded private channels face an uncertain financial future as satellite and digital technology opens up the DOM-TOMs to the output of foreign broadcasters. More worryingly for French policy-makers, if in the future local viewers turn away in large numbers from the output of RFO, then the high cost of maintaining a separate public sector company for small overseas audiences is bound to feature on the media policy agenda in metropolitan France. In this case, the French state will have to decide the extent to which it is prepared to underwrite a publicly funded broadcasting service in the DOM-TOMs to help maintain its cultural and political presence there.

RAYMOND KUHN

See also: francophone radio: DOM-TOMs; francophone television: Europe; parties and movements in francophone countries: DOM-TOMs; television

francophone television: Europe

Television is a vital medium for the dissemination of the French language and francophone culture to European audiences who are resident outside of metropolitan France. Its programme output can help maintain a sense of a francophone community which often looks towards the 'mother country' as a source of cultural values and artefacts. However, the French-speaking audience outside of France is not extensive, and the francophone audiovisual product has to compete with a wide range of non-francophone programming in the fast-expanding multichannel environment of late twentieth-century Europe.

Francophone television in Europe can be divided up into four distinct categories. First, there is the output of French television channels such as TF1 and France Télévision, which can be received by audiences in other European countries via the new distribution systems of cable and satellite or in some cases by traditional terrestrial transmission. Second, in countries such as Belgium and Switzerland, which have their own indigenous French-speaking audiences, French-language channels form part of the national broadcasting system. Third, with national boundaries becoming more permeable as a result of the development of new communication technologies, transnational and pan-European French-language channels such as ARTE and TV5 have entered the market. Finally, pay-TV channels (in which Canal Plus has a stake) are attracting subscribers in various European countries. In this last case, what is being exported is more a French model of television based on the Canal Plus experience rather than French-language product.

In Belgium, the public service broadcaster for French-speaking Wallonia is the RTBF, which is funded from a mix of licence income and advertising revenue and operates two French-language channels. Its official monopoly status was abolished in 1987 and it now faces stiff competition from the commercial channel, RTL-TVi. The latter is owned by the Compagnie Luxembourgeoise de Télédiffusion (CLT), which is the main broadcaster in

Luxembourg. The CLT is in part owned by the French company Havas and has an ownership stake in the French television company M6. Since over 90 per cent of Belgian households are hooked up to cable systems, francophone Belgians can also receive French-language programming from the metropolitan French television channels as well as from ARTE and TV5. TF1, for example, has a large share of the Belgian francophone audience, making it a major competitor with RTBF and RTL-TVi. The pay-TV channel Canal Plus Belgique was started in 1989, and is owned by a consortium comprising RTBF, Canal Plus France and assorted Belgian companies.

In Switzerland, the Société Suisse de Radiodiffusion (SSR) produces programming for each linguistic region, with its studios in Geneva catering for the French-speaking Swiss population. The SSR had a public service monopoly until 1983. However, because of the widespread availability of cable television, francophone Swiss viewers also have access to foreign channels, including those from metropolitan France. Well over half of the viewing time in the French-speaking cantons is devoted to non-Swiss channels. In 1990, for example, the metropolitan French channels – France 1, Antenne 2, France 3, La Cinq and M6 – took over half of the French-speaking audience share, with TF1 alone taking 24 per cent.

The development of cable and satellite technology in the 1980s, and the arrival of digital television in the 1990s, have opened up new opportunities for pan-European francophone output by facilitating a huge expansion in the number of channels and breaking down national boundaries in transmission and reception. In 1996 Canal Plus entered into an agreement with BSkyB (United Kingdom) and Bertelsmann (Germany) to form a European consortium to promote the expansion of Europe-wide digital television. With its technological expertise and production experience, Canal Plus is set to be a major player in the media market of the twenty-first century and, as a result, French television will be at the heart of the European audiovisual revolution. However, the problems for francophone television in Europe remain formidable. On the supply side, the French programme production industry is not geared up to providing huge amounts of original francophone product. In contrast, the United Kingdom has a well-developed audiovisual media sector whose programme output is popular with audiences across continental Europe. Moreover, there are very limited non-European sources of francophone production. Programme imports to Europe from abroad tend to be in English (from the United States) or Spanish/Portuguese (from Latin America). On the demand side, the European francophone community resident outside of metropolitan France is small and concentrated in areas close to French territory.

The French state has sought to promote francophone television in Europe and assist the production base of its audiovisual industries through a combination of financial aid and protectionist measures such as programme quotas. However, France's major partners in the **European Union** have not been sympathetic to its advocacy of regulation and financial support to offset the allegedly undesirable cultural consequences of free trade in audiovisual goods and services. In any case regulation can be only part of the equation. If francophone television is to be successful in securing audiences in the future, this will require not just a larger French-speaking market in Europe but also programmes whose content, form and style make them competitive with non-francophone and particularly anglophone production.

RAYMOND KUHN

See also: francophone television: DOM-TOMs; television

Further reading

Euromedia Research Group (1992) *The Media in Western Europe*, London: Sage (a country-by-country study of Western European media systems).

Siune, K. and Truetzschler, W (eds) (1992) *Dynamics of Media Politics*, London: Sage (thematic study of the media in Western Europe).

francophone writing (fiction, poetry): Belgium

Belgian writing is here defined as the collection of texts (novels, short stories and poetry) produced by authors of Belgian origin, and has been better known through famous figures than through an easily identifiable label (such as 'Belgian literature'). While few would dare propose a definition of what exactly constitutes 'Belgian literature of French expression', Belgian authors have in fact contributed to the history of French literature: for example, Maurice Maeterlinck (recipient of the Nobel prize for literature in 1911), Émile Verhaeren, Henri **Michaux**, Georges **Simenon**, Dominique Rolin, Françoise Mallet-Joris, Pierre Mertens, and the inevitable Tintin, whose adventures scarcely need to be presented. For ideological and political reasons, for want of institutional or academic support (except a Royal Academy of French Language and Literature, avoided by new talents as a stifling institution), and because Belgian publishers were never able to compete with their established and prestigious French neighbours, many Belgian authors have chosen to live in France or to give up their Belgian nationality altogether (Michaux became French in 1955). When they choose to remain in Belgium, Belgian novelists set their novels either in France or behind closed doors with no reference to location. Throughout the history of Belgian literature, the trend of exile to Paris has been so consistent that there is indeed some truth in the adage that 'One French author out of two is Belgian.' Since the 1980s, however, the situation has changed. Thanks to the combined efforts of Belgian publishers (Labor), and to a proactive Ministry of Culture and Social Affairs represented by Marc Quaghebeur (who is not only a diplomat but also an author and critic), Belgian authors have become visible on the international scene as specifically Belgian, though it is no longer felt that such an identity requires a fixed definition outlining exactly what is Belgian and what is not.

The post-1950 literary production remains polymorphous. While many authors of the first half of the century have set their own work within a movement or have been 'labelled' according to French literary taxonomy (naturalism for Camille Lemonnier, symbolism for Georges Rodenbach, and Surrealism for Paul Nougé and Christian Dotremont), contemporary Belgian authors remain idiosyncratic. The 1980s saw a tremendous development as far as Belgian writers were concerned, both with new voices and with writers who had published before and who came back with much-acclaimed novels.

In a deceptively classical style, Jacqueline Harpman explored the abysses of history and memory from *La Mémoire trouble* (Blurred Memory) in 1987, and 1990's *La Fille démantelée* (The Dismantled Daughter), to *Moi qui n'ai pas connu les hommes* (I Who Have Not Known Men) from 1995, a claustrophobic novel set in a wasteland which explores life without memory, and her 1992 collection of short stories, *La Lucarne* (Skylight), in which she rewrote old myths, from the Virgin Mary and Antigone to Joan of Arc.

One of the most prolific and acclaimed Belgian authors, Dominique Rolin, who was awarded the 1952 Femina prize for *Le Souffle* (Breeze), explores love, family and their tragedies – from *Les Marais* (Swamps) of 1942, *Moi qui ne suis qu'amour* (I Who Am Nothing But Love) of 1948, 1960's *Le Lit* (The Bed) and *Le For intérieur* (Heart of Hearts) of 1962, novels influenced by the *nouveau roman*, to 1992's *Deux Femmes un soir* (Two Women One Night), the subtle story of a mother–daughter relationship in which their points of view alternate.

In a much-debated novel (taken to court for its allegedly irreverent comments on Belgian monarchs Leopold III and Baudouin), Pierre Mertens – the author of what had been considered the 'first modern Belgian novel', 1974's *Les Bons Offices* (The Good Services), and recipient of the 1987 Médicis prize for his

Shadowlight (*Les Éblouissements*) – deals with a popular Belgian theme, the interior exile of the tourist, entwined with childhood memories, in *Une Paix royale* (A Royal Peace).

In his 1995 novel, *La Place du mort* (The Passenger Seat), Jean-Luc Outers also deals with memory, but integrates it with a theme central to the Belgian novel of French expression – language itself. In the same year, Louise Lambrichs, whose *Journal d'Hannah* (Hannah's Diary) was elected best novel for 1993 by the French literary journal *Lire*, analyses the dangers of history and memory in *Le Jeu du roman* (The Game of the Novel).

On the more experimental side, Eugène Savitzkaya manipulates the French language to translate the tragedy of the human condition and memory in a world inhabited by decadence, decay and putrefaction – see *Mongolie plaine sale* (Mongolia, dirty plain) from 1976, *La Disparition de maman* (The Vanishing of Mother) of 1982, *Marin mon coeur* (Marin, My Beloved) from 1992, and *En Vie* (Alive) published in 1995. Jean-Philippe Toussaint explores the narrative possibilities of the fragment in *La Salle de bain* (The Bathroom) and *Monsieur: A Novel* (*Monsieur*), published in 1995 and 1996. The most famous writers of the new generation include Pascal de Duve, who explored the tragic ironies of modern life in his 1990 novel (*Izo*), and the playful and tragic possibilities of the French language in his 1993 travel narrative *Cargo Vie* (Cargo Life), before his death from **AIDS** at the age of 29. Amélie Nothomb has become the *enfant terrible* of Belgian literature, a cultural phenomenon, not only with her novels but also with her interviews, in which she has created herself into a myth (coming from a famous family of Belgian diplomats and ministers, she declares that she was an alcoholic between the ages of 3 and 14 and that only anorexia saved her from alcoholism). After her first novel, *Hygiène de l'assassin* (Hygiene of the Murderer), a thriller published in 1992 whose action is the very act of writing, she published *Le Sabotage amoureux* (Amorous Suicide), *Les Combustibles* (Combustibles), and *Les Catilinaires* (Hate Speeches), which was hailed by the popular French literary journal *Lire* as the best novel for 1995. Amélie Nothomb's novels, usually based on the dialogue form, are caustic and captivating domestic tragedies.

JEAN MAINIL

See also: comic strips/cartoonists; francophone cinema: Belgium; francophone performing arts: Belgium; literary prizes; publishing/*l'édition*

Further reading

Biron, M. (1994) *La Modernité belge*, Brussels: Éditions Labor (a theoretical analysis of what led to, and constitutes, Belgian modernity).

Frickx, R. and Trousson, R. (eds) (1988) *Lettres françaises de Belgique: dictionnaire des oeuvres*, Paris: Gembloux (a four-volume dictionary of Belgian literature with alphabetical entries by title with an index by author: volume 1, the novel; volume 2, poetry; an indispensable work of reference).

Quaghebeur, M. (1990) *Lettres belges entre absence et magie*, Bruxelles: Éditions Labor (on poetry).

francophone writing (fiction, poetry): DOM-TOMs

In the Caribbean, the borders of nation-states are incompatible with linguistic and literary frontiers. By concentrating on the (strictly speaking) French territories of Guadeloupe, Martinique and French Guiana that officially acquired the status of overseas departments (*départements d'outre-mer*) in 1946, it is possible to delineate a thriving literary corpus. But no common denominator is easily pinpointed, because Caribbean literatures always question the categories of literary genres, of national or even post-colonial literatures, and invite us to adopt a comparativist approach.

The French language is not a unifying element: Haitian literature of French expression is internationally acclaimed, while not all texts emanating from the French islands are in French: many poems, novels or folk-tales are written in Creole by Hector Poullet and Raphaël Confiant or collected by Ina Césaire. Recent novels have explored the potential of Creolized French: for example Patrick Chamoiseau's (1988) attempt at becoming a *marqueur de parole* in Solibo Magnificent (*Solibo magnifique*) and Daniel Maximin's 1995 prose poem about a hurricane, *Une Île et une nuit* (*One Island and One Night*) .

Caribbean writings from *départements d'outre-mer* are closely related to texts written in other Caribbean islands (in Creole, French, English, Spanish or Dutch), but also to the Creole (though non-Caribbean) literatures of the Indian Ocean (Mauritius and Reunion). Moreover, many authors live and write far from their native islands. Gisèle Pineau, who wrote *La Grande Dérive des esprits* (The Great Drift of the Spirits) and *L'Espérance-Macadam* (Macadam-Hope), was born in Paris; Maryse Condé has lived in Africa – see *Segu* (*Ségou*), and *Heremakhonon* (1976) – in France and in the United States. Always, Caribbean writings redefine fiction and poetry because they bring together literature and politics, history and myths, storytelling and the written word.

Politics and history, turbulent sites of contested cultural reappropriation, constantly mingle with fictional accounts. Many recent novels write a Caribbean history of (de)colonization. Writers denounce the silences of official history – see Dany Bebel-Gisler's 1985 biography of an unknown Guadeloupean woman, *Leonora: The Buried Story of Guadeloupe* (*Léonore: l'histoire enfouie de la Guadeloupe*) or shatter persistent myths: rereading the tragic turning point of 1802 when slavery was re-established by Napoleon after having been abolished in 1794, André Schwarz-Bart's 1972 work *La Mulâtresse solitude*, and Maximin's *Lone Sun* (*L'Isolé Soleil*) and *Soufrières*, ridicule the theory that Caribbean people cannot appreciate their freedom because they never had to fight for it. Novels also provide a Caribbean vision of recent events: Raphaël Confiant's 1988 text, *Le*

Nègre et l'amiral (The Negro and the Admiral) adds a lively Caribbean rendition of **Vichy**-led Martinique to the few and often sketchy accounts left by famous literary figures after their short and unhappy stay in the island on their way to the United States (see, for example, **Lévi-Strauss**'s *Tristes Tropiques*).

Caribbean culture and the way in which it is mediated through written and oral productions is often a controversial site of struggle against neocolonial reflexes, as shown in Bebel-Gisler's *Le Défi culturel guadeloupéen: devenir ce que nous sommes* (The Guadeloupean Cultural Challenge: Becoming Who We Are), published in 1989. Caribbean writing has a long tradition of opposing the racist stereotypes that have survived the heyday of colonial assimilationist policy.

Recent fiction has celebrated heroic *nègres marrons* (maroons), trying to erase the popular image of runaway slaves as mythical villains invoked to scare children (see Édouard Glissant's *Malemort*). In recent fiction and poetry, cultural *marronnage* (marooning) is a conscious tactic of reappropriation, and novelists choose to tap both African storytelling traditions and the Western canon – see Simone Schwarz-Bart's *Between Worlds* (*Ti-Jean l'horizon*) or *The Bridge of Beyond* (*Pluie et vent sur Télumée Miracle*), and Condé's rewriting of *Wuthering Heights*, *La Migration des coeurs* (Migrating Hearts).

What Frantz **Fanon** called *lactification* in his 1952 publication, *Black Skin White Masks* (the tragically alienated desire to mix black blood with the milk of white sexual partners in order to 'save' the race), is still recognizable in derogatory Creole phrases referring to the texture of black people's skin or hair – see Julie Lirus's *Identité antillaise* (Caribbean Identity) – and denounced in Michèle Lacrosil's or Jacqueline Manicom's stories. Most novels published in the 1980s and 1990s, however, welcome racial and cultural hybridity. While they hardly present diversity as a cultural or economic panacea, they move far beyond the tenets of negritude, that focused on black identity and race, neglecting people of mixed-blood, Indian and Chinese origins (see *Aurore*

by the writer and Communist leader of Indian origin, Ernest Moutoussamy). The universe described in Joseph Zobel's 1955 *Black Shack Alley* is still present in collective memories but the grandmother's struggle to help her grandson infiltrate the white educational system is far from recent novelists' preoccupations: Chamoiseau's 1992 Goncourt prizewinning *Texaco* retraces the history of quite contemporary urban developments.

In 1989, when three Martinican thinkers published a lyrical manifesto to celebrate *créolité* as a specific West Indian cultural identity, they did not hesitate to claim that West Indian literature does not exist yet *In Praise of Creoleness* (*Éloge de la créolité*). Readers may have wondered if such a self-disparaging statement was the result of lasting forms of cultural alienation that Chamoiseau, Bernabé and Confiant's literary predecessors had already virulently condemned: Aimé **Césaire**'s 1939 *Return to My Native Land* (*Cahier d'un retour au pays natal*) predates World War II. But the provocative suggestion may also be an invitation to revise our conception of 'literature' in the West Indies. Glissant proposes '*relation*' as a keyword in his *Caribbean Discourse* (*Le Discours antillais*) of 1981, and in his 1990 text, *Poétique de la Relation* (Poetics of Relation). Playing on the French word '*relation*' (meaning 'relationship', but also what is 'related' and what is 'relayed'), he presents us with cross-disciplinary and cross-cultural models. Similarly, *In Praise of Creoleness* invites us to concentrate on the beautifully entangled web of relationships created by our search for a specific French West Indian literature. This web or mosaic finds both thematic and structural representation in novels such as Maryse Condé's *Crossing the Mangrove* (*Traversée de la mangrove*) from 1989, an intriguingly polyphonic text where the voices of first-person male and female narrators of different races and social origins alternate from chapter to chapter. The juxtaposition of separate Caribbean identities does not add up to a coherent whole, but to a complex and sometimes fragmented mosaic, a symbol of the islands' multiracial and multicultural society.

MIREILLE ROSELLO

See also: decolonization; francophone popular music: DOM-TOMs; parties and movements in francophone countries: DOM-TOMs

Further reading

Antoine, R. (1992) *La Littérature franco-antillaise: Haïti, Guadeloupe et Martinique*, Paris: Karthala (a history of the literature produced in these islands from the beginning of the colonial period to the present).

Boyce Davies, C. and Savory Fido, E. (eds) (1990) *Out of the Kumbla: Caribbean Women and Literature*, Trenton: Africa World Press (a collection of interdisciplinary articles by leading specialists of Caribbean studies).

Burton, R. (1995) 'West Indies', in P. France (ed.) *The New Oxford Companion to Literature in French*, Oxford: Clarendon Press (a thorough, chronologically organized survey of Caribbean literature).

Chamoiseau, P. and Confiant, R. (eds) (1991) *Lettres créoles – tracées antillaises et continentales de la littérature, 1635–1976*, Paris: Hatier.

francophone writing (fiction, poetry): Indian Ocean

The principal islands – Madagascar, Mauritius, Reunion and the Seychelles – all have a literary output in French, but its status differs as a result of their varied populations and contrasting colonial history. In all these areas, French as a literary language is rivalled by local languages such as Creole in Reunion, Mauritius and the Seychelles, English and Indian languages in Mauritius, and Malagasy languages in Madagascar. There is nevertheless a well-established tradition of writing in French, going back to the late eighteenth century in the case of Reunion and the early nineteenth century in Mauritius.

The postwar years have seen contrasting developments of these latter two traditions. Mauritian **poetry** has achieved French and international consecration through the figures of Malcolm de Chazal (1902–81), a visionary and aphoristic poet much admired by André Breton and Jean **Paulhan**; and Edouard Maunick (b. 1931), a poet of exile and multicultural island identity and a figurehead of francophone literary circles in Paris. By contrast, the contemporary poets of Reunion have been more concerned to establish and explore their Creole identity, often by writing in Creole or incorporating Creolisms into their use of French. The pioneer of the movement of *créolie* was Jean Albany (1917–84), with his collection *Zamal* of 1951 – the title is the Creole word for 'marijuana', symbolizing the poet's heady memories of his childhood on the island. Others of a more conventional inspiration celebrate Reunionnais decor and culture, such as the archbishop Gilbert Aubry (b. 1942), in *Rivages d'Alizés* (Trade-Wind Shores) of 1971, and *Hymne à la Créolie* (Hymn to Creolia) of 1978; or the long-exiled Jean-Henri Azéma (b. 1913) in *Olographe* (Testament) of 1978. A more militant poetry grew up in the 1970s, aware of the heritage of slavery and contemporary social inequalities, with the monumental epic poem *Vali pour une reine morte* (Lament for a Late Queen) of 1973 by Boris Gamaleya (b. 1930); and the populist and autonomist poetry of Alain Lorraine (b. 1946) in *Tienbo le rein* (Let's Stay as One) of 1975. More recent militant poets, such as Carpanin Marimoutou (b. 1956), have moved from French to Creole, often publishing bilingual editions of their poetry, such as *Romans pou la mèr et la tèr* (Romance for the Sea and the Land) of 1995.

In Madagascar, with the colonial imposition of education in French, a generation of poets grew up who attempted to transpose into French the forms and qualities of the indigenous Malagasy poetic tradition. Three of these, Jean-Joseph Rabéarivelo (1903–37), Jacques Rabémananjara (b. 1913) and Flavien Ranaïvo (b. 1914), were made famous by their inclusion in L. S. Senghor's *Anthologie de la nouvelle poésie nègre et malgache* (Anthology of the

New Negro and Malagasy poetry) in 1948.
The pioneering Rabéarivelo committed suicide
in 1937, but the militant nationalist
Rabémananjara was to dominate the Malagasy
literary scene during the postwar years.
Imprisoned after the uprising of 1947,
Rabémananjara became a spokesman for the
aspirations of his country to independence and
worked closely with Alioune Diop on the revue
Présence africaine. His prison poetry *Antsa*
(Testament) of 1948, *Rites millénaires*
(Millennial Rites) of 1955 and *Lamba* in 1956
are among his most poignant celebrations of
the mystery and beauty of the decor and cus-
toms of his country. After independence in
1958, Rabémananjara became an influential
politician and government minister, but was
forced into exile by the *coup d'état* of 1972
which soon brought to power the Marxist
regime of Ratsiraka. The more discreet figure
of Ranaivo published *L'Ombre et le vent*
(Shadow and Wind) in 1947, *Mes chansons de
toujours* (The songs I always sing) in 1955, and
Le Retour au bercail (Return to the Fold) in
1962, before he too was forced to settle in
France. The period of the People's Republic
was not favourable to writing in French and
very few new poets in French have come to
prominence in the intervening years.

In both Mauritius and Reunion the first
attempts at novel writing date back to a nineteenth century more preoccupied with poets
and poetry, and it is often the case that novelists are also famous as poets. In the postwar
years, the brothers Loys (1915–69) and André
Masson (b. 1921) impose a Mauritian presence
in metropolitan French literature with an
impressively prolific production of novels.
Loys Masson left his native island in 1939,
never to return, but some of his best-known
novels, *L'Étoile et la Clef* (The Star and the
Key) of 1945 and *Le Notaire des Noirs*
(Lawyer to the blacks) of 1961, evoke episodes
of Mauritian society, and the mythical presence
of the island and the sea are recurrent motifs in
his fictions. His brother André remained in
Mauritius but none the less managed to publish
several novels in the 1960s in Paris – *Un temps
pour mourir* (A Time to Die) in 1962, 1963's

Le Chemin de pierre ponce (The Pumice-Stone
Path) and *Le Temps juste* (A Just Time) from
1966 – which evoke metaphysical doubts
through the depiction of Mauritian social
problems such as racial prejudice. The most
notable defenders of the Mauritian novel in
recent years have often been exiles: Jean
Fanchette (b. 1932) with *Alpha du Centaure*
(The Alpha of the Centaur) in 1975; Marie-
Thérèse Humbert (b. 1940) with her autobiographical novel *A l'autre bout de moi* (At the
Other End of Myself) in 1979; and the French
novelist Jean-Marie Le Clézio who rediscovered his Mauritian identity with *Le Chercheur
d'or* (The Gold-Hunter) in 1985. The island
has at the same time experienced a revival of
literature in Creole, be it novels such as René
Asgarally's *Quand montagne prend difé...*
(When the Mountain Catches Fire...) of
1977 or the poems of the dramatist Dev
Virahsawmy.

The mid-1970s in Reunion saw a renaissance of socially committed novels, often written
in Creole or a Creolized French, whose subject
matter was the lives of the poorest members of
Réunionnais society: the most notable of these
are *Les Muselés* (The Silenced) of 1977 by
Anne Cheynet (b. 1938), Daniel Honoré's
Louis Redona of 1980, written in Creole, and
Quartier trois-lettres (Three-Letter District) of
1980 by Axel Gauvin (b. 1944). Gauvin has
continued to publish (in Paris) novels with similar themes of social exclusion and characteristics of formal experiment, which he has subsequently republished in Reunion in Creole:
Faims d'enfance (Childhood Hungers) of 1987
and *L'Aimé* (The Loved One) from 1990. The
implied questioning of Réunionnais identity
has been pursued through historical novels
about the island's often sombre past by Jean-
François Samlong (b. 1949), such as *Terre
arrachée* (Torn Earth) of 1982 and *Madame
Desbassayns* of 1985, and by the metropolitan
Daniel Vaxelaire, in *Chasseur de Noirs* (Slave
Hunter) of 1982 and *L'Affranchi* (The
Freedman) of 1984. The last twenty years have
seen a period of considerable richness in
Reunionnais writing in both French and
Creole, and this looks likely to continue.

The novel in French has not really established itself as a genre for indigenous writers in Madagascar; an exception to this general rule is the recent output of short stories and novels by Michèle Rakotoson (b. 1948), such as *Dadabe* of 1984 and *Le Bain des reliques* (The Bathing of the Relics) of 1988, which evoke from a woman's point of view the social problems of a people emerging from a long period of repression. In general the short story has shown more vitality as a genre, being easier to publish in local newspapers and magazines and able to attract the attention of a wider public through the competitions organized by Radio-France Internationale.

The smaller islands in the region – the Seychelles, the Comores, Mayotte – have shown the first signs of autonomous literary activity during the last twenty years, with their first novels and poetry written in French. In general, however, it is the sustained vitality of the literary output of Reunion and Mauritius which remains the principal contribution of the area to francophone culture, which can arbitrarily be measured by the recognition by Parisian publishing houses of figures such as Malcolm de Chazal, Loys Masson, Marie-Thérèse Humbert, Axel Gauvin or Jean-François Samlong.

PETER HAWKINS

See also: francophone performing arts: Indian Ocean; francophone popular music: DOM-TOMs; parties and movements in francophone countries: DOM-TOMs

Further reading

Joubert, J.-L. (1991) *Littératures de l'Océan Indien*, Paris: EDICEF (essential reading).

francophone writing (fiction, poetry): North Africa

All three Maghrebin countries (Morocco, Algeria and Tunisia) experienced French colonial rule. Morocco and Tunisia gained their independence in 1956, Algeria in 1962. Because of the French policy of assimilation and the length of time (132 years) it was in contact with the French language, Algeria has produced more francophone writers than Morocco or Tunisia. At first, Maghrebin people refused to acknowledge as legitimate the use of French as it was an imposed language, but later accepted its usage, often appropriating it for their own ends. Thus French became the language of anti-colonial struggle, particularly through writing.

The first short story to appear in French in 1891 was *La Vengeance du cheikh* (The Vengeance of the Sheikh) by the Algerian M'hammed Ben Rahhal. However, this early francophone writing was discarded by generations of Maghrebins as assimilationist and over-friendly towards France

It was not until the 1950s that the Maghreb witnessed the birth of a literature written in French that was acknowledged by many as being of quality. The representative writers of this period are Albert Memmi, Driss Chraïbi, Kateb **Yacine** and Mohammed **Dib**, among others. The dynamic and powerful style of these writers earned them the title of forefathers of what is today known as 'francophone Maghrebin literature'.

The early 1950s writers, such as the Algerian Mouloud Feraoun who published *Le Fils du pauvre* (The Pauper's Son) in 1950, and the Moroccan Ahmed Sefrioui with his 1954 novel *La Boîte à merveilles* (The Box of Wonders), were labelled by their peers as ethnographic writers because they provided the reader with a colourful and exotic picture of everyday life in the French colonies. Such writing was essentially directed to a French audience. It was regarded by Maghrebin critics as being politically disengaged, considering that the 1950s were, above all, a period of political unrest throughout the Maghreb. However, in the case of Feraoun, the critics failed to recognize that through the autobiographical narration and the humanist style of *The Pauper's Son* the writer does not simply portray the poverty-stricken Berber region of Kabylia, but shows implicitly that such poverty was a direct consequence of French colonization.

The 1950s was also marked by the revolutionary style of writing of the Tunisian Albert Memmi, the Moroccan Driss Chraïbi and the Algerian Kateb Yacine. They respectively published what were to become canonical texts in francophone Maghrebian literature: *La Statue de sel* (The Statue of Salt) in 1953, *The Simple Past (Le Passé simple)* in 1954 and *Nedjma* in 1956. While Yacine wrote about the metaphorical repeated rape of Algeria, Memmi and Chraïbi respectively attacked the traditional Jewish and Muslim societies from which they feel alienated and which they describe in angry and violent tones.

Of the three writers, it is Chraïbi who drew more attention, both for the quality of his novel and for the aftermath of its publication. His direct attack on Islamic law, which in Chraïbi's view subjugates the individual, gained him the applause of those in France who were for the continuation of colonial rule over a nation who they believed needed to be civilized, and attracted the anger of Moroccans who, during the publication of *The Simple Past*, were struggling for independence and saw the novel as propaganda against their fight.

While the 1950s novels were highly autobiographical, the 1960s saw a more politicized kind of writing, especially in Algeria. With the **Algerian war** of independence, Algerian writers took up arms, and this period saw prolific literary production with revolutionary tones and themes. Thus, Mouloud Mammeri's 1965 novel *L'Opium et le bâton* (The Opium and the Baton) set in a small Kabyle village, became a classical text dealing with the Algerian Revolution and the role of the National Liberation Front (FLN) and the resistance fighters. But, before that, *Les Enfants d'un nouveau monde* (Children of a New World) was published by a woman writer, Assia Djebar. In her 1962 novel, Djebar celebrates the role of women in the war of independence.

From the mid-1960s, a new generation of writers emerged, including Rachid Boudjedra and Mohammed Dib in Algeria, and

Mohammed Khaïr-Eddine in Morocco. They were concerned less with the war than with the situation of the Maghrebin countries in the aftermath of independence. They focused on their own societies, which they criticized for inhibiting freedom of expression and for abusing human rights. Likewise, under the banner of free speech, the Moroccan poet Abdellatif Laâbi founded the literary review *Souffles* (Breaths) in 1966. He was later jailed as a political prisoner but was released in 1988 after Amnesty International intervened on his behalf.

The publications of the 1970s marked a complete break from the previous styles of francophone Maghrebin literature. The writing of this period subverted the French language and gave it new dimensions with highly philosophical tones. Illustrative writers of this period are Abdelkebir Khatibi with his 1971 novel, *La Mémoire tatouée* (The Tattooed Memory), and Abdelwahab Meddeb's 1979 work, *Talismano*. Language, identity, history and sexuality were the key themes of writing of this period. The production of **poetry** gained ground on the novel in the 1970s. Thus, in addition to novelists who are also poets, such as Mohammed Dib and Tahar **Ben Jelloun**, new names became prominent, such as Abdellatif Laâbi (who continued to write from his prison cell), Mohammed Loakira and Mostafa Nissaboury.

Maghrebin women started publishing in French as early as 1947. Religious, social and state censorship often constrain women's writing, which results in some women giving up writing altogether or publishing under pseudonyms, such as Aïcha Lemsine. While, generally, women writers share the same sociopolitical concerns, Assia Djebar stands as the only woman writer whose work experiments with the multiplicity of women's voices in literature and whose use of French is a subversion of what she calls her 'stepmother tongue'.

Despite the controversies surrounding the use of French, women writers continue to use it as a medium to make their voice heard. In fact, in spite of the policy of Arabization in the Maghreb since the 1970s, the 1980s and 1990s produced more names from both sexes on the francophone literary scene. Representative of these periods are women writers such as Béji Hélè, Nina Bouraoui, and male writers such as Rachid Mimouni, and Edmond Amrane El Maleh. On the other hand, of the old generation, Kateb Yacine ceased to write in French as a result of his opposition to the institutionalization of *francophonie*. However, ironically, in 1986 he was awarded the prestigious Prix National des Lettres for his rich contribution to francophone writing.

Though the 1990s represent political and religious threats to Maghrebin writers – especially intense in Algeria – the majority continue to publish. Unlike their predecessors, most of whom lived in France, they have opted to remain in their own countries. This is a brave and risky choice: many writers, like Tahar Djaout in 1993, have been murdered by Islamist opposition groups in Algeria (anyone perceived to be an 'intellectual' is a target). The very real risk of violent death is a high price to pay to keep alive a literature that some critics previously regarded as being of little real value.

LAÏLA IBNLFASSI

See also: autobiography; decolonization; francophone performing arts (North Africa); francophone popular music: North Africa; literary prizes

Further reading

Ibnlfassi, L. and Hitchcott, N. (eds) (1996) *African Francophone Writing: A Critical Introduction*, Oxford: Berg (first selection of critical essays on North and sub-Saharan African literature in English).

Khatibi, A. (1968) *Le Roman maghrébin*, Paris: Éditions du Seuil (full-length study of the North African novel in French).

francophone writing (fiction, poetry): Switzerland

Switzerland and its literature are often viewed as constituting an island in the middle of Europe – an appropriate image, as long as one bears in mind that the closed world of an island is also the symbol of travel, refuge and escapism. Historically speaking the Swiss have always tried to 'escape' their boundaries (in 58 BC Julius Caesar sought to halt their general exodus). The fragmentation of Switzerland, with its late absorption of some of the French-speaking cantons, means that Swiss identity is often constructed in contradistinction to other nationalities.

Historically, perhaps inevitably, French-Swiss literature is strongly linked with France. Indeed the *romand* intelligentsia traditionally went to Paris to study or work. Within Switzerland, France is often accused of claiming as her own the greatest Swiss-French writers, such as Jean-Jacques Rousseau, Mme de Staël, the linguist Saussure, Blaise Cendrars, Robert Pinget, Albert Cohen and Pierre Klossowski. In the same way, most Swiss visual artists are perceived to become 'un-Swissed' once famous (for example, Füseli, **Balthus**, Le Corbusier, Alberto **Giacometti**, Paul Klee, Jean-Luc **Godard**), leaving 'local' and 'minor' artists to remain Swiss.

Charles-Ferdinand Ramuz (1878–1947), whose innovative characteristic is the placing of the reader within the novel by a poetic use of the pronouns 'we' (*nous, on*) and 'you' (*vous*), instigated the rebirth of local literature, his rhythmic, poetical style influencing many later writers beyond the borders of Switzerland. However, his nationality and his affirmation thereof have undoubtedly served to diminish his international standing as a great writer.

The movement of emigration and **immigration** that constituted Switzerland has generated two specific types of literary Swissness: that adopted by the refugee and immigrant (such as Cohen, Anne Cuneo, Klossowski, Benjamin Wilkominski), and that of the 'fifth Switzerland', comprising the Swiss abroad (like

Blaise Cendrars, Edmond Fleg, Clarisse Francillon, Philippe Jaccottet, Pinget, Monique Saint-Hélier), who produced a substantial body of travel and exile literature, as well as some internationally recognized 'French' literature. The insular Swiss have not, as generally believed, generated solely dull and austere work. Playfulness and observation of the outside world are strong preoccupations, as if singularity could be better expressed by toying with otherness (see, for example the work of Amélie Plume). Peasant and workers' roots have also inspired an important strain of Marxist literature (for example, Yves Velan, and Jacques Chessex, who received the Goncourt prize for *L'Ogre* in 1973).

This singularity has led to Swiss-French writers wishing to be seen as individuals rather than as a group, and certain ambiguities towards the notion of nationality can be discerned in their work. Distinctions between writers are today felt to be thematic rather than nationalistic, their Swiss roots often only being identifiable by the fact that they are published by Swiss presses (see, for example Charles-Albert Cingria, Anne Cuneo, Amélie Plume, Gustave Roud, Yvette Z'Graggen). Indeed, except for a substantial corpus of internationally recognized Swiss-French academics and intellectuals (Albert Béguin, Léon Bopp, Marc Eigeldinger, Jean **Piaget**, Marcel Raymond, Denis de Rougemont, Jean Rousset, Jean Starobinski, Jean Ziegler), the international reputation of Swiss-French writing today rests on the unjustly small number taken up by publishers in France (Chessex, Cohen, Jaccottet, Pinget, Velan).

VÉRÈNE GRIESHABER

See also: francophone performing arts: Switzerland; literary prizes

Further reading

Francillon, R. (ed.) (1996–8) *Histoire de la littérature suisse*, 4 vols, Lausanne: Payot (essential background reading).

Frères Jacques, Les

Singers

A legendary quartet of male singers, formed in 1944, whose stage costumes (including leotards, white gloves, top hats and handlebar moustaches) became their distinctive trademark. They perfected their stage performances in variety theatres rather than music halls, combining gesture, mime, movement and lighting in songs which became sketches or playlets. Les Frères Jacques gave their farewell performance at the Champs-Élysées in 1980.

IAN PICKUP

See also: song/*chanson*

Fresson, Bernard

b. 1931, Reims

Actor

A film, television and theatre actor since the 1960s. Fresson has worked with directors, including Jean **Vilar** at the Théâtre National de Paris, **Planchon**, **Maréchal** and **Barsacq**, in productions including Planchon's *Troilus and Cressida*, Fagadau's *Cat on a Hot Tin Roof* and Maréchal's *mise en scène* of de Filippos's *Filumena Marturana*.

ANNIE SPARKS

See also: theatre

Funès, Louis de

b. 1914, Courbevoie;
d. 1983, Nantes

Actor

France's most popular film star of the 1960s. The generally downmarket nature of his films, such as the Gendarmes series directed by Jean

Girault between 1964 and 1982, made great play with a grimacing, irascible body language originally developed in the music hall. The other director for whom he excelled, in a double act with Bourvil, was Gérard Oury (in 1966's *La Grande Vadrouille*). He had begun his career working with more 'respectable' film-makers such as Sacha Guitry and **Autant-Lara** (*La Traversée de Paris*, also with Bourvil, in 1956). His attitude towards authority – hectoring in exercising it, submissive when it was exercised over him – perhaps most fully accounts for his extraordinary popularity with mainstream French audiences.

KEITH READER

See also: cinema

Furet, François

b. 1927, Paris;
d. 1997, Paris

Historian

The best-known recent historian of the French Revolution. Furet's works – above all 1978's *Interpreting the French Revolution* (*Penser la Révolution française*) and, with Mona Ozouf, *Dictionnaire critique de la Révolution française* (1988) – were instrumental in articulating a post-Marxist view in which 1789 was seen as foreshadowing the Russian Revolution of 1917 only in its bloody excesses. For Furet, the positive aspects of the French Revolution found their apotheosis in electoral social democracy – a view given credence by the second **Mitterrand** term and the geopolitical collapse of Communism. A PCF member in his youth, Furet acted as adviser to education minister Edgar Faure in the restructuring of French universities after **May 1968**, and was president successively of the École des Hautes Études en Sciences Sociales and of the Institut Raymond Aron.

KEITH READER

See also: Marxism and Marxian thought; parties and movements

G

Gainsbourg, Serge

b. 1928, Paris;
d. 1991, Paris

Singer-songwriter, real name Lucien
Ginzburg

If any French singer was guaranteed to cause
controversy, it would surely be Gainsbourg.
Although he was mainly known for his music,
his other great passion was painting, which was
his father's profession. After studying fine art in
Paris and a spell as bar pianist, he sang in the
Left Bank cabarets and Théâtre des Trois
Baudets, achieving initial success in 1958 with
Le Poinçonneur des lilas (The Ticket-Puncher
on the Tube).

What is particularly fascinating is the split
personality Gainsbourg developed: on the one
hand, the naive, sensitive artist figure who carefully created words and music; and on the other,
his *alter ego*, whom he named Gainsbarre, an
anti-conformist *provocateur*. Gainsbourg cultivated an unshaven, unkempt look; he led a
hedonistic, self-destructive lifestyle, drinking
and smoking to excess and, as the years wore
on, his nervous twitch and verbal incoherence
became steadily more pronounced. A figure
who sought infamy, Gainsbourg caused a storm
of protest from the military with his 1979 reggae version of the French national anthem, *La
Marseillaise*, *Aux armes et cetaera* (To Arms,
etc.). In 1984 he burned a 500 franc note on

television. Equally provocative was the duet,
Lemon Incest, which he recorded in 1985 with
his daughter, Charlotte.

One of Gainsbourg's more notable obses-
sions was the opposite sex. From an early stage
in his career, female singers such as France **Gall**,
Juliette **Gréco** and Régine recorded his songs.
He was often accused of manipulating, eroticiz-
ing and objectifying women in his life and
work, and he became particularly fascinated
with the sex-kitten image of Brigitte **Bardot**
whom he met in 1967. Together they recorded
Bonnie and Clyde and Gainsbourg paid tribute
to her in *Initials BB*. In *Je t'aime moi non plus*
(I Love You Me Neither), which was censored
by the BBC in 1969, Gainsbourg celebrated
overtly the addictive nature of sex while undermining traditional notions of romantic love.
His subsequent marriage to the English actress
and singer, Jane **Birkin**, created one of the most
famous celebrity couples in France. Although
he appeared at times to be savage and something of a misogynist, he was nevertheless a
romantic who regarded himself as physically
unattractive.

Between 1965 and 1979, a relatively unproductive time in terms of songs, Gainsbourg gave
up concert tours. He did, however, direct, appear
in and write music for several films, and earned
his living by making television commercials.

Musically eclectic and innovative,
Gainsbourg created new musical styles out of
established and current trends, such as **jazz**
(*Black Trombone*). He developed his literary

talent through wordplay, rhyme and alliteration; for example, *La Javanaise*, a song using Javanese or *'av'* slang. He had a particular penchant for franglais and contemporary fashion, as in *Qui est 'in' qui est 'out'* (Who is in Who is Out) and *Ford Mustang*.

Following his death, Gainsbourg achieved the ultimate status of popular icon: an anti-hero, especially for a disenchanted youth and the personification of liberty in its most excessive forms.

CHRIS TINKER

See also: slang/*argot*/*verlan*; song/*chanson*

Major works

Gainsbourg, S. (1994) *Dernières Nouvelles des étoiles*, Paris: Plon, Presses Pocket (collected song lyrics).

Further reading

Verlant, G. (1985) *Gainsbourg*, Paris: Livre de Poche (biographically oriented study).

Gall, France

b. 1947, Paris

Singer

Having had early success as one of the French *yé-yé* (1960s pop) generation, France Gall modified her image successfully in two different reincarnations: first, singing songs by Serge **Gainsbourg** – including *Poupée de cire, poupée de son* (Wax Doll, Rag Doll), which won the **Eurovision Song Contest** in 1965 and sold over a million copies in Japan alone; and second, singing songs by the man who became her husband, the late Michel **Berger**, including *La Déclaration d'amour* (The Declaration of Love) and *Musique*. France Gall is still popular today.

IAN PICKUP

See also: song/*chanson*

Gallimard

Publisher

Gaston Gallimard (1881–1975) co-founded the Éditions de la Nouvelle Revue Française with André Gide and his friends in 1911. The Éditions Gallimard publish some of the greatest works in French literature in different collections, among the most important of which are 'Folio' (accounting for over 30 per cent of turnover) and the renowned 'Bibliothèque de la Pléiade'. The crime novels of the 'Série noire' are also very popular with the reading public.

MARTYN CORNICK

See also: detective fiction

Further reading

Assouline, P. (1984) *Gaston Gallimard, un demi-siècle d'édition française*, Paris: Balland.
Martin, H.-J., Chartier, R. and Vivet, J.-P. (eds) (1986) *Histoire de l'édition française*, vol. 4, *Le Livre concurrencé 1900–1950*, Paris: Promodis (essential reading).

game shows

Ratings rivalry between **TF1** and **France 2** has produced a variety of game shows for prime-time TV. Many are American by-products, such as *Wheel of Fortune* (*Roue de la fortune*) and *Une Famille en or* (both TF1), and *Des Chiffres et des lettres* (France 2). Less slavish towards their Anglo-Saxon prototypes are *Dessinez c'est gagné* and *Que le meilleur gagne* (both

France 2). Live audience participation in most game shows is reduced to applauding.

The two exceptions to the normal kind of game show are *Des Chiffres et des lettres* and *Que le meilleur gagne*. In the former, if participants fail, members of the audience (those with the right answer) are picked out to stand up and read it out – a moment of glory. In the latter, the audience *is* the game, which is one of auto-elimination and self-applause (they clap as they lose). Of the 200-odd participants, only one must remain at the end, and he or she goes on to try to win the prize. The audience shouts '*Au revoir*' as participants are skittled out by failing to answer silly multiple-choice questions. Of all the games this is the only one that in any way resists the codes of game shows. The *compère*, Naguy, is North African (elsewhere on these shows, white males dominate). He insults his participants – especially those who get answers wrong. But the audience hits back: they take pleasure from losing, even deliberately losing to get their moment on the box. Naguy undermines the myth of the all-knowing *compère* – 'it's all written on the card', he announces, thus also ridiculing the myth of knowledge as the key to social and economic mobility to which game shows subscribe. He is not the patriarch nor the *prof* his more elderly counterparts have become. He caricatures the nudge-nudge/wink-wink sexual innuendos so commonplace in the *compère*'s discourse by aping the 'black man as macho/virile' and by deliberately setting up question marks around his own sexuality as much as around that of the male participants in the game.

Dessinez c'est gagné is a reinscription of charades on to a large flip chart, upon which participants draw clues for their team to guess the unnamed word, phrase or whatever. Two teams compete, three to each side – two young contestants plus a well-known TV or media personality. They sit opposite each other on sofas and are surrounded in close proximity by the TV audience. This cosiness is deconstructed by the fact that the teams are single-sexed – male versus female, battle of the sexes – and that ageism and the teacher–pupil dynamic are well in place as the young contestants are sub-

jected to ridicule by the middle-aged *compère*. There appears to be no prize, except the delight of winning, being insulted and being so close to fame. One particular broadcast, however, might not have been so pleasurable: the star in question was the actor Philippe Léotard whose drunkenness was apparent to all. Attempts to laugh off his rudeness and stifle his volubility failed completely – but the spectacle went on, live broadcasting at its best!

SUSAN HAYWARD

See also: stars; television

Garaudy, Roger

b. 1913, Marseille

Writer

A writer and philosopher who might be dubbed the 'Vicar of Bray' of postwar French intellectual life, Garaudy converted to Protestantism in his youth, then for twenty years was a member of the Communist Party's central committee. He subsequently moved, by way of a humanist leftism that led to his expulsion from the party, first to radical **Catholicism** and finally, in 1982, to **Islam**. His ardent Stalinism at the height of the Cold War finds an ominous echo in his recent identification with an anti-Zionism that minimizes (if it does not deny) the Holocaust.

KEITH READER

See also: racism/anti-semitism

García, Victor

b. 1934, Tucumán, Argentina;
d. 1982, Paris

Director

After his arrival in France in 1962, García heavily influenced French theatre with his

Artaudian-style productions, primarily of works by Lorca, **Arrabal, Genet** and Valle-Inclàn. He directed in Spain, the United Kingdom, Portugal and Brazil.

ANNIE SPARKS

See also: Artaud, Antonin; theatre

Further reading

Whitton, D. (1987) *Stage Directors in Modern France*, Manchester: Manchester University Press (a discussion of García's work and influence).

gastronomy

France's reputation as the world centre of gastronomy – loosely defined, perhaps, as the consumption not only of fine food and drink, but of discourses about it – is closely connected with both her geography and her history. At once a Mediterranean and an Atlantic, a northern and a southern country, the range of raw materials to which she has access is probably unrivalled in Europe, and it was after the French Revolution and the bourgeoisie's triumph over the nobility that the multiple ways in which these foodstuffs could be prepared and served spread through society. It is no accident that the first restaurant in the modern sense of the term was opened in Paris in 1782 by a former cook to the count of Provence (later to become Louis XVIII).

Yet *la haute cuisine* as it was known and consumed immediately after the war might well appear monotonous and turgid to a contemporary public. Refrigeration was uncommon, and produce in consequence often far from fresh; it was often as much to mask the less-than-pristine state of fish or meat as to enhance their flavour that the heavy dairy-based sauces characteristic of this type of cooking were used. Even in 1960 there were only seven supermarkets in the whole of France, so the range of raw materials available to the

domestic cook or restaurateur was restricted. The red *Guide Michelin*, like France's leading restaurants dependent on the motor car and the expanding tourist industry, shows certain of their number listing the same specialities literally year in, year out. Crayfish *au gratin*, duckling, truffles and *foie gras* as accompaniments suggest what may now seem the indigestible tone of this cuisine, in which vegetables were relegated to a strictly secondary position. Presentation was as heavy and codified as the dishes themselves; the ceremonial raising of the silver dome that covered the *plat de résistance* was an indispensable part of the dining ritual. The vast majority of French people, of course, had neither cultural nor financial access to this type of cooking. *La cuisine bourgeoise*, often perforce rooted in regional specialities, yielded such dishes as the *tripes à la mode de Caen* characteristic of Normandy or the *quenelles* (sausages of minced pike) of Lyon. Popular restaurants such as the *bistrots* in the Les Halles area of Paris or the *bouchons* of Lyon fed into the loftier gastronomic tradition – a tendency that has continued apace until the present day.

The spread of refrigeration, improved systems of **transport** and the increasing importance of **television** all contributed to the democratization of gastronomy that has been a dominant tendency of the postwar period. Raymond **Oliver**, owner of the celebrated Parisian restaurant, Le Grand Véfour, gave the first live television cookery demonstrations in the 1950s, thereby becoming one of the two key French gastronomic personalities of his time. The other was Fernand Point (1897–1955), whose Restaurant La Pyramide in Vienne (between Lyon and Grenoble) trained many of the greatest chefs of succeeding generations and whose stress on fresh products of the highest quality, always freshly prepared, combined with his innovative use of sauces to mark a welcome break from the often lacklustre cuisine of the bigger hotels.

The spread of colour photography , enlivening the cookery columns of such magazines as *Elle* or *L'Express*, also had a major influence, especially combined with the weekly column in

Elle written by Dr Édouard de Pomiane, France's best-known apostle of the healthy diet until 1964, when he died. More types of food became widely available and more care went into finding healthier ways of preparing them; Oliver and other chefs 'returned from the [1964] Tokyo Olympics infatuated with Japanese cooking' (Mennell 1993), and this was to exercise a major influence on what was later to become known as *la nouvelle cuisine*. The food critics Henri Gault and Christian Millau applied this term (whose first use dates back as far as 1740) to the cooking of such figures as Paul **Bocuse** and Michel **Guérard**, though Point has a strong claim to be its founding father. Through their annual restaurant guide and monthly magazine, Gault and Millau became the dominant figures in French gastronomy. *Nouvelle cuisine* reacted against heavy saucing, lengthy cooking times, excessive reliance on dairy products and the orthodoxies of Parisian and grand hotel dishes, in favour of lighter types of cooking (steaming, under the Oriental influence, was a favourite), the use of unusual herbs and fruits to impart new flavours, and an inventiveness often drawing upon regional and provincial traditions for its inspiration.

Nowadays many of the innovations of *nouvelle cuisine* scarcely seem novel at all. The serving of sorrel with salmon (a Troisgros discovery), the use of a plethora of wild mushrooms, the promotion of once 'vulgar' items such as lentils or spinach to gastronomic glory have all long since become part of the French diner's landscape. The controversy it raised between about 1973 – the date of Gault and Millau's article 'Vive la nouvelle cuisine française' – and 1976, when Guérard's *La Grande Cuisine minceur* was published, was none the less fierce, partisans of the *ancien régime* such as *Le Monde*'s food critic La Reynière (Robert Courtine) or Jean-Robert Pitte often acrimoniously crossing swords with Gault and Millau and 'their' young Turks. *Nouvelle cuisine*'s cause was certainly not helped by the zealotry of some of its practitioners, who dished up combinations of well-nigh Surrealist absurdity (raspberry vinegar

was a favourite component), in visual forms more reminiscent of abstract painting than of still life, and most notoriously all too often in minuscule portions (a cartoon in the English magazine *Punch* memorably distilled this last tendency in depicting a puzzled couple in a *nouvelle cuisine* restaurant asking the waiter: 'Excuse me, have we eaten?'). It was not surprising that no less a figure than Bocuse was to abjure the 'movement', nor that its succession, enthusiastically abetted by Gault and Millau, should have been assumed by *cuisine du terroir*, harking back historically to the supposed heyday of France's peasantry rather than looking exotically to the East for its inspiration. It was the turn of haricot beans, black and white pudding, humbler fish such as the grey mullet, lesser-known varieties of regional cheese all to find stardom. Heartier this type of cooking undoubtedly was, but it in no sense represented a return to the *haute cuisine* of yore, whose omnipresent frying and roasting were largely replaced by grilling and even more casseroling.

The last-named method of cooking, of course, takes time, which is doubtless why it has been raised from the rank of commoner to the nobility; easier by far, if one can afford it, to pay somebody else to prepare a gourmet casserole for you in a restaurant . . . The corollary of this, of course, has been a movement on a vast scale towards various kinds of convenience food for everyday eating. These need not necessarily be bad: the big-name chefs all endorse deep-frozen or vacuum-packed products bearing their name, the best of which are quite as delicious as anything most people could expect to prepare at home, even given unrealistic amounts of time and energy. 'Macdonaldization', however, is spreading apace in France as everywhere else, and for every Bocuse- or Guérard-signed vacuum-packed scallop *ragoût*, numerous tins of cassoulet or sauerkraut in the downmarket William Saurin range are undoubtedly sold in supermarkets. Younger people, their elders often complain, care little for food and less for its traditions, and even actively prefer a *Macdo* to the traditional dishes of their regions. Non-European restaurants – North African ones in particular, generally serving couscous, which occupies a similar place in France to Indian food in Britain – are often popular with younger people, especially students, and their range has been steadily on the increase. Fifteen years ago, a Thai or Indian restaurant was a rarity even in Paris; today, most provincial towns of any size have one or more of each. That, of course, is no less symptomatic than Macdonaldization of the growing internationalization of everything to do with food. Nor, for all the rarity of mad cow disease and the plethora of jokes about it to which English people living in France have been exposed, is anxiety about the quality and purity of one's diet. Excessive use of preservatives, standardized fruit and vegetables grown for appearance not flavour, cheeses with the taste pasteurized out of them – the litany of worries is a familiar one. It is ironic, after two decades and more in which French cuisine returned to the precept of the gastronomic writer Curnonsky (1872-–1956), 'Gastronomy is when things taste like what they are', that the very technical developments that made such a return possible seem to be menacing its survival.

KEITH READER

See also: fast food; wine

Further reading

Fischler, C. (1990/3) *L'Homnivore*, Paris: Odile Jacob/Points (a fascinating socio-anthropological overview, striking a good balance between information and interpretation).

Gillet, P. (1994) *Soyons français à table!*, Paris: Payot/Rivages (contains a helpful glossary of key names and figures).

Guérard, M. (1976) *La Grande Cuisine minceur*, Paris: Robert Laffont (an eloquent plea for the new style of cooking).

Mennell, S. (1985) *All Manners of Food (Eating and Taste in England and France from the Middle Ages to the Present)*, Oxford: Blackwell (the most thorough and

scholarly historical overview readily available).

——(1993) 'Food and Wine', in M. Cook (ed.) *French Culture Since 1945*, Harlow and New York: Longman (a concise distillation of the key developments since the war).

Neirinck, E. and Poulain, J.-P. (1992) *Histoire de la cuisine et des cuisiniers*, Malakoff: Jacques Lanore (a succinct illustrated history, with good biographical and chronological information).

Gatti, Armand

b. 1924, Monaco

Journalist, playwright and director, real name Saveur Dante Gatti

Wartime experiences as a deportee, resistance fighter and prizewinning journalist fuelled many of Gatti's flamboyant political plays. In 1968, he began developing theatre studios for the people of Toulouse and Montreuil, and turned to television, while continuing to develop community theatre projects.

ANNIE SPARKS

See also: theatre

Further reading

Knowles, D. (1989) *Armand Gatti in the Theatre: Wild Duck Against the Wind*, London: Athlone Press (analysis of his life and work).

Gaulle, Charles de

b. 1890, Lille;
d. 1970, Colombey-les-deux-Églises, Haute Marne

Politician

De Gaulle is the outstanding political figure of modern France. Born to a conservative and strongly Catholic family, he embarked on a military career in 1913 and fought in World War I. Between the two wars, he gained a reputation as an unorthodox military thinker and wrote a remarkable study of leadership, *Le Fil de l'épée* (The Sword's Edge). Little known to the general public, he was plucked in May 1940 from obscurity to a junior ministerial post as Under-Secretary for War in the crisis weeks that followed Germany's invasion of France. When the new prime minister, Philippe Pétain, announced that the fighting must stop, de Gaulle flew to London and on 18 June 1940 made the celebrated broadcast inviting those of his compatriots who were able to do so to join him in a Free French movement whose purpose was to continue the struggle against the enemy. This June broadcast is the founding moment of the de Gaulle myth and the basis of his subsequent national legitimacy. At the time, however, it had little impact on a France traumatized by defeat. Even after opposition to the German occupation began to emerge, de Gaulle had great difficulty in getting his authority accepted, not only by other Resistance organizations but also by the United States government, which regarded him as the sort of military dictator against whom the war was being fought. What enabled him to assert his leadership was his single-minded determination not to be pushed aside by the Allied powers and his ability to win the support of the domestic Resistance movement by stressing his commitment to postwar political and social reconstruction. American attempts to exclude him from a role in liberated France failed, and in 1944 he became head of the provisional government of the French Republic, which contained representatives of the major political groupings, including the powerful Communist Party. His government carried out an extensive nationalization programme and organized the referendum of October 1945 on France's constitutional future, which resulted in a massive rejection of a return to the Third Republic and the election of a Constituent Assembly.

The honeymoon between de Gaulle and the political parties did not last long. In January 1946, he stormed out of office and in June made a speech at Bayeux which set out his belief that only a strong presidency, independent of the parties, could give France the strong leadership it needed. This was a challenge to the entrenched Republican doctrine that personal power was incompatible with democracy and that the only genuine Republic was one based on the sovereignty of the National Assembly. The result was open political war between de Gaulle and the parties. In April 1947 he launched a mass political movement, the Rassemblement Pour la France (RPF), which became the spearhead of his campaign to replace the parliamentary constitution of the Fourth Republic. Initially able to capitalize on France's domestic and international difficulties, de Gaulle failed in his ambition of forcing the Fourth Republic to abdicate. In 1954 he withdrew from public life and retreated to his austere country residence at Colombey-les-deux-Églises, where he wrote three highly regarded volumes of war memoirs. It was not the behaviour of a man with a political future.

Yet such a future was to be his. In 1958, faced with the collapse of the authority of the civil government in Algeria and the menace of civil war in France, the bulk of the party leaders turned to him as the one man who could somehow 'win' the war against the Algerian nationalist movement without turning France into a military dictatorship. De Gaulle made his return to power conditional on the right to draw up a constitution which would enable government (by which he meant himself) to govern, and in 1959 became the first president of the Fifth Republic. Between 1958 and 1962 he used referenda to win mass approval for a series of constitutional changes designed first to strengthen the power of the presidency and second to put an end to the ruinous war in Algeria. The decisive year was 1962. Algeria became independent and de Gaulle held, and won, a referendum providing for the direct election of the president. By doing so, he ensured a shift in the balance of political power away from the National Assembly towards the Executive, and in particular the presidency; he also laid the bases for a new party system. With Algeria and a troublesome legislature out of the way, de Gaulle was now able to realize his core ambition of restoring France's status as a major, and independent, player in the international system. To realize the grandeur inherent in his 'certain idea of France', he challenged the right of other powers, be they the Commission of the European Community or the president of the United States, to interfere in French policy. He developed France's independent nuclear deterrent, thwarted Britain's ambitions to join the European Economic Community, withdrew French troops from the integrated command structure of NATO, and launched an attack on the financial pre-eminence of the American dollar. At the same time, he sought to persuade Third World and European countries that France could be an effective champion of their independence against the might of the superpowers and was a strong critic of American involvement in Vietnam. For a man who personified the military virtues of hierarchy and order, de Gaulle showed a singular lack of respect for the conventions of the postwar international order.

De Gaulle's domestic agenda was designed to promote economic modernization and political order. His enthusiasm for state-led technology and industrial modernization was matched by his disdain for what he regarded as the selfish demands of interest groups and the whingeing pieties of opposition liberals. The image he conveyed of caring much more about France than about the French contributed to the unexpectedly good showing of the opposition candidates (notably François **Mitterrand**) in the 1965 presidential elections and to widespread criticisms of his 'solitary exercise of power'. Nothing, however, prepared him – or his political opponents – for the explosion of civil protest which rocked France in **May 1968** and cast an ironic light on his claims to have given France unprecedented political stability. In the short run, de Gaulle was able to ride out the storm, thanks in part to a last, great radio broadcast in which, as in June 1940, he declared his refusal to submit to the pressure of events. But the electoral landslide his support-

ers won in the June elections was a victory much more for law and order than for de Gaulle's heroic vision of France. Less than a year later, he resigned office after the defeat of a referendum on regional reform.

During his lifetime, de Gaulle attracted great devotion from those who regarded him as the two-time (1940 and 1958) saviour of France and as a political genius; he also aroused deep hostility among those, like the followers of Pétain, the French settlers in Algeria, and also the defenders of traditional Republicanism, who paid the price of his success. At the end of the century, there is near consensus in France that he was the country's greatest twentieth-century leader.

PETER MORRIS

See also: Algerian war; constitution of the Fifth Republic; European economic integration; European Union; parties and movements

Major works

Gaulle, C. de (1956–9) *Mémoires de guerre*, Paris: Plon (de Gaulle's own record of his wartime career).
——(1970–1) *Mémoires d'espoir*, Paris: Plon (de Gaulle records his postwar career).
——(1975) *Articles et écrits*, Paris: Plon (a useful anthology).

Further reading

Lacouture, J. (1986) *De Gaulle*, 3 vols, Paris: Éditions du Seuil. Vol. 1 translated P. O'Brian (1993) *De Gaulle: The Rebel, 1890–1944*, New York: W. W. Norton and London: Harvill; vol. 2 translated A. Sheridan (1993) *De Gaulle: The Ruler, 1945–1970*, New York: W.W. Norton and London: Harvill (a magisterial political biography).
Williams, P. M. and Harrison, M. (1973) *Politics and Society in de Gaulle's Republic*, New York (the best English-language introduction).

Gaultier, Jean-Paul

b. 1952, Arcueil

Fashion designer

Known for the irreverence and humour of his designs, Gaultier's forte is the glamorization of street style at couture level. He established his house in 1977 and his first menswear line in 1984. His eclectic references range from punk to Victorian underwear, and his corset designs for Madonna's 'Blonde Ambition' tour received global attention. Gaultier's technical virtuosity, gleaned from his training at traditional French couture houses, allows him to play with conventional ideas of gender and manipulate body forms through careful tailoring. He has hit the headlines frequently with his skirts and corsets for men, and also for his costumes for **Besson**'s *Le Cinquième Élément* (1997).

NICOLA WHITE

See also: fashion

gay activism

Although the 1980s and 1990s have seen the rise of gay activism and increasing coverage in mainstream media, gay activists have long been in existence. **Vichy**-inspired laws for the protection of minors, preventing same-sex relationships with men under 21 years of age, remained on the statute book until 1981 when, in the wake of **Mitterrand**'s election, they were repealed and the age of consent equalized at 15. Any apparent reluctance to change the law between 1945 and 1981 may be seen to be linked to the inherent conservatism of the MRP and Gaullist regimes that followed the war.

The radicalization of 'homosexuals' around the events of **May 1968** led to the establishment of the Comité d'Action Pédérastique Révolutionnaire (CAPR) – a short-lived organization, since the (bourgeois) concept of homosexuality could arguably have no place within a revolutionary context. Some three years later,

in March 1971, the Front Homosexuel d'Action Révolutionnaire (FHAR), in favour of direct action for the achievement of gay liberation, came into being after the disruption of a radio programme on homosexuality. In line with the general decline in radical politics post-May 1968, FHAR ceased to exist in mid-1973.

1974 saw the birth of the Groupe de Libération Homosexuelle (GLH), formed by ex-militants from FHAR. Divisions among its members between reformists and revolutionaries led in 1987 to the establishment of two separate groups – the GLH – Groupe de Base (GLH-GB) comprising reformists, and the GLH – Politique et Quotidien (GLH-PQ), the revolutionaries. The lack of cohesion resulting from such a split led to the creation of a Centre d'Information et de Documentation sur l'Homosexualité (CIDH), providing information as its name suggests. Although the GLH-GB ceased to exist in 1976, the GLH-PQ persisted, forcing the PCF to adopt an anti-discrimination policy in July 1977. Two gay candidates stood in the 1978 parliamentary elections, but their presence could be seen as the last throes of the group.

Survivors from the Marseille GLH-PQ group created the Comité d'Urgence Antirépression Homosexuelle (CUARH) in 1979, a federation of Parisian and regional groups with different religious and political backgrounds. From 1980 to the elections of 1981, CUARH provided a mobilizing force for many gays, organizing a demonstration of some 10,000 participants in April 1981 and launching its own newspaper *Homophonies*.

In the non-political sphere, Catholics had founded David et Jonathan in 1972, with Protestants led by Pastor Joseph Doucé (himself murdered in 1990) founding the Centre du Christ Libérateur in 1976.

Although Mitterrand repealed repressive legislation in 1981 and freed civil servants from the 'good morality' clause which had blocked promotions within the civil service, repression remained elsewhere, for example with elements within the police (and the Senate) resisting the abolition of police squads established to monitor homosexuals. Raids on gay bars continued, though with lessening frequency. Politically, the group Gais pour les Libertés was launched in 1985, enjoying wider political support than the PS's own Homosexualité et Socialisme. Groups on the Right began to find a gay voice around this period, with the establishment in 1984 of the Mouvement des Gays Libéraux (MGL), and even that of an extreme Right group called Gaie France in 1987.

It was around this time that France also began to see cases of what is certainly the most powerful mobilizing activist force around questions of homosexuality, HIV and **AIDS** (though AIDS is not, of course, an exclusively homosexual problem). The activities of ACT-UP (the AIDS Coalition to Unleash Power) provide a focus for the frustration felt by many suffering from the syndrome, seeking as they do to bring the plight of PWAs (people with AIDS) to public attention through rapid action tactics, 'zapping' meetings, boycotting/blockading laboratories, pharmaceutical companies and so on. The reasoning behind their actions is simple: silence equals death, action equals life. Their action is intended to provoke *re*action.

ACT-UP's origins in France may be traced to 1987, when Didier Lestrade – until recently the group's chair, and now editor of the gay monthly *Têtu* – became aware of the concept on a trip to New York. Struck by the simple achievements of direct action, he spent as much time as possible between 1987 and 1989 finding out more about it. At the 1989 Gay Pride march in Paris, fifteen French 'militants' in T-shirts brought over from New York handed out simple photocopied sheets of paper that had been typed in the offices of *Gai Pied*, asking for supporters. On 26 July 1989, the required paperwork founding the organization was lodged with the authorities, and ACT-UP in France was in official existence.

From practically its first action on 2 October 1989 (demonstrating in front of the National Assembly), through protests in front of Notre-Dame against the Catholic church's ban on contraception, pickets of the Ministry of Health and of laboratories known to be conducting

multiple (instead of individual) HIV tests, ACT-UP has ensured that problems around AIDS are not left quietly to go away. Although initially quite small, the group has grown: with 200 militants in Paris alone, ACT-UP is now larger than the New York group, which has itself split because of internal problems.

At the same time as AIDS has served to crystallize activity and activism, the gay community as a whole has become more visible in France, with the 1995 Paris Gay Pride gaining wide coverage in the mainstream press. This visibility, partly arrived at through greater confidence in openness around one's sexuality, is in no small way a tribute to the changes in tolerance and acceptability that have been achieved through the actions of activists since 1945. There is still a long way to go – for example, the recognition of gay partnerships – but progress is slow but sure.

STEVE WHARTON

See also: Catholicism and Protestantism; feminism (movements/groups); gay press; lesbian activism; parties and movements

Further reading

ACT-UP Paris (1994) *Le Sida: combien de divisions?*, Paris: Éditions Dagorno (a good overview of the motivations and activities of ACT-UP, written by those most directly involved).

Darier, E. (1987) 'The Gay Movement in French Society Since 1945', *Modern and Contemporary France* 29 (charts the main historical developments of gay activism up to the mid-1980s).

Martel, F. (1996) *Le Rose et le noir*, Paris: Éditions du Seuil (a controversial account of the modern French gay and lesbian cultural and political scene).

Martet, C. (1993) *Les Combattants du sida*, Paris: Flammarion (the history of ACT-UP in France written by one of its founder members).

gay cinema

In the 1980s and 1990s, representations of central lesbian, gay and bisexual characters have become more common in mainstream French cinema. Examples include: the *La Cage aux Folles* series (I and II directed by Édouard Molinaro in 1978 and 1980; III by Georges Lautner in 1985); *Chacun cherche son chat*, directed by Cédric Klapisch in 1996; *Deux lions au soleil*, directed by Claude Faraldo in 1980; Josiane **Balasko**'s 1995 *French Twist* (*Gazon maudit*); *Tenue de soirée* by Bertrand **Blier** (1986); and Yannick **Bellon**'s *La Triche* from 1984. The context of changing sexual discourses, and the complexities of their reception by gay audiences, mean that they are relevant to any discussion of 'gay cinema'. In addition, classical French cinema has had its gay directors, most notably Marcel Carné. However, a different perspective arises if we understand the term to mean 'films made by lesbians and gay men with lesbian and gay subject-matter' (see Dyer 1990). The history of these films – distinct in France from developments in Anglo-Saxon countries – begins with Cocteau and **Genet**, continues in marginal, politicized filmmaking from 1968 to about 1981, and produces recognized auteurs in the form of **Chéreau, Collard, Téchiné** and Vecchiali.

Male homosexuality, first criminalized by the **Vichy** regime, remained oppressed in the postwar period, and its first cinematic expressions are firmly located in high literary culture. Aestheticism, narcissism, the links between same-sex desire, poetry and death are all on display in Jean Cocteau's *Orphée* (1949), a transposition of the Orpheus and Eurydice myth (starring Cocteau's lover Jean Marais) to postwar Paris and the existentialist heyday. Another reworking of myth, his *Beauty and the Beast* (*La Belle et la bête*) of 1946, can also be read homoerotically, especially as the three protagonists of the final transfiguration are all played by Marais. The elusive symbolism and anti-realism of these films distinguish them in part from the most famous of Genet's sorties into cinema, *Un chant d'amour* of 1950, which is silent, lasts twenty minutes, and was not given a commercial release. Scenes in a prison, where a guard spies on men masturbating in their cells or communicating with each other through the walls, alternate with shots of a garland of flowers being swung from a cell window, and of the men in the film making love. However, Cocteau's influence is not far away: aestheticism in Genet is combined with the homoerotic and a poetry of the sordid, marginal and 'lower depths' to produce one of cinema's most profound meditations on the links society constructs between homosexuality and criminality, power and homophobia.

The oppressive postwar climate for homosexuals began to weaken only in the aftermath of **May 1968**, which also created more spaces for independent and avant-garde film. The 1970s were the heyday of affirmation films from the gay movement. The GLH-PQ (Groupe de Libération Homosexuelle – Politique et Quotidien) organized film festivals in 1977 and 1978 in Paris which embraced **pornography** but also showcased short films such as *Hommes entre eux*, directed by Norbert Terry, and *La Banque du sperme*, by Pierre Chabal and Philippe Genet, which cheerfully played with both porn and political or philosophical preoccupations. Perhaps the most consistent film-maker of this type was Lionel Soukaz, who made two films in collaboration with Guy **Hocquenghem**, *Race d'ep!* (backslang for 'pederast') in 1979, a documentary on 'gay history' rounded off by a cruising dialogue in the Tuileries, and *Toni* in 1980, as well as *Boy Friend 1* and *Boy Friend 2* (1977), *Le Sexe des anges* in 1978 and *Ixe* (1980).

The Socialist government's reforms and the consumerist appropriation of much gay culture in the 1980s meant that, with the diminution of gay militancy, it became less clear what a 'gay cinema' might be. The more positive images to be found in mainstream film were neither a way of placing gay desire dynamically in the forefront of a postmodernist cinema, as with Almodovar's activities in post-Franco Spain, nor were they to be challenged by a 'New Queer Cinema' in the Anglo-Saxon sense, which would provocatively revel in the abject. The lack of a tradition of identity politics in

Republican France meant that directors, audiences and critics, whether straight or gay, often tended to down-play the specificity of gay representation in favour of an individualist, integrative or universalist outlook. Thus Patrice Chéreau's *L'Homme blessé* of 1983, with a script co-written by Hervé **Guibert**, both owes much to Genet in its iconography and decor (the toilets of the Gare du Nord, for example), and at the same time situates itself in a French tradition of portraying the crystallization and consequences of *l'amour fou*, in this case the awakening gay passion of a teenager played by Jean-Hugues Anglade. This approach is also to be found in French 'AIDS films', such as Paul Vecchiali's *Encore* from 1988 and Cyril Collard's *Savage Nights* (*Les Nuits fauves*) of 1992, with their 'bisexual' protagonists, lack of reference to any kind of gay or activist community, and positioning of the illness within existentialist and Romantic narratives of self-discovery. (This is the approach favoured by the 'straight' **AIDS** film that is Xavier Beauvois's *N'oublie pas que tu vas mourir* of 1996.) At their best, however, these French constructions of homosexuality produce the films of André **Téchiné**, whose consistent output since the 1970s depicts in 'relaxed' and empathetic fashion the complex social and historical interactions that go to make up his straight and gay characters, whether the postal worker in 1981's *Hôtel des Amériques*, the young hustler in *J'embrasse pas* (1991) or the adolescent in the 1963 setting of *Les Roseaux sauvages* (1994).

The emphasis on auteurism in critical discourse, and the continued sexism of the French film industry, have militated against the emergence of a distinctive lesbian cinema in France. Chantal Akerman is Belgian. **Women directors** have tended not to identify as a group or (with the exception of **Varda**) as feminist. Mention should be made of Diane **Kurys's** *Coup de foudre* from 1983, a commercial mainstream film portraying the relationship between two women, played by **Miou-Miou** and Isabelle **Huppert**, in 1950s France, but here, typically, any sexual relations between them are merely hinted at and never named.

BILL MARSHALL

See also: existentialism; gay writing

Further reading

Dyer, R. (1990) *Now You See It: Studies on Lesbian and Gay Film*, London: Routledge.

gay press

The launch of the newsletter *Futur* in October 1952 marked perhaps the beginnings of what we now understand as the gay press in twentieth-century France. Drawing on the works of 'homosexual' writers such as Gide (thereby, arguably, acknowledging that literature has long been a privileged means of expressing 'homosexual' desire), *Futur* also aimed to be a newsletter on 'information and sexual freedom' in the wake of the Kinsey Report. Legal battles over the banning of its advertisements, and restrictions on sales to over-18s, were to force its closure in November 1955.

January 1955 saw the launch of *Arcadie*, seeking to enlighten the French with rational scientific arguments concerning homosexuality. From an initial 1,500 subscribers, figures rose to some 10,000 in 1960. It was to be from these ranks that most of new gay organizations emerged in the 1970s and 1980s.

Launched in April 1983, *Gai Pied*, which ceased publication in 1991, offered a weekly overview of the main political, cultural and social events on the gay scene in France and the world. In recognition of the growing power of the so-called 'pink franc', it also carried advertising from the gay commercial scene. Government activity in the early 1990s, which was aimed at reducing the number of *messageries roses* ('lewd' chatlines and small ads), impacted on the publisher's income base to the extent that the magazine ceased publication, to be replaced by the intermittent *La Lettre de Gai Pied*, available on subscription. The company responsible for *Gai Pied*'s publication, Les

Éditions du Triangle Rose, continues its **publishing** activities in other areas, for example with the bilingual *Guide gai* covering the scene in France, Belgium and Switzerland, and Minitel services.

Illico, published monthly in A5 format, offers a good overview of events, with editorial comment and articles on burning issues of the day. Broadsheet format *Exit (le journal)*, published monthly since 1993, carries national and international news and current affairs items.

A more recent arrival has been *Têtu*, the first colour monthly for lesbians and gays, launched in Easter 1995. Edited by Didier Lestrade of ACT-UP, it aims to inform and entertain, calling for greater involvement in activities by members of the lesbian and gay community. Indeed, it was launched with a challenge to gays and lesbians to demonstrate their sexuality concretely by buying the magazine and helping to ensure its survival. Despite an apparently rocky start, sales have grown slowly.

Since the 1950s, then, the gay press has moved from initial tentative moves to explore discussion of homosexuality to a more upfront, open interaction, with events nationally and internationally. The growth in the visibility of the 'pink franc' has aided this phenomenon, which is far from over.

STEVE WHARTON

See also: AIDS; gay activism; lesbian press

gay writing

Although less established as a *genre* than in the Anglo-American world, gay writing – understood here as literature written by or about male homosexuals – is increasingly recognized in France. This is due to a number of factors: literary giants of the earlier part of the twentieth century like Proust, Gide and **Genet** can, notwithstanding their own different positions and allegiances, be identified as key contributors to a specifically gay tradition, alongside a

constellation of other, almost equally eminent – and prolific – writers with at least intermittently specific 'gay themes': Marcel **Jouhandeau**, Henri de Montherlant, Jean Cocteau, Julien Green, Michel **Tournier**, Roger Peyrefitte. A second factor is the substantial oeuvre of more recently established writers, who use particular forms of writing, such as variants on the first-person narrative, journal or diary, and particular themes, such as eroticism, violence and **AIDS**, to explore and question different forms of identity and sexuality. Particularly notable here are Renaud **Camus**, Conrad Detrez, Dominique **Fernandez**, Hervé **Guibert**, Guy **Hocquenghem**, Hugo Marsan and Yves **Navarre**. Third, against this background of real or fictionalized biographies, and of the increasing 'intertextual' cross-fertilization of literary and non-literary genres, the work of eminent critics such as Roland **Barthes** and social analysts such as Michel **Foucault** is being similarly mined for its implications for gay identity and culture. As a wide-ranging account of the different discourses surrounding the evolving notion of homosexuality, from classical to contemporary, Foucault's (1976–84) three-volume *History of Sexuality* (*Histoire de la sexualité*) is, moreover, a landmark for gay studies. Fourth, by emphasizing the gender-relatedness of thinking and production across the humanities, the social sciences and the sciences, feminist, lesbian and queer theorists from both sides of the Atlantic have helped give gender-related writing – *écriture gaie*, by analogy with *écriture féminine* – and particular forms of gendered intertextuality (such as fiction and medicine in 'the AIDS novel') a clearer space and a stronger platform. Finally, there is no doubt that the strength of gay writing in France goes with the heightened gay visibility, energy and creativity in many parts of the globe, from San Francisco to Sydney.

Despite – or perhaps because of – this relative visibility, at least in the cities, the issue of growing up/'coming out' as gay is an important theme. Although evocations of adolescent or post-adolescent sexuality may be accompanied by a 1960s sense of liberated eroticism as in Roger Peyrefitte's 1979 *Roy* (admittedly set in California), such newly discovered sexuality can also be intensely problematic, either because it is associated with young male violence, as in Éric Jourdan's 1984 *Les Mauvais Anges* (The Bad Angels) (banned since 1956) or because it leads to a sense of isolation and rootlessness: Loïc Chotard's first novel *Tiers Monde* (1994) (Third World) follows the desultory, almost despairing, erotico-sentimental *flâneries* of a group of youngsters in a cocooning but anonymous Paris. Equally problematic is the viewing of adolescent sexuality from the perspective of the potentially exploitative older male partner. Even if, as Christopher Robinson has indicated, adolescent sex 'is not, in a French text, automatically a pederastic theme', the older male tends to be either provocatively self-justificatory, as in Tony **Duvert**'s *Journal d'un innocent* (Diary of an Innocent) of 1976; masochistic and wistful, as in Julien Green's 1974 *Youth* (*Jeunesse*); or reproaching himself with the suicide of the younger partner, as in Roger Vrigny's *Le Garçon d'orage* (The Storm-Boy) from 1994. The voyeurism and the power of the older male is, however, repudiated in Guillaume Le Touze's *Comme ton père* (Like Your Father), also of 1994. The dying Giuseppe takes refuge, along with his mother, Claudia, in the retreat of his gay father, Paul, in a remote part of Africa – the fusion of gay, straight and cross-generational bonds gives all the characters new strength and serenity. In Michel Braudeau's 1992 *Le Livre de John* (John's Book) and 1993 *Mon ami Pierrot* (My Friend Pierrot), intimacy between different generations of males raises the issue of homoeroticism in actual or adoptive paternities. The novel of sexual initiation is thus opening up and out into more general questions about male-to-male relationships, masculinity, fatherhood, homosexuality – and gay writing.

Another way of interrogating (gay) male identity is by associating it with violence, whether the violence of social stigmatization, as in Navarre's 1980 Goncourt-winning *Cronos' Children* (*Le Jardin d'acclimatation*), or the violence of self-oppressive masochism, or 'natural' male violence converted into ritual-ized, sadistic male-to-male relationships. Internalized, masochistic violence is shown to be a source of pain, self-reappraisal and creative energy in writers such as Marcel Proust, André Gide, Julien Green and the Japanese writer influential in France, Yukio Mishima (*Confessions of a Mask*). Ritualized or consenting/unconsenting violence, in the *écrivain maudit* tradition exemplified by Sade, Mirbeau and **Bataille**, features in Tony Duvert's *Paysage de fantaisie* (Imagined Country) of 1973; Jean Genet's *Funeral Rites* (*Pompes funèbres*) and *The Thief's Journal* (*Journal du voleur*) from 1947 and 1949; Hervé Guibert's *Vous m'avez fait former des fantômes* (You Made Me Invent Ghosts) from 1987; Pierre Guyotat's 1970 *Éden, Éden, Éden*; and Éric Jourdan's *Charité* (1991), *Révolte* (1991) and *Sang* (1992). Here the main characters, who usually (but not invariably) self-identify as gay, foreground their position of outsiders and outlaws through a violence which can, like gay SM, be seen as either gender-stereotypical or as self-ironizing and subversive. This writing – as, for example, in Guyotat's incorporation of blood and semen – also reflects an attempt to write (with) the male body and 'to put the sex back into homosexuality' in forceful and intentionally shocking ways. A celebrated example of this is Renaud Camus's *Tricks* (1988), whose description of some forty-six one-night stands achieves a certain verbal and psychological violence through relentless repetition, even if actual physical violence is absent from the 'tricks' themselves.

Another form of violence which inevitably questions both identity and its inscriptions (both written and visual) can be found in works which treat AIDS. The most well-known of these are, perhaps, Hervé Guibert's three novels – *To the Friend Who Did Not Save My Life* (*A l'ami qui ne m'a pas sauvé la vie*) of 1990, which, notoriously, evokes Foucault via the character of Muzil; *The Compassion Protocol* (*Le Protocole compassionnel*) from 1991 and *Cytomégalovirus* (1992) – together with his 1992 televised film-journal of his own body with AIDS, *La Pudeur ou l'impudeur* (Modesty or Immodesty). Guibert's surgically

precise self-analyses contrast with the exuberant brinkmanship of Cyril **Collard**'s *Savage
Nights* (*Les Nuits fauves*), both in its novel
(1989) and his highly successful film version,
with himself in the lead role (1992). Different
again are other works by well-known writers,
such as Dominique Fernandez's 1987 *La Gloire
du paria* (The Glory of the Pariah), Guy
Hocquenghem's *Ève* (1987), Yves Navarre's *Ce
sont amis que vent emporte* (It is Friends the
Wind Bears Away) from 1991, and Alain-
Emmanuel Dreuilhe's 1987 *Corps à corps:
journal du sida* (Body to Body – An AIDS
Diary). In most of these, anger at medical inadequacy and social ostracization tends to recede
before the loyalty and devotion provoked
(within the partnerships affected) by the
prospect of death. In Fernandez's *La Gloire du
paria*, moreover, the onset of AIDS reassures
the older, 'neo-romantic' partner, Bernard, that
he is still different, still the eternal rebel, still
the outlaw – a theme repeated in his racy
provocatively decadent historical novel, *Le
Dernier des Médicis* (1994). In *Ève* and *Ce sont
amis que vent emporte* death from AIDS is at
least partly redeemed by the presence of a
healthy daughter or son to continue life in their
father's place. Elsewhere, in Hugo Marsan's
1995 *Les Absents* (The Absent Ones) and Jean-
Noël Pancrazi's 1990 *Les Quartiers d'hiver*
(Winter Quarters), very different clandestine
bars (La Maison Rose and Le Vagabond
respectively) are haunted by a sense of AIDS-
associated death: instead of the visible, lived illness of Guibert, AIDS infiltrates as an image of
nostalgia, inertia and decay. Rather than being
etched in and on the body, AIDS contributes to
the embodiment of an aesthetic.

By endowing both past pleasures and present
intimacies with a sense of irretrievable loss,
AIDS novels also develop two related leitmotifs
of gay, gay-authored or at least sexually ambivalent fiction – the cultivation of a moral, physical
or aesthetic asceticism and of a certain erotico-
philosophical mysticism – evident, for example,
in the very different works of Gide, Green,
Mauriac, Montherlant and even Proust. This
combination of asceticism, eroticism and mysticism also links to the topos of the 'gay martyr',

evoked by the title of **Sartre**'s *Saint Genet*
(1952) and described with relish by Mishima
(the St Sebastian theme) and Jourdan. An initially more positive version of the same combination can be found in novels such as Michel
Tournier's *Les Météores* (1975) where the
homosexual Alexandre seeks to sexualize social
rejection in a hunt for 'exogamic' partners and
to sublimate his sense of abjection through
'endogamic' fraternal union. Alexandre does,
however, achieve neither of these unions, since
he is murdered mid-'*chasse aux garçons*' in
North Africa. Erotico-mystical unions, whether
through brother-twins (*Les Météores*), boy pair-
ings (Jourdan's *Les Mauvais Anges*) or doubling
across generations (the two Adams in
Hocquenghem's *Ève*, and the various Romans
in Jourdan's *Révolte* and *Sang*), fail ultimately
to shield men from the sterility and death which
haunt Marsan's *Les Absents* and Pancrazi's *Les
Quartiers d'hiver*. A more humorous, satirical
version of this erotico-mystical union is to be
found in Conrad Detrez's 1975 *Les Plumes du
coq* (Cockfeathers), where the supposedly
closed world of the Catholic boarding school is
the incongruous launch pad for revolt, violence
and farmyard intimacies. In Renaud Camus's *Le
Chasseur de lumières* (The Light Tracker) of
1993, it is again the setting of the novel, here the
semi-spiritualized countryside of Gascony,
which offers glimpses of erotico-mystical union
between its interlinked characters, notably
between the young *chasseur de lumières* and
landscape photographer Vincent, and the older,
impecunious, semi-aristocratic Adam. Despite
Vincent's reappearance in Camus's *L'Épuisant
Désir de ces choses* (The Draining Desire for
Such Things), contact between the characters is
here even more spasmodic and elusive: mystical
union gives way to self-conscious intertextual
play and eroticism to an unspecified longing in
absence. The combination of asceticism, eroticism and mysticism has itself been absorbed into
a self-conscious narrative style – whether the
baroque extravaganzas of Detrez or the impres-
sionistic kaleidoscopes of Camus.

Given that the interrogation of identity has
been one of the hallmarks of gay writing from
Proust and Gide through to Pancrazi and

Guibert, it is appropriate that this interrogation be accompanied by a corresponding exploration of literary forms, notably the first-person narration. The commodiousness and the flexibility of first-person narrative allows for the identity of author and characters to be inextricably fused and confused – as in Collard's *Les Nuits fauves* – or simultaneously revealed and masked – as in Duvert's *Journal d'un innocent* – or for the writer to be both exposed and distanced as in the multi-person *Roland Barthes par Roland Barthes* (1975) and in nearly all Guibert's oeuvre. The first-person narrative also allows for very different representations of the male body, from René Crevel's surreal *Mon corps et moi* (1925) to Navarre's 1979 wistfully melancholic *Le Temps voulu* (Time Willed), and to Jouhandeau's erotic *Chronique d'une passion* (1949) and *Tirésias* (1954). The first-person narrative also allows for intermittent or extended flashbacks to point to the pain or the pleasures of memory (Camus, Navarre), while the juxtaposition of multiple-person narratives within the one novel creates complementary or divergent perspectives: Le Touze, Marsan, Tournier. When these are combined with a rich vein of third-person narratives, whether formally conventional (Navarre, Pancrazi, Vrigny) or unconventional (Camus, Detrez), or simply flamboyantly erotic (Éric Jourdan's *Sexuellement incorrect* of 1995) it can be seen that gay writing in France is sufficiently substantial and varied for its explorations of the gay self, the gay body and gay identity to offer a map and a platform for the future.

OWEN HEATHCOTE

See also: autobiography; gay cinema; women's/lesbian writing

Further reading

Heathcote, O., Hughes, A. and Williams, J. (eds) (1998) *Gay Signatures*, Oxford: Berg (essays on a range of French gay and lesbian writers and film-makers; a general theoretical and analytical introduction).

Larivière, M. (ed.) (1984) *Les Amours masculines: anthologie de l'homosexualité dans la littérature*, preface by Dominique Fernandez, Paris: Lieu Commun (includes extracts from some fifty twentieth-century writers, mainly French but not exclusively).

Lévy, J. and Nouss, A. (eds) (1994) *Sida-Fiction: essai d'anthropologie romanesque*, Lyon: Presses Universitaires de Lyon (useful, wide-ranging, essentially descriptive survey; bibliography).

Lilly, M. (1993) *Gay Men's Literature in the Twentieth Century*, Basingstoke: Macmillan.

Malinowski, S. (ed.) (1994) *Gay and Lesbian Literature*, Detroit and London: St James Press.

Maxence, J.-L. (1995) *Les Écrivains sacrifiés des années sida*, Paris: Bayard (short, readable review-style accounts of Aron, Collard, Detrez, Dreuilhe, De Duve, Foucault, Guibert and Hocquenghem).

Robinson, C. (1995) *Scandal in the Ink: Male and Female Homosexuality in Twentieth-Century French Literature*, London: Cassell. (very useful overview)

Schehr, L. (1995a) *Alcibiades at the Door: Gay Discourses in French Literature*, Stanford: Stanford University Press (identifies and analyses a homosexual poiesis in Crevel, Sartre, Gide, Barthes and Guibert; bibliography).

——(1995b) *The Shock of Men: Homosexual Hermeneutics in French Writing*, Stanford: Stanford University Press (tests the idea of homosexuality as a mode of interpretation and subversion in Gide, Foucault, Proust, Barthes, Renaud Camus and Tournier; bibliography).

Stambolian, G. and Marks, E. (eds) (1979) *Homosexualities in French Literature*, Ithaca, NY and London: Cornell (early seminal collection of essays).

Geismar, Alain

b. 1939, Paris

Academic

A physicist and *Ingénieur des Mines*, Geismar became a university teacher in Paris in 1963 and general secretary of the higher education teachers' union (SNESup) in 1967. He was catapulted to notoriety as one of the triumvirate (alongside Daniel **Cohn-Bendit** and Jacques Sauvageot) who acted as leaders and spokespersons for the **May 1968** student movement. His 'Maoist' political affiliations in the immediate post-1968 years seem to have had no adverse effect on his subsequent career. He was an official in the Département d'Education Permanente (1974–8) and vice-president of the University of Paris VII (1982–4). In 1985, he became assistant director-general of the Agence de l'Informatique and later acted as an adviser to Jack **Lang**, when he was Minister of Culture.

LAURENCE BELL

See also: parties and movements

Genet, Jean

b. 1910, Paris;
d. 1986, Paris

Writer, dramatist, poet, essayist and political activist

One of the great lyrical writers of modern times, as well as one of the most shocking, Genet spent much of his life creating an image of himself as the archetypal outcast: a thief, a traitor and a homosexual. However, even his most meticulous biographers cannot agree on the sequence – or, indeed, the truth – of the major events in his life. He was certainly abandoned as an infant by his mother, never knew who his father was, and was raised by a foster family in the Morvan. His childhood was much happier and calmer than he would have us

believe, but he had to leave the Régnier family at the age of 13 to learn a trade; after ten days he ran away from the school where he had been sent to learn typography and began a life of petty crime that resulted in him finally being sent to Mettray Reformatory until he was 21. He had his first homosexual experiences there, and in his 1946 novel, *Miracle de la rose*, transformed this borstal into a paradise of mystical and melancholy passions. His first important works are autobiographical novels, even *Querelle de Brest*, the only novel in which 'Genet' is neither a character nor the narrator. These novels can perhaps best be seen as *autofictions*, as the traces of a life that was both lived and invented, both real and imaginary. In them, Genet juxtaposes confession, imagination and scandalous provocation, creating a world in which established social and moral systems are both inverted and (paradoxically) maintained, a fictional world which he called – and which was – his '*chant d'amour*'. In *The Thief's Journal* (*Journal du voleur*), the most evidently autobiographical of his texts, he repeatedly insists that his aim was to make his life a legend: for him, his 'real' life was only ever the preparation for further adventures that would find their full meaning only when written down – and read. In fact, Genet's true triumph over a society he both despised and needed was through language – it was in and by his writing that he defined himself and defied society.

Among his early admirers were Cocteau and **Sartre**, who obtained a presidential pardon for him in 1949. This public recognition, however, amounted in his eyes also to recuperation of him by society, and when it was followed in 1952 by Sartre's monumental biography *Saint Genet*, which presented him as an existentialist hero, he burned all the unpublished manuscripts he had written over the previous five years and thereafter wrote no more fiction. At the heart of his work lies a duality whereby every act elicits and merits both praise and condemnation. But Genet does not seek resolution of such oppositions; rather he envisages a transcendence of them in and through poetry. In the mid-1950s he devoted himself to theatre, repeatedly presenting his vision of a world divided into oppressors and oppressed, the latter able to conceive their function only in terms of the needs and desires of the oppressors. His plays all have a political dimension – notably *The Blacks* (*Les Nègres*), with its exposition of the impotence of the blacks' attempts at revolt, and *The Screens* (*Les Paravents*), set in Algeria, which scandalized French society with its indictment of colonial conflict. While Genet's theatre highlights the urgent reality and importance of struggle, it is also highly ritualized, the distinction between illusion and reality being blurred and language being used less as a means of communication than as a constant fountain of incantation.

In 1964, the suicide of his lover Abdallah (a young tightrope walker) devastated Genet, who once again destroyed his manuscripts and disappeared, reappearing as a political activist, working with the Black Panthers in the United States and then with Yasser Arafat and the PLO. These activities inspired his last finished work, *Prisoner of Love* (*Un Captif amoureux*), a book in which he explicitly swears to tell the whole truth as in a court of law. Much more than a political book, it is a speculation on the nature of truth, a meditation on the interdependence of egoism and altruism, an exploration of different narrative techniques and, above all, a hymn to love, both erotic and fraternal. Here Genet finally presents us with a non-erotic couple, Hamza, a young *feddai*, and his mother, and the book draws together all of Genet's philosophical, political, theological and mythological ideas as well as many biographical references, into a new vision of unity centred on a sense of family and community. In one of the most radical and astonishing reversals of his career, Genet, who had often parodied the cult and iconography of the Virgin Mary, as in his novel *Our Lady of the Flowers* (*Notre-Dame-des-Fleurs*), places at the centre of this, his last book, the Christian image of the *pietà* and the figure of Mary *mater dolorosa*, who in the very moment of her mourning is able to forgive everything and everyone. Several posthumous works have been published, but none has the force or the profound emotion of this work of redemption and reconciliation.

Michael Worton

See also: autobiography; existentialism; gay writing; theatre

Further reading

Brooks, P. and Halpern, J. (eds) (1975) *Jean Genet*, Eaglewood Cliffs, NJ: Prentice Hall (an anthology of essays by such distinguished critics as Sartre, Bataille and Richard Coe).

Moraly, J.-B. (1988) *Jean Genet: la vie écrite*, Paris: Éditions de la Différence (convincingly challenges the legend Genet made of himself and shows how a concern with writing determined all of Genet's life choices).

Sartre, J.-P. (1952), *Saint Genet, comédien et martyr*, Paris: Gallimard. Translated B. Frechtman (1988) *Saint Genet: Actor and Martyr*, London: Heinemann (this 'existential biography', which continues to dominate thinking on Genet, traces what it calls the history of a liberation; for Sartre, Genet underwent three metamorphoses: the child became a thief, the thief became an aesthete, and the aesthete finally became a writer).

Savona, J. (1983) *Jean Genet*, London: Macmillan (an excellent introduction to the theatre, in which each play is analysed separately).

White, E. (1993) *Jean Genet*, London: Chatto & Windus (a monumental and meticulous biography which focuses on Genet's homosexuality; particularly interesting on Genet's responses to painting).

Genette, Gérard

b. 1930

Literary theorist and critic

Genette has published several important essays

on literary forms. His 1972 *Discours du récit* (translated in 1980 as *Narrative Discourse*), which attempts to build a comprehensive theory of narrative, based on copious examples from Proust's work, has been particularly influential in the field of poetics. His original categories for analysing time in the novel and his concept of focalization have, for example, been widely quoted.

BÉATRICE DAMAMME-GILBERT

See also: Barthes, Roland; Greimas, A. J.; linguistic/discourse theory; structuralism

Further reading

Rimmon-Kenan, S. (1983) *Narrative Fiction: Contemporary Poetics*, London and New York: Routledge (refers extensively to Genette's work).

Giacometti, Alberto

b. 1901, Borgonovo, Switzerland; d. 1966, Chur, Switzerland

Artist

Giacometti's early work, after his move to Paris in 1922, was influenced by Brancusi, Cubism via **Lipchitz** and, more significantly, the Surrealist movement. After the war he produced the **sculpture** for which he is best known – his attenuated, almost undifferentiated, bronze figures, isolated or in groups, seen as if from a distance and inviting comparisons, during this postwar period, with concentration camp victims or displaced persons. The critical recognition and international acclaim these works received was largely due to their endorsement by Jean-Paul **Sartre**, who discerned in Giacometti's rejection of the traditional sculptural presentation of the human figure an assertion of the artist's existential freedom and saw in the figures themselves the

spiritual isolation of the human condition as interpreted by **existentialism**.

CAROL WILCOX

Gipsy Kings

Musicians

A paradox of the French pop scene, the Gipsy Kings are a highly talented group of gypsy musicians who sing in Spanish and manage to 'represent' France at some official cultural events. They are based in France and provide evidence of the multicultural heritage of their 'adopted' country, with its tradition of openly welcoming artists of other nationalities. Their latest productions are *Este mundo* (1991) and *Love et liberté* (1993).

GÉRARD POULET

See also: song/*chanson*

Girard, René

b. 1923, Avignon

Philosopher and critic

In novels, primitive mythology and the Bible, Girard discerns an essential association between violence and desire, and an opposition between desire and knowledge. *Deceit, Desire and the Novel: Self and Other in Literary Structures* (*Mensonge romantique, vérité romanesque*) of 1961 examines how literature helps us to understand the unconscious workings of desire. The essayistic *Violence and the Sacred* (*La Violence et le sacré*) from 1972, and 1978's more systematic *Things Hidden Since the Foundation of the World* (*Des Choses cachées depuis la fondation du monde*), present the attenuation of desire through the religious ritual of universal victimage, as embodied in the scapegoat. The singularity of Girard's theme and his confident crossing of generic boundaries distance him from most major schools of contemporary theory.

SEÁN HAND

Giroud, Françoise

b. 1916, Geneva, Switzerland

Journalist, writer and political figure

One of France's leading journalists, Giroud has written for a number of newspapers and magazines, including *Elle*, *Le Nouvel Observateur*, and *L'Express*, which she co-founded with Jean-Jacques **Servan-Schreiber**. In the 1970s, she headed the short-lived Secretariat for Women, established in 1974 by Valéry **Giscard d'Estaing**, before becoming Secreatary of State for Cultural Affairs (1976–7). As well as collections of articles, she has published literary and biographical works, including 1981's *Une Femme honorable* (An Honourable Woman), and *Alma Mahler ou l'art d'être aimée* (Alma Mahler, or the Art of Being Loved).

ALEX HUGHES

See also: feminism (movements/groups); feminist press

Giscard d'Estaing, Valéry

b. 1926, Koblenz, Germany

Politician

Giscard was president of the Republic from 1974 to 1981, and the only Fifth Republic head of state to have gone down to defeat at a presidential election. From an *haut-bourgeois* background, and a graduate of the prestigious École Nationale d'Administration, he rose to prominence as an inspector in the Ministry of Finance, becoming member of parliament for an Auvergne constituency in 1956.

He was Finance Minister from 1962 to 1966, during which period, while loyal to the Fifth Republic, he kept his distance from de **Gaulle** through his membership of the Républicains Indépendants (RI) party. The distinctive Giscardian style – 'French' in its elitist and patrician qualities, 'American' in being technocratically forward-looking and in its economic liberalism – began to emerge in these years. Critical of Gaullist centralization, though he refused to join the vote of censure against the government after **May 1968**, he remained in eclipse until **Pompidou** came to power in 1969, when he returned as Finance Minister, a post he was to occupy for the entire Pompidou presidency.

Giscard's political position is best encapsulated by his October 1972 assertion that France wanted to be governed from the centre, and his 1974 election slogan of 'change without risk'. Such blandness, after the upheavals of the **Algerian war** and 1968, was what a great many French wanted to hear, and his victory over **Mitterrand**, while an extremely narrow one, was far from surprising. As president, he attempted to offset his aristocratic name and demeanour with a series of not always convincing demotic gestures, such as posing in a lounge suit for the official presidential photograph, inviting the Élysée dustmen to breakfast with him and getting himself invited to dine, with ostentatious spontaneity, in the homes of 'ordinary' French men and women. He had to contend in his early years with poor relations with his first prime minister, **Chirac** (replaced by Raymond **Barre** in 1976), and a resurgent Left opposition; but their defeat in the 1978 legislative elections and the Giscard/Barre tandem's image of economic competence strengthened his position. Major reforms under his rule included the breaking-up of the **ORTF** into a number of smaller companies, the legalization of **abortion** and France's entry into the European Monetary System. He felt unable to abolish the death penalty, however, despite proclaimed personal opposition.

As the youngest president this century, Giscard was clearly looking forward to a lengthy period in office, and his defeat by Mitterrand in 1981 – only three years after the collapse of the Union of the Left on which the latter had built his strategy – was all the more traumatic for him in consequence. With neither a House of Lords nor the equivalent of the United States' Carter Foundation to provide a political 'retirement home' for him, he has had to content himself since with the presidency of the Auvergne Regional Assembly, and in 1995 a mortifyingly failed attempt to capture the mayorship of Clermont-Ferrand from the Socialists. His recent publication of an erotic novel has merely reinforced the rather sorry sense of a figure a long way past his sell-by date.

KEITH READER

See also: abortion/contraception; parties and movements

Major works

Giscard d'Estaing, V. (1983) *Démocratie française*, ed. A. Clark, London: Methuen (a well-annotated and well-contextualized republication of Giscard's 1976 political credo).

Further reading

Duhamel, A. (1980) *La République giscardienne: anatomie politique de la France*, Paris: Grasset (the most comprehensive French-language work on the Giscard years).
Frears, J. R. (1981) *France in the Giscard Presidency*, London : Allen and Unwin (a sound overall account).

Glucksmann, André

b. 1937, France

Philosopher

Glucksmann is the best known of the **new**

philosophers of the 1970s. After passing the competitive *agrégation* examination in philosophy in 1961, Glucksmann became a Marxist student militant, gravitating towards the Maoists and taking an active role in the intellectual debates around **May 1968**. In the aftermath of the events, he became one of the leading figures of the **'new philosophers'** movement, comprising former radicals who developed a trenchant right-wing critique of their own former beliefs, drawing inspiration from Solzhenitsyn. He campaigned for causes such as the Vietnamese 'boat people', and is generally credited with promoting the reconciliation of Jean-Paul **Sartre** and Raymond **Aron** in 1978. In the 1990s he wrote forcefully on the treatment of **AIDS** sufferers, and campaigned against the siege of Sarajevo by Bosnian Serbs. His thought focuses on moral issues, rejecting systems of lofty ideals and proposing a permanent revolt against indifference, oppression and other manifestations of evil in society. His best-known book remains *The Master Thinkers* (*Les Maîtres penseurs*) of 1977, whose title became a byword in the postmodernist attack on Marx, Freud and other proponents of systematic thought.

MICHAEL KELLY

See also: educational elitism; Marxism and Marxian thought; revolutionary groups

Godard, Jean-Luc

b. 1930, Paris

Director and critic

Considered by many the greatest film-maker of his generation, certainly the most prolific and influential, Godard has produced an oeuvre of unparalleled range, energy and ambition. With provocative wit and intelligence, as well as an acute sensitivity to beauty and form, he has consistently brought together questions of aesthetics, politics and philosophy. His is the most sustained and challenging analysis in **cinema** of the relations between sound and image, and all his work – critical and filmic – is to some extent essayistic, at once speculative and transitional. When this process fails, it can sometimes expose Godard as politically naive, overintellectual, even nihilistic. However, what made him such a critically important voice during the 1960s and 1970s was the fact that people could identify with this son of the bourgeoisie negotiating the great social and political changes of the Fifth Republic by confronting directly French culture and tradition.

Godard's first film, *Opération béton*, a twenty-minute short made in 1954 about the construction of a dam in Switzerland, was an undistinguished beginning, yet already anticipated the **documentary** aspect of his work. On returning to Paris, where he had studied ethnology at the Sorbonne and attended the cineclubs of the Left Bank, he worked on a series of short films with a group of aspiring film-makers and critics – Jacques **Rivette**, Éric **Rohmer**, François **Truffaut** – who would eventually become known as the **Nouvelle Vague** (New Wave), all united in their contempt of the traditional French *cinéma de qualité*. In 1956, using the pseudonym Hans Lucas, Godard became a regular contributor to the magazines *Arts* and *Cahiers du cinéma* and, inspired by the work of American directors like Hawks and Hitchcock, helped to formulate an aesthetic policy of the auteur. In 1957, he met the film producer Georges de Beauregard, who financed his first feature-length film, *A bout de souffle*, a homage to American 'B' gangster movies starring Jean **Seberg** and Jean-Paul **Belmondo**. Shot by Raoul Coutard in natural light on location in Paris, the film was an unexpected critical and commercial success. Bristling with quotes and references, it used the techniques of hand-held camera and jump-cut to disrupt the act of narration and so create spontaneity. Godard's second film, *Le Petit Soldat* (made in 1960, but not released until 1963), was a fierce exposé of the **Algerian war**, disturbing both for its realistic depiction of horror and for the ambiguous politics of its protagonists. It featured the actress Anna **Karina**, whom Godard later married. So began

a remarkable period of uninterrupted creativity during which Godard developed a fragmented, intensively edited and self-ironic style that broke down the divisions between fiction and documentary, actor and character, narrative and experimental film. The films of this first period (almost all shot by Coutard), include *Vivre sa vie* (1962), an analysis of **prostitution** in twelve tableaux, the classically perfect *Le Mépris* (1963) made in Cinemascope and mischievously employing Brigitte **Bardot**, and *Alphaville, une étrange aventure de Lemmy Caution* (1965), a mixture of film noir and **science fiction**. The poster-bright *Pierrot le fou* (1965), regarded by many as Godard's masterpiece, follows the love–hate relationship between Marianne (Karina) and Ferdinand (Belmondo) and is clearly a reflection of the state of Godard's marriage with Karina, then nearing its end.

Godard was seeking to develop a materialist film poetics, the first signs of which are visible in 1966's *Masculin-Féminin*, starring Jean-Pierre **Léaud**, about the generation of 'the children of Marx and Coca-Cola'. In 1966–67 he made a trilogy exploring modern alienation, in particular the Americanization of French economic and cultural life highlighted by the Vietnam war. *Deux ou trois choses que je sais d'elle* is a social and psychological portrait of Paris and its new suburban sprawl as seen through the eyes of a housewife-cum-prostitute. *La Chinoise*, about a Maoist cell in Paris, is an accurate premonition of the student uprisings of 1968. *Weekend*, a savage indictment of social violence and arguably Godard's most extreme film, offers an apocalyptic vision both of society and of cinema (the closing caption reads '*FIN DU CINÉMA*'). **May 1968** saw Godard leading the protests over the dismissal of Henri **Langlois** from the Cinémathèque Française, and producing a series of *cinétracts*, or impromptu collages, of revolutionary sounds, images and slogans. *Le Gai Savoir* (1968), a treatise on 'progressive' education which heavily foregrounds its means of production, marks the culmination of Godard's self-reflexive film aesthetic. He then began to disavow his earlier work, claiming that it functioned only at the level of theoretical experiment rather than of social and political struggle. His setting up with Jean-Pierre Gorin of the Maoist film collective, the Dziga Vertov Group, marked a complete break with commercial film structures. Joint works like *Pravda, Luttes en Italie, Vent d'est,* (all 1969), and *Vladimir et Rosa* (1971), commissioned by European television although never broadcast, deconstructed in different ways the signs of bourgeois ideology. *Tout va bien* (1972), featuring Yves **Montand** and Jane Fonda as characters and as themselves, is Godard's most authentically Brechtian film, but failed to excite either his increasingly impatient Marxist following or the capitalist film system which had intended to welcome back a prodigal son. Godard had reached an artistic impasse, a fact crudely symbolized by his motorcycle accident in 1971 which left him an invalid for two years. Despite its analytical rigour, his work was becoming less revolutionary than simply didactic, losing its audience in the process. The Group disbanded and Godard left for Grenoble with Anne-Marie **Miéville**, a set photographer on *Tout va bien*, to set up a new production company called Sonimage (romantically conceived as a combination of her 'sound' and his 'image').

Godard then underwent a process of complete self-evaluation unlike that of any other major film-maker. After *Ici et ailleurs* (1974), which used video and previously shot film of Palestine to take personal and political stock of the post-1968 situation, Godard and Miéville returned deliberately in 1973 to basic themes with *Numéro deux*, a stunning exposé of the blockage in French society which incorporated and superimposed video within the cinematic frame. Two major **television** series followed, *Six fois deux (sur et sous la communication)*(1976) and *France/tour/détour/deux/enfants*, (1977/8) which, although meeting with general incomprehension and disapproval, revealed that Godard was seeking above all to resolve the antagonism between video and cinema (Cain and Abel). By the late 1970s, he was back in Switzerland (his country of citizenship). There he made *Slow Motion (Sauve qui peut [la vie])*

(1979), a return to the mainstream and explicitly autobiographical in nature. Produced with a minimal crew and featuring Jacques Dutronc as Godard's *alter ego*, Paul Godard, the film used the video technique of stop-starting images to analyse the relations between female prostitution and male impotence, space and representation. It also included a voice-over sequence with Marguerite **Duras**, illustrating Godard's desire to engage directly with female discourse and, perhaps even more importantly, literature (Godard is himself the author of six published collections of poetry). *Passion* followed (1981), a soaring tale of aesthetics, **painting, class** politics and religion which inspired the even more astonishing *Scénario du film 'Passion'*, a video where Godard explores how *Passion* came into being. *Prénom: Carmen* (1983), which won the Lion d'Or at the 1983 Venice Film Festival, confronts Mérimée with Beethoven to examine the relationship between (pre-)language and identity. Its burlesque figure of Uncle Jean marks the first of Godard's appearances in his own film-fictions. '*Je vous salue, Marie*' (1983), a contemporary reworking of the story of the Nativity, explored the metaphysical themes of love, faith and creativity. Although condemned by the Pope, the film was an honest attempt by Godard (a Protestant) to deal with the question of divine mystery, and its dense soundtrack mixing Dvořák with Bach showcased his total mastery of sound.

An extensive and still evolving phase of personal, historical and philosophical contemplation was initiated by the video Godard made with Miéville in 1986 entitled *Soft and Hard*. Putting aside self-indulgent exercises like *King Lear* and *Soigne ta droite* (both 1987), this fifth period includes works like *Puissance de la parole* (1988), a dazzling video piece exploiting techniques of speed and pulsation; *Nouvelle Vague* (1991), a paean to nature stripped of all but the barest threads of narrative; *Allemagne année 90 neuf zéro*, a meditation for television on the solitude of post-Berlin Wall Germany and Europe; and *JLG/JLG: autoportrait de décembre* (1991), an intimate and elegiac short which is less a self-portrait than a study of childhood, memory and loss. Godard has also experimented with filmed poems, letters, reports, contributions to collective works, historical studies, work notes, fragments of a private diary and dialogues. However, the key work of the recent corpus is the eight-part video *Histoire(s) du cinéma*. Here, Godard, the self-styled artisan, reinvents the cinematic process by means of an extraordinary 'videographic' flux of clips, stills, art reproductions, captions and **photography**. This approach confirms the view of the film critic Serge **Daney** that Godard is less an iconoclast and innovator than a radical reformer tirelessly correcting and redefining. A work of genuine humanist commitment and passion, *Histoire(s) du cinéma* has rarely been seen, suffering the fate of much of Godard's recent output which, if it attracts producers, lacks adequate distribution. In fact, although revered by young film-makers such as Léos **Carax**, Godard is generally known less for his recent work than for his enduring fame as a public figure, the author of axioms like 'cinema is truth 24 times a second', or 'it's not a just image, just an image'. He received the prestigious film award of an honorary César in 1986.

JAMES WILLIAMS

See also: feminist thought; Marxism and Marxian thought; postmodernism; prostitution

Major works

Godard, J.-L. (1980) *Introduction à une véritable histoire du cinéma*, vol. 1, Paris: Éditions Albatros (a first version of the *Histoire(s) du cinéma* project).
——(1985) *Jean-Luc Godard par Jean-Luc Godard*, Paris: Cahiers du Cinéma/Éditions de l'Étoile (a lavishly illustrated compilation of all Godard's film criticism).

Further reading

Bellour, R. and Bandy, M. L. (eds) (1992), *Jean-Luc Godard: Son + Image 1974–1991*, New York: Museum of Modern Art (the best general collection of criticism on Godard's work post-1974).
Douin, J.-L. (1994) *Jean-Luc Godard*, Paris: Rivages (a solid and highly readable overview of Godard's oeuvre).
MacCabe, C. (1980) *Jean-Luc Godard: Images, Sounds, Politics*, London: British Film Institute (an excellent analysis of Godard's work up to the late 1970s).

Goldmann, Jean-Jacques

b. 1951, Paris

Singer-songwriter

Goldmann is a prolific songwriter and a performer. He started his career in 1975 with the group Tai Phong, where he first met the Welsh guitarist Michael Jones. In 1981, Goldmann started a solo and highly successful career for ten years and then formed a new group Fredericks, Goldmann et Jones. A talented musician, he gives the traditional poetical *chanson* a modern musical idiom. Against his own wishes he is perceived as a leading voice of the new moral generation.

GÉRARD POULET

See also: song/*chanson*

Gorz, André

b. 1924, Vienna, Austria

Political philosopher,
real name Gérard Horst

Gorz left his homeland when it was annexed by Hitler in 1938 and it was in 1946, during his exile in Switzerland, that Gorz met Jean-Paul Sartre, thus beginning a long association with *Les Temps modernes*. Gorz's books are concerned mainly with the nature of work in post-industrial societies: he examines the emergence of and tendency towards societies having to contend with mass unemployment in economies experiencing jobless growth. His analysis extends also to changing **class** structures in such societies, and discusses how work should be more equitably distributed. Gorz's name has in more recent years become associated with the ecology movement.

MARTYN CORNICK

See also: employment; green issues

Major works

Gorz, A. (1980) *Ecology as Politics (Écologie et politique)*, Boston: South End Press.
——(1982) *Farewell to the Working Class: An Essay on Post-Industrial Socialism*, London: Pluto.
——(1988) *Métamorphose du travail: quête du sens*, Paris: Galilée.
——(1994) *Capitalism, Socialism, Ecology (Capitalisme, socialisme, écologie)*, trans. C. Turner, London: Verso.

Gracq, Julien

b. 1910, St-Florent-le-Vieil

Writer, real name Louis Poirier

Gracq is the author of novels and essays, was initially close to Surrealism (he was a friend of André Breton) and is noted for his rare poetic style and his individual vision of literature. In 1950 he delivered a violent attack on the Parisian literary establishment in *Literature in the Gut (La Littérature à l'estomac)* and later refused the Goncourt prize awarded for his 1951 novel *The Opposing Shore (Le Rivage des Syrtes)*. Standing apart from all literary trends, his work has moved from fiction towards original forms of personal and reflective writing.

BÉATRICE DAMAMME-GILBERT

See also: literary prizes

Further reading

Murat, M. (1992) *Julien Gracq*, Paris: Pierre Belfond (an approachable and penetrating overview of Gracq's entire work).

Grand Magic Circus, Le

Theatre company

An anarchic, lively company led by Jérôme **Savary**, whose aim was to bring culture to the people by ridiculing the existing cultural establishment. Collectively scripted shows were designed to shock middle-class audiences, and used the music-hall tradition of song, **dance**, stage effects, clowning and pantomime for which shows such as its 1973 *De Moïse à Mao*, and its 1981 *Le Bourgeois Gentilhomme* are particularly famous.

ANNIE SPARKS

See also: theatre

Further reading

Savary, J. (1974) *Album du Grand Magic Circus*, Paris: Belfond.

Grappelli, Stéphane

b. 1908, Paris
d. 1997, Paris

Musician

A legendary jazz violinist who formed an unforgettable partnership with the guitarist Django **Reinhardt** in the 1930s. The two of them were members of the Hot Club de France Quintet which was formed in 1934 and stayed together until the war (when Grappelli came to England). Reformed in 1946, the Quintet continued to perform until Reinhardt's retirement in 1950, since when Grappelli pursued a solo career, working with the likes of Duke Ellington, Oscar Peterson, Barney Kessel, Earl Hines, Yehudi Menuhin and Claude Bolling until his death in December 1997.

IAN PICKUP

See also: jazz

Gréco, Juliette

b. 1926, Montpellier

Singer and actor

Known in her early years as the 'muse of St-Germain-des-Prés', Juliette Gréco began her career in the late 1940s and early 1950s performing songs with words by Jean-Paul **Sartre** and Raymond **Queneau**. Having alienated the French bourgeoisie in her early years, Gréco progressively captivated a wider public, singing songs by **Brel, Prévert**, Guy **Béart, Gainsbourg, Aznavour,** and others. An outstanding stage performer, Gréco projected the image of the archetypal 'liberated' woman. She is also important as an ambassador of French song abroad and (to a lesser extent) as a film star. Gréco was married to Michel **Piccoli**.

IAN PICKUP

See also: song/*chanson*

green issues

Green issues emerged as part of France's social and political agenda in the 1960s, although the debate about the relationship between nature and society is an old one. Modern environmentalism, which followed the growth of the nature protection movements, has been shaped by a number of specific factors, especially the role of the state and the conflicts around **nuclear power**.

The relationship between society and the natural environment has been a much-debated issue for a long time. Indeed, it was pivotal during the Enlightenment period; Rousseau, with his vision of humans as 'good in Nature' in *Le Contrat social* and in *Émile*, differed from the modernism of the Encyclopedists such as Diderot or D'Alembert, for whom 'reason' and 'industry' control 'nature'. In the Romantic period, this debate was continued from all sides. The impulse to 'preserve' nature can be dated back to the creation of the first nature reserve in the forest of Fontainebleau in 1853, after a long campaign by well-known artists and writers such as George Sand and Victor Hugo. Later, the deeply rural character of French society strongly marked the relationship with the natural environment. However, the ambient modernism which, from the 1950s, presided over the '30 Glorious' years of economic growth, and which at first reacted against the 'ruralist' ideology of the collaborationist **Vichy** regime of World War II (which had a wheatsheaf as its symbol), had soon to respond to the deep environmental changes provoked by industrialization and urbanization. These changes, which accelerated the disappearance of traditional rural society, assured the continued popularity of works extolling the values of doomed rural cultures in touch with 'nature' – hence the success of writings by authors such as Pagnol, Genevoix, Giono and Ramuz. On the other hand, it became obvious that the natural and human environments were threatened through pollution and degradation, and that a serious policy response had to be developed.

In this context, two dates are particularly relevant. In 1960, the act creating the national parks was voted in. The first, the Parc National de la Vanoise, was established in the Alps in 1963, to be followed by six other national parks and many regional parks and nature reserves. In 1963, Jean Dorst's book *Avant que nature se meure* (Before Nature Dies) rivalled Carson's *Silent Spring* in the Anglo-Saxon world. At the end of the 1960s and in the early

1970s, green trends were developing in France (as elsewhere), generating debate about the 'limits to growth', the 'hippy' craze, a nostalgia for the *terroirs* and *produits de pays*, and associations for the protection of animals and nature becoming mass movements. The Amis de la Terre (Friends of the Earth) started in 1970; three years later came WWF's French section (Greenpeace France had to wait until 1977). The term *écologiste* (environmentalist) became popular, especially in its familiar, slightly derogatory form of *écolo*.

The main area of conflicts during the 1970s was the development of nuclear power. The 1973 Messmer Plan planned to make of nuclear power the main source of electricity generation (*le tout-nucléaire* policy). This decision was never debated publicly, and local public enquiries for nuclear plants were seen as rubber-stamping procedures. The anti-nuclear movement, therefore, was also a protest against the centralized state. Many environmentalists associated themselves with the libertarian ideals of the **May 1968** movement, pacifism (as the civil nuclear power programme had never been fully separated from the military nuclear programme) and **regionalism** (especially in Brittany).

The high point of anti-nuclear campaigning came in 1977, during the campaign against the Creys-Malville 'fast breeder' reactor near Lyon. With the arrival in power of **Mitterrand** in 1981, a few concessions were made, but the nuclear programme had largely been set in train, and the opposition foundered on the powerful alliance of pro-nuclear interests. Today, France is the country with the highest proportion of electricity generated from nuclear plants. Protests were renewed only when public authorities were accused of providing little or misleading information about the radioactive clouds from the Chernobyl disaster blowing across France in 1986. During the same period, other green issues attracted the attention of activists and the general public, especially urban pollution and the mismanagement of dangerous waste. A number of scandals around the import of hospital waste and illegal chemical dumps erupted across the

1980s. The degrading of the local natural environment by infrastructure encroachment was increasingly resisted – for instance, a new TGV rail track project in the Rhône valley, an area already cramped between existing railways, motorways and canals, and not far from the Côte d'Azur, a fragile environment destroyed by speculative and undercontrolled developments, was strongly opposed in the early 1990s.

From the mid-1970s, a new generation of activists, less marked by the political issues inherited from the 1960s, brought forward the Greens' political project. **Green politics**, which have been marked by deep divisions and a gradual erosion of the electoral and political positions gained in the mid-1980s, have not managed to alter significantly the ways in which green issues are considered. Indeed, 'green' themes are used in widely differing ways. For instance, a conservative-orientated party, the CPNT or Chasse, Pêche, Nature, Traditions (Hunting, Angling, Nature, Traditions), claiming to have an environmental purpose by lobbying for 'traditional' hunting and angling, gained 3.95 per cent of the votes in the 1994 European elections – more than the main Green Party (Les Verts).

The CPNT's relative success is typical of protest politics, but it reveals some of the specific aspects of ideologies on nature which are very different from the usual green image. There are 1.65 million licensed hunters in France, who constitute a powerful and active lobby which claims to have the protection of nature as its main aim. Some recent conflicts illustrate the force of such ideologies: for instance, the seasonal hunting of the *palombe* (a kind of migrant dove) in the southwest region of France is, in principle, forbidden by an EU directive, but is fiercely defended and practised by locals. Indeed, 'ecocentrist' thinking, influential in Anglo-Saxon environmentalism, has had little impact in France, and has been subjected to fierce attacks, for instance by the philosopher Luc Ferry. Alternative lifestyles influenced by green issues have yet to have the same impact in France as they do in the United Kingdom or in Germany, where problems of pollution, energy wastage, losses of wilderness or biological diversity are treated as technical and sociopolitical problems.

FRANÇOIS NECTOUX

Further reading

Hoffmann-Martinot, V. (1991) 'Grüne and Verts: Two Faces of European Ecologism', *West European Politics* 14: 4 (although dealing mainly with green politics, this article also analyses the background in terms of green issues).

Touraine, A. *et al.* (1983) *Anti-Nuclear Protest*, Cambridge: Cambridge University Press (a sociological analysis of the reactions to the most important green issue in France in the 1970s).

green politics

Despite heightened international concern over the environment, the impact of green politics in France has been limited by chronic internal divisions.

The origins of French political ecology lie in the 'new social movements' of the late 1960s, particularly environmentalism, anti-nuclear protest, pacifism and **feminism**. Unresolved tensions within the green movement over appropriate forms of activism – be it through direct action, associations, pressure groups or mainstream politics – have resulted in ambivalent strategies. Structured political parties emerged late. Of the two main parties, the Verts (the Greens) was formed in 1984, and Génération Écologie (GE) in 1990. The former retains strong elements of grassroots democracy and has a radical platform (opposition to French **nuclear power**, to the rush for economic growth, to collaboration with the parties of government, advocacy of cancelling Third World debt). The latter is centralized, focused on its founder, Brice **Lalonde**, reformist in orientation and accepts civil uses of nuclear power (Lalonde was Environment Minister under the

Socialists during 1989–92). However, both parties agree on the need for global environmental strategies, more work-sharing and a deepening of democracy.

Despite the greening of the French public as measured by opinion surveys, between 1974 and 1988 no single ecology party or candidate polled 5 per cent in a major election. The breakthrough came in the 1989 European elections (with 10.6 per cent of votes, the Verts returned nine MEPs), followed by success in the 1992 regional elections, where ecology parties attracted nearly 15 per cent of voters. In both years, ecologists benefited from the popularity of environmental issues and proportional representation. But the 1993 parliamentary elections (only 7.6 per cent of votes in the first round and no seats won) and the 1995 presidential elections (3.3 per cent for Dominique Voynet) constituted serious set-backs. Explanatory factors for these disappointing performances included inexperience in major elections, poor communication of policy, the aftermath of recession, the first-past-the-post electoral system and the resurgence of the Right.

But the major weakness of French political ecology has been its ever-increasing fragmentation, with green politicians more intent on ideological finesse and factional disputes than on formulating environmental policy. These divisions prevented the election of a single green MEP in the 1994 European elections. By that year, there was a green party for most shades of the political spectrum, with the Verts moving leftwards, GE drifting to the centre, CPNT (a hunting lobby) and the Nouveaux Écologistes firmly on the Right, while Antoine **Waechter**'s Mouvement Écologiste Indépendant sought to be on neither Left nor Right. Although this is a fair reflection of the competing constituencies that form the environmental movement, it has led to voter confusion, the marginalization of green parties and the dilution of their influence on decision-makers, despite the continued saliency of national and global environmental problems.

JOSEPH SZARKA

See also: green issues; parties and movements

Further reading

Cole, A. and Doherty, B. (1995) '*Pas comme les autres* – the French Greens at the Cross-Roads', in D. Richardson and C. Rootes (eds) *The Green Challenge: The Development of Green Parties in Europe*, London: Routledge (studies the greens within the context of the French political system).

Sainteny, G. (1992) *Les Verts*, Paris: PUF (detailed history and development of the Verts).

Szarka, J. (1994) 'Green Politics in France', *Parliamentary Affairs* 47, 3 (June) (on electoral performance and political positioning of green parties).

Greimas, A. J.

b. 1917, Tula, Lithuania;
d. 1992

Linguist

An influential French semanticist and semiologist who taught at the École Pratique des Hautes Études and worked in the 1960s alongside **Barthes**, Todorov and **Genette** on the structure of narratives. Two of his theoretical models exploring deep and surface structures, the semiotic square and the actantial model, have been widely used and applied to a range of subdisciplines within semiotics.

BÉATRICE DAMAMME-GILBERT

See also: linguistic/discourse theory; structuralism

Further reading

Rimmon-Kenan, S. (1983) *Narrative Fiction: Contemporary Poetics*, London and New York: Routledge (has several sections on Greimas's work and a bibliography).

Groult, Benoîte

b. 1920, Paris

Journalist, novelist and essayist

The author of novels co-written with her sister Flora in the 1960s – *Diary in Duo* (*Journal à quatre mains*); *Feminine Plural* (*Le Féminin pluriel*); *Il était deux fois* (Twice Upon a Time) – as well as of single-authored fictions – including 1972's *La Part des choses* (All Things Considered), and the erotic novel *Salt on Our Skin* (*Les Vaisseaux du coeur*), published in 1988 – Groult is perhaps best known for two feminist essays. These texts – *Ainsi soit-elle* (So Be She) and *Le Féminisme au masculin* (Feminism in the Masculine Mode) – contributed to the rise of feminist awareness in 1970s France. A dedicated campaigner for equal rights, Groult became president of the Commission for the Feminization of Job Designations in 1985.

ALEX HUGHES

See also: erotic writing; feminist thought; women's/lesbian writing

Grumberg, Jean-Claude

b. 1939, Paris

Playwright

Over three decades, Grumberg has been writing plays, such as *Zone libre* (Free Zone) and *Linge sale* (Dirty Linen), television scripts and a screenplay in 1988 (*Les Années sandwichs*). His work displays differing formats and subjects, employing humour to make social observation.

ANNIE STEPHENSON

See also: theatre

Guattari, Félix

b. 1930, Colombes;
d. 1992, Cour-Cheverny, Loir-et-Cher

Radical psychiatrist and intellectual

Guattari was influenced by the work which he began in the 1950s at Dr Jean Oury's experimental Clinique de la Borde psychiatric hospital at Cour-Cheverny. In 1960, he was active in the creation of the Groupe de Travail de Psychologie et de Sociologie Institutionnelle. He was also the co-author of five important philosophical works with Gilles **Deleuze**, most notably *Anti-Oedipus* (*LAnti-Œdipe*) in 1972. As well as being politically active on the Left, Guattari worked with Deleuze to outline a philosophy of desire and 'molecular' revolution which calls into question the 'molar' organizing tendencies of contemporary societies. In the 1980s he began to write on ecological questions.

JOHN MARKS

See also: psychoanalysis

Guérard, Michel

b. 1933, Vétheuil

Chef

Guérard is the chef who founded *la nouvelle cuisine* (also known as *la cuisine minceur*), a reaction of the health-conscious late 1970s against heavy sauces and a surfeit of dairy products. This style of cooking, practised by Guérard at his restaurant in the southwestern spa town of Eugénie-les-Bains, makes great use of mousses, steamed dishes and low-fat reductions, flavoured with unusual (frequently Oriental) herbs and spices. Guérard's imitators were often derided for their stress on fussy presentation and the supposedly minuscule size of

the portions they offered, but his influence has been the major individual one on French cooking of the past twenty years.

KEITH READER

See also: gastronomy

Guérin, Daniel

b. 1904, Paris;
d. 1988, Paris

Political militant and thinker

Prominent in prewar left-wing politics as a revolutionary syndicalist and dissident Socialist, Guérin developed in the postwar era a form of libertarian socialism marked especially by anti-militarism and anti-colonialism. His writings on Kinsey and Reich, and the accounts of his homosexual activity in autobiographical works such as *Autobiographie de jeunesse* (Autobiography of Youth) and *Le Feu du sang* (Fire in the Blood), of 1972 and 1977 respectively, provide a link between the Socialist tradition and the post-**May 1968** landscape.

BILL MARSHALL

See also: autobiography; gay activism; gay writing; lesbian activism

Guibert, Hervé

b. 1955, Paris;
d. 1991, Paris

Writer and photographer

Hervé Guibert is the author of over twenty novels, plays, collections of stories, photographs and a televised film. Although not prominent until his three 'AIDS novels' and **television** appearances on *Apostrophes* and *Ex-Libris*, his medicalization and mediatization as an 'AIDS writer' also illustrate his main themes: the analytical representation of the external and internal human body; the relation between image/imagination and reality; shifts from the hallucinatory to the punctiliously precise. His combination of extreme restraint and mischievous, provocative excess, notably in his treatment of violence and the erotic, mark him as a fine literary stylist and *moraliste*.

OWEN HEATHCOTE

See also: AIDS; gay writing

Further reading

Boulé, J.-P. (1995a) '*A l'ami qui ne m'a pas sauvé la vie*' *and Other Writings*, Glasgow: University of Glasgow French and German Publications (this focuses on the best known of his 'AIDS novels').

——(1995b) 'Hervé Guibert', *Nottingham French Studies* 34, 1 (edited collection of articles and bibliography).

Guignols de l'info, Les

Television programme

Les Guignols de l'info is a puppet-based satire programme which emulates the United Kingdom's *Spitting Image*. Broadcast nightly on the pay-TV channel **Canal Plus** in an unencrypted form, it pokes fun at politicians, media personalities and show-business stars. It is watched by a smaller, younger and more left-wing audience than its competitor on **TF1**, the *Bébête-Show*. During the 1995 presidential campaign the possible electoral impact of the programme's portrayal of the leading candidates became a topic of media and political debate. The format of *Les Guignols* has been exported to other countries with considerable success.

RAYMOND KUHN

See also: television

Hallier, Jean-Edern

b. 1936, St-Germain en Laye;
d. 1997, Paris

Novelist and publisher

A co-founder of *Tel quel*, Hallier's career as a maverick intellectual was always inclined towards non-conformity, provocation and iconoclasm. A lover of publicity, much of his work was conceived to challenge the status of institutional and political authorities. After **May 1968** such efforts were channelled into the left-wing and humorous monthly *L'Idiot international* (1969–73) and the establishment of his own **publishing** house, Les Éditions Hallier (1974). Having already attacked the regime of **Giscard d'Estaing** in 1979 in *Lettre ouverte au colin froid* (Open Letter to the Cold Hake), during the 1980s Hallier turned his efforts to delving into the past and personal life of his former close friend, François **Mitterrand**.

MARTYN CORNICK

See also: national press in France; Tel Quel group

Major works

Hallier, J.-E. (1972) *La Cause des peuples*, Paris: Éditions du Seuil.

——(1992) *La Force d'âme: l'honneur perdu de François Mitterrand*, Paris: Belles Lettres.

Hallyday, Johnny

b. 1943, Paris

Lyricist and singer,
real name Jean-Philippe Smet

France's best-known rocker, Johnny Hallyday sang mainly French translations of American **rock**, twist, and rhythm and blues songs in the early years of his career, before introducing more French compositions into his repertoire. Seemingly the incarnation of violence and of loneliness in many of his stage performances, Hallyday has perfected his high-tech public appearances for a great (if mainly ageing) band of fans. Despite huge success in France, he has made no impact in the English-speaking world. He married for the fifth time in March 1996.

IAN PICKUP

See also: song/*chanson*

Hardy, Françoise

b. 1944, Paris

Singer-songwriter

An instant star of the pop world at the age of 18 with her first composition, *Tous les garçons et les filles* (All the Boys and Girls), Françoise Hardy has progressed from **rock** and twist, to ballads, and to ever more reflective (often poetic) songs, some of which were written for her by Michel **Berger**, Michel **Jonasz** and others. One of the survivors of the 1960s generation, Hardy is often seen as the incarnation of loneliness. She is married to Jacques Dutronc, the singer and film star.

IAN PICKUP

See also: song/*chanson*

health

Over the postwar period, health has become an important concern for governments in Western industrialized nations. Medical advances and the organized provision of health services may have contributed in no small measure to increasing life expectancy, but the soaring cost of providing medical care has led governments to search for ways of containing expenditure, while maintaining the high standards of provision people have come to expect.

As a proportion of total expenditure on social protection and in relation to gross domestic product (GDP), within the **European Union** (EU) France is among the big spenders on health. In 1993, per capita expenditure on health was higher in France than in any other member-state, although the level of provision in terms of the proportion of medical practitioners, chemists, hospital beds or length of stay in relation to population size was not consistently above average.

Irrespective of whether a high level of spending on health can be interpreted as the cause or effect of declining mortality rates, French women register the greatest life expectancy of all Europeans. The evidence is less positive for men, who display higher mortality rates at all ages, and particularly in the 20–24 age group. The disparity here is explained by the greater propensity of young men to be involved in fatal accidents. Among the older age groups, the main causes of death for men are malignant tumours, followed by circulatory diseases. The order is reversed for women. With Spain, France records the highest incidence of **AIDS** in the Union, with 42.55 cases for 100,000 inhabitants – more than three times the level in the United Kingdom.

The health care system that developed in France in the postwar period to meet the demands of a rapidly growing population and changing lifestyles is based on two fundamental principles, which may help to explain why the system is one of the most costly to operate in Europe. The health service was premised on the freedom for patients to choose their own medical practitioners, consultants and hospitals, and on equality of access to services.

Health is one of the main branches of the French **social security** system. The health insurance funds (*caisses d'assurance maladie*) cover sickness, disability and accidents at work for about 80 per cent of the insured population. The remaining 20 per cent are covered by special schemes or as self-employed workers. In return for employer and employee contributions, which are calculated as a proportion of salary, insured persons and their dependants are eligible for partial reimbursement of medical fees and most pharmaceutical costs incurred in the course of treatment. The amount paid by the patient, known as the *ticket modérateur*, was intended to ensure that patients had a financial involvement in their treatment and developed a sense of responsibility. Payment for in-patient hospital care is made direct by the funds to the hospital. The full cost of medical care during pregnancy is covered by the same funds. In addition, employed persons receive a daily rate to compensate for loss of wages during absences due to illness or industrial accidents.

While the health funds are run by the social partners (employers' and workers' representatives) and are, in theory, responsible for managing their own affairs, the Ministry of Health lays down the conditions for levying contributions and the principles for setting rates of reimbursement, and it decides on the allocation of hospital budgets. Private hospitals (*cliniques*) also fall under the administrative and financial control of the ministry and are obliged to engage in contracts with the funds. Medical practitioners can choose whether to enter into such an agreement, and some 80 per cent of all general practitioners are under contract. In return for doctors observing set fees, their patients are reimbursed at a higher rate. Chemists are subject to a *numerus clausus*. Although similar restrictions are not imposed on medical practitioners, the number of medical students has been limited since the 1970s. While doctors are expected to display moderation, they have retained their freedom to prescribe whatever drugs they consider necessary, and patients can consult any number of doctors if they are not satisfied with their diagnosis or treatment. In line with the principle of solidarity, low income groups and certain categories of chronic illnesses may be exempt from the patient's contribution, but about half the population contribute to supplementary schemes, mutual insurance companies (*mutuelles*) or private insurance schemes, which provide additional cover for their members.

The constraining regulatory function exercised by the state was intended to ensure that both patients and the medical profession assume responsibility for the demand and supply of treatment, but it has not been effective in containing costs. Since the 1980s, schemes have, therefore, been introduced to control hospital budgets and cut administrative overheads; daily charges have been levied for patients in hospital; restrictions have been introduced on exemptions from medical bills; and the level of reimbursement for patients has been reduced. One of the results of retrenchment is that the share of expenditure borne by the health funds has fallen. The burden has shifted more heavily on to private individuals and the supplementary insurance schemes. It is doubtful, however, whether the attempts at reform have resulted in long-term efficiency gains, since policies have been introduced in piecemeal fashion. In any case, they have met with strong opposition from the medical pro-

fession and the social partners, who see reform as a threat to their freedom of action.

LINDA HANTRAIS

See also: alcohol, cigarettes, drugs; demographic developments; social policy

Further reading

European Commission (1995) *Social Protection in Europe*, Luxembourg: Office for Official Publications of the European Communities (a wide-ranging review covering current debates on social protection).

Wilsford, D. (1991) 'The Continuity of Crisis: Patterns of Heath Care Policymaking in France, 1978–1988', in J. S. Ambler (ed.) *The French Welfare State. Surviving Social and Ideological Change*, New York and London: New York University Press (a thorough analysis of an important period of change in the development of the French health care system).

Hersant, Robert

b. 1920, France;
d. 1996

Press baron

A controversial right-wing figure, Hersant successfully circumvented anti-concentration legislation, and in the early 1990s controlled roughly 30 per cent of French dailies, including *Le Figaro*, *France-Soir* and numerous regional titles, as well as advertising agencies, printing plants and radio stations. Despite a suspect past and wartime collaboration, he held political office locally and nationally. His newspaper career began with the creation of the successful motorists' monthly *L'Auto-Journal* in 1950. He built his empire by buying up and ruthlessly restructuring or merging newspapers in difficulty (over fifty titles in forty years). His holdings extended to Belgium, Spain and eastern Europe.

PAM MOORES

See also: advertising; national press in France; regional press in France

Heure de vérité, L'

Television programme

A current affairs programme which started in 1982. Broadcast on Antenne 2 (later France 2) the format was based on a studio interview between a leading politician and three journalists. The peculiarity of the programme lay in its use of public opinion as an active element in the discussion. For example, from 1985 onwards the programme included an instant audience opinion poll on the views expressed by politicians, concluding with a verdict on their ability to produce convincing arguments.

RAYMOND KUHN

See also: television

Hirsch, Robert

b. 1927, L'Isle-Adam

Actor

A Comédie Française sociétaire between 1951 and 1972, noted for his flexibility as an actor and his interpretations of Molière and Marivaux, as well as performances in the lead role of Arturo Ui at the Théâtre National Populaire in 1968, and in Thomas Dörst's 1989 Feuerbach.

ANNIE SPARKS

See also: theatre

Hocquenghem, Guy

b. 1946, Boulogne-Billancourt; d. 1988, Paris

Intellectual, gay activist, writer and journalist

In 1971 Hocquenghem was one of the founders of the FHAR. Although he was a prominent media spokesperson for the cause in the 1970s, he was uncomfortable with the orthodoxies of identity politics. This is clear as early as 1972's Homosexual Desire (Le Désir homosexuel), which is heavily indebted to Deleuze and Guattari, and his iconoclastic social dissidence is developed throughout his theoretical works and five novels.

BILL MARSHALL

See also: gay activism; gay writing; lesbian activism

Major works

Hocquenghem, G. (1993) Homosexual Desire, Durham: Duke University Press.

Further reading

Marshall, B. (1996) Guy Hocquenghem, London: Pluto (essential reading).

horse racing

French horse racing is dominated by its state-run and café-based system of pool betting, the Pari Mutuel Urbain (PMU), which forbids private bookmaking. The weekly gambling highlight is the televised Sunday tiercé, a 1–2–3 forecast bet which attracts some 8 million punters. This may focus on anything from a humble handicap to one of the great events in the racing calendar, such as the Prix de l'Amérique (a showcase for French trotting, the country's most popular form of racing), or the culmination of the European flat-racing season, the Prix de l'Arc de Triomphe.

PHILIP DINE

See also: sport

housing

In the immediate postwar period, a major building programme was launched in France to replace the housing stock destroyed or damaged during hostilities, to cater for the fast-expanding and urbanizing population and to modernize the existing stock. As population growth began to ease in the 1960s, and as the economy went into recession in the mid-1970s, new building slowed down, and policy shifted towards a more targeted approach aimed at encouraging owner-occupation and assisting low-income families. By the 1990s, the majority of housing in France was either pre-1918 or had been built between 1949 and 1967, but over 90 per cent of dwellings were equipped with a telephone, indoor toilet, with access to a bath or shower and hot water, and nearly 80 per cent had central heating.

Despite the high concentration of population in the major cities, particularly in the Paris area, almost 60 per cent of French people live in houses rather than flats, a proportion that is above the European average. Couples with children are more likely to live in houses, which they have acquired by moving to the outskirts of towns where affordable housing is available in the developing residential areas. As arrangements for obtaining mortgages have improved, and home ownership has been encouraged by state-funded mortgage subsidies, more couples have become owner-occupiers, accounting for nearly 60 per cent of occupancies in the 1990s, a level slightly below the European average. Almost 10 per cent of French people own a second home, inherited from a parent or relation in one in four cases. Although less than half of owner-occupiers are paying for a mortgage, the share of the household budget devoted, on average, to housing costs has doubled since the

1960s, accounting for a fifth of consumer spending.

Postwar governments in France have intervened in two main ways to subsidize housing: first, by building social housing (*habitations à loyer modéré*), particularly between the 1950s and 1970s; and second, by paying housing benefits to families in need, as part of family policy. Over 15 per cent of all housing belongs to the social sector, representing a rapidly expanding proportion of rented accommodation, though a lower level than that found in the United Kingdom. From the 1980s, policy shifted from subsidies on buildings to more personalized forms of housing benefit (*aide personnalisée au logement* and *allocation de logement social*), which are paid to low-income families, including young couples without children, young workers and students (about 25 per cent of households). While making an important contribution to the standard of housing for the population in general, these measures have not been able to stem the rising tide of homelessness, estimated to affect some 202,000 people in France in the mid-1990s.

LINDA HANTRAIS

See also: demographic developments; family; social policy

Further reading

INSEE (1993) 'Cadre de vie', *La Société française: données sociales 1993*, Paris: INSEE, (a collection of informative contributions covering various aspects of housing in France).

Humanité, L'

Newspaper

Originally a Socialist newspaper, founded in 1904 by Jean Jaurès, it became Communist in 1920, and has been the official newspaper of the French Communist Party since 1923. Its fate parallels the demise of Communism: peak circulation of over 400,000 copies in 1946 was halved by 1958, and dropped in the 1990s to around 60,000. The last French daily to be directly associated with a political party, its readers are primarily party members and supporters. The party appoints senior executives and editor; many journalists are party members. The stance is partisan, the tone combative. *L'Huma*, as it is commonly known, devotes special attention to social and industrial problems, emphasizing the universal dimension of the workers' struggle.

PAM MOORES

See also: left-wing press; national press in France; parties and movements

Huppert, Isabelle

b. 1955, Paris

Actor

Her career was launched in Goretta's *The Lacemaker* (*La Dentellière*) in 1977). She has made films for many auteurist directors: several for **Chabrol**, including *Violette Nozière* (1977) and *La Cérémonie* in 1995, **Pialat**'s *Loulou* (1980), **Godard**'s *Sauve qui peut (la vie)* (1979) and *Passion* (1981), **Tavernier**'s *Coup de torchon* (1981), **Blier**'s *La Femme de mon pote* (1983). Her favoured persona is that of the rebel with feminist overtones, e.g. the closet lesbian in **Kurys**'s *Coup de foudre* (1983) or the abortionist in Chabrol's *Une affaire de femmes* (1988).

PHIL POWRIE

See also: cinema; stars

Hussards

The name *Hussards* was given to a group of young right-wing writers working in the 1940s and 1950s, and including principally Roger Nimier (1925–62), Antoine Blondin (1922–91) and Jacques Laurent (1919–), though also comprising Michel Déon, Kléber Haedens, Stephen Hecquet, Félicien Marceau and Michel Mohrt. Although often coming from right-wing backgrounds, they were for the most part too young to have active experience of collaboration during the Occupation. They adopted an acerbic right-wing stance in the postwar years as an expression of both disorientation in a world which provided no role for them and contempt for a political system which they saw as corrupt and hypocritical.

Their rebellion against an older generation and the political and moral orthodoxy took the form of ardent anti-republicanism and bitter opposition to what they saw as the 'official philosophy of the regime', **existentialism**. This opposition was translated into polemical texts, like Laurent's *Paul et Jean-Paul* (1951), or intellectual fiction, like Nimier's *Les Épées* (The Swords) and *Le Hussard bleu* (The Blue Hussar) from 1948 and 1950 respectively, which trace the disabused journey of the protagonist, François Sanders, through the Occupation and the French invasion and occupation of Germany in 1945. More importantly, the opposition to republican moral superiority founded on a Resistance past and the high-serious didacticism of existentialism, took the form of fictional experimentation and exploitation of a strain of wistful comedy which both punctured the prevailing pomposity and expressed an underlying sense of frustration. Laurent's 1948 novel *Les Corps tranquilles* (Quiet Bodies) is an ambitious attempt to evoke the interwar years through one of its major intellectual preoccupations – suicide – using a large cast of characters and a structure, indicated by the chemical title, which comes from scientific theory. In this, he joins both **Queneau** and **Vian** in turning the novel away from moral or political thematic concerns to the aesthetic, intellectual and ludic domain which is the heartland of fiction. Similarly, Blondin's 1949 *L'Europe buissonnière* (Europe Plays Truant) depicts World War II in comic terms which owe much to Céline's *Journey to the End of the Night* (*Voyage au bout de la* *nuit*) and his 1952 *Les Enfants du Bon Dieu* (Children of God), evokes the lack of purpose of postwar youth through a whimsical psychological plot in which, literally, history, the cornerstone of existentialism, is rewritten. The *Hussards* constituted a powerful literary group and counterweight to existentialism in the late 1940s and 1950s, mainly, but not exclusively, clustered around the publisher Roland Laudenbach and Les Éditions de la Table Ronde. They also played an important part in postwar journalism, with Nimier as editor of *Opéra*, Laurent as editor of *La Parisienne* (of which he was also proprietor) and *Arts*, and Blondin as leading editorialist of *Rivarol* in its early years, while at the same time becoming one of France's most distinguished sports journalists, writing regularly on rugby and cycling for *L'Équipe*. Their cultural heritage, however, came specifically from the 1920s and the '*années folles*' following World War I, which they sought to replicate after the next world war: hence their devotion to **Morand**, Cocteau, Chardonne and, especially, the memory of Drieu la Rochelle. While this produced genuinely innovative literature in the 1940s and 1950s, it was (arguably) not able to sustain the group's output into de **Gaulle**'s presidency and beyond.

NICHOLAS HEWITT

See also: committed literature; publishing/*l'édition*

Further reading

Hewitt, N. (1996) *Literature and the Right in Post-War France: The Story of the* Hussards, Oxford: Berg (a comprehensive account).

Hyvrard, Jeanne

b. 1945, Paris

Writer

Hyvrard's adoption of a pseudonym and her efforts to protect her privacy led readers of the novels she published in the mid-1970s – *Les Prunes de Cythère* (The Plums of Cythera), *Mother Death* (*Mère la mort*) and *La Meurtritude* (Murderation) – to assume that she, like their narrator/protagonists, was a black woman from the Antilles who had experienced madness and psychiatric incarceration. Hyvrard is in fact white and French, but was inspired to write after working in the Caribbean in the late 1960s. Much of her creative work deals with themes such as women's identity/identity loss, their (oppressive) bond with the mother, their relation to writing, and the (deadly) restraints imposed upon them by patriarchal society and its language. Identified by critics as a kind of *écriture féminine*, her literary style is multivocal, poetic and grammatically unconventional. Apart from novels, Hyvrard has written short stories and, in the 1980s, philosophical essays, including *Canal de la Toussaint* (All Saints' Channel) and *La Pensée corps* (Thinking Through the Body), published respectively in 1986 and 1989.

ALEX HUGHES

See also: Montrelay, Michèle; women's/lesbian writing

I

Ici-Paris

Newspaper

Ici-Paris is one of France's main weekly scandal sheets, euphemistically classified as the 'escapist press' (*presse d'évasion*). Founded in 1945 by Henri and Suzanne de Montfort, as successor to their Resistance newspaper, *Ici-Paris* soon changed to target a lowbrow market, featuring horoscopes, titillating love intrigues, cartoons and society gossip. Locked in permanent battle to outdo its main competitor, **France-Dimanche**, it has consistently plumbed the depths of outrageous, shocking and far-fetched reportage, drawing on bizarre tales of the occult, gory accounts of medical mishaps, exposés of secrets, and in particular the intimate detail of marriages and divorces. It has made a speciality of speculatively probing the private lives of internationally known figures in politics or entertainment, often printing wholly fictitious accounts, and focusing with particular relish on Europe's royal families, especially that of Britain; for example, since the 1960s it has regularly headlined lurid announcements of the (secret) abdication, blindness, terminal illness or death of Queen Elizabeth II. Its circulation rose to a high point of 1.2 million in 1970, but fell in the 1990s to a third of that level. Like *France-Dimanche*, it is now owned by the powerful Hachette **publishing** group.

MICHAEL KELLY

See also: national press in France

iconography

Like other same-suffix terms, iconography designates both the object of investigation and the investigative method itself (for most current scholarly purposes, Panofsky's distinction between iconography as description-cum-classification, and iconology as interpretation, is largely disregarded). Originally devotional or monarchical images, icons (from the Greek *eikon*) gradually acquired the triple functions of identification, mobilization and allegorical narrative. In increasingly secular societies, iconography expresses the beliefs and objectives of different sociocultural groups, from **football** clubs to political parties, and, like other forms of symbolic discourse which connote as well as denote, is capable of overdetermination and ideological recuperation with changing historical circumstances.

The Revolution of 1789 launched, and the nineteenth century consolidated, a particular iconographical and symbolic lexicon (allegorical female figures, Phrygian bonnet, Republican fasces, etc.), energetically idealized in works such as Rude's sculpted *Départ des volontaires* (also known as *La Marseillaise*) and Delacroix's *Liberty Leading the People* (*La Liberté guidant le peuple*). It was, however, the emergence in the 1920s of the antagonistic ideologies of Communism and Fascism which produced the high-water mark of political iconography in twentieth-century France, the period from the Popular Front of 1936–8, through the **Vichy** regime (1940–4) to the postwar 'tripartism' of the victorious Resistance coalition. Vichy's corporatist experiment, enshrined in the motto '*Travail, famille, patrie*' (Work, family, fatherland), was focused upon the cult of the head of state, Marshal Philippe Pétain, iconographically evoked in the military *képi*, and the seven-starred marshal's baton which also constituted the shaft of the double-headed *francisque* (decorative Gallic axe). With its regionalist, culturalist and agriculturalist dimensions, Petainism was a sustained attempt to establish a coherent iconographical system whose very coherence did not reflect, and was doubtless designed in part to mask, its ideological and intellectual contradictions. The mood of national reconstruction and reconciliation, and the re-establishment of Republicanism which accompanied the **Liberation**, were encapsulated in Paul Colin's strikingly 'Christian' Marianne (1944), but this was essentially a resurrection of pre-war symbolism and, like the coalition itself, likely to unravel into its constituent political strands. A 1958 Colin poster combined the triadic arrows of Socialism with a stylized (female) bowsprit; Communism continued to give pride of place to the hammer and sickle, but the Phrygian bonnet also served (both featured on partisan Resistance memorials) and, after 1961, so did **Picasso**'s dove of peace. Gaullism, given its origins, its organizing principles and the personality of its founder, scarcely lent itself to the multiple variations of *maréchaliste* iconography and, apart from the Cross of Lorraine, it is rather a series of discreet photographic images that represent de **Gaulle**'s achievement: the garden and study at Colombey-les-deux-églises, the Algiers prefecture in 1958, the televised appeals to the nation and, after definitive retirement in 1969, the last elegiac photograph of the general and Madame de Gaulle on an Irish beach. The student revolution of **May 1968**, which effectively ended his presidential tenure, generated innumerable posters and graffiti, some of which, replicated by cartoonists such as Sennep, Jean Effel and Jacques Faizant, became collectors' items. 1968 also reactualized certain iconic symbols, notably the Phrygian-bonneted Marianne, since modelled by *vedettes* such as **Bardot** and **Deneuve**. The sexualization is not new; Marianne was always a phantasy figure, who survives in more traditional mode on the postage stamps. But the legacy of the events was literary as much as iconographical, and the 'Occident' symbol of the right-wing student group of that name provided a motif for textual variations by **Ricardou** in *Révolutions minuscules* (Minuscule Revolutions) of 1971.

The tendency for iconography as an accumulation of complex signifying practices to return to its origins, for iconography to regress to icon, to single images whose meaning is transparent and not constructed (the replacement of traditional Socialist symbols by the red rose, a phenomenon typical also of the British Labour Party), accelerated significantly in the 1980s. This arose partly from greater televisual mediation, and partly from the decline of traditional party politics, and stable, overarching, totalizing ideologies with the rise of single-issue groups representing feminists, sexual and ethnic minority rights, ecologists, etc. Whether a 'rainbow coalition' will emerge from 'this division of the French into heterogeneous consumer groups' (translated from Fumaroli 1991) remains to be seen. Moreover, while the extreme right-wing amalgam of Lepenism and Catholic *intégrisme* (pre-Vatican II fundamentalism) briefly juxtaposed images of the Sacred Heart, Joan of Arc and Pétain, iconography traditionally associated with the Left and Centre Left has increasingly been experienced in a nostalgic or caricatural mode: the Bicentenary reenacted 1789 as tourist spectacle and heritage industry; a **Mitterrand** campaign poster with its country village and the candidate's tricolour rosette contained echoes of a previous 'return to the land', which, in the light of subsequent revelations about the late president's wartime role, could be deemed ironic as well as iconic. The powerful marketing imperatives of the **advertising** industry, the transient consecration of *le look*, also played a part in this transformation. As 'icon' and 'iconic' came variously to designate media personalities, **sport** and leisure fashion items (an international brand of training shoes, for example), and the once-sacrosanct base interest rate of the *caisse d'épargne* (Trustees Savings Bank), some commentators adopted the term 'emblematic' – equally evocative, equally vague, but giving fewer hostages to fortune. Paradoxically, but perhaps predictably, in the 1990s traditional French iconography enjoyed greater transnational and crosscultural resonance: Delacroix's *Liberty*, and Géricault's more problematic *Radeau de la méduse* (The Raft of the Medusa) have become established in the representational arsenal of contemporary British cartoonists, a tool for the portrayal of Anglo-Saxon attitudes, social and political, and a graphic expression of underlying ambivalence towards the United Kingdom's nearest European partner.

WILLIAM KIDD

See also: Catholicism and Protestantism; comic strips/cartoonists; Le Pen, Jean-Marie; nationalism; painting; parties and movements

Further reading

Agulhon, M. and Bonte, P. (1992) *Marianne: les visages de la République*, Paris: Gallimard (an anatomy of France's major icon).

Forbes, J. and Kelly, M. (eds) (1995) *French Cultural Studies: An Introduction*, Oxford: Oxford University Press (a collection of essays).

Fumaroli, M. (1991) *L'État culturel: essai sur une religion moderne*, Paris: Folio (a polemical critique of state cultural intervention).

immigration

Immigration has become an issue of major political, social and cultural significance. In recent times, it has been used as both a political football and an umbrella term to refer to a diverse range of issues. The term 'immigration' is therefore ambiguous, since it can embrace both the limited questions of migration flows and the nature of the foreign population in France, and wider issues and debates in contemporary French society, such as French national history and national identity, Islam and secularism, and racism and anti-racism.

Let us briefly consider the recent history of migration flows and immigration policy in France. Until the beginning of the 1970s, immigration was largely confined to the realm of technocrats concerned with the **economy**, the labour force and questions of demography. The state had a minimal role in regulating migration flows (despite the presence of the Office National d'Immigration, established in 1945 precisely for that purpose), and immigration was not a prominent political issue. A more interventionist approach by the state was only deemed necessary when the nature of immigration changed from predominantly European flows to North and sub-Saharan African flows, was believed to have shifted from the temporary residence of single men to the permanent settlement of families, and was consequently deemed to be no longer simply an economic but now a social and cultural question. The new 'problem' of immigration required a new 'solution' which, as in other Western industrial democracies at the time, took the form of immigration controls of non-European foreigners whose presence was conceived as a threat to social cohesion.

Following the suspension of primary immigration in 1974 by **Giscard d'Estaing**, initial efforts to aid the process of integration of immigrants (for example, in the areas of housing and employment) and to recognize cultural difference soon gave way to a more rigorous attempt to control and reverse migration flows from North Africa. This policy was pursued through measures which linked the right of residence to employment, clamped down on illegal immigration (*immigration clandestine*) and established a package of financial aid for repatriation (*aide au retour*).

Despite Socialist claims that they would introduce a new and coherent policy on immigration when they took over power in 1981, the broad lines of **Mitterrand**'s policy of 'integration and control' in the 1980s could be said to be simply a continuation of the approach adopted by Giscard in the 1970s. Measures improving the lives and conditions of immigrants – the right to free association of immigrant groups and the amnesty for illegal immigrants in 1981, the ten-year residence and work permit in 1984 – were offset by tighter controls from 1983 onwards, the refusal to grant immigrants the right to vote in municipal elections (a promise which was contained in Mitterrand's 110-point manifesto programme for the presidential elections of 1981), and the reintroduction of a voluntary repatriation scheme (*aide à la réinsertion*) in 1984. Since 1986, the alternation of right- and left-wing governments has had little bearing on the direction of immigration policy, which has continued to favour restrictive controls on entry and residence, the removal of illegal immigrants, and the tightening up of rules on political asylum.

Despite the fact that the foundations for this politicization of immigration were laid in the 1970s, it was only in the 1980s that immigration became an issue of major political significance: the rise of the extreme right-wing Front National (founded in 1972 by Jean-Marie **Le Pen**), and the parallel rise of new anti-racist organizations (notably SOS Racisme in 1984 and France Plus in 1985), polarized the issue around pro- and anti-immigrant positions; political parties sought to use immigration for electoral ends; the media raised the stakes through their generally emotive treatment of the question; while second-generation youth sought new forms of expression of cultural and political identities. By the middle of the decade it had become difficult to debate immigration in a rational, non-partisan way, because the issues had become obscured by half-truth and distortion, while the term 'immigration' had itself become a euphemism to refer to those of North African origin or 'appearance'. In this atmosphere, the fact that the Portuguese community was roughly the same size as the Algerian community, or that almost half a million *Harkis* (Algerians who fought for France

during the **Algerian war**) and many second-generation immigrants born in France had French nationality, did not disturb the general impression that 'immigration' was a question of what to do about 'others' from the Maghreb. Increasingly, this unholy alliance of euphemism, dubious statistics and cultural stereotyping was bracketed (in political and media discourse) with wider social and political questions, such as the problems of **housing** and **employment** in the **suburbs** of major cities, the crisis in universal values and the 'integration' of society, and the future of secular education (*laïcité*).

In other words, the contemporary politicization of immigration is symptomatic of wider crises affecting France in a post-colonial and postmodern era: migration from the poorer south and the post-Communist East to the richer Western democracies; the breakdown in processes of assimilation of diverse people through the major institutions of the state; the question of cultural difference in a society which has traditionally prided itself on uniformity and equality in the public sphere (*la République une et indivisible*); new forms of racism accompanying the fast-changing political and cultural landscape; the nature of national identity in what is, arguably, a post-national era.

Accompanying the debate on immigration has been a far-reaching reappraisal of French national history and the idea of the nation. For some, it has been an opportunity to view France's past in terms of an historical cultural unity which is threatened by the cultural difference of today's immigrants. For others, it has been a chance to reaffirm the importance of immigration (and hence diversity) in the development of the French nation, and to challenge the mythical cultural homogeneity of a 'pure' France. The historical question of whether the nation is a contractual association of individuals (irrespective of race, religion or origin), or a community of cultural or racial heritage, is at the heart of these debates. This was most evident at the time of the proposed changes to the Nationality Code by the **Chirac** administration in 1986–7. The plan to transform the acquisition of French nationality for second-generation children born in France from an automatic right to a voluntary request was shelved at the time, but became law under the **Balladur** government in 1993. Many saw this as a clear sign that France had abandoned its traditionally open model of the nation based on residence (known as the political model) in favour of the 'German' model based on blood (the ethnic or racial model). The debate on the Code of Nationality demonstrated to what extent 'immigration' raised fundamental questions about the history and institutional fabric of the French nation.

In recent times, immigration has been transformed from a minor non-political issue into a major issue encompassing diverse aspects of French society and history. At stake are fundamental questions concerning France's present and future: Are equality and uniformity the only means by which social solidarity and cohesion can be preserved, or can an acceptance of difference and pluralism provide the answer? Or can France find a satisfactory middle path between the two?

MAX SILVERMAN

See also: beurs; demographic developments; Désir, Harlem, and SOS Racisme; Islam; Judaism; parties and movements; postmodernism; racism/anti-semitism

Further reading

Hargreaves, A. G. (1995) *Immigration, 'Race' and Ethnicity in Contemporary France*, London: Routledge (good overview of current debates and issues).

Ireland, P. (1994) *The Policy Challenge of Ethnic Diversity: Immigrant Politics in France and Switzerland*, Cambridge, MA: Harvard University Press (analysis of immigrants' political mobilization within the context of a national framework of a 'host' society).

Silverman, M. (1992) *Deconstructing the Nation: Immigration, Racism and Citizenship in Modern France*, London: Routledge (immi-

gration treated as a symptom of wider crises in contemporary France).

Weil, P. (1991) *La France et ses étrangers*, Paris: Calmann-Lévy (detailed and comprehensive analysis of French immigration policy).

Indochine

Musicians

An influential, highly instrumental rock group with a harsh, rhythmic, powerful sound, whose career in France took off in the 1980s. Internationally renowned, they export their product – polished, but with a hint of derision in their style – to the rest of Europe, Canada, the Far East and Latin America. Their tours include numbers from their last three albums: *The Birthday Album* (1991), *Un jour dans notre vie* (One Day in Our Life) from 1993 and *Radio Indochine* (1994).

GÉRARD POULET

See also: rock and pop; song/*chanson*

InfoMatin

Newspaper

A new-style newspaper (created 10 January 1994), targeted at a young and busy city-dwelling audience and published on weekdays only, *InfoMatin* survived longer than any other new national title since the advent of **Libération**. A product of market research, it was a small-format news-sheet, weighing just 60 g, and was printed on good-quality paper. Colour on every page and extensive use of photographs emphasized the visual. Serious news coverage was provided in short, accessible articles, and practical advice offered on a wide range of topics. Initially enthusiastic reception soon subsided: André Rousselet came to the paper's rescue in March 1995, but on 8 January 1996 *InfoMatin* was obliged to cease publication.

PAM MOORES

See also: national press in France

informal economy

The term 'informal economy' refers to those activities which are productive of goods or services, but which are ignored by or hidden from the state for tax, **social security** and labour-law purposes, albeit legal in all other ways. Interest was kindled in the informal economy in France by the huge rises in unemployment which took place during the 1970s and 1980s.

Because the term 'informal economy' covers very diverse phenomena, it is necessary to distinguish between paid and unpaid informal economic activity. Paid informal work is often known as clandestine or 'black market' work. The term covers a range of activities from one-off cash-in-hand jobs undertaken for friends or neighbours, to the exploitation of illegal immigrant workers in sweatshops. Unpaid informal work includes voluntary work, work done for family, friends or neighbours and the everyday unpaid domestic work carried out in the home often by women for their families.

It is obviously very difficult to discover the actual amount of informal economic activity taking place in an economy, but estimates are possible. In France, it has been suggested that the paid informal economic sector may be worth anything up to 10 per cent of gross domestic product (GDP). This figure is higher than that for Britain and other northern European states, but lower than the figure for many southern European nations. Furthermore, national studies have revealed that the number of hours the French population spend engaged in unpaid informal work outstrips the amount of time spent on employment and professional activities. Moreover, monetary estimates of the value of unpaid informal work in France indicate that it is worth around 50–65 per cent of GDP.

In France, much interest has been shown in the informal economy, particularly in the early 1980s, before a universal welfare benefit was introduced for the long-term unemployed. Some were surprised that revolution had not broken out on the streets, given the rising numbers of long-term unemployed who had come to the end of their period of entitlement to statutory unemployment benefits (Rosanvallon 1980). The conclusion was therefore drawn that the unemployed, having the time and the incentive to do so, were busying themselves working in the informal economy. However, research found that this was not the case (Barthe 1985). It was discovered that, although the unemployed have the time and the incentive to carry out informal economic activity, various factors prohibit them from undertaking such work. Often the unemployed do not have the skills to work informally, nor can they afford to buy the equipment or raw materials necessary for such work. Equally, if there is no market for their labour in the formal sector, it is likely that there will not be a market in the informal sector either.

JAN WINDEBANK

See also: economy; employment

Further reading

Barthe, M.-A. (1985) 'Chômage, travail au noir et entraide familial', *Consommation* 3 (article reporting a research project into the relationship between unemployment and the informal economy).

Rosanvallon, P. (1980) 'Le Développement de l'économie souterraine et l'avenir des sociétés industrielles', *Le Débat* 2 (theoretical article suggesting the unemployed are active in the paid informal economy).

Windebank, J. (1991) *The Informal Economy in France*, Aldershot: Avebury (a discussion of competing theoretical perspectives concerning the informal economy in France).

Institute of the Arab World

Conceived in the context of the oil crisis under

the presidency of **Giscard d'Estaing** as part of a policy to improve relations with the Arab world, this became one of the Grands Projets built under François **Mitterrand**. The site and architect originally chosen were changed under the auspices of Jack **Lang** at the Ministry of Culture and his adviser Christian Dupavillon. The building, designed by Jean Nouvel and partners, was acclaimed as an architectural masterpiece. Inaugurated in 1987, its facilities include a museum, a library and exhibition space, but its record of activities has been generally disappointing, due to persistent conflicts between the founding partners.

SUSAN COLLARD

See also: architecture under Mitterrand

Ionesco, Eugène

b. 1912, Slatina, Romania;
d. 1994, Paris

Playwright

One of the most internationally famous playwrights of twentieth-century French theatre, Ionesco began writing plays in the 1950s, which by the following decade had become associated with the so-called **Theatre of the Absurd**. Characterized by his rejection of traditional notions of form, structure, character and language, Ionesco's works incarnate his philosophical ideas through employing both absurd and absurdist material and methods of structure and presentation. He defines the Absurd as 'that which is devoid of purpose . . . Cut off from his religious, metaphysical and transcendental roots, man is lost; all his actions become senseless, absurd, useless' (Esslin 1980).

Born to a Romanian father and a French mother, Ionesco grew up in France until 1925, when he returned to Romania, teaching French in a Bucharest *lycée* and writing articles for publication. He returned to Paris in 1940, where he worked in **publishing** until 1949. At this time, he vowed that he detested the theatre,

finding it both embarrassing and false as a medium. It was only after embarking on a series of English lessons that he found himself, almost against his will, writing his first play. Inspired by the nonsensical dialogue of his English primer, Ionesco produced *The Bald Primadonna* (*La Cantatrice chauve*), first staged by Nicolas **Bataille** in 1950. Billed as an 'anti-play', this marked his first challenge to the traditional, bourgeois theatre he detested. After acting for the first time for Bataille in his adaptation of Dostoevsky's *The Possessed*, he went on to write *The Lesson* (*La Leçon*), staged in 1951, which he dubbed a '*farce tragique*', an extremely black comedy, using language as a symbol of power, with seemingly nonsensical communications between characters and grotesque political and power-related imagery. *Jacques or Obedience* (*Jacques ou la Soumission*) followed, re-employing the idea, emphasized through the language, of the individual forced into conformism, with strong sexual imagery to stress the slavery of sexual desire. Then followed *The Chairs* (*Les Chaises*), a set of cabaret-style sketches, and *Victims of Duty* (*Victimes du Devoir*), the latter arguing strongly against considered ideas of drama at the time, and moving away from the theme of language. In *L'Impromptu d'Alma* in 1956 he argued once more against the dramatic dogmas of the day, this time attacking Brechtian drama. In *The Killer* (*Tueur sans gages*), staged in 1959, he developed the character of Bérenger, who was to reappear in several subsequent plays, notably *Rhinocéros*. He epitomized the struggling individual trying to challenge the absurdity of society, a theme which was to dominate much of Ionesco's later work. *Rhinocéros*, staged by **Barrault** at the Théâtre de l'Odéon, in 1960, was perhaps his biggest success, attacking totalitarianism in all its forms and exploring the desire for conformism in human nature. By now, Ionesco was enjoying international success, ironically finding himself part of the regular repertoire of the theatre establishment which he had sought to subvert, and applauded for the way his work redefined the possiblities of theatre. His plays are still regularly performed worldwide.

ANNIE SPARKS

See also: theatre

Further reading

Bradby, D. (1991) *Modern French Drama 1940–1990*, Cambridge: Cambridge University Press (see Chapter 4 for a discussion of Ionesco).

Esslin, M. (1980) *The Theatre of the Absurd*, Harmondsworth: Penguin (a thorough analysis of plays and philosophy; see especially Chapter 3).

Lamont, R. (1995) *Ionesco's Political Imperative*, Michigan: University of Michigan Press.

Irigaray, Luce

b. 1932, Belgium

Psychoanalyst and philosopher

Irigaray is a feminist working in the areas of **psychoanalysis**, philosophy and linguistics. Her work in general has been more warmly received in Italy, Canada, the United States and Britain than in France, although the importance of her studies in sociolinguistics is recognized in France far more than in anglophone circles.

Initially the aspects of Irigaray's work which attracted widespread attention were her critiques of Freud and **Lacan**, and her poetic celebrations of the female body in *This Sex Which is Not One* (*Ce Sexe qui n'en est pas un*). This skewed perspective on her oeuvre led to her being associated with women such as Hélène **Cixous** and Julia **Kristeva** as a 'French feminist' or advocate of *écriture féminine*. In the course of the 1970s and 1980s, these terms came to imply an emphasis on the joys of the female body, particularly in its reproductive capacity, which appeared biologically essentialist, heterosexist and Eurocentric to many other feminists – whether materialist or reformist. They also implied esoteric and thus elitist writing, which was difficult to penetrate, both because of its technicality (the range of psychoanalytical and philosophical reference) and because of its avant-gardist literary qualities. From the late 1980s onwards, a number of works have been published by Margaret Whitford and others which have addressed Irigaray's work with the seriousness and attention to detail which it requires, helping to unpick these misconceptions or oversimplifications.

Unlike Cixous and Kristeva, Irigaray has fairly consistently presented herself as a feminist. The former have both trained as analysts of literature, have produced literary works themselves and, more unusually to an Anglo-Saxon feminist eye, have focused their celebratory analysis of linguistic transgressions and modernist or avant-garde literary practices (which Cixous has called *écriture féminine*) on male-authored texts (with one or two notable exceptions, such as the writings of the Brazilian modernist Clarice Lispector). Irigaray appears to have little interest in literature as such, although her amorous dialogues with philosophers such as Nietzsche – as in her *Marine Lover* (*Amante marine*) – have an undoubted poetical quality. Her mode of reading does not display Kate Millett's hostility to male authors, but it combines amorous dialogue (approaching Cixous's reading practice) with a feminist critique which would be more welcome to an Anglo-Saxon feminist audience than Cixous's readings of Joyce. While, as a practising psychoanalyst, she is not as hostile to Freud as certain radical feminists, her approach is more openly feminist than that of Kristeva, who also practises **psychoanalysis** (see Irigaray's *Speculum of the Other Woman*).

Irigaray's loving words about women's sexual organs and possible relations between women still provoke charges of biologism, despite hopeful pronouncements by her admirers that the debate is dead. Clearly her words are designed to help make women feel more positive about what has been denigrated and degraded in our society. Irigaray is aware that for change to occur a transformation must take place on several levels; she does discuss economic, political and legislative issues. However, her expertise is in philosophy and psychoanalysis, and she has focused on questions of language. Crucially this is not a disembodied language – Irigaray has emphasized our need for a sensible transcendental which would overcome the deathly opposition between body (indeed, all matter) and mind or soul. That opposition, which privileges the mental and spiritual above mere matter, has not only had lethal effects in the biosphere, Irigaray tells us, but is also a question of sex, of downgrading the maternal body in favour of Father, Son and Holy Spirit. Women will only be able to exist as women (as opposed to the opposites of men, the mothers, virgins and whores assigned value in the masculine economy) when they have a place in the Symbolic and Imaginary Orders – when they have their own spiritual and aesthetic place, but also when the spiritual and cultural ceases to be cut off from the (maternal) body.

Irigaray publishes on a range of topics using a range of styles. The articles in *Je, tu, nous*, covering the role of the placenta, sexual practices in the time of AIDS, women and employment, are accessible to a wide audience. Other texts, such as *Elemental Passions* (*Passions élémentaires*), invite the reader to read them over and over again, playing with the dense, polysemic and elliptical pronouncements. Others again, such as her collaborative work on sociolinguistics (see *Sexes et genres*), address an audience of specialists, and use technical language and scholarly style. Irigaray's work can be conceptually divided into three strands:

- the critical strand, in particular her engagement with great figures of philosophy and psychoanalysis;
- the positive, practical strand – detailed suggestions how women's lives might be improved in the short and medium term; and
- the poetic and utopian strand, for example her dreams of a feminine economy.

The first strand has proved most generally palatable, although some feminists find aspects of this work both elitist and too kind to the great misogynists of the past. The second strand has sometimes been found comically detailed by more 'sophisticated' readers. The third strand inevitably provokes questions like 'how' and 'when'. The best answer utopian feminists can suggest is the transformative effect of reading utopian writing – at least as likely as the transformative effect of reading Mallarmé.

JUDITH STILL

See also: feminist thought

Major works

Irigaray, L. (1974) *Speculum de l'autre femme*, Paris: Éditions de Minuit. Translated G. Gill (1985) *Speculum of the Other Woman*, Ithaca: Cornell University Press.

——(1977) *Ce Sexe qui n'en est pas un*, Paris: Éditions de Minuit. Translated C. Porter with C. Burke (1985) *This Sex Which is Not One*, Ithaca: Cornell University Press.

——(1980) *Amante marine de Friedrich Nietzsche*, Paris: Éditions de Minuit. Translated G. Gill (1991) *Marine Lover of Friedrich Nietzsche*, New York: Columbia University Press.

——(1982) *Passions élémentaires*, Paris: Éditions de Minuit. Translated J. Collie and J. Still (1992) *Elemental Passions*, London: Athlone Press.

——(1990a) *Je, tu, nous pour une culture de la différence*, Paris: Grasset. Translated A. Martin (1993) *Je, Tu, Nous: Towards a Culture of Difference*, New York: Routledge.

——(ed.) (1990b) *Sexes et genres à travers les langues: éléments de communication sexuée*, Paris: Grasset.

Further reading

Burke, C., Schor, N. and Whitford, M. (eds)

(1994) *Engaging with Irigaray*, New York: Columbia University Press.

Chanter, T. (1995) *Ethics of Eros: Irigaray's Rewriting of the Philosophers*, New York and London: Routledge (philosophical analysis).

Fuss, D. (1990) *Essentially Speaking*, London: Routledge (an interesting intervention into the essentialism debate although the opposition set up between Irigaray and Monique Wittig is somewhat schematic).

Grosz, E. (1989) *Sexual Subversions: Three French Feminists*, Sydney: Allen and Unwin (an important survey).

Whitford, M. (1991), *Luce Irigaray: Philosophy in the Feminine*, London: Routledge (essential reading for anyone who wishes to take Irigaray seriously).

—— (ed.) (1991) *The Irigaray Reader*, Oxford: Basil Blackwell (a clear, accessible introduction to Irigaray's work).

Islam

Islam is often confused with *islamisme*. The former refers to the religion and cultural practices of Muslims; the latter to a political project associated especially with fundamentalist movements in Iran, Algeria, Egypt and elsewhere. The conflation of these two terms, coupled with the negative historical image of the barbarous Islamic hordes of the Crusades, has led to the popular image of Islam as a threat to the secular and 'modern' foundations of the Republican nation-state. Yet new constructions of Islam in France have challenged this image and, in the process, have reformulated both Islam and Frenchness.

Negative images of Islam in France have been fuelled not only by the rise of Islamic fundamentalism elsewhere in the world but by a number of other contributory factors. Amongst these we should mention the **Algerian war** and the debate around **immigration**. The bitter war fought between 1954 and 1962, which ultimately led to Algerian independence, has left deep scars in the French 'psyche'. The uncertain position of about half a million 'French Muslims', or *Harkis*, in France (those who fought for the French during the war of independence and had to be repatriated to France in 1962 for their own safety) is testimony to the profound ambivalence in France towards Algerian Muslims.

The politicization of immigration over the last twenty-five years has had the effect of extending this ambivalence to all North Africans (Maghrébins) in France. The new discourse of the cultural difference of North Africans in France (frequently based on the criterion of religious difference) is a powerful weapon for those who argue for the incompatibility of French and Muslim identities. Following what is perceived as a crisis in integration of many from immigrant families, Islam has become associated with the 'problems of the **suburbs**', disaffected and delinquent 'second-generation' youth, and uncivilized foreign practices (like ritual slaughter).

Underlying the notion of a dichotomy between Frenchness and Islam is the powerful French tradition of *laïcité* (secularism). With its roots in Republican universalism and Jacobin anti-clericalism, this tradition is central to the profound belief that the modern nation depends on the division between public (political) and private (religious/cultural) spheres. Islam, which does not recognize this division, is therefore interpreted by many as incompatible with the modern French nation. However, in today's post-colonial, postmodern and pluralist climate, not only does this doctrinaire version of *laïcité* appear more and more like an intolerant fundamentalism itself, but the separation of the public and private spheres (and hence political and sociocultural questions) is becoming increasingly difficult to maintain. A number of commentators have suggested that the principles of *laïcité* need to be rethought in order to bring it into line with the contemporary national and international landscape, and to guarantee the possibility of a French Islam.

Many of the issues mentioned above were raised during the famous 'headscarf affair' of 1989, in which three Muslim girls were excluded from their school in Creil near Paris for wearing their Islamic headscarves, hence breaching the code of *laïcité* in state education. Although the event was often presented in the media as a struggle between the fundamentalist obscurantism of a foreign-based Islam and the modern, secular and enlightened French nation-state, the issues were far more complex (see Gaspard and Khosrow-Khavar 1995).

Unlike Christianity and **Judaism**, which (in their different ways and over the years) have reached compromises with the Republican secular tradition and have an institutional presence recognized by the state, Islam has never been granted the same opportunity to find a similar space of its own. Hence, the common perception that Islam functions as a fifth column in France, manipulated by foreign regimes and outside influences (for example, the grand mosque in Paris is under Algerian control), is largely due to the inability of the French state to establish the ground rules for a French Islam.

However, just as Jews are not simply the product of anti-semitism, so too Muslims are not simply the product of anti-Muslim racism. Today, more than ever, Islam in France is far from an unproblematic faith, reducible to extremist fundamentalist politics or the product of negative images. Kepel (1987) and Étienne (1989) have revealed the diversity of practices which go under the name of Islam, and the heterogeneous nature of the so-called 'Muslim community'. Less than 5 per cent of the 2.5–3 million Muslims in France actually pray in a mosque or other place of worship, and most of them are of the older generation. For many young Muslims (for the most part born in France with French nationality, or eventually to acquire it at the age of 18), Islam has been either rejected or reinterpreted in a variety of ways. A number of young people have used Islam strategically, for the purposes of socialization and identity construction. For most, a Muslim heritage today is only one part of the wider process of socialization and identification; in conjunction with other forms of cultural and social identification, Islam contributes towards a hybrid sense of identity which challenges all-embracing religious/cultural stereotypes.

The so-called 'second' or beur generation has not only participated in political struggles to redefine rights and identities (for example, through anti-racist organizations like SOS Racisme and France Plus, and movements for new citizenship), but has also produced a vibrant cultural output, frequently born from the clash or mixing of traditions and identifications. In literature (Hargreaves 1991), music, theatre and the other arts, the new voices in the 1980s and 1990s of the beur generation have presented a challenge to the frequently ethnocentric nature of French cultural production and cultural theory, and rendered problematic some of the unquestioned assumptions underlying concepts of the French nation and national identity. The writers Mehdi **Charef** and Azouz **Begag**, the pop group **Carte de séjour** and the popular music known as raï have all, in their different ways, refashioned the terms 'Muslim' and 'France' to counter the notion of their mutual incompatibility.

Institutional rigidity and negative historical images are therefore being challenged by two processes: the breakdown of the divisions between the political and the sociocultural spheres, and the everyday construction by young French Muslims and cultural practitioners of a hybridized form of identification. Pluralism from above and below might yet lead to the erosion of monolithic stereotypes of Frenchness and Islam.

MAX SILVERMAN

See also: beurs; Désir, Harlem, and SOS Racisme; education, the state and the church; postmodernism; racism/anti-semitism

Further reading

Cesari, J. (1994) *Être musulman en France: associations, militants et mosquées*, Paris: Karthala/IREMAM (comprehensive overview of Muslims in France).

Étienne, B. (1989) *La France et l'Islam*, Paris: Hachette (historical account).

Gaspard, F. and Khosrow-Khavar, F. (1995) *Le*

Foulard et la République, Paris: Éditions du Seuil (account of the 'Creil affair').

Hargreaves, A. G. (1991) *Voices from the North African Immigrant Community in France: Immigration and Identity in Beur Fiction*, Oxford: Berg (discussion of **beur writing**).

Kepel, G. (1987) *Les Banlieues de l'Islam: naissance d'une religion en France*, Paris: Éditions du Seuil.

J

Jabès, Edmond

b. 1912, Cairo, Egypt;
d. 1991, Paris

Poet

Edmond Jabès is the outstanding self-consciously Jewish poet writing in French during the second half of the twentieth century. Born in a French-speaking community, he began writing **poetry** in 1943, having cultivated friendships with Max Jacob and Gabriel Bounoure. After the Suez crisis he left Egypt to settle in Paris and pursued his activity as a writer with renewed vigour. Deeply marked by the trauma of the Holocaust, Jabès tried in his writings to come to terms with the silence and absence of the Hebrew God during the years of persecution and extermination. After an initial collection of poems published in 1959, *Je bâtis ma demeure* (I Build My Dwelling), he developed a poetic style comprising lyrical expression, narrative, meditation, journal entries and aphorisms. The first cycle of six books (1963–5) is called *The Book of Questions/The Book of Yukel/Return to the Book* (*Le Livre des questions/Le Livre de Yukel/Le Retour au livre*), followed by the anagrammatic series *Yaël/Elya/Aély* (1967–72) and closed off by a seventh volume entitled *El, ou le dernier livre* (El, or the Last Book) (1973). 'Livre' occurs consistently in these, as well as in Jabès's later works, such as the three volumes of 1976–80, *The Book of the Resemblances* (*Le Livre des ressemblances*); its specific significance lies in the fact that Jabès thinks of the persistence of Judaism as being informed and confirmed by 'the Book'. Thus, for him the act of writing has become in certain ways the most authentic Jewish (and also human) act in the time of God's eclipse: how to speak the unutterable.

WALTER A. STRAUSS

See also: poetry

Jakobson, Roman

b. 1896, Moscow, Russia;
d. 1982, Boston, USA

Linguist

Jakobson worked successively with the Moscow, Prague and Copenhagen linguistic circles before settling in the United States, and published highly influential essays in a variety of fields: phonology, language acquisition, general linguistics and poetics. His model of the six functions of communication, and his binary analysis of the metaphoric and metonymic poles, have been widely quoted in France, particularly in connection with **structuralism**.

BÉATRICE DAMAMME-GILBERT

See also: Lévi-Strauss, Claude; linguistic/discourse theory.

Further reading

Jefferson, A. and Robey, D. (eds) (1986) *Modern Literary Theory*, London: B. T. Batsford (has several clear sections on Jakobson's poetics and a bibliography).

Jarre, Jean-Michel

b. 1948, Lyon

Composer and musician

Jean-Michel Jarre is France's most famous and commercially successful popular composer and musician of the modern era. His unprecedented success – based on technical and technological innovations with synthesizers, such as his semi-circular 'Magic Keyboard' and his famous Laser Harp – has guaranteed him huge audiences worldwide: for example, 1 million spectators for his Bastille Day concert in the Place de la Concorde in 1979, 150,000 spectators at five concerts in Peking and Shanghai in 1982 (with 30 million watching on television and 500 million listening on radio), and 1.3 million people at his free concert in Houston in 1986 (a feat which won him his second entry in the *Guinness Book of Records*). Worldwide record, tape, CD and video sales are now almost impossible to calculate, but record sales alone were of the order of 32 million by 1986.

Jarre's family contained a number of musicians and it was therefore not surprising that he began to learn the piano at the age of 5. While he was still at the Lycée Michelet, he took lessons in harmony, counterpoint and fugue with Jeannine Rueff of the Paris Conservatory. He also learned to play the electric guitar before gaining his degree and joining the Groupe de Recherches Musicales (Musical Research Group) in 1968. The direction his career was to take was now clear: seeking to create something other than conventional or classical music, he experimented with a new acoustic world that went beyond traditional scales and musical notation. The initial result was *The Cage* (1970), a piece of pure electronic music, followed in 1971 by the audacious but eminently successful introduction of his avant-garde music to the Paris Opera with *AOR*. The experimental *Deserted Palace* followed in 1972.

Jarre now diversified his activities by writing music for films, television, advertisements and other performers, not to mention compositions for ballet and the theatre. His first recording intended for release, the revolutionary *Oxygène*, dates from 1976 and became the best-selling French record of all time, topping the charts worldwide. This instant success brought with it prestigious accolades at home and abroad (the Grand Prix de l'Académie Charles Cros in France, and 'personality of the year' awarded by *People* magazine in the USA), while his achievements were recognized by the world's press ('Jean-Michel Jarre Oxygenius', proclaimed *Interview*; 'A French revolution to rock the world' announced the *Daily Mirror*). The world of popular music had been introduced to new sounds – electronic in origin but vibrant with emotion and rich in their powers of suggestion.

Jarre's second album, *Equinoxe* (1978), confirmed his international status and encouraged him to break new ground in the realm of live performance. The result was the spectacular and highly innovative Bastille Day concert of 1979 which, in addition to attracting the (then) record-breaking number of spectators, was seen by a television audience of some 100 million. On a personal level, this live concert allowed Jarre to realize one of his ambitions: the re-establishment of the free, 'open-house' musical festival. On a commercial level, it also led to the production of France's first 'full-length' video featuring a popular concert (though the duration – forty minutes – may seem short by current standards). Further successes have followed, such as *Magnetic Fields*, *Zoolooks*, *Rendez-Vous*, *Waiting for Cousteau*, and Jarre made a huge impact on the United Kingdom with his much-acclaimed Docklands Concerts (1988). Jarre continues to produce innovative, emotionally charged music of the highest quality and to perform in multimedia concerts which exploit every form of entertainment technology.

IAN PICKUP

See also: concert music

Major works

Jean-Michel Jarre Songbook (1989), Paris: Francis Dreyfus Music (Distribution ID Music) (contains English and French texts which look at Jarre's career in addition to the music of some of his compositions).

jazz

France is considered to be a special place for jazz, because of its extraordinary development there as the most popular form of 'scholarly' music since the 1950s. At the end of World War II, American troops entered France and in their wake came the jazzmen.

Before the war, jazz was already known in France. It had inspired some authentic jazzmen, like the orchestras of Jacques Hélian and Ray Ventura, and Django **Reinhardt** and Stéphane **Grappelli** formed the Quintette du Hot Club de France. This was the beginning of a French tradition of string jazz which is still very much alive. Jazz had also inspired the critical and sometimes controversial writings of Hugues Panassié – for example, his critical 1946 survey, *Douze années de Jazz* (Twelve Years of Jazz) and the influential review *Jazz hot* started in 1935 by Charles Delaunay. At the end of the 1940s, Panassié and Delaunay found themselves on opposite sides: the former defended pure jazz, the latter was open to new trends (such as swing and bebop). In Paris, it was the golden age of St-Germain des Prés, with Boris **Vian** the soul and mentor of the new musical wave. He reigned at the Tabou and other *caves* of the Latin Quarter, where the cellars of some cafés were transformed into temples of jazz. He regularly wrote his *Chroniques*

de jazz, in *Jazz hot* among others, until his premature death. Jazz, for him, was a way of life.

Besides the richness of French critical discourse in the 1960s and 1970s, jazz in France did not exist only in books. French musicians were particularly fertile in adopting this idiom and transforming it beyond its conventional borders. At the beginning, the controversy about the orthodoxy of New Orleans sound, compared to the new bebop closer to Charles Delaunay's and Boris Vian's hearts, was only concerned with conforming to the American model. A considerable number of American jazzmen went on tour in France. Some liked it so much they stayed – Sydney Bechet, for example. But if imitation for some was enough to express their musical talents, others, such as the pianist Bernard Peiffer and the saxophonist Jean Claude Fohrenbach, explored original paths. André Hodeir was to see his own original compositions triumph abroad.

The end of the 1960s coincided with a new page in the history of jazz worldwide in general, and France in particular. The younger generation rejected the old purists; even the beboppers were in decline. Miles Davis and free jazz were the new models. Jam sessions were everywhere and some talented bands systematically explored improvisation, such as the Workshop de Lyon. In the absence of structured codes, and with the generalization of a variety of practices, the improvisations took a new turn. When they met, artists listened to each other, rather than initiating collective improvisation. Often this came through drama or scenic endeavours, for example, La Compagnie Lubat.

The pendulum swung the other way at the end of the 1970s, with a neoclassical revival. Some very talented musicians, still organically linked with the tradition of free jazz, expressed their private world through more independent avenues. As a jazz intrument the violin was transformed, like the guitar, by becoming electric; and there was a whole new generation of jazz violinists whose talents would blossom in the 1980s (Dominique Pifarély, Pierre Blanchard). The strings would swing again (D. Levallet's Swing Strings System). The Hammond organ and the accordion were brilliantly used and the best example of the creative virtue of mixing free improvisation with the rigorous code of old could be found with the associations of Henri Texier (double-bass) and François Jeanneau (saxophone). This was the period of a more intimist form of neo-classical jazz performance in duos and trios, without the drum kit because of the illegal level of decibels at night in urban areas.

In the 1980s the jazz scene saw the revival of big bands, with a prolific number of new talents in this area. This phenomenon culminated in 1986 with the creation of the National Jazz Orchestra (ONJ), proving that since 1981 the cultural administration has been taking music in general, and jazz in particular, very seriously by providing generous subsidies for its development. It also provided the right context for an extraordinary increase in the number of music schools teaching jazz, as well as for a singular development of associations whose main objective was the creation and diffusion of jazz music. Another sign of this revolution was the creation (in 1992) of a substantial jazz department within the respected and scholarly Conservatoire National Supérieur de Musique et de Danse in Paris. The growth of the number of jazz musicians living or expecting to live off their trade in France is significant too – currently estimated at about 3,000. Unsuprisingly, half of them live in Paris, a centre of excellence, with a friendly rivalry between home-grown talents and jazz performers from America, Europe and Africa. It is happening within a fragile commercial world. Jazz counts for 3 per cent of record sales, of which 75 per cent are reissues – a stifling situation for creative artists who can only rely on a few independent producers to express their talents, within a market dominated by a handful of multinational concerns. The growth in the number of festivals is also significant – from 5 in 1975 (e.g. Juan-les-Pins), to 180 musical events exclusively concerned with jazz in Paris and in all regions (e.g. Provence-Côte d'Azur). All this points to the extrodinary vitality of jazz in the 1990s.

GÉRARD POULET

See also: cultural topography (Paris); music venues; regional music

Further reading

Anquetil, P. (1995) 'Géographie du jazz en France aujourd'hui', *Les Cahiers du jazz 6* (an analytical and critical survey of the jazz scene in Paris and the regions).
Bergerot, F. and Merlin, A. (1991) *L'Épopée du jazz 2: au delà du bop*, Paris: Découvertes Gallimard (a remarkably well-illustrated and informative study of postwar jazz in general, with a relevant chapter on jazz in France).

Jonasz, Michel

b. 1947, Drancy

Singer-songwriter

This former member of the group King Set initially wrote songs for others (including Alain Souchon) before becoming a most successful solo performer whose hits include Jean-Claude Vannier's *Super nana* (Fantastic Chick) and his own *J'veux pas qu'tu t'en ailles* (I Don't Want You to Go Away). The anguish which his songs often express (and the influence of blues is most pronounced) is sometimes tinged with humour – a combination of mood also characteristic of Souchon's work.

IAN PICKUP

See also: song/*chanson*

Jospin, Lionel

b. 1937, Meudon

Politician

A civil servant at Foreign Affairs and then a university teacher, Jospin joined the Parti

Socialiste (PS) in 1971. A protégé of **Mitterrand** in the 1970s, he was First Secretary of the PS between 1981 and 1988. Elected to the National Assembly in 1981, 1986 and 1988, and to the European Parliament in 1984, he was Minister of Education from 1988 to 1992. In the absence of other credible Socialist candidates, he emerged from the background to represent the PS in the 1995 presidential election and turned a predicted electoral *débâcle* into an honourable defeat (47.37 per cent of second-ballot votes). His conviction and promise of an honest, 'citizen's' (implicitly post-Mitterrand) approach to government contributed to his victory at the head of a Socialist–Communist–green coalition, which took him to the premiership following the 1997 elections.

LAURENCE BELL

See also: parties and movements

Major works

Jospin, L. (1991) *L'Invention du possible*, Paris: Flammarion (his vision of Socialism and interpretation of the Socialists' experience in power).
——(1995) *1995: 2000 propositions pour la France*, Paris: Stock (Jospin's 1995 campaign platform).

Jouhandeau, Marcel

b. 1888, Guéret;
d. 1979, Rueil-Malmaison

Novelist, essayist and memorialist, real name Marcel Provence

Jouhandeau was a prolific, gay Catholic writer tortured by what Claude Mauriac termed a '*mystique de l'enfer*'. In works such as *Chroniques maritales* (Chronicles of a Marriage), which features his *alter ego* Monsieur Godeau, *Chronique d'une passion* (Chronicle of a Passion), *L'École des garçons* (The School for Boys) and *Du pur amour* (On Pure Love), Jouhandeau examines the moral crisis created by having simultaneously a wife, a male lover and personal, spiritual needs. Accused of compromising himself with the Nazis during the war, and much criticized for his often overbearing candour and egotism – as evidenced in his twenty-seven-volume collection of autobiographical chronicles-cum-reflections, *Journaliers* (1961–1981) – Jouhandeau only achieved popular success with his early novels depicting the inhabitants of 'Chaminadour', an area drawn from his native town of Guéret. However, with the recent republication of 'secret' texts like *Traité de l'abjection* (Treatise on Abjection) and *Tirésias* (both eulogies of anal sex) he can now be better appreciated for exploring, with vivid and compassionate intensity, both the physical and the spiritual dimensions of male gay experience.

JAMES WILLIAMS

See also: Catholicism and Protestantism; gay writing; Vichy

Jourdheuil, Jean

b. 1944, St-Loup

Director and writer

Co-founder of the Théâtre de l'Espérance in 1968, Jourdheuil is noted for his Brechtian approach, written collaborations with Bernard **Chartreux** in the 1970s, and the discovery and translation of writer Heiner Müller. In the 1980s he co-wrote many autobiographical spectacles with Peyret, and is now professor at the University of Paris-X (Nanterre).

ANNIE SPARKS

See also: theatre

Major works

Jourdheuil, J. (1976) *L'Artiste, la politique, la production*, Paris: Union Générale d'Éditions (writings on theatre).

Jouve, Pierre-Jean

b. 1887, Arras;
d. 1976, Paris

Poet, novelist, translator and critic

Jouve's early formation was marked by Romain Rolland and the short-lived Unanimist movement. The next important event was his religious crisis in 1924, which caused him to renounce his early works and enter a new phase of poetic activity (plus the composition of five novels) in which spiritual and erotic sensibility predominates (the influence of Freudian **psychoanalysis** is also significant). His work during and after World War II continues along that same vein – *La Vierge de Paris* (The Virgin of Paris) of 1946, *Hymne* (Hymn) from 1947 and *Diadème* (Diadem) in 1949. The later poems, *Ode* and *Langue* (Language), from 1950 and 1954 respectively, make use of the *verset* (versicle) introduced into French poetry by Claudel and Saint-John **Perse**. A strong theme in Jouve's poetry is the spiritual anguish caused by the sense of nothingness (frequent reference to 'Nada'). Somewhat in contrast with most French poets, whose strongest affinities are with the plastic arts, Jouve maintained a lively attachment to music, publishing important lengthy essays on Mozart's *Don Giovanni* in 1942 and on Berg's *Wozzeck* in 1953. There is also a journal, *En miroir* (In the Looking Glass), published in 1954, and translations from Hölderlin, Shakespeare and St Theresa of Avila. The complete poems are published by Mercure de France (*Poésies*) in four volumes (1964–7).

WALTER A. STRAUSS

See also: poetry

Judaism

Judaism (*judaïsme*) and Jewishness (*judéité*) are treated together here, although strictly speaking the first refers to the religion of Jews, while the second embraces the wider and less stable category of Jewish identity. Today, both are subject to a number of different influences: traditional links between French Jewry and the ideas of French Republicanism; the fate of Jews in France under German Occupation and the **Vichy** regime during World War II, and the continuing repercussions of these events after the war; the centrality of the Holocaust; traditional and contemporary forms of anti-semitism; the history and destiny of Israel; the rise of ethnic particularisms and the reappraisal of monolithic concepts of identity.

Historically, the fate of Jews in France has been closely bound up with Republican ideals. The emancipation of the Jews in 1791 became symbolic of the power of the revolutionary ideal to free individuals from their particular 'parochial' backgrounds and bring them into the realm of 'light' as free and equal citizens. Jews, therefore, came to be associated, like no other group, with the revolutionary Republican and Enlightenment project of assimilation. This was a contract that both sides, Jews and Republicans, entered willingly in the name of freedom and equality. Hence, the Dreyfusards, in championing the falsely accused Jewish army captain, Alfred Dreyfus, at the end of the nineteenth century, were inspired more by pro-Republican than by philosemitic sentiment, and used Dreyfus as a symbol of the universalist and assimilationist Republican message. Jews themselves were far more comfortable fighting for universal human rights than in the name of ethnic difference. Until fairly recently, French Jewry has, in general, been a fervent supporter of the Republican message, which has meant repressing signs of difference in the public sphere (the neutral, egalitarian space of citizenship) and maintaining religious and cultural practices only discreetly in the private sphere.

However, a number of factors have brought about a reappraisal of the position of Judaism and concepts of Jewishness, three of which are considered here. First, the contemporary crisis in Republican institutions and ideals, the breakdown in traditional forms of political mobilization, and the re-emergence of ethnic identities, has led to new forms of Jewish self-perception and new directions for political action. Less and less reticent about expressing their difference, Jews are now just as likely to fight anti-semitism on ethnic lines (that is, as Jews) as on the traditional Republican lines of the Rights of Man (that is, as human beings). The robust challenge to revisionist histories of the war and to the latent (and often overt) anti-semitism of the Front National demonstrates a greater willingness, especially among the generation of Jews born after the war, to reaffirm the Jewish presence in French history and in contemporary France. Hence, the infamous statement by Jean-Marie Le Pen that the Holocaust represented only a 'detail' in the history of the war and the desecration of Jewish graves in Carpentras in 1990 were both met by high-profile campaigns to mobilize popular support behind opposition to anti-semitism.

Second, the betrayal of the Republican contract by the Vichy regime and the continuing refusal (until relatively recently) of political leaders to acknowledge the complicity between France and the Holocaust have contributed to a loss of faith in the universalist egalitarianism of Republicanism, and the desire to be more assertive in protecting Jewish interests. The issue of war crimes in the 1980s and 1990s is, in part, a reflection of this desire: the pursuit (by the lawyer Serge Klarsfeld and others) of the Nazi Klaus Barbie and the French collaborators Paul Touvier, René Bousquet and Maurice Papon not only sought to bring to justice those who had committed crimes against humanity, but also aimed to challenge established myths about French protection of Jews during the war.

Third, the Holocaust itself has become, for many, the major determinant of Jewish identity and has therefore replaced the connections between Jews and the Enlightenment tradition of modernity as the central definer of Jewish history in France. Much cultural output by

Jews since the war (notably that of Paul Celan, Edmond **Jabès**, Claude Lanzmann, Emmanuel **Lévinas**, Patrick **Modiano** and Elie Wiesel) has inevitably dealt with questions of survival and loss, memory, history, identity and representation deriving from the experience of the Holocaust.

For a number of French writers and philosophers (Maurice **Blanchot**, Hélène **Cixous**, Jacques **Derrida**, Jean-François **Lyotard**) Jewish experience of the Holocaust has been developed into a generalized critique of the project of modernity. The term 'Jew', inextricably linked to Auschwitz, is employed allegorically to signify the failure of the modern project of assimilation or eradication of the other, and the postmodern impossibility of the representation of truth, presence and reality. 'Jew' is therefore an affirmation of all that was stigmatized in the age of modernity, including otherness, difference and a non-essentialist concept of unrooted and diasporic identity. Here the specificity of real Jews, Jewish history and identity is replaced by the term 'Jew' as a sign of 'otherness' and postmodern flux.

Hence, Judaism and Jewishness in France today must be seen in the context of both wider historical processes and contemporary developments. In today's climate of a crisis of assimilation and a decline in universal values, Judaism and Jewishness are more overtly particularistic, fighting their corner to reaffirm their past and present existence. Like other ethnicized groups today, Jews are caught between two extremes: on the one hand, fixed and monolithic versions of difference and history; and on the other, more flexible and pluralistic notions of difference and history in which Jewishness is not only itself seen as problematic (for example, the distinction within the Jewish community between Sephardi and Ashkenazi traditions), but constitutes only one aspect of a multilayered identity. Although poles apart in terms of identity-formation, both these positions have at least one thing in common: the view that Jews are not simply determined from the outside (through the look of the non-Jew or the anti-semite, as Jean-Paul **Sartre** famously argued in 1946 in *Anti-Semite and Jew* (*Réflexions sur la* *question juive*), but play an active role in the construction and perpetuation of their own difference.

MAX SILVERMAN

See also: racism/anti-semitism

Further reading

Birnbaum, P. (1992) *Anti-Semitism in France: A Political History from Léon Blum to the Present*, Oxford: Blackwell (a translation from the French of Birnbaum's comprehensive treatment of the subject).

Hayoun, M.-R. (1991) *Le Judaïsme moderne*, Paris: PUF, 'Que sais-je?' (general introduction to modern Judaism).

Lyotard, J.-F. (1988) *Heidegger et 'les juifs'*, Paris: Galilée (postmodern philosophical use of the term 'Jew' to signify otherness).

Juppé, Alain

b. 1945, Mont-de-Marsan, Landes

Politician

One of a generation of technocrats whose political career was tied to that of **Chirac** from the late 1970s, Juppé was deputy mayor of Paris (1983–95), Minister for the Budget and government spokesman (1986–8), and General Secretary of the neo-Gaullist RPR (1988–95). As Minister for Foreign Affairs in the 1993–5 **Balladur** government, his competence was generally appreciated. Elected mayor of Bordeaux and appointed as prime minister by Chirac in 1995, he soon faced protracted strike movements and became deeply unpopular, owing to the apparent readiness of his government to sacrifice employment, welfare provision and public spending to the exigencies of preparing France for a single European currency. He was widely (but somewhat unjustly) blamed for the Right's resounding defeat in 1997, following President Chirac's ill-advised calling of early elections.

LAURENCE BELL

See also: European economic integration; parties and movements

K

Kaas, Patricia

b. 1967, Forbach, Lorraine

Singer

A remarkably mature blues singer for someone of her age, Patricia Kaas is one of the rising stars of the world of French popular music. Already a very successful stage performer (in France and abroad), whose successes include *Mademoiselle chante le blues* (The Young Lady Sings the Blues) and *I Wanna be Loved by You*, Kaas has already been drawn to Hollywood and to a possible film career.

IAN PICKUP

See also: jazz; song/*chanson*

Kacel, Karim

b. 1959, Paris

Singer

The pure product of beur culture, Kacel has created a singular synthesis of all the musical styles he has exposed himself to: **jazz**, classical, rock, funk and soul. Classified at first as the voice of the **suburbs** (*banlieue*), as in his well-known song, *Banlieues* on his 1984 album, *Gens qui rient, gens qui pleurent* (Laughing People,

Crying People), this charismatic performer is becoming a legend in the French pop landscape.

GÉRARD POULET

See also: beur music; beurs; rock and pop; song/*chanson*

Kalisky, René

b. 1936, Brussels;
d. 1981, Brussels

Playwright

Kalisky was a Belgian writer of structured texts during the 1970s, when the mood was generally against text-based theatre and towards **collective creation**. These include *Skandalon*, *La Passion selon Pier Paolo Pasolini* (Passion According to Pier Paolo Pasolini), and *Dave au bord de mer* (Dave at the Seaside), directed by **Vitez** in 1979.

ANNIE SPARKS

See also: francophone performing arts: Belgium; theatre

Karina, Anna

b. 1940, Copenhagen, Denmark

Actor

Karina was **Godard**'s obsessive muse for six years (the time they were married) and seven films, in all of which she is the love object for his camera in one of the great director–actor relationships. *Pierrot le fou* of 1965 – among other things a 'documentary' on the end of their marriage – features her most remarkable performance, though as the prostitute in 1962's *Vivre sa vie* she is also deeply affecting. Her non-Godardian career, with the possible exception of **Rivette**'s *La Religieuse* (1966), was never so successful, and her one attempt at direction (*Vivre ensemble* of 1973) misfired.

KEITH READER

See also: cinema

Khaled, Cheb

b. 1960, Oran

Singer

A paradox of the French pop scene, and known as *le king du raï*, Cheb Khaled exports his rock version of modern raï to the rest of the world from France. His big band was in the USA and UK in 1994. He sings in Arabic, but his message is not fundamentalist and reflects a wider human experience of wine, women and song.

GÉRARD POULET

See also: beur music; francophone popular music: North Africa; rock and pop

Kieslowski, Krzysztof

b. 1941, Warsaw;
d. 1996, Paris

Director

A Polish film director, whose last and most commercially successful films – *La Double Vie de Véronique* (1991) and the *Trois Couleurs* trilogy: *Bleu, Blanc,* and *Rouge* (1993–4) were produced in France, Kieslowski first gained international prominence in 1988 with *Dekalog (The Decalogue)*, ten short television dramas, two of which were expanded and released as feature films – *A Short Film About Love* and *A Short Film About Killing*, both 1988. A graduate of the state-run Lodz film school in Poland, he spent the first part of his career making documentaries that were critical of the Communist-led government in his native country. His abandonment of documentary for feature films marked his disillusionment with political struggle and a turn inward to emotional and spiritual questions.

The interlocking themes of freedom and responsibility, as well as a quasi-mystical sense of fate, subtend Kieslowski's later films. In *Dekalog*, which is based on the Ten Commandments, he depicted the crisis of morality in modern life, in which human passions are thwarted by a highly rationalized – if not always rational – world. The *Trois Couleurs* trilogy interprets the French ideals of *liberté, égalité* and *fraternité* respectively, in a context that is more personal than political. In *Bleu*, a woman must face her new-found 'freedom' after suffering the loss of her husband and child in a car accident. She embarks on a new life steeped in sorrow, but free of the responsibility and restrictions brought by emotional attachments. The film seems to question the value of such freedom, which the protagonist ultimately rejects as she comes to accept a new set of familial commitments. *Blanc*, set in both Poland and France (like *La Double Vie de Véronique*), depicts the corruption of egalitarian ideals in post-Communist Poland, where power differentials – once the privileged domain of politics – are expressed in terms of financial and personal relationships. The theme of imprisonment appears in parallel scenes, in which the protagonist gazes up at his beloved from below. In one scene, it is scorn that denies him access to her bedroom, while in the later one, an emotional reversal has taken place, as the overwhelming attachment she has developed for him leads her literally into prison.

Rouge, the final film in the trilogy, explores the idea of fraternity as it ponders where one life ends and another begins, and the extent to which people's lives affect one another. As in *Dekalog*, many characters reappear briefly from one film to the next in the *Trois Couleurs* trilogy, undermining the conventional assumption that a film must depict a self-contained diegetic universe. In a culmination of this practice, the final scene in *Rouge* unites the protagonists from all three films, giving the sense of a larger community that transcends the lives of individuals.

ELIZABETH EZRA

See also: cinema

Major works

Kieslowski, K. (1993) *Kieslowski on Kieslowski*, ed. D. Stok, London: Faber and Faber.

Kieslowski, K. and Piesiewicz, K. (1991) *Decalogue: The Ten Commandments*, trans. P. Cavendish and S. Bluh, London: Faber and Faber.

Further reading

Positif (1989) December (special section on Kieslowski).

Sight and Sound (1996) May (special section on Kieslowski).

Klein, Yves

b. 1928, Nice;
d. 1962, Paris

Artist

As an artist, Yves Klein resists all classification, despite his involvement with Nouveau Réalisme. Without a formal art education himself, he was raised among painters. His father was a landscape artist and his mother a painter of the *art informel* school. In his own art work Klein could be said to have transcended the opposition between the abstract and the figurative his parents represented: his almost fanatical devotion to Rosicrucianism and the Christian mystical teachings of its sacred text, the *Cosmogonie*, played a crucial role in the development of his artistic theories and practice. These beliefs were complemented by his practice of the spiritual disciplines associated with the art of judo, which he taught for much of his adult life.

In 1955, his monochrome **painting** *Expression de l'univers de la couleur mine orange* was rejected by the Salon des Réalités through a failure to understand Klein's intentions. These were to awaken in the viewer, through contemplation of the luminous intensity and immateriality of the single colour, the pictorial sensibility (*la sensibilité picturale*), which seems to equate to some kind of cosmic consciousness. It was the critic Pierre Restany who took on the role of interpreting and promoting Klein's work, beginning with the 1959 exhibition 'Yves: propositions monochromes'. The highly saturated luminous blue which Klein developed and patented as International Klein Blue (IKB) was used in his 1957 Milan exhibition in which eleven similar-sized blue monochromes were shown. Klein had priced each differently in an attempt to show that the painting's value resided not in its physical appearance but in its immateriality. It was an attempt to bring his art into line with the teachings of the *Cosmogonie*, which prophesied that the end of the age of physical matter and ego consciousness would herald an era of 'pure spirit', the immaterial.

The spiritual quality Klein saw in the colour blue was given further expression in his exhibition 'Pigment pur', which displayed a variety of objects impregnated with blue pigment, and an 'aerostatic sculpture' consisting of 1,001 blue balloons suspended over Paris could be regarded as an early Happening, prefiguring those of the 1960s.

Thanks to his 1958 exhibition 'Le Vide',

Klein has been seen as a precursor of Minimalism. The empty interior and bare white walls of Iris Clert's gallery represented an attempt to raise cosmic awareness by presenting the immateriality of the void itself as an object of contemplation. The void as a theme reappeared in 1965, when Klein published a one-off newspaper featuring a photomontage of himself flying in space with the caption '*Le peintre de l'espace se jette dans le vide*' ('The painter of space flings himself into the void'). This use of the media for artistic ends also identifies him as an early Pop artist.

In 1959, he used the female body as a 'living paintbrush', orchestrating the application of blue paint to the model and producing imprints on paper fixed to a wall. Dubbed *Anthropométries de l'époque bleue* by Pierre Restany, these body prints represented for Klein a concentration of 'vital energy', while others now see them merely as early examples of body art or performance art.

In 1960, Klein produced his triptych *IKB, Monopink, Monogold*, the triad of colours observable at the centre of a flame. Fire as a symbol of the life force was celebrated in his fire-sculptures and tamed in the fire-paintings made by holding sheets of paper to the flames. The process involved in creating these is comparable to that involved not only in his *Anthropométries* but also in his *Cosmogonies de la pluie*, in which rain was allowed to leave its mark on a painted blue canvas. This subordination of the painter's skills to the single creative act arguably prefigures conceptual art of the 1970s.

Klein's ability to anticipate so many later trends is not confined to the field of art. Many of the features of Rosicrucianism that informed his artistic production are reminiscent of the New Age thinking that arose in the decade following his premature death from a heart attack. His eccentric and grandiose plans for a provisional world government led by artists, scientists and the spiritually enlightened were grounded in the same belief system that fuelled his art. For Klein, art and life were one.

CAROL WILCOX

See also: sculpture

Major works

Klein, Y. (1983) *Yves Klein*, Paris: Centre Georges Pompidou (articles by Pierre Restany *et al.*, with good reproductions of Klein's work).

Further reading

Stich, S. (1995) *Yves Klein*, London: Hayward Gallery (gives useful and detailed documentation on the beliefs and values that inform his art).

Weitemeier, H. (1995) *Yves Klein 1928–1962*, Cologne: Benedikt Taschen (a comprehensive account of his art and life).

Kofman, Sarah

b. 1934, Paris;
d. 1995, Paris

Philosopher

A disciple of **Derrida**, Kofman wrote widely on his work and that of Freud and Nietzsche. Key thematic preoccupations of her work are aesthetics as read by and within psychoanalytic theory, and female sexuality in the psychoanalytic context. The latter is the focus of Kofman's 1980 publication, *The Enigma of Woman* (*L'Énigme de la femme: la femme dans les textes de Freud*). This work explores Freud's accounts of female sexuality, and critically deconstructs their ambiguities, obscurities and contradications. Kofman also wrote two autobiographical texts, *Rue Labat, rue Ordener* and *Paroles suffoquées* (Suffocated Words).

ALEX HUGHES

See also: psychoanalysis

Kokkos, Yannis

b. 1944, Athens

Stage designer

A political exile in France since 1963, and designer of sets for plays, operas and musicals. Kokkos's numerous collaborations with **Vitez** at the Théâtre National de Chaillot (1981–8) include the acclaimed *The Satin Slipper* (*Le Soulier de Satin*) by Claudel. He also worked on **Lassalle**'s productions of **Vinaver**'s work.

ANNIE SPARKS

See also: **theatre**

Major works

Kokkos, Y. (1989) *Le Scénographe et le Léon*, Paris: Actes Sud.

Koltès, Bernard-Marie

b. 1948, Metz;
d. 1989, Paris

Playwright

Despite admitting that he detested theatre, Koltès is nevertheless mostly remembered for his theatre works, and since his death from **AIDS** in 1989 he has continued to be one of the most regularly performed contemporary playwrights in French theatre. His works deal with issues topical in modern-day France, ranging from homelessness to inter-family relationships, with varied settings and an admirable command of both language and structure.

Koltès avoids political comment in general, whatever his own views, and links personal life to a series of social and political gestures. All relationships are reduced to the idea of the deal, epitomized in his play *Dans la solitude des champs de coton* (In the Solitude of the Cotton Fields), the tension in buyer–seller

negotiations symbolizing individual and ideological, class and cultural struggle.

Koltès was born to a Catholic family in Alsace, although his soldier father was away for much of the 1950s, fighting in Algeria a war which was to influence his later work. After studying journalism in Strasbourg, and rejecting a career as a professional pianist, Koltès's eyes were opened to new possibilities by travel to the United States: New York became a key influence, appearing as the setting for his later play, *Quai ouest* (Western Docks). While subsidizing his passion for **cinema** with funds from temporary jobs, Koltès also wrote six theatre plays in four years. He performed four of these in Strasbourg with friends, attracting the attention of Herbart Gignoux at the Strasbourg National Drama School. Koltès took the place offered to him there, while continuing to write: influential figures such as Lucien **Attoun** (who broadcast two of his plays on national radio) and director Patrice **Chéreau** thus became aware of Koltès's works.

After a spell writing his first novel, *The Flight on Horseback Far into the Town* (*La Fuite à cheval très loin dans la ville*) – the 1970s were notoriously difficult times for playwrights – Koltès returned to the theatre, writing *Sallinger* and his dramatic monologue, *The Night Just Before the Forests* (*La Nuit juste avant les forêts*), performed in 1977. Travels in South America and Africa incited a particular interest in the plight of the oppressed – *Struggle of the Dogs and the Black* (*Combat de nègre et de chiens*) was one of the results of this. By now, Patrice Chéreau (whom Koltès admired greatly) was directing most of his work, and Chéreau directed all but one of his plays during Koltès's lifetime. This certainly helped to promote Koltès's career, but perhaps prevented him being performed as often as he might have been in France, for fear of comparison: abroad, his work was more regularly staged. Koltès continued to work on famous Chéreau productions at Nanterre during the 1980s, including **Genet**'s *The Screens* (*Les Paravents*) in 1983, and his translation of *A Winter's Tale*. In the last year of his life, Koltès also wrote the figuratively autobiographical, anarchic (yet emotive) *Roberto Zucco* as a response to the incarceration imposed by his illness.

ANNIE SPARKS

See also: Algerian war; collective creation; gay writing; theatre

Further reading

Bradby, D (ed.) (1996) 'Introduction', in *Three Plays by B.-M. Koltès*, London: Methuen (a general introduction to Koltès's drama in English).

Kraemer, Jacques

b. 1938, Metz

Actor, director and playwright

The founder of the Théâtre Populaire de Lorraine, and a proponent of the decentralization movement there until 1984, Kraemer has directed his own and others' works in France and Germany. He is currently the director of the Théâtre de Chartres.

ANNIE SPARKS

See also: theatre

Kristeva, Julia

b. 1941, Bulgaria

Psychoanalyst, literacy theorist and semiotician

Kristeva is known for her work in semiotics, literary theory and **psychoanalysis**. Her work has received a mixed reception from feminists, some regarding her analysis as useful and others accusing her of betraying women.

With regard to literary theory, Kristeva is seen as a founder of the analysis of intertextu-

ality, and of the claim that the text (like the human subject) is not structured (and therefore fixed), but always in a process of structuration. For Kristeva, intertextuality is a conflictual and dynamic process – the clashing of different codes as they cross the text. Kristeva develops the Lacanian and **structuralist** emphasis on language and on the linguistic construction of the subject in her focus on the disruptive or transgressive elements in the work of writers such as Lautréamont or **Bataille**, many of whom have become part of the new (largely male) canon of **poststructuralism**. She believes that no political revolution is possible without a transformation in the structure (or structuring) of the subject, that is to say in the structure of language – hence analyses of high cultural artefacts are not elitist but politically necessary.

Since she trained as a psychoanalyst, her work on literature (and on painting) has become ever more dependent on psychoanalysis, and vice versa. For instance, in *Black Sun: Depression and Melancholia* (*Soleil noir: dépression et mélancolie*) she moves between case histories on the one hand and readings of Nerval or Holbein on the other. One of her major contributions to psychoanalysis has been her emphasis on the semiotic order, which she juxtaposes to a symbolic order. Kristeva's symbolic cannot simply be mapped on to the Lacanian Symbolic, nor is her semiotic order to be understood as an order of signs (semes). For Kristeva, the semiotic may be developmentally described as a pre-Oedipal order dominated by the child's preverbal communion with the mother. However, it is better understood structurally as a continuing stratum of interruptive rhythm, gesture or laughter which disturbs the ordered and logical symbolic order into which we enter at the time of the father's interdiction (the Oedipus complex). That disturbance is evident, for example, in poetic writing. The mother's unrepresentable (unsymbolizable) body is connoted by the *chora*, the locus of the drives underlying the semiotic.

Kristeva, **Barthes**'s '*l'étrangère*', can be seen as marginal to the Parisian scene, as a woman born and brought up in Bulgaria. (It must be remembered, however, that several figures in the Parisian intellectual landscape of the time are 'outsiders' in some sense; for instance, both Hélène **Cixous** and Jacques **Derrida** are Jews born in Algeria.) This marginality is a positive quality according to Barthes's or Kristeva's own perspective. She expands upon this in *About Chinese Women* (*Des Chinoises*), in which she suggests that the double marginality of Chinese women enables her to get a more distanced analytical purchase on the dominant Western patriarchy. In the work, Kristeva advocates the adoption of a position of *oscillation*. The subject should oscillate between the Father and the Mother; between the symbolic, with its purchase on logic, on historical time, and on political action, and the semiotic which disturbs the rigidity and frigidity of the Word. For Kristeva, the dominant position is oppressive, but immersion in wordless *jouissance* or in absolute union with the mother leads to insanity. One of the controversial aspects of *Des Chinoises* is the Orientalism detected therein by Gayatri Spivak, among others. It could be argued that many left-wing Parisian intellectuals (not only the **Tel Quel group** who went on the trip to China with Kristeva) indulged in a kind of Orientalism, as Maoist China took over from the USSR (revealed as a locus of death camps and show trials) as a utopic revolutionary space. Admirers of Kristeva might respond that at least her book is highly self-conscious about its inability to do much more than use the material on Chinese women to draw conclusions about the West. Kristeva's later fascination with the United States has also proved politically controversial – her status as outsider which, from one perspective gives her a positive vantage point, can equally be seen as encouraging a rather naive, not to say ignorant, enthusiasm.

One of the problems underlying much criticism of Kristeva is that any theory deriving from psychoanalysis tends to have a drive towards the universal. Even where Kristeva makes statements allowing for a degree of historical change, her historical and geographical sweep is vast. Those readers who do not reject her work utterly, but are uncomfortable with aspects of the universalism, often rewrite the theory creatively. Thus we find the argument that her theory of *abjection* applies only to the male subject.

However, abjection is a revolt of being against an exorbitant 'something' (not an object), which is neither quite inside nor outside the subject and which both fascinates and disgusts desire. Kristeva's abstract formulation can be rewritten as the boy child's simultaneously horrified and desiring response to his mother's body. However, this Anglo-Saxon concretization does not quite fit the detail of Kristeva's analyses. The abject may be fantasmatically projected by an individual or a society on to the female sex, but also on to the racial outsider. In *Powers of Horror*, Kristeva focuses on anti-semitism, but in later works she analyses a range of nationalisms.

JUDITH STILL

See also: Lacan, Jacques

Major works

Kristeva, J. (1974a) *Des chinoises*, Paris: Des femmes. Translated A. Barrows (1986) *About Chinese Women*, London: Marion Boyars.

——(1974b) *La Révolution du langage poétique: l'avant-garde à la fin du XIXe siècle, Lautréamont et Mallarmé*, Paris: Éditions du Seuil. First part translated M. Waller (1984) *Revolution in Poetic Language*, New York: Columbia University Press.

——(1980) *Pouvoirs de l'horreur: essai sur l'abjection*, Paris: Éditions du Seuil. Translated L. Roudiez (1982) *Powers of Horror: An Essay on Abjection*, New York: Columbia University Press.

——(1987) *Soleil noir: dépression et mélancolie*, Paris: Gallimard. Translated L. Roudiez (1989) *Black Sun: Depression and Melancholia*, New York: Columbia University Press.

——(1988) *Étrangers à nous-mêmes*, Paris: Fayard. Translated L. S. Roudiez, *Strangers to Ourselves*, New York: Columbia University Press.

Further reading

Barthes, R. (1970) 'L'étrangère', *La Quinzaine littéraire* 94.

Fletcher, J. and Benjamin, A. (eds) (1990) *Abjection, Melancholia and Love: The Work of Julia Kristeva*, London and New York: Routledge.

Lechte, J. (1990) *Julia Kristeva*, London and New York, Routledge (clear, accurate and interesting – focuses on Kristeva as semiologist).

Moi, T. (ed.) (1986) *The Kristeva Reader*, Oxford: Blackwell (a useful introduction).

Spivak, G. (1988) 'French Feminism in an International Frame', in *In Other Worlds: Essays in Cultural Politics*, London and New York: Routledge (a hostile reading of *About Chinese Women* and work by H. Cixous).

Kurys, Diane

b. 1948, Lyon

Director, screenwriter and producer

Diane Kurys's semi-autobiographical films use period reconstructions and close social observation to evoke childhood, adolescence and family breakdown from a female point of view. After eight years as an actress, in 1977 Kurys wrote and directed *Peppermint Soda* (*Diabolo menthe*) about growing up in the 1960s. *Coup de foudre* (1983) deals with ambivalent female friendship in postwar France, while 1990's *C'est la vie* (*La Baule Les Pins*) reconstructs a family summer holiday. Although Kurys does not identify herself as a woman director, her films problematize women's subjectivity through predominantly female-centred narratives. Her study of the modern (bourgeois) woman, *Après l'amour* (1992) was followed by a less successful venture into psychodrama, *A la folie* (1994).

CARRIE TARR

See also: cinema; women directors

L

Lacan, Jacques

b. 1901, Paris;
d. 1981, Paris

Psychoanalyst

A traditional psychiatric training and an intense knowledge of Freud's texts, combined with an exposure to the avant-garde culture of Surrealist circles and an absorption of structural linguistics and **anthropology**, produced in Jacques Lacan one of the most original of all psychoanalysts since Freud. His increasingly sophisticated speculations on the signifying processes that compose subjectivity have hardened into a powerful school of analysis whose influence notably reaches into many, if not all, of the human sciences. The collection of his lectures, *Écrits* (1966), remains a key text of structuralist and poststructuralist theory, in spite of (or sometimes because of) its opacity. It manages to retain something of Lacan's exploitation of the oral nature of teaching and his linguistic subversion of the position of master. What saves this from being merely irritatingly pretentious, wit and erudition apart, is that the operations of language are precisely central to Lacan's preoccupations; he thus sought to renew the concrete approach if not the clinical objective of 'the talking cure'. Already in his doctoral dissertation in 1932, 'Paranoid Psychosis and Its Relation to Personality' ('De la psychose paranoïaque dans ses rapports avec la personnalité'), which dutifully reproduces existing theories of paranoia and the requisite academic references, Lacan had none the less presented the patient 'Aimée' less as the object of a psychotic condition than as the subject of a certain discourse (Lacan quotes her literary efforts, which aroused some interest in Surrealist quarters).

In later papers, such as the 1953 'Function and Field of Speech and Language in Psychoanalysis' ('Fonction et champ de la parole et du langage en psychanalyse'), or the 1957 'The Agency of the Letter in the Unconscious' ('L'Agence de la lettre dans l'inconscient'), Lacan identifies his clinical approaches with the analysis of speech as the vehicle through which the human being is brought into an already existing social order and thus as the means and form of expression of the unconscious. This structural and linguistic vision of the emergence of full subjectivity appropriates and transforms particular features of **Lévi-Strauss**, Saussure and **Jakobson**. Subjectivity for Lacan signifies not in the individual's will, but only through the signifying chain to which it must belong, as well as in the unstable relation which it must negotiate between a signifier (or term) and its signified (or concept). Lacanian analysis does not, then, operate with any sense of a final cure; the inevitable immersion of the human in the Symbolic order tends rather towards the point where the subject of a discourse may fully inhabit the *structure* of meaning. This is in direct opposition to the aims of a psychology that would wish to repair and fortify a battered ego, in the belief it is in the ego that personal identity is guarded and developed.

In contrast to such an instrumental approach – seemingly founded in Freud, who had presented the ego as pitted against the id (albeit in a renewable and reversible way) – Lacan began as early as 1936 to emphasize the imaginary identifications which take place prior to full verbalization in the child and which are crucial to the emergence of a first, ideal notion of identity that anticipates the entry into the Symbolic order. This first 'mirror phase', where typically the child notices, celebrates and begins to play with his or her own reflection, for Lacan has the value of showing up the emerging *ego* as the result of an *illusory* identification and sense of wholeness, in contrast to the *subject*, which is a position arising out of the structural acknowledgement of otherness, alienation, lack and disintegration.

This direct confrontation with ego psychology will permit Lacan henceforth to elaborate increasingly schematized relations between the Imaginary, the Symbolic and the Real – this last category being a convenient structural conceptualization of whatever cannot be conceptualized – in place of the dualist clashes between ego and id, conscious and unconscious, in the more biological sections of Freud. It is this structural and linguistic revision which accounts for the famous reformulations and redesignations in Lacan. It is logical, if spectacular, for Lacan to call the unconscious 'the discourse of the other'; the Law, the 'Name- [/No-] of-the-Father' ('The Nom/non-du-Père'); or the phallus, 'the signifier of desire'. For the same reason, his untranslatable neologisms – *méconnaissance*, *hainamouration*, etc. – and their later topological equivalents – knots, chains and other schemata – are all attempts to make manifest the essentially intricated nature of subjectivity.

What the benefit of hindsight shows, finally, is the degree to which Lacan's practice both illustrates and tests the structurality it presents. His systematizations try to embed, yet never fully control, his exploitation of a succession of word systems, each one fashionable and at odds with the others, all the way from Politzer through Kojèvean Hegelianism and Heidegger to topological theory. At best, this approach was inspirational; at worst, opportunistic. Certainly Lacan the sorcerer never stopped being the precocious apprentice.

This intellectual slippage was also played out over the years in his ritualized formation and dissolution of the groups and circles bearing his message. This institutional dramatization of hysteria, still evident in some academic disciples, is one added level on which the phenomenon of Lacan is itself one of the most telling symptoms of French intellectual life in the twentieth century, and especially in the postwar period.

SEÁN HAND

See also: poststructuralism; psychoanalysis; structuralism

Further reading

Benvenuto, B. and Kennedy, R. (1986) *The Works of Jacques Lacan: An Introduction*, London: Free Association Books (clear guidance through major essays and themes).

Bowie, M. (1991) *Lacan*, London: Fontana (an accessible and authoritative introduction).

Mitchell, J. and Rose, J. (eds) (1982) *Feminine Sexuality: Jacques Lacan and the 'École freudienne'*, London: Macmillan (a good presentation of the Lacan seminars most important to feminists).

Roudinesco, E. (1993) *Jacques Lacan: esquisse d'une vie, histoire d'un système de pensée*, Paris: Fayard (the essential biography).

—— (1997) *Jacques Lacan: His Life and Work*, New York: Columbia University Press.

Lacroix, Christian

b. 1951, Arles

Fashion designer

In 1987, Lacroix launched the first French couture house for twenty-six years, with the backing of French textile conglomerate, Agache. His career in fashion began at Hermès and Guy Paulin, followed by a spell as a designer for the house of Patou from 1981. Lacroix is best known for his spectacular shows and his exotic designs, inspired by a wide range of influences. His most spectacular effects are created with luxurious fabrics and surface treatments, such as intricate embroideries. His creations attract sufficient publicity to support the sale of a range of subsidiary products.

NICOLA WHITE

See also: fashion

Lalonde, Brice

b. 1946, Neuilly-sur-Seine

Environmental activist and politician

In the 1970s Lalonde was a leader of the French environmental group Friends of the Earth. He became one of the best-known media personalities for the environmentalists and was chosen as the candidate for a loose green coalition for the 1981 presidential election. He soon took a reformist view of environmental issues, and rejected the radical positions of the green party, Les Verts. In 1988, he took the position of Minister for the Environment in both the **Rocard** Socialist government and the following **Cresson** administration. He created his own green party, Génération Écologie, in 1990, contributing to the division of the green vote. This movement lacked grassroots support and mostly appeared as a vehicle for the political ambitions of its leader and founder. In 1995, Lalonde moved towards the right-wing liberal umbrella political group UDF.

FRANÇOIS NECTOUX

See also: green issues; green politics; parties and movements; Waechter, Antoine

Lang, Jack

b. 1939, Mirecourt

Politician and cultural activist

One of Lang's most remarkable traits, and assets, is his talent for achieving notoriety. He first did so when, as a law student in his home town of Nancy, he launched a student drama festival in 1963, which went professional in 1968. Influenced by Brecht and **Artaud**, it dedicated itself to daringly experimental work, becoming a jamboree of **collective creations** and 1960s counterculture. In 1972, Lang was appointed director of the National Theatre of Chaillot in Paris. With Antoine **Vitez**, he furthered his avant-gardist reputation, but his costly alterations to the building led to his dismissal in 1974. Abandoning **theatre** for university teaching and politics, he was elected to the Paris Council in 1977 as a left-wing independent, but soon went over to the Socialist Party. An ardent Mitterrandist, he became party spokesman and adviser on cultural affairs and was a key figure in **Mitterrand**'s 1981 presidential victory.

Twice Minister of Culture (1981–6 and 1988–93), Lang's greatest achievement was doubling the culture budget for 1982 and giving his neglected department a high political and media profile. Courting the young and fashionable, he gained further notoriety by his flamboyant clothes and hairstyle, his dithyrambs to the president, and a provocative if oblique reference to American 'intellectual and financial imperialism'. He also scandalized traditionalists by supporting unconventional mass-cultural forms, from rock to **rap**, **comic strips** to graffiti. His life-long faith in culture's capacity to energize societies also irritated some.

After the Socialists' defeat in the March 1986 elections, when Lang himself became MP for Blois, he left the ministry but returned after Mitterrand's re-election in 1988, resuming his previous policies, though with more restraint and a more classical emphasis on the heritage. His second ministry was also distinguished by his accumulation of political responsibilities: for the media, the presidential building projects, the Bicentenary (1988–9) and education (1992–3). He was elected mayor of Blois in 1989 and a regional councillor in 1992.

His career then suffered two set-backs. In March 1993, he left the ministry again after the Socialists' electoral disaster. The following December, he lost the parliamentary seat he had regained in March, for exceeding campaign costs. In 1994, he became a Euro MP and in 1995 stood briefly for the Socialist nomination for the presidency, but withdrew in favour of Lionel **Jospin**.

DAVID LOOSELEY

See also: architecture under Mitterrand; cultural policy; parties and movements; rock and pop; universities

Major works

Lang, J. (1995) *Demain les femmes*, Paris: Grasset (reflections on the situation of women).
Lang, J. and Bredin, J.-D. (1978) *Éclats*, Paris: Simoën (Lang's recollections of Nancy and Chaillot).

Further reading

Hunter, M. (1990) *Les Jours les plus Lang*, Paris: Éditions Odile Jacob (a critical assessment of Lang's career).
Looseley, D. L. (1990) 'Jack Lang and the Politics of Festival', *French Cultural Studies* 1, 1: 5–19 (on Lang's theatrical career).
——(1995) *The Politics of Fun: Cultural Policy and Debate in Contemporary France*, Oxford and Washington, DC: Berg (a detailed study of Lang's career at the ministry).

Langlois, Henri

b. 1914, Izmir, Turkey;
d. 1977, Paris

Cultural figure

Langlois was the co-founder and director of the Paris Cinémathèque, with which his name is imperishably associated. His undeniably disorderly and financially imprudent management of the institution was more than offset by the passion with which he hoarded films and by his stimulating programming. The Cinémathèque (housed first in the rue d'Ulm, then in the Palais de Chaillot) was the place where the **Nouvelle Vague** and the *Cahiers du cinéma* critics received their cinematic education.

Criticism of Langlois's methods led to **Malraux**'s decision to dismiss him in February 1968. This sparked off an immense wave of protest; major film-makers banned the screening of their work at the Cinémathèque, outside which there were regular demonstrations, often brutally broken up by the police. Langlois was finally reinstated at the end of April. The 'Langlois affair' clearly appears in retrospect to be a curtain-raiser for **May 1968**.

KEITH READER

See also: cinema

Further reading

Langlois, G. P. and Myrent, G. (1986) *Henri Langlois, premier citoyen du cinéma*, Paris: Denoël (a comprehensive biography, co-authored by Langlois's brother).

language and the French regions

France, despite centuries of policies designed to eradicate varieties other than standard French, preserves within its frontiers several other languages of differing status and with survival prospects ranging from good to dismal. These function as vernaculars, used predominantly in informal situations, and in all cases the norm is bilingualism among speakers of regional languages (with French as the higher-status variety).

The extant regional languages may be subdivided into several separate categories:

1 non-Romance languages which survive as minority languages in certain regions;
2 other Romance dialects;
3 French dialects (dialects of French); and
4 the subsidiary question of *français régional*.

In the case of (1), obvious examples are Breton or Alsatian; other cases are Flemish and Basque. The exact number of speakers of these languages is hard to ascertain reliably: most surveys fail to differentiate between different types of speaker (level of fluency and competence) and many omit data about real language use – about how many people of what age, sex and socioeconomic class speak a language, but also when, to whom and under what circumstances. The most flourishing of the languages in this category is probably Alsatian. It is supported by the hinterland of Germany, is closely related to the dialect spoken in the adjacent Black Forest area, and has an 'official' or written form in *Hochdeutsch* (standard German). A substantial proportion of the inhabitants of Alsace speak Alsatian as a first or second language, with very few monolingual speakers. The status of the other minority languages of this type is more precarious. Basque is more secure than Flemish, which for a variety of reasons is fast disappearing from the corner of northeastern France where it once existed. The position of Breton is uncertain. Despite vigorous efforts, it has not succeeded in re-establishing itself to the extent that (say) its sister Celtic language, Welsh, has, and the relatively small number of speakers, predominantly concentrated in the west and southwest of Brittany, is probably not enough of a critical mass to ensure genuine, vernacular survival.

Under (2), the most striking case is that of Occitan, often erroneously categorized as a 'French dialect', which it is emphatically not. It is a Romance dialect (or possibly language – this distinction is not a matter of typology but of status), related to French, but not 'French' any more than (say) Corsican is. Occitan is the most widely spoken of non-French languages in France and extends across much of southern France with its heartland in the Toulouse–Albi area. How much it is genuinely spoken is another matter altogether. In common with the minority languages of type (1) – perhaps even more so – Occitan has been politicized. It shares with Catalan in Spain a link with the autonomist and regionalist tradition of the postwar period, and its prospects have been improved by internal developments in France (in 1981 the Socialist government proclaimed, even if it never really implemented, *le droit à la différence*, and a measure of regional independence was established) and by external European changes (the role of the EU in breaking down the role of the nation-state and the concomitant rise of the regions as political and economic units). Occitan suffers acutely both from the *exode rural* (depopulation) which is so dramatic a feature of many areas of southern France, and from the aftermath of repressive French government policies in respect of minority (non-French) languages. These go back to the French Revolution and, in the case of Occitan, to the fifteenth century; only since the middle of this century has there been any attempt to modify (let alone reverse) them, and to introduce educational programmes which would enhance rather than eradicate such linguistic varieties. Recent sociolinguistic studies in the Tarn and Cantal reveal a consistent and worrying pattern of use of Occitan diminishing sharply in the younger generations, to an extent that suggests that the language can have no real future as a vernacular. Set against this is a resurgence of interest among the educated (and often urban) middle classes in towns like Montpellier and Toulouse. Whether this constitutes 'real' language survival is a moot point, and there must be the suspicion that this resuscitation programme – largely detached as it is from the language as it is still (just) used by rather different groups – will remain an artificial exercise, the twentieth-century equivalent of Mistral's Félibrige which (ironically) the modern Occitanist movement so derides.

Category (3) refers to dialects which are recognizably related to standard French (originally the French of the Île-de-France) and thus, by definition, dialects of the northern half of France. These are not in a good state of health. It is very rare to hear genuine dialect (or *patois*, though the latter word is laden with values which are singularly unhelpful for objective discussion). Exceptions (perhaps, and then only among the older generations) are enclaves of the northeast and the east of the country. In the main, what is now encountered (by the casual visitor or the sociolinguist alike) is (4), *français régional*, namely French with a discernible and localizable regional accent. In parts of Normandy, for example, vestiges of Norman French survive in the retention of vowel length as a feature permitting audible distinctions between masculine and feminine past-participle endings (*donné* vs *donnée*). In the 'minority language' areas where category (1) applies, the *français régional* will similarly be influenced – sometimes heavily – by the local non-French language spoken, and often even in the case of those who do not speak it, because their French will have been inherited from those who do.

D. A. TROTTER

See also: Deixonne law; linguistic regulation; regional economic development; regional press in France; regional writing: Breton; regional writing: Occitan; regionalism

Further reading

Istituto della Enciclopedia Italiana (1986) *Linguistic Minorities in Countries Belonging to the European Community*, Luxembourg: Commission of the European Communities (statistical information, details of broadcasting and educational provision).
Marcellesi, J. B. (1975) *L'Enseignement des 'langues régionales'*, Langue française 25 (history of reintroduction of regional languages via educational system).

Lartigue, Jacques-Henri

b. 1894, Courbevoie;
d. 1986, Nice

Photographer

Born into a wealthy middle-class family, Lartigue began taking photographs as a child and, while he later became a professional painter and illustrator, photography remained for him the most delightful and important of hobbies. Although he took very few posed portraits, preferring the *instantané* (snapshot), he worked with extraordinary precision, leaving nothing to chance, but his work is characterized by a sense of spontaneity. In 1974, he was chosen by **Giscard d'Estaing** to take the official presidential portrait.

MICHAEL WORTON

See also: photography

Lassalle, Jacques

b. 1936, Clermont-Ferrand

Director and playwright

A director of the Théâtre National de Strasbourg from 1983 to 1991, Lassalle staged and promoted many rediscovered and new writers, and worked with **Vinaver** and set designer **Kokkos**. A director of the *Comédie-Française* from 1991 to 1994, he has since directed elsewhere, and is professor at the Conservatoire National d'Art Dramatique.

ANNIE SPARKS

See also: theatre; theatres, national

Major works

Lassalle, J. (1991) *Pauses*, Paris: Actes Sud (writings on the theatre, presented by Yannic Mancel).

Lavelli, Jorge

b. 1932, Buenos Aires, Argentina

Director

Lavelli is known for his contemporary repertoire. Director of the national Théâtre de la Colline until 1996, he is also known for his direction of opera, and of many Fernando **Arrabal** works.

ANNIE SPARKS

See also: theatre

Major works

Stagé, A. and Lavelli, J. (1979) *Lavelli, opéra et mise à mort*, Paris: Fayard (a discussion of work in the theatre).

Lavilliers, Bernard

b. 1946, St-Étienne

Singer-songwriter

Lavilliers's long career started in the 1970s, when a visit to South America profoundly influenced his style. Like many of his contemporaries, his musical itinerary saw him play blues, rock – in 1976's *Haute Surveillance* (Close Watch), for example – reggae and salsa in *La Salsa* (1980). He established himself in the 1980s; exoticism and protest songs are his hallmark. Charismatic on stage, with his cultivated working-class rocker look, he is a genuine poetic and political animal who never tires

of discovering new musical horizons or exotic experiences, as expressed in his 1994 album, *Champ du possible* (Virtual Horizon).

GÉRARD POULET

See also: rock and pop; song/*chanson*

Le Corbusier

b. 1887, La Chaux-de-Fonds;
d. 1965, Roquebrune Cap-Martin

Architect, urban planner and writer, real name Charles-Édouard Jeanneret

Le Corbusier, an avant-garde Paris architect of Swiss origin, was the leading French member of the worldwide Modern movement in architecture between the 1920s and the 1960s. His villa designs in the 1920s and 1930s (e.g. Villa Savoye, 1931), his books, his housing projects and his city plans (e.g. Plan Voisin, 1925; Algiers, 1930; Radiant City, 1930–) had won him world renown by the 1950s but his practical achievements in France were limited, owing mainly to state indifference and distrust. However, Le Corbusier's designs and theories were based on his rigid concepts of universal relationships between people and space, and these tended to produce standardized designs for mass housing and city planning. He began to make these systems more flexible after the war – his chapel of Notre-Dame-du-Haut at Ronchamp (1955), for example – but a big postwar reconstruction scheme at St-Dié (1945) was rejected by residents and officials alike. Not until the 1950s, when France launched a big wave of high-rise housing in the public sector, were slab designs set in open space, comparable to his *unité d'habitation* (built at Marseille 1947–52), widely adopted on new housing estates. The city of towers and motorways came under criticism from the 1970s, but Le Corbusier's immaculate and persuasive architecture never lost its reputation and continues to influence French students and architects at the end of the century.

ANTHONY SUTCLIFFE

See also: architecture

Major works

Le Corbusier (1946) *Towards a New Architecture*, London: Architectural Press.
——(1947) *The City of Tomorrow and Its Planning*, London: Architectural Press.

Further reading

Fishman, R. (1977) *Urban Utopias in the Twentieth Century*, New York: Basic Books.
Von Moos, S. (1979) *Le Corbusier: Elements of a Synthesis*, Cambridge, MA: MIT Press.

Le Forestier, Maxime

b. 1949, Paris

Singer-songwriter

Having performed with his talented sister (as Max et Cat Le Forestier), Maxime Le Forestier embarked on a solo career and was hugely successful in the early 1970s in particular. Appealing to a largely left-wing, adolescent audience, Le Forestier had hits with, among others, *San Francisco* and the anti-militarist *Parachutiste*. An outstanding lyricist whose professional stance undermines the crass commercialism of show business, he was voted best French male vocalist in 1996, having seen an upturn in his solo career.

IAN PICKUP

See also: song/*chanson*

Le Pen, Jean-Marie

b. 1928, La Trinité-sur-Mer

Politician

Le Pen's political training ground was as a Poujadist deputy (1956–62) and as a vigorous supporter of Algérie Française. After a decade in the political wilderness, in 1972 he became the leader of the Front National, which set out to federate the diverse strands of the French extreme Right, increasingly around the themes of race and **immigration**. Persistence finally paid off with the Front's initial electoral breakthrough in 1983–4, and its presence has since had a profound effect on the tactics and policies of mainstream political parties. The movement, which regularly attracts around 10 per cent of the vote, owes much to Le Pen's personal appeal (15 per cent at the presidential elections of 1988 and 1995).

BRIAN JENKINS

See also: nationalism; racism/anti-semitism

Further reading

Bresson, G. and Lionet, C. (1994) *Le Pen*, Paris: Éditions du Seuil (a recent biography in French).
Marcus, J. (1995) *The National Front and French Politics: The Resistible Rise of Jean-Marie Le Pen*, Basingstoke and London: Macmillan (currently the only book in English exclusively devoted to Le Pen and his movement; lively and accessible).

Le Roy Ladurie, Emmanuel

b. 1929, Moutiers-en-Cinglais, Normandy

Intellectual

Le Roy Ladurie is the leading contemporary inheritor of the *Annales* historical tradition, focusing on long-term cultural attitudes rather than on great men and events. A former Communist Party militant, he first became famous with *Les Paysans de Languedoc* (1966), which traces developments among the peasantry over the 300 years from 1450. He succeeded Fernand **Braudel** at the Collège de France in 1973, but his 'star' status can really be dated from *Montaillou* (1975), which uses the records of the southern French see of Pamiers as the basis for an enthralling anthropological reconstruction. Le Roy Ladurie was director of the Bibliothèque Nationale from 1987 to 1994.

KEITH READER

See also: anthropology and ethnology; libraries; parties and movements

Léaud, Jean-Pierre

b. 1944, Paris

Actor

Actor-protégé of the film-maker François **Truffaut**, he made his debut as a 13-year-old in *Les 400 coups* (1959) as Antoine Doinel and went on to star in Truffaut's Antoine Doinel series, which ended in 1979. Léaud also starred in several **Godard** films during the 1960s when his career was at its height. Very much identified as Truffaut's *alter ego*/pseudo-son, upon the film-maker's death in 1984 Léaud's fortunes went into a decline and he is now seen mostly in small cameo roles.

SUSAN HAYWARD

See also: cinema

Leclerc, Annie

b. 1940, France

Feminist thinker, essayist and writer

In the 1970s, Leclerc wrote various feminist essays, the most widely read of which are *Parole de femme* (Woman's Word) and *Coming to Writing* (*La Venue à l'écriture*), co-authored with Hélène **Cixous** and Madeleine Gagnon. She also collaborated with Marie **Cardinal** in 1977 on *Autrement dit* (In Other Words). Controversy was generated by Leclerc's apparent celebration, in *Parole de femme*, of 'female' values and of a feminine specificity emblematized by the female body. Although born out of a desire to think through sexual difference in such a way as to contribute to the demolition of sexual oppression, Leclerc's essay was denounced by some feminist contemporaries as excessively idealistic/biologistic. In her 1976 essay, 'Protofeminism and Antifeminism' ('Protoféminisme et antiféminisme'), for example, Christine **Delphy** criticized *Parole de femme* for conforming to sexist ideology. Leclerc has also written fictional texts. In 1988, she published *Origines* (Origins), an autobiographical account of her relationship with the writing of Jean-Jacques Rousseau. All of Leclerc's work is highly personal.

ALEX HUGHES

See also: autobiography; feminist thought; women's/lesbian writing

Lecoq, Jacques

b. 1921, Paris

Actor, director and teacher

The founder, in 1956, of his celebrated eponymous international **mime** and theatre school in Paris, and of his own theatre company, Lecoq's teaching and productions focus on physical theatre, which is influenced by his interest in *commedia dell'arte*, clown work and masks.

ANNIE SPARKS

See also: theatre

Further reading

Rolfe, B. (1972) 'The Mime of Jacques Lecoq',

Drama Review 16, 1 (article on Lecoq's methods).

Le Doeuff, Michèle

b. 1948, France

Philosopher

The author of *The Philosophical Imaginary* (*L'Imaginaire philosophique*), a 1980 study of the imagery that philosophical discourse specifically (and unconsciously?) generates for itself, and of translations of Bacon and Shakespeare, Le Doeuff is best known for her 1989 publication, *Hipparchia's Choice* (*L'Étude et le rouet*). This text explores in detail a theme central to Le Doeuff's writing: the treatment of women by and within the philosophical tradition and its discourse. Within it, space is devoted to a discussion of the work of Simone de **Beauvoir** and its relation to that of **Sartre**. Le Doeuff has also worked in the theatre.

ALEX HUGHES

See also: feminist thought

Leduc, Violette

b. 1907, Arras;
d. 1972, Faucon, Provence

Writer

A protégée of Simone de **Beauvoir**, Leduc published her first novel, *In the Prison of Her Skin* (*L'Asphyxie*), in 1946. Much of her writing draws upon her experiences of illegitimacy, ugliness and social/sexual marginalization, and in 1964 she published her first directly autobiographical work, *La Bâtarde*. This text, which became a best seller, was followed by two further autobiographical volumes; *Mad in Pursuit* (*La Folie en tête*), which appeared in 1970, and *La Chasse à l'amour* (In Pursuit of Love), pub-

lished posthumously in 1973. Leduc died of cancer in 1972.

ALEX HUGHES

See also: autobiography; women's/lesbian writing

Further reading

Hughes, A. (1994) *Violette Leduc: Mothers, Lovers and Language*, London: MHRA (a feminist/psychoanalytic reading of three of Leduc's novels).

Lefebvre, Henri

b. 1901, Navarrenx;
d. 1991, Pau

Philosopher

Lefebvre was one of the most productive Marxist philosophers in France. After a religious upbringing in the provinces, he studied at the Sorbonne, where he was involved in avant-garde intellectual groups, eventually emerging as the leading proponent of a humanist Marxism inspired by the alienation theories of the early Marx. At the **Liberation**, he figured as the French Communist Party's leading philosopher, but fell from favour during the Cold War. Increasingly critical of Stalinism, he was expelled from the party in 1958, and went on to play a key role in non-Communist left-wing intellectual circles. As professor of sociology at Strasbourg and then Nanterre, he was one of the inspirations for the situationists and for the student leaders of **May 1968**. Throughout his long life, he was active in many areas of enquiry and debate, and his popularizations of a non-dogmatic Hegelian Marxism, *Dialectical Materialism* (*Le Matérialisme dialectique*) of 1939, and *Marxism* (*Le Marxisme*) of 1948, were best sellers. His best-known work is the three-volume *Critique of Everyday Life* (*Critique de la vie quotidienne*) published between 1947 and 1981, in which he confronts the alienated reality of life in the modern world with, on the one hand the illusory images which seek to justify it and, on the other, the unrealized possibilities within it which are waiting to be set free by radical and emancipatory action.

MICHAEL KELLY

See also: Marxism and Marxian thought; situationism

left-wing press

The events of **May 1968** spawned a plethora of left-wing publications known collectively as *la presse gauchiste*. Despite their ideological differences, these publications had a number of points in common: a commitment to ending the 'bourgeois capitalist system' in France through revolutionary action; a contempt for the ('revisionist' or 'Stalinist') French Communist Party; and a commitment to an alternative network of news and information to combat the lies of the 'bourgeois media'.

The earliest of these radical alternative publications was *Action*, a non-sectarian paper which reflected and served the radical movement of May 1968 and whose first issue appeared on 7 May 1968. From 5 June until 1 July, *Action* appeared five times a week with sales of 30,000 per issue. After the 'events', it faltered and finally ceased publication after the presidential elections of June 1969. The other main left-wing publications can be grouped in three political 'families' – pro-Chinese, Trotskyist and Anarchist – plus those which can be classified as 'non-aligned left'.

Pro-Chinese publications were:

- *L'Humanité Rouge*, first published in February 1969. The organ of the clandestine Parti Communiste Marxiste-Léniniste de France, it aimed to adopt a revolutionary theory and practice by applying the principles of Marxism-Leninism-Mao Tse Tung thought to France. It was the only publica-

tion officially recognized by Beijing and Tirana.
- *La Cause du Peuple* (*La CdP*), a Maoist newspaper of the Gauche Prolétarienne (Proletarian Left). Its articles advocating direct action and violence led to repeated seizures of the paper and imprisonment of two editors. In April 1970, Jean-Paul **Sartre** became director. In May 1971, *La CdP* fused with *J'Accuse*. It officially ceased publication in 1973.
- *Tout* (see below).

Trotskyist publications include:

- *Rouge*, a weekly newspaper of the Ligue Communiste Révolutionnaire.
- *Lutte Ouvrière*, founded in autumn 1968 to succeed *Voix Ouvrière*. It represents a strand within Trotskyism which refused to participate in forming the Fourth International. It supported Arlette Laguiller in presidential elections from 1974.
- *Jeune Révolutionnaire*, a monthly publication of the Alliance des Jeunes pour le Socialisme, representing the 'Lambertist' tendency of the Trotskyist movement.

The two main anarchist publications predate May 1968:

- *Le Monde Libertaire*, the monthly organ of the Anarchist Federation, which offers a traditional anti-Marxist anarchist perspective.
- *Le Combat Syndicaliste*, the publication of the Confédération Nationale du Travail, based in Toulouse.

Other publications include:

- *Cahiers de mai*, created on 15 June 1968, as a non-sectarian periodical offering discussion and popularization of worker struggles. It ceased publication in 1975.
- *Libération*, launched as a radical national left-wing daily in 1973, which is now established as a serious newspaper, but has shed its early radicalism.
- *L'Idiot International*, which was launched

by Jean-Edern **Hallier** in December 1969. It was initially a left-wing monthly. Simone de **Beauvoir** became *directrice* of the journal in September 1970, but resigned in May 1971. Sporadic interruptions of publication have resulted from financial and legal difficulties. It was accused in 1993 of flirting with the radical nationalist Right.

- *Tout*, which was launched in September 1970 by the group Vive la Révolution (VLR) to replace a journal of the same name. It represented a radical fusion of conventional revolutionary politics and the politics of everyday life.

DAVID DRAKE

See also: Marxism and Marxian thought; national press in France; parties and movements; revolutionary groups

legal system

Legal systems have been the object of numerous classifications, and it is now agreed that the French and English systems belong to two distinct legal families: England to the common law system and France to the civil law system. Membership of one of these legal families implies quite distinctive characteristics. In turn, the reasons for the French system's distinctive features are the result of choices made at some time in history.

France, unlike the United Kingdom, is the land of written constitutions. Since 1789, the date of the abolition of the absolute monarchy, France has known seventeen regimes and has proclaimed five different Republics. The present constitution dates from 4 October 1958 and the proclamation of the Fifth Republic. The regime which was meant to create a sort of amended parliamentary order (that is, one with a reinforced executive) turned out to have a strong presidential slant: de **Gaulle** had imposed his personality on the system, and it has survived him. The constitutional text not only establishes and organizes the regulation of the branches of government (executive, legisla-

tive and judicial powers), but it also includes reference to two declarations of rights: the Declaration of Rights of Citizens of 1789 and the Preamble of the 1946 Constitution. These protect both individual freedoms (individual freedom, freedom of movement, freedom of expression, right to property) and social and economic rights (right to strike, right to education, right to social protection, right to work, etc.). These are upheld regularly in decisions of the Conseil Constitutionnel, the court which ensures that statutes respect the constitution.

The court structure in France presents an oddity. There are two court systems operating side by side – the private law courts and the administrative law courts. Originally, French administrative courts were created out of a paradox: if the will of the revolutionaries had been respected, there would never have been any administrative courts in France. They had decided that no court should be allowed to control the actions of the administration in case this was used to promote a counter-revolution. However, complaints against administrative decisions needed to be addressed, and soon a solution was found – these were heard by boards of civil servants or by the minister in charge. This unsatisfactory solution did not survive long, but the idea that the control of administrative decisions should be exercised from within lived on. These ideas were embodied in the Conseil d'État and in the administrative courts. Therefore, while private law courts deal with litigation between private individuals and apply criminal law, administrative courts settle cases between private individuals and the state.

France is said to lack a doctrine of precedent as it exists in the English system: the principles applied in one case are directly linked to the facts of the case and are not recognized as general rules (only parliament can create general rules and principles). The reality is in fact quite different from the theory. Arguably, the principles 'discovered' by judges in cases could be said to be at least as influential as those in English law: case law in France is organized and systematized through principles and, because of the need for legal certainty, the same principles are reapplied. Moreover, the two

French supreme courts, the Conseil d'État (supreme court of the administrative law courts) and the Cour de Cassation (supreme court of the private law courts), ensure the strict application of the principles that they have established previously.

Besides, court decisions in France are extremely short and terse. After a brief summary of the facts and of the parties' arguments (a few lines), the court unveils in one single judgment the interpretation and the principles which led it to the solution. The drafting is very concise indeed and there is no room for creative style, so much so that frequently courts reproduce entire sentences or expressions from previous cases. However, lawyers are wary of even the slightest change in the drafting, since this is often the signal that the case law has changed direction. This way of drafting is unfortunately difficult to reconcile with democratic principles and, unless one is trained to read the signals, it is nearly impossible to understand the import of any decision. This is quite the opposite to English cases: every judge can put forward their opinion of the case (and they often choose to do so) in a style which is much more accessible to the neophyte.

France is renowned for a number of legal creations, and one of these is the movement of codification – an idea implemented by the Revolutionary ideology. Rationality was called upon to shape the form that legislative texts should take: they should be simple, rational and democratic. The codes would implement all three aspects: simple, because all rules of one area of the law would be in one single book (for instance, the famous Civil Code deals with contracts, property, torts, successions, etc.); rational, because the rules in each of the codes would be organized around general principles rather than long and exhaustive lists; democratic, because anyone could look at any of the well- and simply written codes and know instantly the state of the law in these areas. Codes were a brilliant device at the time and codification was imitated in a great number of countries. Even now, the ideas of the Enlightenment can still be felt in the way legislation is drafted in France, in comparison with English statutes. In general, civil-law legislation promotes principles, while common-law statutes establish long and detailed lists and thorough definitions for all important terms used in the legislation. However, this might render it less democratic by increasing the discretion of the courts where provisions are unclear.

SOPHIE BOYRON

Léger, Fernand

b. 1881, Argentan, Orne;
d. 1955, Gif-sur-Yvette, Seine-et-Oise

Artist

Associated with Fauvism and then the Cubist movement, Léger disagreed with analytical Cubism and supported the Section d'Or's emphasis on colour and movement, which is apparent in his own painting, characterized by a bright palette and cylindrical shapes. He met **Le Corbusier** in 1920, and in 1925 produced mural paintings for him at the Decorative Arts Exhibition. He visited the United States several times, including spending his exile there during World War II. After the war he joined the Communist Party. His later work is often concerned with industrial objects and landscapes showing a continuing interest in machines and the modern world. In the 1950s he created a series of stained-glass windows in the Audincourt church (France) and the Courfaivre church (Switzerland), which are part of the postwar decade revival in projects for churches, including, for example, **Matisse**'s chapel in Vence, and Le Corbusier's church in Ronchamp.

DEBRA KELLY

See also: painting

Leiris, Michel

b. 1901, Paris;
d. 1990, St-Hilaire, Essonne

Writer and ethnographer

Though professionally an ethnographer (producing important and, at the time, transgressive work on African and Caribbean cultures), it is for his remarkable autobiographies that Leiris is chiefly praised. These run from the one-volume *Manhood* (*L'Age d'homme*) in 1939, a thematic, psychoanalytic and existential presentation of the self, to the four-volume *The Rules of the Game* (*La Règle du jeu*) from 1948 to 1976, a linguistic and temporal deconstruction of selfhood. Leiris's associations with a succession of political/aesthetic movements (Surrealism, **existentialism**, post-colonialism . . .), borne out in his writing's psychological and formal complexity, mean that he is increasingly viewed as an exemplary intellectual of the postwar period.

SEÁN HAND

See also: anthropology and ethnology; autobiography

Lemahieu, Daniel

b. 1946, Roubaix

Playwright, director and teacher

A writer and translator of plays since the 1970s, Lemahieu has pioneered new writing through workshops with theatre practitioners and students, and as the director of conferences at the Institut d'Études Théâtrales at the new Sorbonne, Paris III. He worked with **Vitez** in the 1980s, and was secretary-general of the Théâtre National de Chaillot from 1985 to 1988. He is also a member of the company Le Théâtre d'Essai.

ANNIE SPARKS

See also: theatre

Léotard, François

b. 1942, Cannes

Politician

Léotard is a key figure in the Parti Républicain, of which he became leader in succession to **Giscard d'Estaing**. A former seminarist, he succeeded Jack **Lang** as Culture Minister in 1986, doubtless helped by his brother Philippe's fame as an actor. His support for **Balladur** against **Chirac** in the 1995 presidential elections cost him political ground in the short term.

KEITH READER

See also: parties and movements

lesbian activism

Throughout the postwar era, lesbians in France have not been noted for their political 'visibility'. This phenomenon is remarked on in the editorial preface to the first volume of the gay and lesbian periodical *Masques*, which invites its readers to reflect on the reasons why the existence of lesbians remains unknown, while that of gays is not (see *Masques*, May 1979). During the 1970s – when the Mouvement de Libération des Femmes (MLF) emerged in the wake of **May 1968**; when politically aware French women, straight and gay alike, were addressing and campaigning around issues such as sexual politics, desire and a woman's right to exercise control over her body/sexuality; and when lesbian groups such as the Gouines Rouges (Red Dykes) came into being within the MLF, organized around figures like Monique **Wittig** and Christine **Delphy** – it did look as if lesbian activism might assume the kind of public profile which the French gay liberation movement was in the process of acquiring. This did not happen, however. According to Janine Mossuz-Lavau's 1991 study, *Les Lois de l'amour: les politiques de la sexualité en France* (The Laws of Love: The Politics of Sexuality in France), various factors explain why not. First, although French lesbian groups of the 1970s made key contributions to the sexual debates of the day, helping not only to refigure the feminist agenda but also to revise public perceptions of sexuality, they never achieved the visibility of gay rights groups. This, claims Mossuz-Lavau, was because they avoided the formal organization of their gay counterparts, and tended to be more short-lived. Second, the lesbian political cause was further devisibilized in the 1970s by virtue of its involvement with the politics of the 'broad church' Front, a movement which, according to many French women, failed to address the specific issue of lesbian oppression. This latter phenomenon generated, in the early 1980s, a kind of lesbian political secession within the MLF, out of which emerged a separatist Lesbian Radical Front whose leading light was Monique Wittig. Many French lesbian women refused, however, to accept its dogmatism, and were even unprepared to find palatable the (political implications of the) label '*lesbienne*', with the result that the Front foundered in 1982. Currently, although the Maison des Femmes contains a lesbian documentation centre (the Archives Lesbiennes or ARCL), France has no autonomous lesbian movement, since even the MIEL – the Mouvement d'Information et d'Expression des Lesbiennes – more or less disappeared in the mid-1990s. Its absence, argues Frédéric Martel (see Martel 1996), means that lesbian politics continues to lack visibility in contemporary France.

ALEX HUGHES

See also: feminism (movements/groups); gay activism; lesbian press

Further reading

Martel, F. (1996) *Le Rose et le noir: les homosexuels en France depuis 1968*, Paris: Éditions du Seuil (excellent, if controversial, account of the gay and lesbian political and cultural scene in contemporary France).

Mossuz-Lavau, J. (1991) *Les Lois de l'amour:*

les politiques de la sexualité en France, Paris: Éditions du Seuil (very useful on the legal and social history of the gay and lesbian movements).

Robinson, C. (1995) *Scandal in the Ink: Male and Female Homosexuality in Twentieth-Century French Literature*, London: Cassell (contains useful insights into the history of the lesbian movement in France).

lesbian press

The best-known lesbian publication of postwar France, and one that is still going strong, is the monthly magazine *Lesbia*. Created in 1982 by Christiane Jouve and Catherine Marjollet, it is focused on cultural rather than political issues and has a slightly 'coffee-table' slant. One of its most regular contributors is the lesbian writer Hélène de Monferrand. *Masques*, a mixed periodical which was launched in 1979 and survived until 1986, published pieces on political and cultural issues pertaining to lesbianism, although it was always more gay-orientated. A split in its editorial team gave birth, briefly, to the lesbian cultural journal *Vlasta*, four issues of which appeared between 1983 and 1985. Feminist publications of the 1970s with a marked lesbian slant include *Le Torchon Brûle* and *Les Cahiers du grif*, published in Brussels.

ALEX HUGHES

See also: feminist press; gay press; lesbian activism; women's/lesbian writing

Further reading

Martel, F. (1996) *Le Rose et le noir: les homosexuels en France depuis 1968*, Paris: Éditions du Seuil (gives an excellent, albeit controversial, account of the gay and lesbian political and cultural scene in contemporary France).

Lévi-Strauss, Claude

b. 1908, Brussels

Anthropologist

Lévi-Strauss's original training was in philosophy, but, like a number of his contemporaries, he quickly became disillusioned with the subject as it was then taught, preferring the concrete and exotic experiences of ethnology to what seemed the rhetorical abstractions of philosophy. After a year in secondary education, he was offered a teaching post in sociology at the University of São Paulo, which enabled him to undertake a series of fieldwork expeditions into the Brazilian interior. During his contact with the indigenous inhabitants, he developed a lasting sense of affinity with his subjects, movingly expressed in his influential **autobiography**, *Tristes tropiques*. The crucial experience, however, were the years he spent teaching in New York during the war, when he met most of the leading American anthropologists of the day, and began what was to be a lifelong friendship and collaboration with the Russian phonologist Roman **Jakobson**. Decisively, Jakobson introduced him to structural linguistics, which inspired him to apply similar techniques of analysis to his own research in anthropology.

Jakobson's influence is discernible in Lévi-Strauss's first major publication, *The Elementary Structures of Kinship* (*Les Structures élémentaires de la parenté*), but equally important was his original interpretation of Marcel Mauss's classic theory of exchange. Lévi-Strauss took from Mauss the idea of gift exchange as a fundamental mechanism of social cohesion in non-Western societies and applied it to the quasi-universal phenomenon of incest prohibition. This negative prohibition also had a positive aspect in that it obliged group A to give its women as spouses to group B, and vice versa, thus creating a stable alliance between the two groups. The prohibition of incest and the relations of kinship that were its result were therefore expressions of a more basic function – the principle of reciprocity. While *Les Structures*

élémentaires was criticized by more empirically minded British and American anthropologists suspicious of its generalizations, the work ensured Lévi-Strauss's international reputation, bringing to French sociological thought a breadth of reference and a degree of theoretical sophistication unknown since Durkheim.

When he was appointed to the École Pratique des Hautes Études in 1950 Lévi-Strauss's new area of specialization was the anthropology of religions. Here his emphasis was on the cognitive structures of non-Western thought rather than aspects of ritual or belief. Hence, in *Totemism* (*Le Totémisme aujourd'hui*) he rejected the concept of totemism as an illusory construct which established an imaginary distinction between 'primitive' and 'civilized' thought. The diverse representations normally categorized as 'totemism' were in fact systems of classification used to map differences in the natural world on to differences in social organization. What was primary was not the belief or practice associated with a particular totem, but its difference from other totems, homologous to the differences between social groups. 'Totemic' systems were therefore like codes, used to express elements of social structure. Lévi-Strauss continued this line of enquiry in *The Savage Mind* (*La Pensée sauvage*), where he described non-Western classifications of the natural world as a 'logic of the concrete', a kind of DIY science (*bricolage*) different from Western science but with its own rigour and coherence. Such classifications proceeded by way of a binary ordering which was a universal feature of the human mind. These two key works of 1962 prepared the way for Lévi-Strauss's *magnum opus*, the four-volume cycle *Mythologiques*, an extensive analysis of over 800 North and South American myths. These myths are treated as a closed system – that is, they are analysed not as isolated stories with such and such a message or meaning, but rather in terms of their structure, their individual modes of combination of a finite set of 'mythemes'. Because the human mind has a limited repertory of logical categories, based on the type of binary oppositions found in language, each myth should, according to Lévi-

Strauss, be a decodable transformation of another myth. Lévi-Strauss's work on myth published since the 1970s is essentially a continuation of the programme set in place in the *Mythologiques*.

The above synopsis represents the core of Lévi-Strauss's contribution to anthropology, but the content of his work is more diverse and its influence more extensive than this. From *Les Structures élémentaires* onwards, it was evident that the kind of anthropology he was proposing had a considerably wider scope than what, in France, had traditionally passed as ethnology. In 1958, the programmatic collection of essays, *Structural Anthropology* (*Anthropologie structurale*), ambitiously placed anthropology at the centre of the human sciences in France, both as a rigorous science of human society and as a privileged mediator of cultural diversity. Combined with the popular success of *Tristes tropiques*, this served to project Lévi-Strauss and his discipline to the forefront of intellectual debate in the 1950s and 1960s. Anthropology thus became the avantgarde of the movement known as **structuralism** and the focus of a new type of humanism; Lévi-Strauss was its figurehead. In 1959 he was elected to the first chair in social anthropology at the Collège de France; the following year he founded *L'Homme*, the first French journal of anthropology. In 1973 he was elected to the **Académie Française**.

Lévi-Strauss is one of the outstanding intellectual figures of this century. Apart from his international reputation in anthropology and more generally as the originator of structuralism, the literary qualities of texts such as *Tristes tropiques*, his numerous interviews, his writings on subjects as diverse as music, literature and the visual arts have all ensured his celebrity beyond academic and intellectual circles in France.

CHRISTOPHER JOHNSON

See also: anthropology and ethnology; linguistic/discourse theory

Major works

Lévi-Strauss, C. (1967) *Les Structures élémentaires de la parenté*, Paris and La Haye: Mouton & Co./Maison des Sciences de l'Homme. Translated J. H. Bell, J. R. von Sturmer and R. Needham (1969) *The Elementary Structures of Kinship*, Boston: Beacon Press.
——(1955) *Tristes tropiques*, Paris: Plon. Translated J. and D. Weightman (1984) *Tristes tropiques*, Harmondsworth: Penguin.
——(1958) *Anthropologie structurale*, Paris: Plon. Translated C. Jacobson and B. Grundfest Schoepf (1977) *Structural Anthropology 1*, Harmondsworth: Penguin.
——(1962a) *Le Totémisme aujourd'hui*, Paris: Presses Universitaires de France. Translated R. Needham (1964) *Totemism*, London: Merlin Press.
——(1962b) *La Pensée sauvage*, Paris: Plon. Translated R. Needham (1966) *The Savage Mind*, Chicago: Chicago University Press.
——(1964–71) *Mythologiques*, 4 vols, Paris: Plon. Translated J. and D. Weightman (1970–81) *Mythologiques: Introduction to a Science of Mythology*, 4 vols, London: Cape.
——(1973) *Anthropologie structurale deux*, Paris: Plon. Translated M. Layton (1978) *Structural Anthropology 2*, Harmondsworth: Penguin.

Further reading

Eribon, D. (1988) *De près et de loin*, Paris: Plon. Translated P. Wissing (1991) *Conversations with Claude Lévi-Strauss*, Chicago: University of Chicago Press (contains much autobiographical information not found in *Tristes tropiques*, casting interesting light on the debates of the 1950s and 1960s).
Hénaff, M. (1991) *Claude Lévi-Strauss*, Paris: Belfond (a clear and accurate overview of Lévi-Strauss's anthropology, with useful synopses of principal texts).

Levinas, Emmanuel

b. 1906, Kovno, Lithuania;
d. 1995, Paris

Philosopher

Levinas's combination of Judaic culture and phenomenological training produced a philosophy based on the primacy of ethics which, in the wake of structuralist determinations, has assumed increasing importance and influence. Born of Jewish parents, Levinas frequently drew on the moral lessons contained in writers such as Tolstoy and Dostoevsky, who were his earliest reading. After studies in Strasbourg, his first publications were essentially an importation of the lessons learned, first from Husserl and then from Heidegger, into French philosophy. This period, running from 1930's *The Theory of Intuition in Husserl's Phenomenology* (*La Théorie de l'intuition dans la phénoménologie de Husserl*) to *Existence and Existents* (*De l'existence à l'existant*) of 1947 and *Discovering Existence with Husserl and Heidegger* (*En découvrant l'existence avec Husserl et Heidegger*) from 1949, already harbours the idea which is to assume increasing importance and radical expression in Levinas's philosophy: the ethical confrontation with the other, whose existence is subordinated to philosophical representation and existential mastery. This preconditional obligation to be for-the-other rather than for-itself leads to two publications which are among the most important philosophical works in French of the postwar period: the 1961 *Totality and Infinity* (*Totalité et infini*) and 1974's *Otherwise Than Being or Beyond Essence* (*Autrement qu'être ou au-delà de l'essence*). In the first, Levinas contrasts the closed and masterful system of philosophical intentionality with the infinity opened up in consciousness by the face-to-face relation: instead of grasping this appearance of the other and absorbing it into a total intelligibility, I must respond to the ethical demand which its apparition produces in me. The implications for a philosophical language no longer devoted to thematization and reduction, and the response, articulated notably by **Derrida**, that this non-conceptual approach in itself constituted a concept and made sense only within the terms of a philosophy it sought to break open, in turn led to the remarkable *Otherwise Than Being or Beyond Essence*. Levinas replaces the concept of otherness with the more immediate and less definable notions of neighbour and proximity, and moves from a scrutiny of the face to an attentiveness to the generous and responsible act of saying, a gesture that establishes immediate contact, exposes me to the other and resists the silence of intellectual mastery. In keeping with this, he also transforms the words and modes of his own philosophical communication: his earlier *descriptions* of eros now become his basic means of *expression*, the high point being the chapter on substitution, with its scandalous evocation of torn skin, exposure and obsession, passivity and persecution. The ethical dimension of such passivity is for Levinas guaranteed by the absolute ethics, or obedience to the Most High, of God's law. For Levinas, God is not the reintroduction of absolute rule, however, but the constant revelation of absolute alterity within the human situation. In similar vein, Levinas's concept of justice is based on the possibility of embodying a prophetic morality which must by its nature lie beyond the machinery of state and politics.

SEÁN HAND

See also: structuralism

Further reading

Hand, S. (ed.) (1989) *The Levinas Reader*, Oxford: Blackwell (essential texts by Levinas, edited and presented with an introduction, headnotes and glossary).

Lévy, Bernard-Henri

b. 1948, Paris

Essayist

Lévy is the most prominent of the intellectuals who have presented their work in the media, especially the press and **television**. A philosopher, trained at the elite École Normale Supérieure, he came to public notice as leading promoter of the **new philosophers** in the 1970s, editing with Grasset a book series in which many of its chief works were published, including his own *Barbarism with a Human Face* (*La Barbarie à visage humain*) in 1977. *The French Ideology* (*L'Idéologie française*), published in 1981, controversially pointed to past Fascist tendencies in the French intellectual Left. An energetic writer with a reputation as a charismatic and charming personality, he has held a number of regular columns in the daily and monthly press, and has made frequent appearances on television, including his own 1990 series, *The Adventures of Freedom* (*Les Aventures de la liberté*). His media presentation of ideas has been particularly criticized by other intellectuals, for its superficiality and self-promotion. He is often referred to as BHL, a reference to the BHV department store. His ideas centre on the role of the intellectual, and on the need for political and social involvement in favour of human rights. He has actively promoted campaigns against racism, Fascism and religious fundamentalism, supporting organizations such as SOS Racisme, and protesting against human rights violations in Bosnia, Rwanda and Algeria.

MICHAEL KELLY

See also: Désir, Harlem, and SOS Racisme; educational elitism; publishing/*l'édition*; racism/anti-semitism

Libération

Newspaper

Taking its name from a Resistance newspaper which continued publication until 1964, *Libération* began in 1973 as a radical daily left-wing newspaper committed to carrying forward the spirit of **May 1968**. Despite a number

of financial crises it has survived, and although still on the Left, it has long abandoned its early radicalism. The first issue of *Libération* appeared on 22 May 1973, although eleven issues had appeared sporadically since 18 April. The newspaper offered a heady mix of irreverent libertarianism and militant workerism and initially refused to carry paid **advertising**, depending instead for its finances on its readers and supporters. The paper belonged to the staff, who were all paid the same wage (equivalent to that of an unskilled factory worker in the Paris area). Although by the end of 1980 sales had risen to around 41,000 (from around 18,000 at the end of 1975), the newspaper's financial position was far from secure and disagreements among the staff about the future direction of the paper were intensifying. On 21 February 1981, a staff meeting agreed to suspend publication of the paper and debate its future development.

When *Libération* reappeared on 13 May 1981, it was clear that the views of Serge July, one of the initiators of the paper, had triumphed. Under July's direction, *Libération* now set out to establish itself as a serious, professional daily paper with a reputation for quality coverage of cultural, literary and political issues. The commitment to workers' control was jettisoned, a traditional structure replaced the non-hierarchical one, a new smaller staff team was constituted through sackings and the employment of journalists from other papers – *Libération* became a limited company. Salary differentials were introduced, and from February 1982 the newspaper accepted advertising in an attempt to extricate itself from its still-precarious financial situation. Politically part of the mainstream Left, *Libération* was sympathetic to (if sometimes critical of) **Mitterrand** and the Socialist government.

The circulation figures of the relaunched *Libération* rose from 53,000 in 1981 to 195,000 in 1992, but sales were still only about half those of its main rivals (*Le Figaro* and *Le Monde*) and a long way off July's long-term aim of 500,000. Moreover, after the expensive failure of a regional newspaper, *Lyon-*

Libération, and radio and audiovisual projects coinciding with a dramatic fall in advertising revenue, in 1992 the paper was once again facing a financial crisis. On 26 September 1994, a revamped *Libération* was launched, but it did not prove to be the hoped-for success. The new format eighty-page newspaper with its Saturday magazine did not impress the existing readership and failed to attract enough new readers; the costs of the relaunch had been underestimated, while the price of newsprint continued to rise. The paper now faced yet another financial crisis and, in February 1996, the Chargeurs group headed by Jérôme Seydoux increased its stake in *Libération* from 12 to 65 per cent, while signing an agreement guaranteeing the paper its editorial independence. At the same time, the stake held by the staff, who had lost their position as majority shareholders in the run-up to the 1994 relaunch, fell to 20 per cent.

DAVID DRAKE

See also: left-wing press; national press in France

Further reading

Samuelson, F. M. (1979) *Il était une fois 'Libé'*, Paris: Éditions du Seuil.

Liberation and épuration

The Liberation of France in the summer of 1944 should be considered in the global context of the Allies' efforts to defeat Hitler. The need for landings in France grew partly from pressures exerted by Soviet Russia to open a second front to relieve their armies on the eastern front. The Allies had been considering landings in France since 1942, but when a mainly Canadian force met with disaster at Dieppe it became clear that such an undertaking would need to be meticulously prepared in advance in order to assemble the appropriate *matériel* and armed forces. Operation Overlord

was finally made ready and launched under the Allied supreme commander, General Dwight D. Eisenhower, on 6 June 1944.

Thus began the Liberation of France, with landings of United States, British, Canadian and some Free French troops on the beaches of the Normandy coast between Cherbourg and Ouistreham, near Caen. In an operation of unprecedented scale and ambition, Allied troops managed to establish bridgeheads, to land sufficient men, armour and equipment to overcome some tenacious German resistance, and to begin the process of forcing the withdrawal of most of the occupying forces from France.

The armed French Resistance (known as FFI – Forces Françaises de l'Intérieur – or more popularly as 'Fifis') came into its own during this period, carrying out sabotage operations and disrupting German troop movements. These efforts sometimes provoked terrible reprisals on the part of the Germans, for instance the massacre at Oradour-sur-Glane, near Limoges. The FFI helped liberate many towns in Normandy and Brittany after the Allies' initial sweep through. The uprising in Paris on 19 August 1944 marked the beginning of the battle to free the French capital. The Free French armoured division under General Leclerc entered Paris at the head of the American armies on 25 August, upon which the Germans surrendered; de **Gaulle** arrived there the same evening, and the next day made a triumphal march down the Champs-Élysées.

Liberation proved more difficult in the southeast of the country, because the Resistance met with several reverses. In the Vercors, for example, around 19 July the poorly equipped forces of the *maquis* were encircled by the Germans and massacred. However, after 15 August, landings in Provence (Operation Anvil) enabled the Allies to proceed up the Rhone valley and, by 12 September, Free French troops under Leclerc and de Lattre de Tassigny met near Dijon. By this time, much of French territory was liberated, except for pockets of German resistance on the Atlantic coast, around Dunkirk and in Alsace-Lorraine.

As far as political authority in liberated areas is concerned, after 12 July 1944 the Allies gave de facto recognition to the Provisional Government of the French Republic (GPRF); as areas were liberated, authority was vested in commissioners of the Republic appointed by the GPRF. On 22 October 1944, the Allies gave *de jure* recognition to the Provisional Government. Among its tasks was to re-establish order in the country by enforcing the authority of the commissioners, disbanding Communist paramilitaries and incorporating the FFI into the regular army. Another task of the GPRF was to set in train the so-called *épuration* (purge). In theory, the purge was to be conducted by tribunals whose task it was to avoid summary justice by guaranteeing basic legal rights to the accused, thereby preventing civil strife and furthering de Gaulle's aim of 'reconciling' the French. However, given the circumstances of the time and the nature and length of the Occupation, there was much enmity between resisters and those adjudged to be compromised by collaboration, leading to the so-called *épuration sauvage*, or the meting out of summary justice.

The purges remain a subject surrounded by confusion and controversy. Some of the confusion arises from the fact that the term tended to be applied not only to the execution of collaborators during the war, but also to the summary executions carried out during the Liberation and the sentences handed down by the tribunals set up for the purpose of bringing collaborators to justice. The controversy was fuelled by the surprisingly rapid re-emergence of the extreme right-wing press after the war, when various papers alluded to a figure of 100,000 victims of summary justice during the Liberation. This figure was exaggerated for political reasons. That summary justice was meted out is not disputed; moreover, several thousand women were subjected to the humiliation of having their heads shaved in public (*les tondues*) for allegedly having had relations with the Germans (known at the time as 'horizontal collaboration'), and in some cases these women served to deflect attention from those who might have been accused of an 'eleventh-hour conversion' to resistance. Around 9,000 people were summarily executed during the Liberation, of which 1,600 cases were decided by improvised tribunals.

The legal purge was based on the French penal code, having provisions to sanction acts of damage to national defence and external security, and of intelligence with the enemy. Over 300,000 cases were opened, of which 170,000 were pursued. Some 95,000 received sentences, with 50,000 having their civic rights suspended. As for the rest, around 25,000 prison sentences were pronounced, a further 13,000 of forced labour and 6,700 death penalties, of which over half were given *in absentia*. Of the 2,800 death sentences, de Gaulle commuted some 73 per cent; in the end, 770 people were shot. In short, there were about 10,000 executions during the purges, of which some 8,000–9,000 amounted to summary justice, and some 1,500 the result of a trial.

Among those executed were politicians Pierre Laval (prime minister at **Vichy**), Joseph Darnand (head of the Milice), Fernand de Brinon (Pétain's ambassador in Paris), journalists like André Suarez, and intellectuals such as Robert Brasillach, editor of the pro-Nazi paper *Je suis partout*. Those guilty of economic collaboration seem to have been treated relatively lightly, mainly because of difficulties arising from legal definition; also, although his firm had contributed substantially to the Germans' war effort, Louis Renault could not be brought to trial since he died in prison in October 1944.

Over the years since the Liberation, the purges have continued to fuel political controversy, and have contributed to what Henry Rousso has called the 'Vichy syndrome', the perpetuation of bitter French memories of World War II. In the climate of the Cold War, they also partly played a role in conferring a veneer of plausibility on the extreme Right.

MARTYN CORNICK

See also: legal system

Further reading

Assouline, P. (1990) *L'Épuration des intel-*

lectuels Brussels: Complexe (a brief account of what happened to those intellectuals accused of 'intelligence with the enemy').

Brossat, A. (1994) *Les Tondues, un carnaval moche* Paris: Hachette-Pluriel (a study of the public degradation of many women during the Liberation).

Footitt, H. and Simmonds, J. (1988) *France 1943–1945*, Leicester: Leicester University Press (history of the Liberation period based on archival sources).

Kedward, H. R. and Wood, N. (eds) (1995) *The Liberation of France: Image and Event*, Oxford: Berg (a solid collection of essays in English on various aspects of the Liberation).

L'Histoire (1994) *La France libérée: 600 jours pour finir la guerre*, special issue, July–August (covers many of the important questions).

Novick, P. (1968) *The Resistance Versus Vichy: The Purge of Collaborators in Liberated France*, New York: Columbia University Press (remains an authoritative and well-informed account of the purges).

Rioux, J.-P. (1987) *The Fourth Republic 1944–1958*, Cambridge: Cambridge University Press (a good starting point for studying the circumstances and effects of the Liberation).

Rousso, H. (1991) *The Vichy Syndrome: History and Memory in France Since 1944*, Cambridge, MA: Harvard University Press (translation of Rousso's path-breaking book, *Le Syndrome de Vichy*, published in French by Éditions du Seuil in 1987).

——(1992) 'L'Épuration en France, une histoire inachevée' *Vingtième siècle* January–March (a thorough review of the statistics and historical issues).

Wieviorka, O. (1994) 'Les Mécanismes de l'épuration', *L'Histoire* 179 (a useful summary of much recent work).

libraries

Embodying ideals of free and open access to culture and literature, libraries have long been central to France's intellectual and cultural activities, and with one in five French people enrolled in a municipal library, they are part of the fabric of everyday life. Their development in all sectors is characterized by a tension between the conflicting roles of safeguarding collections and promoting open access.

Municipal public libraries combine recreational and cultural functions with symbolic notions of citizenship and democracy, a symbolism focused in the revolutionary late 1960s, when library staff saw the potential of libraries to change society and culture. Some felt that libraries, as mass disseminators of information, could be harnessed to challenge the hegemony of *la culture lettrée* (literary culture) and instead promote popular and minority cultures. Many librarians in deprived areas also developed a social role, and were often at the forefront of efforts to combat illiteracy.

In the 1980s, under the presidency of François **Mitterrand**, and under Socialist administrations committed to public cultural projects, generous funding saw library buildings and borrowing rates double in number. More recently, however, municipal libraries are moving away from the principle of free access, with 70 per cent charging a subscription fee in 1996. Furthermore, decentralization of library control to local authorities since the 1980s has, paradoxically, threatened the freedom of libraries, as some extremist local politicians have imposed censorship on their libraries, most notably in the Front National-controlled town of Orange in 1996.

Unusually, some of France's municipal libraries also hold priceless incunabula confiscated in the Revolution and, partly as a result of this, French libraries have traditionally been rather custodial, with modern notions of open access poorly established in parts. However, in other respects, French libraries have gained a reputation for innovation; the *médiathèque* concept has furnished models for international emulation, including the Bibliothèque publique d'Information in the **Pompidou Centre** and the Vidéothèque de Paris in Les Halles.

Elsewhere, libraries permeate every aspect of French life, flourishing in institutions as diverse as cathedrals, prisons, hospitals and **banks**. They also play an important role in exporting French culture, with over 300 libraries in French cultural centres and embassies worldwide. In the education sector, while school libraries have developed from meagre beginnings, university libraries have singularly failed to keep pace with rapid postwar expansion. The 1989 Miquel report into university libraries led to some improvements, but provision remains well short of European counterparts.

The Bibliothèque nationale is regarded as one of the world's greatest libraries, and its significance in French cultural life was clearly demonstrated by the passions aroused by the new Bibliothèque nationale de France (BNF), which opened in 1996. The BNF was the last and most Pharaonic of Mitterrand's Grands Projets, and was marked by his desire to welcome the general public into what had previously been the elitist preserve of specialized researchers, a symbolic returning of the nation's heritage to the people, which Mitterrand declared to be the noblest function to which the Republic could aspire. That France should be witnessing the opening of one of the largest libraries in the world, at a time when the very existence of libraries in the electronic information age is considered anachronistic by some, is appropriate testimony to the continuing status of libraries in French cultural life.

LUCY MCKEEVER

See also: architecture under Mitterrand; cultural policy; electronic revolution; universities

Lindon, Jérôme

b. 1925, Paris

Publisher

As the adventurous literary director of the Éditions de **Minuit** since 1948, Lindon has been a vigorous champion of serious experimental literature. He was the principal editorial force behind the ***nouveau roman***, virtually launching the new literary generation together with Alain **Robbe-Grillet** as literary editor. He is also responsible for the publication of Samuel **Beckett**'s first works in French. Having been a target of the OAS during the **Algerian war**, he has also been militant in arguing against censorship, and for the defence of literature against the forces of the mass market.

PATRICK FFRENCH

See also: publishing/*l'édition*

linguistic/discourse theory

Linguistic thought and theory has long had a firm base in France, but has flourished particularly since the 1950s, initially under the influence of Ferdinand de Saussure's structural and social view of language. Linguistics has had a profound effect on other disciplines, such as anthropology and literary theory, which have borrowed concepts from it to lay the foundations of **structuralism**. Discourse theory is more recent, dating in France from the mid-1960s, and is at the interface of linguistics and other social sciences, such as history, sociology, philosophy and **psychoanalysis**. Its success and extension to a broad range of fields has been remarkable.

Linguistics, coming under the broader heading of the science of language, has a long history in French intellectual thought, although in its modern form, deeply influenced by Saussure's *Course in General Linguistics* (*Cours de linguistique générale*), with an emphasis on synchronic (rather than historical) studies, it is in the second half of the twentieth century that it has grown remarkably. Linguistics is taught widely in French **universities**.

Saussure's ideas, furthered by the work of the Prague Linguistic Circle (especially Roman **Jakobson**) on structural phonology, had a powerful influence over French linguistic theory and teaching in the 1950s. André Martinet's functionalism played a particularly important role in this period. American distributionalism, which had developed independently of Saussure's work, had to wait until the mid- and late 1960s to find followers in France, such as Jean Dubois and Maurice Gross. Generative and transformational theories of grammar by then also started to find favour with French linguists, such as the Belgian-born Nicolas Ruwet. Specifically French are the theory of Lucien Tesnière (on structural syntax) and Gustave Guillaume's 'psychosystematic' approach, but their influence outside France has been limited.

More recently, interest in France has centred on semantics – as, for instance, with Bernard Pottier's componential analysis and Greimas's structural semantics and, even more importantly, on *énonciation* (enunciation), particularly with Émile Benveniste's influential work on deictics and tenses and Antoine Culioli's own theory of enunciation. Oswald Ducrot's important work on pragmatics (particularly on presupposition) has helped bring pragmatic preoccupations to the forefront of French linguistic thought.

The shift away from phonology and syntax, and away from Saussurean *langue* (which concentrates on the abstract system of language), towards considerations of meaning and subjectivity within discourse, indicates the direction linguistic theory has been taking. The success of discourse theory, and particularly of France's own brand of discourse analysis, must be looked at in the context of this changing emphasis within linguistic research.

The term 'discourse' is itself highly ambiguous and has been used in different ways by, for instance, pure linguists, literary theorists, social scientists or psychoanalysts, and there are variations even within practitioners of 'discourse analysis'. What has been termed 'the French school' is also markedly different from American and British research, which has tended to concentrate on ordinary communication, particularly oral interaction, and has relied a great deal on psychological and sociological data. French discourse analysis, on the other hand, has been mainly text-based, looking at the formal properties of language in use from the point of view of its production within historical, institutional and ideological constraints. The vocabulary of certain historical or ideological texts, such as the tracts of May 1968 or documents from the French Revolution, was (for instance) analysed by the laboratory of political lexicology at the École Normale Supérieure de Saint Cloud in the late 1960s. Inspired by the American Z. S. Harris, other research looked at rules governing textual organization. An important and growing area of enquiry has thus been text grammar, which has been applied to a variety of contexts (such as legal, political or journalistic discourse) but also to literary texts. Investigations of narrative, exemplified by the work of Gérard Genette, Roland Barthes or Tzvetan Todorov and Greimas's narrative semiotics, can also all be seen as theories or analyses of discourse. From the 1960s onwards, these investigations have been particularly productive in France, and a number of leading figures have led seminars at the École Pratique des Hautes Études, a graduate school at the forefront of French intellectual thought. Another recent and fertile area of research has been the rhetorical properties of argumentation and persuasion.

Although theories of discourse now cover an extremely wide field, are interdisciplinary in approach, and draw extensively on general theories of meaning such as semiotics, they all owe a great deal initially to basic linguistic concepts such as *signifiant* (signifier) and *signifié* (signified), *syntagme* (syntagm) and *paradigme* (paradigm), sometimes stretching them far from their original context of use. However, the relationship between linguistic science and the host of disciplines which claim to have an interest in language and discourse is far from clear and often controversial.

The direct and indirect influence of linguistics over contemporary French intellectual thought cannot be underestimated, although its nature is sometimes questioned. Two types of examples could be given of this fertilization across a wide range of disciplines: the much-discussed structuralist analysis of Baudelaire's poem *Les Chats* by Roman Jakobson and Claude Lévi-Strauss, published in the anthropological journal *L'Homme* in 1962; and the intellectual trajectories of figures such as

Roland Barthes and Julia **Kristeva**, whose work defies classification but owes an initial debt to linguistic theory. Although theories of discourse undoubtedly used linguistics as a stimulus, conversely, some of the questions which were raised about language from disciplines outside linguistics (such as philosophy, history or psychoanalysis) have enabled linguistic research to address issues of subjectivity and meaning initially omitted from linguistic enquiry.

BÉATRICE DAMAMME-GILBERT

See also: anthropology and ethnology

Further reading

Benveniste, É. (1971) *Problems in General Linguistics*, Coral Gables, FL: University of Miami Press (Benveniste's most influential papers).

Ducrot, O. and Schaeffer, J.-M. (1995) *Dictionnaire encyclopédique des sciences du langage*, Paris: Éditions du Seuil (a new and fully extended edition of their very successful 1972 publication, *Encyclopedic Dictionary of the Sciences of Language*).

Gadet, F. (1989) *Saussure and Contemporary Culture*, London: Hutchinson Radius (a reassessment of Saussure's influence).

linguistic regulation

The continuing intervention of authorities in the structure and status of the language is a unique feature of French, and this extends from individuals and pressure groups to the state itself. The first example of such intervention, the edicts of Francis I – which reduced the role of Latin and culminated in the Ordonnances de Villers-Cotterêts (1539) – struck a blow not only against Latin but also the other vernaculars, by decreeing that all legal decisions should be pronounced, registered and delivered to the parties in the French mother tongue and not otherwise. Parallel with this approach, there

flourished lively debate among scholars and writers to establish a standard written language, as is shown by the development of dictionaries and grammars of French, together with proposals for language reform.

In the seventeenth century, Malherbe proposed a purification and simplification of the language, and Vaugelas in his influential 1647 publication *Remarques sur la langue françoise* (Remarks on the French Language) attempted to impose the usage of the court and contemporary writers as the norm. This tendency to regulate language was marked by the establishment by Richelieu of the **Académie Française** in 1635.

The statutes of the Academy declare that its main function is to labour to provide sure rules for French and to make it pure, eloquent and capable to treat of the arts and sciences. In addition it shall be responsible for composing a dictionary, a grammar, and works on rhetoric and poetics. The first edition of the Academy dictionary did not appear until 1694, and, so far, eight editions have been published. A grammar came out in 1932.

Although the publications of the Academy are accorded status and authority, their influence on the language of the average native speaker is minimal. The grammar was heavily criticized when it appeared and is completely neglected today, but the various editions of the dictionary do register and give acceptance to the evolution of the language, both in lexis and orthography. However, it must be emphasized that the Academy dictionaries are extremely selective, rejecting most technical, vulgar, **slang** and foreign terms to concentrate on the standard literary language.

The Revolution continued the royal policy of prioritizing French: the decree of 2 Thermidor year II (20 July 1794) declared that no public deed could be written other than in the French language throughout the whole territory of the Republic; the decree of 27 Brumaire year III (17 November 1794) required teaching in primary schools to be conducted in French, the local idiom being limited to an auxiliary role.

In the twentieth century, one can discern

three main forces in linguistic regulation: the Academy, the Ministry of Education and the state. Although all are genuinely concerned about the quality and status of French, they approach the subject in different ways and attempt to deal with it by differing actions.

The Academy continues to be concerned with standard written French, admitting modifications after a period of maturation. Its involvement in the spelling reform of 1990 caused it to lose prestige when, after supporting a limited programme of reform, it made a U-turn, deciding that the proposals should not be applied.

The Ministry of Education has come to make up for the Academy's timidity. Two decrees – the first signed by Georges Leygues in 1901, the second under the signature of René Haby in 1976 – proposed a list of *tolérances* (permitted variations against the strict rules of French grammarians) in the various examinations under the control of the ministry. The initiatives are interesting since they provide a backdoor to linguistic reform. They are revealing, also, in providing check-lists of points of special difficulty to learners of French, particularly archaic and illogical features in morphology and syntax. It is sobering to note, however, that the 1976 decree repeats several examples from its predecessor and it is generally agreed that the proposals are not well-known and universally applied. Indeed, the 1990 reform reproduced again some of the 1976 proposals on the reform of diacritics.

In the 1950s, the government sponsored the development of *le français fondamental* (initially, *élémentaire*), a scientific project to provide a restricted vocabulary and grammar for speaking, writing and reading simple French. The programme, under the umbrella of UNESCO, sought to maintain French as a world language and has had some success, in that many courses for beginners were based on the research results.

State concern with language has resulted in the creation of numerous agencies – Office du Vocabulaire Français (1957), Délégation Générale à la Langue Française (1989), replacing the Haut-Commissariat, itself a replacement

for the Haut Conseil de la Langue Française – all concerned with promoting and co-ordinating efforts to spread the use of good French. A particular aspect of this movement is fostered by the Haut-Conseil de la Francophonie (1984) and the Conseil International de la Langue Française (1967), both concerned with French as a world language.

The state has eventually realized the need to support regional languages; the **Deixonne law** (1951) permitted the study of regional languages in schools, which have since acquired enhanced status in school, university and media. In the 1990s, Arabic has become partially accepted in the French system.

The rest of state activity has been the battle against English and franglais. In the 1970s and 1980s, various decrees created commissions to oversee the development of French technical vocabulary and the *Journal officiel* of 18 January 1973 published lists of several hundred approved terms replacing anglicisms, e.g. *industrie du spectacle* (show business), *bouclier thermique* (heat shield) and *tuyère* (nozzle). These efforts culminated in the *Dictionnaire des termes officiels* published in 1994.

In 1975, the *loi Bas-Lauriol* made French obligatory in the publicity and instructions for all goods sold in France, and this was reinforced in 1994. There were a small number of cases of fines being imposed for infringements. The Conseil Constitutionnel (1994), while accepting that the state can prescribe the language to be used in public service and by collectivities, insisted on the individual's rights to use language as he/she wishes. The debate goes on!

JO REED

See also: *anglomanie*/franglais; education ministry; language and the French regions

Further reading

Ager, D. (1990) *Sociolinguistics and Contemporary French*, Cambridge: Cambridge University Press (this reviews many aspects of the language scene in France).

Battye, A. and Hintze, A.-M. (1992) *The French Language Today*, London: Routledge (a comprehensive review of the contemporary idiom).

Délégation Générale à la Langue Française (1994) *Dictionnaire des termes officiels*, Paris: Direction des Journaux Officiels (a dictionary of several thousand technical terms with English equivalents, plus a list of main legislative texts concerning language policy in France, as an appendix).

Lipchitz, Jacques

b. 1891, Druskieniki, Lithuania;
d. 1973, Capri

Artist

After settling in Paris in 1909, Lipchitz became one of the first artists to make **sculpture** based on Cubist principles. His friendship with Juan Gris may have given him the impetus to reintroduce humanity into his sculpture, and his *transparents* of the 1920s marked a further change in style, involving the breaking down of volume by interwoven masses and voids. His postwar sculpture was produced in America, where he had fled following the German invasion and Occupation of France. In New York, his sculpture became more autobiographical and monumental (often the result of commissions) and more biomorphic than abstract or figurative. Regarding Israel as his spiritual home, Lipchitz chose to be buried there.

CAROL WILCOX

literary adaptation

Literary classics and modern novels frequently provided the subject matter of French cinema in the 1950s, while scriptwriters such as Jean Aurenche (1904–), Pierre Bost (1901–75),

Henri Jeanson (1900–67), Roland Laudenbach (1921–) and the Belgian Charles Spaak (1903–75) dominated the industry. Their most popular source was the nineteenth-century canon consisting of Hugo, Dumas, Stendhal, Flaubert, Maupassant and Zola (but not Balzac). From the eighteenth century, Prévost's *Manon Lescaut* (directed by Henri-Georges **Clouzot** in 1949) and Laclos's *Les Liaisons dangereuses* (directed by Roger **Vadim** in 1959 and in Hollywood – as *Dangerous Liaisons* – by Stephen Frears in 1992) have proved popular, not least because they offer major roles for women. Among twentieth-century authors, those like Jean Giono, Georges Bernanos and Marcel Aymé, whose works are based on traditional narrative and evoke an identifiable milieu or like Colette, which turn on gentle eroticism, have proved more popular sources of material than the works of more experimental novelists such as Céline, who has never been adapted for the screen, or Proust who was first (very poorly) adapted by Wajda (*Swann in Love*, 1984). Some individual works have proved perennially adaptable. Following several silent film versions, Hugo's *Les Misérables* has been adapted three times since the war: in 1957 for Jean-Paul Le Chanois with Jean Gabin as Jean Valjean; in 1982 for Robert Hossein, with Lino Ventura; and in 1995 for Claude Lelouch with Jean-Paul **Belmondo**, in a version which transposed the setting to France under German occupation. Similarly, Flaubert's *Madame Bovary*, filmed before the war by **Renoir**, has had a Hollywood version by Vincente Minnelli (1949) with Jennifer Jones as Emma, and a 1991 French version, directed by **Chabrol**, with Isabelle **Huppert** in the same role. These examples illustrate the close relationship between the narrative genres of cinema and of post-Revolutionary literature which flourished until the **Nouvelle Vague** instituted a completely different (more documentary-style) approach to subject matter in films. More recently, literary adaptation has been used to bring about a symbolic fusion between the auteurist traditions of the Nouvelle Vague and the narrative practices of the *tradition de qualité*. Marcel Pagnol's legacy exemplifies this

trend. Prewar, his writings were adapted for
other film-makers – *Marius* for Alexander
Korda (1931), *Fanny* for Marc Allégret (1932)
and *Topaze* for Louis Gasner (1932) – while he
himself filmed adaptations of Jean Giono
(*Jofroi* in 1933; *Regain* in 1937), in whose
works he undoubtedly found a celebration of
an unchanging France that appealed to his own
sense of tradition. After the war, he adapted his
own *Manon des sources* (1952). But, by combining the roles of writer, director, producer
and manager of his own studios, Pagnol served
as a powerful example to Claude **Berri**, who –
as writer/producer/director of Pagnol's *Manon
des sources* in *Jean de Florette* and *Manon des
sources* (both 1986), Zola's *Germinal* (1993),
and Aymé's *Uranus* (1991) – has attempted to
revitalize the popular traditions of adaptation
within an auteurist framework so as to create,
or recreate, a 'cultural heritage'.

JILL FORBES

See also: cinema

literary censorship

Under the climate of moral austerity imposed
during World War II by the **Vichy** regime,
advance censorship of literary and journalistic
material, abolished in 1918, was reinstated.
This ceased after the **Liberation**. However,
'obscene' literary material continued to be subject to a level of official repression which
remained severe for some thirty years. This
abated in and after the 1970s; however, laws
allowing the proscription of literary works
remained in place and were reinforced by new
anti-**pornography** measures introduced in
1994.

A law which pertained to the control of
publications intended for the young, and which
extended restrictions placed upon books
deemed to contravene morality by the 1939
Family Protection Decree, was passed on 16
July 1949, serving as a pretext for proscription.
The 1940s and 1950s witnessed a series of literary prohibitions, the objects of which were

works of erotic literature. Texts affected
included the French translations of Henry
Miller's *Tropic of Cancer*, *Tropic of Capricorn*
and *Sexus*; *I Spit on Your Grave* (*J'irai cracher
sur vos tombes*) by 'Vernon Sullivan' (alias
Boris **Vian**); Pauline Réage's *Story of O*
(*Histoire d'O*); and some of the works by the
Marquis de Sade, published by Jean-Jacques
Pauvert.

A further landmark in the battle to restrict
the publication of erotico-literary material
waged by the French legislature was an administrative edict – an *ordonnance*, which did not
require the sanction of the National Assembly
– of 21 December 1958. The ambit of this document, which was modified by the law of 4
January 1967 and was intended, ostensibly, to
protect French youth, covered books and periodicals destined not only for children and adolescents but also for adults. It made it illegal to
make available to minors any publication that
was licentious, pornographic or violent in
nature. Between 1958 and 1967, a hundred or
so books were banned and, in 1966, both *Le
Figaro* and *Le Nouvel Observateur* ran into
legal difficulties after running advertisements
for books subject to proscription. The sociosexual upheavals generated by **May 1968** did
not, at least not initially, militate against the
restrictions to which erotico-literary material
had become subject. In the closing years of the
1960s, erotic texts by authors such as Sade,
Henry Miller, Guyotat, Réage and Emmanuelle
Arsan were banned. In 1973, a publisher of
erotica, Régine Deforges, was fined 10,000
francs for bringing out works constituting an
'apologia for perversion'. Deforges's trial provoked a storm of protest, which may have contributed to the diminution in literary repression
that took place in France during and after the
mid-1970s. This period is generally considered
to be one in which, as far as matters pertaining
to book **publishing** were concerned, the legislative status quo bowed to the pressure of social
evolution, and to changes in popular conceptions of what did and did not constitute
'obscenity'. This is not to say that the French
legal system has become openly tolerant of
erotica. In 1994, the new French penal code

included a section detailing the sanctions attendant upon the dissemination (to minors) of pornographic material.

ALEX HUGHES

See also: erotic writing; pornography

Further reading

Brécourt-Villars, C. (1985) *Écrire d'amour*, Paris: Ramsay (an anthology of French female-authored erotic texts, which contains an introduction offering useful information regarding the evolution of the erotico-literary tradition in France).

Pauvert, J.-J. (1994) *Nouveaux (et moins nouveaux) visages de la censure*, Paris: Belles Lettres (an historical account of censorship in France).

literary journals

The traditional value placed on the printed word in France was heightened during the transition from war to peace following the August 1944 Liberation, when writers and publishers suspected of collaborating with the Nazis were singled out and tried with vehemence. Long after the Liberation, debates surrounding this postwar purge (*épuration*) and a concomitant politics of writing remain a key to the rise and fall of France's major literary journals and publishing houses.

A prime case in point is the *Nouvelle Revue française* (NRF), conceived in 1908 by André Gide and his circle to assert a high-minded *moeurs littéraires*. Under the editorial guidance of Jacques Rivière and Jean Paulhan, the NRF became France's preeminent literary journal between the wars. After Paulhan resigned in 1940 rather than work under German censors, the NRF's publisher, Gaston Gallimard, allowed the monthly to continue under the direction of the pro-Nazi writer, Pierre Drieu La Rochelle. In exchange, Drieu used his influence with German officials in Paris to keep the

Éditions Gallimard operating. Gallimard avoided prison after the war, but his monthly was forced to suspend publication and did not reappear until 1954.

The vacuum created by censure against the NRF was filled by *Les Temps modernes* (TM), whose director, Jean-Paul Sartre, had been a rising star at Gallimard prior to 1940. Opposed to what he saw as the NRF's growing detachment from the social and political issues of the 1930s, Sartre grounded *Les Temps modernes* on a programme of committed literature (*littérature engagée*) that mobilized prose to drive the writer through language to disclose and correct social and political injustices threatening the freedom of the individual that the monthly sought to protect. Over the next fifty years, dual concerns with social justice and individual freedom made TM a critical voice to be reckoned with in debates ranging from independence for Vietnam and Algeria, racism, nuclear testing, and a viable peace in the Middle East to the events of May 1968, women's liberation, and Jewish identity.

Critique, founded in 1946 under the directorship of Georges Bataille, billed itself as a 'general review of French and foreign publications'. It featured extended reviews of new and recent books on topics ranging from new criticism (*la nouvelle critique*) and phenomenology to linguistics and structuralism. Under Bataille and his successor, Jean Piel, contributors such as Michel Foucault, Jacques Derrida, Emmanuel Levinas, Gilles Deleuze, René Girard and Michel Deguy made *Critique* a prime forum for debate related to literary criticism, philosophy, and the hybrid form of theorizing and social sciences known in French as *les sciences humaines*. Occasional clusters devoted to individual writers (Nietzsche, Roland Barthes) and topics ('Fin-de-siècle Vienna,' 'Anglo-American Philosophy') likewise enhanced multidisciplinary debate within and outside France. The elegant *Critique* logo imprint also graced a book series at Minuit whose authors included Derrida and Deleuze.

While TM and *Critique* served as alternatives to the interwar NRF, neither aspired to the explicit cachet of the avant-garde that *Tel quel* (TQ) cultivated between 1960 and 1982 under the aegis of Philippe **Sollers**. As TQ continually defined and refined its mission, it resembled nothing so much as an avatar of the Surrealist movement of the 1920s. To this end, Sollers and company flaunted eclecticism by fashioning their own set of precursors from the Marquis de Sade, Stéphane Mallarmé, and James Joyce to Raymond Roussel, Antonin **Artaud**, Bataille and Francis **Ponge** while – at moments – asserting the primacy of writing (Sollers, Derrida) and the psychoanalytic notion of subjects in process (Julia **Kristeva**). The journal developed its own book series at the Éditions du **Seuil**, with contributors ranging from Barthes and Derrida to Gérard **Genette**, Tzvetan Todorov, Kristeva and Jean **Ricardou**.

From 1966 to 1976, *Tel quel* engaged in a collective turn toward revolutionary politics that sought (in the student uprisings of May 1968, the French Communist Party, and the Cultural Revolution led in China by Mao Ze Dong) various solutions to the impasse between open creativity and revolutionary politics that had plagued the first generation of Surrealists under André Breton. By 1980, Sollers declared the history of the European avant-garde at an end. In retrospect, it seems that, except for Derrida, most TQ critics failed to account for the philosophical implications of their positions in anything more than a narrow historical context. This was because – as Herman Rapaport notes – they were preoccupied instead with developing formal semiotic methods of analysis and reinventing Marxist Leninism (Rapaport 1994). By 1982, *Tel quel* no longer existed and Sollers was editor-in-chief of *L'Infini*, a journal of less militant ambitions than its predecessor.

Poétique (1970–) was initially an offshoot of *Tel quel* that – much in the tradition of the Russian Formalists, whose writings Todorov had translated in 1965 – devoted itself to the theory, history and analysis of literary forms. The same held true for the origins of *Change*, founded in 1968 by a *collectif permanent* headed at various moments by Jean-Pierre Faye and Jean Paris. Other major postwar journals include *Esprit*, *Présence africaine*, *L'Arc*, *Littérature*, *La Nouvelle Critique* and *Poésie*. More specialized journals in fields related to literary studies range from **Cahiers du cinéma**, **Annales** and *La Nouvelle Revue de la psychanalyse* to *Communications*, *La Revue des sciences humaines*, *Diogène*, and *Le Débat*.

More in line with commercial aspects of book publishing since the 1960s, *La Quinzaine littéraire* and *Le Magazine littéraire* featured one- to two-page reviews of new publications as well as interviews and dossiers. Finally, mass-circulation weeklies such as *Le Nouvel Observateur* and *L'Événement du jeudi* and dailies such as *Le Monde* and **Libération** include reviews of literary and non-fiction titles that are often more informed and substantial than those to be found in equivalent publications outside France.

STEVEN UNGAR

See also: Algerian war; Judaism; racism/anti-semitism; revolutionary groups

Further reading

Assouline, P. (1984) *Gaston Gallimard: un demi-siècle d'édition française*, Paris: Balland; (1988) *Gaston Gallimard: A Half-century in Publishing*, trans. H. J. Salemson, New York: Harcourt Brace Jovanovich.

Boschetti, A. (1988) *The Intellectual Enterprise: Sartre and 'Les Temps modernes'*, Evanston: Northwestern University Press (essential reading).

Rapaport, H. (1994) 'French Theory and Criticism, 5: 1945–1968', and '6: 1968 and After', in M. Groden and M. Kreiswirth (eds) *The Johns Hopkins Guide to Literary Theory and Criticism*, Baltimore: Johns Hopkins University Press.

Simonin, A. (1994) *Les Éditions de Minuit, 1942–1955: le devoir d'insoumission*, Paris: IMEC Éditions (definitive study, sets *Critique* within the history of the publishing house that emerged from the underground following the Liberation).

Suleiman, S. (1987) 'As Is: The First Issue of *Tel quel* is Published', in D. Hollier (ed.) *A New History of French Literature*, Cambridge: Harvard University Press.

literary prizes

Literary prizes (*prix*) and competitions (*concours*) have long been a feature of the French cultural scene, and have proliferated in the present century (there are currently around 1,500). The former are awarded to published texts, while unpublished works and manuscripts are entered for the latter. Juries – often composed of former prizewinners (*lauréats*) – play a central role in the selection process. Their choices ensure that a book will attract the attention of the media and will become a best seller (sums of money actually offered as prize awards are often merely nominal). Unsurprisingly, selections are regularly the focus of controversy.

Prizes are awarded for all kinds of texts, including those relating to the following areas: archaeology, art history, **autobiography**, cartoons, children's writing, criticism, documentary writing, history, humour, law, philosophy, **photography**, **poetry**, new writing, non-French francophone writing, **science fiction**, short-story writing, **theatre**, and translation. Some of the most prestigious French literary prizes are the:

- Femina (created in 1904, with an all-woman jury and two categories: the best French novel of the year, and the best foreign novel translated into French)
- Goncourt (created in 1903, and awardable to works belonging to any category of literary prose, although novels usually win it)
- Interallié (created in 1930 and given to works of literary journalism)
- Médicis (created in 1958, along with the related *prix Médicis étranger* and the *prix Médicis essai*)
- Renaudot
- Grand Prix du Roman.

ALEX HUGHES

See also: francophone writing (fiction, poetry): Belgium; francophone writing (fiction, poetry): DOM-TOMs; francophone writing (fiction, poetry):Indian Ocean; francophone writing (fiction, poetry): Switzerland; publishing/*l'édition*

Livre de poche

Book series

In 1953, Henri Filipacchi (1900–61) launched the series of cheap paperbacks known as 'Le Livre de poche' for the publisher Hachette. The first two-franc edition was Pierre Benoit's novel *Königsmark*. Between 1953 and the end of 1993, 9,500 different titles and 720 million copies had already been published. The best-selling were the *Larousse de poche* in 1968 (6.9 million) and Alain-Fournier's *Le Grand Meaulnes* in 1962 (4.28 million).

MARTYN CORNICK

See also: publishing/*l'édition*

Lyotard, Jean-François

b. 1924, Versailles

Philosopher

Lyotard is famous to an international (especially North American) audience as the author of the cultish *The Post-Modern Condition* (*La Condition postmoderne*) in 1979. In keeping, however, with the multiple nature of **postmodernism**, of which he is seen as one of the prime philosophers, Lyotard's intellectual identities are several. He was an early and active member of the Socialisme ou Barbarie group, which tried to conduct a critique of Marxism from within; Lyotard's political writings on Algeria from 1956 to 1963 are best read in this light. In 1954, he produced the introductory *Phenomenology* (*La Phénoménologie*), which struggled with the tensions inherently separating that philosophical approach from Marxism. This Marxist strain lasted until **May 1968** and the subsequent disillusion felt by many left-wing intellectuals regarding the French Communist Party's collusion in the quelling of the events' revolutionary potential. A second phase – predicted by the non-**Lacan**ian emphasis on figurality in *Discourse, Figure* (*Discours, figure*) of 1971 and the essays collected in *Driftworks* (*Dérive à partir de Marx et Freud*) and *Des dispositifs pulsionnels* (Drive Mechanisms), both from 1973 – was marked by the turbulent *Libidinal Economy* (*Économie libidinale*) of 1974, which broke with Marxism and sought to initiate a neo-Nietzschean politics of libidinal forces by plunging spectacularly into the whole body of language and especially the language of the body. This text's dramatization of intensity, multiplication and ecstasy anticipated the more precisely elaborated thesis of *The Post-Modern Condition*, regarding this age's delegitimation of master narratives and the move to paralogy, or cultivation of paradox and instability over and within consensus. Arising out of this presumed collapse of absolutes and certainties, Lyotard moved in 1979 to a consideration of the possibilities of justice and its formulation in agonistic or endlessly discursive terms in *Just Gaming* (*Au Juste*), a text which logically took the form of a Platonic dialogue. This, in turn, was supposedly superseded, along with all previous moves, by 1983's *The Differend: Phrases in Dispute* (*Le Différend*), Lyotard's most sustained engagement with the history and discipline of philosophy, which claimed to cancel his previous, partial attempts to negotiate the problem of judgement in a postmodern context, and sought to view philosophy itself as a differend (or dispute involving competing genres of discourse) in relation to economic and academic discourses.

SEÁN HAND

See also: Marxism and Marxian thought; post-structuralism

Further reading

Bennington, G. (1988), *Lyotard: Writing the Event*, Manchester: Manchester University Press (an authoritative presentation of Lyotard's strategies).

M

M6

Television channel

This private television company, funded from **advertising** revenue, came into existence in 1987. Its predecessor, TV6, had been established as a dedicated music channel by the Socialist government one year earlier. M6 provides a general entertainment service with an emphasis on comedy, feature films and television series, much of it imported from the United States. Its principal shareholders are the Groupe Lyonnaise des Eaux and the Luxembourg media company, the Compagnie Luxembourgeoise de Télédiffusion. The channel diversified into programme production and other media-related activities in the early 1990s.

RAYMOND KUHN

See also: television

Madelin, Alain

b. 1948, Paris

Politician

Madelin is France's most avowedly 'Thatcherite' political figure, with the possible exception of Jean-Marie **Le Pen**. A Fascist militant in his Paris student days (his long-time political rival François **Léotard** claims to have had his first encounter with him on the wrong end of an iron bar), he soon mellowed into a political career on the right wing of the Parti Républicain that reached its apogee when **Chirac**, as a reward for Madelin's perhaps unexpected support in the 1995 presidential elections, appointed him Finance Minister. Madelin resigned after only a few months in the post, the better to concentrate on his ultimately unsuccessful attempt to win the leadership of the Parti Républicain. His privatizing fervour has also manifested itself in his writings, including *Chers Compatriotes* (My Fellow French) of 1994 and *Quand les autruches relèveront la tête* (When the Ostriches Look up) of 1995.

KEITH READER

See also: parties and movements

Maeght Foundation

The first private museum of modern art in France, and the first building designed expressly for the exhibition of modern art, the Maeght Foundation was opened on 28 July 1964 by André **Malraux**, then Minister for Cultural Affairs. Situated in the hilltop town of St-Paul de Vence, Alpes-Maritimes, it attracts over a quarter of a million visitors each year: its permanent collection comprises over 6,000 works, and it stages frequent temporary exhibitions.

The foundation was established by Aimé Maeght (1906–81), lithographer, gallery owner, art publisher, dealer and collector, and his wife Marguerite. Both were lovers of contemporary art, and formed friendships with many celebrated artists including Georges **Braque** (who designed the chapel's stained-glass windows), Marc **Chagall**, Alberto **Giacometti**, Fernand **Léger**, Henri **Matisse** and Joan Miró; many works by these artists belong to the permanent collection. The main building, designed by the Catalan architect Josep Lluis Sert, houses the majority of the exhibits, while many **sculptures** are situated in the surrounding garden.

COLVILLE WEMYSS

See also: painting

maisons de la culture

A network of multidisciplinary regional arts centres in major cities, initiated in the 1960s by André **Malraux** to decentralize and democratize Parisian high culture. Underfunded, and considered either too subversive or too bourgeois, the network never matched initial ambitions and failed to alter the sociological composition of audiences. From 1969, government priorities shifted and financial problems ensued. In 1990, the surviving establishments were renamed *scènes nationales* (national stages), specializing in performing arts.

DAVID LOOSELEY

See also: cultural policy; theatre

Further reading

Looseley, D. L. (1993) 'Paris Versus the Provinces: Cultural Decentralization Since 1945', in M. Cook (ed.) *French Culture Since 1945*, London: Longman (traces the *maisons*' history).

Malle, Louis

b. 1932, Thumeries/Lille;
d. 1995, Los Angeles, USA

Director

A film-maker for the most part disregarded by critics in his own country (until a belated César awarded in the year of his death), Malle is one of the rare French directors to make a successful career in the USA, where his fine analysis of human beings has won him international acclaim (e.g. *Atlantic City, USA* in 1980). His ability to work with actors is a hallmark of his work, as is his careful *mise-en-scène*. Malle's work is at the vanguard of a moral cinema treating difficult subjects before their time; for example, issues surrounding sexuality (incest, infidelity, child pornography) and political taboos such as the Occupation (in *Lacombe Lucien* of 1973 and *Au Revoir les enfants* of 1987) and the **Algerian war.**

KEITH READER

See also: cinema

Malraux, André

b. 1901, Paris;
d. 1976, Créteil

Writer and politician

Malraux was already an established novelist and intellectual when his encounter with de **Gaulle** in 1945 took him into politics. Appointed Minister of Cultural Affairs in 1959, he is chiefly remembered for cleaning Parisian buildings, the **Malraux act**, and the *maisons de la culture*. Contested during **May 1968**, he resigned in June 1969.

DAVID LOOSELEY

See also: cultural policy; Langlois, Henri

Further reading

Lacouture, J. (1973) *André Malraux*, Paris: Éditions du Seuil (biography).
Looseley, D. L. (1995) *The Politics of Fun: Cultural Policy and Debate in Contemporary France*, Oxford: Berg (examines Malraux the minister).

Malraux act

This law, passed in 1962 and named after André **Malraux** (then Minister of Cultural Affairs), legislated for the protection, development and restructuring of historically significant urban areas (*secteurs sauvegardés*), in the face of modern urban expansion. The act influenced conservation strategies adopted by other European governments of the 1960s, notably that of the UK.

ALEX HUGHES

See also: architecture; conservation zones; renovation projects

Man Ray

b. 1890, Philadelphia, USA;
d. 1976, Paris

Photographer and artist

Trained as a painter, Man Ray discovered the work of **Duchamp** and Picabia at the 1913 Armory Show. The following year he began taking photographs, originally to reproduce his paintings. He went to Paris in 1921 and was part of the Dadaist and then Surrealist movements, whose members he famously photographed. His work includes such celebrated photographic images as *Ingres's Violin (Le Violon d'Ingres)* of 1924 and *Tears (Larmes)* from 1930. He spent 1940 to 1951 in the United States, where he had several one-man shows, painted a great deal and, again, pho-

tographed many of the great writers and painters of the period. He was the inventor of several photographic techniques, particularly using light effects such as solarizations and 'rayographs', a personal variant of the photogram.

DEBRA KELLY

See also: photography

Major works

Man Ray (1963) *Self Portrait*, London: André Deutsch (an autobiography in which he also explains his techniques).

management style

The management style of the French has often been criticized for being overly authoritarian and distant. Indeed, the traditional French approach to management is seen as partly to blame for the confrontational nature of industrial relations in France. In order to understand how this management style developed, it is necessary to trace the history of the French management class, *les cadres*.

Small family-run firms continued to dominate the economy in France until much later than in its main competitor countries, and this had a significant influence on French management style. In such companies, the owner, or *patron*, retained much everyday control of the labour force and the production process. In other words, there was no distinction to be made between the owners of these businesses and their managers. Unsurprisingly, these *petits patrons* were often authoritarian and paternalistic in their dealings with their workforce.

It was only in the larger companies in the 1930s that a new class grew up in French industry situated between the *patronat* on the one hand, and the workers on the other. This new class was that of the *cadres*. This category of employee normally constituted the engineers who took control of production processes, which were becoming ever more complicated and impossible for one person (or a small team of family members) to oversee. However, the development of the *cadre* did nothing to change the authoritarian and distant management style set in place by the *patronat*. Although the *cadre* class expanded to cover areas which did not necessarily demand a technical knowledge, because of its roots in engineering, *cadres* continued to be recruited from the prestigious engineering *grandes écoles*. This meant that French *cadres* were, and still often are today, individuals who have come straight in to their positions from higher education, rather than having served any kind of shop-floor apprenticeship, and whose training is of a type which prizes abstract thinking and logic over interpersonal skills or creativity.

However, more recently, and with the influence of American and latterly Japanese work practices, the French have become aware of the shortcomings of their own management style. This is particularly true for those trying to manage workers in the ever-expanding service sector in which, because of the nature of the tasks to be performed, it is not possible to control the workforce in the same way as on a production line. Rather, it is necessary to motivate them to work harder. In response to this need for a new kind of manager, a number of management schools have been set up in France, offering an education perhaps more suited to contemporary conditions in which marketing and organizational behaviour take pride of place in the curriculum over mathematics and technical specialisms.

JAN WINDEBANK

See also: economy; educational elitism: the *grandes écoles*

Further reading

Barsoux, J.-L. and Lawrence, P. (1990) *Management in France*, London: Cassell Educational (an overview of management practices in France).

Manessier, Alfred

b. 1911, St-Ouen

Artist

Alfred Manessier, a painter usually associated with the École de Paris, demonstrated the clear influence of Cubism and Fauvism until the end of World War II. Returning to Paris from the Normandy coast after the Occupation, he reasserted his pantheistic reification of nature. The extraordinary synthesis of structured surface picture plane derived from Cubism, with the vibrant colour rendered admissible by the Fauves, gave rise to his distinctive 'stained-glass' style, and provided the vehicle for an abstraction more accurately designated 'non-figuration'. Subject matter for these vast sublime paintings is divided between the ecstasies of religious passion and the grandeur of the sea. Avoiding literal figuration, these paintings are none the less profoundly humanist and, above all, affective.

SIMEON HUNTER

See also: painting

Manet, Éduardo

b. 1927, Santiago de Cuba, Cuba

Playwright and novelist

Manet was a director of Cuban theatres and cinemas, until his play *Las Monjas* (The Nuns), directed by **Blin** in France in 1969, sparked off a prolific French writing career. His plays include *Eux ou la prise de pouvoir* (Them or the Seizure of Power), *Un balcon sur les Andes* (Balcony Over the Andes) and *Ma'dea*.

ANNIE SPARKS

See also: theatre

Further reading

Bradby, D. (1991) *Modern French Drama 1940–1990*, Cambridge: Cambridge University Press (essential reading).

Mano Negra

Musicians

A leading indie group of the 1990s at the confluence of rockabilly, hip-hop and punk, **rap**, raï, salsa and many more styles, which they mix with panache. Singing in French, Arabic, English and Spanish, they are generous, unconventional and exuberant performers on the world circuit. Their latest products are *Puta's Fever* (1990) and *Casa Babylone* (1994).

GÉRARD POULET

See also: rock and pop

manufacturing industry

The manufacturing industry was the backbone of the thirty glorious years of French economic growth from 1945 to 1974; since then, however, a deep crisis has affected a number of 'traditional' industries, contributing to increasing unemployment and to the decay of regional infrastructure. Now the fourth industrial power in the world, France has developed some larger world-weight conglomerates, especially in the 1980s, but still lags behind European competitors in this respect.

Manufacturing, excluding activities such as energy and building, only accounts for one-fifth of France's national product and **employment**, and the sector has lost the leading role it had in the economy from 1945 to 1974. During that period, French society underwent deep material changes which helped the development of manufacturing industries catering for the new mass markets – cars, white and brown electrical goods, leisure goods – or infrastructures required by the postwar reconstruction and the sudden transformation of urban areas. France, which had long trailed behind other countries, then entered consumer society with a vengeance. After the 1974 crisis, however, manufacturing industry suffered a succession of problems, which resulted in the closure of many plants, with pockets of mass unemployment particularly concentrated in areas of old industry, such as the north or Lorraine, or in the industrial towns surrounding the Massif Central. In other cases, efforts to increase competitiveness brought considerable loss of jobs – the so-called *dégraissage* (slimming down). In the car industry, for instance, the Renault workforce went down from 223,000 to 138,000 employees between 1980 and 1994.

Manufacturing industry is highly diversified, from traditional shoemaking, say, to high-tech space electronics. Since the mid-1980s, firms have made considerable efforts to penetrate foreign markets, especially European ones. Indeed, some companies are true multinationals, but they are usually only mid-table in world size rankings.

Manufacturing in the past was concentrated in specific areas (the Vosges mountains for textiles mills; the Alpine valleys for aluminium; toy-making and watch assembly a speciality of farmers in the Jura . . .), because of either availability of natural resources or a skilled workforce. This regional distribution has changed dramatically. Regions of heavy traditional industries have suffered badly since the 1970s. Other regions, however, have benefited from recent development, such as those of Toulouse (home of the aerospace industry) or Grenoble, but localization of industries is now more flexible, and manufacturing employment less important than services.

FRANÇOIS NECTOUX

See also: agriculture; economy; transport

Further reading

Szarka, J. (1992) *Business in France: An*

Introduction to the Economic and Social Context, London: Pitman (the chapter on industrial policy and industrial development gives an overall view of the French industry).

Taddeï, D. and Coriat, B. (1993) *Made in France: L'Industrie française dans la competition mondiale*, Paris: Le Livre de Poche (an official report, giving an advanced analysis of current industrial problems).

Marais plan

The area of Right Bank Paris known as the Marais is one of the showpieces of post-World War II urban conservation in France, but at the same time it is where the political weight of popular protest about social change accompanying building restoration has been greatest. It is an area of 126 hectares designated a *secteur sauvegardé* in 1965, at which time its legacy of valuable classical architecture from the seventeenth and eighteenth centuries had become much degraded by subdivision, neglect and the introduction of industrial activities. Many street façades have now been restored by the conservation project known as the Marais plan, and new economic activities have been introduced. However, many of the indigenous residents have been forced to leave. Rents and property prices have risen as a consequence of the conservation work, which has changed the popular perception of the area from a slum to one of urban chic.

ROGER KAIN

See also: conservation zones; Malraux act; renovation projects

Marceau, Félicien

b. 1913, Cortemberg, Belgium

Playwright, essayist and novelist, real name Louis Carette

A member of the **Académie Française** since 1975, and the author of popular plays written during the 1950s and 1960s and directed by **Barsacq**, these include *L'Oeuf* (The Egg) and *La Bonne Soupe* (Good Soup).

ANNIE SPARKS

See also: theatre

Marceau, Marcel

b. 1923, Strasbourg

Mime artist, real name Marcel Mangel

An internationally famed **mime** artist, and the founder of a troupe which performed his *mimodrames*, including *Le Manteau* (The Coat), adapted from Gogol, and *Mont-de-Piété*. Due to lack of subsidy, he moved to Germany, where he developed his renowned solo routines. The city of Paris now finances his mime school.

ANNIE SPARKS

See also: theatre

Marceau, Sophie

b. 1966, Paris

Actor

Her career was launched by Pinoteau's successful *La Boum* (1980) followed by *La Boum 2* (1982), where she typified the 1980s French adolescent, and for which she received a César as most promising actress. Pinoteau picked up her 'story' in *L'Étudiante* (1988). Although she has acted, somewhat unsuccessfully, in auteurist films (such as **Pialat**'s *Police* of 1985), her roles have been mostly confined to big-budget films, like Corneau's *Fort Saganne* (1984), with a penchant for historical films – for example, de Broca's *Chouans!* (1988) and **Tavernier**'s *La Fille de d'Artagnan* (1994). Her part in Mel Gibson's Oscared *Braveheart* (1996) made her an international star.

PHIL POWRIE

See also: cinema; stars

Marcellin, Raymond

b. 1914, Sézanne

Politician

Appointed Minister of the Interior by de **Gaulle** in the major governmental reshuffle after **May 1968**, Marcellin's name was to become a byword for repressive legislation. The *loi anti-casseurs* of 1970 rendered anybody found in the vicinity of a demonstration liable for any violence committed on it – it was repealed in 1982. Marcellin's fervent belief in a Communist/leftist conspiracy to take over France (illustrated throughout his political testament, *L'Ordre public et les groupes révolutionnaires* (Public Order and Revolutionary Groups)) led him to deport more or less instantly any foreigner found taking part in a demonstration on French soil.

KEITH READER

See also: parties and movements; revolutionary groups

Marchais, Georges

b. 1920, La Hoquette, Calvados; d. 1997, Paris

Politician

Originally a machine fitter, Marchais was a Communist member of the National Assembly from 1947 until 1997. A member of the Political Bureau of the Parti Communiste Français from 1959 and general secretary of the party from 1970 to 1994, he publicly condemned the student movement of **May 1968**, criticized Soviet intervention in Czechoslovakia in 1968, backed his party's alliance with the Parti Socialiste from 1972 to 1984 and supported Soviet intervention in Afghanistan in 1979. As the Communist presidential candidate in 1981 he gained 15.34 per cent of the vote. Renowned for his dogmatism and verbal gaffes, he presided over his party's electoral decline in the 1980s and early 1990s, refusing to acknowledge the consequences of the crisis of international Communism.

LAURENCE BELL

See also: parties and movements

Major works

Marchais, G. (1990) *La Démocratie*, Paris: Messidor/Éditions Sociales (a restatement of the traditional French Communist line).

Maréchal, Marcel

b. 1937, Tassin-la-Demi-Lune, Rhône

Actor and director

Known for his love of directing and acting in text-based works from playwrights including Claudel, **Audiberti** and **Novarina**, Maréchal is currently based at Paris's Théâtre du Rond Point with his company, which moved from Lyon to Marseille in the 1970s, and received regional dramatic centre status in 1981.

ANNIE SPARKS

See also: theatre

Major works

Maréchal, M. (1974) *La Mise en théâtre*, Paris: Union Générale d'Éditions (Maréchal's theories).

Marie-Claire

Women's magazine

One of today's best-selling women's magazines in the *haut de gamme* (luxury) monthly category, *Marie-Claire* is aimed at young, professional women.

It was first launched as a weekly magazine, in 1937, by the powerful Prouvost press group. In 1939, the magazine was moved to Lyon, its distribution restricted to the **Vichy** zone. The extension of Nazi rule to the south forced the magazine to cease production in 1943. After 1945, *Marie-Claire*, along with other publications which had continued under Vichy rule, was banned. However, 1954 saw the relaunch of the new *Marie-Claire* as a luxury but affordable monthly, whose professed aim was to promote the interests of modern, young women who had obtained the vote in 1944.

The magazine's luxurious appearance and energetic style appealed to women under 35. Its mixture of **fashion** and beauty items, style and culture pages – together with practical pages on cooking, health and home decoration – made for an approach which worked. By 1957, its annual circulation figure had exceeded a million. However, by 1963, readers were beginning to tire of the same format and content and this marked the beginning of declining circulation figures. By 1968, it was clear that fresher, bolder ideas were needed and in this respect the magazine gave a big nod to new feminist ideas which were gaining currency among young, working women, who had started to question traditional feminine roles. A major innovation was the inclusion of a substantial supplement entitled *Femmes*, which contained news about feminist organizations, events and literature. This approach proved successful for a part of the 1970s, boosting circulation to an extent, but it failed to restore magazine sales to the levels of the late 1950s and early 1960s. Furthermore, it was an approach which was not to last into the 1980s, as a media 'backlash' against feminism was to emerge.

From the mid- to late 1970s, *Marie-Claire*, in common with all other categories of the periodical press, saw sales decrease again as competition from other media, within the context of a stagnating **economy**, drove readers towards alternative sources of information and entertainment. In the 1980s and 1990s, the magazine has maintained its position within the category of luxury women's magazines, despite the threat of legal liquidation in December 1993 from which it was saved by the Marie-Claire Album group in 1994. Since then, its yearly circulation has stabilized between 500,000 and 600,000. As far as style and content are concerned, the magazine has stayed with certain well-developed themes: fashion and beauty, the beautifully illustrated *reportages à l'étranger* (overseas reports), interviews with famous people and topical social issues treated through personal testimonies. Added to these are items on horoscopes, recipes, home, holidays, arts and so on. Along with other magazines in its category, *Marie-Claire* has remained an important channel of information within the cultural universe of French women.

KHURSHEED WADIA

See also: feminism (movements/groups); women's magazines.

marriage/cohabitation

While it remains the dominant model of **family** formation, marriage has become a less stable relationship in France, and it is gradually being replaced by unmarried cohabitation. Since the early 1970s, marriage rates have fallen consistently. By the mid-1990s, France displayed one of the lowest rates in Europe, with 4.4 marriages per 1,000 inhabitants. Fewer of the marriages being contracted were for the first time: more people were remarrying. Couples were also delaying getting married, with the result that mean age at marriage had reached 26.4 years for women and 28.4 years for men. Even though more marriages were ending in divorce, the vast majority of men (84 per cent) and women (88 per cent) were marrying at some point in their lives. The divorce rate had doubled since the beginning of the 1960s: nearly one in every two new marriages would end in divorce.

Falling marriage rates do not, however, mean that couples no longer want to live together. The number of unmarried cohabiting couples has increased significantly, together with the proportion of extramarital births, indicating that the institution of marriage is not seen as the only environment in which couples can live together and raise children. By the early 1990s, about 13 per cent of all cohabiting couples were unmarried, but the proportion of consensual unions in the 20 to 24 age group reached 82 per cent for men and 73 per cent for women. From a level below 6 per cent in the mid-1960s, the proportion of all live births outside marriage had risen to 33 per cent. Whereas, in the 1960s, extramarital conception was usually legitimized by marriage, by the 1990s couples were no longer deciding to get married when they were expecting children, and the children of unmarried cohabitees had acquired the same rights as those of married couples. One in three children conceived outside wedlock was born to a mother aged under 25, but more extramarital births were occurring in reconstituted families, following divorce or separation. The number of births to women living alone remained constant at around 3 to 4 per cent, while a growing proportion of lone parents were likely to be either separated or divorced. Marriage can no longer be seen as a stable and enduring relationship, and unmarried cohabitation even less so. By the early 1990s, 10 per cent of children had experienced life in a lone-parent family and 13 per cent in a reconstituted family.

LINDA HANTRAIS

See also: demographic developments

Further reading

Hantrais, L. and Letablier, M.-T. (1996) *Families and Family Policies in Europe*, London and New York: Longman (an analysis of concepts of marriage and cohabitation within a family-policy framework).

Saboulin, M. de and Thave, S. (1993) 'La Vie en couple marié: un modèle qui s'affaiblit', *La Société française: données sociales 1993*, Paris: INSEE (a succinct account of trends in marriage and cohabitation).

Marxism and Marxian thought

As a corpus of ideas inspired by the writings of Karl Marx and Friedrich Engels, Marxism comprises an economic and social theory, a theory of the politics of class struggle and a materialist philosophy of history. Adopted by the international Communist movement, it has been interpreted and developed in a variety of ways, mainly in response to different perceptions of the needs of the political struggle. Elements of Marxist thought have also been incorporated within theoretical frameworks, deriving from other traditions.

The influence of Marxist thought on French intellectuals was at its height in the two decades following World War II. To a great extent, this was a result of a political rather than a theoretical choice. The French Communists had emerged from the war with their political reputation greatly enhanced, as a result of their leading role in the national resistance against the Nazi occupier. Although their identification with the political interests of the Soviet Bloc was to lead once again to their isolation from mainstream French political life with the development of the Cold War from 1947, their credit remained high with a large number of intellectuals for two main reasons. First, the French Communist Party (PCF) was the largest single party in France and attracted the support of a majority of the working class. Second, the polarization of international politics fostered a climate in which intellectuals felt that they had to take sides in the conflict between East and West; many felt that, overall, the forces for peace, progress and a better economic and social order were on the side of the

Soviet Union, in its battle to defend itself against imperialist designs on the part of the USA.

Although by the early 1950s more intellectuals than ever before were members of the PCF, philosophers such as Louis **Althusser**, writers such as Louis Aragon and Paul **Éluard**, scientists such as Marcel Prenant and Jacques Monod, the mathematician Jean-Louis Desanti, the historian Emmanuel **Le Roy Ladurie**, to mention just a few, or 'fellow travellers' sympathetic to it, such as Jean-Paul **Sartre** and Maurice Merleau-Ponty, there were considerable ambiguities in their relationship with Marxist theory. On the whole, intellectuals joined the party for political reasons, rather than because of any theoretical commitment to Marxism. The party's *ouvriérisme*, or distrust of anyone without working-class credentials, meant that intellectuals constantly had to prove their loyalty to the leadership of the working class, by renouncing the right to independent thinking. What passed for theory in party circles was a version of Marxism simplified into dogma and passed on to party militants in the form of selected extracts and quotations from a limited number of texts by Marx, Engels, Lenin and Stalin, especially the latter's *History of the Communist Party of the Soviet Union (Bolsheviks): Short Course*, which summarized Marxist philosophy in a schematic exposition of the laws and tenets of dialectical and historical materialism.

The loyalty of the Communist intellectuals, along with their willingness to sacrifice theoretical integrity to the requirements of politics, was put to one of its most severe tests at the time of the Lysenko affair in 1948. Lysenko was a biologist who claimed to have disproved the theories of classical genetics, with his work on the transmission of acquired characteristics into new generations of agricultural crops. The political significance of this claim resulted from the endorsement of his thesis by the full weight of the Soviet regime. In French Communist circles, it gave rise to the theory of the 'two sciences', in which Lysenko became the champion of 'proletarian' science, as against the 'bourgeois' science of geneticists like Mendel and

Morgan. The importance of the scientific evidence was minimized in favour of the test of political loyalties and French Communists, including some of the most distinguished scientists of the time, were called upon to toe the party line.

During this period, developments in Marxist theory were taking place, but on the whole from outside the French Communist Party. Previously unpublished texts, such as Marx and Engels' *The German Ideology* and Lenin's *Philosophical Notebooks*, had begun to be published in French in 1937 and 1938. The publication of Marx's *Economic and Philosophical Manuscripts* (1844) in 1937 was to have a significant effect on the development of a new current, which presented Marxism as a humanism, in which the predominant influence was Hegel. Bridges were built between Marxist and non-Marxist philosophers, in which the work to popularize Hegelian philosophy done by Jean Hyppolite and Alexandre Kojève, especially the latter's 1947 *Introduction à la lecture de Hegel* (Introduction to the Reading of Hegel), played an important role. Marx was portrayed as a mainstream philosopher, following in and continuing the Western European philosophical tradition. At the same time, Catholic thinkers, such as the priest, Jean-Yves Calvez, with his 1956 text *La Pensée de Karl Marx*, (The Thought of Karl Marx) attempted to synthesize elements of Christian theology and Marxist thought. Of the group including Georges Politzer, Paul Nizan and Henri **Lefebvre**, which had begun work in the 1930s and drew on psychoanalytical and other theories – such as Politzer's *Critique des fondements de la psychologie (Criticisms of the Foundations of Psychology)*, Lefebvre's *Dialectical Materialism (Le Matérialisme dialectique)* and Lefebvre and Guterman's *La Conscience mystifiée* (The Mystification of Mind) – only Lefebvre, who survived the war, was able to produce substantial new work in the postwar period. Lucien Goldmann, much influenced by Lukács, was to provide a bridge between literature and sociology, with his 'genetic structuralism', in *The Human Sciences and Philosophy (Les Sciences humaines et la* *philosophie*) and *The Hidden God* (*Le Dieu caché*).

Jean-Paul Sartre, claiming that Marxism was 'the indispensable philosophy for our time', (Sartre 1985) was to develop his own original version of this philosophy, culminating in the publication of the *Critique of Dialectical Reason* (*Critique de la raison dialectique*) in 1960, which attempted to theorize the possibilities of individual, group and collective action in history.

In spite of the many significant differences between these different strands of Marxist thought, what they all had in common was an emphasis on the philosophical and ethical elements of Marx's thought; his contribution to economic and political theory was largely ignored. Thus, in these hands, Marxism became primarily an analysis of the alienation of the individual and the possibilities available to the individual to transcend this alienated status. Marx's analysis of the mode of production of the capitalist system, and the class relations which were built upon it, had little or no role to play in work of this type.

Within party ranks, theoretical work was tightly controlled by the party leadership. The works of Maurice **Thorez**, party leader from 1930 to 1964 and subject of a mini personality cult in his own right, were required reading, and all were expected to defend the party analysis of French state monopoly capitalism and Thorez's theory of the progressive impoverishment of the French working class, in the face of all the evidence to the contrary.

With the death of Stalin in 1953 and the revelations and criticisms of the excesses of his regime, first expressed within Communist circles with Khrushchev's secret report to the Twentieth Congress of the Soviet Communist Party in 1956, it appeared that the lid might be lifted and greater intellectual freedom allowed. The Italian response to the revelations, which was to lead toward a more pluralist approach and ultimately to the development of Eurocommunism in the 1970s, found favour with a significant strand of French Communist intellectuals. The French party, however, was reluctant to follow the Italian example and was slow to tackle the issue of de-Stalinization of the party machine. The Soviet suppression of the Hungarian uprising, also in 1956, led to many intellectuals leaving the party. None the less, attempts were made, most notably through the works of party philosopher, Roger **Garaudy** – such as *Humanisme marxiste* (Marxist Humanism), *Perspectives de l'homme* (Perspectives for Mankind), *De l'Anathème au Dialogue* (From Anathema to Dialogue) and *Marxism and the Twentieth Century* (*Marxisme au XXe siècle*) – to appeal to a broader intellectual public and build bridges with humanists, Socialists and Catholics outside the PCF.

If Sartre had been by far the most influential figure in the 1950s, defending the integrity of the intellectual within a loosely Marxist framework, the 1960s were to see an attempted theoretical revolution from within the party, which was to have a profound effect on the newer generation of intellectuals, whose political education had been vouchsafed by the **Algerian war**. Louis Althusser, from his intellectual base at the École Normale Supérieure, put the case for the development and modernization of Marxist theory, through a rereading of the classical texts in the light of contemporary theories: the epistemology of Bachelard, Canguilhem, Cavaillès, the **structuralism** of **Lévi-Strauss** and the **psychoanalysis** of Jacques **Lacan**.

At the same time, he developed new concepts – theoretical practice, the autonomy of theory – which gave a privileged role to theoretical work, and stressed the status of Marxist theory as a science, with its own objective validity, beyond all political considerations. All of this was set against the split in the international Communist movement, following Soviet attempts to disavow the legacy of Stalin, and the inspirational force of the new path followed by the Chinese Maoists.

The events of **May 1968**, when the explosion of the student movement sparked off a country-wide workers' revolt, represented both the high point and the beginning of the end of this type of Maoist-inspired Marxist militancy. Althusserian theory had little (if any) role to play in the actual political events. The Paris Maoists mostly moved on to a factory-based militant politics and the Union of the Left, bringing Socialists and Communists together in 1971, brought the more pedestrian concerns of ballot-box politics to the top of the agenda. Already by the end of the 1970s, even before the collapse of Soviet and eastern European Communist regimes in 1989, Marxism had long ceased to be the indispensable reference for French intellectuals which it had once been. This was in spite of the fact that, during this decade, Marxism had in fact penetrated the academic barrier which had been set against it in previous decades and permeated many of the university bastions which had denied it entry. The decline of the PCF; the failure of the Union of the Left, which split in 1977; the subsequent election of François **Mitterrand** as president of the Republic from 1981 to 1995; and the political domination of the Socialists during this period – all this contributed to the marginalization and demise of Marxist influence, together with the failure of more radical political action to transform in a fundamental manner the French social and political system. Many of the most important intellectual figures of the 1980s and 1990s, such as **Foucault**, acknowledge, but fleetingly – if at all – any debt to Marxist theory.

The key difficulty for French Marxism throughout the postwar period has been the harmonization of theory and practice. Marxism developed as a theorization of the economic exploitation and political oppression of the working class in a bourgeois society dominated by capitalist class relations. It was further developed by Lenin and others into a theory of the strategy and tactics of the international proletarian revolution. On both counts, French Marxists have found it difficult to reconcile the theory with the reality of postwar French politics, in which a belief in the possibility of the proletarian revolution has receded, along with the increased prosperity of an ever smaller working class, albeit increasingly at the expense of an expanding, marginalized subclass of the unemployed and underemployed. On the whole, they have not

looked beyond the borders of France, to take on board the globalization of capitalism and set the specific difficulties of French working-class politics within a wider international framework. As a result, they have been unable to resolve the difficult problem of the divorce between theory and practice.

Margaret Majumdar

See also: class; *Humanité, L'*; parties and movements; *Temps modernes, Les*

Further reading

Anderson, P. (1976) *Considerations on Western Marxism*, London: New Left Books (examines French Marxist thought within the context of the development of Western Marxism).

Caute, D. (1964) *Communism and the French Intellectuals (1914–1960)*, London: André Deutsch (a useful overview for the earlier period).

Furet, F. (1995) *Le Passé d'une illusion: essai sur l'idée communiste au XXe siècle*, Paris: Robert Laffont/Calmann-Lévy (an up-to-date polemic).

Kelly, M. (1982) *Modern French Marxism*, Oxford: Blackwell (an analysis of the most important strands of recent French Marxist thought).

Lagueux, M. (1982) *Le Marxisme des années soixante: une saison dans l'histoire de la pensée critique*, Montreal: Hurtubise (a focused study on 1960s Marxism).

Poster, M. (1975) *Existential Marxism in Post-War France: From Sartre to Althusser*, Princeton: Princeton University Press (an overview of the intellectual history of the period).

Reader, K. (1987) *Intellectuals and the Left in France Since 1968*, Basingstoke and London: Macmillan (a study of the impact of the events of 1968 on the consciousness of Left intellectuals in France).

Maspero, François

b. 1932

Publisher

The doyen of left-wing **publishing** in France, who made available the work of figures as divergent as Mao Ze Dong and Régis **Debray** in affordable editions. He left the Communist Party in 1956 and thereafter was associated with the 'new Lefts' that flourished in and after **May 1968**. His bookshop La Joie de Lire, just off the Boulevard St-Michel, was long renowned as the intellectual epicentre of the revolutionary movements of the time, stocking material often difficult or impossible to obtain elsewhere. His 1989 text *Roissy Express* (*Les Passagers du Roissy Express*) is an itinerary through the working-class **suburbs** (*banlieues*) that were to prove so inflammable in the following decade.

KEITH READER

Mathieu, Georges

b. 1921, Boulogne-sur-mer

Artist

There were two principal intellectual referents for Mathieu's work – the Surrealist concept of 'automatic writing', and Merleau-Ponty's *Phenomenology of Perception* (*Phénoménologie de la perception*) of 1945. Merleau-Ponty's identification of self with body (' . . . *je suis mon corps*') was paramount in defining Mathieu's technique. Working rapidly, on a large scale, Mathieu added suggestive signs or ideograms to his paintings, earning himself the title of '*calligraphe occidental*' (Western calligrapher) from **Malraux**. In 1957, Mathieu made a painting (15 m long) in just one hour prior to an opening, working in the window of a Tokyo gallery before an ecstatic audience. This 'direct universality' of the sign identified with the body was

the particular achievement of an artist whose paintings are also of extreme elegance and restraint compared with their more 'heroic' American counterparts.

SIMEON HUNTER

See also: *art informel*; painting

Matisse, Henri

b. 1869, Le Cateau, Picardy;
d. 1954, Nice

Artist

Matisse, whose reputation as leader of the Fauves soon after the turn of the century secured his enduring membership of the artistic avant-garde, continued to produce important and influential work in the years following World War II. The increasing critical recognition of abstraction as an alternative to the figurative tradition in **painting** would seem to have played a part in the radical simplification of form that characterized Matisse's postwar work, although this development can be seen to have had a more immediate cause.

Ill-health and the after-effects of surgery meant that, from 1941 to 1944, Matisse was often bed-ridden, with the result that the artwork he continued to produce during this period was necessarily small in scale. Numerous drawings produced between 1941 and 1942 were followed by the design and illustration of a number of literary works, whose authors included Montherlant, Pierre **Reverdy** and Baudelaire (*Les Fleurs du mal*). In 1943, Matisse agreed to design and illustrate a book entitled *Jazz* for the Greek publisher Tériade. Physically unable to paint at this stage, he made collages using cut-outs from sheets of paper pre-painted in gouache with motifs drawn from dream, folk art and circus life. These were reproduced via stencils for the book.

Matisse continued to use his *papiers découpés* in his designs for the screen-printed hangings *Oceania, the Sea* and *Oceania, the Sky*, and for the tapestry commissions, *Polynesia, the Sea* and *Polynesia, the Sky* (1946), using the marine imagery of *Jazz* on a much larger scale. His designs for the windows and vestments for the Chapelle du Rosaire at Vence, on which he worked from 1948 to 1951, were also realized through the same process. *Papier découpé* was used as a pictorial medium in its own right from 1950, when Matisse reworked the theme of the Moroccan odalisque. He found that, by cutting directly into the painted surface, he was able to resolve the conflict between line and colour which he had experienced in the execution of his paintings, while the formal simplicity of the imagery imposed by this technique enabled him to resolve what he perceived as the 'fashionable' division between realism and the non-representational. The sharp edges produced by the scissors when cutting out the motif clearly defined not only the figure but also the ground as a positive element, once the motif was collaged on to the support. *La Piscine* (1952), in which this traditional pictorial distinction between figure and ground was so obviously lost, became one of the most 'abstract' of Matisse's works and illustrated his assertion that, for him, expression resided above all in the entire arrangement of the picture – the place occupied by the figures as well as the empty space surrounding them. The same could be said of Matisse's *papiers découpés* of 1952/3, *L'Escargot*, in the Tate Gallery, and *Souvenir de l'Océanie*, where any vestige of recognizable figuration has all but given way to an expression of the rhythms sensed in nature through the simultaneous interplay of colour and form. His 1952 series of *Blue nudes*, which seem to have been carved from blocks of pure colour, recall his **sculptures** of the female form made over forty years earlier.

After his health had recovered enough to allow him to resume oil painting, Matisse produced his last series of *Interiors*. In *Le Silence habité des maisons* of 1947 and his *Grand intérieur rouge* of 1948, in which the figures depicted lack solidity and the formal values of colour and form dominate, he seems to be approaching the abstraction of his *papiers découpés*. These gouache cut-outs, far from being the decorative doodlings of an old man, as has often been suggested, are arguably the culmination of an artistic journey, his way of resolving the conflict between colour and form, abstraction and figuration, which had occupied him throughout his long career.

CAROL WILCOX

See also: painting

Further reading:

Gowing, L. (1979) *Matisse*, London and New York: Thames and Hudson (covers the whole of Matisse's career, stressing the significance of the cut-outs in the last phase).

Néret, G. (1994) *Henri Matisse, Cut-Outs*, Cologne: Benedikt Taschen (brief commentary and good reproductions of Matisse's last works).

Mauclair, Jacques

b. 1919, Paris

Director, writer and playwright

The founder of the Théâtre du Marais in 1971. His vast repertoire of acting and direction has included **Ionesco** works, including *Victims of Duty* (*Victimes du devoir*), and plays by Pirandello, de Filippo and **Adamov**.

ANNIE SPARKS

See also: theatre

Mauriac, Claude

b. 1914, Paris;
d. 1996, Paris

Writer and memorialist

The son of the novelist François Mauriac, at the **Liberation** Claude Mauriac became General de **Gaulle**'s private secretary (1944–9) and editor of the Gaullist intellectual monthly, *Liberté de l'esprit* (1949–53), before gaining a reputation as a novelist. In the 1950s he became associated with those writers experimenting with the ***nouveau roman***, but his major achievement is the cycle of memoirs known as *Le Temps immobile* (Time Immobile), in which the relationship between memory and chronology is explored.

MARTYN CORNICK

Major works

Mauriac, C. (1958) *La littérature contemporaine*, Paris: Albin Michel.
——(1974–88) *Le Temps immobile*, 10 vols, Paris: Grasset.

Mauroy, Pierre

b. 1926, Cartignies

Politician

Rooted in the northern tradition of working-class, municipal Socialism and mayor of Lille from 1973, Mauroy was chosen by **Mitterrand** in 1981 to be his first prime minister and was one of the main architects of the 'Socialist experiment' of the early 1980s. Despite also having been behind the U-turn towards a policy of economic 'rigour', his image is inextricably associated with the supposed errors of the 1981–4 period and with old-style Socialism. As first secretary of the Parti Socialiste between 1988 and 1992, he argued for a form of social democracy which would entertain a 'critical relationship' with capitalism.

LAURENCE BELL

See also: parties and movements

Further reading

Pfister, T. (1985) *A Matignon au temps de l'Union de la Gauche*, Paris: Hachette (an account of Mauroy's premiership by one of his aides).

May 1968

Viewed with hindsight, the events of May and June 1968 mark a turning point in the history of the Fifth Republic, so much so that during the next decade France would undergo a process of irreversible change that constitutes a watershed in modern French history. As opinion polls consistently show, May 1968 is the event most frequently recalled by the French since 1945. Part of the fascination resides in the paradoxical nature of the events themselves: on the one hand, no one could have foreseen the sheer scale of the crisis, despite the signs of discontent which had existed for some time; on the other hand, the events may be said to constitute a 'failed' or a 'non-revolution' which ended up transforming France and particularly the French people in a quite fundamental way. Although interpretations of May are varied, often determined as much by political orientation as by the degree of hindsight characterizing them, one thing is certain: after May 1968 France would not be the same again.

It is important to note the international context in which the events occurred. As David Caute (1988) records, the social and political crises of 1968 were not limited solely to France. French unrest was part of a much wider groundswell of protest across the globe. Indeed, the student movement developed in the United States, where, from the early 1960s onwards, the SDS (Students for a Democratic Society) protested about enduring inequalities there. The event which did most to catalyse the wider spread of student protest was, however, American involvement in the Vietnam war. During April 1967, student draftees in the United States signalled their opposition to the war by burning their draft cards, and almost half a million people took part in anti-war demonstrations and marches. The civil rights movement also added momentum to the protests. Across Europe during 1967 and into 1968, in major cities in Britain, West Germany, Poland, Spain and Czechoslovakia, as well as in France, students protested against what they considered to be state oppression and authority, whether originating at home or inflicted abroad. Already during 1967, French students had begun to protest about general conditions in higher education, especially about the regime prevailing in university residences; although these protests may have appeared trivial, they were symptoms of a profound malaise in French higher education.

In analysing the unrest in France it is commonplace to divide the events into three successive phases: the university or student crisis, 2–12 May; the social crisis, 13–27 May; and finally the political crisis, from 27 May to 23 June. Because of demographic factors (principally the 'baby-boom' generation of the immediate postwar years having attained university age), pressure on the university sector in France had reached a critical point. In just five years, student numbers had doubled from 250,000 in 1963 to over 500,000 in 1968. Dissatisfaction regarding both the curriculum and the distant and authoritarian delivery of teaching, combined with anxieties about disciplines taught and the inadequate preparation of university courses for the world of work, all led to explosive pressures on the system. Symbolic of the half-hearted measures taken to deal with the crisis was the opening in 1963 of Nanterre University, situated to the west of Paris. Designed to relieve ever-growing student numbers at the Sorbonne in central Paris, Nanterre was an impersonal, outwardly soulless concrete and glass development situated in a *bidonville* (a sort of urban wasteland). The student protest movement focused on Nanterre, where the central administrative building was occupied on 22 March 1968. A movement named after this date was created, led by Daniel **Cohn-Bendit**, a sociology student who had followed the protests in Germany. Sharing ideals with two of the most active unions in higher educa-

tion (the students' Union National des Étudiants de France, or UNEF, and the lecturers' Syndicat National de l'Enseignement Supérieur, or SNE-Sup), the movement of 22 March brought together small groups of revolutionary student militants (mainly Trotskyists, Maoists, Revolutionary Communists and anarchists). Among their aims were the rejection of the values of consumer society, opposition to the Vietnam war, and the creation of a new, libertarian society in which power would be decentralized, and in which conventional moral, religious and social constraints would be challenged, if not severed. Protests against the university represented a starting point for these objectives and, although their aims and politics were certainly not universally shared, these militant groups nevertheless struck a chord with the larger student body. At a more general level, the protests reflected young people's increasing dissatisfaction with the values and culture of the society in which they had been brought up: to this extent, May 1968 was a clash of generations, in which youth protested against both parental authority and the monolithic character of Gaullist France.

By 2 May 1968, student disruption of classes had reached such a level that the authorities decided to close Nanterre University. This served only to move the protests from the periphery to the centre of Paris, resulting in students and their leaders occupying the Sorbonne on Friday 3 May. At the request of the university's director, the police moved in, making 500 arrests. However, the unrest spilled over into the Latin Quarter, with students erecting barricades, and the police resorting to the use of tear gas and increasingly violent retaliation, the effect of which was to escalate the protests, causing major disruption in the area and adding weight to the students' cause. In its turn, the Sorbonne was closed on 6 May, and classes suspended. Now the whole student body was free to join in the protests, which began spreading to the provinces. By the end of the week, during the night of 10–11 May the unrest reached a crescendo, with police charging the barricades and demonstrators burning cars and smashing shop windows. At last the prime minister, Georges **Pompidou**, having just returned from a ten-day official visit to Iran and Afghanistan, addressed the situation by appearing to make some relatively minor concessions to student demands. However, the unrest had gathered such momentum that on Monday 13 May (coincidentally the tenth anniversary of the Algiers insurrection which had signalled the beginning of de **Gaulle**'s return to power in 1958), a wave of strikes and demonstrations unfurled, with trade **union** representatives marching with students for the first time. In over 150 provincial towns throughout France, the unrest spread. Thus began the second, social, phase of the crisis.

It was partly the violence of the police repression which caused trade union leaders to join the students, a gesture of solidarity which brought the crisis into the world of work. A huge demonstration of 200,000 people marched to the place Denfert-Rochereau in Paris. Increasingly, strikes took hold across provincial France: on 14 May, the Sud-Aviation factory in Nantes stopped work; on 15–16 May, large car factories in the Paris region were occupied by workers; coal and steel production in the Lorraine was disrupted. As the week went on, more and more workers downed tools or occupied their workplace, with schoolteachers, public service employees, banking and **transport** staff and broadcasters among them. Estimates vary as to the numbers involved; by 18 May there were between 3 million and 6 million strikers, and by 22 May the figure had risen nearer to 10 million. It is not an exaggeration to say that, in the third week of May 1968, France was facing almost total paralysis. What distinguished the strikes from those which had occurred during former periods of social strife in France (e.g. in 1936 or 1947) was that they did not merely encompass employees in the traditional working classes (the car industry, coal and steel) – white-collar workers in both public and private sectors were also extensively involved. Apart from demands for higher wages, much of the social unrest was aimed at improving working conditions, and was especially concerned to modify the rigid hierarchical structures that typified Gaullist

France (what the sociologist Michel Crozier characterized as the 'stalemate society'). Most importantly, employees demanded more consultation with their bosses and a greater degree of devolved responsibility. Of course, such changes have to evolve over the longer term, but during the upheavals of May 1968 demands for greater autonomy (*autogestion*) were made for the first time. Measures would be introduced to achieve greater worker participation during the 1970s and the early years of the **Mitterrand** presidency.

At length Prime Minister Pompidou responded to union demands by convening consultative meetings at the employment ministry in the rue de Grenelle in Paris (25–27 May). As a result of these so-called 'Grenelle negotiations', undertaken by representatives of the employers' organization (the CNPF, or Conseil National du Patronat Français) and the trade unions, Pompidou proposed an increase of 35 per cent in the **minimum wage** (known as the SMIC), a 10 per cent salary increase (to be delivered in two stages), and increased trade-union rights in companies. By the time the Renault workers rejected these proposals on 27 May, after they had been communicated by the leader of the Communist CGT union (Confédération Générale du Travail), the crisis had passed into its final, political, phase.

Coming after General de Gaulle's ineffectual public intervention in the crisis on 24 May (a rather stilted televised broadcast proposing a referendum), and coinciding with the rejection of the Grenelle negotiations, if there was any 'revolutionary' potential in the unrest, then it was at this point that it became most manifest to the Left. At a meeting held at the Charléty sports stadium on 27 May, the possibilities of a united left-wing front were discussed, and it even seemed that Pierre **Mendès France** (a veteran left-wing politician and fervent opponent of de Gaulle), who was present at the rally, might be a candidate to lead the movement. Mendès France, however, remained silent. The next day, François Mitterrand, then leader of the FGDS (the Centre-Left Fédération de la Gauche Démocrate et Socialiste), held a press conference at which he announced his intention to stand as presidential candidate, and put forward the idea of a provisional government headed by Mendès France to fill what many believed had become a vacancy of political power. Mendès France stated that he would be willing to lead the united Left should de Gaulle stand down. The impression that there was indeed a political vacuum was reinforced by de Gaulle's sudden and unexplained absence from Paris. Rumours abounded: where was the saviour of France? It turned out that in the morning of 29 May the president had gone to Baden-Baden in West Germany to consult with General Massu, the army commander there. The reasons behind this visit remain clouded by controversy, but in the immediate aftermath of his return to Paris de Gaulle turned potential disaster into triumph.

On 30 May, after a cabinet meeting, at 4.30 p.m. de Gaulle made a radio broadcast. Using forthright language, raising the spectre of 'totalitarian communism', and declaring that if need be he would take exceptional measures to restore order, de Gaulle postponed the referendum, dissolved the National Assembly and announced a general election for the end of June. The appropriateness of this action seemed to be confirmed when a huge procession, apparently spontaneous, but in fact carefully orchestrated by de Gaulle's entourage, took place the same evening: around 400,000 people marched down the Champs-Élysées in support of the general. Pompidou reshuffled his cabinet, and passed decrees to begin implementing the proposed increase in the minimum wage. Over the next few days and weeks before the elections, work gradually resumed in the factories and, to forestall any further student unrest, on 12 June the government banned all demonstrations and dissolved eleven revolutionary student groups. The elections took place on 23 and 30 June. Any lingering doubts there may have been about the general's actions were dispelled when the Gaullist party, the UDR (the Union pour la Défense de la République), gained a spectacular electoral victory. In the first round, the party gained 46 per cent of the poll, an outright majority over the other main contenders. After the second round

(a week later), the Gaullists were returned with no fewer than 294 seats out of a total of 485, with the other major parties (the Communists and the FGDS) losing at least half the seats they had held before the election. The Gaullist party (renamed the Union des Démocrates pour la République) won an unprecedented victory: for the first time in a century, a single party was able to form the government without the support of any other political formation. The silent majority, so it seemed, had taken revenge on those militating for revolution. However, the events of May and June inflicted a severe shock on French society: the demands which had been made by students and workers could not be ignored, and the reform process began.

In the immediate term, the new government addressed the crisis in the university sector through legislative reforms. In November 1968, the *loi Edgar Faure* set out to overhaul the sector by introducing greater autonomy into **universities**, which were reorganized into more modern teaching and research units incorporating disciplines the student body demanded. Students were given a greater say in management, and a number of new universities were opened to cope with rising demand for places. As for the world of work, employees gained salary increases, better mobility and extended rights in the workplace. The strikes had protested against the hierarchical rigidity of the world of work in France. In the years which followed, the bosses' organization (the CNPF) gradually responded by introducing increased responsibilities for workers; *participation* and *autogestion* became keywords during the 1970s as French industry modernized and adopted fairer working practices. In the political domain, notwithstanding the Gaullist party's triumph over the divided Left, May 1968 marked the beginning of the end of de Gaulle's own long political career. Maurice Couve de Murville was appointed to replace Pompidou as prime minister on 10 July 1968. However, opinion polls showed that it was de Gaulle's own standing and credibility which had suffered, not Pompidou's, and less than a year later, on 27 April 1969 the general was voted out of office in a referendum (53 per cent of the voters saying 'no'). Thus ended the Gaullist Republic: on 15 June 1969, Georges Pompidou was elected president as de Gaulle's successor.

From today's perspective, May 1968 is most usefully studied through a range of interpretations (e.g. Reader and Wadia 1993 and *Pouvoirs* 39). As far as their political consequences are concerned, the events did not constitute a revolution because the regime was neither overturned nor replaced – if anything, in the immediate term, it was reinforced. Yet, if May 1968 did have a revolutionary dimension, it was long-term, and much more traceable in the areas of attitudes, values and culture. **Youth culture** in particular, as it is variously manifested in music, drugs and **fashion,** has tended to follow a pattern set in the late 1960s. The longer-term consequences of May 1968 in France may be traced in the development during the 1970s and 1980s of working practices, left-wing politics, feminism, ecology, decentralization and movements for regional autonomy or separatism. In the words of Laurent Joffrin (1988), 'May 68 changed France. This failed revolution ended up revolutionizing society, and the French do not always realize it.'

MARTYN CORNICK

See also: alcohol, cigarettes, drugs; armed forces; banks; demographic developments; feminism (movements/groups); green issues; parties and movements; regionalism; revolutionary groups

Further reading

Aron, R. (1968) *The Elusive Revolution: Anatomy of a Student Revolt*, trans. G. Clough, London: Pall Mall Press (the classic right-wing liberal interpretation, originally published in French as *La Révolution introuvable* by Fayard).

Bénéton, P. and Touchard, J. (1970) 'Les Interprétations de la crise de mai–juin 1968', *Revue française de science politique*, 20, 3 (a pioneering article offering eight different but interlocking interpretations of the events; a good starting point – also available in translation in Reader and Wadia 1993; see below).

Capdevielle, J. and Mouriaux, R. (1988) *Mai 68, l'entre-deux de la modernité* Paris: Presses de la FNSP (a sophisticated longer-term interpretation by French political scientists).

Caute, D. (1988) *Sixty-Eight: The Year of the Barricades*, London: Hamish Hamilton (one of the best and most readable studies examining the events in a global context).

Combes, P. (1984) *La Littérature et le mouvement de mai 68*, Paris: Seghers (an interesting study of the literary fallout from 1968).

Crozier, M. (1970/5) *La Société bloquée*, Paris: Éditions du Seuil (a key sociological analysis).

Delale, A. and Ragache, G. (1978) *La France de '68*, Paris: Seuil (a well-illustrated survey of the events produced for the tenth anniversary).

Dreyfus-Armand, G. and Gervereau, L. (eds) (1988) *Mai 68: les mouvements étudiants en France et dans le monde*, Nanterre: BDIC (catalogue of an exhibition containing a mine of information and illustrations).

Hoffmann, S. (1974) 'May 1968: Drama or Psychodrama', in *Decline or Renewal? France Since the 1930s*, New York: Viking (one of the best starting points for interpreting the events).

Joffrin, L. (1988) *Mai 68: histoire des événements*, Paris: Points-Éditions du Seuil (one of the most accessible studies in French following the events through their student, social and political phases; contains an excellent bibliography).

Morin, E., Lefort, C. and Castoriadis, C. (1988) *Mai 1968: la brèche*, Brussels: Complexe (new edition of a collection of challenging essays by philosophers including Morin, Lefort and Castoriadis).

Pouvoirs (1986) *Mai 68*, special issue 39 (an excellent collection of texts by participants and academics based on a conference held in Lyon; short, useful, interpretive essays).

Reader, K. A., with Wadia, K. (1993) *The May 1968 Events in France*, Basingstoke: Macmillan (a wide-ranging survey over the major interpretations, including a valuable essay on women and 1968).

Schnapp, A. and Vidal-Naquet, P. (1969) *Journal de la commune étudiante*, Paris: Éditions du Seuil (a large and indispensable collection of documents from the period, illustrating the student angle; excellent introductory essay).

Touraine, A. (1971) *The May Movement: Revolt and Reform* [*Le Mouvement de mai, ou le communisme utopique*], New York: Random House (the influential interpretation of a sociologist).

Weber, H. (1988), *Vingt ans après: que reste-t-il de '68?*, Paris: Éditions du Seuil (the view twenty years on by a participant).

Winock, M. (1995) *La Fièvre hexagonale*, Paris: Points-Éditions du Seuil (Chapter 8 looks at the events in the broader context of over a century of political crises in France; accessible and suggestive).

MC Solaar

b. 1969, Dakar

Singer

France's leading **rap** artist of the 1990s, who invites contemplation rather than conflict. MC Solaar acknowledges the influences of hip-hop, acid **jazz** and West Coast sounds, but what he has given us in his first two CDs – *Qui sème le vent récolte le tempo* (Who Sows the Wind Reaps the Beat) and *Prose Combat*, from 1992 and 1994 respectively – has a very French flavour. In MC Solaar's own words, 'no slang, good subjects and sometimes just poetry'. He has had the merit of taking rap to a wider audience than its roots in disenfranchized *banlieues* (**suburbs**).

GÉRARD POULET

See also: song/*chanson*

Médecins Sans Frontières (MSF)

A private international organization established in 1971 by a group of French doctors who had previously worked for the Red Cross, and were determined to create a non-governmental agency for emergency medical relief. MSF assists victims of natural or man-made disasters, irrespective of race, religion or political affiliation, observing strict impartiality. Funding comes primarily from private donations, also the European Community and UNHCR. In 1979, a rift within MSF led to the creation of new associations, Aide Médicale Internationale in 1979, and Médecins du Monde by Bernard Kouchner in 1980. MSF is also active within France in the fight to secure health care for immigrants, and to assist drug addicts.

PAM MOORES

Melville, Jean-Pierre

b. 1917, Paris;
d. 1973, Paris

Director,
real name Jean-Pierre Grumbach

A film-maker largely credited as being *the* thriller maker of the mid-1950s and 1960s, Melville often used Alain **Delon**, the fetish star of the 1960s (e.g. *Le Samourai* in 1967). He is also heralded as a precursor to the **Nouvelle Vague**, because of both his unorthodox production practices (very much an independent) and his film style (low budgets, grainy realism). His films often treat the question of individual choice in the face of almost impossible odds sometimes due to national conflicts (e.g. *Le Silence de la mer* in 1949).

SUSAN HAYWARD

See also: cinema; stars

Mendès France, Pierre

b. 1907, Paris;
d. 1982, Paris

Politician

Despite, or perhaps because of, a relatively short ministerial career, Pierre Mendès France acquired a durable reputation as the conscience of the French Left. He entered politics as a Radical Socialist in the 1930s and quickly demonstrated the economic competence for which he became famous. His Jewish origins, and outspoken Republicanism, made him a natural target for the anti-semitic, anti-democratic **Vichy** regime which imprisoned him. He escaped to London and emerged in 1945 as a clear-headed modernizing political leader. It was these qualities, rather than any powerful party backing, that led to his appointment as prime minister in 1954 after the French military disaster at **Dien Biên Phu**. Mendès France rapidly extricated France from an impossible military situation in Indochina and began the process of disengagement from Morocco and Tunisia. His modernizing zeal led him to attack out-of-date economic attitudes and privileges. He was, by contrast, lukewarm about the cause of European integration and this contributed to his loss of office in February 1955. He opposed de **Gaulle**'s 1958 return to power on the grounds of democratic principle and never accepted the legitimacy of the Fifth Republic. A prestigious, but ultimately powerless, figure, he lived to see François **Mitterrand** gain the political benefits of his oppositionism.

PETER MORRIS

See also: decolonization; May 1968; parties and movements; racism/anti-semitism

Messiaen, Olivier

b. 1908, Avignon;
d. 1992, Paris

Composer and organist

Messiaen has described himself as a *rythmicien et ornithologue* (rhythm-artist and ornithologist); of course, he is much more than that. His career spans practically the entire twentieth century and marks the continuing importance of French music since Debussy. Yet Messiaen stands more outside than inside the Western tradition. His major interest does not lie in counterpoint or even tonality: both of these fundamental characteristics of Western music involve variation, development and drama, i.e. motion within a time frame. Messiaen's music, on the other hand, strives towards a structure that makes time, or rather timelessness, a subject for contemplation and expression. In this sense, Messiaen should be regarded as the most 'Catholic' (in the sense also of the original meaning, 'universal') composer of our time. His strongest antecedents in the West are plainchant and the Greek modes (arrangements of the musical scale); to a lesser extent, Berlioz; and his more immediate models, Debussy, Stravinsky and Bartók. In addition to these formative influences, there is a strong indebtedness to Hindu rhythms and scales, and pervasive in all his music after 1950 is the presence of birdsong. In order to achieve the kind of circularity and stasis to which his music aspired, Messiaen invented a set of 'modes of limited transpositions', which have been very influential on his best students at the Conservatoire, **Boulez**, Stockhausen, **Xenakis** and Barraqué. Moreover, Messiaen's music is richly textured and coloured harmonically; he believed that chords are 'coloured'. All of these creations are inspired by a devout Catholicism reflected in the titles of his works and their individual movements. These works also strive to reflect the ecstasy of the contemplation of the Incarnation or Resurrection. The piety and occasional 'whiff of incense' have alienated a number of listeners, but his music is steadily gaining admirers, for his sensuousness as well as for his astonishing mastery.

Educated at the Paris Conservatoire (his principal teacher being Paul Dukas), in 1931 he was appointed organist at La Trinité in Paris and he held the post for most of his life. His organ works, notably *Le Livre d'orgue* and *Méditations sur le mystère de la Sainte Trinité*, mark him as one of the most prolific organ composers since Bach. But his most striking successes have been in the orchestra hall: *Turangalîla-Symphonie* in twelve movements, *Oiseaux exotiques, Chronochromie, Et exspecto resurrectionem mortuorum, Des Canyons aux étoiles, Éclairs sur l'au-delà*. There are practically no chamber works, except the remarkable *Quatuor pour la fin du temps* written and performed in a German prisoner-of-war camp in 1941. There is also an important body of piano music, notably the highly influential *Quatre études de rythme*; and several song cycles. In many respects, the crowning achievement of his long career is the long opera *Saint François d'Assise* ('Scènes franciscaines'), performed in 1983 by the Paris Opéra, which crystallizes Messiaen's musical individuality: his concern with 'the presence of the eternal within the temporal, the unmeasurable within the measured, the mysterious within the known' (Griffiths 1985).

WALTER A. STRAUSS

See also: concert music

Further reading

Griffiths, P. (1985) *Olivier Messiaen and the Music of Time*, London: Faber and Faber (the most recent and comprehensive study of Messiaen in English).

Metz, Christian

b. 1931, Béziers;
d. 1993, Paris

Philosopher

An influential film theorist who during the structuralist period of the 1960s attempted to establish a grammar of film – see his *Film Language: A Semiotics of the Cinema* (*Essais sur la signification au cinéma*) of 1968–72. His grammar of film was strongly influenced by Saussure's concept of a linguistic system that functioned as a general science of signs (semiology). His endeavour to uncover the rules governing film language marked an important step forward in film theory, by providing a framework within which to discuss the relationship between film image and representation. Sensing the limitations of this total theory approach, Metz then went on to explore the relevance of **psychoanalysis** to film theory, particularly in relation to spectator positioning, as in *The Imaginary Signifier: Psychoanalysis and the Cinema* (*Le Signifiant imaginaire: psychanalyse et cinéma*) of 1977.

SUSAN HAYWARD

See also: cinema; structuralism

Michaux, Henri

b. 1899, Namur, Belgium;
d. 1984, Paris

Poet

Despite being close in spirit and manner to the Surrealists, Michaux was never part of the movement. His poems, most of them prose poems, are marked by an intense anguish, a fear of existence – but one that usually takes clownish, fantastic and exotic forms. His originality lies in his ability to turn poetry into a form of exorcism by the manipulation of obsessive sounds, word coinages – often displays of linguistic violence, incantatory rhythms: he is constantly attempting to propel himself (and the reader) into an *ailleurs*. This aspiration also accounts for his experimentation with drugs (*Misérable Miracle*, from 1956, is a typical as well as an eloquent comment on these experiences, and there are other accounts of similar drug experiments). Some of the most important titles of his later poetry are: *Épreuves, exorcismes* (Trials, Exorcisms) from 1945; *La Vie dans les plis* (Life in the Folds) in 1949 and *L'Espace du dedans* (The Space Within) of 1966 – all of them bearing revealing titles.

WALTER A. STRAUSS

See also: poetry

Michel, Georges

b. 1926, Paris

Playwright

Michel is known for plays written in the late 1960s about the individual and society, of which *L'Agression* (Aggression) and *La Promenade du dimanche* (Sunday Stroll) were directed at the Théâtre National de Paris. Disappearing during the 1970s, he returned to the theatre in 1986 with *Rhapsodie-Béton* at the Théâtre de la Huchette.

ANNIE SPARKS

See also: collective creation; theatre

Miéville, Anne-Marie

b. 1945, Lausanne, Switzerland

Director

After an unsuccessful singing career in Paris during the 1960s, and after working on two short films with the Swiss film-maker, Francis Reusser, Miéville made personal and professional contact in the early 1970s with Jean-Luc **Godard**. She worked as a set photographer on his *Tout va bien*, co-directed *Ici et ailleurs*, and has collaborated with Godard ever since, most notably on films such as *Numéro deux* and *Sauve qui peut (la vie)*, Godard's television work of the late 1970s, the video piece *Soft and Hard,* and, most recently, *2 x 50 années de cinéma*, a celebration of French **cinema**. Miéville's own films (which she also edits) are mainly intimate and sensitive depictions of domestic crisis. The short *Le Livre de Marie* (1983) traces the effects of divorce on a young girl, while *Lou n'a pas dit non* (1993) studies a couple on the point of breaking up. Other films include *Papa comme maman, L'Amour des femmes, How Can I Live?, Faire la fête, Mon cher sujet* and *Mars et Vénus*.

JAMES WILLIAMS

See also: feminism (movements/groups)

Further reading

Locke, M. and Warren, C. (eds) (1993) *Jean-Luc Godard's 'Hail Mary': Women and the Sacred in Film*, Carbondale and Edwardsville: Southern Illinois University Press (includes readings of *Le Livre de Marie* in the context of Godard's *'Je vous salue, Marie'*, as well as a filmography of Miéville).

mime

Mime, the tradition of physical, non-verbal expression in theatre, has its roots in pantomime and the tradition of characters such as the well-known Pierrot (in his white clown costume with a black tear on his cheek), but today it has become part of the established repertoire of theatrical communication. The importance of the actor, the role of physical theatre and the importance of the gesture in performance are all factors in current theatre practice which have been influenced by mime during the last century in particular. Thus, as well as yielding famous mime artists such as Étienne **Decroux**, Marcel **Marceau** and Jean-Louis **Barrault**, techniques used in mime have also influenced general ideas of theatrical performance, with the emphasis on the physical importance of the stage. Barrault's concept of 'total theatre' and his numerous productions exploring it are notable examples of this, although the tradition of mime in theatre continues to this day through the work of directors such as Jean **Vilar**, Peter **Brook** and Ariane **Mnouchkine**.

Many of the key figures in the movement of mime within the French theatre tradition share a similar background, whether directly or indirectly – that of Copeau's theatre school at the Vieux Colombier, where the famous mime artist and teacher, Decroux, and Dullin, future founder of his own celebrated school, studied. At the time, an increased interest in physical education was in the air outside the theatre world, as well as inside it, with pioneers such as Georges Demeny in France encouraging participation in **sport**. In the early decades of the twentieth century, Copeau had begun experimenting with physical theatre using mime and masks, exploring this with his troupe, which eventually moved down to Burgundy to concentrate on its work. One of the troupe, Charles Dullin, left in 1920, but went on to form his own theatre and theatre school, based largely on the same principles as Copeau's teaching, with the emphasis on *le tréteau nu* (the bare stage) and on the importance of gesture and physical expression. It was here that Decroux (now a teacher of mime), Barrault and **Artaud** were to meet, and that (after the war) Decroux would teach the now-legendary mime artist Marcel Marceau.

Decroux's work was central in pushing back the boundaries of mime with his famous silent mimes, nude on an empty stage, based on many of the principles he had learned himself with Copeau's troupe in Burgundy. His skill helped inspire his pupil Barrault, who went on to become one of the most celebrated mime artists of the century in film roles such as Baptiste in Carné's *Les Enfants du Paradis* (1945), a film in which his teacher Decroux also performed. At the same time, Jean **Dasté**, another protégé of Copeau's, had also founded a troupe, the Comédiens de Grenoble, including among others Jacques **Lecoq**, which also sought to explore the possibilities of mime and masks in performance. Lecoq himself went on to found his famous theatre school in Paris, focusing his training on movement, gesture and body language, although disagreeing in the importance of teaching pure mime as an art form in its own right.

It was Barrault and Decroux who, between them, were largely responsible for formalizing what could be described as modern mime, codifying and defining the 'language' of the body for use within a theatrical context. Marcel Marceau, Decroux's pupil at the Dullin school, was especially impressed by the work of Barrault; the latter's *mimodrames*, such as *As I Lay Dying* (*Autour d'une mère*), were a particular influence on his work. The actor's training imparted to him by Dullin was also to play its role in his development of his renowned character Bip in 1947 and his *mimodrames*. He was also certainly influenced by foreign theatre traditions from the East, as were Mnouchkine and Brook in later decades. Both of these directors focused on physical as well as verbal theatre, looking to popular performers such as the clown figure to inspire wider audiences, and experimenting with Japanese and Indian theatrical traditions, rich in their intricate tradition of gesture and mime. Today mime remains an important ingredient in theatrical expression, both in its own right (as pure mime, in the *mimodrame*) and also as part of the actor's training and tools for expression within the world of 'spoken' French theatre.

ANNIE SPARKS

See also: collective creation; theatre; Théâtre du Soleil

Further reading

Felner, M. (1985) *Apostles of Silence: The Modern French Mime*, London: Associated University Presses (essential reading).

Lecoq, J. (ed.) (1987) *Le Théâtre du geste*, Paris: Bordas (a pictorial study with first-hand accounts by practitioners of the development of mime and physical theatre).

minimum wage

In France, the wage levels of the lowest-paid workers are protected by minimum wage legislation. This minimum wage is known as the *salaire minimum interprofessionel de crois-sance* (SMIC), which replaced the *salaire mini-mum interprofessionel garanti* in 1970 when increases in the minimum wage were fixed to price and average earnings increases. From the mid-1980s onwards, liberal economists and politicians have criticized the SMIC for keeping the wage levels of those with few skills artifi-cially high, which harms employment creation. However, an attempt by the government to reduce the SMIC for young workers in 1994 was brought down by popular protest.

JAN WINDEBANK

See also: employment

Minuit

Publishing house

Les Éditions de Minuit were founded by Pierre de Lescure and Jean Bruller (Vercors) during the Occupation, first publishing Vercors's resis-tance parable, *The Silence of the Sea* (*Le Silence de la mer*) in 1942, among no fewer than twenty-five titles to appear up to August 1944. After Jérôme **Lindon** took over in 1948, Minuit achieved even greater fame for launch-ing the *nouveau romanciers* **Beckett**, **Butor**, **Duras**, Pinget, **Robbe-Grillet** and **Sarraute**. Minuit also has an extensive philosophy cata-logue, including authors such as Jacques **Derrida**, Gilles **Deleuze** and Jean-François **Lyotard**, and publishes the review *Critique*.

MARTYN CORNICK

See also: *nouveau roman*; publishing/*l'édition*

Further reading

Debû-Bridel, J. (1945) *Les Éditions de Minuit, historique et bibliographie*, Paris: Éditions de Minuit.
Simonin, A. (1994) *Les Éditions de Minuit 1942–1955: le devoir d'insoumission*, Paris: IMEC Éditions.

Minute

Newspaper

A provocative, extreme right-wing weekly, launched by Jean-François Devay in 1962. Outspokenly critical of de **Gaulle**'s policy in Algeria, *Minute* has a reputation for polemic and sensational scandal-mongering. Pet themes include a denunciation of the abolition of the death penalty, the supposedly luxurious condi-tions in French prisons and the overgenerous treatment of immigrants. Circulation peaked at 188,084 copies per week in 1978. Despite resurgence of interest following the Socialist victory in 1981, circulation has since fallen dramatically (to below 50,000 copies by 1991). Internal squabbling as to how closely the paper should align itself with the Front National, and competition from *National Hebdo*, have exac-erbated this decline.

PAM MOORES

See also: national press in France; parties and movements

Minyana, Philippe

b. 1946, Metz

Playwright

A former literature and drama teacher, who began writing in 1980. His works include *Premier Trimestre* (First Term), *Titanic*, *Exhibition* and *Drames Brefs 1* (Brief Dramas 1). The Théâtre Ouvert publishes and performs many of his plays.

ANNIE SPARKS

See also: theatre

Miou-Miou

b. 1950, Paris

Actor

Her career began in Faraldo's provocative *Themroc* (1972), which she followed in 1974 with **Blier**'s equally provocative *Les Valseuses*, alongside **Depardieu** and **Dewaere**. Blier made an updated version, *Tenue de soirée*, where she accompanied Depardieu and Michel **Blanc** in 1986. Although most of her roles have been comic, or sexually provocative (as in Deville's 1988 *La Lectrice*), her persona is often that of a sensitive and proud woman, as can be seen in **Kurys**'s *Coup de foudre* (1983) and (especially) in her role as La Maheude, Depardieu's screen wife in **Berri**'s *Germinal* (1993).

PHIL POWRIE

See also: cinema

Mistinguett

b. 1873, Enghien-les-Bains;
d. 1956, Bougival

Music-hall artist,
real name Jeanne Bourgeois

Arguably France's greatest female music-hall performer – she was known as the *Impératrice du Music-Hall* (Empress of the Music Hall) – Mistinguett (originally Miss Tinguette) had an early successful partnership with Maurice **Chevalier** and later with a number of other male performers. The star of a whole series of revues, Mistinguett appeared in North and South America and became a most successful recording artist. Despite the limitations of her singing voice, her humour and powers of mimicry helped to extend her career well beyond World War II. She will be remembered as the incarnation of *la Parisienne* in various guises.

IAN PICKUP

See also: song/*chanson*

Mitchell, Eddy

b. 1942, Paris

Lyricist, singer and television presenter, real name Claude Moine

Originally a member of Les Chaussettes Noires (1961–4), Eddy Mitchell rapidly became one of France's outstanding singers of **rock** and roll from the mid-1960s. Having sung mainly American imports, he increasingly wrote the words of his songs (music by Jean-Pierre Bourtayre and later Pierre Papadiamondis) and broadened his repertoire to embrace country music, rhythm and blues and ballads. Endowed with a good sense of humour, he has appeared in films and as a presenter of films on television.

IAN PICKUP

See also: song/*chanson*

Mitterrand, François

b. 1916, Jarnac, Charente;
d. 1996, Paris

Politician

Often perceived as an enigma, François Mitterrand was the first ever president of a French Republic to complete two terms of office (1981–95). At times reviled by his adversaries and mistrusted by his allies, his death gave rise to genuine scenes of public grief, and brought forth tributes from former adversaries and allies alike. The ambiguity of his public persona undoubtedly owes much to the longevity of his political career, the variety of roles which he came to play and his highly personalized approach to politics.

Born into a provincial, Catholic, conservative, bourgeois milieu, there is little evidence to suggest that, as a law student in Paris in the mid-1930s, Mitterrand broke with the influences of his background. While his interest in the great debates of the day was eclectic, his assessment of their proponents was often based on literary and moral considerations rather than on political ones (indeed, he himself had literary ambitions).

His wartime experience brought about a certain change of direction. Mobilized in 1939, Mitterrand was wounded and captured by the Germans in June 1940. In the hardships and camaraderie of prisoner of war camps in Germany and Poland, he later claimed to have discovered the 'natural' moral principles required to underpin legitimate social organization: equity, social and economic justice, and freedom. On his third attempt, he escaped at the end of 1941 to unoccupied France, where he worked for nearly a year as a functionary in the **Vichy** administration for the War Prisoners Commissariat and was later awarded the *Francisque* medal by the regime. As a result, he was later accused of having harboured Vichyite sympathies. He himself always argued that he used his position in Vichy as a cover for his Resistance activities, notably as the self-styled head of a network for prisoners of war and escapees.

At the **Liberation** the network of contacts and influence he had assiduously developed through his Resistance activity placed Mitterrand in a position to play a political role. Yet he was not affiliated to a party and was reluctant to accept the idea of being led by anyone but himself. He was first elected to parliament in 1946 in the Nièvre on a conservative and markedly anti-Communist platform at a time when the tripartite coalition of Communists, Socialists and Christian Democrats was still in the ascendant. His profile was clearly that of a right-of-centre *bien pensant* Catholic. Once in parliament he allied himself with the Union Démocratique et Socialiste de la Résistance (UDSR), a small, loosely structured party, created by former *résistants*. By 1953 he had become its dominant figure. The hinge role of the UDSR in coalitions gave it an importance beyond its size and enabled him to occupy no less than eleven ministerial posts under the Fourth Republic (1946–58), some of them among the most

senior. His opposition both to Communism and to de **Gaulle**'s Rassemblement du Peuple Français (RPF) placed him at the centre of gravity of Third Force politics.

One of Mitterrand's priorities at this time was the maintenance of France's colonies, particularly in Africa. When the **Algerian war** broke out in 1954 he was Minister of the Interior. Like the vast majority of French people, he did not envisage Algerian independence and only came to accept it reluctantly. His approach to the colonies was, however, reformist and this brought him into conflict with reactionary forces on the Right.

While Mitterrand had entered politics on the Centre Right, his reformism in colonial affairs, his opposition to the RPF, his move away from the institution of the Catholic church and his involvement in the 1956 Front Républicain alliance placed him, towards the end of the Fourth Republic, to the left of centre. He was a competent minister, who did not hesitate to assert his authority, and a skilful orator. His political ambiguity, obvious ambition and cavalier yet aloof manner often inspired cautiousness, if not mistrust. Nevertheless, he would probably have been called to the premiership in due course had the collapse of the Fourth Republic and de Gaulle's return to power not changed the rules of the political game completely.

The feeling that de Gaulle had robbed him of the opportunity to reach the top government position, and that there would be no room for his ambitions in de Gaulle's entourage, undoubtedly determined his decision to adopt an intransigent stance against the new regime of the Fifth Republic and all its works. Paradoxically, however, the presidential and bipartisan logic of the Fifth Republic enabled him to resurrect his political career. His strident opposition also placed him more clearly on the Left.

With the first direct election of the president of the Republic due to take place in 1965, Mitterrand realized that, for a candidate of the Left to stand a chance of success against de Gaulle, he had to be able to obtain the firm backing of the whole of the non-Communist Left and the vote of the Communist electorate, without frightening away too much of the centrist vote. Thus began the historic union of the Left.

Mitterrand drew on and expanded his clan-like network of personal followers (in whom he was able to inspire unstinting loyalty and a belief in his own destiny) to create the Convention des Institutions Républicaines (CIR) in 1964. With none of the substance of a political party, the CIR nevertheless gave the impression that he represented a considerable political force. In the run-up to the election he brought the Socialist Party, the Centre-Left Parti Radical and his own CIR together within the Fédération de la Gauche Démocratique et Socialiste (FGDS) and obtained the support of the Communist Party (PCF) while avoiding making any concessions to it. His 'honourable' defeat in the second ballot (45 per cent) provided momentum for the continuation of this strategy. There seemed to be a happy congruence between the resurrection of the Left and Mitterrand's career ambitions.

Progress in this direction was abruptly halted, however, by the events of **May 1968**. With the Gaullist state briefly appearing to totter, Mitterrand put himself forward as the leader of a provisional government with a view to organizing early presidential elections, in which he announced he would stand. This led many to accuse him of illegality and opportunism. However, de Gaulle reasserted himself and in the subsequent parliamentary elections the parties of the Left, which had responded to the events in a disunited fashion, were roundly defeated. Shortly afterwards, the FGDS broke up and Mitterrand once again found himself in the wilderness.

However, following the humiliating defeat in the 1969 presidential election of the Socialist Defferre, who had stood on a centrist ticket, the union of the Left again seemed the only viable opposition strategy. In order to advance it, the CIR joined the partly renovated Parti Socialiste (PS) in 1971 at its famous Épinay Congress where Mitterrand, by dint of entering into an incongruous pact with the right-of-centre and extreme-Left tendencies of the party, was able to snatch the leadership position.

For Mitterrand, as the joint candidate of the Left, the 1970s were marked by narrow defeat by **Giscard d'Estaing** in the 1974 presidential election, and by his unstinting effort to establish and maintain his control of the PS, which he had taken into a competitive alliance with the PCF. The strategic aim of this alliance was to assert the PS's dominance on the Left and woo a substantial swathe of the Communist electorate. For this reason the PS had to be ideologically positioned as far to the left as was feasible and Mitterrand had to learn to 'speak Socialist'. His diatribes on the corrupting influence of money may have seemed disingenuous to some, but were in fact not incompatible with the social Catholic influence of his early years.

The '110 Propositions' of his 1981 presidential election campaign were to a large extent based on the PS programme of the 1970s. His main campaign poster, however, portrayed him against a rural backdrop, complete with church spire, and bore the reassuring slogan '*La Force tranquille*'.

Once in power, Mitterrand's resolve to execute his programme as promised was made manifest in his appointment of four Communist ministers and in a series of radical measures which included nationalizations, a voluntaristic reflationary growth strategy based on public spending, the enhancement of employees' rights, major decentralization reforms and liberal measures, such as the abolition of the death penalty and the authorization of independent radio stations. However, the reforming energy of the Socialist government soon foundered on the rock of economic failure and massive opposition to plans to integrate private (Catholic) schools into the state sector.

The subsequent U-turn in government policy left the Left in a defensive posture. Hedged in and deeply unpopular, Mitterrand sought to regain the initiative by launching France's first private **television** channel and introducing proportional representation for parliamentary elections (which enabled the extreme-Right Front National to gain thirty-five seats in 1986). But such measures were not enough to prevent the PS from losing its majority in 1986. As a result, Mitterrand was obliged to appoint the neo-Gaullist Jacques **Chirac** as prime minister and embark on the first *cohabitation* of the Fifth Republic. This form of executive power sharing effectively stripped him of control of the domestic policy agenda and confined his initiatives to the field of foreign policy. However, his judicious handling of *cohabitation* obviated a constitutional crisis and earned him the gratitude of the public.

In the 1988 presidential election Mitterrand could convincingly present himself as a statesman able to unite the nation and comfortably beat the apparently volatile and divisive Chirac. In contrast to the ideological turbulence which had marked his first term, Mitterrand's 1988 campaign promised reconciliation. His priorities would be to pursue **European economic integration** and reduce social inequality.

In the 1988–93 period, the PS enjoyed a relative majority and Mitterrand was again able to appoint Socialist prime ministers. Despite this, the functioning of the executive continued to bear some relation to *cohabitation*, in that prime ministers defined the orientation of domestic policy, albeit at the cost of occasional presidential obstruction and criticism (particularly in the case of **Rocard**). There was also a distinct cooling of relations between the PS and Mitterrand, whose presidential style became increasingly regal. In 1991 he dismissed the still-popular Rocard (whom he personally disliked) and appointed France's first ever woman prime minister, Édith **Cresson**, only to have to replace her with the more reassuring **Bérégovoy** in 1992.

Mitterrand preferred, however, to devote his attention to foreign and European affairs. He showed himself to be more Atlanticist than his predecessors, staunchly defending the installation of US cruise missiles in Europe in the early 1980s. He engaged French troops under allied (American) command in the Gulf war in 1991 and co-operated with NATO in Bosnia in 1994. In African policy, his record is questionable, but he himself considered that French policy encouraged the development of democratic practices there (Adler 1995). He was one of the

architects of the 1985 Single European Act and of the Maastricht Treaty, whose ratification he put to a referendum in France in 1992.

More than any of his predecessors, Mitterrand left his mark on the cultural and architectural landscape of Paris, thanks to the Grand Louvre, the Arche de la Défense (constructed for the Bicentenary celebrations of the 1789 Revolution), the Opéra de la Bastille and the grandiose and hyper-modern Bibliothèque Nationale de France.

The PS's catastrophic defeat in the 1993 elections forced Mitterrand into a second *cohabitation*, this time with **Balladur** as premier. In this final period of his presidency, his executive initiatives were few: one can cite French humanitarian intervention in Rwanda in 1994. In the grip of terminal illness, he was dogged by fresh allegations concerning his ideological affiliations in the prewar and Vichy periods. Yet he refused to respond clearly to his detractors and allowed the existence of a 20-year-old daughter by a mistress to become public knowledge, as if he wanted to lay himself bare to the public.

This perhaps provides a key to understanding the man and his career. Possessed of a great belief in his own destiny and legitimacy, he rarely regretted his actions and tended to attribute whatever negative outcomes might be perceived in them as the failure of others to comprehend the rightness of his purpose, as if they did not see the big picture.

Despite his taste for provocation and his readiness to do combat, Mitterrand's mode of leadership was, in essence, reactive. Like de Gaulle, he was a great legitimator of the (virtually) inevitable and contributed to reconciling France with some of the imperatives of the age (decentralization, a more liberal economy, European integration), while at the same time representing aspects of a traditional France, embodied in its literature and (often provincial) culture.

LAURENCE BELL

See also: architecture under Mitterrand; Catholicism and Protestantism; decolonization;

education, the state and the church; foreign policy; nationalization and privatization; parties and movements; radio (private/free)

Further reading

Adler, L. (1995) *L'Année des adieux*, Paris: Flammarion (on his final year).
Clark, A. (1986) *Anthologie Mitterrand*, London: Methuen (a concise biography, followed by a good selection of extracts from Mitterrand's key writings).
Cole, A. (1994) *François Mitterrand: A Study in Political Leadership*, London: Routledge (covers the political context, rather than the man).
Giesbert, F.-O. (1996) *François Mitterrand: une vie*, Paris: Éditions du Seuil (a well-informed third biography of Mitterrand by a leading figure in the press; written in a journalistic style).

Mnouchkine, Ariane

b. 1934, Boulogne-sur-Seine

Director

Ariane Mnouchkine is perhaps the most influential director in France today, noted for her willingness to take risks, to experiment and to combine different theatrical traditions in order to search for a relevant, contemporary voice.

Since her student days, she has worked with the theatre company she founded in 1964 (and now directs), the now internationally renowned **Théâtre du Soleil**, which since 1970 has been based at the Cartoucherie, Vincennes. In terms of style, she is recognized for adopting a non-authoritarian stance: her view of the director's role is to co-ordinate the thoughts and ideas of her company into a coherent form, rather than forcing them to conform to her own prescribed vision. During the last three decades she has aimed to explore the role of the actor and his or her relationship to the audi-

ence, retaining a political message in her productions. A confirmed left-winger, she directs the Théâtre du Soleil along strictly democratic lines. In the 1970s, the company was particularly noted for **collective creations**, such as the renowned *1789* (filmed by Mnouchkine in 1974), for their challenging new approach to performance, and for their staging and innovative methods of relating historical fact.

After other successful collective creation projects, including *1793* and *L'Âge d'or* (The Golden Age) between 1972 and 1975, Mnouchkine turned to film for her new challenge, making *Molière, la vie d'un honnête homme* (Molière, the Life of an Honest Man) between 1976 and 1977 with a cast from the Théâtre du Soleil, using many of the principles acquired in previous stage productions. She went on to adapt Thomas Mann's *Mephisto* in 1979, before returning to text-based productions. Inspired by her knowledge of Eastern theatre, Mnouchkine and the Soleil embarked upon a series of Shakespeare plays which gained her renewed renown for her radical, fresh approach, borrowing from Indian and Japanese performance traditions. She experimented further, between 1990 and 1993, with a series of plays based on Greek tragedies called *Les Atrides*, again exploring existing theatre traditions in a search for a way of conveying a contemporary political message. Mnouchkine's recent work has also attempted to confront twentieth-century concerns, especially in her collaboration with Hélène **Cixous**. Her epic plays, sometimes as much as nine hours long, deal with issues as varied as: the legacy of colonialism in Cambodia, as in 1985's *L'Histoire terrible mais inachevée de Norodom Sihanouk roi du Cambodge* (The Terrible but Unfinished Story of Norodom Sihanouk, King of Cambodia); the partitioning of India in *L'Indiade* (1987); and French government corruption in *La Ville parjure* (Treacherous City), in 1994, into which she incorporates valuable lessons learned from the Soleil's Greek cycle. In 1995, she directed a memorable production of *Tartuffe*, giving Molière's classic contemporary relevance by setting it in the troubled Algeria of the 1990s.

ANNIE SPARKS

See also: theatre

Further reading

Kiernander, A. (1995) *Ariane Mnouchkine and the Théâtre du Soleil*, Cambridge: Cambridge University Press (essential reading).

Modiano, Patrick

b. 1947, Boulogne-sur-Seine

Writer

Modiano's early work – such as *La Place de l'étoile* (1968) and *Les Boulevards de ceinture* (The Ring Road) (1972) – was among the first to deal graphically with the period of the Occupation, before it became virtually *de rigueur* to do so. His screenplay for **Malle**'s *Lacombe Lucien* (1973) brought this theme to an even wider audience. His more recent work, such as *Une jeunesse* (Youth) (1981) or *Un cirque passe* (A Passing Circus) (1992), may have a more contemporary setting, but is unceasingly worked and reworked by memories of the past.

KEITH READER

Mollet, Guy

b. 1905, Flers, Normandy;
d. 1975, Paris

Politician

As leader of the Parti Socialiste-SFIO between 1946 and 1969, Mollet presided over the decline of a party caught between its unrevised revolutionary doctrine and its reformist practice. As prime minister in 1956 he stepped up the repression of the independence movement in French Algeria. In the same year he joined with the British to organize the ill-fated Suez expedition. He facilitated de **Gaulle**'s return to power in the wake of the May 1958 crisis, but in the 1960s took his party into electoral agreements with the Communists in order to combat the Gaullists. His absolute loyalty to the traditions of his own party tended to block any significant renewal of the Left.

LAURENCE BELL

See also: Algerian war; parties and movements

Further reading

Quilliot, R. (1972) *La SFIO et l'exercice du pouvoir*, Paris: Fayard (an insider's account of the SFIO in the period 1944–58).

Monde, Le

Newspaper

An opinion-forming daily of international repute, *Le Monde* is the most comprehensive French newspaper, providing in-depth analysis of national news and unparalleled international coverage. An evening paper, it is an indispensable, authoritative source of information for the ruling classes, intellectuals and highly educated sections of the population, and can be relied upon to publish official reports from organizations otherwise neglected by the press.

Austere in appearance, with a dense layout and rare photographs, its tone is sober, restrained, even dry, and its style polished, elevated and analytical. Committed to a noble conception of journalism, *Le Monde* aspires to balanced, impartial reporting, and does not hesitate to criticize. While independent of political parties, it is the forum for much political debate. It is socially progressive and left of centre, demonstrating a commitment to justice and human rights.

The newspaper was founded by Hubert Beuve-Méry on 18 December 1944 at the instigation of General de **Gaulle**, who felt France should have a newspaper of reference to replace *Le Temps* after the war. Beuve-Méry remained associated with the newspaper until his death in 1989. He wrote his editorials under the pseudonym 'Sirius', and *Le Monde*'s reputation for ironic understatement and cultivation of an allusive, indirect style is generally attributed to his influence.

Following an internal crisis in 1951, *Le Monde* adopted a revolutionary legal framework, giving journalists an important role in decision-making. Priding itself on its financial and political independence, it organized its share ownership to give a stake to founder members, managers, journalists and employees, leaving only a minor shareholding available to external investors. In 1982, prolonged squabbling over who should succeed Jacques Fauvet as director demonstrated the drawbacks of this internal democracy. New appointee André Laurens was quickly replaced by André Fontaine in 1985, for the paper was in crisis, with accumulating deficits and falling readership. *Libération* had won over younger readers, and *Le Figaro* was in the ascendant. Drastic measures were introduced: reductions in staff and salaries, the sale of the famous offices in the rue des Italiens, and an injection of capital from the newly founded readers' association. The traditional presentation of the paper was revamped, new supplements introduced, and more importance attached to the investigative role (well demonstrated by Edwy Plenel's reporting of the Rainbow Warrior affair). Fontaine succeeded in rejuvenating the paper and reversing the decline, but costly investment in new printing facilities at Ivry in 1989 brought further financial problems. Jacques Lesourne, appointed director in 1991, presided over increasing difficulties, and was replaced in 1994 by Jean-Marie Colombani, who undertook further innovation, including the introduction of André Laurens as mediator responsible for improving communications between readers and the editorial team.

Through the main newspaper and associated publications – such as *Le Monde diplomatique*, *Le Monde de l'éducation*, *Le Monde des*

débats, *Le Monde: dossiers et documents* – the title exerts considerable influence. None the less, in 1995 it was only the fourth French daily in terms of circulation, selling 379, 089 copies on average.

PAM MOORES

See also: national press in France

Montand, Yves

b. 1921, Monsumano Alto, Italy;
d. 1991, France

Singer and actor, real name Yvo Livi

Brought up in Marseilles after his parents fled from the Mussolini regime, Yves Montand made his first appearance on stage in 1938, performing songs made famous by Charles **Trenet**, Maurice **Chevalier** and Fernandel. Taken under the wings of Édith **Piaf** in 1944, he developed his own repertoire and emerged as one of France's most admired stage performers of the postwar period, enjoying unprecedented success above all in the 1950s and early 1960s. Meticulous preparation (set, dance, gesture, modulation of the voice) enabled Montand to perform a whole range of songs, some of which reveal a left-wing political commitment (as do some of the many films he made from the late 1960s, notably **Resnais'** *La Guerre est finie* of 1966). He was married to Simone **Signoret**.

IAN PICKUP

See also: song/*chanson*

Montparnasse Tower

A fifty-six-storey office tower, 210 m high, the Tour Maine-Montparnasse was built as part of a development project begun in 1958 which replaced the old railway stations of Maine and Montparnasse by a single new station. The tower formed the focal point of a new centre for business and commercial activity and was intended as a triumphal gesture to symbolize the embracing of modernism by the state as represented by the capital city of Paris. Inaugurated in 1973, it had taken four years to build, with a combination of both public and private investment. Opposition to the tower on aesthetic grounds was not openly expressed until it was near completion.

SUSAN COLLARD

See also: architecture

Montrelay, Michèle

birthdate unknown

Psychoanalyst

Author of *L'Ombre et le nom: sur la féminité* (The Shadow and the Name: On Femininity), published in 1977. This hermetic collection of essays on the subject of feminine difference is deeply indebted to Lacanian thought. It discusses the work of Marguerite Duras, Chantal Chawaf and Jeanne Hyvrard; *écriture féminine* and feminine discourse/language; psychoanalytic theories of the feminine; and women's relation to the female/maternal body.

ALEX HUGHES

See also: feminist thought; psychoanalysis

Morand, Paul

b. 1889, Paris;
d. 1976, Paris

Writer

Morand's career spanned much of the twentieth century. His novels, short stories and travelogues often reflected his exploits as a diplomat and world traveller. His controversial story collection of 1928, *Magie noire* (Black Magic), elicited strong reactions from black intellectu-

als and others concerned about his use of racial stereotypes. Similarly, his virulent satire of the French film industry, *France-la-doulce* (1934), provoked accusations of anti-semitism. His active participation in the Vichy regime (as an ambassador to Berne, and then as director of the bureau of film censorship) led to his ostracization for a period after the war. He was elected to the Académie Française in 1968.

ELIZABETH EZRA

See also: Hussards; racism/anti-semitism

Moreau, Jeanne

b. 1928, Paris

Actor

A stage and screen actor, Moreau became the icon of the Nouvelle Vague as the new liberated androgynous woman. Her career began in 1947, but her big breakthrough into cinema as a screen name came with her decision to work with Louis Malle – most notoriously in *The Lovers* (*Les Amants*) in 1958, where she has an orgasm on screen. She is an international star and has worked with all the major filmmakers. Both an intellectual and a feminist – at least in the roles she portrays – Moreau has exemplary depth in the compassion she brings to her performance. Dedicated to fostering new talent, she has also directed her own films, such as *Lumière* in 1976. Her wide-ranging talent as singer, actor, director, together with her natural performance style and intense curiosity, have brought her roles worldwide.

SUSAN HAYWARD

See also: cinema; stars; theatre

Morin, Edgar

b. 1921, Paris

Sociologist

During the Occupation, Morin entered the Resistance as a Communist, and ended the war in the French army of occupation in Germany, an experience he recorded in his first book, *L'An zéro de l'Allemagne* (Germany Year Zero), published in 1946. From 1949, he disagreed with party policy and was finally expelled from the PCF in 1951 for his opposition to Stalinism; this intellectual itinerary is recounted in his **autobiography** (Morin 1959). Having become a sociologist, from the early 1950s he published a number of works on culture and **cinema**, and a variety of social responses to modernization in France. His complex thought may be traced across a wide range of theoretical works encompassing political and social anthropology, culminating in *La Méthode*, spanning a period of fifteen years.

MARTYN CORNICK

See also: parties and movements

Major works

Morin, E. (1957) *Les Stars*, Paris: Éditions du Seuil.
——(1959) *Autocritique*, Paris: Éditions du Seuil. Republished 1994 with a new preface.
——(1980–95), *La Méthode*, 4 vols, Paris: Éditions du Seuil.
Morin, E., Lefort, C. and Castoriadis, C. (1988) *Mai 68: La Brèche*, Brussels: Complexe (covers May 1968).

Further reading

Kofman, M. (1995) *Edgar Morin*, London, Chicago: Pluto Press (comprehensive monograph).

motor sport

Motor sport in France is governed by the Fédération Française du Sport Automobile (French Motor Sports Federation) and the sport divides into Formula 1 (and, at a lower level, Formula 3,000 and Formula 3), rallying and endurance races. France stages a Grand Prix as part of the world Formula 1 championships and this attracts huge crowds, but the annual Le Mans twenty-four-hour race has seen a decline in its popularity. Renault engines have been most successful in Formula 1 races, as have French drivers such as Jacques Lafitte and France's first Formula 1 champion, Alain Prost. France's best-known rally, the Paris-Dakar (it involves cars, lorries and motorbikes) attracted much controversy. Motorcycle racing and motocross have seen a resurgence in popularity since the late 1960s.

IAN PICKUP

See also: sport

Mouloudji, Marcel

b. 1922, Paris

Singer-songwriter, playwright, novelist and actor

Having appeared in a number of films and having written plays, poems and novels (winning a Pléiade Prize for *Enrico* in 1945), Marcel Mouloudji turned to singing and progressively to songwriting from 1950. He is best remembered as the performer of Boris **Vian**'s *Le Déserteur* (The Deserter) in 1956, which, during the **Algerian war**, was banned from broadcasting and the record withdrawn from sale. Having experienced a barren period, Mouloudji made a successful comeback in 1971, ironically singing another anti-militarist song by Vian, *Allons z'enfants* (Go on, Children).

IAN PICKUP

See also: song/*chanson*

Moustaki, Georges

b. 1934, Alexandria, Egypt

Singer-songwriter,
real name Joseph Mustacchi

Having studied at the Lycée Français (French secondary school) in Alexandria, Moustaki went to Paris in 1951. The turning point in his career was his meeting in 1957 with Edith **Piaf**, for whom he wrote *Milord*. He later wrote for Serge Reggiani – *Sarah* and *Ma liberté* (My Freedom), for instance – before becoming a highly successful performer in his own right: *Joseph* and *Le Métèque* (The Wog), for example. His songs reveal a variety of musical influences, ranging from Oriental to South American.

IAN PICKUP

See also: song/*chanson*

multinational companies

A multinational company is one which owns and/or controls resources engaged in production outside the country in which it is based. Companies need to reach a certain critical size before they can operate multinationally, and French industry has lagged behind its competitors in terms of its degree of multinational activity. French companies were relatively small at the beginning of the postwar period; subsequently only a limited number of very large French companies developed. Multinational companies are necessary for the international strength and prestige of a national economy, but their activities are very difficult for the state to control.

JAN WINDEBANK

See also: economy; manufacturing industry

music festivals

France has a proud tradition of music festivals associated with individual towns: for example, Aix-en-Provence hosts an international music festival (and also film and **dance** festivals); Dijon has a music festival (in addition to a **theatre** and **wine** festival), while Nice puts on a **jazz** festival; Rennes organizes a **rock** festival (Les Trans-Musicales) and Strasbourg a music festival. Paris has its own music festival (La Fête de la Musique) in June. However, since Easter 1977, the most significant music festival to promote essentially French song has been held annually in Bourges, a relatively small town situated to the southeast of Orléans and the southwest of Auxerre.

The so-called Printemps de Bourges (Bourges Spring Festival) began as a French version of popular music festivals held in the English-speaking world, such as the now-defunct rock festival on the Isle of Wight in the United Kingdom. The Printemps de Bourges – which was sponsored by the local *maison de la culture* and was run, as it still is today, by its director Daniel Colling – immediately established itself as *the* music festival; in no small measure, because it gave the outstanding Charles **Trenet** the opportunity to make himself known to a whole new generation of music lovers. From modest beginnings in terms of paying spectators (12,000 in the first year but 45,000 by 1980), the festival was able to claim an aggregate audience of something approaching two million as it reached its twentieth birthday. Perceived from the outset as a venue which attracted an audience interested in French song *per se*, rather than a specific singer-songwriter, the festival has always been an important meeting place, a point of contact and of discussion, as well as offering the opportunity to listen to established stars (Trenet, Guy **Béart**, Georges **Moustaki**, Claude **Nougaro** and Maxime **Le Forestier**, for example), those in the process of establishing themselves (**Renaud** and Alain **Souchon** being the most enduring examples), and others who were looking for a breakthrough (Francis Lalanne, for example).

The Bourges Spring Festival confirms recent trends in French song and in the changing nature of **music venues** since the heyday of the *café-concert*, the revue and the music hall.

While relatively intimate variations of the cabaret and the larger music halls have long since lost their mass appeal (the Paris Olympia being a notable exception), festivals like the one at Bourges and also single concerts in much bigger arenas such as Bercy or the Palais des Congrès (both in Paris) now attract numbers of spectators which were inconceivable, even in the 1950s, to performances which are heavily reliant on the new entertainment technology. What is also apparent is that French audiences now spend more time listening to performers on stage than they spend singing along with – or indeed instead of – the singer or singers in question (though it is still common for live audiences to join in the singing of the biggest hits of the artists concerned). It is the continued success of music festivals such as the Printemps de Bourges, and, indeed, of the increasingly influential Francofolies (a music festival held in La Rochelle in July), which helps to guarantee the ongoing public attendance at live concerts in an age often dominated by television and pop videos.

IAN PICKUP

See also: song/*chanson*

Further reading

Brunschwig, C., Calvet, J.-L. and Klein, J.-C. (1981) *Cent ans de chanson française*, Paris: Éditions du Seuil (an alphabetically arranged reference work).

Fléouter, C. (1988) *Un siècle de chansons*, Paris: PUF (a chronologically arranged analytical section is followed by an alphabetically arranged reference section).

Rioux, L. (1994) *50 ans de chanson française*, Paris: Archipel (a critical study organized chronologically).

music industry

The music industry in France has, as elsewhere, undergone major changes in the wake of the technological revolution and the creation of the worldwide market. If the microphone, the talkies, 78 rpm records, microgroove records, audio cassettes, CDs and video cassettes in turn signalled new stages in audio and audiovisual recording, successive changes in popular musical fashion which originated in France and (more often) abroad have seen the growth of an industry, aimed predominantly at the young, that makes overnight millionaires of performers whose careers are often very ephemeral. The globalization of the music industry saw the arrival – and rapid domination – in France of **multinational companies** at the expense of more modest indigenous ones. By the mid-1970s, Phonogram and EMI were outstripping French firms such as Carrère, Vogue and **Barclay** where the combined sales of singles and LPs were concerned. Symptomatic of the sea change the industry was undergoing was the takeover of the Barclay label by the Polygram Corporation in 1979 at a time when CBS was making great inroads in the market. Since then, Sony and Virgin are two of the multinationals claiming their own huge slice of the market (and the Virgin Megastore in Paris, for example, can hold its own against the indigenous FNAC). If an established French singer such as Jean **Ferrat** can still record on his own label (Disques Temey – a combination of his own real name, Tenenbaum, and that of his artistic director, Gérard Meys), it is significant that the distribution of CDs is carried out by Sony Music. Further examples of the domination of the multinationals are easy to find: **Gainsbourg**'s CDs carry the Polygram label, **Renaud**'s that of Virgin, while those of Francis **Cabrel** and Patricia **Kaas** are labelled 'Columbia', which is 'the exclusive trademark of Sony Music Entertainment Inc'.

If the commercial side of the music industry is now firmly in the hands of the multinationals, French song has for many years had to face the threat to its position in French popular culture posed by Anglo-Saxon music. From the time of the music hall, when a guest star was known as a *vedette américaine*, through the big-band era to that of **rock** and roll, punk, heavy metal and **rap**, English-language songs have had great success in France. The situation on the airwaves was deemed to be so critical in 1993 (the managing director of Skyrock had admitted that 85 per cent of the songs his radio station broadcast were in English) that the Pelchat amendment imposed a minimum quota of 40 per cent – effective from January 1996 – for songs in the French language. Since the quota came into effect, one only has to peruse the programme listings for the **M6** television channel to realize that, if one wishes to listen to songs in French, the middle of the night is usually the best time. Despite such ruses, and despite the significant presence at **music venues** in France of **stars** from abroad, French song continues to flourish, albeit for a discerning minority.

IAN PICKUP

See also: song/*chanson*

Further reading

Delbourg, P. (1994) *Mélodies chroniques: la chanson française sur le gril*, Paris: Le Castor Astral (a highly personal, critical look at French song from 1980 to 1993, based on articles which first appeared in the press).
Hennion, F. (1981) *Les Professionnels du disque*, Paris: Métailié (a sociological study of artistic creation and production in the French popular music industry).

music venues

Changing tastes and the introduction of new technology have radically changed the size and nature of music venues in France since World War II. The **café-concert** had already been largely replaced by the cabaret, while music halls had declined dramatically in numbers with the advent of the **cinema**. However, the late 1950s and 1960s saw the fashion of the Left Bank cabaret in Paris where, in usually cramped and smoke-filled surroundings, a predominantly young, intellectual and often left-

wing audience was able to listen to emerging talents, such as Jean **Ferrat**, Hugues **Aufray**, Serge **Gainsbourg** and Juliette **Gréco**; older artists such as Léo **Ferré** had been performing there since the 1940s. These cabarets, situated in the Latin Quarter and in St-Germain-des-Prés, often had evocative or slightly exotic names: Le Tabou, La Rose Rouge, L'Échelle de Jacob, L'Écluse, La Méthode, La Colombe, La Contrescarpe, Le Cheval d'Or, and so on. The songs of the Left Bank cabarets were often poetic, intellectual and anti-establishment. The cramped surroundings encouraged the use of the piano and, increasingly, the guitar for musical accompaniment.

Variety theatres and music halls were declining in number after the war but three of the most famous – Les Trois Baudets, Bobino and the Olympia – witnessed concerts by almost all the big names of French song of the period. Today, the Olympia (reconstructed in 1997) is the one remaining traditional venue which attracts the biggest stars, both French and foreign; the rebuilt Bobino still welcomes performers of lesser stature. Many cabarets still thrive in Paris, on the Left and the Right Bank, as do establishments which produce extravagant revues such as the Moulin Rouge, the Crazy Horse, L'Éléphant Bleu and La Belle Époque. *Chansonniers* (politically motivated singer-comedians who specialize in satire) can still be seen in such establishments as Le Caveau de la République and Les Deux Ânes. For **jazz** enthusiasts there are many cabarets specializing in traditional and modern jazz, while lovers of classical music are not limited to concert halls: many Parisian churches stage classical concerts (for example, the Église St-Germain-des-Prés, the Église St-Julien-le-Pauvre and the Église de la Madeleine). Opera lovers can listen to performances in such venues as the Opéra Comique and the huge Opéra National de Paris-Bastille.

Technological innovations have also meant that popular music concerts can now be staged in much larger venues than was possible in the past and, after the pioneering concerts mounted at the Palais des Congrès, for example, the huge multisports complex at Bercy is capable of housing some 14,000 or so spectators. Similar concerts are staged at venues in the provinces (such as the enormous Palais des Sports in Toulouse). Much more modestly sized municipal halls offer concerts in provincial towns, many of which host their own **music festivals**.

Visitors to Paris may peruse the full list of music venues in the capital and the surrounding area by consulting *L'Officiel des spectacles*, a modestly priced weekly publication on sale at news-stands.

IAN PICKUP

See also: cultural topography (Paris); song/*chanson*

Further reading

Brunschwig, C., Calvet, J.-L. and Klein, J.-C. (1981) *Cent ans de chanson française*, Paris: Éditions du Seuil (an alphabetically arranged reference work).

N

Namiand, Arlette

b. 1951, France

Playwright and director

A collaborator and dramaturg for Jean-Paul
Wenzel at the Centre Dramatique National
(CDN) at Les Fédérés, Montluçon, Namiand is
the author of many works, some of them per-
formed at the CDN and directed by Wenzel.
They include *Surtout quand la nuit tombe*
(Especially When Night Falls) and *Sang blanc*
(White Blood). Her adaptations include works
by Maupassant and Koestler.

ANNIE SPARKS

See also: theatre

National Cinematographic Centre

The Centre National de la Cinématographie
(CNC) is a state institution created in 1946 and
is the overseeing body for the French film industry. Notionally an autonomous decision-making body, it is composed of different committees
whose remit is to foster the well-being of
France's **cinema** by allocating funds to successful applications. It is charged with maintaining
control over the financing of films, the receipts
from box-office takings and statistics pertaining

to the totality of film practices. The CNC manages funds that support the industry, the
Compte de soutien, which takes two forms: the
soutien automatique (1948) and the **avance sur
recettes** (1960).

SUSAN HAYWARD

See also: cinema

national press in France

The French press reflects the country's geographical, cultural and political diversity in a
wide range of publications, including local,
regional and national newspapers, and a particularly thriving magazine sector which caters for
every specialist interest and leisure pursuit.
However, when compared to other nations, the
French read relatively few dailies: only half as
many as the British and Germans, and a quarter of the number read in Finland and Sweden.
Despite a rich intellectual and political heritage,
international comparisons of the number of
dailies sold per capita place France in a lowly
twenty-third position in the world rankings.
Moreover, approximately 70 per cent of the
total circulation of French dailies is accounted
for by provincial titles.

The Paris-based daily press has declined dramatically since the beginning of the century. In
1914 there were eighty newspapers printing a
total of 5.5 million copies each day. By 1939 the

number of titles had fallen to thirty-one, and by the beginning of the 1990s to just eleven. Meanwhile the total print run of national dailies had fallen to below three million copies, despite the growth in population over this period, despite rising standards of living and educational achievement, and the increasing importance of information in contemporary society. July 1994 saw the collapse of Philippe Tesson's twenty-year-old *Le Quotidien de Paris* (not to be confused with the flimsy right-wing rag since launched under the same title). In 1995, leading national titles *Le Parisien*, *Le Figaro*, *Le Monde*, *France-Soir* and *Libération* all made losses. With the exception of *Le Parisien* (and to some extent this is a Paris-based regional paper rather than a national title), the only national dailies to increase their circulation over recent years are specialist titles: the financial paper *Les Échos*, and sporting daily *L'Équipe*. Since the successful creation of *Libération* in 1973, repeated attempts have been made to launch new dailies. *Le Matin de Paris* lasted longest, from 1977 to 1988, while *Paris: 24 heures* survived only two weeks . . . 1996 began ominously with the disappearance of *InfoMatin*, a promising new title, which had run up losses of 150 million francs in less than two years.

The regional press is stable and prosperous in comparison, but does not offer such diversity in terms of style, ideology and distinctive identity (except in the regional sense). However, the more consensual attitude to politics evident in local newspapers has proved advantageous, since one explanation advanced for the demise of national dailies is public distaste for their partisan stance: certainly the Communist *L'Humanité* and the Catholic *La Croix* have been badly affected by falling sales, and other titles have responded by moderating their political line. Nonetheless, national titles enjoy the greatest prestige and influence both in France and abroad. They are more widely quoted as a source of reference, and provide the in-depth analysis necessary to complement broadcasting, although they are also more severely affected by competition from **television** news in so far as the latter, in France, is

predominantly national and international as opposed to local.

One problem for national dailies is their high cover price. For many years the price of a French newspaper was equal to that of a postage stamp (and this is still the case for many British tabloids in the mid-1990s). However, whereas a French stamp costs 3 francs, the price of *Le Figaro*, *Le Monde* and *Libération* has climbed to 7 francs or more, while provincial newspapers are sold for about 4.5 francs. Since the latter primarily serve relatively distinct geographical areas, they sometimes sign co-operation agreements and benefit from economies of scale, whereas national titles compete directly throughout the country and therefore incur higher costs, particularly for distribution. National distribution via the Nouvelles Messageries de la Presse Parisienne is expensive, and has become the focus of much critical attention. Operating costs in the capital are also high, for property, salaries and transport, and some newspapers have moved their premises out of the congested city centre to the outskirts. *Le Monde* set up a magnificent new printing plant at Ivry in the late 1980s, as did *Le Figaro* at Roissy. However, in view of the falling circulation of national titles, it appears that there may have been overinvestment resulting in surplus capacity. The newspapers are caught in a vicious circle: financial difficulties have prompted them to raise their cover prices, but this in turn has a negative impact on sales. The situation has been exacerbated by increasing competition for **advertising** from television, in the context of a general fall in advertising revenue in the early 1990s. *InfoMatin* deliberately set an attractive cover price of 3 francs (subsequently raised to 3.80 francs), but was none the less unable to achieve the volume of sales necessary to be viable.

There is not a clear division between quality broadsheets and a downmarket 'gutter press' in France. Readers in search of sex and scandal will find no equivalent of Britain's mass circulation tabloids. Even popular style dailies such as *France-Soir* are comparatively sober, and one has to turn to specialist weeklies for unadulterated sensationalism: to the infamous

Le Nouveau Détective, Hachette titles *France-Dimanche* and *Ici Paris*, or Alain Ayache's magazines *Spécial-Dernière* and *Le Meilleur*.

Magazines also fulfil the basic news function assumed in many countries largely by dailies and Sunday newspapers. (There is only one Sunday paper of note, *Le Journal du dimanche*.) Paris-based weekly news magazines such as *L'Express*, *Le Nouvel Observateur*, *Le Point* and *L'Événement du jeudi* provide wide-ranging news coverage and commentary, and are often regarded as another reason for the poor circulation figures of daily newspapers. In 1995, *L'Express* and *Le Nouvel Observateur* both exceeded the sales of any national daily. For busy people who have little time to read a paper, and who are used to the high-quality images seen on television news each evening, the news magazine has the advantage of providing a synthesis of the most important events of the week, together with considered analyses and good-quality photography, all in a convenient format.

PAM MOORES

See also: regional press in France

Further reading

Cayrol, R. (1991) *Les Médias: presse écrite, radio, télévision*, Paris: PUF (a wide-ranging study including introduction to historical development and current state of newspaper industry, and profiles of individual titles).

Charon, J.-M. (1991) *La Presse en France de 1945 à nos jours*, Paris: Éditions du Seuil (a lively analysis of the decline of the national press).

Kuhn, R. (1995) *The Media in France*, London and New York: Routledge (an excellent overview of historical, political and economic aspects of the press; systematic and comprehensive).

Pedley, A. (1993) 'The Media', in M. Cook (ed.) *French Culture Since 1945*, London: Longman (provides useful insights).

nationalism

France occupies a special place in the history of nationhood and nationalism. By the seventeenth century, it was already a 'prototype' nation-state with well-established frontiers and a burgeoning central state apparatus. More significantly, however, the French Revolution is commonly identified as the birthplace of modern nationalism as a political ideology. The revolutionary notion that state legitimacy should be founded on popular consent within a defined territory was the catalyst for the nation-building process in nineteenth-century Europe, and for the subsequent ascendancy of the idea of 'nation' as the dominant principle of state organization worldwide.

At one level, nationalism in France may be seen as a process of social integration which progressively overcame regional and sectional loyalties, and was characterized in particular by the dominant role of the state as an agent of national 'assimilation', from the Third Republic's conversion of 'peasants into Frenchmen' to the nationalizing impetus of Fifth Republic presidentialism.

At another level, however, the idea of nation in France has been profoundly divisive. In 200 years punctuated by war, revolution and changes of regime, diverse ideologies and movements have sought to appropriate the discourse of nationalism and to identify their political aspirations as the authentic expression of 'national' values. This produced a complex dialectical process in which nationalism moved between Left and Right, between anti-state populism and 'state patriotism', between an open, voluntarist ('civic') conception of nationality and a closed, deterministic ('ethnic') version.

During the Nazi occupation, these nuances were simplified and polarized into an opposition between two distinctive national value systems and 'histories', exemplified by **Vichy**'s *Révolution nationale* and the **Liberation** discourse of the Resistance Left. In the postwar era, however, these simple polarities have lost their resonance. France's reduced status in a changed world, the emerging 'bloc' system of the Cold War, the construction of Europe, the painful experience of **decolonization**, produced multiple and contradictory cleavages in the political community of the Fourth Republic. This fragmentation provided the basis for the new synthesis achieved by the Gaullist nationalism of the 1960s, which successfully buried old antagonisms by developing a consensus around presidentialism, economic modernization, and the theme of an 'independent' foreign and defence policy which exploited the space provided in the international bloc system by a period of relative *détente*.

Ironically, it was under de **Gaulle** that France's membership of the European Community, coupled with state-sponsored economic modernization, opened her economy to the accelerating processes of market globalism which have progressively undermined the autonomy of nation-states in the field of economic and other related areas of policy-making. The failure of the French Left's own version of economic nationalism ('Keynesianism in one country') in 1981–2, followed by the collapse of the Communist command-economies and the demise of the bloc system on which France's 'independent' foreign policy was predicated, have deeply undermined the credibility of nationalism as a political programme.

At the same time, the emergence in France of a pluralistic, multiethnic, post-industrial society has weakened the appeal of the historic homogenizing myths of French nationhood. The increasing separation of state and nation has produced something of a crisis of national identity, and the Front National's successful politicization of race and **immigration** may be seen as symptomatic of this deeper malaise. Feeding on nostalgia for lost national status, and on the quest for identity in the face of economic and cultural globalization, it has appropriated a nationalist discourse now largely abandoned by mainstream political parties.

BRIAN JENKINS

See also: economy; European Union; racism/anti-semitism

Further reading

Hoffmann, S. (1974) *Decline or Renewal: France Since the 1930s*, New York, Viking (contains an influential and pioneering essay on the idea of 'nation' in France).

Jenkins, B. (1990) *Nationalism in France: Class and Nation Since 1789*, London, Routledge (an analysis of the ideological dynamics of French nationalism since the Revolution).

Silverman, M. (1992) *Deconstructing the Nation: Immigration, Racism and Citizenship in Modern France*, London, Routledge (situates the contemporary issue of immigration within the framework of the historical French conception of nationality and citizenship).

Weber, E. (1976) *Peasants into Frenchmen: The Modernisation of Rural France 1870–1914*, Stanford, CA: Stanford University Press (the classic study of the development of French national consciousness under the Third Republic).

nationalization and privatization

The evolution of the public sector in France during the last few decades has been turbulent. After the 1945–6 nationalizations, it developed during the 'thirty glorious years' of growth, with the nationalized companies taking a leading role in the modernization of the economy. The extensive new nationalization programme in the financial and industrial sectors implemented in 1981 nearly doubled the size of the commercial public sector. However, since 1986, several privatization programmes have reduced the size and importance of the public sector.

Intervention in the economy by the strong arm of the state, including the public ownership of firms, is not a recent phenomenon. In the 'mercantile' period of the late seventeenth century, in Holland or England, private enterprise was financing new developments, but in France it was under the initiative of the

absolutist royal power that merchants participated in new industrial endeavours, especially
under the direction of Colbert, minister of
Louis XIV (hence the neologism, *Colbertisme*,
meaning state interventionism). The King
owned, or was the patron of, the celebrated
Manufactures Royales (Aubusson, Sèvres,
Gobelins, arsenals, shipyards).

It is not surprising, then, that despite the influence of the liberal ideology of the Revolution,
interventionism reappeared in France at the
beginning of the twentieth century, when a
'technocratic' ideology of 'public service'
developed, according to which efficient and
publicly managed institutions had to be substituted for inefficient markets for the common
good. The economic crisis of the 1920s and
1930s reinforced these views, often supported by
conservative segments of society. From another
angle, Socialists and Marxists were also calling
for the 'collectivization' of means of production,
or at least for their nationalization. The 'Popular
Front' government, which came to power in
1936, conducted the first nationalizations.

A large nationalized sector was created,
during the period September 1944 to May
1946, mostly by de **Gaulle**'s provisional government, either because previous private owners had collaborated with the Nazis (Renault)
or because of the strategic importance of the
company for the reconstruction of France. This
affected energy utilities (Charbonnages de
France, EDF, GDF), **transport** companies (there
was a full nationalization of Air France and
SNCF), industrial firms (Renault, SNECMA),
the Banque de France and the four main
high-street **banks** (Société Générale, Crédit
Lyonnais, and two others later to merge into
the BNP) and most insurance companies.

The public sector continued to extend during the 'thirty glorious years' of growth that
followed the war, either via the creation of new
concerns or via the grouping of smaller, ailing
private industrial companies into a larger public firm (such as Aérospatiale). The public sector was used as the driving force for the rest of
the economy (especially for industrial relations)
and was responsible for a very high proportion
of investments. The public and private sectors

were not always opposed: indeed, numerous
Sociétés d'Économie Mixte (half private, half
public) also developed during the 1960s, especially for local utilities.

The victory of the Left in the 1981 elections
brought a new wave of nationalizations, affecting most of the remaining private financial
institutions such as Suez and Paribas investment banks, and the largest industrial groups
(such as Pechiney, Thomson, Rhône-Poulenc,
etc.). Private shareholders were compensated at
full market price. The strategy was for the state
to control strategic and monopolistic companies in order to influence investment strategies,
create **employment**, improve social relations
and provide the private sector with competitive
examples.

The 1981 nationalizations had mixed
results. The short-term impact was considerable: in 1985, there were over 3,000 nationalized commercial firms, with 1.86 million
employees. In industry alone, nationalized
companies accounted for a fifth of employment, a third of investment and exports, and
nearly a quarter of turnover. The balance sheet
of nationalizations had positive aspects. A
number of loss-making firms were restructured
and reorganized after nationalization, and
from 1985–6 started to be profitable. However,
costs to the public purse were considerable.
Furthermore, the justifiability of the programme was weakened when the Socialists
changed economic strategy in 1983, embracing
the belief that the 'discipline of market forces'
had to be respected by public sector firms as
well as private ones. Consequences were immediate, with companies such as Renault, previously a 'social laboratory', shedding tens of
thousands of employees in order to improve
competitiveness. The position of nationalized
firms was also weakened by the European
Community reinforcement of competition and
anti-monopolistic rule, and its limiting of
opportunities for state capital funding.

In this context, in 1986 the **Chirac** right-
wing government launched an initial wave of
privatizations, shedding its 'Gaullist' inheritance. The denationalization programme was
implemented only partially (for instance, the

Société Générale, Paribas, Saint-Gobain, Matra and **TF1** were sold). Popular at first, it was slowed down by the financial crisis of November 1987, and its implementation was criticized, as part of the capital was set aside for stable institutional investors amid allegations of political favouritism. The 1988 re-election of **Mitterrand** interrupted the privatization process, but only temporarily. The attempt to freeze public and private sectors soon proved unrealistic. In 1991 the Socialist government started to 'part-privatize' firms such as Elf, Total, Rhône-Poulenc, etc. The role of the nationalized industries, increasingly managed as private concerns, was appearing less central to public policies.

Indeed, when the conservative coalition came back to power after the parliamentary elections of 1993, a new, wider privatization programme was launched, which proved to be far less controversial. This time, conditions were regulated by an independent commission. Soon, jewels of the public sector were sold, such as the BNP, the insurance company UAP, Renault, Elf and Usinor-Sacilor. Other groups were in line, such as Aérospatiale and Thomson, but some of those concerned are required to effect first a return to profitability and a complete reorganization. This is the case for Air France and, more particularly, for the Crédit Lyonnais, one of the three largest high-street banks, and one which was rocked by scandals and unsound financial strategies during the late 1980s.

The 1993 privatization plans excluded utilities such as EDF, France Telecom and the Post Office. However, as European competition laws are becoming stricter, the French concept of 'public services' is tending to weaken, and this prepares the opening of public utilities to private capital. It seems that, in the future, little will remain of the 'nationalized' sector which for four decades had been at the heart of the French development model.

FRANÇOIS NECTOUX

See also: *dirigisme*; economy

Further reading

Rand Smith, W. (1990) 'Nationalizations for What? Capitalist Power and Public Enterprise in Mitterrand's France', *Politics and Society,* March (this explains the changes occurring in the 1980s).

Ross, G., Hoffmann, S. and Malzachert, S. (eds) (1987) *The Mitterrand Experiment: Continuity and Change in Socialist France*, Cambridge: Polity Press (an analysis of the context of the 1981 nationalizations).

Navarre, Yves

b. 1940, Condom, Gascony;
d. 1994, Paris

Writer

Navarre's prolific output of novels since the first, *Lady Black*, in 1971, often returns to the same themes of homosexuality, death, melancholy, scarred childhoods, cats, and the oppressions of the bourgeois family. In *Cronos' Children (Le Jardin d'acclimatation)* of 1980, which won the Goncourt prize, a patriarch has his gay son lobotomized. His formally ambitious *Biographie* (Biography) of 1981 provides autobiographical keys to much of this material. Demoralized by illness, a conflict with publishers which had sent him into residence in Montreal, and the loss of friends to **AIDS** – as in 1991's *Ce sont amis que vent emporte* (It is Friends the Wind Bears Away) – he committed suicide.

BILL MARSHALL

See also: autobiography; gay writing; literary prizes

Négresses vertes, Les

Musicians

A popular indie group which appeared on the French scene in 1987 – a hybrid band like **Mano negra**, which out of creative necessity mixes styles and inspirations. Their musical roots are in Memphis, Seville, Algiers and Joinville-le-Pont. They sing in French, accompanied by accordions, drums, piano, guitars and export worldwide their *joie de vivre*. Their lyrics are full of humour and derision. They see the world as a *Famille nombreuse* (Big Family) – the title of their penultimate album. In 1995, they performed their album *ZigZague* in London.

GÉRARD POULET

See also: beur music; rock and pop; song/*chanson*

new philosophers

The 'new philosophers' emerged in 1976–7 as a grouping of intellectuals determined to attack the leading left-wing ideologies and reinstate traditional values as a legitimate focus of commitment.

By the mid-1970s, the idealism and optimism of the **May 1968** movements had largely evaporated. Many intellectuals who had put their hopes in **revolutionary groups**, especially Maoists or Trotskyists, now turned their back on these, and looked for radically different alternatives. Linking up with earlier spiritual traditions and with an older generation of right-wing activists, represented by Maurice Clavel, they launched a political and philosophical attack on the intellectuals of the Left.

They were strongly influenced by reading Solzhenitsyn's *The Gulag Archipelago*, published in French in 1974, and containing a detailed denunciation of Soviet labour camps. The 'new philosophers' saw totalitarianism as the main crime of the Left, and the Communists and Socialists were attacked for their political complicity, in works such as André **Glucksmann**'s *The Cook and the Man-eater* (*La Cuisinière et le mangeur d'hommes*) of 1975 and Bernard-Henri **Lévy**'s *Barbarism*

with a Human Face (*La Barbarie à visage humain*) of 1977. They particularly attacked the most influential theoretical frameworks of the previous decade, especially Marxism and Freudian **psychoanalysis**, both considered totalitarian and inherently oppressive, a case made in Glucksmann's 1977 *The Master Thinkers* (*Les Maîtres penseurs*), and Clavel's *What I Believe* (*Ce que je crois*) of 1976. The criticism was often extended to include large sections of the European intellectual tradition since the eighteenth century, notably the production of large-scale philosophical syntheses, and the reliance on notions of reason, progress and the values of the Enlightenment, all of which could be associated with past or present totalitarian practices. Other writers associated with the group included Guy Lardreau, Christian Jambet, Jean-Paul Dollé, Michel Guérin and Philippe Némo.

The content of their work drew heavily on the Cold War polemics of the 1950s, and on the ideas of Raymond **Aron**, Friedrich Nietzsche and Catholic spiritualism. It was the philosophers and not the philosophy that were new, as several of them agreed. However, their arrival made a considerable public impact, in part because most of them were formerly associated with the radical Left, and in part because they presented the novelty of intellectuals supporting the government, then under **Giscard d'Estaing**'s liberal Right presidency. They helped to set the ideological climate of a close-fought legislative election campaign, and are often thought to have contributed to the surprise victory of the governing coalition in March 1978.

Their impact also derived from a sophisticated awareness of the power of the media, as a result of which their emergence in 1976–7 was given wide coverage in the press and on **television** in France, and taken up by the international media, eager to find a new French avant-garde.

Inevitably, the 'new philosophers' were vehemently attacked by many prominent left-wing intellectuals, who typically saw them as being superficial and opportunistic, scraping together the worn-out clichés and superstitions of the Right and presenting them as a glossy and marketable product. Paradoxically, these attacks served to give the philosophers in question a greater prominence.

What the 'new philosophers' shared was a criticism of the intellectual traditions of the French Left, rather than a positive alternative. Their differences rapidly emerged in the later 1970s, as the French intelligentsia adjusted to the end of the postwar intellectual dominance of the Left. Lévy, the editor of their book series with Grasset, and unofficial leader, formally declared the nonexistence of the 'new philosophy' in April 1978 (in *La Nef 35*).

MICHAEL KELLY

See also: Catholicism and Protestantism; Marxism and Marxian thought

Nichet, Jacques

b. 1942, Albi

Director

A leading figure in the Théâtre de l'Aquarium in the 1970s and the founder of the Maison Antoine **Vitez** international theatre translation centre in 1990. He has been the director of the Centre Dramatique National du Languedoc Roussillon-Montpellier since 1986, where he has developed a contemporary and Mediterranean repertoire, including plays by Lorca, Calderón and de Filippo, and has promoted contemporary comedy.

ANNIE SPARKS

See also: theatre

Noiret, Philippe

b. 1931, Lille

Actor

A stage and screen actor, Noiret gave up the

stage to concentrate on film after the huge success of Louis **Malle**'s *Zazie dans le métro* (1960) launched his cinema career. Ever since his role as Zazie's cabaret-performing uncle, Noiret has tended to play the bumbling avuncular type with a sting in his tail: corrupt policeman, refined murderer on the run, father on a counter-Oedipal trajectory – in films such as Zidi's *Les Ripoux* (1984), Granier-Deferre's *L'Étoile du nord* (1982), **Tavernier**'s *L'Horloger de Saint-Paul* (1973). He has attained full star status in maturity, exemplifying, as a sign of the times, a quiet, but large and preoccupied man whose stature can lead him to take heroic action however small the scale: as in 1989's *Life and Nothing But (La Vie et rien d'autre)*, by Tavernier, for example.

SUSAN HAYWARD

See also: cinema

Nougaro, Claude

b. 1929, Toulouse

Singer-songwriter

This son of an operatic tenor first wrote songs for others, including Marcel **Amont**, before achieving immediate success as a singer in his own right from 1962. A performer who has arguably improved with age, Claude Nougaro is an outstanding lyricist, whose poetic inspiration is complemented by the jazz musicians with whom he surrounds himself. Successes include *Brésilien* (Brazilian), *Chanson pour Marylin* (Song for Marylin) and *Tu verras* (You'll See).

IAN PICKUP

See also: song/*chanson*

nouveau roman

Writers of the *nouveau roman* (new novel) conceive of the novel as a laboratory for research into new forms of writing. Judging the traditional novel to be a form of mystification and aware that fiction is constructed and unreal, they propose alternatives to conventional notions of plot, character, genre, point of view, the relation between narration and description, and even the paragraph and sentence. According to an aphorism advanced by Jean **Ricardou**, the *nouveau roman*'s foremost theorist, a novel recounts not the writing of an adventure, but rather the adventure of writing.

The *nouveau roman* was not an organized school, nor did it have a fixed agenda, a journal, a manifesto or a leader. Rather, it began in the mid-1950s as a convergence of authors working in similar directions. Critical attention, including writings about each other's work, and prestigious **literary prizes** publicized the new trend, as did Ricardou's theoretical essays. Jérôme **Lindon**, head of **Minuit** publishers, solicited their work and brought them together under a banner of sorts. Ricardou organized a colloquium entitled 'Nouveau Roman: hier, aujourd'hui' at Cerisy-la-Salle, Normandy, in 1971. Novelists who adopted the rubric by electing to participate were, in addition to Ricardou: **Butor**, Ollier, Pinget, **Robbe-Grillet**, **Sarraute** and **Simon**. The writers continued to work independently, however, and emphasized different technical concerns. A few others not associated with the movement have nevertheless worked along sympathetic lines, e.g. **Duras** and **Modiano** and film-makers of the **Nouvelle Vague**, especially **Godard** and **Resnais**.

During this first phase in the 1950s and 1960s, the new novelists published their first novels or consolidated their reputations, set out their individual programmes, and began to educate a new reading public. They declared the 'referential illusion' of traditional novels outmoded and systematically subverted the assumption that fiction should or even can transmit predetermined realities and messages. In highly autoreferential novels like Butor's 1956 *Passing Time* (*L'Emploi du temps*), Robbe-Grillet's 1953 *The Erasers* (*Les Gommes*) and 1955 *The Voyeur* (*Le Voyeur*), protagonist and reader are detectives attempting together to decipher puzzles. Conventional

props to understanding are removed and habits deflected by texts that didactically but playfully reveal secrets of their own construction.

A second phase, after 1968 and following the 1971 Cerisy colloquium, saw the most extreme forms of self-consciously textual fiction. Techniques whereby the text is generated from linguistic, imaginary and graphic materials were foregrounded, and stories serve as metaphors for the creative process. Butor's five volumes of *Matière de rêves* (The Stuff of Dreams), published 1975–85, are generated from dream functioning. Robbe-Grillet, Simon and Ricardou wrote stories generated from paintings. Simon played with the productive power of words to produce ever more words and meanings in novels like his 1969 novel, *The Battle of Pharsalus* (*La Bataille de Pharsale*), and his 1975 *The World About Us* (*Leçon de choses*). This period marks a more aggressive challenge to readers' expectations and habits of reading.

The new novelists continued to pursue similar goals into the 1980s and 1990s. Robbe-Grillet and Sarraute have ventured into dismantling another domain of traditionally realistic fiction: the **autobiography**. Simon's work has always been autobiographical, and he continues to challenge the conventions of the genre. Ricardou pursues his blending of theory with fiction, fiction with theory. Butor invents new and ever more poetic genres. Despite seemingly less abstruse content, they continue to complicate the question of who is speaking, the role of language, and how fiction is generated.

The *nouveau roman*'s death was proclaimed almost before its existence was acknowledged, but interest persists, and novels keep appearing. Perhaps this is thanks to interested academics, especially in the United Kingdom and the United States. Perhaps it is because much of the writing is of high quality, always surpassing its own efforts to theorize. Perhaps it is also because, from the beginning, the *nouveau roman* has engaged major theoretical and philosophical questions of its era. The movement's rise coincided with the emergence of **structuralism**, which raised analogous questions in various disciplines. The primacy accorded in structuralism to linguistics (Saussure), where linguistic and other codes are viewed as interrelations of shifting meanings, corresponded to new novelists' emphasis on the independence of language to structure realities. Ethnography (**Barthes, Lévi-Strauss**) and fiction alike investigated the impact of myth on consciousness. Postmodern challenges to humanism and the speaking subject (**Foucault**) found echoes in fictional manipulations of character and disintegration of narrative authority. **Althusser**'s post-Marxist understanding of how ideology mediates consciousness found counterparts in novelists' insistence that language itself contains ideology and that realism, considered natural, is anything but. **Lacan** linked language to the unconscious in ways similar to novelists' use of fantasy to generate fiction (and vice versa). Both the *nouveau roman* and deconstruction (**Derrida**) explored how language itself creates meanings not always in agreement with those the author intends. Thinkers and writers have shared the activist aim of demystifying assumptions, myths, knowledge and desires, showing how these are mediated and thereby mutable.

LYNN A. HIGGINS

Further reading

Barthes, R. (1954) 'Littérature objective', *Critique* 10.

Britton, C. (1992) *The Nouveau Roman: Fiction, Theory, and Politics*, London: Macmillan (an excellent overview and analysis).

Heath, S. (1972) *The Nouveau Roman: A Study in the Practice of Writing*, London: Elek (emphasizes collective goals and techniques).

Higgins, L. A. (1996) *New Novel, New Wave, New Politics: Fiction and the Representation of History in Postwar France*, Lincoln: University of Nebraska Press (analyses formal innovations in metahistoriographic terms).

Oppenheim, L. (ed.) (1986) *Three Decades of the French New Novel*, Urbana and Chicago: University of Illinois Press (proceedings of a colloquium on historical retrospectives by novelists and critics).

Ricardou, J. (1973/1990) *Le Nouveau Roman*, Paris: Éditions du Seuil.

Ricardou, J. and van Rossum-Guyon, F. (eds) (1972) *Nouveau Roman: hier, aujourd'hui*, 2 vols, Paris: UGE.

Robbe-Grillet, A. (1965) *For a New Novel: Essays on Fiction*, trans. Richard Howard, New York: Grove.

Roudiez, L. S. (1991) *French Fiction Revisited*, Elmwood Park, IL: Dalkey Archive Press (an introduction to the oeuvre of individual novelists).

Nouvel Observateur, Le

Newspaper

Le Nouvel Observateur is a left-wing intellectual weekly, created by industrialist Claude Perdriel and editorial director Jean Daniel on 19 November 1964, with moral support from Jean-Paul **Sartre** and Pierre **Mendès France**.

Its origins go back to the political weekly *L'Observateur*, launched in 1950 by former members of the Resistance. Renamed *France-Observateur* in 1954, this became a politically outspoken, polemical title, rallying all factions of the non-Communist Left. It was among the first newspapers to denounce torture in Algeria, and was accused of undermining the morale of French troops. The newspaper's premises were bombed, and the paper seized repeatedly by the authorities. It also played a prominent cultural role, attracting contributions from historians François **Furet** and Denis Richet, sociologist Edgar **Morin**, **Nouvelle Vague** film directors, artists and intellectuals.

Declining interest in politics following the end of the **Algerian war** and internal conflicts led to falling circulation in the early 1960s. *L'Express* was also losing readers, and responded by adopting a new formula. Its editor

Jean Daniel resigned in protest, and joined Claude Perdriel and journalists from *France-Observateur* to create *Le Nouvel Observateur*, which quickly established a distinctive new style, remaining left-wing but independent. The paper was bold and innovative, boasting numerous famous contributors, including **Vilar**, Mendès France, Sartre, **Godard** and **Sagan**. In coverage of **cinema**, music, **theatre**, literature and society, it captured the mood of the times and in less than a year rapidly attracted readers. In **May 1968**, it defended the students' cause, and it was central to campaigns for women's rights, sexual liberation, and the defence of immigrants, among other causes. In the 1970s, leading intellectuals **Malraux**, **Lévi-Strauss** and **Glucksmann** wrote in its columns, and cartoonists such as Claire Bretécher and columnist Delfeil De Ton also displayed their wit (continuing to do so in the 1990s). In 1981, typical non-conformism was demonstrated in extensive coverage of the prospective presidential candidacy of ribald comedian **Coluche**. Ultimately, however, *Le Nouvel Observateur* backed François **Mitterrand**.

In the early 1980s, with the Socialists in power, the paper struggled to find its way. Advertisers withdrew their custom as 'punishment' for having supported the Left. On the other hand, continued critical independence brought a 10 per cent loss of readers. In 1984, Perdriel increased his personal investment and introduced changes: Franz-Olivier Giesbert was appointed editorial director, Jacques Julliard was entrusted with a regular political editorial, and new journalists were taken on. A more commercial news magazine formula was adopted; social, economic and cultural coverage was extended; party politics played down – and circulation was restored.

1988 brought another shock when Giesbert left to join *Le Figaro*. He was replaced by Laurent Joffrin, under whom the weekly continued to develop and prosper, thanks to initiatives such as **television** supplement *TéléObs*. Circulation grew steadily from 69,301 copies in 1966, to 226,000 in 1971, 373,055 in 1980 and 436,560 in 1994. Long-standing contributions from famous editorialists Jean Daniel,

Jacques Julliard and Françoise **Giroud** help to maintain the reputation of the leading intellectual weekly.

PAM MOORES

See also: comic strips/cartoonists; left-wing press; national press in France

Nouvelle Vague

This term, translated as New Wave (originally coined in a non-cinematic context by Françoise **Giroud** in *L'Express*), rapidly came to be used to refer to the young film-makers, usually connected with *Cahiers du cinéma*, who revitalized film production in France in the late 1950s and early 1960s. **Chabrol, Godard, Rivette, Rohmer** and **Truffaut** are its undisputed leaders.

KEITH READER

See also: cinema

Novarina, Valère

b. 1942, Geneva, Switzerland

Playwright and poet

A modern playwright noted for his rich and complex language, his works during the 1980s and 1990s have included *Le Babil des classes dangereuses* (The Babbling of the Dangerous Classes), *Vous qui habitez le temps* (You Who Inhabit Time) and *La Chair de l'homme* (Flesh of Man), which he directed at the Théâtre du Rond Point in 1995.

ANNIE SPARKS

See also: Maréchal, Marcel; theatre

nuclear power

France has one of the largest civil nuclear power systems in the world. After a period of intense opposition from environmentalists and a large fraction of the population, nuclear power is now less of an issue. The technical success of the programme has been achieved through an extreme concentration of responsibilities and economies of scale, at the cost of a very limited debate in the public arena.

Nuclear research in France started with great scientists such as Pierre and Marie Curie or Becquerel. From 1945, the Commissariat à l'Énergie Atomique (CEA) became responsible for nuclear research and development in civil and military matters. Electricity was first commercially generated in 1956, and in the late 1960s six reactors were operating, built on a CEA design close to the United Kingdom's Magnox. The CEA then had the upper hand in all matters nuclear, also mining uranium, building and operating reprocessing and enrichment plants, and controlling a whole high-technology industry. Furthermore, there were few barriers between civil and military developments as the CEA's military wing developed the bombs. The first French (nuclear) A-bomb exploded in the Sahara in 1960, before the development of the Mururoa site in the Pacific.

However, the tide started to turn against the CEA at the end of the 1960s. CEA proprietary technology was abandoned in favour of the PWR design licensed from the USA, which was preferred by the generating board, *Électricité de France* (EDF). The 1974 Messmer Plan programmed the construction of a string of near-identical PWR nuclear reactors in order to eliminate France's reliance on imported oil for electricity generation (hence the expression *le tout-nucléaire*). In less than two decades, the programme was more than fully implemented. In 1994, fifty-seven nuclear reactors were operating on eighteen sites. These reactors were built in record time, and most of them have been working satisfactorily ever since. Nuclear electricity represented nearly 80 per cent of electricity consumed in 1994, and electricity is exported to neighbouring countries, especially the United Kingdom. The key to this success can be attributed to the way the programme has been managed at all levels through its reliance on a single basic design, a series of identical reactors

from a single supplier (Framatome), a single project manager, EDF (also the plants' operator), a well trained workforce and trusted subcontractors. Furthermore, EDF had the full backing of the authorities, and had little need to worry about public enquiries. There was no debate in parliament about the programme up to the early 1980s.

The whole programme has not been accepted easily. Large-scale protests only slightly slowed it down, but they did force EDF to adopt high-profile public relations strategies and contributed significantly to the rise of environmentalism. These protests were particularly virulent in the 1970s, when a majority of the French population opposed the nuclear power programme (in the 1980s, partly because reversal seemed impossible, the opinion polls showed that a majority of the population accepted the programme). These protests affected most sites, and were related not only to worries about long-term safety of reactors and accidental radioactive releases, but also to the perceived consequences of such a large-scale programme, controlled by a small technical elite, for civil liberties and democracy.

The programme also had its technical problems. The most important failure concerns the Super-Phoenix FBR at Creys-Malville, which never operated satisfactorily and is beset with technical problems. The PWRs themselves aged prematurely in the late 1980s and early 1990s, and this necessitated the early replacement of important components. In the future, a difficult phase can be expected between 2005 and 2020, when a large number of reactors will have to be dismantled and replaced in a relatively short space of time. This may prove difficult to implement and even more costly than the Messmer programme.

FRANÇOIS NECTOUX

See also: *dirigisme*; green issues; green politics

Further reading

Goldschmit, B. (1980) *Le Complexe atomique*,

Paris: Fayard (this remains the most detailed analysis of the origins and culture of the French nuclear programme, both civil and nuclear).

Simonnot, P. (1988), *Les Nucléocrates*, Grenoble: Presses Universitaires de Grenoble (an analysis of the elite culture of the French nuclear industry).

Touraine, A., Hegedos, Z., Dubet, F. and Wieviorka, M. (1980) *La Prophètie anti-nucléaire,* Paris: Éditions du Seuil. Translated as *Anti-Nuclear Protest: The Opposition to Nuclear Energy in France,* Cambridge: Cambridge University Press (a sociological analysis of the origins of anti-nuclear movements in the 1970s).

Obaldia, René d'

b. 1919, Hong Kong

Playwright

A 1960s playwright, whose works were successfully directed by **Barsacq**, **Maréchal** and **Lavelli**. *L'Air du large* (Sea Air), *Le Général inconnu* (The Unknown General) and the popular *Du vent dans les branches du sassafras* (Wind in the Sassafras Branches) number among the best known.

ANNIE SPARKS

See also: theatre

Ockrent, Christine

b. 1944, Brussels, Belgium

Broadcaster

Ockrent is France's leading and best-loved current affairs **television** presenter, extravagantly praised by Michel **Foucault** among others. Her programme *A la une sur le 3* attracted large audiences from 1992 onwards. Her skilful interviewing techniques have contributed to her renown at least as much as her marriage to Bernard Kouchner.

KEITH READER

Oliver, Raymond

b. 1909, Langon;
d. 1990, Paris

Chef

From 1948, Oliver was owner of one of Paris's most fashionable restaurants, Le Grand Véfour, in the Palais-Royal. However, his fame springs less from this than from the fact that he was France's first **television** cook. At a time when programmes went out live and equipment lacked the sophistication of today's, this was a bold venture; he quickly became a household word, especially after the success of his best-selling book *Le Cuisinier* (1965). He refused to take part in a televised cooking contest with the British TV chef Fanny Craddock, stating that in his view women were not capable of great cuisine.

KEITH READER

See also: gastronomy

Ophuls, Marcel

b. 1921, Frankfurt, Germany

Director

The son of the film-maker Max Ophuls, Marcel became nationally known for the 1971 **documentary** *The Sorrow and the Pity* (*Le Chagrin* *et la pitié*). This, commissioned by Swiss television, presented a view of life under the Occupation in Clermont-Ferrand that flew in the face of the Gaullist and post-Gaullist myth of omnipresent resistance. Its unflattering portrayal of collaboration (often grounded in indifference) meant that French television refused to screen it for many years, and it remains a key text in the re-examination of the Resistance years. Ophuls's subsequent work – notably *Hotel Terminus* (1989), about the Lyon Gestapo leader Klaus Barbie – has continued in *The Sorrow and the Pity*'s line of lengthy, often gruelling historical interrogation.

KEITH READER

See also: cinema; Gaulle, Charles de; Vichy

Orlan

b. 1947, St-Étienne

Multimedia and performance artist

A multimedia artist since the 1960s, Orlan moved in 1980 to Ivry-sur-Seine in the Paris suburbs. In 1971 she named herself Saint Orlan, and in 1990 began the project *The Reincarnation of Saint Orlan*, in which she transforms plastic surgery carried out on her face and body into performance art; her November 1993 operation, 'Omnipresence', was transmitted live to fourteen art galleries around the world. This ongoing project, which arguably styles feminist critique as art, constitutes a dramatic interrogation of the female human body, human identity and the increasing role of technology in the contemporary visual arts.

KATE INCE

See also: feminism (movements/groups); painting

ORTF (Office de Radio-Télévision Française)

Broadcasting organization

Created by the law of 27 July 1964, the ORTF (the French Radio and Television Office) was a publicly owned commercial enterprise exercising the state's monopoly of radio and **television** broadcasting. Financial problems, its monolithic nature and its reputation of being the mouthpiece of an authoritative Gaullist regime, particularly during and following the events of **May 1968**, made it an early target of **Giscard d'Estaing**'s liberalizing reforms. The law of 7 August 1974 dismantled the ORTF, dividing it into seven autonomous organizations: three television channels, **TF1**, Antenne 2 (now **France 2**) and FR3 (now **France 3**); Radio France; TDF (Télédiffusion de France); the SFP (Société Française de Production) and INA (Institut National des Archives Audiovisuelles).

ALAN PEDLEY

See also: Gaulle, Charles de

OuLiPo

Literary group

Ouvroir de Littérature Potentielle is a literary group that uses principles from logic and mathematics in order to develop experimental writing techniques, and it was founded in Cerisy-la-Salle in 1960. Early organizers included François Le Lionnais, a chemical engineer and mathematician interested in literature, and the writer Raymond **Queneau**, best known for his novels *Zazie dans le métro*, published in 1959 and made into a film by Louis **Malle**, and *Sunday of Life* (*Le Dimanche de la vie*) from 1952, as well as his playful literary variations on a theme in *Exercises in Style* (*Exercices de style*) (1947). The group has also counted among its members Georges **Perec**, known in particular for *Things* (*Les Choses*) (1965) and

Life: A User's Manual (*La Vie mode d'emploi*) from 1978; painter Marcel **Duchamp**; poet and mathematics professor Jacques Roubaud (1932–); American writer Harry Matthews (1930–); and Italian writer Italo Calvino (1923–85).

An *ouvroir* is a sewing room – an appropriate metaphor for the group's practice of stitching together texts from various threads of language. The group's name not only contains the first letters of the words *littérature potentielle*, but also suggests phonetically the same idea: *lipo* is a prefix that means 'a missing thing', so *Où lipo* asks, 'Where [is] the missing thing?' The missing thing is that which exists only as a hypothetical possibility, such as a text that may be created using a particular linguistic constraint. One such constraint that Oulipians have experimented with is the lipogramme, a text that does not contain a particular letter or word, such as Perec's 1969 *A Void* (*La Disparition*), a full-length novel in which there is not a single occurrence of the letter 'e'. OuLiPo also practises combinatorics, in which elements of a text can be rearranged to create a variety of new texts: the most famous example of this is Queneau's *Cent mille milliards de poèmes* (One Hundred Thousand Billion Poems), which actually contains only ten sonnets, each of whose fourteen lines is interchangeable with every other line in every poem of the collection (the title of which reflects the permutations thus generated).

Many of OuLiPo's founding members were involved in the Collège de Pataphysique, a group devoted to promoting the irreverent ideas of Alfred Jarry, author of the play *Ubu roi* (1896). Another of OuLiPo's literary influences was Raymond Roussel, the eccentric early twentieth-century author who wrote many of his works, including the novel *Impressions d'Afrique* (Impressions of Africa) in 1910, using a self-imposed linguistic constraint that he called his 'procédé'.

Oulipians were among the first to recognize the creative potential of computers, which, as early as the first manifesto (1962's 'La Lipo', by François Le Lionnais), were viewed as a tool for generating texts in all their permutations. Queneau and others wrote stories whose maze of possible outcomes allowed readers to choose their own plot, thus anticipating today's hypertext.

ELIZABETH EZRA

Further reading

Bens, J. (1980) *OuLiPo 1960–1963*, Paris: Christian Bourgois (collection of texts).

Motte, W. F., Jr. (1986) *OuLiPo: A Primer of Potential Literature*, Lincoln: University of Nebraska Press (an excellent analytical study).

OuLiPo (1981) *Atlas de littérature potentielle*. Paris: Gallimard (collection of texts).

——(1990) *La Bibliothèque Oulipienne*, Paris: Seghers (collection of texts).

P

painting

The historical conditions pertaining after World War II allowed social and literary contexts for art practice in France radically different from increasingly dominant American paradigms. Memories of the Occupation, collaborationist guilt and, later, difficulties with **decolonization** in Algeria and then Vietnam all acted as contexts for a specific kind of cultural production. The parallel paths traced by **Sartre**, **Genet** and **Giacometti** typify the association of art practice with the literary and the philosophical which has characterized the French cultural scene since the war.

This difference of approach, which from the 1960s became entrenched through an increasing insistence upon 'theory as model' in art practice, has led to difficulties in assimilating French contemporary art practice into the dominant 'Modernist' aesthetic canon, which may be characterized as both apolitical and predominantly abstract. This modernist canon was, after the war, largely American, and to a certain extent this justifies French fears of 'Anglo-Saxon' cultural and economic colonization.

It should be noted that there is a certain difficulty in discussing contemporary French art practice under the heading 'painting', as from about 1960 it becomes almost impossible to distinguish between painting, **sculpture** and installation, these boundaries being first attacked and then effaced. Any selection of 'significant' artists is therefore subjective; it is dependent upon the critical paradigms used to establish criteria for judgement and as such is ultimately arbitrary.

Much of the art production in the immediate postwar period has the war as its referent, if not its subject. Anti-humanist views became plausible in a world which had demonstrated the smallness of human life. The need to renegotiate the position of mankind in relation to the new world order, and the moral duty of *témoignage* (bearing witness), encouraged an initial return to figuration.

The association of Alberto Giacometti's postwar work with **existentialism** is unavoidable. The most direct links are demonstrated by his portrait of Jean Genet, and by Genet's references to Jean-Paul Sartre in his text L'*Atelier de Giacometti* (Giacometti's Workshop), which describes the process of making the portrait. Genet's text insists upon the fragility, isolation and desperation implicit in Giacometti's practice as well as its legibility in the resultant oeuvre.

Wols is also often associated with Sartre, who defended his late paintings as 'inhuman' in their refusal of all organic or geometric forms. His evocative but non-figurative paintings were considered in the light of 'automatism'. That the artist had been incarcerated during the Occupation was seen as deepening his alienation. The late works have also been claimed as precursors for *art informel*.

Jean Fautrier (1898–1964) is perhaps best remembered for his *Otages* series of 1945. He had been staying at the Châtenay-Malabry asylum for safety during the Occupation, in the wooded grounds of which he witnessed Nazi torture and executions. The *Otages* show the mutilated remains of victims, increasingly unrecognizable as the series progresses. They were defended in a catalogue preface by André **Malraux** for bringing this contemporary and painful subject into the public domain, and the paintings were widely criticized for their experimental technique and paradoxical beauty.

Boris Taslitzky (1911–), in the tradition of *témoignage*, made large figurative works, and his position as concentration camp survivor adds authority to his powerful, allegorical *grandes-machines*. *Le Petit Camp à Buchenwald* from 1945, for example, depicts prisoners loading the skeletons of their predecessors on to carts; the incinerator behind indicates their destination. The whole is worked in a traditional oil technique, startlingly vivid in colour, and carefully arranged into the Renaissance pyramid composition. The tension between the exquisite execution, a composition usually reserved for religious or classical subjects, and the grim workaday manner of the prisoners, is disquieting in the extreme.

Even in the next generation, artists like Christian Boltanski (1944–) continue to refer to the legacy of the war. Following the more Duchampian tradition of the found object, he makes elaborate presentations of objects which stand as symbolic displacements of the biographies of their owners. These take on poignancy with reference to the collections of passports, clothing and personal effects, which are the visual trace of Holocaust victims, examples of which Boltanski first saw at Auschwitz.

Nicolas **de Staël** worked without clear allegiance. Most of his work dates from the last decade of his life, and this means that, unlike most artists of his generation, he made paintings which demonstrate a Parisian tendency of the 1950s – to fuse the illusion of space generated through colour with an insistent flatness of picture plane, figuration with abstraction. Perhaps the best example of this richly textured abstraction-with-subject is his *Les Toits* of 1952.

Francis Gruber (1912–48) embraced social realism coupled with historical allegory in his tense, brittle paintings, and the poignant, politicized contemporary motifs are as shocking as they are exquisitely crafted. His painting *Job* (1944) stands as allegory for the Occupation. The socialism/realism debate which had dominated the 1930s was reopened by Louis Aragon, for whom Gruber's work was exemplary. The dry outlines of his figures were to resurface in the work of the younger generation, and especially that of Bernard **Buffet**, of the Homme-Témoin group.

Balthus was a strong proponent of figurative painting in France until 1961, when (on Malraux's recommendation) he became restorer for the Villa Médicis in Rome. His *La Toilette de Cathy* (1933) uses the ultra-traditionalist egg tempura medium to present three figures in a room. The tension of the piece derives from his manner of presenting the figures, Cathy in particular. Her standing, full-frontal nudity is eroticized by the dressing gown resting upon her shoulders, while her gaze is abstracted, almost mutinous. Her maid combs her hair unheeded. And there is a male figure, fully clothed, seated, thoughtful and tense. Balthus's own features are recognizable in this young romantic, for whom the untouchability of such beauty appears difficult to bear.

Two artists more than any other have engendered an 'anxiety of influence' among art-makers of the postwar period. The desire for a synthesis of their respective achievements in the domains of colour and line may be seen as a constant in subsequent art practice.

Henri **Matisse** has left his own special legacy to French art history. It should not be forgotten that, in a career whose impact began at the end of the nineteenth century, much of the work which has been seminal for Modernism (the cut-outs, the Chapel at Vence) was made in the early 1950s.

Pablo **Picasso**, having joined the PCF (French Communist Party) just after the **Liberation** in 1944, went on to paint the peace murals in 1952 at the Chapelle de Vallauris, and in 1949 Aragon chose his *Dove* for use at the International Peace Congress. On the occasion of Stalin's death in 1953, he drew a heroic portrait for the front cover of *Les Lettres* *françaises*. These activities tend to be omitted from histories of Picasso's practice, as they conform neither to the dominant critical paradigm, with its refusal of political content, nor to the illusory perception of his work as incontrovertibly positive.

Antonin **Artaud** fulfilled the roles of both playwright and (towards the end of his life) artist. The Occupation and the dubious **Vichy** regime had raised questions about the status of the 'outsider' in a society which had itself run mad. Artaud made drawings, portraits and jottings during his internment: these challenge the separation of verbal and plastic expression, and were central to the recuperation and extension of 'psychotic' art in the 1950s and 1960s.

Jean **Dubuffet**'s practice would exemplify the next generation's interest in a childlike or unsocialized art. He established the *Compagnie de l'Art Brut* in 1948. Following research into the art of paranoid schizophrenics, his painting *Rue Passagère* (1961) exemplifies the resultant practice of completely filling a composition in order to avoid either uncertainty or agoraphobia. His late work challenges the traditional refusal of line as constructive component in sculpture. His *Jardin d'hiver* (1968–70) invites the viewer literally to enter the picture plane; once inside, a cave or safe place has its contours delineated by his unerring puzzle-like line.

Working with the idea of a transcendence of Western writing and strongly linked with Zen in the 1950s, Jean Degottex (1918–) went on to insist upon the value of material, using tearing, ripping, re-covering and folding in paintings of the 1970s.

Georges **Mathieu**, a key proponent of *art informel*, challenged American action painting with a large-scale gestural painting which, by reference to automatic writing, engendered a kind of Westernized ideogrammatic sign system. Pierre **Soulages** worked in large format and mostly in black on a white ground. The dynamism and tension of the works derives from the texture of thick impasto, and from the 'seams' between the painted surface and its canvas support.

Simon Hantaï (1922–), initially associated with Mathieu and ideogrammatic painting (e.g. *Sexe-Prime* from 1955), made the significant departure in 1960 in producing an all-over painting by repeatedly folding the unstretched canvas, and painting it 'blind', the pattern being revealed when the canvas was unfolded. This technique had the effect of emphasizing the structural elements of the canvas and its physical history. Initially 'organic' in aspect (e.g. *Mariale 3* of 1960), these works have become increasingly geometric in form (e.g. *Tabula* of 1980). These works may be seen as precursors to the work of the **Supports/Surfaces** group, which dominated the 1970s by associating **structuralist** theory with Maoism, and regional identity with the new unifying scientific agenda in the arts.

Lettrisme, founded by Isodore Isou (1925–), may be seen to inherit the ideogrammatic aspect of *art informel*, developing a visual language whose aesthetic it was hoped could be applied in all the arts and liberate meaning in every domain of cultural life. For example, Sabatier's *Robe à lire, roman hypographique* from the fourth Paris Biennale (1965) aimed to extend the semantic possibilities of clothing. The desire for a universal symbolic language, primal and poetic, was seen as a way of escaping from the academicism of figuration and the semantic vacuity of abstraction. Alain Satié's experimental fusions of the figure with the roman alphabet, such as the *Entassements* of 1966, effect a refusal of semantic or narrative closure, while retaining an extreme elegance and an ambiguity of referent.

Situationism, a break away from Lettrisme under Guy Debord, took a more radical view. By asserting that the process of aestheticization was not only to operate in cultural domains but should be regarded as a political step, the situationists hoped to remedy the ills of post-industrial society. Debord's *Society of the spectacle* (*La Société du spectacle*) investigates the passivity of the consumer, and proposes remedies which are progressively more radical, and increasingly architectural. The practices of 'drifting' and the analysis of 'psychogeography' were intended to help establish the criterion for changes in our understanding of the urban landscape. Slogans such as 'The beach is under the pavement' and 'Don't work' appeared around Paris following the formation of the journal Situationist International in 1957.

Ten years later, the group was to play a key role in destabilizing French student politics: the pamphlet *De la misère en milieu étudiant* (On Wretchedness in the Student Domain) was widely distributed after the Situationist takeover of the Strasbourg student body, and had considerable impact on the articulation of 'quality of life' grievances, and possible anarchist solutions. The text recommends, for example, the theft of books as a means of redistributing intellectual wealth. Through its increasing insistence, not on making art objects with exchange values, but rather on altering the way in which existing environmental factors are perceived, arguably a dematerialized art practice in itself, this challenging movement vanished from the gallery-based art scene. Students of **architecture** are still grappling with the legacy of a politicized urban landscape.

Alongside this movement, the Salon de la Jeune Peinture, organized around a more traditional PCF agenda, was particularly active both with respect to the American intervention in French Vietnam (e.g. *Salle rouge pour le Vietnam*), and striking miners in northern France. The policy of consultation and direct involvement with political issues led to strong graphic work in the style dubbed 'socialist realism'.

Under the leadership of Pierre Buraglio, in **May 1968**, the engagement of students occupying the École des Beaux-Arts in the *Atelier Populaire* (People's Workshop) followed this model, negotiating with union representatives at the Peugeot car plant, encouraging occupying workers to paint murals, and distributing powerful screen-printed propaganda.

Daniel Spoerri's (1930–) work clearly demonstrates that subject matter which distinguishes the Nouveaux Réalistes's production from American Pop Art, with which they are often inaccurately assimilated. Spoerri's characteristic *Tableaux Pièges* (1960), in which the remains of breakfast are glued to a tabletop, in turn fixed to a wall, is strongly evocative of Cubist subject matter: much Nouveau Réaliste work contains references to the reality of the fine, as opposed to commercial, art world.

César's (1921–) *Ricard, Compression dirigée d'automobile* (1962) is closer to mainstream Pop subject matter, but the insistence upon the advertised beverage (Pastis) locates the subject firmly in the culture of the Midi.

Arman's (1928–) accumulations invoke historical realities pertaining in the present by synecdoche: in *Home Sweet Home* (1960), gas masks unveil ghosts of World War II, while in *Chopin's Waterloo* (1962) the impossibility of sustaining bourgeois art is implied with reference to the destructive aspect of the Cubist genre: an entire aesthetic battle is laid out on canvas, and if there were any doubt as to the victor, the title makes it clear that the French should be on their guard.

Christo, though probably best known for work executed in America, was closely associated with the Nouveaux Réalistes in the mid-1960s. His 'wrappings' made literal the semantic transformations involved in the re-contextualization of found objects. By making the objects into gifts, the artist forced the spectator to accept the codified responsibilities of the recipient, including the obligation to repay the artist for any unsolicited pleasure gained from such (re)*pre*sentations. That this process occurs at the level of semantics and not materials allows the exchange to remain both cultural and abstract. The increasingly extravagant scale of Christo's oeuvre (which includes the wrapping of both architecture and landscape) has led to certain difficulties. In the case of his 'landscapes', environmental issues as well as those of 'health and safety' have led to litigation, while the now habitual practice of wrapping buildings under renovation has obscured the radical generosity of what has become banal gesture.

Niki de **Saint-Phalle**'s dramatic *Tirs* of the mid-1960s functioned for her as a catharsis following separation from her husband. These works incorporate objects associated with painful memories, together with paintballs, into plaster; the artist invited spectators to shoot at the resultant white collage, causing it to bleed colour, forming a portrait of her past.

Her subsequent relationship with Jean **Tinguely** led to less violent collaborations, such as the 'Stravinsky Fountain' adjacent to the **Pompidou Centre**, and her 'Tarot Garden', a vast architectural-sculpture project in Tuscany. Her early work and close relationship with Tinguely might justify her inclusion in the Nouveau Réaliste group, but her 'feminist' reworking of Gaudi in her architectural 'Tarot Garden' project is unrecognizable under such a historical definition.

One should not allow the spirituality and simplicity of Yves **Klein**'s aesthetic utopia to obscure his thoughtful contribution to art practice, which, in spite of being somewhat marginal to the Nouveau Réaliste project, is none the less beginning to receive its rightful critical acclaim. His monochromes, painted in 'International Klein blue', attempt to dematerialize the art object, a meditative aesthetic experience designed to heighten awareness. His *anthropométries* (prints of the female body using the same binderless pigment) may be seen as significant in their assertion of the post-performance trace as symbolic signifying value, replacing traditional figurative representation. His insistence upon the medieval elements contributes to a rigorously anti-industrial conception of the world, while his ritualized manipulation of these materials as semantic vehicles places him paradoxically within the avant-garde. His performance with blow torch on gilt canvas is particularly seductive, the scorched molten trace invoking not only the elements, the appearance of medieval religious art and an alchemical metamorphosis, but also emphasizing the transience of the creative moment itself. *Leap into the Void*, his photomontage self-portrait, stands as a symbol against materialism for our age.

'Ben' (Vautrier) (1935–) worked on the edge of the Nouveau Réaliste grouping. He is often dismissed as a 'clown', but this should be qualified. He is a Shakespearean clown; he speaks in jest more truths than the official court. His now moss-lined bathtub, inscribed with the words '40 years since **Duchamp** and still no new ideas' (1979) seems particularly poignant.

SIMEON HUNTER

Further reading

La Beaumelle, A. and Pouillon, N. (eds) (1987) *La Collection*, Paris: Centre Georges Pompidou/MNAM (a guide).

Lionel-Marie, A., Llopès, M-C. and Thomas, M. (eds) (1981) *Paris-Paris*, Paris: Centre Georges Pompidou/Éditions Gallimard (a catalogue of a major exhibition).

Morris, F. *et al.* (1993) *Paris Post War*, London: Tate Gallery.

Paris-Match

Magazine

This illustrated weekly news magazine, created by Jean Prouvost in 1949, represents one of the most outstanding successes of the postwar French press.

Prouvost, a textile manufacturer, had built his press empire in the 1930s, publishing popular daily *Paris-Soir* and women's magazine *Marie-Claire*. In 1938 he bought the sports weekly *Match* (created in 1928) and turned it into a general-interest, glossy magazine modelled on American *Life*. Sales soared and by June 1940 the print run reached 1.7 million copies. During the Occupation, publication ceased and, owing to allegations of collaboration against Prouvost, it was not until March 1949 that he was able to relaunch the magazine, now renamed *Paris-Match*.

Following initial difficulties throwing off its previous sporting image, *Paris-Match* rapidly established a reputation for dramatic colour photoreportage of international affairs, particularly the Korean and Indochina wars, but also current affairs at home, scientific exploits, cinema, fashion and show business. The lives of film stars and members of royalty attracted extensive photographic coverage, as did solemn occasions like deaths and funerals of national and international leaders. The magazine's political line was conformist, even chauvinistic and, by 1958, strongly Gaullist. It was the historic edition devoted to the death of General de

Gaulle that brought all-time record sales of just over 2.1 million copies in November 1970.

Average circulation peaked at 1.5 million copies in 1960, but as television grew in popularity the appeal of *Paris-Match*'s images was undermined. Competition from rival news magazines intensified and, from 1969 onwards, sales fell. In 1976 Prouvost sold to Daniel Filipacchi, who relaunched the magazine with a new image and famous slogan: 'Paris-Match – *Le poids des mots, le choc des photos* (Weighty words, photos that shock). Filipacchi also recalled Roger Therond, a member of the magazine's former successful team, as chief editor and director. Circulation soared to over a million copies. Following a decline in the 1980s, circulation stabilized in the 1990s at over 800,000 copies – well ahead of other general-interest weeklies.

Politically, *Paris-Match* is on the Right, but focuses on personalities not policies. Main sections cover news (*L'Actualité*), with explicit and sensational photoreportage on subjects ranging from massacre in Rwanda to the Paris–Dakar rally; and personalities (*Gens*), especially the private lives of the famous, such as the controversial revelations about François **Mitterrand**'s illegitimate daughter Mazarine in November 1994. A fascination for death and disaster has attracted accusations of bad taste, as demonstrated in full-page spreads showing distraught victims of the Paris bombings in 1995. The magazine defends its sensational tactics in self-righteous terms, and enjoys such a long-standing reputation as a pro-establishment institution that it achieves massive boosts in sales without risking lasting damage to its considerable reputation. The cover pages of half a century of *Paris-Match* are like a photo album recording legendary figures and events of postwar history.

PAM MOORES

See also: national press in France

Parisien, Le

Newspaper

A daily newspaper, created in 1944 (entitled *Le Parisien libéré* until 1986), which vies with *Le Figaro* for the title of leading national daily. Popular in style and readership, it uses colour extensively, and favours short, accessible articles. It is often cited because of a famous workers' conflict with founder Émilien Amaury, which lasted over two years (1975–7). On the political Right in Amaury's lifetime, it has since moved to the centre. Publishing separate national, Parisian and local editions for the Île de France, it combines national status with the appeal of a local newspaper. On 24 April 1995, following the first round of the presidential election, it achieved record sales of 659,200 copies.

PAM MOORES

See also: national press in France

parties and movements

Owing to the diversity of its political traditions, throughout the twentieth century France has had a multiparty system. The major differences between the parties have conventionally been understood in terms of a Left/Right divide. However, the substance of this divide has changed over time, and some contemporary commentators question the idea that such a dichotomy is the best way of understanding how partisan politics is now structured (see, for example, Rémond 1993).

Under the Fourth Republic (1946–58) the party system was extremely fragmented. The traditional dividing lines over socioeconomic issues and hostility to, or support for, the church were further complicated by the Cold War pro-Soviet isolationism of the Parti Communiste Français (PCF), at a time when it attracted the support of one in four voters, and the hostility of the followers of General de **Gaulle** to the very nature of the regime.

Contested on its Left and on its Right, the regime depended for its survival on uneasy 'Third Force' coalitions. Yet the differences, both in terms of policy options and sensibilities, between the various 'system' parties (principally the Parti Socialiste-SFIO or PS, the Christian Democratic Mouvement Républicain Populaire, the Parti Radical and traditional conservatives – the latter now represented by the Centre des Indépendants et Paysans – remained considerable and contributed to the instability of the Fourth Republic.

The Fifth Republic has seen a number of important changes both with regard to the configuration of the party system and to the nature of the parties themselves. The major factors which set these changes in train included: de Gaulle's domination of political life in the period from 1958 to 1969, and the creation in 1958 of a new Gaullist Party – the Union pour la Nouvelle République (UNR), later renamed the Union des Démocrates pour la République whose *raison d'être* was to support his presidency; the adoption of a majority, two ballot, voting system for elections to the National Assembly; the introduction of the direct election of the president by universal suffrage in 1962; and a degree of *détente* in East–West relations, which encouraged the PCF to come out of its Cold War isolation and seek an alliance with its erstwhile Socialist rival.

The rallying of the UNR and of certain Independents led by Valéry **Giscard d'Estaing**. (the Républicains Indépendants) around de Gaulle produced a new majoritarian phenomenon: henceforth, the idea that governments could rely on the support of a stable parliamentary majority became firmly rooted. This being the case, the other parties had to choose between allying themselves to the Gaullist-dominated majority, or forming a more resolute and united opposition (on this trend, see Wright 1989). Between 1962 and 1974, a number of changes occurred: opposition conservatives (those Independents who did not follow Giscard d'Estaing) virtually disappeared from the political map, and the Christian Democratic centre joined the right-wing majority, as did part of the Parti Radical, while the

main parties of the Left (PCF, PS and the remainder of the Parti Radical) moved falteringly towards a strategy of unity. The latter development was punctuated by François **Mitterrand**'s unsuccessful but auspicious presidential candidacies of 1965 and 1974, the refounding of the PS in 1971, when Mitterrand simultaneously became a member of the party and its leader, and the signing of the Programme Commun de Gouvernement by the three parties of the Left in 1972. In the course of the 1970s, the PS reversed its postwar electoral decline and assumed the leadership of the Left.

Following the Gaullists' loss of the presidency with the election of Giscard d'Estaing in 1974, their relations with their liberal-conservative and centrist partners were often uneasy, especially after Jacques **Chirac**'s reorganization of the Gaullist Party (henceforth called the Rassemblement pour la République or RPR) in 1976, in a bid to re-establish its dominance on the Right and strengthen his position as a future presidential candidate. President Giscard's response to this was to form the Union pour la Démocratie Française (UDF), a federation comprising his own party (renamed the Parti Républicain in 1977), the heirs of the Christian democratic tradition (now the Centre des Démocrates Sociaux, the Parti Radical and the small Parti Social-Démocrate). While these parties have maintained a degree of autonomy, they have felt it necessary, for electoral and parliamentary reasons, to remain under the UDF umbrella.

By the late 1970s, then, the party system was more polarized than ever before: two coalitions, each comprising two major formations, faced each other across the Left/Right political divide. Bipolarization in this period was not merely a by-product of the electoral system, but also an ideological reality: while the Right was slowly moving away from de Gaulle's idea of the pre-eminence of the state and lukewarm attitude towards private enterprise in favour of a more liberal approach to the economy, the PS, in order to bolster its left-wing credentials and contain its Communist ally, adopted a rhetoric of radical change. Its

1972 and 1980 programmes declared that the Left in power would, by interventionist means, 'change life', bring about a 'break with capitalism' and reorganize all institutions according to the democratic principles of *autogestion* (participation and self-management). Nationalizations and the curbing of market forces figured prominently in the joint programme of the Left. Despite the souring of relations between the PCF and the PS in the late 1970s, as the latter began to outstrip the former electorally, it was with such a programme that the Left came to power in 1981, following Mitterrand's election to the presidency and the subsequent victory of the PS. Just as Gaullism had dominated political life in the 1960s, the PS was to be the dominant party throughout most of the 1980s. However, bipolarization was challenged in this period by a number of factors.

Following the failure of its state-led reflationary economic policy in the period 1981–3, the Socialist government abandoned its former radical redistributionist ambitions and accepted the monetary constraints of the market economy, moved towards much more centrist positions and made 'modernization', 'rationalization' and 'enterprise' its watchwords. Following electoral defeat in 1986 and then the subsequent return to power of a minority Socialist government under the premiership of Michel **Rocard** in 1988, an attempt was made to translate the new, moderate policy stance into a new alliance strategy aimed at wooing centrist *députés* away from their conservative allies (on this period, see Furet *et al.* 1988). This met with little success, and the PS found itself without a clear strategy. Talk in the early 1990s of attracting ex-Communists, ecologists and 'social' centrists into a new broadly based party of the Left produced little in the way of concrete results.

The PS's ideological shift was only reluctantly accepted by a disorientated rank and file, and robbed the party of much of its distinctiveness in the eyes of the electorate. This, combined with the Left's failure to stem the rise of unemployment and a series of financial scandals implicating leading Socialists, led to crushing defeats in the 1992 regional elections, the parliamentary elections of 1993 and the European elections of 1994. However, Lionel **Jospin**'s 'honourable' defeat in the 1995 presidential election showed that the PS still occupied a space on the political spectrum which no other party could fill. Subsequently re-elected as party leader, Jospin set about reasserting the identity of the PS in terms of a modernization of its traditional (broadly speaking, social democratic) convictions.

The PS's alliance difficulties from the mid-1980s to the mid-1990s stemmed in large part from the breakdown of its relations with the PCF in 1984, when the latter refused to endorse the PS's move away from traditional Socialist policies. In addition, with the collapse of the Communist vote in the 1980s, it no longer seemed that the PCF represented a sufficient electoral force for the price paid for its support (in terms of policy concessions) to be worth paying. The decline of the PCF under the leadership of Georges **Marchais** can be attributed largely to its failure to acknowledge the worldwide crisis of Communism and its dogmatic inability to adjust its doctrine and rhetoric to the post-Cold War world. It found itself orphaned by the breakup of the Soviet Union in 1991 and increasingly fell back on the other side of its identity, jacobin nationalism. The replacement of Marchais by the more pragmatic Robert Hue in 1994 did not bring about an immediate renewal, and most commentators viewed the PCF as having been reduced to the role of a protest party. However, in the PS's leaner times, following its electoral routs of 1992–4, the regular 10 per cent of the vote scored by the PCF again made it look worth counting.

The parties of the Right used their period in opposition between 1981 and 1986 to overhaul their ideological profile and adopted a radical neo-liberal stance. The *cohabitation* Chirac government of 1986–8 attempted to apply this vision in the form of privatization, deregulation and a tougher line on law and order issues and **immigration**. Enthusiasm for thoroughgoing neo-liberalism was dampened, however, by the stock market crash of 1987 and the government's liberal-inspired reform plans for **universities** were blocked by massive student protests. The 'neo-liberal revolution' did not touch French culture and institutions to the extent that it did in the United Kingdom. Nevertheless, the voters' desire to punish the PS, combined with the majoritarian logic of the electoral system, brought the Right back to government in 1993 with a huge parliamentary majority, which did not accurately reflect its true standing in the country. The confused debates of the 1995 presidential campaign, in which two rival RPR candidates (Chirac and **Balladur**) vied for the leadership of the Right, caused divisions both between and within the RPR and UDF, and President Chirac's failure to deliver the voluntarist policies he promised in order to combat unemployemnt and social exclusion produced a deep sense of uneasiness in their ranks and made the **Juppé** government deeply unpopular.

The above changes, in the period from the mid-1980s to the mid-1990s, weakened bipolarization since the leaderships of all the main 'system' parties (PS, RPR and UDF) now seemed to be in broad agreement on the major issues (acceptance of the market economy, tempered by a degree of regulation, European integration, the Gaullist legacy in **foreign policy**). Alternatives were voiced elsewhere: by the extreme right-wing, national populist Front National (FN), which challenged the RPR and UDF, and by the ecologists, who kept their distance from the PS.

While the FN had existed since 1972, it was not until disillusionment with the Left's performance set in in the 1980s that it began to have significant electoral success. It was able to play on popular fears concerning unemployment, immigration and the 'identitarian' question with alarming effectiveness. What makes the FN different from previous extreme right-wing movements in France is the solidity of its organization throughout the country, its strategy of accepting the political regime and of contesting elections at all levels, its attempt to pass itself off as an ordinary, respectable party which is not extreme, and its ability to affect mainstream political debate – particularly regarding

immigration and particularly by using modern media methods. With the help of a proportional representation voting system the FN won thirty-five seats in the National Assembly in 1986, only to lose virtually all of them in the 1988 elections, following the reintroduction of the majority voting system. Nevertheless, in presidential elections its leader, Jean-Marie **Le Pen**, won over 14 per cent of the vote in 1988 and over 15 per cent in 1995, and the FN's share of the vote in different elections since 1986 has varied between just under 10 per cent and over 15 per cent in 1995. In 1995, the FN gained overall control of three town councils in the South.

Ecologism began to emerge as a political movement in the 1970s, bringing together grassroots activists who had cut their political teeth in isolated environmentalist protests (for example, against France's extensive **nuclear power** programme) and more politicized post-**May 1968** activists, who were suspicious of the PS's tactical and electoral preoccupations and alienated by the sterile doctrinal debates of the small parties of the extreme Left. From the outset the diversity of the different basic principles associated with ecologism made it difficult to situate on the political spectrum.

The Mouvement Écologique was founded in 1974. However, partly because of the ambiguity of their basic premises and partly because of their inbuilt suspicion of political organizations and leaders, it was not until 1984, with the founding of the Green Party (Les Verts), that the ecologists began to carve out their own political space. Even then they refused to identify themselves in terms of the conventional Left/Right distinction, since they rejected the desire for continued economic growth common to the established parties of both Left and Right.

The first significant electoral success of Les Verts came in the 1989 European elections (10.67 per cent of the vote) under the leadership of Antoine **Waechter**. The following year saw the appearance of a rival green movement, Génération Écologie, created by Brice **Lalonde**. The combined vote of the two movements in the 1992 regional elections was 14.7 per cent, but the high expectations this created were disappointed in the 1993 parliamentary elections, in which they polled only 7.63 per cent. In the 1994 European elections they fell back to 4.96 per cent and in the municipal elections in 1995 they did not get beyond 6 per cent in towns of any size. The inability of the ecologists to make a durable electoral breakthrough seemed to be due to the fact that, with the exception of environmentalism, it was not clear to the bulk of the electorate what they represent. This lack of clarity was exacerbated in the mid-1990s by rivalry between leading personalities and the extreme fragmentation of the movements claiming to represent ecologism.

All of the above factors blurred partisan boundaries. In addition, divisions in the early 1990s over the question of European integration did not correspond to those of the old bipolar system: the PS and the UDF were predominantly in favour of the Maastricht Treaty, while the PCF and the FN were against it, and the RPR and the *Verts* were divided. However, the presidential and parliamentary electoral systems continue to exert polarizing pressure on the party system. This was clearly seen in the 1997 elections, which followed President Chirac's surprise dissolution of parliament. Thanks in large part to the figurehead role of Jospin, the parties of the Left (PS, PCF, J.-P. Chevènement's small Mouvement des Citoyens, the Radicaux-Socialistes and the Verts led by D. Voynet) were able to unite on a vague but decidedly 'social' platform to defeat the parties of the Right, which were divided over the liberal-monetarist implications of the Maastricht Treaty's criteria for the creation of a single European currency. In the coalition government subsequently formed by Jospin, all the components of this *majorité plurielle* were represented. In the wake of these elections, the Parti Républicain was renamed Démocratie Libérale and the 'social' neo-Gaullist Philippe **Séguin** took control of the RPR, promising to democratize an organization whose *raison d'être* had hitherto been unconditional support for Chirac.

It is also arguable that the Left/Right distinction is still relevant with regard to moral and cultural values. The Right is more inclined to embrace traditional values, such as respect for authority, and to emphasize the importance of individual effort and of the **family** as an institution, whereas the Left's identity is more closely tied to broadly libertarian views on issues such as the death penalty, law and order and sexual ethics. When it comes to positioning the parties in relation to what may be called cultural liberalism, the exact location of the Right/Left dividing line may not be crystal clear. However, it is clear that the FN and the ecologists represent the extremities: while the former expresses the traditional positions of the Right in their most trenchant form, the latter most consistently reflect those of the libertarian Left.

Laurence Bell

See also: architecture under Mitterrand; economy; employment; European economic integration; European Union; green issues; green politics; nationalization and privatization

Further reading

Addinall, N. (ed.) (1996) *French Political Parties: A Documentary Guide*, Cardiff: University of Wales Press (an overview, with texts).

Chagnollaud, D. (ed.) (1993) *La Vie politique en France*, Paris: Éditions du Seuil (contains contributions by leading French specialists).

Flood, C. and Bell, L. (eds) (1997) *Political Ideologies in Contemporary France*, London: Cassell (contextualizes the doctrines and underlying assumptions of the major strands of French political life).

Furet, F., Julliard, J. and Rosanvallon, P. (1988) *La République du centre*, Paris: Éditions du Seuil (analysis by major political writers).

Morris, P. (1994) *French Politics Today*, Manchester: Manchester University Press (an approachable overview of politics under the Fifth Republic).

Rémond, R. (1993) 'Droite–gauche: où est la différence?', *L'Histoire* 169 (January).

Wright, V. (1989) *The Government and*

Politics of France, London: Unwin Hyman (a good overall introduction).

parties and movements: DOM-TOMs

Political activity in France's *départements et territoires d'outre-mer* (DOM-TOMs) takes place within an institutional framework of regular elections to the National Assembly and Senate, as well as municipal, departmental and regional councils or territorial assemblies. Residents also cast ballots in French presidential and **European Union** elections. Debates on the exact status of each DOM-TOM – including demands for greater autonomy or independence in some areas – often dominate political life. Especially in New Caledonia, struggles between pro- and anti-independence groups have led to periods of upheaval and violence.

France today claims ten overseas outposts, the remnants of its colonial empire. Martinique and Guadeloupe in the West Indies, French Guiana in South America and Reunion in the Indian Ocean became *départements d'outre-mer* in 1946. In principle, they have the same institutions, laws and administration as metropolitan *départements*. New laws are automatically applicable to the DOMs unless legislative acts explicitly state otherwise. The state is represented by a *préfet*, although since the decentralization programme of the early 1980s, elected *conseils départementaux* and *conseils régionaux* look after most day-to-day administration. French Polynesia, New Caledonia, and Wallis and Futuna, located in the South Pacific, became *territoires d'outre-mer* under provisions of the 1958 constitution. Specific statutes for each TOM, which vary considerably, were adopted by the French parliament. A *Haut-Commissaire* represents the state in New Caledonia and French Polynesia (and a *préfet* in Wallis and Futuna). The territorial assembly in French Polynesia elects a president and government which, since 1984, have enjoyed a great deal of autonomy, although Paris retains control of such crucial areas as defence, mone-

tary policy and international relations. Wallis and Futuna has a territorial assembly, but the traditional 'king' of Wallis and the two 'kings' of Futuna play a significant role in local affairs (particularly in relation to questions of land use and Polynesian culture). Since 1989, New Caledonia has been divided into largely autonomous 'provinces' with elected councils which deal separately with Paris; meeting together, the councils form the territory's Congress, although it has few powers. The Terres Australes et Antarctiques (TAAF), which include the French zone of Antarctica (Terre Adélie) and several sub-Antarctic islands, are also a TOM; without a permanent population, it is administered by a senior bureaucrat (assisted by appointed councils) in Reunion. The two other French outposts, St-Pierre-et-Miquelon in the northwestern Atlantic, and Mayotte in the southwestern Indian Ocean, are *collectivités territoriales*; the former is essentially a DOM, the latter a TOM. Both have *préfets* and elected assemblies.

All of the metropolitan political parties are represented in the DOM-TOMs, although they do not have the same proportional strength as in the metropole. The Parti Communiste Réunionnais, for instance, has remained a powerful rallying point for dissidents, despite the decline of the French Communist Party; the Front National secured more support in New Caledonia in the 1980s than did its counterpart in mainland France. The Rassemblement pour la République monopolizes politics in Mayotte and Wallis and Futuna. The Parti Socialiste has not been particularly strong in the DOM-TOMs, even though such local parties as the Parti Progressiste Martiniquais have lent support to the Socialists in parliament. The pro-independence movement has fragmented into groups representing various ideological tendencies, regional interests or religious and social bases. Throughout the DOM-TOMs, trade unions, religious groups and other associations are a dynamic presence on the political scene as well.

The issue of the DOM-TOMs' relationship with metropolitan France has dominated much political activity. Most parties champion greater administrative autonomy from Paris, all the while calling for the maintenance of (and usually for an increase in) the government transfers, subsidies, **social security** payments and salary bonuses for public servants on which the largely unproductive local economies depend. Some parties, which usually garner the majority of the vote, strongly defend the attachment of the DOM-TOMs to mainland France as a guarantee of economic prosperity, public order and international security. Pointing out that residents of the DOM-TOMs are fully fledged French citizens with the right of abode in the metropole and duly elected representatives in government, they reject the claim that the DOM-TOMs represent cases of persistent colonialism and insist that incorporation is a different form of **decolonization**.

Opposition groups argue that the DOM-TOMs are indeed vestiges of colonialism which, immediately or in due course, ought to gain independence. Independence movements are absent only in the smallest DOM-TOMs, St-Pierre-et-Miquelon, Wallis and Futuna, and Mayotte. In Martinique and French Guiana, and especially in Guadeloupe and Reunion, there was considerable *indépendantiste* activity in the 1970s, but thereafter it diminished markedly because of government crackdowns on militant extraparliamentary protests, the administrative decentralization of the 1980s, and the waning of the radical views with which pro-independence positions were linked. In 1981, Aimé **Césaire**, poet of *négritude* and long-time *député* from Martinique, called for a moratorium on debates concerning status, and many politicians in the DOMs seem to have heeded his counsel. Small *indépendantiste* groups remain active but have failed to gain political power.

In New Caledonia, the struggle between *indépendantistes* and 'loyalists' reached new heights in the 1980s. Most *indépendantistes* came from the indigenous Melanesian population (Kanaks), who had been reduced to a demographic minority by the immigration of Europeans, Asians and Polynesians. The expansion of pastoral, mining and settler interests had led to the dispossession of Melanesians from much of their ancestral land. Not until the late

1950s were all Melanesians granted the suffrage. Long-term European settlers (Caldoches) and more recent European migrants continued to monopolize political power and pocket the profits from the territory's rich nickel mines. Deep-seated Melanesian grievances fuelled pro-independence sentiment and led to the formation of a Front Indépendantiste, which briefly gained control of the territorial assembly in the early 1980s. In 1984, a coalition of political parties, a trade union and a women's group formed the Front de Libération Nationale Kanak et Socialiste (FLNKS) under the leadership of Jean-Marie Tjibaou; the FLNKS and a smaller pro-independence party won the support of four-fifths of Kanaks. The majority of the Caldoches joined the Rassemblement pour la Calédonie dans la République (RPCR), led by Jacques Lafleur; the RPCR secured the support of other ethnic groups, worried about their future in an independent 'Kanaky'. In 1985, a proposal by the government to move towards New Caledonian 'independence-in-association' with France satisfied none of the parties and aggravated political polarization. The next few years saw occasional boycotting of elections by the FLNKS and violence – physical harassment, riots, hostage-takings, and attacks by newly formed militias – carried out by both Kanaks and Caldoches; the police and army often responded with heavy-handed tactics. Tensions increased further during the period of *cohabitation* after 1986, when Jacques **Chirac**'s government cast its lot with the 'loyalists' and, particularly, with the RPCR, which was affiliated with Chirac's own party. A particularly tragic episode of hostage-taking by a Kanak group on the island of Ouvéa, followed by a bloody military attempt to free the hostages, occurred in the midst of the presidential campaign of 1988. Subsequently, the new government of Michel **Rocard** succeeded in convincing the FLNKS and the RPCR to sign the Matignon Accords, which divided New Caledonia into three 'provinces' (two of which came under Kanak control, although the major city, Nouméa, and its region remained under Caldoche control). The agreement foreshadowed a supposedly final vote on the future of the territory to be held in 1998; suffrage will be restricted to voters already registered in 1988 and their children who attain voting age. Renegade Kanak *indépendantistes* rejected the accords and Tjibaou was assassinated; some Caldoches also opposed the compromise. Both the FLNKS and the RPCR have since been racked by internecine quarrels. The state has injected much money into the territory and tried to maintain peace. Yet unrest festers, tensions between ethnic groups remain high, economic problems loom and New Caledonia's future status is uncertain.

In French Polynesia, several independence parties, the most important of which is now the Tavini Huira'atira under Oscar Temaru, were organized in the 1970s and 1980s. They also condemned French nuclear testing in the territory, denounced the 'artificial' transfer economy and demanded greater recognition of Maori language and culture. However, *indépendantistes* succeeded in getting only one-fifth of votes in most elections. Opponents of independence divided into a number of small parties, but the Tahoera'a Huira'atira, under Gaston Flosse, became the leading party in the territory. Flosse negotiated with Paris for a new statute for French Polynesia in 1984; according to the anti-*indépendantistes*, it gives the territory an acceptable measure of self-government and such symbols of national identity as a flag (although it is always flown alongside the French tricolour). Nevertheless, riots broke out in Papeete in 1987, provoked by labour disputes but touching on the question of independence. In 1995, President Chirac's decision to end a two-year moratorium on nuclear tests sparked major riots in Tahiti, and Temaru (who emerged as the primary spokesman for the anti-nuclear and pro-independence movement) renewed calls for independence. Chirac declared in February 1996 that testing had definitively terminated, and he promised extra funds to French Polynesia to make up for the financial shortfall the cessation of testing would undoubtedly create.

Mayotte presents a different debate scenario on the status question. When the other three islands of the Comoros archipelago voted to become independent in 1974, Mayotte voted overwhelmingly against independence. A very small group in the island now promotes unification with the Federal Islamic Republic of the Comoros, but the majority support candidates who favour complete integration of Mayotte with the metropole through *départementalisation*. Because of its economic underdevelopment and the cultural differences between mainland France and Mayotte – where almost all of the population is Muslim, and fewer than a third of Mahorais speak French – authorities in Paris have refused to sanction such an arrangement.

Many issues in DOM-TOM politics which do not directly relate to the status of the outposts nevertheless are linked with their colonial heritage. Disparities in income between ethnic groups and geographical areas – with indigenous populations and residents of outer islands and rural hinterlands disadvantaged when compared with Europeans and inhabitants of larger cities – evoke regular criticism, especially from leftist groups. Political activists demand greater recognition of local cultures, such as Creole languages and cultures in Reunion and the West Indies. Calls for increased government financial commitments come from across the political spectrum, since high labour costs and international competition make it vital to obtain high subsidies and guaranteed prices for such primary products as bananas from the Antilles, geranium from Reunion, vanilla from Tahiti and ylang-ylang from Mayotte. Politicians agree in urging Paris to align minimum wages, family allocations and other social security payments with those of the metropole, although levels for all these transfers lag behind those current in mainland France.

Nevertheless, much of local politics revolves around 'bread-and-butter' issues of access to education and employment, provisions for public services and regional development. Office-holders, particularly mayors – who are frequently also elected to departmental, regional or territorial bodies, or parliament – hold great power of influence and patronage; municipal governments count among the largest employers throughout the DOM-TOMs, for instance, and mayors have an important say in dispensing jobs. Consequently, politics in the DOM-TOMs bears many traits of clientelism and patronage (and gives rise to accusations of nepotism, voting fraud and corruption). Such politicians as Césaire, Tjibaou, Lafleur, Flosse and Temaru have defined ideologies, acted as powerbrokers in their respective areas, served as intermediaries between the DOM-TOMs and Paris, and wielded considerable economic clout because of their links with business and the administration. Even leaders of pro-independence *groupuscules* play a larger role on the small stages of the DOM-TOMs than they might elsewhere.

ROBERT ALDRICH

See also: parties and movements

Further reading

Aldrich, R. (1993) *France and the South Pacific Since 1940*, London: Macmillan (includes several chapters on politics).

Aldrich, R. and Connell, J. (1992) *France's Overseas Frontier: Départements et Territoires d'Outre-Mer*, Cambridge: Cambridge University Press (comprehensive study of DOM-TOMs with a chapter on politics).

Belorgey, G. and Bertrand, G. (1994) *Les DOM-TOM*, Paris: Éditions La Découverte (most recent general study in French).

Constant, F. (1988) *La Retraite aux flambeaux: société et politique en Martinique*, Paris: Éditions Caribéennes (study of Martinique, particularly local political issues and clientelism).

Hintjens, H. M. (1995) *Alternatives to Independence: Explorations in Post-Colonial Relations*, Aldershot: Dartmouth (includes chapters on Caribbean DOMs, French Guyana and Reunion).

Miles, W. E. S. (1986) *Elections and Ethnicity in French Martinique: A Paradox in Paradise*, New York: Praeger (a study of politics in Martinique).

Pasqua, Charles

b. 1927, Grasse

The son of a Corsican policeman, Pasqua can claim Gaullist affiliations since the time of the Resistance. He rose to public prominence as Minister of the Interior in the **Chirac** government of 1986–8, resuming this post under **Balladur** (1993–5). His tough approach to **immigration**, and to law and order issues, identified him firmly with the right wing of the neo-Gaullist RPR, and he achieved a degree of notoriety in 1988 by claiming that the Front National 'shared the same values' as the mainstream Right. In the RPR's factional infighting before the 1995 presidential elections, he associated himself with the Balladur candidacy, and this eliminated him from consideration for a ministerial post following Chirac's presidential victory.

BRIAN JENKINS

See also: Gaulle, Charles de; parties and movements

Further reading

Desjardins, T. (1994) *Pasqua*, Paris: Éditions No. 1 (currently the most recent of several biographies in French) .

Knapp, A. (1994) *Gaullism Since de Gaulle*, Dartmouth (currently the most comprehensive and up-to-date study in English of the Gaullist inheritance in its RPR phase).

Patachou

b. 1918, Paris

Singer, real name Henriette Ragon

Having opened a cabaret-restaurant, Chez Patachou, in Montmartre in 1948, and having enjoyed the support of one of her clients, Maurice **Chevalier**, this reincarnation of the female monologuists of the turn-of-the-century music halls discovered and encouraged Georges **Brassens** (also being the first to perform some of his songs). Patachou was later to perform songs by (among others) Guy **Béart**, Léo Ferré, Charles **Aznavour** and Serge **Gainsbourg**. She retired as a singer in the early 1960s. Since then, she has been compère at the restaurant-cabaret of the Eiffel Tower and appeared in the film *Faubourg Saint-Martin* (1987).

IAN PICKUP

See also: song/*chanson*

Paulhan, Jean

b. 1884, Nîmes;
d. 1968, Boissise-la-Bertrand

Writer and editor

Paulhan is notable primarily for his role as editor of the *Nouvelle Revue française* or NRF (1925–40; with Marcel Arland, 1953–68), considered by many to be the most prestigious French literary review of the twentieth century. It was at the NRF, and as adviser to Gaston **Gallimard**, that he helped to launch many authors who subsequently gained lasting renown. His own complex work ranges over a wide diversity of subjects, including explorations of the relationship between language and ideas – see *Les Fleurs de Tarbes* (The Flowers of Tarbes) of 1941 – and **art criticism**.

MARTYN CORNICK

See also: literary journals; publishing/*l'édition*

Major works

Paulhan, J. (1966–70) *Oeuvres*, Paris: Cercle du Livre Précieux.

Further reading

Cornick, M. (1995) *Intellectuals in History: The 'Nouvelle Revue française' Under Jean Paulhan*, Amsterdam: Rodopi (a study of the influence of history and politics over the intellectuals of the review).

Peduzzi, Richard

b. 1943, Argentan

Stage designer

Peduzzi is known for his architectural style, and his collaboration with **Chéreau** since 1969 on acclaimed productions including *Peer Gynt* in 1981 and *Hamlet* in 1988. He has worked with other directors in film and theatre, including **Bondy**, on his 1988 version of Shakespeare's *A Winter's Tale*.

ANNIE SPARKS

See also: theatre

Penchenat, Jean-Claude

b. 1937, Nice

Actor and director

A founder member of the **Théâtre du Soleil**, who played an active role in **collective creation** productions such as *1789* and *L'Age d'or*. In 1975, he left to form his own company, the Théâtre du Campagnol, a Centre Dramatique National since 1983, mixing collective creations with text-based productions.

ANNIE SPARKS

See also: theatre; theatres, national

Further reading

Bradby, D. (1991) *Modern French Drama 1940–1990*, 2nd edition, Cambridge: Cambridge University Press (see the section on collective creation).

Perec, Georges

b. 1936, Paris;
d. 1982, Ivry

Novelist, autobiographer and director

When he died at the age of 46, Perec, of Polish-Jewish parentage, had produced a disconcertingly varied body of work. Since then, partly through posthumous publications, he has come to be regarded as one of the most influential creators of his time. The first of two landmarks in his literary career was the publication, in 1965, of *Things: A Chronicle of the Nineteen Sixties* (*Les Choses: une histoire des années soixante*), a sociologically inspired novel about consumerism, written without dialogue but including numerous hidden quotations, including some from Flaubert's *Sentimental Education*, an earlier ironic study of deluded youth. The second was *Life: A User's Manual* (*La Vie mode d'emploi*), an extraordinary creative feat where the entire contents of a Parisian apartment block are conjured up in words and stories, each chapter focusing on the same instant in the lives of the inhabitants of one apartment at a time. Like his mentor, Raymond **Queneau**, Perec saw that eclectic erudition, combined with a highly speculative stance and a strong sense of form, could produce works which defied all established categories. While fiction and storytelling were always important to him, he identified three other themes as being of equal significance: first, the quest for ways of exploring and recording everyday reality, which inspired *Espèces d'espaces* (Kinds of Space) and *Tentative d'épuisement d'un lieu parisien* (Attempt to Exhaust a Parisian Space); second,

autobiography and memory, which led to *W or the Childhood Memory* (*W ou le souvenir d'enfance*), a work haunted by his mother's destruction in the Nazi holocaust, and *Je me souviens* (I Remember) a list of 480 'collective' or generational memories; and third, games and formal constraints, which inspired Perec, avid maker of crosswords and co-author of a treatise on the Japanese game of Go, to become a fervent member of **OuLiPo**, and to write *A Void* (*La Disparition*), a full-length novel written without the letter 'e'. Always creative and stimulating, Perec's works, including films such as *Un Homme qui dort* (A Man Asleep) and *Récits d'Ellis Island* (Ellis Island Stories – with Robert Bober), generally weave his various interests into new patterns, combining a playful lightness of touch with themes whose seriousness and importance have been increasingly recognized.

MICHAEL SHERINGHAM

See also: autobiography

Further reading

Bellos, D. (1993) *Georges Perec: A Life in Words*, London: Harvill (essential background reading).

Périer, François

b. 1919, Paris

Actor, real name Gabriel Pillu

Périer has played a wide range of roles in Parisian boulevard theatres, at the Théâtre National Populaire and the **Comédie-Française**, as well as on radio and **television**. Influenced throughout his career by **Sartre**, he appeared in the 1948 production of *Dirty Hands* (*Les Mains sale*) .

ANNIE SPARKS

See also: theatre

Perrein, Michèle

b. 1929, La Réole, Gironde

Novelist and essayist

The author of some fifteen novels, which typically dissect women's identity and situation in realist mode and are often set in provincial France, Perrein trained and worked as a journalist. Literature became her full-time career after the success (in 1970) of her eighth novel *La Chineuse* (The Tease), an exploration, in fictional form, of sex/gender difference set in southeast Asia. The winner of various **literary prizes** – including the Prix Interallé, awarded in 1984 for *Les Cotonniers de Bassalane* (The Cotton Plants of Bassalane) – she has also written plays and feminist essays.

ALEX HUGHES

See also: women's/lesbian writing

Further reading

Parker, G. (1990) 'Michèle Perrein: The Parenthesis as Metaphor of the Female Condition', in M. Atack and P. Powrie (eds) *Contemporary French Fiction by Women*, Manchester: Manchester University Press (a wide-ranging essay on Perrein's fiction).

Perse, Saint-John

b. 1887 St-Léger-les-Feuilles, Guadeloupe;
d. 1975, Presqu'île-de-Giens, France

Poet and diplomat, real name Alexis Saint-Léger Léger

Born in the Antilles and trained in France for the diplomatic service (holding a post in the Ministry of Foreign Affairs, performing diplomatic service in China, and closely associated with Aristide Briand), he wrote poetry only rarely – *Éloges* in 1911, under his civil name, and *Anabasis* (*Anabasie*) in 1924, using his pseudonym for the first time. *Anabasis* was translated by T. S. Eliot in 1938. Stripped of his French citizenship by the **Vichy** regime in 1940, he emigrated to the United States and worked in the Library of Congress. From 1940 on, he published a series of remarkable long prose poems, powerfully rhythmical and with strong epic and lyrical profiles, reminiscent of Pindar, the scriptures and Claudel. The cycle begins with *Exile* (*Exil*) in 1942, a collection containing his first 'elemental' poems, 'Pluies' and 'Neiges'. There followed the enormous epics *Winds* (*Vents*) in 1946 and *Seamarks* (*Amers*) in 1957. In 1960 he was awarded the Nobel prize for literature; Saint-John Perse expressed his strong humanistic faith in the coexistence of science and poetry in his acceptance speech.

Later volumes are devoted to a celebration of Dante (1965); a scientific/ poetic work called *Birds* (*Oiseaux*) in 1962, for which Georges **Braque** made memorable illustrations; and a work on old age, *Chronicle* (*Chronique*) (1960). The final work, in 1977, is called *Songs of an Equinox* (*Chant d'un équinoxe*). All the poems are available in the Pléiade edition of 1972.

Perse returned to France in 1957 and died there. He is remembered not only as a major poet but as a distinguished diplomat and adviser to statesmen.

WALTER A. STRAUSS

See also: poetry

pétanque

Pétanque (a combination of two Provençal words, *pieds tanqués*, meaning 'feet tied together') or *boules*, as it is also known, is a (southern) French game which involves throwing metal balls at a jack (*cochonnet*), usually on dusty surfaces of village squares (grass is unsuitable). The game generates high passion among its enthusiasts and there is a French and World Championship. The game has crossed the Channel and there is a very active British Pétanque Association.

IAN PICKUP

See also: sport

Further reading

Freeman, G. (1987) *Pétanque, the French Game of Boules*, Leatherhead: Carreau Press (an authoritative, illustrated examination of the game's history, rules, tactics and organization in the United Kingdom).

Philipe, Gérard

b. 1922, Cannes;
d. 1959, Paris

Actor

A stage and screen actor, Philipe was also strongly committed politically to the causes of the Left. His career began during the Occupation (1940–4), but he was really one of the first of the new generation of actors of the 1950s. He was a sign of the times of the new focus on youth and beauty evident in Yves Allégret's film *Les Orgueilleux* of 1953. His performance style was a radical departure from that of his flamboyant predecessors in its muted naturalness, and his understated style and performativity from the interior, mixed with his elegance and beauty, gave him an aura that no one resisted. When Théâtre National Populaire (TNP) theatre director Jean **Vilar** first spotted him in 1950, he declared he had met the real El Cid. His untimely death from cancer provoked unprecedented national mourning.

SUSAN HAYWARD

See also: cinema; *cinéma de qualité*; theatre

photography

Since the mid-nineteenth century, when Baudelaire defined it as a mere secretarial aid to the sciences and arts like printing or short-hand, photography has occupied an ambiguous and somewhat precarious place in French artistic life and thought. In the first half of the twentieth century, visual culture continued to be dominated by **painting**: photographic pictorialism, with its dusky half-tones evoking the stifling atmosphere of the turn of the century, was a shadow of impressionism, and even much of the radical work of Surrealist photographers like Hans Bellmer and Brassaï (which travestied and reconstructed banal reality) was predicated on the work of painters. However, with the founding in 1937 of the American magazine *Life*, the new concept of the photojournalist was born. In France, Eugène Atget and **Lartigue** had already been linking *reportage-photo* to a more aesthetic concept of photography, whereby photographs were seen as both documents and lyrical objects in their own right, and the existence of two magazines, *Regards* and **Paris-Match**, both keen on emulating *Life*, encouraged photographers to make their images more incisive and more informative.

After the war, photography acquired new prestige and a new dynamism, for the public was thirsty for images that bore the marks of authenticity; photographers now considered their primary function to be to document the world for those who could not witness it first hand. In 1945, the Rapho agency grouped together many photographers such as **Doisneau** and **Ronis**, whose work was informed by a humanist approach to the witnessing of world events. Then, in 1947, **Cartier-Bresson** and Robert Capa set up the Magnum agency, an international co-operative of photographers who felt concerned with the human suffering and misery caused by war, and with social and racial injustice, and who expressed their concern through their cameras and pictures. Convinced that much postwar political history would be decided in the developing countries, the Magnum photographers travelled the world, sending back their candid shots to be developed in Paris and then distributed throughout the world. The influence of Magnum can be seen in the vast 1955–6 'Family of Man' exhibition of 503 photos by 273 photographers, put on in Paris and New York. In the 1950s, *Life* and *Paris-Match* functioned as a sort of conscience of the world, presenting the last images of the war, of the subsequent activities of reconstruction and then of the traumas of **decolonization**. Throughout this period, photography was seen as the capturing of a 'decisive moment' of reality – as Cartier-Bresson famously defined it in the preface to his 1952 book, *Images à la sauvette* (Stolen Images) .

Both 'art photographers' and 'photojournalists' were now broadening the range of their subject matter and experimenting with the technical possibilities of the medium, and public interest in this art form was so great that in 1961 Michel **Tournier** was entrusted with setting up and presenting a series of monthly television programmes which showed great photographers at work; *Chambre noire* (The Darkroom) ran for four years until 1965. A dominant feature of the 1960s was the move towards 'subjective photography', a move fostered and encouraged by many intellectuals who began to question the humanistic premises of Magnum-type photography. For instance, in *Mythologies*, **Barthes** denounced what he saw as attitudes of benevolent distance and attacked photojournalistic work for its sentimental humanism and, ultimately, its complicity with injustice. In 1965, Pierre **Bourdieu** argued that, despite the fact that photography may appear to be spontaneous, accessible to all and therefore highly personal, it is one of the most structured and systematic of all cultural activities.

Photography was now increasingly at the centre of avant-garde art and intellectual debate, as well as having achieved true popular acceptance not only as a documentary medium but also as an art form. In a significant symbolic gesture, after the events of **May 1968**, the Bibliothèque Nationale separated its photographic gallery from the main buildings, redesigning it to open directly on to the street. The public visibility of photography was fur-

ther increased in 1969 by the founding by Lucien Clergue and others of the Rencontres Internationales de Photographie in Arles, probably the world's premier competition, and then by the inauguration in 1976 of the Mois de la Photo, held every second year in Paris. In 1973, the prestigious magazine *Chroniques de l'art vivant* devoted a whole issue to photography, and by 1988 interest in photography of all types was so great that the magazine *Le Photographe* was founded. Finally, the almost inevitable institutionalization took place in 1982 with the creation of the École Nationale de la Photographie (ENP) in Arles and the equally inevitable social consecration by prizes was effected in 1984 when the Société des Gens d'Image founded the Prix Niepce for photographs and the Prix Nadar for books.

In 1980, Barthes published *Camera Lucida* (*La Chambre claire*), a highly personal essay in which he insisted on the magical quality of photography which permits a new relationship with the past, the present and the future. Barthes's poetic meditation on loss, and his notion that time is both reinforced and undone in what he calls the photographic ecstasy, have influenced both the theory and practice of photography, and much of the most exciting contemporary photography is now concerned with interiority – rejecting reportage but also wishing to intensify the presence of the material world, it presents itself as 'fiction-photography' in which the image is an explicitly staged *mise-en-scène*.

MICHAEL WORTON

Further reading

Barthes, R. (1980) *La Chambre claire: note sur la photographie*, Paris: Éditions de l'Étoile, Gallimard, Le Seuil. Translated R. Howard (1982) *Camera Lucida*, London: Jonathan Cape.

Bourdieu, P., Boltanski, L. and Castel, R. (1965) *Un art moyen; essais sur les usages sociaux de la photographie*, Paris: Les Éditions de Minuit. Translated S. Whiteside (1990) *Photography: A Middle-Brow Art*, Cambridge: Polity Press.

Deedes-Vincke, P. (1992) *Paris: The City and Its Photographers*, Boston, Toronto and London: Bulfinch Press (a thoughtful and eminently readable study of the history of French photography and the part played in it by Paris; includes 100 well-chosen illustrations).

Gouvion Saint Cyr, A. de, Lemagny, J.-C. and Sayag, A. (1988) *Art and Nature: Twentieth-Century French Photography*, London: Trefoil Publications/Barbican Art Gallery (lavishly illustrated, with short but insightful essays; published to accompany the 1988 'Images de France' exhibition held in London).

Piaf, Édith

b. 1915, Paris;
d. 1963, Paris

Lyricist and singer, real name
Édith Giovanna Gassion

One of France's most internationally acclaimed popular singers of the postwar period, Édith Piaf will best be remembered for her mournful songs which articulate female pain, hardship and suffering, often caused by love. Her life is the very stuff of popular myths and legends: allegedly born under a gas lamp in the rue de la Villette in Paris and cradled by a passing gendarme, Piaf – the daughter of street performers – was temporarily blinded at the age of 8, but was 'miraculously' cured, having prayed to St Theresa. Later brought up amongst pimps and prostitutes, living mainly in the Pigalle quarter of Paris, Piaf was discovered singing in the street in 1935 by Louis Leplée, the owner of a chic cabaret, Gerny's. He took her on immediately and presented her under the name *la môme Piaf* (The Piaf Kid; *piaf* is slang for 'sparrow').

Her career seemed to be taking off dramatically when, in April 1936, the first of a series of tragedies that were to punctuate Piaf's life was to strike: her mentor, Louis Leplée, was murdered in his apartment. Piaf herself came under suspicion, was held for police questioning for two days and then released. Offered protection by the lyric writer Raymond Asso, who guided her career until the outbreak of World War II, Piaf now tasted huge success in France before touring America for the first time in 1947 (with the **Compagnons de la chanson**). It was there that she met the great French boxer Marcel Cerdan, who was to become the world middleweight champion the following year. He was also to become the great love of her life, but tragedy struck again on 27 October 1949, when Cerdan was killed in a plane crash.

The rest of Piaf's life was filled with tour after tour, the pain caused by rheumatoid arthritis which was visibly to deform her, drug-induced illness, her divorce from the singer Jacques Pills in 1956 (they had married four years earlier), her relationship with the young Georges **Moustaki** (among others) and, finally, her marriage in 1962 to the much younger Théo Sarapo (who died at the age of 34 in a car crash in 1970). Piaf herself died on 9 October 1963 – though the official date is 11 October on her death certificate, as her body was spirited by ambulance from the south of France to Paris, where she had always wanted to die. One final irony associated with Piaf is that she had been a friend of the playwright Jean Cocteau, who wrote a one-act play for her. When he learned of her death, he was preparing to write a tribute to her, but he too died the same day. Best remembered in the English-speaking world for *Milord*, *If You Love Me, Really Love Me* (*Hymne à l'amour*) and the standard *No, No Regrets* (*Non, je ne regrette rien*), Édith Piaf sang and recorded a huge number of songs, characterized by her doleful voice, with its rolled 'r' sounds and the vibrato which was also accentuated with the passing of the years. A charismatic stage performer (characteristically dressed in black) who eventually mastered the art of gesture, Piaf remains a much-admired and much-discussed figure today.

IAN PICKUP

See also: song/*chanson*

Major works

Piaf, Édith (1994) *L'Hymne à l'amour*, Paris: Livre de poche (the words of the songs recorded by Piaf).

Further reading

Duclos, P. and Martin, G. (1993) *Piaf*, Paris: Éditions du Seuil (a well-researched biography).

Piaget, Jean

b. 1896, Neuchâtel, Switzerland;
d. 1980, Geneva

Psychologist

A developmental psychologist, specializing in the maturation of children's intelligence, but trained as a biologist, Piaget first became interested in psychology through observing the intellectual development of his own children, who provide the evidence for his earliest studies, such as *The Language and Thought of the Child* (*Le Langage et la pensée chez l'enfant*) (1923). His analysis of the emergent process of reasoning in children through a mechanism of 'reflexive abstraction' based on their interaction with the material world led him to a generalized theory of knowledge which he called *Genetic Epistemology* (*Épistémologie génétique*) (1970). His thinking has been widely influential in educational theory and has inspired controversial new methods of teaching basic logical and mathematical skills to primary school children.

PETER HAWKINS

Pialat, Maurice

b. 1925, Puy-de-Dôme

Director

His career started in 1960 with intense psychological dramas in a realist idiom, such as *L'Enfance nue* (1969) and *La Gueule ouverte* (1974, with **Baye** and Philippe Léotard). In the 1980s, his films used **stars** and reached a wider public: *Loulou* (in 1980), with **Depardieu**); *A nos amours* (1983), with **Bonnaire**, seen as a key film of the 1980s; *Police* (1985), with Depardieu and **Marceau**; and *Sous le soleil de Satan* (1987), with Bonnaire and Depardieu.

PHIL POWRIE

See also: cinema

Further reading

Magny, J. (1992) *Maurice Pialat*, Paris: Cahiers du Cinéma (thematic analysis).
Toffetti, S. (ed.) (1992) *Maurice Pialat: l'enfant sauvage*, Turin: Lindau (a collection of homages, articles, interviews).

Picasso, Pablo

b. 1881, Malaga, Spain;
d. 1973, Mougins, France

Artist

The twentieth century's most celebrated artist, Picasso's prolific production includes **sculpture**, printmaking, ceramics, stage design, book illustrations and writing, as well as paintings and drawings. Although Spanish by birth, Picasso lived and worked most of his adult life in France and was closely associated with the Parisian avant-garde before World War I. In 1907, he created the founding work of Cubism, *Les Demoiselles d'Avignon*. In the 1920s, he was associated with the Surrealist movement.

He never returned to Spain after the Spanish Civil War in 1936, and spent World War II continuing to work in occupied Paris. From 1948 onwards, he lived mainly in the south of France in Vallauris and near Mougins.

Picasso's father, a painter and teacher of drawing himself, encouraged his son's precocious talent. In 1895, his father took up a post in Barcelona, an important city at the turn of the century for European intellectual life which had cultural and artistic links with France. Picasso first visited Paris in 1900, and in 1904 he settled in Montmartre, then the centre of Bohemian artistic life. His early work is categorized in two periods, the Blue Period (1901–4) which includes the famous *Self-Portrait* of 1901, and the Rose Period (1904–6), identified by its acrobats and harlequins.

It is impossible to exaggerate the impact and achievements of Cubism, which provoked the most radical change in art since the Renaissance. The influences on *Les Demoiselles d'Avignon* (1907) both of Paul Cézanne and of primitive African art, in which most of the Parisian avant-garde were interested, have been much commented on. Georges **Braque** was introduced to Picasso by Guillaume Apollinaire at this time, and the two of them worked closely together during this period. It should be noted, however, that Picasso was never part of a 'group' or 'school', and did not, for example, exhibit at the first large Cubist exhibition at the 1911 Salon des Indépendants. From 1909 onwards, Picasso began to sell canvases despite hostility from the public and the art establishment. The artistic avant-garde was largely dispersed by the outbreak of World War I, with many French artists leaving for the Front, and foreigners, including Picasso, were regarded with suspicion. Cubism came under attack as anti-French in a wave of popular and cultural xenophobia, due in part to the German nationality of one of the century's most influential art dealers, Daniel-Henry Kahnweiler. Towards the end of the war, Picasso entered into a new realist and neoclassical style of working in tune with the postwar revival of classicism in Paris. He was already becoming rich, enjoying a com-

fortable lifestyle, and he spent much of his time on the French Riviera. His classicism was imbued with the Mediterranean culture which continued to exert a fascination over him.

In 1923, Picasso met André Breton, leader of the Surrealist movement, who greatly admired his work and was the first to reproduce *Les Demoiselles d'Avignon*, in his magazine *La Révolution surréaliste* in 1925. In the same year, Picasso created another canvas which shocked the critics, *The Three Dancers*, and agreed to participate for the first time in a group exhibition, the first Surrealist exhibition at the Galerie Pierre. Throughout his career, Picasso painted portraits, often of his two wives and several mistresses, and the late 1920s and early 1930s saw a number of realist portraits. A renewed interest in sculpture is evident in the etchings of the *Vollard Suite*, on which Picasso worked from 1930 to 1937 and in which his personal mythology – with its mixture of pagan and Christian elements, bulls and minotaurs, nymphs, fauns and satyrs, and the theme of the artist and his model – became firmly established. The culmination of his work before World War II is *Guernica* (1937), a response to the bombing by Franco's German allies of the ancient Basque capital of Guernica on market day. With its palette of black, white and grey, and its **iconography** of twisted human and animal figures, *Guernica* is considered by many to be one of the century's most important anti-war paintings. Before the outbreak of World War II, the painting travelled to Norway, London and New York (where it hung in the Museum of Modern Art from 1940), returning to Madrid only in 1981 to mark the artist's hundreth birthday.

Picasso remained mainly in Paris during World War II, refusing many offers of refuge. His presence was considered by many a symbol of the Resistance, and thousands of people went to visit him at the **Liberation**. A photograph taken at a private reading of Picasso's play, *Desire Caught by the Tail (Le Désir attrapé par la queue)* – organized by Michel **Leiris** in 1944, produced by Albert **Camus**, with Jean-Paul **Sartre**, Simone de **Beauvoir**, Jacques **Lacan** and Pierre **Reverdy**, among others

– bestows upon the event a symbolic value. In the same year, *L'Humanité* announced on its front page that Picasso had joined the French Communist Party, although this is usually seen as an act of solidarity with fellow artists rather than motivated by deep political conviction. *The Charnel House* (1945), linked in its style to *Guernica*, was painted after the revelations of the Nazi concentration camps. In 1949, Picasso was asked by the Communist Party to design a poster for the World Peace Congress in Paris. His *Dove* appeared all over the walls of European cities. In 1950, he was awarded the Lenin Peace Prize. In 1951, he produced a large, overtly political painting (*Massacre in Korea*) and, in 1952, the huge murals *Peace* and *War* in an abandoned chapel at Vallauris, then named the Temple of Peace. In 1953, he produced his infamous portrait of Stalin which scandalized the party. As the Cold War hardened, he withdrew his support for the cultural activities of the French Communists.

In 1948, Picasso had moved to Vallauris in the south of France, a village full of ceramicists and potters, where he became passionately involved in ceramics, combining sculpture, **painting** and drawing. His frequent presence on the beach soon became well-known and he attracted a huge crowd of admirers. In the post-1945 period, he produced a range of work which was both retrospective and innovative. He continued with his own well-established themes while beginning a dialogue with the great masters of the past, including Delacroix, Velazquez and Manet in the 1950s. In 1955 the film-maker Henri-Georges **Clouzot** made the film *The Picasso Mystery* (*Le Mystère Picasso*), which recorded his process of creation. The 1960s saw a controversial change in style, in which the familiar Picassian mythology is apparent, together with the figures of the old man, the musketeer, the king and the painter, but in which the technique appears clumsy. His output remained prolific, with over 1,000 paintings, drawings and graphics produced in the last five years of his life, including 165 large- and medium-sized canvases for an exhibition of his recent work shown at the Palais des Papes in Avignon in 1970.

DEBRA KELLY

See also: parties and movements

Further reading

Bernadec, M.-L. and du Bouchet, P. (1993) *Picasso: Master of the New*, trans. C. Lovelace, London: Thames and Hudson (an engaging introduction to his work with good illustrations and explanations of technique and an evocative document section, despite a sometimes curious style).

Daix, P. (1993) *Picasso: Life and Art*, trans. O. Emmet, London: Thames and Hudson (a thorough one-volume discussion of his life, career and work by a writer, critic and Picasso scholar who knew him for twenty-five years).

Gallwitz, K. (1985) *Picasso: The Heroic Years*, New York: Abbeville Press (a revised and updated version of the 1971 *Picasso at 90* which concentrates on the post-1945 period).

Richardson, J. (1991) *A Life of Picasso*, vol. 1, *1881–1906*, vol. 2 (1996), *1907–1917: The Painter of Modern Life*, London: Jonathan Cape (the first two volumes of a four-volume monumental work).

Piccoli, Michel

b. 1925, Paris

Actor

A stage and screen actor and a great risk-taker in the roles he accepts and the film-makers and theatres he works for (avant-garde **theatre**, art **cinema**, unknown directors). Not all choices have been successes, but Piccoli has obtained the status of a great performer and gained national acclaim. He willingly uses his fame to help projects get off the ground, to foster new talent and to undertake risky productions (such as Faraldo's *Themroc* in 1972). His performance style exudes moral and physical strength, which he contains or releases depending on the role. As an actor he has a great range (from classical to comedy) and in any given role he can embody and sustain many contradictory characteristics: subtlety, vulgarity, insolence, robustness and vulnerability, as in **Godard**'s *Le Mépris* (1963).

SUSAN HAYWARD

Planchon, Roger

b. 1931, St Chamond

Director, actor and playwright

One of the major figures in the **director's theatre** of the postwar period, Planchon is best remembered as one of France's greatest **theatre** directors since the war, noted for his ability to combine, like his hero Brecht, concrete realism with heavily sign-laden anti-naturalistic qualities. He was one of the most successful proponents of a new blend of social-historical theatre to emerge in France during the years of decentralization in the 1950s and 1960s, drawing on the traditions of Brecht and Büchner as well as the Elizabethan theatre to form an epic style designed to appeal to all classes and backgrounds.

Planchon, however, was not an essentially political director, maintaining that campaigning would never change the fact that theatre audiences were predominantly middle-class. However, it is still true that his efforts to take theatre to the people of Villeurbanne (near Lyon) with his theatre company (Théâtre de la Cité) were remarkably successful. The son of a café-owner, the young Planchon earned his keep with a part-time bank job, while exploring the works of **Artaud** (another great influence on his work), **Bataille** and **Genet**, and indulging a love of **cinema** and modern **poetry**. His theatre career began in 1950, when he staged a winning burlesque production in a local theatre competition. With the money, the

group set themselves up as the Théâtre de la Comédie, and in 1952 moved into new premises in an old printworks, with a small theatre seating around 100 people, staging classics from Shakespeare to Calderón, and a variety of plays from the New Theatre. **Adamov**, in particular, proved a good choice for Planchon to direct, given their shared interest in Artaud. Adamov was so impressed with their work that he went on to write for Planchon's company.

In 1954, the Berliner Ensemble visited Paris. This marked the beginning of Planchon's fascination with Brechtian theatre. After meetings with Brecht, together with analysis of his production techniques and views on the role of the director as interpreter of a huge network of stage signs, Planchon staged several Brecht plays, including *The Good Woman of Szechuan* in 1958 and *Fear and Misery in the Third Reich* in 1956. At the same time, he had also become interested in the young playwright **Vinaver**, whose *Today or the Koreans (Aujourd'hui ou les Coréens)* he staged at the same time. Planchon's production prompted Adamov to bestow upon him *Paolo Paoli*, the first truly Brechtian-style play to be written in France; it became the first play the company took to Paris, and persuaded the Communist mayor of Villeurbanne to allow them a permanent base for the company. In October 1957, the company staged its first production there (Shakespeare's *Henry IV*, following popular local request); then, a year later, Alexandre Dumas's *The Three Musketeers (Les Trois Mousquetaires)*, and Planchon's first Molière production, *George Dandin*, noted for the Brechtian style of the production, with characters firmly in their historical and social background. Planchon was now considered leader of the Brechtian contingent in France, as much for his interpretations of the classics as for his Brecht productions. Between 1958 and 1961, his company made several trips to Paris, as well as continuing to play to packed houses within the Villeurbanne community. By 1963, it had been awarded the status of a Centre Dramatique National. Planchon began writing his own material, while Robert Gilbert, one of the original members of the company, helped him run the centre. Planchon's plays (more successful with the critics than the public), many of them staged in Villeurbanne, were noted for their combination of historical background and individual experience or real event, usually set in a provincial, peasant community and using a rich mix of emotion, imagery and epic range.

In 1962, Planchon staged his renowned *Tartuffe* in Villeurbanne, revived for five seasons running, and went on to direct a series of classics throughout the 1960s, including *Troilus and Cressida*, *Richard III* and Racine's *Bérénice*, confirming his status as a major director. In 1973, winning his theatre the title of Théâtre National Populaire, the third national theatre, Planchon took on the young Patrice **Chéreau** as artistic director. Chéreau worked with him until 1981, and was followed by Georges Lavaudant from 1986 to 1990. Throughout the 1970s, Planchon continued to direct plays by authors such as Vinaver and Pinter, as well as much of his own work. He also acted in films, and made his own, new version of *Dandin*, and encouraged regional dramatic centres to involve themselves with multimedia, creating in 1990 the European Cinematographic Centre in the Rhône-Alpes.

ANNIE SPARKS

See also: theatres, national

planning system

Dubbed a 'flexible' or 'indicative' planning system, this was developed after World War II in order to co-ordinate and organize the reconstruction and modernization of the socio-economic life of France, helping to establish medium-term investment and budgetary strategies for the public sector and firms. It was created by Jean Monnet, adviser to de **Gaulle** and one of the historical 'fathers' of Europe. It is managed by the Commissariat Général du Plan, a small administrative body which co-ordinates the works of sectorial commissions linking representatives of the 'social partners' (unions and management) to experts and administrations. It operated successfully during the 1960s period of high growth, but it has lost importance since the late 1970s. Nowadays, it has limited relevance to governmental strategies, but still helps to feed the public debate on future orientations of French economy and society.

FRANÇOIS NECTOUX

See also: *dirigisme*; economy; public works; regional economic development

Further reading

Estrin, S. and Holmes, P. (1983) *French Planning in Theory and Practice*, London: Allen and Unwin (a detailed analysis of the 'golden age' of French economic planning and the subsequent crisis).

Machin, H. (1989) 'Economic Planning: Policy-Making or Policy Preparation?', in P. Golt (ed.) *Policy-Making in France from de Gaulle to Mitterrand*, London: Pinter (a shorter, broader account of the evolution of planning within the context of policy-making).

poetry

French poetry of the 1945–60 period remained largely dominated, on the one hand, by a number of poets emerging from the interwoven if divergent traditions of late nineteenth-century symbolism (Mallarmé, Rimbaud and Laforgue), Surrealism, Cubism, the absurd and **existentialism**, whose careers were just reaching their peak – poets such as Pierre **Reverdy**, André Breton, Pierre-Jean **Jouve**, Paul **Éluard**, Jacques **Prévert**, Saint-John **Perse** and Raymond **Queneau**. On the other hand, a number of poets whose work received significant acclaim during this period – René **Char**, Francis **Ponge**, Henri **Michaux**, André Frénaud, Eugène Guillevic, Edmond **Jabès**, Aimé **Césaire** – continued to publish well into the 1980s and beyond. The 1960–95 period saw the further emergence of powerful new poetic voices whose work also draws considerable international critical attention – poets such as Yves **Bonnefoy**, André **du Bouchet**, Philippe Jaccottet, Édouard Glissant, Salah Stétié, Bernard Noël, Michel **Deguy**, Lorand Gaspar and Jacques Réda. The same period, however, witnessed the increasing critical recognition given to women poets more frequently supported by important smaller **publishing** houses (Folle Avoine, Rougerie, Belfond, Des Femmes, Obsidiane, Ulysse Fin de Siècle) – poets such as Andrée Chedid, Marie-Claire Bancquart, Jeanne **Hyvrard**, Anne-Marie Albiach, Joyce Mansour, Marie Étienne, Jacqueline Risset, Anne Teyssiéras, Denise Le Dantec, Esther Tellermann, Céline Zins and others. Other younger voices, meanwhile, continued to impose their wide-ranging and ever-renewed modes and tonalities: Richard Rognet, Emmanuel Hocquard, Benoit Conort, Jean-Claude Pinson, Yves Leclair, Jean-Claude Schneider, François Boddaert, Yves Di Manno, Jean-Charles Vegliante, Pascal Boulanger, Jean-Louis Chrétien.

The fifteen or so years following World War II allowed for a final flowering of the work of many great poets of modernity. Pierre Reverdy's *Le Chant des morts* (The Song of the Dead), or his 1966 posthumously published *Sable mouvant* (Shifting Sands), illustrated by **Picasso**, revealed the paradox of the mind's search for a transmutation of the chaos of the real into a harmonious 'anti-nature' that still allows for the fullest sense of our being. Paul Éluard's poems manifest his Surrealist beginnings, the power of desire, love and sense of 'fraternity', yet in an often more discreetly, yet lyrically distilled manner. The leading exponent of Surrealism, André Breton, published collections such as *Les États généraux* (Estates General), *Ode à Charles Fourier* and *Constellations*, and various volumes gathered and expanded his earlier poetry in the years preceding his death in 1966. His work, like Éluard's, Perse's, Prévert's and Queneau's, is now available in the prestigious Pléiade editions and eloquently reveals the intensity of his

exploration of 'the real functioning of the mind' in pursuit of 'a certain point in the mind from where life and death, the real and the imaginary, . . . cease to be perceived in contradiction'. Tristan Tzara, too, pushed his poetic output to fresh limits, beyond Dada's explosive revolt and the Surrealist mode of the beautiful 1931 Approximate Man (*L'Homme approximatif*) over twenty collections appeared from 1946 on, including the 1955 *A haute flamme* (Full Heat), the 1958 *La Rose et le chien* (The Rose and the Dog) and, in the year of Tzara's death (1963), his *Lampisteries/Sept manifestes Dada*, where the full weight of his early refusals and his sense of some 'moral absolute' can be meditated in the light of a need for sociopolitical action. Pierre-Jean Jouve's work, which goes back as far as 1909, was radically rethought from 1924 on, after his spiritual crisis and conversion to Catholicism. His postwar publications include *Hymne* (Hymn), *Diadème* (Diadem) and *Ténèbre* (Darkness) and Mercure de France gathered together in the 1960s all of a considerable poetic output in which Eros and Thanatos's struggle for supremacy, and guilt and suffering, define a tragic human condition. Saint-John Perse published major volumes in the thirty years preceding his death in 1975: *Winds* (*Vents*), *Seamarks* (*Amers*), *Chronicle* (*Chronique*) and *Birds* (*Oiseaux*). The supple rhythms of his long, atemporal yet sensually attuned, life-affirming, 'heroic' poems earned him the Nobel prize for literature. 1945 was the year when Jacques Prévert – the sales of whose poetry are second only to Victor Hugo's – burst upon the literary scene with *Words* (*Paroles*) and a voice at once satirical and tender, polemical and rejoicing in the marvels of the humdrum. The taut yet oddly easeful manner of Prévert, his theatre and film involvements, led to his work's being interpreted by musicians and singers such as Yves **Montand** and Juliette **Gréco**. The postwar production of Raymond Queneau blossomed with volumes such as *Petite Cosmogonie portative (Little Portable Cosmogony)*, *Cent mille milliards de poèmes* (One Hundred Thousand Billion Poems) and *Morale élémentaire*. (Elementary Morals). Both ludic and serious, Queneau's lyricism of language, rather than of sentiment, offers an at once gentle and tongue-in-cheek response to the absurd and affiliated him to the **OuLiPo** group. Other poets of considerable force and great modal variance, such as Jules **Supervielle**, Marie Noël and Jean Cocteau, also deserve attention in this postwar period.

René Char, Francis Ponge and Henri Michaux already had recognized poetic status by the end of World War II. In the forty years that followed, all three, along with André Frénaud and Edmond Jabès, both deceased in the early 1990s, and Aimé Césaire and Eugène Guillevic, established oeuvres of great range, depth and pertinence. Char, in both prose and verse poetry of exceptionally intense metaphoric and aphoristic density, maintains great aesthetic power while never yielding up ethical, philosophical or, indeed, simple quotidian urgency. Volumes such as the 1955 *Recherche de la base et du sommet* (Search for Top and Bottom), the 1975 *Aromates Chasseurs* (Hunting Aromatics) and the 1988 *Éloge d'une Soupçonnée* (In Praise of her Suspected) demonstrate unusual creative vision caught between 'fury and mystery'. Ponge, in collections such as the 1952 *Expressive Rage* (*La Rage de l'expression*), the 1967 *Soap* (*Le Savon*) and the 1977 *How a Fig of Words and Why* (*Comment une figue de paroles et pourquoi*), becomes the lifelong meditator of the logic of language's relation to things. Praised by **Sartre**, **Robbe-Grillet** and **Sollers**, Ponge exceeds such affinities in his poetics of *objeu* and *objoie*, and in his shifting from an aesthetics of closure and textual 'infallibility' to one of osmosis, unfinishedness and simple *parole*. Henri Michaux, a painter as well as a poet, gives us an oeuvre of great modal range: personal travel, fantastic imaginary journeying, exploration of the psyche's shifting states (often via hallucinogens), serene meditative texts where the corporeal and the near-mystic pulse in union. *Épreuves, exorcismes* (Trials, Exorcisms), *L'Infini turbulent* (Infinite Turbulence), *Chemins cherchés, chemins perdus* (Sought Paths, Lost Paths) and many other texts reveal a poet of rare self-penetration. Césaire's work,

from the 1946 *Les Armes miraculeuses* (Miraculous Weapons) to the 1994 *Poetry* (*La Poésie*), bears the mark of his long sociopolitical struggles, yet leaps clear of any reductive tendentiousness in its espousal of cosmic freedom, spurting 'presence', 'communication via a hiccuping of essentialness'. The extensive writings of Edmond Jabès include the trilogies *The Book of Questions* (*Le Livre des questions*), *The Book of Margins* (*Le Livre des marges*) and *Threshold; Sand* (*Le Seuil; le sable*). His is a work of ontological and textual exile, a work of nomadic errancy of mind and body, soul and expression. His books are filled with questions, elliptical dialogues, enigmas, mutating aphorisms, yet it is via such unsettledness, such endless mental drift, that some possible self-coincidence may be sought. André Frénaud – from *Les Roi Mages* (The Magi Kings) and *Il n'y a pas de paradis* (There Is no Paradise) to the 1982 *Haeres* and the 1986 *Nul ne s'égare* (No One Goes Astray) – offers a poetry at once of stridency and contemplation, of stark lucidity tipping into irony and derision, and of the ardour of 'visitation', intuition and glimpsed ecstasy. The dialectics of 'quest' and 'question' obtains synthesis only via sheer persistence. Eugène Guillevic's poetry, from the 1942 *Terraqué* on, has become progressively distilled and transparent and, in the mid-1990s, his relatively prolific work has reached a considerable public. Volumes such as *Avec* (With), *Du domaine* (Of the Domain), *Le Chant* (Song), *Maintenant* (Now) and *Possibles Futurs* (Possible Futures) display a continued fascination with the way things, consciousness and speech interconnect. The self-reflexive gaze of the poet is far from idly narcissistic and, indeed, the work of the 1980s and 1990s is increasingly centred upon principles of love, reconciliation and unity-in-difference.

Other contemporary poetic voices have reached maturity and received wide critical acclaim in the 1975–95 period. Yves Bonnefoy is the author of collections such as *On the Motion and Immobility of Douve* (*Du mouvement et de l'immobilité de Douve*) and *In the Lure of the Threshold* (*Dans le leurre du seuil*), has written brilliantly on modern poetry and art, and is a major translator of Shakespeare and Yeats. André du Bouchet has also translated Shakespeare and Joyce, has given us penetrating criticism and has created an exemplary poetic oeuvre in which the influences of Mallarmé, Reverdy and various poets of *L'Éphémère* are absorbed, meditated and surpassed. Philippe Jaccottet, too, translates – Rilke, Höderlin, Musil, Gongora, Homer – and offers us reflections, diaries, chronicles in addition to a sober yet exquisitely transparent and sensitive poetic oeuvre. Jacques **Dupin** has written widely on modern art (on **Giacometti**, Miró, Riopelle, Tàpies) and his powerful, vehement and thickly metaphoric poetry reveals the tensions of the visceral and the mental, pulsion and meditation. Andrée Chedid's work – poetic, dramatic and novelistic – is attuned both ethically and ontologically. Her 1995 *Beyond Words* (*Par delà les mots*) confirms her preferred unaestheticizing alertness to factors of love and compassion, humanity and healing, in the face of existential difficulty and dilemma. Michel Deguy, a poet-philosopher, has generated an abundant and much-admired oeuvre centred upon a meditation on figuration, metaphor, representation, our being as *être-comme*, as *poiein* – much of this in relation to other writers and artists such as Baudelaire, Rimbaud, Mann, Du Bellay or Marivaux. Salah Stétié's considerable and at once concretely and spiritually powerful work is coloured by his Lebanese origins and his immense knowledge of both Western and Eastern literature. In his writing, a great aesthetic sensibility is counterpoised by an urgent ethico-ontological vision. Other postwar poets who merit the considerable reputation and recognition accorded them include Bernard Noël, with a vast oeuvre of at once personal and sociopolitical richness; Édouard Glissant, with his teeming Antillean sensitivities; Jacques Réda and his remarkable poetry of Paris and beyond; Jude Stéfan, with his flashing provocations; and Lorand Gaspar, with his serene modulations of bareness and plenitude.

Only since the 1990s has the poetry of many more women been increasingly accessible to a larger public. Some works are manifestly philosophical or socioethical in orientation (including those of Céline Zins, Marie Étienne, Françoise Hàn and Jeanne Hyvrard), while others veer towards a certain formalism or dense self-reflexiveness (see the earlier writings of Jacqueline Risset, and the work of Anne-Marie Albiach); yet others draw more manifestly on lived experience, and are marked by a contemplated concreteness (see the work of Jeannine Baude, Heather Dohollau, Marie-Claire Bancquart, Anne Teyssiéras, Denise le Dantec, Esther Tellermann). Poets as distinct as Richard Rognet, Yves Leclair, Jean-Claude Pinson, François Boddaert and Yves Di Manno have also come to the fore in the 1980s and 1990s. As with their sister poets, their preoccupations and their manners create a rich and dynamic young mosaic.

MICHAEL BISHOP

Further reading

Bishop, M. (1985) *The Contemporary Poetry of France*, Amsterdam and Atlanta: Rodopi (eight studies of poets from Frénaud to Bonnefoy).

——(1995) *Contemporary French Women Poets*, 2 vols, Amsterdam and Atlanta: Rodopi (sixteen individual studies and global assessments).

Cardinal, R. (ed.) (1977) *Sensibility and Creation*, London and New York: Croom Helm/Barnes and Noble (twelve studies from Valéry to Dupin, plus an introduction).

Caws, M. A. (ed.) (1974) *About French Poetry from Dada to 'Tel Quel'*, Detroit: Wayne State University Press (seventeen critical essays).

Leuwers, D. (1990) *Introduction à la Poésie moderne et contemporaine*, Paris: Bordas (this offers a good general contextualization).

Richard, J.-P. (1964) *Onze études sur la poésie moderne*, Paris: Éditions du Seuil (seminal critical assessments).

Stamelman, R. (1990) *Lost Beyond Telling*, Ithaca, NY and London: Cornell University

Press (an analysis of the poetics of death and absence, from Baudelaire to Jabès).

PHIL POWRIE

See also: cinema

Point, Le

Magazine

A weekly current affairs magazine founded in 1972 by breakaway journalists from *L'Express*. Foremost among these was Claude Imbert, who has remained at *Le Point*. His outspoken editorials, rich in cultural allusions, focusing on moral and philosophical issues, are central to the publication's identity. Faithful to the American news magazine tradition, *Le Point* offers a clear synthesis of the week's events. Serious (even austere), conservative (but independent), it appeals to middle and senior managers and professionals. Since 1992 it has collaborated with *L'Express* for commercial, technical and administrative purposes, while retaining a distinct identity. Circulation in the 1990s is around 300,000 copies per week.

PAM MOORES

See also: national press in France

Poiré, Jean-Marie

b. 1945, Paris

Director

A director of comic films, Poiré's career is closely linked to that of Le Splendid café theatre troupe. He directed the film versions of two of their best shows, *Le Père Noël est une ordure* (1982) and *Papy fait de la résistance* (1983), and they have appeared in most of his subsequent films – particularly **Balasko**, who acted in his first two films as well; Christian Clavier, who (with Jean Reno) appeared in *Operation Corned Beef* (1991); and the more successful *Les Visiteurs* (1993), which was the second most popular postwar film in France with 13 million spectators.

Poivre d'Arvor, Patrick

b. 1947, Reims

Broadcaster and author

'PPDA' is all but synonymous with **television** news broadcasting in France, thanks to his lengthy stewardship (since 1987) of **TF1**'s *Journal de 20 heures*, despite an unfortunate interruption in 1996 when he was suspended for a period following a fracas with tabloid journalists and paparazzi. He is also a prolific author, notably of *Les Loups et la bergerie* (The Wolves and the Sheepfold), a thriller set around the imagined kidnapping of Philippe Léotard – actor, singer and brother of the former French Minister for Culture – in the run-up to the 1995 presidential elections.

KEITH READER

Poliakoff, Serge

b. 1909, Moscow;
d. 1969, Paris

Artist

A painter of the School of Paris, Poliakoff met the artists Kandinsky and the Delaunays, who taught him to use colour without reference to the object. A member of the postwar non-figurative group of painters, his early abstract compositions present a fragmented pictorial space with sharp-edged forms in contrasting *drapeau* (flag) colours (*Espace orangé*). In his later paintings, he uses fewer interlocking shapes and colour gradation, as in his 1956 *Composition*, to create spatial unity and balance.

ELZA ADAMOWICZ

See also: painting

Politis

Magazine

An independent, non-sectarian left-wing journal initially financed by individual subscription. Launched in January 1988 by Bernard Langlois as a weekly publication, *Politis-le Citoyen* later changed its title to *Le Nouveau Politis*. It aimed to combat 'the prevailing stultifying consensus' on key social and economic issues, and from January 1989 adopted a strong ecological focus. Despite a series of acute financial crises, in March 1992 a 100-page monthly was produced to supplement the sixteen-page weekly. Production of the monthly was abandoned in September 1993 and the weekly was expanded to thirty-two pages. In 1996, the weekly print run is 25,000.

DAVID DRAKE

See also: left-wing press

Pompidou, Georges

b. 1911, Montboudif, Cantal; d. 1974, Paris

Politician

Prime minister (1962–8) and president (1969–74), Pompidou is often held up as an example of 'Republican' egalitarianism, since he was the grandson of an Auvergnat peasant and son of a primary school teacher. He studied at the École Normale Supérieure and later entered Rothschilds **bank**, where he managed the finances of the Gaullist Party. Having been President de **Gaulle**'s chief of staff in the period 1958–62, he was then appointed prime minister by the latter (much to the annoyance of the bulk of non-Gaullist parliamentarians, who viewed him as an outsider without a parliamentary background). As prime minister, he accepted a role subordinate to that of de Gaulle, but played an important role in consolidating and controlling the Gaullist Party and promoted a new generation of Gaullists (**Chirac** and **Balladur**, for example).

Faced with the events of **May 1968**, Pompidou kept a cooler head than de Gaulle, but was rewarded for the landslide electoral victory of the Gaullist Party in June 1968 by being dismissed from the premiership, since he now appeared as a rival to the general. Following de Gaulle's resignation in 1969, he was elected president, ensuring both Gaullist continuity in power and a confirmation of the presidentialist functioning of the Fifth Republic. Indeed, he expanded the scope of the presidency, since he maintained a special interest in areas which had concerned him as premier, notably the pursuit of rapid industrial expansion, which was criticized by the opposition for favouring the business world and for its laissez-faire lack of attention to social consequences. His appointment of **Chaban-Delmas** as prime minister (with his reformist theme of the 'New Society', which supposed a significant level of state intervention) seemed to promise some response to the aspirations expressed in May 1968. However, pressure from the conservative Right of the Gaullist Party led him to dismiss Chaban in 1972 and replace him with a more servile successor (Pierre Messmer).

Under Pompidou, the style of the presidency was less aloof and somewhat more relaxed. **Foreign policy** became less strident and de Gaulle's veto on British membership of the European Economic Community was abandoned. Although Pompidou put the question of British, Irish and Danish EEC membership to a referendum in 1972, this was in large part an attempt to drive a wedge between the increasingly united Left opposition parties.

Pompidou's presidency was curtailed by terminal cancer which was, however, hidden from the public until its visible signs and his increasingly infrequent public appearances could no longer be denied. He died in office in April 1974, leaving no obvious Gaullist heir. He is remembered as a political conservative with a marked taste for modern art and French literature (he published a study of Racine's *Britannicus* in 1944, a study of Taine in 1947 and an anthology of French poetry in 1961). He was responsible for the construction of the resolutely modernist **Pompidou Centre**, an arts complex and library which is, however, known to most Parisians simply as 'Beaubourg', after the street which it displaced.

LAURENCE BELL

See also: parties and movements

Further reading

Muron, L. (1994) *Pompidou: le président oublié*, Paris: Flammarion (a re-examination of Pompidou's record).

Rials, S. (1977) *Les Idées politiques du Président Georges Pompidou*, Paris: Presses Universitaires de France (an analysis of the political ideas underlying Pompidou's policies).

Roussel, E. (1984) *Georges Pompidou*, Paris: Lattès (a biography based on extensive documentation and interviews with two hundred personalities).

Pompidou Centre and the Forum des Halles

Instigated by the president in 1969, this was the realization of **Pompidou**'s long-held private ambition, encouraged by **Le Corbusier** and **Malraux**, to build a museum of modern art in the centre of Paris. Architects Renzo Piano and Richard Rogers were selected not by monarchical fiat but by France's first international architectural competition. The site on the *plateau Beaubourg* was chosen in the context of the plans to develop the area of Les Halles after the destruction of the Pavillons Baltard. This development project caused great conflict between central and local authorities, but agreement was finally reached on plans for the Forum des Halles after the reform which gave Paris an elected mayor. It was completed in 1988.

SUSAN COLLARD

See also: architecture; art galleries/museums

Ponge, Francis

b. 1899, Montpellier;
d. 1988, Bar-sur-le-Loup, Alpes Maritimes

Poet and theorist

Ponge was for a brief while close to the Surrealists, and all his life close to painters (such as **Braque** and Fautrier). He found his poetic voice early, as well as his subject matter. The focus of all his poetry is *things*: the title of his first major collection (1942), *The Nature of Things* (*Le Parti pris des choses*), could easily be a general title for all his prose poems (which he called *proèmes*). His originality lies in a 'materialistic' lyricism: it is the creative task of human beings to provide a voice for the mute things that surround them. This quest is bound up with 1952's *Expressive Rage* (*La Rage de l'expression*), in which Ponge allows the reader to observe the making of poems – close, patient observation, precise articulation, with the help of Littré's etymological dictionary, which Ponge uses with great verbal ingenuity and a playful wit. In 1961's *Le Grand Recueil* (The Great Collection) – in three volumes: *Lyres*, *Méthodes* and *Pièces* – these notions are more fully deployed and elaborated; and this is followed by a similar volume, *Nouveau Recueil* (New Collections), in 1967. There are also long poems on soap, meadows and figs – 1967's *Soap* (*Le Savon*); *The Making of the 'Pré'* (*La Fabrique du pré*) from 1971; and *How a Fig of Words and Why* (*Comment une figue de paroles et pourquoi*) from 1977 – which, among other volumes, give ample evidence of Ponge's originality and inventiveness and his contagious humour. His motto is 'l'objet c'est la poétique' (the object is poetics, poetics is the object), and the objective is to create objeux (object-games).

WALTER A. STRAUSS

See also: poetry

pop video

The *vidéoclip* appeared in the 1980s and has had a considerable impact on the aesthetic and commercial aspects of pop music everywhere. The industry in France is highly creative (success depends on visual imagery), and this can be seen daily on *Boulevard des clips* on **M6**. This prolific genre is claimed to be the eighth art (**cinema** being the seventh) in the first *vidéoclip* encyclopedia, published in 1993.

GÉRARD POULET

See also: rock and pop; television; video imports

pornography

The French pornography industry, at any rate since the de **Gaulle** and **Pompidou** years, has flourished with comparatively few constraints of censorship. The first chains of sex shops opened in 1970, under the aegis of the journalist, Resistant and former Trotskyist, the Comte de Polignac. The liberalization of censorship under the **Giscard d'Estaing** presidency led to a mushrooming of cinemas showing an unrelieved diet of porn films, which were entitled to the same financial assistance as any other kind of film and had the advantage of being substantially cheaper to make. By the end of 1974, pornographic films represented 47 per cent of the total French cinematic output. The following year, they were declared ineligible for state financial support, and cinemas screening them became liable to a much higher rate of taxation.

There are now no more than a handful of porn cinemas in Paris; consumers of the moving image overwhelmingly favour the video cassette. These can not only be bought, but also viewed in booths in the rue St-Denis and its equivalents in provincial towns, often with the aid of a 'smart card' that enables the punter to 'zap' between the programmed variety of genres and films on offer. Video seems to have led to an increase in the number of female viewers, which rose from 5 per cent in 1980 to just short of 20 per cent in 1987. The only films to have fallen foul of the law appear to be not even those depicting bestiality – legal, provided that the animal is not mistreated(!) – but those showing pregnant women engaged in sexual activity, which has been judged to fall under the prohibition on images depicting the 'degradation of the human person'.

Most video cassettes and porn magazines currently sold in France come, unsurprisingly, from the United States, though there are a growing number from Oriental and eastern European countries. The only new French genre would seem to be the 'amateur' cassette (equivalent to the British 'readers' wives'), which made its appearance in small advertisements in 1984. Faligot and Kauffer (1987) state, a trifle idealistically, that this type of film 'takes its place in a typical trend of the 1980s, the search for a different kind of conviviality'. The differently focused concerns of feminism in France, and the traditionally laxer attitudes of Catholic cultures towards the depiction of sexual activity, have meant that pornography in France has not faced the same problems of censorship and cultural hostility as in Britain and much of the United States.

KEITH READER

See also: feminism (movements/groups); prostitution

Further reading

Faligot, R. and Kauffer, R. (1987) *Porno Business*, Paris: Fayard (a history of the industry with a degree of sociological analysis).

postmodernism

Postmodernism is an intellectual phenomenon which, in France, must be considered in a cultural and a philosophical sense. As Jean-Philippe

Mathy points out in his recent study, *French Intellectuals and America*, postmodernism has arguably become for French intellectuals a way of talking about, or even a synonym for, America, and in particular the relationship between French and American culture. In terms of general journalistic and cultural debate, discussions of postmodernism can also be considered as the latest version of debates on mass cultural forms in France. These forms can sometimes be directly linked to the USA. An obvious example would be the building of the Disneyland **theme park** in Marne-la-Vallée near Paris. Disneyland's 'postmodern' celebration of surface, inauthenticity and artifice represents for many critics the unacceptable face of corporate cultural imperialism. However, it might even be argued that Paris *intra muros* has itself become a postmodern city which acts as a museum and tourist theme park.

One explanation of the vibrancy of these types of debate in France may indeed be the tension between the Republican tradition of Enlightenment values and an enthusiastically modernizing postwar France. The question of education in both an institutional and a broadly cultural sense is extremely important. For example, in *La Défaite de la pensée* Alain **Finkielkraut** talks of *le postmoderne* as a general blurring of the boundaries between high and low cultural genres, a vague, eclectic, self-service, 'anything-goes' attitude which contradicts the Enlightenment project of Republican education. Gilles Lipovetsky, on the other hand, celebrates consumerism, **advertising** and **fashion** as a way of democratizing access to information and education.

The question of postmodernism has also appeared in the domain of philosophy and theory. In this realm, the two main thinkers of postmodernity in France are Jean-François **Lyotard** and Jean **Baudrillard**. In *The Postmodern Condition* (*La Condition postmoderne*), Lyotard rejects the notion of society as a totality, a form of 'unicity'. He also rejects Habermas's commitment to the Enlightenment as an 'unfinished project' of communication, education and consensus. In *The Postmodern Explained* (*Le Postmoderne expliqué aux enfants*) he goes further, declaring war on the notion of totality, citing the horror of Auschwitz as the crime which opens the era of postmodernity. Lyotard argues that the Enlightenment consciously thinks of itself as inaugurating a *project,* which, as far as education is concerned, draws inspiration and legitimation from two major 'metanarratives'. First, the conviction that knowledge is the right of the people in their quest for education and emancipation. The educational policy of the Third Republic, for example, finds its legitimation in this particular narrative. Second, the idea that the subject of knowledge is the abstract system of *'l'esprit spéculatif'.* Lyotard rejects as antiquated the notion of education as the process by which knowledge is transmitted to an elite which will in turn be capable of leading society towards emancipation. He claims that in a post-industrial, postmodern society these 'metanarratives' can no longer be a source of legitimation. Rather than relying upon metanarratives, contemporary legitimation should rely on a subtler agonistic world of 'language games'. To illustrate this idea, Lyotard borrows an image from Wittgenstein of language as an old city, a labyrinth of alleys and small squares. Lyotard believes that the decline of metanarratives will lead to new 'languages' being added, like suburbs, to the old city. This commitment to new language games may now appear to be overly optimistic. He has also been accused of promoting this 'performative' notion of language as a form of free-market politics. In general terms, it should be noted that Lyotard's notion of the postmodern condition has much in common with the rejection of the perceived constraints of modernity and Enlightenment thinking evinced by almost an entire generation of French postwar thinkers such as **Foucault, Derrida** and **Lacan**. These thinkers have tended to consider modernity as being dominated by too stable a notion of the subject. In this way, Lyotard links the postmodern 'moment' to the Kantian notion of the sublime. In the same way that the later Kant acknowledges the possibility that there might be productive conflict between the faculties, so Lyotard asserts that we should not expect a straightforward reconciliation between language games.

Baudrillard is often identified with post-modernism, although when questioned about his 'postmodern' credentials he is evasive, admitting only to being anti-modernist. He argues that the contemporary era tends towards the 'hyperreal'. The distinction between the real and the virtual has been lost, and we now live in a world of simulation. In effect, Baudrillard portrays Europe and America as two very different types of 'moder-nity'. European modernity is rooted in a sense of history and of the dialectic, whereas the American version of modernity entails a utopi-an break with history. Baudrillard's mode of writing may justifiably be described as 'post-modern', in that he has largely rejected the pos-sibility of representation. Writing should be a way of transforming and inventing reality, a 'fatal strategy' which seeks to push things to their limit. He has therefore gradually refined a style of fiction-theory, which owes much to sci-ence fiction, especially J. G. Ballard. *The Gulf War Did Not Take Place* (*La Guerre du Golfe n'a pas eu lieu*) is an example of this fiction-theory which caused great controversy and crystallized some elements of the debate on postmodernism. In a series of newspaper arti-cles, Baudrillard argued intially that the Gulf War would not take place, and subsequently that it *did* not take place. In simple terms, he argues that the Gulf war is only the latest in a series of media events. Reporting on the event becomes inextricably linked with the event itself, leading to a circular process of reporting on reporting. In short, Baudrillard argues that the Gulf war did not achieve reality for the viewing masses in the United States and Europe. His point is therefore partly moral. How will we recognize a real war when it comes along? Reporting on the Gulf war is absorbed into the hyperreal flow of news events for which, as McLuhan argued in the 1960s, the medium has become the message. Critics have rejected Baudrillard's stance as exaggerated and defeatist, an example of the way in which postmodernism leads to a dan-gerous relativism.

Postmodernism in the hands of Baudrillard and Lyotard is intimately related to the notion of **poststructuralism**. Both styles of thought employ metaphors and strategies of flatness and dispersion. They are both, in this sense, pluralistic and 'horizontal' forms of thought which seek to question the 'vertical' assump-tions of hierarchy, history and established prin-ciples of identity.

JOHN MARKS

Further reading

Baudrillard, J. (1991) *La Guerre du Golfe n'a pas eu lieu*, Paris: Galilée. Translated with an introduction P. Patton (1995) *The Gulf War Did Not Take Place*, Bloomington and Indianapolis: Indiana University Press.

Lipovetsky, G. (1983) *L'Ère du vide: essais sur l'individualisme contemporain*, Paris: Gallimard (eulogy of the consumerist indi-vidual).

Lyotard, J.-F. (1979) *La Condition postmod-erne: rapport sur le savoir*, Paris: Éditions de Minuit. Translated G. Bennington (1984) *The Postmodern Condition: A Report on Knowledge*, Manchester: Manchester University Press.

——(1986) *Le Postmoderne expliqué aux enfants: correspondence 1982–1985*, Paris: Galilée. Translated and edited J. Pefanis and M. Thomas (1993) *The Postmodern Explained: Correspondence, 1982–1985*, Minneapolis: University of Minnesota Press.

Mathy, J.-P. (1993) *Extrême Occident: French Intellectuals and America*, Chicago: University of Chicago Press.

poststructuralism

Poststructuralism is a movement which may be defined by its emphasis on the heterogeneity and instability of language, discourse and sub-jectivity found in the writings of a number of prominent French theorists. It came to the fore in the late 1960s and 1970s, and continued to exert an influence on critical theory and practice in the 1980s and 1990s.

The history of the reception of poststructuralism as an intellectual movement has been international, but as a movement it remains a thoroughly French phenomenon. Poststructuralism is associated with the names of three of the most renowned postwar French thinkers, Jacques **Derrida**, Michel **Foucault** and Jacques **Lacan**, the extent of whose influence on the numerous disciplines of the human sciences since the 1960s it is hard to overestimate. During the 1960s, these disciplines had undergone the equally forceful impact of **structuralism**, a movement spearheaded by theorists such as Roland **Barthes**, Gérard **Genette**, A. J. **Greimas** and Claude **Lévi-Strauss**. The following account will look in turn at the three main areas of intellectual enquiry on which poststructuralism has had the greatest impact: the subject; language, meaning and textuality; and discourse.

Poststructuralist thought makes use of the term 'subject', rather than 'individual' or 'self', both concepts laden with the presuppositions of Renaissance and Enlightenment humanism. The anti-humanist character of poststructuralism testifies to its continuity with structuralism's use of the linguistic theory of Ferdinand de Saussure, whose privileging of 'langue' (the language system) over 'parole' (the individual act of language) relegates the speaking subject to the sidelines of social, linguistic activity. Although they concur about and develop this decentring of the humanist individual or self, Derrida, Foucault and Lacan displace the subject differently.

The writings of Derrida and Foucault contain no 'theory' of the subject. They recast subjectivity as, respectively, a metaphysically underpinned structure destabilized by the restless differing and deferral of linguistic meaning (*différance*), and a product of the Enlightenment's formation of the human sciences undermined, like other of those sciences' central concepts, by the anti-humanist thrust of the philosophy of Marx, Nietzsche, Freud and their successors. According to Foucault, subjec-

tivity, the concept of 'man' that is the linch-pin of the human sciences, is situated amidst the discontinuities out of which new discourses constantly arise.

The work of Lacan, in contrast to that of Derrida and Foucault, does contain a theory of the subject, as one might expect of the leading figure and theorist of **psychoanalysis** since Freud. According to most commentators (a notable exception is the Slovenian political theorist Slavoj Žižek), it is the blend of Saussurean and post-Saussurean linguistics with psychoanalytic theory which makes Lacan a poststructuralist.

The centrality of language to Lacan's account of the subject is evident in his concept of the Symbolic Order, the sociolinguistic domain in which every subject must take up a position, masculine or feminine. In Lacanian theory the phallus as signifier of loss and separation is indubitably master in the house of language that is the Symbolic Order, a mastery Derrida terms 'phallogocentrism'. A constant of Lacan's account of subjectivity is the imperious reign of the phallus *as a signifier*, a phenomenon consequent upon the cross-fertilization of Freudian and Saussurean theory Lacan sets out in his 1957 essay 'The Agency of the Letter in the Unconscious or Reason Since Freud' ('L'Agence de la lettre dans l'inconscient ou la raison depuis Freud'). The consequences of the two changes Lacan brings about here – the inversion of the positions of signifier and signified and the placing of a bar between them – should not be underestimated. It is by means of these swiftly effected transformations of Saussure's conception of the sign that the signifier acquires the preponderance and autonomy it enjoys in Lacan's subsequent work. The superiority and independence Lacan grants to the signifier, and the continual demonstration of these qualities in his own difficult, poetic prose (a practice of writing Lacan intended to imitate the infinite slipperiness of the unconscious and of desire) are probably the best justifications for classing Lacan as a poststructuralist thinker and writer.

One other theorist who should not be omitted from a summary of poststructuralist thinking about the subject is the psychoanalyst and linguistician Julia **Kristeva**. Her work makes use of a concept of the Symbolic Order which resembles Lacan's. But, whereas Lacan's theorization of the subject revolves around the triad of Symbolic, Imaginary and Real, Kristeva's is structured around the dyad of symbolic and 'semiotic'. The semiotic describes the interruption and destabilization of symbolic meaning by the rhythms, stresses and melodies of the prelinguistic primary processes theorized by psychoanalysis. Another name Kristeva uses for this dialectical structuring of subjectivity and language is the 'subject in process'.

It is through the exploration of the most radical implications of Saussure's theory of the sign for the issues of language, meaning and textuality that some of the central ideas of poststructuralism can be grasped. It would be an exaggeration and a misrepresentation to say, as many commentators have done, that poststructuralism grants total autonomy to the signifier, thereby somehow mysteriously causing material objects and reality to dissolve into a nebulous network of textuality. However poststructuralism certainly does privilege the signifier over the signified, a privileging taken to its extreme in Lacan's inversion of Saussure's diagram of the sign.

The implications of Derrida's deconstruction of the sign are arguably even more far-reaching. His reading of Saussure attempts to show how the bar separating signifier and signified is a limit which cannot hold. Every signified one arrives at turns out to be subject to the differing and deferring play of signifiers that is *différance*. In this conception of language and textuality, fixed, stable meaning is not even a possibility. Derrida's insistence on this impossibility of arresting signification, a linguistic restlessness his own writing can sometimes be seen struggling with, contrasts starkly with Lacan's concept of the quilting point (*point de capiton*), a name for the point at which meaning is arrested and stabilized, albeit only temporarily.

Among the most stylish and impassioned performances of the instability of language and signification vital to all poststructuralist

thought are the writings of Roland Barthes which follow his structuralist phase, in particular *S/Z*, *The Pleasure of the Text* (*Le Plaisir du texte*) and *Roland Barthes par Roland Barthes*. Many ideas central to poststructuralism can be found in the sense Barthes gives to the notion of 'text', and the use he makes of this notion. The binary opposition of theory and practice is deconstructed in Barthes's insistence that 'text' is only to be found in a *practice* of writing and reading. (This emphasis on the practice of writing was an idea central to the activities of the **Tel Quel** group prominent in France in the late 1960s). Barthes sums up 'text' as follows:

> the discourse on the Text should itself be nothing other than text, research, textual activity, since the Text is that *social* space which leaves no language safe, outside, nor any subject of the enunciation in position as judge, master, analyst, confessor, decoder. The theory of the Text can coincide only with a practice of writing.
>
> (Barthes 1977: 164)

The change that can be observed in Barthes's thinking about the processes of language and meaning between the 1966 essay 'Introduction to the Structural Analysis of Narratives' ('Introduction à l'analyse structurale du récit') and 1970's *S/Z* (although commentators disagree about to what extent the latter is a structuralist or poststructuralist book) is perhaps the best illustration of the continuity and the seismic shift that exist between structuralism and poststructuralism.

A phenomenon which should be mentioned alongside the radical implications of poststructuralist thought for linguistic and textual theory is *écriture féminine*. The feminist writings of Hélène **Cixous** and Luce **Irigaray**, which are central to this movement, postdate the 1966 and 1967 publications of Derrida, Lacan and Foucault which may be said to have initiated poststructuralism, and convey much of the flavour of poststructuralist writings on language and textuality, concentrating in particular on their relationships to sexuality and the female body.

Discourse as a poststructuralist concept is associated above all with the name of Foucault, who, although called a structuralist by some, refused this categorization. Foucault was in many ways using the term 'discourse' against other poststructuralists' theorization of language and textuality: Derrida is clearly implicated in the criticism of 'the reduction of discursive practices to textual traces' Foucault made in 'The Order of Discourse' ('L'Ordre du discours'), his 1970 inaugural lecture to the Collège de France. Saussure's distinction between 'langue' and 'parole' had differentiated the language system from actual speech acts, but left room for the fully social definition of language found in Foucault's description of discourses as 'practices that systematically form the objects of which they speak' (Foucault 1989). Discursive practices occupy the same terrain as all the rules, systems and procedures which determine, and are determined by, the different forms of our knowledge. The object of Foucault's 'archaeologies' was to articulate these unthought and unspoken rules and procedures. The shift which may be observed between these studies and Foucault's later work is a shift to the analysis of how discursive rules are linked to the exercise of power. The configuration of discourses, knowledge and power can be seen in the way discursive practices select, exclude and dominate in order to ensure the continuity of the social system or the institution, while themselves undergoing reformulation in the process.

Further key terms in Foucault's work include 'genealogy', his method of studying history through the analysis of discourses, and 'episteme', a name for the open fields of relationships in which discourses are located. Despite observable shifts in his thinking between his early studies of madness and medical perception and his later work on the relationship of power and knowledge, with its idea that power is productive as much as it is repressive, Foucault's work always stressed difference, heterogeneity and discontinuity, emphases central to poststructuralism. There is no space in this account even to summarize the contribution to poststructuralism of other thinkers whose work, like Foucault's, had as much impact on the social sciences as on literary criticism and philosophy. It is a testimony to the importance of poststructuralism as a movement that its influence was felt, and continues to be felt, across such a wide range of disciplines.

KATE INCE

See also: Deleuze, Gilles; Guattari, Félix; Marxism and Marxian thought; postmodernism

Further reading

Barthes, R. (1977) *Image, Music, Text*, trans. S. Heath, London: Fontana.

Foucault, M. (1977) *Language, Counter-Memory, Practice*, ed. and trans. D. F. Bouchard and S. Simon, Oxford: Blackwell.

——(1989) *The Archaeology of Knowledge*, trans. A. M. Sheridan Smith, London: Routledge.

Harari, J. V. (ed.) (1980) *Textual Strategies: Perspectives in Post-Structuralist Criticism*, London: Methuen (contains a rich selection of poststructuralist criticism by major writers, and a valuable bibliography).

Kamuf, P. (ed.) (1991) *Between the Blinds: A Derrida Reader*, London and New York: Harvester Wheatsheaf (the most useful edited selection of Derrida's writings).

Lacan, J. (1977) *Écrits*, a selection, trans. A. Sheridan, London: Routledge.

Moi, T. (1985) *Sexual/Textual Politics: Feminist Literary Theory*, London and New York: Methuen.

Sarup, M. (1988) *An Introductory Guide to Post-Structuralism and Postmodernism*, London: Harvester Wheatsheaf (a clearly written and sensibly organized volume).

Young, R. (ed.) (1981) *Untying the Text: A Post-Structuralist Reader*, Boston, London and Henley: Routledge & Kegan Paul (a very useful selection of criticism with an invaluable introduction and editorial matter).

Prévert, Jacques

b. 1900, Neuilly;
d. 1977, Omonville-le-Petit,
Normandy

Songwriter and poet

Jacques Prévert, a one-time member of the
Surrealist movement in the late 1920s and film
scriptwriter, made his reputation as a poet in
1945, with the highly successful collection
Paroles (Words). This work was followed by
Spectacle (1951), *La Pluie et le beau temps*
(Rain and Fine Weather) in 1955 and *Fatras*
(Hotchpotch) in 1966. Prévert made his mark in
the world of French song as early as 1936 when
his *Chasse à la baleine* (Whale Hunt) was sung
by Agnès Capri. The words of his poems were
usually put to music by Joseph Kosma – the
most famous of which was *Les Feuilles mortes*
(Autumn Leaves). Singers who performed musical settings of his poems include **Montand**, Les
Frères Jacques, **Gréco** and **Mouloudji**.

IAN PICKUP

See also: song/*chanson*

prostitution

Since 1946, prostitution in France has been
legal but unregulated; soliciting and procuring
(*proxénétisme*) are, however, illegal. The former can elicit a nominal fine; the latter can be
punished with heavy fines and imprisonment,
particularly if underage women are involved.
The rue St-Denis, in Paris, is certainly France's
most notorious *quartier chaud* (red-light district). Currently, however, its status as such is
threatened by council policy aimed at removing
putes from the centre of Paris.

In 1995, it was estimated that there were
some 15,000–30,000 French women working
as professional prostitutes (95 per cent of
whom were beholden to pimps, or *proxénètes*),
with a further 60,000 working in the sex industry on a more casual basis. Currently, popular

wisdom has it that women working the traditional prostitute's 'beat', the pavement, are
these days losing their customers to what are
known as *occasionnelles*: part-time student sex
workers who advertise their services and their
highly educated charms via electronic small
ads. Rivalry also exists between women prostitutes and the Brazilian transvestites who
worked Paris's Bois de Boulogne until a permanent night-curfew forced them into other parts
of the city, putting a stop to an open display of
vice that had become something of a tourist
spectacle. If traditional red-light areas such as
the Bois are being cleaned up and/or are even
succumbing to gentrification – this is the case
as far as parts of Pigalle are concerned – some
of Paris's run-down **suburbs**, especially those
with a markedly immigrant population, offer
punters access to round-the-clock, cheap sex.

Women working in the more far-flung sectors of Paris, for example on its outer ring of
boulevards named after Napoleon's marshals,
are known as *marèches*. Another area in which
prostitution is rife is that adjacent to the gare St
Lazare.

ALEX HUGHES

See also: immigration; pornography

Psych et Po

Feminist group

One of the principal groupings within the
Mouvement de Libération des Femmes (MLF),
Psych et Po (short for 'Psychanalyse et
Politique') claimed to have laid the foundations
for a science of women in which its theory and
practice of women's liberation are located at
the intersection of **psychoanalysis** and political
action. Under the tutelage of Antoinette
Fouque, Psych et Po emerged from a study
group at the University of Paris-Vincennes, in
1968, drawing most of its members from
Maoist groups such as Gauche Prolétarienne.

Psych et Po's theory of women's oppression
and liberation developed from Jacques **Lacan's**

theory which holds that one's masculine or feminine identity is constructed in the realms of the Symbolic (the conceptual framework within which human beings think, speak, act). Furthermore, within this Symbolic Order, both masculinity and femininity are expressed through the acceptance of masculine behaviour, attributes and values derived from the masculine libidinal economy (organization of life forces and energy). Psych et Po's criticism of Lacanian theory was that it recognized only a masculine libidinal economy. The group asserted that a feminine libidinal economy, which had never functioned, also existed but had remained suppressed. Women had never, therefore, existed as real women and had never expressed themselves freely.

In order for them to do so, masculinity had to be weakened in a number of ways. First, women had to undergo psychoanalysis to understand and fight their own misogyny. Only then could they develop and assert true femininity. This process required space controlled by women, and it was to this end that Psych et Po established ventures such as the Des Femmes publishing house, bookshops in Paris, Lyon and Marseille and a number of periodicals devoted to the promotion of women's writing. Writing was a particularly important means of deriding and thus threatening masculinity and of extolling feminine attributes and values. Second, women had to gain 'erotic independence' (the practice of women's homosexuality) as a further means of undermining masculinity. Third, feminism, premised upon equal rights which, according to Psych et Po, was interested only in promoting women to positions of male power as opposed to attaining fundamental change, had to be challenged. Following this logic, Psych et Po staged and won a legal battle in 1979 to own copyright of the title MLF, thus effectively enabling itself to become the only legal voice of the French women's movement.

A campaign mounted by feminists against Psych et Po, from 1979, went some way towards discrediting the group and reviving, to some extent, a united front of feminists. If, however, Psych et Po had lost its way by the mid-1980s, it was because it had failed to capitalize from the Socialist victory of 1981 and the establishment of the Ministry for Women's Rights.

KHURSHEED WADIA

See also: *écriture féminine*; feminism (movements/groups); publishing/*l'édition*

Further reading

Duchen, C. (1986) *Feminism in France: From May '68 to Mitterrand*, London: Routledge & Kegan Paul (to date, the best account, in English, of second wave feminist thought and activism in France).

Fouque, A. (1992) *Women in Movements: Yesterday, Today, Tomorrow and Other Writings*, Paris: Des Femmes USA (a selection of Fouque's writings translated into English).

psychoanalysis

A discipline invented by the Viennese Sigmund Freud towards the end of the nineteenth century, and based upon the discovery and theorization of the unconscious mind. In the early twentieth century the ideas and therapeutic practice associated with psychoanalysis spread to most parts of the Western world. Its impact on Western intellectual life and the practice of the human sciences in the West was to make it one of the most influential disciplines of the century.

Psychoanalysis had established firm foundations in France by 1945. However, in the decades after World War II France was home to the rise of the dominant figure in psychoanalysis after Freud, and the leading inheritor of the tradition Freud had established, Jacques **Lacan**. In view of Lacan's dominance of French postwar psychoanalysis, this account will briefly summarize the main implications of Lacan's 'return' to Freud's theories and then give an overview of the institutional struggles within psychoanalysis in France since 1945 and the people involved in them.

The 'return' to Freud's discoveries and theories which Lacan proclaimed his work represented was no simple repetition, but a development and a reinvention which was the mainstay of his fifty-year career. Between 1895 and Freud's death in 1939, psychoanalysis had become a fully developed science of the human mind and human sexuality, based on the concepts of the unconscious and of the Oedipus complex. Lacan's career in fact overlapped with Freud's, as Lacan completed his doctorate in 1932 and delivered an early version of his important paper, 'The Mirror-Phase' ('Le Stade du miroir'), at the International Psychoanalytic Congress in Marienbad in 1936, before Freud's last publications, which included the 1938 paper 'The Splitting of the Ego in the Process of Defence'. But, beginning in earnest after World War II, Lacan's work was to develop in ways which would mark out its difference from Freud's, and its originality.

Lacan's single most important departure from Freudian theory was his unceasing emphasis on the importance of language to the human psyche. His originality in this regard stemmed from his use of the linguistics of Ferdinand de Saussure and Roman **Jakobson**, expounded in his 1953 and 1957 essays 'The Function and Field of Speech and Language in Psychoanalysis' ('Fonction et champ de la parole et du langage en psychanalyse') and 'The Agency of the Letter in the Unconscious or Reason Since Freud' ('L'Agence de la lettre dans l'inconscient ou la raison depuis Freud'). For Lacan, this turn to linguistics followed from his conviction that psychoanalysis was concerned above all with the understanding of human speech. A link may be seen here with a truth apparent to any practising psychoanalyst, which is that analytic interpretations are indissociable from the unconscious as it is mediated by language – the recounted dreams, phantasies and observations of the patient. 'The unconscious is structured like a language', probably the best known of Lacan's dictums, betrays his lifelong attempt to formulate the laws of intersubjective speech, a striving after

logic destined always to be destabilized by the signifying chain of unconscious desire which runs through that speech, as it does through all language.

In the early 1950s, Lacan began to mimic the wit, ambiguity and poeticity of unconscious language in his writing style, a rhetorical strategy which has gained him the reputation of being notoriously difficult to read. The contrast between Lacan's complex and allusive wordplay and Freud's pellucid prose points up another decisive difference between the two thinkers. As Malcolm Bowie puts it, 'where Freud cultivates clarity in the presentation of his ideas, Lacan cultivates obscurity' (1991). Despite his elegant command of rhetorical devices and the skill at telling stories demonstrated in his case histories, Freud always observed the imperative of clear communication incumbent upon scientists. Lacan, on the other hand, preferred to be a stylist and a guru. His astonishing skill at manipulating the French language (spoken and written) assured him a huge and admiring following, above all in the public seminars he delivered in Paris every week from 1951.

This summary of the continuity and differences between Freudian and Lacanian psychoanalysis concludes with a brief comparison of some of the chief concepts of each thinker (see Grosz 1990: Chapters 2–5; Bowie 1991). Lacan replaces Freud's notion of the Oedipus complex with his concept of the Symbolic Order, one of a triad of interrelated terms central to Lacanian theory, Symbolic, Imaginary and Real. Where Freud describes the maturation of infantile sexuality through the Oedipal crisis (which takes place differently for boys and girls, and is the moment of the construction of sexual difference), and retains a biological emphasis, Lacan stresses the symbolic, non-biological construction of sexual identity. For Lacan, the Imaginary corresponds to the pre-Oedipal period in which the child recognizes its own unity but not its separation from the mother's body. The Imaginary also describes subsequent operations of the ego such as identification and falling in love. The sense of wholeness and completion bestowed on the subject by such states is relentlessly undermined by the loss, division and lack internal to the Symbolic Order (that the child's recognition of its image at the mirror stage is a *mis*recognition is a vital example of this). Lacan's emphasis is always on Symbolic processes at the expense of Imaginary ones, as his persistent exploration of the role of language in the psyche would suggest. The Real, the last of Lacan's triad of terms, is neither Symbolic nor Imaginary, but is that upon which language is at work, a material vortex which escapes all signifying processes. 'The Real never fits comfortably into any conceptualization. Hence Lacan's point that the Real is impossible to grasp; it must be different from what words say it is' (Wright 1986).

Throughout the Occupation of France by the Nazis during World War II, the public activity of the Société psychanalytique de Paris (SPP), then under the directorship of Marie Bonaparte, was suspended, a contrast to the Nazification of psychoanalysis which took place in Germany. Elisabeth Roudinesco suggests that, in France, 'starting with 1945, the history of the implantation of Freudianism is a closed book. The historian leaves the terrain of the grandiose adventure of the pioneers for the less heroic turf of the negotiation of conflicts' (1990). There began a phase of struggles inside psychoanalytic institutions which was not peculiar to France, an emergence of national traditions of psychoanalysis which could happen only because Freud's doctrine was by now internationally established. Psychoanalysis would, nevertheless, undergo enormously different forms of integration and development in the different countries to which it had travelled.

The path taken by French psychoanalysis in the late 1940s and 1950s was in marked contrast to its development and subsequent character in the United States. American psychoanalysis prioritized the ego over the unconscious and, rather than being analytic or theoretical, was predominantly adaptive in nature. The association recognized before all others by American psychoanalysts was the American Psychoanalytic Association, 'the largest and most individualistic federative member of the international movement' (Roudinesco 1990). It was on this international movement, the International Psychoanalytic Association (IPA), that the careers of Lacan and other dominant figures in French psychoanalysis would leave their mark. Apart from Lacan himself, the principal players in the institutional drama of French psychoanalysis during the 1950s were Sacha Nacht, a Romanian Jew who had emigrated to Paris in 1919, and Daniel Lagache, an academic liberal. Nacht had a particular reverence for medicine partly shared by Lagache, who favoured the integration of psychoanalysis into psychology via the structures of academia. While the different stances of these two men were ultimately to prove equally acceptable to the IPA, Lacan's was not.

For much of the 1950s, the SPP vied with an organization founded in June 1953, the Société française de Psychanalyse (SFP). This association brought together a younger generation of analysts, the 'juniors', which included men such as Jean Laplanche, Jean-Bertrand Pontalis and Serge Leclaire. The SFP was officially dissolved in 1965 after some of its supporters had reaffiliated to the IPA, under the demand that they do so or declare loyalty to Lacan, whom the IPA refused to readmit. In 1963, Laplanche and Pontalis, along with other prominent psychoanalysts such as Didier Anzieu and Wladimir Granoff, participated in the foundation of an organization called the Association psychanalytique de France, which was recognized by the IPA. This decisive split in French psychoanalysis, which Lacan referred to as his 'excommunication' from the IPA, saw the foundation, in June 1964, of his École freudienne de Paris (EFP).

It was under the auspices of the École freudienne in the 1960s that the heyday of Lacanian psychoanalysis occurred. Between 1964 and 1969, thanks to Louis **Althusser** (whose theory of ideology was more marked by Freudian and Lacanian psychoanalysis than any other Marxist thinker of his time) Lacan gave his seminar in the Salle Dussane of the École Normale Supérieure, bastion of the

French academic elite. Lacan was involved in the structuralist enterprise of this decade through his work on linguistics and borrowings from the anthropologist Claude Lévi-Strauss. At the same time, philosophy, and in particular the philosopher Jacques Derrida, began to interrogate psychoanalysis from the deconstructive perspective emerging alongside poststructuralist thought. The work of the Bulgarian émigrée Julia Kristeva incorporated psychoanalysis into linguistics and poetics. And the 1969 encounter of the therapist Félix Guattari (a former analysand of Lacan's) with the philosopher Gilles Deleuze was to produce, in 1972, a co-authored volume significant in the history of French psychoanalysis for its denunciation of Freudian Oedipalism. In its place, Deleuze and Guattari's L'Anti-Oedipe proposed a 'schizo-analysis' based on the machine-like and plural character of non-Oedipal desire. Finally in this period, the centrality of psychoanalysis to Parisian intellectual life was nowhere more apparent than in its influence on the wave of feminist activity which followed the May 1968 events and was testified to in the name of the prominent feminist organization Psych et Po.

The ejection of Lacan's seminar from its favoured location in the École Normale Supérieure in March 1969 was one of numerous insults he turned to his advantage, but from the late 1960s the position of the École freudienne became less secure. Conflict emerged between Lacan and Serge Leclaire, who had remained a loyal (although not obsequious) disciple since being sent to Lacan for a training analysis by Françoise Dolto in the late 1940s. (Dolto herself had always been active in Lacan's circle, while retaining an intellectual and theoretical independence derived from her own clinical experience, which was predominantly with children. She remained a close personal friend of Lacan's until his death.) Leclaire was the initiator of the foundation of a department of psychoanalysis at the University of Vincennes (Paris VIII), an experiment born out of the upheaval of 1968, and one to which Lacan was hostile. In the 1970s women, who had always been numerous in the École

Freudienne, played a more public role. In 1974, Catherine Clément prepared a special issue of the journal L'Arc paying homage to Lacan, and written exclusively by women. But in the same year Luce Irigaray's Speculum of the Other Woman (Speculum de l'autre femme) included a critique of Lacan, making greater use of a Derridean approach in its interrogation of the occlusion of la femme in Western metaphysical philosophy. Another leading woman analyst, Michèle Montrelay, was to be a leading upholder of juridically correct procedure during the dissolution of the École freudienne in 1979–80.

Major factors in the collapse of the École freudienne were Lacan's withdrawal from the public activity of his school from 1978, and internal dissent about the passe (the procedure Lacan had introduced as the route from a training analysis to fully qualified status) from 1977. The crisis became public on 30 September 1979, and a legal battle ensued which lasted into 1980. Symbolic dissolution of the school had followed Lacan's letter of 5 January 1980 instructing that it take place, but several meetings of the entire membership of the school were required in order to dissolve it juridically. Lacanian psychoanalysis had already divided into four currents of differing degrees of stability by the time of Lacan's death on 9 September 1981.

The legal heir to Lacan's École freudienne was Jacques-Alain Miller, a follower since 1963–4 and his son-in-law since 1966. The beginnings of 'Millerism' can perhaps be dated from the transcription to writing of Lacan's seminars, a task Miller undertook to do wholesale when his first attempt in 1972, on volume 11, The Four Fundamental Concepts of Psychoanalysis (Les quatre concepts fondamentaux de la psychanalyse), met with Lacan's approval. Miller's instrumental role in the publication of the seminars was arguably equivalent to that of co-author, and a notarized document of 13 November 1980 appointed him executor of the oral and written work of Lacan – its legal owner. The 1980s can be called the decade of Millerian Lacanianism, a much more collective enterprise than its predecessor, which was always inextricably linked to the person and teaching of Lacan. Elisabeth Roudinesco's view is that 'the Millerian network is above all concerned with preventing the IPA from appropriating the doctrine of a deceased master whose teaching it rejected while he was alive' (1990). 'Millerism' has, however, been but a dominant current in an enormous splintering process which produced no less than sixteen French Freudian institutions by the mid-1980s. The prevalent mood of psychoanalysis in France since Lacan's death has been one of dissidence, while its prevalent institutional process has been decentralization. However, neither of these apparently negative aspects detracts from a strong intellectual and institutional footing which will secure psychoanalysis a place in French intellectual life for the foreseeable future.

KATE INCE

See also: feminism (movements/groups)

Further reading

Bowie, M. (1991) *Lacan*, London: Fontana Modern Masters (an absorbing, elegantly written guide to Lacan's work).

Freud, S. (1953–74) *The Standard Edition of the Complete Psychological Works of Sigmund Freud*, 24 vols, London: The Hogarth Press.

Grosz, E. (1990) *Jacques Lacan: A Feminist Introduction*, London and New York: Routledge (a lucid guide to Lacan and Freud, written from a feminist philosophical perspective).

Lacan, J. (1977) *Écrits*, a selection, trans. A. Sheridan, London: Routledge (see also the complete *Écrits* [1966], Paris: Éditions du Seuil.

Laplanche, J. and Pontalis, J.-B. (1973) *The Language of Psychoanalysis*, London: Hogarth Press. Translated D. Nicholson-Smith (1967) from *Vocabulaire de la Psychanalyse*, Paris: Presses Universitaires de France (an invaluable encyclopedia-style

guide to some 400 of the key concepts of psychoanalysis).

Roudinesco, E. (1990) *Jacques Lacan & Co: A History of Psychoanalysis in France 1925–1985*, London: Free Association Books. Translated J. Mehlman (1966) from *La Bataille de cent ans: histoire de la psychanalyse en France, 2*, Paris: Éditions du Seuil (an indispensable source to the often dramatic history of psychoanalytic figures and institutions in twentieth-century France).

Wright, E. (1984) *Psychoanalytic Criticism: Theory in Practice*, London: Methuen (a valuable guide to the work of Freud and Lacan, its relevance to criticism, and to a broader range of psychoanalytic theory and critical practice).

——(1986) 'Modern Psychoanalytic Criticism', in A. Jefferson and D. Robey (eds) *Modern Literary Theory: A Comparative Introduction*, London: Batsford.

public works

France is known as a country which invests heavily in public works, understood here as infrastructure or grand architectural projects funded by the state. Particularly during the **Mitterrand** years, various landmark projects were undertaken in Paris such as the Pyramide at the Louvre, the Grande Arche at La Défense and the new Bibliothèque Nationale (National Library). Equally, France has invested heavily in the **transport** infrastructure. Perhaps the most famous of such projects is the *train à grande vitesse* (high-speed train), the TGV, a showcase high-speed railway service which links the furthest corners of France with Paris.

JAN WINDEBANK

See also: architecture; architecture under Mitterrand

publishing/l'édition

Régis **Debray**, in his analysis of the three phases

of intellectual power in twentieth-century France, classifies the second period (1920–60) as the 'publishing cycle' (Debray 1979). Owing to considerable improvements in literacy levels, as well as the introduction by the French Third Republic from the 1880s onwards of a national education policy, publishing came to be established as a viable and modern commercial venture after the beginning of the twentieth century. It was during the interwar period, however, that the major French publishing houses flourished. Their success and growth is epitomized in the rivalry between the two leading houses of the 1920s and 1930s, Grasset and **Gallimard**. Bernard Grasset, who first established his firm in 1907, gained renown by launching the novelists known as 'the four Ms', André **Maurois**, François Mauriac, Henry de Montherlant and Paul **Morand**, the last of whom Grasset tempted over from Gallimard. He added authors such as André **Malraux**, Jean Cocteau and Pierre Drieu de Rochelle to his catalogue, although these and others did not publish exclusively with Grasset. Similarly, Gaston Gallimard's involvement with the Éditions de la *Nouvelle Revue française* dated from before 1914; it was during the interwar period that Éditions Gallimard, with its advisers such as Jean **Paulhan**, published and established the literary reputations of authors like André Gide, Marcel Proust, Jean Giono, Saint-Exupéry and Paul Valéry. Later in the 1930s, the Gallimard house discovered the talents of Albert **Camus** and Jean-Paul **Sartre**. The period 1920–60 also saw the creation of other major publishing houses such as **Seuil** and **Minuit**, as well as the expansion of established firms like **Flammarion**. In the 1950s, as literary tastes

evolved, and as consumer demand expanded with demographic growth, other ventures such as **Livre de poche** (1953) and 'J'ai lu' (1958) were created in order to cater for a developing popular culture in France.

In the 1990s, publishing remains a multibillion-franc sector, even though for some time reading as a leisure activity has been facing strong competition from other media such as **television**, **cinema**, music and personal computers. Over the period 1960 to 1994, as a proportion of total consumer spending, expenditure on leisure activities *including* reading has increased from 6 per cent to 7.4 per cent, falling back from a peak of 7.7 per cent in 1990 (INSEE, 1996). Within this proportion, book buying as a form of leisure consumption has fallen markedly. However, this has not prevented the French publishing industry from increasing both its production of titles and its turnover in most years, as Table 1 below shows. Of almost 41,000 titles published in 1993, some 8,400 were classified as literary, 2,800 as applied science, 2,600 as geography or history. The sector is now dominated by large groups which tend increasingly to have multimedia interests; in 1993, the largest was Groupe de la Cité with a turnover of around 7,000 million francs, followed by Groupe Gallimard, Masson, Flammarion, Hâtier and Seuil.

Finally, mention should be made of FNAC (Fédération Nationale d'Achats), a major chain of bookshops in France. The attraction of *la FNAC* for many French people, for whom a visit to the local store (now established in most major towns) has become a sort of ritual, is that, in addition to the generous stocks of illustrated comic books (*bandes dessinées*) on open

Table 1

Year	1985	1987	1990	1991	1993
Titles published	29,068	30,982	39,054	39,492	40,916
Turnover (billions of francs)	12.9	—	14.5	13	14.2

Source: Syndicat National de l' Édition, quoted in *Quid* (1995)

shelf access, the latest CDs, cameras and personal stereos may be tried and purchased.

MARTYN CORNICK

See also: comic strips/cartoonists; literary journals; literary prizes

Further reading

Debray, R. (1979) *Le Pouvoir intellectuel en France*, Paris: Ramsay. Translated D. Macey *Writers, Teachers, Celebrities*, London: Verso (examines publishing in the context of twentieth-century French intellectual history and society).

INSEE (1996) *Données sociales*, Paris: INSEE (for studies on consumer spending).

Martin, H.-J., Chartier, R. and Vivet, J.-P. (eds) (1986) *Histoire de l'édition française*, vol. 4, *Le Livre concurrencé 1900–1950*, Paris: Promodis (indispensable for the interwar period).

Quid (1995) Paris: Laffont (encyclopedia containing the latest publishing statistics).

Q

Queneau, Raymond

b. 1903, Le Havre;
d. 1976, France

Writer and literary theorist

One of the most influential novelists and literary theorists in the postwar period, Queneau had already acquired a solid reputation in the interwar years and the Occupation through novels such as *Le Chiendent* (Couchgrass) from 1933, and *Pierrot mon ami* (Pierrot My Friend) of 1942. A former Surrealist, he was part of the renewal of influence of the group in the early postwar years. Through works like *Zazie dans le métro* (1959) and 1965's *The Blue Flowers (Les Fleurs bleues)*, he combined French spoken language with a rigorous mathematical structure to create complex and intellectually demanding fiction, theoreticized in his two collections of essays, *Bâtons, chiffres et lettres* (Sticks, Figures and Letters) and *Bords* (Edges), published in 1953 and 1960 respectively.

NICHOLAS HEWITT

See also: OuLiPo

R

racism/anti-semitism

Racism has changed considerably over the last fifty years. The major transformation is the change from modern forms of racism, underpinned by the concept of the biological hierarchy of races, to postmodern forms, underpinned by the concept of cultural difference.

Since the war, scientific theories of the hierarchy of races have been discredited and 'race' itself, as a means of categorizing human groups and understanding human behaviour, has been delegitimized. However, the delegitimization of 'race' has not brought about the disappearance of racism. Today, racism in France tends to take the form of the stigmatization of groups defined in cultural rather than biological terms, and through the discourse of their difference and incompatibility, rather than their inferiority and their need to be assimilated or eradicated.

This change can be related to the crisis of modernity in contemporary Western democracies brought about by the growing awareness of the relativism of Western values, the development of post-industrial and post-national forms of organization of society, the globalization of communications and culture, and the rise in new forms of identity formation based on ethnicity. In France, the crisis is perceived as a breakdown in the traditional processes of integration (through schools, trade **unions**, political parties, etc.) leading to the fragmentation of society and the creation of a new 'space' for the clash of ethnic/cultural particularisms (Wieviorka 1991). In this climate of cultural relativism, the notion of difference is used both for the purposes of individual and group identity, and for the stigmatization of others.

Probably the two most significant examples of contemporary racism are anti-semitism and anti-immigrant racism. In general, anti-semitism today differs from its modern genocidal form in that it involves an increase in symbolic violence aimed at cultural signs of Jewishness. Hence, the increase in recent years in the desecration of Jewish graves (the most-publicized example of which was the incident in Carpentras in May 1990), the desecration of synagogues, anti-semitic graffiti and tracts, and revisionist history denying the Holocaust.

The same might be said of the racism associated with new forms of **immigration** from North Africa, for here too visible signs of cultural difference (headscarves, mosques, ritual slaughter) are the object of racial violence. In this case, cultural difference is conflated with that of national difference: nations are viewed as culturally homogeneous entities whose distinctive identity is threatened by mixing and infiltration. The debates around immigration and national identity are the major areas through which this racism is expressed. Clearly, Jean-Marie **Le Pen**'s Front National is the most prominent exponent of this form of racism, but the ideas are not confined to the fringes of French political and social life.

The use of code words as a means of stigmatizing certain groups (immigration, national preference, cultural difference, and so on) is indicative of the shift in contemporary racist terminology and practice. It has been called a neo-racism or a 'racism without races' (Balibar and Wallerstein 1988). This has posed innumerable problems for anti-racist organizations. First, the right to difference (*le droit à la différence*) was once their own slogan for challenging ethnocentric, assimilationist and racist practices, and has since been turned against them by the New Right for the ends of separation and exclusion of particular groups. Second, their attempt to demonize Le Pen by equating his ideas with Fascism fails to ring true when his 'respectable' discourse of cultural/national difference contains few traces of Fascist ideology.

Although the concrete results of racist action are (today as in the past) discrimination and violence, its underlying forms are profoundly related to contemporary social and political processes.

MAX SILVERMAN

See also: Désir, Harlem, and SOS Racisme; Islam; Judaism; nationalism; parties and movements

Further reading

Balibar, E. and Wallerstein, I. (1988) *Race, nation, classe: les identités ambiguës*, Paris: La Découverte.

Silverman, M. (1992) *Deconstructing the Nation: Immigration, Racism and Citizenship in Modern France*, London: Routledge (analysis of links between 'race', culture and nation in contemporary France).

Taguieff, P.-A. (1988) *La Force du préjugé: essai sur le racisme et ses doubles*, Paris: La Découverte (analysis of the overlapping features of racist and anti-racist discourses in the modern period).

——(ed.) (1991) *Face au racisme*, 2 vols, Paris: La Découverte (diverse contributions on theory and practice of racism and anti-racism).

Wieviorka, M. (1991) *L'Espace du racisme*, Paris: Éditions du Seuil.

radio (private/free)

The law of 9 November 1981 authorized the creation of private local radio (*radios libres*) in France, so heralding the end of the state monopoly of broadcasting. President **Mitterrand**'s blow for freedom was intended to encourage non-profit-making local associations, hence the initial prohibition of **advertising**. The law of 1 August 1984 changed all this by belatedly allowing *la pub*. By 1989, there were 3,000 private local radio stations in France, transmitting on FM. They have become the victims of their own commercial success, however, and have gradually organized themselves into national networks or been taken over by larger concerns like **RTL** or **Europe 1**. With very few exceptions, while remaining private, they can no longer be considered very free or local.

These new private radio stations are specialist (mainly in popular music) and increasingly eating into the general-interest (both public and private) audiences. NRJ has become France's third most popular radio station (according to 1995 estimates), with an 11 per cent share. Originally targeting the 15–34 age range, it has managed to attract older listeners by diversifying its offerings (e.g. quiz programmes). Three other privately owned stations of a similar nature also attract over 5 per cent of the national audience: Fun Radio (France's sixth most popular station), very much for the teenager; Nostalgie (seventh) targeting the 25–45 year-olds, offering game shows and appealing very much to the emotions; Skyrock (ninth), the noisiest and most provocative of these music stations. Another successful private station is Chérie FM (eleventh), which targets adults who like tuneful and romantic music. In twelfth position comes RFM, which concentrates on traditional favourites such as **Piaf**, **Brel** and **Brassens**.

The other privately owned FM network

stations in France cover a variety of interests. Fourvière, based in Lyon, is an ecumenical Christian radio station. Montmartre targets the over-50s and specializes in unashamedly old-fashioned French songs; it has recently been taken over by RMC (Radio Monte-Carlo, the *périphérique* station created during World War II, occupying tenth place in the national listening league table). Radio Classique specializes in classical music. TSF targets those who enjoy listening to a wide range of music and songs, from traditional French songs to **folk** and hard **rock**. Finally, mention should be made of Sud Radio, the smallest of the non-specialized *radios périphériques*, transmitting from Andorra, but with studios in Toulouse. Created in 1939, it has had a chequered career.

In 1989, to encourage genuine private local radio, the government introduced legislation offering state subsidies to stations complying with CSA regulations and in receipt of an advertising income not exceeding 20 per cent of their turnover. On a less positive note, more recent government legislation (January 1996) insists that private popular music stations (NRJ, Skyrock, RFM, Europe 2, RTL 2) must broadcast a minimum of 40 per cent of francophone songs, in a vain attempt to stem the tide of Anglo-Saxon culture.

ALAN PEDLEY

See also: francophone radio: Europe; radio (state-owned); television

Further reading

Boon, M., Ryst, A. and Vinay, C. (1990) *Lexique de l'audiovisuel*, Paris: Dalloz (a mine of information).
Guide de la radio (1995), Paris: Télérama.

radio (state-owned)

About 20 per cent of the total radio audience in France listens to some of the 466,000 hours of programmes broadcast each year by Radio France, the state-owned company. It was created in 1974 when the **ORTF** was divided into seven autonomous organizations. Although the state officially enjoyed a broadcasting monopoly until 1982, a number of francophone radio stations, known collectively as *radios périphériques*, operating from outside France's frontiers (notably **RTL, Europe 1** and RMC), had been available to the bulk of the French listening public through long-wave transmission since the 1940s and 1950s. Radio has thus been a highly competitive business in France for a long time. Since the creation of local radio stations, both public and private, brought about by the decentralizing policies of the early 1980s, competition has become even keener. The overall tendency is indeed increasingly a move away from generalist, national (whether state-owned or private) radio, to localized, specialized stations.

Radio France, whose chairman and managing director (currently Jean Boyon) is appointed by the CSA (Conseil Supérieur de l'Audiovisuel), runs several centrally operated stations from its Paris base. It is financed almost entirely (88.5 per cent in 1992) by the licence fee, *la redevance* (700F in 1997). Commercial **advertising** is not allowed on state-owned radio in France, but collective and public-interest advertising is authorized and contributed 4.6 per cent of Radio France's 1992 revenue. Its headquarters in the impressive Maison de la Radio houses sales and information services, as well as a Museum of Radio. Its main mission is to provide a public service for the French listening public, through entertainment and information. It also supports two national orchestras, the Orchestre National de France and Orchestre Philharmonique de Radio France, as well as a choir, the Choeur de Radio France. It has a full-time personnel of over 3,100, 14 per cent of whom are journalists.

Radio France's flagship, enjoying 11.2 per cent of the national audience according to a recent estimate, is **France-Inter**. Created in 1947 as Paris-Inter, it assumed its present title in 1964. It is a general-interest station, offering a wide range of programmes, each of which has its regular daily or weekly slot. A daily dose of satirical humour is offered at 11 a.m. (French time) on weekdays by *Rien à cirer*; *Le Téléphone sonne* provides informed discussion (with listener participation) of an issue of current concern at 7.20 p.m. on weekdays; *Les Guetteurs du siècle*, an in-depth interview of a personality, is hosted by Jacques Chancel every Sunday at 6 p.m.; *Le Masque et la plume* offers a lively debate on the arts on Sunday evenings at 10 p.m.; *En avant la zizique* champions the French song just after midnight on weekdays. A number of these programmes (in addition to *Inter-Treize*, a daily news programme) are broadcast in the presence of a live audience. France-Inter broadcasts twenty-four hours a day on long wave (ensuring good reception well beyond the national frontiers), medium wave and FM stereo.

While France-Inter's audience is in slow decline (down 2.4 per cent over the period 1989–95), France Info (FM only), a nonstop news service created in 1987, has been recently showing a healthy annual increase in its audience (up 2.1 per cent 1994–5). The first such station to be set up in Europe, it currently attracts over 10 per cent of the total national radio audience. Like its British counterpart Radio 5, it also offers sports coverage.

France Culture (FM stereo, twenty-four hours a day), created in 1963, lives up to its name, offering intellectually challenging programmes to seriously-minded listeners. It broadcasts six news bulletins each day, ten hours of radio drama each week, along with debates, discussions, documentaries and news magazines. **France Musique** (FM stereo, twenty-four hours a day), also created in 1963, offers mainly classical music but also **jazz**, interspersed with a good deal of discussion. The station broadcasts a thousand concerts each year and five news bulletins per day.

Radio Bleue (medium wave, 7a.m.–7 p.m.), created in 1980, targets the over-50s. Its song output is reputedly 100 per cent French. FIP (FM and medium wave, 7 p.m.–4 p.m. or 6 p.m.) targets the motorist and offers music, traffic and weather news and urgent personal messages. Created in 1971, this station originally served only the Paris region; in 1992, it

became a national network. Formerly known as Victor, France Culture Europe (FM, twenty-four hours a day) broadcasts via satellite (Eutelsat 11-F6) to the whole of Europe and is a mixture of mainly France Culture (75 per cent) and France Musique (20 per cent). Hector also broadcasts via satellite (1 a.m.–7 a.m.) and carries France Musique's programmes. Finally, Sorbonne Radio France (medium wave) broadcasts university lectures during term time from 10 a.m. to 1 p.m. and 2 p.m. to 5 p.m. The best guide to radio programmes, wavelengths and FM frequencies in France is the weekly audiovisual magazine, *Télérama*.

Radio France also runs thirty-nine local radio stations, created in the 1980s, to compete with the local private stations, the *radios libres* (mainly ex-pirate radio stations) authorized by the newly elected Socialist government in their *Loi sur la communication audiovisuelle du 29 juillet 1982*. Three pilot stations were initially set up in 1980: Fréquence Nord (Lille), Radio Mayenne (Laval) and Melun FM. The remaining thirty-six were created in the years 1982–8, conveniently supporting the Socialists' decentralization reforms introduced in 1981. There are four regional programme-production workshops, at Nantes, Bordeaux, Nice and Strasbourg. Administration is also distributed over a number of regional centres, namely at Avignon, Besançon, Nantes, Bordeaux and Paris. The thirty-nine stations broadcast a variety of programmes, from **soap** operas to **documentaries**. Many of these regional productions are later broadcast on all the other stations. Many programmes are of an interactive nature. The stations function twenty-four hours a day on FM, geographically covering about 50 per cent of the country.

ALAN PEDLEY

See also: francophone radio: Europe; radio (private/free)

Further reading

Boon, M., Ryst, A. and Vinay, C. (1990)

Lexique de l'audiovisuel, Paris: Dalloz.

Guide de la radio (1995), Paris: Télérama (a very informative, comprehensive guide).

INA/CSA (1994) *Les Chiffres clés de la radio*, Paris: La Documentation Française.

rap

Appearing in France in 1983, rap has become an important trend on the popular music scene, but was only heard on the airwaves in 1993, when *Je danse le Mia* by IAM became a huge success.The root of this art form is the hip-hop culture in the United States and suggests an oppressed black minority. In France, rap could not really have existed without the presence of black and beur immigrants. If it was originally a protest song against the injustices of urban society, French rap has developed another dimension: fun and pun.

GÉRARD POULET

See also: beur music; beurs; MC Solaar; song/*chanson*

Rappeneau, Jean-Paul

b. 1932, Auxerre

Director and scriptwriter

He began his career as a director, but spent the 1960s mostly as a scriptwriter. Two of his six 1960s films were scripted with **Malle**, including *Zazie dans le métro* (1960). He turned to directing again in the 1970s, making films with **Belmondo** (*Les Mariés de l'an II* in 1970), **Montand** (*Le Sauvage* in 1975) and **Adjani** (*Tout feu, tout flamme* in 1982). He made one of the best sellers of the 1990s, *Cyrano de Bergerac* (1990), with **Depardieu**, followed by another heritage film in 1995, *The Horseman on the Roof* (*Le Hussard sur le toit*), with **Binoche**.

PHIL POWRIE

See also: cinema

Redonnet, Marie

b. 1948, France

Playwright and writer

Having begun to write in the late 1970s, after the death of her father, Redonnet is the author of plays, short stories and a series of novels, including: the trilogy, *Splendid Hôtel* (1986), *Forever Valley* (1987) and *Rose Mélie Rose* (1987); *Silsie* (1990); and *Nevermore* (1994). The denuded, pared-down style of her writing and its staging of strange, fairy-tale worlds have caused it to be likened to that of Samuel **Beckett**. Key themes within Redonnet's work are identity and maturation – especially in relation to women – and inter-/intra-generational relationships.

ALEX HUGHES

See also: women's/lesbian writing

Further reading

Fallaize, E. (1992) 'Filling in the Blank Canvas: Memory, Identity and Inheritance in the Work of Marie Redonnet', *Forum for Modern Language Studies* 28 (highly lucid account of key thematic issues in Redonnet's work).

regional economic development

The uneven economic development of France's regions and the growing concentration of population and wealth in the Paris region after World War II brought policy changes, grouped under the concept of *aménagement du territoire* (town and country planning), which aims at 're-equilibrating' the various regions. These policies had mixed results, although they helped in directing the flow of investment and contributed to a greater awareness of regional issues. Recently, regional planning has found a new lease of life, because of the need to organize relations better between central government, regional authorities and Europe.

In 1947, J. F. Gravier's book, *Paris et le désert français*, had a considerable impact, showing the widening gap between the Paris region, increasingly populous and wealthy, and those rural areas relying on family agriculture and small scale rural industries (such as most of the Massif Central, the Provence back-country, and large areas in the west of France), losing their younger generations to rural exodus and slowly dying out. Later, the geographical distribution of economic activities and, especially, industry appeared to change things dramatically. A number of regions with older, heavy industries started to decline. New areas of economic growth were attracting investments, population and infrastructure, with large regional capitals such as Toulouse or Grenoble acting as magnets. The crisis from the mid-1970s accentuated regional imbalances. Some old industrial regions went into terminal crisis, and some rural areas (for instance, in the south of the Massif Central in regions such as the Lozère) were close to becoming real deserts. Indeed, the Paris/Île-de-France region has twice the gross product per person per year of peripheral regions such as Corsica and the Pas de Calais, with considerable differentials also as far as unemployment rates, education levels, etc. are concerned.

In the face of this uneven socioeconomic development, regional planning has been organized since the early 1960s around an autonomous agency (DATAR) and regional commissions, sometimes the responsibility of a minister.

Contrary to economic planning, regional planning is still a tool of public policy. The 1982 Defferre law on decentralization gave local authorities new political powers, with wider budgetary and investment responsibilities, requiring co-ordination with central government, especially through regional planning.

European economic integration has a growing impact on regional development: because some peripheral areas (such as Brittany or the Pyrenees) were left out of the richer, fast-growing middle Europe, this led regional planners to establish strategies, and devote resources to a better integration in Europe, complementing the European Union's own structural policies for poorer areas. Regional planning has also been drafted since the mid-1980s into implementing policies against social exclusion evident in many deprived urban areas.

FRANÇOIS NECTOUX

See also: *dirigisme*; economy; regionalism

Further reading

Gravier, J.-F. (1971a) *Économie et organisation régionales*, Paris: Masson et Cie.
——(1971b) *La Question régionale*, Paris: Flammarion.
——(1983) *L'Espace vital*, Paris: Flammarion.
Loughlin, J. and Mezey, S. (eds) (1995) *The End of the French Unitary State? Ten Years of Regionalisation in France 1982–1992*, Ilford: Frank Cass (an analysis of the consequences of decentralization, including regional development).
Scargill, I. (1995) ' "L'Aménagement du Territoire": The Great Debate', *Modern and Contemporary France* NS3: 1 (a brief assessment of the impact of regional planning on regional development).

regional music

The postwar cliché on French cultural life in general and musical enterprises in particular was encapsulated by the formula, *Paris et le désert français* (Paris and the French cultural desert). If, in terms of creation, Paris remains the centre of attraction, a systematic policy of cultural regionalization since 1958 under various governments (whether conservative or Socialist) has eventually brought about, with various degrees of success, some significant changes in the musical life of the regions, evident in terms of creativity and diffusion. Bridging the cultural gap between Paris and the regions was an essential element of the *aménagement du territoire* (town and country planning). Under **Giscard d'Estaing** (1974–81) and **Mitterrand** (1981–95) French cultural practices changed towards a greater consumption of all kinds of music (classical, opera, **jazz**, **rock and pop** and *chansons*) and the capitals of the twenty-five regions became cultural centres of excellence. As far as music is concerned, some had a greater impact than others in certain genres. But it is as if every regional capital has been concerned with furnishing itself with an original cultural symbol of identification: Bourges and its 'Printemps' (spring festival) and La Rochelle and its 'Francofolies' (French extravaganza) are the two main events in the domain of rock, pop and *variétés* in France.

Opera in the provinces was revived in the 1970s by Rolf Liebermann. Twelve towns host this symbol of highbrow culture, and Bordeaux, Lyon, Toulouse, Strasbourg and Nancy outshine some Parisian productions with their creations. Rock has its capitals sometimes unknown to a wider public: Rennes, Valenciennes, Nancy. Singers like **Nougaro** and **Cabrel** have been able to record their soundtracks and *vidéoclips* in Toulouse (at the Condorcet Studio and, after 1984, the Polygone). As far as classical music is concerned, the models have been the regional orchestras of Lille (with Jean-Claude Casadesus) and Toulouse (with Michel Plasson). From the 1970s, jazz saw the emergence of numerous regional associations defined as centres of creation and diffusion and subsidized as such; some of these musical cooperatives have been active since then, such as the ARFI (Lyon) and the GRIM (Marseille), while some are seen more as teaching centres (the JAM in Montpellier and Caen Jazz Action). Each region develops its own voluntarist policy for the development of all forms of music, attempting to avoid the inherent danger of insularity. At the end of the 1990s, Paris is no longer surrounded by a cultural desert and

some might argue that it is now only the first of the provinces.

Regional music could also be understood as the expression of the musical cultural consciousness of the regions, involving the re-creation from a traditional heritage, of music for a modern audience. We must refer to 'real' regions rather than their administrative divisions (e.g. the Occitan, Catalan and Basque territories, Brittany, Aquitaine, Auvergne, Limousin, Berry, Provence and Picardy.) Then we get into **folk-music** territory.

GÉRARD POULET

See also: folk music; language and the French regions; music festivals; music industry; music venues; regionalism; song/*chanson*

regional press in France

Only a quarter of the 10 million daily newspapers produced in France are Paris-based; only 10 of the nation's 75 daily titles are produced in the capital. The relative strength of the provincial press seems to run counter to the traditionally centralized nature of French institutions. The balance between national and regional dailies has been shifting slowly but constantly, during the twentieth century, away from a Parisian to a provincial dominance. Just before World War II, parity had been reached, each sector providing about 5.5 million copies per day. By the 1990s, while the number of copies of regional dailies had risen to over 7 million, the total of Paris dailies had dropped to well under 3 million.

In a situation of generally declining newspaper readership, this provincial success story appears all the more remarkable. Provincial media consumers in France perhaps need the more locally focused regional papers to counteract the impact of the largely national and international bias of **television**. Another factor worth mentioning is that the more densely populated regions of France are, the less their inhabitants read. This tendency is demonstrated by the fact that, whereas 52.8 per cent of the inhabitants of the provinces read a daily paper, the figure for the Paris region is only 35.4 per cent.

Apart from *Le Parisien*, which produces a 'national' edition, *Aujourd'hui*, the capital's papers are all-embracing, single-edition publications. By contrast, many provincial dailies publish several differentiated local editions. *Ouest-France*, for example, publishes forty editions. This flexibility gives regional papers a distinct advantage over Paris papers, catering for the never-satiated appetite of the French for *faits-divers* and the *rubrique des chiens écrasés* (human interest stories).

Three other factors account for the relatively healthy state of the regional press in France. First, production processes, both in terms of composition and printing, have tended to be more technologically developed in the provinces. Regional papers tend, for example, to be far more colourful than Paris papers. Second, provincial papers have suffered less than their Parisian counterparts from the decline in **advertising** revenue caused by the ever-increasing share that television has been claiming over the past few years. The more specifically targeted adverts in local papers continue to provide a regular income. Finally, the average price of a provincial daily is considerably lower than the typical Paris daily: *Ouest-France*, for example, only costs about two thirds of the price of *Le Monde* and *Le Figaro*.

Whereas only 8 Paris-based dailies sell more than 100,000 copies, 19 regional dailies have circulations in that range. By far the leading title is *Ouest-France*, based in Rennes and like so many French dailies founded in August 1944, which not only outsells all other provincial dailies, but all Parisian ones too, with over 750,000 copies. This paper's penetration extends well beyond the borders of the old province of Brittany and benefits from the fact that it serves a region boasting the highest level of newspaper readership in France (62.4 per cent). While far behind *Ouest-France*, seven other titles nevertheless have circulation figures of over 250,000: *La Voix du Nord* (based in Lille, founded in 1941); *Sud-Ouest* (Bordeaux,

1944), which took over *La Petite Gironde* (founded in the nineteenth century but, like all other papers (whether in Paris or in the provinces) which continued to appear under Germany occupation, forced to close after the **Liberation**); *Le Progrès* (Lyon, 1859), *Le Dauphiné Libéré* (Grenoble, 1944) and *La Montagne* (Clermont-Ferrand, 1919).

Three other titles top the 200,000 mark: *L'Est Républicain* (Nancy, 1889); *La Dépêche du Midi* (Toulouse, 1870) and *Les Dernières Nouvelles d'Alsace* (Strasbourg, 1877), which enjoys the unique distinction of being read by an absolute majority of the inhabitants of the region it serves. The following eight titles have circulations of between 100,000 and 200,000: *Le Républicain Lorrain* (Metz, 1919); *Midi libre* (Montpellier, 1944), *Le Télégramme* (Morlaix, 1944); *Le Provençal* (Marseille, 1944); *L'Alsace* (Mulhouse); *Paris-Normandie* (Rouen, 1944); *L'Union* (Reims) and *Le Courrier de l'ouest* (Angers).

This overall diversity of titles does not mean, however, that there is any degree of choice for the individual reader in any given locality. Very few towns in fact offer a choice of regional daily titles. Thanks to mergers, takeovers or closures due to ever-increasing problems caused by a variety of factors (diminishing advertising revenues, increasing production costs, increased prices deterring would-be purchasers leading to falling sales, strikes, distribution problems and competition from television as a provider of information and entertainment), the number of provincial titles has fallen from 175 to 65 in fifty years.

Readership figures can obviously only be estimates, but in most cases they can be calculated as being three (or occasionally four) times the circulation figures. In addition to the non-purchasing readers in families and workplaces, it must be noted that most cafés in France make free copies of local papers available for their clients.

As for the identity of readers, the following differences are worth noting: provincial papers attract a higher female readership (49 per cent) than Parisian papers (41 per cent); provincial papers also attract a higher proportion of readers aged 50 and over (46.5 per cent) than Parisian papers (35.3 per cent) and a low proportion of readers aged 35 and below (28.6 per cent as opposed to 36.6 per cent).

It is worth making a final point with regard to the distribution of newspapers in France: they are virtually never delivered to readers' homes by newsagents (although of course they can be obtained by subscription through the post). Distribution difficulties probably account for the scarcity of Sunday papers both in Paris (two titles only) and in the provinces, where only twenty-two titles are available, selling a total of just over 3 million copies.

ALAN PEDLEY

See also: national press in France; regionalism

Further reading

Albert, P. (1990) *La Presse française*, Paris: La Documentation Française.
Cayrol, R. (1991) *Les Médias*, Paris: PUF.
Mathien, M. (1986) *La Presse quotidienne régionale*, Paris: PUF (a short but comprehensive guide).

regional writing: Breton

The dominant current in literature in Breton, from the 1920s to the 1970s, has been the Skol Walarn, the brainchild and lifelong struggle of Roparz Hemon, associated with his review, *Gwalarn*, and its successor *Al Liamm*. Hemon denounced clichés of sacrifice and faith, the stereotype of a primitive, rural, Catholic other. He called for a national literature open to the modern world, a literature modern in all respects, that would make Breton worthy of being part and parcel of European culture. It would have to be written not in imitation of village speech but in a literary form intelligible to all educated readers of Breton, a high-culture tongue capable of functioning in all the ways that French is wont to do.

Fañch Elies (Abeozen), Hemon and Maodez Glanndour are the leading poets. Hemon's *Barzhonegoù* (Poems) contain noble meditations on the destiny of the warrior and the poet who struggle for the eternal Brittany. Glanndour composes powerful, complex, rich Christian verse which evokes the simple, quotidian reality of Breton life, always suffused with the sacred, and calls for overcoming worldly deception through a quest of the spirit to God. Anjela Duval, a peasant who began to write in her fifties, in *Kan an douar* (Song of the Earth) and *Traoñ an dour* (The Dale of Water), displays comparable mastery in portraying *Dinglichkeit*. The '1960s poets' created a literature of **postmodernism**: a turning away from high art towards a more popular register in texts committed to the politics of rebellion. Paol Keineg's *Barzhonegoù-trakt* (Tract Poems), *Mojennoù gwir* (True Stories), and *Iwerzhon ar C'hreistez, Iwerzhon an Hanternoz* (Southern Ireland, Northern Ireland) contain dense, powerful, nightmare evocations of insanity and physical torture, the poet's lot and the lot of his fellow Celts.

In the immediate postwar years, the leading novelists were Youenn Drezen, whose 1940 *Itron Varia Garmez* (Our Lady of Carmel) is a strike novel in the line of Zola, the hero of which is a would-be artist who cannot complete his sculpture, held back by political injustice and his own illness. The three-volume 1972–4 *Skol-louarn Veig Trebern* (Little Hervé Trebern Plays Hookey) recounts in the picaresque mode the adventures of two 8-year-olds, in about 1910, who enjoy a month-long truancy from school. Hemon wrote *Nenn Jani* in the realist mode, telling of little people leading little lives in Brest; *Tangi Kerviler* in the fantastic and utopian register, and *Mari-Vorgan* (The Mermaid), a powerful, symbolic evocation of a ship's doctor (the unreliable homodiegetic narrator) who goes mad, under the sway of passion for a hallucinatory creature who may or may not be real. More recently, Per Denez plays with narrative structures and furthers a trend towards something approaching magical realism in the 1979 *Diougan Gwenc'hlan* (Gwenc'hlan's Prophecy), a tale of a modern man possessed by the ghost of an ancestor, and *Blue Like Blue Eyes Which Were Not My Own* (*Glas evel daoulagad c'hlas na oant ket ma re*), a powerful story of murder, obsession and madness.

The **theatre** has traditionally played a vital role in Brittany. Jarl Priel and Hemon composed a number of plays. The most brilliant dramatist, however, is Pierre-Jakez Hélias, famous for his 'testimony' *The Horse of Pride* (*Le Cheval d'orgueil*). Hélias's dramas, first performed and published in French, include finely crafted demystifications of rural life such as *Mevel ar Gosker* (The Top Hand of Kosker Farm) and *Katrina Lenn-zu* (Katrina of the Black Pond), and poetic visions for today of history and legend, like *An Isild a-heul* (The Second Iseult).

WILLIAM CALIN

See also: regional writing: Occitan; regionalism

Further reading

Denez, P. (1971) 'Modern Breton Literature,' in J. E. Caerwyn Williams (ed.) *Literature in Celtic Countries*, Cardiff: University of Wales Press (an informative and committed essay).

Favereau, F. (1991) *Littérature et écrivains bretonnants depuis 1945*, in *Skol Vreizh* 20 (the most complete and up-to-date survey, with a full bibliography).

Galand, R. (1990) *Stratégie de la lecture*, New York: P. Lang (perceptive essays on Breton and French literature).

Movannou, F. and Piriou, Y.-B. (1987) 'La Littérature de langue bretonne au XXe siècle', in J. Balcou and Y. Le Gallo (eds) *Histoire littéraire et culturelle de la Bretagne*, Paris: Champion, vol. 3, pp. 175–252 (elegant presentation, especially for the earlier periods).

regional writing: Occitan

Literature in Occitan (Provençal) since World War II is of a quality and richness unequalled since the age of the troubadours. The leading writers from southern France have, in general, adhered to the programme enunciated by the Institut d'Estudis Occitans (Institute for Occitan Studies) associated with the review *Oc*. In brief, the new writing is grounded in modernity: realist and post-realist novels of modern life; hard, arcane **poetry** in the line of Valéry and **Perse**; and a serious modern **theatre** treating serious questions in a modern way. Implied is the repudiation of folklore and nostalgia for a Catholic, rural past, the latter associated with the Provençal epigones who claim the heritage of Mistral and the Felibrige.

Two of the leading poets are René Nelli and Bernard Manciet. Nelli's 1981 *Òbra poëtica occitana* (Poetical Works in Occitan) is a meditation on *fin' amor* (courtly love) and Catharism, with the accompanying alienation, longing and terror, wrought in a new Mediterranean classicism, a fusion of antiquity and the high art of the troubadours. Manciet's masterpiece is the 1989 *Enterrament a Sabres* (Burial in Sabres), a magnificent, baroque evocation of an old lady in the village, one-half Gascon notable, one-half local witch, and her fierce erotic and intellectual duel with God, an encounter highlighting the village, the Gascon people, and the history of the race. Since 1968, one trend has been a more simple, populist, rhetorical and politically committed 'Poetry of Decolonization', best represented in the work of Yves Rouquette and his brother, Jean Larzac. Larzac, an ordained priest, declaims against French capitalism and Paris; he also utters, in powerful sacred verse, his desire for the absent God Unknown.

By general accord, Jean Boudou (Joan Bodon) is the best of the novelists. *La Grava sul camin* (The Gravel on the Roadbed) tells, in the behaviourist mode of Hemingway or **Camus**, the botched life of a young farm labourer returned from the camps in Germany. No less powerful is the first person story of an intellectual dying of cancer in *Lo Libre dels grands jorns* (The Book of the Last Days). In this novel and in *La Santa Estèla del Centenari* (The Felibrige Centennial), however, Boudou breaks away from realism into a more fantastic mode comparable to magical realism. Similarly, Robert Lafont, after *Vida de Joan Larsinhac* (The Life of Jean Larsignac), a stark tale of urban realism, in *L'Icòna dins l'iscla* (The Icon on the Island), writes a futurist post-nuclear holocaust fantasy, recounting the horrible life and death of some of the last Europeans on a Greek island near Crete. His masterpiece, nevertheless, is the 1983 *La Festa* (The Festival), a two-volume *nouveau roman* located in both the eighteenth and twentieth centuries and spanning much of European topography and history. The youngest novelist is Jean-Claude Forêt, whose 1990 *La Peira d'asard* (The Stone of Chance), also a form of *nouveau roman*, is composed in three distinct languages: modern literary Languedocian, spoken northern Auvergnat and standard medieval Occitan.

The theatre remains inevitably the most difficult genre to conquer in a minority language. Lafont is the leading dramatist, with a number of fine plays in Occitan, such as *La Loba* (The She-Wolf), retelling the story of the troubadour Peire Vidal, and others in French and Occitan, dramas in the modern style, like *La Croisade* (The Crusade), with a political message.

Writers in the Provençal or Felibrige or Mistralian school include the poet Max-Philippe Delavouët, author of the five-volume *Pouèmo*, and the novelists Bernard Giély and Charles Galtier.

WILLIAM CALIN

See also: Catholicism and Protestantism; regional writing: Breton; regionalism

Further reading

Gardy, P. (1992) *Une Écriture en archipel*, Église-neuve-d'Isaac: Fédérop (essays by a leading academic critic and scholar).

Kirsch, F. P. (1965) *Studien zur langue-dokischen und gaskognischen Literatur der Gegenwart*, Vienna, Braumüller (study of the non-Mediterranean strain in the tradition).

Lafont, R. and Anatole, C. (1970) *Nouvelle Histoire de la littérature occitane*, 2 vols, Paris, PUF (the standard modern literary history).

regionalism

Regionalism has been a constant element of French political and cultural discourse for the past half-century, reflecting a long-standing opposition between capital and provinces, between governing and governed. It is also the focus for an unresolved debate about the dictates of national unity and the demands for individual and local freedoms.

It is a commonplace of modern French history that successive governments have regarded the concept of *la république une et indivisible* as sacrosanct. Whether its purpose was to weld together the constituent parts of a country as geographically, culturally and linguistically diverse as France or to assert national identity in the face of the monolithic power blocks of the United States and the Soviet Union, the indivisible Republic symbolized the coming-together of state and nation.

The legacy of historic centralization, brought about by the age-old concentration of political and economic power in Paris, can be found in the rigidly hierarchical administrative system founded after the Revolution of 1789. The establishment of the *commune* as the basic unit of French administration, together with the *département* as the main territorial division, formed the basis of a centralized system of administration which changed little until well after the end of World War II. The appointment to each *département* of a *préfet* as the authoritative representative of central government imposed a quasi-military discipline on the relationship between the capital and the provinces, ensuring that the term *administration locale* was more appropriate than *gouvernement local*.

The stability of a predominantly rural population meant that, until World War II, there was little pressure for change. From 1945 onwards, however, unprecedented population growth, together with industrial advances, began to lay bare the uneven economic development of the provinces. In the thirty years (*les trente glorieuses*) from 1946 to 1975, the population grew from 40.5 million to 52.75 million. The dramatic increases in living standards during this period, however, tended to mask regional imbalances. As the period of expansion drew to a close in the mid-1970s, the first signs of a determination to proclaim regional identities, as opposed to a single national identity, began to emerge. Regions such as Brittany, underindustrialized and with a surplus of farm labour, and the south, suffering from foreign competition in agriculture and with declining traditional industries, were those in which the impetus for change and the assertion of regional identity were most in evidence.

The first concerted initiatives for regional reform were private ventures: the grouping-together of local chambers of commerce such as the Comité d'Étude et de Liaison des Intérêts Bretons (CELIB) in 1952 was widely imitated, and was rapidly followed by the official recognition of Comités d'Expansion Économique. The impact of these *comités* was sufficient to bring about a new territorial division, superimposed on the departmental system, of twenty-two *circonscriptions d'action régionale*, eventually to be called, simply, *régions*.

It is clear that the impetus behind the changes, which were not accompanied by any attempt to democratize local decision-making, was essentially economic, and gave currency to the phrase *l'aménagement du territoire* (town and country planning). However, the period since the mid-1950s has also seen the resurgence of a belief in regional identity. Geographically peripheral regions such as Brittany, Alsace, Provence, the Basque country and Corsica have seen a ground swell of support for, and pride in, local and regional values and traditions.

The failure of the state to respond to the aspirations which such values represent was perhaps one element of the social and political turbulence of **May 1968**. De **Gaulle**'s failure to advance the cause of regional reform in the referendum-cum-plebiscite of 1969 led not only to his own political demise but to a decade of inaction. However, following François **Mitterrand**'s victory in the presidential election of 1981, and the decision to place regional reform at the heart of his legislative programme, the pace of reform quickened. The law of July 1982 enshrined two major innovations: the principle of direct election to regional assemblies, and the curtailment of the power of the *préfet*, whose role was limited to an *a posteriori* evaluation of the legitimacy of local decisions. The attribution of a *statut particulier* (special statute) for Corsica, providing for generous representation on its regional assembly, and for Paris, Lyon and Marseille, offering directly elected *conseils d'arrondissements* (district councils), completed the main elements of the reform. These latter measures also ensured that, for the first time in postwar France, a breach was created in the principle of *la république indivisible*.

It should be noted that these reforms, for all their genuinely innovatory features, did not release the hitherto untapped sources of enthusiasm and dynamism among the electorate that had been predicted at the time of their promulgation. Neither can it be said, however, that the major political shifts signalled by the legislative elections of 1993 and presidential election of 1995 revealed a desire to roll back the reforms of the 1980s, widely seen as a sensible modernization of an archaic and overly rigid system. Indeed, it may reasonably be claimed that the relationship between Paris and the regions has undergone its first significant modification for two centuries. The role of the **European Union** in seeking to promote inter-regional contact and co-operation, both within and across national boundaries, seems likely to attenuate further the influence of France's historic centralization.

PETER WAGSTAFF

See also: agriculture; constitution of the Fifth Republic; demographic developments; language and the French regions; regional economic development; regional writing: Breton; regional writing: Occitan

Further reading

Bodineau, P. and Verpeaux, M. (1993) *Histoire de la décentralisation*, Paris: PUF (a broad-ranging but useful summary).

Scargill, I. (1995) 'L'Aménagement du territoire: the great debate', *Modern and Contemporary France*, NS3, 1 (an analysis of the prospects for regional development until the end of the twentieth century and beyond).

Schmidt, V. A. (1990) *Democratizing France: The Political and Administrative History of Decentralization*, Cambridge: Cambridge University Press (a meticulous assessment of the origins of the centralization/decentralization debate).

Wagstaff, P. (1994) 'Regionalism in France', *Europa*, 1, 2/3 (a survey of the relationship between Paris and the provinces, and a consideration of the impact of European Union regional policy).

Reinhardt, Django

b. 1910, Charleroi, Belgium;
d. 1953, Fontainebleau

Musician and composer,
real name Jean-Baptiste Reinhardt

Reinhardt, who led the Quintette du Hot Club de France (1934–9), devised his singular technique on guitar after losing two fingers of his left hand in a childhood accident. The success of the Quintette's swing sound played off Reinhardt's gypsy-prince charisma against the lush melodics of Stéphane **Grappelli**'s violin, as in the classic *Nuages*. After touring the United States in 1946 at the invitation of Duke Ellington, Reinhardt toured throughout Europe with a new Quintette until he died of a stroke at the age of 43.

STEVEN UNGAR

See also: jazz

Further reading

Delaunay, C. (1982) *Django Reinhardt*, New York: Da Capo (biography).

Fairweather, D. (1995) 'Django Reinhardt', in I. Carr, D. Fairweather and and B. Priestley (eds) *Jazz: The Rough Guide*, New York: Penguin (contextualizing introduction).

Renaud

b. 1952, Paris

Singer-songwriter and actor,
real name Renaud Séchan

In turn anarchistic, irreverent and amusing, this left-wing exponent of contemporary French **slang** – in songs which often espouse the cause of the working class and the underprivileged – projects the image of a latter-day Aristide Bruant, of an urban hooligan who can also be considered to be the creator of an imported form of song, the suburban western. Successes include *Hexagone* (France), *Miss Maggie* (an attack on Margaret Thatcher) and *Morgane de toi* (In Love with You). Renaud played the role of Lantier in **Berri**'s *Germinal*.

IAN PICKUP

See also: song/*chanson*

Renaud, Madeleine

b. 1900, Paris;
d. 1994, Paris

Actor

Renaud left the **Comédie-Française** in 1946 to found the prestigious Renaud–**Barrault** company with her husband Jean-Louis Barrault. She is most remembered for her 1960s interpretations of Winnie in **Beckett**'s *Happy Days* (*Oh les beaux jours*) and Maude in *Harold and Maude*, and appeared in **Genet's** *The Screens* (*Les Paravents*) and many **Duras** productions.

ANNIE SPARKS

See also: theatre

Further reading

Loriot, N. (1993) *Madeleine Renaud*, Paris: Presse de la Renaissance.

Renoir, Jean

b. 1894, Paris;
d. 1979, Beverly Hills, USA

Director

Renoir's great period in film-making predates World War II. However, in the 1950s, he was canonized by the *Cahiers du cinéma* group as an auteur and his reputation as a reference point in contemporary **cinema** marks him out as an ongoing influence.

The son of Auguste Renoir (whose paintings he sold in order to finance film projects he had difficulty funding), critics have persisted in seeing the influence of the father in his film images. In fact, Renoir is far more in the realist tradition and he has been hailed, justifiably, as the precursor of neo-realism. In this respect, Renoir preferred location shooting to studio wherever possible, and synchronized rather than post-synch sound. He mostly avoided **stars**, and worked with professional and non-professional actors with equal ease. In terms of production practices, he believed in the principle of collective team work (thus, for example, actors would learn to wield cameras, camera operators would have small acting parts, and so on). These hallmarks to his films and production practices are ones that readily identify his work as belonging to a French tradition that still holds sway today and which has been particularly influential with **Nouvelle Vague** film-makers.

A pacifist, humanist and man of the Left, Renoir made what could be termed a moral cinema, one that asks us to examine our own sets of values and prejudices. His prewar films are especially enlightened in their observations of the working and proletarian classes. *Toni* (1934), *Le Crime de M Lange* (1935) and *La Bête humaine* (1938) are among some of his most sensitive treatments of the struggles and hardships of these classes and also reveal the solidarity of the working classes in an unheroized way. Sexuality, desire and love's potential to exacerbate as well as heal divisions between the sexes are key issues in all his films. Renoir was also a great champion of Republican ideals and his films have consistently analysed human behaviour, particularly in relation to **class** and to individual as well as group aspirations, such as *La Vie est à nous* (1936) and *La Marseillaise* (1937). His most controversial films – *La Grande Illusion* (1937) and *La Règle du jeu* (1939) – examine questions of class boundaries and the artificial nature of national identities. Both were condemned by the authorities in 1940 as demoralizing and pacifist and banned during the Occupation.

Renoir went to Hollywood after the Occupation of France by Germany. He became an American citizen in 1944, although he retained dual citizenship. Of the 37 films he made during his career, 13 were made postwar and of those only 5 were made in France. The most successful of these attest to his continuing love of the theatre and group work – *French Cancan* (1954) and *Le Petit Théâtre de Jean Renoir* (1969). As a testimony to his international status among film-makers, he was awarded an Oscar for life achievement in 1975.

SUSAN HAYWARD

renovation projects

Architectural and urban conservation is an

area of cultural affairs in which France can claim to have established a 'model and exemplar' for other European countries to follow (see Kain 1982, 1993). At the end of World War II, France had already enjoyed almost exactly a century of European supremacy in this field, during which one of the first European 'lists' of protected historic buildings was drawn up (1837) and the idea of extending protection to the buildings and streets which surrounded a listed building was first enacted (Kain 1986).

In the immediate post-World War II period, France, in common with most other European countries, suffered chronic housing shortages (due in part to the fact that about a quarter of the total housing stock was either war-damaged or destroyed). The 1950s solution was 'comprehensive redevelopment' involving slum removal and rehousing in the now notorious *grands ensembles* of high-rise apartments on the peripheries of cities (see Scargill 1983; Pariset 1991). Properties demolished could be both slum housing in social amenity terms and of significant historical and/or architectural value, notwithstanding their run-down physical condition.

It was against this background of the mass destruction of the historic quarters of French cities in the name of housing improvement that, in 1962 – at precisely the time that this activity was at its apogee – the French government once again enacted reforms which were radical not only for France but for the whole of Europe (see Kain 1981). An act, known since as the **Malraux act** after André **Malraux** (then Minister of Cultural Affairs, and its chief sponsor), provided for the designation of *secteurs sauvegardés* (**conservation zones**) within historic towns and gave powers for state intervention to enhance their historic qualities.

The Malraux act involved much more than the mere repair and preservation of old buildings. It also envisaged the demolition of eyesores within *secteurs sauvegardés*; the conversion of old buildings to adapt them to modern uses; the upgrading of housing by providing baths, sanitation and proper sewage disposal; the management of traffic and parking; and, most

radically, provision for the integration of new buildings with the old where restoration was not practicable. Of fundamental significance were attempts to introduce new economic activities to help retain populations and provide some positive functional role for *secteurs sauvegardés* within the wider urban context. It was certainly not the intention that they become open-air museums of historic architecture, but that their historic qualities be retained in a restructured functional context.

From the perspective of today we can judge that the *secteur sauvegardé* approach to urban and architectural conservation, while undoubtedly producing some spectacular individual beauties, has not brought about the general renaissance of the French urban past that André Malraux had planned. Designation has been slow (only some 75 *secteurs sauvegardés* exist out of about 400 initially envisaged), and the work of enhancement has progressed equally slowly and has been dogged by political problems, not least the fact that local communities had little say in what the central, Paris-based authorities intended to happen in each town. There has also been equally powerful popular political protest at the social changes that conservation in *secteurs sauvegardés* encouraged. However, any criticism should take account of the fact that the political and economic worlds of the present and thirty years ago are very different, particularly in the sense that the threats to historic quarters of towns today come less from the comprehensive redevelopers than from the inexorable processes of physical decay fuelled by economic stagnation and decline in inner-city areas. Nevertheless, the very limited public participation and an equally low order of local input to the decision-making process in *secteurs sauvegardés* are now politically unacceptable (Tuppen 1988).

In 1975, in what proved to be an analysis of the first importance, Nora and Eveno (1976) reported to the French government that, despite all the attempts in the thirty years since the end of World War II, 39 per cent of the national housing stock was still substandard. Their report underlined the (perhaps not unexpected) fact that it was the lowest income sector of the population, particularly the elderly, who suffered the worst conditions and who were effectively trapped. Nora and Eveno highlighted the scale of the reservoir of old, and often 'historic' housing stock for rehabilitation, and argued for rehabilitation rather than renewal on social and economic grounds, as well as for reasons of cultural heritage conservation.

The indictment of the failings of postwar housing improvement in France by the Nora-Eveno report and the recognition of the political opposition and the social problems consequent on the *secteur sauvegardé* approach brought about a radical change of government policy in the late 1970s. First, in 1976, a new single body, the Fonds d'Aménagement Urbain, was instituted to be responsible for the administration of all government funding of urban works; part of its brief was to establish a socially just approach to restoration. Opérations Programmées d'Amélioration de l'Habitat (OPAH) introduced in 1977 were designed both to avoid the local opposition which was slowing down work so much in the *secteurs sauvegardés* and to do something more in quantitative terms to improve the poor housing stock of French towns. The aims of OPAH are much more modest than those of the *secteurs sauvegardés*, and the areas they cover much smaller – perhaps about 300 dwellings on average. Gone also is the sweeping curetage of 'alien' structures built in recent times to return a *secteur sauvegardé* to a 'pure' state in which it was known to have (or more likely imagined to have) existed at a particular time in its past. Instead, the object with OPAH is to upgrade existing buildings to statutory norms of amenity and effect necessary structural repairs to buildings, providing that the continued survival of the indigenous population can be assured (see Kain 1993).

In practice, however, reality does not match up to these ideals. The voluntary principle which underpins them means that municipalities can declare OPAH but are not obliged to do so. Furthermore, even where an OPAH has been declared, owners are not required to do work on their properties. In the three OPAH of Bordeaux, for example, Michel Genty (1989) finds that all the restoration activity of the 1980s has resulted in only a modest number of rehabilitations of low-rented dwellings. By contrast, some 500 dwellings a year for uncontrolled letting have been produced and this process is bringing about substantial changes in the socioeconomic structure of these historic areas. In place of low-income families, there is a temporary and transient population of students, single people and childless couples who value a city-centre living environment, appreciate the historic aura engendered by the old buildings and are prepared and able to pay for it. *Plus ça change?*

ROGER KAIN

See also: architecture

Further reading

Genty, M. (1989) 'Stratégies immobilières et mutations résidentielles dans les quartiers historiques de Bordeaux', *Revue Géographique des Pyrénées et du Sud-Ouest* 60 (detailed historical piece).

Kain, R. J. P. (1982) 'Europe's Model and Exemplar Still? – The French Approach to Urban Conservation, 1962–1981', *Town Planning Review* 55.

——(1986) 'Développement des politiques de restauration du patrimoine historique des villes d'Europe occidentale', in P. Claval (ed.) *Géographie Historique des Villes d'Europe Occidentale*, Paris: Université de Paris-Sorbonne.

——(1993) 'Conserving the cultural heritage of historic buildings and towns in France since 1945' in M. Cook (ed.) *French Culture since 1945*, Exeter: University of Exeter Press, (a well-illustrated overview).

Nora, P. and Eveno, B. (1976) *L'Amélioration de l'habitat ancien*, Paris: La Documentation Française (a government publication that led to major social and policy discussion.)

Pariset, J.-D. (1991) *Reconstructions et modernisations: la France après les ruines*

1918 . . . 1945 . . . ,   Paris: Archives Nationales.

Scargill, I. (1983) *Urban France*, London: Croom Helm (a study of urban France).

Tuppen, J. (1988) *France Under Recession 1981–1986*, Basingstoke: Macmillan (a study of social conditions).

Resnais, Alain

b. 1922, Vannes

Director

Resnais's use of close-ups, tracking shots and subjective montage makes his style among the most distinctive in contemporary French cinema. He has always worked from pre-written screenplays – a *metteur-en-scène* in the full sense of the word – in which the exploration of time, place, memory and imagination looms large. Those factors, of course, are associated not only with the **Nouvelle Vague**, of whom Resnais is a close cousin, but also with the *nouveau roman*, and it is not surprising that his first two feature films, after a remarkable series of **documentaries** including the harrowing concentration-camp record *Nuit et Brouillard* (1955), should have been scripted by *nouveaux romanciers*. *Hiroshima mon amour* (1959) adapts a Marguerite **Duras** screenplay about a French actor whose love affair with a Japanese in Hiroshima rekindles the memory of her German lover, killed during the war. If the audacious equation of personal with historical trauma is Durassian, the slow tempo of filming, and cuts back and forth between remembered past and lived present, became recognized as Resnais's trademarks. *Last Year in Marienbad* (*L'Année dernière à Marienbad*) of 1961, from a **Robbe-Grillet** script, carries the earlier film's experimentation with time several stages further, to the point where past, present and future, remembered and imagined, cease to be clearly distinguishable. The flurry of possible interpretations this provoked contributed

as much as the unforgettable performance of Delphine **Seyrig** to the film's reputation.

Resnais's subsequent work has often had a more overtly political dimension, as with *Muriel* (1963), dealing with among other things the aftermath of the **Algerian war**, or *La Guerre est finie* (1966), in which Yves **Montand** plays a disabused Spanish Republican veteran. He has tackled the problems posed by accelerated social mobility in **Giscard d'Estaing**'s France (*Mon oncle d'Amérique*, with **Depardieu**, in 1980), the question of the boundary between life and death (*L'Amour à mort* in 1984) and latterly adaptations of bourgeois theatre (1986's *Mélo*, after Henri Bernstein, and the Alan Ayckbourn-scripted duo *Smoking/No Smoking* of 1993). His current companion Sabine Azéma has prominent roles in the three last-named.

For all this wide range of subject matter, Resnais's films are generally instantly recognizable as his. No other film-maker is quite so readily associated with the inescapability and elusiveness of memory, a theme dominant in contemporary French culture, as the obsession with the Occupation and Resistance and the centrality of **psychoanalysis** both show (in different ways). By turns solemn and humorous, his films almost always repay repeated viewings.

KEITH READER

See also: cinema

Further reading

Higgins, L. A. (1996) *New Novel, New Wave, New Politics*, Lincoln and London: University of Nebraska Press (this integrates Resnais's earlier work suggestively with the cultural and political climate of its period).

Monaco, J. (1978) *Alain Resnais*, London and New York: Secker and Warburg/Oxford University Press (a well-documented study of the role of imagination).

Oms, M. (1988) *Alain Resnais*, Paris and Marseille: Rivages (a handy guide with full cinematography and bibliography).

restaurant guides

The first and most famous of France's restaurant guides was the red *Guide Michelin*, which made its first appearance in 1900 and whose annual awarding of stars up to a maximum of three still causes much suspense and heart-searching. *Michelin* was long associated with the rich traditional style of *la haute cuisine*, to which the polemical embracing of *nouvelle cuisine* by the *Guide Gault-Millau* (founded in 1972) represented something of a riposte. *Gault-Millau* awards *toques* (chef's hats) up to a maximum of four, along with marks out of twenty. Unlike *Michelin*, which contents itself with a brief list of the principal dishes of each listed restaurant, *Gault-Millau* provides often lengthy discursive accounts of the specialities, atmosphere, decor and development of its choices. A more recent wave of guides catering for the young and/or financially challenged includes the 'Petit futé' series, dealing not only with restaurants but also with shops, accommodation and a variety of services on a town-by-town basis, and the 'Guides du routard', whose *Libération*-like use of language and happy-go-lucky cover designs clearly target the discriminating backpacker market. Other noteworthy guides include the *Bottin gourmand* (founded in 1983), the *Guide Kléber* (1954–82) and that produced by the motoring magazine, *Auto-Journal*, available from news-stands rather than booksellers. However, the unquestioned market leaders would appear to be *Michelin*, with a circulation of 500,000, and *Gault-Millau* (200,000).

KEITH READER

See also: gastronomy

restaurants du coeur

These are soup kitchens, first established by comedian **Coluche** in 1985 to provide free meals for the hungry over the winter months. Friends in show business and politics joined Coluche in a massive media appeal. The chari-

ty's name and logo (a heart between a knife and fork) summarize the philosophy of appealing to public generosity, the food industry and government in order to make available surplus food supplies and to mobilize volunteers in an annual, nationwide operation. After her husband's death, Véronique Colucci maintained the initiative; assistance now also includes hostel accommodation for the homeless. During the winter 1995–6, over 50 million meals were provided.

PAM MOORES

See also: street papers

Rétoré, Guy

b. 1924, Paris

Producer and director

The founder of the Théâtre de l'Est de Paris (TEP) in 1950 with the Guilde, an amateur-turned professional troupe, and an advocate of *théâtre populaire*, Rétoré is famous for his 1970s production of classics, and contemporary writings from **Bonal** and **Besnehard**. The Guilde became the TEP in 1963, and the TEP became a national theatre (Théâtre National de la Colline) in 1987, under the direction of Jorge **Lavelli**.

ANNIE SPARKS

See also: theatre; theatres, national

Reverdy, Pierre

b. 1889, Narbonne;
d. 1960, Solesmes

Poet

Reverdy formed friendships with Apollinaire and Jacob and with painters (particularly Cubists) and founded the review *Nord-Sud*. His **poetry** was always private, centred on solitude, with strong emphasis on enclosures ('Le monde est ma prison' is a line from the poem 'Outre Mesure') and spaces that separate and isolate. There is in those poems a quiet anguish and a sense of dread, which point toward a continuing spiritual crisis. After 1926, he lived in retirement near the famous Abbey of Solesmes, as if to resolve a religious problem by living in the vicinity of a monastery. His most famous collections are *Ferraille* (Scrap-Iron) of 1937, *Plupart du temps* (Most of the Time) from 1944, and 1949's *Main d'oeuvre* (Workmanship), along with prose works such as 1956's *En vrac* (Loosely Packed).

WALTER A. STRAUSS

revolutionary groups

Increasing dissatisfaction with the French Communist Party, culminating in the events of **May 1968**, led to the emergence of a number of self-styled revolutionary groups on the Left. These rejected any suggestion of an electoral or parliamentary road to social change, seen as doomed to neutralization or 'recuperation' by the bourgeois state and the **class** interests underlying it, and favoured direct action – factory occupations, general strikes, sometimes even the taking of hostages. Groups of so-called Maoist inspiration fell into two categories : the unreconstructed Sinophile Stalinists of the Parti Communiste Français (Marxiste-Léniniste) and the anarcho-spontaneists in such groups as Vive la Révolution or the Nouvelle Résistance Populaire, for whom France was occupied by the forces of capital much as she had been by those of Germany in the war years. The murder of Maoist militant Pierre Overney by a security guard at the Renault factory near Paris in 1972 led to the demise of the credibility of such revolutionary rhetoric; it would now be virtually impossible to describe oneself as a 'Maoist' in France, or indeed anywhere in Europe. The Trotskyist groups, the most enduring of which remains the Ligue Communiste Révolutionnaire, led by Alain

Krivine, were much more critical of individual acts of violence, advocating a Leninist strategy within an internationalist perspective that refused identification with any existent forms of Socialism. Less attention-attracting than the different varieties of Maoism, they remain active and substantially loyal to their earlier principles and programmes today.

KEITH READER

See also: Marxism; parties and movements

Further reading

Bourseiller, C. (1996) *Les Maoistes*, Paris: Plon (an absorbing narrative which concludes that Maoism meant so many different things in different places that it cannot really be said to have existed at all).

Reyes, Alina

b. 1956, Soulac

Writer

Alina Reyes's first novel, the prizewinning *The Butcher* (*Le Boucher*), traces the sexual initiation of a young woman with a lyrical and visceral sensuality which Reyes later applies to other female voyages of self-discovery: for example, Lucie/Mélusine in *Lucie's Long Voyage* (*Lucie au long cours*) and Lucile/Alice in *Au corset qui tue* (At the Sign of the Corset That Kills). Women's self-discovery creates life, future and freedom from initially unappealing flesh, from the remote past, from enclosed spaces or from a seemingly hostile natural environment. Openness is also suggested by multiple narratives within narratives and Reyes's luminous style. *Behind Closed Doors* (*Derrière la porte*) uses the tropes of **pornography** to deconstruct the mechanisms of male and female desire.

OWEN HEATHCOTE

See also: erotic writing; women's/lesbian writing

Further reading

Heathcote, O. (1994) 'Is There Abuse in the Text? Legitimate and Illegitimate Violence in *La Question*, *Les Chiens*, *Le Boucher* and *Mémoires d'une fouetteuse*', in R. Günther and J. Windebank (eds) *Violence and Conflict in French Culture*, Sheffield: Sheffield Academic Press (a consideration of the gender-political implications of Reyes's first novels).

ICA audio cassette 736: Alina Reyes, Kate Campbell, 14 November 1991 (interview and discussion).

Reza, Yasmina

birthdate unknown

Playwright

An actor graduate of **Lecoq**'s school, Reza has written film scripts, adaptations and plays, including *Conversations après un enterrement* (Conversations After a Funeral); *La Traversée d'hiver* (Getting Through the Winter), '*Art*' [sic], her most successful **theatre** work to date, and *L'Homme du hasard* (Man of Fate). Patrice Kerbrat directs much of her work.

ANNIE SPARKS

Rezvani, Serge

b. 1928, place unknown

Playwright and writer

A writer of Persian and Russian origins, which influence his forty-plus works. His plays include the famous *Capitaine Shell, Capitaine*

Ecco, *Le Palais d'hiver* (The Winter Palace) and *Le Camp du drap d'or* (Camp of the Golden Flag). *Les Années lumière* (The Light Years), an autobiographical novel, is his best-known work.

ANNIE SPARKS

See also: theatre

Ricardou, Jean

b. 1932, Cannes

Writer and critic

Ricardou's writings blend poetic fiction with guidelines to instruct the reader and theories of textual production showing how texts are generated from narrative and linguistic mechanisms. As organizer of numerous colloquia, Ricardou brought novelists and critics together and made the **nouveau roman** more visible.

LYNN A. HIGGINS

Further reading

Higgins, L. A. (1984) *Parables of Theory: Jean Ricardou's Metafiction*, Birmingham, AL: Summa (the first book on Ricardou's fiction and theory).

Sirvent, M. (ed.) (1991) *Studies in Twentieth-Century Literature* 15, 2 (a cluster of articles including interview and bibliographies).

Richard, Jean-Pierre

b. 1922, Paris

Critic

A literary critic of the so-called Geneva School of criticism, Jean-Pierre Richard's first major publication, *Poésie et profondeur* (Poetry and

Profundity), appeared in 1955. After this, he went on to produce several more books on **poetry**. His work is characterized principally by techniques of close reading, that is, of subjecting segments of text to particularly detailed interpretive scrutiny. This penetrating approach may be most readily appreciated in his *Proust et le monde sensible* (Proust and the World of the Senses) of 1974, *Microlectures* (Microreadings) in 1979, and *Onze études sur la poésie moderne* (Eleven Studies on Modern Poetry) in 1981. He has also published works on the novelist Céline and the poet Mallarmé.

MARTYN CORNICK

Major works

Richard, J.-P. (1961) *L'Univers imaginaire de Mallarmé*, Paris: Éditions du Seuil.
——(1979) *Microlectures*, Paris: Éditions du Seuil.
——(1996) *Terrains de lecture*, Paris: Gallimard.

Ricoeur, Paul

b. 1913, France

Philosopher

Paul Ricoeur is one of the most respected French philosophers. Trained at the Sorbonne, he blended Husserl's phenomenology with his Protestant faith, and developed an ethical philosophy much influenced by the Socialist ideas of André Philip. After the war, he incorporated elements of Freudian **psychoanalyis** into his thought and, during regular visits to the United States, explored analytical philosophy, becoming a channel through which the 'linguistic turn' of English-speaking philosophers was introduced into French thought. He also joined Mounier's review *Esprit*, for which he wrote the philosophy column. After the events of **May 1968**, he supported university reform and

moved from the Sorbonne to become rector of Nanterre, but resigned after sustained attacks from radical students and staff. Thereafter, he mainly taught in the United States, at Yale and Chicago, while still working in Paris as a CNRS director of research, and from 1974 as editor of the prestigious *Moral and Metaphysical Review* (*Revue de métaphysique et de morale*). His three-volume *Time and Narrative* (*Temps et récit*) published between 1983 and 1985 examines how time and narrative are interlinked in historical, literary and philosophical writing, and has become the most influential of Ricoeur's works, which are widely read in the English-speaking world.

MICHAEL KELLY

See also: Catholicism and Protestantism

Rita Mitsouko, Les

Musicians

A rock double act which began in the 1980s – Rita is the singer Catherine Ringer, and Mitsouko is Fred Chichin the musician – and was successful throughout the 1990s. Their whole repertory is definitely eclectic, they have been iconoclastic on the world stage, and their musical style is baroque in the sense of being grotesque, whimsical, imaginative and at times disturbing. Their videos earned them the Prix Euro MTV in 1994, when the album *Système D* was released.

GÉRARD POULET

See also: pop video; rock and pop

Rivette, Jacques

b. 1928, Rouen

Director

Rivette followed the path from *Cahiers du cinéma* criticism to direction in 1958, when he began shooting *Paris nous appartient*, whose length meant that it was not ready for release until 1961. The original version of *Out One* (1974) lasted twelve hours and forty minutes; understandably, it was only ever screened once. Rivette uses exceptional length to explore and distort the possibilities of narrative and the spectator's sense of time within the **cinema** – a distortion mirrored in the relationship between painter (**Piccoli**) and model (Emmanuelle **Béart**) in *La Belle Noiseuse* of 1991. He attained perhaps unwanted notoriety when his 1966 Diderot adaptation *La Religieuse* was for a while banned by the French censor.

KEITH READER

See also: cinema

Robbe-Grillet, Alain

b. 1922, Brest

Writer and director

By generating fictions from linguistic play and from often sado-erotic fantasy, Robbe-Grillet's self-reflecting novels and films show how imagination is shaped by language and popular culture. He reveals subjective states through description of the visual world. As an editor at **Minuit**, he has influenced contemporary fiction.

LYNN A. HIGGINS

See also: *nouveau roman*

Further reading

Leki, I. (1983) *Alain Robbe-Grillet*, Boston: Twayne (introduction to Robbe-Grillet's work; contains bibliography).

Morrissette, B. (1975) *The Novels of Robbe-Grillet*, Ithaca, NY: Cornell University Press (a novel-by-novel study by Robbe-Grillet's first exegete).

Robuchon, Joël

b. 1945, France

Chef

Perhaps the outstanding French chef to concentrate his activity in the kitchens of his own restaurant (the Jamin, in Paris), Robuchon is famed for the rigour and precision of his cooking. He obtained the coveted three Michelin stars only three years after opening the restaurant in 1981, and represents the opposite tendency to the 'galloping gourmet' media stardom of such as Paul **Bocuse**.

KEITH READER

See also: gastronomy

Rocard, Michel

b. 1930, Courbevoie, near Paris

Politician

A Socialist minister (1981–5) and prime minister (1988–91) and several times would-be presidential candidate, Rocard was for many years a rival of **Mitterrand** and leader of a minority tendency within the Parti Socialiste. Undoubtedly influenced by his Protestant background and backed by intellectuals such as Jacques Julliard and Alain **Touraine**, and publications such as *Le Nouvel Observateur*, Rocard sought to define Socialism as an ethic of responsibility and autonomy. His brief period as party leader (1993–4) and his presidential ambitions were brought to an end by the PS's catastrophic defeat in the 1994 European elections.

LAURENCE BELL

See also: parties and movements

Major works

Rocard, M. (1987) *Le Coeur à l'ouvrage*, Paris: Odile Jacob (an autobiography, followed by Rocard's political prescriptions).

Further reading

Schneider, R. (1987) *Michel Rocard*, Paris: Stock (a favourable biography by a political columnist).

Rochefort, Christiane

b. 1917, Paris

Writer

Through play with language, genre and parody, Rochefort demystifies institutions such as marriage and social services. Her feminist, humorous, utopian and anarchic vision constitutes a passionate plea for an end to exploitation of all kinds. Rochefort's 1959 *The Warrior's Rest* (*Le Repos du guerrier*), her first novel, made into a film by Roger **Vadim** in 1962, shocked in its portrayal of eroticism.

LYNN A. HIGGINS

See also: feminism (movements/groups); women's/lesbian writing

Further reading

Constant, I. (1996) *Les Mots étincelants de Christiane Rochefort: langages d'utopie*, Amsterdam: Rodopi (the first book on Rochefort, this studies her novels in the context of utopias; contains bibliography).

rock and pop

Since the late 1950s and early 1960s the French pop scene has seen significant developments as well as the steamrolling invasion – as everywhere else – of Anglo-American pop music in its various, successive or overlapping forms: rock and roll, rockabilly, West Coast, progressive rock, decadent rock, punk rock, hard rock, blues rock, indie pop, reggae, soul, disco, rap. As consumers of pop music, the French listen to more 'Anglo-Saxon' music than their own, which could explain the lowly status of French rock and pop.

The first French rock and roll number in France was written as a humorous parody of a genre with no apparent future by Boris **Vian** and performed by Henri **Salvador** (*Rock'n'Roll Mops*). But in the 1960s Elvis Presley had his followers; their temple was Le Golf Drouot in Paris. This venue saw the start of the careers of **Hallyday**, **Mitchell** and Dutronc. Rock and roll music represented a political stance for a young and largely working-class generation and a medium for individual liberation; it was cleverly harnessed by managers and producers of show business and generated the *yé-yé* phenomenon. The radio programme *Salut les copains* (Hello, buddies) on **Europe 1** was their rallying point.

In the 1970s, rock music pervaded the sounds of the **folk music** revival. Pure French rock generated an extraordinary number of groups who came and went, producing endless carbon copies of British or American models. At the end of the 1970s disco music reigned – but, with a few exceptions, French rock was in the doldrums.

Since the 1980s, authentic rock groups like Telephone (highly popular at home and abroad), Starshooter, Marquis de Sade, **Indochine**, Les **Rita Mitsouko** and Les **Négresses vertes** have shown that French rock and pop is thriving, and have at last found international recognition even if in France itself it has generally been American and British artists who have attracted the biggest crowds. The cultural establishment gave the home product a helping hand. In 1984, Jack **Lang**, then Minister of Culture, officially inaugurated the first Zenith, at the Porte de Bagnolet, a new venue for rock and pop concerts, with Jacques Higelin, the charismatic rock figure, topping the bill. For a while, in 1989, there was even a *Chargé de mission pour le rock et les variétés* (a rock and pop official representative) within his ministry. Also significant is the huge contribution to the French pop scene from multiple ethnic communities and their musical hybrids (**jazz**, rock, funk, reggae, raï): **Carte de séjour**, Karim **Kacel**, Cheb **Khaled**, **Mano Negra**, Kassav's and West Indian Zouk. French pop music's success lies in the future reconciliation of rhythms and sounds coming from other continents and cultures.

GÉRARD POULET

See also: beur music; music venues; video imports

Further reading

Poulet, G. (1993) 'Popular Music', in M. Cook (ed.) *French Culture Since 1945*, London: Longman (an informative and serious attempt to cover the various facets of rock, pop and *variétés* in postwar France).

Rohmer, Éric

b. 1920, Nancy

Director, real name Maurice Schérer

The only **Nouvelle Vague** director whose films are still regularly distributed in English-speaking countries, Rohmer has maintained remarkable success through filming on often impossibly tight budgets, using 16 mm film stock or video – as for *The Green Ray* (*Le Rayon vert*) of 1986, shown on French television before its cinema premiere – and confining himself to a miniaturist canvas in which ambiguities and misunderstandings between (generally would-be) lovers predomi-

nate. His literary antecedents are such as Marivaux or Jane Austen; in the **cinema**, though he has posterity (Christian Vincent or the American Whit Stillman both owe an obvious debt), ancestors are harder to find.

His first feature, *Le Signe du lion* of 1959 (but not released until 1962), is harsher than his subsequent work. It tells of the agony of a Bohemian musician (a distant cousin of **Renoir**'s Octave in *La Règle du jeu*?) left stranded and impoverished in a pitiless August Paris. Thereafter, his feature films fell generally into two series, *Six contes moraux* (Six Moral Tales) and *Comédies et proverbes* (Comedies and Proverbs). Best known in the first series is *My Night with Maud* (*Ma nuit chez Maud*) of 1969, in which Jean-Louis **Trintignant**'s sophistically Catholic engineer hesitates between the supposedly nice girl in the pew next door and the worldly wise divorcée Maud. Few other films have focused so closely on people talking themselves into love yet out of bed together; it is not surprising that Rohmer's major critical work, in collaboration with **Chabrol**, was a study of that arch-exponent of Catholic sexual guilt, Hitchcock.

The talkiness and insecurity masquerading as sophistication of Rohmer's characters is marked in more recent films, such as 1982's *Le Beau Mariage* and 1984's *Les Nuits de la pleine lune*, in both of which the bourgeois institutions of marriage and monogamy prove more resistant to attacks upon them than might be imagined. His most recent series, *Contes des quatre saisons* (Tales of the Four Seasons), displays, along with the somewhat prurient attitude towards young women for which he has earned predictable feminist criticism, a turn towards belief – however ironic – in destiny and the miraculous already foreshadowed in *The Green Ray*. Félicie's reuniting with the father of her child at the end of *Conte d'hiver* (1992) is among the most moving moments in Rohmer's entire oeuvre.

KEITH READER

Further reading

Bonitzer, P. (1991) *Éric Rohmer*, Paris: Cahiers du Cinéma (a subtle philosophical and thematic study).

Magny, J. (1995) *Éric Rohmer*, Paris: Rivages (includes a full and up-to-date filmography and bibliography).

romantic novels

Modern romantic novels (*romans à l'eau de rose*) comprise 15 per cent of all paperback sales in France. They are produced on a monthly basis to a standard format and length, much like magazines, and sell in supermarkets, railway station kiosks and corner shops as well as by mail order. Harlequin, owned by the Canadian media group Torstar, is the market leader and accounts for well over 60 per cent of sales of romantic novels. It began publication in 1978 with four novels per month and its translations of English-language contemporary romances were so successful that in six years it had reached a sales peak of 20 million books and a readership of 6 million. Harlequin's success stimulated emulation and a number of French publishers followed with locally written contemporary romances, notably J'Ai Lu (who also publish Barbara Cartland), Presses de la Cité, Jean-Claude Lattès and Tallendier.

The romantic novel is a love story, narrating the birth of an affective and sexual bond between a man and a woman. The narrative programme is organized by an initial meeting of the protagonists, usually producing a conflict between attraction and repulsion. There then follows the overcoming of obstacles, both internal and external, and a resolution which culminates in a happy ending. The roots of the theme can be traced back to Ancient Greek mythology, via medieval romances, the classics *L'Astrée*, *La Princesse de Clèves*, *Manon Lescaut*, *The New Heloise* (*La Nouvelle Héloïse*) and *The Lady of the Camellias* (*La Dame aux camélias*). Its modern form, however, is more usefully seen as emerging in the mass market for literature that developed in the course of the nineteenth century, in the *roman-feuilleton* (serial novel) appearing in the popular press, via Georges Ohnet's *Le Maître de forges* (The Ironmaster) and continued into this century by Delly, du Veuzit, Bernage, Magali and Anne and Serge Golon's *Angélique*, writers whose books dominated the field till the arrival of Harlequin. Thereafter, the dominant model of the successful romantic novel has been derived from the Anglo-Saxon world, originally based on the books of the UK publisher Mills and Boon. The bulk are based on the contemporary workplace, though recently the romantic novel publishers have added series that evoke **detective fiction**. The central focus of the narrative, however, remains the love conflict of the two main characters, although the social profile and position of the heroine, as well as sub-themes, evolve to reflect the constantly changing expectations and aspirations of women in our times.

GEORGE PAIZIS

Further reading

Bettinotti, J. (1990) *La Corrida de l'amour*, Montreal: XYZ (a study of Harlequins intended to discover how the texts function).

Coquillat, M. (1988) *Romans d'amour*, Paris: Odile Jacob (an attack on the contemporary romantic novel from a traditional feminist point of view).

Péquignot, B. (1991) *La Relation amoureuse*, Paris: L'Harmattan (a sociological study of the modern genre).

Le Roman sentimental, actes du colloque (1990/1) 2 vols, Limoges: PULIM (a variety of articles on romantic fiction).

Ronis, Willy

b. 1910, Paris;
d. 1972, Paris

Photographer

From the beginning of his career, Ronis was ideologically attracted by assignments of a social nature, covering strikes and union activity for the Parti Communiste and, like **Doisneau**, charting the urbanization of the **suburbs** (in his case, those of Ménilmontant and Belleville). In the 1960s, he produced photographic illustrations for many news stories on Algeria and eastern Europe.

MICHAEL WORTON

See also: photography

Rouault, Georges

b. 1871, Paris;
d. 1958, Paris

Artist

Considered one of the greatest spiritual painters of the twentieth century, Rouault was a devout Christian and religious subjects dominate his work, particularly depictions of Christ. As a boy he was apprenticed to a restorer of stained glass and his paintings often resemble stained-glass windows with their simple shapes, outlined with thick black lines filled with rich colours. He remained outside the main currents of the art of the period.

DEBRA KELLY

See also: painting

Rouch, Jean

b. 1917, Paris

Documentarist

An ethnographic documentarist who started his film career making **documentaries** in Nigeria (in the 1950s) and whose belief in filming only what he saw – what he initially called *cinéma-direct* – marks Rouch as one of the founders of the *cinéma-vérité* group of film-

makers. Lightweight 16 mm camera and recording equipment for direct sound are the tools of his committed politicized cinema that strives to record as close as possible the real. For Rouch, the personages on screen are the authors of their own scripts and verbal testimonies, and the footage must remain uncut (see *Moi, un Noir* from 1957). If this documentary style has its limitations by dint of its lack of editing, Rouch was to discover with *Chronique d'un été* (1961) that there are, equally, ideological problems inherent in any attempts at objectivity once the decision to edit footage has been made.

SUSAN HAYWARD

See also: cinema

Roudy, Yvette

b. 1929, Pessac, Gironde

Politician

Roudy will be best remembered as France's first Minister for Women's Rights (1981–6), responsible for initiatives and reforms favouring women. Of these, the 1982 law on state-reimbursed **abortion** and that of 1983, establishing equality at work between the sexes, were the most notable.

A **mitterrandiste**, her career has spanned a period of over thirty years, in which time she has occupied high offices, both within the Socialist Party and those of deputy, MEP and mayor.

KHURSHEED WADIA

See also: abortion/contraception; feminism (movements/groups); parties and movements

Major works

Roudy, Y. (1985) *A cause d'elles*, Paris: Albin Michel (an autobiographical work).

Rouge

Newspaper

Founded in September 1968 by militants from the ex-Jeunesse Communiste Révolutionnaire, *Rouge* was initially published fortnightly but became weekly while supporting Alain Krivine, the Trotskyist candidate in the 1969 presidential election campaign. It has remained the newspaper of the French Section of the Fourth International through its various name changes (currently the Ligue Communiste Révolutionnaire). It was published daily for twenty issues during Krivine's 1974 presidential campaign and was launched as a daily paper in March 1976, but financial problems forced it back to weekly publication. In 1996, *Rouge* had a weekly print run of 7,000.

DAVID DRAKE

See also: left-wing press; May 1968; revolutionary groups

Roy, Claude

b. 1915, Paris;
d. 1997, Paris

Writer

A poet, novelist and critic, Roy began his career in right-wing circles, being attracted in particular to Charles Maurras's nationalist Action Française movement and writing for the reviews and newspapers in its orbit. After being denounced in the collaborationist press, in 1942 Roy turned to the Resistance, joining the French Communist Party a year later. However, when the Soviets invaded Hungary in 1956, Roy entered a period of dissidence from Communism which culminated in his resignation from the party in 1958. His intellectual itinerary is charted in a series of autobiographical memoirs – *Moi je* (Me, I) from 1969, *Nous* (Us) in 1972 and *Somme toute* (When All's Said and Done) in 1976 – and in later years in his *Livres de bord* (Notebooks). He has also produced children's books and travel writing; his work reflects a penchant for the lapidary phrase and a particular fascination for Chinese culture.

MARTYN CORNICK

See also: autobiography; parties and movements

Major works

Roy, C. (1970) *Poésies*, Paris: Gallimard.
——(1979) *Sur la Chine*, Paris: Gallimard.

RTL (Radio-Télévision Luxembourg)

Radio station

Attracting nearly 18 per cent of the listening public, RTL enjoys the status of not only France's most popular radio station, but also its oldest *radio périphérique*. Created in 1933, its transmitters are in Luxembourg, although its studios are in Paris. Broadcasting on long wave, the station is available to a large proportion of listeners in western Europe. Its programmes are wide-ranging: news, debates, interviews, documentaries, quizzes and variety shows (hosted by such popular presenters as Patrick Sabatier and Philippe Bouvard), and listener participation (by telephone) plays an important role. In 1995, a subsidiary popular music station, RTL 2 (FM), was created.

ALAN PEDLEY

See also: radio (private/free)

rugby

With its stronghold in southwest France (Toulouse, Agen, Béziers, Biarritz, and so on), rugby has remained an important sport in

France, with its national championship and the country's participation in the Five Nations' Tournament (which it dominated in the 1960s) and the World Cup. Only the Racing Club in Paris has been able to break the southwest's stranglehold on the national championship in recent times, but the country unites behind its national team which had unusually limited success in the 1990s until its third place in the Rugby World Cup in South Africa (1995). Rugby League – *le Rugby à XIII* or *le Jeu à XIII* in French – is also at its strongest in the southwest but consistently fails to reach the heights of its British counterpart. Outstanding French players of the fifteen-a-side game include Pierre Albaladejo, Serge Blanco, Jean-Pierre Rives and Jean-Pierre Romeu.

IAN PICKUP

See also: sport

Rykiel, Sonia

b. 1939

Fashion designer

Rykiel studied modelling and decorated the windows at La Grande Maison des Blancs as an intern. She designed the famous *pour girl sweater*, an oversized sweater for women which launched her career as a designer when it was featured on the cover of **Elle**. In 1968, she opened her boutique and started to design original sweaters. She invented the outside seams and still designs clothes for various foreign fashion houses. She has created over 4,000 knitwear designs and is among the most successful and popular French ready-to-wear designers.

JOËLLE VITIELLO

See also: fashion

S

Sagan, Françoise

b. 1935, Cajarc, Lot

Writer and playwright

A popular novelist, Sagan has also written plays, short stories and volumes of **autobiography**. Of her numerous fictions, which frequently focus on women's experience of the pleasures and pain of love, two early novels – *Bonjour tristesse* (1954) and *A Certain Smile* (*Un certain sourire*) from 1956 – are the best known. The first, written when Sagan was in her teens, won the *Prix des Critiques*, and established Sagan's international reputation. Sagan's work is usually considered as 'light'; however, her novels offer, arguably, significant insights into feminine psychology.

ALEX HUGHES

See also: literary prizes; women's/lesbian writing

Saint Laurent, Yves

b. 1936, Oran, Algeria

Fashion designer

Saint Laurent studied fashion design in Paris. In 1953, he was hired by Christian **Dior** and devel-oped the 'trapeze' silhouette. In 1962, after being drafted by the French army for the French–Algerian conflict, he opened his fashion house. After introducing successively the cowboy and the sailor look, Saint Laurent turned to contemporary art and in 1965 launched his Mondrian dress. In 1966, he opened his first ready-to-wear boutique, Saint Laurent Rive Gauche. He mass-produced his clothes to make them accessible, and developed accessories, a men's line and perfumes.

JOËLLE VITIELLO

See also: Algerian war; fashion

Saint-Phalle, Niki de

b. 1930, Paris

Artist

Niki de Saint-Phalle first attracted attention with her 'rifle-shot' reliefs incorporating containers of paint which, when shot at by the viewer, would stain the surface – a parody of abstract *art informel* painting. A member of the *Nouveau Réalisme* group founded in 1960, she used *objets trouvés* to create playful reliefs and sculptures. The representation of women was the theme of her series of *Brides* and *Nanas*, huge, gaudily painted female figures, which culminated in a monumental, hollow, reclining woman, 28 m long, containing 'rooms' which were entered via the vagina. This collaboration with Jean **Tinguely** was followed by others, notably the Stravinsky fountain outside the **Pompidou Centre**. In 1979, she began work on her Gaudi-inspired Tarrochi Garden in Tuscany.

CAROL WILCOX

See also: sculpture

Salacrou, Armand

b. 1899, Rouen;
d. 1989, Le Havre

Playwright

Salacrou's home town, Le Havre, provides the focus for many of his plays. His works since 1940 are notable for their **Sartrean** outlook, such as *Les Nuits de Colère* (Nights of Anger) and *Dieu le savait* (God Knew), and for their satire of the bourgeoisie, like *Histoire de rire* (History of Laughter) and *Une femme trop honnête* (The Over-Honest Woman).

ANNIE SPARKS

See also: theatre

Further reading

Ubersfeld, A. (1969) *A. Salacrou*, Paris: Seghers (thorough critique of his work).

Sallenave, Danièle

b. 1940, Angers

Writer, academic and literary theorist

Sallenave's early publications, including *Paysage de ruines avec personnages* (Ruined Landscape with Figures) and *Le Voyage* *d'Amsterdam* (Amsterdam Journey), bear witness to her theoretical interest in narrative and semiotic innovation. However, her best-known novel, *Les Portes de Gubbio* (Gubbio's Gateways), published in 1980 and awarded the Prix Renaudot, represents a return to a more traditional, less experimental form of novelistic practice. Sallenave has also worked in the medium of the **theatre**.

ALEX HUGHES

See also: literary prizes; women's/lesbian writing

Salvador, Henri

b. 1917, Cayenne, French Guiana

Singer-songwriter and musician

Having gone to Paris at the age of 7, Henri Salvador joined Ray Ventura's big band, Les Collégiens (The College Boys), touring with them in 1941 in South America, where he stayed until 1945, having become a star in his own right. Back in France, Salvador established himself as a singer (particularly in the 1960s), comic actor and parodist, though his first love was and remains **jazz**. This French version of Sammy Davis Junior was the highly respected guest of honour at the eleventh 'Victoires de la Musique' (French Pop Music Awards) in 1996.

IAN PICKUP

See also: song/*chanson*

Sanson, Véronique

b. 1949, Paris

Singer-songwriter

Adopting a style which blends **jazz**, blues and **rock**, Véronique Sanson has, from the early 1970s, remained in the forefront of French popular music. Having benefited from the guidance of Michel **Berger** on her first two records, and having been married to the musician Stephen Stills, she successfully split her time for a number of years between France and the United States. A distinctive (if ultimately repetitive) style on the piano is allied to a voice influenced by the phrasing of American blues singers. One of her more unusual successes is her album *Symphonique Sanson* (1989), with the Prague Symphony Orchestra.

IAN PICKUP

See also: song/*chanson*

Sardou, Michel

b. 1947, Paris

Singer-songwriter

A third-generation member of a family of French show-business artists, Michel Sardou has scarcely been out of the limelight since 1970. He is often associated with right-wing and unfashionable views – as in *Les Ricains* (The Yanks), a song highlighting the French debt to the USA during World War II, which was released when it was fashionable to decry American involvement in Vietnam. Sardou has regularly expressed controversial opinions, which have none the less won him a large and faithful following. He had notable successes at Bercy in 1991 and 1993 and at the Olympia in 1995, and has written songs with Jacques Revaux, Pierre Billon and Pierre **Delanoë**.

IAN PICKUP

See also: song/*chanson*

Sarraute, Nathalie

b. 1902, Ivanovo-Voznessensk, Russia

Writer

In his preface to her 1948 novel, *Portrait of a*

Man Unknown (*Portrait d'un inconnu*), **Sartre** situated Sarraute's writing by observing that the novel genre, like postwar France itself, was entering a period of self-reflection. Sarraute's work was well under way by the time the **nouveau roman** emerged, and her approach contributed to its development. Like others among the new novelists, Sarraute sees the novel as a quest for (rather than a representation of) reality; unlike them, the reality she seeks is that of psychological interiority.

In her 1956 essay collection, *The Age of Suspicion* (*L'Ère du soupçon*), Sarraute outlines her goals for renewing the novel: she seeks to remove conventional narrative props that would construct a reassuringly familiar world. Her desire to establish unmediated encounters between the reader and another consciousness is the driving force behind her formal innovations.

In Sarraute's novels, the only plot consists of proto-events without label or description, devoid of distancing past tenses or narrative viewpoint. Most significant are her reforms of characterization, introduced in her 1939 collection of texts, *Tropisms* (*Tropismes*), reissued in 1957. The term 'tropism', borrowed from biology, refers to an organism's instinctive turning towards light or heat. Sarraute's tropisms chart the involuntary impulses, emotions and perceptions below the surface of consciousness. She invented the techniques of 'subconversations' and 'predialogue' in an attempt to capture these unarticulated and uncodified movements of subjectivity. Recognizing the inadequacy of traditional modes of writing to capture these fragmentary, interior voices, Sarraute explores the limits of intelligibility. She replaces names and descriptions with imagery and metaphors to evoke the liquidity of laughter, for example, or the cutting edge of interpersonal hostility.

Sarraute's career is unified by her search for techniques capable of communicating her conception of subjectivity. After *Tropisms*, her 1953 novel, *Martereau* (*Martereau*), and the 1959 *The Planetarium* (*Le Planétarium*) convey the inner experience of anonymous characters in their familial and social interactions.

Her 1963 novel *The Golden Fruits* (*Les Fruits d'or*), the 1968 novel *Between Life and Death* (*Entre la Vie et la mort*), and her 1972 *Do You Hear them?* (*Vous les entendez?*) explore, from within, the creative process itself. Several radio and stage plays investigate the capacity of spoken dialogue to incorporate the voices hidden below conscious awareness. Finally, her 1983 fictionalized **autobiography**, *Childhood* (*Enfance*), examines the tropisms of a particular child. Sarraute here rejoins other *nouveaux romanciers* such as **Robbe-Grillet**, **Duras** and **Simon**, who problematized and renewed the autobiographical genre in the 1980s.

LYNN A. HIGGINS

See also: women's/lesbian writing

Further reading

Besser, G. R. (1979) *Nathalie Sarraute*, Boston: Twayne (an overview of Sarraute's career, its major themes and stages, in the context of the experimental modern novel; contains bibliography).

L'Esprit créateur (1996) *Nathalie Sarraute ou le texte du for intérieur*, special issue 36, 2.

Minogue, V. (1981) *Nathalie Sarraute and the War of the Words: A Study of Five Novels*, Edinburgh: Edinburgh University Press (an analysis of Sarraute's work with language).

Sarrazin, Albertine

b. 1937, Algiers;
d. 1967, Montpellier

Writer

The author of a series of autobiographical fictions chronicling her disrupted and disruptive life – she was a foundling child whose difficulties with her adoptive family led to a stint at reform school, followed by a series of sojourns in prison, punctuated by several escapes – Sarrazin's work captured the attention of French critics and readers when it began to appear in the mid-1960s. Best known for novels telling of prison life and its aftermath – *Astragal* (*L'Astragale*) in 1965, *The Runaway* (*La Cavale*) in 1969 and *La Traversière* (The Crossing) in 1966 – Sarrazin was also a prolific producer of diaries, poems and letters. Many of these were published posthumously in the 1970s, after their author died prematurely.

ALEX HUGHES

See also: autobiography; women's/lesbian writing.

Sarrazin, Maurice

b. 1925, Toulouse

Actor, director and troupe leader

A pioneer of postwar theatre decentralization, and a founder of the Grenier de Toulouse in 1945, which took numerous classical productions on tour and gave **Gatti** a stage for his work.

ANNIE SPARKS

See also: theatre

Major works

Sarrazin, M. (1970) *Comédien dans une troupe*, Toulouse: Grenier de Toulouse (an autobiographical account of his work).

Sartre, Jean-Paul

b. 1905, Paris;
d. 1980, Paris

Philosopher and writer

Sartre ranks alongside André **Malraux**, Simone de **Beauvoir**, Albert **Camus** and Marguerite

Duras among writers born between 1900 and 1915 whose experiences of war and revolution deeply affected French literature between 1945 and 1970. More doggedly than these others, Sartre cultivated the role of the committed – also known as 'engaged' – intellectual who spoke out on contemporary issues without acceding to party line, ideology, or doctrine. Between 1945 and 1980, the force of Sartre's public presence built in large part on his sustained explorations of formats and genres ranging from essay, letter and treatise to **theatre** and film. It was no coincidence that Sartre's refusal of the 1964 Nobel prize extended the very oppositional position that the award committee had sought to recognize.

Sartre emerged following the **Liberation** as though on a mission to ensure that literature in postwar France would be fashioned by intellectuals for whom culture was inextricably linked to concerns for social and political freedom. In fact, this postwar vision evolved out of narrower conceptions of literature and the writer that had propelled Sartre to prominence as a novelist and literary critic in the late 1930s. Sartre was initially converted to activism by his 1940 prisoner-of-war experience of literature's capacity to disclose the simultaneous freedom and responsibility of all men and women. Four years later, Sartre sought the best possible format to convey this capacity to as wide a public as possible following the Liberation of France.

When the first issue of *Les Temps modernes* appeared on 15 October 1945 under the joint direction of Sartre, de Beauvoir and Maurice Merleau-Ponty, it was less of a literary monthly in the mould of the *Nouvelle Revue française* than a descendant of the left-wing weeklies *Marianne* and *Vendredi*. But, unlike its interwar predecessors, *Les Temps modernes* inscribed essays on politics and literature within a programme of **committed literature** (*littérature engagée*) that called for the writer to disclose and correct the full range and variety of injustice he or she encountered. While this double injunction to disclosure and correction made his monthly a forum for debate and consciousness-raising, Sartre's efforts on behalf of *Les Temps modernes* were only one aspect of a

broad personal programme of writing that included essays, fiction, theatre, screenplays and biography.

The cost of Sartre's commitment to high visibility in public was the inevitability of conflict. When Albert Camus published *The Rebel* (*L'Homme révolté*) in 1951, Sartre could no longer set aside the growing differences that placed his involvement with political revolution increasingly at odds with what he perceived as the disinterested and ahistorical notion of rebellion set forth in the book by his former colleague and friend. Sartre's break with Camus was acrimonious and – because of Camus's death in a January 1960 automobile accident – definitive.

From 1945 through to the mid-1970s, Sartre was seemingly everywhere at the same time, as though compelled to execute his decision to act in and on history on the most public of stages. On one front, he was a tireless voice in debate on issues ranging from the 1956 anti-Communist uprising in Hungary, to torture and the violation of human rights by French soldiers, police and intelligence agents during the **Algerian war**. When circumstances required it, Sartre was not above taking to the streets to picket, protest and gather signatures in support of a chosen cause of the moment. On another front, he travelled to China, Poland, Yugoslavia and Cuba to meet with political leaders and local intellectuals.

Most of all, Sartre continued to write: newspaper and magazine articles, prefaces and editorials, as well as plays and film scripts. The thirty years that Sartre devoted on and off to his 3,000-page, three-volume study of Gustave Flaubert, *The Family Idiot* (*L'Idiot de la famille*), illustrate the extent to which his desire to write as a witness (and historical conscience) of postwar France forced him to postpone and even to abandon a number of long-term intellectual projects. Inevitably some of these projects resurfaced where Sartre and his readers least expected to find them.

The appearance of *Words* (*Les Mots*) in 1964, in the wake of the deaths of Camus and Merleau-Ponty, marked a turn towards introspection beyond self-critique. Driven more by self-hatred than by self-centredness, *Words* was a kind of test case for the broad analyses that Sartre soon applied at length with regard to the life of the nineteenth-century novelist, Gustave Flaubert. *The Family Idiot* combined Sartre's interests in the irreducible specificity of Flaubert as an individual or, *universel singulier*, with what looked very much like a Freudian enquiry into the effects of early trauma on adult creativity. Moreover it confirmed that the bitterness with which Sartre had judged Flaubert in his *What is Literature?* (*Qu'est-ce que la littérature?*) of 1948 was part of his lifelong ambivalence toward a tutor figure whom he admired but could not but also condemn.

Words recalled Sartre's early literary and philosophical ambitions at least as much as his commitment to **Marxism** and politics over the previous twenty years. After the fact, even the ponderous 1960 *Critique of Dialectical Reason* (*Critique de la raison dialectique*) seemed less to resolve than to reconfigure the theoretical implications of Sartre's evolution from committed writing to the action in and on history that he referred to as *praxis*. By the time he wrote *Words*, Sartre was no longer simply the good dialectician thinking against himself in an exercise of auto-critique. Nor was he an essayist in the mould of a Montaigne reflecting on his mortality and the world around him. From the early 1960s until his death in April 1980, Sartre led a life of increasing contradiction between his efforts to resolve literary and philosophical issues that had long preoccupied him and attempts to assert militancy in social and political causes imposed by the force of circumstance.

So while Sartre hawked *La Cause du peuple* on the streets of Paris in the hope that his arrest by police might bring mass-media exposure to the newspaper he sought to sponsor on behalf of young post-**May 1968** militants, his writing focused increasingly on the nineteenth century in order to understand how Flaubert's progression through childhood, adolescence and young adulthood resulted in an alienation that Sartre saw objectified in *Madame Bovary*. For Sartre, *The Family Idiot* was less an escape from the present than the very contemporary project of a total biography that sought to link the immediate environment represented by Flaubert's family and a literary generation marked by the failed revolution of 1848. Sartre never completed the close reading of *Madame Bovary* that he had planned as the fourth volume of his study. After the fact, it is reasonable to wonder if the ambition of a total biography was an impossibility whose failure Sartre foresaw from the start as a counterpart to the privilege and success that he had enjoyed as a product of the upper middle class that he came to loathe.

The shortcomings of *The Family Idiot* that derive from Sartre's long-term obsession with Flaubert are offset by placing this final project of total understanding in the guise of biography within a series of biographical studies that Sartre devoted to Charles Baudelaire, Stéphane Mallarmé and Jean **Genet**. In each case, and including *The Family Idiot*, Sartre attempted to trace the genesis of identity in a trauma that eventually turned the individual to rebel against the bourgeois environment into which he or she had been born. In retrospect, these biographies can be read as attempts at self-analysis and self-understanding that evolved through and beyond the ostensible mixture of **autobiography** and fiction visible in *The Words*.

It is curious and fitting that ongoing interest in Sartre is devoted to the full range of his writings from *The Transcendence of the Ego* (*La Transcendance de l'égo*) and *Nausea* (*La Nausée*) published between the wars, to the posthumous *War Diaries* (*Carnets de la drôle de guerre*) and unfinished second volume of the *Critique of Dialectical Reason*. For beyond the writings it is also very much the example of Sartre's life – and often that of decisions that he later regretted – that continues to draw readers to see in his personal itinerary a clear sense of what committed literature can (and cannot) accomplish.

STEVEN UNGAR

See also: existentialism; existentialist theatre

Further reading

Cohen-Solal, A. (1986) *Sartre: A Life*, New York: Pantheon (a biography).

Goldthorpe, R. (1984) *Sartre: Literature and Theory*, Cambridge: Cambridge University Press (a good general study).

Hollier, D. (1986) *The Politics of Prose: Essay on Sartre*, trans. J. Mehlman, Minneapolis: University of Minnesota Press (highly provocative synthesis of Sartre's corpus).

Howells, C. (1988) *Sartre: The Necessity of Freedom*, Cambridge: Cambridge University Press (a philosophical study).

LaCapra, D. (1978) *A Preface to Sartre*, Ithaca, NY: Cornell University Press (a general introduction).

Scriven, M. (1984) *Sartre's Existential Biographies*, London: Macmillan (illuminating study of the biographical works in particular).

Ungar, S. (1987) 'Rebellion or Revolution?', in D. Hollier (ed.) *A New History of French Literature*, Cambridge, MA: Harvard University Press (studies prehistory of *Les Temps modernes* through Sartre's evolution towards collective action between 1940 and 1953).

Sautet, Claude

b. 1924, Montrouge

Director

Sautet is something of a 'sleeper': although he has been an important film-maker in France for all but forty years, his work has only just begun to become known in English-speaking countries. His dissection of bourgeois social relations relied heavily on his work with **Montand**, **Piccoli** and (above all) Romy Schneider, who starred in five of his films. His most recent work has featured Emmanuelle **Béart**, who stars with Daniel **Auteuil** in *Un coeur en hiver* (1992) and with Michel **Serrault** in *Nelly et Monsieur Arnaud* (1995).

KEITH READER

See also: cinema

Savary, Jérôme

b. 1942, Buenos Aires, Argentina

Director, actor and writer

Noted since 1988 for his theatrical spectacles as director at the Théâtre de Chaillot, Savary is the founder of the famous **Grand Magic Circus** company in 1965, famed for its provocative, experimental approach.

ANNIE SPARKS

See also: theatre

Major works

Savary, J. (1985) *La Vie privée d'un magicien ordinaire*, Paris: Ramsay (an autobiographical account of his work).

science fiction

Science fiction, properly speaking, explores the limits and possibilities of scientific discoveries and, as such, was born with the impact of modern science on life. The underlying theme of the genre is change and it projects mankind's possible evolution on the basis of what is now known. In contrast to previous works of fantasy or utopia – More's *Utopia*, some pamphlets by Cyrano de Bergerac, Voltaire's *Micromégas*, works which were of a primarily philosophical preoccupation – modern science fiction is based on contemporary scientific and social theories and thus serves to explore new dimensions of human experiences, dreams and nightmares. The application of science to modern life meant that science fiction entered into the domain of mass preoccupation, and the science fiction genre explored not only its beneficial possibilities but also its destructive powers. The pioneering founder of the genre is the Frenchman Jules Verne, whose fantastic adventures, written in the nineteenth century, introduced the excitement of science to a mass audience. His first major success *Five Weeks in a Balloon* (*Cinq semaines en ballon*) of 1863, and his most famous *Twenty Thousand Leagues Under the Sea* (*Vingt mille lieues sous les mers*) from 1870, brought together traditional themes and fantasies, narrated within the boundaries of contemporary scientific probability. However, science fiction has not attracted a mass audience in the modern postwar period. Popularity reached its peak in the 1950s when the term *science-fiction* came to replace *anticipation*, under the influence of Boris **Vian**, Gérard Klein and others, and serious interest was paid to it in periodicals like *Les **Temps modernes*** and *Esprit*. Publishers dedicated series to the genre – notably 'Fleuve noir-Anticipation', 'Le Rayon fantastique' and Denoël's 'Présence du futur' – and this period saw the birth of the work of writers such as Klein, Carsac and Sternberg, but the enthusiasm of French readers was and still is primarily inspired by the quality of works of science fiction written by American writers.

GEORGE PAIZIS

See also: literary journals

Further reading

Europe (1977) *La Science-Fiction*, special issue, August/September.

Gattégno, J. (1971) *La Science-Fiction*, Paris: PUF 'Que sais-je' (essential reading).

Klein, G. (1966) *En un autre pays: anthologie de la science-fiction française*, Paris: Seghers (dated, but the classic in the field).

Science-fiction (1984–5), Paris: Denoël (published between January 1984 and September 1985, so relatively recent, but hard to find).

sculpture

The abstraction/figuration debate associated with postwar **painting** did not generate the same degree of antagonism within the field of sculpture. Sculptural abstraction seemed to have gone as far as it could with Constructivism, and the ideals of progress associated with it were unable to survive the horrors of war. Those who continued in this tradition tended to move into **architecture**. The most important figurative sculptors working in France in the immediate postwar years were **Giacometti** and, to a lesser extent, Germaine Richier, but they expressed themselves in such a personal way that no 'school' of sculpture could develop from their work. While they may have had imitators, they had no successors.

Giacometti's postwar sculpture is rooted in the prewar period. The opportunity for self-examination that the war years offered him, along with many other sculptors, resulted in a transformation that allowed him to confront a changed world. In the aftermath of a war involving genocide, death camps and the Holocaust, man's humanity was called into question and only figuration that disturbed and questioned was henceforth credible. There are resonances of the death camps and the economic deprivation of the postwar years in Giacometti's attenuated figures, but also reflected are the feelings of alienation and the inability to communicate present in **Sartre**'s analysis of the human condition. Sartre's critical endorsement of Giacometti in the catalogue of his 1948 New York exhibition at the Pierre Matisse gallery helped him to become one of the most celebrated of postwar sculptors, not only in France but internationally. These postwar sculptures were also about perception. Giacometti was seeking a sculptural means of representing the figure as it is perceived in reality, in space, as leaving or having left a much larger visual field. The phenomenological undertones here link him to the philosopher Merleau-Ponty, with whom Sartre was also associated.

Germaine Richier's postwar figurative sculpture has often been compared to Giacometti's.

Like him, she was able to reconsider her approach to sculpture during the war. She was aware of his work and, like him, she had undergone the influence of prewar Surrealist discourse. In her *Mante religieuse* of 1946, the hybrid woman/insect figure, comparable to Giacometti's *Femme égorgée*, embodies an existential nightmare evoking the thirst for destruction which the war years had witnessed.

During this period, **Picasso**'s innovative prewar sculpture found a public for the first time, not least thanks to Brassai's book of photographs, *Les Sculptures de Picasso* (Picasso's Sculptures), published in the late 1940s. His application of collage techniques to three-dimensional work had led him to break down the prevailing hierarchy of materials. This was to influence much subsequent post-1945 sculpture. Although the ground for this had already been broken by **Duchamp** and his 'ready mades', Picasso's use of the *objet trouvé* was different. Duchamp's true successors were the Surrealists, who exploited the associations triggered off by the juxtapositions of disparate objects. Picasso, on the other hand, was more interested in the forms created by discarded objects, evident in his practice of casting in bronze his final assemblage of found objects after covering them in plaster. This division, between sculpture that demands a formal reading and that which works by association, still persists.

Jean **Arp**'s postwar sculptures also worked as plastic statements rather than through association, despite his previous involvement with Surrealism. His biomorphic shapes can be read as distillations of natural forms, body parts, and so on. Here seemed to be an example of sculpture that was arguably 'abstract' but not descended from Constructivism. However, Arp's very originality isolated him and although, like Giacometti, he had imitators, his postwar work produced no real successors, although its echoes can be found in the sculpture of Anish Kapoor working in England and some of the more recent work of Claes Oldenburg in the United States.

The first generation of entirely new names in sculpture in postwar France were to become, for the most part, members of that (fairly disparate) group of artists dubbed by the critic Pierre Restany Nouveaux Réalistes. César established his reputation in 1960 with his series of *Compressions*, works consisting of scraps of multicoloured metal from old cars. This was followed in 1967 with his *Expansions*, for which he exploited the properties of the new material polyurethane. The actual creation of these sculptures was turned into a series of Happenings.

Nouveau Réalisme was, loosely speaking, the French equivalent of British or American Pop Art of the 1960s, although the individualism of its main players ensured that it was a short-lived movement. Apart from César, those working in three dimensions included Arman, who is best known for his accumulations of everyday objects of the same type – echoes here of Warhol – as well as for his assemblages of objects cut into strips. He has cast some pieces in bronze, a practice which recalls Jasper Johns's beer cans as well as Picasso.

Niki de **Saint-Phalle** was also at work in the 1960s, creating her *Nanas*, figures made of polystyrene painted in primary colours. The use of this new material, associated with mass production and a product of the industrial/consumer age, together with the sexual and feminist overtones in her work, identifies her with the issues of that decade and popular culture in particular. But Saint-Phalle seems also to have been inspired by another artist whose roots go back to the prewar period, Jean **Dubuffet**. His painted objects of expanded polystyrene made in the 1960s were to develop into often monumental sculptures of steel and fibreglass.

The work of Daniel Spoerri and much of the creative output of Yves **Klein**, also one-time Nouveaux Réalistes, can be loosely classified as sculpture whose idiom is that of Pop Art. Spoerri's *tableaux pièges*, debris randomly displayed in glass-sided boxes, and Yves Klein's sponges and 'aerostatic sculptures', crossed the boundaries that traditionally separated high art from popular art.

Jean **Tinguely**, also a so-called Nouveau Réaliste, is usually regarded as a kineticist whose sculptures are descendants of Dada rather than Constructivism. His motorized assemblages, often inviting public participation, sometimes 'self-destructing', seem to be mocking technology rather than honouring it. He is one of the few kinetic sculptors to have survived that period.

Minimalism, which dominated sculpture internationally in the 1970s, like its Conceptualist offshoot, was largely an American/British phenomenon, as is the ambiguously titled Land Art. **Christo** invented *empaquetage* (packaging) soon after arriving in France in 1958, and has been identified with the Land Art movement, but his interventions in the landscape, unlike those of other Land Artists, take place not in a wilderness far from public view but precisely where they can disturb. Through his temporary transformations he appears to be questioning and making us look again at what we take for granted environmentally (for example, the Pont-Neuf for Parisians). A similar motive seems to be behind the work of the French sculptor Jean-Pierre Raynaud, whose most famous work is the construction of his own house – a domestic space conforming to none of the traditional criteria, forcing one to move around, live and breathe differently. Through his cheap, white, commonplace china tiles, he orders his space, showing the poetic side of untransformed objects.

In the late 1970s and early 1980s, sculpture worldwide began to demonstrate a multiplicity of styles. Within the context of French sculpture, this postmodern stylistic pluralism and love of pastiche is evident in the archaeological collages of Anne and Patrick Poirier. Bernard Pagès also appears to be quoting from the past when he deals with the theme of the column, although this may also be seen as an attempt to rediscover the instinct of the first builders. Postmodern eclecticism, in France as elsewhere, subverts any attempt to map current sculptural trends.

CAROL WILCOX

Further reading

Cabanne, P. (1993) *Arman*, Paris: ELA (a good account not only of Arman's sculpture but that of other Nouveaux Réalistes).

Restany, P. (1975) *César*, Paris: Éditions André Sauret (Restany's introduction to César's sculpture consists of a typically partisan overview of postwar French sculpture, with special reference to the Nouveaux Réalistes he promoted).

Sebbar, Leïla

b. 1941, Aflou, Algeria

Writer

Brought up in Algeria where her French mother and Algerian father taught French, and educated at university in France, Leïla Sebbar differs from beur writers in ethnic origin, class, education and age, but her influential novels, short stories, journalism and letters also explore questions of exile and identity in postcolonial France. Her work particularly foregrounds the perspectives of marginalized Algerian, beur and mixed-'race' female characters, culminating in the emblematic heroine of 1982's *Shérazade Missing: Aged 17, Dark Hair, Green Eyes* (*Shérazade, 17 ans, brune, frisée, les yeux verts*), the nomadic beurette whose unconventional identity quest informs a series of novels.

CARRIE TARR

See also: beur writing; beurs; francophone writing (fiction, poetry): North Africa

Seberg, Jean

b. 1938, Marshalltown, USA;
d. 1979, Paris

Actor

Famed above all else for her role opposite Jean-Paul **Belmondo** in **Godard**'s *A bout de souffle* (1959), Seberg had already appeared in Otto Preminger's adaptation of the Françoise **Sagan** novel, *Bonjour tristesse* in 1958. Her brand image as the young American woman in France was further consolidated during her marriage to the novelist Romain Gary. Her career did not sustain its early momentum and her radical views earned her persecution from the FBI – she committed suicide.

KEITH READER

See also: cinema; stars

Séguin, Philippe

b. 1943, Tunis

Politician

The RPR's leading Eurosceptic, but of a totally different stripe to the politicians on the British Right who bear that name. Séguin took control of the RPR after its defeat in the legislative elections of 1997. Like de **Gaulle**, he is imbued with a belief in the importance of the nation on the one hand, and the state on the other. His brand of what might be called 'social Gaullism' is thus a long way removed from the privatizing zeal of a **Balladur** or a **Madelin**, and in many respects is more attuned to elements on the Left.

KEITH READER

See also: parties and movements

Serrault, Michel

b. 1928, Brunoy

Actor

Noted for the precision of his acting, in many boulevard theatre productions as well as for mime work with **Decroux**, cabaret and sketch-es, Serrault played in 1,700 performances of *La Cage aux Folles* in the 1970s, and in **Planchon**'s famous 1986 *L'Avare*. He also starred in Molinaro's film of *La Cage aux folles* (1980) and in Claude **Sautet**'s *Nelly et Monsieur Arnaud* (1995).

ANNIE SPARKS

See also: cinema; theatre

Serreau, Coline

b. 1947, Paris

Director, screenwriter, actor and playwright

A trained musician, trapeze artist and actress, Coline Serreau achieved celebrity in 1985 with the hilarious César-winning hit, *Trois Hommes et un couffin*, remade in Hollywood as *Three Men and a Baby*, in which confirmed bachelors develop maternal instincts. Her earliest films are indebted to the women's movement, exploring women's desires in *Mais qu'est-ce qu'elles veulent?* (1976) and utopian alternatives to the nuclear family in *Pourquoi pas!* (1977). Subsequent films like *Romuald et Juliette* (1989) and *La Crise* (1992) provide acute comic observations of contemporary bourgeois mores without the earlier feminist edge. She has also written and performed in successful stage comedies, including *Quisaitout et Grosbêta*, which received four Molières in 1994.

CARRIE TARR

See also: cinema; theatre; women directors

Serres, Michel

b. 1930

Philosopher and science historian

Michel Serres's voluminous writings bear four

principal traits. First, the early articles on literature and science, published in five volumes under the title of *Hermes* (*Hermès*), studied the dynamics of exchange in relation to language, place and subjects. Therein Serres detected how the laws of thermodynamics that characterize scientific theory and practice in the nineteenth century have earlier literary expression in the classical age but also inflect writings in human sciences. Second, his major two-volume and crowning study, *Le Système de Leibniz* (Leibniz's System), shows how the monad co-ordinates the birth of an 'inner realm' of subjective experience to the world at large: Leibniz breaks decisively with the relativism and reason in ways that open experience to what is imponderable in language. Third, Serres has studied social, aesthetic and literary relations through the dynamics of parasitism, understood here as a productive symbiosis. Most recently, his work has embraced ecology in its broadest sense. He argues that human expression must embody relations of equilibrium and balance that serve as models for human activity in the next century. Serres's work is both a great reflection on the history of science in all disciplines and a history of a consciousness that moves from science to aesthetics and ethics at large.

TOM CONLEY

Servan-Schreiber, Jean-Jacques

b. 1924, Paris

Journalist and politician

Co-founder (with Françoise **Giroud**) of *L'Express* in 1953, he was successively general secretary of the Radical Socialist Party (1969) and a member of parliament (1970). The author of *The American Challenge* (*Le Défi américain*) in 1967, he was on all fronts a proponent of social change and modernization and a leading voice raised against Gaullist anti-Americanism. Politicians as different as

Giscard d'**Estaing** and Michel **Rocard** bear the trace of his influence.

KEITH READER

See also: Gaulle, Charles de; parties and movements

Further reading

Ross, K. (1995) *Fast Cars, Clean Bodies*, Cambridge, MA and London: MIT Press/October Books (a fascinating reading of the period of modernization of which Servan-Schreiber and Giroud are shown to have been key proponents).

service industry

The service industry in France employs two-thirds of the country's workforce, in a wide range of activities. It is currently affected by a series of changes and conflicts. On the one hand, the concentration and 'rationalization' of activities oppose large-scale networks to traditional, small-scale providers who fight for survival with little success. On the other, the considerable importance of 'public services' is now threatened by a process of liberalization and market deregulation.

The service industry is a heterogeneous, unevenly developed sector, grouping activities with little in common. These range from personal services and traditional retail activities or religious organizations to large-scale 'public services' such as **health**, education, public **transport**, police, and also fast-changing activities such as financial services, mass-retailing *hypermarchés* (giant supermarkets), media and telecommunications, transport and services to enterprises, increasingly integrated or controlled in large corporate entities. All these activities have gone through an accelerated modernization process, which has brought in its wake considerable social, economic and cultural upheaval. Trade has been particularly affected. The dense network of retail shops and associated support crafts (*artisans*) – which, up to the 1960s, constituted the socioeconomic backbone of rural areas and generated a large proportion of urban **employment** – is now largely destroyed. The continued urbanization of the country and industrial mass production coincided with changes in trade patterns: *hypermarchés* and shopping malls have now swamped the outskirts of urban areas. *Hypermarchés*, which sell anything from food to computers, are an established part of French culture, and groups such as Mammouth, Leclerc, Continent and Intermarché have become household names. In 1993, they controlled 55 per cent of retail trade, including 74 per cent of all food sold – a considerable proportion for a country priding itself on food traditions.

The crisis affecting traditional service trades, *artisans* and shopkeepers has given rise to a number of populist protest movements, always anti-state (their main target is usually tax offices) and conservative-leaning (sometimes belonging to the extreme Right). The Poujadiste movement (from the name of its founder, Robert Poujade) in the 1950s, and the corporatist shopkeepers union CID-UNATI, which organized violent protests in the late 1960s, are the best-known examples of such protest movements. These movements did not significantly alter trends, and neither have the legal limits imposed since 1973 (the Royer act) on the installation of *hypermarchés*.

Another important change concerns 'public services'. Many of these, such as health, education and social services, are controlled by central administrations, and their employees (such as teachers) have civil servant status. Other service industries (such as the post or telecommunications), although commercial in nature, are considered as 'public services'. The concept of public service, which has been part of the political culture of the ordinary citizen, is losing its relevance: since the mid-1980s, deregulation and competition rules, partly pushed by the **European Union**'s increasingly insistent free-market programme, are transforming the nature of these services and are enlarging the scope for market-based provision, as shown particularly in areas such as telecommunications.

FRANÇOIS NECTOUX

See also: *dirigisme*; economy

Further reading

Eck, J.-F. (1992) *Histoire de l'économie française depuis 1945*, Paris: Armand Colin (this covers the development of the service industries in not too complicated language)

Seuil

Publishing house

Éditions du Seuil was founded in 1935 by Henri Sjöberg, who was joined by Jean Bardet and Paul Flamand later in 1937. In 1945, it established itself by publishing the work of several authors with reputations as 'left-wing catholics'. It gained further renown during the 1960s and 1970s for publishing the work of literary and critical theorists such as Roland **Barthes**, Tzvetan Todorov and Gérard **Genette** in collections such as 'Critique'. In 1971, Seuil launched a series of cheap editions, 'Points', and it has interests in the reviews *Communications*, *Esprit*, *La Recherche* and *L'Histoire*.

MARTYN CORNICK

See also: publishing/*l'édition*

Further reading

Sur le Seuil, 1935–1979 (1979), Paris: Éditions du Seuil.
Martin, H.-J., Chartier, R. and Vivet, J.-P. (eds) (1986) *Histoire de l'édition française*, vol. 4, *Le Livre concurrencé 1900–1950*, Paris: Promodis (essential reading).

Seyrig, Delphine

b. 1932, Beirut, Lebanon;
d. 1990, Paris

Actor

Also known as Beltiane, Seyrig is one of
France's great but underestimated actors.
Renowned for her extraordinary voice and
delivery, her stylized performance was both
gracious and intense. An international star, she
was at ease on both stage and screen. She took
on primarily contemporary **theatre** roles (plays
by **Beckett**, Stoppard and **Cixous**) and equally
challenging parts in auteur cinema (**Resnais**,
Duras, Buñuel, Ottinger). Her film roles delve
into questions of the unconscious and memory
(Resnais's *L'Année dernière à Marienbad* of
1961), expose bourgeois hypocrisy – Buñuel's
The Discreet Charm of the Bourgeoisie (*Le
Charme discret de la bourgeoisie*) of 1972 –
and speak out strongly for the feminist cause,
which is a rare phenomenon among French
screen **stars** (for example, Duras's *India Song*
of 1975, and Chantal Akerman's *Jeanne
Dielman, 23 quai du commerce 1080 Bruxelles*
of 1975).

SUSAN HAYWARD

See also: cinema; francophone cinema: Belgium

Sheila

b. 1946, Créteil

Singer, real name Annie Chancel

The archetypal 'manufactured' pop star, Sheila
had her career carefully plotted for her by the
impresario Claude Carrère. Marketed as the
girl next door, a fashionable but respectable
French teenager, Sheila had a string of hit
recordings in the 1960s when she mimed her
records on television (her first live concert
appearance was at the Zénith over twenty
years after her career was first launched). Hit

songs include *L'École est finie* (School is Out),
Ma première surprise-partie (My First Party)
and *C'est toi que j'aime* (You're the One That I
Love).

IAN PICKUP

See also: song/*chanson*

short-story writing

Although a surprisingly high number of modern French writers have at some stage in their
literary careers been drawn to short fiction,
with the likes of Colette, Jean-Paul **Sartre** and
Albert **Camus** achieving notable success, the
nouvelle (short story) in the twentieth century
has generally been regarded (not least by the
French themselves) as a disappointment, especially when compared to the 'golden age' of
French short-story writing in the nineteenth
century. Yet there is much to savour in the
realm of postwar short fiction, where a number
of key trends stand out in terms of both literary
quality and cultural significance. Three such
trends are highlighted here.

Between the mid-1950s and the mid-1960s,
during the period dominated by the deconstructive energies of the *nouveau roman*, writers like Marguerite **Duras**, Nathalie **Sarraute**,
Samuel **Beckett** and Alain **Robbe-Grillet** gave
short fiction a new 'point' – a new function,
import and relevance – as an experimental
form. That none of these writers chose to call
their texts *nouvelles* reflects a core dissatisfaction with the very idea of genre, which has continued ever since to find one of its strongest
expressions in the domain of short fiction.
Indeed, young writers in the 1980s and 1990s
have tended increasingly to think of themselves
as authors of *récits brefs* (short fictions) or even
textes courts (short texts). The contemporary
writer insists on being generically as well as
ideologically 'unprogrammable'.

This principle of 'unprogrammability', of
resistance to wholesale political, philosophical
and artistic theories, has become a salient feature of the French postmodern sensibility. The

connection between this and short fiction was strongly suggested, in fact, at an early stage in the emergence of French **postmodernism**, when in 1979 Jean-François **Lyotard** defined the postmodern attitude as one of incredulity towards 'grand narratives' (grandiose theories claiming universal significance). Accordingly, we are invited to enter the era of the *petit récit*, or 'little narrative'. And, while it would be an oversimplification to draw too direct a link between the general politics of the *petit récit* and the more circumscribed poetics of the *récit bref*, the gradual emergence of a postmodern sensibility has undoubtedly fostered a renewed sense – not unlike that found during the mid-1950s – of the contemporary 'point' of short fiction. Besides remaining attractive as a site of generic overlap (with the prose poem, the autobiographical fragment, the essay, and even certain kinds of novel writing, for instance), short fiction in the late twentieth century comes helpfully fitted with a kind of default option known as the *nouvelle-instant*. This is the French term for the main Modernist variant of the *nouvelle*, typically focused on a single event set within a limited time and space, and frequently geared towards an 'epiphany', a moment of illumination or insight. Despite a decline of belief among writers in the depth and power of the individual moment, the *nouvelle-instant* has proved readily adaptable to embodying postmodern interest in the value of the local, the provisional and the plural.

The most well-known French short-story writers since the demise of the *nouveau roman* are probably Jean-Marie Le Clézio and Michel **Tournier**, though it is significant that both made their names primarily as novelists. Anyone who bothers to look beyond the big names, however, will soon discover that one of the main trends in French short fiction during this period has been the growing contribution of women writers. Reasons for this development range from material constraints on women writers who are also holding down full-time jobs to identification with both the marginal status of short fiction as genre and the marginal figures so often brought to life in the stories themselves. Indeed the theme of the outcast, the misfit, frequently embodied in the figure of the child, has been the mainstay of the many volumes of *nouvelles* written by the most important short-story writer in France over the 1980s and 1990s, male or female: Annie Saumont. Drawing inspiration from modern American short fiction in particular, Saumont writes soberly and unsentimentally about moments of human disarray. Among other established women writers who have specialized with great success in the domain of short fiction, the names of Christiane Baroche and Claude Pujade-Renaud immediately spring to mind. The range of exciting talent within the emerging generation of women writers makes short-listing a far more difficult task, but the volumes of short fiction already published by Régine Detambel, Liliane Giraudon, Linda Lê and Catherine Lépront suggest that these are among the most promising.

The third significant trend which deserves to be reported concerns the popularity and vitality of short fiction in the non-metropolitan francophone world. Whereas French attitudes towards short fiction veer predominantly between indifference and disdain, outside of France the genre has come to command levels of respect comparable with those found in most anglophone cultures. In Quebec, as in Ireland, short fiction tends to be regarded as a co-ordinate of identity, a means of differentiating a minority culture from its 'big brother(s)'. Thus, within a particular kind of symbolic universe, 'small' or 'short' once more assumes a point, indeed a very political kind of pointedness. The situation is somewhat different in Africa and the Caribbean, where the growth of interest in short fiction is explained partly by the genre's perceived affinities with indigenous oral traditions (as attested in the work of Francis Bebey and Birago Diop in Africa, and of Gisèle Pineau and Sylviane Telchid in Guadeloupe), and partly by the impact of short-story competitions promising financial reward and eventual publication.

In the age of the so-called 'three-minute culture', where, from sound bites to **pop videos**, so many of the messages aimed at us are designed to provide a quick fix, is short fiction part of the problem or part of the solution? The very 'point' of the best short fiction written in French since the 1960s has been to enhance rather than diminish our powers of critical attention.

JOHNNIE GRATTON

See also: francophone writing (fiction, poetry): DOM-TOMs; women's/lesbian writing

Further reading

Cottenet-Hage, M. and Imbert, J.-P. (eds) (1996) *Parallèles: anthologie de la nouvelle féminine de langue française*, Quebec: L'Instant même (seventeen stories by women writers from Colette to the present, each accompanied by a critical commentary).

Gratton, J. and Le Juez, B. (eds) (1994) *Modern French Short Fiction*, Manchester: Manchester University Press (an anthology of stories from the 1830s to the present, with an informative introduction in English).

Grojnowski, D. (1993) *Lire la nouvelle*, Paris: Dunod (an accessible, reliable introductory guide to the history, poetics and thematics of short fiction).

Pujade-Renaud, C. and Zimmermann, D. (eds) (1993) *131 nouvellistes contemporains*, Levallois-Perret: Manya (the views of over a hundred writers on the significance of short fiction in the 1990s: invaluable insights).

Signoret, Simone

b. 1921, Wiesbaden, Germany;
d. 1985, Paris

Actor, real name Simone Henriette Kaminker

Signoret changed her name during the Occupation (1940–4). A committed woman of the Left (which saw her banned from the United States in the 1950s), she had both **star** and anti-star qualities. Her multifaceted nature made her attractive to men and women alike. Her incendiary eyes, long slim legs, heavy voice and lisp were matched by her image of independent womanhood. While her roles place her as victim – for example, Yves Allégret's *Dédée d'Anvers* (1947) and **Becker**'s *Casque d'Or* (1952) – in her performance style she acts as agent of desire. One of the few women stars to sustain a film career into old age, she was still delivering stunning performances when blind and ravaged by the effects of cancer, as in Moshe Misrahi's *La Vie devant soi* (1977).

SUSAN HAYWARD

See also: cinema

Simenon, Georges

b. 1903, Liège, Belgium;
d. 1989, Belgium

Writer

Simenon is the prolific author of approximately 200 works. Between the early 1930s and 1970s, he wrote mainly **detective fiction** based on the adventures of his now famous detective Maigret. From the early 1970s, Simenon's production concentrated on autobiographical narratives – for example, his 1981 publication *Mémoires intimes* (Intimate Memoirs) – and testimonials of historical events taking place in the 1930s and 1940s, like *Mes apprentissages* (My Apprenticeship). Simenon's novels have been adapted for the screen by **Renoir**, Duvivier and Leconte, and for television series.

JEAN MAINIL

See also: francophone writing (fiction, poetry): Belgium

Simon, Claude

b. 1913, Tananarive, Madagascar

Writer

Grounded in family legends, visual arts and personal experience of the Spanish Civil War and the 1940 fall of France, Simon's radically disrupted narratives problematize the notion of historical fiction. His protagonists struggle to know the world and the past against the unreliable meanings produced by language and memory. Simon's 1985 Nobel prize for literature honoured his broadly humanistic though despairing and pessimistic vision of the twentieth century.

LYNN A. HIGGINS

See also: *nouveau roman*

Further reading

Britton, C. (ed.) (1993) *Claude Simon*, London: Longman (a collection of reprinted essays by leading Simon scholars; contains bibliography).

situationism

The intellectual and political movement dubbed situationism, a descendant of Dada and Surrealism, worked against the passivity of the 'society of the spectacle' (the title of Guy Debord's 1967 text, *La Société du spectacle*), and aimed at nothing less than the revolutionary overthrow of bourgeois art, politics and society from within. The Situationist International, founded in 1957, lasted until 1969 and was rent by expulsions and dissensions, notwithstanding which the work of its best-known members, Debord and Raoul Vaneigem, had a major influence in **May 1968** and has attracted renewed interest in the wake of **postmodernism** and of Debord's 1994 suicide.

KEITH READER

See also: revolutionary groups

Further reading

Plant, S. (1992) *The Most Radical Gesture: The Situationist International in a Post-Modern Age*, London and New York: Routledge (the only major study in English).

slang/argot/verlan

Argot or slang goes back to the secret language of the medieval underworld, the *jargon* of the criminal classes, for which documentation exists as early as the fifteenth century. By the nineteenth century, *argot* had become widespread, confused with the spoken vernacular, particularly of the working classes.

Essentially, *argots* are social dialects, usually belonging to an urbanized group: they include the speech of trades and professions, student groups, the army, and in the late twentieth century, the younger inhabitants of certain *banlieues* (**suburbs**).

Argot is a parasitic development of language in so far as it consists in the substitution of parts of the spoken lexis according to predetermined rules: the basic phonic system, the syntax and morphology are not affected, except for word formation.

One attractive aspect of *argot* is the free development of metaphors, such as *la cafetière* (coffee pot) = head (cf. 'mug' in English); *le mouton* (sheep) = police informer (cf. 'grass', 'snout'); *les rosbifs* (roast-beefs) = the Brits; *se poivrer* (be peppered) = get drunk (cf. 'get ratted', 'tight'). Such metaphorical creation is ongoing and subject to quite rapid attrition, so that the new vocabulary of one generation may seem very dated to the next. It is noteworthy that in the choice of metaphors, as in much of *argot*, there is a strong pejorative tonality and often a coarse humour.

Other typical devices in lexical creation are:

- truncation, e.g. *jar* = *jargon* (slang); *clandé* = *maison clandestine* (brothel); *charr* = *charriage* (bluff, joke); *ricain* = *américain*; and
- parasitic suffixation, the addition of an

unnecessary suffix, more to disguise a word than to modify it, e.g. *fortiche* = *fort* (strong); *raidillard* = *raide* (1,000-franc note); *matouser* = *mater* (spy on). In many cases, other transformations take place, e.g. *clodo* – *clochard* (tramp, bum); *perniflard* = *Pernod*; *rencard* = *rendez-vous*; *cinoche* = *cinéma*. Again, we may note a pejorative tonality in such suffixes, e.g. *-ard, -aille, -oche, – -ouser*.

The best-known type of *argot* is *verlan*, dating from the 1950s, although the feature of inverting syllables is found early in the nineteenth century: *verlan* is thus the inversion of *l'envers* (reverse, back to front). This is significantly different from English back slang, e.g. *yob, kool*.

Although *verlan* can seem to be easy to decipher (e.g. *féca* = *café*), some examples are less obvious – e.g. *meuf* = *femme*, and **beur** (born in France of North African immigrant parents) is explained as an inversion of *Arabe* but with a change of vowel. Moreover, a major communicatory difficulty resides in the uncertainty as to which words are *verlan* forms; as a result such speech can retain something of the secret code of *argot*.

Other forms of *argot* exist: *largonji* = *jargon* in which 'l' replaces the initial consonant, which is placed at the end of the word, e.g. *lacsé* = *sac* (bag); *en loucedé* = *en douce* (quietly); *le loucherbem* (butchers' slang) is a particular form of *largonji*; *le javanais* uses the parasitic infix *-av-*, e.g. *baveau* = *beau* (handsome), *javardin* = *jardin* (garden).

Argot words can achieve respectability, e.g. *cambrioleur* (burglar) and *rossignol* (skeleton key), but most remain on the fringe of the system. Note, however, the many writers from the nineteenth century onwards (Balzac, Hugo, Zola, Céline, San Antonio) who make regular use of *argot*.

JO REED

See also: beurs; linguistic regulation

Further reading

Guiraud, P. (1969) *L'Argot*, Paris: PUF (a useful introduction).

soap

Soap opera is not France's forte. After the failure of two 1980 attempts, *Châteauvallon* and *En cas de bonheur*, July 1991 witnessed the launch of a third attempt to get soap right – *Riviera*, a collaborative production between **TF1** and an American company (EC Television). Due to run for a trial year, by January 1992 it had disappeared off the screen. The only other attempts, though they are much disliked by their target teenage audience, are the Americanized teen soaps produced by the major independent children's TV production company Club Dorothée. These programmes are pastel-shaded versions of an imagined French-Californian space (e.g. *Hélène et les garçons, Les Filles d'à côté*). Furthermore, because they are a hybrid between soap and sitcom, they fail to satisfy the codes and conventions of either genre and so cannot be taken seriously as either.

The soap of the 1990s was the supposedly French soap *Riviera*, which was in actuality a multinational affair. A third of the mostly very rich 'soap community' were American; production practices were also American. To keep production costs down, and with an eye to English-speaking markets, the soap was shot in English and dubbed in French. This marketing strategy did not pay off. If English audiences do not like dubbed products, French audiences like French soap masquerading as an American product even less. Undoubtedly the over-Americanization of the product in terms of its look and its consequent lack of cultural specificity caused it to fail with French audiences. However, *Riviera* did have strengths and should not be deemed a total failure. The strengths lay in its narrative strategies. The storyline focuses around the wealthy de Courcey family (whose business is perfumery and whose name dominates Riviera society) and their arch-rival, Diego Marquez (an *arriviste*), a property speculator who plots the family's downfall (*la vieille France* clashes with the *nouveaux riches*). Meantime, Marquez's wife strives to be accepted by the upper echelons of society, and both husband and wife fail in their ambitions. Woven into this fabric are further intrigues: an illegitimate son, incestuous love, orphaned twins with identity crises, sibling rivalry and, finally, Oedipal triangles between father, son and daughter. Everyone in *Riviera* has a secret, a past or an illicit passion – true melodrama French-style. *Riviera* succeeds also in achieving spectator identification, in so far as the various storylines of crises, crime and mystery do intrigue the viewer, thanks to a multiplicity of subjective points of view. Further practices to stitch the audience into the plot are the representations of gender in the form of stereotypes (including the battle of the sexes) and representations of sexuality (especially as taboo) which both repel and attract the viewer. Thus we see men as wheeler-dealers and women as schemers – stereotypes we love to hate. That men are morally and sexually weaker is a generic fiction of soap, but one that pleases the female viewer, as must the representation of women in control of their own sexuality. Enigma is the soap of the masses. However, hybridity as exemplified (culturally and linguistically) by *Riviera* counters too many generic codes to permit the suspension of disbelief and, ultimately, lack of familiarity breeds discontent.

SUSAN HAYWARD

See also: romantic fiction; television; video imports

social policy

Social policy covers a broad field of analysis, from the formulation of policy objectives, and measures to achieve them, through to the provision of social protection and minimum standards of income. Social policy is not, however, a neutral or autonomous area of public policy.

Its parameters vary according to the ideology of the governments in power and their priorities, and they in turn cannot act independently of domestic and, increasingly, international pressures. Nor can social policy be properly understood in isolation from economic policy: it may be constrained by economic forces, or it may serve to modify or counteract the adverse effects of the economic system.

France has long been recognized as a highly centralized and bureaucratic state, with a concern for social justice, equality and solidarity as a legacy of its Republican tradition. The **social security** institutions which developed over the postwar period as the main vehicle for the delivery of social policy are, however, characterized by their decentralization, autonomy, pluralism and corporatism. Proposals from ministers for social reform, whatever the political persuasion of the government in power, rarely meet with consensus; strikes and protest movements have become common features of the social landscape, signalling the opposition to change by strong interest groups intent on defending their acquired social rights.

In the phase of postwar reconstruction, the social security system was able to develop in a climate of economic growth. Its primary aim was to protect an expanding labour force and to enable workers and their families to maintain their standard of living, rather than tackling residual problems of poverty. The decision, taken after a long process of negotiation, to opt for an employment-related insurance system meant that national solidarity and universality were not dominant guiding principles. Occupational groups were allowed to retain their own well-established insurance schemes. Although coverage was gradually extended to the whole of the non-working population and to socio-occupational groups not initially entitled to protection under the general scheme or schemes operating for particular categories of **employment**, different conditions and levels of benefits applied. Nor was unemployment integrated into the social security system; a separate employment insurance scheme was instituted only in 1958 for workers in industry and commerce (*associations pour l'emploi dans l'industrie et le commerce*, ASSEDIC).

Despite anomalies in coverage, by the late 1970s, it could be claimed, with some justification, that the French population was protected from the risks of ill-health, disability, old age, unemployment and **family** responsibilities. Social policy had been less successful in reducing social inequalities, particularly with regard to old age, where income inequality was greater than among the working population. From the mid-1970s, policy-makers were, however, facing new social problems, as the country went into economic recession. At the same time, the growing population in retirement was imposing an increasing burden on the working population in the absence of fully funded pension schemes. Rising unemployment created a severe drain on resources, social security slid into deficit, and new forms of poverty and social exclusion began to emerge.

The social policies pursued by the left-wing governments of the early 1980s involved high levels of spending: the Left had pledged themselves to increase the **minimum wage** and minimum income for older people, to raise family allowances, **housing** and unemployment benefits, to lower retirement age and reduce working hours. A period of sounder financial management followed in response to the funding problems that ensued. By the end of the decade, additional sources of income were, however, still needed to ease the ever-growing deficit without imposing a heavier burden on employers: one of the solutions was to raise a tax across all sources of income (*contribution sociale généralisée*, CSG), and this was followed in 1996 by an additional levy (*remboursement de la dette sociale*, RDS).

By the early 1990s, spending on benefits and social services had reached over 30 per cent of gross domestic product (GDP), representing a substantial increase since the early 1970s. The share of the social budget devoted to old age accounted for nearly 43 per cent of the total, and **health** for almost 27 per cent. Despite attempts to spread the burden of contributions, employers still paid by far the largest share – over 50 per cent – as part of the wage package. A number of the policies introduced to alleviate unemployment involved exempting employers from social insurance contributions as an incentive to take on unemployed people. A more innovative work-related scheme (*revenu minimum d'insertion*, RMI) was introduced in 1988, to lessen the impact of unemployment: it provided a minimum income for unemployed people aged over 25 in return for an agreement to undertake some form of training or work placement to facilitate their re-entry into the labour market.

The growing awareness by governments of new sources of poverty and social exclusion, combined with the need to meet the demand for a high standard of social benefits and services, while containing spending, has led to a shift in the focus of social policy towards a more solidaristic approach, based on social justice. This does not mean that retrenchment of social spending has disappeared from the social policy agenda or that proposals for radical reform of the social protection system will receive unqualified support from the social partners, but it does imply that central government is exercising stronger control over the policy-making process and seeking to instil a greater sense of social responsibility among the population at large.

LINDA HANTRAIS

See also: demographic developments; economy; women and social policy

Further reading

Ambler, J. S. (ed.) (1991) *The French Welfare State: Surviving Social and Ideological Change*, New York and London: New York University Press (a collection of thoroughly argued chapters on various aspects of French social policy).

Hantrais, L. (1996) 'France: Squaring the Welfare Triangle', in V. George and P. Taylor-Gooby (eds) *European Welfare Policy: Squaring the Welfare Circle*, London: Macmillan (a critical appraisal of social policy developments in France since the early 1980s).

social security

Although cover has been extended and provisions have been improved since World War II, the French social security system has not achieved the objectives set out by its founder, Pierre Laroque, in 1945. The system was to be based on the principles of equality, solidarity and social democracy, enabling universal access to benefits and services, redistribution of income, and participation by representatives of employers and employees in its management, without undue bureaucratic interference from the state.

The system was designed to protect workers and their families against a number of contingencies that might pose a threat to their well-being. Three major areas of risk were covered: sickness, maternity, invalidity, industrial accidents and diseases; old age; and **family** responsibilities. Unemployment assistance was not an integral part of social security in the 1940s, and separate schemes have since developed to cater for the growing number of unemployed people and for other population groups not adequately covered by employment-related insurance.

Social security is funded largely by contributions from employers and employees, proportional to income up to a ceiling, rather than from taxation. Access to benefits is related to contributions in line with the insurance principle, except in the case of **health** care, family allowances and other derived rights, which are paid, or reimbursed in the case of medical services, at fixed rates. Non-contributory benefits are generally means-tested.

The French system is difficult to classify in terms of welfare regimes: in some respects it is universalistic, like the British system as conceived by Beveridge; in others it functions as a corporatist employment-insurance system, like that developed in Germany under Bismarck. The anomalies can be largely explained by the fact that the system resulted from a compro-

mise in response to the pressures exerted by different interest groups, intent on preserving the advantages they derived from existing arrangements. Thus, although a general scheme was established for employees in commerce and industry, innumerable special and supplementary schemes (including *mutuelles*) were allowed to continue. The whole population is, in theory, now protected, but the standard of cover and level of benefits are variable, particularly with regard to pensions.

Since employers and employees were the main contributors to the schemes, their representatives were made responsible for managing the funds. Between the 1950s and 1970s – when the population was growing rapidly, the **economy** was thriving and unemployment was minimal – social security operated efficiently. Since the mid-1970s, deficits have become endemic, and the government has sought ways to cut back spending and reduce the burden on employers from high labour costs, while also coping with the growing problems of unemployment and social exclusion.

LINDA HANTRAIS

See also: social policy

Further reading

Chatagner, F. (1993) *La Protection sociale*, Paris: Le Monde-Éditions (a lively account of the issues surrounding social security provision in France).
Revue française des affaires sociales (1995) *Les 50 ans de la sécurité sociale: pourquoi une protection sociale?*, special issue, 49, 4 (a collection of informative articles reviewing the French social security system).

Sollers, Philippe

b. 1936, Bordeaux

Writer and critic

After the conventional and sentimental *Une curieuse solitude* (1958), Sollers gained notoriety as editor of **Tel quel**. The structurally austere late 1960s novels *Drame* (Drama) and *Nombres* (Numbers) were followed by the humorous and formally more anarchic *Lois* (Laws) in 1972 and the unpunctuated 'epic' *Paradis* (Paradise) in 1981. In an apparent volte-face Sollers abandoned experimental form with the 1983 work *Femmes* (Women), a vast *roman-à-clé* of the previous decade, and a critical meditation on society and sexuality. Since then, as novelist and reviewer in *Le Monde*, Sollers articulates an increasingly ironic perspective on all forms of orthodoxy, social, literary and intellectual, while affirming the transcendent value of art.

PATRICK FFRENCH

See also: *nouveau roman*; poststructuralism; structuralism

song/chanson

La chanson française (French song) is an important element of French popular culture which combines lyric expression, satirical, political and social commentary with music which is usually relatively simple, often linking verses to a repeated chorus or refrain. Allegedly in crisis today because of the high volume of anglophone music played on French radio and **television** (though a minimum 40 per cent quota of songs in French was imposed by legislation brought into force in January 1996), French song has none the less produced a number of outstanding performers and singer-songwriters since World War II.

The origins of French song can be traced back to the troubadours, medieval poets of southern France, and to their northern equivalents, the *trouvères*. There has always been a strong oral tradition in France and song has been used since the medieval period as a vehicle for lyric expression. As a means of articulating emotion, as a popular method of commemorating events of national importance or of

expressing satirical or political views, it has always been an important form of popular entertainment. Song flourished, then, through the centuries and by the time of the Third Republic, the **café-concert**, or **caf'conc'** as it was known familiarly, had become one of the most popular forms of public entertainment and was to remain so until World War I. The next notable development in the history of popular song was the advent of the music hall in Paris in the early years of this century and this provoked a trend still apparent today: the audience now listens more than it sings along with the performer on stage. The music hall saw the rise to stardom of legendary names: **Mistinguett**, Maurice **Chevalier**, Rose Amy, Tino Rossi, Josephine **Baker**, Alibert and so on. However, with the advent of the **cinema**, two-thirds of Parisian concert halls were converted into cinemas between 1910 and 1920.

Anglo-Saxon influences were by now bringing themselves to bear in the world of French popular music and of French popular entertainment in general. Not only in the cinema but also in the music hall, American popular culture made its mark. In music, ragtime, **jazz** and blues exerted a strong ongoing influence, as did a whole succession of popular dances. The world of music was now changing beyond recognition: the microphone, the silent cinema, the talkies, television, long-playing records and, more recently, digitally recorded CDs and *vidéo-clips*, have all provoked a metamorphosis in the French **music industry**.

The most striking result of technological innovations and inventions is that, by the end of World War II, the world is a shrinking place in which communication has improved beyond recognition and in which the fashions of one continent are immediately accessible to the inhabitants of another. During the immediate aftermath of the big-band era, during and after the period which saw the birth and immediate explosion of rock and roll (the late 1950s and the early 1960s), during the period which saw the re-emergence of **folk music** and the vogue of the protest song (the 1960s in particular), popular music became increasingly a global phenomenon and French song was increasingly open to alluring Anglo-Saxon influences at a time when American (and also British) culture in its various manifestations became a real threat to the homogeneity of Gallic traditions.

French song, though, was in good health at the end of World War II. Charles **Trenet** had already charmed the French public with an often poetic, more wholesome form of song which replaced the vulgar excesses of the songs which were characteristic of the heyday of the music hall. While Trenet's career reached new heights in the 1950s, Édith **Piaf** followed in his footsteps by helping to reverse the trend of Anglo-Saxonization: she made a huge impact not only in France but also in America, where she toured (initially with Les **Compagnons de la chanson**) from the late 1940s. In her entourage at various points were several composers who were later to become outstanding performers in their own right (**Montand, Moustaki** and **Aznavour**, for example).

French song was soon to be transformed, however, particularly for young people, with the advent of rock and roll, which was to inspire a new form of music in France, known – quite revealingly – as *yé-yé* (1960s pop). Aspiring young French singers adopted Anglo-Saxon names (Johnny **Hallyday**, Eddy **Mitchell, Sheila,** Richard Anthony) and 'cover versions' of American (and later British) songs became the vogue. The electric guitar (sometimes supplemented by the saxophone and occasionally the trumpet, a legacy of jazz and the big-band era) now became the most popular instrument, and loud, catchy music with extremely simple lyrics captivated the young and horrified the old.

Alongside the influx of Anglo-Saxon music, French song was, none the less, enjoying something of a new golden age: while cabarets on the Left Bank gave birth to a more intellectual form of song known as the *chanson rive gauche*, performers such as Montand and later **Bécaud** were to maintain French traditions (though they did allow jazz, swing and other imported influences to be incorporated in their songs). Even more significantly, however, two outstandingly original talents rejuvenated French song from the late 1950s: Georges

Brassens and the adopted Belgian singer-songwriter Jacques **Brel** wrote and recorded songs of the highest quality and, in the case of Brel, took performance to new heights.

French popular music has subsequently undergone the influence of punk, heavy metal, reggae, **rap**, Afro-Caribbean and North African elements, and so on, but a distinctly Gallic tradition has been maintained in the realm of the politically committed or provocative song (**Ferrat, Renaud** and **Gainsbourg**, for example), in the realm of lyric expression (**Souchon** and **Cabrel**, to name but two) and in the domain of live performance in venues as big as Bercy (**Sardou's** 1991 and 1993 concerts providing examples to set alongside the more Americanized, but technically brilliant concerts of Hallyday). Although casual listening to French airways will not make it immediately apparent, French song is still in good health today, though the genuine article does have to be sought out with patience.

IAN PICKUP

See also: music festivals; music venues; rock and pop

Further reading

Brunschwig, C., Calvet, J.-L. and Klein, J.-C. (1981) *Cent ans de chanson française*, Paris: Éditions du Seuil 'Collection points' (an alphabetically arranged reference work).

Fléouter, C. (1988) *Un siècle de chansons*, Paris: PUF (a chronologically arranged analytical section is followed by an alphabetically arranged reference section).

Klein, J.-C. (1991) *La Chanson française à l'affiche: histoire de la chanson française du café-concert à nos jours*, Paris: Éd. du May (an illustrated history of *chanson* in the last century).

Rioux, L. (1994) *50 ans de chanson française*, Paris: Archipel (a critical study organized chronologically).

Souchon, Alain

b. 1945, Casablanca, Morocco

Singer-songwriter

Having failed to make an impact for many years, Alain Souchon suddenly found fame in the mid-1970s when he teamed up with Laurent Voulzy to write songs. Souchon's somewhat elliptical texts, which juxtapose what are often wistful images, are complemented perfectly by Voulzy's music. His stage and recording persona is that of a perpetual adolescent lost in an adult world and nostalgic for times past. His successes include *Bidon* (Phoney), *Dix ans* (Ten Years Old), *Allô maman bobo* (Hello Mummy Hurt), *Casablanca* and *S'asseoir par terre* (To Sit Down on the Ground). An original and enduring talent.

IAN PICKUP

See also: song/*chanson*

Soulages, Pierre

b. 1919, Rodez

Artist

Soulages was influenced by the ancient Gallic megaliths and Romanesque buildings of his native Rouergue. His palette is dominated by black and white, and his early figurative paintings present outlines of bare dark trees. In his first non-figurative compositions, black or brown shapes, painted with broad energetic brush strokes, appear on a white ground; he was interested in calligraphic signs and rhythmic shapes. From 1950, bright colours were added, giving depth to the black and, in the 1960s, his compositions evolve from strong contrasts in light and shade to graded tones from deep black to pale grey. His latest compositions are large paintings in luminous black paint.

ELZA ADAMOWICZ

See also: painting

Soustelle, Jacques

b. 1912, Montpellier, Hérault; d. 1990

Ethnographer and politician

As a young graduate of the École Normale Supérieure in the 1930s, Soustelle supported the left-wing Popular Front, but became a companion of de **Gaulle** in London during the war. During the Fourth Republic, Soustelle supported Gaullism as an activist and *député* in Lyon, helping de Gaulle regain power in 1958. Having served as governor-general in Algeria and been won over by arguments for *l'Algérie française*, he subsequently bitterly opposed de Gaulle's policy of abandonment. Tainted by contacts with the extreme Right, Soustelle fled France, returning only after the amnesty of 1968. In 1984, he was elected to the **Académie Française**. Rising to intellectual and political distinction from humble Protestant origins, Soustelle exemplified the social mobility allowed by **educational elitism**, and his split with de Gaulle epitomized the divisive effects of the **Algerian war**.

HUGH DAUNCEY

See also: decolonization; parties and movements

spelling reform

French spelling vies with English in terms of inconsistency and difficulty, for native speaker and foreign learner alike. Contemporary modifications in spelling are the product of a historical process which it is necessary to understand in order to get to grips with twentieth-century spelling reform.

Standard French is considered to have

thirty-six phonemes, whereas the written code possesses as many as forty-three signs (the twenty-six letters of the alphabet together with diacritic forms); in addition, through historical evolution, French contains numerous compound graphemes, e.g. *ch*, *gn*, *au*, *eau*, *ain*. This means that a particular sound may have several written forms, e.g. [s] in *sac*, pre*ss*e, *sci*-ence, na*ti*on, si*x*, le*ç*on; likewise a written letter or letters can have several values, including zero, e.g. *s* in *sac*, *rose*, *femmes*.

Ideas for spelling reform, or for making the orthographic system consistent, began to flourish with the development of printed texts and the consequent evolution of an accepted literary French. As early as the sixteenth century, printers and scholars engaged in debate and experiment to establish a norm for texts in the vernacular: until this time, Latin had been the language of scholars and the essential written language, but French had many features alien to Latin. G. Tory, for example, recommends the use of the cedilla, apostrophe and accents, and other sixteenth-century printers rapidly develop proposals for a modern orthographic system, including the separation of 'i' and 'j', 'u' and 'v'.

The seventeenth century recognized a traditional spelling lingering on with certain writers and officials, together with the new, reformed orthography. However, the first edition of the Academy dictionary (1694) declared that it wished to follow *l'ancienne orthographe*. Scholars such as Richelet, and writers like Corneille, continued to argue for (and to use) a spelling code in which the written form attempts to reproduce the spoken form as closely as possible, reducing double consonants, eliminating parasitic letters and making full use of the diacritics.

The various editions of the Academy dictionaries have authorized various spelling reforms – in particular the third edition (1740), which modified up to 6,000 words and gave French its modern shape by eliminating some superfluous letters; one example is the replacement of preconsonantal *s* by a circumflex on the preceding vowel. The 1835 edition replaces *oi* by *ai* in many words, e.g. *français* (French),

paraître (appear) and, more importantly, in all conditional and imperfect endings. The eighth edition (1932–5), replaces the apostrophe in nouns such as *grand'mère* (grandmother) by a hyphen and modifies some 500 words in total.

In the twentieth century, there have been numerous projects for spelling reform – Dauzat (1939), Beslais (1952), Thimonnier (1967), Conseil Supérieur de la Langue Française (1990) – all of which have revealed the inconsistencies of French but failed to provide acceptable solutions. Certain phenomena are regularly cited: double consonants, Greek features (*th*, *rh*, *ph*, *y*), mute consonants, hyphen, circumflex and other diacritics, as well as individual anomalies.

The failure of the Academy to adopt the limited programme of reforms in 1990 is testimony to the stability of French spelling, however eccentric, but this should not conceal the fact that French has come to accept many changes and will continue to do so.

Jo Reed

See also: Académie Française; linguistic regulation

sport

Modern sports, like the industrialization and urbanization of which they were historically an expression, came late to France, but have since been widely disseminated, developing in ways which reflect the demographic, economic and even political character of French society. Having been introduced from Britain in the 1880s, the first modern sports (**rugby**, **football**, **athletics**) were initially the preserve of fashionable Parisian society, as exemplified by Baron Pierre de Coubertin, the founder of the modern Olympic Games. However, as the appeal of these sporting imports spread, they were democratized, commercialized, ever more intensely mediated, and joined by indigenous sports, such as France's first and still most important sporting spectacle, professional **cycling**, epitomized since 1903 by the **Tour de**

France, an event perfectly adapted to the demographic reality of a nation of many small rural or semi-rural communities as well as a few major conurbations.

State involvement in the organization of sport dates back to the 1901 law on associations, which requires formal registration of sports (and all other) clubs. Such associations, which may be single-sport but are more often multi-sport, must be affiliated to the appropriate national federation(s), which in turn come under the umbrella of the Comité National Olympique et Sportif Français (CNOSF). Each governing body is authorized to administer its own sport, receiving significant funding to enable it to carry out its responsibilities. Such is the federations' power that no sportsman or sportswoman may participate in formally constituted matches, leagues or championships without previously having been granted a *licence* by the appropriate federation. The numbers of such *licenciés* (licence-holders) indicate that football is the most popular team sport in France, with tennis, skiing and cycling being the major individual sports (both in competitive and leisure terms), followed by 'minority' interests like judo, basketball, rugby, horse riding, sailing and golf. The democratization in the 1970s and 1980s of hitherto socially exclusive sports like **tennis** and skiing reflects a general rise in disposable incomes available for leisure expenditure, together with improvements in sports and travel infrastructures. It also underlines the success of state initiatives such as the now firmly established *classes de neige* (skiing classes for schoolchildren), which began in the 1950s.

Spectator sport similarly reflects a preoccupation with soccer, with the televised performances of the leading clubs and, especially, of the national side in international competitions representing a regular high point for viewing figures. (Half of all French TV viewers are believed to have watched Michel Platini's team in the 1986 World Cup semi-final.) François **Mitterrand**, as president of the Republic, maintained a tradition first established by Charles de **Gaulle** of identifying the nation with top-level sport by regularly attending the final of the French football knockout cup. His re-establishment in 1991 of a full ministry for youth and sport underlined the renewed importance attached to sport under his presidency, as did the doubling of the weighting attached to the physical education component of the *baccalauréat* school-leaving examination in 1995.

De Gaulle's own well publicized attachment to rugby union – a sport rooted firmly in southwest France, where it has given rise to a unique, and regularly applauded, style of play which is the source of considerable local (specifically municipal) pride – was part of the transformation of a regional passion into a national preoccupation made possible by the massive expansion of televised sports coverage from the 1950s onwards. (Today's TV highlights also include particularly the Open tennis championships at Roland Garros and the 'the hell of the north', the Paris–Roubaix cycle race). The appointment, under Georges **Pompidou**'s presidency, of Jacques **Chaban-Delmas** (a former rugby and tennis international) to the post of prime minister is likewise of significance as regards the process of national identification with sports stars, as is the massive coverage provided by both a specialist press (notably *L'Équipe* and *Le Miroir des sports*) and the general national (and especially regional) press. Indeed, such is French sport's sociological significance that it has periodically attracted the attention of distinguished commentators from **Barthes** to **Bourdieu**.

Such diverse factors as long-term structural unemployment, the television-led emergence of the home as the primary cultural space, the collapse of established social hierarchies including particularly traditional gender roles, the advent of *le sport-business* (typified, in spite of recent set-backs, by Bernard **Tapie**) and even administrative decentralization can all be linked to changes in French leisure patterns. The rise of the so-called 'Californian' sports (such as windsurfing and hang-gliding) and the 'informal' use of new sporting spaces (such as street basketball or skateboarding) reflect profound changes in French society, as they do in other developed industrial nations. The centralized and hierarchical model of sports administration is increasingly challenged by the development of sporting activity outside the formal structures of the federations (including jogging, aerobics and modern dance), as part of broader social changes often characterized as the privatization of leisure. In these circumstances, the vexed question of whether (as has sometimes been optimistically suggested) sport may provide a privileged mechanism for the integration of alienated youth of ethnic minority origin remains undecided.

PHILIP DINE

See also: horse racing; motor sport; *pétanque*; regional press in France; sport and education; sports funding; winter sports

Further reading

Dine, P. (1995) 'The Tradition of Violence in French Sport', in R. Günther and R. Windebank (eds) *Violence and Conflict in Modern French Culture*, Sheffield: Sheffield Academic Press (an examination of continuities and changes in French sporting practices).

Greaves, A. (1993) 'Sport in France', in M. Cook (ed.) *French Culture Since 1945*, London: Longman (an overview of the topic which is particularly incisive on links with the national education system).

Holt, R. (1981) *Sport and Society in Modern France*, London: Macmillan (the classic English-language account of the rise of French sport).

Hubscher, R., Durry, J., Jeu, B. and Garrier, G. (1992) *L'Histoire en mouvements: le sport dans la société française (XIXe–XXe siècle)*, Paris: Armand Colin (a major collaborative survey of the history and sociology of sport in France).

sport and education

Since World War II, the French Ministry of Education and the Ministry of Youth, Sport and Leisure have strengthened considerably the role of sport in the lives of French youth and have developed professional qualifications in sport and exercise science in **universities** (Sciences et Techniques des Activités Physiques et Sportives). Sporting facilities have been radically improved in educational and municipal establishments throughout the country.

Historically, physical education in France was associated with the military, although as early as 1817 the government was supporting a mixed civil and military training centre (the Gymnase Normal Civil et Militaire). It was only in 1937, however, that the first Ministère des Sports (sports ministry) was created, along with sports diplomas. This new ministry was responsible for sport and physical education in educational establishments (gymnastics had been compulsory in secondary schools since a decree of 1869). The **Vichy** government reinforced the trend with a Commissariat for general education and sport and, in the aftermath of the war, the Institut National du Sport (National Institute for Sport) was created in 1945.

In 1958, the Fifth Republic formed the so-called Commissariat à la Jeunesse et aux Sports (Youth and Sports Commission) before transforming it into a ministry in 1966. In 1968 it became a Secrétariat d'État (ministry of state). Sport was, then, being increasingly recognized as an important element in the curriculum (as witnessed, for example, in the official instructions issued to educational establishments in 1967 which proclaimed the crucial role of sport and competition in the pursuit of 'material and spiritual progress').

Another highly significant development of national importance was the merging in 1976 of the Écoles Normales Supérieures d'Éducation Physique (the top-level teacher-training establishments for physical education) and the Institut National des Sports (National Institute of Sport), which became the prestigious Institut National du Sport et de l'Éducation Physique, or INSEP (the National Institute of Sport and Physical Education). This institute now attracts the elite of French sportsmen and sportswomen and has done much to improve France's standing in the world of sport.

The Ministère des Sports oversees school, university and civil sport from international level down to that of the *départements*; it maintains close relations with the federations which control individual sports. Each federation has a national technical director (DTN) who is at the top of a pyramid which goes all the way down to individual clubs. School sport has its national 'union' at primary and secondary level (Union Sportive des Écoles Primaires, Union Nationale du Sport Scolaire), while universities have their own sports federation (Fédération Nationale du Sport Universitaire). Despite the undoubted improvements in organization, training and sports facilities, France had limited success in competitive sport before the outstanding achievements at the Atlanta Olympic Games in 1996. The country has also made great strides in **tennis**, has maintained its high standards in **rugby** and improved them significantly in **football**.

IAN PICKUP

See also: athletics; cycling; motor sport; *pétanque*; sport; Tour de France; water sports; winter sports

Further reading

Dicosport 1996 (1996), Paris: Dicosport/Éditions Presse Audiovisuelle (a dictionary of French and world sport published annually).
Thomas, R. (1981) *L'Éducation physique*, Paris: PUF (an account of the history, development and organization of physical education in France).

sports funding

French sport relies upon both public and private funding, with a central role played by local government. The principle of state involvement in the organization and funding of sport became firmly established as part of the broader process of economic and social reconstruction which occurred after World War II. The present Ministère de la Jeunesse et des Sports administers the financial support given to the national federations responsible for overseeing individual sports. While seldom exceeding 0.2 per cent of total government expenditure, this funding has provided both a lifeline for the weaker organizations and a means of exerting influence on sports development for the government. At present, state support may make up anything between 10 and 90 per cent of the revenue of an individual federation, depending on its ability to generate additional income from subscriptions, sponsorship and **television** rights, with the average figure being in the region of 40 per cent. (These and other statistics cited are derived from Miège 1993.) Since the early 1960s, such aid has taken two main forms: personnel and grants. Some 1,700 technical advisers are made available to individual federations at both national and local levels. The salaries of these civil servants, like the awards made by the ministry to cover the federations' operating costs and their support for top-level performers, are financed jointly through direct taxation and the Fonds National pour le Développement du Sport (FNDS), a specifically targeted levy on alcohol sales and gambling (principally **horse racing** and the national lottery, including its version of the football pools, the *loto sportif*). Since the administrative decentralization of 1983, the state has ceased to be directly involved in the financing of capital projects, with the exception of major initiatives such as the loss-making Albertville Olympic Games in 1992 and the new national stadium in the Paris **suburbs**. The *régions* and the *départements* have thus joined the *communes* in what has long been a privileged field of local government action, with an average 7 per cent of municipal funds currently devoted to sport, and over one-third of the total sports budget coming from the municipalities. The involvement of the *régions* and the *départements*, at under 4 per cent, remains modest, but is rapidly expanding. However, this apparently solid structure is under strain as a result of a general crisis of commercialization, with entrepreneurial attitudes replacing a traditional associative ethos reliant upon voluntary involvement. The funding of professional sport has similarly been subject to stress, as evidenced by both regular administrative reforms and the periodic financial crises of major clubs (most notably Bernard **Tapie**'s Olympique de Marseille).

PHILIP DINE

See also: sport

Further reading

Conseil National de la Vie Associative (1993) *Les Associations à l'épreuve de la décentralisation: Bilan 1991–1992*, Paris: La Documentation Française (a detailed report on the impact of a decade of decentralization on French associations, including particularly sports clubs).

Miège, C. (1993) *Les Institutions sportives*, Paris: PUF (an introductory survey of the administrative structures of French sport).

Stäel, Nicolas de

b. 1914, St Petersburg, Russia;
d. 1955, Antibes

Artist

Nicolas de Staël's painting helped to define the lyrical and expressive form of abstraction that evolved in Paris and elsewhere in the postwar years. A Russian émigré, orphaned soon after his family was forced into exile, he was adopted by Russian expatriates living in Brussels, where he studied at the Académie Royale des Beaux-Arts. After serving in the Foreign Legion, he moved to France in 1940, settling for a time in Nice, where, through his companion, Jeannine Guillou, he made the acquaintance of a group of abstract artists including Magnelli, Marie Raymond (Yves **Klein**'s mother) and Sonia and Robert Delaunay. Their

influence led him to abandon the figurative painting he had practised before the war in favour of abstraction.

After settling in Paris in 1943, he began to show his work in exhibitions alongside abstractionists such Domela, Kandinsky and Magnelli. His *Compositions* (1943/4) distinguished him from the 'geometric' abstractionists represented by Mondrian's successors – Magnelli and **Vasarély**, for example – and identified him with the expressive and lyrical form of abstraction that was evolving as an alternative. While these early, rather decorative, works lacked a certain assurance, from 1946 onwards Staël proved that abstract painting could express mood while remaining self-referential. His *De la danse* (1946) has been hailed as an expression of 'pure painting', with its subtle and sombre beiges and grey-blues translating his subjective state at the time. The misery of these early years, which had been marked by penury and the death of Jeannine, began to dissipate with his marriage to Françoise Chapouton and growing artistic success. In 1948, he acquired French citizenship.

The influence of his friend Georges **Braque**, and his admiration for the painterly qualities in the work of artists such as Rembrandt, may have led him to focus on colour and texture, while a fellow Russian émigré, André Lanskoy, is said to have taught him, through example, the technique of applying thick paint with a palette knife to produce the rich, tactile surfaces that distinguish his work of the late 1940s. The expressive qualities of texture, also seen in Jean Fautrier's *Otages* of 1945, was to become a recognizable characteristic of the lyrical form of abstraction with which Staël is associated.

From 1952, figurative elements began to appear in his paintings – still lifes, landscapes, the human body. A floodlit football match at the Parc des Princes in 1952 inspired his *Footballeurs* series, which provoked enthusiasm in the public and condemnation from the defenders of abstract art. Yet his human figures are treated as compact masses of colour, without a psychological or even an anatomical presence, and are analysable in purely formal terms, while his seascapes *Marine claire* and

Marine foncée (both 1955) also serve to show that the distinction between abstract and representational art is, in many respects, meaningless.

The last five years of Staël's life were marked by international acclaim, with important exhibitions in New York, London and other European cities. He committed suicide in March 1955 while working on paintings for two exhibitions planned for the summer. Since his death, his paintings have continued to be exhibited on a regular basis throughout Europe and America.

CAROL WILCOX

See also: painting

Further reading

Chastel, A. (ed.) (1972) *Staël*, Paris: Maeght (this wide range of reproductions of Staël's work is prefaced by a leading French art historian).

Dumur, G. (1989) *Nicolas de Staël*, Paris: Flammarion (an interesting evaluation of Staël's life and work, even if the style is rather flowery).

stars

Star studies have been an important part of film studies since the late 1970s, but tend to focus on Hollywood stars. There are therefore problems of definition in relation to French stars, who do not work in a studio system, and who cross over popular genres (comedies, police thrillers) and auteurist art films. If box office is used to justify star status, then the French star system is overwhelmingly masculine and dominated by popular genres, with an emphasis on comedy. In the postwar period, Louis de **Funès** and Bourvil, whose greatest joint success was Oury's comedy *La Grande Vadrouille* (1966), dominated the 1960s, just as **Belmondo** and **Delon** dominated the 1970s in a mixture of comic action films and thrillers.

During the 1980s and since, **Depardieu** has topped the league as the main male French star, whose appearance can ensure a film's success, such as in Dupeyron's *Drôle d'endroit pour une rencontre* in 1988. A 1990 poll by *Télérama*, however, placed Gabin at the top, followed by Gérard **Philipe**, and included **Montand** in its first six, suggesting that box office is not the only condition for stardom. The same poll listed the following women as stars, in rank order: Romy Schneider, Michèle Morgan, Simone **Signoret**, Isabelle **Adjani**, Catherine **Deneuve**, Brigitte **Bardot**. While Schneider has always been popular with French audiences, it is curious that Bardot should figure so low (only 8 per cent voted her as their favourite), since she seems the epitome of the female star, her retirement patterned on Garbo's. The 1990 poll also asked respondents who the stars of tomorrow might be, and these (including Sophie **Marceau**, Emmanuelle **Béart** and Juliette **Binoche**) seem more likely candidates for star status. Stardom might therefore seem to be ephemeral, but this is contradicted by the first list of stars given in the same poll, since Schneider's decade was the 1970s (she died in 1982), and Signoret's decade straddled the 1960s and 1970s (she died in 1985). Another criterion is international status. Those who might be considered major stars in 1996 – Adjani, Binoche and Depardieu – have all been in Hollywood films (although Depardieu was a star before *Green Card*). Conversely, **Ardant** has been in a number of European films since *Swann in Love*, often by well-known directors: Tato's *Desiderio* (1984, in Italy), Scola's *La Famiglia* (1987, in Italy/France), Von Trotta's adaptation of Chekhov's *Three Sisters*, *Paura e amore* (1988, in Italy/Germany/France), Peploe's *Afraid of the Dark* (1991, in France/Great Britain) and Bellocchio's *Il Sogno della Farfalla* (1992, in Italy/France/Switzerland); but despite this, and despite her association with **Truffaut**, Ardant is not seen as a star. It would therefore seem that to be a star in the French system, you have to act in Hollywood films. The second major point to emerge is that stars, like the desires which give rise to them, fade, although at different speeds of light.

PHIL POWRIE

See also: cinema

Further reading

Morin, E. (1961) *The Stars*, New York: Grove
Press (a standard introduction; originally
published in French in 1957).

street papers

Macadam Journal, Le Réverbère, La Rue and
Faim de siècle, launched in rapid succession in
1993, followed by *Le Lampadaire* in 1994, are
the main French street papers, commonly
referred to as *la presse SDF*. SDF means people
sans domicile fixe (of no fixed abode). These
alternative newspapers, championing the cause
of the homeless, are sold in the streets by homeless vendors in return for a percentage of the
cover price, normally 60 per cent. Their aim is
to provide a source of revenue, and act as an
instrument of social integration for vendors,
giving them self-respect and facilitating contacts with the public.

PAM MOORES

See also: *restaurants du coeur*

structuralism

An influential intellectual movement dominant
in France from the late 1950s to the early
1970s. The origins of structuralism are multiple, and some commentators (such as **Piaget**
and **Serres**) rightly insist on its transdisciplinary
basis (e.g. in physics, mathematics and biology). However, the main path of assimilation of
structuralism into the human sciences in France
was via linguistic theory, and in this version at
least it could more precisely be called linguistic
structuralism.

The basic elements of linguistic structuralism can be found in the pioneering work of the
Swiss linguist Ferdinand de Saussure, the
Course in General Linguistics (*Cours de linguistique générale*), published in 1916.
Saussure distinguished between two aspects or
levels of language, *langue* and *parole*. *Parole*
refers to the external and contingent aspect of
language production in activities such as
speech and writing, while *langue* – the principal object of linguistic science – is the set of
patterns or rules which precedes and makes
possible the realization of language in *parole*.
For Saussure, *langue* is a system, in which it is
the relations between elements, and not the elements themselves, that are responsible for
meaning. On the semantic level, an individual
word (e.g. 'horse') only makes sense in terms of
its difference from other, related concepts (e.g.
donkey, ass, unicorn, automobile, etc.). On the
phonetic level, difference of meaning is generated by the substitution of minimally distinct
units of sound: 'horse', 'Norse', 'course', etc.
From this differential explanation of signification follows the central postulate of Saussure's
linguistic theory, the arbitrariness of the sign.
Word and concept (or 'signifier' and 'signified')
have no essential connection other than their
habitual association within the system of
langue. An important aspect of Saussure's distinction between *langue* and *parole* is that it
also implies a distinction between the individual and the collective. Saussure reiterates that
langue is by nature a social construct, whereas
parole, the exercise or execution of *langue*, is
individual and variable.

Probably the most important mediation of
Saussurean linguistics in postwar French
thought came from the anthropologist Claude
Lévi-Strauss. Inspired by the phonological theory of the Russian linguist Roman **Jakobson**, in
his first book, *The Elementary Structures of
Kinship* (*Les Structures élémentaires de la parenté*), Lévi-Strauss argued that it is possible to
isolate a small number of elementary and
invariant structures from which the diversity of
observable kinship structures might be derived.
He then went on to extend his application of
the linguistic model to other areas of social life.
Already in the *Cours* Saussure had indicated
that linguistics dealt with only one of a number

of sign systems used in human society, and for this reason he suggested that the study of language should ultimately be part of a more general science of signs – semiology. Lévi-Strauss developed this idea in his inaugural lecture at the Collège de France in 1960, where he defined social anthropology as a semiology, that is, the study of signs in social life. The different social practices and institutions studied by anthropologists are homologous in that, like language, they are symbolic systems with their own inherent significations, ensuring communication between members of the group. Social phenomena as diverse as kinship structures, totemism or myth could therefore be analysed in the same way as a language. Lévi-Strauss's most elaborate application of the linguistic model can be found in his extensive work on myth, most remarkably in the four-volume cycle *Mythologiques*, published between 1964 and 1971. According to Lévi-Strauss, traditional interpretations of myth concentrated on the meaning of isolated elements or themes, whereas each myth should be considered as an integrated system. Just as linguists isolated the minimal constitutive units of language (phonemes, morphemes, etc.), so the mythologist could isolate the most basic elements of a myth (mythemes). As a system, the signification of the myth came not from any individual element or mytheme, but from the differential relations between these elements, more precisely their mode of combination. As in language, this combination of elements was not arbitrary, and followed certain definite rules. The aim of structural analysis was therefore to determine the rules of combination that would constitute the structure of the myth.

An important feature of Lévi-Strauss's definition of structure is that, like Saussure's *langue*, it is independent of the conscious intentions and interpretations of the individual member of the social group. This does not mean that structure is unconscious in the Freudian sense, that is, the subject of censorship or repression; rather, it is unconscious in the same way that the implicit rules of a language are not conscious to the average speaker of the language. As Lévi-Strauss asserted, it is not individuals that speak through myths but myths that speak through individuals.

Lévi-Strauss's application of linguistic theory to social and cultural formations caught the imagination of a new generation of thinkers in search of new models and more rigorous methods of analysis. This was in a context where the human sciences, and anthropology in particular, were increasingly seen as a more scientific alternative to the old humanism. Few disciplines were left untouched by structuralist theory. In **psychoanalysis**, Jacques **Lacan**'s proposed return to Freud was combined with a theory of the unconscious based on Saussurean linguistics. In history, Fernand **Braudel** described his analysis of long-term social and economic trends as 'structural history'. For the philosopher and historian Michel **Foucault**, structuralism announced the dissolution of 'man', a comparatively recent construct of Western philosophy and science. In the field of literary studies, Roland **Barthes** proposed a semiology of contemporary social and cultural forms, applying structural analysis to items of popular culture such as fashion writing. Related to the linguistic turn in literary studies was a revival of interest in theories of rhetoric and narrative discourse, which also drew on the earlier work of the Russian Formalists; this trend was evident in the work of **Genette**, **Greimas** and Todorov.

The differences between thinkers categorized as 'structuralist' were often very great, and many of these thinkers themselves resisted such assimilation and categorization. Significantly, Lévi-Strauss was doubtful of the validity of applications of structural analysis to literature, considering this an inappropriate extension of methods specific to the object of his own discipline, anthropology. Yet, despite such restrictions, and despite the heterogeneity of the thinkers involved, it can be said that during the period in question structuralism became the dominant paradigm in French intellectual life. This success cannot be attributed solely to the intrinsic merits of structuralist theory itself, which was open to criticism on a number of levels, even in its original, Lévi-Straussian interpretation; it was equally a function of the context in which structuralism first came to prominence. As a movement, it participated in the climate of reaction against the philosophical humanism which had dominated intellectual discussion in France since the war. After the war, Jean-Paul **Sartre**'s version of **existentialism** had emerged as the philosophy most suited to the urgent moral questions – questions of individual choice, responsibility and commitment – which the experience of war had rendered so immediate. However, as these conflicts receded into the past and France proceeded along the path of postwar reconstruction, to many the solutions offered by existentialism seemed less relevant and even inadequate to the moral, political and economic complexities of the post-colonial world. Increasingly, intellectuals turned to the specialized knowledge of the human and social sciences for answers which philosophy itself could not provide. This was also a period of major advances in the natural sciences, in new disciplines such as cybernetics, information theory and molecular biology. The Sartrean version of existentialism was primarily concerned with the immediate experience of the individual subject in-the-world, rather than with scientific objectifications of the world, the subject or the society inhabited by the subject. As Lévi-Strauss pointed out some years later, one of the significant weaknesses of Sartre's thought was his failure to engage with contemporary science, which is precisely what structuralism had done. In addition to its assimilation of the methods of structural linguistics, structuralism also drew its inspiration from the recent achievements of the new sciences mentioned above. Whatever the ultimate limitations of this kind of interdisciplinarity, it at least gave the impression of a ferment of ideas which appeared to be absent in existentialism.

Inevitably, a polemic developed between the two movements, crystallizing around the figures of Sartre and Lévi-Strauss. In *Tristes tropiques*, Lévi-Strauss had already attacked the subjectivist bias of phenomenology and existentialism. A philosophy based on personal experience, he claimed, can never tell us anything essential about society or humanity, but is simply a dramatization of the individual. A few years later, in *The Savage Mind* (*La Pensée*

sauvage), he questioned the obsession of philosophers like Sartre with history, arguing that their conception of the historical process was purely relative. The societies studied by ethnologists also possessed a history, but chose to represent it differently, constructing their social identity around the repetition of archetypal situations rather than in relation to a linear sequence of events. Sartre's response to structuralism, both in this local debate and more generally, was to criticize the abstraction of structural analysis, which ignored the dialectical realities of concrete relations and of the historical process. In his view, the priority structuralism gave to autonomous and unconscious structures dehumanized the subject and excluded the possibility of individual agency. On a more general level, he saw structuralism as a symptom of the political stasis of France under de **Gaulle**'s Fifth Republic and as the intellectual incarnation of modern technocratic ideology.

Sartre's resistance was by no means isolated. He was joined by French intellectuals of diverse persuasions (Marxist, Christian and others), who saw in structuralism a philosophy inimical to the interests of an authentic humanism. Despite their often valid criticisms, it was evident that the tide had turned in favour of the human sciences as exemplified in the anthropology of Lévi-Strauss. The events of **May 1968** seemed to offer momentary vindication of Sartre's position, as for many structuralism had become synonymous with the conservative elements of the discredited regime: one commentator memorably remarked that *les structures ne descendent pas dans la rue* ('structures do not take to the streets'). The triumph was short-lived, however, and by the late 1960s the position of structuralism seemed assured as it finally received academic consecration in the post-1968 expansion of the university system.

To an extent it could be said that the decline of structuralism came from within: that is, it came from those who had enthusiastically assimilated its lessons and had come to recognize its inherent limitations. The diverse applications of linguistic structuralism could often be reductive and in the worse cases degenerated into the mechanical repetition of a preset formula. While Lévi-Strauss continued to refine his own version of structural analysis in the relatively specialized domain of mythology, by the early 1970s thinkers such as Barthes had abandoned structuralism. It remains that structuralism represented a crucial phase in postwar French thought, and it is a measure of its historical importance that the heterogeneous movement which succeeded it is commonly referred to as **poststructuralism**.

CHRISTOPHER JOHNSON

See also: anthropology and ethnology; Derrida; linguistic/discourse theory

Further reading

Descombes, V. (1979) *Le Même et l'autre: quarante-cinq ans de philosophie française (1933–1978)*, Paris: Éditions de Minuit. Translated L. Scott-Fox and J. M. Harding (1980) *Modern French Philosophy*, Cambridge: Cambridge University Press (essential for an understanding of the philosophical debates surrounding structuralism).

Dosse, F. (1991/2) *Histoire du structuralisme*, 2 vols, Paris: Éditions la Découverte (an exhaustive if sometimes rather anecdotal survey of the personalities, issues and debates of the structuralist period).

Lévi-Strauss, C. (1955) *Tristes tropiques*, Paris: Plon. Translated J. and D. Weightman (1984) *Tristes tropiques*, Harmondsworth: Penguin.

——(1962) *La Pensée sauvage*, Paris: Plon. Translated R. Needham (1966) *The Savage Mind*, Chicago: Chicago University Press.

——(1964–71) *Mythologiques*, 4 vols, Paris: Plon. Translated J. and D. Weightman (1970–81) *Mythologiques: Introduction to a Science of Mythology*, 4 vols, London: Cape.

——(1967) *Les Structures élémentaires de la parenté*, Paris and La Haye: Mouton & Co/Maison des Sciences de l'Homme. Translated J. H. Bell, J. R. von Sturmer and

R. Needham (1969) *The Elementary Structures of Kinship*, Boston: Beacon Press.

——(1973) *Anthropologie structurale deux*, Paris: Plon. Translated M. Layton (1978) *Structural Anthropology 2*, Harmondsworth: Penguin.

Saussure, F. de (1986) *Cours de linguistique générale*, Paris: Payot. Translated R. Harris (1983) *Course in General Linguistics*, London: Duckworth.

Sturrock, J. (ed.) (1979) *Structuralism and Since: From Lévi-Strauss to Derrida*, Oxford: Oxford University Press (an authoritative collection of essays on the main luminaries of structuralist thought).

student revolt of 1986

In late 1986, a bill before parliament (containing proposals that might have significantly increased university registration fees and introduced measures of selective entry) provoked widespread strikes in educational institutions, and brought students from **universities** and *lycées* alike on to the streets in their hundreds of thousands, in the common cause of protest at the infringement of the Republican constitutional right to free access to non-fee-paying higher education. It was the largest and best co-ordinated student protest since the events of **May 1968**, to which some commentators began to liken it. When clashes between demonstrators and police in Paris led to the death of a student, the legislation was withdrawn. The Junior Minister for Research and Higher Education responsible, Alain Devaquet, resigned.

RON HALLMARK

See also: education ministry; education, secondary: *collèges, lycées*

Further reading

Various (1987) 'Université: le séisme: les dossiers complets de la crise', *Le Monde de l'éducation* 134 (January): 3–20 (a full exploration of the issues).

suburbs

The *banlieue*, as the urban periphery outside the urban core is called, has a history going back to the redevelopment of city centres and influx of rural migrants in the second half of the nineteenth century. Later, in the interwar period, urban peripheries expanded haphazardly with little planning. The term 'red belt', referring to the Communist-voting suburbs to the northeast of Paris, dates from this period. It was coined by Paul-Vaillant Couturier in articles that appeared in the Communist newspaper *L'Humanité* in 1924–6 and eventually became a reality after the 1935 municipal elections. Today, the tight network of Communist associations and culture has come to an end as the *banlieue* becomes truly part of urban civilization, an integral extension rather than an appendage of the city.

It was at the beginning of the 1960s that Sarcelles, then a dormitory suburb in the Paris agglomeration, gave its name to *sarcellite*, an illness equated with the concrete gigantism and poor living conditions of the HLM (*habitat à loyer modéré*). 'Banlieue' has increasingly operated, as the inner city has done in Britain, as the simplified shorthand for a cluster of social ills and problematic inhabitants. The coupling of security and foreigner, delinquency and **immigration**, violence and suburbs, has reinforced the sense of the suburb as being outside of normal society, a place of exclusion for the dangerous classes. Thus *banlieue* merges seamlessly into *cités* (estates), ghettos and *quartiers difficiles* (problem areas).

Disturbances in Vénissieux (1981) and Vaulx-en-Velin (1990) – both suburbs of Lyon – and in Sartrouville (1991) and Mantes-la-Jolie (1991) maintained the suburb in the forefront of media attention and public policy. From 1983, the 'Banlieue 89' programme, launched by Roland Castro and Michel Cantal-Dupart, began its work on creating a new

urbanism. The projects in the 'Banlieue' programme, of which 200 had been undertaken in the 1980s, combined design, sociability and cultural activities; they sought to recentre places which had been peripheral and connect them together. However, the 'Banlieue 89' programme exuded an unwarranted optimism in the power of improvements in the built environment to provide an answer to inequalities and economic and social exclusion.

Not only has the *banlieue* come to occupy centre stage politically, but it has also gained prominence cinematically in the 1990s. Whereas in the 1960s the *banlieue* was an unusual setting, with the exception of a few films such as *Deux ou trois choses que je sais d'elle* directed by Jean-Luc **Godard** (1966), which examined women's **prostitution**, and *La Dernière Femme* (1976) by Marco Ferreri, in the mid-1990s a new wave of French film adopted the themes of life in the *banlieue* – youth in their dealings with parents and the law, and relationships between different ethnic minorities – as central concerns. Kassovitz's *La Haine* (1995) highlighted the lives of youths from different ethnic backgrounds who, bored and hassled on their estate, escape to the bright lights of Paris, for which they do not possess the necessary *savoir faire*. Other accounts, such as the voyage undertaken by François **Maspero** and Anaik Frantz through the Parisian *banlieue*, follow the route of the RER (express metro), presenting portraits of landscape which, though sometimes very desolate, are always peopled with real figures.

ELEONORE KOFMAN

See also: *cinéma de banlieue*; parties and movements

Further reading

Jazouli, A. (1992) *Années de banlieue*, Paris: Éditions du Seuil (polemical sociological analysis)

Maspero, F. and Frantz A. (1993) *Roissy Express: A Journey Through the Paris*

Suburbs, London: Verso (French edition [1990] *Les Passagers du Roissy Express*, Paris: Seuil) (a lively and thoughtful narrative account).

Supervielle, Jules

b. 1884, Montevideo, Uruguay;
d. 1960, Paris

Poet, writer and dramatist

Supervielle was educated in France and lived in France after World War II. In his **poetry** as well as in his fiction, he is noted for his gracious intimacy, his ability to link himself to nature and the universe with fresh eyes, and without grandiloquence. His friendships with Gide, Valéry and Rilke were crucial in his formation, yet he maintained a fine balance between his Uruguayan and French cultural legacies. Primarily his works win readers by their charm and simplicity. There are many volumes of poetry, from *Gravitations* (1926) to 1959's *Le Corps tragique* (The Tragic Body), plus several collections of fiction, notably the appropriately entitled *Premiers pas de l'univers* (First Steps in the Universe) from 1950.

WALTER A. STRAUSS

Supports/Surfaces

The Supports/Surfaces group, which existed as a coherent avant-garde between 1971 and 1972, was associated with the structuralist review *Tel quel* and its pro-Maoist faction, the Mouvement de Juin '71. Marcelin Pleynet acted as 'bridge' between art and literature through his position as art critic and editor of *Tel quel*. Pleynet's *Painting and System* (*Système de la Peinture*), which provides a model for interpreting the history of art with reference to Marx and Freud, was applauded by the artists of the Supports/Surfaces group.

The Supports/Surfaces artists made two important contributions to art practice: they attacked the Greenbergian Modernist paradigm (which insists upon abstraction and the sublime as qualitative measures of 'Modern' art) by revealing the extent to which the surface picture plane is itself constructed (falsifying); and insisted upon the semantic value of plastic practice. These projects were wrapped up in Far Left political rhetoric by the group's journal, *Peinture, cahiers théoriques*. That the plastic works resemble American minimal art of the preceding decade has made it difficult to assimilate them within an international art market which demands aesthetic innovation, while rejecting politics and philosophy as determinants for value in art practice.

Bioulès's *Sans titre* of 1971 (a diptych in which each panel is divided in two, coloured white, blue/white, red) would provide an example in which the refusal of the *écran pictural* is achieved through the use of acrylic washes, absorbed by the fine linen surface, emphasizing 'objecthood', and denying the assumption of colour as transcendent surface.

Bioulès ultimately resigned over the strict imposition of a posited 'dialectical materialism', which he felt limited Freudian interpretations of his pulsion towards colour.

Louis Cane's *Toiles découpées* from 1970 (large felt squares, with the centre cut to form a protrusion on the floor and a 'frame' on the wall) negotiate the **Matisse** inheritance and its Freudian corollary through 'cutting', as well as invoking Stella's shaped canvases (and thereby asserting the 'objecthood' of the work, its material reality as opposed to its transcendent aesthetic value). They question through their three-dimensional quality not only the Renaissance *Véduta* (window on the world) as structure in **painting** but also the Modernist critical intolerance of **sculpture**'s physicality. For a political interpretation to be defended, it is necessary to see Cane's earlier *Tampons* (rubber stamp marks which read 'Louis Cane, artiste peintre') of 1967 as positing the artist as artisan-worker: the repetitive manual operation is seen as analogous to the 'skilled ouvrier' emergent under **Pompidou**, their identity disappearing in the almost infinite repetition of their 'Fordist' mechanized gesture.

Dezeuze was already a long way into his systematic investigations by the time he made his *Échelle de bois verte et brune* (Brown and Green Wooden Ladder) in 1971. The disruption of the categories painting/sculpture/architectural space may once again be seen as a refusal of Modernist critical preoccupations with transcendence and its analogous exclusion of non-codified genres. The concern with relocating the stretcher as structurally meaningful is clearer here than in almost any Supports/Surfaces work: the absorption of wood dyes for colour, affirming the rejection of the primacy of the surface screen (which is absent), the rolled-up part of the piece insisting upon a refusal of narrative closure, a refusal of mastery, the undetermined presence of excess.

Valensi's *tressages* (weavings) and *objet d'analyses* (analytical objects) of 1970 engage strongly with questions of language, text(ile), intertextuality and refusal of narrative closure. Particularly, this artist may be seen to take on board the notion of 'system' as a scientific approach to a research-based art, seeking to explore the effects of stitching, knotting, weaving and layering materials traditionally associated with painting. There is no place here for 'bourgeois' aesthetic bliss. This work is functional, not in the propagandizing manner of socialist realism, but rather after the fashion of science ameliorating understanding in the domain of the arts, a position very much at one with the contradictory French cultural context of its moment.

Viallat's *Disparitions multiples* (Multiple Disappearances) of 1970 engages with not only a refusal of the surface through the use of absorbed colours, not only with the refusal of closure which is implicit in the multilayered recto–verso work, not only with the refusal of surface narrative through the use of his repetitive non-referential form, but also with the notion of an acquired material narrative, liberated through this series of refusals.

His *Pochoir de filet sur toile métis* of 1972 cross-references his rope/knot pieces with his 'disparition' pieces by using the trace of an absent knotted rope net to indicate the absence of his non-referential forms (the marks forming in effect the tessellated outline of the usual pattern). His recuperation of materials and liberation of their narrative value uses a Derridean displacement to effect a structural revelation of semantic excess usually covered by painting.

Viallat never made any specific claims for the political value of his work, and this proved to be a stumbling block for his participation in the group. It should be noted that it was a political commitment to a culturally distinct Midi, rather than an absence of political stance, which was at stake. This 'other' political domain is expressed most clearly not in his painted/theoretical works but rather in his drawings, where the representation of bullfighting is central. Viallat's separation of politics from art is reflected in his separation of art and drawing, where the former is deemed intellectual and theoretical, and the latter an expression of reality as lived by the artist.

These examples of the Supports/Surfaces group's practice are intended to be representative rather than exhaustive. It should be noted that, while the group formally existed only between 1971 and 1972, its impact on French art practice was dominant throughout the 1970s. Its significance may be measured by the strength of its legacy, a legacy of postmodern art practice which works freely with shattered cultural narrative, as if its previous seeming coherence had never needed to be questioned.

SIMEON HUNTER

See also: Derrida; painting

T

Tapie, Bernard

b. 1945, Paris

Businessman and politician

Tapie was the archetypal 'Socialist' millionaire, at least until his fall from grace in 1994. The owner (among other things) of France's biggest manufacturer of sporting footwear, his support for **Mitterrand** (who appointed him minister with special responsibility for cities) and demolition of Jean-Marie **Le Pen** in a televised debate made him one of the Left's leading standard-bearers in Marseille, one of whose constituencies he represented in parliament and whose football team he owned. Disgraced successively by his involvement in match-rigging and by a spectacular bankruptcy, he began serving a prison sentence in 1997. He embarked upon a screen acting career in Claude Lelouch's *Hommes, femmes: mode d'emploi* (1996), for which he agreed to accept a percentage of the takings by way of payment.

KEITH READER

See also: parties and movements; sport

Tardieu, Jean

b. 1903, Ain;
d. 1995, Paris

Playwright and poet

Tardieu is known for his translation of Hölderlin's poetry in the 1930s, and after the war for short absurdist plays, experimenting with language and form. These include *Le Guichet* (The Ticket Office), *La Serrure* (The Lock) and *Le Sonate et les trois messieurs* (The Sonata and the Three Gentlemen).

ANNIE SPARKS

See also: theatre; Theatre of the Absurd

Further reading

Esslin, M. (1968) *The Theatre of the Absurd*, London: Pelican (Chapter 5 discusses Tardieu's drama in relation to this movement).

Tati, Jacques

b. 1908, Le Pecq, Yvelines;
d. 1982, Paris

Director and actor

Tati is one of the great French comedians, with an original comic style close to **mime**. He made only nine films, and is best remembered for his incarnation of the accident-prone Hulot, first in the anthology of gags *Mr Hulot's Holiday* (*Les Vacances de M. Hulot*) in 1953, followed by a critique of the gadgets in modern life in *Mon Oncle* (1958), which received a Special Jury prize at Cannes and an Oscar. His greatest film is *Playtime* (1967), a powerful portrait of Americanized France.

PHIL POWRIE

See also: cinema

Tavernier, Bertrand

b. 1941, Lyon

Director

Tavernier's films, many of them scripted by the key scriptwriters of the 1950s, Aurenche and Bost, hark back to the French quality tradition. His career took off with *L'Horloger de Saint-Paul* (1973), starring Noiret, which won the Prix Delluc. Subsequent films were either similar social analyses, e.g. the drug squads in *L627* (1991), or historical films, such as his nostalgic *Un dimanche à la campagne* (1984) set in 1912, which won a César, or 1989's *Life and Nothing Else But* (*La Vie et rien d'autre*), set in World War I, again starring Noiret.

PHIL POWRIE

See also: cinema; *cinéma de qualité*

Further reading

Douin, J.-L (1988) *Tavernier*, Paris: Édilig (analysis of the films).

Téchiné, André

b. 1943, Valence-d'Agen

Director

'A man of taste and culture rather than the creator of a universe' (according to the Larousse *Dictionnaire du cinéma*), Téchiné remains one of contemporary French cinema's outstanding directors of female actors, and it was for him that Catherine Deneuve gave two of her best performances in *Hôtel des Amériques* (1981) and *Ma saison préférée* (1993). He used Jeanne Moreau to good effect in the Brechtian *Souvenirs d'en France* (1975), and showed a sensitivity to adolescent – especially homosexual – anxieties in the autobiographically based *Les Roseaux sauvages* (1994).

KEITH READER

See also: cinema; gay cinema

Tel Quel group

This group of writers and critics associated with the review *Tel quel* was particularly influential in the late 1960s and early 1970s and proposed a radical theory and practice of writing.

The review *Tel quel* was created in 1960 at Éditions du Seuil as a rival to the *Nouvelle Revue française*, but soon began, under the dominance of Philippe Sollers, to celebrate the (then) literary avant-garde *nouveau roman*. By 1966, *Tel quel* had divested itself of this influence, developed its own experimental literary practice in the novel (Sollers, Jean-Louis Baudry, Jacques Henric) and in poetry (Marcelin Pleynet, Denis Roche), and become a vital context for innovative critical practices such as those of structuralist critics Genette and Barthes (who would remain a close ally of the group until his death). A key moment was the 1965 publication, in the 'Tel quel' series, of translations of the Russian Formalists, affirming the autonomy of literary practice. The limitations of structuralism and Formalism were soon bypassed, however, when in 1968 the review radicalized itself, articulating a complex theoretical 'programme', which appealed to the burgeoning theoretical apparatuses of Althusser, Lacan, Derrida and Kristeva (who became one the principal forces of the group with Sollers and Pleynet). Linking textual revolution to social revolution, also in 1968 the group engaged in an uneasy alliance with the Communist Party, only to move away from this position, in a spectacular and somewhat hysterical manner, and towards Maoism in 1971 (culminating in a trip to China in 1974 which was to puncture the ideological fantasy of China as revolutionary utopia). After 1971, the group's rhetoric became increasingly anarchic and terroristic, as if under the delayed pressure of the events of **May 1968**. A symptom of this was the more Rabelaisian or Joycean style of the group's fiction, and a critical focus on writers such as Joyce and Céline in the 1970s. With the growing importance of **psychoanalysis** and of the work of **Lacan**, the review became more and more critical of political systems, and emphasized the subjective dimension in literature and thought. This implied the abandonment of the group's political positions and a focus on forms of subjective excess or *jouissance*, notably in relation to sexuality and religion. This focus on the subject as exception also resulted in the dispersal of the group. In 1983, the review changed name and publisher to *L'Infini* at **Gallimard,** and is still published at present, with Sollers in overall control, affirming literature as an exceptional force resistant to cultural or social homogeneity.

PATRICK FFRENCH

See also: literary journals; Marxism and Marxian thought; poststructuralism

Further reading

ffrench, P. (1995) *The Time of Theory: A History of 'Tel quel'*, Oxford: Oxford University Press (a critical analysis of the literary theory proposed by the Tel Quel group in its context).

Forest, P. (1995) *Histoire de 'Tel quel'*, Paris: Éditions du Seuil (a highly detailed account of the history of *Tel quel*).

Sollers, P. (1983) *Théorie des exceptions*, Paris: Gallimard.

Tel quel (1960–82) Paris: Éditions du Seuil (quarterly review).

——(1968) *Théorie d'ensemble*, Paris: Éditions du Seuil.

television

For most of the postwar period French television was organized as a state monopoly which in practice was closely controlled by the government. From the middle of the 1980s, private sector competition was introduced, new channels were established and the balance of the system tilted towards commercial players. French television increasingly operates as part of a European audiovisual market, which opens up commercial opportunities for some companies but also poses problems for the defence of French content and culture.

French television was officially established in 1935, though regular broadcasts did not take place until after the end of World War II. The medium was slow to make an impact on French society and it was not until the late 1950s that a television set began to be perceived as an essential household item. By the end of the 1960s, television viewing had become a routinized part of leisure activity.

Its hold on the nation's attention has increased ever since, with the result that, in line with other western European countries, France has fully embraced the audiovisual era. The number of households with at least one television set has attained saturation level (over 95 per cent), while about 65 per cent also possess a video cassette recorder. The provision of national terrestrial networks has increased from 1 in the early 1960s to 6 by the mid-1990s, while cable offers its subscribers at least another 20 channels. The amount of television programming available' on terrestrial television alone has jumped from 2,760 hours per year in 1960 to over 50,000 hours in 1993. In return, by the mid-1990s a French adult watched television for an average of more than three hours per day.

During its formative years, French television

was organized as a state monopoly. The state broadcasting corporation, the **ORTF**, grew incrementally to manage three television channels by the early 1970s. After the Giscardian reform of 1974 these channels became separately constituted programme companies – TF1, Antenne 2 and FR3 – competing against each other for audiences within the state sector. The monopoly was finally abolished in 1982 by the Socialist government of Pierre **Mauroy**. This opened up the broadcasting system to private competition. In 1984 a new terrestrial pay-TV channel, **Canal Plus**, was launched under the control of Havas, which at that time still enjoyed close links with the state. In 1986 two new privately run commercial channels, La **Cinq** and TV6 (later renamed **M6**), came into existence. In the same year the conservative government of Jacques **Chirac** took the controversial step of privatizing the main national channel, TF1, which thus became the first public channel in Europe to be hived off to the private sector. Only a few years after the abolition of the state monopoly, therefore, the balance in programme supply between private and public sector channels had shifted overwhelmingly to the benefit of the former.

During the 1990s, however, public sector provision has been strengthened, while that of the private sector has been reduced. In 1992, La Cinq went into liquidation and ceased transmission. The privatization of TF1 had resulted in too many channels competing for **advertising** revenue and La Cinq suffered accordingly, failing to secure either a mass public or a sufficiently upmarket audience to attract advertisers. In 1989, Antenne 2 and FR3, since renamed **France 2** and **France 3**, were linked at the top under a single chairperson to improve the running of public sector television. In 1992 the Franco-German cultural channel **ARTE** was launched with state support on the terrestrial network vacated by La Cinq. Finally, in 1994 a public sector educational and training channel, La Cinquième, was established. It broadcast during the day on the same network used by ARTE in the evening. In addition, private **cable and satellite television** channels came on stream in the 1980s and

1990s, though their impact on the audience was limited, as many viewers seemed content with the output of the terrestrial channels and disinclined to pay additional subscription costs.

By the mid-1990s, the French television system was highly diverse. Programming was delivered through the new technologies of cable and satellite as well as via traditional terrestrial transmission, while digital television was beginning to make an impact by 1996. There was a mix of public and private channels, with the privatized TF1 securing the highest audience ratings. Different regulatory regimes were in force, ranging from detailed public service obligations in the case of France 2 and France 3, to a much lighter set of provisions for Canal Plus and the cable channels. A variety of funding mechanisms existed (licence revenue, advertising, viewer subscription and sponsorship), with many channels being financed from a mix of sources. Niche channels on cable (film, music, sport, news) complemented the mixed programme output of the terrestrial networks, while subscribers to Canal Plus enjoyed a programme diet based largely on recently released feature films and 'live' **sport**.

For a long part of its history French television was subject to a high degree of political interference. During the Fourth Republic (1946–58), this had little effect on the public since television had not yet become a mass medium. However, during de **Gaulle**'s presidency (1958–69) television news was censored and controlled to further the interests of the Gaullist regime, with considerable success in the early years. Government censorship and direct control were relaxed during the post-de Gaulle presidencies, largely because they were increasingly ineffective as a means of audience persuasion. The expansion of the system also made detailed control of news output impractical.

However, the tradition of a close relationship between the state and television, especially the public sector channels, has never been wholly relinquished. Appointments to top posts in public television are still made in part on the basis of political criteria. Moreover, the rapid turnover in the composition and powers of regulatory authorities in the 1980s was a stark reminder of the continuing partisan politicization of the audiovisual system despite its economic liberalization.

In contrast, there is some evidence of a less deferential attitude on the part of broadcasters towards politicians than was the case in the past. Satirical programmes such as the *Bébête-Show* and *Les Guignols de l'info*, which use puppet characters to poke fun at political figures, demonstrate a change in journalistic culture. This in turn reflects a more cynical public attitude towards politicans, fuelled by several corruption scandals in the 1980s and 1990s.

Up until the abolition of the monopoly, the programme output of French television was strictly regulated to conform with obligations laid down by the state and included in the operating conditions (*cahiers des charges*) of the programme companies. Since 1982, regulation has been a key issue on the media policy agenda, with the powers and composition of the regulatory authority at the heart of the political debate.

One of the innovations of the Socialists' 1982 statute (*loi Fillioud*) was the creation of a High Authority for Audiovisual Communication. Headed by the well-known former journalist, Michèle Cotta, the High Authority symbolized the desire of the government to attenuate its links with broadcasting. However, the role of the High Authority was limited and on certain key decisions, such as the allocation of licences to La Cinq and TV6, it was not consulted in advance. When the conservative government came to power in 1986 it introduced new legislation (*loi Léotard*) which among other things abolished the High Authority and replaced it with a National Commission for Communication and Liberties.

Sullied in the eyes of the Socialists because of its overtly partisan decisions, this commission was scrapped in 1989 following Mitterrand's second presidential victory and the subsequent election of a Socialist government. Its replacement, the Conseil Supérieur de l'Audiovisuel (Higher Audiovisual Council), has survived the conservative parliamentary

victory of 1993 and Chirac's accession to the presidential office in 1995. Composed of nine members – three appointed by the president of the Republic, three by the president of the National Assembly and three by the president of the Senate – the Council ensures that regulations on ownership, financing and programme content are respected by the television companies, particularly those in the public sector.

It is impossible to generalize about the programme output of French television. The growth in the number of channels and the banalization of television viewing have certainly amplified the role of the medium as a vehicle for popular culture. In its early years French television sought to elevate audience tastes with a programme diet which contained many worthy, serious and culturally demanding programmes. During the early years of de Gaulle's presidency, for example, television was intended to disseminate the best of French high culture to the growing nationwide audience. In the 1990s, much of the output is geared to mass taste, with the viewer regarded as a consumer to be satisfied rather than a pupil to be educated. **Game shows**, light entertainment programmes, **soap** operas and films fill the screen.

Yet, while a contrast is evident between the mission of the television system in the 1990s and that of the 1960s, it should not be overdrawn. Game shows and low-quality programming existed in the era of **Malraux**, while government backing for ARTE shows the commitment of the French state in the 1990s to serious cultural programming. The essential difference between the formative years and the present day is that in a multichannel system there is bound to be more programming catering for popular tastes than in the early elitist years of a single-channel state monopoly. The increasing confinement of high cultural programming to specialist channels or the fringes of the public sector networks is the consequence of a market-oriented system replacing a paternalistic state-dominated one.

Increasingly, French television is becoming part of a wider European and even global audiovisual market. Technology has played a part in this, with satellite transmission opening up the French system to foreign channels and vice versa. New patterns of media ownership have reinforced this internationalization of the medium. Canal Plus, for example, has successfully exported its pay-TV format to other countries where it has taken a stake in subscription television. Pursuing a corporate strategy based on vertical integration, Canal Plus has built up a powerful domestic base in the technological and production sectors from which to move out and conquer foreign markets. In particular, Canal Plus is at the forefront of the development of digital television in France and this experience will allow it to be a major player at the European level in this new form of broadcasting.

As national boundaries in Europe become more permeable and major national actors are transformed into transnational and global media players, French television faces problems as well as opportunities. The growth of television within France and elsewhere in Europe gives French production and programme companies the chance to expand and promote French output. But because of the size of the domestic (and European francophone) audience, of necessity French television has to rely on imports and the reproduction of foreign programme formats for some of its content. Regulatory quotas on programming may help offset some of the undesirable consequences of a free market in audiovisual goods and services in the eyes of French elites. Yet the objectives of greater consumer choice, high quality output and the defence of French culture are increasingly difficult to reconcile in a system where an optimal relationship between state, television and audience has never been satisfactorily achieved.

RAYMOND KUHN

See also: francophone television: DOM-TOMs; francophone television: Europe; Giscard d'Estaing, Valéry

Further reading

Barbrook, R. (1995) *Media Freedom*, London: Pluto (a history of the French media which uses different explanatory models based on the concept of media freedom).

Bourdon, J. (1990) *Histoire de la télévision sous de Gaulle*, Paris: Anthropos/INA (an excellent detailed study of the relationship between television and the Gaullist presidency).

Franceschini, L. (1995) *La Régulation audiovisuelle en France*, Paris: PUF (a short legal study of broadcasting regulation).

Kuhn, R. (1995) *The Media in France*, London: Routledge (the first full-length study of the French media in English).

Michel, H. (1995) *Les Grandes Dates de la télévision française*, Paris: PUF (a short historical overview of the medium).

Thomas, R. (1976) *Broadcasting and Democracy in France*, London: Crosby Lockwood Staples (a part-historical, part-thematic account of the multifaceted relationship between broadcasting and democracy in France up until the 1974 Giscardian reform).

television/spectacle guides

Television guides are France's most popular and profitable publications, with a dozen titles selling a total of 15 million copies per week. The leading title, *Télé 7 jours*, created in 1960, accounts for 3 million copies, with *Télé star*, *Télé Z*, *Télé poche* and *Télé loisirs* close on its heels. *Télérama* has a distinctive upmarket reputation: in addition to the full range of radio and television programmes, it covers music, literature and especially **cinema**, providing critical reviews for a discriminating public. Weekly spectacle guides, primarily *L'Officiel des spectacles* and *Pariscope* for the capital, and provincial titles such as *Lyon poche*, also devote large sections to cinema listings, in addition to providing information on theatre, concerts, exhibitions, museums, cabaret, festivals, restaurants, etc.

PAM MOORES

See also: television

Temps modernes, Les

Journal

Launched in 1944 by Jean-Paul **Sartre**, Simone de **Beauvoir** and Maurice Merleau-Ponty, this independent left-wing monthly sought to promote in peacetime the spirit of unity among opponents of Nazi forces and those who had collaborated with them during the Occupation. Taking its name from Charlie Chaplin's 1936 film, *Les Temps modernes*'s programme of **committed literature** (*littérature engagée*) spoke to and for a generation of activist-intellectuals whose experience of world war spawned a desire to act in and on history. Under Sartre's editorship through the late 1970s, it advocated **decolonization** in Vietnam and Algeria, a just peace in the Middle East and the emergent feminist movement in France.

STEVEN UNGAR

See also: Algerian war

Further reading

Boschetti, A. (1988) *The Intellectual Enterprise: Sartre and 'Les Temps modernes'*, Evanston: Northwestern University Press (essential reading).

tennis

French tennis improved its world ranking quite dramatically in the 1980s, with the emergence of players such as Yannick Noah and Henri Leconte. Indoor facilities in France are vastly superior to those of the United Kingdom, and outdoors clay and hard courts are the order of the day. The revamped Roland Garros stadium in Paris stages the French Open championships,

where Noah became the first French postwar champion in 1983.

IAN PICKUP

See also: sport

Terzieff, Laurent

b. 1935, Toulouse

Actor and director,
real name Laurent Tchermerzine

A director of international avant-garde works, and discoverer of many new plays, Terzieff has also interpreted many powerful roles for directors such as **Barrault**, **Serreau** and **Brook**. His acting style, stage and screen, is noted for its physicality and characterization skills.

ANNIE SPARKS

See also: theatre

Further reading

Mauriac, C. (1980) *Laurent Terzieff*, Paris: Stock (biography).

TF1

Television channel

The national television company Télévision Française 1 (TF1) came into existence in 1975 as a result of the break-up of the state broadcasting organization, the **ORTF**. The channel remained part of the public sector until its privatization by the conservative government in 1987. Since then, it has established itself as the leading mass-audience channel in France, with an emphasis on entertainment programming and news. Its principal shareholder is the Bouygues construction group. The company has diversified into programme production and thematic channels, including ownership of the rolling news channel on cable, La Chaîne d'Information (LCI).

RAYMOND KUHN

See also: cable and satellite television; television

theatre

Theatre in France has always been renowned as providing a home and encouragement for the avant-garde, and continues to do so today, whether it be for Peter **Brook**'s experimental theatre at the Bouffes du Nord in Paris or in the new forms of writing evident in contemporary productions. Traditions and the state attitude to theatre in twentieth-century France have been markedly different from those seen in English-speaking countries, with active encouragement of the avant-garde in recent decades, especially in terms of the development of the director's and actor's input into theatrical creation.

From the nineteenth century's Parisian *boulevard* theatres, with their melodramas and light (usually romantic) comedies, it might seem as if nothing has changed much to this day, if one takes into consideration the capital's private theatres, which advertise their star-laden entertainment across town. However, in France, they are under increasing threat from well-funded public theatre, developed in France since World War II. While theatres such as the **Comédie-Française** date back much further than the postwar period, it is during this time that the nature of publicly funded theatre in France has changed dramatically. Following a markedly different line from the private theatres, its brief today is to make theatre a public service, providing France not only with a staple diet of well-produced classics, but also with a home for experimental and contemporary work. As part of the wave of decentralization which swept France during the 1950s, therefore, a number of Centres Dramatiques Nationaux (or CDNs; National Drama

Centres) were set up regionally, to be financed with a combination of state and local money. Jeanne Laurent made funds available to the first of these in 1946, the Centre Dramatique National de l'Est in Colmar, and, a year later, to Jean **Dasté**'s company the Comédie de St Étienne, which moved to St Étienne, since Grenoble (its home town) refused to help fund it as a regional centre. It toured in its region with a lively selection of fun, 'popular' theatre productions intended both to encourage new audiences to theatre and to return to popular performance traditions. It became a model for other new CDNs, such as the Centre Dramatique de l'Ouest and the Grenier de Toulouse, both of which became CDNs in 1949, and the Comédie de Provence.

During this period, when public theatre was mainly preoccupied with politicizing theatre (such as the work of **Vilar**) by taking it to the people, often to new, working-class audiences, the result was that on the whole directors stuck mainly with well-known classics, in an attempt to attract these audiences and to appeal to their theatrical tastes, with little opportunity for experimentation with new ideas or contemporary texts. It was therefore in the small theatres of Paris's Left Bank that avant-garde authors such as **Beckett**, **Ionesco** and **Adamov** were given their first performances, which, while viewed at first very much as avant-garde, quickly achieved worldwide renown. By the 1960s, they had been accepted as modern classics, and were performed in Paris at theatres such as the Odéon, under the direction of **Barrault**, as well as worldwide. Their effect on French theatrical writing was profound in the decades to follow, and they continue to influence many contemporary writers, such as Philippe **Minyana**, who freely acknowledges his fascination with Beckett's work.

Meanwhile in the public theatre world, as the number of CDNs grew, so did the power of the directors running them, who were not only in financial charge of running these theatres, but also controlled creative decision-making and practice. This factor is certainly one of the main reasons for the extreme importance the director has developed in the postwar French theatre world.

Following on from the practices of Copeau and the Cartel before the war, through to the influence of Brechtian theatre upon the increased importance of the director, and the ideas of avant-garde theorists such as **Artaud**, the role of director became an intrinsic one not only in terms of choreographing the work of the author, but also for his or her own artistic input. Today this role is considered in many ways equal to, if not more important than, that of the author: talk of **Mnouchkine**'s *Tartuffe* or **Chéreau**'s *Dans la solitude des champs de coton* (In the Solitude of the Cotton Fields) is still common practice, referring to the director as creator in much the same way as in the **cinema** world.

Thus, from the 1950s onwards, the fact that directors of CDNs were usually also responsible for directing artistic projects meant that they had free rein to decide exactly how state money should be spent creatively, and used this position to mount productions on which they were able to impose their personal mark. As a result of state funding, they were also more free to experiment with the boundaries of theatre practice alongside the staple diet of classics they presented, experimenting with staging non-theatrical texts, adapted from novels or other art forms, or simply mounting classics upon which it was easy to impose their own ideas and make their own mark. Some directors such as **Planchon**, for example, were criticized for using state money to fund productions of their own plays.

The tradition of non-text productions was further enhanced during the 1970s by practices such as **collective creation**, of which the **Théâtre du Soleil** was one of the main proponents. The company became renowned for its revolutionary approach to performance, turning away from the text, experimenting with performance traditions worked on collectively by the entire company and focusing on the actor and scene as much as on the spoken word. The result was legendary productions such as *1789* and *L'Age d'or* (The Golden Age). Combined with collective creation and the increased interest in actor, scene and non-spoken means of communication, the power of **director's theatre** resulted in a severe lack of contemporary texts being produced, particularly from the late 1960s to the end of the 1970s. With some exceptions, the 1970s were a desert as far as playwrights were concerned: if they wanted to see their plays produced, often the only way to do so was to mount them personally.

It was only in the 1980s that theatre found itself returning to texts as a basis for production. Many theatre companies had become disillusioned with the impracticalities of collective creation, but, having learned valuable lessons about staging, the role of the actor and non-text-based performance from their experiments, their renewed work on text was in many ways enriched. Good examples of this include Ariane Mnouchkine's Shakespearean cycle and her collaboration with feminist playwright Hélène **Cixous**, both projects relying on influences from Eastern theatre tradition.

During the 1970s, despite the predominant lack of interest in text, a new generation of playwrights had nevertheless emerged, loosely banded together under the umbrella term the **Théâtre du Quotidien**, although each adopted a very individual approach. Influenced in some ways by the playwrights of the **Theatre of the Absurd**, works such as **Wenzel**'s *Loin d'Hagondange* (Far from Hagondange) and Michel **Deutsch**'s *Convoi* (Convoy) returned the emphasis to language, using it to highlight the alienation of the protagonists, and using fragmented structure to pinpoint the confusion of the world in which they were forced to forge their existence. However, at the same time, inheriting in some part the tradition of performance-led work, the plays of the Quotidien also relied heavily on performance to convey their message, leaving plenty of scope for actors and directors to interpret the language and fragmented structure.

Michel **Vinaver** is perhaps the most famous playwright of the 1970s, and continues to write today. Like the playwrights of the Quotidien, Vinaver also experimented with structure and particularly viewpoint in works such as *Overboard* (*Par-dessus bord*) and *Portrait d'une femme* (Portrait of a Woman), and his plays have proved influential to many young writers.

During the 1980s, the works of Bernard-Marie **Koltès**, perhaps the best-known playwright in the contemporary repertoire, became known through their stagings by star director Patrice Chéreau. Koltès, who died in 1989, could be considered (alongside Vinaver) to be the best-known contemporary playwright in the 1990s and his plays enjoy regular performance in France today.

The theatre-going public as a whole, especially in Paris, is not a purely bourgeois and conservative one; there exists today a divide in the theatre world between the boulevard theatres of the private theatre sector, still catering to this bourgeois 'market' as they did in the nineteenth century, and the audiences of publicly funded theatre, which, thanks to generous subsidies during the **Mitterrand** years, has been able to experiment and explore the possibilities of theatre as a medium, attracting an intellectual audience in the process.

Despite spending cuts by the **Chirac** regime in 1996, the extent of funding in France makes the French theatre scene a markedly different one from that of the United Kingdom. In France, public theatre has, during a period of substantial financial support, found itself the home to huge, spectacular (but frequently loss-making) productions, and with the resources to house experimental and contemporary works. Thus the avant-garde in some ways could be considered now to have moved into the very establishment which it once sought to undermine: the private theatres today are under such financial constraints that it is they who resort to sure-fire successes, often with stars in their line-up, in a bid to cover their costs at least.

Public theatre, at least for the time being, is well resourced, and continues to stage a varied mixture of productions, both text- and non-text-based. Today in France there are 33 Centres Dramatiques Nationaux, 6 of these devoted to youth theatre. Each consists of a theatre venue with a permanent troupe attached to it, with 44 per cent of costs met by

the state, 20 per cent by local government and the rest (36 per cent) engendered by the theatres themselves through either sponsorship or revenue, according to 1994 Ministry of Culture statistics (Direction du théâtre et des spectacles 1994). In addition to the CDNs, there are also 9 Centres Dramatiques Régionaux (Regional Drama Centres) with specific local missions, and 61 *scènes nationales*, formerly **maisons de la culture**, which have a wide, multidisciplined brief aimed at cultural development and the search for new audiences, and prioritizing contemporary works. These are financed half by the Ministry of Culture and half by local government.

ANNIE SPARKS

See also: arts funding; Avignon and summer arts festivals; circus; mime; Theatre of Cruelty; theatres, national; theatres, private

Further reading

Bradby, D. (1991) *Modern French Drama 1940–1990*, Cambridge: Cambridge University Press (a detailed history of postwar theatre practices, traditions and exponents).

Corvin, M. (ed.) (1995) *Le Dictionnaire du théâtre*, 2 vols, Paris: Bordas (an encyclopedia of French theatre in French).

Couty, D. and Rey, A. (eds) (1995) *Le Théâtre*, Paris: Bordas (a general history of practices and traditions, with particularly textual and pictorial material on twentieth-century practitioners such as the Théâtre du Soleil).

Whitton D. (1987) *Stage Directors in Modern France*, Manchester: Manchester University Press (a useful English-language introduction to individual directors).

Théâtre du Quotidien

This name signifies a genre of theatre produced by a significant number of playwrights in the 1970s in France. Their plays dealt with everyday life on stage, as the word *quotidien* suggests, relying on everyday language and events to make more general, often violent statements about aspects of society. The movement was inspired by German and Austrian theatre and cinema of the time, and by the numerous German translations appearing in French theatres which told of the lives of everyday people in ordinary situations, usually in fragmented form. The same fragmented form and departure from linear plot was evident in many French plays of the 1970s, which explored the way everyday language can often be imprisoning to the people who use it. Nonlinear structure was also a feature of these texts, suspending emotional engagement, and allowing the permeation of larger, more violent messages told through the relationship between characters and their environment. Notable playwrights of the movement were René **Kalisky**, Michel **Deutsch** and Jean-Paul **Wenzel**. The sociopolitical content of their work, often violently exposed in their tales of heightened everyday reality, appealed to directors of the day, who continued to seek to politicize theatre and reach out to ordinary people through their productions, while also searching for works leaving them room to imprint their own creative voice. Using fragmentary structure, playwrights of the movement experimented with time and space – in plays such as Deutsch's *Convoi* (Convoy), and many of **Vinaver**'s works. Well-rounded characters in the Théâtre du Quotidien were to some extent abandoned, as was linear plot, inasmuch as the characters in these plays are often trapped by the language of the everyday, which leaves them unable to articulate emotions. Their existence, in dramatic terms, is rooted in the message or theme they embody and epitomize, rather than in their essence as naturalistic characters: the plays of the Théâtre du Quotidien were sociopolitically motivated, evoking emotion or sympathy only while exposing wider social issues.

ANNIE SPARKS

See also: theatre; director's theatre

Further reading

Bradby, D. (1991) *Modern French Drama 1940–1990*, Cambridge: Cambridge University Press (includes a chapter on playwrights of the 1970s).

Sarrazac, J.-P. (1981) *L'Avenir du drame*, Paris: L'Aire (a discussion of tendencies in plays during this period).

Théâtre du Soleil

Founded in 1963 by Ariane **Mnouchkine** and friends from the Sorbonne, the Théâtre du Soleil has become one of the most influential theatre groups in France, famous for innovations in theatrical tradition, structure, form and working methods. Christened 'Soleil' at a time when state-run, decentralized theatre was full of heavy and bureaucratically named companies, the Théâtre du Soleil set out to seek new ways of presenting political and aesthetic messages to a mass audience made up of the working class as well as the bourgeoisie. It was keen to explore uncharted means of theatrical representation, drawing on existing European theatre traditions such as the *commedia dell' arte*, old French farce, even Roman and medieval theatre, for inspiration. Physical, exuberant performances dominated its versions of Gautier's *Fracasse* and Wesker's *The Kitchen*, in which the actors added an expressionist, physical interpretation of their characters to an otherwise naturalistic play, which appealed to packed audiences in occupied factories during revolutionary 1968. The company also produced an acclaimed production of Shakespeare's *A Midsummer Night's Dream*, combining physical and emotional vibrancy. *Les Clowns* in 1969 was a further attempt to explore the role of the performer – a series of autobiographical pieces based on individual and group improvisations, the first of the company's celebrated **collective creations**.

Now including designer Guy-Claude François in the team, the Théâtre du Soleil set up in the Cartoucherie in 1970, a disused cartridge factory in Vincennes, where they experimented further with theatre space and actor–audience relations. The result was the hugely successful *1789*, combining historical research with exuberant theatrical spectacle, plural viewpoints of individual events with multi-staging and audience involvement. Many were so excited by it that they would remain after the performance to discuss the ideas it raised.

1793, which followed, also combined historical documentation with political comment and multiple viewpoints, while *L'Age d'or* (The Golden Age), which came next, turned to contemporary reality for inspiration, which meant extra efforts were needed to prevent the piece from becoming social documentary. Using masks and gesture, the company told stories based around real events, showing capitalism at work using essentially theatrical means.

By 1975, the now state-subsidized company still found that its lengthy rehearsal and research periods were leading to financial problems. Jean-Claude **Penchenat** left to form the Théâtre du Campagnol, while remaining members moved on to play in Mnouchkine's film venture, *Molière*. The company returned to theatre with *Mephisto*, Mnouchkine's adaptation of Mann's novel in 1979, exploring the political role of a theatre company, interspersing 'rehearsal' scenes with political discussion. Reversible seats allowed the audience to watch Nazi Germany from a dual perspective, to highlight the gulf between personal and official viewpoints and culture.

The company cleared its debts with subsidy from the new Socialist government in 1981, embarking on a Shakespearean cycle inspired by theatrical traditions from India and Japan, followed by the four-play cycle *Les Atrides* in the early 1990s, experimenting with Greek tragedy. Both cycles sought to find contemporary relevance for the classics while experimenting with performance traditions. During the 1980s and 1990s, Mnouchkine has also worked extensively with feminist author Hélène **Cixous**, whose epic *Sihanouk* in 1985, *L'Indiade* in 1987 and *La Ville parjure ou les Érinyes* (Treacherous City) in 1994 have proved memorable epic productions, dealing with contemporary social and political issues. The latter, for example, took on the controversial issue of blood contamination and consequent infection with **AIDS**; Cixous set the play, however, in an undefined time scale, between ancient times and the modern day, employing the Furies (the *Érinyes* of the play's title from Greek myth) to seek revenge on behalf of the victims. The trial before society which ensues in the play is fruitless: no one will take responsibility. This two-part epic was performed the following year in alternation with *Tartuffe* at the 1995 Avignon festival. Mnouchkine's new production, and her first full-scale production of a Molière play, took on the issue of contemporary war-ridden Algeria, endowing Molière's classic with a biting relevance to the present day.

ANNIE SPARKS

See also: Algerian war; Avignon and summer arts festivals; theatre

Further reading

Kiernander, A. (1995) *Ariane Mnouchkine and the Théâtre du Soleil*, Cambridge: Cambridge University Press.

Theatre of Cruelty

Antonin **Artaud**'s notion of a 'theatre of cruelty' is central to his collection of essays entitled *The Theatre and Its Double* (*Le Théâtre et son double*), first published in 1938. Artaud's overall aim in these essays was to rewrite the conventions of theatre. He sought to subvert the classical conception of drama, which gave priority to the playwright, the text and the dramatic canon, and to develop instead a theatre which pushed the audience towards the painful collective release of their subconscious, through cruelty. Cruelty in the theatre, for Artaud, did not refer simply to the staging of criminal or violent acts, but involved exposing the audience to the contradictory thrills and dangers of existence. As a result, the audience would be forced to confront the dark side of their own cultural inheritance, and ultimately the eroticism and violence which lay repressed within their own subconscious. Artaud drew a close parallel between cruelty on stage and the Plague, both of which were able to subvert and destroy conventional social hierarchies, and thereby allow actor and spectator a privileged insight into their essential complexity.

In an attempt to rewrite stage conventions, Artaud proposed a new theatrical 'language' which sought to bypass the spoken word or 'logocentrism' of the Aristotelian theatre. Artaud's theatre was to depend on the synthesis of music, **dance, mime** and set, which together would form a concrete theatrical language able to penetrate the spectator's subconscious through the senses. Following his observation of the sharp, angular movements of the Balinese actors in Paris in 1931, movements which provided an economy of direct, unmediated communication between actor and spectator, Artaud developed an interest in the dramatic possibilities of gesture. Despite Artaud's detailed specifications, however, the Theatre of Cruelty failed to achieve the impact or success which Artaud had hoped for during his lifetime. Indeed, his only full-length play, *The Cenci* (*Les Cenci*), written in 1935, was plagued by financial difficulties and derided by a number of critics as a failure, before being withdrawn after only two weeks. **Derrida**, in *Writing and Difference* (*L'Écriture et la différence*) sees in Artaud's writing an implicit critique of Western metaphysics as a whole. Artaud, says Derrida, attempted to destroy the legacy of God the Father, who was the originator of all language and 'logocentrism'. This attempted parricide led to the closure of all representation, and the impossibility of all repetition, within Artaud's theatre.

It was only after the posthumous publication of Artaud's essays in English in 1958 that Artaud's reputation eventually grew. There are clear thematic links between Artaud's theatre and the French New Theatre of the 1950s, associated with writers such as **Beckett,**

Ionesco and **Genet**, and practitioners like **Blin** and **Barrault**. Artaud's theatre also influenced the development of film. For instance, Claudel wrote in 1930 in his essay *Le Drame et la musique* (Drama and Music) that the screen, rather like the stage, could unlock the door to the troubled world of the human unconscious, and that cinema and theatre would establish an alliance firmly based within America. Artaud's theatre, equally, encouraged the development of a new **director's theatre**. One exponent of this kind of theatre, Roger **Planchon**, follows Artaud in suggesting that the modern director is no longer subservient to the playwright. In his preface to the 1986 edition of Molière's *L'Avare*, he suggests that the director resembles a museum curator, who by restoring and displaying relics from the past instils in them an essential ambiguity, such that it is no longer clear who is responsible for the 'relic' as it is now perceived.

GERARD PAUL SHARPLING

See also: theatre

Further reading

Barber, S. (1993) *Antonin Artaud: Blows and Bombs,* London: Faber (an authoritative account of Artaud's life and works, with a chapter on the emergence and the demise of the Theatre of Cruelty).

Theatre of the Absurd

'Theatre of the Absurd' is a term used to refer to the work of a collection of individual playwrights writing in the 1950s and 1960s, whose radical approach to drama intrinsically questioned the nature of **theatre**. Leading proponents of the movement were **Beckett, Ionesco, Adamov** and **Genet**, all of whose works were produced in the 1950s in small, Parisian avantgarde theatres. They were by no means part of a self-acknowledged group. The various writers of the Theatre of the Absurd can be said, however, to be linked by their philosophy of pessimism and despair, and their identification of the absurdity of the human condition. Unlike Giraudoux and existentialist playwrights such as **Sartre** and **Camus**, who used the accepted framework of theatre practice as a vehicle for their intellectual ideas, dramatists of the Absurd were united by their successful, revolutionary attempts to make both their theatrical methods and their subject matter absurd. Hence the plays of the Theatre of the Absurd do not discuss the futility of the human condition: they show it, using a complex web of stage imagery and poetry. Rejecting standard theatrical devices such as linear plot and straightforward characterization, the plays of the Absurd encapsulate their philosophy in their approach to staging and text as much as in theme. Working on a more primal, psychological level than their existentialist forebears, playwrights such as Beckett and Ionesco undermined conventions, experimenting with structure to such an extent that at first their plays may appear to have no cohesive structure at all. In *Waiting for Godot* (*En attendant Godot*), for example, it appears that nothing happens. There is no development of action. The characters are clown-like figures rather than psychologically rounded characters acting according to their own reason – there is no reason in their world.

It is by virtue of their ability to transfer the *néant* of their philosophy into concrete stage images that the playwrights of the Absurd can be seen to be particularly distinguished. Structure, character and language are used to embody their ideas, rather than to act as a vehicle for them. Unlike the works of the poetic avant-garde also operating in Paris in the 1950s and 1960s, the playwrights of the Absurd regularly used language to offend or shock in a way which often appeared nonsensical (hence reflecting their general *Weltanschauung*). As well as manifesting black humour, many Absurdist plays aim also to confuse and confront expectations and concepts of form. This aggressive desire to shock was intended to evoke an emotional rather than a reasoned response. Ionesco's unpublished alternative

endings for *The Bald Primadonna* (*La Cantatrice Chauve*), for example, required either the author to come on stage and harangue the audience verbally, or extras placed in the audience to get up and cause disruption.

By the 1960s, the plays of authors such as Beckett and Ionesco, which had caused a stir from their beginnings on Paris's Left Bank, had achieved international recognition. By 1960, **Barrault** was able to stage Ionesco's *Rhinocéros* at the Théâtre de l'Odéon in Paris, and schedule **Blin**'s revival of Beckett's *Waiting for Godot* in 1961. The plays of the Absurd are now considered contemporary classics worldwide and part of the established modern repertoire.

ANNIE SPARKS

See also: existentialism; existentialist theatre; theatre

theatres, national

Of the five national theatres run on state subsidy in France, four are in Paris: the **Comédie-Française**, the Théâtre National de l'Odéon – Théâtre de l'Europe, the Théâtre de la Colline and the Théâtre National de Chaillot. The fifth, in Strasbourg, is the Théâtre National de Strasbourg. As well as these five institutions, the state also funds forty-two regional **theatre** centres, known as Centres Dramatiques Nationaux et Régionaux (National or Regional Drama Centres), which consist of a permanent venue and team, and run themselves along the lines of commercial theatre, each as its own business seeking funding outside the state as well as receiving an average of 44 per cent of income from the state.

The joint mission of all the national theatres is threefold: to present major works from the accepted repertoire in new and interesting ways; to promote contemporary creation (including non-text-based theatre as well as new authors); and to try to appeal to as wide a public as possible, with ticket prices fixed by the state to keep prices down. They often manage to accomplish the latter through productions and national and international exchanges. Each national theatre is headed by a director chosen by the Ministry of Culture. Although sharing a common mission, the repertoire of the various national theatres differs slightly.

Of the five national theatres, the Comédie-Française is the most famous and certainly the oldest institution. It is obliged to show a minimum of four different works per week, and often even two plays a day. It is the only institution to have a permanent troupe of actors (*pensionnaires* and *sociétaires*): all the other national theatres maintain a permanent administrative staff, but hire actors according to their needs. Recent directors have been Jean-Pierre **Vincent** (1983–6), Antoine **Vitez** (1988–90), Jacques **Lassalle** (1990–3) and Jean-Pierre Miquel (1993–). The theatre under their leadership has witnessed the growing importance of modern authors such as **Genet, Sartre, Camus** and **Césaire**, in addition to the classic repertoire. The Vieux Colombier, the revived theatre of Copeau fame, operating under the direction of the Comédie-Française since 1993, aims to mix more contemporary works with the classics. In October 1996, the Comédie-Française also opened another smaller performance space, the Carrousel du Louvre, in the gallery beneath the Louvre's pyramid, which concentrates on small-scale classic and modern productions, and incorporates literary discussion nights, a video theatre run in connection with **ARTE** showing recordings of historic productions, and a video archive.

Functioning as a subsidiary under the umbrella of the Comédie-Française since 1968, the Théâtre de l'Odéon provides the home for a wide-ranging national and international classic and contemporary repertoire. In 1983, the Théâtre de l'Europe company arrived at the Odéon to perform for six months of the year, under the direction of Giorgio Strehler: in 1990, the company took up permanent residence at the Odéon (and it was renamed Le Théâtre National de l'Odéon – Théâtre de l'Europe to reflect this), with the Catalan Lluis Pasqual at the helm. He was replaced by Georges Lavaudant in 1996. The theatre's

brief, to produce itself and to welcome companies from all over the world, has led to some memorable productions over the years from (among others) the Deutsche Schaubühne, the Royal Shakespeare Company, the **Théâtre du Soleil**, the Théâtre National Populaire (TNP) and the Théâtre de Nanterre-Amandiers. Prior to 1990, it also hosted productions by the Comédie-Française's Jeune Théâtre National (National Youth Theatre). The Petit Odéon, the smaller of its two auditoria, has been home to numerous contemporary works from playwrights including Heiner Müller.

Following in the wake of the Théâtre de L'Est de Paris (East Paris Theatre), and founded in 1988, the Colline is the newest of the national theatres. Its two auditoria, the main theatre and the studio, stage twentieth-century French and international classics, ranging from **Audiberti** to Tony Kushner in the 1996–7 season, for example. In 1996, Alain Françon took over from Argentinian director Jorge **Lavelli** as director.

The Théâtre National de Chaillot was also founded in 1968 in the Chaillot palace in Paris, taking over from **Vilar**'s (1951–63) and Georges Wilson's (1963–8) Théâtre National Populaire. The label of Théâtre National Populaire passed on to **Planchon**'s theatre in Villeurbanne three years later, while the Théâtre National de Chaillot, under the direction of Wilson, began to work towards the requirements of its new national theatrical mission. This was, essentially, to provide a home for the popular theatre repertoire in Paris, with a wide-ranging programme designed to appeal to the widest public possible. In 1973, Jack **Lang** nominated Vitez and Du Pavillon as co-directors to undertake a radical revamp of the main auditorium, although the following year Michel Guy, the Secretary of State for Culture, vetoed the nomination. Perinetti became director, until 1981, when Jack Lang was able to reinstate Vitez until his move to the Comédie-Française in 1988. Jérôme **Savary** was elected in his place.

The Théâtre National de Strasbourg divides its energies between performing the established repertoire and research and creation, part of which involves the work of its renowned theatre school, L'École Nationale Supérieure d'Art Dramatique. Its director is Jean-Louis Martinelli, who has been in the position since 1993: well-known predecessors include Vincent (1975–83) and Lassalle (1985–90), both of whom went on to become the director (*administrateur général*) of the Comédie-Française.

ANNIE SPARKS

See also: arts funding; theatres, private

Further reading

Abirached, R. (1992) *Le Théâtre et le prince 1981–1991*, Paris: Plon (see the chapter on public theatres).

La Mode d'emploi (1994), Paris: Direction du Théâtre et des Spectacles (a booklet published by the Ministère de la Culture et de la Francophonie, detailing national theatres, their mission, and factual information about the National Drama Centres).

Temkine, R. (1992) *Le Théâtre en l'état*, Paris: Éditions Théâtrales (deals with public theatre's historical and contemporary context and role).

theatres, private

The private theatre tradition in France – theatres that operate independently and are not reliant to any significant degree on state funding or governorship – owes its origins to the popular boulevard theatres of the Parisian Right Bank during the nineteenth century, home to a genre of light, romantic comedy which continues to this day to be the staple diet of Parisian 'boulevard' theatre-goers. While the private theatres of Paris are certainly responsible for a more varied selection of works than this, it is this kind of play which draws large audiences. For this reason there is also a long-standing tradition of 'star' performers in private theatre productions, important in drawing the crowds. Many famous film actors return occasionally to the stage, bringing an audience to the theatre to see them as much as the play. For example, contemporary playwright Éric Emmanuel Schmitt's philosophical play *Variations énigmatiques*, staged at the Théâtre Marigny in the autumn of 1996, became the success of the season, due in no small part to the fact that it starred Alain **Delon** in his great theatrical comeback after twenty years off the stage, and fellow film actor Francis Huster.

According to 1994 figures, private theatres numbered 48 in France, 47 of which were in Paris (the other being the Théâtre du VIIIème in Lyon). Private theatres are self-governing, usually with a theatre practitioner at the helm, even if the building itself is let by a third party (insurance companies are often the landlords of private theatres). Few private theatres are actually owned by the people who run them – the Poche, Variétés and Palais Royal theatres being the best-known exceptions. Most theatres pay rent to the landlord, calculated according to the number of seats in the venue. Seat prices in private theatre are usually higher than in state-run theatres, due to the dual commercial pressures of higher rates of VAT on private theatre seats and the lack of subsidy. However, it would be wrong to suggest that private theatre receives no subsidy at all. That said, there is very little money allocated to them in comparison with the national theatres and Centres Dramatiques Nationaux (CDNs). In 1994, for example, the Direction du Théâtre et des Spectacles, the government department responsible for distributing money to theatres, gave only 47.3 million francs to private theatre (including street theatre and **circus** companies), while the five national theatres received 316.6 million francs and the CDNs a similar figure (Direction du Théâtre et des Spectacles 1994). Government money also partly funds the *Fonds du Soutien* (Support Fund) to which many private theatres subscribe. It aims to support private theatres needing to redress the balance between outgoings and receipts on a particular production. To qualify for membership and support from this fund, theatres must have over 200 seats: those with between 200 and 500 seats usually receive the most help. The amount of aid given also varies according to the play: new French creations attract more help than classics or one-person shows. The fund also allocates money for renovation of theatre buildings, as well as to help support a production which has been slow to be successful, but which is succeeding at last, and to mount any of the first three plays written by a new French author. The City of Paris also helps subsidize a number of theatres and productions, and aims to encourage theatre-going with its annual two-for-the-price-of-one ticket deal for many productions in the capital. In recent years, the private theatre sector, which accounts for half the total theatre-going in France, has faced increasing competition from the public sector, which (thanks to government funding) can produce often elaborate creations while still being able to keep ticket prices at reasonable levels. Private theatre, on the other hand, has suffered from inflationary costs and thus has to be especially careful in its choice of play, taking into account production costs and the need for long runs. Many more private theatres are also turning to the *Fonds du Soutien* for aid. Whereas the 1950s and 1960s saw the small private theatres of the Left Bank innovating with the launch of **Beckett**, **Ionesco** and other avant-garde work, in the 1990s private theatres are less able to experiment, needing to rely on classics, a star performer or a show with low costs, such as a one-person show, often even to come close to break-even point. Private theatre is, however, fighting back against the competition from state-funded theatre by attempting to save money on productions and make itself competitive once more. Increasingly, theatres are working on co-productions together, pooling resources, risks and potential profits, with the hope of redeveloping an arena for innovation and experimentation in the future.

ANNIE SPARKS

See also: theatres, national

Further reading

La Mode d'emploi (1994) Paris: Direction du Théâtre et des Spectacles (a government department booklet on theatre expenditure).
Temkine, R. (1992) *Le Théâtre en l'état*, Paris: Éditions Théâtrales (see the chapter on private theatre).

theme parks

There are around sixty theme parks in France, many of which were built in the 1980s and early 1990s, as their popularity soared. The most successful parks include the Schtroumpf (Smurf)-themed park near the German border, and Futuroscope, a science park opened in 1987 near Poitiers, which includes an Imax 3D cinema (600 sq m) that projects 70 mm films depicting the wonders of the natural world (between 1993 and 1995, attendance at this park more than doubled, from 1.3 million to 2.8 million visitors). The ever-popular Parc Astérix, located in the Ermenoville forest 60 km from Paris, is based on the Belgian comic strip of the same name. But, like the ancient Gauls depicted in the Astérix comics, it must contend with fierce competition from a formidable invading force: the American Disney Corporation.

The biggest and best known of France's theme parks, Disneyland Paris was originally called EuroDisney. The name change, effected in 1995, signalled an attempt to reverse initially disappointing attendance figures both by linking the park to its successful Californian predecessor and by invoking the romantic appeal of Paris (though the park is actually situated in Marne-la-Vallée, 32 km away). The new name, at once more American and more French, suggests the conflict inherent in its dual identity.

From its inception, the park was viewed by French intellectuals (such as Ariane **Mnouchkine**, who likened it to *un Chernobyl culturel*) as an emblem of American cultural imperialism. Many of the employees, and the intellectuals who championed their cause, objected to the imposition of a regimented American work ethic, manifested in the strict dress code and grooming guidelines, the enforced cheerfulness and the corporate environment. Equally unpopular was the park's ban on alcohol, which followed the company policy in the American parks, but which was not appreciated by the French, who were accustomed to drinking wine or beer with meals. This ban was eventually lifted.

Theme parks have often been compared to world fairs. Although the comparison may be justified to a certain extent, theme parks and world fairs adhere to different temporal and spatial logics. Whereas world fairs literally occupy a city for their duration, they are ephemeral by design: when their time is up, they are razed to the ground, leaving few traces of their existence. On the other hand, theme parks, as self-contained artificial cities, are pushed outside the borders of the real city, but they are permanent (for as long as they are profitable). A fixture of leisure time, peripheral to the city and peripheral to work, theme parks serve as a constant reminder of both.

ELIZABETH EZRA

See also: comic strips/cartoonists

Thorez, Maurice

b. 1900, Noyelles-Godault,
Pas-de-Calais;
d. 1964 en route to Russia

Politician

Originally a miner, Thorez joined the Parti Communiste Français (PCF) at an early age. As party leader from 1930 and a member of parliament from 1932 onwards, he played an important role in preventing the PCF from becoming a marginal revolutionary sect and backed the 1936 Front Populaire anti-Fascist alliance. He spent most of World War II in the Soviet Union and advocated resistance in France. He was a senior minister in the period 1944–7. Known as 'the son of the people', he was the object of a personality cult in PCF ranks and was a combative proponent of PCF Cold War isolationism.

LAURENCE BELL

See also: Marchais, Georges; parties and movements

Further reading

Robrieux, P. (1978) *Maurice Thorez: vie secrète et vie publique*, Paris: Fayard (a biography by the author of a four-volume history of the PCF).

Tinguely, Jean

b. 1925, Fribourg, Switzerland;
d. 1991, Berne

Sculptor

Tinguely was the creator of both static **sculpture** and motorized constructions, including machines designed to produce paintings, self-destroying machines (one of the most famous of which, *Homage to New York*, self-destructed in the gardens of the Museum of Modern Art in New York in 1960) and large percussion sculptures known as 'sound reliefs'. Tinguely was interested from his student days in movement as an artistic medium, and in 1955 he participated in an important exhibition of kinetic and mobile art in Paris. The same year he met Yves **Klein**, with whom he collaborated in 1958. His friendship with Klein and other artists led to the founding of New Realism (*Nouveau Réalisme*) which sought to reassess artistic form and material. In the 1960s, he produced sculptures made of scrap metal and junk material, especially in the *Baluba* series. In 1983, the Stravinsky Fountain, on which he collaborated with Niki de **Saint-Phalle**, was inaugurated beside the **Pompidou Centre**, on the roof of the Institute for Acoustic and Musical Research (IRCAM) directed by Pierre **Boulez.**

DEBRA KELLY

See also: sculpture

Toubon law

Passed in August 1994 and named after Jacques Toubon, Minister of Culture and Francophonie in the **Balladur** government of 1993–5, this law replaced the Bas-Lauriol law of 1975, which had proved difficult to apply and which had few effective sanctions. Both laws represent official policy towards the status of the French language, insisting on its use by public servants in five domains: official government documents, media, commerce, advertising and education. Condemned by the Socialist Party as dictatorial, the law's provisions were modified by the Constitutional Council to enable ordinary citizens to continue using terms like *le hot-dog* and *le Shuttle*, although the main target had been franglais: **advertising** slogans like *Just roule cool.*

DENNIS AGER

See also: *anglomanie*/franglais

Tour de France

The Tour de France is the most famous and the most lucrative road race in world cycling. Held annually since 1903 (apart from interruptions during World Wars I and II), the Tour has become increasingly commercialized and politicized as towns, regions and even neighbouring countries vie for the right to be included in the route and offer large sums of money to be selected as the finishing point of one of the stages. The Tour includes mountain stages (some of which are in the Alps and the Pyrenees) and time trials; it has a points and team classification (teams representing cycle manufacturers and other sponsors work as a

unit protecting their leader) and an overall winner based on the aggregated times of all the stages. The leader at any one point and at the end – when the race finishes on the Champs Élysées – wears the coveted 'yellow jersey' (*le maillot jaune*). It is an annual sporting spectacle of huge proportions, which has entrants from throughout the world.

IAN PICKUP

See also: cycling; sport

Touraine, Alain

b. 1925, Hermanville-sur-Mer

Sociologist

After entering the École Normale Supérieure in 1945, Touraine left temporarily to work as a miner in northeast France (1947–8). Finishing his studies under the influence of the sociologist Georges Friedmann, Touraine's early work analysed the stagnation of the industrial working **class.** As his fieldwork and analyses evolved, he pointed successively to developments in socioeconomic activity, which indicated that in a post-industrial society social organization would respond to the expanding 'tertiary' (or service) sector which would gradually replace the traditional industrial landscape. Especially after **May 1968,** he traced the emergence of new social movements which would shape a new society: these include the women's movement, regionalists, autonomists and ecologists.

MARTYN CORNICK

See also: educational elitism; green issues

Major works

Touraine, A. (1967) *La Conscience ouvrière*, Paris: Éditions du Seuil.
——(1971a) *The May Movement: Revolt and Reform*, New York: Random House (French edition [1972] *Le Mouvement de mai, ou le*

communisme utopique, Paris: Éditions du Seuil).

——(1971b) *The Post-Industrial Society: Tomorrow's Social History, Classes, Conflicts and Culture in the Programmed Society*, New York: Random House (French edition [1971] *La Société post-industrielle*, Paris: Denoël).

——(1983) *L'Après socialisme*, Paris: Hachette.

——(1992) *Critique de la modernité*, Paris: Fayard.

——(1993) *Towards a New Economic Order*, Cambridge: Polity.

Tournier, Michel

b. 1924, Paris

Writer

Tournier is one of the most important modern European novelists. While writing within the tradition of the realist novel, he constantly engages in intertextual play, each of his novels being a rewriting of previous texts or crucial myths. As befits a writer who was trained as a philosopher, his subjects are always vast ones: the human couple, the problem of solitude, deviant sexuality, Nazism, religious belief, the purpose of art. In his fiction and journalism, he constantly intervenes forcefully into debates on politics, sexuality and **immigration**, as well as writing extensively on **painting** and **photography**. His best-known novel is the Goncourt prizewinner *The Erl King* (*Le Roi des Aulnes*).

MICHAEL WORTON

See also: gay writing; literary prizes

Further reading

Worton, M. (ed.) (1995), *Michel Tournier*, London: Longman (a collection of essays).

trade

Trade is a feature of all societies and all economies. However, during the postwar period, the term 'trade' for Western countries such as France has become synonymous with 'foreign trade'. The increase in importance of foreign trade is one of the main features of the postwar economic development of France, and France is one of the top five exporting economies in the world.

From the moment that France accepted Marshall Aid after World War II, the country was drawn into the process of globalization of trade led by the United States. This was to have dramatic consequences for the French **economy** and economic policy-making. France has traditionally had a reputation for being protectionist. Particularly in the 1950s and 1960s, the state saw it as its duty to protect fledgling industries from foreign competition. This was possible because much French production was for the home market and therefore France did not need to open the doors of its economy to foreign competition in order to be allowed to enter foreign markets itself. However, with the coming of the European Economic Community (EEC) and the lowering of protectionist barriers for manufactured goods between member-states in 1968, the ability of French governments to protect French industry was eroded. Consequently, trade increased between member-states.

Furthermore, with the increase in oil prices brought about by the 1974 oil crisis, France had to offset the high costs of its imported energy needs with exports of manufactured goods and services. Indeed, from the 1970s onwards, the balance of trade has been a major preoccupation of French governments, since the French economy has more often been in the red than in the black. The French have attempted to reduce their dependence on imported energy by developing the nuclear industry. None the less, the main problem for France concerning foreign trade now comes from the competition which the country faces from the newly industrializing nations of the Pacific Rim. Unfortunately, French industry specializes in the production of the same kind of goods as are produced by these countries, but costs in France are much higher. France therefore aspires to be an economy specializing in high-technology products, like Germany and Japan.

JAN WINDEBANK

See also: European Union; manufacturing industry; multinational companies

transport

Transport networks in France have been shaped to respond to the central role of Paris. However, since the 1970s, the need for better connections with the rest of Europe, as well as regional development policies, have helped to develop more balanced networks. Road is increasingly France's favoured mode of transport, but rail has maintained a strong presence.

Until very recently, railway and road networks had a striking shape: organized as a 'star' structure, centring on Paris and radiating across France, this illustrated the concentration of population and power in the Île-de-France. Before the 1980s, it was sometimes easier when travelling by train from the west of France to the Rhône valley to go to Paris first, and then down again, avoiding the badly served Massif Central.

However, France has a very high density of small *départementales* (county roads) and narrower *chemins communaux* (parish lanes) which spread through some 36,500 municipalities. The wider *Routes Nationales* constitute the primary road network and became a symbol of the growth of travel by car when, in the 1950s, the first cheap models, such as the Citroën 2CV or the Renault 4, became popular. Some of these roads have now become part of popular culture. Charles **Trenet**'s hit song, *Nationale 7*, celebrated the national road that follows the Rhone valley towards the Côte d'Azur, and is the emblem of holidays and freedom. The French motorway network was developed from the mid-1960s; it now covers nearly 9,000 km (nearly three times the length of motorways in Great Britain). Most motor-

ways were built by part-public, part-private consortia, which collect tolls from motorway users.

The car has become a way of life for most of the French population, deeply affecting socio-cultural behaviour. From the beginnings of the car era, the mythology of speed and individual freedom associated with the possession and control of a vehicle have become major cultural themes. The novelist Paul **Morand**, in *L'Homme pressé* (*Man in a Hurry*), extolled the virtues of speed at any price. More recently, Françoise **Sagan**, in *Avec mon Meilleur Souvenir* (*With my Best Memory*), wrote about racing cars and the excitement of speeding. The car itself is seen as a highly symbolically charged object, the epitome of modern values; this was particularly well expressed by Roland **Barthes**'s *Mythologies* in the analysis of the Citroën DS19, a car which appeared in 1955 with a striking 'designer' shape.

The cost of a car civilization has been considerable, with France having one of the highest road accident rates in Europe (13,787 people were killed in 1975, the worst year). Since then, the toll has fallen (around 8,500 deaths in 1994, against 1,700 in Great Britain). Traffic jams hit car commuters day after day, as do the mass departures for summer or weekend holidays for which France is famous. Traffic jams and accidents are also now part of the culture – as is evidenced by the themes of films, such as Jean-Luc **Godard**'s *Week-End* or Claude **Sautet**'s *Les Choses de la vie*.

Other means of transport also took their place in the culture of modernity, when, just before World War I, it transpired for the first time that the whole world was accessible. Since then, the romantic appeal of transcontinental rail travel and ocean liners has died out – the French merchant fleet has dwindled. Apart from ferries in the Channel and Mediterranean Sea, only some holiday cruise ships have upheld the tradition of the great liners such as the series of *Normandie* and *France* which competed with the *Queen Mary* and *Queen Elizabeth* for the Blue Ribbon across the Atlantic Ocean. Similarly, rail had considerable appeal before losing out to the car. It became the most powerful means of transport between the two world wars, hence the use of railway sabotage by the French Resistance during World War II, reconstituted in René **Clément's** film *La Bataille du rail* (1946).

Steam engines now inspire nostalgia rather than awe, despite the fact that the trainspotter does not exist in French popular culture. Many local and regional railway lines disappeared in the 1960s and 1970s. However, the train has survived as an efficient interregional and international passenger transport system, through the *train à grande vitesse* (TGV) programme. Launched in 1981 on the Paris–Lyon line, the TGV regained the world rail-speed record in 1990, with over 500 kph, which is faster than passenger aeroplanes in 1960. TGV lines have now spread across most regions and compete with internal air flights – indeed, Paris is now 110 minutes away from Lyon, instead of 240 minutes, as in 1960. The Eurostar services between London, Paris, Lille and Brussels have also been immensely successful despite early problems.

France has been one of the pioneer countries for air flight. The first winged device to lift up in the air with a helix and propeller was built and flown by Clément Ader near Paris in 1890, and Louis Blériot first flew over the Channel in 1909. It inspired many dreams, and Antoine de Saint-Exupéry wrote novels imagining the new professional pilot as modern knight.

A last major component of the transport system comprises the urban transport systems (tube, trains, buses and tramways). The most important covers the Paris region, an integrated system of underground railways (the *Métro*) and a fast regional transit system, the RER (*Réseau Express Régional*), feeding on each other and on the SNCF commuter network. Urban transport in Paris is relatively cheap, with popular season tickets (the *Carte Orange*). The system is heavily subsidized by the state, and a special tax is imposed upon the employers to fund the transport system. However, this does not prevent the car from being an urban nuisance, with air pollution and loss of time becoming real problems.

FRANÇOIS NECTOUX

See also: green issues; motor sport

Further reading

Baleste, M. (1992) *L'Économie française*, Paris: Masson (regularly re-edited, this work describes the various transport networks).

Trenet, Charles

b. 1913, Narbonne

Singer-songwriter

The most influential French singer-songwriter of the prewar and postwar periods, Charles Trenet enjoyed a seemingly never-ending career which stretched from 1933 to 1992 and includes some 350 compositions, excluding his musical settings of works by Verlaine, Rimbaud and others. Having started as a duettist with Johnny Hess (as Charles et Johnny, 1933–7), and characteristically singing songs which offer an escape in time and in space, Trenet was forced to interrupt his career in order to do his military service. Relaunched as a solo performer in 1938 and nicknamed *le fou chantant* (the singing madman), Trenet incorporated swing, **jazz**, the waltz and tango, not to mention tropical rhythms, in a repertoire which rejuvenated French song after its decline into the vulgar innuendo of the **café-concert** and later cabarets.

A wordsmith of unusual talent whose songs captivated the imagination of the French prewar generation, Trenet was sung by Maurice **Chevalier** as early as 1937 – as in *Y'a d'la joie* (There is Joy), a song performed much later by Georges **Brassens**, who enthusiastically acknowledged the immense formative influence of the composer of this piece. Writing often poetic texts which sometimes bear the imprint of Surrealism, or which sketch an everyday scene or the portrait of a woman, Trenet created sounds (onomatopoeia being a favourite device) which merge seamlessly with his music. A prolific composer whose output was scarcely diminished during the war years, Trenet continued to record and to undertake stage performances, refusing to abandon the Americanized rhythms which were scarcely designed to please the German forces of the Occupation. With an ever-broadening repertoire (tender love songs and parodies co-existing alongside swing numbers), Trenet increased his popularity in France significantly before reaching international stardom with arguably his most famous composition, *(Somewhere) Beyond the Sea (La Mer)*, in 1945.

Sung by an ever-increasing number of stars (including Yves **Montand**, Les **Compagnons de la chanson**, Juliette **Gréco** and Tino Rossi), Trenet continued to enjoy huge success in France until the end of the 1950s, when his output of songs declined as he travelled extensively abroad. If foreign tours diminished to some extent his creative verve during the 1960s, Trenet reacquainted himself with a French audience at the Olympia in 1971 and 1975 (the latter allegedly being his farewell performance) before triumphing at the 'Printemps de Bourges' (Bourges Spring Festival) – an annual **music festival** staged at Easter from 1977 where, despite the increasing melancholy which characterized his later work, he captivated a new, young audience. Persuaded to come out of retirement in 1988 (for a concert at the Châtelet) and in 1989 (for a final recital at the Palais des Congrès), Trenet made his last impact on record sales in 1992 when he released thirteen songs. It would be almost impossible fully to assess the importance of Trenet in the field of French song in the twentieth century. In addition to his influence as indicated above, it would be necessary to add the names of **Aznavour**, Bécaud, **Jonasz**, **Souchon** and many more to the list of distinguished performers and singer-songwriters who are clearly indebted to him. Suffice it to say that, without him, French song as we know it today would never have existed.

IAN PICKUP

See also: music venues; song/*chanson*

Major works

Trenet, C. (1993) *Le Jardin extraordinaire*, Paris: Livre de Poche (this contains all the songs written by Trenet; edited by Pierre Saka).

Further reading

Pérez, M. (1964) *Charles Trenet*, Paris: Seghers (an account of Trenet's career until the 1960s).

Trintignant, Jean-Louis

b. 1930, Pont St-Esprit

Actor

Primarily a screen actor, his career took off, curiously given his timid persona, in two notorious Roger **Vadim** films – *And God Created Woman (Et Dieu créa la femme)* in 1956 and *Les Liaisons dangereuses* (1959). Trintignant is the master of the understated virtual non-performance, yet the roles he has most consistently played are ones of extremes in terms of emotions or issues of political or personal power, such as Costa-Gavras's *Z* (1969) and Bertolucci's *The Conformist* (1970). The larger and more impassioned the character he is to inhabit, the greater the minimalist performance and the wider the range of modulation of his voice – he can exude terror or hatred, love or seduction through an almost silent enunciation.

SUSAN HAYWARD

See also: cinema

Truffaut, François

b. 1932, Paris;
d. 1984, Paris

Director

One of the key figures of the **Nouvelle Vague**
(New Wave), Truffaut is almost certainly the
postwar French film director whose work is
most widely known in English-speaking countries. He had an unhappy and neglected
Parisian childhood against which he reacted by
continually playing truant from school to go to
the **cinema**; unlike most of his New Wave contemporaries, he received virtually no formal
education. The ciné-clubs of the **Liberation**
were his 'university', and it was there that he
met the critic André **Bazin**, who rescued him
from the French equivalent of borstal and
became an educator and father figure to him
much as Truffaut himself was later to become
to Jean-Pierre **Léaud**.

Truffaut first made his mark with his film
criticism, above all for *Cahiers du cinéma*.
Abrasive, often abusive, his favourite target
was the high-budget, studio-filmed *cinéma de
qualité* that had been dominant in France since
the end of the war, with such figures as **Autant-
Lara** or Jean Delannoy. For Truffaut, this was
tired, lacklustre film-making, which he contrasted unfavourably to the work of the major
Hollywood auteurs like Fuller, Hawks and
Hitchcock. His own work as a director was to
bear the twofold hallmark of concise vivacity,
often with an improvised feel, and a strongly
personal thematic vision characteristic of those
film-makers.

These qualities are in evidence from his first
feature, *The Four Hundred Blows* (*Les quatre
cents coups*) of 1959, autobiographical in
inspiration and starring the young Léaud as
Truffaut's *alter ego*, Antoine Doinel. The naturalness and verve of Léaud's performance and
the location shooting in the streets of Paris
(often reminiscent of the Italian neo-realists) –
and, above all else, the film's at once plangent
and humorous evocation of adolescent experience – made it an instant success. Doinel/Léaud

was to return in three subsequent features –
Stolen Kisses (*Baisers Volés*) in 1968, *Domicile
conjugal* (1970) and *L'Amour en fuite* (1979) –
which take him through a failed marriage and
much career hesitation before he realizes his
vocation as a writer. The tone of these films is
mellower, and the use of cinematic technique
less adventurous, than in *Les quatre cents
coups*, and Truffaut's work from the late 1960s
is often thought less important than his earlier
films.

Shoot the Pianist (*Tirez sur le pianiste*),
from 1960, combines the iconography of the
gangster movie with a use of cinematic techniques from the silent age to tell the melancholy tale of a pianist (Charles **Aznavour**)
haunted by a secret from his past. Charlie
Kohler/Aznavour's move from concert pianist
to piano player in an underworld café parallels
the film's amalgam of high and popular culture, which is taken yet further in *Jules et Jim*
(1962). Jeanne **Moreau** here gives the most
memorable performance of her career, as the
woman loved by two men – one French, one
German – whose friendship is thereby strengthened rather than destroyed. The film received a
standing ovation at the Cannes festival, and
became, along with the de **Beauvoir**–**Sartre**
couple, a founding myth of the desire for emotional and sexual independence from bourgeois
convention that preceded the impact of feminism.

The brio and exhilaration with which
Truffaut uses the camera in these earlier works
gives place with his most **Chabrol**ian film, *La
Peau douce* (1964), to a more sober and
restrained style, which highlights the preoccupation with friendship, love, and above all
death, so characteristic of his work. Those who
know him primarily through the bittersweet
playfulness of *Baisers volés* or the comedy of
La Nuit américaine (1973), which takes place
on a film set, may find this last assertion surprising, but it is not prompted merely by
Truffaut's own early death from a brain
tumour. *La Mariée était en noir* (1968), *La
Sirène du Mississippi* (1969) and *Une belle fille
comme moi* (1972) all centre on actually or
potentially homicidal women. *L'Homme qui*

aimait les femmes (1977) ends with the death – literally caused by his pursuit of women – of its central character. *La Chambre verte* (1978) has Truffaut himself in the lead role, as a journalist who specializes in obituaries and has set up the room of the title as a shrine to the memory of his dead wife.

This is not to suggest that Truffaut was in any sense a purely introspective or egotistical film-maker, for history plays a more important role in his work than may at first appear. The love triangle in *Jules et Jim* is also an allegory of Franco-German cultural and political relationships from the beginning of the century through World War I to the early days of the Nazi regime. *The Last Metro* (*Le Dernier Métro*) from 1980 – his most commercially successful film – takes place in a Paris theatre under the Occupation. The theatricality of the setting, abetted by the much-touted pairing of Catherine **Deneuve** and Gérard **Depardieu**, often seems to relegate the deadly seriousness of the period to second place, for which the film was much criticized. Truffaut was also involved with the two major French political crises of his own lifetime, as opponent of the **Algerian war** and as supporter of the **May 1968** movement. The credits of *Baisers volés* are superimposed on a view of the Paris Cinémathèque, and the film is dedicated, in a clear allusion to the 'Langlois affair' of February, to Henri **Langlois**.

Nevertheless, it seems true to say that Truffaut's later work periodically suffers from a frivolity and lack of substance far removed from the gracefully deadly seriousness of the early masterpieces. For these, for his always sensitive direction of actors, for his seminal work as critic and campaigning figure of the New Wave, for the manner in which he (more than any other film-maker) came to represent French cinema throughout the world, he remains one of the key figures in the French culture of his time.

KEITH READER

See also: cinema

Major works

Truffaut, F. (1975) *Les Films de ma vie*, Paris: Flammarion (Truffaut's autobiographical cinematic testament).

Further reading

Bonnafons, É. (1981) *François Truffaut*, Lausanne: L'Age d'Homme (a thorough thematic account).

Insdorf, A. (1978) *François Truffaut*, Boston: Twayne (particularly good on the importance of women and the influence of Hitchcock).

TV5

Television channel

TV5 was established in 1983 by a consortium of five francophone public service broadcasters from France, Belgium and Switzerland. In 1986, a Quebec **television** company joined the consortium. Renamed TV5-Europe in 1988, the venture is the first pan-European francophone channel. It is broadcast on cable and satellite with the aim of promoting francophone culture in all its aspects. Its programming is based on the output of the members of the consortium, supplemented by its own production and co-productions. Its round-the-clock output can be received in Africa as well as Europe.

RAYMOND KUHN

See also: cable and satellite television; francophone television: Europe

U

unions

France is one of the industrialized countries with the lowest level of unionization, and the unions are divided, particularly at political level. Nevertheless, their influence is considerable and they play a far more important political and social role than the low number of card-holders would seem to indicate.

The first trade union 'confederation' was the CGT (Confédération Générale du Travail), launched in 1895. Since then, unions have become embedded in the institutional framework as a 'social partner' to employers' associations and government, and they are one of the main channels for the resolution of conflicts in society. The right to belong to a union is written into the Preamble to the French Constitution, as is the right to strike. It is a long way from the past: during the nineteenth century, attempts to form workers' associations were severely repressed, and it was only after a long struggle that limited rights to form associations were won in 1864, and full rights recognized in 1884. In the late nineteenth and early twentieth centuries, the CGT was the only 'confederation' (except the far smaller Christian CFTC), but it divided after the break-up between Communists and Socialists in 1920. In 1936, the two CGTs re-merged, but in 1947, with the Cold War starting, a strong minority split up to form the social democratic CGT-FO (later the FO, the Force Ouvrière) supported and funded at first by the United States, with the CGT

increasingly under Communist influence. This was not the only split. In 1964, a majority of the CFTC, now a large 'confederation', decided to shed the religious dimension of the union, and became the CFDT (Confédération Française Démocratique du Travail), with a minority continuing the CFTC. Therefore, there are four main 'confederations': CGT, CFDT, FO and CFTC. But if that is not complicated enough, there is also a 'confederation' for middle management, the CGC (Confédération Générale des Cadres), and a number of independent, professionally based unions, for instance in education (FEN and FSU), in the police, etc.

This fragmentation appears disastrous, given that less than 8 per cent of the workforce hold a union card. Some sectors are well unionized (such as education and public transport), but others have only a residual membership (like trade and tourism). Membership has fallen steadily since the 1970s, as traditionally unionized industries suffered from the economic crisis, and the sociopolitical climate of France changed. Resort to strike action has become less frequent: between 3 million and 5 million work days were lost through strike in the 1970s every year, under 1 million since the late 1980s, and just under half a million in 1994. However, some national conflicts, such as those which occurred at the end of 1996 in protest against **social security** reforms and threats to public sector employment, still attract strong support.

The main 'confederations' also achieve much

power and influence through *organismes paritaires* (public bodies managed by both employers and employees), such as social security funds, the participation in many consultative bodies, and official recognition of sectorial agreements, obtained through collective bargaining. Elected shop stewards and union representatives are protected by law and have paid time off work for union business, as the elected members of consultative workers' councils (*comités d'entreprise*). Nevertheless, all these institutional arrangements cannot hide the gradual disaffection of employees, although periodic crises show that unions still have an important role to play in the French sociopolitical framework.

FRANÇOIS NECTOUX

See also: economy; parties and movements; social policy

Further reading

Rand Smith, W. R. (1987) *Crisis in the French Labour Movement*, London: Macmillan (this presents an interesting analysis of long-term causes of disaffection with unions).

Szarka, J. (1992) *Business in France: An Introduction to the Economic and Social Context*, London: Pitman (Chapter 6 assesses industrial relations and the role of trade unions).

universities

Entrusted with the dual role of teaching and research, and cast as the agents of mass state higher education in France, the universities are open to all holders of the *baccalauréat*, or an equivalent qualification, and charge only minimal registration fees. They are the providers in higher education terms of the 'free state education' which is guaranteed at all levels as a basic human right by the constitution. Government policy and increasing demand has meant that these institutions have been asked to expand dramatically, both in number and in size, since the 1960s: in 1995–6 they were struggling to cope with over 1.5 million registered students. Since funding and staffing have failed to keep pace with such increases, considerable strains have been imposed on the system, and a constant series of reforms has been tried in an endeavour to alleviate them. For its part, the student body, in the spirit of **May 1968**, has been active and vocal in its denunciation of inadequate study conditions and state neglect.

Universities in France boast a proud tradition, stretching back to medieval times when Paris (1211), Toulouse (1229) and Montpellier (1289) were among the earliest and most prestigious institutions in Europe. Since World War II, however, they have been propelled into the role of purveyors of mass higher education.

To all intents and purposes, the universities in their modern form date from the legislation which came out of the events of May 1968. The *loi d'orientation sur l'enseignement supérieur* (Higher Education Reform Act), passed later that year, abolished the seventeen existing university groupings, founded for the most part at the end of the nineteenth century on the basis of no more than one per *académie* out of the remaining imperial faculties. In their place, more than seventy new pluridisciplinary institutions were created, with greater autonomy (especially financial and administrative) and governed by bodies which guaranteed a voice to all categories of staff and students. Divided no longer into faculties, but into self-administering Unités d'Enseignement et de Recherche (UER), these new universities were designed to break down traditional academic barriers and overcome vested interests. Degree programmes were organized into three successive tiers (*cycles*), of which the first two lasted for two years; the third was more open-ended. The first tier was conceived as a broadly based introduction to an area of study and to working methods, and led to the award of the Diplôme d'Études Universitaires Générales (DEUG). The second tier developed more specialized study, and led to a first degree (*licence*) after one year and a Master's (*maîtrise*), including some initiation to research method, after a second year. The third tier covered high specialization and doctoral research. Universities were given some control over the design of their curricula, but only within agreed limits, imposed to protect the national character of the awards. Teaching was dispensed via lectures, seminars or practical classes, as appropriate, in units of about ninety minutes per week (*unités de valeur – UV*).

These structures are still broadly speaking in place, despite some changes in emphasis and terminology introduced by subsequent reforms. In 1984, the UER were redesignated UFR (Unités de Formation et de Recherche), in keeping with the emphasis on career preparation in the Savary act, and in 1992 the units were replaced, theoretically, by more broadly based modules, to introduce measures of compensation between individual course units. However, despite its apparent centrally inspired uniformity, in practice the system remains somewhat diverse; since being granted autonomy, some universities have in the past used it to delay, even to avoid applying, the various reforms urged upon them by government. In administrative terms, however, they come within the direct purview of the **education ministry**, which controls staff appointments, pays salaries (generally speaking, all permanent teachers are civil servants), sanctions the national diplomas the institutions are entitled to award, and provides the majority of their recurrent funding. These matters are incorporated in the four-year contracts signed with the ministry. In addition, the Recteur d'Académie acts as chancellor of the universities within his or her administrative district.

Reforms over the last twenty years have been dominated by two overriding concerns: the need to combat the high failure rate, in the the first *cycle* in particular, and the desire to make syllabuses and qualifications more relevant to subsequent **employment.**

The first of these concerns derives from figures which suggest that up to 40 per cent of university entrants fail to achieve even the first-level qualification, the DEUG. With selective entry having been repeatedly ruled out, various alternative formulae have been tried, often

with some short-term success, within the limits of the resources available: better briefing on courses and careers before registration; reformed programmes which introduce greater measures of subject and career counselling and possibilities of change of direction early in the course; the employment of senior students to act as 'tutors' to newcomers; the creation of *antennes* (outposts) in local towns, where the transition between the more protective environment of the *lycée* and the disorientating, impersonal campus might be made more easily by those without university experience in the family.

The second preoccupation is linked to the first, in so far as clear definition of career possibilities is perceived as enhancing motivation, and thereby reducing failure. It has repeatedly been stated that the extended programmes of university study are too long and too abstract for a significant (and increasing) proportion of those embarking upon them. Hence, major attempts have been made to adapt. Firstly this has involved the development of shorter, professionally orientated alternatives, both inside and outside the universities, whether it be two-year intensive courses in technical subjects leading to a Diplôme Universitaire de Technologie, in the Instituts Universitaires de Technologie or expansion of advanced post-*baccalauréat* technical education at the *lycée* (Sections de Techniciens Supérieurs). More significantly, perhaps, professionally orientated diplomas have been introduced into the second and third *cycles*. These range from the specialist commercial qualification, the Maîtrise de Sciences de Gestion, first introduced in 1970, to the diploma of *ingénieur-maître* awarded by the Instituts Universitaires Professionnalisés established by Lionel **Jospin** in 1991. What these prestigious programmes have in common, however – apart, that is, from purporting to be in the mould of the *grandes écoles*, with input from industrialists and compulsory practical placements – is the fact that they select the best applicants from among those already embarked upon higher education. By virtue of the selective process, they do not of course recruit the intellectually weaker students, who are therefore obliged to fall back upon non-selective, traditional abstract studies to which they are least suited. In this way, such developments have, ironically, helped to defeat the objective of adapting the universities' offering to a more diverse audience.

Given the government's aim of ensuring that 80 per cent of the age group achieve the *baccalauréat* by the year 2000, with consequent effects upon demand for university places, the problems of the university system seem destined to last well into the twenty-first century – especially in a climate of government austerity policies designed to cut public spending.

RON HALLMARK

See also: education, secondary: *collèges, lycées,* etc.; educational elitism; student revolt of 1986

Further reading

Firth, K (1989) 'French Universities: The Difficult Road to Reform', *Modern Languages* 70, 1 (March) (this article reviews the problems at the beginning of Jospin's term as minister).

Ministère de l'Éducation Nationale, de l'Enseignement Supérieur et de la Recherche (1996) *Après le BAC: réussir ses études. Le guide des études supérieures 1996*, Paris: Les Dossiers ONISEP (an up-to-date official guide to courses, choices, institutions and careers).

Vasconcellos, M. (1993) *Le Système éducatif*, Paris: Éditions La Découverte (includes a good chapter on higher education, viewed in critical perspective).

Utrillo, Maurice

b. 1883, Paris;
d. 1955, Dax

Artist

Born in Montmartre, Utrillo is celebrated as the painter of Parisian street scenes. His life was disrupted by acute alcoholism, and his mother, the painter Suzanne Valadon, first encouraged him to paint to distract him from drinking. His work is also notorious because of the number of fakes which appeared on the market from 1918 onwards, with a whole flood in 1955, mainly in America.

DEBRA KELLY

See also: painting

V

Vadim, Roger

b. 1928, Paris

Director

Vadim rose to fame overnight in 1956, when he directed Brigitte **Bardot** in *And God Created Woman* (*Et Dieu créa la femme*). This film's sexual frankness and use of a young and (then) little-known lead female actor caused Vadim briefly to be assimilated to the **Nouvelle Vague**. His modern-day adaptation of Laclos's *Les Liaisons dangereuses* (1959), with Gérard **Philipe** and Jeanne **Moreau**, however, was seen as a retrograde step, and his more recent work (in the United States as well as in France) has done more for his reputation as a womanizer than as a leading cinematic auteur.

KEITH READER

See also: cinema

Varda, Agnès

b. 1928, Brussels, Belgium

Director

A naturalized French citizen, Varda is a film-maker who describes herself as an auteur and her work as *artisanale*. She never repeats the same style nor the same narrative – an approach that makes producers reluctant to finance her. Yet she is known as the mother of the **Nouvelle Vague** (New Wave). More significantly, five of her feature films have received international prizes.

Varda places her work at the interface between factual fiction and fictional fact, and speaks of filming the subjectivity of the individual as it relates to the objectivity of the environment – the individual is placed and viewed in the context of society. This means that her films are generally exceptionally topical (for example, in the 1960s she covered cancer; the 1970s feminism; and the 1980s social decline).

Varda may never repeat, but there are several distinctive features to her film-making: use of counterpoint, distanciation, and what she terms *cinécriture* (cine-writing). Varda was the first to understand how to transcribe counterpoint (in the Faulknerian sense of sustaining two narratives side by side) into the cinematic form that would express, simultaneously, individual and social problems. Her contrapuntal editing style is unique and one that the Nouvelle Vague film-makers adapted to their own work (**Resnais** and **Godard**). Her detachment from the story in favour of an attachment to film technique is crucial to her use of counterpoint. Both the subjective/individual and the objective/social must be observed impassively for a realism to emerge out of the collision of the two narratives. Hence Varda's frequent references to her **cinema** in terms of violence.

Ever since her first film, *La Pointe courte*

(1954), Varda has deliberately chosen to distanciate, to make what she calls cold films. She achieves this distanciation through truncation of space, time and narration. She subverts the codes and conventions of classical cinema, deconstructs genres to reconstruct them as other, for example, *One Sings, the Other Doesn't* (*L'Une chante, l'autre pas*) of 1977, a musical on women's reproductive rights, and *Vagabond* (*Sans toit ni loi*) of 1985, a woman's road movie. Her film practices function to counter spectator identification. Held at a distance, it is for the spectator to evaluate the film.

Similarly, her *cinécriture* draws attention to the process of film-making. Varda sees it as closely allied to the technique of **painting** in its structural composition, texture and tonality – for example, she talks of cinepainting the texture of solitude in *Vagabond*. Thus film language itself counterpoints the narratives at the same time as film language is counterpointed within itself through its textures (use of colour, textual references to **photography, sculpture**) and intertexts.

Varda is a feminist and most of her films address the way in which women are fixed in traditional cinema as eternal, unchanging, as object of and for the male gaze – therefore as ahistoric and other. In her film-making practices, Varda counters this naturalization of women by cine-writing the process of their invisibilization, as in *Le Bonheur* (1965). Varda speaks of her film work in terms of asking questions and of doing so in disturbing ways. To this effect she uses cinematic language disruptively, intent on denaturalizing dominant male ideology and opening up institutional myths.

SUSAN HAYWARD

See also: feminism (movements/groups); women directors

Vartan, Sylvie

b. 1944, Iskretz, Bulgaria

Singer

One of the manufactured stars of the *yé-yé* (1960s pop) generation, whose first hit *Quand le film est triste* (When the Film is Sad) dates from 1961, Sylvie Vartan enjoyed popular success before she had mastered the rudiments of her profession. A national celebrity whose hairstyle and dresses were copied by a whole generation, she achieved even greater fame as the wife of Johnny **Hallyday** (who married for the fifth time in 1996). Subsequent dedicated training in the art of live performance transformed her into a more traditional ballad singer and star of spectacular revues.

IAN PICKUP

See also: song/*chanson*

Vasarély, Victor

b. 1908, Pécs, Hungary

Artist

Through his work and theory Vasarély is considered to be one of the fathers of the 1960s Op Art movement. Significantly, his art studies in Budapest were Bauhaus-influenced. Upon settling in France in 1930, he worked in the field of graphic art until his rediscovery of **painting** in 1943. From 1947, his focus was geometrical abstraction. His carefully calculated paintings explore optical ambiguities such as figure-ground alternations which produce illusory movement. The Fondation Vasarély, which he designed himself as a centre for research and creativity, was opened in 1976 in Aix-en-Provence.

CAROL WILCOX

See also: painting

Vauthier, Jean

b. 1910, Grâce-Hollogne;

d. 1992, Paris

Playwright

Part of the 1950s poetic avant-garde movement, Vauthier's works – such as *Captain Bada*
of 1949 (famously directed by **Maréchal** in
1966) and *The New Madragore*, his adaptation
of a Machiavelli text – are notable for their use
of language and sense of adventure.

ANNIE SPARKS

See also: theatre

Further reading

Abirached, R. (1973) *Jean Vauthier*, Paris:
Seghers (a biography).

Veil, Simone

b. 1927, Nice

Politician

A concentration-camp survivor prominently
associated with the left wing of the RPR. As
Health Minister under **Giscard**, she piloted
through parliament the *loi Veil* which legalized
abortion in 1975 – a measure that along with
her Jewishness has attracted to her particularly
vicious opprobrium from **Le Pen** and the
extreme right in general. She became a member
of the European Parliament in 1979 and subsequently its speaker (1979–82) but her domestic
political ambitions would seem to have been
curtailed by her support for **Balladur** for the
1995 Gaullist presidential nomination.

KEITH READER

Vian, Boris

b. 1920, Ville-d'Avray;

d. 1959, Paris

Singer-songwriter, musician and
writer

Something of an artistic all-rounder, Boris Vian
was a dedicated member of the Collège de
Pataphysique (Pataphysics College), **jazz** critic
and musician, (pornographic) novelist, translator, playwright, poet, (unsuccessful) singer and
(successful) songwriter (writing 400–500
songs).

A lifelong jazz enthusiast, Vian played the
trumpet at the Tabou club and wrote for the
revue *Jazz-Hot* but in order to make ends meet
he translated James Cain, August Strindberg
and the memoirs of Omar Bradley. His songwriting activity included collaboration with
Henri **Salvador**, with whom he wrote some
eighty humorous songs, many of which are
parodies of **rock** songs – these include *Le Blues
du dentiste* (The Dentist's Blues), *Frock and
Roll* and *Rock and Rollmops*. Many of his personal phobias surfaced in his songs: the snob-
bery he associated with St-Germain-des-Prés, as
in *J'suis snob* (I'm a Snob), taxation, in
Complainte des contribuables (The Taxpayers'
Lament) and also, for example, the military, in
Les Joyeux Bouchers (The Joyful Butchers).

Despite his prodigious output, Vian did not
have great success as a singer himself (though
he did appear at *Les Trois Baudets* in the mid-
1950s and he did go on a tour organized by the
impresario Jacques Canetti). To compound his
problems, when the most famous contemporary performer of his songs, Marcel **Mouloudji**,
recorded what was to become arguably Vian's
most famous song, the anti-militarist *Le
Déserteur* (1954), the record was banned from
broadcasting and withdrawn from sale as a
result of its controversial nature (it was hardly
designed to meet with the approval of the
authorities, as it advocated a refusal of military
service at a time when the **Algerian war** was
raging).

As is the case with so many non-conformist
figures, Boris Vian did not find fame until after
his death in 1959. His novels began to sell well
by the mid-1960s and he found posthumous

recognition in the world of song when Serge Reggiani began his singing career with a record dedicated to him – *Arthur, où t'as mis le corps?* (Arthur, Where Have You Put the Body?) – and when Jean **Ferrat** paid tribute to him in his 1967 composition *Pauvre Boris* (Poor Boris). Cover versions of *Le Déserteur* were made by Richard Anthony and, in a more anodine English version, by Peter, Paul and Mary (**Renaud** wrote his own slang, more vulgar version in his 1983 song, entitled simply *Déserteur*). The career of the previously ill-fated Mouloudji was given new impetus with the release of yet another anti-militarist Vian song, *Allons z'enfants* (Go on, Children), as late as 1971.

A key importer, with **Queneau**, of **science fiction** into France, Vian was also an important novelist: *L'Écume des jours* (1947), *L'Automne à Pékin* (1947), *L'Herbe rouge* (1950) and *L'Arrache-coeur* (1953) are works of considerable complexity and intertextual resonance.

Boris Vian will be best remembered as the author of *J'irai cracher sur vos tombes* (I Will Go and Spit on Your Graves) from 1946, a novel attributed to Vernon Sullivan, and as the author and composer of *Le Déserteur*.

IAN PICKUP/NICK HEWITT

See also: cultural topography (Paris); song/*chanson*; Theatre of the Absurd

Major works

Vian, B. (1966) *Textes et chansons*, Paris: Julliard.
——(1966) *En avant la zizique*, Paris: Albin Michel (the title of this work, which contains Vian's thoughts on song, was also used for Eve Grilliquez's prizewinning show which was produced at the Gaîté-Montparnasse in 1970).

Vichy

'Vichy' or the 'Vichy regime' are names by which the French state during World War II is known. It was formed after the German military victory over combined French, Belgian and British forces in May/June 1940, coming into being on 10 July 1940 when the National Assembly voted to place Marshal Philippe Pétain at the head of the French state. The Franco-German armistice of 22 June divided France into several zones, the largest two of which were the northern, occupied zone, and the southern (or so-called 'free') zone, whose government was based at the spa town of Vichy in central France, chosen for the quality of its facilities. To all intents and purposes Vichy was a sovereign state, with a legally constituted government and state apparatus whose ministries were lodged in the town's hotels. It even appointed an ambassador to represent its interests to the German occupying authorities in Paris.

Vichy was authoritarian and reactionary, yet (despite appearances) it was not a Fascist regime in the same sense as Nazism or Italian Fascism (this aspect of Vichy continues to be debated among historians). Because of the armistice conditions as they applied specifically to France, the Vichy regime was unique. Its character was reflected in the person and cult of its leader, Marshal Pétain, known as the 'hero of Verdun' (in honour of the fact that, during World War I, under Pétain's command the French army stubbornly resisted a ferocious German offensive at a terrible cost in lives). Aged 84 in 1940, Pétain, who was greeted initially as a saviour by the majority of the French population, reinforced the specifically *French* identity of the regime. In the aftermath of humiliating defeat, the figure of Pétain was seized upon by Vichy apologists and propagandists as representing the very essence of France, as the antithesis of all that had been supposedly corrupt in the Third Republic in general, and the left-wing Popular Front government of 1936–8 in particular. The presence of Pétain conferred a semblance of unity on a country which in reality was physically divided up into 'zones', some of which were 'forbidden' to the French people, and one of which became a Nazi *Gau*. Vichy drew heavily on right-wing, reactionary and (sometimes extreme) nationalist and counter-revolutionary traditions (e.g. the Action Française), but by no means exclusively; in the words of Stanley Hoffmann (1974), Vichy was a 'pluralist dictatorship' which also attracted personalities and influences from other groupings such as veterans' organizations, political 'non-conformists' of the 1930s, and even former radicals and renegade left-wingers.

From the very beginning it was made explicit that under Pétain's paternalistic authority the regime intended to effect a 'National Revolution' which would strive to expunge from France the allegedly corrupt Republican heritage. Using the slogan '*Travail, Famille, Patrie*' (used by the veterans' leader Colonel de La Rocque in his book *Service public* in 1934) to replace the Republican motto of '*Liberté, Égalité, Fraternité*', the government introduced measures to transform the structures of French society which extended beyond institutional domains into everyday socioeconomic activities, religion and culture. In addition to its wish to promote a 'return to the earth' (symbolic of the regime's preference for traditional values and rejection of all that was cosmopolitan and therefore decadent), efforts were made to eradicate elements of what was considered to be 'anti-France': in constructing this new French identity, not only were ties to be cut with the immediate past regarding both domestic and international politics, but those influences deemed to be most damaging to the 'real' France were to be expunged. Thus the enemies of the regime were clearly identified by Vichyite propaganda: Anglo-Saxons, Communists, freemasons and Jews.

In October 1940, after Pétain met Hitler at Montoire, the strategy of 'Collaboration' was formally adopted by the Vichy government. As official texts show, this policy was followed because during the first year of the Occupation the regime was convinced that eventually the Germans would defeat Britain and dominate the continent. The policy of Collaboration was designed to ensure a leading place for France in the 'new Europe'. As the war went on, however, German victory against the Allies became

less certain. Particularly after the return to power of Pierre Laval, Pétain's prime minister, in April 1942, and after the occupation of the southern zone by the Germans in November 1942, Vichy was increasingly and irreversibly drawn into the machinery of the Nazi war effort. This extended well beyond the economic domain. In particular, the two sets of anti-Jewish statutes put into place by Vichy in October 1940 and June 1941, laws which drew on a specifically French anti-semitic tradition dating back to the Dreyfus affair of 1894–9 and beyond, and which predated the measures introduced by the Germans, eventually eased the implementation of the Nazis' Final Solution in France. It was French authorities which carried out censuses of the Jewish population, and French police (co-ordinated with the Nazis by police chief René Bousquet) who co-operated in many of the round-ups of Jews, the most infamous of which was the *rafle du Vélodrome d'hiver* (a Paris sports stadium) on 16–17 July 1942. In total, some 76,000 Jews (of whom 24,000 were French) were deported from French railheads to the Nazi death camps in eastern Europe: only 3 per cent survived.

For a long time after the war, this complicity in Nazi genocide was masked by what Henry Rousso (1991) has called 'the Vichy syndrome', according to which painful memories of the difficult choices arising from the Occupation, and especially the memory of the fate inflicted on the Jews, were pushed to the back of the collective conscious. However, the path-breaking work of historians such as Robert Paxton (1972) opened the way towards a reappraisal of France's role in the Occupation, and work undertaken by researchers at the CNRS Institut d'Histoire du Temps Présent began to present the realities of the war in France in a clearer light. Public and press reaction to revelations that President **Mitterrand** began his political career under Vichy, and that he had connections with René Bousquet after the war (Péan 1994), suggests that the 'dark years' of the Vichy period in France continue to trouble notions of contemporary French identity.

MARTYN CORNICK

See also: Judaism; racism/anti-semitism

Further reading

Amouroux, H. (1976–93) *La Grande Histoire des Français sous l'Occupation*, 10 vols, Paris: Laffont (a great fresco investigating everyday life under the Occupation).

Azéma, J.-P. and Bédarida, F. (eds) (1993) *La France des années noires*, 2 vols, Paris: Éditions du Seuil (a thorough and illustrated collection of essays summarizing recent research on the 'dark years' of the Occupation).

Burrin, P. (1996) *Living with Defeat: France Under German Occupation 1940–1944* (*La France à l'heure allemande* [1995]), London: Arnold (using the concept of *accommodation*, this examines how the French coped with the Nazi Occupation).

Hoffmann, S. (1974) *Decline and Renewal? France Since the 1930s*, New York: Viking Press (contains path-breaking analyses of the composition of the Vichy regime).

Kedward, H. R. (1985) *Occupied France*, Oxford: Blackwell (the best brief introduction).

Laborie, P. (1990) *L'Opinion française sous Vichy*, Paris: Éditions du Seuil (study of opinion and how it reacted to policy and events in the context of the unfolding war).

Marrus, M. and Paxton, R. O. (1981) *Vichy France and the Jews*, New York: Basic Books (classic study of how Vichy's anti-semitic attitudes and policies affected the Jews in France and contributed to the Final Solution).

Paxton, R. O. (1972) *Vichy France: Old Guard, New Order 1940–44*, New York: Knopf (based on German archives, the classic study on the nature of the Vichy regime).

Péan, P. (1994) *Une jeunesse française: François Mitterrand, 1934–1947*, Paris: Fayard (revelations on Mitterrand's early political career under Vichy).

Rousso, H. (1990) 'Qu'est-ce que la Révolution nationale?', *L'Histoire* January (brief summary of the character of Vichy's 'National Revolution').

——(1991) *The Vichy Syndrome: History and Memory in France Since 1944* (*Le Syndrome de Vichy* Paris: Seuil [1987]), Cambridge, MA: Harvard University Press (translation of Rousso's path-breaking book published in French in 1987 on the legacies of Vichy).

Weisberg, R. H. (1996) *Vichy France and the Holocaust in France*, Amsterdam: Harwood Academic Publishers (a thorough account of the complicity of Vichy's legal system in the Holocaust).

Wieviorka, A. (1992) *Déportation et génocide: entre la mémoire et l'oubli*, Paris: Plon (detailed synthesis of research on the French contribution to the Final Solution).

video imports

Anglo-American **pop video** represents a very small part of total audiovisual output in France, most notably in evidence on the cable music channels MCM and MTV. However, it forms an important part of the media consumption of many young people. Though listening to anglophone music is scarcely a new phenomenon in France, in 1994 the sensitivity of French elites to perceived Anglo-American domination in the audiovisual field and the alleged weakening of French cultural identity led the conservative government to include a minimum quota of 40 per cent francophone production in music output on radio (*la loi Carignon*).

RAYMOND KUHN

See also: rock and pop; television

Vilar, Jean

b. 1912, Sète;
d. 1971, Sète

Director and actor

Jean Vilar is one of the most influential figures in twentieth-century French theatre, thanks not only to his abilities as an artist, but also to his vision of a 'popular' theatre, or theatre of the people, and his founding of the acclaimed Avignon theatre festival, which celebrated its fiftieth birthday in July 1997.

A student with Dullin in the 1930s, he acted with and co-directed the touring company La Roulotte after the war, launching his directing career with Strindberg's *Dance of Death* in 1942, and keenly supporting dramatists of the so-called New Theatre such as **Adamov** in the small avant-garde theatres of Paris. In 1943 he set up his own professional company, the Compagnie de Sept at the Théâtre de Poche, Paris, where he enjoyed recognition for his productions of Molière's *Dom Juan* in 1945, T. S. Eliot's *Murder in the Cathedral* the following year, as well as works by, among others, Koestler and Adamov. He also acted in Carné's and **Prévert's** 1946 film *Les Portes de la nuit*, and for Jouvet's theatre productions of Claudel and **Sartre**.

In 1947, he founded the Avignon festival. Vilar was notable for his political commitment to the social role of theatre and to the necessity of taking theatre to the provinces. The open air performances in the Cour d'Honneur of the Palais des Papes were a huge success, the lack of scenic devices on offer only adding to the drama of the spectacle. Indeed, when Vilar was installed at the Théâtre National Populaire at Chaillot in 1951, thanks to the success of his work in Avignon and Paris, he was to introduce the same open staging there, doing away with a traditional proscenium arch, re-evoking the open expanse of the Avignon stage in the 3,000-seat theatre.

Here he mounted numerous productions of the classics, employing his belief in minimalist staging in an open space, stating his objectives as '*un public de masse, un répertoire de haute culture, une régie qui n'embourgeoise pas, ne falsifie pas les oeuvres*' ('a mass public, a repertoire of production which does not render works middle-class or falsify them' – see Bradby 1991). He attracted new, working-class audiences for his plays by organizing theatre trips through factories and **unions**, keeping ticket prices low and rejecting traditional Parisian theatre-going rituals (evening dress and late-starting performances, for example) By the early 1960s, he had staged contemporary works by such as Brecht, Calderón and Bolt alongside those of Sophocles and Aristophanes. However, it proved difficult to make a financial success of new works in such a large theatre. In 1963, he resigned from Chaillot, moving on to stage operas in Venice and Milan, completing a study for **Malraux** on the possibilities of popular opera, and reorganizing the Opéra and Opéra-Comique in 1967. He also staged plays in Geneva and Paris, including his own play *The Oppenheimer File* (*Le Dossier d'Oppenheimer*) at the Théâtre de l'Athénée in 1965, in which he played the lead. Vilar also worked hard to expand the Avignon festival, with a series of debates (Rencontres d'Avignon), in 1966 extending the festival to a fortnight. By 1969, it had expanded to include music, **cinema** and other arts. The fringe 'Off' festival was created in 1970, a year before his death.

ANNIE SPARKS

See also: Avignon and summer arts festivals; theatre

Major works

Vilar, J. (1975) *Le Théâtre, service public*, Paris: Gallimard (Vilar's theatrical testament).

Further reading

Bradby, D. (1991) *Modern French Drama 1940–1990*, Cambridge: Cambridge University Press.

Wehle, P. (1991) *Le Théâtre Populaire selon Jean Vilar*, Paris: Actes Sud (a major study).

Vinaver, Michel

b. 1927, Paris

Playwright, novelist and critic

One of the most frequently performed contemporary playwrights in France today, Michel Vinaver has enjoyed a career as a writer spanning five decades, as well as rising to the top of his commercial profession as managing director of the French wing of a multinational company, a position he gave up at the beginning of the 1980s in order to pursue his career as a playwright. His writings have many points in common with the **Théâtre du Quotidien**, in terms of language, subject matter and experimentation with different structures, time and form.

He began writing in the 1950s: after a series of novels, his first play, *Today or the Koreans* (*Aujourd'hui ou les Coréens*), was staged by **Planchon** in 1956 to critical acclaim, dealing with a group of soldiers and a group of villagers in the Korean war. His subsequent plays, *Les Huissiers* (The Ushers) in 1958 and *Iphigénie Hôtel* a year later, dealt with the sensitive issue of the **Algerian war,** but *Iphigénie Hôtel* was only finally staged by **Vitez** in 1977, and *Les Huissiers* three years later by Chevassieux. During the 1960s, he withdrew from writing to concentrate on his work in French business, experiences which fuelled his fascination with economic, political and social realities and how they affect the lives of everyday people. *Overboard (Pardessus-Bord)* was his next work (1969), staged by Planchon in 1973, followed by *Situation Vacant (La Demande d'emploi)*, staged in 1973, *Smile on the End of a Line (Les Travaux et les jours)* in 1977, and *Bending Over Backwards (A la renverse)* three years later. They, like all Vinaver's plays, explore these themes through everyday settings, dialogue and situations, presented often using various overlapping time scales: in *Pardessus-Bord*, for example, he analyses the effect on everyday people of modernizing industry, and in *The Television Programme* (*L'émission de télévision*), written in 1988, the destructive role of the televisual medium. Vinaver does not, however, intend his works to be taken as realism, but rather to question the bigger issues arising from situation and dialogue. An element of strangeness is lent to the 'reality' he presents by experiments with time, structure and language; by deliberately layering and juxtaposing these elements to create dramatic tension, he aims to make the audience question the unrolling events, and by throwing together opposing elements of 'reality', he raises questions about its very nature.

There is also a rich layering of themes in Vinaver's work. The problems facing workers in France are certainly a main theme in many of his plays. However, the multitude of preoccupations present in everyday life, expressed through everyday language, are just as important.

Aside from his playwriting, Vinaver has also taken an active role as a critic and campaigner on behalf of the playwright. In 1987, he published a report commissioned by the Ministry of Culture entitled *Le Compte rendu d'Avignon* (The Avignon Report), which detailed the plight of writers in the **theatre** world and the need for more theatre texts to be published.

ANNIE SPARKS

Major works

Vinaver, M. (1986) *Théâtre complet*, 2 vols, Arles: L'Aire/Actes Sud.

Further reading

Bradby, D. (1993) *The Theatre of Michel Vinaver*, Michigan: University of Michigan Press (key reading on Vinaver's work).
Ubersfeld, A. (1989) *Vinaver dramaturge*, Paris: Librairie Théâtrale (sociological approach).

Vincent, Jean-Pierre

b. 1942, Paris

Actor and director

Vincent was a collaborator of **Chéreau** and **Jourdheuil** in the 1960s, famed for his political, contemporary approach, and a director of the Théâtre National de Strasbourg (1975–83) and the **Comédie-Française** (1983–6). He now teaches and directs, and became director of the Théâtre des Amandiers-Nanterre in 1990.

ANNIE SPARKS

See also: theatre; theatres, national

Further reading

Gunthert, A. (1983) *Le Voyage du TNS*, Paris: Solin (account of his time at the Théâtre National de Strasbourg).

Virilio, Paul

b. 1932

Epistemologist and media analyst

Paul Virilio's crucial 1984 study *War and Cinema* (*Logistique de la perception*) stands unparalleled in its implications for philosophy, history and aesthetics. He argues that at the time of its birth the international film industry (in France and the United States) quickly realized that, once mobilized, its images could determine collective perception and experience. Film and publicity would provide the model for what would soon become history. The two determining events of the twentieth century, World Wars I and II, were mapped out by a cinematic institution that shaped their advent. International collusions were built in the development of the media. In all of his writing – visionary, delphic, speculative – Virilio studies how articulations of space and language plot out subjectivity. He appeals to the architectural theories and practice of Fascist Italy, to the military practices (what he calls 'bunker archaeologies') of Nazi Germany, and to the history of air power (and its innovations in cartography) to show how humans can no longer think of the relation of space and language – a ground for philosophy and religion – in ways that preceded modernism. His writings are salubriously chilling in their outlook.

TOM CONLEY

Vitez, Antoine

b. 1930, Paris;
d. 1990, Paris

Director, translator and teacher

An influential theatre director, Vitez is noted for his attempts to find new ways of staging language and text, for his Communist beliefs, and for his belief in '*un théâtre élitaire pour tous*' ('an elitist theatre for all'). His directing career began in 1966, at the *Maison de la Culture* in Caen. In 1972, he became well-known for his productions at the Quartiers d'Ivry theatre in the Communist Parisian suburb of Ivry-sur-Seine, where he staged famous classic productions alongside contemporary works, notably by **Vinaver**, **Kalisky** and Pommeret. It was here too, in 1976, that *Catherine*, his famous adaptation of Aragon's novel, *Les Cloches de Bâle* (The Bells of Basle), demonstrated his interest in experimenting with the staging of non-dramatic texts. Alongside these productions, he also staged other forms of theatre, including puppet shows and political farce. In 1981, he became director of the Théâtre de Chaillot. Celebrated productions such as *Hamlet* (in 1982), the complete version of Claudel's *The Satin Slipper* (*Le Soulier de Satin*) in 1987, and contemporary works such as Kalisky's *Falsch* (1983) were the result of his work with the team of stage designer **Kokkos**, composer Georges Aperghis and lighting director Patrice Trotter. In 1988, he became general administrator of the **Comédie-Française**, where his last production was Brecht's *Life of Galileo* in 1990, the year of his death. He is also noted for his teaching of acting, both at Jacques **Lecoq**'s school (1966–70) and the Conservatoire National d'Art Dramatique (1968–81), where he encouraged a destructured rather than psychological approach to interpretation. He is also remembered for his regard for Russian and Greek theatre repertoires, and was responsible for numerous translations and productions from these throughout his career. The national centre for translation, the Maison Antoine Vitez, was named in his honour.

ANNIE SPARKS

See also: director's theatre; theatre

Further reading

Ubersfeld, A. (1995) *Vitez, metteur en scène et poète*, Paris: Les Quatre Vents (a very useful guide).

Vogue

Magazine

Possibly the most influential of exclusive, 'pure fashion' magazines of this century, *Vogue* has devoted itself to fashion, art and design and society. It refuses to place itself in the category of 'women's magazines'.

It was originally founded in the United States, in 1892, as a fashion weekly for society women. In 1909, it was taken over by William Condé Nast, who transformed it into the high-quality publication it is today. The internationalization of the fashion industry after 1918 saw the establishment of *Vogue* in west European capitals. *Vogue Paris* was founded in June 1920, although the magazine's Paris operation did not begin until 1921 (the first few issues were printed in London), under its first French editor, Cosette Vogel. From the beginning, the magazine deliberately segregated itself and an elite clientele from the producers and consumers of women's magazines, and offered its readers the highest standards (in magazine publishing) of art, **photography**, illustration, typography and writing. Hence, its pages have over the years presented or discussed the works of Cecil Beaton, **Picasso**, **Sartre**, de **Beauvoir**, **Godard**, **Duras** and others.

One of the magazine's enduring claims has been that fashion in *Vogue* represents the drama of contemporary life, and in this respect it has aimed to reflect, through its images and text, social, political and economic changes which have occurred in France through the magazine's history. Thus, for example, while working women and a futuristic but practical look became preoccupying themes in the 1960s, the 1970s brought ideas of liberation and casual fashion to the magazine's pages. Since the 1980s, it has been more schizophrenic, in that fashion has been both aggressive and whimsical, uninterested in women as real people (witness the techno-styles of designers such as Jean-Paul **Gaultier** and purely ornamental, 'baby-doll' designs of Christian **Lacroix**) while, through its textual content, the magazine has subscribed to a certain post/anti-feminist thinking but has welcomed **AIDS** awareness, environmental concern and other progressive issues which do not challenge its own *raison d'être*.

Today, *Vogue* continues to target an exclusive clientele of sophisticated women, although since the 1960s there has been a gradual move away from older readers with established wealth to a younger, more active set of women aspiring to a certain affluence and culture. This approach appears to have borne success: *Vogue*'s annual circulation figure has increased from 24,508 in 1950 to 84,826 in 1994 and, unlike the periodical press in general, the magazine appears not to have suffered greatly from the economic austerity of the late 1970s and 1980s. *Vogue Paris* appears ten times yearly.

KHURSHEED WADIA

See also: fashion; women's magazines

Further reading

Presse et statistiques (1994), Paris: SJTI (statistical information relating to the press).

Train, S. (1995) 'Ils ont fait Vogue', *Vogue, Le fabuleux album des 75 ans*, special issue 763 (seventy-fifth anniversary edition which charts, nostalgically, the history of French *Vogue* through text and the expected high-quality visuals).

Waechter, Antoine

b. 1949, Mulhouse

Environmental activist and politician

A founder of the main French Green Party, *Les Verts*, in 1984 and its main leader and speaker for the following ten years, Waechter became known for his uncompromising, earnest views. He represents a radical, fundamentalist approach to **green politics**, refusing alliances with other political groups. He was the Green candidate in the 1988 presidential elections, and an MEP from 1989 to 1991. His views were defeated within the Green Party in 1994, by an alliance of less 'fundamentalist' activists, and he left to create his own movement, the Mouvement Écologiste Indépendant, which has not been successful in attracting support.

FRANÇOIS NECTOUX

See also: green issues; Lalonde, Brice; parties and movements

water sports

A variety of water sports are popular in France and each has its national federation (Fédération Française de . . .): Canoë-Kayak (canoeing), Natation (swimming), Ski Nautique (waterskiing), Surf et Skate (surfing and skateboarding), Voile et Planche à Voile (sailing and windsurfing), Water-Polo. Sailing is particularly popular and France has produced sailors of world stature such as Alain Colas and the incomparable Éric Tabarly.

IAN PICKUP

Wenzel, Jean-Paul

b. 1947, St Étienne

Playwright, actor and director

After national theatre school in Strasbourg, Wenzel acted for **Brook**, and helped create the company **Théâtre du Quotidien** in 1975, before writing plays such as *Loin d'Hagondange* (Far from Hagondange) and *La Fin des Monstres* (End of the Monsters). A supporter of decentralization, Wenzel often collaborates with the Théâtre Ouvert and directs the Centre Dramatique National at Montluçon, Les Fédérés.

ANNIE SPARKS

See also: Attoun, Lucien; theatre

wine

It is commonly said that France is the home of the best food and drink – particularly wine – in the world. With a tradition which goes back to the Gauls and an unrivalled reputation which goes back many centuries, in the last century the French wine industry had to recover from a devastating blow caused by the phylloxera louse. A native of America, the *Phylloxera vastatrix* crossed the Atlantic in the mid- to late nineteenth century (probably through the ignorance or negligence of an unsuspecting botanist) and found the roots of European vines much to its liking. The result was the almost total devastation of France's (and ultimately Europe's) vineyards. The solution eventually adopted in France as elsewhere, after the failure of different chemical treatments, was the grafting of European vines on to American root stock unaffected by phylloxera (a practice still followed today). In France, only Bollinger's *Vieilles Vignes* champagne is produced from pre-phylloxera, ungrafted vines.

Although the development of the global market has meant greater competition for the French wine industry abroad (and the country imports twice the quantity of wine it exports; something in excess of 800 million litres per year), Germany, the United Kingdom, the Benelux countries and the United States remain its best customers and France retains a tight grip on the top end of the market (claret or Bordeaux, Burgundy and Champagne, for example, are recognized words across the world). Some 1.5 million hectares (3.35 per cent of France's arable land) are planted with vines, and some 6 million French people work in (or make direct or indirect profit from) the wine industry.

The varieties of vines grown in France vary significantly from region to region: while the Bordeaux region is planted with Cabernet Sauvignon, Cabernet Franc and Merlot for its red wine, and Sauvignon (dry) and Sémillon (sweet) for its white wines, Burgundy cultivates Pinot Noir and (for its lesser wines) Gamay grapes for reds and Chardonnay, and (for its lesser wines) Aligoté grapes for its whites. Whereas the red Beaujolais wines are produced from Gamay grapes, the Rhône area shows greater variety: Syrah grapes for red wine and Viognier, and Roussanne and Marsanne grapes

for white wine, are to be found in the north of the region, while in the south there is a mixture including Syrah, Grenache, Mourvèdre and Cinsaut for reds. The Nantes area cultivates Muscadet and (for its lesser wines) Gros Plant grapes for its distinctive whites, while further south in the Loire region (around Anjou and Saumur) Cabernet grapes produce the well-known *rosé* wines – Groslot and Gamay grapes (for the reds) and the Chenin Blanc variety (for whites). The Pinot Noir variety is also the source of red wines in Alsace and of white wines in the Champagne region. Other varieties of grapes cultivated in France include Pinot Gris, Pinot Blanc, Pinot Meunier, Riesling, Muscat and Sylvaner.

The two most prestigious regions of France for still wine are the Bordeaux region (which stretches from Saint Estèphe in the north to Sauternes and the area which produces *Graves* wines in the south), and Burgundy, which goes from Chablis in the north to the Beaujolais vineyards in the south. Both of these regions illustrate well the prestigious French wine classification system which is based on what is known as the *Appellation d'Origine Contrôlée* (AOC, the label of origin which is also something of a guarantee of quality and of a specific method of cultivation and production; it is reserved for a tiny fraction of the national production). The hierarchy of wine in the Bordeaux region moves upwards from the straightforward *Appellation Bordeaux Contrôlée* through the various *crus bourgeois* (bourgeois growths or vintages) to the so-called *crus classés* (classed growths) which relate to a particular chateau or commune. These, in ascending order, are *bons crus* (good vintages), *crus supérieurs* (superior or higher growths), *grands crus* (great growths), the *crus exceptionnels* (exceptional growths) and, at the very pinnacle, the *crus hors classe* (the most exceptional growths, which in the 1978 classification number only eight chateau wines, four from the Haut-Médoc, one from the Graves area, two from St Émilion and one Pomerol). The very mention of a wine from the highest category (the incomparable Château Lafite-Rothschild from the Haut Médoc, for example) is guaranteed to capture the attention of any oenologist. Bordeaux produces twice as much red wine as white and it is on the former that its reputation is primarily founded.

Burgundy, second in importance only to Bordeaux as a wine-producing area, is composed of five different zones – if we include Beaujolais in the south with the Mâcon vineyards, those of the Côte Chalonnaise (or Région de Mercurey), the Côte d'Or (composed of the Côte de Beaune and the Côte de Nuit) and finally Chablis. If a typical claret is light, dry, not too heavy in alcohol and redolent of the oak casks in which it is matured, then the red and white wines of Burgundy show tremendous variety, from dark, often full-bodied, velvety reds which do not have the dryness of a claret, to crisp, dry white wines which are, none the less, full-bodied and (at their best) full of ageing potential. Burgundy wine may be purchased, at the bottom end of the market, as *Bourgogne Grand Ordinaire*, while a slightly superior wine is the so-called *Bourgogne Passe-Tout Grains*, followed by the plainer-sounding *AC Bourgogne*. Further up the market are the *Bourgogne Hautes Côtes de Beaune*, the *Bourgogne Hautes Côtes de Nuit*, *Côtes de Beaune Villages*, *Côtes de Nuit Villages* and the commune wines which bear the name of a village on the AC (*Appellation Contrôlée*) label. Burgundy also has its own list of *grands crus*.

Although this account has focused on the two great wine-growing areas of France, it must not be forgotten that Épernay and Reims are the major towns of the prestigious Champagne region, known throughout the world for its sparkling whites, while *vins de pays* (country wines) of very acceptable quality are produced in such areas as the Rhone, Roussillon, Minervois and the Gard, for example. Add the *Appellation Contrôlée* wines of Alsace, Lorraine, the Jura and Touraine (among others) and it becomes clear that, in addition to the huge amount of 'plonk' or table wine (*vin ordinaire* or *vin de table*) which it produces, France retains its reputation for quality and variety unrivalled by any other country in the world.

IAN PICKUP

See also: gastronomy

Further reading:

Lichine, A. (1980) *Encyclopédie des vins et des alcools de tous les pays*, Paris: Laffont 'Bouquins' (an alphabetically arranged encyclopedia of wines and spirits by a well-known oenologist and wine merchant).

Plessis, L. (1979) *Le Vin à la maison*, Paris: Flammarion (an introductory guide to French wines).

Rainbird, G. (1984) *Le Vin dans le monde*, Paris: Compagnie Internationale du Livre (an illustrated guide to wine, almost half of which is devoted to France).

Robinson, J. (1979) *The Wine Book*, London: A & C Black/Fontana (an English-language guide to 'better buying and drinking for less money').

winter sports

The French Alps attract countless French and foreign skiers every year, and the facilities offered are probably second to none (if somewhat expensive). France has hosted the Winter Olympics (Chamonix in 1924, Grenoble in 1968 and Albertville in 1992) and produced world and Olympic champions, of whom the best known are Jean-Claude Killy and Marielle Goitschel. France has also had world champions in figure skating – including Alain Calmat, who went on to become Minister of Sport (the first former top-level sportsman to do so). Another popular winter sport in France is ice hockey: there is a national championship which in the 1950s and 1960s was dominated by the Chamonix Hockey Club.

IAN PICKUP

See also: sport

Wittig, Monique

b. 1935, Alsace

Novelist, playwright and feminist theorist

The work of Monique Wittig is widely known for its original combination of literary innovations and radical lesbian politics. A prominent figure in the French feminist movement of the early 1970s, Wittig emigrated to the United States in 1976. As a writer, her main concern is to dismantle language in its patriarchal forms and to reconstruct it from a lesbian perspective. To this end, she appropriates and transforms works by male authors, conventional genres and patriarchal mythologies. Unlike the practitioners of *écriture féminine*, however, Wittig does not celebrate 'the feminine', but aims to abolish sex and gender categories, as discussed in her theoretical work *The Straight Mind and Other Essays*.

Her first novel, *The Opoponax* (*L'Opoponax*), for which Wittig won the Prix Médicis, describes the experiences of a group of girls and the love between two of the protagonists. Apparent in this text are themes central in Wittig, such as the obliteration of lesbians from patriarchal culture and the conflict between feminine socialization and female subjectivity. In the modern epic *Les Guérillères*, female warriors wage a guerrilla war against the patriarchal order. The text charts different stages in feminism, representing the female culture which emerges after the destruction of patriarchy as a transitional phase, superseded by a genderless society. *The Lesbian Body* (*Le Corps lesbien*) is an incantation of lesbian passion, reminiscent of the poetry of Sappho. Here Wittig breaks down heterosexual constructs of the female body and recreates it as the subject of desire for another woman. Co-authored with Sande Zeig, *Lesbian Peoples: Material for a Dictionary* (*Brouillon pour un dictionnaire des amantes*) rewrites history from a lesbian perspective through redefinitions of words and provides a key to the terminology used in Wittig's other works. *Across the Acheron*

(*Virgile, non*), a subversive reworking of Dante's *The Divine Comedy*, is set in contemporary San Francisco and stages Wittig's journey through the hell of women's oppression, her excursions to the limbo of the lesbian bar scene and her arrival in a paradise of freedom. *The Constant Journey* (*Le Voyage sans fin*), a play written and produced with Sande Zeig, is based on Cervantes' *Don Quixote*. It presents an all-female cast, with Quichotte as a feminist struggling against patriarchal society. The striking dissociation between action and dialogue demonstrates the originality of Wittig's technical experimentation. Her work has inspired feminists and lesbians worldwide and has influenced contemporary writers like Michèle Causse and Nicole Brossard.

RENATE GÜNTHER

See also: feminism (movements/groups); feminist thought; literary prizes; women's/lesbian writing

Further reading

Crowder, D. G. (1983) 'Amazons and Mothers? Monique Wittig, Hélène Cixous and Theories of Women's Writing', *Contemporary Literature* 24, 2 (a lucid study of Wittig's work in its French feminist context).

Duffy, J. H. (1990) 'Monique Wittig', in M. Tilby (ed.) *Beyond the Nouveau Roman*, Oxford: Berg (a comprehensive account of Wittig's literary and theoretical texts).

Ostrovsky, E. (1991) *A Constant Journey: The Fiction of Monique Wittig*, Carbondale: Southern Illinois University Press (an in-depth study of themes and literary techniques with an excellent bibliography).

Wols

b. 1913, Berlin;
d. 1951, Champigny-sur-Marne,
(near Paris)

Artist and photographer,
real name Alfred Otto Wolfgang
Schulze

Of German nationality, Wols (his pseudonym taken from a torn fragment of a telegramme sent to him) was a student at the Berlin Bauhaus and went to Paris in 1933, where he was influenced by Surrealism. In 1937 he had a one-man exhibition of his photographs in Paris and was commissioned to photograph the fashion pavilion at the International Exhibition. His career as a photographer ended when he was interned in 1939 as an enemy alien, although he was freed a year later. In the early 1940s, he began to draw and paint in a style described by **Sartre** (who much admired the unease his works provoked) as 'automatism'. His first exhibition in December 1945 showed tiny drawings and watercolours displayed in illuminated boxes which appear to the viewer like microscopic forms or far-away worlds. He was admired by the artist George **Mathieu**, and he helped pioneer **L'Art Informel** and Tachism in the 1950s.

DEBRA KELLY

See also: painting; photography

women and employment

By the mid-1990s, over 11 million French women were economically active, representing almost 45 per cent of the labour force. The real take-off for the growth of women's labour market participation is generally situated in the early 1970s, when the **economy** was about to enter a period of restructuring. Since then, while male economic activity rates have declined, women have continued to increase their share of the labour force and have benefited from the overall shift in **employment** from the industrial to the service sector.

In relation to its European neighbours, France displays relatively high levels of full-time continuous female economic activity, particularly for women in the 25–49 age group,

when they are also likely to be engaged in rearing children. In the mid-1990s, after the Nordic countries, France showed the highest activity rates in the **European Union** for women in this age group, with over 76 per cent of French women participating in the labour force, almost regardless of the presence of young children.

The postwar constitution of 1946 enshrined the principle of equal rights in France, but women's incorporation into the labour force has continued to be on different terms from those for men. More girls than boys gain school-leaving qualifications and a university education, but they experience greater difficulty in finding jobs. Despite the strong commitment of French women to employment, they tend to be segregated into less secure and less well-paid jobs, and they are more likely than men to be unemployed.

By the mid-1990s, over 80 per cent of women in employment were working in the service sector, where they had benefited from the expansion of jobs in retailing, education, **health** and welfare, but they continued to be concentrated in a relatively small number of low-status positions, particularly in clerical work and direct services to clients. A higher proportion of women than men (14.8 per cent compared with 12.6 per cent) were employed in the public sector – where more flexible working conditions and greater security of employment generally compensated for lower salaries – than in the private sector.

Part-time work is less widespread in France than in the United Kingdom, accounting for 28 per cent of female economic activity in 1995 (compared to the United Kingdom's 44 per cent). Although part-time workers are entitled, *pro rata*, to the same rights as full-time workers, the attitude towards part-time work is ambiguous. While offering a convenient solution to the problem of combining paid and unpaid work, it is not infrequently imposed by employers requiring a flexible labour force.

LINDA HANTRAIS

See also: demographic developments; women and social policy

Further reading

Hantrais, L. (1990) *Managing Professional and Family Life: A Comparative Study of British and French Women*, Aldershot and Vermont: Dartmouth (a comparison of women's employment patterns in relation to family life).

INSEE (1995) *Les Femmes*, Paris: INSEE, 'Collection Contours et Caractères' (a useful analysis of characteristics of women's employment).

women and politics

Since French women won the right to vote and to stand for election (in October 1944), their participation in politics has evolved considerably. If a principal indicator of political participation is voting, then in the 1990s French women participate at the same rate as men. However, as far as participation in political decision-making is concerned, little has changed since 1944.

Traditionally, women voters have been associated with abstentionism and conservatism. Until 1969, female abstention rates were 7–12 percentage points higher than male abstention rates. Women's participation was also distinct from that of men in that they voted, in greater numbers, for the Right. For instance, this gender gap was at its greatest in the first round of the presidential elections of 1965, when the Left's candidate, François **Mitterrand**, obtained 39 per cent of the women's vote compared with 51 per cent of the men's vote. The explanations for these early differences between male and female voting are that women were political beginners and were apprehensive about exercising their newly won rights and that they were more easily influenced in their choice of conservative candidates by the Catholic church.

This traditional model of the female voter began to fragment in the 1970s as, progressively, more women left the private sphere of home and family to enter the workforce or higher education, and the gap between male and female participation decreased. By the legislative elections of 1993 the difference in abstention rates was negligible, with 24 per cent of women abstaining compared with 23 per cent of men. The early 1970s also marked the radicalization of the female electorate. By the 1986 legislative elections, women and men voted equally for the Left, while by the second round of the 1988 presidential elections, women had overtaken men, for the first time, in voting for the Left.

While women accounted for 53 per cent of the electorate and nearly 45 per cent of the workforce in 1994, they only represented 6 per cent of *députés* and 5.5 per cent of *sénateurs* in parliament, placing France near the bottom of the league of **European Union** countries. Women's exclusion from political power has been put down to historical precedents such as property-based suffrage which (from 1789) prevented women from voting and representing others, to Catholicism's view of women's role and responsibilities, to the refusal of political parties to promote women and to the rules of the electoral system itself.

Since 1994, the fiftieth anniversary of women's political rights, a feminist campaign for political 'parity' (the equal representation of women and men in all elected assemblies) has gathered momentum. The argument that parity is the only way to renew French democracy has gained favour in a large section of the political class.

KHURSHEED WADIA

See also: Catholicism and Protestantism; feminism (movements/groups); parties and movements; women and employment

Further reading

Allwood, G. (1995) 'The Campaign for Parity

in Political Institutions in France' in D. Knight and J. Still (eds) *Women and Representation*, Nottingham: WIF Publications (an account of the campaign for gender parity in French political institutions).

Mossuz-Lavau, J. (1995) 'Les Françaises aux urnes (1945–1994)', *Modern and Contemporary France* 3, 2 (an overview of the voting patterns and political behaviour of French women over fifty years).

women and social policy

In France, women have gained access to welfare, both indirectly as the dependants of male breadwinners and as mothers, and directly as workers in their own right. Since the 1970s, the focus has been on policies to help women reconcile **family** life and **employment**.

The **social security** system which developed in France in the postwar period was premised on the principle of employment-related insurance rights, implying that regular employment should be rewarded by access to sickness benefits, occupational pensions and other forms of social protection. Since few women were gainfully employed outside the home, their access to welfare depended essentially on derived rights in their capacity as wives and mothers. The origins of family allowances at the turn of the century lay in the wage supplements paid to workers in industry to compensate fathers for their family responsibilities. The model of the family supported in **social policy** was centred on the mother as home-maker. More generous provision was made for mothers of three or more children, with the pro-natalist aim of increasing family size.

By the 1970s, women's rights had moved on to the political agenda. Married women and women with children were joining the labour force in large numbers. Governments therefore came under increasing pressure to respond to the demands of women for protection as paid workers. Economically active women were already entitled to social security cover in their own right, and they had long been eligible to receive maternity pay. Innovative schemes were introduced, particularly in the public sector, to improve work-time organization and working conditions. Under the Socialist government, the 1983 *loi* **Roudy** reinforced and extended women's rights. French women are legally protected against unfair dismissal and loss of status due to pregnancy. They are guaranteed reinstatement after paid maternity leave, which is taken into account in calculating pensionable service. Part-time workers are eligible to receive *pro rata* benefits.

Increasingly, policy has been adapted to take account of women's dual roles as workers and mothers, and to encourage them to combine paid and unpaid work. State provision for **child care** and nursery schooling is extensive in France, and allowances are paid towards childminding costs. Parental leave, with pay for parents of two or more children, is available for up to three years and can be shared between men and women. Take-up of leave has, however, remained low, and French women in the 25–49 age bracket seem to prefer to pursue continuous full-time employment careers, which give them full entitlement to welfare in their own right.

LINDA HANTRAIS

See also: demographic developments; Roudy, Yvette; women and employment

Further reading

Hantrais, L. (1993) 'Women, Work and Welfare in France', in J. Lewis (ed.) *Women and Social Policies in Europe*, Aldershot: Edward Elgar (a survey of the postwar development of women and welfare).

Hantrais, L. and Letablier, M.-T. (1996) *Families and Family Policies in Europe*, London and New York: Longman (an international comparison of welfare provision for women).

women directors

Women have found it difficult to succeed as directors in the French film industry and, typically, begin their careers in some other branch. Jacqueline Audry (1908–77) was a script-girl and editor before making her first feature, *Les Malheurs de Sophie*, in 1946. Her adaptations of Colette's *Gigi* (1948), *Minne, l'ingénue libertine* (1950) and *Mitsou* (1956) rework earlier literary genres but with *La Garçonne* (1957) and *Le Secret du chevalier d'éon* (1960), and her masterpiece *Olivia* (1951), are also proto-feminist questionings of gender roles. Yannick **Bellon** edited films and directed a large number of shorts, but did not make her first feature, *Quelque part, quelqu'un*, until 1972. Thereafter, she specialized in 'women's interest' films which considered topics such as rape, breast cancer and adultery in fictions which were often inspired by true stories: *La Femme de Jean* (1974), *L'Amour violé* (1978), *L'Amour nu* (1981). Nadine Trintignant (*Mon amour, mon amour*, in 1967) and Nina Companeez (*Faustine et le bel été*, 1971) were both editors, while many other women have come to film directing via acting: Juliet Berto, with *Neige* (1981), *Cap Canaille* (1983) and *Havre* (1986); Anna **Karina**, with *Vivre ensemble* (1973); and Jeanne **Moreau**, with *Lumière* (1976) and *L'Adolescente* (1978).

Agnès **Varda**, who trained as a photographer, was the only woman to emerge to prominence in the late 1950s, despite the emphasis placed by the **Nouvelle Vague** on independent film-making and low budgets. Her shorts – *La Pointe courte* (1954), *Opéra-Mouffe* (1958) – were followed by three feature films *Cléo de 5 à 7* (1962), *Le Bonheur* (1965) and *Les Créatures* (1966). *Cléo* was praised as a technical *tour de force* matching 'real time' with 'diegetic time' (both two hours), but all were subsequently criticized for depicting women as narcissistic and overdependent on men, and the two latter films for using a palette reminiscent of soap-powder commercials. However, after 1968 it became clear that Varda's strength was to place two different visions of the world in a continuum. Thus, in *One Sings, the Other*

Doesn't (*L'Une chante, l'autre pas*) in 1977, an overtly feminist companion-piece to *Cléo*, the highly coloured and deliberately escapist world of the spectacle, similar to that imagined by Varda's husband Jacques **Demy** in musicals such as *Les Parapluies de Cherbourg* and *Les Demoiselles de Rochefort*, is contrasted with the grainy, black-and-white world of documentary photography, while her 1985 masterpiece, *Vagabonde* (*Sans toit ni loi*), is a radical questioning of the nature of 'woman', part road movie, part *film noir* and part TV **documentary**. Similar concerns underpin her brilliant series of documentaries dating from the 1970s and 1980s – *Daguerréotypes* (1975), *Réponse de femmes* (1975), *Mur murs* (1982), *Les Dites cariatides* (1984), all of which bear the marks of her encounter with the American women's movement in the late 1960s, as does *Jane B par Agnès V* (1988) which is simultaneously a self-portrait, a portrait of a celebrated female icon, and a documentary about the actress Jane **Birkin**.

Like Varda, but to an even greater extent, Marguerite **Duras** questioned the values of a male-dominated film industry by means of a thoroughgoing minimalism based on extremely low budgets, actors who worked without fees, and very limited crews. Indeed, Duras's most radical film *Le Camion* (1979), in some respects a post-1968 reworking of **Godard**'s *La Chinoise* as '*un film en train de se faire*', is principally composed of a conversation between herself and Gérard **Depardieu**, in the living room of her own house, about what the film was 'supposed to be' (the conversation takes place in the conditional), intercut from time to time with shots of an articulated lorry at an unidentified crossroads in the Paris suburbs. Duras came to film directing after a long and successful career as a novelist and playwright and having written the screenplay for Alain **Resnais**'s first feature film *Hiroshima mon amour* (1959). The orientalism of Duras's novels, and the lyricism of her compositions, are magisterially incorporated into her film masterpiece *India Song* (1975), which evokes, in an extraordinary montage of theatrical gesture and music, the life of Anne-Marie Stretter

(Delphine **Seyrig**) and her lovers in pre-inde-pendence India (in fact, a chateau in the Paris outskirts). But the film is also radically chal-lenged by its companion piece and diptych, *Son nom de Venise dans Calcutta désert* (1976), which deploys the same soundtrack as *India Song*, edited over different images.

In investigating the relationship between sound and image, between the body and its representation, and between silence and speech, the films of Varda and Duras show the influence of feminist theory in the 1970s. More recently, women directors such as Coline **Serreau**, Diane **Kurys** and Josiane **Balasko** have been less concerned with the thematics of fem-inism than to make their mark in mainstream or popular genres, especially in comedy. After a documentary about women, *Mais qu'est-ce qu'elles veulent?* (1976), Serreau shifted to comic mode (albeit with a radical edge) with *Pourquoi pas?* (1977), before the immense suc-cesses of *Trois hommes et un couffin* (1985) and *Romuald et Juliette* (1989), both of which reveal her talent for acute social observation and her brilliant direction of actors, and to harder-hitting social commentary in *La Crise* (1992). Kurys has likewise made a name as a witty observer of social mores, from the auto-biographical *Peppermint Soda* (*Diabolo men-the*) in 1977 and *C'est la vie* (*La Baule les Pins*) in 1990, to the more romanticized *Coup de foudre* (1983) or *Après l'amour* (1992). Balasko was a star of the **café-theatre** and remains an impressive theatrical writer and performer. Her first film as director, *Sac de noeuds* (1985), casting herself and Isabelle **Huppert** as a *couple infernal*, did not meet with the success it deserved, whereas the more sac-charine *French Twist* (*Gazon maudit*) of 1995 dressed up lesbian themes for a mass audience and was extravagantly praised. Balasko's great originality, evident in her contribution to **Blier**'s *Trop belle pour toi* (1989), is to chal-lenge typecasting, especially as regards gender roles. In this she contrasts strongly with Chantal Akerman, a Belgian who worked mainly in France in the 1970s and 1980s, who linked the lesbian themes of *Je, tu, il, elle* (1974) to a thoroughgoing critique of the role

of women in society, *Jeanne Dielman, 23, quai du Commerce 1080 Bruxelles* (1975), and her own relationship, as Belgian Jew, to metropoli-tan French culture in *News from Home* (1976) and *Les Rendez-Vous d'Anna* (1978).

Despite mainstream successes, however, the precarious professional and artistic position of women in the film industry continues to be reflected in their interest in the socially margin-al and to inspire some of their most interesting contemporary film-making. Thus Claire **Denis**'s three key films are oblique essays on race and sex in the context of the French colo-nial heritage: *Chocolat* (1988), in which a white French girl revisits and recalls the Cameroon of her colonial upbringing; *S'en fout la mort* (1990), set in the immigrant milieux of the Paris **suburbs**; and the magnificent *J'ai pas sommeil* (1993), in which a young girl from the Baltic states encounters the cosmopolitan world of the 18th *arrondissement* in Paris.

JILL FORBES

See also: cinema; feminism (move-ments/groups); francophone cinema: Belgium; gay cinema

women's magazines

Women's magazines represent a unique cultur-al space for women. Within this space, women express themselves publicly but also encounter the values and beliefs of femininity which influ-ence the way they think, speak and act.

Women's magazines fall within two main categories: the *haut de gamme* (luxury) maga-zines such as **Marie-Claire** and *Elle*; and *maga-zines populaires*, such as *Femme actuelle* and *7 jours madame*, at the cheaper end of the market.

The luxury magazines consider themselves forward-looking publications, responding to a desire on the part of modern, professional women for luxury, new lifestyles and informa-tion upon which they can make free choices. Hence, their glossy pages contain articles on prominent personalities (politicians, artists, entrepreneurs), reports on topical issues, high-quality photographs and illustrations on **fashion**, beauty and home decoration. In the 1960s and 1970s, in particular, these magazines proclaimed themselves a vanguard for change, by discussing and campaigning around feminist issues such as **abortion/contraception**, women's rights and equal opportunities in the workplace. Since the economically austere years of the 1980s, they have become less keen to protest in favour of collective women's rights and have instead focused attention upon the successes of individual women, especially those who have managed to combine the ideals of femininity with public prominence. New additions to this category in the 1980s, such as *Madame Figaro*, have been particularly aggressive in marketing the 'new feminine woman'.

On the other hand, the *magazines populaires* have never attempted to relay progressive thinking. They have traditionally targeted a provincial readership of full-time mothers and housewives, or women working in manual or less well-paid white-collar occupations, giving practical advice on beauty, fashion, home crafts and personal relationships, with the aim of showing readers how an often humdrum existence can be made more fulfilling. They have offered their readers a more intimate, if not introverted world in which an exchange of information takes place between women. The 1980s brought a downturn in the fortunes of the *magazines populaires* as they faced competition from technically advanced media which offered the public wider perspectives on French society and the world outside it. This forced them to make the first changes: for instance, the use of quadrochromatic colour, varied format and page layout and a livelier journalistic style. While these measures stopped further decline, they were not innovative enough to promote growth, except in the case of new titles such as *Femme actuelle* and *Prima*.

In spite of the fact that women's magazines in both categories have suffered a decline in the 1980s, they remain the jewel in the crown of the French periodical press; not only because of their high sales but also because their readers are important consumers of beauty, fashion,

household and other products. This makes women's magazines the highest earners of **advertising** revenue within the French magazine market.

K_HURSHEED_ W_ADIA_

See also: feminist press; national press in France

Further reading

Bonvoisin, S.-M. and Maignien, M. (1986) *La presse féminine*, Paris: PUF (a useful introduction to the women's periodical press).
Presse et statistiques (1994), Paris: SJTI (statistical information relating to the press).

women's/lesbian writing

In postwar France, no single model of female-authored writing has predominated. Different sociohistorical moments have generated different types of writing, confirming the point made by Irma Garcia that women's literary creativity is bound up, inextricably, with history and with women's place within it (see Garcia 1981).

The discussion that follows covers some of the variant forms and styles of women's writing produced at different points within the postwar era, and also addresses two specific (if, in the French context, marginal) modes of women's writing: that produced by women within the North African community in France and writing by lesbians.

In 1944, women in France belatedly obtained the vote. By 1946, thirty-nine women MPs held seats in the National Assembly. In the late 1940s, therefore, it seemed as if the **Liberation** France had recently won might be being extended to her *citoyennes*. In fact, legal/political emancipation did not, in the course of the 1950s and early 1960s, bring with it the autonomy and independence many *Françaises* craved. For one thing, the financial affairs of married women remained under their husbands' control. Until 1965, French women required their spouse's permission to hold down a job, open a bank account and dispose of property. Additionally, and perhaps more importantly, because contraception did not become legally available until 1967 and the right to abortion was only accorded in 1975, French women of the postwar era had little control over their sexuality and their reproductive processes.

The 1950s and 1960s saw the publication of a good many female-authored works of French literature. A number of these texts, written by authors such as Françoise Mallet-Joris and Benoîte and Flora **Groult** and intended for an exclusively feminine readership, offer a somewhat tame account of the realities of French women's lives. Others, however – unsurprisingly, given the sociosexual climate within which they came into being – envision the feminine condition in a more honest, and less positive, fashion. This latter category of texts includes works by women authors such as Simone de **Beauvoir**, Marguerite **Duras**, Claire **Etcherelli**, Violette **Leduc**, Christiane **Rochefort**, Albertine **Sarrazin** and Françoise **Sagan**. In their writings – which range from the exclusively fictional to the directly autobiographical, and predominantly belong to the realist genre – these *écrivaines* represent the *condition féminine* either as resting on a desperate *chasse à l'amour* that brings dependency in its wake and/or is rarely permanently satisfied (see the prose fictions of Beauvoir and Sagan, and the autobiographical writings of Leduc), or as a deeply acculturated mode of being that offers little chance of escape from pre-ordained roles (see Sagan, Beauvoir, Rochefort and Duras's *Moderato Cantabile*), or as a form of second-class citizenship equivalent, or even inferior, to that enjoyed by the socially marginal (cf. Etcherelli's *Elise, or the Real Life (Élise, ou la vraie vie)*, or as a state that is so generally unsatisfactory that it impels the female subject into various forms of revolt (see the autobiographical works of Sarrazin and Leduc). It is certainly the case that the more insightful female-authored literary creations of the 1950s and the early to mid-1960s offer depictions of the feminine condition that can be categorized as more or less 'feminist'. However, their 'polit-

ical' impact is limited, by virtue of the fact that they tend simply to signal the negative aspects of women's lives (in order implicitly to highlight and critique their sources/causes), and generally hesitate to offer radical solutions or imagine alternative ways of female being.

In the wake of **May 1968**, the French feminist movement – largely quiescent during the 1940s and 1950s, in spite of the publication in 1949 of de Beauvoir's *Second Sex* – received a new lease of life. One of the consequences of its renascence, and of the sociosexual upheavals that hit France in the 1970s, was a kind of feminine re-entry into, or remoulding of, the sociosymbolic *champ culturel* (cultural arena). This phenomenon, argues Marcelle Marini, was made possible by the supportive, creative, female-centred 'space' the Mouvement de la Libération des Femmes allowed women writers and artists to access in the post-1968 period (Marini 1992).

During the 1970s, a new generation of *écrivaines*, inspired by the revolutionary times in which they were writing and also, in certain cases, by a burgeoning body of French feminist theoretical work, brought into being a corpus of literary texts which tended to the experimental, the poetic and/or the highly personal, and within which their own preoccupations as women subjects were manifestly – and courageously – on display. Produced by the likes of Hélène **Cixous**, Chantal **Chawaf**, Jeanne **Hyvrard**, Christiane Rochefort, Emma Santos, Monique **Wittig** and Marie **Cardinal**, these texts addressed themes such as desire, eroticism, sexuality, sexual difference, bodily being, feminine relationships, madness, and the alliance of language and patriarchy. Often, in terms of their stylistic and linguistic composition, they departed from traditional or conventional literary forms – a phenomenon which has encouraged contemporary (feminist) literary critics to categorize the works of Cixous, Chawaf, Hyvrard and even Cardinal as exercises in, and affirmations of, a kind of *écriture féminine* (an avant-garde writing mode deemed to be feminine-gendered, and to relate in some way to the female body). In addition, many of the female-authored literary productions of the 1970s bore witness either to the anger French women of the period felt at their oppression by and within patriarchy and its linguistic order (see the work of Cardinal, Santos and Hyvrard), or to a desire to imagine new worlds/realities wherein sexual politics, human relationships and language might be remoulded, to the detriment of the patriarchal hegemony (see the writings of Wittig and Rochefort's *Archaos*). In this particular literary era, then, textual experimentation, and an imagination that was not only gynocentric but was often also distinctly utopian in its tenor, were the hallmarks of French women's incursions into the literary domain.

Latterly, in an era that is conceivably 'post-feminist' and is certainly significantly less dominated by issues of gender politics than the 1970s, French women's writing seems to have changed course or, at least, to have diversified. Many of the feminist *écrivaines* whose literary careers began in the late 1960s and early 1970s and who were associated for one reason or another with *écriture féminine* have continued to publish in the 1980s and 1990s; however – as is evidenced by the work of other key women writers of the contemporary period, such as Marguerite Duras, Danièle **Sallenave**, Florence Delay and Annie **Ernaux** – the post-1980 publications of Cixous, Chawaf and Wittig are by no means representative of women's literary creativity in the late twentieth century. Duras's 1980s publications certainly address 'the feminine' in so far as they regularly focus on female desire/eroticism, but, with the possible exception of *The Lover* (*L'Amant*), they eschew in so doing the celebratory style associated with *écriture féminine*. Neither Sallenave nor Delay appears particularly preoccupied with representing the *condition féminine*; the work of both women has on the other hand been linked with a *retour au romanesque* (i.e. with a move towards a kind of writing which is manifestly less experimental and self-referential than that of the *nouveau romanciers*). For all that she refuses to accept that gender issues play a dominant role within her literary oeuvre, Ernaux's work is more gynocentric than that of her contemporaries and, by virtue of this fact, stands in some kind of relation to those literary texts born out of

1970s French neo-feminism. It does not, however, display the lyrical, experimental qualities or the *affirmation d'une écriture spécifiquement féminine* that characterized French women's writing in the post-1968 era. Ernaux's autobiographical fictions, especially those in which her family history constitutes a key focus, foreground a realist, documentary, almost anthropological style, which leaves her reader with the sense that he or she is being offered insights not only into the personal trajectory of Ernaux herself but also into diverse aspects of French society and its social mores.

A not insignificant body of texts has been produced in the 1980s by women writers who either are **beurs** or who, born in North Africa, live and work in France. Authors belonging to this category include Leïla **Sebbar** (who is not herself a beur but has written several texts in which the fate of second-generation North African women is a central focus), Farida **Belghoul**, Sakina Boukhedenna, Djura, Leïla Houari, Tassadit Imache, Antoinette Ben Kerroum, Soraya Nini and Ferrudja Kessas. Like the writings of contemporaries such as Ernaux, their highly personal, autobiographically inflected literary creations often display a distinctly documentary quality. Themes and topics addressed within them include:

- the experience of cultural alienation/schizophrenia (an experience encountered by the heroines of beur novels not only in France but also in their so-called *pays d'origine*;
- the need for and pursuit of freedom, access to which is often associated with education and with the literary act; and
- the relation to her body of the female beur subject (the body being the symbolic focus *par excellence* of a parental, especially paternal, authority that is generally represented as oppressive and resented).

In postwar France, a manifest lesbian politico-theoretical and literary culture has been largely lacking. The reasons for this are three-fold. First, with the exception of the essays Monique Wittig published in the 1970s and early 1980s, little theoretico-analytical, conceptual

French feminist work has displayed a strong lesbian dimension. Second, lesbian political activism – partly because, historically, the lesbian movement has existed within the women's movement rather than as a separate entity – has not enjoyed the visibility of gay politics. Third, those texts within France's literary 'canon' in which lesbianism is an issue/theme have in the main been male-authored, date back to the nineteenth and early twentieth centuries, and lack the 'authentic' perspective on female homosexuality present, arguably, in the work of Colette (see Marks 1979). It is highly probable that these phenomena have adversely affected lesbian creativity in the modern era. It is certainly true that in the 1960s and 1970s fictional and autobiographical accounts of lesbian love were written by Leduc, Wittig and Rochefort. The writings of these authors, whether or not they bear witness to a political consciousness inspired by the feminist revolution of the early 1970s, have engendered the existence of a powerful corpus of texts wherein lesbian eroticism and desire are given a female-authored voice and gender positions are addressed and reworked in an increasingly radical way. Newer additions to this corpus include the novels of Jocelyne François, Hélène de Monferrand and Mireille Best. However, as Elula Perrin argues, in the *late* twentieth century French lesbian literary artefacts are something of a rarity (see Perrin 1995), a fact which suggests that in today's France the lesbian creative voice which emerges from the work of the women cited above is being stifled by and within a (deeply misogynistic) cultural climate that has failed to accommodate it.

ALEX HUGHES

See also: abortion/contraception; autobiography; beur writing; beurs; feminism (movements/groups); feminist thought; *nouveau roman*

Further reading

Attack, M. and Powrie, P. (eds) (1990) *Contemporary French Fiction by Women: Feminist Perspectives*, Manchester: Manchester University Press (an accessible volume of essays on a range of modern women writers).

Bonn, C. (1994) 'Romans féminins de l'immigration d'origine maghrébine', *Nouvelles Écritures féminines* 118 (a useful survey of the forms and themes of female-authored beur literature).

Fallaize, E. (1993) *French Women's Writing*, Basingstoke and London: Macmillan (a useful survey of contemporary writers such as Chawaf, Hyvrard and Cardinal).

Garcia, I. (1981) *Promenade femmilière*, Paris: Des femmes (a useful survey of key themes and styles in French *écriture féminine*).

Holmes, D. (1996) *French Women's Writing 1848–1994*, London: The Athlone Press (a historically organized study, with interesting essays focused on key women writers).

Marini, M. (1992) 'La Place des femmes dans la production culturelle', in G. Duby and M. Perrot, (eds) *Histoire des femmes*, vol. 5, Paris: Plon (an excellent essay focusing on the effect that May 1968 and the feminist revolution emergent from it had upon women's creativity in France).

Marks, E. (1979) 'Lesbian Intertextuality', in G. Stambolian and E. Marks (eds) *Homosexualities and French Literature*, Ithaca, NY and London: Cornell University Press (a stimulating examination of the 'lesbian continuum' within French literature).

Perrin, E. (1995) *Coup de gueule pour l'amour des femmes*, Paris: Ramsay (a highly personal account of the state of lesbian politics and lesbian cultural activity in modern and contemporary France).

Sartori, E. and Zimmerman, D. (eds) (1991) *French Women Writers: A Bio-Bibliographical Source Book*, New York: Greenwood Press (a collection of well-referenced essays on French women authors through the ages).

Sellers, S. (1991) *Writing and Sexual Difference*, Basingstoke and London: Macmillan (particularly useful for understanding *écriture féminine*).

Xenakis, Iannis

b. 1922, Brãila, Romania

Composer

Educated at the Athens Polytechnic, Xenakis settled in France in 1947, working as an architect with **Le Corbusier** until 1959. He is best known for his 'stochastic' music, an application of probability theory to structure rather than to the actual production of sounds. He was strongly influenced by Varèse, with whom Xenakis shares a predilection for percussive sonorities and a fascination with the spatial deployment of music – for example, musicians placed within the audience, and electronic techniques. Xenakis's work requires of its audience a different attitude towards listening. His works range from chamber to orchestral and choral works: *Herma* (piano), *Eonta* (piano and brass), *Pithoprakta* (orchestra) and incidental music for the *Oresteia*.

WALTER A. STRAUSS

See also: concert music

Yacine, Kateb

b. 1929, Constantine, Algeria;
d. 1989, Grenoble

Playwright and director

A well-known North African playwright and director, Yacine has worked in French since the 1950s. His texts in French, noted for their liveliness, movement and flexibility, and for dealing with Algeria, revolutions, national identity, etc., include *Polygone étoilé* (Starry Zone) and *L'Homme aux sandales de caoutchouc* (The Man in Rubber Sandals). He has also written many plays in Arab dialect.

ANNIE SPARKS

See also: francophone performing arts: North Africa; theatre

Further reading

Arnaud, J. (1986) *La Littérature maghrébine de langue française*, Paris: Publisud, vol. 2 (study of Arabic literature, including a section on Yacine).

Yourcenar, Marguerite

b. 1903, Belgium;
d. 1987, Maine, USA

Writer

Yourcenar was a half-Belgian, half-French writer, who in 1980 became the first woman to be elected to the **Académie Française**; she had been elected to its Belgian counterpart nine years before. Her best-known work, published in 1951, *Memoirs of Hadrian* (*Mémoires d'Hadrien*), is a first person fictional portrait of the Roman emperor. Since 1939, she had lived in the United States with her long-term partner, Grace Frick, but lesbianism is less prominent in her writing than male homosexuality, an important theme in *Mémoires d'Hadrien* and *Alexis* (1929), whose central character reveals his sexual problems in a long letter to his wife. Yourcenar's geographical marginality to French culture was mirrored by her distance from its dominant intellectual movements, most notably the *nouveau roman*. She was at work on the third and final volume of her **autobiography** at the time of her death.

KEITH READER

See also: women's/lesbian writing

youth culture

La culture jeune is a somewhat slippery term, usually denoting the leisure practices or (more broadly) the references, icons and values deemed to be specific to the 12–25 age group. As in other Western societies, youth culture in France is closely associated with the audiovisual media and leisure technologies.

The democratization of postwar secondary education in France and the raising of the school-leaving age to 16 in 1959 had the effect of extending the period of adolescence. This, together with France's 'baby boom' and economic recovery, opened a new teenage consumer market in the late 1950s increasingly centred on pop music, which the transistor radio and vinyl record made easily available to the young person with more disposable income and leisure than the average adult. These developments benefited a new generation of French singer-songwriters such as **Brel** and **Brassens**, but their chief impact was to facilitate the emergence of a French form of American rock and roll known as *yé-yé*, performed by teen idols like Johnny **Hallyday** and Françoise **Hardy** and disseminated by the radio programme and magazine, *Salut les copains*. Although *yé-yé* seemed little more than a derivative and trivial commodity, as early as 1963 the sociologist Edgar **Morin** noted its deeper significance as mirror and stimulant of a new sense of youth identity. *Yé-yé*, he argued, was the voice of a virtually homogeneous 'class' founded not on socioeconomic status but on a community of age, taste, ritual and language. It was also profoundly ambivalent: while it helped prepare French youth for life in the consumer society, its validation of gratuitous pleasure and play also contained the seeds of rebellion against the adult world.

Although the homogeneity argument was questionable, Morin's detection of revolt at the heart of French youth culture proved prophetic, as youth protests against Gaullist society, fanned by Anglo-American counterculture, culminated in the 'cultural revolution' of **May 1968**, whose polymorphous values impregnated the music, **comic strips**, fashions and lifestyles of many young people in France. However, the very forces which had generated the youth phenomenon soon changed it. The development of new technologies such as video

and the Walkman, and the universalization of the post-1960s values of youthfulness, pluralism and pleasure, transformed Western youth culture generally into a multinational, multi-million-dollar industry. Punk notwithstanding, adolescent dissent was packaged and marketed during the 1970s, while disillusionment and recession steadily defused 1960s radicalism. In France as elsewhere, once immutable cultural hierarchies began shifting, so that by the 1980s even the government, under **Mitterrand**, had set about legitimizing youth cultural practices previously considered unworthy or positively antisocial, such as **fashion**, comic strips, **pop video**, **rock and pop**, **rap** and graffiti. Concurrently, the pop market was becoming segmented, embracing an ever wider variety of styles.

During the 1980s, the rise of racism and **AIDS**, ongoing dissatisfaction with educational reform and the popularity of worldwide humanitarian causes all helped generate a new social awareness in French youth, variously exemplified in the student protests of November–December 1986, SOS Racisme, new 'alternative' entertainers like the singer **Renaud** and the comedian **Coluche**, and an enthusiasm for world music. Such phenomena testified to a reinvented sense of youth solidarity, coupled with a new, multicultural sensibility which generated various musical innovations, such as the French rap of **MC Solaar** or the fusion of rock with languages and rhythms from the Maghreb and elsewhere.

As a result of these changes, and of the progressive domestication and commodification of cultural life in the multimedia age, the existence of a homogeneous youth culture today is less widely accepted than it was in the 1960s, though some argue that even then what was perceived as a common culture was merely that of a privileged minority. Nevertheless, surveys published in 1990 and 1995 still suggest a degree of commonality in French adolescents' cultural practices. One finding is the decline of reading, despite a rise in the level of educational attainment. When young people do read, it is most often comic strips. Correspondingly, audiovisual practices have risen. In 1994, 92 per cent of the 12–25 age group had access to a hi-fi system; 79 per cent a personal stereo and a VCR; and 39 per cent a TV-linked video game.

This does not, however, mean the complete domestication of young people's cultural experience, since sociability – going to cafés, roaming the streets, seeing friends – remains crucial. By far the most popular outing for the 12–25 age group in 1994 was to the **cinema** (90 per cent), while other favourites were fun fairs (60 per cent), nightclubs (57 per cent) and amusement parks (41 per cent). Opera productions, however, attracted only 3 per cent and classical music concerts 7 per cent. 'Rock', in fact, remains the preferred music of 54 per cent of the young. Here, too, there is evidence of increasing sociability: 24 per cent of 15–25s attended a rock concert in 1988, and 41 per cent in 1994. Yet it is far from certain that rock constitutes the homogeneous culture Morin had found in *yé-yé*. First, 'rock' is a deceptively singular term which masks a plurality of tastes and, second, young people's cultural consumption is differentiated by their cultural inheritance, gender and social position.

Although a certain homogeneity is produced by the shared experiences of schooling, cultural practices soon diverge once education ends.

DAVID LOOSELEY

See also: beur music; concert music; Désir, Harlem, and SOS Racisme; education, secondary: *collèges*, *lycées*, etc.; racism/antisemitism

Further reading

Donnat, O. and Cogneau, D. (1990) *Les Pratiques culturelles des Français 1973–1989*, Paris: La Découverte/Documentation Française (survey sponsored by the government).

Guy, J.-M. (ed.) (1995) *Les Jeunes et les sorties culturelles*, Paris: Ministry of Culture (another government-sponsored survey).

Nouvelle Enquête sur les pratiques culturelles des Français (1990), Paris: Documentation Française (another government survey).

Yonnet, P. (1985) *Jeux, modes et masses: la société française et le moderne*, Paris: Gallimard (a useful sociological study).

Index

Page numbers in **bold** indicate references to the main entry.

Cartier-Bresson, Henri **91**, 201, 421, 422

Cartland, Barbara 474

cartoons and cartoonists 66–7, 98, **116–19**, 292, 348

   see also animation

Cartoucherie, Vincennes 115, 525–6

Casadesus, Jean-Claude 456

Casarès, Maria **91**

Cassavetes, John 105

Castermann (publisher) 116

Castro, Fidel 120, 193

Castro, Roland 512

Cathelat, Bernard 4

Catholicism **92–3**, **94–5**

   cultural movements 112

   and Marxist thought 359, 360

   and music 122, 370

   new philosophers 394

   newspapers 128, 389

   opponents to Church 212, 261

   politicians 375, 376, 377, 560

   schools 178, 179

   and women 560

   writers 254, 306, 429

Caubère, Philippe **95**

Cause du Peuple, La 328

Causse, Michèle 558

Caute, David 199, 364

Cavaillès, Jean 360

Cavanna, François 98

Celan, Paul 308

Céline, Louis Ferdinand (Louis Destouches) 132, 344, 470, 495, 517

Cendrars, Blaise 249, 250

censorship

   journalism 345

   laws 187, 345–6

   libraries 339

   pornography 435

   stands against 90, 119, 340

   see also film, censorship; literary censorship

Centre D'Études Féminines 209

Centre National de la Bande Dessinée et de l'Image 116

Centres Dramatiques Nationaux et Régionaux 53, 522, 528, 555

ceramics 163, 424, 426

Cerdan, Marcel 423

Cerruti, fashion house 201

Certeau, Michel de 39, **95**

Césaire, Aimé **95–6**, 142, 199, 244, 415, 417, 428–9, 430, 529

Cévennes region: Protestantism 93

Cézanne, Paul 425

Chabal, Pierre 262

Chaban-Delmas, Jacques **96**, 100, 147, 433, 503

Chabrol, Claude 55, 81, 87, **96**, 104, 113, 288, 344, 398, 473, 538

Chad: intervention in conflict (1984) 145

Chagall, Marc **96**, 351

Chalem, Denise 97

Chamoiseau, Patrick 243, 244

Champagne

   agriculture 7

   wine 556, 557

Chandler, Raymond 155

Chanel, Coco 97

   fashion house 200–1, 201

Change 347

Chaplin, Charlie 521

Chaplin, Geraldine 107

Char, René 75, **97**, 123, 164, 193, 428–9, 430

Chardonne, Jacques 289

Charef, Mehdi 64–5, 68, 69, **97–8**, 300

Charlie Hebdo 98

Charpentier, Pascal 234

Chartreux, Bernard 98, 306

Chatiliez, Étienne 111

Chawaf, Chantal **97–8**, 172–3, 382, 565–6

Chazal, Malcolm de 245, 247

Chechnick, Jeremiah 114

Chedid, Andrée 429, 431

Chekhov, Anton: *Platonov* 99

Chemetov, Paul 21, 23, 62

Chéreau, Patrice **99**, 262, 314, 418, 428, 552

   films 3, 38, 105, 263

   theatre 42, 91, 154, 158, 159, 227, 314, 523, 524

Chérie FM 451

Chernobyl disaster 278

Chessex, Jacques 250

Chevalier, Maurice **99–100**, 375, 381, 417, 499, 536

Chevènement, Jean-Pierre 191, 413

Cheynet, Anne 246

Chibane, Malik 65

child care **100**, 184, 561

Child, Loudolf 137